Merriam-Webster's Notebook French-English Dictionary

Merriam-Webster, Incorporated
Springfield, Massachusetts, U.S.A.

Preface

MERRIAM-WEBSTER'S NOTEBOOK FRENCH-ENGLISH DICTIONARY is a concise reference for the core vocabulary of French and English. Its 40,000 entries and over 50,000 translations provide up-to-date coverage of the basic vocabulary and idioms in both languages. In addition, the book includes vocabulary specific to the Canadian province of Quebec.

IPA (International Phonetic Alphabet) pronunciations are given for all words. Included as well are tables of irregular verbs in both languages and the most common French abbreviations.

This book shares many details of presentation with our larger *Merriam-Webster's French-English Dictionary,* but for reasons of conciseness it also has a number of features uniquely its own. Users need to be familiar with the following major features of this dictionary.

Main entries follow one another in strict alphabetical order, without regard to intervening spaces or hyphens.

Homographs (words spelled the same but having different meanings or parts of speech) are run on at a single main entry if they are closely related. Run-on homograph entries are replaced in the text by a boldfaced swung dash (as **devoir** . . . *vt* . . . — **~** *nm* . . .). Homographs of distinctly different origin (as **date**[1] and **date**[2]) are given separate entries.

Run-on entries for related words that are not homographs may also follow the main entry. Thus we have the main entry **calculer** *vt* followed by run-on entries for — **calcul** *nm,* — **calculateur, -trice** *adj,* and — **calculatrice** *nf.* However, if a related word falls later in the alphabet than a following unrelated main entry, it will be entered at its own place; **ear** and its run-on — **eardrum** precede the main entry **earl** which is followed by the main entry **earlobe.**

Variant spellings appear at the main entry separated by *or* (as **judgment** *or* **judgement; paralyze** *or Brit* **paralyse;** or **lis** *or* **lys).**

Inflected forms of English verbs, adjectives, adverbs, and nouns are shown when they are irregular (as **wage** . . . **waged; waging, ride** . . . **rode; ridden; good** . . . **better; best;** or **fly** . . . *n, pl* **flies)** or when there might be doubt about their spelling (as **ego** . . . *n, pl* **egos).** Inflected forms of French irregular verbs are shown in the section Conjugation of French Verbs on page 3a; numerical references to this table are included at the main entry (as **tenir** {92} *vt*). Irregular plurals of French nouns or adjectives are shown at the main entry (as **mondial, -diale** *adj, mpl* **-diaux).**

Cross-references are provided to lead the user to the appropriate main entry (as **mice** → **mouse** or **fausse** → **faux**[2]).

Pronunciation information is either given explicitly or implied for all English and French words. A full list of the pronunciation symbols used appears on page 8a.

The grammatical function of entry words is indicated by an italic **functional label** (as *vt, adj,* or *nm*). Italic **usage labels** may be added at the entry or sense as well (as **artilleur** . . . *nm Can* **:** pitcher (in baseball); **center** *or Brit* **centre** . . . *n* . . .; or **tuyau** . . . *nm* . . . **2** *fam* **:** tip, advice). These labels are also included in the translations (as **bet** . . . *n* **:** pari *m,* gageure *f Can).*

Usage notes are occasionally placed before a translation to clarify meaning or use (as **moins** . . . *prep* . . . **2** (*in expressions of time*) **:** to, of).

Synonyms may appear before the translation word(s) in order to provide context for the meaning of an entry word or sense (as **poursuivre** . . . *vt* . . . **2** CONTINUER **:** carry on with; or **meet** . . . *vt* . . . **2** SATISFY **:** satisfaire).

Bold notes are sometimes used before a translation to introduce a plural sense or a common phrase using the main entry word (as **meuble** . . . *nm* . . . **2 ~s** *nmpl* **:** furniture; or **call** . . . *vt* . . . **3 ~ off :** annuler). Note that when an entry word is repeated in a bold note, it is replaced by a swung dash

Contents

ISBN 0-87779-673-4

Made in the United States of America
34QWD05

Conjugation of French Verbs

Simple Tenses

Tense	Regular Verbs Ending in -ER parler		Regular Verbs Ending in -IR grandir	
PRESENT INDICATIVE	je parle tu parles il parle	nous parlons vous parlez ils parlent	je grandis tu grandis il grandit	nous grandissons vous grandissez ils grandissent
PRESENT SUBJUNCTIVE	je parle tu parles il parle	nous parlions vous parliez ils parlent	je grandisse tu grandisses il grandisse	nous grandissions vous grandissiez ils grandissent
PRETERIT INDICATIVE	je parlai tu parlas il parla	nous parlâmes vous parlâtes ils parlèrent	je grandis tu grandis il grandit	nous grandîmes vous grandîtes ils grandirent
IMPERFECT INDICATIVE	je parlais tu parlais il parlait	nous parlions vous parliez ils parlaient	je grandissais tu grandissais il grandissait	nous grandissions vous grandissiez ils grandissaient
IMPERFECT SUBJUNCTIVE	je parlasse tu parlasses il parlât	nous parlassions vous parlassiez ils parlassent	je grandisse tu grandisses il grandît	nous grandissions vous grandissiez ils grandissent
FUTURE INDICATIVE	je parlerai tu parleras il parlera	nous parlerons vous parlerez ils parleront	je grandirai tu grandiras il grandira	nous grandirons vous grandirez ils grandiront
CONDITIONAL	je parlerais tu parlerais il parlerait	nous parlerions vous parleriez ils parleraient	je grandirais tu grandirais il grandirait	nous grandirions vous grandiriez ils grandiraient
IMPERATIVE	parle, parlez	parlons parlez	grandis, grandissez	grandissons grandissez
PRESENT PARTICIPLE (GERUND)	parlant		grandissant	
PAST PARTICIPLE	parlé		grandi	

Perfect Tenses

The *perfect* tenses are formed with *avoir* and the past participle:

PRESENT PERFECT
: j'ai parlé, nous avons parlé, etc. (*indicative*)
j'aie parlé, nous ayons parlé, etc. (*subjunctive*)

PAST PERFECT
: j'avais parlé, nous avions parlé, etc. (*indicative*)
j'eusse parlé, nous eussions parlé, etc. (*subjunctive*)

PRETERIT PERFECT
: j'eus parlé, nous eûmes parlé, etc.

FUTURE PERFECT
: j'aurai parlé, nous aurons parlé, etc.

CONDITIONAL PERFECT
: j'aurais parlé, nous aurions parlé, etc.
or
j'eusse parlé, nous eussions parlé, etc.

PAST IMPERATIVE
: aie parlé, ayons parlé, ayez parlé

The perfect tenses of the following verbs are formed with *être*:

aller, arriver, décéder, devenir, échoir, éclore, entrer, mourir, naître, partir, repartir, rentrer, rester, retourner, sortir, tomber, venir, revenir, parvenir, survenir

For example, the present perfect of *arriver* would be as follows:
je suis arrivé, nous sommes arrivés, etc. (*indicative*)

Irregular Verbs

The *imperfect subjunctive*, the *conditional*, and the first and second person plural of the *imperative* are not included in the model conjugations list but can be derived from other verb forms.

The *imperfect subjunctive* is formed by using the second person singular of the preterit indicative, removing the final *s*, and adding the following suffixes: *-sse, -sses, -t* (and adding a circumflex accent on the preceding vowel), *-ssions, -ssiez, -ssent*. *Servir* is conjugated as follows:

PRETERIT INDICATIVE, SECOND PERSON SINGULAR — servis – *s* = servi

IMPERFECT SUBJUNCTIVE — je servisse, tu servisses, il servît, nous servissions, vous servissiez, ils servissent

The *conditional* is formed by using the stem of the future indicative and adding the following suffixes: *-ais, -ais, -ait, -ions, -iez,- aient*. *Prendre* is conjugated as follows:

FUTURE INDICATIVE — je prendrai – *ai* = prendr

CONDITIONAL — je prendrais, tu prendrais, il prendrait, nous prendrions, vous prendriez, ils prendraient

The first and second person plural of the *imperative* are the same as the corresponding forms of the present indicative.

Model Conjugations of Irregular Verbs

The model conjugations below include the following simple tenses: the *present indicative* (*IND*), the *present subjunctive* (*SUBJ*), the *preterit indicative* (*PRET*), the *imperfect indicative* (*IMPF*), the *future indicative* (*FUT*), the second person singular form of the *imperative* (*IMPER*), the *present participle* or *gerund* (*PRP*), and the *past participle* (*PP*). Each set of conjugations is preceded by the corresponding infinitive form of the verb, shown in bold type. Only tenses containing irregularities are listed, and the irregular verb forms within each tense are displayed in bold type.

Also note that some conjugated verbs are labeled *defective verb*. This refers to a verb lacking one or more of the usual forms of grammatical inflection (tense, mood, etc.), for example, in French, the verbs *bruire* and *ouïr*.

Each irregular verb entry in the French-English section of this dictionary is cross-referred by number to one of the following model conjugations. These cross-reference numbers are shown in curly braces { } immediately preceding the entry's functional label.

The three main categories of verbs are:

1) Verbs ending in -ER
2) Verbs ending in -IR

Present indicative endings for verbs in these categories are:

-is, -is, -it, -issons, -issez, -issent

For example, *j'arrondis, nous arrondissons,* etc. for infinitive *arrondir*

3) Verbs ending in -IR/-OIR/-RE

Present indicative endings for verbs in these categories are:

-e, -es, -e, -ons, -ez, -ent

For example, *j'accueille, nous accueillons,* etc. for infinitive *accueillir*

or

-s(x), -s(x), -t(d), -ons, -ez, -ent

For example, *je rends, nous rendons,* etc. for infinitive *rendre*

Note that in the third group there are two different sets of endings for both the present indicative and preterit indicative depending on the verb in question, as shown above for the present indicative. For clarity, these forms are included in the model conjugations in an attempt to prevent the reader from inadvertently choosing the wrong endings.

4a Conjugation of French Verbs

1 **absoudre :** *IND* **j'absous, tu absous, il absout, nous absolvons, vous absolvez, ils absolvent;** *SUBJ* **j'absolve, tu absolves, il absolve, nous absolvions, vous absolviez, ils absolvent;** *PRET (not used)*; *IMPF* **j'absolvais, tu absolvais, il absolvait, nous absolvions, vous absolviez, ils absolvaient;** *IMPER* **absous;** *PRP* **absolvant;** *PP* **absous**

2 **accroire** *(defective verb) Used only in the infinitive*

3 **accueillir :** *IND* **j'accueille, tu accueilles, il accueille,** nous accueillons, vous accueillez, ils accueillent; *PRET* **j'accueillis, tu accueillis, il accueillit, nous accueillîmes, vous accueillîtes, ils accueillirent;** *FUT* **j'accueillerai, tu accueilleras, il accueillera, nous accueillerons, vous accueillerez, ils accueilleront;** *IMPER* **accueille**

4 **advenir** *(defective verb) Used only in the infinitive and in the following tenses* **:** *IND* **il advient;** *SUBJ* **il advienne;** *PRET* **il advint;** *IMPF* **il advenait;** *FUT* **il adviendra;** *PRP* **advenant;** *PP* **advenu**

5 **aller :** *IND* **je vais, tu vas, il va, nous allons, vous allez, ils vont;** *SUBJ* **j'aille, tu ailles, il aille, nous allions, vous alliez, ils aillent;** *FUT* **j'irai, tu iras, il ira, nous irons, vous irez, ils iront;** *IMPER* **va**

6 **annoncer :** *IND* j'annonce, tu annonces, il annonce, **nous annonçons,** vous annoncez, ils annoncent; *PRET* **j'annonçai, tu annonças, il annonça, nous annonçâmes, vous annonçâtes, ils annoncèrent;** *IMPF* **j'annonçais, tu annonçais, il annonçait,** nous annoncions, vous annonciez, **ils annonçaient;** *PRP* **annonçant**

7 **apparaître :** *IND* **j'apparais, tu apparais, il apparaît, nous apparaissons, vous apparaissez, ils apparaissent;** *SUBJ* **j'apparaisse, tu apparaisses, il apparaisse, nous apparaissions, vous apparaissiez, ils apparaissent;** *PRET* **j'apparus, tu apparus, il apparut, nous apparûmes, vous apparûtes, ils apparurent;** *IMPF* **j'apparaissais, tu apparaissais, il apparaissait, nous apparaissions, vous apparaissiez, ils apparaissaient;** *IMPER* **apparais;** *PRP* **apparaissant;** *PP* **apparu**

8 **appeler :** *IND* **j'appelle, tu appelles, il appelle,** nous appelons, vous appelez, **ils appellent;** *SUBJ* **j'appelle, tu appelles, il appelle,** nous appelions, vous appeliez, **ils appellent;** *FUT* **j'appellerai, tu appelleras, il appellera, nous appellerons, vous appellerez, ils appelleront;** *IMPER* **appelle**

9 **asseoir :** *IND* **j'assieds** *or* **j'assois, tu assieds** *or* **tu assois, il assied** *or* **il assoit, nous asseyons** *or* **nous assoyons, vous asseyez** *or* **vous assoyez, ils asseyent** *or* **ils assoient;** *SUBJ* **j'asseye** *or* **j'assoie, tu asseyes** *or* **tu assoies, il asseye** *or* **il assoie, nous asseyions** *or* **nous assoyions, vous asseyiez** *or* **vous assoyiez, ils asseyent** *or* **ils assoient;** *PRET* **j'assis, tu assis, il assit, nous assîmes, vous assîtes, ils assirent;** *IMPF* **j'asseyais** *or* **j'assoyais, tu asseyais** *or* **tu assoyais, il asseyait** *or* **il assoyait, nous asseyions** *or* **nous assoyions, vous asseyiez** *or* **vous assoyiez, ils asseyaient** *or* **ils assoyaient;** *FUT (not used)*; *IMPER* **assieds** *or* **assois;** *PRP* **asseyant** *or* **assoyant;** *PP* **assis**

10 **avoir :** *IND* **j'ai, tu as, il a, nous avons, vous avez, ils ont;** *SUBJ* **j'aie, tu aies, il ait, nous ayons, vous ayez, ils aient;** *PRET* **j'eus, tu eus, il eut, nous eûmes, vous eûtes, ils eurent;** *IMPF* **j'avais, tu avais, il avait, nous avions, vous aviez, ils avaient;** *FUT* **j'aurai, tu auras, il aura, nous aurons, vous aurez, ils auront;** *IMPER* **aie, ayons, ayez;** *PRP* **ayant;** *PP* **eu**

11 **balayer :** *IND* **je balaie** *or* je balaye, **tu balaies** *or* tu balayes, **il balaie** *or* il balaye, nous balayons, vous balayez, **ils balaient** *or* ils balayent; *SUBJ* **je balaie** *or* je balaye, **tu balaies** *or* tu balayes, **il balaie** *or* il balaye, nous balayions, vous balayiez, **ils balaient** *or* ils balayent; *FUT* **je balaierai** *or* je balayerai, **tu balaieras** *or* tu balayeras, **il balaiera** *or* il balayera, **nous balaierons** *or* nous balayerons, **vous balaierez** *or* vous balayerez, **ils balaieront** *or* ils balayeront; *IMPER* **balaie** *or* balaye

12 **battre :** *IND* **je bats, tu bats, il bat,** nous battons, vous battez, ils battent; *PRET* **je battis, tu battis, il battit, nous battîmes, vous battîtes, ils battirent;** *IMPER* **bats;** *PP* **battu**

13 **boire :** *IND* je bois, tu bois, il boit, **nous buvons, vous buvez, ils boivent;** *SUBJ* **je boive, tu boives, il boive, nous buvions, vous buviez, ils boivent;** *PRET* **je bus, tu bus, il but, nous bûmes, vous bûtes, ils burent;** *IMPF* **je buvais, tu buvais, il buvait, nous buvions, vous buviez, ils buvaient;** *PRP* **buvant;** *PP* **bu**

14 **bouillir :** *IND* **je bous, tu bous, il bout,** nous bouillons, vous bouillez, ils bouillent; *PRET* **je bouillis, tu bouillis, il bouillit, nous bouillîmes, vous bouillîtes, ils bouillirent;** *IMPER* **bous**

15 **braire** *(defective verb) Used only in the infinitive and in the following tenses* **:** *IND* **il brait, ils braient;** *IMPF* **brayait, brayaient;** *FUT* **il braira, ils brairont**

16 **bruire** *(defective verb) Used only in the infinitive and in the following tenses* **:** IND **il bruit, ils bruissent;** SUBJ *(not used)*; *PRET (not used)*; IMPF **il bruissait, ils bruissaient;** PRP **bruissant;** PP **bruit**

17 **changer :** *IND* je change, tu changes, il change, **nous changeons,** vous changez, ils changent; *PRET* **je changeai, tu changeas, il changea, nous changeâmes, vous changeâtes, ils changèrent;** *IMPF* **je changeais, tu changeais, il changeait,** nous changions, vous changiez, **ils changeaient;** *PRP* **changeant**

18 **choir** *(defective verb) Used only in the following tenses* **:** IND **je chois, tu chois, il choit, ils choient;** *SUBJ (not used)*; *PRET* **il chut;** *IMPF (not used)*; *FUT* il choira; *IMPER (not used)*; *PRP (not used)*; *PP* **chu**

19 **clore** *(defective verb) Used only in the following tenses* **:** *IND* je clos, tu clos, **il clôt, ils closent;** *SUBJ* **je close, tu closes, il close, nous closions, vous closiez, ils closent;** *PRET (not used)*; *IMPF (not used)*; *FUT (used but regularly formed)*; *PRP* **closant;** *PP* **clos**

20 **congeler :** *IND* **je congèle, tu congèles, il congèle,** nous congelons, vous congelez, **ils congèlent;** *SUBJ* **je congèle, tu congèles, il congèle,** nous congelions, vous congeliez, **ils congèlent;** *FUT* **je congèlerai, tu congèleras, il congèlera, nous congèlerons, vous congèlerez, ils congèleront;** *IMPER* **congèle**

21 **conquérir :** *IND* **je conquiers, tu conquiers, il conquiert,** nous conquérons, vous conquérez, **ils conquièrent;** *SUBJ* **je conquière, tu conquières, il conquière,** nous conquérions, vous conquériez, **ils conquièrent;** *PRET* **je conquis, tu conquis, il conquit, nous conquîmes, vous conquîtes, ils conquirent;** *FUT* **je conquerrai, tu conquerras, il conquerra, nous conquerrons, vous conquerrez, ils conquerront;** *IMPER* **conquiers;** *PP* **conquis**

22 **coudre :** *IND* je couds, tu couds, il coud, **nous cousons, vous cousez, ils cousent;** *SUBJ* **je couse, tu couses, il couse, nous cousions, vous cousiez, ils cousent;** *PRET* **je cousis, tu cousis, il cousit, nous cousîmes, vous cousîtes, ils cousirent;** *IMPF* **je cousais, tu cousais, il cousait, nous cousions, vous cousiez, ils cousaient;** *PRP* **cousant;** *PP* **cousu**

23 **courir :** *IND* **je cours, tu cours, il court,** nous courons, vous courez, ils courent; *PRET* **je courus, tu courus, il courut, nous courûmes, vous courûtes, ils coururent;** *FUT* **je courrai, tu courras, il courra, nous courrons, vous courrez, ils courront;** *IMPER* **cours;** *PP* **couru**

24 **croire :** *IND* je crois, tu crois, il croit, **nous croyons, vous croyez,** ils croient; *SUBJ* je croie, tu croies, il croie, **nous croyions, vous croyiez,** ils croient; *PRET* **je crus, tu crus, il crut, nous crûmes, vous crûtes, ils crurent;** *IMPF* **je croyais, tu croyais, il croyait, nous croyions, vous croyiez, ils croyaient;** *PRP* **croyant;** *PP* **cru**

25 **croître :** *IND* **je croîs, tu croîs, il croît, nous croissons, vous croissez, ils croissent;** *SUBJ* **je croisse, tu croisses, il croisse, nous croissions, vous croissiez, ils croissent;** *PRET* **je crûs, tu crûs, il crût, nous crûmes, vous crûtes, ils crûrent;** *IMPF* **je croissais, tu croissais, il croissait, nous croissions, vous croissiez, ils croissaient;** *IMPER* **croîs;** *PRP* **croissant;** *PP* **crû**

26 **décevoir :** *IND* **je déçois, tu déçois, il déçoit,** nous décevons, vous décevez, **ils déçoivent;** *SUBJ* **je déçoive, tu déçoives, il déçoive,** nous décevions, vous déceviez, **ils déçoivent;** *PRET* **je déçus, tu déçus, il déçut, nous déçûmes, vous déçûtes, ils déçurent;** *IMPER* **déçois;** *PP* **déçu**

27 **déchoir** *(defective verb) Used only in the following tenses* **:** *IND* je déchois, tu déchois, il déchoit *or* **il déchet, nous déchoyons, vous déchoyez, ils déchoient;** *SUBJ* je déchoie, tu déchoies, il déchoie, **nous déchoyions, vous déchoyiez, ils déchoient;** *PRET* **je déchus, tu déchus, il déchut, nous déchûmes, vous déchûtes, ils déchurent;** *IMPF (not used)*; *FUT (used but regularly formed)*; *IMPER (not used)*; *PRP (not used)*; *PP* **déchu**

28 **devoir :** *IND* **je dois, tu dois, il doit,** nous devons, vous devez, **ils doivent;** *SUBJ* **je doive, tu doives, il doive,** nous devions, vous deviez, **ils doivent;** *PRET* **je dus, tu dus, il dut, nous dûmes, vous dûtes, ils durent;** *IMPER* **dois;** *PRP* **dû**

29 **dire :** *IND* je dis, tu dis, il dit, **nous disons, vous dites, ils disent;** *SUBJ* **je dise, tu dises, il dise, nous disions, vous disiez, ils disent;** *PRET* **je dis, tu dis, il dit, nous dîmes, vous dîtes, ils dirent;** *IMPF* **je disais, tu disais, il disait, nous disions, vous disiez, ils disent;** *PRP* **disant;** *PP* **dit**

30 **dormir :** *IND* **je dors, tu dors, il dort,** nous dormons, vous dormez, ils dorment; *PRET* **je dormis, tu dormis, il dormit, nous dormîmes, vous dormîtes, ils dormirent;** *IMPER* **dors**

31 **échoir** *(defective verb) Used only in the following tenses* **:** *IND* **il échoit, ils échoient;** *SUBJ* **il échoie;** *PRET* **il échut, ils échurent;** *IMPF (not used)*; *FUT* il échoira *or* **il écherra;** ils échoiront *or* **ils écherront;** *IMPER (not used)*; *PRP* **échéant;** *PP* **échu**

32 **éclore** *(defective verb) Used only in the following tenses* **:** *IND* **il éclot;** *PP* **éclos**

33 **écrire :** *IND* j'écris, tu écris, il écrit, **nous écrivons, vous écrivez, ils écrivent;** *SUBJ* **j'écrive, tu écrives, il écrive, nous écrivions, vous écriviez, ils écrivent;** *PRET* **j'écrivis, tu écrivis, il écrivit, nous écrivîmes, vous écrivîtes, ils écrivirent;** *IMPF* **j'écrivais, tu écrivais, il écrivait, nous écrivions, vous écriviez, ils écrivaient;** *PRP* **écrivant;** *PP* **écrit**

34 **enclore** *(defective verb) Used only in the following tenses* **:** *IND* j'enclos, tu enclos, il enclot, **nous enclosons, vous enclosez, ils enclosent;** *SUBJ* **j'enclose, tu encloses, il enclose, nous enclosions, vous enclosiez, ils enclosent;** *PRET (not used)*; *IMPF (not used)*; *FUT (used but regularly formed)*; *IMPER* enclos; *PRP* **enclosant;** *PP* **enclos**

35 **ensuivre (s')** (*defective verb*) *Used only in the following tenses* : *IND* **il s'ensuit;** *SUBJ* **il s'ensuive;** *PRET* **il s'ensuivit;** *IMPF* **il s'ensuivait;** *FUT* **il s'ensuivra;** *PP* **s'ensuivi**

36 **envoyer** : *IND* **j'envoie, tu envoies, il envoie,** nous envoyons, vous envoyez, **ils envoient;** *SUBJ* **j'envoie, tu envoies, il envoie,** nous envoyions, vous envoyiez, **ils envoient;** *FUT* **j'enverrai, tu enverras, il enverra, nous enverrons, vous enverrez, ils enverront;** *IMPER* **envoie**

37 **éteindre** : *IND* **j'éteins, tu éteins, il éteint, nous éteignons, vous éteignez, ils éteignent;** *SUBJ* **j'éteigne, tu éteignes, il éteigne, nous éteignions, vous éteigniez, ils éteignent;** *PRET* **j'éteignis, tu éteignis, il éteignit, nous éteignîmes, vous éteignîtes, ils éteignirent;** *IMPF* **j'éteignais, tu éteignais, il éteignait, nous éteignions, vous éteigniez, ils éteignaient;** *IMPER* **éteins;** *PRP* **éteignant;** *PP* **éteint**

38 **être** : *IND* **je suis, tu es, il est, nous sommes, vous êtes, ils sont;** *SUBJ* **je sois, tu sois, il soit, nous soyons, vous soyez, ils soient;** *PRET* **je fus, tu fus, il fut, nous fûmes, vous fûtes, ils furent;** *IMPF* **j'étais, tu étais, il était, nous étions, vous étiez, ils étaient;** *FUT* **je serai, tu seras, il sera, nous serons, vous serez, ils seront;** *IMPER* **sois;** *PRP* **étant;** *PP* **été**

39 **exclure** : *IND* **j'exclus, tu exclus, il exclut, nous excluons, vous excluez, ils excluent;** *PRET* **j'exclus, tu exclus, il exclut, nous exclûmes, vous exclûtes, ils exclurent;** *IMPER* **exclus;** *PP* **exclu**

40 **extraire** : *IND* j'extrais, tu extrais, il extrait, **nous extrayons, vous extrayez,** ils extraient; *SUBJ* j'extraie, tu extraies, il extraie, **nous extrayions, vous extrayiez,** ils extraient; *PRET* (*not used*); *IMPF* **j'extrayais, tu extrayais, il extrayait, nous extrayions, vous extrayiez, ils extrayaient;** *PRP* **extrayant;** *PP* **extrait**

41 **faillir** (*defective verb*) *Used only in the infinitive and as a PP* **failli**

42 **faire** : *IND* je fais, tu fais, il fait, **nous faisons, vous faites, ils font;** *SUBJ* **je fasse, tu fasses, il fasse, nous fassions, vous fassiez, ils fassent;** *PRET* **je fis, tu fis, il fit, nous fîmes, vous fîtes, ils firent;** *IMPF* **je faisais, tu faisais, il faisait, nous faisions, vous faisiez, ils faisaient;** *FUT* **je ferai, tu feras, il fera, nous ferons, vous ferez, ils feront;** *PRP* **faisant;** *PP* **fait**

43 **falloir** (*defective verb*) *Used only in the following tenses* : *IND* **il faut;** *SUBJ* **il faille;** *PRET* **il fallut;** *IMPF* **il fallait;** *FUT* **il faudra;** *IMPER* (*not used*); *PRP* (*not used*); *PP* **fallu**

44 **forfaire** (*defective verb*) *Used only in the infinitive and in the following tenses* : *IND* **il forfait;** *PP* **forfait**

45 **frire** (*defective verb*) *Used only in the following tenses* : *IND* **je fris, tu fris, il frit;** *FUT* je frirai, tu friras, il frira, nous frirons, vous frirez, ils friront; *IMPER* **fris;** *PP* **frit**

46 **fuir** : *IND* je fuis, tu fuis, il fuit, **nous fuyons, vous fuyez, ils fuient;** *SUBJ* je fuie, tu fuies, il fuie, **nous fuyions, vous fuyiez, ils fuient;** *PRET* je fuis, tu fuis, il fuit, **nous fuîmes, vous fuîtes, ils fuirent;** *IMPF* **je fuyais, tu fuyais, il fuyait, nous fuyions, vous fuyiez, ils fuyaient;** *PRP* **fuyant;** *PP* **fui**

47 **gésir** (*defective verb*) *Used only in the following tenses* : *IND* **je gis, tu gis, il gît, nous gisons, vous gisez, ils gisent;** *IMPF* **je gisais, tu gisais, il gisait, nous gisions, vous gisiez, ils gisaient;** *PRP* **gisant**

48 **haïr** : *IND* **je hais, tu hais, il hait, nous haïssons, vous haïssez, ils haïssent;** *SUBJ* **je haïsse, tu haïsses, il haïsse, nous haïssions, vous haïssiez, ils haïssent;** *PRET* **je haïs, tu haïs, il haït, nous haïmes, vous haïtes, ils haïrent;** *IMPF* **je haïssais, tu haïssais, il haïssait, nous haïssions, vous haïssiez, ils haïssaient;** *IMPER* **hais;** *PRP* **haïssant;** *PP* **haï**

49 **instruire** : *IND* j'instruis, tu instruis, il instruit, **nous instruisons, vous instruisez, ils instruisent;** *SUBJ* **j'instruise, tu instruises, il instruise, nous instruisions, vous instruisiez, ils instruisent;** *PRET* **j'instruisis, tu instruisis, il instruisit, nous instruisîmes, vous instruisîtes, ils instruisirent;** *IMPF* **j'instruisais, tu instruisais, il instruisait, nous instruisions, vous instruisiez, ils instruisaient;** *PRP* **instruisant;** *PP* **instruit**

50 **joindre** : *IND* **je joins, tu joins, il joint, nous joignons, vous joignez, ils joignent;** *SUBJ* **je joigne, tu joignes, il joigne, nous joignions, vous joigniez, ils joignent;** *PRET* **je joignis, tu joignis, il joignit, nous joignîmes, vous joignîtes, ils joignirent;** *IMPF* **je joignais, tu joignais, il joignait, nous joignions, vous joigniez, ils joignaient;** *IMPER* **joins;** *PRP* **joignant;** *PP* **joint**

51 **lire** : *IND* je lis, tu lis, il lit, **nous lisons, vous lisez, ils lisent;** *SUBJ* **je lise, tu lises, il lise, nous lisions, vous lisiez, ils lisent;** *PRET* **je lus, tu lus, il lut, nous lûmes, vous lûtes, ils lurent;** *IMPF* **je lisais, tu lisais, il lisait, nous lisions, vous lisiez, ils lisaient;** *PRP* **lisant;** *PP* **lu**

52 **mener** : *IND* **je mène, tu mènes, il mène,** nous menons, vous menez, **ils mènent;** *SUBJ* **je mène, tu mènes, il mène,** nous menions, vous meniez, **ils mènent;** *FUT* **je mènerai, tu mèneras, il mènera, nous mènerons, vous mènerez, ils mèneront;** *IMPER* **mène**

53 **mettre** : *IND* **je mets, tu mets, il met,** nous mettons, vous mettez, ils mettent; *PRET* **je mis, tu mis, il mit, nous mîmes, vous mîtes, ils mirent;** *IMPER* **mets;** *PP* **mis**

54 **moudre** : *IND* je mouds, tu mouds, il moud, **nous moulons, vous moulez, ils moulent;** *SUBJ* **je moule, tu moules, il moule, nous moulions, vous mouliez, ils moulent;** *PRET* **je moulus, tu moulus, il moulut, nous moulûmes, vous moulûtes, ils moulurent;** *IMPF* **je moulais, tu moulais, il moulait, nous moulions, vous mouliez, ils moulaient;** *PRP* **moulant;** *PP* **moulu**

55 **mourir** : *IND* **je meurs, tu meurs, il meurt,** nous mourons, vous mourez, **ils meurent;** *SUBJ* **je meure, tu meures, il meure,** nous mourions, vous mouriez, **ils meurent;** *PRET* **je mourus, tu mourus, il mourut, nous mourûmes, vous mourûtes, ils moururent;** *FUT* **je mourrai, tu mourras, il mourra, nous mourrons, vous mourrez, ils mourront;** *IMPER* **meurs;** *PRP* **mourant;** *PP* **mort**

56 **mouvoir** : *IND* **je meus, tu meus, il meut,** nous mouvons, vous mouvez, **ils meuvent;** *SUBJ* **je meuve, tu meuves, il meuve,** nous mouvions, vous mouviez, **ils meuvent;** *PRET* **je mus, tu mus, il mut, nous mûmes, vous mûtes, ils murent;** *IMPER* **meus;** *PP* **mû**

57 **naître** : *IND* **je nais, tu nais, il naît, nous naissons, vous naissez, ils naissent;** *SUBJ* **je naisse, tu naisses, il naisse, nous naissions, vous naissiez, ils naissent;** *PRET* **je naquis, tu naquis, il naquit, nous naquîmes, vous naquîtes, ils naquirent;** *IMPF* **je naissais, tu naissais, il naissait, nous naissions, vous naissiez, ils naissaient;** *IMPER* **nais;** *PRP* **naissant;** *PP* **né**

58 **nettoyer** : *IND* **je nettoie, tu nettoies, il nettoie,** nous nettoyons, vous nettoyez, **ils nettoient;** *SUBJ* **je nettoie, tu nettoies, il nettoie,** nous nettoyions, vous nettoyiez, **ils nettoient;** *FUT* **je nettoierai, tu nettoieras, il nettoiera, nous nettoierons, vous nettoierez, ils nettoieront;** *IMPER* **nettoie**

59 **oindre** (*defective verb*) *Used only in the infinitive and as a PP* **oint**

60 **ouïr** (*defective verb*) *Used only in the infinitive and as a pp* **ouï**

61 **paître** (*defective verb*) *Used only in the following tenses* : *IND* **je pais, tu pais, il paît, nous paissons, vous paissez, ils paissent;** *SUBJ* **je paisse, tu paisses, il paisse, nous paissions, vous paissiez, ils paissent;** *PRET* (*not used*); *IMPF* **je paissais, tu paissais, il paissait, nous paissions, vous paissiez, ils paissaient;** *FUT* (*used but regular*); *IMPER* **pais;** *PRP* **paissant;** *PP* (*not used*)

62 **parfaire** (*defective verb*) *Used only in the infinitive and in the following tenses IND* **il parfait;** *PP* **parfait**

63 **perdre** : *IND* je perds, tu perds, **il perd**, nous perdons, vous perdez, ils perdent; *PRET* **je perdis, tu perdis, il perdit, nous perdîmes, vous perdîtes, ils perdirent;** *PP* **perdu**

64 **piéger** : *IND* **je piège, tu pièges, il piège, nous piégeons,** vous piégez, **ils piègent;** *SUBJ* **je piège, tu pièges, il piège,** nous piégions, vous piégiez, **ils piègent;** *PRET* **je piégeai, tu piégeas, il piégea, nous piégeâmes, vous piégeâtes, ils piégèrent;** *IMPF* **je piégeais, tu piégeais, il piégeait,** nous piégions, vous piégiez, **ils piégeaient;** *IMPER* **piège;** *PRP* **piégeant;** *PP* **piégé**

65 **plaindre** : *IND* je plains, tu plains, il plaint, **nous plaignons, vous plaignez, ils plaignent;** *SUBJ* **je plaigne, tu plaignes, il plaigne, nous plagnions, vous plagniez, ils plaignent;** *PRET* **je plaignis, tu plaignis, il plaignit, nous plaignîmes, vous plaignîtes, ils plaignirent;** *IMPF* **je plaignais, tu plaignais, il plaignait, nous plaignions, vous plaigniez, ils plaignaient;** *PRP* **plaignant;** *PP* **plaint**

66 **plaire** : *IND* je plais, tu plais, **il plaît, nous plaisons, vous plaisez, ils plaisent;** *SUBJ* **je plaise, tu plaises, il plaise, nous plaisions, vous plaisiez, ils plaisent;** *PRET* **je plus, tu plus, il plut, nous plûmes, vous plûtes, ils plurent;** *IMPF* **je plaisais, tu plaisais, il plaisait, nous plaisions, vous plaisiez, ils plaisaient;** *PRP* **plaisant;** *PP* **plu**

67 **pleuvoir** (*defective verb*) *Used in the infinitive and in the following tenses IND* **il pleut, ils pleuvent** (*only in the figurative*); *SUBJ* **il pleuve, ils pleuvent** (*only in the figurative*); *PRET* **il plut;** *IMPF* **il pleuvait, ils pleuvaient** (*only in the figurative*); *FUT* **il pleuvra;** *IMPER* (*not used*); *PRP* **pleuvant;** *PP* **plu**

68 **pourvoir** : *IND* **je pourvois, tu pourvois, il pourvoit, nous pourvoyons, vous pourvoyez, ils pourvoient;** *SUBJ* **je pourvoie, tu pourvoies, il pourvoie, nous pourvoyions, vous pourvoyiez, ils pourvoient;** *PRET* **je pourvus, tu pourvus, il pourvut, nous pourvûmes, vous pourvûtes, ils pourvurent;** *IMPF* **je pourvoyais, tu pourvoyais, il pourvoyait, nous pourvoyions, vous pourvoyiez, ils pourvoyaient;** *FUT* **je pourvoirai, tu pourvoiras, il pourvoira, nous pourvoirons, vous pourvoirez, ils pourvoiront;** *IMPER* **pourvois;** *PRP* **pourvoyant;** *PP* **pourvu**

69 **pouvoir** : *IND* **je peux** *or* **je puis, tu peux, il peut,** nous pouvons, vous pouvez, **ils peuvent;** *SUBJ* **je puisse, tu puisses, il puisse, nous puissions, vous puissiez, ils puissent;** *PRET* **je pus, tu pus, il put, nous pûmes, vous pûtes, ils purent;** *FUT* **je pourrai, tu pourras, il pourra, nous pourrons, vous pourrez, ils pourront;** *IMPER* (*not used*); *PP* **pu**

70 **prendre** : *IND* je prends, tu prends, **il prend, nous prenons, vous prenez, ils prennent;** *SUBJ* **je prenne, tu prennes, il prenne, nous prenions, vous preniez, ils prennent;** *PRET* **je pris, tu pris, il prit, nous prîmes,**

vous prîtes, ils prirent; *IMPF* **je prenais, tu prenais, il prenait, nous prenions, vous preniez, ils prenaient;** *PRP* **prenant;** *PP* **pris**

71 **prévaloir :** *IND* **je prévaux, tu prévaux, il prévaut,** nous prévalons, vous prévalez, ils prévalent; *PRET* **je prévalus, tu prévalus, il prévalut, nous prévalûmes, vous prévalûtes, ils prévalurent;** *FUT* **je prévaudrai, tu prévaudras, il prévaudra, nous prévaudrons, vous prévaudrez, ils prévaudront;** *IMPER* **prévaux;** *PP* **prévalu**

72 **rassir** (*defective verb) Used only in the infinitive and as a* *PP* **rassis**

73 **ravoir** (*defective verb) Used only in the infinitive*

74 **résoudre :** *INF* **je résous, tu résous, il résout, nous résolvons, vous résolvez, ils résolvent;** *SUBJ* **je résolve, tu résolves, il résolve, nous résolvions, vous résolviez, ils résolvent;** *PRET* **je résolus, tu résolus, il résolut, nous résolûmes, vous résolûtes, ils résolurent;** *IMPF* **je résolvais, tu résolvais, il résolvait, nous résolvions, vous résolviez, ils résolvaient;** *IMPER* **résous;** *PRP* **résolvant;** *PP* **résolu**

75 **résulter** (*defective verb) Used only in the infinitive and in the following tenses* **:** *IND* **il résulte;** *PRP* **résultant**

76 **rire :** *IND* **je ris, tu ris, il rit, nous rions, vous riez, ils rient;** *SUBJ* je rie, tu ries, il rie, **nous riions, vous riiez,** ils rient; *PRET* **je ris, tu ris, il rit, nous rîmes, vous rîtes, ils rirent;** *IMPER* **ris;** *PP* **ri**

77 **rompre :** *IND* je romps, tu romps, **il rompt**, nous rompons, vous rompez, ils rompent; *PRET* **je rompis, tu rompis, il rompit, nous rompîmes, vous rompîtes, ils rompirent;** *PP* **rompu**

78 **saillir :** *IND* **je saille, tu sailles, il saille,** nous saillons, vous saillez, ils saillent; *PRET* **je saillis, tu sallis, il saillit, nous saillîmes, vous saillîtes, ils saillirent;** *FUT* **je saillerai, tu sailleras, il saillera, nous saillerons, vous saillerez, ils sailleront;** *IMPER* **saille**

79 **savoir :** *IND* **je sais, tu sais, il sait,** nous savons, vous savez, ils savent; *SUBJ* **je sache, tu saches, il sache, nous sachions, vous sachiez, ils sachent;** *PRET* **je sus, tu sus, il sut, nous sûmes, vous sûtes, ils surent;** *FUT* **je saurai, tu sauras, il saura, nous saurons, vous saurez, ils sauront;** *IMPER* **sache, sachons, sachez;** *PRP* **sachant;** *PP* **su**

80 **seoir** (*defective verb) Used only in the following tenses* **:** *IND* **il sied, ils siéent;** *SUBJ* **il siée, ils siéent;** *PRET* (*not used*); *IMPF* **il seyait, ils seyaient;** *FUT* **il siéra, ils siéront;** *IMPER* (*not used*); *PRP* **séant** *or* **seyant;** *PP* (*not used*)

81 **servir :** *IND* **je sers, tu sers, il sert,** nous servons, vous servez, ils servent; *PRET* **je servis, tu servis, il servit, nous servîmes, vous servîtes, ils servirent;** *FUT* **je servirai, tu serviras, il servira, nous servirons, vous servirez, ils serviront;** *IMPER* **sers;** *PP* **servi**

82 **sortir :** *IND* **je sors, tu sors, il sort,** nous sortons, vous sortez, ils sortent; *PRET* **je sortis, tu sortis, il sortit, nous sortîmes, vous sortîtes, ils sortirent;** *FUT* **je sortirai, tu sortiras, il sortira, nous sortirons, vous sortirez, ils sortiront;** *IMPER* **sors;** *PRP* **sortant;** *PP* **sorti**

83 **souffrir :** *IND* **je souffre, tu souffres, il souffre,** nous souffrons, vous souffrez, ils souffrent; *PRET* **je souffris, tu souffris, il souffrit, nous souffrîmes, vous souffrîtes, ils souffrirent;** *FUT* **je souffrirai, tu souffriras, il souffrira, nous souffrirons, vous souffrirez, ils souffriront;** *IMPER* **souffre;** *PP* **souffert**

84 **sourdre** (*defective verb) Used only in the infinitive and in the following tenses* **:** *IND* **il sourd, ils sourdent;** *IMPF* **il sourdait, ils sourdaient**

85 **stupéfaire** (*defective verb) Used only in the following tense* *PP* **stupéfié**

86 **suffire :** *IND* je suffis, tu suffis, il suffit, **nous suffisons, vous suffisez, ils suffisent;** *SUBJ* **je suffise, tu suffises, il suffise, nous suffisions, vous suffisiez, ils suffisent;** *PRET* **je suffis, tu suffis, il suffit, nous suffîmes, vous suffîtes, ils suffirent;** *IMPF* **je suffisais, tu suffisais, il suffisait, nous suffisions, vous suffisiez, ils suffisaient;** *PRP* **suffisant;** *PP* **suffi**

87 **suggérer :** *IND* **je suggère, tu suggères, il suggère,** nous suggérons, vous suggérez, **ils suggèrent;** *SUBJ* **je suggère, tu suggères, il suggère,** nous suggérions, vous suggériez, **ils suggèrent;** *IMPER* **suggère**

88 **suivre :** *IND* **je suis, tu suis, il suit,** nous suivons, vous suivez, ils suivent; *PRET* **je suivis, tu suivis, il suivit, nous suivîmes, vous suivîtes, ils suivirent;** *IMPER* **suis;** *PP* **suivi**

89 **suppléer :** *IND* **je supplée, tu supplées, il supplée, nous suppléons, vous suppléez, ils suppléent;** *SUBJ* **je supplée, tu supplées, il supplée, nous suppléions, vous suppléiez, ils suppléent;** *PRET* **je suppléai, tu suppléas, il suppléa, nous suppléâmes, vous suppléâtes, ils suppléèrent;** *FUT* **je suppléerai, tu suppléeras, il suppléera, nous suppléerons, vous suppléerez, ils suppléeront;** *IMPER* **supplée;** *PP* **suppléé**

90 **surseoir :** *IND* **je sursois, tu sursois, il sursoit, nous sursoyons, vous sursoyez, ils sursoient;** *SUBJ* **je sursoie, tu sursoies, il sursoie, nous sursoyions, vous sursoyiez, ils sursoient;** *PRET* **je sursis, tu sursis, il sursit, nous sursîmes, vous sursîtes, ils sursirent;** *IMPF* **je sursoyais, tu sursoyais, il sursoyait, nous sursoyions, vous sursoyiez, ils sursoyaient;** *FUT* **je surseoirai, tu surseoiras, il surseoira, nous surseoirons, vous surseoirez, ils surseoiront;** *IMPER* **sursois;** *PRP* **sursoyant;** *PP* **sursis**

91 **taire :** *IND* je tais, tu tais, **il tait, nous taisons, vous taisez, ils taisent;** *SUBJ* **je taise, tu taises, il taise, nous taisions, vous taisiez, ils taisent;** *PRET* **je tus, tu tus, il tut, nous tûmes, vous tûtes, ils turent;** *IMPF* **je taisais, tu taisais, il taisait, nous taisions, vous taisiez, ils taisaient;** *PRP* **taisant;** *PP* **tu**

92 **tenir :** *IND* **je tiens, tu tiens, il tient,** nous tenons, vous tenez, **ils tiennent;** *SUBJ* **je tienne, tu tiennes, il tienne,** nous tenions, vous teniez, **ils tiennent;** *PRET* **je tins, tu tins, il tint, nous tînmes, vous tîntes, ils tinrent;** *FUT* **je tiendrai, tu tiendras, il tiendra, nous tiendrons, vous tiendrez, ils tiendront;** *IMPER* **tiens;** *PP* **tenu**

93 **tressaillir :** *IND* **je tressaille, tu tressailles, il tressaille,** nous tressaillons, vous tressaillez, ils tressaillent; *PRET* **je tressaillis, tu tressaillis, il tressaillit, nous tressaillîmes, vous tressaîllites, ils tressaillirent;** *FUT* **je tressaillirai, tu tressailliras, il tressaillira, nous tressaillirons, vous tressaillirez, ils tressailliront;** *IMPF* **tressaille;** *PP* **tressailli**

94 **vaincre :** *IND* **je vaincs, tu vaincs, il vainc, nous vainquons, vous vainquez, ils vainquent;** *SUBJ* **je vainque, tu vainques, il vainque, nous vainquions, vous vainquiez, ils vainquent;** *PRET* **je vainquis, tu vainquis, il vainquit, nous vainquîmes, vous vainquîtes, ils vainquirent;** *IMPF* **je vainquais, tu vainquais, il vainquait, nous vainquions, vous vainquiez, ils vainquaient;** *IMPER* **vaincs;** *PRP* **vainquant;** *PP* **vaincu**

95 **valoir :** *IND* **je vaux, tu vaux, il vaut,** nous valons, vous valez, ils valent; *SUBJ* **je vaille, tu vailles, il vaille,** nous valions, vous valiez, **ils vaillent;** *PRET* **je valus, tu valus, il valut, nous valûmes, vous valûtes, ils valurent;** *FUT* **je vaudrai, tu vaudras, il vaudra, nous vaudrons, vous vaudrez, ils vaudront;** *IMPER* **vaux;** *PP* **valu**

96 **vérifier :** *SUBJ* je vérifie, tu vérifies, il vérifie, **nous vérifiions, vous vérifiiez,** ils vérifient; *IMPF* je vérifiais, tu vérifiais, il vérifiait, **nous vérifiions, vous vérifiiez,** ils vérifiaient

97 **vêtir :** *IND* **je vêts, tu vêts, il vêt,** nous vêtons, vous vêtez, ils vêtent; *PRET* **je vêtis, tu vêtis, il vêtit, nous vêtîmes, vous vêtîtes, ils vêtirent;** *FUT* **je vêtirai, tu vêtiras, il vêtira, nous vêtirons, vous vêtirez, ils vêtiront;** *IMPER* **vêts;** *PP* **vêtu**

98 **vivre :** *IND* **je vis, tu vis, il vit,** nous vivons, vous vivez, ils vivent; *PRET* **je vécus, tu vécus, il vécut, nous vécûmes, vous vécûtes, ils vécurent;** *IMPER* **vis;** *PP* **vécu**

99 **voir :** *IND* je vois, tu vois, il voit, **nous voyons, vous voyez,** ils voient; *SUBJ* je voie, tu voies, il voie, **nous voyions, vous voyiez,** ils voient; *PRET* **je vis, tu vis, il vit, nous vîmes, vous vîtes, ils virent;** *IMPF* **je voyais, tu voyais, il voyait, nous voyions, vous voyiez, ils voyaient;** *FUT* **je verrai, tu verras, il verra, nous verrons, vous verrez, ils verront;** *PRP* **voyant;** *PP* **vu**

100 **vouloir :** *IND* **je veux, tu veux, il veut,** nous voulons, vous voulez, **ils veulent;** *SUBJ* **je veuille, tu veuilles, il veuille,** nous voulions, vous vouliez; **ils veuillent;** *PRET* **je voulus, tu voulus, il voulut, nous voulûmes, vous voulûtes, ils voulurent;** *FUT* **je voudrai, tu voudras, il voudra, nous voudrons, vous voudrez, ils voudront;** *IMPER* **veux** *or* **veuille;** *PP* **voulu**

Irregular English Verbs

INFINITIVE	PAST	PAST PARTICIPLE
arise	arose	arisen
awake	awoke	awoken *or* awaked
be	was, were	been
bear	bore	borne
beat	beat	beaten *or* beat
become	became	become
befall	befell	befallen
begin	began	begun
behold	beheld	beheld
bend	bent	bent
beseech	beseeched *or* besought	beseeched *or* besought
beset	beset	beset
bet	bet	bet
bid	bade *or* bid	bidden *or* bid
bind	bound	bound
bite	bit	bitten
bleed	bled	bled
blow	blew	blown
break	broke	broken
breed	bred	bred
bring	brought	brought
build	built	built
burn	burned *or* burnt	burned *or* burnt
burst	burst	burst
buy	bought	bought
can	could	—
cast	cast	cast
catch	caught	caught
choose	chose	chosen
cling	clung	clung
come	came	come
cost	cost	cost
creep	crept	crept
cut	cut	cut
deal	dealt	dealt
dig	dug	dug
do	did	done
draw	drew	drawn
dream	dreamed *or* dreamt	dreamed *or* dreamt
drink	drank	drunk *or* drank
drive	drove	driven
dwell	dwelled *or* dwelt	dwelled *or* dwelt
eat	ate	eaten
fall	fell	fallen
feed	fed	fed
feel	felt	felt
fight	fought	fought
find	found	found
flee	fled	fled
fling	flung	flung
fly	flew	flown
forbid	forbade	forbidden
forecast	forecast	forecast
forego	forewent	foregone
foresee	foresaw	foreseen
foretell	foretold	foretold
forget	forgot	forgotten *or* forgot
forgive	forgave	forgiven
forsake	forsook	forsaken
freeze	froze	frozen
get	got	got *or* gotten
give	gave	given
go	went	gone
grind	ground	ground
grow	grew	grown
hang	hung	hung
have	had	had
hear	heard	heard
hide	hid	hidden *or* hid
hit	hit	hit
hold	held	held
hurt	hurt	hurt
keep	kept	kept
kneel	knelt *or* kneeled	knelt *or* kneeled
know	knew	known
lay	laid	laid
lead	led	led
leap	leaped *or* leapt	leaped *or* leapt
leave	left	left
lend	lent	lent
let	let	let
lie	lay	lain
light	lit *or* lighted	lit *or* lighted
lose	lost	lost

INFINITIVE	PAST	PAST PARTICIPLE
make	made	made
may	might	—
mean	meant	meant
meet	met	met
mow	mowed	mowed *or* mown
pay	paid	paid
put	put	put
quit	quit	quit
read	read	read
rend	rent	rent
rid	rid	rid
ride	rode	ridden
ring	rang	rung
rise	rose	risen
run	ran	run
saw	sawed	sawed *or* sawn
say	said	said
see	saw	seen
seek	sought	sought
sell	sold	sold
send	sent	sent
set	set	set
shake	shook	shaken
shall	should	—
shear	sheared	sheared *or* shorn
shed	shed	shed
shine	shone *or* shined	shone *or* shined
shoot	shot	shot
show	showed	shown *or* showed
shrink	shrank *or* shrunk	shrunk *or* shrunken
shut	shut	shut
sing	sang *or* sung	sung
sink	sank *or* sunk	sunk
sit	sat	sat
slay	slew	slain
sleep	slept	slept
slide	slid	slid
sling	slung	slung
smell	smelled *or* smelt	smelled *or* smelt
sow	sowed	sown *or* sowed
speak	spoke	spoken
speed	sped *or* speeded	sped *or* speeded
spell	spelled	spelled
spend	spent	spent
spill	spilled	spilled
spin	spun	spun
spit	spit *or* spat	spit *or* spat
split	split	split
spoil	spoiled	spoiled
spread	spread	spread
spring	sprang *or* sprung	sprung
stand	stood	stood
steal	stole	stolen
stick	stuck	stuck
sting	stung	stung
stink	stank *or* stunk	stunk
stride	strode	stridden
strike	struck	struck
swear	swore	sworn
sweep	swept	swept
swell	swelled	swelled *or* swollen
swim	swam	swum
swing	swung	swung
take	took	taken
teach	taught	taught
tear	tore	torn
tell	told	told
think	thought	thought
throw	threw	thrown
thrust	thrust	thrust
tread	trod	trodden *or* trod
wake	woke	woken *or* waked
waylay	waylaid	waylaid
wear	wore	worn
weave	wove *or* weaved	woven *or* weaved
wed	wedded	wedded
weep	wept	wept
will	would	—
win	won	won
wind	wound	wound
withdraw	withdrew	withdrawn
withhold	withheld	withheld
withstand	withstood	withstood
wring	wrung	wrung
write	wrote	written

Abbreviations in This Work

adj adjective
adv adverb
adv phr adverbial phrase
Bel Belgium
Brit Great Britain
Can Canada
conj conjunction
conj phr conjunctive phrase
esp especially
etc et cetera
f feminine
fam familiar or colloquial
fpl feminine plural
interj interjection
m masculine
mf masculine or feminine
mpl masculine plural
n noun
nf feminine noun
nfpl feminine plural noun
nfs & pl invariable singular or plural feminine noun
nm masculine noun
nmf masculine or feminine noun
nmfpl plural noun invariable for gender
nmfs & pl noun invariable for both gender and number
nmpl masculine plural noun
nms & pl invariable singular or plural masculine noun
npl plural noun
ns & pl noun invariable for plural
pl plural
pp past participle
prep preposition
prep phr prepositional phrase
pron pronoun
qqch quelque chose (something)
qqn quelqu'un (someone)
s singular
s.o. someone
sth something
Switz Switzerland
usu usually
v verb (transitive and intransitive)
v aux auxiliary verb
vi intransitive verb
v impers impersonal verb
vr reflexive verb
vt transitive verb

Pronunciation Symbols

VOWELS

æ ask, bat, glad
ɑ cot, bomb
ɑ̃ *French* chant, ennui
a *New England* aunt, *British* ask, glass
e *French* été, aider, chez
ɛ egg, bet, fed
ɛ̃ *French* lapin, main
ə about, javelin, Alabama
ə when italicized as in *ə*l, *ə*m, *ə*n, indicates a syllabic pronunciation of the consonant as in bottle, prism, button
i very, any, thirty
iː eat, bead, bee
ɪ id, bid, pit
o Ohio, yellower, potato
oː oats, own, zone, blow
ɔ awl, maul, caught, paw
ɔ̃ *French* ombre, mon
ʊ sure, should, could
u *French* ouvert, chou, rouler
uː boot, two, coo
ʌ under, putt, bud
y *French* pur, *German* fühlen
eɪ eight, wade, bay
aɪ ice, bite, tie
aʊ out, gown, plow
ɔɪ oyster, coil, boy
ər further, stir
ø *French* deux, *German* Höhe
œ *French* bœuf, *German* Gött
œ̃ *French* lundi, parfum

CONSONANTS

b baby, labor, cab
d day, ready, kid
ʤ just, badger, fudge
ð then, either, bathe
f foe, tough, buff
g go, bigger, bag
h hot, aha
j yes, vineyard
k cat, keep, lacquer, flock
l law, hollow, boil
m mat, hemp, hammer, rim
n new, tent, tenor, run
ŋ rung, hang, swinger
ɲ *French* digne, agneau
p pay, lapse, top
r rope, burn, tar
s sad, mist, kiss
ʃ shoe, mission, slush
t toe, button, mat
t̬ indicates that some speakers of English pronounce this sound as a voiced alveolar flap, as in later, catty, battle
ʧ choose, batch
θ thin, ether, bath
v vat, never, cave
w wet, software
ɥ *French* cuir, appui
x *German* Bach, *Scottish* loch
z zoo, easy, buzz
ʒ azure, beige
h, k, p, t when italicized indicate sounds which are present in the pronunciation of some speakers of English but absent in the pronunciation of others, so that *whence* [ˈ*h*wɛn*t*s] can be pronounced as [ˈhwɛns], [ˈhwɛnts], [ˈwɛnts], or [ˈwɛns].

OTHER SYMBOLS

ˈ high stress **pen**manship
ˌ low stress penman**ship**
ʼ aspiration; when used before French words in *h-*, indicates absence of liaison, as in *le héros* [lə ʼero]
( ) indicate sounds that are present in the pronunciation of some speakers of French but absent in that of others, as in *cenellier* [s(ə)nɛlje], *but* [by(t)]

French-English

A

a [a] *nm* : a, first letter of the alphabet
à [a] *prep* **1** : to **2 ~ deux heures** : at two o'clock **3 ~ la** : in the manner of, like **4 ~ l'heure** : per hour **5 ~ mon avis** : in my opinion **6 ~ pied** : on foot **7 ~ vendre** : for sale **8 la femme aux yeux verts** : the woman with green eyes **9 un ami ~ moi** : a friend of mine **10 voler aux riches** : steal from the rich
abaisser [abese] *vt* **1** : lower, reduce **2** HUMILIER : humble — **s'abaisser** *vr* **1** : lower oneself **2 ~ à** : stoop to
abandonner [abɑ̃dɔne] *vt* : abandon — **s'abandonner** *vr* **1** : neglect oneself **2 ~ à** : give oneself up to — **abandon** [abɑ̃dɔ̃] *nm* **1** : abandonment, neglect **2** DÉSINVOLTURE : abandon
abasourdir [abazurdir] *vt* : stun
abat–jour [abaʒur] *nms & pl* : lampshade
abats [aba] *nmpl* **1** : entrails **2 ~ de volaille** : giblets
abattant [abatɑ̃] *nm* : flap, leaf
abattis [abati] *nmpl* : giblets
abattoir [abatwar] *nm* : slaughterhouse
abattre [abatr] {12} *vt* **1** : knock down, cut down **2** ÉPUISER : wear out **3** DÉMORALISER : dishearten — **s'abattre** *vr* **1** : fall, crash **2 ~ sur** : descend on — **abattement** [abatmɑ̃] *nm* **1** : reduction, allowance **2** : despondency — **abattu, -tue** [abaty] *adj* : downcast
abbaye [abei] *nf* : abbey — **abbé** [abe] *nm* **1** : abbot **2** PRÊTRE : priest
abcès [apsɛ] *nm* : abscess
abdiquer [abdike] *v* : abdicate — **abdication** [abdikasjɔ̃] *nf* : abdication
abdomen [abdɔmɛn] *nm* : abdomen — **abdominal, -nale** [abdɔminal] *adj, mpl* **-naux** [-no] : abdominal
abécédaire [abesedɛr] *nm* : primer, speller
abeille [abɛj] *nf* : bee
aberrant, -rante [abɛrɑ̃, -rɑ̃t] *adj* : absurd — **aberration** [abɛrasjɔ̃] *nf* : aberration
abêtir [abetir] *vt* : make stupid
abhorrer [abɔre] *vt* : abhor
abîme [abim] *nm* : abyss, depths — **abîmer** [abime] *vt* : spoil, damage — **s'abîmer** *vr* **1** : be spoiled **2** : sink, founder
abject, -jecte [abʒɛkt] *adj* : despicable, abject
abjurer [abʒyre] *vt* : renounce, abjure
abnégation [abnegasjɔ̃] *nf* : self-denial
aboiement [abwamɑ̃] *nm* : barking — **abois** [abwa] *nmpl* **aux ~** : at bay
abolir [abɔlir] *vt* : abolish — **abolition** [abɔlisjɔ̃] *nf* : abolition
abominable [abɔminabl] *adj* : abominable
abonder [abɔ̃de] *vi* : abound — **abondamment** [abɔ̃damɑ̃] *adv* : abundantly — **abondance** [abɔ̃dɑ̃s] *nf* : abundance — **abondant, -dante** [abɔ̃dɑ̃, -dɑ̃t] *adj* : abundant
abonner [abɔne] *vt* : subscribe to — **abonné, -née** [abɔne] *n* : subscriber —**abonnement** [abɔnmɑ̃] *nm* : subscription
aborder [abɔrde] *vt* **1** : approach **2** : tackle, deal with — *vi* : (reach) land — **abord** [abɔr] *nm* **1** : approach **2 d'~** : at first **3 ~s** *nmpl* : surroundings — **abordable** [abɔrdabl] *adj* **1** : approachable **2** : affordable — **abordage** [abɔrdaʒ] *nm* : boarding
aborigène [abɔriʒɛn] *nmf* : aborigine, native — **~** *adj* : aboriginal
abortif, -tive [abɔrtif, -tiv] *adj* : abortive
aboutir [abutir] *vi* **1** : succeed **2 ~ à** : result in — **aboutissement** [abutismɑ̃] *nm* : result
aboyer [abwaje] {58} *vi* : bark
abraser [abraze] *vt* : abrade — **abrasif, -sive** [abrazif, -ziv] *adj* : abrasive
abréger [abreʒe] {64} *vt* : shorten, abridge — **abrégé** [abreʒe] *nm* : summary — **abrègement** [abrɛʒmɑ̃] *nm* : abridgment
abreuver [abrœve] *vt* **1** : water **2 ~ de** : shower with — **s'abreuver** *vr* : drink — **abreuvoir** [abrœvwar] *nm* : watering place
abréviation [abrevjasjɔ̃] *nf* : abbreviation
abri [abri] *nm* **1** : shelter **2 à l'~** : under cover — **abriter** [abrite] *vt* **1** : shelter **2** HÉBERGER : house
abricot [abriko] *nm* : apricot
abrier [abrije] {96} *vt Can* : cover
abroger [abrɔʒe] {17} *vt* : repeal
abrupt, -brupte [abrypt] *adj* **1** ESCARPÉ : steep **2** BRUSQUE : abrupt
abrutir [abrytir] *vt* : make stupid — **abruti, -tie** [abryti] *n fam* : fool, idiot
absenter [apsɑ̃te] *v* **s'absenter** *vr* : leave, go away — **absence** [apsɑ̃s] *nf* : absence — **absent, -sente** [apsɑ̃, -sɑ̃t] *adj* : absent — **~** *n* : absentee
absolu, -lue [apsɔly] *adj* : absolute — **absolu** *nm* : absolute — **absolument** [-lymɑ̃] *adv* : absolutely
absolution [apsɔlysjɔ̃] *nf* : absolution
absorber [apsɔrbe] *vt* **1** : absorb **2** : take (medicine) — **absorbant, -bante** [apsɔrbɑ̃, -bɑ̃t] *adj* **1** : absorbent **2** : engrossing — **absorption** [apsɔrpsjɔ̃] *nf* : absorption
absoudre [apsudr] {1} *vt* : absolve
abstenir [apstənir] {92} *v* **s'abstenir** *vr* **1** : abstain **2 ~ de** : refrain from — **abstinence** [apstinɑ̃s] *nf* : abstinence
abstraction [apstraksjɔ̃] *nf* **1** : abstraction **2 faire ~ de** : set aside — **abstraire** [apstrɛr] {40} *vt* : abstract — **abstrait, -traite** [apstrɛ, -trɛt] *adj* : abstract — **abstrait** *nm* : abstract
absurde [apsyrd] *adj* : absurd — **absurdité** [apsyrdite] *nf* : absurdity
abuser [abyze] *vt* : deceive — *vi* **~ de 1** : misuse **2** : exploit — **s'abuser** *vr* : be mistaken — **abusif, -sive** [abyzif, -ziv] *adj* **1** EXAGÉRÉ : excessive **2** IMPROPRE : incorrect
académie [akademi] *nf* : academy — **académique** [akademik] *adj* : academic
Acadien, -dienne [akadjɛ̃, -djɛn] *n* **1** : Acadian **2** : Cajun — **acadien, -dienne** *adj* **1** : Acadian **2** : Cajun
acajou [akaʒu] *nm* : mahogany
acariâtre [akarjatr] *adj* : cantankerous
accabler [akable] *vt* **1** ÉCRASER : overwhelm **2** : condemn — **accablant, -blante** [akablɑ̃, -blɑ̃t] *adj* : overwhelming — **accablement** [akabləmɑ̃] *nm* : despondency
accalmie [akalmi] *nf* : lull
accaparer [akapare] *vt* : monopolize
accéder [aksede] {87} *vi* **1 ~ à** : reach, obtain **2 ~ à** : accede to
accélérer [akselere] {87} *v* : accelerate — **accélérateur** *nm* : accelerator — **accélération** [akselerasjɔ̃] *nf* : acceleration
accent [aksɑ̃] *nm* **1** : accent **2** : stress, emphasis — **accentuer** [aksɑ̃tɥe] *vt* **1** : accent, stress **2** : emphasize — **s'accentuer** *vr* : become more pronounced
accepter [aksɛpte] *vt* : accept, agree to — **acceptable** [aksɛptabl] *adj* : acceptable — **acceptation** [aksɛptasjɔ̃] *nf* : acceptance
acception [aksɛpsjɔ̃] *nf* : sense, meaning
accès [aksɛ] *nm* **1** : access **2** : entry **3** CRISE : fit, attack — **accessible** [aksɛsibl] *adj* : accessible
accession [aksɛsjɔ̃] *nf* **~ à** : accession to, attainment of
accessoire [aksɛswar] *nm* **1** : accessory **2** : prop — **~** *adj* : incidental, secondary
accident [aksidɑ̃] *nm* : accident — **accidenté, -tée** [aksidɑ̃te] *adj* **1** : damaged, injured **2** : rough, uneven — **~** *n* : accident victim — **accidentel, -telle** [aksidɑ̃tɛl] *adj* : accidental — **accidentellement** [-tɛlmɑ̃] *adv* : accidentally
acclamer [aklame] *vt* : acclaim, cheer — **acclamation** [aklamasjɔ̃] *nf* : cheering
acclimater [aklimate] *vt* : acclimatize — **s'acclimater** *vr* : adapt
accolade [akɔlad] *nf* **1** ÉTREINTE : embrace **2** : brace sign, bracket
accommoder [akɔmɔde] *vt* : accommodate — **s'accommoder** *vr* **~ de** : put up with — **accommodant, -dante** [akɔmɔdɑ̃, -dɑ̃t] *adj* : obliging — **accommodement** [akɔmɔdmɑ̃] *nm* : compromise
accompagner [akɔ̃paɲe] *vt* : accompany — **accompagnement** [akɔ̃paɲmɑ̃] *nm* : accompaniment
accomplir [akɔ̃plir] *vt* : accomplish — **s'accomplir** *vr* : take place — **accompli, -plie** [akɔ̃pli] *adj* : finished — **accomplissement** [akɔ̃plismɑ̃] *nm* : accomplishment
accordéon [akɔrdeɔ̃] *nm* : accordion
accorder [akɔrde] *vt* **1** : reconcile **2** OCTROYER : grant, bestow — **s'accorder** *vr* : be in agreement — **accord** [akɔr] *nm* **1** : agreement **2** : approval, consent **3** : chord (in music)
accoster [akɔste] *vt* : approach — *vi* : dock, land
accotement [akɔtmɑ̃] *nm* : shoulder (of a road)
accoucher [akuʃe] *vt* : deliver (a baby) — *vi* **1** : be in labor **2 ~ de** : give birth to — **accouchement** [akuʃmɑ̃] *nm* : childbirth
accouder [akude] *v* **s'accouder** *vr* **~ à** *or* **~ sur** : lean (one's elbows) on — **accoudoir** [akudwar] *nm* : armrest
accoupler [akuple] *vt* : couple, link — **s'accoupler** *vr* : mate — **accouplement** [akupləmɑ̃] *nm* **1** : coupling **2** : mating
accourir [akurir] {23} *vi* : come running
accoutrement [akutrəmɑ̃] *nm* : outfit
accoutumer [akutyme] *vt* : accustom — **s'accoutumer** *vr* **~ à** : get accustomed to — **accoutumé, -mée** [akutyme] *adj* : customary
accréditer [akredite] *vt* **1** : accredit **2** : substantiate (a rumor, etc.)
accroc [akro] *nm* **1** : rip, tear **2** OBSTACLE : hitch, snag
accrocher [akrɔʃe] *vt* **1** SUSPENDRE : hang up **2** : hook, hitch **3** HEURTER : bump into **4 ~ l'œil** : catch the eye — *vi* : catch, snag — **s'accrocher** *vr* : hang on, cling — **accrochage** [akrɔʃaʒ] *nm* **1** : hanging, hooking **2** : collision **3** QUERELLE : dispute — **accrocheur, -cheuse** [akrɔʃœr, -ʃøz] *adj* **1** OPINIÂTRE : tenacious **2** ATTRAYANT : eye-catching
accroire [akrwar] {2} *vt* **en faire ~ à** : take in, dupe
accroître [akrwatr] {25} *vt* : increase — **s'accroître** *vr* : grow — **accroissement** [akrwasmɑ̃] *nm* : growth, increase
accroupir [akrupir] *v* **s'accroupir** *vr* : squat
accueillir [akœjir] {3} *vt* : greet — **accueil** [akœj] *nm* : welcome, reception — **accueillant, -lante** [akœjɑ̃, -jɑ̃t] *adj* : welcoming, hospitable
acculer [akyle] *vt* : corner
accumuler [akymyle] *vt* : accumulate — **s'accumuler** *vr* : pile up — **accumulation** [akymylasjɔ̃] *nf* : accumulation
accuser [akyze] *vt* **1** : accuse **2 ~ réception de** : acknowledge receipt of — **accusateur, -trice** [akyzatœr, -tris] *adj* : incriminating — **accusation** [akyzasjɔ̃] *nf* : accusation — **accusé, -sée** *n* : defendant, accused
acerbe [asɛrb] *adj* : acerbic
acéré, -rée [asere] *adj* : sharp
acharner [aʃarne] *v* **s'acharner** *vr* **1** S'OBSTINER : persevere **2 ~ sur** : persecute, hound — **acharné, -née** [aʃarne] *adj* : relentless — **acharnement** [aʃarnəmɑ̃] *nm* : relentlessness
achat [aʃa] *nm* **1** : purchase **2 faire des ~s** : go shopping
acheminer [aʃmine] *vt* **1** : transport **2** : forward (mail) — **s'acheminer** *vr* **~ vers** : head for — **acheminement** [aʃminmɑ̃] *nm* : dispatch, routing
acheter [aʃte] {20} *vt* : buy, purchase — **acheteur, -teuse** [aʃtœr, -tøz] *n* : buyer
achever [aʃve] {52} *vt* : complete, finish — **s'achever** *vr* : draw to a close — **achèvement** [aʃɛvmɑ̃] *nm* : completion
acide [asid] *adj & nm* : acid — **acidité** [asidite] *nf* : sourness, acidity
acier [asje] *nm* : steel — **aciérie** [asjeri] *nf* : steelworks
acné [akne] *nf* : acne
acolyte [akɔlit] *nm* : accomplice
acompte [akɔ̃t] *nm* : deposit, installment
à–côté [akote] *nm, pl* **à–côtés** : extra, perk
à–coup [aku] *nm, pl* **à–coups** : jerk, jolt
acoustique [akustik] *adj* : acoustic — **~** *nf* : acoustics
acquérir [akerir] {21} *vt* **1** : acquire **2** : purchase — **acquéreur, -reuse** [akerœr, -røz] *n* : buyer
acquiescer [akjese] {6} *vi* : agree
acquis, -quise [aki, -kiz] *adj* **1** : acquired **2** : established — **acquis** *nms & pl* : knowledge — **acquisition** [akizisjɔ̃] *nf* : acquisition
acquitter [akite] *vt* **1** : acquit **2** PAYER : pay — **s'acquitter** *vr* **~ de 1** : carry out **2** : pay off — **acquit** [aki] *nm* : receipt — **acquittement** [akitmɑ̃] *nm* : payment (of a debt)
acre [akr] *nf* : acre *Can*
âcre [akr] *adj* : acrid — **âcreté** [akrəte] *nf* : bitterness
acrobate [akrɔbat] *nmf* : acrobat — **acrobatie** [akrɔbasi] *nf* : acrobatics — **acrobatique** [akrɔbatik] *adj* : acrobatic
acrylique [akrilik] *adj & nm* : acrylic
acte [akt] *nm* **1** : action, deed **2** : act (in theater) **3** : certificate, document **4 ~s** *nmpl* : proceedings
acteur, -trice [aktœr, -tris] *n* : actor, actress *f*
actif, -tive [aktif, -tiv] *adj* : active — **actif** *nm* **1** : assets *pl* **2** : active voice
action [aksjɔ̃] *nf* **1** : action, act **2** EFFET : effect **3** : share (in finance) — **actionnaire** [aksjɔnɛr] *nmf* : shareholder — **actionner** [aksjɔne] *vt* **1** : engage, set in motion **2** : sue
activer [aktive] *vt* **1** : activate **2** HÂTER : speed up — **s'activer** *vr* : bustle about
activiste [aktivist] *adj & nmf* : activist — **activisme** [aktivism] *nm* : activism
activité [aktivite] *nf* : activity
actualité [aktɥalite] *nf* **1** : current events *pl* **2 ~s** *nfpl* : news — **actualiser** [aktɥalize] *vt* : update, modernize
actuel, -tuelle [aktɥɛl] *adj* : current, present — **actuellement** [-tɥɛlmɑ̃] *adv* : at present
acuité [akɥite] *nf* : acuteness
acupuncture [akypɔ̃ktyr] *nf* : acupuncture
adage [adaʒ] *nm* : adage
adapter [adapte] *vt* : adapt, fit — **s'adapter** *vr* : adapt — **adaptation** [adaptasjɔ̃] *nf* : adaptation — **adaptateur** [adaptatœr] *nm* : adapter
additif [aditif] *nm* : additive
addition [adisjɔ̃] *nf* **1** : addition **2** NOTE : bill, check — **additionnel, -nelle** [adisjɔnɛl] *adj* : additional — **additionner** [adisjɔne] *vt* : add (up)
adepte [adɛpt] *nmf* : follower
adéquat, -quate [adekwa, -kwat] *adj* **1** SUFFISANT : adequate **2** APPROPRIÉ : appropriate
adhérer [adere] {87} *vi* **1** : adhere **2 ~ à** : join — **adhérence** [aderɑ̃s] *nf* : adhesion, grip — **adhérent, -rente** [aderɑ̃, -rɑ̃t] *adj* : adhering, sticking — **~** *n* : member
adhésif, -sive [adezif, -ziv] *adj* : adhesive — **adhésif** *nm* : adhesive — **adhésion** [adezjɔ̃] *nf* **1** : adhesion **2** : adherence, support **3** AFFILIATION : membership
adieu [adjø] *nm, pl* **adieux** : farewell, goodbye
adjacent, -cente [adʒasɑ̃, -sɑ̃t] *adj* : adjacent
adjectif [adʒɛktif] *nm* : adjective
adjoindre [adʒwɛ̃dr] {50} *vt* **1** : appoint **2** : add, attach — **s'adjoindre** *vr* **~ qqn** : take s.o. on, hire s.o. — **adjoint, -jointe** [adʒwɛ̃, -ʒwɛ̃t] *adj & n* : assistant
adjonction [adʒɔ̃ksjɔ̃] *nf* : addition
admettre [admɛtr] {53} *vt* : admit
administrer [administre] *vt* : administer — **administrateur, -trice** [administratœr, -tris] *n* : director, administrator — **administratif, -tive** [administratif, -tiv] *adj* : administrative — **administration** [administrasjɔ̃] *nf* : administration
admirer [admire] *vt* : admire — **admirable** [admirabl] *adj* : admirable — **admirateur, -trice** [admiratœr, -tris] *n* : admirer — **admiratif, -tive** [admiratif, -tiv] *adj* : admiring — **admiration** [admirasjɔ̃] *nf* : admiration
admissible [admisibl] *adj* : acceptable, eligible — **admission** [admisjɔ̃] *nf* : admittance
admonester [admɔnɛste] *vt* : admonish
ADN [adeɛn] *nm* (*acide désoxyribonucléique*) : DNA
adolescence [adɔlesɑ̃s] *nf* : adolescence — **adolescent, -cente** [-lesɑ̃, -sɑ̃t] *adj & n* : adolescent
adopter [adɔpte] *vt* : adopt — **adoptif, -tive** [adɔptif, -tiv] *adj* : adoptive, adopted — **adoption** [adɔpsjɔ̃] *nf* : adoption
adorer [adɔre] *vt* : adore, worship — **adorable** [adɔrabl] *adj* : adorable
adosser [adose] *vt* : lean — **s'adosser** *vr* **~ à** *or* **~ contre** : lean back against
adoucir [adusir] *vt* **1** : soften **2** : alleviate, ease — **s'adoucir** *vr* : become milder, mellow — **adoucissement** [adusismɑ̃] *nm* **1** : softening **2** : alleviation

adresser [adrese] *vt* : address — **adresse** [adrɛs] *nf* **1** : address **2** HABILETÉ : skill — **s'adresser** *vr* **~ à** : speak to

adroit, -droite [adrwa, -drwat] *adj* HABILE : skillful

adulte [adylt] *adj & nmf* : adult

adultère [adyltɛr] *nm* : adultery — **~** *adj* : adulterous

advenir [advənir] {4} *v impers* **1** : happen, occur **2 ~ de** : become of

adverbe [advɛrb] *nm* : adverb

adversaire [advɛrsɛr] *nmf* : opponent — **adverse** [advɛrs] *adj* : opposing — **adversité** [advɛrsite] *nf* : adversity

aérer [aere] {87} *vt* : air out — **s'aérer** *vr* : get some fresh air

aérien, -rienne [aerjɛ̃, -rjɛn] *adj* : air, aerial

aérobic [aerɔbik] *nm* : aerobics

aérodynamique [aerɔdinamik] *adj* : aerodynamic

aérogare [aerɔgar] *nf* : air terminal

aéroglisseur [aerɔglisœr] *nm* : hovercraft

aéroport [aerɔpɔr] *nm* : airport

aérosol [aerɔsɔl] *nm* : aerosol

affable [afabl] *adj* : affable

affaiblir [afeblir] *vt* : weaken — **s'affaiblir** *vr* **1** : become weak **2** ATTÉNUER : fade

affaire [afɛr] *nf* **1** : affair **2** CAS : matter **3** ENTREPRISE : business **4** TRANSACTION : deal **5 ~s** *nfpl* : belongings **6 ~s** *nfpl* : business **7 avoir ~ à** : deal with — **affairer** [afere] *v* **s'affairer** *vr* : be busy — **affairé, -rée** [afere] *adj* : busy

affaisser [afese] *v* **s'affaisser** *vr* : collapse, give way — **affaissement** [afɛsmɑ̃] *nm* : sagging, sinking

affaler [afale] *v* **s'affaler** *vr* : collapse

affamé, -mée [afame] *adj* : famished

affecter [afɛkte] *vt* **1** : affect **2** NOMMER : appoint **3** ASSIGNER : allocate **4** FEINDRE : feign — **affectation** [afɛktasjɔ̃] *nf* **1** : appointment **2 ~ des fonds** : allocation of funds — **affecté, -tée** [afɛkte] *adj* : mannered, affected

affectif, -tive [afɛktif, -tiv] *adj* : emotional

affection [afɛksjɔ̃] *nf* **1** : affection **2** : ailment — **affectionner** [afɛksjɔne] *vt* : be fond of — **affectueux, -tueuse** [afɛktɥø, -tɥøz] *adj* : affectionate — **affectueusement** [-tɥøzmɑ̃] *adv* : fondly

afférent, -rente [aferɑ̃, -rɑ̃t] *adj* **~ à** : pertaining to

affermir [afɛrmir] *vt* : strengthen

affiche [afiʃ] *nf* : poster, notice — **affichage** [afiʃaʒ] *nm* **1** : posting, publicizing **2 ~ numérique** : digital display — **afficher** [afiʃe] *vt* **1** : post, put up **2** : show, display

affilée [afile] **d'~** *adv phr* : in a row

affiler [afile] {96} *vt* : sharpen

affilier [afilje] *vt* : affiliate — **s'affilier** *vr* **~ à** : join

affiner [afine] *vt* : refine

affinité [afinite] *nf* : affinity

affirmatif, -tive [afirmatif, -tiv] *adj* : affirmative — **affirmative** *nf* : affirmative

affirmer [afirme] *vt* : affirm, assert — **s'affirmer** *vr* : assert oneself — **affirmation** [afirmasjɔ̃] *nf* : assertion

affliger [afliʒe] {17} *vt* : afflict, distress — **affliction** [afliksjɔ̃] *nf* : affliction — **affligeant, -geante** [afliʒɑ̃, -ʒɑ̃t] *adj* : distressing

affluer [aflye] *vi* **1** COULER : flow **2 ~ vers** : flock to — **affluence** [aflyɑ̃s] *nf* **1** : crowd **2 heure d'~** : rush hour — **affluent** [aflyɑ̃] *nm* : tributary

afflux [afly] *nm* : influx, rush

affoler [afɔle] *vt* EFFRAYER : terrify — **s'affoler** *vr* : panic — **affolé, -lée** [afɔle] *adj* : frightened — **affolement** [afɔlmɑ̃] *nm* : panic

affranchir [afrɑ̃ʃir] *vt* **1** LIBÉRER : liberate, free **2** : stamp (a letter) — **affranchissement** [afrɑ̃ʃismɑ̃] *nm* **1** : liberation **2** : stamping, postage

affréter [afrete] {87} *vt* : charter

affreux, -freuse [afrø, -frøz] *adj* : horrible — **affreusement** [afrøzmɑ̃] *adv* : horribly

affronter [afrɔ̃te] *vt* : confront — **s'affronter** *vr* : confront each other — **affront** [afrɔ̃] *nm* : affront — **affrontement** [afrɔ̃tmɑ̃] *nm* : confrontation

affûter [afyte] *vt* : sharpen — **affût** [afy] *nm* **être à l'~ de** : be on the lookout for

afin [afɛ̃] *adv* **1 ~ de** : in order to **2 ~ que** : so that

africain, -caine [afrikɛ̃, -kɛn] *adj* : African

agacer [agase] {6} *vt* : irritate — **agaçant, -çante** [agasɑ̃, -sɑ̃t] *adj* : annoying — **agacement** [agasmɑ̃] *nm* : annoyance

âge [aʒ] *nm* **1** : age (of a person) **2** : age, era — **âgé, -gée** [aʒe] *adj* **1** VIEUX : elderly **2 ~ de 10 ans** : 10 years old

agence [aʒɑ̃s] *nf* : agency, office

agencer [aʒɑ̃se] {6} *vt* : arrange, lay out — **agencement** [aʒɑ̃smɑ̃] *nm* : layout

agenda [aʒɛ̃da] *nm* : appointment book

agenouiller [aʒnuje] *v* **s'agenouiller** *vr* : kneel

agent, -gente [aʒɑ̃, -ʒɑ̃t] *n* **1** : agent **2 ~ de police** : police officer

agglomération [aglɔmerasjɔ̃] *nf* : urban area

agglutiner [aglytine] *vt* : stick together

aggraver [agrave] *vt* : aggravate, make worse — **s'aggraver** *vr* EMPIRER : worsen — **aggravation** [agravasjɔ̃] *nf* : worsening

agile [aʒil] *adj* : agile — **agilité** [aʒilite] *nf* : agility

agir [aʒir] *vi* **1** : act **2** SE COMPORTER : behave **3** : take effect (of medication) — **s'agir** *vr* **il s'agit de** : it is a question of — **agissements** [aʒismɑ̃] *nmpl* : schemes, dealings

agiter [aʒite] *vt* **1** SECOUER : shake **2** TROUBLER : disturb — **s'agiter** *vr* **1** : bustle about **2** : fidget — **agitation** [aʒitasjɔ̃] *nf* **1** : agitation **2** : (political) unrest — **agité, -tée** [aʒite] *adj* **1** : restless **2** : rough, choppy

agneau [aɲo] *nm, pl* **agneaux** : lamb

agonie [agɔni] *nf* : (death) throes *pl* — **agoniser** [agɔnize] *vi* : be dying

agrafe [agraf] *nf* **1** : hook, fastener **2** : staple — **agrafer** [agrafe] *vt* **1** : fasten **2** : staple — **agrafeuse** [agraføz] *nf* : stapler

agrandir [agrɑ̃dir] *vt* : enlarge — **s'agrandir** *vr* : expand, grow — **agrandissement** [agrɑ̃dismɑ̃] *nm* : enlargement, expansion

agréable [agreabl] *adj* : nice, pleasant — **agréablement** [-abləmɑ̃] *adv* : pleasantly

agréer [agree] *vt* **1** : accept **2 veuillez ~ l'expression de mes sentiments distingués** : sincerely yours — **agréé, agréée** [agree] *adj* : authorized

agrégé, -gée [agreʒe] *n France* : certified teacher or professor — **agrégation** [agregasjɔ̃] *nf France* : qualifying exam for teachers or professors

agrément [agremɑ̃] *nm* **1** : charm, appeal **2 voyage d'~** : pleasure trip — **agrémenter** [agremɑ̃te] *vt* : embellish

agrès [agrɛ] *nmpl* : (gymnastic) apparatus

agresser [agrese] *vt* : attack, assault — **agresseur** [agrɛsœr] *nm* : attacker — **agressif, -sive** [agrɛsif, -siv] *adj* : aggressive — **agression** [agrɛsjɔ̃] *nf* **1** : attack **2** : aggression — **agressivité** [agresivite] *nf* : aggressiveness

agricole [agrikɔl] *adj* : agricultural — **agriculteur, -trice** [agrikyltœr, -tris] *n* : farmer — **agriculture** [agricyltyr] *nf* : agriculture, farming

agripper [agripe] *vt* : clutch, grab — **s'agripper** *vr* **~ à** : cling to, clutch

agrumes [agrym] *nmpl* : citrus fruits

aguets [agɛ] **aux ~** *adv phr* : on the lookout

ah [a] *interj* : oh!, ah!

ahuri, -rie [ayri] *adj* : dumbfounded — **ahurissant, -sante** [ayrisɑ̃, -sɑ̃t] *adj* : astounding

aider [ede] *vt* : help — **aide** *nf* **1** : aid **2 à l'~ de** : with the help of — **aide** *nmf* : assistant

aïe [aj] *interj* : ouch!, ow!

aïeux [ajø] *nmpl* : ancestors

aigle [ɛgl] *nm* : eagle

aigre [ɛgr] *adj* : sour, tart — **aigre–doux, -douce** [ɛgrədu, -dus] *adj* : bittersweet — **aigreur** [ɛgrœr] *nf* : sourness — **aigri** [egri] *adj* : embittered

aigu, -guë [egy] *adj* **1** : sharp, keen **2** VIF : acute **3** STRIDENT : shrill

aiguille [egɥij] *nf* **1** : needle **2** : hand (of a clock)

aiguillon [egɥijɔ̃] *nm* **1** : goad **2** : stinger (of an insect)

aiguiser [egize] *vt* **1** : sharpen **2 ~ l'appétit** : whet the appetite

ail [aj] *nm* : garlic

aile [ɛl] *nf* **1** : wing **2** : fender (of an automobile) — **ailier** [elje] *nm* : wing, end (in sports)

ailleurs [ajœr] *adv* **1** : elsewhere **2 d'~** : besides, moreover **3 par ~** : furthermore

aimable [ɛmabl] *adj* : kind — **aimablement** [ɛmabləmɑ̃] *adv* : kindly

aimant[1], **-mante** [ɛmɑ̃, -mɑ̃t] *adj* : loving, caring

aimant[2] *nm* : magnet

aimer [eme] *vt* **1** : love, like **2 ~ mieux** : prefer

aine [ɛn] *nf* : groin

aîné, -née [ene] *adj* **1** : older, oldest **2** : senior — **~** *n* **1** : elder child, eldest child **2 aînés** *nmpl* : elders **3 il est mon aîné** : he's older than me

ainsi [ɛ̃si] *adv* **1** : in this way, thus **2 ~ que** : just as **3 ~ que** : as well as **4 et ~ de suite** : and so on **5 pour ~ dire** : so to speak

air [ɛr] *nm* **1** : air **2** MÉLODIE : tune **3** EXPRESSION : air, look **4 avoir l'~** : look, seem

aire [ɛr] *nf* **1** : area **2 ~ d'atterrissage** : landing strip

aisance [ezɑ̃s] *nf* **1** : ease **2** PROSPÉRITÉ : affluence — **aise** *nf* **1** : ease **2 être à l'~** : be comfortable — **aisé, -sée** [eze] *adj* **1** : easy **2** RICHE : well-off — **aisément** [ezemɑ̃] *adv* : easily

aisselle [ɛsɛl] *nf* : armpit

ajourner [aʒurne] *vt* : adjourn — **ajournement** [aʒurnəmɑ̃] *nm* : adjournment

ajouter [aʒute] *vt* : add — **ajout** [aʒu] *nm* : addition

ajuster [aʒyste] *vt* : adjust — **ajustement** [aʒystəmɑ̃] *nm* : adjustment

alarmer [alarme] *vt* : alarm — **s'alarmer** *vr* : become alarmed — **alarmant, -mante** [alarmɑ̃, -mɑ̃t] *adj* : alarming — **alarme** [alarm] *nf* : alarm

album [albɔm] *nm* : album

alcool [alkɔl] *nm* : alcohol — **alcoolique** [alkɔlik] *adj & nmf* : alcoholic — **alcoolisé, -sée** [alkɔlize] *adj* : alcoholic — **alcoolisme** [-kɔlism] *nm* : alcoholism

alcôve [alkov] *nf* : alcove

aléa [alea] *nm* : risk — **aléatoire** [aleatwar] *adj* **1** : risky, uncertain **2** : random

alentour [alɑ̃tur] *adv* : around, surrounding — **alentours** [alɑ̃tur] *nmpl* **aux ~ de** : around, in the vicinity of

alerter [alɛrte] *vt* : alert, warn — **alerte** [alɛrt] *adj* : alert, lively — **alerte** *nf* : alert, warning

algèbre [alʒɛbr] *nf* : algebra

algérien, -rienne [alʒerjɛ̃, -rjɛn] *adj* : Algerian

algue [alg] *nf* : seaweed

alias [aljas] *adv* : alias

alibi [alibi] *nm* : alibi

aliéner [aljene] {87} *vt* : alienate — **aliénation** [aljenasjɔ̃] *nf* : alienation

aligner [aliɲe] *vt* : align — **s'aligner** *vr* : fall into line — **alignement** [aliɲmɑ̃] *nm* : alignment

alimenter [alimɑ̃te] *vt* **1** : feed **2** APPROVISIONNER : supply — **aliment** [alimɑ̃] *nm* : food — **alimentation** [alimɑ̃tasjɔ̃] *nf* **1** : diet, nourishment **2 magasin d'~** : grocery store

alinéa [alinea] *nm* : paragraph

alité, -tée [alite] *adj* : bedridden

allaiter [alete] *vt* : nurse, breast-feed — **allaitement** [alɛtmɑ̃] *nm* : breast-feeding

allant [alɑ] *nm* : drive, spirit

allécher [aleʃe] {87} *vt* : allure, tempt — **alléchant, -chante** [aleʃɑ̃, -ʃɑ̃t] *adj* : tempting

allée [ale] *nf* **1** : path, lane, walk **2** : aisle **3 ~s et venues** : comings and goings

allégation [alegasjɔ̃] *nf* : allegation

allégeance [aleʒɑ̃s] *nf* : allegiance

alléger [aleʒe] {64} *vt* **1** : lighten **2** SOULAGER : alleviate

allègre [alɛgr] *adj* : cheerful, lively — **allégresse** [alegrɛs] *nf* : elation

alléguer [alege] {87} *vt* : allege

allemand, -mande [almɑ̃, -mɑ̃d] *adj* : German — **allemand** *nm* : German (language)

aller [ale] {5} *vi* **1** : go **2** MARCHER : work **3** : proceed, get along **4 ~ à** : fit, suit **5 allons–y** : let's go **6 comment allez–vous?** : how are you? **7 elle va bien** : she is fine — *v aux* : be going to, be about to — **s'en ~** *vr* : go away — **~** *nm* **1** *or* **~ simple** : one-way (ticket) **2 aller–retour** : round-trip (ticket)

allergie [alɛrʒi] *nf* : allergy — **allergique** [alɛrʒik] *adj* : allergic

alliage [aljaʒ] *nm* : alloy

allier [alje] {96} *vt* : combine — **s'allier** *vr* **~ à** : become allied with — **alliance** [aljɑ̃s] *nf* **1** : alliance **2** : wedding ring **3 par ~** : by marriage — **allié, -liée** *n* : ally

alligator [aligatɔr] *nm* : alligator

allô [alo] *interj* : hello

allocation [alɔkasjɔ̃] *nf* **1** : allocation **2 ~ de chômage** : unemployment benefit

allocution [alɔkysjɔ̃] *nf* : short speech, address

allonger [alɔ̃ʒe] {17} *vt* **1** : lengthen **2** ÉTIRER : stretch (out) — *vi* : get longer — **s'allonger** *vr* SE COUCHER : lie down

allouer [alwe] *vt* : allocate

allumer [alyme] *vt* **1** : light, ignite **2** : turn on, switch on — **s'allumer** *vr* : come on, light (up) — **allumage** *nm* **1** : lighting **2** : (automobile) ignition — **allumette** [alymet] *nf* : match

allure [alyr] *nf* **1** APPARENCE : appearance **2** : speed, pace **3 à toute ~** : at full speed

allusion [alyzjɔ̃] *nf* : allusion

almanach [almana] *nm* : almanac

alors [alɔr] *adv* **1** : then **2 ~ que** : while, when **3 ~ que** : even though **4 et ~?** : so?, so what? **5 ou ~** : or else

alouette [alwɛt] *nf* : lark

alourdir [alurdir] *vt* : weigh down — **s'alourdir** *vr* : become heavy

alphabet [alfabɛ] *nm* : alphabet — **alphabétique** [alfabetik] *adj* : alphabetical

alpin, -pine [alpɛ̃, -pin] *adj* : alpine — **alpinisme** [alpinism] *nm* : mountain climbing

altérer [altere] {87} *vt* **1** : distort **2** ABÎMER : spoil — **s'altérer** *vr* : deteriorate

alterner [altɛrne] *v* : alternate — **alternatif, -tive** [altɛrnatif, -tiv] *adj* : alternative — **alternative** [altɛrnativ] *nf* : alternative

altesse [altɛs] *nf* **son Altesse** : His (Her) Highness

altier, -tière [altje, -tjɛr] *adj* : haughty

altitude [altityd] *nf* : altitude

altruisme [altrɥism] *nm* : altruism

aluminium [alyminjɔm] *nm* : aluminum

amabilité [amabilite] *nf* : kindness

amadouer [amadwe] *vt* : cajole

amaigrir [amegrir] *vt* : make thin — **amaigrissement** [amegrismɑ̃] *nm* : weight loss

amalgame [amalgam] *nm* : mixture

amande [amɑ̃d] *nf* **1** : almond **2** : kernel (of a fruit or nut)

amant, -mante [amɑ̃, -mɑ̃t] *n* : lover

amarrer [amare] *vt* : moor — **amarrage** [amaraʒ] *nm* : mooring

amas [ama] *nm* : pile, heap — **amasser** [amase] *vt* ACCUMULER : amass — **s'amasser** *vr* : pile up

amateur [amatœr] *nm* **1** : enthusiast **2** : amateur

ambages [ɑ̃baʒ] **sans ~** *adv phr* : plainly

ambassade [ɑ̃basad] *nf* : embassy — **ambassadeur, -drice** [ɑ̃basadœr, -dris] *n* : ambassador

ambiance [ɑ̃bjɑ̃s] *nf* : atmosphere — **ambiant, -biante** [ɑ̃bjɑ̃, -bjɑ̃t] *adj* : surrounding

ambigu, -guë [ɑ̃bigy] *adj* : ambiguous — **ambiguïté** [ɑ̃bigɥite] *nf* : ambiguity

ambitieux, -tieuse [ɑ̃bisjø, -sjøz] *adj* : ambitious — **ambition** [ɑ̃bisjɔ̃] *nf* : ambition

ambivalent, -lente [ɑ̃bivalɑ̃, -lɑ̃t] *adj* : ambivalent

ambre [ɑ̃br] *nm* : amber

ambulant, -lante [ɑ̃bylɑ̃, -lɑ̃t] *adj* : itinerant — **ambulance** [ɑ̃bylɑ̃s] *nf* : ambulance

ambulatoire [ɑ̃bylatwar] *adj* : ambulatory

âme [am] *nf* **1** : soul **2 état d'~** : state of mind

améliorer [ameljɔre] *vt* : improve — **s'améliorer** *vr* : get better — **amélioration** [ameljɔrasjɔ̃] *nf* : improvement

aménager [amenaʒe] {17} *vt* : fit out — **aménagement** [amenaʒmɑ̃] *nm* **1** : fitting out **2** : development (of a region, etc.)

amender [amɑ̃de] *vt* : amend — **amende** [amɑ̃d] *nf* : fine — **amendement** [amɑ̃dmɑ̃] *nm* : amendment

amener [amne] {52} *vt* **1** : bring **2** OCCASIONNER : cause

amenuiser [amənɥize] *v* **s'amenuiser** *vr* : dwindle

amer, -mère [amɛr] *adj* : bitter — **amèrement** [amɛrmɑ̃] *adv* : bitterly

américain, -caine [amerikɛ̃, -kɛn] *adj* : American

amérindien, -dienne [amerɛ̃djɛ̃, -djɛn] *adj* : Native American

amertume [amɛrtym] *nf* : bitterness

ameublement [amœbləmɑ̃] *nm* **1** : furnishing **2** MEUBLES : furniture

ami, -mie [ami] *n* **1** : friend **2** *or* **petit ~** : boyfriend **3** *or* **petite ~e** : girlfriend

amiable [amjabl] *adj* **à l'~** : amicable

amiante [amjɑ̃t] *nm* : asbestos

amibe [amib] *nf* : amoeba

amical, -cale [amikal] *adj, mpl* **-caux** [-ko] : friendly

amidon [amidɔ̃] *nm* : starch — **amidonner** [amidɔne] *vt* : starch

amincir [amɛ̃sir] *vt* : make thinner — **s'amincir** *vr* : get thinner

amiral [amiral] *nm, pl* **-raux** [-ro] : admiral

amitié [amitje] *nf* **1** : friendship **2 ~s** *nfpl* : best regards

ammoniaque [amɔnjak] *nf* : ammonia

amnésie [amnezi] *nf* : amnesia

amnistie [amnisti] *nf* : amnesty

amoindrir [amwɛ̃drir] *vt* : lessen — **s'amoindrir** *vr* : diminish

amollir [amɔlir] *vt* : soften

amonceler [amɔ̃sle] {18} *vt* : accumulate — **s'amonceler** *vr* : pile up — **amoncellement** [amɔ̃sɛlmɑ̃] *nm* : pile, heap

amont [amɔ̃] *nm* **en ~** : upstream

amorce [amɔrs] *nf* **1** DÉBUT : beginning(s) **2** APPÂT : bait **3** : detonator, fuse — **amorcer** [amɔrse] {6} *vt* **1** COMMENCER : begin **2** APPÂTER : bait **3** : boot (a computer) — **s'amorcer** *vr* : begin

amorphe [amɔrf] *adj* : listless

amorti [amɔrti] *nm Can* : bunt (in baseball)

amortir [amɔrtir] *vt* : cushion, deaden — **amortisseur** [amɔrtisœr] *nm* : shock absorber

amour [amur] *nm* : love — **amoureusement** [amurøzmɑ̃] *adv* : lovingly — **amoureux, -reuse** [amurø, -røz] *adj* **1** : loving **2 être ~** : be in love — **~** *n* : lover — **amour–propre** [amurprɔpr] *nm* : self-esteem

amovible [amɔvibl] *adj* : removable

amphibien [ɑ̃fibjɛ̃] *nm* : amphibian

amphithéâtre [ɑ̃fiteatr] *nm* **1** : amphitheater **2** : lecture hall

ample [ɑ̃pl] *adj* : ample — **ampleur** [ɑ̃plœr] *nf* : extent, range

amplifier [ɑ̃plifje] {96} *vt* **1** : amplify **2** : expand — **s'amplifier** *vr* : increase — **amplificateur** [ɑ̃plifikatœr] *nm* : amplifier

ampoule [ɑ̃pul] *nf* **1** : lightbulb **2** CLOQUE : blister **3** : vial (in medicine)

amputer [ɑ̃pyte] *vt* **1** : amputate **2** : cut drastically — **amputation** [ɑ̃pytasjɔ̃] *nf* **1** : amputation **2** : drastic cut

amuse–gueule [amyzgøl] *nms & pl* : appetizer

amuser [amyze] *vt* : amuse — **s'amuser** *vr* **1** : play **2** : enjoy oneself — **amusant, -sante** [amyzɑ̃, -zɑ̃t] *adj* : amusing — **amusement** [amyzmɑ̃] *nm* : amusement

amygdale [amidal] *nf* : tonsil
an [ɑ̃] *nm* **1** : year **2 le Nouvel An** : New Year's Day
analgésique [analʒezik] *adj & nm* : analgesic
analogie [analɔʒi] *nf* : analogy — **analogue** [analɔg] *adj* : similar
analphabète [analfabɛt] *adj* : illiterate — **analphabétisme** [analfabetism] *nm* : illiteracy
analyse [analiz] *nf* **1** : analysis **2** : (blood) test — **analyser** [analize] *vt* : analyze — **analytique** [analitik] *adj* : analytic, analytical
ananas [anana(s)] *nms & pl* : pineapple
anarchie [anarʃi] *nf* : anarchy
anatomie [anatɔmi] *nf* : anatomy — **anatomique** [anatɔmik] *adj* : anatomic(al)
ancêtre [ɑ̃sɛtr] *nmf* : ancestor
anchois [ɑ̃ʃwa] *nms & pl* : anchovy
ancien, -cienne [ɑ̃sjɛ̃, -sjɛn] *adj* **1** : former **2** VIEUX : ancient, old — **anciennement** [ɑ̃sjɛnmɑ̃] *adv* : formerly — **ancienneté** [ɑ̃sjɛnte] *nf* **1** : oldness **2** : seniority
ancre [ɑ̃kr] *nf* : anchor — **ancrer** [ɑ̃kre] *vt* : anchor
andouille [ɑ̃duj] *nf fam* **1** : andouille (sausage) **2** *fam* : fool, sap
âne [an] *nm* : ass, donkey
anéantir [aneɑ̃tir] *vt* **1** DÉTRUIRE : annihilate **2** ACCABLER : overwhelm — **anéantissement** [aneɑ̃tismɑ̃] *nm* : annihilation
anecdote [anɛkdɔt] *nf* : anecdote
anémie [anemi] *nf* : anemia — **anémique** [anemik] *adj* : anemic
ânerie [anri] *nf* : stupid mistake or remark
anesthésie [anɛstezi] *nf* : anesthesia — **anesthésique** [anɛstezik] *adj & nm* : anesthetic
aneth [anɛt] *nm* : dill
ange [ɑ̃ʒ] *nm* : angel — **angélique** [ɑ̃ʒelik] *adj* : angelic
anglais, -glaise [ɑ̃glɛ, -glɛz] *adj* : English — **anglais** *nm* : English (language)
angle [ɑ̃gl] *nm* **1** : angle **2** : corner
anglophone [ɑ̃glɔfɔn] *adj* : English-speaking
anglo–saxon, -saxonne [ɑ̃glɔsaksɔ̃, -saksɔn] *adj* : Anglo-Saxon
angoisser [ɑ̃gwase] *vt* : distress — **angoissant, -sante** [ɑ̃gwasɑ̃, -sɑ̃t] *adj* : agonizing — **angoisse** [ɑ̃gwas] *nf* : anguish
anguille [ɑ̃gij] *nf* : eel
anguleux, -leuse [ɑ̃gylø, -løz] *adj* : angular
animal [animal] *nm, pl* **-maux** [-mo] : animal
animateur, -trice [animatœr, -tris] *n* **1** : moderator **2** : (television show) host
animer [anime] *vt* : enliven — **s'animer** *vr* : come to life — **animation** [animasjɔ̃] *nf* : animation — **animé, -mée** [anime] *adj* : animated, lively
animosité [animɔzite] *nf* : animosity
anis [ani(s)] *nm* : anise
ankyloser [ɑ̃kiloze] *v* **s'ankyloser** *vr* : stiffen (up)
anneau [ano] *nm, pl* **-neaux** : ring
année [ane] *nf* **1** : year **2 ~ bissextile** : leap year
annexe [anɛks] *adj* **1** : adjoining, attached **2** : related — **~** *nf* : annex — **annexer** [anɛkse] *vt* : annex
annihiler [aniile] *vt* : annihilate — **annihilation** [aniilasjɔ̃] *nf* : annihilation
anniversaire [anivɛrsɛr] *nm* **1** : anniversary **2** : birthday
annoncer [anɔ̃se] {6} *vt* **1** : announce **2** DÉNOTER : indicate — **s'annoncer** *vr* : appear (to be) — **annonce** [anɔ̃s] *nf* **1** : announcement **2** : advertisement — **annonceur, -ceuse** [anɔ̃sœr, -søz] *n* **1** : advertiser **2** *Can* : (radio) announcer
annoter [anɔte] *vt* : annotate — **annotation** [anɔtasjɔ̃] *nf* : annotation
annuaire [anɥɛr] *nm* **1** : yearbook **2 ~ téléphonique** : telephone directory
annuel, -nuelle [anɥɛl] *adj* : annual — **annuellement** [anɥɛlmɑ̃] *adv* : annually
annulaire [anylɛr] *nm* : ring finger
annuler [anyle] *vt* **1** : cancel **2** RÉVOQUER : annul — **annulation** [anylasjɔ̃] *nf* **1** : cancellation **2** : annulment
anodin, -dine [anɔdɛ̃, -din] *adj* **1** : insignificant **2** : harmless
anomalie [anɔmali] *nf* : anomaly
anonyme [anɔnim] *adj* : anonymous — **anonymat** [anɔnima] *nm* : anonymity
anorexie [anɔrɛksi] *nf* : anorexia
anormal, -male [anɔrmal] *adj, mpl* **-maux** [-mo] : abnormal
anse [ɑ̃s] *nf* **1** : handle **2** : cove
antagoniste [ɑ̃tagɔnist] *adj* : antagonistic
antan [ɑ̃tɑ̃] **d'~** *adj phr* : of yesteryear
antarctique [ɑ̃tarktik] *adj* : antarctic
antécédent, -dente [ɑ̃tesedɑ̃, -dɑ̃t] *adj* : previous — **antécédents** *nmpl* : (medical) history, (criminal) record
antenne [ɑ̃tɛn] *nf* : antenna
antérieur, -rieure [ɑ̃terjœr] *adj* **1** PRÉCÉDENT : previous **2** : front (of a part, etc.) — **antérieurement** [ɑ̃terjœrmɑ̃] *adv* : previously
anthologie [ɑ̃tɔlɔʒi] *nf* : anthology
anthropologie [ɑ̃trɔpɔlɔʒi] *nf* : anthropology
antibiotique [ɑ̃tibiɔtik] *adj & nm* : antibiotic
anticiper [ɑ̃tisipe] *vt* : anticipate — *vi* : think ahead — **anticipation** [ɑ̃tisipasjɔ̃] *nf* : anticipation
anticorps [ɑ̃tikɔr] *nms & pl* : antibody
antidote [ɑ̃tidɔt] *nm* : antidote
antigel [ɑ̃tiʒɛl] *nm* : antifreeze
antilope [ɑ̃tilɔp] *nf* : antelope
antipathie [ɑ̃tipati] *nf* : antipathy
antique [ɑ̃tik] *adj* : ancient, antique — **antiquité** [ɑ̃tikite] *nf* **1** : antiquity **2** : antique
antisémite [ɑ̃tisemit] *adj* : anti-Semitic
antiseptique [ɑ̃tisɛptik] *adj & nm* : antiseptic
antonyme [ɑ̃tɔnim] *nm* : antonym
antre [ɑ̃tr] *nm* : den, lair
anus [anys] *nms & pl* : anus
anxieux, anxieuse [ɑ̃ksjø, -sjøz] *adj* : anxious — **anxiété** [ɑ̃ksjete] *nf* : anxiety
août [u(t)] *nm* : August
apaiser [apeze] *vt* : appease — **s'apaiser** *vr* : quiet down — **apaisement** [apɛzmɑ̃] *nm* : calming (down)
apanage [apanaʒ] *nm* : prerogative
apathie [apati] *nf* : apathy — **apathique** [apatik] *adj* : apathetic
apercevoir [apɛrsəvwar] {26} *vt* : perceive, see — **s'apercevoir** *vr* **1 ~ de** : notice **2 ~ que** : realize that — **aperçu** [apɛrsy] *nm* : general idea, outline
apéritif [aperitif] *nm* : aperitif
à–peu–près [apøprɛ] *nms & pl* : approximation
apeuré, -rée [apœre] *adj* : frightened
apitoyer [apitwaje] {58} *v* **s'apitoyer** *vr* **~ sur** : feel sorry for — **apitoiement** [apitwamɑ̃] *nm* : pity
aplanir [aplanir] *vt* **1** : level **2** : resolve (a problem) — **s'aplanir** *vr* : flatten out
aplatir [aplatir] *vt* : flatten
aplomb [aplɔ̃] *nm* **1** : aplomb, composure **2 d'~** : steady, balanced
apocalypse [apɔkalips] *nf* : apocalypse
apogée [apɔʒe] *nm* : peak
apostrophe [apɔstrɔf] *nf* : apostrophe — **apostropher** [apɔstrɔfe] *vt* : address rudely
apothéose [apɔteoz] *nf* : crowning moment
apôtre [apotr] *nm* : apostle
apparaître [aparɛtr] {73} *vi* : appear — *v impers* **il apparaît que** : it seems that
apparat [apara] *nm* **1** : pomp **2 d'~** : ceremonial
appareiller [apareje] *vi* : set sail — *vt* : match up — **appareil** [aparɛj] *nm* **1** : apparatus, appliance **2** : telephone **3 ~ auditif** : hearing aid **4 ~ digestif** : digestive system **5 ~ photo** : camera
apparence [aparɑ̃s] *nf* **1** : appearance **2 en ~** : outwardly — **apparent, -rente** [aparɑ̃, -rɑ̃t] *adj* : apparent — **apparemment** [aparamɑ̃] *adv* : apparently
apparenté, -tée [aparɑ̃te] *adj* : related
apparition [aparisjɔ̃] *nf* **1** MANIFESTATION : appearance **2** SPECTRE : apparition
appartement [apartəmɑ̃] *nm* : apartment
appartenir [apartənir] {92} *vi* **~ à** : belong to — *v impers* **il m'appartient de** : it's up to me to — **appartenance** [apartənɑ̃s] *nf* : membership, belonging
appâter [apate] *vt* **1** : bait **2** : lure, entice — **appât** [apa] *nm* : bait, lure
appauvrir [apovrir] *vt* : impoverish — **s'appauvrir** *vr* : become impoverished
appeler [aple] {8} *vt* **1** : call **2** NÉCESSITER : call for, require **3 en ~ à** : appeal to — *vi* : call — **s'appeler** *vr* : be named, be called — **appel** [apɛl] *nm* **1** : call **2** : appeal
appendice [apɛ̃dis] *nm* : appendix — **appendicite** [apɛ̃disit] *nf* : appendicitis
appentis [apɑ̃ti] *nm* : shed
appesantir [apəzɑ̃tir] *vt* : weigh down — **s'appesantir** *vr* **1** : grow heavier **2 ~ sur** : dwell on
appétit [apeti] *nm* **1** : appetite **2 bon ~!** : enjoy your meal! — **appétissant, -sante** [apetisɑ̃, -sɑ̃t] *adj* : appetizing
applaudir [aplodir] *v* : applaud — **applaudissements** [aplodismɑ̃] *nmpl* : applause
appliquer [aplike] *vt* : apply — **s'appliquer** *vr* **1** : apply oneself **2 ~ à** CONCERNER : apply to — **applicateur** [aplikatœr] *nm* : applicator — **application** [aplikasjɔ̃] *nf* : application — **appliqué, -quée** [aplike] *adj* : industrious, painstaking
appoint [apwɛ̃] *nm* **1** : contribution, support **2 d'~** : extra **3 faire l'~** : make exact change — **appointements** [apwɛ̃tmɑ̃] *nmpl* : salary
apporter [apɔrte] *vt* **1** AMENER : bring **2** FOURNIR : provide — **apport** [apɔr] *nm* : contribution
apposer [apoze] *vt* : put, affix
apprécier [apresje] {96} *vt* **1** : appreciate **2** : appraise — **appréciation** [apresjasjɔ̃] *nf* : assessment, appraisal
appréhender [apreɑ̃de] *vt* **1** ARRÊTER : apprehend, arrest **2** : dread — **appréhension** [apreɑ̃sjɔ̃] *nf* : apprehension
apprendre [aprɑ̃dr] {70} *vt* **1** : learn **2** ENSEIGNER : teach
apprenti, -tie [aprɑ̃ti] *n* : apprentice — **apprentissage** [aprɑ̃tisaʒ] *nm* **1** : apprenticeship **2** : learning
apprêter [aprete] *v* **s'apprêter** *vr* : get ready
apprivoiser [aprivwaze] *vt* : tame
approbateur, -trice [aprɔbatœr, -tris] *adj* : approving — **approbation** [aprɔbasjɔ̃] *nf* : approval
approcher [aprɔʃe] *vt* : approach — *vi* : draw near — **s'approcher** *vr* **~ de** : come up to — **approchant, -chante** [aprɔʃɑ̃, -ʃɑ̃t] *adj* : similar — **approche** [aprɔʃ] *nf* : approach
approfondir [aprɔfɔ̃dir] *vt* **1** : deepen **2** PÉNÉTRER : delve into — **approfondi, -die** [aprɔfɔ̃di] *adj* : thorough
approprier [aprɔprije] {96} *v* **s'approprier** *vr* : appropriate — **approprié, -priée** [aprɔprije] *adj* : appropriate
approuver [apruve] *vt* : approve (of)
approvisionner [aprɔvizjɔne] *vt* : supply — **s'approvisionner** *vr* : stock up — **approvisionnement** [aprɔvizjɔnmɑ̃] *nm* : supply, provision
approximation [aprɔksimasjɔ̃] *nf* : approximation — **approximatif, -tive** [aprɔksimatif, -tiv] *adj* : approximate — **approximativement** [-tivmɑ̃] *adv* : approximately
appuyer [apɥije] {58} *vt* **1** : rest, lean **2** SOUTENIR : support — *vi* **~ sur** : push, press — **s'appuyer** *vr* **1 ~ à** *or* **~ contre** : lean against **2 ~ sur** : rely on — **appui** [apɥi] *nm* : support
âpre [apr] *adj* : bitter, harsh
après [aprɛ] *adv* : afterwards — **~** *prep* **1** : after **2** : beyond **3 ~ tout** : after all **4 d'~** : according to — **après–demain** [aprɛdmɛ̃] *adv* : the day after tomorrow — **après–midi** [aprɛmidi] *nmfs & pl* : afternoon
à–propos [aprɔpo] *nm* **1** : aptness **2** : presence of mind
apte [apt] *adj* : capable — **aptitude** [aptityd] *nf* : aptitude
aquarelle [akwarɛl] *nf* : watercolor
aquarium [akwarjɔm] *nm* : aquarium
aquatique [akwatik] *adj* : aquatic
aqueduc [akdyk] *nm* : aqueduct
arabe [arab] *adj* : Arab, Arabic — **~** *nm* : Arabic (language)
arachide [araʃid] *nf* : peanut
araignée [areɲe] *nf* : spider
arbitraire [arbitrɛr] *adj* : arbitrary
arbitre [arbitr] *nm* **1** : arbitrator **2** : referee **3 libre ~** : free will — **arbitrer** [arbitre] *vt* **1** : arbitrate **2** : referee
arborer [arbɔre] *vt* : bear, display
arbre [arbr] *nm* **1** : tree **2** : shaft
arbrisseau [arbriso] *nm* : shrub
arbuste [arbyst] *nm* : bush
arc [ark] *nm* **1** : arc, curve **2** : bow (in archery)
arcade [arkad] *nf* : arch, archway
arc–boutant [arkbutɑ̃] *nm, pl* **arcs–boutants** : flying buttress
arc–en–ciel [arkɑ̃sjɛl] *nm, pl* **arcs–en–ciel** : rainbow
archaïque [arkaik] *adj* : archaic
arche [arʃ] *nf* **1** : arch **2** : ark
archéologie [arkeɔlɔʒi] *nf* : archaeology
archet [arʃɛ] *nm* : bow (in music)
archevêque [arʃəvɛk] *nm* : archbishop
archipel [arʃipɛl] *nm* : archipelago
architecture [arʃitɛktyr] *nf* : architecture — **architecte** [arʃitɛkt] *nmf* : architect
archives [arʃiv] *nfpl* : archives
arctique [arktik] *adj* : arctic
ardent, -dente [ardɑ̃, -dɑ̃t] *adj* **1** : burning **2** PASSIONNÉ : ardent — **ardemment** [ardamɑ̃] *adv* : ardently — **ardeur** [ardœr] *nf* **1** CHALEUR : heat **2** : ardor
ardoise [ardwaz] *nf* : slate
ardu, -due [ardy] *adj* : arduous
arène [arɛn] *nf* **1** : arena **2 ~s** : bullring, amphitheater — **aréna** [arena] *nm Can* : arena
arête [arɛt] *nf* **1** : fish bone **2** : ridge, bridge (of the nose)
argent [arʒɑ̃] *nm* **1** : money **2** : silver **3 ~ comptant** : cash — **argenté, -tée** [arʒɑ̃te] *adj* **1** : silver-plated **2** : silvery — **argenterie** [arʒɑ̃tri] *nf* : silverware
argile [arʒil] *nf* : clay
argot [argo] *nm* : slang
argument [argymɑ̃] *nm* : argument — **argumentation** [argymɑ̃tasjɔ̃] *nf* : rationale — **argumenter** [argymɑ̃te] *vi* : argue
aride [arid] *adj* : arid
aristocrate [aristɔkrat] *nmf* : aristocrat — **aristocratique** [-kratik] *adj* : aristocratic — **aristocratie** [aristɔkrasi] *nf* : aristocracy
arithmétique [aritmetik] *nf* : arithmetic
armature [armatyr] *nf* : framework
armer [arme] *vt* **1** : arm **2** : cock (a gun) — **arme** [arm] *nf* **1** : weapon **2 ~s** *nfpl* : coat of arms — **armée** [arme] *nf* : army — **armement** [arməmɑ̃] *nm* : armament
armistice [armistis] *nm* : armistice
armoire [armwar] *nf* **1** : cupboard **2** : wardrobe, closet
armoiries [armwari] *nfpl* : coat of arms
armure [armyr] *nf* : armor
arnaquer [arnake] *vt fam* : swindle — **arnaque** [arnak] *nf fam* : swindle
aromate [arɔmat] *nm* : spice, herb
arôme [arom] *nm* **1** : aroma **2** : flavor — **aromatique** [arɔmatik] *adj* : aromatic — **aromatiser** [arɔmatize] *vt* : flavor
arpenter [arpɑ̃te] *vt* **1** : pace up and down **2** MESURER : survey
arqué, -quée [arke] *adj* : curved, arched
arrache–pied [araʃpje] **d'~** *adv phr* : relentlessly
arracher [araʃe] *vt* **1** : pull up or out **2** DÉCHIRER : tear off **3** : snatch, grab
arranger [arɑ̃ʒe] {17} *vt* **1** : arrange **2** RÉPARER : fix **3** CONVENIR : suit, please **4** RÉGLER : settle — **s'arranger** *vr* **1** : come to an agreement **2** : get better — **arrangement** [arɑ̃ʒmɑ̃] *nm* : arrangement
arrestation [arɛstasjɔ̃] *nf* : arrest
arrêter [arete] *vt* **1** : stop **2** FIXER : fix **3** APPRÉHENDER : arrest **4** DÉTERMINER : decide on — **s'arrêter** *vr* **1** : stop, cease **2 ~ de faire** : stop doing — **arrêt** [arɛ] *nm* **1** : stopping, halt **2** : decree **3 ~ d'autobus** : bus stop
arrhes [ar] *nfpl France* : deposit
arrière [arjɛr] *adj* : back, rear — **~** *nm* **1** : back, rear **2 en ~** : backwards **3 en ~ de** : behind — **arriéré, -rée** [arjere] *adj* **1** : overdue **2** : backward — **arriéré** *nm* **1** : arrears *pl* **2** : backlog — **arrière–goût** [arjɛrgu] *nm, pl* **arrière–goûts** : aftertaste — **arrière–grand–mère** [arjɛrgrɑ̃mɛr] *nf, pl* **arrière–grands–mères** : great-grandmother — **arrière–grand–père** [arjɛrgrɑ̃pɛr] *nm, pl* **arrière–grands–pères** : great-grandfather — **arrière–pays** [arjɛrpei] *nms & pl* : hinterland — **arrière–pensée** [arjɛrpɑ̃se] *nf, pl* **arrière–pensées** : ulterior motive — **arrière–plan** [arjɛrplɑ̃] *nm, pl* **arrière–plans** : background
arrimer [arime] *vt* **1** : stow **2** FIXER : secure, fix
arriver [arive] *vi* **1** : arrive, come **2** RÉUSSIR : succeed **3** SE PASSER : happen, occur **4 ~ à** ATTEINDRE : reach — **arrivée** [arive] *nf* **1** : arrival **2** *or* **ligne d'~** : finish line — **arriviste** [arivist] *adj* : pushy — **~** *nmf* : upstart
arrogant, -gante [arɔgɑ̃, -gɑ̃t] *adj* : arrogant — **arrogance** [arɔgɑ̃s] *nf* : arrogance
arroger [arɔʒe] {17} *v* **s'arroger** *vr* : claim (without right)
arrondir [arɔ̃dir] *vt* **1** : make round **2** : round off (a number)
arrondissement [arɔ̃dismɑ̃] *nm* : district
arroser [aroze] *vt* **1** : water **2** : baste (in cooking) **3** CÉLÉBRER : drink to — **arrosoir** [arozwar] *nm* : watering can
arsenal [arsənal] *nm, pl* **-naux** [-no] **1** : shipyard **2** : arsenal
arsenic [arsənik] *nm* : arsenic
art [ar] *nm* : art
artère [artɛr] *nf* **1** : artery **2** : main road
arthrite [artrit] *nf* : arthritis
artichaut [artiʃo] *nm* : artichoke
article [artikl] *nm* **1** : article **2 ~s de toilette** : toiletries
articuler [artikyle] *vt* : articulate — **articulation** [artikylasjɔ̃] *nf* **1** : articulation **2** : joint (in anatomy)
artifice [artifis] *nm* : trick, device
artificiel, -cielle [artifisjɛl] *adj* : artificial — **artificiellement** [-sjɛlmɑ̃] *adv* : artificially
artillerie [artijri] *nf* : artillery
artilleur [artijœr] *nm Can* : pitcher (in baseball)
artisan, -sane [artizɑ̃, -zan] *n* : artisan, craftsman — **artisanal, -nale** *adj, pl* **-naux** : made by craftsmen, homemade — **artisanat** [artizana] *nm* **1** : artisans *pl* **2** : arts and crafts *pl*
artiste [artist] *nmf* : artist — **artistique** [artistik] *adj* : artistic
as [as] *nm* : ace
ascendant, -dante [asɑ̃dɑ̃, -dɑ̃t] *adj* : ascending — **ascendant** *nm* **1** : influence **2 ~s** *nmpl* : ancestors — **ascendance** [asɑ̃dɑ̃s] *nf* : ancestry
ascenseur [asɑ̃sœr] *nm* : elevator
ascension [asɑ̃sjɔ̃] *nf* : ascent
ascète [asɛt] *nmf* : ascetic — **ascétique** [asetik] *adj* : ascetic
asiatique [azjatik] *adj* : Asian
asile [azil] *nm* **1** : (political) asylum **2** ABRI : refuge
aspect [aspɛ] *nm* **1** : aspect **2** ALLURE : appearance
asperge [aspɛrʒ] *nf* : asparagus
asperger [aspɛrʒe] {17} *vt* : sprinkle, spray
aspérité [asperite] *nf* : bump, protrusion
asphalte [asfalt] *nm* : asphalt
asphyxier [asfiksje] {96} *vt* : asphyxiate, suffocate — **s'asphyxier** *vr* : suffocate — **asphyxie** [asfiksi] *nf* : asphyxiation
aspirer [aspire] *vt* **1** : suck up (a liquid) **2** : inhale — *vi* **~ à** : aspire to — **aspiration** [aspirasjɔ̃] *nf* **1** AMBITION : aspiration **2** : suction **3** : inhaling — **aspirateur**

[aspiratœr] *nm* **1** : vacuum cleaner **2 passer l'~** : vacuum

aspirine [aspirin] *nf* : aspirin

assagir [asaʒir] *vt* : calm, quiet — **s'assagir** *vr* : quiet down

assaillir [asajir] {93} *vt* : attack — **assaillant, -lante** [asajɑ̃, -jɑ̃t] *n* : attacker

assainir [asenir] *vt* : purify, clean up

assaisonner [asɛzɔne] *vt* : season — **assaisonnement** [ɑsɛzɔnmɑ̃] *nm* : seasoning

assassiner [asasine] *vt* : murder, assassinate — **assassin** *nm* : murderer, assassin

assaut [aso] *nm* **1** : assault **2 prendre d'~** : storm

assécher [aseʃe] {87} *vt* : drain

assembler [asɑ̃ble] *vt* : assemble — **s'assembler** *vr* : gather — **assemblée** [asɑ̃ble] *nf* **1** RÉUNION : meeting **2** : (political) assembly

asséner [asene] {87} *vt* : strike (a blow)

assentiment [asɑ̃timɑ̃] *nm* : assent, consent

asseoir [aswar] {9} *vt* : seat, sit — **s'asseoir** *vr* : sit down

assermenté, -tée [asɛrmɑ̃te] *adj* : sworn

assertion [asɛrsjɔ̃] *nf* : assertion

asservir [asɛrvir] *vt* : enslave

assez [ase] *adv* **1** SUFFISAMMENT : enough **2** : rather, quite

assidu, -due [asidy] *adj* : diligent — **assiduité** [asidɥite] *nf* : diligence

assiéger [asjeʒe] {64} *vt* : besiege

assiette [asjɛt] *nf* : plate, dish — **assiettée** [asjete] *nf* : plateful

assigner [asiɲe] *vt* : assign, allot — **assignation** [asiɲasjɔ̃] *nf* **1** : allocation **2** : summons, subpoena

assimiler [asimile] *vt* **1** : assimilate **2 ~ à** : equate with, compare to — **assimilation** [asimilasjɔ̃] *nf* : assimilation

assis, -sise [asiz] *adj* : seated, sitting down

assise *nf* **1** : foundation, base **2 ~s** *nfpl* : court

assister [asiste] *vt* : assist — *vi* **~ à** : attend — **assistance** [asistɑ̃s] *nf* **1** : assistance **2** : audience — **assistant, -tante** [asistɑ̃, -tɑ̃t] *n* : assistant

associer [asɔsje] {96} *vt* **1** : associate **2 ~ qqn à** : include s.o. in — **s'associer** *vr* : join together — **association** [asɔsjasjɔ̃] *nf* : association — **associé, -ciée** [asɔsje] *n* : associate

assoiffé, -fée [aswafe] *adj* : thirsty

assombrir [asɔ̃brir] *vt* : darken — **s'assombrir** *vr* : darken

assommer [asɔme] *vt* **1** : stun, knock out **2** *fam* : bore stiff — **assommant, -mante** [asɔmɑ̃, -mɑ̃t] *adj* : boring

assortir [asɔrtir] *vt* : match — **assorti, -tie** [asɔrti] *adj* **1** : matched **2** : assorted — **assortiment** [asɔrtimɑ̃] *nm* : assortment

assoupir [asupir] *v* **s'assoupir** *vr* : doze off

assouplir [asuplir] *vt* : make supple, soften — **s'assouplir** *vr* : loosen up

assourdir [asurdir] *vt* **1** : deafen **2** ÉTOUFFER : muffle

assouvir [asuvir] *vt* : appease

assujettir [asyʒetir] *vt* **1** : subjugate **2 ~ à** : subject to

assumer [asyme] *vt* : assume, take on

assurer [asyre] *vt* **1** : assure **2** FOURNIR : provide **3** : insure (one's property, etc.) — **s'assurer** *vr* **~ de** : make sure of — **assurance** [asyrɑ̃s] *nf* **1** : assurance **2** : insurance **3 ~-vie** : life insurance — **assuré, -rée** [asyre] *adj* : confident, certain — **assurément** [asyremɑ̃] *adv* : certainly

astérisque [asterisk] *nm* : asterisk

asthme [asm] *nm* : asthma

asticot [astiko] *nm* : maggot

astiquer [astike] *vt* : polish

astre [astr] *nm* : star

astreindre [astrɛ̃dr] {37} *vt* : compel — **astreignant, -gnante** [astrɛɲɑ̃, -ɲɑ̃t] *adj* : demanding

astrologie [astrɔlɔʒi] *nf* : astrology

astronaute [astrɔnot] *nmf* : astronaut

astronomie [astrɔnɔmi] *nf* : astronomy

astuce [astys] *nf* **1** : cleverness **2** TRUC : trick **3** PLAISANTERIE : joke — **astucieux, -cieuse** [astysjø, -sjøz] *adj* : astute, clever — **astucieusement** [-sjøzmɑ̃] *adv* : cleverly

atelier [atəlje] *nm* **1** : studio **2** : workshop

athée [ate] *adj* : atheistic — **~** *nmf* : atheist

athlète [atlɛt] *nmf* : athlete — **athlétique** [atletik] *adj* : athletic — **athlétisme** [atletism] *nm* : athletics

atlantique [atlɑ̃tik] *adj* : Atlantic

atlas [atlas] *nm* : atlas

atmosphère [atmɔsfɛr] *nf* : atmosphere — **atmosphérique** [atmɔsferik] *adj* : atmospheric

atome [atom] *nm* : atom — **atomique** [atɔmik] *adj* : atomic

atomiseur [atɔmizœr] *nm* : atomizer

atout [atu] *nm* **1** : trump (card) **2** AVANTAGE : asset

âtre [atr] *nm* : hearth

atroce [atrɔs] *adj* : atrocious — **atrocité** [atrɔsite] *nf* : atrocity

atrophier [atrɔfje] {96} *v* **s'atrophier** *vr* : atrophy

attabler [atable] *v* **s'attabler** *vr* : sit down at the table

attacher [ataʃe] *vt* : tie (up), fasten — **s'attacher** *vr* **1** : fasten **2 ~ à** : attach oneself to **3 ~ à** : apply oneself to — **attachant, -chante** [ataʃɑ̃, -ʃɑ̃t] *adj* : appealing, likeable — **attache** [ataʃ] *nf* **1** : fastener **2** LIEN : tie, bond — **attaché, -chée** [ataʃe] *n* : attaché — **attachement** [ataʃmɑ̃] *nm* : attachment

attaquer [atake] *v* : attack — **s'attaquer** *vr* **~ à** : attack — **attaque** [atak] *nf* : attack

attarder [atarde] *v* **s'attarder** *vr* : linger — **attardé** [atarde] *adj* **1** : late **2** : retarded **3** DÉMODÉ : old-fashioned

atteindre [atɛ̃dr] {37} *vt* **1** : reach, attain **2** FRAPPER : strike, hit **3** AFFECTER : affect — **atteinte** [atɛ̃t] *nf* **1** : attack **2 hors d'~** : out of reach **3 porter ~ à** : undermine

atteler [atle] {8} *vt* : harness — **s'atteler** *vr* **~ à** : apply oneself to — **attelage** [atlaʒ] *nm* : team (of animals)

attelle [atɛl] *nf* : splint

attenant, -nante [atnɑ̃, -nɑ̃t] *adj* : adjoining

attendre [atɑ̃dr] {63} *vt* **1** : wait for **2** ESPÉRER : expect — *vi* **1** : wait **2 faire ~ qqn** : keep s.o. waiting **3 en attendant** : in the meantime — **s'attendre** *vr* **~ à** : expect

attendrir [atɑ̃drir] *vt* **1** ÉMOUVOIR : move **2** : tenderize (meat) — **s'attendrir** *vr* : be moved — **attendrissant, -sante** [atɑ̃drisɑ̃, -sɑ̃t] *adj* : moving, touching

attendu, -due [atɑ̃dy] *adj* **1** : expected **2** : long-awaited — **attendu** *prep* **~ que** : since, considering that

attente [atɑ̃t] *nf* **1** : wait **2** ESPOIR : expectation

attenter [atɑ̃te] *vi* **~ à** : make an attempt on — **attentat** [atɑ̃ta] *nm* : attack

attention [atɑ̃sjɔ̃] *nf* **1** : attention **2 ~!** : look out!, beware! **3 faire ~** : pay attention — **attentionné, -née** [atɑ̃sjɔne] *adj* : considerate — **attentif, -tive** [atɑ̃tif, -tiv] *adj* **1** : attentive **2** : careful **3 être ~ à** : pay attention to — **attentivement** [-tivmɑ̃] *adv* : attentively

atténuer [atenɥe] *vt* **1** : tone down **2** : ease, allay — **s'atténuer** *vr* : subside

atterrer [atere] *vt* : dismay, appall

atterrir [aterir] *vi* : land — **atterrissage** [aterisaʒ] *nm* : landing

attester [atɛste] *vt* : attest, testify to — **attestation** [atɛstasjɔ̃] *nf* **1** : affidavit **2** : certificate

attirail [atiraj] *nm fam* : gear, paraphernalia

attirer [atire] *vt* : attract, draw — **attirance** [atirɑ̃s] *nf* : attraction — **attirant, -rante** [atirɑ̃, -rɑ̃t] *adj* : attractive

attiser [atize] *vt* : stir up, kindle

attitré, -trée [atitre] *adj* **1** : authorized **2** HABITUEL : regular

attitude [atityd] *nf* : attitude

attouchement [atuʃmɑ̃] *nm* : touching, fondling

attraction [atraksjɔ̃] *nf* : attraction (in science)

attrait [atrɛ] *nm* : appeal, attraction

attraper [atrape] *vt* : catch

attrayant, -trayante [atrɛjɑ̃, -trɛjɑ̃t] *adj* ATTIRANT : attractive

attribuer [atribɥe] *vt* : attribute, assign — **s'attribuer** *vr* : claim for oneself — **attribut** [atriby] *nm* : attribute — **attribution** [atribysjɔ̃] *nf* : allocation, allotment

attrister [atriste] *vt* : sadden

attrouper [atrupe] *v* **s'attrouper** *vr* : gather — **attroupement** [atrupmɑ̃] *nm* : crowd

au [o] → **à, le**

aubaine [obɛn] *nf* : good fortune, godsend

aube [ob] *nf* : dawn, daybreak

aubépine [obepin] *nf* : hawthorn

auberge [obɛrʒ] *nf* **1** : inn **2 ~ de jeunesse** : youth hostel — **aubergiste** [obɛrʒist] *nmf* : innkeeper

aubergine [obɛrʒin] *nf* : eggplant

auburn [obœrn] *adj* : auburn

aucun, -cune [okœ̃, -kyn] *adj* **1** : no, not any **2 plus qu'aucun autre** : more than any other — **~** *pron* **1** : none, not any **2** : any, anyone **3 d'aucuns** : some (people) — **aucunement** [okynmɑ̃] *adv* : not at all

audace [odas] *nf* **1** : audacity **2** COURAGE : boldness — **audacieux, -cieuse** [odasjø, -jøz] *adj* **1** : audacious **2** HARDI : daring

au-dedans [odədɑ̃] *adv* **1** : inside **2 ~ de** : within

au-dehors [odəɔr] *adv* **1** : outside **2 ~ de** : outside (of)

au-delà [odəla] *adv* **1** : beyond **2 ~ de** : beyond

au-dessous [odsu] *adv* **1** : below **2 ~ de** : below, under

au-dessus [odsy] *adv* **1** : above **2 ~ de** : above, over

au-devant [odvɑ̃] *adv* **1** : ahead **2 aller ~ de** : go to meet

audible [odibl] *adj* : audible

audience [odjɑ̃s] *nf* **1** : audience **2 ~s publiques** : public hearings

audio [odjo] *adj* : audio — **audiovisuel, -suelle** [odjɔvizɥɛl] *adj* : audiovisual

auditeur, -trice [oditœr, -tris] *n* : listener

audition [odisjɔ̃] *nf* **1** : hearing **2** : audition (in theater) — **auditionner** [odisjɔne] *v* : audition — **auditoire** [oditwar] *nm* : audience — **auditorium** [oditɔrjɔm] *nm* : auditorium

auge [oʒ] *nf* : trough

augmenter [ogmɑ̃te] *v* : increase — **augmentation** [ogmɑ̃tasjɔ̃] *nf* : increase, raise

augurer [ogyre] *vt* : augur — **augure** [ogyr] *nm* : omen

aujourd'hui [oʒurdɥi] *adv & nm* : today

aumône [omon] *nf* : alms *pl*

aumônier [omonje] *nm* : chaplain

auparavant [oparavɑ̃] *adv* : before(hand)

auprès [oprɛ] *adv* **~ de 1** : beside, near, next to **2** : compared with **3 ambassadeur ~ des Nations Unies** : ambassador to the United Nations

auquel, -quelle [okɛl] → **lequel**

auréole [oreɔl] *nf* **1** : halo **2** TACHE : ring

auriculaire [orikylɛr] *nm* : little finger

aurore [ɔrɔr] *nf* AUBE : dawn

ausculter [oskylte] *vt* : examine (with a stethoscope)

auspices [ospis] *nmpl* **sous les ~ de** : under the auspices of

aussi [osi] *adv* **1** : too, also, as well **2** TELLEMENT : so **3 ~ ... que** : as ... as

aussitôt [osito] *adv* **1** : immediately **2 ~ que** : as soon as

austère [ostɛr] *adj* : austere — **austérité** [osterite] *nf* : austerity

austral, -trale [ostral] *adj, mpl* **-trals** : southern

australien, -lienne [ostraljɛ̃, -jɛn] *adj* : Australian

autant [otɑ̃] *adv* **1** *or* **~ de** : as much, as many, so much, so many **2 ~ que** : as much as, as many as, as far as **3 d'~ plus** : all the more **4 pour ~** : for all that

autel [otɛl] *nm* : altar

auteur [otœr] *nm* **1** : author **2** : person responsible, perpetrator

authentique [otɑ̃tik] *adj* : authentic

auto [oto] *nf* : car, automobile

autobiographie [otɔbjɔgrafi] *nf* : autobiography

autobus [otɔbys] *nm* : bus

autocar [otɔkar] *nm* : bus, coach

autochtone [otɔktɔn] *adj & nmf* : native

autocollant, -lante [otɔkɔlɑ̃, -lɑ̃t] *adj* : self-adhesive — **autocollant** *nm* : sticker

autocuiseur [otɔkɥizœr] *nm* : pressure cooker

autodéfense [otɔdefɑ̃s] *nf* : self-defense

autodidacte [otɔdidakt] *adj* : self-taught

autodiscipline [otɔdisiplin] *nf* : self-discipline

autographe [otɔgraf] *nm* : autograph

automation [otɔmasjɔ̃] *nf* : automation — **automatique** [otɔmatik] *adj* : automatic — **automatiquement** [-tikmɑ̃] *adv* : automatically

automatiser [otɔmatize] *vt* : automate — **automatisation** [otɔmatizasjɔ̃] *nf* : automation

automne [otɔn] *nm* : autumn, fall

automobile [otɔmɔbil] *adj* : automotive — **~** *nf* : automobile, car — **automobiliste** [otɔmɔbilist] *nmf* : motorist, driver

autonome [otɔnɔm] *adj* : autonomous — **autonomie** [otɔnɔmi] *nf* : autonomy

autoportrait [otɔpɔrtrɛ] *nm* : self-portrait

autopsie [otɔpsi] *nf* : autopsy

autoriser [otɔrize] *vt* : authorize — **autorisation** [otɔrizasjɔ̃] *nf* **1** : authorization **2** PERMIS : permit

autorité [otɔrite] *nf* : authority — **autoritaire** [otɔritɛr] *adj* : authoritarian

autoroute [otɔrut] *nf* **1** : highway, freeway **2 ~ à péage** : turnpike

auto-stop [otɔstɔp] *nm* **faire de l'~** : hitchhike — **auto-stoppeur, -peuse** [otɔstɔpœr, -pøz] *n* : hitchhiker

autosuffisant, -sante [otɔsyfizɑ̃, -zɑ̃t] *adj* : self-sufficient

autour [otur] *adv* **1 ~ de** : around, about **2 tout ~** : all around

autre [otr] *adj* **1** : other, different **2 ~ chose** : something else — **~** *pron* : other, another

autrefois [otrəfwa] *adv* : in the past, formerly

autrement [otrəmɑ̃] *adv* **1** : differently **2** SINON : otherwise **3 ~ dit** : in other words

autruche [otryʃ] *nf* : ostrich

autrui [otrɥi] *pron* : others

auvent [ovɑ̃] *nm* : awning

auxiliaire [oksiljɛr] *adj & nmf* : auxiliary, assistant — **~** *nm* : auxiliary (verb)

auxquels, -quelles [okɛl] → **lequel**

avachi, -chie [avaʃi] *adj* : shapeless, limp

aval [aval] *nm* **en ~** : downstream

avalanche [avalɑ̃ʃ] *nf* : avalanche

avaler [avale] *vt* : swallow

avancer [avɑ̃se] {6} *vt* : move forward, put ahead — *vi* **1** : advance, go forward **2** : be fast (of a watch) — **s'avancer** *vr* **1** : move forward **2** : progress — **avance** [avɑ̃s] *nf* **1** : advance **2** : lead **3 à l'~** *or* **d'~** : in advance **4 en ~** : early — **avancé, -cée** [avɑ̃se] *adj* : advanced — **avancement** [avɑ̃smɑ̃] *nm* : promotion

avant [avɑ̃] *adv* **1** : before **2** : first **3 ~ de** : before **4 ~ que** : before, until — **~** *adj* : front — **~** *nm* **1** : front **2** : forward (in sports) **3 en ~** : forward, ahead **4 en ~ de** : ahead of — **~** *prep* **1** : before, by **2 ~ tout** : above all

avantager [avɑ̃taʒe] {17} *vt* **1** FAVORISER : favor **2** : flatter — **avantageux, -geuse** [avɑ̃taʒø, -ʒøz] *adj* : profitable, worthwhile — **avantage** [avɑ̃taʒ] *nm* **1** : advantage **2 ~s sociaux** : fringe benefits

avant-bras [avɑ̃bra] *nms & pl* : forearm

avant-dernier, -nière [avɑ̃dɛrnje, -njɛr] *adj* : next to last

avant-garde [avɑ̃gard] *nf, pl* **avant-gardes** : avant-garde

avant-goût [avɑ̃gu] *nm, pl* **avant-goûts** : foretaste

avant-hier [avɑ̃tjɛr] *adv* : the day before yesterday

avant-midi [avɑ̃midi] *nfs & pl Can, nms & pl Bel* : morning

avant-poste [avɑ̃pɔst] *nm, pl* **avant-postes** : outpost

avant-première [avɑ̃prəmjɛr] *nf, pl* **avant-premières** : preview

avant-propos [avɑ̃prɔpo] *nms & pl* : foreword

avant-toit [avɑ̃twa] *nm* : eaves *pl*

avare [avar] *adj* : miserly — **~** *nmf* : miser

avarié [avarje] *adj* : spoiled, rotten

avec [avɛk] *prep* : with — **~** *adv fam* : with it, with them

avenant, -nante [avnɑ̃, -nɑ̃t] *adj* : pleasant

avènement [avɛnmɑ̃] *nm* **1** : accession (to a throne) **2** DÉBUT : advent

avenir [avnir] *nm* **1** : future **2 à l'~** : in the future

avent [avɑ̃] *nm* **l'~** : Advent

aventure [avɑ̃tyr] *nf* **1** : adventure **2** : love affair — **aventurer** [avɑ̃tyre] *vt* : risk — **s'aventurer** *vr* : venture — **aventureux, -reuse** [avɑ̃tyrø, -røz] *adj* : adventurous

avenu [avny] *adj m* **nul et non ~** : null and void

avenue [avny] *nf* : avenue

avérer [avere] {87} *v* **s'avérer** *vr* : turn out to be

averse [avɛrs] *nf* : shower, storm

aversion [avɛrsjɔ̃] *nf* : aversion, dislike

avertir [avɛrtir] *vt* **1** : warn **2** INFORMER : inform — **avertissement** [avɛrtismɑ̃] *nm* : warning — **avertisseur** [avɛrtisœr] *nm* **1** : (car) horn **2** : alarm

aveu [avø] *nm, pl* **-veux** : confession, admission

aveugle [avœgl] *adj* : blind — **~** *nmf* : blind person — **aveuglant, -glante** [avœglɑ̃, -glɑ̃t] *adj* : blinding — **aveuglement** [avœgləmɑ̃] *nm* : blindness — **aveuglément** [avœglemɑ̃] *adv* : blindly — **aveugler** [avœgle] *vt* : blind

aviateur, -trice [avjatœr, -tris] *n* : pilot — **aviation** [avjasjɔ̃] *nf* : aviation

avide [avid] *adj* **1** CUPIDE : greedy **2 ~ de** : eager for — **avidité** [avidite] *nf* **1** CUPIDITÉ : greed **2** : eagerness

avilir [avilir] *vt* : debase

avion [avjɔ̃] *nm* : airplane

aviron [avirɔ̃] *nm* RAME : oar

avis [avis] *nm* **1** : opinion **2** ANNONCE : notice **3** CONSEIL : advice — **aviser** [avize] *vt* : inform, notify — **avisé, -sée** [avize] *adj* : sensible

aviver [avive] *vt* : revive

avocat[1]**, -cate** [avɔka, -kat] *n* : lawyer, attorney

avocat[2] *nm* : avocado

avoine [avwan] *nf* : oats *pl*

avoir [avwar] {10} *vt* **1** POSSÉDER : have **2** OBTENIR : get **3 ~ dix ans** : be ten years old **4 ~ à** : have to **5 ~ mal** : be hurt — *v impers* **1 il y a** : there is, there are **2 qu'est-ce qu'il y a?** : what's wrong? — *v aux* : have — **~** *nm* : assets *pl*

avoisiner [avwazine] *vt* : be near, border on — **avoisinant, -nante** [avwazinɑ̃] *adj* : neighboring

avorter [avɔrte] *vi* : abort — **avortement** [avɔrtəmɑ̃] *nm* : abortion

avouer [avwe] *vt* : admit, confess to — **s'avouer** *vr* : confess, own up

axe [aks] *nm* **1** : axis **2 ~ routier** : major road — **axer** [akse] *vt* : center, focus

axiome [aksjom] *nm* : axiom

azote [azɔt] *nm* : nitrogen

azur [azyr] *nm* : sky blue

B

b [be] *nm* : b, second letter of the alphabet

babeurre [babœr] *nm* : buttermilk

babiller [babije] *vi* : babble, chatter — **babillage** [babijaʒ] *nm* : babbling — **babillard** [babijar] *nm Can* : bulletin board

babiole [babjɔl] *nf* : trinket

babouin [babwɛ̃] *nm* : baboon

baby-sitter [bebisitœr] *nmf, pl* **baby-sitters** *France* : baby-sitter — **baby-**

sitting [bebisitiŋ] *nm* **faire du ~** *France* : baby-sit

baccalauréat [bakalɔrea] *nm* **1** *France* : school-leaving certificate **2** *Can* : bachelor's degree

bâche [baʃ] *nf* : tarpaulin

bâcler [bakle] *vt* : rush through

bacon [bekɔn] *nm* : bacon

bactéries [bakteri] *nfpl* : bacteria

badaud, -daude [bado, -dod] *n* : (curious) onlooker

badge [badʒ] *nm* : badge

badiner [badine] *vi* **1** : joke, jest **2 ~ avec** : toy with — **badinage** [badinaʒ] *nm* : banter, joking

bafouer [bafwe] *vt* : ridicule, scorn

bafouiller [bafuje] *v* : mumble, stammer — **bafouillage** [bafujaʒ] *nm* : mumbling, gibberish

bagage [bagaʒ] *nm* : baggage, luggage

bagarrer [bagare] *vi* : fight — **se bagarrer** *vr* : fight, brawl — **bagarre** [bagar] *nf* : fight, brawl

bagatelle [bagatɛl] *nf* : trifle, trinket

bagne [baɲ] *nm* : labor camp

bagnole [baɲɔl] *nf fam* : jalopy

bague [bag] *nf* : ring

baguette [bagɛt] *nf* **1** : stick, rod, baton **2** : baguette (loaf of French bread) **3 ~ de tambour** : drumstick **4 ~s** *nfpl* : chopsticks

baie [bɛ] *nf* **1** : bay **2** : berry

baigner [beɲe] *vt* : bathe, wash — *vi* : soak, steep — **se baigner** *vr* **1** : take a bath **2** : go swimming — **baignade** [bɛɲad] *nf* : swimming — **baigneur, -gneuse** [bɛɲœr, -ɲøz] *n* : swimmer, bather — **baignoire** [bɛɲwar] *nf* : bathtub

bail [baj] *nm, pl* **baux** [bo] : lease

bâiller [baje] *vi* **1** : yawn **2** : be ajar (of a door) — **bâillement** [bajmɑ̃] *nm* : yawn

bâillonner [bajɔne] *vt* : gag, muzzle — **bâillon** [bajɔ̃] *nm* : gag

bain [bɛ̃] *nm* : bath

bain–marie [bɛ̃mari] *nm, pl* **bains–marie** : double boiler

baïonnette [bajɔnɛt] *nf* : bayonet

baiser [beze] *vt* : kiss — **~** *nm* : kiss

baisser [bese] *vt* : lower, reduce (volume, light, etc.) — *vi* : drop, decline — **se baisser** *vr* : bend down — **baisse** [bɛs] *nf* : fall, drop

bal [bal] *nm* : ball, dance

balader [balade] *v* **se balader** *vr* **1** : go for a walk **2** : go for a drive — **balade** [balad] *nf* **1** : stroll, walk **2** : drive, ride

balafre [balafr] *nf* : gash, slash

balai [balɛ] *nm* : broom, brush

balancer [balɑ̃se] {6} *vt* **1** : sway, swing (one's arms, etc.) **2** : balance (an account) **3** *fam* : chuck, junk — **se balancer** *vr* : rock, sway — **balance** [balɑ̃s] *nf* : scales *pl*, balance

balancier [balɑ̃sje] *nm* : pendulum

balançoire [balɑ̃swar] *nf* **1** : child's swing **2** BASCULE : seesaw

balayer [baleje] {11} *vt* **1** : sweep **2** : scan (in computer science) — **balayage** [balɛjaʒ] *nm* : sweeping — **balayeuse** [balɛjøz] *nf* **1** : street-cleaning truck **2** *Can* : vacuum cleaner

balbutier [balbysje] {96} *v* : stammer, stutter — **balbutiement** [balbysimɑ̃] *nm* **1** : stammering, stuttering **2 ~s** *nmpl* : beginnings

balcon [balkɔ̃] *nm* : balcony

baldaquin [baldakɛ̃] *nm* : canopy

baleine [balɛn] *nf* : whale

balise [baliz] *nf* : buoy, beacon — **baliser** [balize] *vt* : mark with beacons

balistique [balistik] *adj* : ballistic

balivernes [balivɛrn] *nfpl* : nonsense

ballade [balad] *nf* : ballad

balle [bal] *nf* **1** : ball (in sports) **2** : bullet **3** *France fam* : franc

balle–molle [balmɔl] *nf Can* : softball

ballet [balɛ] *nm* : ballet — **ballerine** [balrin] *nf* : ballerina

ballon [balɔ̃] *nm* **1** : (foot)ball **2** : balloon — **ballon–panier** [balɔ̃panje] *nm Can* : basketball (game)

ballot [balo] *nm* BALUCHON : pack, bundle

ballotter [balɔte] *vt* SECOUER : shake, toss about — *vi* : toss, roll around

balloune [balun] *nf Can* : balloon

balnéaire [balneɛr] *adj* : seaside

balourd, -lourde [balur, -lurd] *adj* : awkward, clumsy

baluchon [balyʃɔ̃] *nm* : pack, bundle

balustrade [balystrad] *nf* : guardrail

bambin, -bine [bɑ̃bɛ̃, -bin] *n* : child, toddler

bambou [bɑ̃bu] *nm* : bamboo

ban [bɑ̃] *nm* **1** : round of applause **2 ~s** *nmpl* : banns **3 mettre au ~** : ostracize

banal, -nale [banal] *adj, mpl* **-nals** : commonplace, trite — **banalité** [banalite] *nf* : triviality

banane [banan] *nf* : banana

banc [bɑ̃] *nm* **1** : bench **2** : school (of fish) **3 ~ de sable** : sandbank **4 ~ de neige** *Can* : snowbank

bancaire [bɑ̃kɛr] *adj* : banking, bank

bancal, -cale [bɑ̃kal] *adj, mpl* **-cals** : wobbly, rickety

bandage [bɑ̃daʒ] *nm* **1** : bandaging **2** PANSEMENT : bandage

bande [bɑ̃d] *nf* **1** : gang, group, pack (of animals) **2** : tape, (reel of) film **3 ~ dessinée** : comic strip

bandeau [bɑ̃do] *nm, pl* **-deaux 1** : blindfold **2** : headband

bander [bɑ̃de] *vt* **1** : bandage **2 ~ les yeux à** : blindfold

banderole [bɑ̃drɔl] *nf* : banner, pennant

bandit [bɑ̃di] *nm* VOLEUR : bandit, robber

bandoulière [bɑ̃duljɛr] *nf* : shoulder strap

banlieue [bɑ̃ljø] *nf* : suburbs *pl*

bannière [banjɛr] *nf* : banner

bannir [banir] *vt* : banish, exile

banque [bɑ̃k] *nf* **1** : bank **2 travailler dans la ~** : work in banking — **banqueroute** [bɑ̃krut] *nf* : bankruptcy

banquet [bɑ̃kɛ] *nm* : banquet, feast

banquette [bɑ̃kɛt] *nf* : bench, seat (in a booth or vehicle)

banquier, -quière [bɑ̃kje, -kjɛr] *n* : banker

baptême [batɛm] *nm* : baptism — **baptiser** [batize] *vt* : baptize, christen

bar [bar] *nm* **1** : sea bass **2** CAFÉ : bar

baragouin [baragwɛ̃] *nm* : gibberish — **baragouiner** [baragwine] *vi* : talk gibberish, jabber

baraque [barak] *nf* **1** : hut, shack **2** : stall, booth (at a fair, etc.)

barbare [barbar] *adj* : barbaric — **~** *nmf* : barbarian

barbe [barb] *nf* : beard

barbecue [barbəkju] *nm* : barbecue

barbelé, -lée [barbəle] *adj* **fil barbelé** : barbed wire

barbiche [barbiʃ] *nf* : goatee

barbier [barbje] *nm Can* : barber

barbouiller [barbuje] *vt* **1** : smear **2** GRIBOUILLER : scribble

bardeau [bardo] *nm, pl* **-deaux** : shingle

barème [barɛm] *nm* : scale, table, list

baril [baril] *nm* TONNELET : barrel, keg

bariolé, -lée [barjɔle] *adj* : multicolored

barman [barman] *nm, pl* **-mans** *or* **-men** : bartender

baromètre [barɔmɛtr] *nm* : barometer

baron, -ronne [barɔ̃, -rɔn] *n* : baron *m*, baroness *f*

barque [bark] *nf* : small boat

barrage [baraʒ] *nm* **1** : dam **2 ~ routier** : roadblock

barre [bar] *nf* **1** : bar, rod **2** NIVEAU : mark, level **3 prendre la ~** : take the helm — **barreau** [baro] *nm, pl* **-reaux 1** : bar **2** : rung — **barrer** [bare] *vt* **1** : bar, block **2** : cross out (a word) **3** : steer (a boat) **4** *Can* : lock

barricader [barikade] *vt* : barricade — **barricade** [barikad] *nf* : barricade

barrière [barjɛr] *nf* : barrier

baryton [baritɔ̃] *nm* : baritone

bas *nms & pl* **1** : bottom, lower part **2** : stocking **3 à ~** : down with **4 en ~** : below **5 en ~ de** : at the bottom of — **~** *adv* **1** : low **2 parler tout ~** : whisper, speak softly — **bas, basse** [ba, baz (*before a vowel or mute h*), bas] *adj* **1** : low **2** VIL : base, vile

basané, -née [bazane] *adj* : tanned, sunburned

bascule [baskyl] *nf* **1** BALANCE : balance, scales *pl* **2** BALANÇOIRE : seesaw — **basculer** [baskyle] *vi* : tip, topple

base [baz] *nf* **1** : base **2** FONDEMENT : basis **3 ~ de données** : database

baseball *or* **base–ball** [bɛzbol] *nm* : baseball — **baseballeur, -leuse** [bɛzbolœr, -løz] *n Can* : baseball player

baser [baze] *vt* FONDER : base, found

basilic [bazilik] *nm* : basil

basilique [bazilik] *nf* : basilica

basket [baskɛt] *or* **basket–ball** [baskɛtbol] *nm* : basketball — **basketteur, -teuse** [baskɛtœr, -tøz] *n* : basketball player

basque [bask] *adj & nm* : Basque

basse [bas] *nf* : bass (in music)

bassin [basɛ̃] *nm* **1** : basin (in geography) **2** : pond, pool **3** : pelvis — **bassine** [basin] *nf* : bowl

basson [basɔ̃] *nm* : bassoon

bataille [bataj] *nf* : battle, fight — **batailler** [bataje] *vi* : fight, struggle (hard) — **batailleur, -leuse** [batajœr, -jøz] *adj* : quarrelsome — **~** *n* : fighter

bâtard, -tarde [batar, -tard] *adj & n* : bastard

bateau *nm, pl* **-teaux 1** : boat, ship **2 ~ à voiles** : sailboat

batifoler [batifɔle] *vi* : frolic

bâtir [batir] *vt* **1** CONSTRUIRE : build, erect **2** FAUFILER : baste, tack — **bâtiment** [batimɑ̃] *nm* **1** : building, structure **2** NAVIRE : ship — **bâtisseur, -seuse** [batisœr, -søz] *n* : builder

bâton [batɔ̃] *nm* **1** : rod, stick, staff **2** *Can* : bat (in sports) **3 ~ de rouge** : lipstick

battre [batr] {12} *vt* **1** FRAPPER : hit, strike **2** VAINCRE : defeat **3** : shuffle (cards) — *vi* : beat (of the heart) — **se battre** *vr* : fight — **battant, -tante** [batɑ̃, -tɑ̃t] *adj* **1** : beating, pounding **2 pluie battante** : pouring rain — **batte** [bat] *nf* : bat (in sports) — **battement** [batmɑ̃] *nm* **1** : beating **2 ~ de cœur** : heartbeat — **batterie** [batri] *nf* **1** : battery (of a car) **2** ENSEMBLE : set, group **3** : drums, drum set — **batteur** [batœr, -tøz] *nm* **1** : whisk, eggbeater **2** : drummer **3** : batter (in sports)

baume [bom] *nm* : balm

baux → **bail**

bavard, -varde [bavar, -vard] *adj* : talkative — **~** *n* : chatterbox — **bavarder** [bavarde] *vi* **1** : chatter **2** : gossip — **bavardage** [bavardaʒ] *nm* : idle talk, chatter

bave [bav] *nf* : dribble, spittle — **baver** [bave] *vi* **1** : dribble, drool **2** COULER : leak — **bavoir** [bavwar] *nm* : (baby's) bib

bavure [bavyr] *nf* **1** : smudge **2** GAFFE : blunder

bazar [bazar] *nm* **1** : bazaar **2** *fam* : clutter, mess

beau [bo] (**bel** [bɛl] *before vowel or mute h*), **belle** [bɛl] *adj, mpl* **beaux** [bo] **1** : beautiful, handsome **2** : good (of a performance, etc.) **3** : considerable (in quantity) **4 ~ temps** : nice weather — **~** *adv* **1 avoir ~** : do (something) in vain **2 il fait ~** : it's nice outside

beaucoup [boku] *adv* **1** : much, a lot **2 ~ de** : much, many, a lot of **3 de ~** : by far

beau–fils [bofis] *nm, pl* **beaux–fils 1** : son-in-law **2** : stepson — **beau–frère** [bofrɛr] *nm, pl* **beaux–frères 1** : brother-in-law **2** : stepbrother — **beau–père** [bopɛr] *nm, pl* **beaux–pères 1** : father-in-law **2** : stepfather

beauté [bote] *nf* : beauty

beaux–arts [bozar] *nmpl* : fine arts

beaux–parents [boparɑ̃] *nmpl* : in-laws

bébé [bebe] *nm* : baby, infant

bec [bɛk] *nm* **1** : beak, bill **2** *fam* : mouth **3** EMBOUCHURE : mouthpiece **4** : point (of a pen) **5** : spout, lip (of a jug, etc.) **6** *Can fam* : kiss

bêche [bɛʃ] *nf* : spade — **bêcher** [beʃe] *vt* : dig (up)

bedaine [bədɛn] *nf fam* : paunch

bée *adj* [be] → **bouche**

beffroi [befrwa] *nm* : belfry

bégayer [begeje] {11} *v* : stutter, stammer

béguin [begɛ̃] *nm fam* : crush, infatuation

beige [bɛʒ] *adj & nm* : beige

beignet [bɛɲɛ] *nm* **1** : doughnut **2** : fritter — **beigne** [bɛɲ] *nm Can* : doughnut

bel [bɛl] → **beau**

bêler [bele] *vi* : bleat — **bêlement** [bɛlmɑ̃] *nm* : bleat

belette [bəlɛt] *nf* : weasel

belge [bɛlʒ] *adj* : Belgian

bélier [belje] *nm* : ram

belle [bɛl] *adj* → **beau**

belle–famille [bɛlfamij] *nf, pl* **belles–familles** : in-laws *pl* — **belle–fille** [bɛlfij] *nf, pl* **belles–filles 1** : daughter-in-law **2** : stepdaughter — **belle–mère** [bɛlmɛr] *nf, pl* **belles–mères 1** : mother-in-law **2** : stepmother — **belle–sœur** [bɛlsœr] *nf, pl* **belles–sœurs** : sister-in-law

belligérant, -rante [beliʒerɑ̃, -rɑ̃t] *adj & n* : belligerent

belliqueux, -queuse [bɛlikø, -køz] *adj* GUERRIER : warlike

bémol [bemɔl] *adj & nm* : flat (in music)

bénédiction [benediksjɔ̃] *nf* : blessing, benediction

bénéfice [benefis] *nm* **1** AVANTAGE : benefit, advantage **2** GAIN : profit — **bénéficiaire** [benefisjɛr] *nmf* : beneficiary — **bénéficier** [benefisje] {96} *vi* **~ de** : benefit from — **bénéfique** [benefik] *adj* : beneficial

bénévole [benevɔl] *adj* : voluntary — **~** *nmf* : volunteer

bénin, -nigne [benɛ̃, beniɲ] *adj* **1** : slight, minor **2** : benign (of a tumor)

bénir [benir] *vt* : bless — **bénit, -nite** [beni, -nit] *adj* : blessed

benjamin, -mine [bɛ̃ʒamɛ̃, -min] *n* CADET : youngest child

béquille [bekij] *nf* **1** : crutch **2** : kickstand

bercer [bɛrse] {6} *vt* **1** : rock (a baby) **2** APAISER : soothe, lull — **se bercer** *vr* : rock, swing — **berceau** [bɛrso] *nm, pl* **-ceaux** : cradle — **berceuse** [bɛrsøz] *nf* **1** : lullaby **2** : rocking chair

béret [berɛ] *nm* : beret

berge [bɛrʒ] *nf* RIVE : bank (of a river, etc.)

berger, -gère [bɛrʒe, -ʒɛr] *n* : shepherd, shepherdess *f* — **berger** *nm* : sheepdog

berline [bɛrlin] *nf* : sedan

berlingot [bɛrlɛ̃go] *nm* **1** : carton (for milk, etc.) **2** : hard candy

berner [bɛrne] *vt* : fool, deceive

besogne [bəzɔɲ] *nf* : task, job

besoin [bəzwɛ̃] *nm* **1** : need **2 avoir ~ de** : need **3 dans le ~** : needy

bestiole [bɛstjɔl] *nf* : bug, tiny creature

bétail [betaj] *nm* : livestock, cattle *pl*

bête [bɛt] *nf* ANIMAL : animal, creature — **~** *adj* : stupid, silly — **bêtement** [bɛtmɑ̃] *adv* : foolishly — **bêtise** [betiz] *nf* **1** : stupidity **2** : stupid thing, nonsense

béton [betɔ̃] *nm* : concrete

bette [bɛt] *nf* : Swiss chard

betterave [bɛtrav] *nf* : beet

beugler [bøgle] *vi* **1** : moo, bellow **2** : blare (of a radio, etc.) — *vt* : bellow out

beurre [bœr] *nm* : butter — **beurrer** [bœre] *vt* : butter

bévue [bevy] *nf* : blunder

biais [bjɛ, bjɛz] *nm* **1** : means, way **2 de ~** : diagonally — **biaiser** [bjeze] *vi* : hedge, dodge the issue

bibelot [biblo] *nm* : trinket, curio

biberon [bibrɔ̃] *nm* : baby bottle

Bible [bibl] *nf* **la ~** : the Bible — **biblique** [biblik] *adj* : biblical, scriptural

bibliographie [biblijɔgrafi] *nf* : bibliography

bibliothèque [biblijɔtɛk] *nf* **1** : library **2** : bookcase — **bibliothécaire** [biblijɔtekɛr] *nmf* : librarian

bicarbonate [bikarbɔnat] *nm* **~ de soude** : baking soda

biceps [bisɛps] *nms & pl* : biceps

biche [biʃ] *nf* : doe

bicoque [bikɔk] *nf* : shack, shanty

bicyclette [bisiklɛt] *nf* : bicycle

bidon [bidɔ̃] *nm* : can, flask

bien [bjɛ̃] *adv* **1** : well, satisfactorily **2** TRÈS : very, quite **3** RÉELLEMENT : definitely, really **4** VOLONTIERS : readily, happily **5 ~ des fois** : many times **6 ~ que** : although **7 ~ sûr** : of course — **~** *adj* **1** : good, fine, satisfactory **2** : well, in good health **3** BEAU : good-looking **4** RESPECTABLE : nice **5** : comfortable (of shoes, etc.) — **~** *nm* **1** : good **2 ~s** *nmpl* : possessions, property — **~** *interj* : OK, all right, very well — **bien–aimé, -aimée** [bjɛ̃neme] *adj & n* : beloved — **bien–être** [bjɛ̃nɛtr] *nm* **1** : well-being **2** : comfort

bienfaisance [bjɛ̃fəzɑ̃s] *nf* : charity, kindness — **bienfaisant, -sante** [bjɛ̃fəzɑ̃, -zɑ̃t] *adj* **1** : charitable **2** BÉNÉFIQUE : beneficial — **bienfait** [bjɛ̃fɛ] *nm* AVANTAGE : benefit — **bienfaiteur, -trice** [bjɛ̃fɛtœr, -tris] *n* : benefactor

bientôt [bjɛ̃to] *adv* : soon, shortly

bienveillance [bjɛ̃vɛjɑ̃s] *nf* : kindness, benevolence — **bienveillant, -lante** [bjɛ̃vejɑ̃, -jɑ̃t] *adj* : kind, benevolent

bienvenu, -nue [bjɛ̃vny] *adj* : welcome — **~** *n* **soyez le ~** : you are welcome (here) — **bienvenue** *nf* : welcome

bière [bjɛr] *nf* : beer

biffer [bife] *vt* : cross out

bifteck [biftɛk] *nm* : steak

bifurquer [bifyrke] *vi* : to fork — **bifurcation** [bifyrkasjɔ̃] *nf* : fork (in a road)

bigot, -gote [bigo, -ɔt] *adj* : overly devout — **~** *n* : (religious) zealot

bigoudi [bigudi] *nm* : hair curler

bijou [biʒu] *nm, pl* **-joux 1** : jewel **2** MERVEILLE : gem — **bijouterie** [biʒutri] *nf* **1** BIJOUX : jewelry **2** : jewelry store — **bijoutier, -tière** [biʒutje, -tjɛr] *n* : jeweler

bilan [bilɑ̃] *nm* **1** : assessment **2** : balance sheet (in finance)

bilatéral, -rale [bilateral] *adj, mpl* **-raux** [-ro] : bilateral

bile [bil] *nf* **1** : bile **2 se faire de la ~** : worry

bilingue [bilɛ̃g] *adj* : bilingual

billard [bijar] *nm* : billiards *pl*

bille [bij] *nf* **1** : (playing) marble **2** : billiard ball

billet [bijɛ] *nm* **1** : bill, banknote **2** TICKET : ticket **3 ~ doux** : love letter — **billetterie** [bijɛtri] *nf* **1** GUICHET : ticket office **2** : automatic teller machine

billion [biljɔ̃] *nm* : trillion (US), billion (Brit)

bimensuel, -suelle [bimɑ̃sɥɛl] *adj* : semimonthly

binette [binɛt] *nf* : hoe

biochimie [bjɔʃimi] *nf* : biochemistry

biographie [bjɔgrafi] *nf* : biography — **biographe** [bjɔgraf] *nmf* : biographer — **biographique** [bjɔgrafik] *adj* : biographical

biologie [bjɔlɔʒi] *nf* : biology — **biologique** [bjɔlɔʒik] *adj* : biological

bis [bis] *adv* **1** : twice (in music) **2** : A (in an address) — **~** *nm & interj* : encore

biscotte [biskɔt] *nf* : cracker

biscuit [biskɥi] *nm* **1** : cookie **2** : sponge cake

bise [biz] *nf* **1** : north wind **2** *fam* : kiss, smack

biseau [bizo] *nm* **1** : bevel **2 en ~** : beveled

bisexuel, -sexuelle [bisɛksɥɛl] *adj* : bisexual

bison [bizɔ̃] *nm* : bison, buffalo

bissextile [bisɛkstil] *adj* **année ~** : leap year

bistouri [bisturi] *nm* : lancet

bistro *or* **bistrot** [bistro] *nm* : café

bit [bit] *nm* : bit (unit of information)

bizarre [bizar] *adj* : bizarre, strange — **bizarrement** [-zarmɑ̃] *adv* : oddly, strangely

blafard, -farde [blafar, -fard] *adj* : pale, pallid

blague [blag] *nf* PLAISANTERIE : joke — **blaguer** [blage] *vi* PLAISANTER : joke, kid around — **blagueur, -gueuse** [blagœr, -gøz] *n* : joker

blaireau [blɛro] *nm, pl* **-raux** : badger

blâmer [blame] *vt* : blame, criticize — **blâme** [blam] *nm* DÉSAPPROBATION : blame, censure
blanc, blanche [blɑ̃, blɑ̃ʃ] *adj* **1** : white **2** PÂLE : pale **3** : pure, innocent **4 page blanche** : blank sheet — **blanc** *nm* **1** : white **2** INTERVALLE : gap, blank space
blanchir [blɑ̃ʃir] *vt* **1** : whiten, bleach **2** : launder (one's clothes) **3** : blanch (vegetables) — *vi* : turn white — **blanchissage** [blɑ̃ʃisaʒ] *nm* : laundering — **blanchisserie** [blɑ̃ʃisri] *nf* : laundry
blasé, -sée [blaze] *adj* : blasé, jaded
blason [blazɔ̃] *nm* : coat of arms
blasphème [blasfɛm] *nm* : blasphemy
blatte [blat] *nf* : cockroach
blazer [blazɛr] *nm* : blazer
blé [ble] *nm* : wheat
blême [blɛm] *adj* : pale, wan
blesser [blese] *vt* : injure, wound — **blessé, -sée** [blese] *n* : casualty, injured person — **blessure** [blesyr] *nf* : injury, wound
bleu, bleue [blø] *adj* **1** : blue **2** : very rare (of steak, etc.) — **bleu** *nm* **1** : blue **2** : bruise
bleuet [bløɛ] *nm Can* : blueberry
blindé, -dée [blɛ̃de] *adj* : armored — **blindé** *nm* : armored vehicle
bloc [blɔk] *nm* **1** : block **2 en ~** : as a whole
blocage [blɔkaʒ] *nm* **1** : obstruction **2** : freezing (of prices, etc.)
blocus [blɔkys] *nm* : blockade
blond, blonde [blɔ̃, blɔ̃d] *adj & n* : blond
blonde *nf Can fam* : girlfriend
bloquer [blɔke] *vt* **1** : block (an entrance) **2** : jam on (the brakes) **3** : freeze (a bank account, etc.), stop (a check) — **se bloquer** *vr* : jam, stick
blottir [blɔtir] *v* **se blottir** *vr* : cuddle, snuggle
blouse [bluz] *nf* **1** CHEMISIER : blouse **2** SARRAU : smock
blouson [bluzɔ̃] *nm* : jacket
blue–jean [bludʒin] *nm, pl* **blue–jeans** : jeans *pl*
bluffer [blœfe] *vi* : bluff — **bluff** [blœf] *nm* : bluff
bobine [bɔbin] *nf* : reel, spool
bocal [bɔkal] *nm, pl* **-caux** [bɔko] : jar
bœuf [bœf] *nm, pl* **bœufs** [bø] : beef
bohème [bɔɛm] *adj* : bohemian — **bohémien, -mienne** [bɔemjɛ̃, -mjɛn] *n* : gypsy
boire [bwar] {13} *vt* **1** : drink **2** ABSORBER : absorb — *vi* : drink
bois [bwa] *nms & pl* **1** : wood **2** FORÊT : woods *pl* **3 ~ de chauffage** : firewood **4 ~** *nmpl* : antlers — **boisé, -sée** [bwaze] *adj* : wooded — **boisé** *nm Can* : woods *pl*
boisseau [bwaso] *nm* : bushel
boisson [bwasɔ̃] *nf* **1** : drink, beverage **2 en ~** *Can* : drunk
boîte [bwat] *nf* **1** : (tin) can **2** : box **3 ~ de nuit** : nightclub
boiter [bwate] *vi* : limp — **boiteux, -teuse** [bwatø, -tøz] *adj* **1** : lame **2** BRANLANT : wobbly, shaky — **boitiller** [bwatije] *vi* : limp slightly, hobble
boîtier [bwatje] *nm* : casing, housing
bol [bɔl] *nm* **1** : bowl **2** : bowlful
bombarder [bɔ̃barde] *vt* : bomb, bombard — **bombardement** [bɔ̃bardəmɑ̃] *nm* : bombing, bombardment — **bombardier** [bɔ̃bardje] *nm* : bomber (plane)
bombe [bɔ̃b] *nf* **1** : bomb **2** ATOMISEUR : aerosol spray
bomber [bɔ̃be] *vt* : puff out, swell
bon, bonne [bɔ̃ (bɔn *before a vowel or mute h*), bɔn] *adj* **1** : good **2** CORRECT : correct, proper **3 ~ marché** : inexpensive **4 ~ sens** : common sense **5 pour de ~** : for good, for keeps — **bon** *adv* **faire ~** : be nice — **~** *nm* **1** : good thing **2** : voucher, bond
bonbon [bɔ̃bɔ̃] *nm* : candy
bond [bɔ̃] *nm* **1** SAUT : bound, leap **2** : bounce (of a ball)
bondé, -dée [bɔ̃de] *adj* : crammed, packed
bondir [bɔ̃dir] *vi* : jump, leap
bonheur [bɔnœr] *nm* **1** : happiness, pleasure **2 par ~** : luckily
bonhomme [bɔnɔm] *nm, pl* **bonshommes** **1** *fam* : fellow, guy **2 ~ de neige** : snowman
bonjour [bɔ̃ʒur] *nm* **1** : hello, good morning, good afternoon **2** *Can* : good-bye
bonne [bɔn] *nf* DOMESTIQUE : maid
bonnement [bɔnmɑ̃] *adv* **tout ~** : quite simply
bonnet [bɔnɛ] *nm* : cap, hat
bonneterie [bɔnɛtri] *nf* : hosiery
bonsoir [bɔ̃swar] *nm* : good evening, good night
bonté [bɔ̃te] *nf* : goodness, kindness
bord [bɔr] *nm* **1** : edge, rim **2** : bank, shore **3 à ~** : on board, aboard **4 au ~ de** : on the verge of
bordeaux [bɔrdo] *nm* : Bordeaux, claret (wine)
bordée [bɔrde] *nf* **1** : volley **2 ~ de neige** *Can* : snowstorm
bordel [bɔrdɛl] *nm fam* **1** : brothel **2** PAGAILLE : mess, shambles
border [bɔrde] *vt* **1** : border, line **2** : tuck in
bordereau [bɔrdəro] *nm, pl* **-reaux** [-ro] **1** : note (in finance) **2 ~ de dépôt** : deposit slip
bordure [bɔrdyr] *nf* : border, edge
borne [bɔrn] *nf* **1** : milestone, landmark **2 ~s** *nfpl* : limits — **borné, -née** [bɔrne] *adj* : narrow-minded — **borner** [bɔrne] *vt* RESTREINDRE : limit, restrict — **se borner** *vr* : confine oneself
bosquet [bɔske] *nm* : grove, copse
bosse [bɔs] *nf* **1** : hump (of a person or animal) **2 se faire une ~** : get a bump — **bosseler** [bɔsle] {8} *vt* : dent (a bumper, etc.) — **bosser** [bɔse] *vi France fam* : work, slave away
botanique [bɔtanik] *nf* : botany — **~** *adj* : botanical
botte [bɔt] *nf* **1** : boot **2** : bunch (of radishes), sheaf (of hay) — **botter** [bɔte] *vt* : kick (in sports)
bottin [bɔtɛ̃] *nm* : (telephone) directory
bouche [buʃ] *nf* **1** : mouth **2** ENTRÉE : opening, entrance **3 ~ bée** : flabbergasted **4 ~ d'incendie** : fire hydrant — **bouchée** [buʃe] *nf* : mouthful
boucher[1] [buʃe] *vt* : stop up, block — **se boucher** *vr* : become blocked — **bouchon** [buʃɔ̃] *nm* **1** : cork, stopper **2** : float (in fishing) **3** EMBOUTEILLAGE : traffic jam
boucher[2], **-chère** [buʃe, -ʃɛr] *n* : butcher — **boucherie** [buʃri] *nf* : butcher's shop
boucler [bukle] *vt* **1** : buckle (a belt), fasten (a seat belt) **2** : complete (a task) — *vi* : curl — **boucle** [bukl] *nf* **1** : buckle **2** : curl **3 ~ d'oreille** : earring — **bouclé, -clée** [bukle] *adj* : curly
bouclier [buklije] *nm* : shield
bouddhiste [budist] *adj & nmf* : Buddhist — **bouddhisme** [budism] *nm* : Buddhism
bouder [bude] *vt* : avoid — *vi* : sulk, pout — **bouderie** [budri] *nf* : sulkiness — **boudeur, -deuse** [budœr, -døz] *adj* : sulky
boudin [budɛ̃] *nm* : blood sausage
boue [bu] *nf* : mud — **boueux, boueuse** [buø, buøz] *adj* : muddy
bouée [bwe] *nf* : buoy
bouffant, -fante [bufɑ̃, -fɑ̃t] *adj* : baggy (of pants) — **bouffi, -fie** [bufi] *adj* : puffy, swollen
bouffe [buf] *nf fam* : grub, chow — **bouffer** [bufe] *vt fam* : eat, gobble up
bouffée [bufe] *nf* **1** : puff, gust **2** : surge, fit (of rage, etc.)
bouffon, -fonne [bufɔ̃, bufɔn] *adj* : comical — **bouffon** *nm* : clown, buffoon
bougeoir [buʒwar] *nm* : candlestick
bouger [buʒe] {17} *vt* : move — *vi* : budge, stir
bougie [buʒi] *nf* **1** : candle **2** : spark plug (of a car)
bougonner [bugɔne] *vi* : grumble — **bougon, -gonne** [bugɔ̃, -gɔn] *adj* : grumpy
bouillabaisse [bujabɛs] *nf* : fish soup
bouillir [bujir] {14} *vi* **1** : boil **2** : seethe (with anger, etc.) — **bouillie** [buji] *nf* : baby cereal, gruel — **bouilloire** [bujwar] *nf* : kettle, teakettle — **bouillon** [bujɔ̃] *nm* **1** : broth, stock — **bouillonner** [bujɔne] *vi* **1** : bubble, foam **2** → **bouillir 2**
boulanger, -gère [bulɑ̃ʒe, -ʒɛr] *n* : baker — **boulangerie** [bulɑ̃ʒri] *nf* : bakery
boule [bul] *nf* **1** : ball **2 ~ de neige** : snowball
bouleau [bulo] *nm, pl* **-leaux** : birch
bouledogue [buldɔg] *nm* : bulldog
boulet [bulɛ] *nm* **1** : cannonball **2** : ball and chain
boulette [bulɛt] *nf* **1** : pellet **2** : meatball
boulevard [bulvar] *nm* : boulevard
bouleverser [bulvɛrse] *vt* **1** : upset, turn upside down **2** PERTURBER : overwhelm — **bouleversant, -sante** [bulvɛrsɑ̃, -sɑ̃t] *adj* : distressing, upsetting — **bouleversement** [bulvɛrsəmɑ̃] *nm* : upheaval, upset
boulon [bulɔ̃] *nm* : bolt
boulot [bulo] *nm fam* **1** : work, task **2** EMPLOI : job — **boulot, -lotte** [bulo, -lɔt] *adj* : plump, chubby
boum [bum] *nm* **1** : bang **2** : boom (of business, etc.)
bouquet [bukɛ] *nm* : bouquet, bunch (of flowers)
bouquin [bukɛ̃] *nm fam* : book — **bouquiniste** [bukinist] *nmf* : secondhand bookseller
bourbier [burbje] *nm* : swamp, quagmire
bourde [burd] *nf* : blunder
bourdon [burdɔ̃] *nm* : bumblebee — **bourdonnement** [burdɔnmɑ̃] *nm* : buzz, hum, droning — **bourdonner** [burdɔne] *vi* : buzz, hum
bourgeois, -geoise [burʒwa, -ʒwaz] *adj & n* : bourgeois — **bourgeoisie** [burʒwazi] *nf* : bourgeoisie
bourgeon [burʒɔ̃] *nm* : bud — **bourgeonner** [burʒɔne] *vi* : bud
bourgogne [burgɔɲ] *nm* : Burgundy (wine)
bourrage [buraʒ] *nm* : filling, stuffing
bourreau [buro] *nm, pl* **-reaux** **1** : executioner **2 ~ de travail** : workaholic
bourrer [bure] *vt* : fill, stuff, cram — *vi* : be filling — **se bourrer** *vr* : stuff oneself
bourru, -rue [bury] *adj* : gruff, surly
bourse [burs] *nf* **1** PORTE-MONNAIE : purse **2** : scholarship **3 la Bourse** : the stock market — **boursier, -sière** [bursje, -sjɛr] *adj* : stock, stock-market
boursoufler [bursufle] *vt* : puff up, cause to swell — **se boursoufler** *vr* : blister — **boursouflure** [bursuflyr] *nf* : blister (of paint, etc.)
bousculer [buskyle] *vt* **1** : jostle, shove **2** PRESSER : rush — **se bousculer** *vr* : jostle — **bousculade** [buskylad] *nf* : rush, scramble
bousiller [buzije] *vt fam* : bungle, botch
boussole [busɔl] *nf* : compass
bout [bu] *nm* **1** EXTRÉMITÉ : end, tip **2** MORCEAU : bit **3 au ~ de** : after **4 à ~ portant** : point-blank
bouteille [butɛj] *nf* : bottle
boutique [butik] *nf* : shop, boutique
bouton [butɔ̃] *nm* **1** : button **2** BOURGEON : bud **3** : pimple **4** *or* **~ de porte** : doorknob — **boutonner** [butɔne] *vt* : button — **boutonnière** *nf* : buttonhole
bovins [bɔvɛ̃] *nmpl* : cattle
bowling [buliŋ] *nm* : bowling
box [bɔks] *nm, pl* **boxes** : stall (for a horse)
boxe [bɔks] *nf* : boxing — **boxer** [bɔkse] *vi* : box — **boxeur** [bɔksœr] *nm* : boxer, fighter
boyau [bwajo] *nm, pl* **boyaux** **1** INTESTIN : intestine, gut **2** : inner tube (of a tire)
boycotter [bɔjkɔte] *vt* : boycott — **boycottage** [bɔjkɔtaʒ] *nm* : boycott
bracelet [braslɛ] *nm* : bracelet
braconner [brakɔne] *vi* : poach (of game)
braguette [bragɛt] *nf* : fly (of pants, etc.)
braille [braj] *nm* : braille
brailler [braje] *vi fam* : bawl, howl
braire [brɛr] {15} *vi* : bray
braise [brɛz] *nf* : embers *pl*
brancard [brɑ̃kar] *nm* CIVIÈRE : stretcher
branche [brɑ̃ʃ] *nf* **1** : branch **2** : sidepiece (of eyeglasses) — **branché, -chée** [brɑ̃ʃe] *adj fam* : trendy — **brancher** [brɑ̃ʃe] *vt* **1** : connect (a utility) **2** : plug in (a device)
branchie [brɑ̃ʃi] *nf* : gill (of a fish)
brandir [brɑ̃dir] *vt* : brandish, wave
branler [brɑ̃le] *vi* : wobble, be loose — **branlant, -lante** [brɑ̃lɑ̃, -lɑ̃t] *adj* : unsteady — **branle** [brɑ̃l] *nm* **mettre en ~** : set in motion
braquer [brake] *vt* **1** DIRIGER : aim **2** : turn (a steering wheel) **3** *fam* : point a gun at **4 ~ qqn contre qqch** : turn s.o. against sth
bras [bra] *nms & pl* : arm — **brasser** [brase] *vt* **1** : mix **2** : brew (beer) — **brasserie** [brasri] *nf* **1** : brewery **2** : restaurant — **brassière** [brasjɛr] *nf Can* : bra, brassiere
brave [brav] *adj* **1** GENTIL : good, nice **2** COURAGEUX : brave — **bravement** [busɔl] *adv* : bravely, boldly — **braver** [brave] *vt* : brave
break [brɛk] *nm France* : station wagon — **~** *nm Can* : break, rest
brebis [brəbi] *nf* : ewe
brèche [brɛʃ] *nf* : gap
bredouiller [brəduje] *v* : mumble, mutter
bref, brève [brɛf, brɛv] *adj* : brief, short — **bref** [brɛf] *adv or* **en ~** : briefly, in short
brésilien, -lienne [breziljɛ̃, -ljɛn] *adj* : Brazilian
bretelle [brətɛl] *nf* **1** : strap **2** : (access) ramp **3 ~s** *nfpl* : suspenders
breton, -tonne [brətɔ̃, brətɔn] *n* : Breton
breuvage [brœvaʒ] *nm* : beverage
brevet [brəvɛ] *nm* **1** : patent **2** : diploma, certificate — **breveter** [brəvte] {8} *vt* : patent
bribes [brib] *nfpl* : bits, pieces
bric–à–brac [brikabrak] *nms & pl* : odds and ends
bricoler [brikɔle] *vi* : do odd jobs, putter — *vt* : fix up — **bricolage** [brikɔlaʒ] *nm* : do-it-yourself work — **bricoleur, -leuse** [brikɔlœr, -løz] *n* : handyman
bride [brid] *nf* : bridle — **brider** [bride] *vt* **1** : bridle (a horse) **2** CONTENIR : keep in check
bridge [bridʒ] *nm* : bridge (card game)
brièveté [brijɛvte] *nf* : brevity — **brièvement** [brijɛvmɑ̃] *adv* : briefly
brigade [brigad] *nf* : brigade, squad
briller [brije] *vi* : shine — **brillant, -lante** [brijɑ̃, -jɑ̃t] *adj* **1** : bright, shiny **2** REMARQUABLE : brilliant, outstanding — **brillant** *nm* : gloss, shine
brimer [brime] *vt* : bully
brin [brɛ̃] *nm* **1** : blade (of grass), sprig **2** : little bit, iota **3** : strand (of thread, etc.)
brindille [brɛ̃dij] *nf* : twig
bringue [brɛ̃g] *nf fam* : binge
brio [brijo] *nm* **1** : brilliance, panache **2 avec ~** : brilliantly
brioche [brijɔʃ] *nf* **1** : brioche **2** *fam* : paunch
brique [brik] *nf* : brick
briquet [brikɛ] *nm* : (cigarette) lighter
brise [briz] *nf* : breeze
briser [brize] *vt* **1** : break, smash **2** DÉTRUIRE : ruin, wreck — **se briser** *vr* : shatter, break
britannique [britanik] *adj* : British
broche [brɔʃ] *nf* **1** : brooch **2** : spit, skewer (in cooking) — **brochette** [brɔʃɛt] *nf* : skewer
brochure [brɔʃyr] *nf* : brochure, pamphlet
brocoli [brɔkɔli] *nm* : broccoli
broder [brɔde] *vt* : embroider — **broderie** [brɔdri] *nf* : embroidery
bronchite [brɔ̃ʃit] *nf* : bronchitis
bronze [brɔ̃z] *nm* : bronze — **bronzage** [brɔ̃zaʒ] *nm* : suntan — **bronzé, -zée** [brɔ̃ze] *adj* : suntanned — **bronzer** [brɔ̃ze] *vi* : get a suntan
brosse [brɔs] *nf* : brush — **brosser** [brɔse] *vt* **1** : brush **2** : paint (a picture) — **se brosser** *vr* **~ les cheveux** : brush one's hair
brouette [bruɛt] *nf* : wheelbarrow
brouiller [bruje] *vt* **1** : mix up, scramble **2** TROUBLER : blur, cloud — **se brouiller** *vr* **1** : quarrel **2** : cloud over (of the weather) — **brouillard** [brujar] *nm* : fog, mist — **brouillon, -lonne** [brujɔ̃, -jɔn] *adj* : disorganized, untidy — **brouillon** *nm* : rough draft
broussailles [brusaj] *nfpl* : undergrowth
brousse [brus] *nf* **la ~** : bush, wilderness
brouter [brute] *vi* : graze
broyer [brwaje] {58} *vt* : grind, crush
bru [bry] *nf* : daughter-in-law
bruine [brɥin] *nf* : drizzle — **bruiner** [brɥine] *vi* : drizzle
bruire [brɥir] {16} *vi* : rustle, murmur, hum — **bruissement** [brɥismɑ̃] *nm* : rustling, murmuring — **bruit** [brɥi] *nm* **1** : noise **2** VACARME : commotion, fuss **3** RUMEUR : rumor
brûler [bryle] *vt* **1** : burn, scald **2** : run (a red light) — *vi* : burn (up) — **se brûler** *vr* : burn oneself — **brûlant, -lante** [brylɑ̃, -lɑ̃t] *adj* **1** : burning hot **2** : ardent — **brûleur** [brylœr] *nm* : burner — **brûlure** [brylyr] *nf* **1** : burn **2 ~s d'estomac** : heartburn
brume [brym] *nf* : mist, haze — **brumeux, -meuse** [brymø, -møz] *adj* : misty, foggy
brun, brune [brœ̃, bryn] *adj* : brown — **brun** *n* : brunet — **~** *nm* : brown — **brunette** [brynɛt] *nf* : brunette
brusque [brysk] *adj* : brusque, abrupt — **brusquement** [bryskəmɑ̃] *adv* : abruptly, suddenly — **brusquer** [bryske] *vt* : rush, hurry
brut, brute [bryt] *adj* **1** : raw, crude **2** : dry (of wine) **3 poids ~** : gross weight
brutal, -tale [brytal] *adj, mpl* **-taux** [bryto] : brutal — **brutalement** [-talmɑ̃] *adv* **1** : brutally **2** : suddenly — **brutaliser** [brytalize] *vt* : abuse, mistreat — **brutalité** [brytalite] *nf* : brutality — **brute** [bryt] *nf* : brute
bruyant, bruyante [brɥijɑ̃, -jɑ̃t] *adj* : noisy, loud — **bruyamment** [brɥijamɑ̃] *adv* : noisily, loudly
bruyère [bryjɛr] *nf* : heather
buanderie [byɑ̃dri] *nf* **1** : laundry room **2** *Can* : self-service laundry
buccal, -cale [bykal] *adj, mpl* **-caux** [byko] : oral
bûche [byʃ] *nf* : log — **bûcher** [byʃe] *vi fam* : work, slave away — **bûcheron, -ronne** [byʃrɔ̃, -rɔn] *n* : logger, lumberjack
budget [bydʒɛ] *nm* : budget — **budgétaire** [bydʒetɛr] *adj* : budgetary — **budgétiser** [bydʒezite] *vt* : budget
buée [bɥe] *nf* : steam, mist
buffet [byfɛ] *nm* **1** : sideboard **2** : buffet
buffle [byfl] *nm* : buffalo
buisson [bɥisɔ̃] *nm* : bush, shrub
bulbe [bylb] *nm* : bulb (of a plant)
bulldozer [byldozɛr] *nm* : bulldozer
bulle [byl] *nf* : bubble
bulletin [byltɛ̃] *nm* **1** : report, bulletin **2 ~ de vote** : ballot
bureau [byro] *nm, pl* **-reaux** **1** : office, study **2** SECRÉTAIRE : desk **3** : department, bureau
bureaucrate [byrokrat] *nmf* : bureaucrat — **bureaucratie** [byrokrasi] *nf* : bureaucracy — **bureaucratique** [-kratik] *adj* : bureaucratic
bus [bys] *nm* AUTOBUS : bus
buste [byst] *nm* **1** : chest, bust **2** : bust (in sculpture)
but [by(t)] *nm* **1** : aim, goal **2** *Can* : base (in baseball)
buter [byte] *vi* **~ contre** *or* **~ sur** : stumble on, trip over — *vt* : antagonize — **se buter** *vr* : become obstinate — **buté, -tée** [byte] *adj* : obstinate
butin [bytɛ̃] *nm* : loot
butte [byt] *nf* **1** : small hill, mound **2 être en ~ à** : come up against
buveur, -veuse [byvœr, -vøz] *n* : drinker

C

c [se] *nm* : c, third letter of the alphabet

ça [sa] *pron* **1** : that, this **2** : it **3 ~ va?** : how's it going? **4 ~ y est** : there, that's it

cabane [kaban] *nf* : cabin, hut — **cabanon** [kabanɔ̃] *nm* : shed

cabaret [kabarɛ] *nm* : nightclub

cabine [kabin] *nf* **1** : cabin, cab (of a truck, etc.) **2 ~ téléphonique** : telephone booth **3 ~ de pilotage** : cockpit

cabinet [kabinɛ] *nm* **1** : office **2** : cabinet (in government) **3 ~ de toilette** *France* : toilet

câble [kabl] *nm* **1** : cable **2** : cable television

cabosser [kabɔse] *vt* : dent

cabriole [kabrijɔl] *nf* : somersault

cacahouète [kakaɥɛt] *nf* : peanut

cacao [kakao] *nm* : cocoa

cache–cache [kaʃkaʃ] *nms & pl* : hide-and-seek

cachemire [kaʃmir] *nm* : cashmere

cacher [kaʃe] *vt* : hide, conceal — **se cacher** *vr* : hide

cachet [kaʃɛ] *nm* **1** COMPRIMÉ : tablet, pill **2** *or* **~ de la poste** : postmark **3** : fee **4** : character, style — **cacheter** [kaʃte] {8} *vt* : seal

cachette [kaʃɛt] *nf* : hiding place

cachot [kaʃo] *nm* : dungeon

cachottier, -tière [kaʃɔtje, -tjɛr] *adj* : secretive — **cachotterie** [kaʃɔtri] *nf* : little secret

cacophonie [kakɔfɔni] *nf* : cacophony

cactus [kaktys] *nms & pl* : cactus

cadavre [kadavr] *nm* : corpse

cadeau [kado] *nm, pl* **-deaux** : gift, present

cadenas [kadna] *nm* : padlock — **cadenasser** [-nase] *vt* : padlock

cadence [kadɑ̃s] *nf* : cadence, rhythm

cadet, -dette [kadɛ, -dɛt] *adj* : younger, youngest — **~** *n* **1** : younger, youngest (son, daughter, child) **2** : junior

cadran [kadrɑ̃] *nm* **1** : dial, face **2** *Can fam* : alarm clock

cadre [kadr] *nm* **1** : frame **2** : setting, surroundings *pl* **3** STRUCTURE : framework **4** : executive

caduc, -duque [kadyk] *adj* **1** : obsolete **2** : deciduous

cafard [kafar] *nm* **1** : cockroach **2 avoir le ~** : have the blues

café [kafe] *nm* **1** : coffee **2** : café, bar — **caféine** [kafein] *nf* : caffeine — **cafetière** [kaftjɛr] *nf* : coffeepot — **cafétéria** [kafeterja] *nf* : cafeteria

cage [kaʒ] *nf* **1** : cage **2 ~ d'escalier** : stairwell

cageot [kaʒo] *nm* : crate

cagnotte [kaɲɔt] *nf* : pool, kitty

cagoule [kagul] *nf* : hood

cahier [kaje] *nm* : notebook, exercise book

cahoter [kaɔte] *vi* : bump along — **cahoteux, -teuse** [kaɔtø, -tøz] *adj* : bumpy

cailler [kaje] *vi* **1** : curdle **2** : clot (of blood) — **caillot** [kajo] *nm* : clot

caillou [kaju] *nm, pl* **-loux** : pebble, stone

caisse [kɛs] *nf* **1** BOÎTE : box, crate **2** *or* **~ enregistreuse** : cash register **3 ~ d'épargne** : savings bank **4 ~ populaire** *Can* : cooperative bank — **caissier, -sière** [kesje, -sjɛr] *n* **1** : cashier **2** : (bank) teller

cajoler [kaʒɔle] *vt* **1** : fuss over, cuddle **2** ENJÔLER : cajole

cajun [kaʒœ̃] *adj* : Cajun

cake [kɛk] *nm* : fruitcake

calamité [kalamite] *nf* : calamity

calcaire [kalkɛr] *nm* : limestone — **~** *adj* : chalky

calciner [kalsine] *vt* : char

calcium [kalsjɔm] *nm* : calcium

calculer [kalkyle] *vt* : calculate — **calcul** [kalkyl] *nm* **1** : calculation, sum **2** : arithmetic **3 ~ bilaire** : gallstone — **calculateur, -trice** [kalkylatœr, -tris] *adj* : calculating — **calculatrice** *nf* : calculator

cale [kal] *nf* **1** : wedge **2** : hold (of a ship)

calé, -lée [kale] *adj fam* : brainy

calèche [kalɛʃ] *nf* : (horse-drawn) carriage

caleçon [kalsɔ̃] *nm* **1** : boxer shorts *pl* **2** : leggings *pl* **3** *or* **~s de bain** : swimming trunks

calembour [kalɑ̃bur] *nm* : pun

calendrier [kalɑ̃drije] *nm* : calendar

calepin [kalpɛ̃] *nm* : notebook

caler [kale] *vt* : wedge — *vi* : stall (of an engine)

calibre [kalibr] *nm* **1** : caliber **2** : grade, size — **calibrer** [kalibre] *vt* : calibrate, grade

califourchon [kalifurʃɔ̃] **à ~s** *adv phr* : astride

câliner [kaline] *vt* : cuddle — **se câliner** *vr* : cuddle (up)

calmant, -mante [kalmɑ̃, -mɑ̃t] *adj* : soothing — **calmant** *nm* : sedative

calmar [kalmar] *nm* : squid

calme [kalm] *nm* **1** : calm **2 du ~!** : quiet down! — **~** *adj* : calm — **calmer** [kalme] *vt* : calm, soothe — **se calmer** *vr* : calm down

calomnie [kalɔmni] *nf* : slander, libel — **calomnier** [kalɔmnje] {96} *vt* : slander, libel

calorie [kalɔri] *nf* : calorie

calorifère [kalɔrifɛr] *nm* : heater, stove

calquer [kalke] *vt* **1** : trace (a drawing) **2** : copy, imitate — **calque** [kalk] *nm* : (exact) copy

calvaire [kalvɛr] *nm* : ordeal, suffering

calvitie [kalvisi] *nf* : baldness

camarade [kamarad] *nmf* **1** : friend **2 ~ de classe** : classmate — **camaraderie** [kamaradri] *nf* : friendship

cambrer [kɑ̃bre] *vt* : curve, arch

cambrioler [kɑ̃brijɔle] *vt* : burglarize — **cambriolage** [kɑ̃brijɔlaʒ] *nm* : burglary — **cambrioleur, -leuse** [kɑ̃brijɔlør, -løz] *n* : burglar

cambrure [kɑ̃bryr] *nf* : arch, curve

camelot [kamlo] *nm Can* : paperboy

camelote [kamlɔt] *nf fam* : trash, junk

caméra [kamera] *nf* : movie or television camera

camion [kamjɔ̃] *nm* : truck — **camionnette** [kamjɔnɛt] *nf* : van — **camionneur, -neuse** [kamjɔnœr, -nøz] *n* : truck driver

camoufler [kamufle] *vt* : camouflage — **camouflage** [kamuflaʒ] *nm* : camouflage

camp [kɑ̃] *nm* **1** : camp **2** PARTI : side, team

campagne [kɑ̃paɲ] *nf* **1** : country, countryside **2** : campaign (in politics, etc.) — **campagnard, -gnarde** [kɑ̃paɲar, -ɲard] *adj* : country, rustic

camper [kɑ̃pe] *vi* : camp — **campement** [kɑ̃pmɑ̃] *nm* : encampment — **campeur, -peuse** [kɑ̃pœr, -pøz] *n* : camper — **camping** [kɑ̃piŋ] *nm* **1** : camping **2** : campground

campus [kɑ̃pys] *nm* : campus

canadien, -dienne [kanadjɛ̃, -djɛn] *adj* : Canadian — **canadien–français, canadienne–française** *adj, pl* **canadiens–français, canadiennes–françaises** : French-Canadian

canal [kanal] *nm, pl* **-naux** [kano] **1** : canal **2** : channel

canapé [kanape] *nm* : sofa, couch

canard [kanar] *nm* : duck

canari [kanari] *nm* : canary

cancer [kɑ̃sɛr] *nm* : cancer — **cancéreux, -reuse** [kɑ̃serø, -røz] *adj* : cancerous

candeur [kɑ̃dœr] *nf* : ingenuousness

candidat, -date [kɑ̃dida, -dat] *n* : candidate — **candidature** [kɑ̃didatyr] *nf* : candidacy

candide [kɑ̃did] *adj* : ingenuous, naïve

cane [kan] *nf* : (female) duck — **caneton** [kantɔ̃] *nm* : duckling

canette [kanɛt] *nf* **1** : (small) bottle **2** : can (for a beverage)

caniche [kaniʃ] *nm* : poodle

canicule [kanikyl] *nf* : heat wave

canif [kanif] *nm* : pocketknife

canine [ˈkeɪˌnaɪn] *nf* : canine (tooth)

caniveau [kanivo] *nm, pl* **-veaux** : gutter (in a street)

canne [kan] *nf* **1** : cane **2 ~ à pêche** : fishing rod **3 ~ à sucre** : sugarcane

canneberge [kanbɛrʒ] *nf* : cranberry

cannelle [kanɛl] *nf* : cinnamon

cannibale [kanibal] *nmf* : cannibal

canoë [kanɔe] *nm* : canoe

canon [kanɔ̃] *nm* **1** : cannon **2** : barrel (of a gun) **3** : canon, rule

canot [kano] *nm* **1** *France* : boat **2** *Can* : canoe **3 ~ de sauvetage** : lifeboat

cantaloup [kɑ̃talu] *nm* : cantaloupe

cantine [kɑ̃tin] *nf* : canteen, cafeteria

cantique [kɑ̃tik] *nm* : hymn

canton [kɑ̃tɔ̃] *nm* **1** *France* : district, canton **2** *Can* : township

canular [kanylar] *nm* : hoax

canyon [kaɲɔ̃] *nm* : canyon

caoutchouc [kautʃu] *nm* **1** : rubber **2 ~s** *nmpl* : galoshes — **caoutchouteux, -teuse** [kautʃutø, -tøz] *adj* : rubbery

cap [kap] *nm* **1** PROMONTOIRE : cape **2** ÉTAPE : milestone

capable [kapabl] *adj* : capable

capacité [kapasite] *nf* **1** : capacity **2** APTITUDE : ability

cape [kap] *nf* : cape, cloak

capitaine [kapitɛn] *nm* : captain

capital, -tale [kapital] *adj, mpl* **-taux** [-to] **1** : major, crucial **2 peine capitale** : capital punishment — **capital** *nm, pl* **-taux** : capital, assets *pl* — **capitale** *nf* : capital (city)

capitalisme [kapitalism] *nm* : capitalism — **capitaliste** [kapitalist] *adj* : capitalist(ic)

capiteux, -teuse [kapitø, -tøz] *adj* : heady

caporal–chef [kapɔralʃɛf] *nm, pl* **caporaux–chefs** [-ro] : corporal

capot [kapo] *nm* : hood (of an automobile) — **capoter** [kapɔte] *vt* : overturn, capsize

caprice [kapris] *nm* : whim — **capricieux, -cieuse** [kaprisjø, -sjøz] *adj* : temperamental

capsule [kapsyl] *nf* **1** : capsule **2** : cap (of a bottle)

capter [kapte] *vt* **1** : pick up (radio signals) **2 ~ l'attention de** : capture the attention of

captif, -tive [kaptif, -tiv] *adj & n* : captive — **captiver** [kaptive] *vt* : captivate — **captivité** [kaptivite] *nf* : captivity

capture [kaptyr] *nf* **1** : capture, seizure **2** ATTRAPE : catch — **capturer** [kaptyre] *vt* : capture, catch

capuche [kapyʃ] *nf* : hood — **capuchon** [kapyʃɔ̃] *nm* **1** : hood **2** : cap, top (of a pen, etc.)

caqueter [kakte] {8} *vi* : cackle

car[1] [kar] *nm* : bus, coach

car[2] *conj* : for, because

carabine [karabin] *nf* : rifle

caractère [karaktɛr] *nm* **1** : letter, character **2** TEMPÉRAMENT : character, nature — **caractériser** [karakterize] *vt* : characterize — **caractéristique** [karakteristik] *adj & nf* : characteristic

carafe [karaf] *nf* : carafe, decanter

caramel [karamɛl] *nm* **1** : caramel **2 ~ mou** : fudge

carapace [karapas] *nf* : shell

carat [kara] *nm* : carat, karat

caravane [karavan] *nf* **1** : caravan **2** : trailer

carbone [karbɔn] *nm* : carbon — **carboniser** [karbɔnize] *vt* : burn, char

carburant [karbyrɑ̃] *nm* : fuel — **carburateur** [karbyratœr] *nm* : carburetor

carcasse [karkas] *nf* : carcass

cardiaque [kardjak] *adj* : cardiac

cardigan [kardigɑ̃] *nm* : cardigan

cardinal, -nale [kardinal] *adj, mpl* **-naux** [-no] : cardinal, chief — **cardinal** *nm, pl* **-naux 1** : cardinal (in religion) **2** : cardinal number

carence [karɑ̃s] *nf* : lack, deficiency

caresser [karese] *vt* **1** : caress **2** : cherish, dream of — **caresse** [karɛs] *nf* : caress

cargaison [kargɛzɔ̃] *nf* : cargo, freight — **cargo** [kargo] *nm* : freighter

caricature [karikatyr] *nf* : caricature

carie [kari] *nf* : tooth decay, cavity

carillon [karijɔ̃] *nm* : bell, chime — **carillonner** [karijɔne] *v* : chime

carnage [karnaʒ] *nm* : carnage, bloodshed

carnaval [karnaval] *nm, pl* **-vals** : carnival

carnet [karnɛ] *nm* **1** : notebook **2** : book (of stamps, tickets, etc.)

carotte [karɔt] *nf* : carrot

carré, -rée [kare] *adj* **1** : square **2** : straightforward — **carré** *nm* : square

carreau [karo] *nm, pl* **-reaux 1** : tile **2** VITRE : windowpane **3** : diamond (in playing cards) **4 à ~x** : checkered

carrefour [karfur] *nm* : intersection, crossroads

carreler [karle] {8} *vt* : tile — **carrelage** [karlaʒ] *nm* : tiled floor

carrément [karemɑ̃] *adv* **1** : bluntly, directly **2** : downright

carrière [karjɛr] *nf* **1** : career **2** : stone quarry

carrosse [karɔs] *nm* : (horse-drawn) coach

carrure [karyr] *nf* : build (of the body)

carte [kart] *nf* **1** : card **2** : (road) map **3** : menu (in a restaurant) **4** *or* **~ à jouer** : playing card **5 ~ de crédit** : credit card **6 ~ des vins** : wine list **7 ~ postale** : postcard

cartilage [kartilaʒ] *nm* : cartilage, gristle

carton [kartɔ̃] *nm* **1** : cardboard **2** : cardboard box

cartouche [kartuʃ] *nf* : cartridge

cas [ka] *nms & pl* **1** : case **2 en aucun ~** : on no account **3 en ~ de** : in case of

cascade [kaskad] *nf* **1** : cascade, torrent **2** : waterfall

case [kaz] *nf* **1** : box (on a form) **2 ~ postale** *Can* : post office box

caserne [kazɛrn] *nf* **1** *France* : barracks *pl* **2 ~ de pompiers** *France* : fire station

casier [kazje] *nm* **1** : pigeonhole **2 ~ judiciaire** : police record

casino [kazino] *nm* : casino

casque [kask] *nm* **1** : helmet **2** : headphones *pl* — **casquette** [kaskɛt] *nf* : cap

casser [kase] *v* : break — **se casser** *vr* **1** : break (one's leg, etc.) **2 cassetoi!** *fam* : get out of here! — **cassable** [kasabl] *adj* : breakable — **casse–croûte** [kaskrut] *nms & pl* **1** : snack **2** *Can* : snack bar — **casse–noix** [kasnwa] *nms & pl* : nutcracker

casserole [kasrɔl] *nf* : saucepan

casse–tête [kastɛt] *nms & pl* **1** : puzzle **2** PROBLÈME : headache

cassette [kasɛt] *nf* : cassette

cassonade [kasɔnad] *nf* : brown sugar

cassure [kasyr] *nf* : break

castor [kastɔr] *nm* : beaver

catalogue [katalɔg] *nm* : catalog

cataracte [katarakt] *nf* : cataract

catastrophe [katastrɔf] *nf* : catastrophe — **catastrophique** [katastrɔfik] *adj* : catastrophic

catéchisme [kateʃism] *nm* : catechism

catégorie [kategɔri] *nf* : category — **catégorique** [kategɔrik] *adj* : categorical

cathédrale [katedral] *nf* : cathedral

catholique [katɔlik] *adj* : Catholic — **catholicisme** [katɔlisism] *nm* : Catholicism

catimini [katimini] **en ~** *adv phr* : on the sly

cauchemar [kɔʃmar] *nm* : nightmare

cause [koz] *nf* **1** : cause, reason **2** : (legal) case **3 à ~ de** : because of, on account of — **causer** [koze] *vt* PROVOQUER : cause — *vi* : chat — **causerie** [kozri] *nf* : talk, chat

caution [kosjɔ̃] *nf* **1** : surety, guarantee **2 libérer sous ~** : release on bail

cavalerie [kavalri] *nf* : cavalry — **cavalier, -lière** [kavalje, -ljɛr] *n* : rider, horseman *m*, horsewoman *f* — **cavalier** *nm* : knight (in chess)

cave [kav] *nf* : cellar

caverne [kavɛrn] *nf* GROTTE : cavern, cave

caviar [kavjar] *nm* : caviar

cavité [kavite] *nf* : cavity, hollow

CD [sede] *nm* (compact disc) : CD

ce [sə] (**cet** [sɛt] *before a vowel or mute h*), **cette** [sɛt] *adj, pl* **ces** [se] **1** : this, that, these, those **2 cette foisci** : this time **3 cette idée!** : what an idea! — **ce** (**c'** [s] *before a vowel*) *pron* **1** : it, that, these, those **2 ~ que, ~ qui, ~ dont** : what, which **3 c'est** : it is **4 ce sont** : they are **5 c'est cela** : that's right

ceci [səsi] *pron* : this

cécité [sesite] *nf* : blindness

céder [sede] {87} *vt* : give up, yield — *vi* : give in

cédille [sedij] *nf* : cedilla

cèdre [sɛdr] *nm* : cedar

cégep [seʒɛp] *nm* (*c*ollège d'*e*nseignement *g*énéral *e*t *p*rofessionnel) *Can* : junior college

ceinture [sɛ̃tyr] *nf* **1** : belt **2 ~ de sauvetage** : life belt **3 ~ de sécurité** : safety belt

cela [səla] *pron* : that, it

célébrer [selebre] {87} *vt* : celebrate — **célébration** [selebrasjɔ̃] *nf* : celebration — **célèbre** [selɛbr] *adj* : famous — **célébrité** [selebrite] *nf* **1** : fame, renown **2** : celebrity (person)

céleri [sɛlri] *nm* : celery

céleste [selɛst] *adj* : heavenly

célibataire [selibatɛr] *adj* : single, unmarried — **~** *nmf* : single person

celle, celles → **celui**

cellule [selyl] *nf* : cell

celui [səlɥi], **celle** [sɛl] *pron, pl* **ceux** [sø], **celles** [sɛl] : the one(s), those — **celui–ci** [səlɥisi], **celle–ci** [sɛlsi] *pron, pl* **ceux–ci** [søsi], **celles–ci** [sɛlsi] **1** : this (one), these **2** : the latter — **celui–là** [səlɥila], **celle–là** [sɛlla] *pron, pl* **ceux–là** [søla], **celles–là** [sɛlla] **1** : that (one), those **2** : the former

cendre [sɑ̃dr] *nf* : ash — **cendrier** [sɑ̃drije] *nm* : ashtray

censé, -sée [sɑ̃se] *adj* **être ~ faire** : be supposed to do

censurer [sɑ̃syre] *vt* : censor, ban — **censure** [sɑ̃syr] *nf* **1** : censorship **2** : censure

cent [sɑ̃] *adj* : a hundred, one hundred — **~** *nm* **1** : hundred **2** : cent **3 pour ~** : percent — **centaine** [sɑ̃tɛn] *nf* : about a hundred — **centenaire** [sɑ̃tnɛr] *adj* : hundred-year-old — **~** *nm* : centennial — **centième** [sɑ̃tjɛm] *adj & nmf & nm* : hundredth

centigrade [sɑ̃tigrad] *adj* : centigrade

centime [sɑ̃tim] *nm* : centime

centimètre [sɑ̃timɛtr] *nm* **1** : centimeter **2** : tape measure

central, -trale [sɑ̃tral] *adj, mpl* **-traux** [sɑ̃tro] : central — **central** *nm* **~ téléphonique** : telephone exchange — **centrale** *nf* **1** : power plant **2 ~ syndicale** : labor union —**centraliser** [sɑ̃tralize] *vt* : centralize

centre [sɑ̃tr] *nm* **1** : center **2 ~ commercial** : shopping center — **centrer** [sɑ̃tre] *vt* : center — **centre–ville** [sɑ̃trəvil] *nm, pl* **centres–villes** : downtown

cependant [səpɑ̃dɑ̃] *conj* : however, yet

céramique [seramik] *nf* : ceramics

cerceau [sɛrso] *nm, pl* **-ceaux** : hoop

cercle [sɛrkl] *nm* **1** : circle **2** : group (of friends, etc.)

cercueil [sɛrkœj] *nm* : coffin

céréale [sereal] *nf* : cereal

cérémonie [seremɔni] *nf* **1** : ceremony **2 sans ~** : informally

cerf [sɛr] *nm* : stag

cerf–volant [sɛrvɔlɑ̃] *nm, pl* **cerfs–volants** : kite

cerise [səriz] *nf* : cherry — **cerisier** [sərizje] *nm* : cherry tree

cerner [sɛrne] *vt* **1** : surround **2** DÉFINIR : define, determine — **cerne** [sɛrn] *nm* **avoir des ~s** : have rings under one's eyes

certain, -taine [sɛrtɛ̃, -tɛn] *adj* **1** : certain, sure **2** : certain, some — **certainement** [sɛrtɛnmɑ̃] *adv* : certainly — **certains, certaines** [sɛrtɛ̃, -tɛn] *pron pl* : some (people), certain (ones)

certes [sɛrt] *adv* : of course, indeed

certifier [sɛrtifje] {96} *vt* : certify — **certificat** [sɛrtifika] *nm* : certificate

certitude [sɛrtityd] *nf* : certainty

cerveau [sɛrvo] *nm, pl* **-veaux** : brain

ces → **ce**

cesser [sese] *v* : cease, stop — **cesse** [sɛs]

nf **sans ~** : constantly — **cessez-le-feu** [seselfø] *nms & pl* : cease-fire
c'est-à-dire [sɛtadir] *conj* : that is (to say)
cet, cette → **ce** — **ceux** → **celui** — **ceux-ci** → **celui-ci** — **ceux-là** → **celui-là**
chacun, chacune [ʃakœ̃, -kyn] *pron* **1** : each (one) **2** : everybody, everyone
chagrin [ʃagrɛ̃] *nm* PEINE : grief, sorrow — **chagriner** [ʃagrine] *vt* : grieve, distress
chahut [ʃay] *nm* : uproar, din
chaîne [ʃɛn] *nf* **1** : chain **2** : (television) channel **3** : (stereo) system — **chaînon** [ʃɛnɔ̃] *nm* : link
chair [ʃɛr] *nf* **1** : flesh **2** : meat **3 ~ de poule** : goose bumps
chaire [ʃɛr] *nf* **1** : (university) chair **2** : pulpit
chaise [ʃɛz] *nf* **1** : chair, seat **2 ~ roulante** : wheelchair
chaland [ʃalɑ̃] *nm* : barge
châle [ʃal] *nm* : shawl
chalet [ʃalɛ] *nm* **1** : chalet **2** *Can* : cottage
chaleur [ʃalœr] *nf* **1** : heat **2** : warmth — **chaleureux, -reuse** [ʃalœrø, -røz] *adj* : warm, friendly
chaloupe [ʃalup] *nf* : rowboat
chamailler [ʃamaje] *v* **se chamailler** *vr* : bicker
chambarder [ʃɑ̃barde] *vt fam* : mess up
chambre [ʃɑ̃br] *nf* **1** : room, bedroom **2** : (legislative) chamber, house
chameau [ʃamo] *nm, pl* **-meaux** : camel
champ [ʃɑ̃] *nm* **1** : field **2 ~ de bataille** : battlefield **3 ~ de courses** : racetrack
champagne [ʃɑ̃paɲ] *nm* : champagne
champêtre [ʃɑ̃pɛtr] *adj* : rural
champignon [ʃɑ̃piɲɔ̃] *nm* : mushroom
champion, -pionne [ʃɑ̃pjɔ̃, -pjɔn] *n* : champion — **championnat** [ʃɑ̃pjɔna] *nm* : championship
chance [ʃɑ̃s] *nf* **1** : luck, fortune **2** POSSIBILITÉ : chance, possibility **3 par ~** : fortunately
chanceler [ʃɑ̃sle] {8} *vi* : stagger — **chancelant, -lante** [ʃɑ̃slɑ̃, -lɑ̃t] *adj* : unsteady
chancelier [ʃɑ̃səlje] *nm* : chancellor
chanceux, -ceuse [ʃɑ̃sø, -søz] *adj* : lucky
chandail [ʃɑ̃daj] *nm* : sweater
chandelle [ʃɑ̃dɛl] *nf* : candle — **chandelier** [ʃɑ̃dəlje] *nm* : candlestick
changer [ʃɑ̃ʒe] {17} *vt* **1** REMPLACER : change **2** MODIFIER : alter — *vi* **1 ~ de** : change **2 ~ d'avis** : change one's mind — **se changer** *vr* : change one's clothes — **change** [ʃɑ̃ʒ] *nm* : exchange (in finance) — **changement** [ʃɑ̃ʒmɑ̃] *nm* : change
chanson [ʃɑ̃sɔ̃] *nf* : song — **chant** [ʃɑ̃] *nm* **1** : song, hymn **2** : singing
chantage [ʃɑ̃taʒ] *nm* : blackmail
chanter [ʃɑ̃te] *v* **1** : sing **2 faire ~** : blackmail — **chanteur, -teuse** [ʃɑ̃tœr, -tøz] *n* : singer
chantier [ʃɑ̃tje] *nm* **1** : (construction) site **2 ~ naval** : shipyard
chantonner [ʃɑ̃tɔne] *v* : hum
chanvre [ʃɑ̃vr] *nm* : hemp
chaos [kao] *nm* : chaos — **chaotique** [kaɔtik] *adj* : chaotic
chapeau [ʃapo] *nm, pl* **-peaux** : hat, cap
chapelet [ʃaplɛ] *nm* : rosary
chapelle [ʃapɛl] *nf* : chapel
chapelure [ʃaplyr] *nf* : bread crumbs *pl*
chaperon [ʃaprɔ̃] *nm* : chaperon
chapiteau [ʃapito] *nm, pl* **-teaux** : circus tent
chapitre [ʃapitr] *nm* **1** : chapter (of a book) **2** : subject matter
chaque [ʃak] *adj* : each, every
char [ʃar] *nm* **1** : chariot **2** : cart, wagon, float (in a parade) **3 ~ d'assaut** : tank
charabia [ʃarabja] *nm fam* : gibberish
charbon [ʃarbɔ̃] *nm* **1** : coal **2 ~ de bois** : charcoal
charcuterie [ʃarkytri] *nf* **1** : delicatessen **2** : cooked pork products
charger [ʃarʒe] {17} *vt* **1** : load **2** : charge (a battery) **3 ~ de** : put in charge of — **se charger** *vr* **~ de** : take care of — **charge** [ʃarʒ] *nf* **1** : load **2** RESPONSABILITÉ : responsibility **3** : (electrical) charge **4** FONCTION : office **5 ~s** : costs **6 à la ~ de** : dependent on — **chargé, -gée** [ʃarʒe] *adj* : busy — **chargement** [ʃarʒəmɑ̃] *nm* **1** : loading **2** : load, cargo
chariot [ʃarjo] *nm* : cart, wagon
charisme [karism] *nm* : charisma — **charismatique** [-rismatik] *adj* : charismatic
charité [ʃarite] *nf* : charity — **charitable** [ʃaritabl] *adj* : charitable
charlatan [ʃarlatɑ̃] *nm* : charlatan
charmer [ʃarme] *vt* : charm — **charmant, -mante** [ʃarmɑ̃, -mɑ̃t] *adj* : charming, delightful — **charme** [ʃarm] *nm* : charm, attraction — **charmeur, -meuse** [ʃarmœr, -møz] *adj* : charming — **~** *n* : charmer
charnière [ʃarnjɛr] *nf* : hinge
charnu, -nue [ʃarny] *adj* : fleshy
charpente [ʃarpɑ̃t] *nf* **1** : framework **2** : build (of the body) — **charpentier** [ʃarpɑ̃tje] *nm* : carpenter
charrette [ʃarɛt] *nf* : cart
charrue [ʃary] *nf* : plow
charte [ʃart] *nf* : charter — **charter** [ʃarte] *nm* : charter flight
chas [ʃa] *nm* : eye (of a needle)
chasser [ʃase] *vt* **1** : hunt **2** EXPULSER : chase away — **chasse** [ʃas] *nf* **1** : hunting **2** POURSUITE : chase **3** *or* **~ d'eau** : flush (of a toilet) — **chasse-neige** [ʃasnɛʒ] *nms & pl* : snowplow — **chasseur, -seuse** [ʃasœr, -søz] *n* : hunter
châssis [ʃasi] *nm* : frame (of a window)
chaste [ʃast] *adj* : chaste — **chasteté** [ʃastəte] *nf* : chastity
chat, chatte [ʃa, ʃat] *n* : cat
châtaigne [ʃatɛɲ] *nf* : chestnut
château [ʃato] *nm, pl* **-teaux** **1** : castle **2 ~ fort** : stronghold
châtier [ʃatje] {96} *vt* : chastise — **châtiment** [ʃatimɑ̃] *nm* : punishment
chaton [ʃatɔ̃] *nm* : kitten
chatouiller [ʃatuje] *vt* : tickle — **chatouilleux, -leuse** [ʃatujø, -jøz] *adj* : ticklish
châtrer [ʃatre] *vt* : castrate
chatte → **chat**
chaud, chaude [ʃo, ʃod] *adj* : warm, hot — **chaud** [ʃo] *adv* **1 avoir ~** : feel warm or hot **2 il fait ~** : it's warm, it's hot — **~** *nm* : heat, warmth — **chaudière** [ʃodjɛr] *nf* : boiler — **chaudron** [ʃodrɔ̃] *nm* : cauldron
chauffage [ʃofaʒ] *nm* : heating
chauffard [ʃofar] *nm* : reckless driver
chauffer [ʃofe] *vt* : heat, warm — *vi* : warm up — **se chauffer** *vr* : warm (oneself) up
chauffeur [ʃofœr] *nm* : driver, chauffeur
chaussée [ʃose] *nf* : roadway
chausser [ʃose] *vt* **1** : put on (shoes) **2 ~ du 7** : take size 7 (in shoes) — **chaussette** [ʃosɛt] *nf* : sock — **chausson** [ʃosɔ̃] *nm* **1** : slipper **2 ~ aux pommes** : apple turnover — **chaussure** [ʃosyr] *nf* : shoe, footwear
chauve [ʃov] *adj* : bald — **chauve-souris** [ʃovsuri] *nf, pl* **chauves-souris** : bat (animal)
chauvin, -vine [ʃovɛ̃, -vin] *adj* : chauvinistic
chaux [ʃo] *nf* **1** : lime **2 lait de ~** : whitewash
chavirer [ʃavire] *v* : capsize
chef [ʃɛf] *nm* **1** : leader, head, chief **2** *or* **~ cuisinier** : chef **3 ~ d'orchestre** : conductor **4 en ~** : (in) chief — **chef-d'œuvre** [ʃɛdœvr] *nm, pl* **chefs-d'œuvre** : masterpiece
chemin [ʃəmɛ̃] *nm* **1** : road, path **2 ~ de fer** : railroad
cheminée [ʃəmine] *nf* **1** : fireplace **2** : chimney
cheminer [ʃəmine] *vi* **1** : walk along **2** PROGRESSER : progress
chemise [ʃəmiz] *nf* **1** : shirt **2** DOSSIER : folder **3 ~ de nuit** : nightgown — **chemisier** [ʃəmizje] *nm* : blouse
chenal [ʃənal] *nm, pl* **-naux** [ʃəno] : channel
chêne [ʃɛn] *nm* : oak
chenille [ʃənij] *nf* : caterpillar
chèque [ʃɛk] *nm* : check
cher, chère [ʃɛr] *adj* **1** : dear, beloved **2** COÛTEUX : expensive — **~** *n* **mon cher, ma chère** : my dear — **cher** *adv* **coûter ~** : cost a lot
chercher [ʃɛrʃe] *vt* : look for, seek — **chercheur, -cheuse** [ʃɛrʃœr, -ʃøz] *n* : researcher
chérir [ʃerir] *vt* : cherish — **chéri, -rie** [ʃeri] *adj & n* : darling, dear
chétif, -tive [ʃetif, -tiv] *adj* : puny, weak
cheval [ʃəval] *nm, pl* **-vaux** [ʃəvo] **1** : horse **2** *or* **cheval-vapeur** : horsepower
chevalerie [ʃəvalri] *nf* : chivalry
chevalet [ʃəvalɛ] *nm* : easel
chevalier [ʃəvalje] *nm* : knight
chevaucher [ʃəvoʃe] *vt* **1** : straddle **2** : overlap — **se chevaucher** *vr* : overlap
chevelure [ʃəvlyr] *nf* : hair — **chevelu, -lue** [ʃəvly] *adj* : hairy
chevet [ʃəvɛ] *nm* : bedside
cheveu [ʃəvø] *nm, pl* **-veux** **1** POIL : hair **2 ~x** *nmpl* : (head of) hair
cheville [ʃəvij] *nf* : ankle
chèvre [ʃɛvr] *nf* : goat — **chevreau** [ʃəvro] *nm, pl* **-vreaux** : kid (goat)
chevreuil [ʃəvrœj] *nm* : roe deer
chevron [ʃəvrɔ̃] *nm* : rafter
chez [ʃe] *prep* **1** : at (the house of) **2** PARMI : among, in **3 ~ soi** : at home
chez-soi [ʃeswa] *nms & pl* : home
chic [ʃik] *adj s & pl* **1** : stylish **2** SYMPATHIQUE : nice
chicane [ʃikan] *nf* : squabble
chicorée [ʃikɔre] *nf* **1** : endive **2** : chicory (for coffee)
chien, chienne [ʃjɛ̃, -ʃjɛn] *n* : dog, bitch *f*
chiffon [ʃifɔ̃] *nm* : rag — **chiffonner** [ʃifɔne] *vt* : crumple
chiffre [ʃifr] *nm* **1** : figure, numeral **2** : amount, sum (in finance) **3** CODE : code **4 ~ d'affaires** : turnover — **chiffrer** [ʃifre] *vt* : calculate, assess — **se chiffrer** *vr* **~ à** : amount to
chignon [ʃiɲɔ̃] *nm* : (hair) bun
chimie [ʃimi] *nf* : chemistry — **chimique** [ʃimik] *adj* : chemical — **chimiste** [ʃimist] *nmf* : chemist
chimpanzé [ʃɛ̃pɑ̃ze] *nm* : chimpanzee
chinois, -noise [ʃinwa, -nwaz] *adj* : Chinese — **chinois** *nm* : Chinese (language)
chiot [ʃjo] *nm* : puppy
chips [ʃips] *nfpl* : potato chips
chirurgie [ʃiryrʒi] *nf* : surgery — **chirurgical, -cale** [ʃiryrʒikal] *adj, mpl* **-caux** [-ko] : surgical — **chirurgien, -gienne** [ʃiryrʒjɛ̃, -ʒjɛn] *n* : surgeon
chlore [klɔr] *nm* : chlorine
choc [ʃɔk] *nm* **1** : shock **2** : impact, crash
chocolat [ʃɔkɔla] *nm* : chocolate
chœur [kœr] *nm* **1** : choir **2** : chorus
choir [ʃwar] {18} *vi* : drop, fall
choisir [ʃwazir] *vt* : choose — **choix** [ʃwa] *nm* **1** : choice **2 de ~** : choice, first-rate
cholestérol [kɔlɛstɛrɔl] *nm* : cholesterol
chômage [ʃomaʒ] *nm* : unemployment — **chômeur, -meuse** [ʃomœr, -møz] *n* : unemployed person
choquer [ʃɔke] *vt* : shock, offend — **choquant, -quante** [ʃɔkɑ̃, -kɑ̃t] *adj* : shocking
choral, -rale [kɔral] *adj, mpl* **-rals** or **-raux** [kɔro] : choral — **chorale** *nf* : choir
chose [ʃoz] *nf* **1** : thing **2** AFFAIRE : matter
chou [ʃu] *nm, pl* **choux** : cabbage — **chouchou, -choute** [ʃuʃu, -ʃut] *n fam* : pet, favorite — **choucroute** [ʃukrut] *nf* : sauerkraut
chouette [ʃwɛt] *nf* : owl — **~** *adj fam* : terrific, neat
chou-fleur [ʃuflœr] *nm, pl* **choux-fleurs** : cauliflower
choyer [ʃwaje] {58} *vt* : pamper
chrétien, -tienne [kretjɛ̃, -tjɛn] *adj & n* : Christian — **christianisme** [kristjanism] *nm* : Christianity
chrome [krom] *nm* **1** : chromium **2 ~s** *nmpl* : chrome
chronique [krɔnik] *adj* : chronic — **~** *nf* : (newspaper) column, (televison) report — **chroniqueur, -queuse** [krɔnikœr, -køz] *n* : columnist
chronologie [krɔnɔlɔʒi] *nf* : chronology — **chronologique** [krɔnɔlɔʒik] *adj* : chronological
chronomètre [krɔnɔmɛtr] *nm* : stopwatch — **chronométrer** [krɔnɔmetre] {87} *vt* : time
chuchoter [ʃyʃɔte] *v* : whisper — **chuchotement** [ʃyʃɔtmɑ̃] *nm* : whisper
chum [tʃɔm] *nm Can fam* : boyfriend
chut [ʃyt] *interj* : sh!, hush!
chute [ʃyt] *nf* **1** : fall **2** *or* **~ d'eau** : waterfall **3 ~ de pluie** : rainfall
ci [si] *adv* **1 ce livreci** : this book **2 cette foisci** : this time **3 ceux-ci** : these ones **4 par-ci par-là** : here and there — **~** *pron* **1 ~ et ça** : this and that **2** → **comme** — **ci-après** [siaprɛ] *adv* : hereafter — **ci-bas** [siba] *adv* : below
cible [sibl] *nf* : target
ciboule [sibul] *nf* : scallion — **ciboulette** [sibulɛt] *nf* : chive
cicatrice [sikatris] *nf* : scar — **cicatriser** [sikatrize] *v* **se cicatriser** *vr* : heal (up)
ci-contre [sikɔ̃tr] *adv* : opposite
ci-dessous [sidəsu] *adv* : below
ci-dessus [sidəsy] *adv* : above
cidre [sidr] *nm* : cider
ciel [sjɛl] *nm* **1** *pl* **ciels** : sky **2** *pl* **cieux** [sjø] : heaven
cierge [sjɛrʒ] *nm* : candle (in a church)
cigare [sigar] *nm* : cigar — **cigarette** [sigarɛt] *nf* : cigarette
cigogne [sigɔɲ] *nf* : stork
ci-inclus, -cluse [siɛ̃kly, -klyz] *adj* : enclosed — **ci-inclus** [siɛ̃kly] *adv* : enclosed
ci-joint, -jointe [siʒwɛ̃, -ʒwɛ̃t] *adj* : enclosed — **ci-joint** [siʒwɛ̃] *adv* : enclosed, herewith
cil [sil] *nm* : eyelash
cime [sim] *nf* : summit, peak
ciment [simɑ̃] *nm* : cement
cimetière [simtjɛr] *nm* : cemetery
cinéaste [sineast] *nmf* : film director
cinéma [sinema] *nm* **1** : movie theater **2 aller au ~** : go to the movies
cinglant, -glante [sɛ̃glɑ̃, -glɑ̃t] *adj* : cutting, biting
cinq [sɛ̃k] *adj* **1** : five **2** : fifth (in dates) — **~** *nms & pl* : five
cinquante [sɛ̃kɑ̃t] *adj & nms & pl* : fifty — **cinquantaine** [sɛ̃kɑ̃tɛn] *nf* **une ~ de** : about fifty — **cinquantième** [sɛ̃kɑ̃tjɛm] *adj & nmf & nm* : fiftieth
cinquième [sɛ̃kjɛm] *adj & nmf & nm* : fifth
cintre [sɛ̃tr] *nm* : coat hanger
cirage [siraʒ] *nm* : shoe polish
circoncire [sirkɔ̃sir] {86} *vt* : circumcise — **circoncision** [sirkɔ̃sizjɔ̃] *nf* : circumcision
circonférence [sirkɔ̃ferɑ̃s] *nf* : circumference
circonflexe [sirkɔ̃flɛks] *adj* **accent ~** : circumflex (accent)
circonscrire [sirkɔ̃skrir] {33} *vt* : limit, contain — **circonscription** [sirkɔ̃skripsjɔ̃] *nf* : district, ward
circonspect, -specte [sirkɔ̃spɛ, -spɛkt] *adj* : cautious, circumspect
circonstance [sirkɔ̃stɑ̃s] *nf* : circumstance, occasion
circuit [sirkɥi] *nm* **1** : circuit **2** *or* **coup de ~** *Can* : home run (in baseball)
circulaire [sirkylɛr] *adj & nf* : circular
circuler [sirkyle] *vi* **1** : circulate **2** SE DÉPLACER : move (along) **3** : run (of buses, etc.) **4 faire ~ des bruits** : spread rumors — **circulation** [sirkylasjɔ̃] *nf* **1** : circulation **2** : traffic
cire [sir] *nf* : wax — **ciré** [sire] *nm* : oilskin — **cirer** [sire] *vt* : wax, polish
cirque [sirk] *nm* **1** : circus **2** *fam* : chaos
cisailles [sizaj] *nfpl* : shears
ciseau [sizo] *nm, pl* **-seaux** **1** : chisel **2 ~x** *nmpl* : scissors — **ciseler** [sizle] {20} *vt* : chisel
citadelle [sitadɛl] *nf* : citadel
citadin, -dine [sitadɛ̃, -din] *n* : city dweller
citation [sitasjɔ̃] *nf* **1** : quotation **2** : summons (in law)
cité [site] *nf* **1** : city **2 ~ universitaire** *France* : college dormitories *pl* **3 ~ universitaire** *Can* : college campus
citer [site] *vt* **1** : quote **2** MENTIONNER : name, cite
citerne [sitɛrn] *nf* : tank, reservoir
citoyen, citoyenne [sitwajɛ̃, -jɛn] *n* : citizen — **citoyenneté** [sitwajɛnte] *nf* : citizenship
citron [sitrɔ̃] *nm* : lemon — **citronnade** [sitrɔnad] *nf* : lemonade
citrouille [sitruj] *nf* : pumpkin
civière [sivjɛr] *nf* : stretcher
civil, -vile [sivil] *adj* **1** : civil **2** : secular — **~** *n* : civilian — **civilisation** [sivilizasjɔ̃] *nf* : civilization — **civiliser** [sivilize] *vt* : civilize — **civilité** [sivilite] *nf* : civility
civique [sivik] *adj* : civic
clair, claire [klɛr] *adj* **1** : clear **2** LUMINEUX : bright **3** PÂLE : light-colored — **clair** *adv* : clearly — **clair** [klɛr] *nm* **1 ~ de lune** : moonlight **2 mettre au ~** : make clear — **clairement** [klɛrmɑ̃] *adv* : clearly — **clairière** [klɛrjɛr] *nf* : clearing
clairon [klɛrɔ̃] *nm* : bugle
clairsemé, -mée [klɛrsəme] *adj* : scattered, sparse
clamer [klame] *vt* : proclaim — **clameur** [klamœr] *nf* : clamor
clan [klɑ̃] *nm* : clan, clique
clandestin, -tine [klɑ̃dɛstɛ̃, -tin] *adj* **1** : clandestine **2 passager ~** : stowaway
clapier [klapje] *nm* : (rabbit) hutch
clapoter [klapɔte] *vi* : lap (of waves)
claque [klak] *nf* **1** : slap, smack **2 ~s** *nfpl Can* : rubbers, galoshes — **claquement** [klakmɑ̃] *nm* : bang(ing), slam(ming) — **claquer** [klake] *vt* **1** GIFLER : slap **2** : slam (a door) — *vi* **1 faire ~ ses doigts** : snap one's fingers **2 il claque des dents** : his teeth are chattering — **claquettes** [klakɛt] *nfpl* : tap dancing
clarifier [klarifje] {96} *vt* : clarify — **clarification** [-rifikasjɔ̃] *nf* : clarification
clarinette [klarinɛt] *nf* : clarinet
clarté [klarte] *nf* **1** : light, brightness **2** NETTETÉ : clarity
classe [klas] *nf* **1** : class, category **2** : classroom **3 aller en ~** : go to school — **classement** [klasmɑ̃] *nm* **1** : classification **2** RANG : ranking, place — **classer** [klase] *vt* : class, classify — **se classer** *vr* : rank — **classeur** [klasœr] *nm* **1** : binder **2** : filing cabinet
classifier [klasifje] {96} *vt* : classify — **classification** [klasifikasjɔ̃] *nf* : classification
classique [klasik] *adj* : classic(al) — **~** *nm* : classic (of a book, etc.)
clause [kloz] *nf* : clause
claustrophobie [klostrɔfɔbi] *nf* : claustrophobia
clavecin [klavsɛ̃] *nm* : harpsichord
clavicule [klavikyl] *nf* : collarbone
clavier [klavje] *nm* : keyboard
clé *or* **clef** [kle] *nf* **1** : key **2** : clef (in music) **3 ~ anglaise** : monkey wrench — **~** *adj* : key
clément, -mente [klemɑ̃, -mɑ̃t] *adj* **1** : lenient **2** DOUX : mild, clement — **clémence** [klemɑ̃s] *nf* : leniency
clémentine [klemɑ̃tin] *nf* : tangerine
clenche [klɑ̃ʃ] *nf* : latch
clergé [klɛrʒe] *nm* : clergy
clérical, -cale [klerikal] *adj, mpl* **-caux** [-ko] : clerical
cliché [kliʃe] *nm* : cliché
client, cliente [kliɑ̃, kliɑ̃t] *n* **1** : customer, client **2** : patient — **clientèle** [kliɑ̃tɛl] *nf* **1** : customers *pl* **2** : practice (of a doctor)
cligner [kliɲe] *vi* **1 ~ de l'œil** : wink **2 ~ des yeux** : blink — **clignotant** [kliɲɔtɑ̃] *nm* : blinker, directional signal — **clignoter** [kliɲɔte] *vi* **1** : flicker, flash **2** → **cligner 2**
climat [klima] *nm* : climate — **climatisation** [klimatizasjɔ̃] *nf* : air-conditioning — **climatisé, -sée** [klimatize] *adj* : air-conditioned — **climatiseur** [klimatizœr] *nm* : air conditioner
clin [klɛ̃] *nm* **1 ~ d'œil** : wink **2 en un ~ d'œil** : in a flash
clinique [klinik] *nf* : clinic — **~** *adj* : clinical
cliquer [klike] *vi* : click (on a computer)
cliqueter [klikte] {8} *vi* : clink, jingle, clack — **cliquetis** [klikti] *nm* : jingle, clatter

clochard, -charde [klɔʃar, -ʃard] *n* : tramp

cloche [klɔʃ] *nf* : bell — **clocher** [klɔʃe] *nm* : belfry, steeple

cloison [klwazɔ̃] *nf* : partition — **cloisonner** [klwazɔne] *vt* : partition (off)

cloître [klwatr] *nm* : cloister

cloque [klɔk] *nf* : blister

clore [klɔr] {19} *vt* : close, conclude — **clos, close** [klo, -kloz] *adj* : closed, shut — **clôture** [klotyr] *nf* **1** : fence **2** : end, closure — **clôturer** [klotyre] *vt* **1** : enclose **2** : bring to a close

clou [klu] *nm, pl* **~s 1** : nail **2** : high point **3** FURONCLE : boil **4 ~ de girofle** : clove — **clouer** [klue] *vt* **1** : nail **2** : pin down

clown [klun] *nm* : clown

club [klœb] *nm* : club

coaguler [kɔagyle] *v* : coagulate — **se coaguler** *vr* : coagulate, clot

coalition [kɔalisjɔ̃] *nf* : coalition

coasser [kɔase] *vi* : croak

cobaye [kɔbaj] *nm* : guinea pig

cocaïne [kɔkain] *nf* : cocaine

cocasse [kɔkas] *adj* : comical

coccinelle [kɔksinɛl] *nf* : ladybug

cocher [kɔʃe] *vt* : check (off)

cochon [kɔʃɔ̃] *nm* **1** : pig **2 ~ d'Inde** : guinea pig — **cochonnerie** [kɔʃɔnri] *nf* : junk, trash

cocktail [kɔktɛl] *nm* : cocktail

coco [kɔko] *nm or* **noix de ~** : coconut — **cocotier** [kɔkɔtje] *nm* : coconut palm

cocon [kɔkɔ̃] *nm* : cocoon

cocotte [kɔkɔt] *nf* : casserole dish

code [kɔd] *nm* **1** : code **2 ~ postal** : zip code — **coder** [kɔde] *vt* : code, encode

coéquipier, -pière [kɔekipje, -jɛr] *n* : teammate

cœur [kœr] *nm* **1** : heart **2** : center, core **3** : hearts *pl* (in playing cards) **4** COURAGE : courage **5 à ~ joie** : to one's heart's content **6 avoir mal au ~** : feel sick, feel nauseous **7 de bon ~** : willingly

coffre [kɔfr] *nm* **1** : (toy) chest **2** COFFRE-FORT : safe **3** : trunk (of a car) — **coffre–fort** [kɔfrəfɔr] *nm, pl* **coffres–forts** : safe — **coffret** [kɔfrɛ] *nm* : small box, case

cognac [kɔɲak] *nm* : cognac

cogner [kɔɲe] *vt* : knock, bang — *vi* : knock — **se cogner** *vr* **1** : bump oneself **2 ~ la tête** : hit one's head

cohabiter [kɔabite] *vi* : live together

cohérent, -rente [kɔerɑ̃, -rɑ̃t] *adj* : coherent — **cohérence** [-erɑ̃s] *nf* : coherence

cohue [kɔy] *nf* : crowd

coiffe [kwaf] *nf* : headdress — **coiffer** [kwafe] *v* **se coiffer** *vr* : do one's hair — **coiffeur, -feuse** [kwafœr, -føz] *n* : hairdresser — **coiffure** [kwafyr] *nf* **1** : hairdo **2** : hairdressing

coin [kwɛ̃] *nm* **1** : corner **2** ENDROIT : place, spot

coincer [kwɛ̃se] {6} *vt* **1** : wedge, jam **2** *fam* : corner, nab — *vi* : get stuck

coïncider [kɔɛ̃side] *vi* : coincide — **coïncidence** [kɔɛ̃sidɑ̃s] *nf* : coincidence

col [kɔl] *nm* **1** : collar **2** : neck (of a bottle)

colère [kɔlɛr] *nf* **1** : anger **2 se mettre en ~** : get angry — **coléreux, -reuse** [kɔlerø, -røz] *adj* : bad-tempered, irritable — **colérique** [kɔlerik] *adj* : bad-tempered

colimaçon [kɔlimasɔ̃] *nm* **1** : snail **2 escalier en ~** : spiral staircase

colique [kɔlik] *nf* **1** : diarrhea **2** *or* **~s** *nfpl* : colic

colis [kɔli] *nms & pl* : parcel, package

collaborer [kɔlabɔre] *vi* : collaborate — **collaborateur, -trice** [kɔlabɔratœr, -tris] *n* : colleague — **collaboration** [-bɔrasjɔ̃] *nf* : collaboration

collant, -lante [kɔlɑ̃, -lɑ̃t] *adj* : sticky — **collant** *nm* **1** : panty hose *pl* **2 ~s** *mpl* : tights

collation [kɔlasjɔ̃] *nf* : snack

colle [kɔl] *nf* **1** : paste, glue **2** : trick question

collecte [kɔlɛkt] *nf* : collection — **collecter** [kɔlɛkte] *vt* : collect (funds) — **collectif, -tive** [kɔlɛktif, -tiv] *adj* : collective, joint — **collection** [kɔlɛksjɔ̃] *nf* : collection — **collectionner** [kɔlɛksjɔne] *vt* : collect — **collectionneur, -neuse** [kɔlɛksjɔnœr, -nøz] *n* : collector

collège [kɔlɛʒ] *nm* **1** *France* : junior high school **2** *Can* : vocational college — **collégial, -giale** [kɔleʒjal] *adj, mpl* **-giaux** [-ʒjo] : collegiate — **collégien, -gienne** [kɔleʒjɛ̃, -ʒjɛn] *n France* : schoolboy *m*, schoolgirl *f*

collègue [kɔlɛg] *nmf* : colleague

coller [kɔle] *vt* : stick, glue — *vi* **~ à** : stick to, adhere to

collet [kɔlɛ] *nm* **1** : collar (of a shirt) **2 être ~ monté** : be prim and proper

collier [kɔlje] *nm* **1** : necklace **2** : (animal) collar

colline [kɔlin] *nf* : hill

collision [kɔlizjɔ̃] *nf* **1** : collision **2 entrer en ~ avec** : collide with

colloque [kɔlɔk] *nm* : symposium

colombe [kɔlɔ̃b] *nf* : dove

colon [kɔlɔ̃] *nm* : settler

côlon [kolɔ̃] *nm* : colon (in anatomy)

colonel [kɔlɔnɛl] *nm* : colonel

colonie [kɔlɔni] *nf* **1** : colony **2 ~ de vacances** : summer camp — **colonial, -niale** [kɔlɔnjal] *adj, mpl* **-niaux** [-njo] : colonial — **coloniser** [kɔlɔnize] *vt* : colonize, settle

colonne [kɔlɔn] *nf* **1** : column **2 ~ vertébrale** : spine, backbone

colorer [kɔlɔre] *vt* : color, tint — **colorant** [kɔlɔrɑ̃] *nm* : dye, stain — **coloré, -rée** [kɔlɔre] *adj* **1** : colorful **2** : colored — **colorier** [kɔlɔrje] {96} *vt* : color (a drawing) — **coloris** [kɔlɔri] *nm* : shade, color

colporter [kɔlpɔrte] *vt* : hawk, peddle — **colporteur, -teuse** [kɔlpɔrtœr, -tøz] *n* : peddler

coma [kɔma] *nm* : coma

combattre [kɔ̃batr] {12} *v* : fight — **combat** [kɔ̃ba] *nm* **1** : fight(ing) **2 ~ de boxe** : boxing match — **combattant, -tante** [kɔ̃batɑ̃, -tɑ̃t] *n* **1** : combatant, fighter **2 ancien combattant** : veteran — **combatif, -tive** [kɔ̃batif, -tiv] *adj* : combative

combien [kɔ̃bjɛ̃] *adv* **1** : how much, how many **2 ~ de** : how much, how many **3 ~ de fois** : how often **4 ~ de temps** : how long

combiner [kɔ̃bine] *vt* **1** : combine **2** PRÉPARER : work out, devise — **combinaison** [kɔ̃binɛzɔ̃] *nf* **1** : combination **2** : coveralls *pl*, suit — **combiné** [kɔ̃bine] *nm* : (telephone) receiver

combler [kɔ̃ble] *vt* **1** : fill (in) **2** : satisfy, fulfill — **comble** [kɔ̃bl] *adj* : packed — **~** *nm* **le ~ de** : the height of

combustible [kɔ̃bystibl] *adj* : combustible — **~** *nm* : fuel — **combustion** [kɔ̃bystjɔ̃] *nf* : combustion

comédie [kɔmedi] *nf* : comedy — **comédien, -dienne** [kɔmedjɛ̃, -djɛn] *n* : actor *m*, actress *f*

comestible [kɔmɛstibl] *adj* : edible

comète [kɔmɛt] *nf* : comet

comique [kɔmik] *adj* : comic, funny — **~** *nmf* : comedian, comic

comité [kɔmite] *nm* : committee

commander [kɔmɑ̃de] *vt* **1** : command **2** : order (a meal, etc.) — **commandant** [kɔmɑ̃dɑ̃] *nm* **1** : commander **2** : major (in the army) **3 ~ de bord** : captain — **commande** [kɔmɑ̃d] *nf* **1** : order **2 ~ à distance** : remote control — **commandement** [kɔmɑ̃dmɑ̃] *nm* **1** : command, authority **2** : commandment (in religion)

comme [kɔm] *adv* : how — **~** *conj* **1** : as, like **2** : since **3** : when, as **4 ~ ci, ~ ça** : so-so **5 ~ il faut** : properly — **~** *prep* : like, as

commémorer [kɔmemɔre] *vt* : commemorate — **commémoration** [kɔmemɔrasjɔ̃] *nf* : commemoration

commencer [kɔmɑ̃se] {6} *v* : begin, start — **commencement** [kɔmɑ̃smɑ̃] *nm* : beginning, start

comment [kɔmɑ̃] *adv* **1** : how **2** : what **3 ~ ça va?** : how is it going?

commenter [kɔmɑ̃te] *vt* : comment on — **commentaire** [kɔmɑ̃tɛr] *nm* **1** : comment **2** : commentary

commérages [kɔmeraʒ] *nmpl fam* : gossip

commerce [kɔmɛrs] *nm* : business, trade — **commercer** [kɔmɛrse] {6} *vi* : trade, deal — **commerçant, -çante** [kɔmɛrsɑ̃, -sɑ̃t] *n* : merchant, storekeeper — **commercial** [kɔmɛrsjal] *adj, mpl* **-ciaux** [-sjo] : commercial — **commercialiser** [kɔmɛrsjalize] *vt* : market

commère [kɔmɛr] *nf fam* : gossip (person)

commettre [kɔmɛtr] {53} *vt* : commit

commis [kɔmi] *nm* **1** : clerk **2 ~ voyageur** : traveling salesman

commissaire [kɔmisɛr] *nm* : superintendent, commissioner — **commissariat** [kɔmisarja] *nm* **~ de police** : police station

commission [kɔmisjɔ̃] *nf* **1** : committee **2 ~s** *nfpl* : shopping

commode [kɔmɔd] *adj* **1** : handy **2 pas ~** : awkward — **~** *nf* : chest of drawers — **commodité** [kɔmɔdite] *nf* : convenience

commotion [kɔmɔsjɔ̃] *nf* **~ cérébrale** : concussion

commun, -mune [kɔmœ̃, -myn] *adj* **1** : common, shared **2** : usual, ordinary — **commun** *nm* **1 en ~** : in common **2 hors du ~** : out of the ordinary

communauté [kɔmynote] *nf* **1** : community **2** : commune — **communautaire** [kɔmynotɛr] *adj* : communal

communication [kɔmynikasjɔ̃] *nf* **1** : communication **2 ~ téléphonique** : telephone call

communion [kɔmynjɔ̃] *nf* : communion

communiquer [kɔmynike] *v* : communicate — **communiqué** [kɔmynike] *nm* : press release

communisme [kɔmynism] *nm* : communism — **communiste** [kɔmynist] *adj & nmf* : communist

commutateur [kɔmytatœr] *nm* : (electric) switch

compact, -pacte [kɔ̃pakt] *adj* : compact, dense — **compact** *nm* : compact disc

compagnie [kɔ̃paɲi] *nf* **1** : company **2 tenir ~ à qqn** : keep s.o. company — **compagne** [kɔ̃paɲ] *nf* : (female) companion, partner — **compagnon** [kɔ̃paɲɔ̃] *nm* : companion

comparer [kɔ̃pare] *vt* : compare — **comparaison** [kɔ̃parɛzɔ̃] *nf* : comparison

compartiment [kɔ̃partimɑ̃] *nm* : compartment

compas [kɔ̃pa] *nms & pl* : compass

compassion [kɔ̃pasjɔ̃] *nf* : compassion

compatible [kɔ̃patibl] *adj* : compatible — **compatibilité** [kɔ̃patibilite] *nf* : compatibility

compatir [kɔ̃patir] *vi* : sympathize — **compatissant, -sante** [kɔ̃patisɑ̃, -sɑ̃t] *adj* : compassionate

compatriote [kɔ̃patrijɔt] *nmf* : compatriot

compenser [kɔ̃pɑ̃se] *vt* : compensate for — **compensation** [kɔ̃pɑ̃sasjɔ̃] *nf* : compensation

compétent, -tente [kɔ̃petɑ̃, -tɑ̃t] *adj* : competent — **compétence** [-petɑ̃s] *nf* : competence

compétiteur, -trice [kɔ̃petitœr, -tris] *n* : competitor, rival — **compétitif, -tive** [kɔ̃petitif, -tiv] *adj* : competitive — **compétition** [kɔ̃petisjɔ̃] *nf* : competition

complaisant, -sante [kɔ̃plɛzɑ̃, -zɑ̃t] *adj* **1** AIMABLE : obliging, kind **2** INDULGENT : indulgent

complément [kɔ̃plemɑ̃] *nm* : complement — **complémentaire** [kɔ̃plemɑ̃tɛr] *adj* : complementary

complet, -plète [kɔ̃plɛ, -plɛt] *adj* **1** : complete **2** PLEIN : full (of a hotel, etc.) — **complet** *nm* : suit — **complètement** [kɔ̃plɛtmɑ̃] *adv* : completely — **compléter** [kɔ̃plete] {87} *vt* : complete

complexe [kɔ̃plɛks] *adj & nm* : complex — **complexité** [kɔ̃plɛksite] *nf* : complexity

complication [kɔ̃plikasjɔ̃] *nf* : complication

complice [kɔ̃plis] *adj* : knowing (of a look, etc.) — **~** *nmf* : accomplice

compliment [kɔ̃plimɑ̃] *nm* : compliment — **complimenter** [kɔ̃plimɑ̃te] *vt* : compliment

compliquer [kɔ̃plike] *vt* : complicate — **compliqué, -quée** [kɔ̃plike] *adj* : complicated

complot [kɔ̃plo] *nm* : plot — **comploter** [kɔ̃plɔte] *v* : plot, scheme

comporter [kɔ̃pɔrte] *vt* **1** CONTENIR : include **2** : entail (risks, etc.) — **se comporter** *vr* : behave — **comportement** [kɔ̃pɔrtəmɑ̃] *nm* : behavior

composer [kɔ̃poze] *vt* **1** : compose (music) **2** : constitute, make up **3** : dial (a number) — **se composer** *vr* **~ de** : consist of — **composant** [kɔ̃pozɑ̃] *nm* ÉLÉMENT : component — **composé, -sée** [kɔ̃poze] *adj* : compound — **composé** *nm* : compound — **compositeur, -trice** [kɔ̃pozitœr, -tris] *n* : composer — **composition** [kɔ̃pozisjɔ̃] *nf* : composition

compote [kɔ̃pɔt] *nf* **~ de pommes** : apple sauce

compréhensif, -sive [kɔ̃preɑ̃sif, -siv] *adj* : understanding — **compréhension** [kɔ̃preɑ̃sjɔ̃] *nf* : understanding, comprehension

comprendre [kɔ̃prɑ̃dr] {70} *vt* **1** : consist of, comprise **2** : understand **3 mal ~** : misunderstand

compression [kɔ̃prɛsjɔ̃] *nf* : compression

comprimer [kɔ̃prime] *vt* : compress — **comprimé** [kɔ̃prime] *nm* : tablet, pill

compris, -prise [kɔ̃pri, -priz] *adj* **1** INCLUS : included **2 y compris** : including

compromettre [kɔ̃prɔmɛtr] {53} *vt* : compromise — **compromis** [kɔ̃prɔmi] *nm* : compromise

comptable [kɔ̃tabl] *nmf* : accountant — **comptabilité** [kɔ̃tabilite] *nf* : accounting

comptant [kɔ̃tɑ̃] *adv* **payer ~** : pay cash

compte [kɔ̃t, -tes] *nm* **1** : (bank) account **2 au bout du ~** : in the end **3 ~ à rebours** : countdown **4 se rendre ~ de** : realize — **compter** [kɔ̃te] *vt* **1** : count **2** ESPÉRER : expect **3 ~ faire** : intend to do — *vi* **1** CALCULER : count **2** IMPORTER : matter **3 ~ sur** : count on

compte–rendu [kɔ̃trɑ̃dy] *nm, pl* **comptes–rendus** : report

compteur [kɔ̃tœr] *nm* : meter

comptoir [kɔ̃twar] *nm* : counter, bar

comte, comtesse [kɔ̃t, -tɛs] *n* : count *m*, countess *f*

comté [kɔ̃te] *nm* : county

concave [kɔ̃kav] *adj* : concave

concéder [kɔ̃sede] {87} *vt* : grant, concede

concentrer [kɔ̃sɑ̃tre] *vt* : concentrate — **se concentrer** *vr* **1** : concentrate **2 ~ sur** : center on — **concentration** [kɔ̃sɑ̃trasjɔ̃] *nf* : concentration

concept [kɔ̃sɛpt] *nm* : concept — **conception** [kɔ̃sɛpsjɔ̃] *nf* : conception

concerner [kɔ̃sɛrne] *vt* **1** : concern **2 en ce qui me concerne** : as far as I'm concerned — **concernant** [kɔ̃sɛrnɑ̃] *prep* : concerning, regarding

concert [kɔ̃sɛr] *nm* **1** : concert **2 de ~** : together — **se concerter** [kɔ̃sɛrte] *vr* : consult, confer — **concerté, -tée** [kɔ̃sɛrte] *adj* : concerted

concession [kɔ̃sesjɔ̃] *nf* : concession — **concessionnaire** [kɔ̃sesjɔnɛr] *nmf* : dealer, agent

concevoir [kɔ̃səvwar] {26} *vt* **1** : conceive (a child) **2** IMAGINER : conceive of, design

concierge [kɔ̃sjɛrʒ] *nmf* : janitor

concilier [kɔ̃silje] {96} *vt* : reconcile — **conciliant, -liante** [kɔ̃siljɑ̃, -ljɑ̃t] *adj* : conciliatory

concis, -cise [kɔ̃si, -siz] *adj* : concise — **concision** [kɔ̃sizjɔ̃] *nf* **avec ~** : concisely

conclure [kɔ̃klyr] {39} *vt* : conclude — **concluant, -cluante** [kɔ̃klyɑ̃, -klyɑ̃t] *adj* : conclusive — **conclusion** [kɔ̃klyzjɔ̃] *nf* : conclusion

concombre [kɔ̃kɔ̃br] *nm* : cucumber

concorder [kɔ̃kɔrde] *vi* : agree, match — **concordant, -dante** [kɔ̃kɔrdɑ̃, -dɑ̃t] *adj* : in agreement

concourir [kɔ̃kurir] {23} *vi* **1** : compete **2 ~ à** : work toward — **concours** [kɔ̃kur] *nm* : competition, contest

concret, -crète [kɔ̃krɛ, -krɛt] *adj* : concrete — **concrétiser** [kɔ̃kretize] *vt* : give shape to — **se concrétiser** *vr* : materialize

concurrencer [kɔ̃kyrɑ̃se] {6} *vt* : rival, compete with — **concurrence** [kɔ̃kyrɑ̃s] *nf* : competition, rivalry — **concurrent, -rente** [kɔ̃kyrɑ̃, -rɑ̃t] *adj* : competing, rival — **~** *n* : competitor

condamner [kɔ̃dane] *vt* **1** : condemn **2** : sentence (in law) — **condamnation** [kɔ̃danasjɔ̃] *nf* **1** : condemnation **2** PEINE : sentence

condenser [kɔ̃dɑ̃se] *vt* : condense — **condensation** [kɔ̃dɑ̃sasjɔ̃] *nf* : condensation

condescendant, -dante [kɔ̃desɑ̃dɑ̃, -dɑ̃t] *adj* : condescending

condiment [kɔ̃dimɑ̃] *nm* : condiment

condition [kɔ̃disjɔ̃] *nf* **1** : condition **2 ~s** *nfpl* : conditions, circumstances **3 sous ~ que** : provided that — **conditionnel, -nelle** [kɔ̃disjɔnɛl] *adj* : conditional

condoléances [kɔ̃dɔleɑ̃s] *nfpl* : condolences

conduire [kɔ̃dɥir] {49} *vt* **1** : drive **2 ~ à** : lead to — **se conduire** *vr* : behave — **conducteur, -trice** [kɔ̃dyktœr, -tris] *n* : driver — **conducteur** *nm* : conductor (of electricity) — **conduite** [kɔ̃dɥit] *nf* **1** : behavior, conduct **2** TUYAU : pipe **3 ~ à droite** : right-hand drive

cône [kon] *nm* : cone

confection [kɔ̃fɛksjɔ̃] *nf* **1** : making **2 la ~** : the clothing industry — **confectionner** [kɔ̃fɛksjɔne] *vt* : make (a meal, a garment, etc.)

confédération [kɔ̃federasjɔ̃] *nf* : confederation

conférence [kɔ̃ferɑ̃s] *nf* **1** : conference **2** COURS : lecture — **conférencier, -cière** [kɔ̃ferɑ̃sje, -sjɛr] *n* : lecturer

conférer [kɔ̃fere] {87} *v* : confer

confession [kɔ̃fesjɔ̃] *nf* **1** : confession **2** : denomination — **confesser** [kɔ̃fese] *vt* : confess

confettis [kɔ̃feti] *nmpl* : confetti

confiant, -fiante [kɔ̃fjɑ̃, -fjɑ̃t] *adj* **1** : confident, trusting **2** ASSURÉ : self-confident — **confiance** [kɔ̃fjɑ̃s] *nf* **1** : confidence, trust **2 ~ en soi** : self-confidence

confidence [kɔ̃fidɑ̃s] *nf* **1** : confidence **2 faire des ~s à** : confide in — **confident, -dente** [kɔ̃fidɑ̃, -dɑ̃t] *n* : confidant, confidante *f* — **confidentiel, -tielle** [kɔ̃fidɑ̃sjɛl] *adj* : confidential

confier [kɔ̃fje] {96} *vt* **1 ~ à qqn** : confide to s.o. **2 ~ (qqch) à qqn** : entrust (sth) to s.o. — **se confier** *vr* **~ à qqn** : confide in s.o.

confiner [kɔ̃fine] *vt* : confine — **confins** [kɔ̃fɛ̃] *nmpl* : limits, confines

confirmer [kɔ̃firme] *vt* : confirm — **confirmation** [kɔ̃firmasjɔ̃] *nf* : confirmation

confiserie [kɔ̃fizri] *nf* **1** : candy store **2** : candy

confisquer [kɔ̃fiske] *vt* : confiscate

confiture [kɔ̃fityr] *nf* : jam, preserves *pl*

conflit [kɔ̃fli] *nm* : conflict

confondre [kɔ̃fɔ̃dr] {63} *vt* **1** : confuse, mix up **2** ÉTONNER : baffle

conformer [kɔ̃fɔrme] *v* **se conformer** *vr* **~ à** : conform to — **conforme** [kɔ̃fɔrm] *adj* **1 ~ à** : in keeping with **2 ~ à** : true to — **conformément** [kɔ̃fɔrmemɑ̃] *adv* **~ à** : in accordance with — **conformité** [kɔ̃fɔrmite] *nf* : conformity

confort [kɔ̃fɔr] *nm* : comfort — **confortable** [kɔ̃fɔrtabl] *adj* : comfortable

confrère [kɔ̃frɛr] *nm* : colleague

confronter [kɔ̃frɔ̃te] *vt* **1** : confront **2** COMPARER : compare

confus [kɔ̃fy] *adj* **1** : confused **2** : embarrassed — **confusion** [kɔ̃fyzjɔ̃] *nf* **1** DÉSORDRE : confusion **2** GÊNE : embarrassment **3** ERREUR : mix-up

congé [kɔ̃ʒe] *nm* **1** VACANCES : vacation **2** : leave, time off — **congédier** [kɔ̃ʒedje] {96} *vt* : dismiss (an employee)

congeler [kɔ̃ʒle] {20} *vt* : freeze — **congélateur** [kɔ̃ʒelatœr] *nm* : freezer

congestion [kɔ̃ʒɛstjɔ̃] *nf* : congestion — **congestionner** [kɔ̃ʒɛstjɔne] *vt* : congest

congrès [kɔ̃grɛ] *nm* : congress, conference

conifère [kɔnifɛr] *nm* : conifer

conjecturer [kɔ̃ʒɛktyre] *v* : conjecture — **conjecture** [kɔ̃ʒɛktyr] *nf* : conjecture

conjoint, -jointe [kɔ̃ʒwɛ̃, -ʒwɛ̃t] *adj* : joint — ~ *n* ÉPOUX : spouse — **conjointement** [-ʒwɛ̃tmɑ̃] *adv* ~ **avec** : in conjunction with

conjonction [kɔ̃ʒɔ̃ksjɔ̃] *nf* : conjunction

conjoncture [kɔ̃ʒɔ̃ktyr] *nf* : circumstances *pl*, juncture

conjugaison [kɔ̃ʒygɛzɔ̃] *nf* : conjugation

conjugal, -gale [kɔ̃ʒygal] *adj, mpl* **-gaux** [-go] : marital

conjuguer [kɔ̃ʒyge] *vt* : conjugate (a verb)

connaître [kɔnɛtr] {7} *vt* **1** : know **2** ÉPROUVER : experience — **se connaître** *vr* **1** : know each other **2 s'y ~ en** : know about, be an expert in — **connaissance** [kɔnɛsɑ̃s] *nf* **1** : knowledge **2** : acquaintance **3** CONSCIENCE : consciousness **4 à ma ~** : as far as I know **5 faire ~ avec qqn** : meet s.o. **6 ~s** *nfpl* : knowledge, learning — **connaisseur, -seuse** [kɔnɛsœr, -søz] *n* : expert

connecter [kɔnɛkte] *vt* : connect

connexe [kɔnɛks] *adj* : related

connu, -nue [kɔny] *adj* : well-known

conquérir [kɔ̃kerir] {21} *vt* **1** : conquer **2** : win over — **conquérant, -rante** [kɔ̃kerɑ̃, -rɑ̃t] *n* : conqueror — **conquête** [kɔ̃kɛt] *nf* : conquest

consacrer [kɔ̃sakre] *vt* **1** : consecrate **2 ~ à** : devote to — **se consacrer** *vr* **~ à** : dedicate oneself to

conscience [kɔ̃sjɑ̃s] *nf* **1** : conscience **2** : consciousness — **consciemment** [kɔ̃sjamɑ̃] *adv* : consciously — **consciencieux, -cieuse** [kɔ̃sjɑ̃sjø, -sjøz] *adj* : conscientious — **conscient, -ciente** [kɔ̃sjɑ̃, -sjɑ̃t] *adj* : conscious, aware

consécutif, -tive [kɔ̃sekytif, -tiv] *adj* : consecutive — **consécutivement** [-tivmɑ̃] *adv* : consecutively

conseil [kɔ̃sɛj] *nm* **1** : (piece of) advice **2** : council **3 ~ d'administration** : board of directors — **conseiller** [kɔ̃seje] *vt* **1** : advise **2** RECOMMANDER : recommend — **conseiller, -lère** [kɔ̃seje, -jɛr] *n* **1** : counselor, advisor **2** : councillor

consentir [kɔ̃sɑ̃tir] {82} *vi* **~ à** : consent to, agree to — **consentant, -tante** [kɔ̃sɑ̃tɑ̃, -tɑ̃t] *adj* : willing — **consentement** [kɔ̃sɑ̃tmɑ̃] *nm* : consent

conséquence [kɔ̃sekɑ̃s] *nf* **1** : consequence **2 en ~** : consequently — **conséquent, -quente** [kɔ̃sekɑ̃, -kɑ̃t] *adj* : consistent, logical — **conséquent** *nm* **par ~** : consequently

conservateur, -trice [kɔ̃sɛrvatœr, -tris] *adj* : conservative — **~ *n*** **1** : conservative **2** : curator — **conservation** [kɔ̃sɛrvasjɔ̃] *nf* : conservation

conservatoire [kɔ̃sɛrvatwar] *nm* : academy, conservatory

conserver [kɔ̃sɛrve] *vt* GARDER : keep, retain — **se conserver** *vr* : keep, stay fresh — **conserve** [kɔ̃sɛrv] *nf* **1** : canned food **2 en ~** : canned

considérable [kɔ̃siderabl] *adj* : considerable

considérer [kɔ̃sidere] {87} *vt* **1** : consider **2** ESTIMER : think highly of — **considération** [kɔ̃siderasjɔ̃] *nf* **1** : consideration **2** ESTIME : respect

consigner [kɔ̃siɲe] *vt* : check (luggage, etc.) — **consigne** [kɔ̃siɲ] *nf* **1** ORDRE : instructions *pl* **2** : checkroom

consister [kɔ̃siste] *vi* **1 ~ en** : consist of **2 ~ dans** : lie in **3 ~ à faire** : consist in doing — **consistance** [kɔ̃sistɑ̃s] *nf* : consistency — **consistant, -tante** [kɔ̃sistɑ̃, -tɑ̃t] *adj* **1** ÉPAIS : thick **2** NOURRISSANT : substantial

consoler [kɔ̃sɔle] *vt* : console, comfort — **consolation** [kɔ̃sɔlasjɔ̃] *nf* : consolation

consolider [kɔ̃sɔlide] *vt* : consolidate

consommer [kɔ̃sɔme] *vt* : consume — *vi* : have a drink — **consommateur, -trice** [kɔ̃sɔmatœr, -tris] *n* : consumer — **consommation** [kɔ̃sɔmasjɔ̃] *nf* **1** : consumption **2** BOISSON : drink — **consommé** [kɔ̃sɔme] *nm* : clear soup

consonne [kɔ̃sɔn] *nf* : consonant

conspirer [kɔ̃spire] *vi* : conspire, plot — **conspiration** [kɔ̃spirasjɔ̃] *nf* : conspiracy

constant, -tante [kɔ̃stɑ̃, -tɑ̃t] *adj* : constant, continual — **constamment** [kɔ̃stamɑ̃] *adv* : constantly

constater [kɔ̃state] *vt* REMARQUER : notice — **constatation** [kɔ̃statasjɔ̃] *nf* : observation

constellation [kɔ̃stelasjɔ̃] *nf* : constellation

consternation [kɔ̃stɛrnasjɔ̃] *nf* : dismay — **consterner** [kɔ̃stɛrne] *vt* : dismay

constipation [kɔ̃stipasjɔ̃] *nf* : constipation — **constiper** [kɔ̃stipe] *vt* : constipate

constituer [kɔ̃stitɥe] *vt* **1** COMPOSER : constitute **2** ÉLABORER : set up, form — **constitution** [kɔ̃stitysjɔ̃] *nf* **1** : constitution **2** ÉTABLISSEMENT : setting up — **constitutionnel, -nelle** [kɔ̃stitysjɔnɛl] *adj* : constitutional

constructeur, -trice [kɔ̃stryktœr, -tris] *n* : builder — **constructif, -tive** [kɔ̃stryktif, -tiv] *adj* : constructive — **construction** [kɔ̃stryksjɔ̃] *nf* : building, construction — **construire** [kɔ̃strɥir] {49} *vt* : construct, build

consulat [kɔ̃syla] *nm* : consulate

consultant, -tante [kɔ̃syltɑ̃, -tɑ̃t] *n* : consultant — **consultation** [kɔ̃syltasjɔ̃] *nf* : consultation (with a doctor, etc.) — **consulter** [kɔ̃sylte] *vt* **1** : consult **2** : refer to — **se consulter** *vr* : confer

consumer [kɔ̃syme] *vt* : burn, destroy

contact [kɔ̃takt] *nm* **1** : contact, touch **2 couper le ~** : switch off the ignition **3 rester en ~** : keep in touch — **contacter** [kɔ̃takte] *vt* : get in touch with, contact

contagieux, -gieuse [kɔ̃taʒjœ, -ʒjøz] *adj* : contagious

contaminer [kɔ̃tamine] *vt* **1** : contaminate **2** INFECTER : infect — **contamination** [-minasjɔ̃] *nf* : contamination

conte [kɔ̃t] *nm* **1** : tale, story **2 ~ de fées** : fairy tale

contempler [kɔ̃tɑ̃ple] *vt* : contemplate — **contemplation** [-tɑ̃plasjɔ̃] *nf* : contemplation

contemporain, -raine [kɔ̃tɑ̃pɔrɛ̃, -rɛn] *adj & n* : contemporary

contenir [kɔ̃tnir] {92} *vt* **1** : hold, contain **2** RETENIR : restrain — **se contenir** *vr* : control oneself — **contenance** [kɔ̃tnɑ̃s] *nf* ALLURE : bearing, attitude

content, -tente [kɔ̃tɑ̃, -tɑ̃t] *adj* : content, pleased — **contentement** [kɔ̃tɑ̃tmɑ̃] *nm* : satisfaction — **contenter** [kɔ̃tɑ̃te] *vt* : satisfy, please — **se contenter** *vr* **~ de** : be contented with

contentieux [kɔ̃tɑ̃sjø] *nm* **1** : dispute **2** : legal department

contenu [kɔ̃tny] *nm* : contents *pl*

conter [kɔ̃te] *vt* : tell (a story)

contester [kɔ̃tɛste] *vt* : contest, dispute — *vi* : protest — **contestation** [kɔ̃tɛstasjɔ̃] *nf* **1** DISPUTE : dispute **2** : (political) protest

conteur, -teuse [kɔ̃tœr, -tøz] *n* : storyteller

contexte [kɔ̃tɛkst] *nm* : context

contigu, -guë [kɔ̃tigy] *adj* : adjacent

continent [kɔ̃tinɑ̃] *nm* : continent — **continental, -tale** [-nɑ̃tal] *adj, mpl* **-taux** [-to] : continental

continuer [kɔ̃tinɥe] *vt* **1** : continue **2** PROLONGER : extend — *vi* : continue, go on — **continu, -nue** [kɔ̃tiny] *adj* : continuous — **continuation** [kɔ̃tinɥasjɔ̃] *nf* : continuation — **continuel, -nuelle** [kɔ̃tinɥɛl] *adj* : continuous, continual — **continuellement** [kɔ̃tinɥɛlmɑ̃] *adv* : continually — **continuité** [kɔ̃tinɥite] *nf* : continuity

contorsion [kɔ̃tɔrsjɔ̃] *nf* : contortion — **contorsionner** [kɔ̃tɔrsjɔne] *v* **se contorsionner** *vr* : contort oneself

contour [kɔ̃tur] *nm* : outline, contour — **contourner** [kɔ̃turne] *vt* **1** : bypass **2** : get around (a difficulty, etc.)

contraceptif, -tive [kɔ̃trasɛptif, -tiv] *adj* : contraceptive — **contraceptif** *nm* : contraceptive — **contraception** [kɔ̃trasɛpsjɔ̃] *nf* : contraception

contracter [kɔ̃trakte] *vt* **1** : contract (a muscle) **2** : incur (a debt) **3** : catch (a cold, etc.) — **contraction** [kɔ̃traksjɔ̃] *nf* : contraction, tensing

contradiction [kɔ̃tradiksjɔ̃] *nf* : contradiction — **contradictoire** [kɔ̃tradiktwar] *adj* : contradictory

contraindre [kɔ̃trɛ̃dr] {65} *vt* **~ à** : compel to, force to — **contrainte** [kɔ̃trɛ̃, -trɛ̃t] *nf* : constraint, coertion

contraire [kɔ̃trɛr] *adj & nm* : contrary, opposite — **contrairement** [kɔ̃trɛrmɑ̃] *adv* **~ à** : contrary to

contrarier [kɔ̃trarje] {96} *vt* : annoy, vex — **contrariant, -riante** [kɔ̃trarjɑ̃, -rjɑ̃t] *adj* : annoying — **contrariété** [kɔ̃trarjete] *nf* : annoyance

contraste [kɔ̃trast] *nm* : contrast

contrat [kɔ̃tra] *nm* : contract

contravention [kɔ̃travɑ̃sjɔ̃] *nf* : (parking) ticket

contre [kɔ̃tr] *prep* **1** : against **2** : versus (in law) **3** : (in exchange) for **4 trois ~ un** : three to one — **~** *nm* **le pour et le ~** : the pros and cons — **~** *adv* **1 par ~** : on the other hand **2 parler ~** : speak in opposition — **contre–attaque** [kɔ̃tratake] *nf, pl* **contre–attaques** : counterattack — **contrebande** [kɔ̃trəbɑ̃d] *nf* : smuggling — **contrebandier, -dière** [kɔ̃trəbɑ̃dje, -djer] *n* : smuggler — **contrebas** [kɔ̃trəba] **en ~** *adv phr* : (down) below — **contrebasse** [kɔ̃trəbas] *nf* : double bass — **contrecarrer** [kɔ̃trəkare] *vt* : thwart — **contrecœur** [kɔ̃trəkœr] **à ~** *adv phr* : unwillingly — **contrecoup** [kɔ̃trəku] *nm* : consequence — **contredire** [kɔ̃trədir] {29} *vt* : contradict — **se contredire** *vr* : contradict oneself — **contrefaire** [kɔ̃trəfɛr] {42} *vt* : counterfeit, forge — **contrefaçon** [kɔ̃trəfasɔ̃] *nf* : counterfeiting, forgery — **contrefort** [kɔ̃trəfɔr] *nm* **1** : buttress **2 ~s** *nmpl* : foothills — **contremaître** [kɔ̃trəmɛtr, -mɛtres] *n* : foreman — **contrepartie** [kɔ̃trəparti] *nf* **1** : compensation **2 en ~** : in return — **contrepoids** [kɔ̃trəpwa] *nm* : counterbalance — **contrer** [kɔ̃tre] *vt* : counter — **contresens** [kɔ̃trəsɑ̃s] **à ~** *adv phr* : the wrong way — **contretemps** [kɔ̃trətɑ̃] *nm* : hitch, setback — **contrevenir** [kɔ̃trəvnir] {92} *vi* **~ à** : contravene

contribuer [kɔ̃tribɥe] *vi* : contribute — **contribuable** [kɔ̃tribɥabl] *nmf* : taxpayer — **contribution** [kɔ̃tribysjɔ̃] *nf* : contribution

contrit, -trite [kɔ̃tri, -trit] *adj* : contrite

contrôle [kɔ̃trol] *nm* **1** : checking, inspection **2 ~ de soimême** : self-control — **contrôler** [kɔ̃trole] *vt* **1** : check, inspect **2** MAÎTRISER : supervise, control — **contrôleur, -leuse** [kɔ̃trolœr, -løz] *n* : (ticket) inspector, (bus) conductor

controverse [kɔ̃trɔvɛrs] *nf* : controversy — **controversé, -sée** [kɔ̃trɔvɛrse] *adj* : controversial

contusionner [kɔ̃tyzjɔne] *vt* : bruise — **contusion** [kɔ̃tyzjɔ̃] *nf* : bruise

convaincre [kɔ̃vɛ̃kr] {94} *vt* : convince — **convaincant, -cante** [kɔ̃vɛ̃kɑ̃, -kɑ̃t] *adj* : convincing

convalescence [kɔ̃valesɑ̃s] *nf* : convalescence

convenir [kɔ̃vnir] {92} *vt* : agree, admit — *vi* **~ à** : suit, fit — *v impers* **il convient de** : it is advisable to — **convenable** [kɔ̃vnabl] *adj* **1** ACCEPTABLE : adequate **2** : proper, decent — **convenance** [kɔ̃vnɑ̃s] *nf* **1 à votre ~** : at your convenience **2 ~s** *nfpl* : conventions, proprieties

convention [kɔ̃vɑ̃sjɔ̃] *nf* **1** USAGE : custom **2** ACCORD : agreement **3** ASSEMBLÉE : convention, assembly — **conventionnel, -nelle** [kɔ̃vɑ̃sjɔnɛl] *adj* : conventional

convenu, -nue [kɔ̃vny] *adj* : agreed

converger [kɔ̃vɛrʒe] {17} *vi* : converge, meet

conversation [kɔ̃vɛrsasjɔ̃] *nf* : conversation — **converser** [kɔ̃vɛrse] *vi* : converse

convertir [kɔ̃vɛrtir] *vt* : convert — **conversion** [kɔ̃vɛrsjɔ̃] *nf* : conversion

conviction [kɔ̃viksjɔ̃] *nf* CERTITUDE : conviction

convier [kɔ̃vje] {96} *vt* : invite

convive [kɔ̃viv] *nmf* : guest (at a meal)

convoi [kɔ̃vwa] *nm* **1** : convoy **2** *or* **~ funèbre** : funeral procession

convoiter [kɔ̃vwate] *vt* : covet

convoquer [kɔ̃vɔke] *vt* **1** : convene **2** : summon

convulsion [kɔ̃vylsjɔ̃] *nf* : convulsion

coopérer [kɔɔpere] {87} *vi* : cooperate — **coopératif, -tive** [kɔɔperatif, -tiv] *adj* : cooperative — **coopération** [-perasjɔ̃] *nf* : cooperation — **coopé-rative** *nf* : cooperative

coordination [kɔɔrdinasjɔ̃] *nf* : coordination — **coordonner** [kɔɔrdɔne] *vt* : coordinate

copain, -pine [kɔpɛ̃, -pin] *n* **1** : friend, buddy **2** *or* **petit copain, petite copine** : boyfriend *m*, girlfriend *f*

copeau [kɔpo] *nm, pl* **-peaux** : chip (of wood, etc.)

copie [kɔpi] *nf* **1** : copy, duplicate **2** DEVOIR : paper, schoolwork — **copier** [kɔpje] {96} *vt* **1** : copy **2 ~ sur** : copy from, crib from

copieux, -pieuse [kɔpjø, -pjøz] *adj* : plentiful, copious

copilote [kɔpilɔt] *nmf* : copilot

copine → **copain**

copropriété [kɔprɔprijete] *nf* **1** : joint ownership **2 immeuble en ~** : condominium

coq [kɔk] *nm* : rooster

coque [kɔk] *nf* **1** : hull (of a boat) **2 œuf à la ~** : soft-boiled egg

coquelicot [kɔkliko] *nm* : poppy

coquet, -quette [kɔke, -kɛt] *adj* **1** ÉLÉGANT : stylish **2** : attractive **3** *fam* : tidy, considerable

coquille [kɔkij] *nf* **1** : shell **2** FAUTE : misprint **3 ~ Saint-Jacques** : scallop — **coquillage** [kɔkijaʒ] *nm* **1** : shellfish **2** COQUILLE : shell

coquin, -quine [kɔkɛ̃, -kin] *adj* : mischievous — **~** *n* : rascal, scamp

cor [kɔr] *nm* **1** : horn (in music) **2** : corn (on one's foot)

corail [kɔraj] *nm, pl* **-raux** [kɔro] : coral

Coran [kɔrɑ̃] *nm* : Koran

corbeau [kɔrbo] *nm, pl* **-beaux** : crow

corbeille [kɔrbɛj] *nf* **1** : basket **2 ~ à papier** : wastepaper basket

corbillard [kɔrbijar] *nm* : hearse

corde [kɔrd] *nf* **1** : rope **2** : string **3 ~s vocales** : vocal cords — **cordage** [kɔrdaʒ] *nm* **1** : rope **2 ~s** *nmpl* : rigging

cordial, -diale [kɔrdjal] *adj, mpl* **-diaux** [-djo] : cordial — **cordialement** [-djalmɑ̃] *adv* : cordially

cordon [kɔrdɔ̃] *nm* **1** : cord (in anatomy) **2 ~ de soulier** : shoelace — **cordonnerie** [kɔrdɔnri] *nf* : shoe repair shop — **cordonnier, -nière** [kɔrdɔnje, -njɛr] *n* : shoemaker, cobbler

coréen, -réenne [kɔreɛ̃, -reɛn] *adj* : Korean — **coréen** *nm* : Korean (language)

coriace [kɔrjas] *adj* : tough

corne [kɔrn] *nf* **1** : antler, horn **2** : horn (instrument) **3 ~ de brume** : foghorn

cornée [kɔrne] *nf* : cornea

corneille [kɔrnɛj] *nf* : crow

cornemuse [kɔrnəmyz] *nf* : bagpipes *pl*

cornet [kɔrnɛ] *nm* **1** : cone **2 ~ de crème glacée** : ice-cream cone

corniche [kɔrniʃ] *nf* : cliff road

cornichon [kɔrniʃɔ̃] *nm* : pickle

corporation [kɔrpɔrasjɔ̃] *nf* : corporation

corporel, -relle [kɔrpɔrɛl] *adj* : bodily

corps [kɔr] *nm* **1** : body **2** : corps (in the army, etc.) **3** : professional body **4 prendre ~** : take shape

corpulent, -lente [kɔrpylɑ̃, -lɑ̃t] *adj* : stout

correct, -recte [kɔrɛkt] *adj* : correct — **correctement** [-rɛktəmɑ̃] *adv* : correctly — **correcteur, -trice** [kɔrɛktœr, -tris] *adj* : corrective — **correction** [kɔrɛksjɔ̃] *nf* **1** : correction **2** : grading, marking **3** PUNITION : beating

corrélation [kɔrelasjɔ̃] *nf* : correlation

correspondre [kɔrɛspɔ̃dr] {63} *vi* **1** : correspond, write **2** : communicate (by telephone, etc.) **3 ~ à** : correspond to — **correspondance** [kɔrɛspɔ̃dɑ̃s] *nf* **1** : correspondence **2** : connection (of a plane, etc.) — **correspondant, -dante** [kɔrɛspɔ̃dɑ̃, -dɑ̃t] *n* **1** : correspondent **2** : person being called (on the telephone)

corrida [kɔrida] *nf* : bullfight

corridor [kɔridɔr] *nm* : corridor

corriger [kɔriʒe] {17} *vt* **1** : correct **2** : grade, mark

corroborer [kɔrɔbɔre] *vt* : corroborate

corroder [kɔrɔde] *vt* : corrode

corrompre [kɔrɔ̃pr] {77} *vt* **1** : corrupt **2** SOUDOYER : bribe — **corrompu, -pue** [kɔrɔ̃py] *adj* : corrupt

corrosif, -sive [kɔrɔzif, -ziv] *adj* : corrosive — **corrosion** [kɔrɔzjɔ̃] *nf* : corrosion

corruption [kɔrypsjɔ̃] *nf* **1** : corruption **2** : bribery

corsage [kɔrsaʒ] *nm* **1** : blouse **2** : bodice (of a dress)

corsé, -sée [kɔrse] *adj* : full-bodied (of wine), strong (of coffee, etc.)

corser [kɔrse] *v* **se corser** *vr* : get more complicated

cortège [kɔrtɛʒ] *nm* : procession

corvée [kɔrve] *nf* : chore

cosmétique [kɔsmetik] *nm* : cosmetic — **~** *adj* : cosmetic

cosmique [kɔsmik] *adj* : cosmic

cosmopolite [kɔsmɔpɔlit] *adj* : cosmopolitan

cosmos [kɔsmos] *nm* : universe, cosmos

cosse [kɔs] *nf* : pod, husk

costaud, -taude [kɔsto, -tod] *adj fam* : sturdy, burly

costume [kɔstym] *nm* **1** : costume **2** COMPLET : suit — **costumer** [kɔstyme] *v* **se costumer** *vr* **~ en** : dress up as

cote [kɔt] *nf* **1** : (stock) quotation **2** CLASSEMENT : rating **3** : call number (of a library book) **4** NIVEAU : level

côte [kot] *nf* **1** : coast **2** : rib (in anatomy) **3** : chop, cutlet **4** PENTE : hill **5 ~ à ~** : side by side

côté [kote] *nm* **1** : side **2** : way, direction **3 à ~** : nearby **4 à ~ de** : next to **5 de ~** : sideways **6 de mon ~** : for my part **7 mettre de ~** : put aside

coteau [kɔto] *nm, pl* **-teaux** : hill, hillside

côtelé, -lée [kotle] *adj* **velours côtelé** : corduroy

côtelette [kotlɛt] *nf* : chop

coter [kɔte] *vt* : quote (in finance)

coterie [kɔtri] *nf* : clique

côteux, -teuse [kotø, -tøz] *adj Can* : hilly

côtier, -tière [kotje, -tjɛr] *adj* : coastal

cotiser [kɔtize] *vi* : subscribe, pay one's dues — **cotisation** [kɔtizasjɔ̃] *nf* : dues *pl*, fee

coton [kɔtɔ̃] *nm* : cotton

côtoyer [kotwaye] {58} *vt* **1** : skirt, run alongside of **2** FRÉQUENTER : mix with

cou [ku] *nm* : neck

coucher [kuʃe] *vt* **1** : put to bed **2** : lay down flat — *vi* : sleep, spend the night — **se coucher** *vr* **1** : lie down, go to bed **2** : set (of the sun) — **~** *nm* **1** : bedtime **2 ~ du soleil** : sunset — **couche** [kuʃ] *nf* **1** : layer, stratum **2** : coat (of paint) **3** : (baby) diaper **4 fausse ~** : miscarriage — **couchette** [kuʃɛt] *nf* : berth, bunk

coucou [kuku] *nm* : cuckoo

coude [kud] *nm* **1** : elbow **2** COURBE : bend, angle **3 ~ à ~** : shoulder to shoulder

cou–de–pied [kudpje] *nm, pl* **cous–de–pied** : instep

coudre [kudr] {22} *v* : sew

couler [kule] *vt* **1** : sink **2** : cast (metal) — *vi* **1** : flow, run **2** : leak (of a faucet) **3** : sink (of a boat)

couleur [kulœr] *nf* **1** : color **2** : suit (of cards)

coulisser [kulise] *vi* : slide (in a groove) — **coulisses** [kulis] *nfpl* : backstage, wings

couloir [kulwar] *nm* **1** : corridor **2** : lane (in transportation)

coup [ku] *nm* **1** : knock, blow **2** CHOC : shock **3** : stroke, shot (in sports) **4** : (political) coup **5 ~ de feu** : gunshot **6 ~ de foudre** : love at first sight **7 ~ de pied** : kick **8 ~ de poing** : punch **9 ~ de soleil** : sunburn **10 ~ de téléphone**

: telephone call 11 **~ d'œil** : glance 12 **tout à ~** : suddenly

coupable [kupabl] *adj* : guilty — **~** *nmf* : culprit

coupant, -pante [kupã, -pãt] *adj* 1 : sharp 2 CAUSTIQUE : cutting, curt

couper [kupe] *vt* 1 : cut, cut up 2 : cut off, block 3 CROISER : intersect 4 DILUER : dilute — *vi* : cut — **se couper** *vr* 1 : cut oneself 2 : intersect — **coupe** [kup] *nf* 1 : fruit dish 2 : cup (in sports) 3 *or* **~ de cheveux** : haircut 4 *or* **~ transversale** : cross section — **coupe–ongles** [kupɔ̃gl] *nms & pl* : nail clippers — **coupe–papier** [kuppapje] *nms & pl* : letter opener

couple [kupl] *nm* : couple — **coupler** [kuple] *vt* : pair (up)

coupon [kupɔ̃] *nm* : coupon

coupure [kupyr] *nf* 1 : cut 2 BILLET : banknote

cour [kur] *nf* 1 : court (of law) 2 : courtyard 3 : courtship 4 **~ de récréation** : playground

courage [kuraʒ] *nm* : courage — **courageux, -geuse** [kuraʒø, -ʒøz] *adj* : courageous

courant, -rante [kurã, -rãt] *adj* 1 : (electric) current 2 COMMUN : common, usual — **courant** *nm* 1 : (electric) current 2 : course (of the day, etc.) 3 **~ d'air** : draft 4 **être au ~ de** : know all about — **couramment** [kuramã] *adv* 1 : fluently 2 SOUVENT : commonly

courbature [kurbatyr] *nf* : stiffness, ache — **courbaturé, -rée** [kurbatyre] *adj* : aching

courber [kurbe] *vt* : bend, curve — **se courber** *vr* : bend, curve — **courbe** [kurb] *nf* : curve

coureur, -reuse [kurœr, -røz] *n* : runner

courge [kurʒ] *nf* : gourd — **courgette** [kurʒɛt] *nf* : zucchini

courir [kurir] {23} *vt* 1 : run in, compete in 2 FRÉQUENTER : frequent 3 PARCOURIR : roam through 4 : run (a risk, etc.) — *vi* 1 : run 2 SE PRESSER : rush

couronner [kurɔne] *vt* : crown — **couronne** [kurɔn] *nf* 1 : crown 2 : wreath — **couronnement** [kurɔnmã] *nm* 1 : coronation 2 : crowning achievement

courrier [kurje] *nm* 1 : mail, correspondence 2 **~ électronique** : electronic mail, e-mail — **courriel** [kurjɛl] *nm Can* : electronic mail

courroie [kurwa] *nf* : strap, belt

cours [kur] *nm* 1 : course, class 2 : flow, current 3 **au ~ de** : in the course of, during 4 **~ d'eau** : river, stream 5 **~ du soir** : night school 6 **en ~** : in progress

course [kurs] *nf* 1 : running 2 COMPÉTITION : race, competition 3 COMMISSION : errand 4 **faire des ~s** : go shopping

court, courte [kur, kurt] *adj* : short — **court** [kur] *adv* 1 **à ~ de** : short of 2 **s'arrêter ~** : stop short 3 **tout ~** : simply — **court** *nm* : court (in sports) — **court–circuit** [kursirkɥi] *nm, pl* **courts–circuits** : short circuit

courtier, -tière [kurtje, -tjɛr] *n* : broker, agent

courtiser [kurtize] *vt* : court, woo

courtois, -toise [kurtwa, -twaz] *adj* : courteous — **courtoisie** [kurtwazi] *nf* : courtesy

cousin, -sine [kuzɛ̃, -zin] *n* : cousin

coussin [kusɛ̃] *nm* : cushion

coût [ku] *nm* : cost — **coûtant** [kutã] **à prix ~** *adv phr* : at cost

couteau [kuto] *nm, pl* **-teaux** 1 : knife 2 **~ de poche** : pocketknife

coûter [kute] *vt* 1 : cost 2 **~ cher** : be expensive 3 **ça coûte combien?** : how much is it? — *vi* : cost — **coûteux, -teuse** [kutø, -tøz] *adj* : costly

coutume [kutym] *nf* : custom — **coutumier, -mière** [kutymje, -mjɛr] *adj* : customary

couture [kutyr] *nf* 1 : sewing 2 : dressmaking 3 : seam (of a garment) — **couturier** [kutyrje] *nm* : fashion designer — **couturière** [kutyrjɛr] *nf* : dressmaker

couvée [kuve] *nf* : brood

couvent [kuvã] *nm* : convent

couver [kuve] *vt* 1 : hatch 2 PROTÉGER : overprotect 3 : be coming down with (an illness) — *vi* 1 : smolder 2 : be brewing

couvercle [kuvɛrkl] *nm* 1 : lid, cover 2 : top (of a spray can, etc.)

couvert, -verte [kuvɛr, -vɛrt] *adj* 1 : covered 2 NUAGEUX : overcast — **couvert** *nm* 1 : place setting (at a table) 2 **~s** *nmpl* : flatware 3 **à ~** : under cover — **couverture** [kuvɛrtyr] *nf* 1 : cover (of a book, etc.) 2 : blanket 3 : roofing 4 : news coverage

couveuse [kuvøz] *nf* : incubator

couvrir [kuvrir] {83} *vt* : cover — **se couvrir** *vr* 1 : dress warmly 2 : become overcast 3 **~ de** : be covered with — **couvre–feu** [kuvrəfø] *nm, pl* **couvre–feux** : curfew — **couvre–lit** [kuvrəli] *nm, pl* **couvre–lits** : bedspread

cow–boy [kɔbɔj] *nm, pl* **cow–boys** : cowboy

coyote [kɔjɔt] *nm* : coyote

crabe [krab] *nm* : crab

cracher [kraʃe] *v* : spit

craie [krɛ] *nf* : chalk

craindre [krɛ̃dr] {65} *vt* 1 REDOUTER : fear, be afraid of 2 **~ que** : regret that, fear that — **crainte** [krɛ̃t] *nf* 1 : fear, dread 2 **de ~ que** : for fear that — **craintif, -tive** [krɛ̃tif, -tiv] *adj* : fearful, timid

crampe [krãp] *nf* : cramp

crampon [krãpɔ̃] *nm* : clamp — **cramponner** [krãpɔne] *v* **se cramponner** *vr* **~ à** : cling to

cran [krã] *nm fam* : courage, guts

crâne [kran] *nm* : skull

crapaud [krapo] *nm* : toad

craquer [krake] *vi* 1 : crack, snap, creak 2 SE DÉCHIRER : tear, rip 3 *fam* : break down — **craquement** [krakmã] *nm* : crack, creak

crasse [kras] *nf* : filth — **crasseux, -seuse** [krasø, -søz] *adj* : filthy

cratère [kratɛr] *nm* : crater

cravache [kravaʃ] *nf* : horsewhip

cravate [kravat] *nf* : necktie

crayon [krɛjɔ̃] *nm* 1 : pencil 2 **~ à bille** : ballpoint pen

créancier, -cière [kreɑ̃sje, -sjɛr] *n* : creditor

créateur, -trice [kreatœr, -tris] *adj* : creative — **~** *n* : creator — **création** [kreasjɔ̃] *nf* : creation — **créativité** [kreativite] *nf* : creativity

créature [kreatyr] *nf* : creature

crèche [krɛʃ] *nf France* : nursery

crédible [kredibl] *adj* : credible — **crédibilité** [-dibilite] *nf* : credibility

crédit [kredi] *nm* 1 : credit 2 **~s** *nmpl* : funds — **créditer** [kredite] *vt* : credit — **créditeur, -trice** [kreditœr, -tris] *n* : creditor

crédule [kredyl] *adj* : credulous — **crédulité** [-dylite] *nf* : credulity

créer [kree] {89} *vt* : create

crémaillère [kremajɛr] *nf* **pendre la ~** : have a housewarming (party)

crème [krɛm] *nf* 1 : cream 2 **~ glacée** *Can* : ice cream — **crémerie** [krɛmri] *nf France* : dairy shop — **crémeux, -meuse** [kremø, -møz] *adj* : creamy

créneau [kreno] *nm, pl* **-neaux** 1 : slot, gap 2 **faire un ~** : back into a parking space

crêpe [krɛp] *nf* : pancake, crepe — **~** *nm* : crepe (fabric)

crépiter [krepite] *vi* : crackle — **crépitement** [krepitmã] *nm* 1 : crackling 2 : patter (of rain)

crépu, -pue [krepy] *adj* : frizzy

crépuscule [krepyskyl] *nm* : twilight, dusk

cresson [kresɔ̃] *nm* : watercress

crête [krɛt] *nf* 1 : crest, peak 2 : comb (of a rooster)

crétin, -tine [kretɛ̃, -tin] *n* : idiot

creuser [krøze] *vt* : dig, hollow out — **se creuser** *vr* **~ la tête** *fam* : rack one's brains — **creux, creuse** [krø, krøz] *adj* 1 : hollow 2 : sunken (of eyes) — **creux** *nm* 1 CAVITÉ : hollow, cavity 2 : pit (of the stomach)

crevaison [krəvɛzɔ̃] *nf* : flat tire

crevasse [krəvas] *nf* : crevice, crack

crever [krəve] {52} *vt* 1 : burst, puncture 2 *fam* : wear out — *vi* 1 : burst 2 **~ de faim** : be starving — **crevé, -vée** [krəve] *adj* 1 : punctured, flat (of a tire) 2 *fam* : dead tired

crevette [krəvɛt] *nf* : shrimp, prawn

cri [kri] *nm* 1 : cry, shout 2 **le dernier ~** : the latest thing — **criant, criante** [krijã, krijãt] *adj* : glaring, obvious — **criard, criarde** [krijar, krijard] *adj* 1 : shrill 2 : gaudy

cribler [krible] *vt* 1 : sift, screen 2 **~ de** : riddle with — **crible** [kribl] *nm* : sieve

cric [krik] *nm* : (car) jack

cricket [krikɛt] *nm* : cricket (sport)

crier [krije] {96} *vi* : shout, yell — *vt* : shout (out)

crime [krim] *nm* 1 : crime 2 MEURTRE : murder — **criminel, -nelle** [kriminɛl] *adj* : criminal — **~** *n* 1 : criminal 2 MEURTRIER : murderer

crinière [krinjɛr] *nf* : mane

criquet [krikɛ] *nm* : locust (insect)

crise [kriz] *nf* 1 : crisis 2 ACCÈS : fit, outburst 3 **~ cardiaque** : heart attack

crispé, -pée [krispe] *adj* : tense, clenched

crisser [krise] *vi* : screech, squeal (of tires)

cristal [kristal] *nm, pl* **-taux** [kristo] : crystal

critère [kritɛr] *nm* : criterion

critique [kritik] *adj* : critical — **~** *nf* 1 : criticism 2 : critique, review — **~** *nmf* : critic, reviewer — **critiquer** [kritike] *vt* : criticize

croasser [krɔase] *vi* : caw, croak

croc [kro] *nm* : fang

crochet [krɔʃɛ] *nm* 1 : hook 2 : square bracket 3 **faire du ~** : crochet 4 **faire un ~** : make a detour — **crochu, -chue** [krɔʃy] *adj* : hooked

crocodile [krɔkɔdil] *nm* : crocodile

croire [krwar] {24} *vt* 1 : believe 2 PENSER : think, believe — *vi* **~ à** *or* **~ en** : believe in

croisade [krwazad] *nf* : crusade

croiser [krwaze] *vt* 1 : cross 2 : intersect 3 RENCONTRER : pass, meet 4 : crossbreed — *vi* : cruise (of a ship) — **se croiser** *vr* 1 : cross, cut across 2 : pass each other — **croisement** [krwazmã] *nm* 1 : junction 2 : crossbreeding — **croiseur** [krwazœr] *nm* : cruiser (ship) — **croisière** [krwazjɛr] *nf* : cruise

croître [krwatr] {25} *vi* : grow, increase — **croissant, -sante** [krwasã, -sãt] *adj* : growing, increasing — **croissant** *nm* : croissant — **croissance** [krwasãs] *nf* : growth, development

croix [krwa] *nf* : cross

croquer [krɔke] *vt* : crunch, munch — *vi* **~ dans** : bite into (an apple, etc.) — **croquant, -quante** [krɔkã, -kãt] *adj* : crunchy — **croque–monsieur** [krɔkməsjø] *nms & pl* : grilled ham and cheese sandwich

croquis [krɔki] *nm* : sketch

crosse [krɔs] *nf* : butt (of a gun)

crotte [krɔt] *nf* : droppings *pl*, dung — **crottin** [krɔtɛ̃] *nm* : (horse) manure

crouler [krule] *vi* S'EFFONDRER : crumble, collapse

croupir [krupir] *vi* 1 : stagnate 2 **~ dans** : wallow in

croustillant, -lante [krustijã, -jãt] *adj* : crisp, crispy

croûte [krut] *nf* 1 : (pie) crust 2 : scab — **croûton** [krutɔ̃] *nm* 1 : crust (of bread) 2 : crouton

croyance [krwajãs] *nf* : belief — **croyant, croyante** [krwajã, -jãt] *n* : believer

cru, crue [kry] *adj* 1 : raw, uncooked 2 OSÉ : crude 3 : harsh (of light, etc.) — **cru** *nm* 1 VIGNOBLE : vineyard 2 : vintage (of wine)

cruauté [kryote] *nf* : cruelty

cruche [kryʃ] *nf* : jug, pitcher

crucial, -ciale [krysjal] *adj, mpl* **-ciaux** [-sjo] : crucial

crucifier [krysifje] {96} *vt* : crucify — **crucifix** [krysifi] *nms & pl* : crucifix — **crucifixion** [krysifiksjɔ̃] *nf* : crucifixion

crudités [krydite] *nfpl* : raw vegetables

crue [kry] *nf* : rise in water level

cruel, cruelle [kryɛl] *adj* : cruel — **cruellement** [-ɛlmã] *adv* : cruelly

crustacés [krystase] *nmpl* : shellfish

crypte [kript] *nf* : crypt

cube [kyb] *adj* : cubic — **~** *nm* : cube — **cubique** [kybik] *adj* : cubic

cueillir [kœjir] {3} *vt* : pick, gather — **cueillette** [kœjɛt] *nf* : picking, gathering

cuillère *or* **cuiller** [kɥijɛr] *nf* 1 : spoon 2 : spoonful 3 **~ à thé** *or* **~ à café** : teaspoon — **cuillerée** [kɥijere] *nf* 1 : spoonful 2 **~ à café** : teaspoonful

cuir [kɥir] *nm* 1 : leather 2 **~ chevelu** : scalp

cuire [kɥir] {49} *vt* : cook, bake — *vi* : cook

cuisine [kɥizin] *nf* 1 : kitchen 2 : cooking, cuisine 3 **faire la ~** : cook — **cuisiner** [kɥizine] *v* 1 : cook 2 *fam* : interrogate, grill — **cuisinier, -nière** [kɥizinje, -njɛr] *n* : chef, cook — **cuisinière** *nf* : stove

cuisse [kɥis] *nf* 1 : thigh 2 : leg (in cooking)

cuisson [kɥisɔ̃] *nf* : cooking, baking

cuit, cuite [kɥi, kɥit] *adj* 1 : cooked 2 **bien ~** : well-done

cuivre [kɥivr] *nm* 1 : copper 2 *or* **~ jaune** : brass 3 **~s** *nmpl* : brass (musical instruments)

culbute [kylbyt] *nf* 1 : somersault 2 CHUTE : tumble, fall

cul–de–sac [kydsak] *nm, pl* **culs–de–sac** : dead end

culinaire [kylinɛr] *adj* : culinary

culminer [kylmine] *vi* : culminate, peak — **culminant, -nante** [kylminã, -nãt] *adj* **point culminant** : high point

culot [kylo] *nm fam* **avoir du ~** : have a lot of nerve

culotte [kylɔt] *nf* 1 PANTALON : pants *pl* 2 : panties *pl*

culpabilité [kylpabilite] *nf* : guilt

culte [kylt] *nm* 1 VÉNÉRATION : worship, cult 2 : religion

cultiver [kyltive] *vt* : cultivate, grow — **cultivateur, -trice** [kyltivatœr, -tris] *n* AGRICULTEUR : farmer — **cultivé, -vée** [kyltive] *adj* 1 : cultivated 2 : cultured, educated

culture [kyltyr] *nf* 1 CONNAISSANCES : culture 2 : cultivation, growing 3 : crop 4 **~ physique** : physical education — **culturel, -relle** [kyltyrɛl] *adj* : cultural — **culturisme** [kyltyrism] *nm* : bodybuilding

cumuler [kymyle] *vt* 1 : accumulate 2 : hold concurrently — **cumulatif, -tive** [kymylatif, -tiv] *adj* : cumulative

cupide [kypid] *adj* : greedy — **cupidité** [kypidite] *nf* : greed

cure [kyr] *nf* : treatment, cure

curé [kyre] *nm* : pastor, parish priest

curer [kyre] *v* **se curer** *vr* : clean (one's nails, teeth, etc.) — **cure–dent** *or* **cure–dents** [kyrdã] *nm, pl* **cure–dents** : toothpick

curieux, -rieuse [kyrjø, -rjøz] *adj* 1 : curious 2 ÉTRANGE : strange, odd — **~** *n* : onlooker — **curieusement** [kyrjøzmã] *adv* : curiously, strangely — **curiosité** [kyrjɔzite] *nf* : curiosity

curry [kyri] *nm* : curry

curseur [kyrsœr] *nm* : cursor

cuver [kyve] *vi* : ferment — **cuve** [kyv] *nf* : vat, tank — **cuvée** [kyve] *nf* : vintage — **cuvette** [kyvɛt] *nf* : basin

cyanure [sjanyr] *nm* : cyanide

cycle [sikl] *nm* : cycle — **cyclique** [siklik] *adj* : cyclic, cyclical

cycliste [siklist] *nmf* : cyclist, bicyclist — **cyclisme** [siklism] *nm* : cycling, bicycling

cyclomoteur [siklɔmɔtœr] *nm* : moped

cyclone [siklon] *nm* : cyclone

cygne [siɲ] *nm* : swan

cylindre [silɛ̃dr] *nm* : cylinder — **cylindrique** [silɛ̃drik] *adj* : cylindrical

cymbale [sɛ̃bal] *nf* : cymbal

cynique [sinik] *adj* : cynical — **~** *nmf* : cynic — **cynisme** [sinism] *nm* : cynicism

cyprès [siprɛ] *nm* : cypress

D

d [de] *nm* : d, fourth letter of the alphabet

dactylographier [daktilɔgrafje] {96} *vt* : type — **dactylo** [daktilo] *or* **dactylographe** [daktilɔgraf] *nmf* : typist

daigner [deɲe] *vt* : deign

daim [dɛ̃] *nm* 1 : deer 2 : suede

dalle [dal] *nf* : slab, paving stone

daltonien, -nienne [daltɔnjɛ̃, -njɛn] *adj* : color-blind

dame [dam] *nf* 1 : lady 2 : queen (in games) 3 **~s** *nfpl or* **jeu de ~s** : checkers — **damier** [damje] *nm* : checkerboard

dandiner [dãdine] *v* **se dandiner** *vr* : waddle

danger [dãʒe] *nm* : danger — **dangereux, -reuse** [dãʒrø, -røz] *adj* : dangerous

dans [dã] *prep* 1 : in 2 : into, inside 3 : from, out of 4 **~ la journée** : during the day 5 **~ les 20 ans** : in about 20 years 6 **monter ~ l'auto** : get into the car

danser [dãse] *v* : dance — **danse** [dãs] *nf* : dance, dancing — **danseur, -seuse** [dãsœr, -søz] *n* : dancer

dard [dar] *nm* 1 : stinger (of an insect) 2 *Can* : dart

date [dat] *nf* : date — **dater** [date] *vi* 1 : be dated, be old-fashioned 2 **~ de** : date from

datte [dat] *nf* : date (fruit)

dauphin [dofɛ̃] *nm* : dolphin

davantage [davãtaʒ] *adv* 1 PLUS : more 2 : (any) longer

de [də] (**d'** *before vowels and mute h*) *prep* 1 : of 2 (*before infinitive*) : to, of 3 **de l', de la, du, des** : some, any 4 **~ Molière** : by Molière 5 **~ Montréal** : from Montreal 6 **moins ~ cinq** : less than five

dé [de] *nm* 1 : die, dice *pl* 2 **~ à coudre** : thimble

déambuler [deãbyle] *vi* : stroll, wander about

débâcle [debakl] *nf* : fiasco

déballer [debale] *vt* : unpack, unwrap

débandade [debãdad] *nf* : stampede

débarquer [debarke] *vt* : unload (goods) — *vi* : disembark (of passengers) — **débarquement** [debarkəmã] *nm* 1 : unloading 2 : landing

débarrasser [debarase] *vt* : clear, rid — **se débarrasser** *vr* **~ de** : get rid of

débarrer [debare] *vt Can* : unlock

débattre [debatr] {12} *vt* : debate, discuss — **se débattre** *vr* : struggle — **débat** [deba] *nm* 1 : debate, discussion 2 **~s** *nmpl* : proceedings

débaucher [deboʃe] *vt* 1 CORROMPRE : corrupt 2 LICENCIER : lay off — **débauche** [deboʃ] *nf* : debauchery

débiliter [debilite] *vt* : debilitate — **débile** [debil] *adj fam* : stupid

débiter [debite] *vt* 1 : debit 2 VENDRE : sell, retail 3 FOURNIR : produce 4 : recite, reel off — **débit** [debi] *nm* 1 : debit 2 : turnover (of merchandise, etc.) 3 : (rate of) flow — **débiteur, -trice** [debitœr, -tris] *n* : debtor

déblayer [debleje] {11} *vt* : clear (away)

débloquer [deblɔke] *vt* : free, release

déboires [debwar] *nmpl* ENNUIS : difficulties

déboîter [debwate] *vt* : dislocate (a joint) — *vi* : pull out, change lanes

débonnaire [debɔnɛr] *adj* : easygoing, good-natured

déborder [debɔrde] *vi* : overflow — *vt* 1 : extend beyond 2 SUBMERGER : overwhelm — **débordé, -dée** [debɔrde] *adj* : overwhelmed

déboucher [debuʃe] *vt* : open, unblock — *vi* **~ sur** : open onto, lead to — **débouché**

[debuʃe] nm 1 : outlet, market 2 : opportunity, prospect
débourser [deburse] vt : pay out
debout [dəbu] adv 1 : standing up 2 : upright, on end 3 : up, out of bed
déboutonner [debutɔne] vt : unbutton, undo
débraillé, -lée [debraje] adj : disheveled
débrancher [debrɑ̃ʃe] vt : unplug, disconnect
débrayer [debreje] {11} vi 1 : disengage the clutch 2 : go on strike — **débrayage** [debrɛjaʒ] nm 1 : disengaging the clutch 2 : strike, walkout
débris [debri] nms & pl 1 : fragment 2 ~ nmpl : rubbish, scraps
débrouiller [debruje] vt DÉMÊLER : disentangle — **se débrouiller** vr : manage, cope — **débrouillard, -larde** [debrujar, -jard] adj : resourceful
débuter [debyte] v : begin — **début** [deby] nm 1 : beginning 2 ~s nmpl : debut, early stages — **débutant, -tante** [debytɑ̃, -tɑ̃t] n : beginner, novice
décacheter [dekaʃte] {8} vt : unseal, open
décadence [dekadɑ̃s] nf : decadence — **décadent, -dente** [dekadɑ̃, -dɑ̃t] adj : decadent
décaféiné, -née [dekafeine] adj : decaffeinated
décalage [dekalaʒ] nm 1 : gap, interval 2 ~ **horaire** : time difference
décamper [dekɑ̃pe] vi : clear out
décaper [dekape] vt 1 : clean, scour 2 : strip (paint, etc.) — **décapant** [dekapɑ̃] nm : paint stripper
décapotable [dekapɔtabl] adj & nf : convertible
décapsuleur [dekapsylœr] nm : bottle opener
décéder [desede] {87} vi : die — **décédé, -dée** [desede] adj : deceased
déceler [desle] {20} vt 1 DÉCOUVRIR : detect 2 RÉVÉLER : reveal
décembre [desɑ̃br] nm : December
décence [desɑ̃s] nf : decency
décennie [deseni] nf : decade
décent, -cente [desɑ̃, -sɑ̃t] adj : decent
déception [desɛpsjɔ̃] nf : disappointment
décerner [desɛrne] vt : award
décès [desɛ] nm : death
décevoir [desəvwar] {26} vt : disappoint — **décevant, -vante** [desəvɑ̃, -vɑ̃t] adj : disappointing
déchaîner [deʃene] vt : unleash — **se déchaîner** vr : erupt, burst out — **déchaîné, -née** [deʃene] adj : raging, unbridled — **déchaînement** [deʃɛnmɑ̃] nm : outburst
décharger [deʃarʒe] {17} vt 1 : unload 2 : discharge (a firearm, etc.) 3 SOULAGER : relieve, unburden — **décharge** [deʃarʒ] nf 1 : discharge 2 : garbage dump
décharné, -née [deʃarne] adj : gaunt
déchausser [deʃose] v **se déchausser** vr : take off one's shoes
déchéance [deʃeɑ̃s] nf : decay, decline
déchet [deʃɛ] nm 1 : scrap 2 ~s : waste, refuse
déchiffrer [deʃifre] vt : decipher
déchiqueter [deʃikte] {8} vt : tear into pieces
déchirer [deʃire] vt : tear up, tear apart — **déchirant, -rante** [deʃirɑ̃, -rɑ̃t] adj : heartrending — **déchirure** [deʃiryr] nf : tear
déchoir [deʃwar] {27} vi : fall, decline (in prestige)
décider [deside] vt 1 : decide 2 CONVAINCRE : persuade 3 ~ de : decide on, determine — **se décider** vr : make up one's mind — **décidé, -dée** [deside] adj 1 : decided, settled 2 DÉTERMINÉ : determined — **décidément** [desidemɑ̃] adv : definitely, really
décimal, -male [desimal] adj, mpl **-maux** [-mo] : decimal — **décimale** nf : decimal
décision [desizjɔ̃] nf 1 : decision 2 : decisiveness — **décisif, -sive** [desizif, -ziv] adj : decisive
déclarer [deklare] vt 1 PROCLAMER : declare 2 : register, report — **se déclarer** vr : break out (of fire, etc.) — **déclaration** [deklarasjɔ̃] nf : declaration, statement
déclencher [deklɑ̃ʃe] vt 1 : set off, trigger 2 LANCER : launch — **déclenchement** [deklɑ̃ʃmɑ̃] nm : onset, outbreak
déclic [deklik] nm : click
décliner [dekline] v : decline — **déclin** [deklɛ̃] nm : decline
décoller [dekɔle] vt : unstick, remove — vi : take off (of an airplane, etc.) — **décollage** [dekɔlaʒ] nm : takeoff
décolleté, -tée [dekɔlte] adj : low-cut
décolorer [dekɔlɔre] vt : bleach — **se décolorer** vr : fade
décombres [dekɔ̃br] nmpl : rubble, debris
décommander [dekɔmɑ̃de] vt : cancel
décomposer [dekɔ̃poze] vt : decompose — **décomposition** [dekɔ̃pozisjɔ̃] nf : decomposition, rotting
décompter [dekɔ̃te] vt 1 : count, calculate 2 DÉDUIRE : deduct — **décompte** [dekɔ̃t] nm 1 : count, breakdown 2 DÉDUCTION : deduction
déconcerter [dekɔ̃sɛrte] vt : disconcert
décongeler [dekɔ̃ʒle] {20} v : thaw, defrost
déconnecter [dekɔnɛkte] vt : disconnect
déconseiller [dekɔ̃seje] vt : dissuade, advise against — **déconseillé, -lée** [dekɔ̃seje] adj : inadvisable
décontracté, -tée [dekɔ̃trakte] adj : relaxed, casual
décorer [dekɔre] vt ORNER : decorate — **décor** [dekɔr] nm 1 : decor 2 : scenery (in theater, etc.) — **décoration** [dekɔrasjɔ̃] nf : decoration — **décorateur, -trice** [dekɔratœr, -tris] n : interior decorator — **décoratif, -tive** [dekɔratif, -tiv] adj : decorative
décortiquer [dekɔrtike] vt : shell, hull
découler [dekule] vi : result, follow
découper [dekupe] vt 1 : cut up, carve 2 : cut out (a picture)
décourager [dekuraʒe] {17} vt : discourage — **se décourager** vr : lose heart — **découragement** [dekuraʒmɑ̃] nm : discouragement
décousu, -sue [dekuzy] adj 1 : unstitched 2 : disjointed, disconnected
découvrir [dekuvrir] {83} vt 1 : discover 2 : uncover — **se découvrir** vr : clear up (of weather) — **découvert** [dekuvɛr] nm : overdraft (in banking) — **découverte** [dekuvɛrt] nf : discovery
décrépit, -pite [dekrepi, -pit] adj : decrepit
décret [dekrɛ] nm : decree, edict — **décréter** [dekrete] {87} vt : decree
décrire [dekrir] {33} vt : describe
décrocher [dekrɔʃe] vt 1 : unhook, take down 2 fam : get, land (a job, etc.) — vi fam : drop out, give up
décroître [dekrwatr] {25} vi : decrease, decline
déçu, -çue [desy] adj : disappointed
dédaigner [dedeɲe] vt : disdain, scorn — **dédaigneux, -neuse** [dedɛɲø, -ɲøz] adj : disdainful, scornful — **dédain** [dedɛ̃] nm MÉPRIS : disdain, scorn
dédale [dedal] nm : maze, labyrinth
dedans [dədɑ̃] adv 1 : inside, in 2 en ~ : on the inside, within — ~ nm : inside, interior
dédicace [dedikas] nf : dedication — **dédicacer** [dedikase] {6} vt : inscribe, dedicate
dédier [dedje] {96} vt : dedicate
dédommager [dedɔmaʒe] {17} vt : compensate — **dédommagement** [dedɔmaʒmɑ̃] nm INDEMNITÉ : compensation
déduire [dedɥir] {49} vt 1 : deduct 2 CONCLURE : deduce, infer — **déduction** [dedyksjɔ̃] nf : deduction
déesse [deɛs] nf : goddess
défaillir [defajir] {93} vi : weaken, fail — **défaillance** [defajɑ̃s] nf : failing, weakness
défaire [defɛr] {42} vt 1 : undo 2 : unpack — **se défaire** vr 1 : come undone 2 ~ de : part with — **défait, -faite** [defɛ, -fɛt] adj 1 : undone 2 : defeated — **défaite** nf : defeat
défaut [defo] nm 1 IMPERFECTION : flaw, defect 2 FAIBLESSE : shortcoming 3 MANQUE : lack 4 **faire** ~ : be lacking
défavoriser [defavɔrize] vt : put at a disadvantage — **défavorable** [defavɔrabl] adj : unfavorable
défectueux, -tueuse [defɛktɥø, -tɥøz] adj : defective, faulty — **défectuosité** [defɛktɥozite] nf 1 : defectiveness 2 DÉFAUT : defect, fault
défendre [defɑ̃dr] {63} vt 1 : defend 2 PROTÉGER : protect, uphold 3 INTERDIRE : forbid — **se défendre** vr : defend oneself — **défendeur, -deresse** [defɑ̃dœr, -drɛs] n : defendant
défense [defɑ̃s] nf 1 : defense 2 INTERDICTION : prohibition 3 : tusk (of an elephant, etc.) — **défenseur** [defɑ̃sœr] nm : defender — **défensif, -sive** [defɑ̃sif, -siv] adj : defensive — **défensive** nf : defensive
défi [defi] nm : challenge, dare
déficit [defisit] nm : deficit
défier [defje] {96} vt 1 : challenge, dare 2 BRAVER : defy
défigurer [defigyre] vt 1 : disfigure 2 ~ **les faits** : distort the facts
défiler [defile] vi 1 : march, parade 2 : stream past 3 : scroll (on a computer) — **défilé** [defile] nm 1 : parade, procession 2 : stream (of visitors, etc.)
définir [definir] vt : define — **défini, -nie** [defini] adj 1 : defined 2 : definite — **définitif, -tive** [definitif, -tiv] adj : definitive, final — **définition** [definisjɔ̃] nf : definition — **définitivement** [definitivmɑ̃] adv : definitively, for good
défoncer [defɔ̃se] {6} vt : smash, break down
déformer [defɔrme] vt : deform, distort — **déformation** [defɔrmasjɔ̃] nf : distortion
défraîchi, -chie [defreʃi] adj : faded, worn
défrayer [defreje] {11} vt : pay (s.o.'s expenses)
défunt, -funte [defœ̃, -fœ̃t] adj & n : deceased
dégager [degaʒe] {17} vt 1 : free 2 DÉBARRASSER : clear (the way, etc.) 3 EXTRAIRE : bring out 4 ÉMETTRE : emit — **se dégager** vr 1 : clear (up) 2 : emanate 3 ~ de : get free of — **dégagé, -gée** [degaʒe] adj 1 : clear, open 2 : free and easy
dégâts [dega] nmpl : damage
dégeler [deʒle] {20} v : thaw — **dégel** [deʒɛl] nm : thaw
dégénérer [deʒenere] {87} vi : degenerate
dégingandé, -dée [deʒɛ̃gɑ̃de] adj : lanky
dégivrer [deʒivre] vt : defrost
dégonfler [degɔ̃fle] vt : deflate — **se dégonfler** vr : deflate, go flat
dégoûter [degute] vt : disgust — **se dégoûter** vr ~ de : get sick of — **dégoût** [degu] nm : disgust — **dégoûtant, -tante** [degutɑ̃, -tɑ̃t] adj : disgusting
dégoutter [degute] vi : drip
dégrader [degrade] vt : degrade
dégrafer [degrafe] vt : unhook
degré [dəgre] nm 1 : degree 2 : step (of a staircase) 3 **par** ~**s** : gradually
dégueulasse [degœlas] adj fam : disgusting
déguiser [degize] vt : disguise — **se déguiser** vr ~ **en** : dress up as — **déguisement** [degizmɑ̃] nm : disguise
déguster [degyste] vt 1 : taste 2 SAVOURER : savor, enjoy
dehors [dəɔr] adv 1 : outside 2 **en** ~ : (toward the) outside 3 **en** ~ **de** : outside of, apart from — ~ nms & pl : outside, exterior
déjà [deʒa] adv : already
déjeuner [deʒœne] nm 1 : lunch 2 Can : breakfast — ~ vi 1 : have lunch 2 Can : have breakfast
déjouer [deʒwe] vt : thwart
delà [dəla] adv → **au–delà, par–delà**
délabrer [delabre] v **se délabrer** vr : become dilapidated — **délabrement** [delabrəmɑ̃] nm : dilapidation, disrepair
délai [delɛ] nm 1 : time limit 2 : extension (of time) 3 : waiting period
délaisser [delese] vt 1 ABANDONNER : abandon, desert 2 : neglect
délasser [delase] vt : relax — **se délasser** vr : relax
délayer [deleje] {11} vt 1 DILUER : dilute 2 : drag out (a speech, etc.)
déléguer [delege] {87} vt : delegate — **délégué, -guée** [delege] n : delegate — **délégation** [delegasjɔ̃] nf : delegation
délibérer [delibere] {87} vi : deliberate — **délibéré, -rée** [delibere] adj 1 : deliberate 2 DÉCIDÉ : determined
délicat, -cate [delika, -kat] adj 1 : delicate 2 : tactful 3 EXIGEANT : fussy — **délicatement** [delikatmɑ̃] adv 1 : delicately 2 : finely, precisely — **délicatesse** [delikatɛs] nf 1 : delicacy 2 : tactfulness
délice [delis] nm : delight — **délicieux, -cieuse** [delisjø, -sjøz] adj : delicious, delightful
délier [delje] {96} vt 1 : untie 2 ~ **de** : release from
délimiter [delimite] vt : demarcate
délinquant, -quante [delɛ̃kɑ̃, -kɑ̃t] adj & n : delinquent
délire [delir] nm 1 : delirium 2 **en** ~ : delirious, frenzied — **délirant, -rante** [delirɑ̃, -rɑ̃t] adj 1 : delirious 2 : frenzied — **délirer** [delire] vi 1 : be delirious 2 : rave
délit [deli] nm : crime, offense
délivrer [delivre] vt 1 : set free 2 : issue, award 3 ~ **de** : relieve of — **délivrance** [delivrɑ̃s] nf 1 : freeing, release 2 : delivery, issue 3 SOULAGEMENT : relief
déloger [delɔʒe] {17} vt 1 : evict 2 : remove, dislodge
déloyal, -loyale [delwajal] adj, mpl **-loyaux** [-jo] 1 : disloyal 2 : unfair — **déloyauté** [delwajote] nf : disloyalty
delta [dɛlta] nm : delta
déluge [delyʒ] nm 1 : deluge, flood 2 AVERSE : downpour
demain [dəmɛ̃] adv & nm : tomorrow
demander [dəmɑ̃de] vt 1 : ask for, request 2 : ask (about) 3 NÉCESSITER : call for, require — **se demander** vr : wonder — **demande** [dəmɑ̃d] nf 1 : request 2 : application (form) 3 **l'offre et la** ~ : supply and demand
démanger [demɑ̃ʒe] {17} vi : itch — **démangeaison** [demɑ̃ʒɛzɔ̃] nf : itch, itching
démarche [demarʃ] nf 1 ALLURE : gait, walk 2 REQUÊTE : step, action
démarrer [demare] v : start (up) — **démarreur** [demarœr] nm : starter
démêler [demele] vt : disentangle — **démêlé** [demele] nm 1 : quarrel 2 ~**s** nmpl : problems, trouble
déménager [demenaʒe] {17} v : move, relocate — **déménagement** [demenaʒmɑ̃] nm : moving, relocation
démence [demɑ̃s] nf : madness, insanity
démener [demne] {52} v **se démener** vr : struggle, thrash about
dément, -mente [demɑ̃, -mɑ̃t] adj : insane, demented
démentir [demɑ̃tir] {82} vt : refute, deny — **démenti** [demɑ̃ti] nm : denial
démesuré, -rée [deməzyre] adj : excessive, immoderate
démettre [demɛtr] {53} vt : dismiss, fire — **se démettre** vr 1 : resign 2 : dislocate (one's shoulder, etc.)
demeurer [dəmœre] vi 1 (with **être**) : remain 2 (with **avoir**) : reside — **demeure** [dəmœr] nf : residence
demi, -mie adj 1 : half 2 **et** ~ : and a half, half past — ~ n : half — **demi** nm France : half-pint (of beer) — **à** ~ adv phr : half, halfway
démission [demisjɔ̃] nf : resignation — **démissionner** [demisjɔne] vi : resign
démocratie [demɔkrasi] nf : democracy — **démocratique** [demɔkratik] adj : democratic
démodé, -dée [demɔde] adj : old-fashioned, out-of-date
demoiselle [dəmwazɛl] nf 1 : young lady 2 ~ **d'honneur** : bridesmaid
démolir [demɔlir] vt : demolish — **démolition** [demɔlisjɔ̃] nf : demolition
démon [demɔ̃] nm : demon
démonstration [demɔ̃strasjɔ̃] nf : demonstration — **démonstrateur, -trice** [demɔ̃stratœr, -tris] n : demonstrator — **démonstratif, -tive** [demɔ̃stratif, -tiv] adj : demonstrative
démonter [demɔ̃te] vt : dismantle, take down
démontrer [demɔ̃tre] vt : demonstrate, show
démoraliser [demɔralize] vt : demoralize
démunir [demynir] vt : deprive
dénégation [denegasjɔ̃] nf : denial
dénicher [deniʃe] vt : unearth
dénier [denje] {96} vt : deny
dénigrer [denigre] vt : disparage
dénombrer [denɔ̃bre] vt : count, enumerate
dénommer [denɔme] vt : name, call — **dénomination** [denɔminasjɔ̃] nf : name, designation
dénoncer [denɔ̃se] {6} vt : denounce, inform on — **dénonciation** [denɔ̃sjasjɔ̃] nf : denunciation
dénoter [denɔte] vt : denote
dénouement [denumɑ̃] nm : outcome
dénouer [denwe] vt : untie, undo
denrée [dɑ̃re] nf 1 : commodity 2 ~**s alimentaires** : foods
dense [dɑ̃s] adj : dense — **densité** [dɑ̃site] nf : density, denseness
dent [dɑ̃] nf 1 : tooth 2 : cog (of a wheel), prong (of a fork) — **dentaire** [dɑ̃tɛr] adj : dental
dentelé, -lée [dɑ̃tle] adj : jagged, serrated
dentelle [dɑ̃tɛl] nf : lace
dentiste [dɑ̃tist] nmf : dentist — **dentier** [dɑ̃tje] nm : dentures pl — **dentifrice** [dɑ̃tifris] nm : toothpaste — **dentition** [dɑ̃tisjɔ̃] nf : teeth pl
dénuder [denyde] vt 1 : make bare 2 : strip (off)
dénué, -nuée [denɥe] adj ~ **de** : devoid of, lacking in
déodorant [deɔdɔrɑ̃] adj & nm : deodorant
dépanner [depane] vt 1 : fix, repair 2 : help out (s.o.) — **dépanneur** [depanœr] nm Can : convenience store
dépareillé, -lée [depareje] adj : odd, not matching
départ [depar] nm 1 : departure 2 : start (in sports)
département [departəmɑ̃] nm : department
départir [departir] {82} v **se départir** vr ~ **de** : abandon, depart from
dépassé, -sée [depase] adj : outdated, outmoded
dépasser [depase] vt 1 : pass, go past 2 EXCÉDER : exceed 3 SURPASSER : surpass 4 **cela me dépasse!** : that's beyond me! — vi : stick out — **dépassement** [depasmɑ̃] nm : passing
dépayser [depeize] vt 1 : disorient 2 : provide with a change of scenery
dépecer [depəse] {6} and {52} vt : cut up, tear apart
dépêcher [depeʃe] vt : dispatch — **se dépêcher** vr : hurry up — **dépêche** [depɛʃ] nf : dispatch
dépeindre [depɛ̃dr] {37} vt : depict, describe
dépendre [depɑ̃dr] {63} vi ~ **de** : depend on — vt : take down — **dépendance** [depɑ̃dɑ̃s] nf : dependence — **dépendant, -dante** [depɑ̃dɑ̃, -dɑ̃t] adj : dependent
dépenser [depɑ̃se] vt 1 : spend (money) 2 : use up, expend (energy) — **se dépenser** vr : exert oneself — **dépens** [depɑ̃] nmpl **aux** ~ **de** : at the expense of — **dépense** [depɑ̃s] nf 1 : spending, expenditure 2 : expense — **dépensier, -sière** [depɑ̃sje, -sjɛr] adj : extravagant
dépérir [deperir] vi 1 : wither (of a plant) 2 : waste away (of a person)
dépister [depiste] vt 1 : detect, discover 2 : track down (a criminal)
dépit [depi] nm 1 : spite 2 **en** ~ **de** MALGRÉ : in spite of, despite
déplacer [deplase] {6} vt : move, shift — **se déplacer** vr : move about — **déplacé, -cée** [deplase] adj : out of place
déplaire [deplɛr] {66} vi 1 : be disliked 2

~ **à** : displease — **déplaisant, -sante** [deplɛzɑ̃, -zɑ̃t] *adj* : unpleasant
dépliant [deplijɑ̃] *nm* : brochure, pamphlet
déplier [deplije] {96} *vt* : unfold
déplorer [deplɔre] *vt* : deplore — **déplorable** [deplɔrabl] *adj* : deplorable
déployer [deplwaje] {58} *vt* **1** : deploy **2** DÉPLIER : unfold, spread out
déposer [depoze] *vt* **1** : put down **2** : deposit (a sum of money) **3** : drop off, leave **4** : register, file (a complaint) — *vi* : testify — **se déposer** *vr* : settle
dépôt [depo] *nm* **1** : deposit **2** ENTREPÔT : warehouse, store **3** : (train) station **4** ~ **d'ordures** : (garbage) dump — **dépotoir** [depɔtwar] *nm* : dump
dépouiller [depuje] *vt* ~ **qqn de** : deprive s.o. of
dépourvu, -vue [depurvy] *adj* ~ **de** : without, lacking in — **au dépourvu** *adv phr* : by surprise
déprécier [depresje] {96} *vt* **1** : devalue **2** : disparage — **se déprécier** *vr* : depreciate — **dépréciation** [depresjasjɔ̃] *nf* : depreciation
dépression [depresjɔ̃] *nf* : depression
déprimer [deprime] *vt* : depress — **déprimant, -mante** [deprimɑ̃, -mɑ̃t] *adj* : depressing — **déprimé, -mée** [deprime] *adj* : depressed, dejected
depuis [dəpɥi] *prep* **1** : since **2** : from **3** ~ **deux ans** : for two years — ~ *adv* : since (then) — **depuis que** *adv phr* : (ever) since
député, -tée [depyte] *n* : representative (in government)
déraciner [derasine] *vt* : uproot
dérailler [deraje] *vi* : derail — **déraillement** [derajmɑ̃] *nm* : derailment
déraisonnable [derɛzɔnabl] *adj* : unreasonable
déranger [derɑ̃ʒe] {17} *vt* **1** : bother, disturb **2** DÉRÉGLER : disrupt, upset — **se déranger** *vr* : put oneself out — **dérangement** [derɑ̃ʒmɑ̃] *nm* **1** : trouble, bother **2** : (stomach) upset
déraper [derape] *vi* **1** GLISSER : skid, slip **2** : get out of hand (of a situation)
dérégler [deregle] {87} *vt* **1** : put out of order **2** : upset, disturb — **se dérégler** *vr* : go wrong
dérision [derizjɔ̃] *nf* : derision, mockery — **dérisoire** [derizwar] *adj* : ridiculous, pathetic
dériver [derive] *vt* **1** : divert **2** ~ **de** : derive from — *vi* : drift, be adrift — **dérivé** [derive] *nm* **1** : derivation (of a word) **2** : by-product
dernier, -nière [dɛrnje, -njɛr] *adj* **1** : last, previous **2** : latest (of a novel, etc.) **3** : final, last **4** : lowest (of a step, etc.) — ~ *n* **1** : last (one) **2 ce dernier, cette dernière** : the latter — **dernièrement** [dɛrnjɛrmɑ̃] *adv* : recently
dérobé, -bée [derɔbe] *adj* : hidden — **à la dérobée** *adv phr* : on the sly
dérouler [derule] *vt* : unwind, unroll — **se dérouler** *vr* : take place — **déroulement** [derulmɑ̃] *nm* : development, progress
dérouter [derute] *vt* : disconcert, confuse — **déroute** [derut] *nf* : rout
derrière [dɛrjɛr] *adv & prep* : behind — ~ *nm* **1** : back, rear **2** *fam* : buttocks *pl*, bottom
des → **de**
dès [dɛ] *prep* **1** : from **2** ~ **lors** : from then on **3** ~ **que** : as soon as
désaccord [dezakɔr] *nm* : disagreement
désagréable [dezagreabl] *adj* DÉPLAISANT : disagreeable, unpleasant
désagréger [dezagreʒe] {64} *vt* : break up — **se désagréger** *vr* : disintegrate
désagrément [dezagremɑ̃] *nm* : annoyance
désapprouver [dezapruve] *vt* : disapprove of — **désapprobation** [dezaprɔbasjɔ̃] *nf* : disapproval
désarmer [dezarme] *vt* : disarm — **désarmement** [dezarməmɑ̃] *nm* : disarmament
désarroi [dezarwa] *nm* : confusion, distress
désastre [dezastr] *nm* : disaster — **désastreux, -treuse** [dezastrø, -trøz] *adj* : disastrous
désavantage [dezavɑ̃taʒ] *nm* : disadvantage — **désavantager** [dezavɑ̃taʒe] {17} *vt* : put at a disadvantage — **désavantageux, -geuse** [dezavɑ̃taʒø, -ʒøz] *adj* : disadvantageous
désaveu [dezavø] *nm, pl* **-veux** : repudiation, denial
désavouer [dezavwe] *vt* RENIER : deny, repudiate
descendre [desɑ̃dr] {63} *vt* **1** : go down (the stairs, etc.) **2** : take (sth) down — *vi* **1** : go down, come down **2** : get off (of a passenger) **3** ~ **de** : be descended from — **descendant, -dante** [desɑ̃dɑ̃, -dɑ̃t] *n* : descendant — **descente** [desɑ̃t] *nf* **1** : descent **2** : (police) raid **3** PENTE : slope
description [dɛskripsjɔ̃] *nf* : description — **descriptif, -tive** [dɛskriptif, -tiv] *adj* : descriptive
désemparé, -rée [dezɑ̃pare] *adj* **1** : distraught **2** : in distress
déséquilibrer [dezekilibre] *vt* : unbalance — **déséquilibre** [dezekilibr] *nm* : imbalance
désert, -serte [dezɛr, -zɛrt] *adj* : desert, deserted — **désert** *nm* : desert
déserter [dezɛrte] *v* : desert — **déserteur** [dezɛrtœr] *nm* : deserter
désespérer [dezɛspere] {87} *vi* : despair — *vt* : drive to despair — **dé-sespéré, -rée** [dezɛspere] *adj* : desperate — **désespoir** [dezɛspwar] *nm* : desperation, despair
déshabiller [dezabije] *vt* : undress — **se déshabiller** *vr* : get undressed
déshonneur [dezɔnœr] *nm* : dishonor, disgrace — **déshonorant, -rante** [dezɔnɔrɑ̃, -rɑ̃t] *adj* : dishonorable — **déshonorer** [dezɔnɔre] *vt* : dishonor, disgrace
déshydrater [dezidrate] *vt* : dehydrate
désigner [deziɲe] *vt* **1** : designate, indicate **2** NOMMER : appoint
désillusion [dezilyzjɔ̃] *nf* : disillusionment — **désillusionner** [dezilyzjɔne] *vt* : disillusion
désinfecter [dezɛ̃fɛkte] *vt* : disinfect — **désinfectant** [dezɛ̃fɛktɑ̃] *nm* : disinfectant
désintégrer [dezɛ̃tegre] {87} *v* **se désintégrer** *vr* : disintegrate
désintéressé, -sée [dezɛ̃terese] *adj* : impartial, disinterested
désinvolte [dezɛ̃vɔlt] *adj* : casual, offhand — **désinvolture** [dezɛ̃vɔltyr] *nf* : offhand manner
désirer [dezire] *vt* : want, desire — **désir** [dezir] *nm* : desire — **désireux, -reuse** [dezirø, -røz] *adj* : anxious, eager
désobéir [dezɔbeir] *vi* : disobey — **désobéissance** [dezɔbeisɑ̃s] *nf* : disobedience — **désobéissant, -sante** [dezɔbeisɑ̃, -sɑ̃t] *adj* : disobedient
désobligeant, -geante [dezɔbliʒɑ̃, -ʒɑ̃t] *adj* : disagreeable
désoler [dezɔle] *vt* : distress — **se désoler** *vr* : be upset — **désolé, -lée** [dezɔle] *adj* **1** : desolate **2 être** ~ : be sorry
désopilant, -lante [dezɔpilɑ̃, -lɑ̃t] *adj* : hilarious
désordonné, -née [dezɔrdɔne] *adj* **1** : disorganized **2** : untidy — **désordre** [dezɔrdr] *nm* **1** : disorder **2** : untidiness
désorganiser [dezɔrganize] *vt* : disorganize
désorienté, -tee [dezɔrjɑ̃te] *adj* : disoriented, confused
désormais [dezɔrmɛ] *adv* : henceforth, from now on
désosser [dezɔse] *vt* : bone (a fish)
desquels, desquelles → **lequel**
dessécher [deseʃe] {87} *vt* : dry up, parch
desserrer [desere] *vt* : loosen
dessert [desɛr] *nm* : dessert
desservir [desɛrvir] {81} *vt* **1** : serve (by providing transportation) **2** : clear (the table) **3** : do a disservice to
dessin [desɛ̃] *nm* **1** : drawing **2** : design, pattern **3** CONTOUR : outline **4** ~ **animé** : (animated) cartoon — **dessinateur, -trice** [desinatœr, -tris] *n* **1** : artist **2** : designer — **dessiner** [desine] *vt* **1** : draw **2** : outline — *vi* : draw, sketch — **se dessiner** *vr* **1** : stand out **2** APPARAÎTRE : appear, take shape
dessous [dəsu] *adv* : underneath — ~ *nms & pl* **1** : underneath, underside **2** ~ *nmpl* : underwear, lingerie **3 en** ~ : underneath, down below **4 en** ~ **de** : below — **dessous–de–verre** [d(ə)ɛsudvɛr] *nms & pl* : coaster
dessus [dəsy] *adv* : on top, on (it) — ~ *nms & pl* **1** : top **2** : upper (of a shoe) **3** : upper floor, upstairs **4 en** ~ : on top, above
destiner [dɛstine] *vt* **1** : destine **2** ~ **qqch à qqn** : intend sth for s.o. — **destin** [dɛstɛ̃] *nm* : fate, destiny — **destinataire** [dɛstinatɛr] *nmf* : addressee — **destination** [dɛstinasjɔ̃] *nf* : destination — **destinée** [dɛstine] *nf* : fate, destiny
destruction [dɛstryksjɔ̃] *nf* : destruction — **destructeur, -trice** [dɛstryktœr, -tris] *adj* : destructive
désuet, -suète [dezɥɛ, -zɥɛt] *adj* : outdated, obsolete — **désuétude** [dezɥetyd] *nf* **tomber en** ~ : fall into disuse
désunir [dezynir] *vt* : separate, divide
détacher [detaʃe] *vt* **1** : detach, tear off **2** : untie, unfasten — **se détacher** *vr* **1** : come undone **2** ~ **de** : grow apart from — **détaché, -chée** [detaʃe] *adj* : detached
détailler [detaje] *vt* **1** : sell retail **2** ÉNUMÉRER : detail, itemize — **détail** [detaj] *nm* **1** : detail **2** : retail
détecter [detɛkte] *vt* : detect — **détecteur** [detɛktœr] *nm* : detector, sensor — **détection** [detɛksjɔ̃] *nf* : detection — **détective** [detɛktiv] *nm* : detective
détendre [detɑ̃dr] {63} *vt* **1** : slacken, loosen **2** : relax, ease — **se détendre** *vr* **1** : become slack **2** : relax, unwind — **détendu, -due** [detɑ̃dy] *adj* : relaxed
détenir [detnir] {92} *vt* **1** POSSÉDER : hold, possess **2** : detain (a suspect)
détente [detɑ̃t] *nf* **1** REPOS : relaxation **2** : trigger (of a firearm)
détenteur, -trice [detɑ̃tœr, -tris] *n* : holder
détention [detɑ̃sjɔ̃] *nf* **1** : possession **2** EMPRISONNEMENT : detention
détenu, -nue [detny] *n* : prisoner
détergent [detɛrʒɑ̃] *nm* : detergent
détériorer [deterjɔre] *vt* : damage — **se détériorer** *vr* : deteriorate — **détérioration** [deterjɔrasjɔ̃] *nf* : deterioration
déterminer [detɛrmine] *vt* : determine — **se déterminer** *vr* ~ **à** : make up one's mind to — **détermination** [detɛrminasjɔ̃] *nf* : determination — **déterminé, -née** [detɛrmine] *adj* **1** : determined, resolute **2** : specified, definite
déterrer [detere] *vt* : dig up, unearth
détester [detɛste] *vt* : detest — **détestable** [detɛstabl] *adj* : hateful
détoner [detɔne] *vi* : explode — **détonation** [detɔnasjɔ̃] *nf* : explosion
détourner [deturne] *vt* **1** : divert, reroute **2** : hijack (an airplane) **3** : embezzle (funds) — **détour** [detur] *nm* : detour — **détourné, -née** [deturne] *adj* : indirect, roundabout — **détournement** [deturnəmɑ̃] *nm* **1** : diversion, rerouting **2** : hijacking **3** : embezzlement
détraquer [detrake] *vt* **1** : put out of order, break **2** *fam* : upset (one's stomach) — **se détraquer** *vr* : break down, go wrong
détresse [detrɛs] *nf* : distress
détriment [detrimɑ̃] *nm* **au** ~ **de** : at the cost of
détritus [detrity(s)] *nmpl* : waste, rubbish
détroit [detrwa] *nm* : strait
détruire [detrɥir] {49} *vt* : destroy
dette [dɛt] *nf* : debt
deuil [dœj] *nm* : bereavement, mourning
deux [dø] *adj* **1** : two **2** : second (in dates) **3** ~ **fois** : twice — ~ *nm* **1** : two **2 tous les** ~ : both (of them) — **deuxième** [døzjɛm] *adj & nmf* : second — **deuxièmement** [døzjɛmmɑ̃] *adv* : secondly, second
deux–points [døpwɛ̃] *nms & pl* : colon
dévaliser [devalize] *vt* : rob (a bank, etc.)
dévaloriser [devalɔrize] *vt* **1** : reduce the value of **2** : belittle (s.o.)
devancer [dəvɑ̃se] {6} *vt* **1** : be ahead of **2** ANTICIPER : anticipate
devant [dəvɑ̃] *adv* : in front, ahead, before — ~ *nm* : front — ~ *prep* **1** : in front of **2** : ahead of
devanture [dəvɑ̃tyr] *nf* **1** : storefront **2** : shopwindow
dévaster [devaste] *vt* : devastate
développer [devlɔpe] *vt* : develop — **se développer** *vr* : develop — **développement** [devlɔpmɑ̃] *nm* : development
devenir [dəvnir] {92} *vi* **1** : become **2 qu'est-ce que tu deviens?** : what are you up to?
déverser [devɛrse] *vt* : pour (out) — **se déverser** *vr* ~ **dans** : flow into
déviation [devjasjɔ̃] *nf* **1** : deviation **2** DÉTOUR : detour — **dévier** [devje] {96} *vt* : deflect, divert (traffic) — *vi* **1** : veer, swerve **2** ~ **de** : deviate from
deviner [dəvine] *vt* **1** : guess **2** APERCEVOIR : perceive **3** PRÉDIRE : foretell
devinette [dəvinɛt] *nf* : riddle
devis [dəvi] *nms & pl* : estimate
devise [dəviz] *nf* **1** : motto **2** : currency (money)
dévisser [devise] *vt* : unscrew
dévoiler [devwale] *vt* : unveil, reveal
devoir [dəvwar] {28} *vt* : owe — *v aux* **1** : have to, should **2** (*expressing obligation*) : must — ~ *nm* **1** : duty **2** ~**s** *nmpl* : homework
dévorer [devɔre] *vt* : devour
dévot, -vote [devo, -vɔt] *adj* : devout, pious — **dévotion** [devosjɔ̃] *nf* : devotion, piety
dévouer [devwe] *vt* : devote — **se dévouer** *vr* : devote oneself — **dévoué, -vouée** [devwe] *adj* : devoted — **dévouement** [devumɑ̃] *nm* : dedication, devotion
dextérité [dɛksterite] *nf* : dexterity, skill
diabète [djabɛt] *nm* : diabetes — **diabétique** [djabetik] *adj & nmf* : diabetic
diable [djabl] *nm* : devil — **diabolique** [djabɔlik] *adj* : diabolical
diagnostic [djagnɔstik] *nm* : diagnosis — **diagnostiquer** [djagnɔstike] *vt* : diagnose
diagonal, -nale [djagɔnal] *adj, mpl* **-naux** [-no] : diagonal — **diagonale** *nf* **1** : diagonal **2 en** ~ : diagonally
diagramme [djagram] *nm* : graph, chart
dialecte [djalɛkt] *nm* : dialect
dialogue [djalɔg] *nm* : dialogue
diamant [djamɑ̃] *nm* : diamond
diamètre [djamɛtr] *nm* : diameter
diaphragme [djafragm] *nm* : diaphragm
diapositive [djapɔzitiv] *nf* : slide, transparency
diarrhée [djare] *nf* : diarrhea
dictateur [diktatœr] *nm* : dictator
dicter [dikte] *vt* : dictate — **dictée** [dikte] *nf* : dictation
dictionnaire [diksjɔnɛr] *nm* : dictionary
dièse [djɛz] *nm* **1** : sharp (in music) **2** : pound sign
diesel [djezɛl] *adj & nm* : diesel
diète [djɛt] *nf* RÉGIME : diet
dieu [djø] *nm, pl* **dieux 1** : god **2 Dieu** : God
diffamer [difame] *vt* : slander, libel — **diffamation** [difamasjɔ̃] *nf* : slander, libel
différence [diferɑ̃s] *nf* **1** : difference **2 à la** ~ **de** : unlike — **différencier** [diferɑ̃sje] {96} *vt* : differentiate — **différend** [diferɑ̃] *nm* : disagreement — **différent, -rente** [diferɑ̃, -rɑ̃t] *adj* : different — **différer** [difere] {87} *vt* : defer, postpone — *vi* : differ, vary
difficile [difisil] *adj* : difficult — **difficilement** [difisilmɑ̃] *adv* : with difficulty — **difficulté** [difikylte] *nf* : difficulty
difforme [difɔrm] *adj* : deformed, misshapen — **difformité** [difɔrmite] *nf* : deformity
diffuser [difyze] *vt* **1** : broadcast **2** PROPAGER : spread, distribute — **diffusion** [difyzjɔ̃] *nf* **1** : broadcasting **2** : distribution
digérer [diʒere] {87} *vt* **1** : digest **2** *fam* : put up with — **digestif, -tive** [diʒɛstif, -tiv] *adj* : digestive — **digestion** [diʒɛstjɔ̃] *nf* : digestion
digital, -tale [diʒital] *adj, mpl* **-taux** [-to] : digital
digne [diɲ] *adj* **1** : dignified **2** ~ **de** : worthy of — **dignité** [diɲite] *nf* : dignity
digue [dig] *nf* : dike
dilapider [dilapide] *vt* : squander
dilater [dilate] *vt* : dilate — **se dilater** *vr* : dilate
dilemme [dilɛm] *nm* : dilemma
diluer [dilɥe] *vt* : dilute
dimanche [dimɑ̃ʃ] *nm* : Sunday
dimension [dimɑ̃sjɔ̃] *nf* : dimension
diminuer [diminɥe] *vt* RÉDUIRE : lower, reduce — *vi* : diminish, decrease — **diminution** [diminysjɔ̃] *nf* : reduction, decreasing
dinde [dɛ̃d] *nf* : (female) turkey — **dindon** [dɛ̃dɔ̃] *nm* : (male) turkey
dîner [dine] *vi* **1** : dine, have dinner **2** *Can* : have lunch — ~ *nm* **1** : dinner **2** *Can* : lunch — **dîneur, -neuse** [dinœr, -nœz] *n* : diner (person)
dinosaure [dinozɔr] *nm* : dinosaur
diplomate [diplɔmat] *adj* : diplomatic, tactful — ~ *nmf* : diplomat — **diplomatie** [diplɔmasi] *nf* : diplomacy — **diplomatique** [diplɔmatik] *adj* : diplomatic
diplôme [diplom] *nm* : diploma — **diplômé, -mée** [diplome] *adj* : qualified, certified — ~ *n* : graduate
dire [dir] {29} *vt* **1** : say **2** : tell **3 qu'en dis–tu?** : what do you think? **4 vouloir** ~ : mean — **se dire** *vr* **1** : tell oneself **2 comment se dit ... en français?** : how do you say ... in French? — ~ *nm* **1** : statement **2 au** ~ **de** : according to
direct, -recte [dirɛkt] *adj* : direct — **direct** *nm* **1** : express train **2 en** ~ : live, in person — **directement** [-təmɑ̃] *adv* : directly, straight
directeur, -trice [dirɛktœr, -tris] *adj* : directing, guiding — ~ *n* **1** : manager, director **2 directeur général** : chief executive officer
direction [dirɛksjɔ̃] *nf* **1** : direction **2** GESTION : management **3** : steering (mechanism)
directive [dirɛktiv] *nf* : order
dirigeant, -geante [diriʒɑ̃, -ʒɑ̃t] *adj* : ruling — ~ *n* : leader, director
diriger [diriʒe] {17} *vt* **1** : direct, manage **2** CONDUIRE : steer **3** MENER : conduct **4** ~ **sur** : aim at — **se diriger** *vr* ~ **vers** : head toward
discerner [disɛrne] *vt* : discern — **discernement** [disɛrnəmɑ̃] *nm* : discernment
disciple [disipl] *nm* : disciple
discipline [disiplin] *nf* : discipline — **discipliner** [disipline] *vt* : discipline
discorde [diskɔrd] *nf* : discord
discours [diskur] *nms & pl* : speech
discréditer [diskredite] *vt* : discredit
discret, -crète [diskrɛ, -krɛt] *adj* : discreet — **discrétion** [diskresjɔ̃] *nf* **1** : discretion **2 à** ~ : unlimited, as much as one wants
discrimination [diskriminasjɔ̃] *nf* : discrimination
disculper [diskylpe] *vt* : clear, exonerate
discussion [diskysjɔ̃] *nf* : discussion
discuter [diskyte] *vt* **1** : discuss, debate **2** CONTESTER : question — *vi* **1** : talk **2** PROTESTER : argue **3** ~ **de** : discuss
diseuse [dizøz] *nf* ~ **de bonne aventure** : fortune-teller
disgrâce [disgras] *nf* : disgrace
disloquer [dislɔke] *vt* LUXER : dislocate
disparaître [disparɛtr] {7} *vi* **1** : disappear **2** MOURIR : die — **disparition** [disparisjɔ̃] *nf* **1** : disappearance **2** MORT : extinction, death
disparité [disparite] *nf* : disparity
disparu, -rue [dispary] *adj* : missing — ~ *n* **1** : missing person **2** : dead person
dispenser [dispɑ̃se] *vt* **1** : exempt, excuse **2** DISTRIBUER : dispense — **se dispenser** *vr* ~ **de** : avoid — **dispense** [dispɑ̃s] *nf* : exemption
disperser [dispɛrse] *vt* : disperse, scatter — **se disperser** *vr* : disperse
disponible [dispɔnibl] *adj* : available — **disponibilité** [dispɔnibilite] *nf* : availability

disposer [dispoze] *vt* **1** PLACER : arrange **2** INCITER : incline, dispose — *vi* **~ de** : have at one's disposal — **disposé, -sée** [dispoze] *adj* **1** : arranged **2 ~ à** : disposed to, willing to — **dispositif** [dispozitif] *nm* **1** : device, mechanism **2** PLAN : plan of action — **disposition** [dispozisjɔ̃] *nf* **1** : arrangement, layout **2** APTITUDE : aptitude **3** TENDANCE : tendency **4 à la ~ de** : at the disposal of **5 ~s** *nfpl* : steps, measures

disproportionné, -née [disprɔpɔrsjɔne] *adj* : disproportionate

disputer [dispyte] *vt* **1** : compete in, play **2** *fam* : tell off **3** *Can* : scold — **se disputer** *vr* : quarrel, fight — **dispute** [dispyt] *nf* : argument, quarrel

disqualifier [diskalifje] {96} *vt* : disqualify

disque [disk] *nm* **1** : (phonograph) record **2** : disk — **disquette** [diskɛt] *nf* : floppy disk

disséminer [disemine] *vt* : scatter

dissentiment [disɑ̃timɑ̃] *nm* : dissent

dissertation [disɛrtasjɔ̃] *nf* : essay (in school)

dissimuler [disimyle] *vt* : conceal, hide — **se dissimuler** *vr* : hide oneself — **dissimulation** [disimylasjɔ̃] *nf* **1** : deceit **2** : concealment

dissiper [disipe] *vt* **1** : disperse **2** : squander (one's fortune) — **se dissiper** *vr* : clear (up), vanish

dissolu, -lue [disɔly] *adj* : dissolute — **dissolution** [disɔlysjɔ̃] *nf* **1** : dissolution, breakup **2** : dissolving — **dissolvant** [disɔlvɑ̃] *nm* **1** : solvent **2** : nail polish remover

dissoudre [disudr] {1} *vt* : dissolve — **se dissoudre** *vr* : dissolve

dissuader [disɥade] *vt* : dissuade, deter

distance [distɑ̃s] *nf* : distance — **distant, -tante** [distɑ̃, -tɑt] *adj* : distant

distiller [distile] *vt* : distill

distinct, -tincte [distɛ̃, -tɛ̃kt] *adj* : distinct — **distinctif, -tive** [distɛ̃ktif, -tiv] *adj* : distinctive — **distinction** [distɛ̃ksjɔ̃] *nf* : distinction

distinguer [distɛ̃ge] *v* : distinguish — **distingué, -guée** [distɛ̃ge] *adj* : distinguished

distraction [distraksjɔ̃] *nf* **1** : distraction **2** PASSE-TEMPS : recreation

distraire [distrɛr] {40} *vt* **1** : distract **2** DIVERTIR : amuse, entertain — **se distraire** *vr* : amuse oneself — **distrait, -traite** [distrɛ, -trɛt] *adj* : distracted, absentminded

distribuer [distribɥe] *vt* **1** : distribute **2** : deliver (mail) — **distributeur** [distribytœr] *nm* **1** : distributor **2** *or* **~ automatique** : dispenser, vending machine — **distribution** [distribysjɔ̃] *nf* **1** : distribution **2** : casting, cast (of actors)

district [distrikt] *nm* : district

dit, dite [di, dit] *adj* **1** : agreed upon, stated **2** : called, known as

divaguer [divage] *vi* : rave

divan [divɑ̃] *nm* : couch

divergence [-vɛrʒɑ̃s] *nf* : difference — **diverger** [divɛrʒe] {17} *vi* : diverge

divers, -verse [divɛr, -vɛrs] *adj* **1** VARIÉ : diverse **2** PLUSIEURS : various — **diversifier** [divɛrsifje] {96} *vt* : diversify — **diversion** [divɛrsjɔ̃] *nf* : diversion — **diversité** [divɛrsite] *nf* : diversity, variety

divertir [divɛrtir] *vt* : amuse, entertain — **se divertir** *vr* : amuse oneself — **divertissement** [divɛrtismɑ̃] *nm* : entertainment, pastime

dividende [dividɑ̃d] *nm* : dividend

divine, -vine [divɛ̃, -vin] *adj* : divine — **divinité** [divinite] *nf* : divinity

diviser [divize] *vt* : divide — **se diviser** *vr* : divide — **division** [divizjɔ̃] *nf* : division

divorcer [divɔrse] {6} *vi* : get a divorce — **divorce** [divɔrs] *nm* : divorce

divulguer [divylge] *vt* : divulge, disclose

dix [dis, *before a consonant* di, *before a vowel or mute h* diz] *adj* **1** : ten **2** : tenth (in dates) — **~** *nms & pl* : ten

dix–huit [dizɥit] *adj* **1** : eighteen **2** : eighteenth (in dates) — **~** *nms & pl* : eighteen — **dix–huitième** [dizɥitjɛm] *adj & nmf & nm* : eighteenth

dixième [dizjɛm] *adj & nmf & nm* : tenth

dix–neuf [diznœf] *adj* **1** : nineteen **2** : nineteenth (in dates) — **~** *nms & pl* : nineteen — **dix–neuvième** [diznœvjɛm] *adj & nmf & nm* : nineteenth

dix–sept [disɛt] *adj* **1** : seventeen **2** : seventeenth (in dates) — **~** *nms & pl* : seventeen — **dix–septième** [disɛtjɛm] *adj & nmf & nm* : seventeenth

dizaine [dizɛn] *nf* : ten, about ten

docile [dɔsil] *adj* : obedient

dock [dɔk] *nm* : dock

docteur [dɔktœr] *nm* : doctor

doctrine [dɔktrin] *nf* : doctrine

document [dɔkymɑ̃] *nm* : document — **documentation** [dɔkymɑ̃tasjɔ̃] *nf* : literature, leaflets *pl* — **documenter** [dɔkymɑ̃te] *v* **se documenter** *vr* **~ sur** : research

dodu, -due [dɔdy] *adj* : plump, chubby

dogme [dɔgm] *nm* : dogma

doigt [dwa] *nm* **1** : finger **2 ~ de pied** : toe — **doigté** [dwate] *nm* TACT : tact

dollar [dɔlar] *nm* : dollar

domaine [dɔmɛn] *nm* **1** : domain **2** PROPRIÉTÉ : estate

dôme [dom] *nm* : dome

domestique [dɔmɛstik] *adj* **1** : domestic **2** : domesticated — **~** *nmf* : servant — **domestiquer** [dɔmɛstike] *vt* APPRIVOISER : domesticate

domicile [dɔmisil] *nm* : residence, home

dominer [dɔmine] *v* : dominate — **dominant, -nante** [dɔminɑ̃, -nɑ̃t] *adj* : dominant

dommage [dɔmaʒ] *nm* **1** PRÉJUDICE : harm, injury **2** DÉGÂTS : damage **3 c'est ~** : that's too bad

dompter [dɔ̃te] *vt* : tame

don [dɔ̃] *nm* : gift — **donateur, -trice** [dɔnatœr, -tris] *n* : donor, giver — **donation** [dɔnasjɔ̃] *nf* : donation

donc [dɔ̃k] *conj* **1** : so, therefore, consequently **2** : so, then

donner [dɔne] *vt* **1** : give **2** : produce, yield **3** MONTRER : indicate, show **4** CAUSER : cause **5** : deal (cards) — *vi* **1** : produce a crop **2 ~ dans** : fall into **3 ~ sur** : overlook — **se donner** *vr* **~ à** : devote oneself to — **donne** [dɔn] *nf* : deal (in card games) — **donné, -née** [dɔne] *adj* **1** : given **2 c'est ~** : it's a bargain — **donnée** *nf* **1** : fact **2 ~s** *nfpl* : data — **donneur, -neuse** [dɔnœr, -nøz] *n* **1** : donor **2** : (card) dealer

dont [dɔ̃] *pron* : of which, of whom, whose

doré, -rée [dɔre] *adj* **1** : gilt **2** : golden

dorénavant [dɔrenavɑ̃] *adv* : henceforth

dorer [dɔre] *vt* **1** : gild **2** BRUNIR : tan — *vi* : brown (in cooking)

dorloter [dɔrlɔte] *vt* : pamper

dormir [dɔrmir] {30} *vi* : sleep, be asleep

dortoir [dɔrtwar] *nm* : dormitory

dorure [dɔryr] *nf* : gilding, gilt

dos [do] *nms & pl* : back

dose [doz] *nf* : dose — **doser** [doze] *vt* : measure out (a dose of medicine)

dossier [dosje] *nm* **1** : file, record **2** : back (of a chair)

doter [dɔte] *vt* **1** : endow **2** ÉQUIPER : equip

douane [dwan] *nf* **1** : customs **2** : (import) duty — **douanier, -nière** [dwanje, -njɛr] *adj* : customs — **douanier** *nm* : customs officer

double [dubl] *adv & adj* : double — **~** *nm* **1** : double **2** : copy, duplicate — **doublement** [dubləmɑ̃] *adv* : doubly — **doubler** [duble] *vt* **1** : double **2** : line (fabric) **3** : dub (a film, etc.) **4** DÉPASSER : pass, overtake — *vi* : double — **doublure** [dublyr] *nf* **1** : lining **2** : understudy

douce → **doux** — **doucement** [dusmɑ̃] *adv* **1** : gently, softly **2** LENTEMENT : slowly — **douceur** [dusœr] *nf* **1** : softness, smoothness **2** : gentleness, mildness

douche [duʃ] *nf* : shower — **doucher** [duʃe] **se doucher** *vr* : take a shower

doué, douée [dwe] *adj* **1** : gifted, talented **2 ~ de** : endowed with

douille [duj] *nf* : electric socket

douillet, -lette [dujɛ, -jɛt] *adj* CONFORTABLE : cozy

douleur [dulœr] *nf* **1** : pain **2** CHAGRIN : grief — **douloureux, -reuse** [dulurø, -røz] *adj* : painful

douter [dute] *vt* **1** : doubt **2 ~ de** : question — **se douter** *vr* **~ de** : suspect — **doute** [dut] *nm* : doubt — **douteux, -teuse** [dutø, -tøz] *adj* : doubtful

doux, douce [du, dus] *adj* **1** : sweet **2** : soft (of skin) **3** : mild, gentle

douze [duz] *adj* **1** : twelve **2** : twelfth (in dates) — **~** *nms & pl* : twelve — **douzaine** [duzɛn] *nf* : dozen — **douzième** [duzjɛm] *adj & nmf & nm* : twelfth

doyen, doyenne [dwajɛ̃, -jɛn] *n* : dean

dragon [dragɔ̃] *nm* : dragon

draguer [drage] *vt* : dredge

drainer [drene] *vt* : drain — **drainage** [drɛnaʒ] *nm* : drainage, draining

drame [dram] *nm* **1** : drama **2** : tragedy — **dramatique** [dramatik] *adj* : dramatic — **dramatiser** [dramatize] *vt* : dramatize — **dramaturge** [dramatyrʒ] *nmf* : playwright

drap [dra] *nm* **1** : sheet **2** : woolen fabric

drapeau [drapo] *nm, pl* **-peaux** : flag

draper [drape] *vt* : drape

drastique [drastik] *adj* : drastic

dresser [drese] *vt* **1** LEVER : raise **2** ÉRIGER : put up, erect **3** ÉTABLIR : draft, draw up **4** : train (an animal) **5 ~ les oreilles** : cock one's ears — **se dresser** *vr* **1** : stand up **2** : rise up, tower

dribbler [drible] *vi* : dribble (in sports)

drogue [drɔg] *nf* : drug — **drogué, -guée** [drɔge] *n* : drug addict — **droguer** [drɔge] *vt* : drug — **se droguer** *vr* : take drugs

droit [drwa] *nm* **1** : right **2** : fee, tax, duty **3 le ~** : law **4 ~s d'auteur** : copyright — **~** *adv* : straight, directly — **droit, droite** [drwa, drwat] *adj* **1** : right, right-hand **2** : straight, direct **3** VERTICAL : upright, vertical **4** HONNÊTE : honest — **droite** *nf* **1** : right, right-hand side **2 la ~** : the right (in politics) — **droitier, -tière** [drwatje, -tjɛr] *adj* : right-handed — **droiture** [drwatyr] *nf* : uprightness, integrity

drôle [drol] *adj* : funny — **drôlement** [drolmɑ̃] *adv* **1** : amusingly **2** BIZARREMENT : strangely, oddly **3** *fam* : really, awfully

dru, drue [dry] *adj* : thick (of hair, etc.)

du → **de, le**

dû, due [dy] *adj* **1** : due, owing **2 ~ à** : due to — **dû** *nm* : due

duc [dyk] *nm* : duke — **duchesse** [dyʃɛs] *nf* : duchess

duel [dɥɛl] *nm* : duel

dûment [dymɑ̃] *adv* : duly

dune [dyn] *nf* : dune

duo [dyo] *nm* **1** : duet **2** : duo, pair

dupe [dyp] *nf* : dupe — **duper** [dype] *vt* : dupe, deceive

duplex [dyplɛks] *nm* : duplex (apartment)

duplicata [dyplikata] *nms & pl* : duplicate

duquel → **lequel**

dur, dure [dyr] *adj* **1** : hard, stiff **2** DIFFICILE : difficult **3** SÉVÈRE : harsh — **dur** *adv* : hard

durable [dyrabl] *adj* : durable, lasting

durant [dyrɑ̃] *prep* **1** : for (a period of time) **2** : during

durcir [dyrsir] *v* : harden — **se durcir** *vr* : harden — **durcissement** [dyrsismɑ̃] *nm* : hardening

durée [dyre] *nf* : duration, length

durement [dyrmɑ̃] *adv* : harshly, severely

durer [dyre] *vi* : last, go on

dureté [dyrte] *nf* **1** : hardness **2** SÉVÉRITÉ : harshness

duvet [dyvɛ] *nm* **1** : down (fabric) **2** : sleeping bag

dynamique [dinamik] *adj* : dynamic

dynamite [dinamit] *nf* : dynamite — **dynamiter** [dinamite] *vt* : dynamite, blast

dynastie [dinasti] *nf* : dynasty

E

e [ø] *nm* : e, fifth letter of the alphabet

eau [o] *nf, pl* **eaux** **1** : water **2 ~ de Cologne** : cologne **3 ~ douce** : freshwater **4 ~ de Javel** : bleach **5 ~ oxygénée** : hydrogen peroxide — **eau–de–vie** *nf, pl* **eaux–de–vie** : brandy

ébahir [ebair] *vt* : astound, dumbfound

ébaucher [eboʃe] *vt* : sketch out, outline — **s'ébaucher** *vr* : form, take shape — **ébauche** [eboʃ] *nf* : outline, sketch

ébène [ebɛn] *nf* : ebony — **ébéniste** [ebenist] *nmf* : cabinetmaker

éblouir [ebluir] *vt* : dazzle, stun

ébouler [ebule] *v* **s'ébouler** *vr* : cave in, collapse

ébouriffer [eburife] *vt* : tousle, ruffle

ébranler [ebrɑ̃le] *vt* **1** : shake **2** : weaken, undermine

ébrécher [ebreʃe] {87} *vt* : chip, nick — **ébréchure** [ebreʃyr] *nf* : chip, nick

ébriété [ebrijete] *nf* : inebriation, drunkenness

ébullition [ebylisjɔ̃] *nf* : boil, boiling

écailler [ekaje] *vt* **1** : scale (fish) **2** : open (a shell) **3** : chip (paint) — **s'écailler** *vr* : flake off — **écaille** [ekaj] *nf* **1** : scale (of a fish) **2** : tortoiseshell **3** FRAGMENT : flake, chip

écarlate [ekarlat] *adj & nf* : scarlet

écarquiller [ekarkije] *vt* **~ les yeux** : open one's eyes wide

écarter [ekarte] *vt* **1** : spread, open **2** ÉLOIGNER : move apart **3** EXCLURE : rule out **4** DÉTOURNER : divert, distract — **s'écarter** *vr* **1** : move away **2** SE SÉPARER : part, open — **écart** [ekar] *nm* **1** : distance, gap **2** VARIATION : difference **3** : lapse (of conduct) **4** DÉVIATION : swerve **5 à l'~** : apart, away — **écarté, -tée** [ekarte] *adj* **1** ISOLÉ : remote **2** : wide apart — **écartement** [ekartəmɑ̃] *nm* : gap

ecclésiastique [eklezjastik] *nm* : clergyman

écervelé, -lée [esɛrvəle] *adj* : scatterbrained

échafaud [eʃafo] *nm* : scaffold — **échafaudage** [eʃafodaʒ] *nm* : scaffolding

échalote [eʃalɔt] *nf* **1** : shallot **2** *Can* : scallion

échanger [eʃɑ̃ʒe] {17} *vt* : exchange — **échange** [eʃɑ̃ʒ] *nm* **1** : exchange **2** : trade, commerce — **échangeur** [eʃɑ̃ʒœr] *nm* : (highway) interchange

échantillon [eʃɑ̃tijɔ̃] *nm* : sample

échapper [eʃape] *vi* **1 ~ à** : escape (from) **2 laisser ~** : let out **3 l'~ belle** : have a narrow escape — *vt Can* : drop — **s'échapper** *vr* : escape

écharde [eʃard] *nf* : splinter

écharpe [eʃarp] *nf* **1** : scarf **2 en ~** : in a sling

échasse [eʃas] *nf* : stilt

échauffer [eʃofe] *v* **s'échauffer** *vr* : warm up

échéance [eʃeɑ̃s] *nf* **1** : due date **2** OBLIGATION : financial obligation, payment **3 à longue ~** : in the long run — **échéant** [eʃeɑ̃] **le cas ~** *adv phr* : if need be

échec [eʃɛk] *nm* **1** : failure, setback **2 ~s** *nmpl* : chess **3 ~ et mat** : checkmate **4 en ~** : in check

échelle [eʃɛl] *nf* **1** : ladder **2** MESURE : scale — **échelon** [eʃlɔ̃] *nm* **1** : rung **2** NIVEAU : level — **échelonner** [eʃlɔne] *vt* : space out, spread out

échevelé, -lée [eʃəvle] *adj* : disheveled

échiquier [eʃikje] *nm* : chessboard

écho [eko] *nm* : echo — **échographie** [ekografi] *nf* : ultrasound

échoir [eʃwar] {31} *vi* **1** : fall due **2 ~ à qqn** : fall to s.o.

échouer [eʃwe] *vi* : fail (of an exam) — **s'échouer** *vr* : run aground

éclabousser [eklabuse] *vt* : splash, spatter — **éclaboussure** [eklabusyr] *nf* : splash

éclairer [eklere] *vt* **1** : light (up) **2** INFORMER : enlighten **3** EXPLIQUER : clarify — *vi* : give light — **s'éclairer** *vr* **1** : light up **2** : become clearer — **éclair** [eklɛr] *nm* **1** ÉCLAT : flash **2** : (flash of) lightning — **éclairage** [eklɛraʒ] *nm* : lighting, illumination — **éclaircie** [eklɛrsi] *nf* **1** : sunny spell **2** : clearing, glade — **éclaircir** [eklɛrsir] *vt* **1** : lighten **2** CLARIFIER : clarify **3** : thin (in cooking) — **s'éclaircir** *vr* : clear (up) — **éclaircissement** [eklɛrsismɑ̃] *nm* : explanation, clarification

éclaireur, -reuse [eklɛrœr, -røz] *n* : boy scout *m*, girl scout *f* — **éclaireur** *nm* : (military) scout

éclater [eklate] *vi* **1** : burst, explode **2** : break up, splinter — **éclat** [ekla] *nm* **1** : splinter, chip **2** : brilliance, shine **3** : splendor **4 ~ de rire** : burst (of laughter) — **éclatant, -tante** [eklatɑ̃, -tɑ̃t] *adj* **1** BRILLANT : brilliant **2 un succès éclatant** : a resounding success — **éclatement** [eklatmɑ̃] *nm* **1** : explosion, bursting **2** : rupture, split

éclipse [eklips] *nf* : eclipse — **éclipser** [eklipse] *v* **s'éclipser** *vr* : slip away

éclore [eklɔr] {32} *vi* **1** : hatch **2** : open out, blossom — **éclosion** [eklozjɔ̃] *nf* **1** : hatching **2** : blossoming

écluse [eklyz] *nf* : lock (of a canal)

écœurer [ekœre] *vt* : sicken, disgust — **écœurant, -rante** [ekœrɑ̃, -rɑ̃t] *adj* **1** : cloying, sickening **2** DÉGUEULASSE : disgusting

école [ekɔl] *nf* **1** : school **2 ~ secondaire** *Can* : high school **3 ~ maternelle** *Can* : kindergarten — **écolier, -lière** [ekɔlje, -ljɛr] *n* : schoolboy *m*, schoolgirl *f*

écologie [ekɔlɔʒi] *nf* : ecology — **écologique** [ekɔlɔʒik] *adj* : ecological

économie [ekɔnɔmi] *nf* **1** : economy **2** : economics **3 ~s** *nfpl* : savings — **économe** [ekɔnɔm] *adj* : thrifty, economical — **~** *nmf* : bursar — **économique** [ekɔnɔmik] *adj* : economic — **économiser** [ekɔnɔmize] *v* : save — **économiste** [ekɔnɔmist] *nmf* : economist

écorce [ekɔrs] *nf* **1** : bark (of a tree) **2** : peel (of a fruit)

écorcher [ekɔrʃe] *vt* **1** DÉPOUILLER : skin **2** ÉGRATIGNER : scratch, graze — **écorchure** [ekɔrʃyr] *nf* : graze, scratch

écossais, -saise [ekɔsɛ, -sɛz] *adj* **1** : Scottish **2** : tartan, plaid

écosser [ekɔse] *vt* : shell (peas, etc.)

écosystème [ekɔsistɛm] *nm* : ecosystem

écouler [ekule] *vt* : sell, dispose of — **s'écouler** *vr* **1** : flow (out) **2** PASSER : pass, elapse — **écoulement** [ekulmɑ̃] *nm* : flow

écourter [ekurte] *vt* : cut short, curtail

écouter [ekute] *vt* : listen to — *vi* : listen — **écouteur** [ekutœr] *nm* **1** : (telephone) receiver **2 ~s** *nmpl* : headphones

écoutille [ekutij] *nf* : hatch (of a ship)

écran [ekrɑ̃] *nm* : screen

écraser [ekraze] *vt* **1** : crush, squash, mash **2** : run over (an animal, etc.) **3** ACCABLER : overwhelm — **s'écraser** *vr* : crash (of a plane, etc.) — **écrasant, -sante** [ekrazɑ̃, -zɑ̃t] *adj* : crushing, overwhelming

écrémé, -mée [ekreme] *adj* **lait écrémé** : skim milk

écrevisse [ekrəvis] *nf* : crayfish

écrier [ekrije] {96} *v* **s'écrier** *vr* : exclaim

écrin [ekrɛ̃] *nm* : case, box

écrire [ekrir] {33} *v* : write — **s'écrire** *vr* : be spelled — **écrit** [ekri] *nm* **1** : writing(s) **2** : document **3 par ~** : in writing — **écriteau** [ekrito] *nm, pl* **-teaux** : notice, sign — **écriture** [ekrityr] *nf* : writing — **écrivain** [ekrivɛ̃] *nm* : writer — **écrivaillon** [ekrivajɔ̃] *nm fam* : hack writer

écrou [ekru] *nm* : (metal) nut

écrouler [ekrule] *v* **s'écrouler** *vr* : collapse — **écroulement** [ekrulmɑ̃] *nm* : collapse

écueil [ekœj] *nm* RÉCIF : reef

écume [ekym] *nf* **1** : foam, froth **2** : scum (in cooking) — **écumer** [ekyme] *vi* : foam, froth — **écumeux, -meuse** [ekymø, -møz] *adj* : foamy

écureuil [ekyrœj] *nm* : squirrel

écurie [ekyri] *nf* : stable

écusson [ekysɔ̃] *nm* : badge

édenté, -tée [edɑ̃te] *adj* : toothless

édifice [edifis] *nm* : building — **édifier** [edifje] {96} *vt* CONSTRUIRE : build

éditer [edite] *vt* **1** : publish **2** : edit — **éditeur, -trice** [editœr, -tris] *n* **1** : publisher **2** : editor — **édition** [edisjɔ̃] *nf* **1** : publishing **2** : edition (of a book) — **éditorial** [editɔrjal] *nm, pl* **-riaux** [-rjo] : editorial

édredon [edrədɔ̃] *nm* : comforter

éducation [edykasjɔ̃] *nf* **1** ENSEIGNEMENT : education **2** : upbringing (of children) **3 avoir de l'~** : have good manners — **éducatif, -tive** [edykatif, -tiv] *adj* : educational — **éduquer** [edyke] *vt* **1** : educate **2** ÉLEVER : bring up

effacer [efase] {6} *vt* : erase, delete — **s'effacer** *vr* **1** : fade **2** S'ÉCARTER : stand aside

effectif, -tive [efɛktif, -tiv] *adj* : real, actual — **effectivement** [efɛktivmɑ̃] *adv* **1** : indeed, in fact **2** RÉELLEMENT : really

effectuer [efɛktɥe] *vt* EXÉCUTER : carry out, make

efféminé, -née [efemine] *adj* : effeminate

effervescent, -cente [efɛrvesɑ, -sɑ̃t] *adj* : effervescent

effet [efɛ] *nm* **1** RÉSULTAT : effect, result **2 en ~** : indeed, actually **3 faire bon ~** : make a good impression

efficace [efikas] *adj* : efficient — **efficacité** [efikasite] *nf* **1** : efficiency **2** : effectiveness

effilocher [efilɔʃe] *vt* : shred, fray — **s'effilocher** *vr* : fray

effleurer [eflœre] *vt* **1** FRÔLER : touch lightly, graze **2 ça m'a effleuré l'esprit** : it crossed my mind

effondrer [efɔ̃dre] *v* **s'effondrer** *vr* : collapse — **effondrement** [efɔ̃drəmɑ̃] *nm* : collapse

efforcer [efɔrse] {6} *v* **s'efforcer** *vr* : strive, endeavor

effort [efɔr] *nm* : effort

effrayer [efreje] {11} *vt* : frighten — **effrayant, -frayante** [efrɛjɑ̃, -jɑ̃t] *adj* : frightening

effréné, -née [efrene] *adj* : wild, unrestrained

effriter [efrite] *vt* : crumble — **s'effriter** *vr* : crumble

effroi [efrwa] *nm* : terror, dread

effronté, -tée [efrɔ̃te] *adj* : impudent

effroyable [efrwajabl] *adj* : dreadful

égal, -gale [egal] *adj, mpl* **égaux** [ego] **1** : equal **2** RÉGULIER : regular, even **3 ça m'est ~** : it makes no difference to me — **~** *n* : equal — **également** [egalmɑ̃] *adv* **1** : equally **2** AUSSI : also, as well — **égaler** [egale] *vt* : equal — **égaliser** [egalize] *vt* **1** : equalize **2** : level (out) — **égalité** [egalite] *nf* : equality

égard [egar] *nm* **1** : regard, consideration **2 à cet ~** : in this respect **3 à l'~ de** : with regard to

égarer [egare] *vt* **1** : lead astray **2** PERDRE : lose, misplace — **s'égarer** *vr* **1** : lose one's way **2** : be misplaced

égayer [egeje] {11} *vt* : cheer up

églefin [egləfɛ̃] *nm* : haddock

église [egliz] *nf* : church

ego [ego] *nm* : ego — **égoïsme** [egɔism] *nm* : selfishness — **égoïste** [egɔist] *adj* : selfish

égorger [egɔrʒe] {17} *vt* : cut the throat of

égotisme [egɔtism] *nm* : egotism — **égotiste** [egɔtist] *adj* : egotisic(al)

égoutter [egute] *vt* : allow to drip, drain — **s'égoutter** *vr* : drain — **égout** [egu] *nm* : sewer — **égouttoir** [egutwar] *nm* : (dish) drainer

égratigner [egratiɲe] *vt* : scratch, graze — **égratignure** [egratiɲyr] *nf* : scratch

eh [e] *interj* **1** : hey! **2 ~ bien** : well

éhonté, -tée [eɔ̃te] *adj* : shameless, brazen

éjaculer [eʒakyle] *v* : ejaculate

éjecter [eʒɛkte] *vt* **1** : eject **2** *fam* : kick out

élaborer [elabɔre] *vt* : develop, put together — **élaboration** [elabɔrasjɔ̃] *nf* : elaboration, development

élan[1] [elɑ̃] *nm* **1** : momentum **2** : rush, surge (of energy, etc.)

élan[2] *nm* : elk

élancé, -cée [elɑ̃se] *adj* : slender

élancer [elɑ̃se] {6} *v* **s'élancer** *vr* SE PRÉCIPITER : dash, rush — **élancement** [elɑ̃smɑ̃] *nm* : shooting pain

élargir [elarʒir] *vt* : widen, broaden — **s'élargir** *vr* : expand, become broader — **élargissement** [elarʒismɑ̃] *nm* : widening, expanding

élastique [elastik] *adj* : elastic, flexible — **~** *nm* **1** : elastic **2** : rubber band

électeur, -trice [elɛktœr, -tris] *n* : voter — **élection** [elɛksjɔ̃] *nf* : election — **électoral, -rale** [elɛktɔral] *adj, mpl* **-raux** [-ro] : electoral, election — **électorat** [elɛktɔra] *nm* : electorate

électricité [elɛktrisite] *nf* : electricity — **électricien, -cienne** [elɛktrisjɛ̃, -sjɛn] *n* : electrician — **électrique** [elɛktrik] *adj* : electric(al)

électrocuter [elɛktrɔkyte] *vt* : electrocute

électron [elɛktrɔ̃] *nm* : electron — **électronique** [elɛktrɔnik] *adj* : electronic — **~** *nf* : electronics

élégance [elegɑ̃s] *nf* : elegance — **élégant, -gante** [elegɑ̃, -gɑ̃t] *adj* : elegant

élément [elemɑ̃] *nm* **1** : element **2** COMPOSANT : component, part — **élémentaire** [elemɑ̃tɛr] *adj* : elementary, basic

éléphant [elefɑ̃] *nm* : elephant

élevage [ɛlvaʒ] *nm* : breeding

élévation [elevasjɔ̃] *nf* **1** : elevation **2** AUGMENTATION : rise, increase

élève [elɛv] *nmf* : pupil, student

élever [elve] {52} *vt* **1** : raise **2** ÉRIGER : erect **3** ÉDUQUER : bring up (a child) — **s'élever** *vr* **1** : rise (up) **2 ~ à** : amount to — **élevé, -vée** [elve] *adj* **1** : high, elevated **2 bien ~** : well-mannered — **éleveur, -veuse** [elvœr, -vøz] *n* : breeder

éligible [eliʒibl] *adj* : eligible

éliminer [elimine] *vt* : eliminate — **élimination** [eliminasjɔ̃] *nf* : elimination

élire [elir] {51} *vt* : elect

élite [elit] *nf* : elite

elle [ɛl] *pron* **1** : she, it **2** : her **3 elles** *pron pl* : they, them — **elle–même** [ɛlmɛm] *pron* **1** : herself, itself **2 elles–mêmes** *pron pl* : themselves

éloge [elɔʒ] *nm* : eulogy, praise

éloigner [elwaɲe] *vt* **1** ÉCARTER : push aside, move away **2** DÉTOURNER : divert, turn away — **s'éloigner** *vr* : move or go away — **éloigné, -gnée** [elwaɲe] *adj* : distant, remote — **éloignement** [elwaɲmɑ̃] *nm* : distance, remoteness

éloquence [elɔkɑ̃s] *nf* : eloquence — **éloquent, -quente** [elɔkɑ̃, -kɑ̃t] *adj* : eloquent

élu, -lue [ely] *adj* : elected — **~** *n* : elected representative

élucider [elyside] *vt* : elucidate

éluder [elyde] *vt* : elude

émacié, -ciée [emasje] *adj* : emaciated

émail [emaj] *nm, pl* **émaux** [emo] : enamel

émanciper [emɑ̃sipe] *vt* : emancipate — **émancipation** [emɑ̃sipasjɔ̃] *nf* : emancipation

émaner [emane] *vi* **~ de** : emanate from

emballer [ɑ̃bale] *vt* **1** EMPAQUETER : pack, wrap **2** *fam* : thrill — **s'emballer** *vr* **1** : race (of an engine), bolt (of a horse) **2** *fam* : get carried away — **emballage** [ɑ̃balaʒ] *nm* : packing, wrapping

embarcadère [ɑ̃barkadɛr] *nm* : wharf, pier

embarcation [ɑ̃barkasjɔ̃] *nf* : small boat

embardée [ɑ̃barde] *nf* : swerve (of a car)

embargo [ɑ̃bargo] *nm* : embargo

embarquer [ɑ̃barke] *vt* **1** : embark **2** CHARGER : load — *vi* : board — **s'embarquer** *vr* : board — **embarquement** [ɑ̃barkəmɑ̃] *nm* **1** : boarding **2** : loading (on board)

embarrasser [ɑ̃barase] *vt* **1** ENCOMBRER : clutter **2** ENTRAVER : hinder **3** GÊNER : embarrass — **s'embarrasser** *vr* **~ de** : burden oneself with — **embarras** [ɑ̃bara] *nms & pl* **1** : difficulty **2** : embarrassment — **embarrassant, -sante** [ɑ̃barasɑ̃, -sɑ̃t] *adj* **1** : embarrassing, awkward **2** ENCOMBRANT : cumbersome

embaucher [ɑ̃boʃe] *vt* : hire — **embauche** [ɑ̃boʃ] *nf* : hiring, employment

embaumer [ɑ̃bome] *vt* **1** : embalm **2** : scent, make fragrant

embellir [ɑ̃belir] *vt* **1** ENJOLIVER : beautify **2** EXAGÉRER : embellish

embêter [ɑ̃bete] *vt* **1** : annoy, bother **2** LASSER : bore — **s'embêter** *vr* : be bored — **embêtant, -tante** [ɑ̃bɛtɑ̃, -tɑ̃t] *adj* : annoying — **embêtement** [ɑ̃bɛtmɑ̃] *nm* : hassle, bother

emblée [ɑ̃ble] **d'~** *adv phr* : right away

emblème [ɑ̃blɛm] *nm* : emblem

embobiner [ɑ̃bɔbine] *vt fam* : bamboozle, trick

emboîter [ɑ̃bwate] *vt* : fit together — **s'emboîter** *vr* **~ dans** : fit into

embonpoint [ɑ̃bɔ̃pwɛ̃] *nm* : stoutness, corpulence

embouchure [ɑ̃buʃyr] *nf* **1** : mouth (of a river) **2** : mouthpiece

embourber [ɑ̃burbe] *v* **s'embourber** *vr* : get bogged down

embouteillage [ɑ̃butejaʒ] *nm* : traffic jam

emboutir [ɑ̃butir] *vt* HEURTER : crash into, ram

embranchement [ɑ̃brɑ̃ʃmɑ̃] *nm* : junction, fork

embraser [ɑ̃braze] *vt* : set on fire — **s'embraser** *vr* : catch fire

embrasser [ɑ̃brase] *vt* **1** : kiss **2** ÉTREINDRE : embrace, hug — **s'embrasser** *vr* : kiss

embrasure [ɑ̃brazyr] *nf* : doorway

embrayage [ɑ̃brɛjaʒ] *nm* : clutch (of an automobile) — **embrayer** [ɑ̃breje] {11} *vi* : engage the clutch

embrocher [ɑ̃brɔʃe] *vt* : skewer (meat on a spit)

embrouiller [ɑ̃bruje] *vt* **1** : tangle up **2** COMPLIQUER : confuse — **s'embrouiller** *vr* : get mixed up

embryon [ɑ̃brijɔ̃] *nm* : embryo

embûche [ɑ̃byʃ] *nf* : trap, pitfall

embuer [ɑ̃bɥe] *vt* : mist up

embuscade [ɑ̃byskad] *nf* : ambush

éméché, -chée [emeʃe] *adj fam* : tipsy

émeraude [emrod] *nf* : emerald

émerger [emɛrʒe] {17} *vi* : emerge — **émergence** [emɛrʒɑ̃s] *nf* : emergence

émeri [emri] *nm* : emery

émerveiller [emɛrveje] *vt* : amaze — **s'émerveiller** *vr* **~ de** : marvel at — **émerveillement** [emɛrvɛjmɑ̃] *nm* : amazement, wonder

émettre [emɛtr] {53} *vt* **1** : produce, give out **2** : issue (a check) **3** TRANSMETTRE : transmit, broadcast **4** EXPRIMER : express — **émetteur** [emetœr] *nm* **1** : transmitter **2** : issuer

émeute [emøt] *nf* : riot — **émeutier, -tière** [emøtje] *n* : rioter

émietter [emjete] *vt* : crumble, break up — **s'émietter** *vr* : crumble

émigrer [emigre] *vi* **1** : emigrate **2** : migrate — **émigrant, -grante** [emigrɑ̃, -grɑ̃t] *n* : emigrant — **émigration** [emigrasjɔ̃] *nf* : emigration — **émigré, -grée** [emigre] *n* : emigrant, émigré

éminence [eminɑ̃s] *nf* : eminence — **éminent, -nente** [eminɑ̃, -nɑ̃t] *adj* : eminent

émission [emisjɔ̃] *nf* **1** : emission **2** : transmission (of a message) **3** : program, broadcast **4** : issue (of a stamp, etc.)

emmagasiner [ɑ̃magazine] *vt* : store (up)

emmêler [ɑ̃mele] *vt* **1** : tangle **2** EMBROUILLER : muddle, mix up

emménager [ɑ̃menaʒe] {17} *vi* : move in

emmener [ɑ̃mne] {52} *vt* : take

emmitoufler [ɑ̃mitufle] *vt* : wrap up, bundle up — **s'emmitoufler** *vr* : bundle (up)

émoi [emwa] *nm* : excitement, turmoil

émotif, -tive [emɔtif, -tiv] *adj* : emotional — **émotion** [emosjɔ̃] *nf* : emotion — **émotionnel, -nelle** [emosjɔnɛl] *adj* : emotional

émousser [emuse] *vt* : blunt, dull

émouvoir [emuvwar] {56} *vt* : move, affect — **s'émouvoir** *vr* **1** : be moved **2 ~ de** : be concerned about — **émouvant, -vante** [emuvɑ̃, -vɑ̃t] *adj* : moving

empailler [ɑ̃paje] *vt* : stuff

empaqueter [ɑ̃pakte] {8} *vt* : package, wrap up

emparer [ɑ̃pare] *v* **s'emparer** *vr* **~ de** : seize, take hold of

empathie [ɑ̃pati] *nf* : empathy

empêcher [ɑ̃peʃe] *vt* **1** : prevent, stop **2 il n'empêche que** : nevertheless — **s'empêcher** *vr* : refrain, stop oneself — **empêchement** [ɑ̃pɛʃmɑ̃] *nm* : hitch, difficulty

empereur [ɑ̃prœr] *nm* : emperor

empester [ɑ̃pɛste] *vt* : stink up — *vi* : stink

empêtrer [ɑ̃petre] *v* **s'empêtrer** *vr* : become entangled

emphase [ɑ̃faz] *nf* : pomposity

empiéter [ɑ̃pjete] {87} *vi* **~ sur** : infringe on

empiffrer [ɑ̃pifre] *v* **s'empiffrer** *vr fam* : stuff oneself

empiler [ɑ̃pile] *vt* : pile, stack — **s'empiler** *vr* : pile up

empire [ɑ̃pir] *nm* **1** : empire **2 sous l'~ de** : under the influence of

empirer [ɑ̃pire] *v* : worsen

emplacement [ɑ̃plasmɑ̃] *nm* : site, location

emplette [ɑ̃plɛt] *nf* **1** ACHAT : purchase **2 faire ses ~s** : go shopping

emplir [ɑ̃plir] *vt* : fill — **s'emplir** *vr* : fill up

employer [ɑ̃plwaje] {58} *vt* **1** UTILISER : use **2** : employ, provide a job for — **s'employer** *vr* : be used — **emploi** [ɑ̃plwa] *nm* **1** : use **2** TRAVAIL : employment, job **3 ~ du temps** : schedule, timetable — **employé, -ployée** [ɑ̃plwaje] *n* : employee — **employeur, -ployeuse** [ɑ̃plwajœr, -plwajøz] *n* : employer

empocher [ɑ̃pɔʃe] *vt* : pocket

empoigner [ɑ̃pwaɲe] *vt* : grasp, seize

empoisonner [ɑ̃pwazɔne] *vt* : poison — **empoisonnement** [ɑ̃pwazɔnmɑ̃] *nm* : poisoning

emporter [ɑ̃pɔrte] *vt* **1** : take (away) **2** ENTRAÎNER : carry away **3 l'~ sur** : beat, get the better of — **s'emporter** *vr* : lose one's temper

empreinte [ɑ̃prɛ̃t] *nf* **1** : print, imprint **2 ~ digitale** : fingerprint

empresser [ɑ̃prese] *v* **s'empresser** *vr* **1 ~ auprès de** : be attentive toward **2 ~ de** : be in a hurry to — **empressé, -sée** [ɑ̃prese] *adj* : attentive, eager (to please) — **empressement** [ɑ̃prɛsmɑ̃] *nm* **1** : attentiveness **2** : eagerness

emprise [ɑ̃priz] *nf* : influence, hold

emprisonner [ɑ̃prizɔne] *vt* : imprison — **emprisonnement** [ɑ̃prizɔnmɑ̃] *nm* : imprisonment

emprunter [ɑ̃prœ̃te] *vt* **1** : borrow **2** PRENDRE : take, follow — **emprunt** [ɑ̃prœ̃] *nm* : loan

ému, -mue [emy] *adj* : moved, touched

en [ɑ̃] *prep* **1** : in, into **2 aller ~ Belgique** : go to Belgium **3 ~ guerre** : at war **4 ~ vacances** : on vacation **5 ~ voiture** : by car **6 fait ~ plastique** : made of plastic — **~** *pron* **1** (*expressing quantity*) : some, any **2** (*representing a noun governed by* de) : it, them **3 qu'~ ferons-nous?** : what will we do of it? **4 j'~ viens** : I've just come from there

encadrer [ɑ̃kadre] *vt* **1** : frame **2** ENTOURER : surround **3** SURVEILLER : supervise — **encadrement** [ɑ̃kadrəmɑ̃] *nm* : frame

encaisser [ɑ̃kese] *vt* **1** : cash (a check), collect (money) **2** *fam* : take, tolerate

encastrer [ɑ̃kastre] *vt* : embed, build in

enceinte [ɑ̃sɛ̃t] *adj* : pregnant — **~** *nf* **1** : wall, enclosure **2 ~ acoustique** : speaker

encens [ɑ̃sɑ̃] *nm* : incense

encercler [ɑ̃sɛrkle] *vt* : surround, encircle

enchaîner [ɑ̃ʃene] *vt* **1** : chain (up) **2** LIER : link, connect — **s'enchaîner** *vr* : be connected — **enchaînement** [ɑ̃ʃɛnmɑ̃] *nm* **1** SÉRIE : series, sequence **2** LIEN : chain, link

enchanter [ɑ̃ʃɑ̃te] *vt* **1** ENSORCELER : enchant, bewitch **2** RAVIR : delight — **enchanté, -tée** [ɑ̃ʃɑ̃te] *adj* **1** : enchanted **2 ~ de vous connaître** : delighted/pleased to meet you — **enchantement** [ɑ̃ʃɑ̃tmɑ̃] *nm* **1** : enchantment **2** : delight — **enchanteur, -teresse** [ɑʃɑ̃tœr, -trɛs] *adj* : enchanting

enchère [ɑ̃ʃɛr] *nf* **1** : bid, bidding **2 vente aux ~s** : auction

enchevêtrer [ɑ̃ʃəvɛtre] *vt* : tangle — **s'enchevêtrer** *vr* : become tangled

enclencher [ɑ̃klɑ̃ʃe] *vt* : engage (a mechanism) — **s'enclencher** *vr* : engage, interlock

enclin, -cline [ɑ̃klɛ̃, -klin] *adj* **~ à** : inclined to

enclore [ɑ̃klɔr] {34} *vt* : enclose

enclos [ɑ̃klo] *nm* : enclosure

enclume [ɑ̃klym] *nf* : anvil

encoche [ɑ̃kɔʃ] *nf* : notch

encolure [ɑ̃kɔlyr] *nf* : neck (of a dress, etc.)

encombrer [ɑ̃kɔ̃bre] *vt* **1** : clutter (up) **2** OBSTRUER : block, hamper — **s'encombrer** *vr* **~ de** : burden oneself with — **encombrant, -brante** [ɑ̃kɔ̃brɑ̃, -brɑ̃t] *adj* : cumbersome — **encombre** [ɑ̃kɔ̃br] **sans ~** *adv phr* : without a hitch — **encombrement** [ɑ̃kɔ̃brəmɑ̃] *nm* **1** : clutter, congestion **2** EMBOUTEILLAGE : traffic jam

encontre [ɑ̃kɔ̃tr] **à l'~ de** *prep phr* : against, contrary to

encore [ɑ̃kɔr] *adv* **1** TOUJOURS : still **2** : more, again **3 ~ que** : although **4 pas ~** : not yet **5 si ~** : if only

encourager [ɑ̃kuraʒe] {17} *vt* : encourage — **encouragement** [ɑ̃kuraʒmɑ̃] *nm* : encouragement

encourir [ɑ̃kurir] {23} *vt* : incur

encrasser [ɑ̃krase] *vt* **1** SALIR : dirty **2** OBSTRUER : clog up

encre [ɑ̃kr] *nf* : ink — **encrer** [ɑ̃kre] *vt* : ink — **encrier** [ɑ̃krije] *nm* : inkwell

encyclopédie [ɑ̃siklɔpedi] *nf* : encyclopedia

endetter [ɑ̃dete] *v* **s'endetter** *vr* : get into debt

endeuillé, -lée [ɑ̃dœje] *adj* : in mourning, bereaved

endive [ɑ̃div] *nf* : endive, chickory

endoctriner [ɑ̃dɔktrine] *vt* : indoctrinate — **endoctrinement** [ɑ̃dɔktrinmɑ̃] *nm* : indoctrination

endommager [ɑ̃dɔmaʒe] {17} *vt* : damage

endormir [ɑ̃dɔrmir] {30} *vt* : put to sleep — **s'endormir** *vr* : fall asleep — **endormi, -mie** [ɑ̃dɔrmi] *adj* **1** : asleep **2** : sleepy

endosser [ɑ̃dose] *vt* **1** : take on, assume **2** : endorse (a check)

endroit [ɑ̃drwa] *nm* **1** : place, spot **2 à l'~** : right side up

enduire [ɑ̃dɥir] {49} *vt* : coat, cover — **enduit** [ɑ̃dɥi] *nm* : coating

endurance [ɑ̃dyrɑ̃s] *nf* : endurance

endurcir [ɑ̃dyrsir] *vt* : toughen, harden — **s'endurcir** *vr* : harden

endurer [ɑ̃dyre] *vt* : endure

énergie [enɛrʒi] *nf* : energy — **énergique** [enɛrʒik] *adj* : energetic

énerver [enɛrve] *vt* : irritate, annoy — **s'énerver** *vr* : get worked up

enfance [ɑ̃fɑ̃s] *nf* : childhood — **enfant** [ɑ̃fɑ̃] *nmf* : child — **enfanter** [ɑ̃fɑ̃te] *vt* : give birth to — **enfantillage** [ɑ̃fɑ̃tijaʒ] *nm* : childishness — **enfantin, -tine** [ɑ̃fɑ̃tɛ̃, -tin] *adj* **1** : childlike **2** : childish

enfer [ɑ̃fɛr] *nm* : hell

enfermer [ɑ̃fɛrme] *vt* : shut up, lock up — **s'enfermer** *vr* **1** : shut oneself away **2 ~ dans** : retreat into

enfiler [ɑ̃file] *vt* **1** : slip on, put on (a garment) **2** : string, thread (a needle)

enfin [ɑ̃fɛ̃] *adv* **1** : finally, at last **2** : lastly **3 ~, je crois** : at least I think so **4 mais ~, donne-le-moi!** : come on, give it to me!

enflammer [ɑ̃flame] *vt* **1** : ignite, set fire to **2** : inflame (in medicine) — **s'enflammer** *vr* : catch fire

enfler [ɑ̃fle] *v* : swell — **s'enfler** *vr* : swell up — **enflure** [ɑ̃flyr] *nf* : swelling

enfoncer [ɑ̃fɔ̃se] {6} *vt* **1** : drive or push in **2** DÉFONCER : break down — *vi* : sink — **s'enfoncer** *vr* **1** : sink in **2** CÉDER : give way

enfouir [ɑ̃fwir] *vt* **1** : bury **2** CACHER : hide

enfreindre [ɑ̃frɛ̃dr] {37} *vt* : infringe

enfuir [ɑ̃fɥir] {46} v **s'enfuir** vr : flee
engager [ɑ̃gaʒe] {17} vt 1 OBLIGER : bind, commit 2 RECRUTER : hire 3 COMMENCER : start 4 ~ **qqn à** : urge s.o. to 5 ~ **une vitesse** : put a car in gear — **s'engager** vr 1 : commit oneself 2 : enlist (in the army) 3 ~ **dans** : enter, turn into (a street) — **engagé, -gée** [ɑ̃gaʒe] adj 1 : committed 2 Can fam : busy — **engageant, -geante** [ɑ̃gaʒɑ̃, -ʒɑ̃t] adj : engaging — **engagement** [ɑ̃gaʒmɑ̃] nm 1 PROMESSE : commitment 2 PARTICIPATION : involvement
engin [ɑ̃ʒɛ̃] nm : machine, device
engloutir [ɑ̃glutir] vt 1 : gobble up, devour 2 : engulf, swallow up
engorger [ɑ̃gɔrʒe] {17} vt : block, jam up
engouement [ɑ̃gumɑ̃] nm : infatuation
engouffrer [ɑ̃gufre] vt : devour
engourdir [ɑ̃gurdir] vt : numb — **s'engourdir** vr : go numb — **engourdi, -die** [ɑ̃gurdi] adj : numb
engraisser [ɑ̃grese] vt : fatten — vi : put on weight — **engrais** [ɑ̃grɛ] nm : fertilizer, manure
engrenage [ɑ̃grənaʒ] nm : gears pl
engueuler [ɑ̃gœle] vt fam : yell at, bawl out
énième [enjɛm] adj : nth, umpteenth
enivrer [ɑ̃nivre] vr : intoxicate, make drunk — **s'enivrer** vr : get drunk
enjamber [ɑ̃ʒɑ̃be] vt 1 : step over 2 : span — **enjambée** [ɑ̃ʒɑ̃be] nf : stride
enjeu [ɑ̃ʒø] nm, pl **-jeux** : stake (in games)
enjôler [ɑ̃ʒole] vt : cajole, wheedle
enjoliver [ɑ̃ʒɔlive] vt : embellish — **enjoliveur** [ɑ̃ʒɔlivœr] nm : hubcap
enjoué, -jouée [ɑ̃ʒwe] adj : cheerful
enlacer [ɑ̃lase] {6} vt : embrace, hug
enlaidir [ɑ̃ledir] vt : make ugly — vi : grow ugly
enlever [ɑ̃lve] {52} vt 1 : remove, take away 2 KIDNAPPER : abduct — **enlèvement** [ɑ̃lɛvmɑ̃] nm 1 : removal 2 : abduction
enliser [ɑ̃lize] v **s'enliser** vr : sink, get stuck
ennemi, -mie [ɛnmi] n : enemy
ennui [ɑ̃nɥi] nm 1 PROBLÈME : trouble, problem 2 : boredom — **ennuyant, -nuyante** [ɑ̃nɥijɑ̃, ɑ̃nɥijɑ̃t] adj Can 1 : annoying 2 : boring — **ennuyer** [ɑ̃nɥije] {58} vt 1 AGACER : annoy 2 : bore — **s'ennuyer** vr : be bored — **ennuyeux, -nuyeuse** [ɑ̃nɥijø, ɑ̃nɥijøz] adj 1 : annoying 2 : boring
énoncer [enɔ̃se] {6} vt : express, state — **énoncé** [enɔ̃se] nm 1 : statement 2 LIBELLÉ : wording
énorme [enɔrm] adj : enormous, huge — **énormément** [enɔrmemɑ̃] adv ~ **de** : a great number of
enquête [ɑ̃kɛt] nf 1 INVESTIGATION : investigation, inquiry 2 SONDAGE : survey — **enquêter** [ɑ̃kete] vi : investigate
enraciner [ɑ̃rasine] vt : root — **s'enraciner** vr : take root
enrager [ɑ̃raʒe] {17} vi : be furious — **enragé, -gée** [ɑ̃raʒe] adj 1 : rabid (of an animal) 2 : furious (of a person)
enrayer [ɑ̃reje] {11} vt 1 : check, curb 2 BLOQUER : jam
enregistrer [ɑ̃rəʒistre] vt 1 : record 2 INSCRIRE : register 3 : check in (baggage) — **enregistrement** [ɑ̃rəʒistrəmɑ̃] nm 1 : registration 2 : (tape) recording
enrhumer [ɑ̃ryme] v **s'enrhumer** vr : catch a cold
enrichir [ɑ̃riʃir] vt : enrich — **s'enrichir** vr : grow rich — **enrichissement** [ɑ̃riʃismɑ̃] nm : enrichment
enrober [ɑ̃rɔbe] vt : coat
enrôler [ɑ̃role] vt : enroll, enlist — **s'enrôler** vr : enlist
enroué, -rouée [ɑ̃rwe] adj : hoarse
enrouler [ɑ̃rule] vt : wind, coil — **s'enrouler** vr ~ **dans** : wrap oneself in (a blanket)
ensanglanté, -tée [ɑ̃sɑ̃glɑ̃te] adj : bloody, bloodstained
enseignant, -gnante [ɑ̃sɛɲɑ̃, -ɲɑ̃t] adj : teaching — ~ n : teacher
enseigne [ɑ̃sɛɲ] nf : sign
enseigner [ɑ̃seɲe] v : to teach — **enseignement** [ɑ̃sɛɲmɑ̃] nm 1 : teaching 2 : education
ensemble [ɑ̃sɑ̃bl] adv : together — ~ nm 1 : group, set 2 TOTALITÉ : whole 3 : (musical) ensemble 4 : suit, outfit 5 **dans l'~** : on the whole
ensemencer [ɑ̃səmɑ̃se] {6} vt : sow
ensoleillé, -lée [ɑ̃sɔleje] adj : sunny
ensorceler [ɑ̃sɔrsəle] {8} vt : bewitch, charm
ensuite [ɑ̃sɥit] adv 1 : then, next 2 : afterwards, later
ensuivre [ɑ̃sɥivr] {35} v **s'ensuivre** vr : ensue, follow
entailler [ɑ̃taje] vt : gash, cut — **entaille** [ɑ̃taj] nf 1 : cut, gash 2 ENCOCHE : notch
entamer [ɑ̃tame] vt 1 : cut into, eat into 2 : start, enter into (negotiations)
entasser [ɑ̃tase] vt 1 : pile (up) 2 SERRER : cram — **s'entasser** vr : pile up
entendre [ɑ̃tɑ̃dr] {63} vt 1 : hear 2 COMPRENDRE : understand 3 VOULOIR : intend — **s'entendre** vr 1 : agree 2 ~ **avec** : get along with — **entendement** [ɑ̃tɑ̃dmɑ̃] nm : understanding — **entendu, -due** [ɑ̃tɑ̃dy] adj 1 : agreed, understood 2 **bien ~** : of course — **entente** [ɑ̃tɑ̃t] nf 1 : harmony 2 ACCORD : agreement, understanding
entériner [ɑ̃terine] vt : ratify
enterrer [ɑ̃tere] vt : bury — **enterrement** [ɑ̃tɛrmɑ̃] nm 1 : burial 2 FUNÉRAILLES : funeral
en–tête [ɑ̃tɛt] nm, pl **en–têtes** : heading
entêter [ɑ̃tete] v **s'entêter** vr : be obstinate, persist — **entêté, -tée** [ɑ̃tete] adj : stubborn, obstinate — **entêtement** [ɑ̃tɛtmɑ̃] nm : stubbornness
enthousiasme [ɑ̃tuzjasm] nm : enthusiasm — **enthousiasmer** [ɑ̃tuzjasme] vt : fill with enthusiasm, excite — **enthousiaste** [ɑ̃tuzjast] adj : enthusiastic — ~ nmf : enthusiast, fan
entier, -tière [ɑ̃tje, -tjɛr] adj : entire, whole — **entier** nm **en ~** : totally, in its entirety — **entièrement** [ɑ̃tjɛrmɑ̃] adv : entirely, wholly
entité [ɑ̃tite] nf : entity
entonnoir [ɑ̃tɔnwar] nm : funnel (utensil)
entorse [ɑ̃tɔrs] nf : sprain
entortiller [ɑ̃tɔrtije] vt : twist, wind
entourer [ɑ̃ture] vt : surround — **entourage** [ɑ̃turaʒ] nm : circle (of friends or family)
entracte [ɑ̃trakt] nm : intermission
entraide [ɑ̃trɛd] nf : mutual aid
entrailles [ɑ̃traj] nfpl 1 : entrails 2 PROFONDEURS : depths
entrain [ɑ̃trɛ̃] nm : liveliness, spirit
entraîner [ɑ̃trene] vt 1 EMPORTER : carry away 2 OCCASIONNER : lead to, involve 3 FORMER : train, coach — **s'entraîner** vr : train, practice — **entraînant, -nante** [ɑ̃trɛnɑ̃, -nɑ̃t] adj : lively — **entraînement** [ɑ̃trɛnmɑ̃] nm 1 : training, coaching 2 PRATIQUE : practice — **entraîneur, -neuse** [ɑ̃trɛnœr, -nøz] n : trainer, coach
entraver [ɑ̃trave] vt : hinder — **entrave** [ɑ̃trav] nf : hindrance
entre [ɑ̃tr] prep 1 : between 2 PARMI : among
entrecôte [ɑ̃trəkot] nf : rib steak
entrecroiser [ɑ̃trəkrwaze] v **s'entrecroiser** vr : intersect
entrée [ɑ̃tre] nf 1 : entrance, entry 2 ACCÈS : admission 3 BILLET : ticket 4 : first course (of a meal) 5 : entry (in a text), input (of information)
entre–jambes [ɑ̃trəʒɑ̃b] nms & pl : crotch (of clothing)
entrelacer [ɑ̃trəlase] {6} vt : intertwine
entremêler [ɑ̃trəmele] vt : mix together
entremets [ɑ̃trəmɛ] nms & pl : dessert
entreposer [ɑ̃trəpoze] vt : store — **entrepôt** [ɑ̃trəpo] nm : warehouse
entreprendre [ɑ̃trəprɑ̃dr] {70} vt : undertake, start — **entreprenant, -nante** [ɑ̃trəprənɑ̃, -nɑ̃t] adj : enterprising — **entrepreneur, -neuse** [ɑ̃trəprənœr, -nøz] n : contractor — **entreprise** [ɑ̃trəpriz] nf 1 : enterprise, undertaking 2 : business, firm
entrer [ɑ̃tre] vi 1 : enter, go in, come in 2 **ça n'entre pas** : it doesn't fit 3 ~ **dans** : join, go into — vt 1 : bring in, take in 2 : enter, input (data, etc.)
entre–temps [ɑ̃trətɑ̃] adv : meanwhile
entretenir [ɑ̃trətnir] {92} vt 1 MAINTENIR : maintain 2 ~ **qqn de** : speak to s.o. about — **s'entretenir** vr 1 ~ **avec** : consult with, converse with 2 ~ **de** : discuss, talk about — **entretenu, -nue** [ɑ̃trətny] adj : kept, maintained — **entretien** [ɑ̃trətjɛ̃] nm 1 : maintenance 2 CONVERSATION : talk, interview
entrevoir [ɑ̃trəvwar] {99} vt 1 : glimpse, make out 2 PRÉSAGER : foresee, anticipate — **entrevue** [ɑ̃trəvy] nf : meeting, interview
entrouvert, -verte [ɑ̃truvɛr, -vɛrt] adj & adv : half open, ajar
énumérer [enymere] {87} vt : enumerate — **énumération** [-merasjɔ̃] nf : enumeration
envahir [ɑ̃vair] vt 1 : invade 2 : overcome (fear, etc.)
envelopper [ɑ̃vlɔpe] vt 1 : envelop 2 RECOUVRIR : wrap up, cover — **enveloppe** [ɑ̃vlɔp] nf : envelope
envergure [ɑ̃vɛrgyr] nf 1 : wingspan 2 IMPORTANCE : breadth, scope
envers [ɑ̃vɛr] prep : toward, to — ~ nm 1 REVERS : back, reverse 2 **à l'~** : inside out, upside down, backward
envie [ɑ̃vi] nf 1 : envy 2 DÉSIR : desire, wish — **envier** [ɑ̃vje] {96} vt : envy — **envieux, -vieuse** [ɑ̃vjø, -vjøz] adj : envious
environ [ɑ̃virɔ̃] adv : about, approximately — **environnement** [ɑ̃virɔnmɑ̃] nm : environment, surroundings — **environnant, -nante** [ɑ̃virɔnɑ̃, -nɑ̃t] adj : surrounding — **environs** [ɑ̃virɔ̃] nmpl 1 : surroundings 2 **aux ~ de** : around, about
envisager [ɑ̃vizaʒe] {17} vt : consider, imagine
envoi [ɑ̃vwa] nm 1 : sending, dispatching 2 COLIS : parcel, package
envoler [ɑ̃vɔle] v **s'envoler** vr 1 : take off (of a plane) 2 : fly away (of a bird) — **envol** [ɑ̃vɔl] nm : takeoff — **envolée** [ɑ̃vɔle] nf 1 : flight 2 AUGMENTATION : rise, surge
envoyer [ɑ̃vwaje] {36} vt 1 : send (out) 2 LANCER : throw 3 ~ **par la poste** : mail — **envoyé, -voyée** [ɑ̃vwaje] n : envoy
enzyme [ɑ̃zim] nf : enzyme
épagneul, -gneule [epaɲœl] n : spaniel
épais, -paisse [epɛ, -pɛs] adj : thick — **épaisseur** [epɛsœr] nf 1 : thickness 2 : layer —**épaissir** [epesir] v **s'épaissir** vr : thicken
épancher [epɑ̃ʃe] vt : give vent to — **s'épancher** vr : pour one's heart out
épanouir [epanwir] v **s'épanouir** vr 1 : bloom 2 S'ÉCLAIRER : light up 3 SE DÉVELOPPER : develop, flourish — **épanouissement** [epanwismɑ̃] nm : blossoming
épargner [eparɲe] vt 1 ÉCONOMISER : save 2 : spare (s.o.'s life, etc.) — **s'épargner** vr : spare oneself — **épargne** [eparɲ] nf 1 : saving 2 : savings pl
éparpiller [eparpije] vt : scatter, disperse — **s'éparpiller** vr : dissipate — **épars, -parse** [epar, -pars] adj : scattered
épater [epate] vt fam : amaze — **épatant, -tante** [epatɑ̃, -tɑ̃t] adj fam : amazing
épaule [epol] nf : shoulder — **épaulette** [epolɛt] nf : shoulder strap
épave [epav] nf : wreck (of a ship)
épée [epe] nf : sword
épeler [eple] {8} vt : spell
éperdu, -due [epɛrdy] adj 1 : intense, passionate 2 ~ **de peur** : overcome with fear — **éperdument** [epɛrdymɑ̃] adv : frantically, desperately
éperon [eprɔ̃] nm : spur — **éperonner** [eprɔne] vt : spur (on)
éphémère [efemɛr] adj : ephemeral
épi [epi] nm 1 : ear, cob 2 : tuft (of hair)
épice [epis] nf : spice — **épicé, -cée** [epise] adj : spicy — **épicer** [epise] {6} vt : spice — **épicerie** [episri] nf 1 : grocery store 2 **~s** nfpl : groceries pl — **épicier, -cière** [episje, -sjɛr] n : grocer
épidémie [epidemi] nf : epidemic — **épidémique** [-demik] adj : epidemic
épiderme [epidɛrm] nm : skin
épier [epje] {96} vt 1 : spy on 2 ATTENDRE : watch out for
épilepsie [epilɛpsi] nf : epilepsy — **épileptique** [epilɛptik] adj & nmf : epileptic
épiler [epile] vt : remove hair from, pluck
épilogue [epilɔg] nm 1 : epilogue 2 : conclusion, outcome
épinards [epinar] nmpl : spinach
épine [epin] nf 1 : thorn 2 ~ **dorsale** : spine, backbone — **épineux, -neuse** [epinø, -nøz] adj : thorny
épingle [epɛ̃gl] nf 1 : pin 2 ~ **à cheveux** : hairpin 3 ~ **de sûreté** : safety pin
épique [epik] adj : epic
épisode [epizɔd] nm : episode
épitaphe [epitaf] nf : epitaph
épithète [epitɛt] nf : epithet
éplucher [eplyʃe] vt 1 PELER : peel 2 EXAMINER : scrutinize
éponge [epɔ̃ʒ] nf : sponge — **éponger** [epɔ̃ʒe] {17} vt : sponge up, mop up
épopée [epɔpe] nf : epic
époque [epɔk] nf 1 : age, era 2 : time, period
épouse [epuz] nf → **époux** — **épouser** [epuze] vt : marry, wed
épousseter [epuste] {8} vt : dust
époustouflant, -flante [epustuflɑ̃, -flɑ̃t] adj fam : amazing
épouvantable [epuvɑ̃tabl] adj : dreadful, horrible
épouvantail [epuvɑ̃taj] nm : scarecrow
épouvanter [epuvɑ̃te] vt : terrify — **épouvante** [epuvɑ̃t] nf : horror
époux, -pouse [epu, -puz] n : spouse, husband m, wife f
éprendre [eprɑ̃dr] {70} v **s'éprendre** vr **de** : fall in love with
épreuve [eprœv] nf 1 ESSAI : test 2 : ordeal, trial 3 : event (in sports) 4 : proof, print (in printing)
éprouver [epruve] vt 1 : test, try 2 RESSENTIR : feel, experience 3 AFFECTER : distress
épuiser [epɥize] vt : exhaust — **épuisé, -sée** [epɥize] adj 1 : exhausted 2 : out of stock — **épuisement** [epɥizmɑ̃] nm : exhaustion
épurer [epyre] vt 1 : purify, refine 2 : purge (in politics) — **épuration** [epyrasjɔ̃] nf 1 : purification 2 : purge
équateur [ekwatœr] nm : equator
équation [ekwasjɔ̃] nf : equation
équerre [ekɛr] nf 1 : square 2 **d'~** : square, straight
équestre [ekɛstr] adj : equestrian
équilibre [ekilibr] nm : equilibrium, balance — **équilibré, -brée** [ekilibre] adj : well-balanced — **équilibrer** [ekilibre] vt : balance
équinoxe [ekinɔks] nm : equinox
équipage [ekipaʒ] nm : crew
équiper [ekipe] vt : equip, outfit — **équipe** [ekip] nf : team — **équipement** [ekipmɑ̃] nm : equipment — **équipier, -pière** [ekipje, -pjɛr] n : team member
équitable [ekitabl] adj : fair, equitable — **équitablement** [-tabləmɑ̃] adv : fairly
équitation [ekitasjɔ̃] nf : horseback riding
équité [ekite] nf : equity, fairness
équivalence [ekivalɑ̃s] nf : equivalence — **équivalent, -lente** [ekivalɑ̃, -lɑ̃t] adj : equivalent — **équivalent** nm : equivalent — **équivaloir** [ekivalwar] {95} vi ~ **à** : be equivalent to
équivoque [ekivɔk] adj 1 : equivocal, ambiguous 2 DOUTEUX : questionable
érable [erabl] nm : maple
éradiquer [eradike] vt : eradicate
érafler [erafle] vt : scratch — **éraflure** [eraflyr] nf : scratch, scrape
ère [ɛr] nf : era
érection [erɛksjɔ̃] nf : erection
éreinter [erɛ̃te] vt 1 ÉPUISER : exhaust 2 CRITIQUER : criticize — **s'éreinter** vr : wear oneself out — **éreintant, -tante** [erɛ̃tɑ̃, -tɑ̃t] adj : exhausting
ergoter [ɛrgɔte] vi : quibble
ériger [eriʒe] {17} vt : erect — **s'ériger** vr ~ **en** : set oneself up as
ermite [ɛrmit] nm : hermit
éroder [erɔde] vt : erode — **érosion** [erozjɔ̃] nf : erosion
érotique [erɔtik] adj : erotic — **érotisme** [erɔtism] nm : eroticism
errer [ɛre] vi : wander, roam — **erreur** [ɛrœr] nf : error, mistake — **erroné, -née** [ɛrɔne] adj : erroneous
érudit, -dite [erydi, -dit] adj : scholarly — ~ n : scholar — **érudition** [erydisjɔ̃] nf : learning, scholarship
éruption [erypsjɔ̃] nf 1 : eruption 2 : rash (in medicine)
escabeau [ɛskabo] nm, pl **-beaux** 1 : stool 2 ÉCHELLE : stepladder
escadre [ɛskadr] nf : squadron — **escadrille** [ɛskadrij] nf : squadron — **escadron** [ɛskadrɔ̃] nm : squadron, squad
escalader [ɛskalade] vt : climb — **escalade** [ɛskalad] nf : (rock) climbing
escale [ɛskal] nf : stopover
escalier [ɛskalje] nm 1 : stairs pl, steps pl 2 ~ **de secours** : fire escape 3 ~ **mécanique** : escalator
escalope [ɛskalɔp] nf : cutlet
escamoter [ɛskamɔte] vt 1 : fold away, retract 2 ÉVITER : evade — **escamotable** [ɛskamɔtabl] adj : retractable, foldaway
escargot [ɛskargo] nm : snail
escarmouche [ɛskarmuʃ] nf : skirmish
escarpé, -pée [ɛskarpe] adj : steep
esclaffer [ɛsklafe] v **s'esclaffer** vr : burst out laughing
esclave [ɛsklav] adj & nmf : slave — **esclavage** [ɛsklavaʒ] nm : slavery
escompter [ɛskɔ̃te] vt 1 : discount 2 ESPÉRER : count on, expect — **escompte** [ɛskɔ̃t] nm : discount
escorter [ɛskɔrte] vt : escort — **escorte** [ɛskɔrt] nf : escort
escrime [ɛskrim] nf : fencing
escroc [ɛskro] nm : swindler, crook — **escroquer** [ɛskrɔke] vt : swindle, defraud — **escroquerie** [ɛskrɔkri] nf : swindle, fraud
eskimo [ɛskimo] → **esquimau**
ésotérique [ezɔterik] adj : esoteric
espace [ɛspas] nm : space — **espacer** [ɛspase] {6} vt : space (out)
espadon [ɛspadɔ̃] nm : swordfish
espadrilles [ɛspadrij] nfpl Can : sneakers pl
espagnol, -gnole [ɛspaɲɔl] adj : Spanish — **espagnol** nm : Spanish (language)
espèce [ɛspɛs] nf 1 : species 2 SORTE : sort, kind 3 **~s** nfpl : cash
espérer [ɛspere] {87} vt 1 : hope for 2 ESCOMPTER : expect — **espérance** [ɛsperɑ̃s] nf : hope
espiègle [ɛspjɛgl] adj : mischievous
espion, -pionne [ɛspjɔ̃, -pjɔn] n : spy — **espionnage** [ɛspjɔnaʒ] nm : espionage — **espionner** [ɛspjɔne] vt : spy on
espoir [ɛspwar] nm : hope
esprit [ɛspri] nm 1 : mind 2 ATTITUDE : spirit 3 HUMOUR : wit 4 FANTÔME : ghost
esquimau, -maude [ɛskimo, -mod] adj, mpl **-maux** [-mo] : Eskimo
esquisse [ɛskis] nf : sketch — **esquisser** [ɛskise] vt : sketch
esquiver [ɛskive] vt : avoid, dodge — **esquive** [ɛskiv] nf : dodge
essai [esɛ] nm 1 TENTATIVE : attempt, try 2 ÉPREUVE : trial, test 3 : (literary) essay
essaim [esɛ̃] nm : swarm
essayer [eseje] {11} vt : try
essence [esɑ̃s] nf : gasoline — **essentiel, -tielle** [esɑ̃sjɛl] adj : essential — **essentiel** nm : main part, essentials pl — **essentiellement** [-sjɛlmɑ̃] adv : essentially
essieu [esjø] nm, pl **-sieux** : axle
essor [esɔr] nm 1 : flight (of a bird) 2 : expansion, growth
essouffler [esufle] vt : make breathless — **s'essouffler** vr : get out of breath
essuyer [esɥije] {58} vt 1 : wipe, dry 2 SUBIR : suffer, endure — **essuie–glace** [esɥiglas] nm, pl **essuie–glaces** : windshield wiper — **essuie–mains** [esɥimɛ̃] nms & pl : hand towel — **essuie–tout** [esɥitu] nms & pl : paper towel
est [ɛst] adj : east, eastern — ~ nm 1 : east 2 **l'Est** : the East

estampe [ɛstɑ̃p] *nf* : engraving, print — **estampille** [ɛstɑ̃pij] *nf* : stamp

esthétique [ɛstetik] *adj* : aesthetic — **esthéticien, -cienne** [ɛstetisjɛ̃, -sjɛn] *n* : beautician

estimer [ɛstime] *vt* **1** : assess, evaluate **2** CALCULER : estimate **3** RESPECTER : esteem **4** CONSIDÉRER : consider — **estimation** [ɛstimasjɔ̃] *nf* : estimate — **estime** [ɛstim] *nf* : esteem, respect

estival, -vale [ɛstival] *adj, mpl* **-vaux** [-vo] : summer

estomac [ɛstɔma] *nm* : stomach

estrade [ɛstrad] *nf* : platform, stage

estragon [ɛstragɔ̃] *nm* : tarragon

estropié, -piée [ɛstrɔpje] *adj* : crippled, maimed

estuaire [ɛstɥɛr] *nm* : estuary

esturgeon [ɛstyrʒɔ̃] *nm* : sturgeon

et [e] *conj* : and

étable [etabl] *nf* : cowshed

établi [etabli] *nm* : workbench

établir [etablir] *vt* **1** : establish, set up **2** : draw up (a list, etc.) — **s'établir** *vr* : become established, get set up — **établissement** [etablismɑ̃] *nm* : establishment

étage [etaʒ] *nm* **1** : story, floor **2** : tier, level — **étagère** [etaʒɛr] *nf* : shelf, bookshelf

étai [etɛ] *nm* : prop, support

étain [etɛ̃] *nm* **1** : tin **2** : pewter

étaler [etale] *vt* **1** : display **2** ÉTENDRE : spread (out) **3** ÉCHELONNER : space out, stagger — **s'étaler** *vr* **1** S'ÉTENDRE : spread out **2** *fam* : fall flat, sprawl — **étalage** [etalaʒ] *nm* **1** : display **2** DEVANTURE : shopwindow **3 faire ~ de** : flaunt

étalon [etalɔ̃] *nm* **1** : stallion **2** MODÈLE : standard

étancher [etɑ̃ʃe] *vt* **1** : stem, staunch **2** : quench (thirst) — **étanche** [etɑ̃ʃ] *adj* : watertight, waterproof

étang [etɑ̃] *nm* : pond

étape [etap] *nf* **1** ARRÊT : stop, halt **2** : stage (of development)

état [eta] *nm* **1** : state, condition **2** : statement (of expenses, etc.) **3** : (social) status **4** MÉTIER : profession, trade

étau [eto] *nm, pl* **-taux** : vise

étayer [eteje] {11} *vt* : prop up

été [ete] *nm* : summer

éteindre [etɛ̃dr] {37} *vt* **1** : put out, extinguish **2** : turn off, switch off — **s'éteindre** *vr* **1** : go out, die out **2** MOURIR : die

étendard [etɑ̃dar] *nm* : standard, flag

étendre [etɑ̃dr] {63} *vt* **1** ÉTALER : spread (out) **2** : hang up (laundry) **3** ALLONGER : stretch (out) **4** ACCROÎTRE : extend — **s'étendre** *vr* **1** : stretch **2** SE COUCHER : lie down **3** CROÎTRE : spread — **étendu, -due** [etɑ̃dy] *adj* : extensive, wide — **étendue** *nf* **1** : area **2** : extent

éternel, -nelle [etɛrnɛl] *adj* : eternal — **éternellement** [-nɛlmɑ̃] *adv* : eternally, forever — **éternité** [etɛrnite] *nf* : eternity

éternuer [etɛrnɥe] *vi* : sneeze — **éternuement** [etɛrnymɑ̃] *nm* : sneeze

éther [etɛr] *nm* : ether

éthique [etik] *adj* : ethical — **~** *nf* : ethics

ethnique [ɛtnik] *adj* : ethnic

étincelle [etɛ̃sɛl] *nf* : spark — **étinceler** [etɛ̃sle] {8} *vi* : sparkle

étiquette [etikɛt] *nf* **1** : label **2** PROTOCOLE : etiquette — **étiqueter** [etikte] {8} *vt* : label

étirer [etire] *vt* : stretch — **s'étirer** *vr* : stretch (out)

étoffe [etɔf] *nf* : material, fabric

étoile [etwal] *nf* : star — **étoilé, -lée** [etwale] *adj* : starry

étonner [etɔne] *vt* : astonish — **s'étonner** *vr* : be surprised — **étonnant, -nante** [etɔnɑ̃, -nɑ̃t] *adj* : astonishing — **étonnement** [etɔnmɑ̃] *nm* : surprise, astonishment

étouffer [etufe] *vt* **1** : stifle **2** ASPHYXIER : smother **3** : deaden (sound, etc.) — **s'étouffer** *vr* **1** : choke **2** : suffocate

étourderie [eturdəri] *nf* : thoughtlessness

étourdir [eturdir] *vt* **1** ASSOMMER : stun **2** : make dizzy — **étourdi, -die** [eturdi] *adj* : absentminded, scatterbrained — **étourdissant, -sante** [eturdisɑ̃, -sɑ̃t] *adj* **1** BRUYANT : deafening **2** : stunning — **étourdissement** [eturdismɑ̃] *nm* VERTIGE : dizziness

étourneau [eturno] *nm, pl* **-neaux** [-no] : starling

étrange [etrɑ̃ʒ] *adj* : strange — **étrangement** [etrɑ̃ʒmɑ̃] *adv* : oddly, strangely — **étrangeté** [etrɑ̃ʒte] *nf* : strangeness, oddity — **étranger, -gère** [etrɑ̃ʒe, -ʒɛr] *adj* **1** : foreign (of a country, etc.) **2** : unfamiliar, strange — **~** *n* **1** : foreigner **2** : stranger **3 à l'étranger** : abroad

étrangler [etrɑ̃gle] *vt* **1** : strangle **2** SERRER : constrict — **s'étrangler** *vr* : choke

être [ɛtr] {38} *vi* **1** : be, exist **2 ~ à** : belong to — *v aux* : have — **~** *nm* **1** : being **2** PERSONNE : person

étreindre [etrɛ̃dr] {37} *vt* **1** : embrace, hug **2** SERRER : grip — **étreinte** [etrɛ̃t] *nf* **1** : embrace, hug **2 sous l'~ de** : in the grip of

étrenner [etrene] *vt* : use for the first time

étrier [etrije] *nm* : stirrup

étriqué, -quée [etrike] *adj* **1** : skimpy **2** MESQUIN : petty

étroit, -troite [etrwa, -trwat] *adj* **1** : narrow **2** SERRÉ : tight — **étroitesse** [etrwatɛs] *nf* : narrowness

étude [etyd] *nf* **1** : study, studying **2** BUREAU : office — **étudiant, -diante** [etydjɑ̃, -djɑ̃t] *adj & n* : student — **étudier** [etydje] {96} *v* : study

étui [etɥi] *nm* : case

euphémisme [øfemism] *nm* : euphemism

euphorie [øfɔri] *nf* : euphoria

euro [øro] *nm* : euro (monetary unit)

européen, -péenne [ørɔpeɛ̃, -peɛn] *adj* : European

eux [ø] *pron* : they, them — **eux–mêmes** [ømɛm] *pron pl* : themselves

évacuer [evakɥe] *vt* : evacuate — **évacuation** [evakɥasjɔ̃] *nf* : evacuation

évader [evade] *v* **s'évader** *vr* : escape — **évadé, -dée** [evade] *n* : fugitive

évaluer [evalɥe] *vt* : evaluate, assess — **évaluation** [evalɥasjɔ̃] *nf* : evaluation, assessment

évangile [evɑ̃ʒil] *nm* **1** : gospel **2 l'Évangile** : the Gospel

évanouir [evanwir] *v* **s'évanouir** *vr* : faint — **évanouissement** [evanwismɑ̃] *nm* : fainting, faint

évaporer [evapɔre] *v* **s'évaporer** *vr* : evaporate — **évaporation** [evapɔrasjɔ̃] *nf* : evaporation

évasif, -sive [evazif,-ziv] *adj* : evasive — **évasion** [evazjɔ̃] *nf* : escape

éveiller [eveje] *vt* **1** RÉVEILLER : awaken **2** : arouse (curiosity, etc.) — **s'éveiller** *vr* **1** : wake up **2** : be aroused — **éveil** [evɛj] *nm* **1** : awakening **2 en ~** : on the alert — **éveillé, -lée** [eveje] *adj* **1** : awake **2** ALERTE : alert

événement [evɛnmɑ̃] *nm* : event

éventail [evɑ̃taj] *nm* **1** : fan **2** GAMME : range, spread

éventaire [evɑ̃tɛr] *nm* : stall, stand

éventé, -tée [evɑ̃te] *adj* : stale, flat

éventrer [evɑ̃tre] *vt* : tear open

éventualité [evɑ̃tɥalite] *nf* : eventuality, possibility — **éventuel, -tuelle** [evɑ̃tɥɛl] *adj* : possible — **éventuellement** [-tɥɛlmɑ̃] *adv* : possibly

évêque [evɛk] *nm* : bishop

évertuer [evɛrtɥe] *v* **s'évertuer** *vr* : strive, do one's best

éviction [eviksjɔ̃] *nf* : eviction

évidemment [evidamɑ̃] *adv* : obviously, of course

évidence [evidɑ̃s] *nf* : obviousness — **évident, -dente** [evidɑ̃, -dɑ̃t] *adj* : obvious, evident

évider [evide] *vt* : hollow out

évier [evje] *nm* : sink

évincer [evɛ̃se] {6} *vt* : oust

éviter [evite] *vt* **1** : avoid **2 ~ à qqn de faire qqch** : save s.o. from (doing) sth

évoluer [evɔlɥe] *vi* **1** : evolve, develop **2** SE DÉPLACER : maneuver, move about — **évolution** [evɔlysjɔ̃] *nf* **1** : evolution **2** CHANGEMENT : development, change

évoquer [evɔke] *vt* : evoke, call to mind

exacerber [ɛgzasɛrbe] *vt* : exacerbate

exact, exacte [ɛgzakt] *adj* **1** : exact **2** JUSTE : correct **3** PONCTUEL : punctual — **exactement** [ɛgzaktəmɑ̃] *adv* : exactly — **exactitude** [ɛgzaktityd] *nf* **1** : accuracy **2** PONCTUALITÉ : punctuality

ex aequo [ɛgzeko] *adv* : equal

exagérer [ɛgzaʒere] {87} *vt* : exaggerate — *vi* : go too far, overdo it — **exagération** [ɛgzaʒerasjɔ̃] *nf* : exaggeration — **exagéré, -rée** [ɛgzaʒere] *adj* : exaggerated, excessive

exalter [ɛgzalte] *vt* **1** : excite, stir **2** GLORIFIER : exalt — **s'exalter** *vr* : get excited

examiner [ɛgzamine] *vt* : examine — **examen** [ɛgzamɛ̃] *nm* : examination

exaspérer [ɛgzaspere] {87} *vt* : exasperate — **exaspération** [ɛgzasperasjɔ̃] *nf* : exasperation

exaucer [ɛgzose] {6} *vt* : grant

excaver [ɛkskave] *vt* : excavate — **excavation** [ɛkskavasjɔ̃] *nf* : excavation

excéder [ɛksede] {87} *vt* **1** : exceed **2** EXASPÉRER : exasperate — **excédent** [ɛksedɑ̃] *nm* : surplus, excess — **excédentaire** [ɛksedɑ̃tɛr] *adj* : surplus, excess

exceller [ɛksele] *vi* : excel — **excellence** [ɛkselɑ̃s] *nf* : excellence — **excellent, -lente** [ɛkselɑ̃, -lɑ̃t] *adj* : excellent

excentrique [ɛksɑ̃trik] *adj & nmf* : eccentric — **excentricité** [ɛksɑ̃trisite] *nf* : eccentricity

excepter [ɛksɛpte] *vt* : except, exclude — **excepté** [ɛksɛpte] *prep* SAUF : except, apart from — **exception** [ɛksɛpsjɔ̃] *nf* **1** : exception **2 à l'~ de** : except for — **exceptionnel, -nelle** [ɛksɛpsjɔnɛl] *adj* : exceptional

excès [ɛksɛ] *nm* **1** : excess **2 ~ de vitesse** : speeding — **excessif, -sive** [ɛksɛsif, -siv] *adj* : excessive

exciter [ɛksite] *vt* **1** : excite **2** STIMULER : stimulate — **s'exciter** *vr* : get excited — **excitant, -tante** [ɛksitɑ̃, -tɑ̃t] *adj* : exciting — **excitation** [ɛksitasjɔ̃] *nf* : excitement

exclamer [ɛksklame] *v* **s'exclamer** *vr* : exclaim — **exclamation** [ɛksklamasjɔ̃] *nf* : exclamation

exclure [ɛksklyr] {39} *vt* **1** : exclude **2** EXPULSER : expel — **exclusif, -sive** [ɛksklyzif, -ziv] *adj* : exclusive — **exclusivement** [-sivmɑ̃] *adv* : exclusively — **exclusion** [ɛksklyzjɔ̃] *nf* **1** : exclusion **2** EXPULSION : expulsion — **exclusivité** [ɛksklyzivite] *nf* **1** : exclusive rights *pl* **2 en ~** : exclusively

excréments [ɛkskremɑ̃] *nmpl* : excrement, feces

excroissance [ɛkskrwasɑ̃s] *nf* : outgrowth

excursion [ɛkskyrsjɔ̃] *nf* : excursion, trip

excuser [ɛkskyze] *vt* : excuse — **s'excuser** *vr* : apologize — **excuse** [ɛkskyz] *nf* **1** : excuse **2 ~s** *nfpl* : apology

exécrer [ɛgzekre] {87} *vt* : abhor, loathe — **exécrable** [ɛgzekrabl] *adj* : atrocious, awful

exécuter [ɛgzekyte] *vt* **1** : execute **2** EFFECTUER : perform — **s'exécuter** *vr* : comply — **exécutant, -tante** [ɛgzekytɑ̃, -tɑ̃t] *n* : performer — **exécutif, -tive** [ɛgzekytif, -tiv] *adj* : executive — **exécution** [ɛgzekysjɔ̃] *nf* : execution

exemple [ɛgzɑ̃pl] *nm* **1** : example **2 par ~** : for example, for instance — **exemplaire** [ɛgzɑ̃plɛr] *adj* : exemplary — **~** *nm* **1** : copy **2** : specimen, example

exempt, exempte [ɛgzɑ̃, ɛgzɑ̃t] *adj* : exempt — **exempter** [ɛgzɑ̃te] *vt* : exempt — **exemption** [ɛgzɑ̃psjɔ̃] *nf* : exemption

exercer [ɛgzɛrse] {6} *vt* **1** : exercise, train **2** : exert (control, influence, etc.) **3** : practice (a profession) — **s'exercer** *vr* : practice — **exercice** [ɛgzɛrsis] *nm* **1** : exercise **2 en ~** : in office

exhaler [ɛgzale] *vt* **1** : exhale **2** ÉMETTRE : utter, breathe

exhaustif, -tive [ɛgzostif, -tiv] *adj* : exhaustive

exhiber [ɛgzibe] *vt* : exhibit, show off — **exhibition** [ɛgzibisjɔ̃] *nf* : display, exhibition

exhorter [ɛgzɔrte] *vt* : exhort, urge

exiger [ɛgziʒe] {17} *vt* : demand, require — **exigeant, -geante** [ɛgziʒɑ̃, -ʒɑ̃t] *adj* : demanding, choosy — **exigence** [ɛgziʒɑ̃s] *nf* : demand, requirement

exigu, -guë [ɛgzigy] *adj* : cramped, tiny

exil [ɛgzil] *nm* : exile — **exilé, -lée** [ɛgzile] *n* : exile — **exiler** [ɛgzile] *vt* : exile — **s'exiler** *vr* : go into exile, isolate oneself

exister [ɛgziste] *vi* : exist — **existant, -tante** [ɛgzistɑ̃, -tɑ̃t] *adj* : existing — **existence** [ɛgzistɑ̃s] *nf* : existence

exode [ɛgzɔd] *nm* : exodus

exonérer [ɛgzɔnere] {87} *vt* : exempt — **exonération** [ɛgzɔnerasjɔ̃] *nf* : exemption

exorbitant, -tante [ɛgzɔrbitɑ̃, -tɑ̃t] *adj* : exorbitant

exotique [ɛgzɔtik] *adj* : exotic

expansion [ɛkspɑ̃sjɔ̃] *nf* : expansion — **expansif, -sive** [ɛkspɑ̃sif, -siv] *adj* : expansive

expatrier [ɛkspatrije] {96} *vt* : expatriate — **s'expatrier** *vr* : emigrate — **expatrié, -triée** [ɛkspatrije] *adj & n* : expatriate

expédient, -diente [ɛkspedjɑ̃, -djɑ̃t] *adj* : expedient — **expédient** *nm* : expedient

expédier [ɛkspedje] {96} *vt* : send, dispatch — **expéditeur, -trice** [ɛkspeditœr, -tris] *n* : sender — **expéditif, -tive** [ɛkspeditif, -tiv] *adj* : quick — **expédition** [ɛkspedisjɔ̃] *nf* **1** : sending, shipment **2** VOYAGE : expedition

expérience [ɛksperjɑ̃s] *nf* **1** : experience **2** ESSAI : experiment — **expérimental, -tale** [ɛksperimɑ̃tal] *adj, mpl* **-taux** [-to] : experimental — **expérimentation** [ɛksperimɑ̃tasjɔ̃] *nf* : experimentation — **expérimenté, -tée** [ɛksperimɑ̃te] *adj* : experienced — **expérimenter** [ɛksperimɑ̃te] *vt* : test, experiment with

expert, -perte [ɛkspɛr, -pɛrt] *adj & n* : expert — **expertise** [ɛkspɛrtiz] *nf* **1** : expert appraisal **2** COMPÉTENCE : expertise

expier [ɛkspje] {96} *vt* : atone for

expirer [ɛkspire] *vi* **1** : breathe out **2** : expire (of a contract) — *vt* : exhale — **expiration** [ɛkspirasjɔ̃] *nf* **1** ÉCHÉANCE : expiration **2** : exhalation (of breath)

explication [ɛksplikasjɔ̃] *nf* : explanation — **explicatif, -tive** [ɛksplikatif, -tiv] *adj* : explanatory

explicite [ɛksplisit] *adj* : explicit

expliquer [ɛksplike] *vt* : explain — **s'expliquer** *vr* **1** : explain oneself **2** : be explained

exploiter [ɛksplwate] *vt* **1** : exploit **2** : work (a field, a mine, etc.), run (a business, etc.) — **exploit** [ɛksplwa] *nm* : exploit — **exploitation** [ɛksplwatasjɔ̃] *nf* **1** : exploitation **2** : running, management (of a farm, mine, etc.) **3 ~ agricole** : (small) farm

explorer [ɛksplɔre] *vt* : explore — **explorateur, -trice** [ɛksplɔratœr, -tris] *n* : explorer — **exploration** [ɛksplɔrasjɔ̃] *nf* : exploration

exploser [ɛksploze] *vi* **1** : explode **2** : burst out, flare up (with anger, etc.) — **explosif, -sive** [ɛksplozif, -ziv] *adj* : explosive — **explosif** *nm* : explosive — **explosion** [ɛksplozjɔ̃] *nf* **1** : explosion **2** : outburst (of anger, joy, etc.)

exporter [ɛkspɔrte] *vt* : export — **exportateur, -trice** [ɛkspɔrtatœr, -tris] *adj* : exporting — **~** *n* : exporter — **exportation** [ɛkspɔrtasjɔ̃] *nf* : export, exportation

exposer [ɛkspoze] *vt* **1** : exhibit **2** EXPLIQUER : explain **3** ORIENTER : orient **4** : expose (to danger), risk (one's life, reputation, etc.) — **s'exposer** *vr* : expose oneself — **exposant, -sante** [ɛkspozɑ̃, -zɑ̃t] *n* : exhibitor — **exposé** [ɛkspoze] *nm* **1** : lecture, talk **2** : account, report — **exposition** [ɛkspozisjɔ̃] *nf* **1** : exhibition **2** PRÉSENTATION : exposition **3** ORIENTATION : orientation, aspect

exprès [ɛksprɛ] *adv* **1** : on purpose, intentionally **2** SPÉCIALEMENT : specially — **exprès, -presse** [ɛksprɛs] *adj* **1** : express, explicit **2** : special delivery — **express** [ɛksprɛs] *adj* : express — **~** *nm* **1** : express (train) **2** *or* **café ~** : espresso — **expressément** [ɛksprɛsemɑ̃] *adv* : expressly — **expressif, -sive** [ɛksprɛsif, -siv] *adj* : expressive — **expression** [ɛksprɛsjɔ̃] *nf* : expression

exprimer [ɛksprime] *vt* **1** : express **2** EXTRAIRE : squeeze, extract — **s'exprimer** *vr* : express oneself

expulser [ɛkspylse] *vt* : expel, evict — **expulsion** [ɛkspylsjɔ̃] *nf* : expulsion, eviction

exquis, -quise [ɛkski, -kiz] *adj* : exquisite

extase [ɛkstaz] *nf* : ecstasy — **extasier** [ɛkstazje] {96} *v* **s'extasier** *vr* : be in ecstasy — **extatique** [ɛkstatik] *adj* : ecstatic

extension [ɛkstɑ̃sjɔ̃] *nf* **1** : stretching (of a muscle, etc.) **2** ÉLARGISSEMENT : extension, expansion — **extensif, -sive** [ɛkstɑ̃sif, -siv] *adj* : extensive

exténuer [ɛkstenɥe] *vt* : exhaust, tire out — **exténuant, -ante** [ɛkstenɥɑ, -ɥɑ̃t] *adj* : exhausting

extérieur, -rieure [ɛksterjœr] *adj* **1** : exterior, outside **2** APPARENT : apparent **3** ÉTRANGER : foreign — **extérieur** *nm* **1** : exterior **2 à l'~** : abroad — **extérieurement** [ɛksterjœrmɑ̃] *adv* **1** : externally **2** APPAREMMENT : outwardly — **extérioriser** [ɛksterjɔrize] *vt* : show, express

exterminer [ɛkstɛrmine] *vt* : exterminate — **extermination** [ɛkstɛrminasjɔ̃] *nf* : extermination

externe [ɛkstɛrn] *adj* : external

extinction [ɛkstɛ̃ksjɔ̃] *nf* **1** : extinction **2** : extinguishing — **extincteur** [ɛkstɛ̃ktœr] *nm* : fire extinguisher

extirper [ɛkstirpe] *vt* : eradicate

extorquer [ɛkstɔrke] *vt* : extort — **extorsion** [ɛkstɔrsjɔ̃] *nf* : extortion

extra [ɛkstra] *adj* **1** : first-rate **2** *fam* : fantastic — **~** *nms & pl* **1** : extra person **2** : extra thing or amount

extraction [ɛstraksjɔ̃] *nf* : extraction

extrader [ɛkstrade] *vt* : extradite

extraire [ɛkstrɛr] {40} *vt* : extract — **extrait** [ɛkstrɛ] *nm* **1** : extract, essence **2** : excerpt (of a speech, etc.)

extraordinaire [ɛkstraɔrdinɛr] *adj* : extraordinary

extraterrestre [ɛkstratɛrɛstr] *adj & nmf* : extraterrestrial

extravagant, -gante [ɛkstravagɑ̃, -gɑ̃t] *adj* : extravagant — **extravagance** [-vagɑ̃s] *nf* : extravagance

extraverti, -tie [ɛkstravɛrti] *adj* : extroverted — **~** *n* : extrovert

extrême [ɛkstrɛm] *adj* : extreme — **~** *nm* : extreme — **extrêmement** [ɛkstrɛmmɑ̃] *adv* : extremely — **extrémité** [ɛkstremite] *nf* : extremity

exubérant, -rante [ɛgzyberɑ̃, -rɑ̃t] *adj* : exuberant — **exubérance** [-berɑ̃s] *nf* : exuberance

exulter [ɛgzylte] *vi* : exult

exutoire [ɛgzytwar] *nm* : outlet

F

f [ɛf] *nm* : f, sixth letter of the alphabet

fable [fabl] *nf* : fable

fabriquer [fabrike] *vt* **1** : make, manufacture **2** INVENTER : fabricate — **fabricant, -cante** [fabrikɑ̃, -kɑ̃t] *n* : manufacturer — **fabrication** [fabrikasjɔ̃] *nf* : manufacture, making — **fabrique** [fabrik] *nf* : factory

fabuleux, -leuse [fabylø, -løz] *adj* : fabulous

façade [fasad] *nf* : façade, front

face [fas] *nf* **1** VISAGE : face **2** CÔTÉ : side **3 en ~** : opposite **4 ~ à ~** : face-to-face **5 faire ~ à** : face — **facette** [fasɛt] *nf* : facet

facétieux, -tieuse [fasesjø, -sjøz] *adj* : facetious

fâcher [faʃe] *vt* : anger — **se fâcher** *vr* : get

angry — **fâché, -chée** [faʃe] *adj* : angry — **fâcheux, -cheuse** [faʃø, -ʃøz] *adj* : unfortunate

facile [fasil] *adj* **1** : easy **2** : easygoing — **facilement** [fasilmɑ̃] *adv* : easily — **facilité** [fasilite] *nf* **1** : easiness **2** APTITUDE : aptitude — **faciliter** [fasilite] *vt* : facilitate

façon [fasɔ̃] *nf* **1** : way, manner **2 ~s** *nfpl* : behavior, manners **3 de ~ à** : so as to **4 de toute ~** : in any case **5 faire des ~s** : put on airs — **façonner** [fasɔne] *vt* **1** FORMER : shape **2** FABRIQUER : manufacture

fac–similé [faksimile] *nm, pl* **fac–similés** : facsimile, copy

facteur[1], **-trice** [faktœr, -tris] *n* : mailman

facteur[2] *nm* : factor

faction [faksjɔ̃] *nf* **1** GROUPE : faction **2** : guard (duty)

factuel, -tuelle [faktɥɛl] *adj* : factual

facture [faktyr] *nf* : bill, invoice — **facturer** [faktyre] *vt* : bill

facultatif, -tive [fakyltatif, -tiv] *adj* : optional

faculté [fakylte] *nf* **1** : faculty, ability **2** LIBERTÉ : option **3** : faculty (of a university)

fade [fad] *adj* : bland

faible [fɛbl] *adj* **1** : weak, feeble **2** : small (in quantity) **3** PÂLE : faint, light — **~** *nmf* : weakling — **~** *nm* : weakness — **faiblesse** [fɛblɛs] *nf* : weakness — **faiblir** [feblir] *vi* **1** : weaken **2** DIMINUER : die down

faïence [fajɑ̃s] *nf* : earthenware

faillir [fajir] {41} *vi* **~ à** : fail to — *vt* **1** : narrowly miss **2 ~ faire qqch** : nearly do sth — **faille** [faj] *nf* **1** : fault (in geology) **2** FAIBLESSE : flaw — **faillible** [fajibl] *adj* : fallible — **faillite** [fajit] *nf* **1** ÉCHEC : failure **2 faire ~** : go bankrupt

faim [fɛ̃] *nf* **1** : hunger **2 avoir ~** : be hungry

fainéant, -néante [feneɑ̃, -neɑ̃t] *adj* : lazy — **~** *n* : loafer, idler

faire [fɛr] {42} *vt* **1** : do **2** : make **3** : equal, amount to **4** DIRE : say **5 cela ne fait rien** : it doesn't matter **6 ~ du football** : play football **7 ~ mal à** : hurt **8 ~ soleil** : be sunny **9 ~ un rêve** : have a dream — **se faire** *vr* **1 ~ à** : get used to **2 s'en faire** : worry — **faire–part** [fɛrpar] *nms & pl* : announcement (of marriage, etc.) — **faisable** [fəzabl] *adj* : feasible

faisan, -sane [fəzɑ̃] *n* : pheasant

faisceau [fɛso] *nm, pl* **-ceaux** : beam (of light)

fait, faite [fɛ, fɛt] *adj* **1** : made, done **2** : ripe (of cheese) **3 tout fait** : ready-made — **fait** *nm* **1** : fact **2** ÉVÉNEMENT : event **3 au ~** : by the way **4 sur le ~** : red-handed

faîte [fɛt] *nm* **1** SOMMET : summit, top **2** APOGÉE : pinnacle

falaise [falɛz] *nf* : cliff

falloir [falwar] {43} *v impers* **1 comme il faut** : proper(ly) **2 il fallait le faire** : it had to be done **3 il fallait me le dire!** : you should have said so! **4 il faut partir** : we must go **5 il faut que je …** : I need to … — **s'en falloir** *vr* **1 peu s'en faut** : very nearly **2 tant s'en faut** : far from it

falsifier [falsifje] {96} *vt* : falsify

famé, -mée [fame] *adj* **mal famé** : disreputable

famélique [famelik] *adj* : starving

fameux, -meuse [famø, -møz] *adj* **1** CÉLÈBRE : famous **2** *fam* : first-rate

familial, -liale [familjal] *adj, mpl* **-liaux** [-ljo] : family — **familiale** *nf* : station wagon

familiariser [familjarize] *v* **se familiariser** *vr* : familiarize oneself — **familiarité** [familjarite] *nf* : familiarity — **familier, -lière** [familje, -ljɛr] *adj* **1** : familiar **2** : informal

famille [famij] *nf* : family

famine [famin] *nf* : famine

fanatique [fanatik] *adj* : fanatic(al) — **~** *nmf* : fanatic — **fanatisme** [-natism] *nm* : fanaticism

faner [fane] *v* **se faner** *vr* : fade

fanfare [fɑ̃far] *nf* **1** : fanfare **2** : brass band

fanfaron, -ronne [fɑ̃farɔ̃, -rɔn] *adj* : boastful — **~** *n* : braggart

fantaisie [fɑ̃tezi] *nf* **1** : fantasy **2** CAPRICE : whim — **fantaisiste** [fɑ̃tezist] *adj* : fanciful

fantasme [fɑ̃tasm] *nm* : fantasy — **fantasmer** [fɑ̃tasme] *vi* : fantasize — **fantasque** [fɑ̃task] *adj* **1** CAPRICIEUX : whimsical **2** BIZARRE : strange, weird — **fantastique** [fɑ̃tastik] *adj* : fantastic

fantoche [fɑ̃tɔʃ] *adj & nm* : puppet

fantôme [fɑ̃tom] *nm* : ghost

faon [fɑ̃] *nm* : fawn

farce [fars] *nf* **1** : practical joke **2** : farce (in theater) — **farceur, -ceuse** [farsœr, -søz] *n* : prankster

farcir [farsir] *vt* : stuff (in cooking)

fard [far] *nm* : makeup

fardeau [fardo] *nm, pl* **-deaux** : load, burden

farfelu, -lue [farfəly] *adj fam* : wacky

farine [farin] *nf* : flour

farouche [faruʃ] *adj* **1** SAUVAGE : wild **2** TIMIDE : shy **3** ACHARNÉ : fierce

fascicule [fasikyl] *nm* **1** : section (of a book) **2** LIVRET : booklet

fasciner [fasine] *vt* : fascinate — **fascinant, -nante** [fasinɑ̃, -nɑ̃t] *adj* : fascinating — **fascination** [fasinasjɔ̃] *nf* : fascination

fascisme [faʃism] *nm* : fascism — **fasciste** [faʃist] *adj & nmf* : fascist

faste[1] [fast] *adj* : lucky

faste[2] *nm* : pomp, splendor

fastidieux, -dieuse [fastidjø, -djøz] *adj* : tedious

fatal, -tale [fatal] *adj, mpl* **-tals 1** MORTEL : fatal **2** INÉVITABLE : inevitable — **fatalement** [fatalmɑ̃] *adv* : inevitably — **fatalité** [fatalite] *nf* **1** SORT : fate **2** : inevitability

fatidique [fatidik] *adj* : fateful

fatiguer [fatige] *vt* **1** : fatigue, tire **2** ENNUYER : annoy **3** : strain (an engine, etc.) — *vi* : grow tired — **se fatiguer** *vr* : wear oneself out — **fatigant, -gante** [fatigɑ̃, -gɑ̃t] *adj* **1** : tiring **2** ENNUYEUX : tiresome — **fatigue** [fatig] *nf* : fatigue — **fatigué, -guée** [fatige] *adj* : tired

faubourg [fobur] *nm* : suburb

faucher [foʃe] *vt* **1** : mow, cut **2** *fam* : swipe, pinch — **fauché, -chée** [foʃe] *adj fam* : broke, penniless

faucille [fosij] *nf* : sickle

faucon [fokɔ̃] *nm* : falcon, hawk

faufiler [fofile] *vt* : baste (in sewing) — **se faufiler** *vr* : weave one's way

faune [fon] *nf* : fauna, wildlife

faussaire [fosɛr] *nmf* : forger

fausse → **faux**[2]

fausser [fose] *vt* **1** : distort **2** DÉFORMER : bend — **faussement** [fosmɑ̃] *adv* **1** : falsely **2** : wrongfully — **fausseté** [foste] *nf* **1** : falseness **2** DUPLICITÉ : duplicity

faute [fot] *nf* **1** : fault **2** ERREUR : mistake **3 ~ de** : for lack of

fauteuil [fotœj] *nm* **1** : armchair **2 ~ roulant** : wheelchair

fautif, -tive [fotif, -tiv] *adj* **1** COUPABLE : at fault **2** ERRONÉ : faulty

fauve [fov] *nm* : big cat

faux[1] [fo] *nfs & pl* : scythe

faux[2], **fausse** [fos] *adj* **1** : false **2** INCORRECT : wrong **3** FALSIFIÉ : counterfeit, fake **4 fausse couche** : miscarriage **5 faire un faux pas** : stumble **6 faux nom** : alias — **~** *nm* : forgery — **~** *adv* : out of tune — **faux–filet** [fofilɛ] *nm, pl* **faux–filets** : sirloin — **faux–monnayeur** [fomɔnejœr] *nm, pl* **faux–monnayeurs** : forger

faveur [favœr] *nf* **1** : favor **2 en ~ de** : in favor of — **favorable** [favɔrabl] *adj* : favorable — **favori, -rite** [favɔri, -rit] *adj & n* : favorite — **favoris** [favɔri] *nmpl* : sideburns — **favoriser** [favɔrize] *vt* **1** : favor **2** ENCOURAGER : promote — **favoritisme** [favɔritism] *nm* : favoritism

fax [faks] *nm* : fax — **faxer** [fakse] *vt* : fax

fébrile [febril] *adj* : feverish

fécond, -conde [fekɔ̃, -kɔ̃d] *adj* : fertile — **féconder** [fekɔ̃de] *vt* : fertilize, impregnate — **fécondité** [fekɔ̃dite] *nf* : fertility

fécule [fekyl] *nf* : starch — **féculent, -lente** [fekylɑ̃, -lɑ̃t] *adj* : starchy — **féculent** [fekylɑ̃] *nm* : starchy food

fédéral, -rale [federal] *adj, mpl* **-raux** [-ro] : federal — **fédération** [federasjɔ̃] *nf* : federation

fée [fe] *nf* : fairy — **féerie** [fe(e)ri] *nf* : enchantment — **féerique** [fe(e)rik] *adj* : magical, enchanting

feindre [fɛ̃dr] {37} *vt* : feign — *vi* : pretend — **feinte** [fɛ̃t] *nf* : trick, ruse

fêler [fele] *vt* : crack

féliciter [felisite] *vt* : congratulate — **félicitations** [felisitasjɔ̃] *nfpl* : congratulations

félin, -line [felɛ̃, -lin] *adj & nm* : feline

fêlure [felyr] *nf* : crack

femelle [fəmɛl] *adj & nf* : female

féminin, -nine [feminɛ̃, -nin] *adj* : feminine — **féminisme** [feminism] *nm* : feminism — **féministe** [feminist] *adj & nmf* : feminist — **féminité** [feminite] *nf* : femininity

femme [fam] *nf* **1** : woman **2** ÉPOUSE : wife **3 ~ au foyer** : homemaker **4 ~ d'affaires** : businesswoman

fendre [fɑ̃dr] {63} *vt* : split, break — **se fendre** *vr* : crack

fenêtre [fənɛtr] *nf* : window

fenouil [fənuj] *nm* : fennel

fente [fɑ̃t] *nf* **1** : slit, slot **2** FISSURE : crack

féodal, -dale [feɔdal] *adj, mpl* **-daux** [-do] : feudal

fer [fɛr] *nm* **1** : iron **2 ~ à cheval** : horseshoe **3 ~ à repasser** : iron (for clothes)

férié, -riée [ferje] *adj* **jour férié** : holiday

ferme [fɛrm] *adj* : firm — **~** *adv* : firmly, hard — **~** *nf* : farm — **fermement** [fɛrməmɑ̃] *adv* : firmly

fermé, -mée [fɛrme] *adj* **1** : closed, shut (off) **2** EXCLUSIF : exclusive

fermenter [fɛrmɑ̃te] *vi* : ferment — **fermentation** [fɛrmɑ̃tasjɔ̃] *nf* : fermentation

fermer [fɛrme] *vt* **1** : close, shut **2** : close down (a factory, etc.) **3** ÉTEINDRE : turn off **4 ~ à clef** : lock up — **se fermer** *vr* : close (up)

fermeté [fɛrməte] *nf* : firmness

fermeture [fɛrmətyr] *nf* **1** : closing, shutting **2 ~ à glissière** : zipper

fermier, -mière [fɛrmje, -mjɛr] *n* : farmer

fermoir [fɛrmwar] *nm* : clasp

féroce [ferɔs] *adj* : ferocious — **férocité** [ferɔsite] *nf* : ferocity, ferociousness

ferraille [fɛraj] *nf* : scrap iron

ferronnerie [fɛrɔnri] *nf* **1** : ironworks **2** : wrought iron

ferroviaire [fɛrɔvjɛr] *adj* : rail, railroad

ferry–boat [fɛribot] *nm, pl* **ferry–boats** : ferry

fertile [fɛrtil] *adj* : fertile — **fertiliser** [fɛrtilize] *vt* : fertilize — **fertilité** [fɛrtilite] *nf* : fertility

fervent, -vente [fɛrvɑ̃, -vɑ̃t] *adj* : fervent — **~** *n* : enthusiast — **ferveur** [fɛrvœr] *nf* : fervor

fesses [fɛs] *nfpl* : buttocks — **fessée** [fese] *nf* : spanking — **fesser** [fese] *vt* : spank

festin [fɛstɛ̃] *nm* : feast

festival [fɛstival] *nm, pl* **-vals** : festival — **festivités** [fɛstivite] *nfpl* : festivities

fête [fɛt] *nf* **1** : holiday **2** : party **3** FOIRE : fair **4 de ~** : festive **5 faire la ~** : have a good time — **fêter** [fete] *vt* : celebrate

fétiche [fetiʃ] *nm* : fetish

fétide [fetid] *adj* : fetid

feu[1] [fø] *nm, pl* **feux 1** : fire **2** *or* **~ de circulation** : traffic light **3** : burner (of a stove) **4** : light (for a cigarette, etc.) **5** TIR : fire, shooting **6 ~ de joie** : bonfire **7 feux d'artifice** : fireworks **8 mettre le ~ à** : set fire to **9 prendre ~** : catch fire

feu[2], **feue** [fø] *adj* : late, deceased

feuille [fœj] *nf* **1** : leaf **2** : sheet (of paper, etc.) — **feuillage** [fœjaʒ] *nm* : foliage — **feuillet** [fœjɛ] *nm* : page, leaf — **feuilleter** [fœjte] {8} *vt* : leaf through — **feuilleton** [fœjtɔ̃] *nm* : series, serial

feutre [føtr] *nm* : felt — **feutré, -trée** [føtre] *adj* : muffled, hushed

fève [fɛv] *nf* : broad bean

février [fevrije] *nm* : February

fiable [fjabl] *adj* : reliable — **fiabilité** [fjabilite] *nf* : reliability

fiancer [fijɑ̃se] {6} *v* **se fiancer** *vr* : get engaged — **fiançailles** [fijɑ̃saj] *nfpl* : engagement — **fiancé, -cée** [fijɑ̃se] *n* : fiancé *m*, fiancée *f*

fibre [fibr] *nf* **1** : fiber **2 ~ de verre** : fiberglass — **fibreux, -breuse** [fibrø, -brøz] *adj* : fibrous

ficelle [fisɛl] *nf* : string, twine — **ficeler** [fisle] {8} *vt* : tie up

fiche [fiʃ] *nf* **1** : index card **2** FORMULAIRE : form **3** : (electric) plug

ficher [fiʃe] *vt* **1** : drive (in) **2** *fam* : do **3** *fam* : give **4 ~ qqn dehors** *fam* : kick s.o. out — **se ficher** *vr* **1 ~ de** *fam* : make fun of **2 je m'en fiche** *fam* : I don't give a damn

fichier [fiʃje] *nm* : file, index

fichu[1], **-chue** [fiʃy] *adj fam* **1** : lousy, awful **2** CONDAMNÉ : done for

fichu[2] *nm* : scarf, kerchief

fiction [fiksjɔ̃] *nf* : fiction — **fictif, -tive** [fiktif, -tiv] *adj* : fictional, fictitious

fidèle [fidɛl] *adj* : faithful — **~** *nmf* **1** : follower **2** : regular (customer) **3 les ~s** : the faithful — **fidèlement** [-dɛlmɑ̃] *adv* : faithfully — **fidélité** [fidelite] *nf* : fidelity

fier[1] [fje] *v* **se fier** *vr* **~ à** : trust, rely on

fier[2], **fière** [fjɛr] *adj* : proud — **fièrement** [fjɛrmɑ̃] *adv* : proudly — **fierté** [fjɛrte] *nf* : pride

fièvre [fjɛvr] *nf* : fever — **fiévreux, -vreuse** [fjevrø, -vrøz] *adj* : feverish

figer [fiʒe] {17} *v* **se figer** *vr* : coagulate

figue [fig] *nf* : fig

figure [figyr] *nf* **1** VISAGE : face **2** PERSONNAGE : figure **3** ILLUSTRATION : illustration — **figurant, -rante** [figyrɑ̃, -rɑ̃t] *n* : extra (in theater) — **figurer** [figyre] *vi* : appear — *vt* : represent — **se figurer** *vr* : imagine

fil [fil] *nm* **1** : thread **2** : wire **3 au ~ de** : in the course of **4 coup de ~** *fam* : phone call **5 ~ dentaire** : dental floss — **file** [fil] *nf* **1** : line, file, row **2** : lane (of a highway) **3 en ~** *or* **à la ~** : one after another — **filer** [file] *vt* **1** : spin (yarn) **2** SUIVRE : shadow **3** *fam* : give — *vi* **1** : run (of stockings) **2** *fam* : dash off **3** *fam* : fly by, slip away **4 ~ bien** *Can fam* : be doing fine

filet [filɛ] *nm* **1** : net **2** : fillet (of beef, etc.) **3** : trickle (of water)

filial [filjal] *nf* : subsidiary (company)

filière [filjɛr] *nf* : (official) channels *pl*

filigrane [filigran] *nm* : watermark

fille [fij] *nf* **1** : girl **2** : daughter — **fillette** [fijɛt] *nf* : little girl

filleul, -leule [fijœl] *n* : godchild, godson *m*, goddaughter *f*

film [film] *nm* : film — **filmer** [filme] *vt* : film

filon [filɔ̃] *nm* : vein, lode

fils [fis] *nm* : son

filtre [filtr] *nm* : filter — **filtrer** [filtre] *vt* **1** : filter **2** : screen (visitors, etc.) — *vi* : filter through

fin[1], **fine** [fɛ̃, fin] *adj* **1** : fine **2** MINCE : thin **3** : excellent (in quality) **4** : sharp, keen **5** *Can* : nice — **fin** *adv* : finely

fin[2] *nf* **1** : end **2 à la ~** : in the end **3 prendre ~** : come to an end **4 sans ~** : endless(ly)

final, -nale [final] *adj, mpl* **-nals** *or* **-naux** [fino] : final — **finale** *nf* : finals *pl* (in sports) — **finalement** [finalmɑ̃] *adv* **1** : finally **2** : after all — **finaliste** [finalist] *nmf* : finalist

finance [finɑ̃s] *nf* **1** : finance **2 ~s** *nfpl* : finances — **financer** [finɑ̃se] {6} *vt* : finance — **financier, -cière** [finɑ̃sje,-sjɛr] *adj* : financial

finesse [finɛs] *nf* **1** : finesse, delicacy **2** PERSPICACITÉ : shrewdness

finir [finir] *vt* : finish — *vi* **1** : finish **2 en ~ avec** : be done with **3 ~ par faire** : end up doing — **fini, -nie** [fini] *adj* **1** : finished **2** : finite — **finition** [finisjɔ̃] *nf* : finish

fiole [fjɔl] *nf* : vial

firme [firm] *nf* : firm

fisc [fisk] *nm* : tax collection agency — **fiscal, -cale** [fiskal] *adj, mpl* **-caux** [fisko] : fiscal — **fiscalité** [fiskalite] *nf* : tax system

fissure [fisyr] *nf* : crack

fiston [fistɔ̃] *nm fam* : son, youngster

fixe [fiks] *adj* **1** IMMOBILE : fixed **2** INVARIABLE : invariable, set — **fixer** [fikse] *vt* **1** ATTACHER : fix, fasten **2** DÉCIDER : determine **3** ÉTABLIR : establish **4 ~ son regard sur** : stare at — **se fixer** *vr* **1** : settle down **2** SE DÉCIDER : decide

flacon [flakɔ̃] *nm* : small bottle

flageller [flaʒɛle] *vt* : flog, whip

flagrant [flagrɑ̃] *adj* **1** : flagrant **2 en ~ délit** : red-handed

flairer [flɛre] *vt* **1** : sniff, smell **2** DISCERNER : detect, sense — **flair** [flɛr] *nm* **1** : sense of smell **2** INTUITION : intuition

flamand, -mande [flamɑ̃, -mɑ̃d] *adj* : Flemish

flamant [flamɑ̃] *nm* : flamingo

flambant, -bante [flɑ̃bɑ̃, -bɑ̃t] *adj* **flambant neuf** : brand-new

flambeau [flɑ̃bo] *nm, pl* **-beaux** : torch

flamber [flɑ̃be] *vi* : burn, blaze — **flambée** [flɑ̃be] *nf* **1** : blaze, fire **2** : outburst (of anger, etc.)

flamboyer [flɑ̃bwaje] {58} *vi* : blaze, flame — **flamboyant, -boyante** [flɑ̃bwajɑ̃, -bwajɑ̃t] *adj* : blazing

flamme [flam] *nf* **1** : flame **2** FERVEUR : passion, fervor **3 en ~s** : on fire

flan [flɑ̃] *nm* : baked custard

flanc [flɑ̃] *nm* : side, flank

flancher [flɑ̃ʃe] *vi fam* **1** : give in **2** : give out, fail

flanelle [flanɛl] *nf* : flannel

flâner [flane] *vi* **1** SE BALADER : stroll **2** PARESSER : loaf around

flanquer [flɑ̃ke] *vt* **1** : flank **2 ~ par terre** : fling to the ground **3 ~ un coup à** *fam* : punch

flaque [flak] *nf* : puddle, pool

flash [flaʃ] *nm, pl* **flashs** *or* **flashes** [flaʃ] **1** : flash (in photography) **2** : news flash

flasque [flask] *adj* : flabby, limp

flatter [flate] *vt* **1** : flatter **2** CARESSER : stroke — **se flatter** *vr* : pride oneself — **flatterie** [flatri] *nf* : flattery — **flatteur, -teuse** [flatœr, -tøz] *adj* : flattering — **~** *n* : flatterer

fléau [fleo] *nm, pl* **fléaux** : calamity, scourge

flèche [flɛʃ] *nf* **1** : arrow **2** : spire (of a church) — **fléchette** [fleʃɛt] *nf* : dart

fléchir [fleʃir] *vt* PLIER : bend, flex — *vi* **1** : bend, give way **2** FAIBLIR : weaken

flegme [flɛgm] *nm* : composure — **flegmatique** [flɛgmatik] *adj* : phlegmatic

flemme [flɛm] *nf France fam* : laziness

flétan [fletɑ̃] *nm* : halibut

flétrir [fletrir] *v* **se flétrir** *vr* : wither, fade

fleur [flœr] *nf* **1** : flower **2 en ~** : in blossom — **fleuri, -rie** [flœri] *adj* **1** : flowered **2** : flowery — **fleurir** [flœrir] *vi* **1** : flower, blossom **2** PROSPÉRER : flourish — **fleuriste** [flœrist] *nmf* : florist

fleuve [flœv] *nm* : river

flexible [flɛksibl] *adj* : flexible — **flexibilité** [flɛksibilite] *nf* : flexibility — **flexion** [flɛksjɔ̃] *nf* : bending, flexing

flic [flik] *nm fam* : cop

flirter [flœrte] *vi* : flirt

flocon [flɔkɔ̃] *nm* **1** : flake **2 ~ de neige** : snowflake **3 ~s de maïs** : cornflakes

floraison [flɔrɛzɔ̃] *nf* : flowering, blossoming — **floral, -rale** [flɔral] *adj, mpl* **-raux** [flɔro] : floral — **flore** [flɔr] *nf* : flora — **florissant, -sante** [flɔrisɑ̃, -sɑ̃t] *adj* : flourishing

flot [flo] *nm* **1** : flood, stream **2 à ~** : afloat

flotter [flɔte] *vi* **1** : float **2** : flutter (of a flag) — **flotte** [flɔt] *nf* : fleet — **flotteur** [flɔtœr] *nm* : float

flou, floue [flu] *adj* **1** : blurred **2** : vague, hazy (of ideas, etc.)

fluctuer [flyktɥe] *vi* : fluctuate — **fluctuation** [flyktɥasjɔ̃] *nf* : fluctuation

fluide [flɥid] *adj* **1** : fluid **2** : flowing freely

— ~ *nm* : fluid — **fluidité** [flɥidite] *nf* : fluidity

fluor [flyɔr] *nm* : fluorine

fluorescent, -cente [flyɔresɑ̃, -sɑ̃t] *adj* : fluorescent — **fluorescence** [-sɑ̃s] *nf* : fluorescence

flûte [flyt] *nf* **1** : flute **2** : baguette — ~ *interj* ~ **alors**! : nonsense!

fluvial, -viale [flyvjal] *adj, mpl* **-viaux** [-vjo] : river

flux [fly] *nm* **1** : flow **2** MARÉE : flood tide **3 le** ~ **et le reflux** : the ebb and flow

fœtus [fetys] *nms & pl* : fetus

foi [fwa] *nf* **1** : faith **2 bonne** ~ : honesty, sincerity **3 digne de** ~ : reliable **4 ma** ~ ! : well!

foie [fwa] *nm* : liver

foin [fwɛ̃] *nm* : hay

foire [fwar] *nf* : fair, market

fois [fwa] *nf* **1** : time, occasion **2 à la** ~ : at the same time, together **3 des** ~ : sometimes **4 il était une** ~ : once upon a time

foison [fwazɔ̃] **à** ~ *adv phr* : in abundance — **foisonner** [fwazɔne] *vi* : abound

fol → **fou**

folâtrer [fɔlatre] *vi* : frolic — **folâtre** [fɔlatr] *adj* : playful, frisky

folie [fɔli] *nf* **1** : craziness, madness **2 à la** ~ : madly

folklore [fɔlklɔr] *nm* : folklore — **folklorique** [fɔlklɔrik] *adj* : folk (of music, dance, etc.)

folle → **fou** — **follement** [fɔlmɑ̃] *adv* : madly, wildly

foncer [fɔ̃se] {6} *vt* : darken — *vi* ~ **sur** : rush at — **foncé, -cée** [fɔ̃se] *adj* : dark (of colors)

foncier, -cière [fɔ̃sje, -sjɛr] *adj* **1** : land, property **2** FONDAMENTAL : fundamental — **foncièrement** [fɔ̃sjɛrmɑ̃] *adv* : fundamentally

fonction [fɔ̃ksjɔ̃] *nf* **1** : function **2** EMPLOI : job, post **3 faire** ~ **de** : serve as **4 en** ~ **de** : according to **5** ~ **publique** : civil service — **fonctionnaire** [fɔ̃ksjɔnɛr] *nmf* : official, civil servant — **fonctionnel, -nelle** [fɔ̃ksjɔnɛl] *adj* : functional — **fonctionnement** [fɔ̃ksjɔnmɑ̃] *nm* : functioning, working — **fonctionner** [fɔ̃ksjɔne] *vi* : function, work

fond [fɔ̃] *nm* **1** : bottom, back **2** CŒUR : heart, root **3** ARRIÈRE-PLAN : background **4 à** ~ : thoroughly **5 au** ~ : in fact **6 au** ~ **de** : at the bottom of, in the depths of

fondamental, -tale [fɔ̃damɑ̃tal] *adj, mpl* **-taux** [-to] : fundamental — **fondamentalement** [-talmɑ̃] *adv* : basically

fonder [fɔ̃de] *vt* **1** : found **2** BASER : base — **se fonder** *vr* ~ **sur** : be based on — **fondateur, -trice** [fɔ̃datœr, -tris] *n* : founder — **fondation** [fɔ̃dasjɔ̃] *nf* : foundation — **fondé, -dée** [fɔ̃de] *adj* : well-founded — **fondement** [fɔ̃dmɑ̃] *nm* **1** : foundation **2 sans** ~ : groundless

fondre [fɔ̃dr] {63} *vt* **1** : melt, smelt **2** : cast (a statue, etc.) — *vi* **1** : melt **2** ~ **en larmes** : dissolve into tears

fonds [fɔ̃] *nms & pl* **1** : fund **2** ~ *nmpl* : funds, capital **3** *or* ~ **de commerce** : business

fontaine [fɔ̃tɛn] *nf* **1** : fountain **2** SOURCE : spring

fonte [fɔ̃t] *nf* **1** : melting, smelting **2** : thawing (of snow) **3** : cast iron

football [futbol] *nm* **1** : soccer **2** *Can* : football **3** ~ **américain** *France* : football — **footballeur, -leuse** [futbolœr, -løz] *n* : soccer player, football player

footing [futiŋ] *nm France* : jogging

forage [fɔraʒ] *nm* : drilling

forçat [fɔrsa] *nm* : convict

force [fɔrs] *nf* **1** : force **2** PUISSANCE : strength **3 à** ~ **de** : as a result of **4 les** ~**s armées** : the armed forces — **forcé, -cée** [fɔrse] *adj* **1** : forced **2** INÉVITABLE : inevitable — **forcément** [fɔrsemɑ̃] *adv* : inevitably — **forcer** [fɔrse] {6} *vt* **1** : force, compel **2** : force open **3** : strain, overtax (one's voice, etc.) — *vi* : overdo it — **se forcer** *vr* : force oneself

forer [fɔre] *vt* : drill, bore

forêt [fɔrɛ] *nf* : forest — **foresterie** [fɔrɛstəri] *nf* : forestry — **forestier, -tière** [fɔrɛstje, -tjɛr] *adj* : forest

forfaire [fɔrfɛr] {44} *vi* ~ **à** : fail in

forfait [fɔrfɛ] *nm* **1** : fixed price **2 déclarer** ~ : withdraw — **forfaitaire** [fɔrfɛtɛr] *adj* : inclusive

forge [fɔrʒ] *nf* : forge — **forger** [fɔrʒe] {16} *vt* : forge — **forgeron** [fɔrʒərɔ̃] *nm* : blacksmith

formaliser [fɔrmalize] *v* **se formaliser** *vr* : take offense

formalité [fɔrmalite] *nf* : formality

format [fɔrma] *nm* : format — **formater** [fɔrmate] *vt* : format (a computer disk)

formation [fɔrmasjɔ̃] *nf* **1** : formation **2** APPRENTISSAGE : education, training — **forme** [fɔrm] *nf* **1** : form, shape **2** ~**s** *nfpl* : (human) figure **3** ~**s** *nfpl* : proprieties **4 en** ~ : fit, in shape — **formel, -melle** [fɔrmɛl] *adj* **1** : formal **2** CATÉGORIQUE : definitive — **formellement** [-mɛlmɑ̃] *adv* : strictly, absolutely — **former** [fɔrme] *vt* **1** : form **2** : train, educate, develop

formidable [fɔrmidabl] *adj* **1** : tremendous **2** *fam* : great, terrific

formulaire [fɔrmylɛr] *nm* : form, questionnaire

formule [fɔrmyl] *nf* **1** : formula **2** MÉTHODE : way, method **3** FORMULAIRE : form **4** ~ **de politesse** : polite phrase, closing (of a letter) — **formuler** [fɔrmyle] *vt* : formulate, express

fort, forte [fɔr, fɔrt] *adj* **1** PUISSANT : strong **2** : loud **3** CONSIDÉRABLE : large **4** DOUÉ : gifted — **fort** [fɔr] *adv* **1** : strongly, loudly, hard **2** TRÈS : very — **fort** *nm* **1** : fort, fortress **2** : strong point — **forteresse** [fɔrtərɛs] *nf* : fortress — **fortifier** [fɔrtifje] {96} *vt* : fortify, strengthen — **fortification** [fɔrtifikasjɔ̃] *nf* : fortification

fortuit, -tuite [fɔrtɥi, -tɥit] *adj* : fortuitous, chance

fortune [fɔrtyn] *nf* : fortune — **fortuné, -née** [fɔrtyne] *adj* : wealthy

forum [fɔrɔm] *nm* : forum

fosse [fos] *nf* **1** : pit **2** TOMBE : grave **3** ~ **septique** : septic tank — **fossé** [fose] *nm* **1** : ditch, trench **2** ~ **de générations** : generation gap — **fossette** [fosɛt] *nf* : dimple

fossile [fosil] *nm* : fossil

fou [fu] (**fol** [fɔl] *before a vowel or mute h*), **folle** [fɔl] *adj* **1** : mad, crazy **2** *fam* : tremendous — ~ *n* : crazy person, lunatic — **fou** *nm* **1** : fool, jester **2** : bishop (in chess)

foudre [fudr] *nf* : lightning — **foudroyant, -droyante** [fudrwajɑ̃, fudrwajɑ̃t] *adj* **1** : overwhelming **2** SOUDAIN : sudden — **foudroyer** [fudrwaje] {58} *vt* : strike down

fouet [fwɛ] *nm* **1** : whip **2** : whisk **3 de plein** ~ : head-on — **fouetter** [fwete] *vt* : whip

fougère [fuʒɛr] *nf* : fern

fougue [fug] *nf* : ardor, spirit — **fougueux, -geuse** [fugø, -gøz] *adj* : fiery

fouiller [fuje] *vt* **1** : search **2** CREUSER : excavate, dig — *vi* ~ **dans** : rummage through — **fouille** [fuj] *nf* **1** : search **2** ~**s** *nfpl* : excavations — **fouillis** [fuji] *nm* : jumble

fouiner [fwine] *vi fam* : snoop around

foulard [fular] *nm* : scarf

foule [ful] *nf* **1** : crowd **2 une** ~ **de** : masses of, lots of

fouler [fule] *vt* : press, tread on — **se fouler** *vr* : sprain (one's ankle, etc.) — **foulée** [fule] *nf* **dans la** ~ **de** : in the aftermath of — **foulure** [fulyr] *nf* : sprain

four [fur] *nm* **1** : oven **2** *fam* : flop (in theater, etc.)

fourbu, -bue [furby] *adj* : exhausted

fourche [furʃ] *nf* **1** : pitchfork **2** : fork (of a road) — **fourchette** [furʃɛt] *nf* : fork

fourgon [furgɔ̃] *nm* : van, truck — **fourgonnette** [furgɔnɛt] *nf* : minivan

fourmi [furmi] *nf* : ant — **fourmilière** [furmiljɛr] *nf* : anthill — **fourmiller** [furmije] *vi* **1** : swarm **2** ~ **de** : be teeming with

fourneau [furno] *nm, pl* **-neaux** [furno] **1** : stove **2** CUISINIÈRE : furnace

fournée [furne] *nf* : batch

fournir [furnir] *vt* **1** : supply, provide (with) **2** ~ **un effort** : make an effort — **fourni, -nie** [furni] *adj* : thick, bushy — **fournisseur, -seuse** [furnisœr, -søz] *n* : supplier — **fournitures** [furnityr] *nfpl* : equipment, supplies

fourrage [furaʒ] *nm* : fodder — **fourrager** [furaʒe] {17} *vi* : forage

fourré [fure] *nm* : thicket

fourreau [furo] *nm, pl* **-reaux** : sheath

fourrer [fure] *vt* **1** : stuff, fill **2** *fam* : thrust, stick — **fourre–tout** [furtu] *nms & pl* : tote bag, carryall

fourrière [furjɛr] *nf* : pound (for animals or vehicles)

fourrure [furyr] *nf* : fur

fourvoyer [furvwaje] {58} *v* **se fourvoyer** *vr* **1** : lead astray **2** ~ **dans** : get involved in

foyer [fwaje] *nm* **1** : hearth **2** DOMICILE : home **3** RÉSIDENCE : residence, hall **4** : foyer (of a theater) **5 lunettes à double** ~ : bifocals

fracas [fraka] *nms & pl* : crash, din — **fracasser** [frakase] *vt* : shatter, smash

fraction [fraksjɔ̃] *nf* : fraction

fracture [fraktyr] *nf* : fracture — **fracturer** [fraktyre] *vt* : fracture

fragile [fraʒil] *adj* **1** : fragile **2** FAIBLE : frail — **fragilité** [fraʒilite] *nf* **1** : fragility **2** FAIBLESSE : frailty

fragment [fragmɑ̃] *nm* : fragment

frais, fraîche [frɛ, frɛʃ] *adj* **1** : fresh **2** : cool (of weather) **3 peinture fraîche** : wet paint — **frais** *nm* **1 mettre au** ~ : put in a cool place **2 prendre le** ~ : take a breath of fresh air **3 frais** *nmpl* : expenses, fees — ~ [frɛ] *adv* **1** : freshly **2 il fait** ~ : it's cool outside — **fraîcheur** [frɛʃœr] *nf* **1** : freshness **2** : coolness — **fraîchir** [frɛʃir] *vi* : cool off (of weather)

fraise [frɛz] *nf* : strawberry

framboise [frɑ̃bwaz] *nf* : raspberry

franc, franche [frɑ̃, frɑ̃ʃ] *adj* **1** HONNÊTE : frank **2** VÉRITABLE : utter, downright — **franc** [frɑ̃] *nm* : franc

français, -çaise [frɑ̃sɛ, -sɛz] *adj* : French — **français** *nm* : French (language)

franchement [frɑ̃ʃmɑ̃] *adv* **1** SINCÈREMENT : frankly **2** NETTEMENT : clearly **3** VRAIMENT : downright, really

franchir [frɑ̃ʃir] *vt* **1** : cross (over) **2** : cover (a distance)

franchise [frɑ̃ʃiz] *nf* **1** SINCÉRITÉ : frankness **2** EXONÉRATION : exemption, allowance **3** : franchise

franco–canadien, -dienne [frɑ̃kokanadjɛ̃, -djɛn] *adj* : French-Canadian

francophone [frɑ̃kɔfɔn] *adj* : French-speaking

frange [frɑ̃ʒ] *nf* **1** : fringe **2** : bangs (of hair)

frapper [frape] *vt* **1** : strike, hit **2** IMPRESSIONNER : impress — *vi* : bang, knock — **frappant, -pante** [frapɑ̃, -pɑ̃t] *adj* : striking

fraternel, -nelle [fratɛrnɛl] *adj* : fraternal, brotherly — **fraterniser** [fratɛrnize] *vi* : fraternize — **fraternité** [fratɛrnite] *nf* : fraternity, brotherhood

fraude [frod] *nf* : fraud — **frauder** [frode] *v* : cheat — **fraudeur, -deuse** [frodœr, -døz] *n* : cheat, swindler — **frauduleux, -leuse** [frodylø, -løz] *adj* : fraudulent

frayer [freje] {11} *v* **se frayer** *vr* ~ **un chemin** : make one's way

frayeur [frɛjœr] *nf* : fright

fredonner [frədɔne] *vt* : hum

frégate [fregat] *nf* : frigate

frein [frɛ̃] *nm* **1** : brake **2 mettre un** ~ **à** : curb, block — **freiner** [frene] *vt* : slow down, check — *vi* : brake

frêle [frɛl] *adj* : frail

frelon [frəlɔ̃] *nm* : hornet

frémir [fremir] *vi* **1** FRISSONNER : shiver **2** TREMBLER : quiver, flutter **3** : simmer (in cooking)

frêne [frɛn] *nm* : ash (tree or wood)

frénésie [frenezi] *nf* : frenzy — **frénétique** [frenetik] *adj* : frantic, frenzied

fréquenter [frekɑ̃te] *vt* **1** : frequent **2** : attend (school, etc.) **3** COTOYER : associate with, see — **fréquemment** [frekamɑ̃] *adv* : frequently — **fréquence** [frekɑ̃s] *nf* : frequency — **fréquent, -quente** [frekɑ̃, -kɑ̃t] *adj* : frequent — **fréquentation** [frekɑ̃tasjɔ̃] *nf* **1** : frequenting **2** PRÉSENCE : attendance **3** RELATION : acquaintance

frère [frɛr] *nm* **1** : brother **2** : friar

fresque [frɛsk] *nf* : fresco

fret [frɛ] *nm* : freight

fretin [frətɛ̃] *nm* **menu** ~ : small fry

friable [frijabl] *adj* : crumbly

friand, friande [frijɑ̃, -jɑ̃d] *adj* ~ **de** : fond of

friandise [frijɑ̃diz] *nf* **1** : delicacy **2** ~**s** *nfpl* : sweets

fric [frik] *nm fam* : dough, cash

friction [friksjɔ̃] *nf* **1** : friction **2** MASSAGE : massage — **frictionner** [friksjɔne] *vt* : rub, massage

frigide [friʒid] *adj* : frigid

frigo [frigo] *nm fam* : fridge

frileux, -leuse [frilø, -løz] *adj* **1** : sensitive to cold **2** PRUDENT : cautious

frimer [frime] *vi fam* : show off

fringale [frɛ̃gal] *nf* **avoir la** ~ *fam* : be ravenous

fringant, -gante [frɛ̃gɑ̃, -gɑ̃t] *adj* : dashing

fripon, -ponne [fripɔ̃, -pɔn] *adj* : mischievous — ~ *n* : rascal

fripouille [fripuj] *nf fam* : scoundrel

frire [frir] {45} *v* : fry

friser [frize] *vt* **1** BOUCLER : curl **2** : border on, be close to — *vi* : curl — **frisé, -sée** [frize] *adj* : curly, curly-haired

frisquet, -quette [friskɛ, -kɛt] *adj* : chilly, nippy

frisson [frisɔ̃] *nm* : shiver, shudder — **frissonner** [frisɔne] *vi* : shiver, shudder

friture [frityr] *nf* **1** : frying **2** : deep fat, oil **3** : fried food — **frites** [frit] *nfpl* : french fries

frivole [frivɔl] *adj* : frivolous — **frivolité** [frivɔlite] *nf* : frivolity

froid, froide [frwa, frwad] *adj* : cold — **froid** [frwa] *adv* **il fait** ~ : it's cold (outside) — ~ *nm* **1** : cold **2 être en** ~ **avec** : be on bad terms with **3 prendre** ~ : catch cold — **froidement** [frwadmɑ̃] *adv* : coldly, coolly — **froideur** [frwadœr] *nf* : coldness, coolness

froisser [frwase] *vt* **1** : crumple, crease **2** BLESSER : offend — **se froisser** *vr* **1** : crease, crumple (up) **2** ~ **un muscle** : strain a muscle

frôler [frole] *vt* : brush against, touch lightly

fromage [frɔmaʒ] *nm* **1** : cheese **2** ~ **blanc** : cottage cheese — **fromagerie** [frɔmaʒri] *nf* : cheese shop

fronce [frɔ̃s] *nf* : gather, crease — **froncement** [frɔ̃smɑ̃] *nm* ~ **de sourcils** : frown

froncer [frɔ̃se] {6} *vt* **1** : gather (fabric) **2** ~ **les sourcils** : frown

fronde [frɔ̃d] *nf* **1** : rebellion, revolt **2** LANCE-PIERRES : slingshot

front [frɔ̃] *nm* **1** : forehead **2** : front (in politics, war, etc.) **3** AUDACE : audacity, cheek **4 de** ~ : head-on **5 faire** ~ **à** : confront — **frontal, -tale** [frɔ̃tal] *adj, mpl* **-taux** [frɔ̃to] : frontal — **frontalier, -lière** [frɔ̃talje, -ljɛr] *adj* : frontier — **frontière** [frɔ̃tjɛr] *nf* : frontier, border

frotter [frɔte] *vt* **1** : rub **2** NETTOYER : polish, scrub — *vi* : rub — **frottement** [frɔtmɑ̃] *nm* **1** : rubbing **2** ~**s** *nmpl* : friction, disagreement

frousse [frus] *nf fam* : scare, fright

fructueux, -tueuse [fryktɥø, -tɥøz] *adj* : fruitful

frugal, -gale [frygal] *adj, mpl* **-gaux** [frygo] : frugal — **frugalité** [frygalite] *nf* : frugality

fruit [frɥi] *nm* **1** : fruit **2** ~**s de mer** : seafood — **fruité, -tée** [frɥite] *adj* : fruity — **fruitier, -tière** [frɥitje, -tjɛr] *adj* : fruit

frustrer [frystre] *vt* **1** : frustrate **2** ~ **de** : deprive of — **frustrant, -trante** [frystrɑ̃, -trɑ̃t] *adj* : frustrating — **frustration** [frystrasjɔ̃] *nf* : frustration

fugace [fygas] *adj* : fleeting

fugitif, -tive [fyʒitif, -tiv] *n* : fugitive, runaway

fugue [fyg] *nf* **1 faire une** ~ : run away **2** ~ **amoureuse** : elopement

fuir [fɥir] {46} *vi* **1** : flee **2** SUINTER : leak — *vt* : avoid, shun — **fuite** [fɥit] *nf* **1** : flight, escape **2** : leak (of water, information, etc.)

fulgurant, -rante [fylgyrɑ̃, -rɑ̃t] *adj* : dazzling, vivid

fulminer [fylmine] *vi* : be enraged

fumer [fyme] *vt* : smoke — *vi* **1** : smoke **2** : give off steam — **fumé, -mée** [fyme] *adj* **1** : smoked **2** : tinted (of glass, etc.) — **fumée** *nf* **1** : smoke **2** VAPEUR : steam — **fumeur, -meuse** [fymœr, -møz] *n* : smoker

fumier [fymje] *nm* : dung, manure

fumigation [fymigasjɔ̃] *nf* : fumigation

funambule [fynɑ̃byl] *nmf* : tightrope walker

funèbre [fynɛbr] *adj* **1** : funeral **2** LUGUBRE : gloomy — **funérailles** [fyneraj] *nfpl* : funeral — **funéraire** [fynerɛr] *adj* : funeral

funeste [fynɛst] *adj* DÉSASTREUX : disastrous

fur [fyr] **au** ~ **et à mesure** *adv phr* : little by little

furet [fyrɛ] *nm* : ferret

fureter [fyrte] {20} *vi* : pry

fureur [fyrœr] *nf* **1** : rage, fury **2 faire** ~ : be all the rage

furibond, -bonde [fyribɔ̃, -bɔ̃d] *adj* : furious — **furie** [fyri] *nf* : fury, rage — **furieux, -rieuse** [fyrjø, -jøz] *adj* : furious

furoncle [fyrɔ̃kl] *nm* : boil

furtif, -tive [fyrtif, -tiv] *adj* : furtive, sly

fusain [fyzɛ̃] *nm* : charcoal

fuseau [fyzo] *nm, pl* **-seaux** **1** : spindle **2** ~ **horaire** : time zone

fusée [fyze] *nf* **1** : rocket **2** ~ **éclairante** : flare

fuselé, -lée [fyzle] *adj* : slender, tapering

fusible [fyzibl] *nm* : fuse

fusil [fyzi] *nm* : gun, rifle — **fusillade** [fyzijad] *nf* : gunfire — **fusiller** [fyzije] *vt* : shoot

fusion [fyzjɔ̃] *nf* : fusion — **fusionner** [fyzɔnje] *v* : merge

fût [fy] *nm* : barrel, cask

futé, -tée [fyte] *adj* : cunning, crafty

futile [fytil] *adj* : futile — **futilité** [fytilite] *nf* : futility

futur, -ture [fytyr] *adj & nm* : future

fuyant, fuyante [fɥijɑ̃, fɥijɑ̃t] *adj* : elusive, shifty

G

g [ʒe] *nm* : g, seventh letter of the alphabet

gabarit [gabari] *nm* **1** : size, dimensions *pl* **2** *fam* : caliber, type

gâcher [gaʃe] *vt* : spoil, ruin

gâchette [gaʃɛt] *nf* : trigger

gâchis [gaʃi] *nm* **1** DÉSORDRE : mess **2** GASPILLAGE : waste

gadget [gadʒɛt] *nm* : gadget

gadoue [gadu] *nf* : mud, muck

gaffe [gaf] *nf fam* : blunder — **gaffer** [gafe] *vi fam* : blunder, goof (up)

gage [gaʒ] *nm* **1** : security **2** GARANTIE : pledge, guarantee **3** ~**s** *nmpl* : wages, pay **4 en** ~ **de** : as a token of **5 mettre en** ~ : pawn — **gager** [gaʒe] {17} *vt* **1** : bet, wager **2** : guarantee (a loan, etc.) — **gageure** [gaʒœr] *nf* **1** : challenge **2** *Can* : bet, wager

gagner [gaɲe] *vt* **1** : win **2** : earn (one's living, etc.) **3** : gain (speed, etc.) **4** : save (time, space, etc.) **5** ATTEINDRE : reach — *vi* **1** : win **2** ~ **en** : increase in **3 y** ~ : be better off — gagnant, -gnante [gaɲɑ̃, -ɲɑ̃t] *adj* : winning — ~ *n* : winner — gagne–pain [gaɲpɛ̃] *nms & pl* : job, livelihood

gai, gaie [gɛ] *adj* : cheerful, merry — gaieté [gete] *nf* : cheerfulness

gaillard, -larde [gajar, -jard] *adj* 1 : sprightly 2 GRIVOIS : ribald — ~ *nmf* : vigorous person

gain [gɛ̃] *nm* 1 : earnings *pl* 2 PROFIT : gain 3 ÉCONOMIE : saving

gaine [gɛn] *nf* 1 : girdle 2 : sheath (of a dagger)

gala [gala] *nm* : gala, reception

galant, -lante [galɑ̃, -lɑ̃t] *adj* : courteous, gallant

galaxie [galaksi] *nf* : galaxy

galbe [galb] *nm* : curve, shapeliness

galerie [galri] *nf* 1 : gallery 2 : balcony (in a theater) 3 : roof rack (of an automobile)

galet [galɛ] *nm* : pebble

galette [galɛt] *nf* : flat round cake

gallois, -loise [galwa, -lwaz] *adj* : Welsh — gallois *nm* : Welsh (language)

gallon [galɔ̃] *nm* : gallon

galoper [galɔpe] *vi* : gallop — galop [galo] *nm* : gallop

galopin [galɔpɛ̃] *nm* : rascal

galvaniser [galvanize] *vt* : galvanize

galvauder [galvode] *vt* : sully, tarnish

gambade [gɑ̃bad] *nf* : leap, skip — gambader [gɑ̃bade] *vi* : leap about

gamelle [gamɛl] *nf* : mess kit

gamin, -mine [gamɛ̃, -min] *adj* : mischievous — ~ *n* : kid, youngster

gamme [gam] *nf* 1 : scale (in music) 2 SÉRIE : range, gamut

ganglion [gɑ̃glijɔ̃] *nm* avoir des ~s : have swollen glands

gangrène [gɑ̃grɛn] *nf* : gangrene

gangster [gɑ̃gstɛr] *nm* : gangster

gant [gɑ̃] *nm* 1 : glove 2 ~ de toilette : washcloth

garage [garaʒ] *nm* : garage — garagiste [garaʒist] *nmf* 1 : garage owner 2 : (garage) mechanic

garant, -rante [garɑ̃, -rɑ̃t] *n* : guarantor — garant *nm* : guarantee (in law) — garantie [garɑ̃ti] *nf* : guarantee, warranty — garantir [garɑ̃tir] *vt* 1 : guarantee 2 ~ de : protect from

garçon [garsɔ̃] *nm* 1 : boy, young man 2 SERVEUR : waiter 3 ~ manqué : tomboy

garder [garde] *vt* 1 : keep 2 SURVEILLER : watch over 3 ~ de : protect from — se garder *vr* 1 : keep 2 ~ de : be careful not to — garde [gard] *nm* 1 : guard 2 ~ du corps : bodyguard — ~ *nf* 1 : nurse 2 : (military) guard 3 : custody, care 4 de ~ : on duty 5 mettre en ~ : warn 6 prendre ~ : be careful — garde–fou [gardəfu] *nm, pl* garde–fous : railing — garde–manger [gardəmɑ̃ʒe] *nms & pl* : pantry — garderie [gardəri] *nf* : day-care center — garde–robe [gardərɔb] *nf, pl* garde–robes : wardrobe, closet — gardien, -dienne [gardjɛ̃, -djɛn] *n* 1 : warden, custodian 2 PROTECTEUR : guardian — gardien *nm* 1 ~ de but : goalkeeper 2 ~ de la paix *France* : police officer — gardienne *nf* ~ d'enfants : day-care worker

gare[1] [gar] *nf* 1 : station 2 ~ routière *France or* ~ d'autobus *Can* : bus station

gare[2] *interj* 1 ~ à toi! : watch out! 2 sans crier ~ : without warning

garer [gare] *vt* STATIONNER : park — se garer *vr* 1 : park 2 S'ÉCARTER : move away

gargariser [gargarize] *v* se gargariser *vr* : gargle

gargouiller [garguje] *vi* : gurgle, rumble

garnement [garnəmɑ̃] *nm* : rascal

garnir [garnir] *vt* 1 REMPLIR : fill 2 COUVRIR : cover 3 DÉCORER : decorate, trim — garni, -nie [garni] *adj* : served with vegetables

garnison [garnizɔ̃] *nf* : garrison

garniture [garnityr] *nf* 1 : filling (in cooking) 2 DÉCORATION : trimming, garnish

gars [ga] *nm fam* 1 : boy, lad 2 TYPE : guy, fellow

gaspiller [gaspije] *vt* : waste, squander — gaspillage [gaspijaʒ] *nm* : waste

gastrique [gastrik] *adj* : gastric

gastronomie [gastrɔnɔmi] *nf* : gastronomy

gâteau [gato] *nm, pl* -teaux 1 : cake 2 ~ sec *France* : cookie

gâter [gate] *vt* 1 : pamper 2 ABÎMER : spoil, ruin — se gâter *vr* 1 : go bad 2 SE DÉTÉRIORER : deteriorate

gâterie [gatri] *nf* : little treat, delicacy

gâteux, -teuse [gatø, -tøz] *adj* : senile

gauche [goʃ] *adj* 1 : left 2 MALADROIT : clumsy — ~ *nf* 1 : left 2 la ~ : the left (wing) — gaucher, -chère [goʃe, -ʃɛr] *adj* : left-handed — gaucherie [goʃri] *nf* : awkwardness

gaufre [gofr] *nf* : waffle — gaufrette [gofrɛt] *nf* : wafer

gausser [gose] *v* se gausser *vr* ~ de : deride, make fun of

gaver [gave] *v* se gaver *vr* : stuff oneself

gay [gɛ] *adj* : gay (homosexual)

gaz [gaz] *nms & pl* : gas

gaze [gaz] *nf* : gauze

gazer [gaze] *vi fam* ça gaze? : how are things going?

gazette [gazɛt] *nf* : newspaper

gazeux, -zeuse [gazø, -zøz] *adj* : fizzy, carbonated

gazon [gazɔ̃] *nm* 1 : grass, turf 2 PELOUSE : lawn

gazouiller [gazuje] *vi* 1 : chirp 2 : gurgle, babble (of a baby)

geai [ʒɛ] *nm* : jay

géant, géante [ʒeɑ̃, -ɑ̃t] *adj* : giant, gigantic — ~ *n* : giant

geler [ʒəle] {20} *v* : freeze — *v impers* on gèle! : it's freezing! — gel [ʒɛl] *nm* 1 : frost 2 : gel 3 : freezing (of prices, etc.) — gélatine [ʒelatin] *nf* : gelatin — gelée *nf* 1 : (hoar)frost 2 : jelly — gelure [ʒəlyr] *nf* : frostbite

gémir [ʒemir] *vi* : groan, moan — gémissement [ʒemismɑ̃] *nm* : groan(ing), moan(ing)

gemme [ʒɛm] *nf* : gem

gênant, -nante [ʒenɑ̃, -nɑ̃t] *adj* 1 : embarrassing 2 ENCOMBRANT : cumbersome 3 ENNUYEUX : annoying

gencives [ʒɑ̃siv] *nfpl* : gums

gendarme [ʒɑ̃darm] *nm* : police officer — gendarmerie [ʒɑ̃darməri] *nf* 1 *France* : police force 2 *France* : police station 3 *Can* : federal police force

gendre [ʒɑ̃dr] *nm* : son-in-law

gène [ʒɛn] *nm* : gene

généalogie [ʒenealɔʒi] *nf* : genealogy

gêner [ʒene] *vt* 1 : embarrass, make uncomfortable 2 DÉRANGER : bother 3 ENCOMBRER : hamper — se gêner *vr* : put oneself out — gêne [ʒɛn] *nf* 1 : inconvenience 2 : embarrassment 3 : (physical) discomfort — gêné, -née [ʒene] *adj* 1 : embarrassed 2 *Can* : shy

général, -rale [ʒeneral] *adj, mpl* -raux [-ro] : general — général *nm, pl* -raux : general — généralement [-ralmɑ̃] *adv* : generally, usually — généraliser [ʒeneralize] *v* : generalize — se généraliser *vr* : become widespread — généraliste [ʒeneralist] *nmf* : general practitioner — généralité [ʒeneralite] *nf* : majority

générateur [ʒeneratœr] *nm* : generator

génération [ʒenerasjɔ̃] *nf* : generation

génératrice [ʒeneratris] *nf* : (electric) generator

générer [ʒenere] {87} *vt* : generate

généreux, -reuse [ʒenerø, -røz] *adj* : generous — généreusement [-røzmɑ̃] *adv* : generously

générique [ʒenerik] *adj* : generic — ~ *nm* : credits *pl* (in movies)

générosité [ʒenerɔzite] *nf* : generosity

génétique [ʒenetik] *adj* : genetic — ~ *nf* : genetics

génie [ʒeni] *nm* 1 : genius 2 INGÉNIERIE : engineering — génial, -niale [ʒenjal] *adj, mpl* -niaux [-njo] 1 : brilliant 2 *fam* : fantastic, great

génisse [ʒenis] *nf* : heifer

génital, -tale [ʒenital] *adj, mpl* -taux [-to] : genital

genou [ʒənu] *nm, pl* -noux 1 : knee 2 se mettre à ~x : kneel down

genre [ʒɑ̃r] *nm* 1 SORTE : kind, type 2 ATTITUDE : style, manner 3 : gender (in grammar)

gens [ʒɑ̃] *nmfpl* 1 : people 2 ~ d'affaires : businesspeople 3 jeunes ~ : teenagers

gentil, -tille [ʒɑ̃ti, -tij] *adj* 1 : kind, nice 2 SAGE : well-behaved — gentillesse [ʒɑ̃tijɛs] *nf* : kindness, niceness — gentiment [ʒɑ̃timɑ̃] *adv* : nicely, kindly

géographie [ʒeɔgrafi] *nf* : geography — géographique [ʒeɔgrafik] *adj* : geographic(al)

geôlier, -lière [ʒolje, -ljɛr] *n* : jailer

géologie [ʒeɔlɔʒi] *nf* : geology — géologique [ʒeɔlɔʒik] *adj* : geologic(al)

géométrie [ʒeɔmetri] *nf* : geometry — géométrique [ʒeɔmetrik] *adj* : geometric(al)

géranium [ʒeranjɔm] *nm* : geranium

gérant, -rante [ʒerɑ̃, -rɑ̃t] *n* : manager

gerbe [ʒɛrb] *nf* 1 : sheaf (of wheat) 2 : bunch (of flowers, etc.)

gercer [ʒɛrse] {6} *v* se gercer *vr* : chap, crack — gerçure [ʒɛrsyr] *nf* : crack (in the skin)

gérer [ʒere] {87} *vt* : manage

germain, -maine [ʒɛrmɛ̃, -mɛn] *adj* cousin germain : first cousin

germe [ʒɛrm] *nm* 1 : germ 2 POUSSE : sprout — germer [ʒɛrme] *vi* 1 : sprout, germinate 2 : form (of ideas, etc.)

gésier [ʒezje] *nm* : gizzard

gésir [ʒezir] {47} *vi* : lie, be lying

gestation [ʒɛstasjɔ̃] *nf* : gestation

geste [ʒɛst] *nm* : gesture, movement

gestion [ʒɛstjɔ̃] *nf* : management — gestionnaire [ʒɛstjɔnɛr] *nmf* : administrator

geyser [ʒezɛr] *nm* : geyser

gibet [ʒibɛ] *nm* : gallows

gibier [ʒibje] *nm* 1 : game (animals) 2 *fam* : prey

giboulée [ʒibule] *nf* : sudden shower

gicler [ʒikle] *vi* : spurt, squirt, spatter — giclée [ʒikle] *nf* : spurt, squirt

gifle [ʒifl] *nf* : slap (in the face) — gifler [ʒifle] *vt* : slap

gigantesque [ʒigɑ̃tɛsk] *adj* : gigantic, huge

gigot [ʒigo] *nm* : leg (of lamb) — gigoter [ʒigɔte] *vi fam* : wriggle, fidget

gilet [ʒilɛ] *nm* 1 : vest 2 : cardigan (sweater) 3 ~ de sauvetage : life jacket

gin [dʒin] *nm* : gin

gingembre [ʒɛ̃ʒɑ̃br] *nm* : ginger

girafe [ʒiraf] *nf* : giraffe

giratoire [ʒiratwar] *adj* sens ~ : rotary, traffic circle

girofle [ʒirɔfl] *nm* clou de ~ : clove

girouette [ʒirwɛt] *nf* : weather vane

gisement [ʒizmɑ̃] *nm* : deposit (in geology)

gitan, -tane [ʒitɑ̃, -tan] *n* : Gypsy

gîte [ʒit] *nm* 1 : shelter, lodging 2 le ~ et le couvert : room and board

givre [ʒivr] *nm* : frost — givrer [ʒivre] *v* se givrer *vr* : frost (up)

glabre [glabr] *adj* : hairless

glacer [glase] {6} *vt* 1 : freeze, chill 2 : frost (a cake) — glaçage [glasaʒ] *nm* : frosting — glace [glas] *nf* 1 : ice 2 *France* : ice cream 3 MIROIR : mirror 4 VITRE : glass — glacé, -cée [glase] *adj* 1 : icy, chilly 2 : iced — glacial, -ciale [glasjal] *adj, mpl* -cials *or* -ciaux [-sjo] : icy, frigid — glacier [glasje] *nm* : glacier — glacière [glasjɛr] *nf* : cooler, icebox — glaçon [glasɔ̃] *nm* 1 : block of ice 2 : icicle 3 : ice cube

glaise [glɛz] *nf* : clay

gland [glɑ̃] *nm* 1 : acorn 2 : tassel (ornament)

glande [glɑ̃d] *nf* : gland

glapir [glapir] *vi* : yelp

glas [gla] *nm* sonner le ~ : toll the bell

glauque [glok] *adj* : gloomy, dreary

glisser [glise] *vi* 1 : slide, slip 2 DÉRAPER : skid — *vt* : slip, slide — se glisser *vr* ~ dans : slip into, creep into — glissant, -sante [glisɑ̃, -sɑ̃t] *adj* : slippery — glissement [glismɑ̃] *nm* 1 : sliding, gliding 2 ÉVOLUTION : shift — glissière [glisjɛr] *nf* 1 : slide, groove, chute 2 à ~ : sliding — glissoire [gliswar] *nf* : slide

globe [glɔb] *nm* 1 : globe 2 ~ oculaire : eyeball 3 le ~ terrestre : the earth — global, -bale [glɔbal] *adj, mpl* -baux [glɔbo] : overall, total — globalement [glɔbalmɑ̃] *adv* : as a whole

gloire [glwar] *nf* 1 : glory, fame 2 MÉRITE : credit — glorieux, -rieuse [glɔrjø, -rjøz] *adj* : glorious — glorifier [glɔrifje] {96} *vt* : glorify

glossaire [glɔsɛr] *nm* : glossary

glousser [gluse] *vi* 1 : cluck 2 : chuckle — gloussement [glusmɑ̃] *nm* 1 : cluck, clucking 2 : chuckling

glouton, -tonne [glutɔ̃, -tɔn] *adj* : gluttonous, greedy — ~ *n* : glutton — gloutonnerie [glutɔnri] *nf* : gluttony

gluant, gluante [glyɑ̃, glyɑ̃t] *adj* : sticky

glucose [glykoz] *nm* : glucose

gobelet [gɔblɛ] *nm* : tumbler, beaker

gober [gɔbe] *vt* 1 : swallow whole 2 *fam* : swallow, fall for

godasse [gɔdas] *nf fam* : shoe

goéland [gɔelɑ̃] *nm* : gull

goguenard, -narde [gɔgnar, -nard] *adj* : mocking

goinfre [gwɛ̃fr] *nm fam* : pig, glutton

golf [gɔlf] *nm* : golf

golfe [gɔlf] *nm* : gulf, bay

gomme [gɔm] *nf* 1 : gum, resin 2 : eraser 3 ~ à mâcher : chewing gum — gommer [gɔme] *vt* : erase

gond [gɔ̃] *nm* : hinge

gondole [gɔ̃dɔl] *nf* : gondola

gondoler [gɔ̃dɔle] *v* se gondoler *vr* : warp, buckle

gonfler [gɔ̃fle] *vt* 1 : swell 2 : blow up, inflate (a balloon, etc.) 3 GROSSIR : exaggerate — *vi* : swell — se gonfler *vr* 1 : swell up 2 ~ de : swell up with, be filled with — gonflé, -flée [gɔ̃fle] *adj* : swollen, bloated — gonflement [gɔ̃fləmɑ̃] *nm* : swelling

gorge [gɔrʒ] *nf* 1 : throat 2 POITRINE : bosom, chest 3 : gorge (in geography) — gorgée [gɔrʒe] *nf* : mouthful, sip — gorger [gɔrʒe] {17} *v* se gorger *vr* : gorge oneself

gorille [gɔrij] *nm* : gorilla

gosier [gozje] *nm* : throat

gosse [gɔs] *nmf France fam* : kid, youngster

gothique [gɔtik] *adj* : Gothic

goudron [gudrɔ̃] *nm* : tar — goudronner [gudrɔne] *vt* : tar (a road)

gouffre [gufr] *nm* : gulf, abyss

goujat [guʒa] *nm* : boor

goulot [gulo] *nm* 1 : neck (of a bottle) 2 ~ d'étranglement : bottleneck

goulu, -lue [guly] *adj* : greedy

gourde [gurd] *nf* 1 : flask 2 : gourd 3 *fam* : dope, dumbbell

gourdin [gurdɛ̃] *nm* : cudgel, club

gourmand, -mande [gurmɑ̃, -mɑ̃d] *adj* GLOUTON : greedy — ~ *n* : glutton — gourmandise [gurmɑ̃diz] *nf* 1 : greed 2 ~s *nfpl* : sweets, delicacies

gousse [gus] *nf* ~ d'ail : clove of garlic

goût [gu] *nm* 1 : taste 2 SAVEUR : flavor 3 GRÉ : fondness, liking 4 de bon ~ : tasteful — goûter [gute] *vt* : taste — *vi* 1 : have an afternoon snack 2 ~ à *or* ~ de : try out, sample — ~ *nm* : afternoon snack

goutte [gut] *nf* : drop (of water, etc.) — gouttelette [gutlɛt] *nf* : droplet — goutter [gute] *vi* : drip — gouttière [gutjɛr] *nf* : gutter (on a roof)

gouvernail [guvɛrnaj] *nm* 1 : rudder 2 BARRE : helm

gouverner [guvɛrne] *vt* : govern, rule — gouvernante [guvɛrnɑ̃t] *nf* 1 : governess 2 : housekeeper — gouvernement [guvɛrnəmɑ̃] *nm* : government — gouvernemental, -tale [-mɑ̃tal] *adj* : governmental — gouverneur [guvɛrnœr] *nm* : governor

grâce [gras] *nf* 1 : gracefulness 2 FAVEUR : favor 3 PARDON : mercy, pardon 4 de bonne ~ : willingly 5 ~ à : thanks to — gracier [grasje] {96} *vt* : pardon — gracieux, -cieuse [grasjø, -sjøz] *adj* 1 : graceful 2 AIMABLE : gracious 3 GRATUIT : free

grade [grad] *nm* 1 : rank 2 monter en ~ : be promoted

gradin [gradɛ̃] *nm* 1 : tier 2 ~s *nmpl* : bleachers, stands

graduel, -duelle [gradɥɛl] *adj* : gradual — graduellement [-dɥɛlmɑ̃] *adv* : gradually

graduer [gradɥe] *vt* 1 : graduate (a measuring instrument) 2 : increase gradually

graffiti [grafiti] *nmpl* : graffiti

grain [grɛ̃] *nm* 1 : (cereal) grain 2 : speck, particle (of sand, salt, dust, etc.) 3 ~ de café : coffee bean 4 ~ de poivre : peppercorn 5 ~ de beauté : mole — graine [grɛn] *nf* : seed

graisse [grɛs] *nf* 1 : fat 2 LUBRIFIANT : grease — graisser [grɛse] *vt* : lubricate, grease — graisseux, -seuse [grɛsø, -søz] *adj* : greasy

grammaire [gramɛr] *nf* : grammar — grammatical, -cale [gramatikal] *adj, mpl* -caux [-ko] : grammatical

gramme [gram] *nm* : gram

grand, grande [grɑ̃, grɑ̃d] *adj* 1 : tall 2 GROS : big, large 3 IMPORTANT : great, important 4 : elder, older, grown-up — grand [grɑ̃] *adv* 1 : wide 2 ~ ouvert : wide-open — grand–chose [grɑ̃ʃoz] *pron* pas ~ : not much — grandeur [grɑ̃dœr] *nf* 1 DIMENSION : size 2 : greatness — grandiose [grɑ̃djoz] *adj* : grandiose — grandir [grɑ̃dir] *vt* 1 : make (look) taller 2 EXAGÉRER : exaggerate — *vi* 1 : grow 2 AUGMENTER : increase — grand–mère [grɑ̃mɛr] *nf, pl* grands–mères : grandmother — grand–père [grɑ̃pɛr] *nm, pl* grands–pères : grandfather — grands–parents [grɑ̃parɑ̃] *nmpl* : grandparents

grange [grɑ̃ʒ] *nf* : barn

granit *or* **granite** [granit] *nm* : granite

granulé [granyle] *nm* : tablet (in medicine) — granuleux, -leuse [granylø, -løz] *adj* : granular

graphique [grafik] *adj* : graphic — ~ *nm* : graph, chart

grappe [grap] *nf* : cluster (of grapes, etc.)

grappin [grapɛ̃] *nm* 1 : grapnel 2 mettre le ~ sur : get one's hooks into

gras, grasse [gra, gras] *adj* 1 : fatty 2 GROS : fat (of persons) 3 HUILEUX : greasy, oily 4 VULGAIRE : crude, coarse 5 : bold (of type) — gras *nm* 1 : (animal) fat 2 : grease — grassouillet, -lette [grasujɛ, -jɛt] *adj* : pudgy, plump

gratifier [gratifje] {96} *vt* ~ de : reward with — gratification [gratifikasjɔ̃] *nf* : bonus

gratin [gratɛ̃] *nm* : dish baked with cheese or crumb topping

gratis [gratis] *adv* : free

gratitude [gratityd] *nf* : gratitude

gratte–ciel [gratsjɛl] *nms & pl* : skyscraper

gratter [grate] *vt* : scratch, scrape — se gratter *vr* : scratch oneself

gratuit, -tuite [gratɥi, -tɥit] *adj* 1 : free 2 : gratuitous — gratuitement [-tɥitmɑ̃] *adv* : free (of charge)

gravats [grava] *nmpl* : rubble

grave [grav] *adj* 1 : serious, grave 2 SOLENNEL : solemn 3 voix ~ : deep voice — gravement [gravmɑ̃] *adv* : seriously

graver [grave] *vt* 1 : engrave 2 : carve 3 ENREGISTRER : cut, record

gravier [gravje] *nm* : gravel

gravillon [gravijɔ̃] *nm* : (fine) gravel, grit

gravir [gravir] *vt* : climb (up)

gravité [gravite] *nf* 1 : gravity (in physics) 2 IMPORTANCE : seriousness — graviter [gravite] *vi* : gravitate

gravure [gravyr] *nf* 1 : engraving 2 : print (of a picture), plate (in a book)

gré [gre] *nm* 1 VOLONTÉ : will 2 GOÛT : taste, liking 3 à votre ~ : as you wish

grec, grecque [grɛk] *adj* : Greek — grec *nm* : Greek (language)

greffe [grɛf] *nf* 1 : graft (in botany) 2 : graft, transplant (in medicine) — greffer [grɛfe] *vt* 1 : graft 2 : transplant (an organ)

greffier, -fière [grɛfje, -fjɛr] *n* : clerk of court

grêle[1] [grɛl] *adj* **1** : lanky, lean **2** AIGU : shrill

grêle[2] *nf* : hail — **grêler** [grele] *v impers* **il grêle** : it's hailing — **grêlon** [grɛlɔ̃] *nm* : hailstone

grelot [grəlo] *nm* : small bell — **grelotter** [grəlɔte] *vi* : shiver

grenade [grənad] *nf* **1** : pomegranate **2** : grenade (weapon)

grenier [grənje] *nm* : attic, loft

grenouille [grənuj] *nf* : frog

grès [grɛ] *nm* **1** : sandstone **2** POTERIE : stoneware

grésiller [grezije] *vi* : crackle, sizzle

grève [grɛv] *nf* **1** RIVAGE : shore **2** : strike — **gréviste** [grevist] *nmf* : striker

gribouiller [gribuje] *v* : scribble — **gribouillage** [gribujaʒ] *nm* : scribble, scrawl

grief [grijɛf] *nm* : grievance — **grièvement** [grijɛvmɑ̃] *adv* : seriously, severely

griffe [grif] *nf* **1** : claw **2** : signature, label (of a product) — **griffer** [grife] *vt* : scratch — **griffonner** [grifɔne] *vt* : scribble, jot down

grignoter [griɲɔte] *vt* **1** : nibble **2** AMOINDRIR : erode, eat away (at)

gril [gril] *nm* **1** : broiler **2** : grill (for cooking) — **grillade** [grijad] *nf* : grilled meat, grill

grille [grij] *nf* **1** : metal fencing, gate, bars *pl* **2** : grate (of a sewer, etc.) **3** : grid (in games) — **grillage** [grijaʒ] *nm* : wire fencing

griller [grije] *vt* **1** : toast, grill, broil **2** : burn out (a fuse, etc.) — *vi* : broil — **grille–pain** [grijpɛ̃] *nms & pl* : toaster

grillon [grijɔ̃] *nm* : cricket

grimace [grimas] *nf* : grimace — **grimacer** [grimase] {6} *vi* : grimace

grimper [grɛ̃pe] *v* : climb

grincer [grɛ̃se] {6} *vi* **1** : creak, grate **2** ~ **des dents** : grind one's teeth — **grincement** [grɛ̃smɑ̃] *nm* : creak, squeak

grincheux, -cheuse [grɛ̃ʃø, -ʃøz] *adj* : grumpy

grippe [grip] *nf* **1** : flu, influenza **2 prendre qqn en ~** : take a sudden dislike to s.o. — **grippé, -pée** [gripe] *adj* **être ~** : have the flu

gris, grise [gri, griz] *adj* **1** : gray **2** MORNE : dull, dreary **3** *fam* : tipsy — **gris** *nm* : gray — **grisaille** [grizaj] *nf* **1** : grayness (of weather) **2** MONOTONIE : dullness

griser [grize] *vt* : intoxicate — **grisant, -sante** [grizɑ̃, -zɑ̃t] *adj* : intoxicating, heady

grisonner [grizɔne] *vi* : turn gray, go gray

grive [griv] *nf* : thrush

grivois, -voise [grivwa, -waz] *adj* : bawdy

grogner [grɔɲe] *vi* **1** : growl **2** : grumble — **grognement** [grɔɲmɑ̃] *nm* **1** : growling **2** : rumbling, roar — **grognon, -gnonne** [grɔɲɔ̃, -ɲɔn] *adj* : grumpy, grouchy

groin [grwɛ̃] *nm* : snout

grommeler [grɔmle] {8} *v* : mutter

gronder [grɔ̃de] *vt* : scold — *vi* **1** : rumble, roar **2** GROGNER : growl — **grondement** [grɔ̃dmɑ̃] *nm* **1** : roar, rumble **2** GROGNEMENT : growling

gros, grosse [gro, gros] *adj* **1** : big, large **2** ÉPAIS : thick **3** CORPULENT : fat **4** GRAVE : serious **5** LOURD : heavy **6** ~ **lot** : jackpot — **gros** [gro] *adv* BEAUCOUP : a lot — ~ *nm* **1 en ~** : roughly, in general **2 le ~ de** : the bulk of

groseille [grozɛj] *nf* **1** : currant **2** ~ **à maquereau** : gooseberry

grossir [grosir] *vt* **1** AUGMENTER : increase **2** EXAGÉRER : exaggerate **3** AGRANDIR : magnify — *vi* **1** : put on weight **2** : grow larger — **grossesse** [groses] *nf* : pregnancy — **grosseur** [grosœr] *nf* **1** : fatness **2** VOLUME : size **3** : lump (in medicine) — **grossier, -sière** [grosje, -sjɛr] *adj* **1** APPROXIMATIF : coarse, rough **2** VULGAIRE : crude, vulgar **3** FLAGRANT : gross, glaring — **grossièrement** [grosjɛrmɑ̃] *adv* **1** APPROXIMATIVEMENT : roughly **2** VULGAIREMENT : crudely — **grossièreté** [grosjɛrte] *nf* **1** : coarseness **2** : rudeness — **grossiste** [grosist] *nmf* : wholesaler

grosso modo [grosomodo] *adv* : more or less, roughly

grotesque [grɔtɛsk] *adj* **1** : grotesque **2** RIDICULE : absurd, ridiculous

grotte [grɔt] *nf* : cave

grouiller [gruje] *vi* ~ **de** : swarm with — **se grouiller** *vr fam* : hurry, get a move on

groupe [grup] *nm* **1** : group **2** ~ **sanguin** : blood type — **groupement** [grupmɑ̃] *nm* : grouping, group — **grouper** [grupe] *vt* : group — **se grouper** *vr* : gather, get together

gruau [gryo] *nm Can* : oatmeal

grue [gry] *nf* : crane

grumeau [grymo] *nm, pl* **-meaux** : lump (in sauce, etc.)

gruyère [gryjɛr] *nm* : Gruyère (cheese)

gué [ge] *nm* : ford, crossing

guenilles[gənij] *nfpl* : rags and tatters

guenon [gənɔ̃] *nf* : female monkey

guépard [gepar] *nm* : cheetah

guêpe [gɛp] *nf* : wasp — **guêpier** [gepje] *nm* **1** : wasps' nest **2** : tight spot, trap

guère [gɛr] *adv* **ne . . . guère** : hardly, scarcely, rarely

guérilla [gerija] *nf* : guerilla warfare — **guérillero** [gerijero] *nm* : guerilla

guérir [gerir] *vt* : cure, heal — *vi* : get better, heal — **guérison** [gerizɔ̃] *nf* **1** : cure, healing **2** RÉTABLISSEMENT : recovery

guérite [gerit] *nf* : sentry box

guerre [gɛr] *nf* : war — **guerrier, -rière** [gɛrje, -jɛr] *adj* : warlike — ~ *n* : warrior

guetter [gete] *vt* **1** : watch (intently) **2** ATTENDRE : watch out for **3** MENACER : threaten — **guet** [gɛ] *nm* **faire le ~** : be on the lookout — **guet–apens** [gɛtapɑ̃] *nm, pl* **guets–apens** : ambush

gueule [gœl] *nf* **1** : mouth (of an animal, a tunnel, etc.) **2** *fam* : face **3 ta ~!** *fam* : shut up! **4** ~ **de bois** : hangover — **gueuler** [gœle] *v fam* : bawl, bellow

gui [gi] *nm* : mistletoe

guichet [giʃɛ] *nm* **1** : window, counter **2** : box office **3** ~ **automatique** : automatic teller machine — **guichetier, -tière** [giʃtje, -tjɛr] *n* : counter clerk, teller

guide [gid] *nm* **1** : guide **2** : guidebook — **guider** [gide] *vt* : guide — **guides** *nfpl* : reins

guidon [gidɔ̃] *nm* : handlebars *pl*

guignol [giɲɔl] *nm* **1** : puppet show **2 faire le ~** : clown around

guillemets [gijmɛ] *nmpl* : quotation marks

guilleret, -rette [gijrɛ, -rɛt] *adj* : sprightly, perky

guillotine [gijɔtin] *nf* : guillotine

guimauve [gimov] *nf* : marshmallow

guindé, -dée [gɛ̃de] *adj* : stiff, prim

guirlande [girlɑ̃d] *nf* **1** : garland **2** ~**s de Noël** : tinsel

guise [giz] *nf* **1 à ta ~** : as you wish **2 en ~ de** : by way of

guitare [gitar] *nf* : guitar — **guitariste** [gitarist] *nmf* : guitarist

gymnase [ʒimnaz] *nm* : gymnasium — **gymnaste** [ʒimnast] *nmf* : gymnast

gymnastique [ʒimnastik] *nf* : gymnastics

gynécologie [ʒinekɔlɔʒi] *nf* : gynecology — **gynécologue** [ʒinekɔlɔg] *nmf* : gynecologist

H

h [aʃ] *nm* : h, eighth letter of the alphabet

habile [abil] *adj* : skillful, clever — **habilement** [abilmɑ̃] *adv* : skillfully, cleverly — **habileté** [abilte] *nf* : skill, cleverness

habilité, -tée [abilite] *adj* ~ **à** : entitled to

habiller [abije] *vt* : dress, clothe — **s'habiller** *vr* **1** : get dressed **2** ~ **en** : dress up as — **habillé, -lée** [abije] *adj* **1** : dressed **2** ÉLÉGANT : dressy — **habillement** [abijmɑ̃] *nm* : clothes *pl*, clothing

habit [abi] *nm* **1** : outfit, costume **2** : (religious) habit **3** *or* ~ **de soirée** : evening dress, tails *pl* **4** ~**s** *nmpl* : clothes

habiter [abite] *vt* : live in, inhabit — *vi* : live, reside — **habitant, -tante** [abitɑ̃, -tɑ̃t] *n* **1** : inhabitant **2** : occupant — **habitat** [abita] *nm* **1** : habitat **2** : housing — **habitation** [abitasjɔ̃] *nf* **1** : house, home **2 conditions d'~** : living conditions

habitude [abityd] *nf* **1** : habit **2** COUTUME : custom **3 comme d'~** : as usual **4 d'~** : usually — **habitué, -tuée** [abitɥe] *n* : regular (customer) — **habituel, -tuelle** [abitɥɛl] *adj* : usual, regular — **habituellement** [-tɥɛlmɑ̃] *adv* : usually — **habituer** [abitɥe] *vt* : accustom — **s'habituer** *vr* ~ **à** : get used to

hache ['aʃ] *nf* : ax — **haché, -chée** ['aʃe] *adj* **1** : chopped, minced, ground **2** SACCADÉ : jerky — **hacher** ['aʃe] *vt* : chop, mince, grind — **hachette** [aʃɛt] *nf* : hatchet — **hachis** ['aʃi] *nms & pl* : ground or minced food — **hachoir** ['aʃwar] *nm* **1** : meat grinder **2** : chopper, cleaver **3** : cutting board

hagard, -garde ['agar, -gard] *adj* : distraught, wild

haie ['ɛ] *nf* **1** : hedge **2** : hurdle (in sports) **3** : line, row (of persons)

haillons ['ajɔ̃] *nmpl* : rags, tatters

haïr ['air] {48} *vt* : hate — **haine** ['ɛn] *nf* : hatred, hate — **haineux, -neuse** ['ɛnø, -nøz] *adj* : full of hatred

haïtien, -tienne [aisjɛ̃, -sjɛn] *adj* : Haitian

hâle ['al] *nm* : suntan — **hâlé, -lée** ['ale] *adj* : (sun)tanned

haleine [alɛn] *nf* **1** : breath **2 hors d'~** : out of breath

haleter ['alte] {20} *vi* : pant, gasp — **haletant, -tante** ['altɑ̃, -tɑ̃t] *adj* : panting, breathless — **halètement** ['alɛtmɑ̃] *nm* : gasp

hall ['ol] *nm* : hall, lobby

halle ['al] *nf France* : covered market

hallucination [alysinasjɔ̃] *nf* : hallucination

halte ['alt] *nf* **1** ARRÊT : stop, halt **2** : stopping place **3** ~ **routière** *Can* : rest area (on a highway)

haltère [altɛr] *nm* : dumbbell — **haltérophilie** [alterɔfili] *nf* : weightlifting

hamac ['amak] *nm* : hammock

hamburger ['ɑ̃bœrgœr] *nm* : hamburger (cooked)

hameçon [amsɔ̃] *nm* : fishhook

hamster ['amstɛr] *nm* : hamster

hanche ['ɑ̃ʃ] *nf* : hip

handball ['ɑ̃dbal] *nm* : handball

handicap ['ɑ̃dikap] *nm* : handicap — **handicapé, -pée** ['ɑ̃dikape] *adj* : handicapped — ~ *n* : handicapped person — **handicaper** ['ɑ̃dikape] *vt* : handicap

hangar ['ɑ̃gar] *nm* **1** : (large) shed **2** *or* ~ **d'aviation** : hangar

hanter ['ɑ̃te] *vt* : haunt — **hantise** ['ɑ̃tiz] *nf* : dread

happer ['ape] *vt* **1** : seize, snatch **2 être happé par** : be hit by (a car, etc.)

harceler ['arsəle] {8 *and* 20} *vt* : harass — **harcèlement** ['arsɛlmɑ̃] *nm* : harassment

hardi, -die ['ardi] *adj* : bold, daring — **hardiesse** ['ardjɛs] *nf* : boldness, audacity — **hardiment** ['ardimɑ̃] *adv* : boldly

hareng ['arɑ̃] *nm* : herring

hargne ['arɲ] *nf* : aggressiveness — **hargneux, -neuse** ['arɲø, -ɲøz] *adj* : aggressive, bad-tempered

haricot ['ariko] *nm* **1** : bean **2** ~ **vert** : string bean

harmonica [armɔnika] *nm* : harmonica

harmonie [armɔni] *nf* : harmony — **harmonieux, -nieuse** [armɔnjø, -njøz] *adj* : harmonious — **harmoniser** [armɔnize] *vt* : harmonize — **s'harmoniser** *vr* : go well together

harnais ['arnɛ] *nm* : harness — **harnacher** ['arnaʃe] *vt* : harness (an animal)

harpe ['arp] *nf* : harp

harpon ['arpɔ̃] *nm* : harpoon — **harponner** ['arpɔne] *vt fam* : nab, collar

hasard ['azar] *nm* **1** : chance, luck **2** ~**s** *nmpl* : hazards, danger **3 au ~** : at random — **hasarder** ['azarde] *vt* : risk, venture — **se hasarder** *vr* ~ **à faire** : risk doing — **hasardeux, -deuse** ['azardø, -døz] *adj* : risky

hâte ['at] *nf* **1** : haste, hurry **2 avoir ~ de** : be eager to — **hâter** ['ate] *vt* : hasten, hurry — **se hâter** *vr* : hurry — **hâtif, -tive** ['atif, -tiv] *adj* **1** : hasty, rash **2** PRÉCOCE : early

hausser ['ose] *vt* **1** : raise **2** ~ **les épaules** : shrug one's shoulders — **se hausser** *vr* : stand up, reach up — **hausse** ['os] *nf* **1** : rise, increase **2 à la ~** *or* **en ~** : rising, up

haut, haute ['o, 'ot] *adj* **1** : high **2** : high-ranking — **haut** ['o] *adv* **1** : high **2** FORT : loud, loudly — ~ *nm* **1** SOMMET : top **2 des ~s et des bas** : ups and downs **3 en ~** : upstairs **4 en ~ de** : on top of **5 un mètre de ~** : one meter high — **hautain, -taine** ['otɛ̃, -tɛn] *adj* : haughty — **hautbois** ['obwa] *nms & pl* : oboe — **hautement** ['otmɑ̃] *adv* : highly — **hauteur** ['otœr] *nf* **1** : height **2** ARROGANCE : haughtiness — **haut–le–cœur** ['olkœr] *nms & pl* **avoir des ~** : retch, gag — **haut–parleur** ['oparlœr] *nm, pl* **haut–parleurs** : loudspeaker

hâve ['av] *adj* : gaunt

havre ['avr] *nm* : haven

hayon ['ajɔ̃] *nm* : tailgate

hé ['e] *interj* : hey

hebdomadaire [ɛbdɔmadɛr] *adj & nm* : weekly

héberger [ebɛrʒe] {17} *vt* : accommodate, put up — **hébergement** [ebɛrʒəmɑ̃] *nm* : accommodations *pl*

hébété, -tée [ebete] *adj* : dazed — **hébétude** [ebetyd] *nf* : stupor

hébreu[ebrø] *adj m, pl* **-breux** : Hebrew — ~ *nm* : Hebrew (language) — **hébraïque** [ebraik] *adj* : Hebrew, Hebraic

hein ['ɛ̃] *interj* : eh?, what?

hélas ['elas] *interj* : alas!

héler ['ele] {87} *vt* : hail, summon

hélice [elis] *nf* : propeller

hélicoptère [elikɔptɛr] *nm* : helicopter

hémisphère [emisfɛr] *nm* : hemisphere

hémorragie [emɔraʒi] *nf* : bleeding, hemorrhage

hémorroïdes [emɔrɔid] *nfpl* : hemorrhoids

hennir ['enir] *vi* : neigh — **hennissement** ['enismɑ̃] *nm* : neighing

hépatite [epatit] *nf* : hepatitis

herbe [ɛrb] *nf* **1** : grass **2** : herb (in cooking) **3 en ~** : budding **4 mauvaise ~** : weed — **herbage** [ɛrbaʒ] *nm* : pasture — **herbeux, -beuse** [ɛrbø, -bøz] *adj* : grassy — **herbicide** [ɛrbisid] *nm* : weed killer

héréditaire [ereditɛr] *adj* : hereditary — **hérédité** [eredite] *nf* : heredity

hérésie [erezi] *nf* : heresy

hérisser ['erise] *vt* **1** : ruffle up (fur, feathers, etc.) **2** ~ **qqn** *fam* : irritate s.o. — **se hérisser** *vr* **1** : stand on end **2** *fam* : bristle (with annoyance) — **hérisson** ['erisɔ̃] *nm* : hedgehog

hériter [erite] *vi* ~ **de** : inherit — *vt* : inherit — **héritage** [eritaʒ] *nm* **1** : inheritance **2** : (cultural) heritage — **héritier, -tière** [eritje, -tjɛr] *n* : heir, heiress *f*

hermétique [ɛrmetik] *adj* **1** ÉTANCHE : airtight, watertight **2** OBSCUR : obscure

hernie ['ɛrni] *nf* : hernia

héroïne [erɔin] *nf* **1** : heroine **2** : heroin — **héroïque** [erɔik] *adj* : heroic — **héroïsme** [erɔism] *nm* : heroism

héron ['erɔ̃] *nm* : heron

héros ['ero] *nm* : hero

hésiter [ezite] *vi* : hesitate — **hésitant, -tante** [ezitɑ̃, -tɑ̃t] *adj* : hesitant — **hésitation** [ezitasjɔ̃] *nf* : hesitation

hétérogène [eterɔʒɛn] *adj* : heterogeneous

hétérosexuel, -sexuelle [eterɔsɛksyɛl] *adj & n* : heterosexual

hêtre ['ɛtr] *nm* : beech

heure [œr] *nf* **1** : time **2** : hour **3** ~ **de pointe** : rush hour **4** ~**s supplémentaires** : overtime **5 quelle ~ est-il?** : what time is it? **6 tout à l'~** : later on

heureux, -reuse [œrø, -røz] *adj* **1** : happy **2** SATISFAIT : glad, pleased **3** CHANCEUX : fortunate, lucky — **heureusement** [œrøzmɑ̃] *adv* : fortunately, luckily

heurter ['œrte] *vt* **1** : strike, collide with **2** OFFENSER : offend, go against — *vi* : hit, collide — **se heurter** *vr* ~ **à** : come up against — **heurt** ['œr] *nm* **1** : collision, crash **2** CONFLIT : conflict

hexagone [ɛgzagɔn] *nm* : hexagon

hiberner [ibɛrne] *vi* : hibernate

hibou ['ibu] *nm, pl* **-boux** [ibu] : owl

hic ['ik] *nm fam* **1** : snag **2 voilà le ~** : that's the trouble

hideux, -deuse ['idø, -døz] *adj* : hideous

hier [ijɛr] *adv* : yesterday

hiérarchie ['jerarʃi] *nf* : hierarchy — **hiérarchique** ['jerarʃik] *adj* : hierarchical

hilarité [ilarite] *nf* : hilarity, mirth — **hilarant, -rante** [ilarɑ̃, -rɑ̃t] *adj* : hilarious — **hilare** [ilar] *adj* : mirthful, merry

hindou, -doue [ɛ̃du] *adj* : Hindu

hippie *or* **hippy** ['ipi] *nmf, pl* **-pies** : hippie

hippique [ipik] *adj* : equestrian, horse — **hippodrome** [ipɔdrom] *nm* : racecourse

hippopotame [ipɔpɔtam] *nm* : hippopotamus

hirondelle [irɔ̃dɛl] *nf* : swallow

hirsute [irsyt] *adj* : hairy, shaggy

hispanique [ispanik] *adj* : Hispanic

hisser ['ise] *vt* : hoist, haul up — **se hisser** *vr* : raise oneself up

histoire [istwar] *nf* **1** : history **2** RÉCIT : story **3** AFFAIRE : affair, matter **4** ~**s** *nfpl* : trouble, problems — **historien, -rienne** [istɔrjɛ̃, -rjɛn] *n* : historian — **historique** [istɔrik] *adj* : historical, historic

hiver [ivɛr] *nm* : winter — **hivernal, -nale** [ivɛrnal] *adj, mpl* **-naux** [-no] : winter, wintry

hocher ['ɔʃe] *vt* ~ **la tête** : nod, shake one's head

hochet ['ɔʃɛ] *nm* : rattle

hockey ['ɔkɛ] *nm* : hockey

hollandais, -daise ['ɔlɑ̃dɛ, -dɛz] *adj* : Dutch

holocauste [ɔlɔkost] *nm* : holocaust

homard ['ɔmar] *nm* : lobster

homélie [ɔmeli] *nf* : homily

homéopathie [ɔmeɔpati] *nf* : homeopathy

homicide [ɔmisid] *nm* : homicide

hommage [ɔmaʒ] *nm* **1** : homage **2 rendre ~ à** : pay tribute to

homme [ɔm] *nm* **1** : man **2 l'~** : man, mankind **3** ~ **d'affaires** : businessman

homme–grenouille [ɔmgrənuj] *nm, pl* **hommes–grenouilles** : frogman

homogène [ɔmɔʒɛn] *adj* : homogeneous

homologue [ɔmɔlɔg] *nmf* : counterpart

homologuer [ɔmɔlɔge] *vt* : ratify, approve

homonyme [ɔmɔnim] *nm* **1** : homonym **2** : namesake

homosexuel, -sexuelle [ɔmɔsɛksɥɛl] *adj & n* : homosexual — **homosexualité** [ɔmɔsɛksɥalite] *nf* : homosexuality

honnête [ɔnɛt] *adj* **1** : honest **2** JUSTE : reasonable, fair — **honnêtement** [ɔnɛtmɑ̃] *adv* **1** : honestly **2** DÉCEMMENT : fairly, decently — **honnêteté** [ɔnɛtte] *nf* : honesty

honneur [ɔnœr] *nm* **1** : honor **2** MÉRITE : credit

honorer [ɔnɔre] *vt* **1** : honor **2** : be a credit to **3** PAYER : pay (a debt) — **honorable** [ɔnɔrabl] *adj* **1** : honorable **2** CONVENABLE : respectable, decent — **honorablement** [-rabləmɑ̃] *adv* **1** : honorably **2** SUFFISAMMENT : respectably, decently — **honoraire** [ɔnɔrɛr] *adj* : honorary — **honoraires** *nmpl* : fees — **honorifique** [ɔnɔrifik] *adj* : honorary

honte ['ɔ̃t] *nf* **1** : shame **2 avoir ~** : be ashamed — **honteux, -teuse** ['ɔ̃tø, -tøz] *adj* **1** : ashamed **2** DÉSHONORANT : shameful

hôpital [ɔpital] *nm, pl* **-taux** [-to] : hospital

hoquet ['ɔkɛ] *nm* **1** : hiccup **2 avoir le ~** : have the hiccups — **hoqueter** ['ɔkte] {8} *vi* : hiccup

horaire [ɔrɛr] *adj* : hourly — ~ *nm* : timetable, schedule

horizon [ɔrizɔ̃] *nm* **1** : horizon **2** : view, vista — **horizontal, -tale** [ɔrizɔ̃tal] *adj, mpl* **-taux** [-to] : horizontal

horloge [ɔrlɔʒ] *nf* : clock — **horloger, -gère** [ɔrlɔrʒe, -ʒɛr] *n* : watchmaker
hormone [ɔrmɔn] *nf* : hormone
horoscope [ɔrɔskɔp] *nm* : horoscope
horreur [ɔrœr] *nf* **1** : horror **2 avoir ~ de** : detest — **horrible** [ɔribl] *adj* : horrible — **horrifiant, -fiante** [ɔrifjɑ̃, -fjɑ̃t] *adj* : horrifying — **horrifier** [ɔrifje] {96} *vt* : horrify
hors ['ɔr] *prep* **1** : except for, save **2 ~ de** : out of, outside, beyond **3 être ~ de soi** : be beside oneself — **hors–bord** ['ɔrbɔr] *nms & pl* **1** : outboard motor **2** : speedboat — **hors–d'œuvre** ['ɔrdœvr] *nms & pl* : hors d'oeuvre — **hors–la–loi** ['ɔrlalwa] *nms & pl* : outlaw
horticulture [ɔrtikyltyr] *nf* : horticulture
hospice [ɔspis] *nm France* **1** : home (for the elderly, etc.) **2** : hospice
hospitalier, -lière [ɔspitalje, -jɛr] *adj* **1** : hospital **2** ACCUEILLANT : hospitable — **hospitaliser** [ɔspitalize] *vt* : hospitalize — **hospitalité** [ɔspitalite] *nf* : hospitality
hostie [ɔsti] *nf* : host (in religion)
hostile [ɔstil] *adj* : hostile — **hostilité** [ɔstilite] *nf* **1** : hostility **2 ~s** *nfpl* : hostilities, war
hot–dog ['ɔtdɔg] *nm, pl* **hot–dogs** : hot dog
hôte, hôtesse [ot, otɛs] *n* : host, hostess *f* — **hôte** *nmf* : guest
hôtel [otɛl] *nm* **1** : hotel **2 ~ de ville** : town hall — **hôtelier, -lière** [otəlje, -jɛr] *adj* : hotel — **~** *n* : hotel manager, innkeeper — **hôtellerie** [otɛlri] *nf* : hotel business
hôtesse [otɛs] *nf* **1** → **hôte 2** : receptionist **3 ~ de l'air** : stewardess
hotte ['ɔt] *nf* **1** : basket (carried on the back) **2** : hood (of a chimney or stove)
houblon ['ublɔ̃] *nm* : hops *pl*
houe ['u] *nf* : hoe
houille ['uj] *nf* : coal — **houiller, -lère** ['uje, -jɛr] *adj* : coal, coal-mining — **houillère** *nf* : coal mine
houle ['ul] *nf* : swell, surge
houlette ['ulɛt] *nf* **sous la ~ de** : under the guidance of
houleux, -leuse ['ulø, -løz] *adj* : stormy
houppe ['up] *or* **houppette** ['upɛt] *nf* : powder puff
hourra ['ura] *nm & interj* : hurrah
housse ['us] *nf* : cover, dust cover
houx ['u] *nms & pl* : holly
huard *or* **huart** ['yar] *nm Can* : loon
hublot ['yblo] *nm* : porthole
huche ['yʃ] *nf* **~ à pain** : bread box
huer ['ɥe] *vt* : boo — *vi* : hoot — **huées** ['ɥe] *nfpl* : boos, booing
huile [ɥil] *nf* **1** : oil **2** : oil painting — **huiler** [ɥile] *vt* : oil — **huileux, -leuse** [ɥilø, -løz] *adj* : oily — **huilier** [ɥilje] *nm* : cruet
huis [ɥi] *nm* **à ~ clos** : behind closed doors
huissier [ɥisje] *nm* **1** : usher **2** *or* **~ de justice** : bailiff
huit ['ɥit, *before consonant* 'ɥi] *adj* **1** : eight **2** : eighth (in dates) — **~** *nms & pl* : eight —**huitaine** ['ɥitɛn] *nf* **une ~ (de jours)** : about a week — **huitième** ['ɥitjɛm] *adj & nmf & nm* : eighth
huître [ɥitr] *nf* : oyster
hululer ['ylyle] *vi* : hoot — **hululement** ['ylylmɑ̃] *nm* : hoot (of an owl)
humain, -maine [ymɛ̃, -mɛn] *adj* **1** : human **2** BIENVEILLANT : humane — **humain** *nm* : human being — **humanitaire** [ymanitɛr] *adj* : humanitarian — **humanité** [ymanite] *nf* : humanity
humble [œbl] *adj* : humble — **humblement** [œbləmɑ̃] *adv* : humbly
humecter [ymɛkte] *vt* : dampen, moisten
humer ['yme] *vt* **1** : breathe in, inhale **2** : smell
humeur [ymœr] *nf* **1** : mood, humor **2** CARACTÈRE : temperament
humide [ymid] *adj* **1** : moist, damp **2** : humid — **humidité** [ymidite] *nf* **1** : dampness **2** : humidity
humilier [ymilje] {96} *vt* : humiliate — **s'humilier** *vr* : humble oneself — **humiliant, -liante** [ymiljɑ̃, -jɑ̃t] *adj* : humiliating — **humiliation** [ymiljasjɔ̃] *nf* : humiliation — **humilité** [ymilite] *nf* : humility
humour [ymur] *nm* **1** : humor, wit **2 avoir de l'~** : have a sense of humor — **humoriste** [ymɔrist] *nmf* : humorist — **humoristique** [ymɔristik] *adj* : humorous
huppé, -pée ['ype] *adj fam* : posh, high-class
hurler ['yrle] *vt* : yell out — *vi* **1** : howl, roar **2** CRIER : yell, shout — **hurlement** ['yrləmɑ̃] *nm* : howl, yell
hutte ['yt] *nf* : hut
hybride [ibrid] *adj & nm* : hybrid
hydratant, -tante [idratɑ̃, -tɑ̃t] *adj* : moisturizing — **hydratant** *nm* : moisturizer
hydrate [idrat] *nm* **~ de carbone** : carbohydrate
hydraulique [idrolik] *adj* : hydraulic
hydroélectrique *or* **hydro–électrique** [idrɔelɛktrik] *adj* : hydroelectric
hydrogène [idrɔʒɛn] *nm* : hydrogen
hyène [jɛn] *nf* : hyena
hygiène [iʒjɛn] *nf* : hygiene — **hygiénique** [iʒjenik] *adj* : hygienic
hymne [imn] *nm* **1** : hymn **2 ~ nationale** : national anthem
hyperactif, -tive [ipɛraktif, -tiv] *adj* : hyperactive
hypermétrope [ipɛrmetrɔp] *adj* : farsighted
hypertension [ipɛrtɑ̃sjɔ̃] *nf* : high blood pressure
hypnotiser [ipnɔtize] *vt* : hypnotize — **hypnose** [ipnoz] *nf* : hypnosis
hypocrisie [ipɔkrizi] *nf* : hypocrisy — **hypocrite** [ipɔkrit] *adj* : hypocritical — **~** *nmf* : hypocrite
hypothèque [ipɔtɛk] *nf* : mortgage — **hypothéquer** [ipɔteke] {87} *vt* : mortgage
hypothèse [ipɔtɛz] *nf* : hypothesis — **hypothétique** [ipɔtetik] *adj* : hypothetical
hystérie [isteri] *nf* : hysteria — **hystérique** [isterik] *adj* : hysterical

I

i [i] *nm* : i, ninth letter of the alphabet
iceberg [ajsbɛrg] *nm* : iceberg
ici [isi] *adv* **1** : here **2** : now **3 d'~ là** : by then **4 par ~** : this way
icône [ikon] *nf* : icon
idéal, idéale [ideal] *adj, mpl* **idéals** *or* **idéaux** [ideo] : ideal — **idéal** *nm* : ideal — **idéaliser** [idealize] *vt* : idealize — **idéaliste** [idealist] *adj* : idealistic — **~** *nmf* : idealist
idée [ide] *nf* : idea
identifier [idɑ̃tifje] {96} *vt* : identify — **s'identifier** *vr* **~ à** : identify with — **identification** [idɑ̃tifikasjɔ̃] *nf* : identification — **identique** [idɑ̃tik] *adj* : identical — **identité** [idɑ̃tite] *nf* : identity
idéologie [ideɔlɔʒi] *nf* : ideology — **idéologique** [ideɔlɔʒik] *adj* : ideological
idiome [idjom] *nm* : idiom (language) — **idiomatique** [idjɔmatik] *adj* : idiomatic
idiot, -diote [idjo, -djɔt] *adj* : idiotic — **~** *n* : idiot, fool — **idiotie** [idjɔsi] *nf* : idiocy
idole [idɔl] *nf* : idol — **idolâtrer** [idɔlatre] *vt* : idolize
idyllique [idilik] *adj* : idyllic
igloo [iglu] *nm* : igloo
ignifuge [iɲifyʒ] *adj* : fireproof
ignoble [iɲɔbl] *adj* : base, vile
ignorance [iɲɔrɑ̃s] *nf* : ignorance — **ignorant, -rante** [iɲɔrɑ̃, -rɑ̃t] *adj* : ignorant — **ignorer** [iɲɔre] *vt* **1** : be unaware of **2** : ignore
il [il] *pron* **1** : he, it **2** (*as subject of an impersonal verb*) : it **3 ils** *pron pl* : they **4 il y a** : there is, there are
île [il] *nf* : island, isle
illégal, -gale [ilegal] *adj, mpl* **-gaux** [-go] : illegal — **illégalité** [ilegalite] *nf* : illegality
illégitime [ileʒitim] *adj* : illegitimate — **illégitimité** [ileʒitimite] *nf* : illegitimacy
illettré, -trée [iletre] *adj & n* : illiterate
illicite [ilisit] *adj* : illicit
illimité, -tée [ilimite] *adj* : boundless, unlimited
illisible [ilizibl] *adj* : illegible
illogique [ilɔʒik] *adj* : illogical
illuminer [ilymine] *vt* : illuminate, light up — **illumination** [ilyminasjɔ̃] *nf* : illumination
illusion [ilyzjɔ̃] *nf* : illusion — **illusoire** [ilyzwar] *adj* : illusory
illustration [ilystrasjɔ̃] *nf* : illustration — **illustre** [ilystr] *adj* : illustrious, renowned — **illustré, -trée** [ilystre] *adj* : illustrated — **illustrer** [ilystre] *vt* : illustrate
îlot [ilo] *nm* **1** : small island **2** : block (of houses)
ils [il] → **il**
image [imaʒ] *nf* **1** : image **2** DESSIN : picture
imaginer [imaʒine] *vt* **1** : imagine **2** INVENTER : devise, think up — **s'imaginer** *vr* : picture oneself — **imaginaire** [imaʒinɛr] *adj* : imaginary — **imaginatif, -tive** [imaʒinatif, -tiv] *adj* : imaginative — **imagination** [imaʒinasjɔ̃] *nf* : imagination
imbattable [ɛ̃batabl] *adj* : unbeatable
imbécile [ɛ̃besil] *adj* : stupid, idiotic — **~** *nmf* : fool, idiot — **imbécillité** [ɛ̃besilite] *nf* : idiocy, stupidity
imbiber [ɛ̃bibe] *vt* : soak — **s'imbiber** *vr* : get soaked
imbuvable [ɛ̃byvabl] *adj* : undrinkable
imiter [imite] *vt* **1** COPIER : imitate, mimic **2** : look (just) like — **imitateur, -trice** [imitatœr, -tris] *n* **1** : imitator **2** : impersonator — **imitation** [imitasjɔ̃] *nf* **1** : imitation **2** : impersonation
immaculé, -lée [imakyle] *adj* : immaculate
immangeable [ɛ̃mɑ̃ʒabl] *adj* : inedible
immanquable [ɛ̃mɑ̃kabl] *adj* **1** : impossible to miss **2** INÉVITABLE : inevitable
immatriculer [imatrikyle] *vt* : register — **immatriculation** [imatrikylasjɔ̃] *nf* **1** : registration **2 plaque d'~** : license plate
immature [imatyr] *adj* : immature — **immaturité** [imatyrite] *nf* : immaturity
immédiat, -diate [imedja, -djat] *adj* : immediate — **immédiatement** [-djatmɑ̃] *adv* : immediately
immense [imɑ̃s] *adj* : immense — **immensité** [imɑ̃site] *nf* : immensity
immerger [imɛrʒe] {17} *vt* : immerse, submerge — **immersion** [imɛrsjɔ̃] *nf* : immersion
immeuble [imœbl] *nm* : building
immigrer [imigre] *vi* : immigrate — **immigrant, -grante** [imigrɑ̃, -grɑ̃t] *adj & n* : immigrant — **immigration** [imigrasjɔ̃] *nf* : immigration — **immigré, -grée** [imigre] *n* : immigrant
imminent, -nente [iminɑ̃, -nɑ̃t] *adj* : imminent — **imminence** [iminɑ̃s] *nf* : imminence
immiscer [imise] {6} *v* **s'immiscer** *vr* **~ dans** : interfere with
immobile [imɔbil] *adj* : motionless
immobilier, -lière [imɔbilje, -ljɛr] *adj* : real estate, property
immobiliser [imɔbilize] *vt* **1** : immobilize **2** ARRÊTER : bring to a halt — **s'immobiliser** *vr* : stop — **immobilité** [imɔbilite] *nf* : immobility, stillness
immodéré, -rée [imɔdere] *adj* : immoderate, excessive
immonde [imɔ̃d] *adj* : foul, filthy
immoral, -rale [imɔral] *adj, mpl* **-raux** [-ro] : immoral — **immoralité** [imɔralite] *nf* : immorality
immortalité [imɔrtalite] *nf* : immortality — **immortel, -telle** [imɔrtɛl] *adj* : immortal
immuable [imɥabl] *adj* : unchanging
immuniser [imynize] *vt* : immunize — **immunisation** [-nizasjɔ̃] *nf* : immunization — **immunité** [imynite] *nf* : immunity
impact [ɛ̃pakt] *nm* : impact
impair, -paire [ɛ̃pɛr] *adj* : odd, uneven — **impair** *nm* : blunder
impardonnable [ɛ̃pardɔnabl] *adj* : unforgivable
imparfait, -faite [ɛ̃parfɛ, -fɛt] *adj* : imperfect — **imparfait** *nm* : imperfect (tense)
impartial, -tiale [ɛ̃parsjal] *adj, mpl* **-tiaux** [-sjo] : unbiased, impartial — **impartialité** [ɛ̃parsjalite] *nf* : impartiality
impartir [ɛ̃partir] *vt* : grant, bestow
impasse [ɛ̃pas] *nf* **1** : impasse, deadlock **2** CUL-DE-SAC : dead end
impassible [ɛ̃pasibl] *adj* : impassive
impatient, -tiente [ɛ̃pasjɑ̃, -sjɑ̃t] *adj* : impatient — **impatiemment** [ɛ̃pasjamɑ̃] *adv* : impatiently — **impatience** [-sjɑ̃s] *nf* : impatience — **impatienter** [ɛ̃pasjɑ̃te] *vt* : annoy — **s'impatienter** *vr* : lose patience
impeccable [ɛ̃pekabl] *adj* : impeccable, faultless
impénétrable [ɛ̃penetrabl] *adj* **1** : impenetrable **2** : inscrutable
impénitent, -tente [ɛ̃penitɑ̃, -tɑ̃t] *adj* : unrepentant
impensable [ɛ̃pɑ̃sabl] *adj* : unthinkable
impératif, -tive [ɛ̃peratif, -tiv] *adj* : imperative — **impératif** *nm* : imperative (mood)
impératrice [ɛ̃peratris] *nf* : empress
imperceptible [ɛ̃pɛrsɛptibl] *adj* : imperceptible
imperfection [ɛ̃pɛrfɛksjɔ̃] *nf* : imperfection
impérial, -riale [ɛ̃perjal] *adj, mpl* **-riaux** [-rjo] : imperial — **impérialisme** [ɛ̃perjalism] *nm* : imperialism
impérieux, -rieuse [ɛ̃perjø, -jøz] *adj* **1** : imperious **2** PRESSANT : urgent
impérissable [ɛ̃perisabl] *adj* : imperishable
imperméable [ɛ̃pɛrmeabl] *adj* : waterproof — **~** *nm* : raincoat
impersonnel, -nelle [ɛ̃pɛrsɔnɛl] *adj* : impersonal
impertinent, -nente [ɛ̃pɛrtinɑ̃, -nɑ̃t] *adj* : impertinent — **impertinence** [-tinɑ̃s] *nf* : impertinence
imperturbable [ɛ̃pɛrtyrbabl] *adj* : unflappable
impétueux, -tueuse, [ɛ̃petɥø, -tɥøz] *adj* : impetuous
impitoyable [ɛ̃pitwajabl] *adj* : merciless, pitiless
implacable [ɛ̃plakabl] *adj* : implacable
implanter [ɛ̃plɑ̃te] *vt* **1** : establish **2** : implant (in medicine) — **s'implanter** *vr* : be set up — **implantation** [ɛ̃plɑ̃tasjɔ̃] *nf* : establishment
implication [ɛ̃plikasjɔ̃] *nf* : implication
implicite [ɛ̃plisit] *adj* : implicit
impliquer [ɛ̃plike] *vt* **1** : implicate **2** SUPPOSER : imply **3** ENTRAÎNER : entail, involve — **s'impliquer** *vr* : become involved
implorer [ɛ̃plɔre] *vt* : implore
imploser [ɛ̃ploze] *vi* : implode
impoli, -lie [ɛ̃pɔli] *adj* : impolite, rude — **impolitesse** [ɛ̃pɔlitɛs] *nf* : rudeness
impopulaire [ɛ̃pɔpylɛr] *adj* : unpopular
importer[1] [ɛ̃pɔrte] *vi* **1** : matter, be important **2 n'importe qui** : anyone, anybody **3 n'importe quoi** : anything **4 peu importe** : no matter — **importance** [ɛ̃pɔrtɑ̃s] *nf* : importance — **important, -tante** [ɛ̃pɔrtɑ̃, -tɑ̃t] *adj* **1** : important **2** LARGE : considerable — **important** *nm* **l'~** : the important thing, the main thing
importer[2] *vt* : import — **importateur, -trice** [ɛ̃pɔrtatœr, -tris] *n* : importer — **importation** [ɛ̃pɔrtasjɔ̃] *nf* **1** : importing **2** : import
importun, -tune [ɛ̃pɔrtœ̃, -tyn] *adj* : troublesome, unwelcome — **~** *n* : nuisance, pest — **importuner** [ɛ̃pɔrtyne] *vt* : pester
imposer [ɛ̃poze] *vt* **1** : impose **2** TAXER : tax — **s'imposer** *vr* **1** : be essential **2** : stand out — **imposable** [ɛ̃pozabl] *adj* : taxable — **imposant, -sante** [ɛ̃pozɑ̃, -zɑ̃t] *adj* : imposing
impossible [ɛ̃pɔsibl] *adj* : impossible — **~** *nm* **l'~** : the impossible — **impossibilité** [ɛ̃pɔsibilite] *nf* : impossibility
imposteur [ɛ̃pɔstœr] *nm* : impostor
impôt [ɛ̃po] *nm* : tax, duty
impotent, -tente [ɛ̃pɔtɑ̃, -tɑ̃t] *adj* : infirm, disabled
impraticable [ɛ̃pratikabl] *adj* : impassable (of a road, etc.)
imprécis, -cise [ɛ̃presi, -siz] *adj* : imprecise — **imprécision** [ɛ̃presizjɔ̃] *nf* : imprecision
imprégner [ɛ̃preɲe] {87} *vt* IMBIBER : impregnate, soak — **s'imprégner** *vr* **~ de** : become filled with
impression [ɛ̃presjɔ̃] *nf* **1** : impression **2** : printing — **impressionnable** [ɛ̃presjɔnabl] *adj* : impressionable — **impressionnant, -nante** [ɛ̃presjɔnɑ̃, -nɑ̃t] *adj* : impressive — **impressionner** [ɛ̃presjɔne] *vt* : impress
imprévisible [ɛ̃previzibl] *adj* : unpredictable
imprévoyance [ɛ̃prevwajɑ̃s] *nf* : lack of foresight — **imprévu, -vue** [ɛ̃prevy] *adj* : unforeseen, unexpected
imprimer [ɛ̃prime] *vt* **1** : print **2** : imprint — **imprimante** [ɛ̃primɑ̃t] *nf* : printer — **imprimé, -mée** [ɛ̃prime] *adj* : printed (of fabric, etc.) — **imprimerie** [ɛ̃primri] *nf* **1** : printing **2** : print shop — **imprimeur, -meuse** [ɛ̃primœr, -møz] *n* : printer
improbable [ɛ̃prɔbabl] *adj* : improbable, unlikely — **improbabilité** [-babilite] *nf* : unlikelihood
impromptu, -tue [ɛ̃prɔ̃pty] *adj* : impromptu
impropre [ɛ̃prɔpr] *adj* **1** INCORRECT : incorrect **2** INADAPTÉ : unsuitable
improviser [ɛ̃prɔvize] *v* : improvise — **improvisation** [ɛ̃prɔvizasjɔ̃] *nf* : improvisation
improviste [ɛ̃prɔvist] **à l'~** *adv phr* : unexpectedly
imprudent, -dente [ɛ̃prydɑ̃, -dɑ̃t] *adj* : rash, careless — **imprudemment** [ɛ̃prydamɑ̃] *adv* : carelessly — **imprudence** [ɛ̃prydɑ̃s] *nf* : carelessness
impudent, -dente [ɛ̃pydɑ̃, -dɑ̃t] *adj* : impudent — **impudence** [ɛ̃pydɑ̃s] *nf* : impudence
impudique [ɛ̃pydik] *adj* : immodest, indecent
impuissance [ɛ̃pɥisɑ̃s] *nf* **1** : helplessness **2** : (physical) impotence — **impuissant, -sante** [ɛ̃pɥisɑ̃, -sɑ̃t] *adj* **1** : helpless **2** : impotent (in medicine)
impulsion [ɛ̃pylsjɔ̃] *nf* **1** : impulse **2** POUSSÉE : impetus — **impulsif, -sive** [ɛ̃pylsif, -siv] *adj* : impulsive — **impulsivité** [ɛ̃pylsivite] *nf* : impulsiveness
impuni, -nie [ɛ̃pyni] *adj* : unpunished — **impunément** [ɛ̃pynemɑ̃] *adv* : with impunity — **impunité** [ɛ̃pynite] *nf* : impunity
impur, -pure [ɛ̃pyr] *adj* : impure — **impureté** [ɛ̃pyrte] *nf* : impurity
imputer [ɛ̃pyte] *vt* : impute
inabordable [inabɔrdabl] *adj* : inaccessible
inacceptable [inaksɛptabl] *adj* : unacceptable
inaccessible [inaksesibl] *adj* : inaccessible
inaccoutumé, -mée [inakutyme] *adj* : unaccustomed
inachevé, -vée [inaʃve] *adj* : unfinished
inaction [inaksjɔ̃] *nf* : inaction, inactivity — **inactif, -tive** [inaktif, -tiv] *adj* : inactive — **inactivité** [inaktivite] *nf* : inactivity
inadapté, -tée [inadapte] *adj* **1** : maladjusted **2 ~ à** : unsuited to, unsuitable for
inadéquat, -quate [inadekwa, -kwat] *adj* : inadequate
inadmissible [inadmisibl] *adj* : unacceptable
inadvertance [inadvɛrtɑ̃s] *nf* **par ~** : inadvertently
inaltérable [inalterabl] *adj* : stable, unchanging
inamovible [inamɔvibl] *adj* : fixed, permanent
inanimé, -mée [inanime] *adj* **1** : inanimate **2** INCONSCIENT : unconscious
inaperçu, -çue [inapɛrsy] *adj* : unseen, unnoticed
inapplicable [inaplikabl] *adj* : inapplicable
inapte [inapt] *adj* : unfit, unsuited
inarticulé, -lée [inartikyle] *adj* : inarticulate
inassouvi, -vie [inasuvi] *adj* : unsatisfied, unfulfilled
inattaquable [inatakabl] *adj* **1** : irreproachable **2** IRRÉFUTABLE : irrefutable

inattendu, -due [inatɑ̃dy] *adj* : unexpected
inattention [inatɑ̃sjɔ̃] *nf* 1 : inattention 2 **faute d'~** : careless error — **inattentif, -tive** [inatɑ̃tif, -tiv] *adj* : inattentive, distracted
inaudible [inodibl] *adj* : inaudible
inaugurer [inogyre] *vt* : inaugurate — **inaugural, -rale** [inogyral] *adj, mpl* **-raux** [-ro] : inaugural — **inauguration** [inogyrasjɔ̃] *nf* : inauguration
incalculable [ɛ̃kalkylabl] *adj* : incalculable, countless
incapable [ɛ̃kapabl] *adj* : incapable, unable — **incapacité** [ɛ̃kapasite] *nf* : incapacity, inability
incarcérer [ɛ̃karsere] {87} *vt* : incarcerate
incarner [ɛ̃karne] *vt* : play (a role)
incassable [ɛ̃kasabl] *adj* : unbreakable
incendie [ɛ̃sɑ̃di] *nm* : fire — **incendiaire** [ɛ̃sɑ̃djɛr] *adj* : inflammatory
incendier [ɛ̃sɑ̃dje] {96} *vt* : set on fire
incertain, -taine [ɛ̃sɛrtɛ̃, -tɛn] *adj* 1 : uncertain 2 VAGUE : indistinct — **incertitude** [ɛ̃sɛrtityd] *nf* : uncertainty
incessant, -sante [ɛ̃sesɑ̃, -sɑ̃t] *adj* : incessant
inceste [ɛ̃sɛst] *nm* : incest — **incestueux, -tueuse** [ɛ̃sɛstɥø, -tɥøz] *adj* : incestuous
inchangé, -gée [ɛ̃ʃɑ̃ʒe] *adj* : unchanged
incidence [ɛ̃sidɑ̃s] *nf* : effect, impact
incident [ɛ̃sidɑ̃] *nm* : incident
incinérer [ɛ̃sinere] {87} *vt* 1 : incinerate 2 : cremate — **incinérateur** [ɛ̃sineratœr] *nm* : incinerator — **incinération** [ɛ̃sinerasjɔ̃] *nf* 1 : incineration 2 : cremation
incision [ɛ̃sizjɔ̃] *nf* : incision
inciter [ɛ̃site] *vt* : incite
incliner [ɛ̃kline] *vt* 1 PENCHER : tilt, bend 2 INCITER : incline, prompt — *vi* **~ à** : be inclined to — **s'incliner** *vr* 1 : tilt, lean 2 **~ devant** : bow to — **inclinaison** [ɛ̃klinɛzɔ̃] *nf* : incline, slope — **inclination** [ɛ̃klinasjɔ̃] *nf* 1 : nod, bow 2 TENDANCE : inclination, tendency
inclure [ɛ̃klyr] {39} *vt* 1 : include 2 JOINDRE : enclose — **inclus, -cluse** [ɛ̃kly, -klyz] *adj* : inclusive — **inclusion** [ɛ̃klyzjɔ̃] *nf* : inclusion
incognito [ɛ̃kɔɲito] *adv & adj* : incognito
incohérent, -rente [ɛ̃kɔerɑ̃, -rɑ̃t] *adj* : incoherent — **incohérence** [ɛ̃kɔerɑ̃s] *nf* : incoherence
incolore [ɛ̃kɔlɔr] *adj* : colorless
incommensurable [ɛ̃kɔmɑ̃syrabl] *adj* : immeasurable
incommode [ɛ̃kɔmɔd] *adj* 1 : inconvenient 2 INCONFORTABLE : uncomfortable — **incommoder** [ɛ̃kɔmɔde] *vt* : inconvenience
incomparable [ɛ̃kɔ̃parabl] *adj* : incomparable
incompatible [ɛ̃kɔ̃patibl] *adj* : incompatible
incompétent, -tente [ɛ̃kɔ̃petɑ̃, -tɑ̃t] *adj* : incompetent — **incompétence** [ɛ̃kɔ̃petɑ̃s] *nf* : incompetence
incomplet, -plète [ɛ̃kɔ̃plɛ, -plɛt] *adj* : incomplete
incompréhensible [ɛ̃kɔ̃preɑ̃sibl] *adj* : incomprehensible — **incompréhension** [ɛ̃kɔ̃preɑ̃sjɔ̃] *nf* : lack of understanding — **incompris, -prise** [ɛ̃kɔ̃pri, -priz] *adj* : misunderstood
inconcevable [ɛ̃kɔ̃svabl] *adj* : inconceivable
inconciliable [ɛ̃kɔ̃siljabl] *adj* : irreconcilable
inconditionnel, -nelle [ɛ̃kɔ̃disjɔnɛl] *adj* : unconditional — **~** *n* : enthusiast
inconduite [ɛ̃kɔ̃dɥit] *nf* : misconduct
inconfort [ɛ̃kɔ̃fɔr] *nm* : discomfort — **inconfortable** [ɛ̃kɔ̃fɔrtabl] *adj* : uncomfortable
incongru, -grue [ɛ̃kɔ̃gry] *adj* 1 : incongruous 2 : unseemly, inappropriate
inconnu, -nue [ɛ̃kɔny] *adj* : unknown — **~** *n* 1 : unknown (person) 2 ÉTRANGER : stranger
inconscient, -ciente [ɛ̃kɔ̃sjɑ̃, -sjɑ̃t] *adj* 1 : unaware 2 : unconscious — **inconsciemment** [ɛ̃kɔ̃sjamɑ̃] *adv* 1 : unconsciously 2 : thoughtlessly — **inconscience** [ɛ̃kɔ̃sjɑ̃s] *nf* 1 : unconsciousness 2 : thoughtlessness
inconsidéré, -rée [ɛ̃kɔ̃sidere] *adj* : thoughtless
inconsistant, -tante [ɛ̃kɔ̃sistɑ̃, -tɑ̃t] *adj* : flimsy, weak
inconsolable [ɛ̃kɔ̃sɔlabl] *adj* : inconsolable
inconstant, -stante [ɛ̃kɔ̃stɑ̃, -stɑ̃t] *adj* : fickle
incontestable [ɛ̃kɔ̃tɛstabl] *adj* : unquestionable, indisputable — **incontesté, -tée** [ɛ̃kɔ̃tɛste] *adj* : undisputed
incontournable [ɛ̃kɔ̃turnabl] *adj* : essential, that cannot be ignored
inconvenant, -nante [ɛ̃kɔ̃vnɑ̃, -nɑ̃t] *adj* : improper, unseemly — **inconvenance** [ɛ̃kɔ̃vnɑ̃s] *nf* : impropriety
inconvénient [ɛ̃kɔ̃venjɑ̃] *nm* : disadvantage, drawback
incorporer [ɛ̃kɔrpɔre] *vt* : incorporate
incorrect, -recte [ɛ̃kɔrɛkt] *adj* 1 ERRONÉ : incorrect 2 INCONVENANT : improper — **incorrectement** [ɛ̃kɔrɛktəmɑ̃] *adv* : wrongly
incorrigible [ɛ̃kɔriʒibl] *adj* : incorrigible
incrédule [ɛ̃kredyl] *adj* : incredulous
incriminer [ɛ̃krimine] *vt* : incriminate — **incrimination** [ɛ̃kriminasjɔ̃] *nf* : incrimination
incroyable [ɛ̃krwajabl] *adj* : unbelievable, incredible — **incroyant, -croyante** [ɛ̃krwajɑ̃, -jɑ̃t] *n* : unbeliever
inculper [ɛ̃kylpe] *vt* : indict, charge — **inculpation** [ɛ̃kylpasjɔ̃] *nf* : indictment, charge — **inculpé, -pée** [ɛ̃kylpe] *n* : accused, defendant
inculquer [ɛ̃kylke] *vt* : instill
inculte [ɛ̃kylt] *adj* 1 : uncultivated 2 : uneducated
incurable [ɛ̃kyrabl] *adj* : incurable
incursion [ɛ̃kyrsjɔ̃] *nf* : incursion, foray
indécent, -cente [ɛ̃desɑ̃, -sɑ̃t] *adj* : indecent — **indécence** [ɛ̃desɑ̃s] *nf* : indecency
indéchiffrable [ɛ̃deʃifrabl] *adj* : indecipherable
indécis, -cise [ɛ̃desi, -siz] *adj* 1 : indecisive 2 INCERTAIN : undecided — **indécision** [ɛ̃desizjɔ̃] *nf* : indecision
indéfini, -nie [ɛ̃defini] *adj* 1 : indefinite 2 VAGUE : ill-defined — **indéfinissable** [ɛ̃definisabl] *adj* : indefinable
indélébile [ɛ̃delebil] *adj* : indelible
indélicat, -cate [ɛ̃delika, -kat] *adj* 1 : indelicate 2 MALHONNÊTE : dishonest
indemne [ɛ̃dɛmn] *adj* : unharmed
indemnité [ɛ̃dɛmnite] *nf* 1 : indemnity 2 ALLOCATION : allowance — **indemniser** [ɛ̃dɛmnize] *vt* : indemnify, compensate
indéniable [ɛ̃denjabl] *adj* : undeniable
indépendant, -dante [ɛ̃depɑ̃dɑ̃, -dɑ̃t] *adj* : independent — **indépendamment** [ɛ̃depɑ̃damɑ̃] *adv* : independently — **indépendance** [-pɑ̃dɑ̃s] *nf* : independence
indescriptible [ɛ̃dɛskriptibl] *adj* : indescribable
indésirable [ɛ̃dezirabl] *adj* : undesirable
indestructible [ɛ̃dɛstryktibl] *adj* : indestructible
indéterminé, -née [ɛ̃detɛrmine] *adj* : indeterminate, unspecified
index [ɛ̃dɛks] *nm* 1 : index 2 : forefinger, index finger — **indexer** [ɛ̃dekse] *vt* : index
indication [ɛ̃dikasjɔ̃] *nf* 1 : indication 2 RENSEIGNEMENT : information 3 **~s** *nfpl* : instructions, directions — **indicateur, -trice** [ɛ̃dikatœr, -tris] *adj* → **panneau, poteau** — **~** *n* : informer — **indicateur** *nm* 1 GUIDE : guide, directory 2 : gauge, meter — **indicatif, -tive** [ɛ̃dikatif, -tiv] *adj* : indicative — **indicatif** *nm* : indicative (mood)
indice [ɛ̃dis] *nm* 1 SIGNE : sign, indication 2 : clue 3 : index (of prices, etc.) 4 ÉVALUATION : rating
indicible [ɛ̃disibl] *adj* : inexpressible
indien, -dienne [ɛ̃djɛ̃, -djɛn] *adj* : Indian
indifférent, -rente [ɛ̃diferɑ̃, -rɑ̃t] *adj* : indifferent — **indifférence** [ɛ̃diferɑ̃s] *nf* : indifference
indigène [ɛ̃diʒɛn] *adj* : indigenous, native — **~** *nmf* : native
indigent, -gente [ɛ̃diʒɑ̃, -ʒɑ̃t] *adj* : destitute
indigestion [ɛ̃diʒɛstjɔ̃] *nf* : indigestion — **indigeste** [ɛ̃diʒɛst] *adj* : indigestible
indignation [ɛ̃diɲasjɔ̃] *nf* : indignation — **indigne** [ɛ̃diɲ] *adj* 1 : unworthy 2 MÉPRISABLE : shameful — **indigné, -gnée** [ɛ̃diɲe] *adj* : indignant — **indigner** [ɛ̃diɲe] *vt* : outrage — **s'indigner** *vr* : be indignant — **indignité** [ɛ̃diɲite] *nf* 1 : unworthiness 2 : indignity
indigo [ɛ̃digo] *adj & nm* : indigo
indiquer [ɛ̃dike] *vt* 1 : indicate, point out 2 DIRE : give, state — **indiqué, -quée** [ɛ̃dike] *adj* 1 : given, specified 2 RECOMMANDÉ : advisable 3 APPROPRIÉ : appropriate
indirect, -recte [ɛ̃dirɛkt] *adj* : indirect — **indirectement** [-rɛktəmɑ̃] *adv* : indirectly
indiscipliné, -née [ɛ̃disipline] *adj* : undisciplined, unruly
indiscrétion [ɛ̃diskresjɔ̃] *nf* : indiscretion — **indiscret, -crète** [ɛ̃diskrɛ, -krɛt] *adj* : indiscreet
indispensable [ɛ̃dispɑ̃sabl] *adj* : indispensable
indisponible [ɛ̃dispɔnibl] *adj* : unavailable
indisposer [ɛ̃dispoze] *vt* : upset, make ill — **indisposé, -sée** [ɛ̃dispoze] *adj* : unwell — **indisposition** [ɛ̃dispozisjɔ̃] *nf* : ailment, indisposition
indissociable [ɛ̃disɔsjabl] *adj* : inseparable
indistinct, -tincte [ɛ̃distɛ̃(kt), -tɛ̃kt] *adj* : indistinct
individu [ɛ̃dividy] *nm* : individual — **individualité** [ɛ̃dividɥalite] *nf* : individuality — **individuel, -duelle** [ɛ̃dividɥɛl] *adj* 1 : individual 2 PARTICULIER : personal, private — **individuellement** [ɛ̃dividɥɛlmɑ̃] *adv* : individually
indolent, -lente [ɛ̃dɔlɑ̃, -lɑ̃t] *adj* : lazy — **indolence** [ɛ̃dɔlɑ̃s] *nf* : laziness
indolore [ɛ̃dɔlɔr] *adj* : painless
indomptable [ɛ̃dɔ̃tabl] *adj* : indomitable
indu, -due [ɛ̃dy] *adj* : unseemly, ungodly
induire [ɛ̃dɥir] {49} *vt* 1 INCITER : incite, induce 2 CONCLURE : infer, conclude
indulgence [ɛ̃dylʒɑ̃s] *nf* : indulgence — **indulgent, -gente** [ɛ̃dylʒɑ̃, -ʒɑ̃t] *adj* : indulgent
indûment [ɛ̃dymɑ̃] *adv* : unduly
industrie [ɛ̃dystri] *nf* : industry — **industrialiser** [ɛ̃dystrijalize] *vt* : industrialize — **industriel, -trielle** [ɛ̃dystrijɛl] *adj* : industrial — **industrieux, -trieuse** [ɛ̃dystrijø, -trijøz] *adj* : industrious
inébranlable [inebrɑ̃labl] *adj* : unshakeable
inédit, -dite [inedi, -dit] *adj* 1 : unpublished 2 ORIGINAL : novel, original
inefficace [inefikas] *adj* 1 : inefficient 2 : ineffective — **inefficacité** [inefikasite] *nf* 1 : inefficiency 2 : ineffectiveness
inégal, -gale [inegal] *adj, mpl* **-gaux** [-go] 1 : unequal 2 IRRÉGULIER : uneven — **inégalé, -lée** [inegale] *adj* : unequaled — **inégalité** [inegalite] *nf* 1 : inequality 2 IRRÉGULARITÉ : unevenness, irregularity
inéligible [ineliʒibl] *adj* : ineligible
inéluctable [inelyktabl] *adj* : inescapable
inepte [inɛpt] *adj* : inept
inépuisable [inepɥizabl] *adj* : inexhaustible
inerte [inɛrt] *adj* 1 : inert, lifeless 2 APATHIQUE : apathetic — **inertie** [inɛrsi] *nf* 1 : inertia 2 APATHIE : apathy
inespéré, -rée [inɛspere] *adj* : unhoped for, unexpected
inestimable [inɛstimabl] *adj* : inestimable
inévitable [inevitabl] *adj* : inevitable — **inévitablement** [-tabləmɑ̃] *adv* : inevitably
inexact, -exacte [inɛgza(kt), -ɛgzakt] *adj* : inaccurate, incorrect
inexcusable [inɛkskyzabl] *adj* : inexcusable
inexistant, -tante [inɛgzistɑ̃, -tɑ̃t] *adj* : nonexistent
inexpérience [inɛksperjɑ̃s] *nf* : inexperience — **inexpérimenté, -tée** [inɛksperimɑ̃te] *adj* : inexperienced
inexplicable [inɛksplikabl] *adj* : inexplicable — **inexpliqué, -quée** [inɛksplike] *adj* : unexplained
inexprimable [inɛksprimabl] *adj* : inexpressible
infaillible [ɛ̃fajibl] *adj* : infallible
infâme [ɛ̃fam] *adj* : vile — **infamie** [ɛ̃fam] *adj* : infamy
infanterie [ɛ̃fɑ̃tri] *nf* : infantry
infantile [ɛ̃fɑ̃til] *adj* : infantile, childish
infarctus [ɛ̃farktys] *nm or* **~ myocarde** : heart attack
infatigable [ɛ̃fatigabl] *adj* : tireless
infect, -fecte [ɛ̃fɛkt] *adj* : revolting, foul — **infecter** [ɛ̃fɛkte] *vt* 1 : infect 2 : contaminate — **s'infecter** *vr* : become infected — **infectieux, -tieuse** [ɛ̃fɛksjø, -tjøz] *adj* : infectious — **infection** [ɛ̃fɛksjɔ̃] *nf* 1 : infection 2 PUANTEUR : stench
inférieur, -rieure [ɛ̃ferjœr] *adj & n* : inferior — **infériorité** [ɛ̃ferjɔrite] *nf* : inferiority
infernal, -nale [ɛ̃fɛrnal] *adj, mpl* **-naux** [-no] : infernal
infertile [ɛ̃fɛrtil] *adj* : infertile — **infertilité** [-tilite] *nf* : infertility
infester [ɛ̃fɛste] *vt* : infest
infidèle [ɛ̃fidɛl] *adj* : unfaithful — **infidélité** [ɛ̃fidelite] *nf* : infidelity
infiltrer [ɛ̃filtre] *vt* : infiltrate — **s'infiltrer** *vr* **~ dans** : seep into, penetrate — **infiltration** [ɛ̃filtrasjɔ̃] *nf* : infiltration
infime [ɛ̃fim] *adj* : minute, tiny
infini, -nie [ɛ̃fini] *adj* : infinite — **infini** *nm* 1 : infinity 2 **à l'~** : endlessly — **infinité** [ɛ̃finite] *nf* 1 : infinity 2 : infinite number
infinitif [ɛ̃finitif] *nm* : infinitive
infirme [ɛ̃firm] *adj* : disabled, infirm — **~** *nmf* : disabled person — **infirmerie** [ɛ̃firməri] *nf* : infirmary — **infirmier, -mière** [ɛ̃firmje, -mjɛr] *n* : nurse — **infirmité** [ɛ̃firmite] *nf* : disability
inflammable [ɛ̃flamabl] *adj* : inflammable, flammable — **inflammation** [ɛ̃flamasjɔ̃] *nf* : inflammation
inflation [ɛ̃flasjɔ̃] *nf* : inflation — **inflationniste** [ɛ̃flasjɔnist] *adj* : inflationary
inflexible [ɛ̃flɛksibl] *adj* : inflexible, unbending — **inflexion** [ɛ̃flɛksjɔ̃] *nf* 1 : inflection (of the voice) 2 : nod (of the head)
infliger [ɛ̃fliʒe] {17} *vt* 1 : inflict 2 : impose (a penalty, etc.)
influence [ɛ̃flyɑ̃s] *nf* : influence — **influencer** [ɛ̃flyɑ̃se] {6} *vt* : influence — **influent, -fluente** [ɛ̃flyɑ̃, -flyɑ̃t] *adj* : influential — **influer** [ɛ̃flye] *vi* **~ sur** : have an influence on
informateur, -trice [ɛ̃fɔrmatœr, -tris] *n* : informant, informer
informaticien, -cienne [ɛ̃fɔrmatisjɛ̃, -sjɛn] *n* : computer programmer
information [ɛ̃fɔrmasjɔ̃] *nf* 1 : information 2 **~s** *nfpl* : news — **informatif, -tive** [ɛ̃fɔrmatif, -tiv] *adj* : informative
informatique [ɛ̃fɔrmatik] *adj* : computer — **~** *nf* : computer science — **informatiser** [ɛ̃fɔrmatize] *vt* : computerize
informe [ɛ̃fɔrm] *adj* : shapeless
informer [ɛ̃fɔrme] *vt* : inform — **s'informer** *vr* : inquire
infortune [ɛ̃fɔrtyn] *nf* : misfortune — **infortuné, -née** [ɛ̃fɔrtyne] *adj* : unfortunate
infraction [ɛ̃fraksjɔ̃] *nf* : breach (in law)
infranchissable [ɛ̃frɑ̃ʃisabl] *adj* 1 : insurmountable 2 IMPRACTICABLE : impassable
infrarouge [ɛ̃fraruʒ] *adj* : infrared
infrastructure [ɛ̃frastryktyr] *nf* : infrastructure
infructueux, -tueuse [ɛ̃fryktɥø, -tɥøz] *adj* : fruitless
infuser [ɛ̃fyze] *v* 1 : infuse 2 : brew (tea, etc.) — **infusion** [ɛ̃fyzjɔ̃] *nf* : infusion
ingénieur, -nieure [ɛ̃ʒenjœr] *n* : engineer — **ingénierie** [ɛ̃ʒeniri] *nf* : engineering
ingénieux, -nieuse [ɛ̃ʒenjø, -njøz] *adj* : ingenious — **ingéniosité** [ɛ̃ʒenjɔzite] *nf* : ingenuity
ingénu, -nue [ɛ̃ʒeny] *adj* : ingenuous, naive
ingérence [ɛ̃ʒerɑ̃s] *nf* : interference
ingratitude [ɛ̃gratityd] *nf* : ingratitude — **ingrat, -grate** [ɛ̃gra, -grat] *adj* 1 : ungrateful 2 : thankless
ingrédient [ɛ̃gredjɑ̃] *nm* : ingredient
inhabitable [inabitabl] *adj* : uninhabitable — **inhabité, -tée** [inabite] *adj* : uninhabited
inhabituel, -tuelle [inabitɥɛl] *adj* : unusual
inhaler [inale] *vt* : inhale — **inhalation** [-alasjɔ̃] *nf* : inhaling
inhérent, -rente [inerɑ̃, -rɑ̃t] *adj* : inherent
inhiber [inibe] *vt* : inhibit — **inhibition** [inibisjɔ̃] *nf* : inhibition
inhumain, -maine [inymɛ̃, -mɛn] *adj* : inhuman — **inhumanité** [inymanite] *nf* : inhumanity
inhumer [inyme] *vt* : bury — **inhumation** [inymasjɔ̃] *nf* : burial
initial, -tiale [inisjal] *adj, mpl* **-tiaux** [-sjo] : initial — **initiale** *nf* : initial
initiative [inisjativ] *nf* : initiative
initier [inisje] {96} *vt* : initiate — **initiateur, -trice** [inisjatœr, -tris] *n* 1 : initiator 2 NOVATEUR : innovator — **initiation** [inisjasjɔ̃] *nf* : initiation
injecter [ɛ̃ʒɛkte] *vt* : inject — **injection** [ɛ̃ʒɛksjɔ̃] *nf* : injection
injonction [ɛ̃ʒɔ̃ksjɔ̃] *nf* : order, injunction
injure [ɛ̃ʒyr] *nf* : insult, abuse — **injurier** [ɛ̃ʒyrje] {96} *vt* : insult — **injurieux, -rieuse** [ɛ̃ʒyrjø, -rjøz] *adj* : insulting, abusive
injuste [ɛ̃ʒyst] *adj* : unjust, unfair — **injustice** [ɛ̃ʒystis] *nf* : injustice
injustifié, -fiée [ɛ̃ʒystifje] *adj* : unjustified
inlassable [ɛ̃lasabl] *adj* : tireless
inné, -née [ine] *adj* : innate, inborn
innocent, -cente [inɔsɑ̃, -sɑ̃t] *adj & n* : innocent — **innocence** [inɔsɑ̃s] *nf* : innocence — **innocenter** [inɔsɑ̃te] *vt* : clear, exonerate
innombrable [inɔ̃brabl] *adj* : innumerable, countless
innover [inɔve] *v* : innovate — **innovateur, -trice** [inɔvatœr, -tris] *adj* : innovative — **~** *n* : innovator — **innovation** [inɔvasjɔ̃] *nf* : innovation
inoccupé, -pée [inɔkype] *adj* : unoccupied
inoculer [inɔkyle] *vt* : inoculate — **inoculation** [-kylasjɔ̃] *nf* : inoculation
inodore [inɔdɔr] *adj* : odorless
inoffensif, -sive [inɔfɑ̃sif, -siv] *adj* : inoffensive, harmless
inonder [inɔ̃de] *vt* : flood, inundate — **inondation** [inɔ̃dasjɔ̃] *nf* : flood
inopiné, -née [inɔpine] *adj* : unexpected
inopportun, -tune [inɔpɔrtœ̃, -tyn] *adj* : untimely
inoubliable [inublijabl] *adj* : unforgettable
inouï, inouïe [inwi] *adj* : incredible, unheard of
inquiet, -quiète [ɛ̃kjɛ, -kjɛt] *adj* : anxious, worried — **inquiétant, -tante** [ɛ̃kjetɑ̃, -tɑ̃t] *adj* : worrisome — **inquiéter** [ɛ̃kjete] {87} *vt* 1 : worry 2 DÉRANGER : bother, disturb — **s'inquiéter** *vr* : be worried — **inquiétude** [ɛ̃kjetyd] *nf* : worry, anxiety
inquisition [ɛ̃kizisjɔ̃] *nf* : inquisition
insaisissable [ɛ̃sezisabl] *adj* : elusive
insalubre [ɛ̃salybr] *adj* : unhealthy
insanité [ɛ̃sanite] *nf* : insanity
insatiable [ɛ̃sasjabl] *adj* : insatiable
insatisfait, -faite [ɛ̃satisfɛ, -fɛt] *adj* : dissatisfied — **insatisfaction** [ɛ̃satisfaksjɔ̃] *nf* : dissatisfaction
inscrire [ɛ̃skrir] {33} *vt* 1 ÉCRIRE : write down 2 ENREGISTRER : register, enroll — **s'inscrire** *vr* : register, enroll — **inscription** [ɛ̃skripsjɔ̃] *nf* 1 : inscription 2 : registration, enrollment
insecte [ɛ̃sɛkt] *nm* : insect — **insecticide** [ɛ̃sɛktisid] *nm* : insecticide
insécurité [ɛ̃sekyrite] *nf* : insecurity
insensé, -sée [ɛ̃sɑ̃se] *adj* : crazy, foolish
insensible [ɛ̃sɑ̃sibl] *adj* : insensitive — **insensibilité** [ɛ̃sɑ̃sibilite] *nf* : insensitivity
inséparable [ɛ̃separabl] *adj* : inseparable
insérer [ɛ̃sere] {87} *vt* : insert
insidieux, -dieuse [ɛ̃sidjø, -djøz] *adj* : insidious
insigne [ɛ̃siɲ] *nm* 1 : badge 2 *or* **~s** *nmpl* : insignia
insignifiant, -fiante [ɛ̃siɲifjɑ̃, -fjɑ̃t] *adj* : insignificant — **insignifiance** [-ɲifjɑ̃s] *nf* : insignificance
insinuation [ɛ̃sinɥasjɔ̃] *nf* : insinuation —

insinuer [ɛ̃sinɥe] *vt* : insinuate — **s'insinuer** *vr* ~ **dans** : insinuate oneself into, penetrate

insipide [ɛ̃sipid] *adj* : insipid

insister [ɛ̃siste] *vi* **1** : insist **2** ~ **sur** : emphasize, stress — **insistance** [ɛ̃sistɑ̃s] *nf* : insistence — **insistant, -tante** [ɛ̃sistɑ̃, -tɑ̃t] *adj* : insistent

insociable [ɛ̃sɔsjabl] *adj* : unsociable

insolation [ɛ̃sɔlasjɔ̃] *nf* : sunstroke

insolent, -lente [ɛ̃sɔlɑ̃, -lɑ̃t] *adj* : insolent — **insolence** [ɛ̃sɔlɑ̃s] *nf* : insolence

insolite [ɛ̃sɔlit] *adj* : unusual, bizarre

insoluble [ɛ̃sɔlybl] *adj* : insoluble

insolvable [ɛ̃sɔlvabl] *adj* : insolvent

insomnie [ɛ̃sɔmni] *nf* : insomnia

insondable [ɛ̃sɔ̃dabl] *adj* **1** : bottomless **2** IMPÉNÉTRABLE : unfathomable

insonoriser [ɛ̃sɔnɔrize] *vt* : soundproof

insouciant, -ciante [ɛ̃susjɑ̃, -sjɑ̃t] *adj* : carefree — **insouciance** [ɛ̃susjɑ̃s] *nf* : carefree attitude

insoutenable [ɛ̃sutnabl] *adj* **1** : untenable **2** INTOLÉRABLE : unbearable

inspecter [ɛ̃spɛkte] *vt* : inspect — **inspecteur, -trice** [ɛ̃spɛktœr, -tris] *n* : inspector — **inspection** [ɛ̃spɛksjɔ̃] *nf* : inspection

inspirer [ɛ̃spire] *vt* : inspire — *vi* : inhale — **s'inspirer** *vr* ~ **de** : be inspired by — **inspirant, -rante** [ɛ̃spirɑ̃, -rɑ̃t] *adj* : inspirational — **inspiration** [ɛ̃spirasjɔ̃] *nf* **1** : inspiration **2** : breathing in

instable [ɛ̃stabl] *adj* **1** BRANLANT : unsteady **2** : unstable, unsettled — **instabilité** [ɛ̃stabilite] *nf* : instability

installer [ɛ̃stale] *vt* : install, set up — **s'installer** *vr* : settle (in) — **installation** [ɛ̃stalasjɔ̃] *nf* **1** : installation **2** ~**s** *nfpl* : installations, facilities

instance [ɛ̃stɑ̃s] *nf* **1** AUTORITÉ : authority **2** : legal proceedings **3 en** ~ : pending

instant [ɛ̃stɑ̃, -tɑ̃t] *nm* : instant, moment — **instantané, -née** [ɛ̃stɑ̃tane] *adj* : instantaneous, instant — **instantané** *nm* : snapshot

instar [ɛ̃star] **à l'**~ **de** *prep phr* : following the example of, like

instaurer [ɛ̃store] *vt* : institute, establish — **instauration** [ɛ̃storasjɔ̃] *nf* : institution

instigateur, -trice [ɛ̃stigatœr, -tris] *n* : instigator — **instigation** [ɛ̃stigasjɔ̃] *nf* : instigation

instinct [ɛ̃stɛ̃] *nm* : instinct — **instinctif, -tive** [ɛ̃stɛ̃ktif, -tiv] *adj* : instinctive, instinctual

instituer [ɛ̃stitɥe] *vt* **1** : institute, establish **2** NOMMER : appoint — **institut** [ɛ̃stity] *nm* : institute — **instituteur, -trice** [ɛ̃stitytœr, -tris] *n* : schoolteacher — **institution** [ɛ̃stitysjɔ̃] *nf* : institution

instruction [ɛ̃stryksjɔ̃] *nf* **1** : instruction, education **2** ~**s** *nfpl* : instructions — **instruire** [ɛ̃strɥir] {49} *vt* **1** : instruct **2** ~ **de** : inform of — **s'instruire** *vr* **1** : educate oneself **2** ~ **de** : find out about — **instruit, -truite** [ɛ̃strɥi, -trɥit] *adj* : learned, educated

instrument [ɛ̃strymɑ̃] *nm* : instrument — **instrumental, -tale** [ɛ̃strymɑ̃tal] *adj, mpl* **-taux** [-to] : instrumental

insu [ɛ̃sy] **à l'**~ **de** *prep phr* : without the knowledge of, unknown to

insuffisant, -sante [ɛ̃syfizɑ̃, -zɑ̃t] *adj* : insufficient, inadequate — **insuffisance** [ɛ̃syfizɑ̃s] *nf* : inadequacy

insulaire [ɛ̃sylɛr] *adj* : island, insular — ~ *nmf* : islander

insuline [ɛ̃sylin] *nf* : insulin

insulter [ɛ̃sylte] *vt* : insult — **insulte** [ɛ̃sylt] *nf* : insult

insupportable [ɛ̃sypɔrtabl] *adj* : unbearable

insurger [ɛ̃syrʒe] {17} *v* **s'insurger** *vr* : rebel, rise up — **insurgé, -gée** [ɛ̃syrʒe] *n* : insurgent, rebel

insurmontable [ɛ̃syrmɔ̃tabl] *adj* : insurmountable

insurrection [ɛ̃syrɛksjɔ̃] *nf* : insurrection

intact, -tacte [ɛ̃takt] *adj* : intact

intangible [ɛ̃tɑ̃ʒibl] *adj* : intangible

intarissable [ɛ̃tarisabl] *adj* : inexhaustible

intégral, -grale [ɛ̃tegral] *adj, mpl* **-graux** [-gro] **1** : complete **2** : unabridged — **intégralité** [ɛ̃tegralite] *nf* : whole — **intégrant, -grante** [ɛ̃tegrɑ̃, -grɑ̃t] *adj* **faire partie intégrante de** : be an integral part of

intègre [ɛ̃tɛgr] *adj* : honest, upright

intégrer [ɛ̃tegre] {87} *vt* : integrate — **s'intégrer** *vr* : integrate

intégrité [ɛ̃tegrite] *nf* : integrity

intellect [ɛ̃telɛkt] *nm* : intellect — **intellectuel, -tuelle** [ɛ̃telɛktɥɛl] *adj & n* : intellectual

intelligent, -gente [ɛ̃teliʒɑ̃, -ʒɑ̃t] *adj* : intelligent — **intelligence** [ɛ̃teliʒɑ̃s] *nf* **1** : intelligence **2** COMPRÉHENSION : understanding — **intelligible** [ɛ̃teliʒibl] *adj* : intelligible, comprehensible

intempéries [ɛtɑ̃peri] *nfpl* : bad weather

intempestif, -tive [ɛ̃tɑ̃pɛstif, -tiv] *adj* : untimely

intense [ɛ̃tɑ̃s] *adj* : intense — **intensément** [ɛ̃tɑ̃semɑ̃] *adv* : intensely — **intensif, -sive** [ɛ̃tɑ̃sif, -siv] *adj* : intensive — **intensifier** [ɛ̃tɑ̃sifje] {96} *vt* : intensify — **intensité** [ɛ̃tɑ̃site] *nf* : intensity

intenter [ɛ̃tɑ̃te] *vt* : initiate, pursue (legal action)

intention [ɛ̃tɑ̃sjɔ̃] *nf* : intention, intent — **intentionnel, -nelle** [ɛ̃tɑ̃sjɔnɛl] *adj* : intentional

interactif, -tive [ɛ̃tɛraktif, -tiv] *adj* : interactive — **interaction** [ɛ̃tɛraksjɔ̃] *nf* : interaction

intercaler [ɛ̃tɛrkale] *vt* : insert

intercéder [ɛ̃tɛrsede] {87} *vi* : intercede

intercepter [ɛ̃tɛrsɛpte] *vt* : intercept

interchangeable [ɛ̃tɛrʃɑ̃ʒabl] *adj* : interchangeable

intercontinental, -tale [ɛ̃tɛrkɔ̃tinɑ̃tal] *adj, mpl* **-taux** [-to] : intercontinental

interdire [ɛ̃tɛrdir] {29} *vt* **1** : ban, prohibit **2** EMPÊCHER : prevent — **interdiction** [ɛ̃tɛrdiksjɔ̃] *nf* : ban, prohibition — **interdit, -dite** [ɛ̃tɛrdi, -dit] *adj* **1** : prohibited **2** STUPÉFAIT : dumbfounded

intéresser [ɛ̃terese] *vt* **1** : interest **2** CONCERNER : concern — **s'intéresser** *vr* ~ **à** : be interested in — **intéressant, -sante** [ɛ̃terɛsɑ̃, -sɑ̃t] *adj* **1** : interesting **2** AVANTAGEUX : attractive, worthwhile — **intéressé, -sée** *adj* **1** : self-interested **2** CONCERNÉ : concerned — ~ *n* : interested party — **intérêt** [ɛ̃terɛ] *nm* : interest

interface [ɛ̃tɛrfas] *nf* : interface

interférence [ɛ̃tɛrferɑ̃s] *nf* : interference — **interférer** [ɛ̃tɛrfere] {87} *vi* : interfere

intérieur, -rieure [ɛ̃terjœr] *adj* **1** : inner, inside **2** : internal, domestic (in politics) — **intérieur** *nm* **1** : inside (of a drawer, etc.) **2** : interior, home **3 à l'**~ : indoors **4 d'**~ : indoor — **intérieurement** [ɛ̃terjœrmɑ̃] *adv* : inwardly, internally

intérim [ɛ̃terim] *nm* **1** : interim (period) **2** : temporary activity — **intérimaire** [ɛ̃terimɛr] *adj* : temporary, acting — ~ *nmf* : temporary employee

interjection [ɛ̃tɛrʒɛksjɔ̃] *nf* : interjection

interlocuteur, -trice [ɛ̃tɛrlɔkytœr, -tris] *n* : speaker

intermède [ɛ̃tɛrmɛd] *nm* : interlude

intermédiaire [ɛ̃tɛrmedjɛr] *adj* : intermediate — ~ *nmf* : intermediary, go-between

interminable [ɛ̃tɛrminabl] *adj* : interminable

intermittent, -tente [ɛ̃tɛrmitɑ̃, -tɑ̃t] *adj* : intermittent, sporadic — **intermittence** [ɛ̃tɛrmitɑ̃s] *nf* **par** ~ : intermittently

international, -nale [ɛ̃tɛrnasjɔnal] *adj, mpl* **-naux** [-no] : international

interne [ɛ̃tɛrn] *adj* : internal

interner [ɛ̃tɛrne] *vt* **1** : intern (in politics) **2** : confine (in medicine)

interpeller [ɛ̃tɛrpəle] *vt* **1** : shout at, call out to **2** INTERROGER : question

interphone [ɛ̃tɛrfɔn] *nm* : intercom

interposer [ɛ̃tɛrpoze] *v* **s'interposer** *vr* : intervene

interpréter [ɛ̃tɛrprete] {87} *vt* **1** : interpret **2** : perform, play (a role) — **interprétation** [ɛ̃tɛrpretasjɔ̃] *nf* : interpretation — **interprète** [ɛ̃tɛrprɛt] *nmf* **1** : interpreter **2** REPRÉSENTANT : spokesperson **3** : performer (in theater, etc.)

interroger [ɛ̃terɔʒe] {17} *vt* : interrogate, question — **s'interroger** *vr* ~ **sur** : wonder about — **interrogateur, -trice** [ɛ̃terɔgatœr, -tris] *adj* : questioning — **interrogatif, -tive** [ɛ̃terɔgatif, -tiv] *adj* : interrogative — **interrogation** [ɛ̃terɔgasjɔ̃] *nf* **1** : interrogation **2** : test (in school) — **interrogatoire** [ɛ̃terɔgatwar] *nm* : interrogation, questioning

interrompre [ɛ̃tɛrɔ̃pr] {77} *v* : interrupt — **s'interrompre** *vr* : break off — **interrupteur** [ɛ̃teryptœr] *nm* : switch — **interruption** [ɛ̃terypsjɔ̃] *nf* **1** : interruption **2 sans** ~ : continuously

intersection [ɛ̃tɛrsɛksjɔ̃] *nf* : intersection

interurbain, -baine [ɛ̃tɛryrbɛ̃, -bɛn] *adj* : long-distance — **interurbain** *nm* **l'**~ : long-distance telephone service

intervalle [ɛ̃tɛrval] *nm* **1** : space, gap **2** : interval (of time) **3 dans l'**~ : in the meantime

intervenir [ɛ̃tɛrvənir] {92} *vi* **1** : intervene **2** SURVENIR : take place **3** : operate (in medicine) — **intervention** [ɛ̃tɛrvɑ̃sjɔ̃] *nf* **1** : intervention **2** OPÉRATION : (medical) operation

intervertir [ɛ̃tɛrvɛrtir] *vt* : invert, reverse

interview [ɛ̃tɛrvju] *nf* : interview — **interviewer** [ɛ̃tɛrvjuve] *vt* : interview

intestin [ɛ̃tɛstɛ̃] *nm* : intestine — **intestinal, -nale** [ɛ̃tɛstinal] *adj, mpl* **-naux** [-no] : intestinal

intime [ɛ̃tim] *adj* **1** : intimate **2** PERSONNEL : private — ~ *nmf* : close friend

intimider [ɛ̃timide] *vt* : intimidate — **intimidant, -dante** [ɛ̃timidɑ̃, -dɑ̃t] *adj* : intimidating — **intimidation** [-midasjɔ̃] *nf* : intimidation

intimité [ɛ̃timite] *nf* : intimacy

intituler [ɛ̃tityle] *vt* : call, title — **s'intituler** *vr* : be called

intolérable [ɛ̃tɔlerabl] *adj* : intolerable, unbearable — **intolérant, -rante** [ɛ̃tɔlerɑ̃, -rɑ̃t] *adj* : intolerant — **intolérance** [-rɑ̃s] *nf* : intolerance

intonation [ɛ̃tɔnasjɔ̃] *nf* : intonation

intoxiquer [ɛ̃tɔksike] *vt* EMPOISONNER : poison — **intoxication** [ɛ̃tɔksikasjɔ̃] *nf* : poisoning

intransigeant, -geante [ɛ̃trɑ̃ziʒɑ, -ʒɑ̃t] *adj* : uncompromising

intransitif, -tive [ɛ̃trɑ̃zitif, -tiv] *adj* : intransitive

intraveineux, -neuse [ɛ̃travɛnø, -nøz] *adj* : intravenous

intrépide [ɛ̃trepid] *adj* : intrepid, fearless

intriguer [ɛ̃trige] *vt* : intrigue, puzzle — *vi* : plot, scheme — **intrigue** [ɛ̃trig] *nf* **1** : intrigue **2** : plot (of a story)

intrinsèque [ɛ̃trɛ̃sɛk] *adj* : intrinsic

introduire [ɛ̃trɔdɥir] {49} *vt* **1** : introduce **2** : show in, bring in **3** INSÉRER : insert **4** : enter, input (data) — **s'introduire** *vr* : penetrate, get in — **introduction** [ɛ̃trɔdyksjɔ̃] *nf* **1** : introduction **2** : insertion

introuvable [ɛ̃truvabl] *adj* : unobtainable, nowhere to be found

introverti, -tie [ɛ̃trɔvɛrti] *adj* : introverted — ~ *n* : introvert

intrusion [ɛ̃tryzjɔ̃] *nf* : intrusion — **intrus, -truse** [ɛ̃try, -tryz] *n* : intruder

intuition [ɛ̃tɥisjɔ̃] *nf* : intuition — **intuitif, -tive** [ɛ̃tɥitif, -tiv] *adj* : intuitive

inuit [inɥi] *adj* : Inuit

inusable [inyzabl] *adj* : durable

inusité, -tée [inyzite] *adj* : unusual, uncommon

inutile [inytil] *adj* **1** : useless **2** SUPERFLU : needless — **inutilement** [inytilmɑ̃] *adv* : pointlessly, needlessly — **inutilisable** [inytilizabl] *adj* : unusable — **inutilité** [inytilite] *nf* : uselessness

invalide [ɛ̃valid] *adj* : disabled — ~ *nmf* : disabled person — **invalidité** [ɛ̃validite] *nf* : disability

invariable [ɛ̃varjabl] *adj* : invariable

invasion [ɛ̃vazjɔ̃] *nf* : invasion

inventaire [ɛ̃vɑ̃tɛr] *nm* **1** : inventory **2 faire l'**~ : take stock

invention [ɛ̃vɑ̃sjɔ̃] *nf* : invention — **inventer** [ɛ̃vɑ̃te] *vt* : invent — **inventeur, -trice** [ɛ̃vɑ̃tœr, -tris] *n* : inventor — **inventif, -tive** [ɛ̃vɑ̃tif, -tiv] *adj* : inventive

inverse [ɛ̃vɛrs] *adj* : reverse, opposite — ~ *nm* : reverse, opposite — **inversement** [ɛ̃vɛrsəmɑ̃] *adv* : conversely — **inverser** [ɛ̃vɛrse] *vt* : reverse, invert

invertébré, -brée [ɛ̃vɛrtebre] *adj* : invertebrate — **invertébré** *nm* : invertebrate

investigation [ɛ̃vɛstigasjɔ̃] *nf* : investigation

investir [ɛ̃vɛstir] *v* : invest — **investissement** [ɛ̃vɛstismɑ̃] *nm* : investment — **investisseur, -seuse** [ɛ̃vɛstisœr, -søz] *n* : investor

invétéré, -rée [ɛ̃vetere] *adj* : inveterate

invincible [ɛ̃vɛ̃sibl] *adj* : invincible

invisible [ɛ̃vizibl] *adj* : invisible

inviter [ɛ̃vite] *vt* : invite — **invitation** [ɛ̃vitasjɔ̃] *nf* : invitation — **invité, -tée** [ɛ̃vite] *n* : guest

involontaire [ɛ̃vɔlɔ̃tɛr] *adj* : involuntary

invoquer [ɛ̃vɔke] *vt* : invoke

invraisemblable [ɛ̃vrɛsɑ̃blabl] *adj* : improbable, unlikely

invulnérable [ɛ̃vylnerabl] *adj* : invulnerable

iode [jɔd] *nm* : iodine

ion [jɔ̃] *nm* : ion

iris [iris] *nm* : iris

irlandais, -daise [irlɑ̃dɛ, -dɛz] *adj* : Irish

ironie [irɔni] *nf* : irony — **ironique** [irɔnik] *adj* : ironic(al)

irradier [iradje] {96} *vt* : irradiate — *vi* : radiate

irrationnel, -nelle [irasjɔnɛl] *adj* : irrational

irréalisable [irealizabl] *adj* : unworkable

irréconciliable [irekɔ̃siljabl] *adj* : irreconcilable

irrécupérable [irekyperabl] *adj* : irretrievable, beyond repair

irréel, -réelle [ireɛl] *adj* : unreal

irréfléchi, -chie [irefleʃi] *adj* : thoughtless, rash

irréfutable [irefytabl] *adj* : irrefutable

irrégulier, -lière [iregylje, -ljɛr] *adj* : irregular — **irrégularité** [iregylarite] *nf* : irregularity

irrémédiable [iremedjabl] *adj* : irreparable

irremplaçable [irɑ̃plasabl] *adj* : irreplaceable

irréparable [ireparabl] *adj* : irreparable

irréprochable [ireprɔʃabl] *adj* : irreproachable, blameless

irrésistible [irezistibl] *adj* : irresistible

irrésolu, -lue [irezɔly] *adj* **1** INDÉCIS : irresolute **2** : unresolved (of a problem)

irrespectueux, -tueuse [irɛspɛktɥø, -tɥøz] *adj* : disrespectful

irresponsable [irɛspɔ̃sabl] *adj* : irresponsible — **irresponsabilité** [irɛspɔ̃sabilite] *nf* : irresponsibility

irrigation [irigasjɔ̃] *nf* : irrigation — **irriguer** [irige] *vt* : irrigate

irriter [irite] *vt* : irritate — **s'irriter** *vr* : get irritated — **irritable** [iritabl] *adj* : irritable — **irritation** [iritasjɔ̃] *nf* : irritation

irruption [irypsjɔ̃] *nf* : bursting in

islam [islam] *nm* : Islam — **islamique** [islamik] *adj* : Islamic

isoler [izɔle] *vt* **1** : isolate **2** : insulate — **s'isoler** *vr* : isolate oneself — **isolation** [izɔlasjɔ̃] *nf* : insulation — **isolement** [izɔlmɑ̃] *nm* **1** : isolation **2** ISOLATION : insulation — **isolément** [izɔlemɑ̃] *adv* : separately, individually

israélien, -lienne [israeljɛ̃, -ljɛn] *adj* : Israeli

issu, -sue [isy] *adj* ~ **de 1** : descended from **2** : resulting from

issue *nf* **1** SORTIE : exit **2** SOLUTION : solution **3** FIN : ending, outcome

isthme [ism] *nm* : isthmus

italien, -lienne [italjɛ̃, -ljɛn] *adj* : Italian — **italien** *nm* : Italian (language)

italique [italik] *nm* : italics *pl*

itinéraire [itinerɛr] *nm* : itinerary

itinérant, -rante [itinerɑ̃, -rɑ̃t] *adj* : itinerant

ivoire [ivwar] *adj & nm* : ivory

ivre [ivr] *adj* : drunk — **ivresse** [ivrɛs] *nf* : drunkenness — **ivrogne, ivrognesse** [ivrɔɲ, -ɲɛs] *n* : drunkard

J

j [ʒi] *nm* : j, 10th letter of the alphabet

jacasser [ʒakase] *vi* : chatter, jabber

jachère [ʒaʃɛr] *nf* : fallow land

jacinthe [ʒasɛ̃t] *nf* : hyacinth

jadis [ʒadis] *adv* : in times past, formerly

jaillir [ʒajir] *vi* **1** : spurt out, gush (out) **2** APPARAÎTRE : spring up, emerge

jais [ʒɛ] *nms & pl* **1** : jet (stone) **2 de** ~ : jet-black

jalon [ʒalɔ̃] *nm* : marker, milestone — **jalonner** [ʒalɔne] *vt* **1** : mark out (a route, etc.) **2** LONGER : line

jaloux, -louse [ʒalu, -luz] *adj* : jealous — **jalouser** [ʒaluze] *vt* : be jealous of — **jalousie** [ʒaluzi] *nf* **1** : jealousy **2** : venetian blind

jamais [ʒamɛ] *adv* **1** : ever **2 ne ...** ~ : never **3 à** ~ *or* **pour** ~ : forever

jambe [ʒɑ̃b] *nf* : leg

jambon [ʒɑ̃bɔ̃] *nm* : ham

jante [ʒɑ̃t] *nf* : rim (of a wheel)

janvier [ʒɑ̃vje] *nm* : January

japonais, -naise [ʒapɔnɛ, -nɛz] *adj* : Japanese — **japonais** *nm* : Japanese (language)

japper [ʒape] *vi* : yap, yelp

jaquette [ʒakɛt] *nf* **1** : dust jacket **2** : jacket (for women)

jardin [ʒardɛ̃] *nm* **1** : garden **2** ~ **d'enfants** *France* : kindergarten **3** ~ **zoologique** : zoo — **jardinage** [ʒardinaʒ] *nm* : gardening — **jardiner** [ʒardine] *vi* : garden — **jardinier, -nière** [ʒardinje, -njɛr] *n* : gardener — **jardinière** *nf* : plant stand, window box

jargon [ʒargɔ̃] *nm* **1** : jargon **2** CHARABIA : gibberish

jarre [ʒar] *nf* : (earthenware) jar

jarret [ʒarɛ] *nm* **1** : back of the knee **2** : shank (in cooking) — **jarretelle** [ʒartɛl] *nf* : garter belt — **jarretière** [ʒartjɛr] *nf* : garter

jaser [ʒaze] *vi* **1** : chatter, prattle **2** MÉDIRE : gossip

jatte [ʒat] *nf* : bowl, basin

jauge [ʒoʒ] *nf* **1** : capacity **2** INDICATEUR : gauge — **jauger** [ʒoʒe] {17} *vt* : gauge

jaune [ʒon] *adj* : yellow — ~ *nm* **1** : yellow **2** *or* ~ **d'œuf** : egg yolk — **jaunir** [ʒonir] *v* : turn yellow — **jaunisse** [ʒonis] *nf* : jaundice

Javel [ʒavɛl] *nf* → **eau**

javelot [ʒavlo] *nm* : javelin

jazz [dʒaz] *nm* : jazz

je [ʒə] (**j'** *before vowel or mute h*) *pron* : I

jean [dʒin] *nm* **1** : denim **2** : (blue) jeans *pl*

jeep [dʒip] *nf* : jeep

jersey [ʒɛrzɛ] *nm* : jersey (fabric)

Jésus [ʒezy] *nm* : Jesus

jeter [ʒəte] {8} *vt* **1** LANCER : throw **2** : throw away **3** ÉMETTRE : give off **4** ~ **l'éponge** : throw in the towel **5** ~ **un coup d'œil** : take a look at **6** ~ **un sort** : cast a spell — **se jeter** *vr* **1** ~ **dans** : flow into **2** ~ **sur** : pounce on — **jet** [ʒɛ] *nm* **1** : jet, spurt **2** LANCER : throw, throwing **3** : jet (airplane) **4** ~ **d'eau** : fountain — **jetable** [ʒətabl] *adj* : disposable — **jetée** [ʒəte] *nf* : pier, jetty

jeton [ʒətɔ̃] *nm* : token, counter

jeu [ʒø] *nm, pl* **jeux 1** DIVERTISSEMENT : play **2** : game **3** : set (of chess, etc.), deck (of playing cards) **4** ~ **de dames** : checkers **5** ~ **de mots** : pun **6 en** ~ : at stake **7 le** ~ : gambling

jeudi [ʒødi] *nm* : Thursday

jeun [ʒœ̃] **à** ~ *adv phr* : on an empty stomach

jeune [ʒœn] *adj* **1** : young **2** CADET : younger **3** RÉCENT : new, recent — ~

nmf **1** : young person **2 les ~s** : young people

jeûner [ʒøne] *vi* : fast — **jeûne** [ʒøn] *nm* : fast

jeunesse [ʒœnɛs] *nf* **1** : youth **2** : youthfulness **3** JEUNES : young people

joaillier, -lière [ʒɔaje, -jɛr] *n* : jeweler — **joaillerie** [ʒɔajri] *nf* **1** : jewelry store **2** : jewelry

job [dʒɔb] *nm fam* : job

jockey [ʒɔkɛ] *nm* : jockey

jogging [dʒɔgiŋ] *nm* **1** : jogging **2** : sweat suit

joie [ʒwa] *nf* : joy

joindre [ʒwɛ̃dr] {50} *vt* **1** : join, link, combine **2** INCLURE : enclose, attach **3** CONTACTER : reach, contact — **se joindre** *vr* **1** : join together **2 ~ à** : join in — **joint** [ʒwɛ̃] *nm* **1** : joint **2** : seal, washer

joker [ʒɔkɛr] *nm* : joker (in playing cards)

joli, -lie [ʒɔli] *adj* **1** BEAU : pretty, attractive **2** : nice — **joliment** [ʒɔlimɑ̃] *adv* **1** : nicely **2** *fam* : really, awfully

jonc [ʒɔ̃] *nm* **1** : reed, rush **2** : (wedding) band

joncher [ʒɔ̃ʃe] *vt* **~ de** : strew with, litter with

jonction [ʒɔ̃ksjɔ̃] *nf* : junction

jongler [ʒɔ̃gle] *vi* : juggle — **jongleur, -gleuse** [ʒɔ̃glœr, -gløz] *n* : juggler

jonquille [ʒɔ̃kij] *nf* : daffodil

joue [ʒu] *nf* : cheek

jouer [ʒwe] *vi* **1** : play **2** : act, perform **3** PARIER : gamble **4 faire ~** : flex — *vt* **1** : play **2** PARIER : bet, wager **3** : perform — **jouet** [ʒwɛ] *nm* : toy, plaything — **joueur, joueuse** [ʒwœr, ʒwøz] *n* **1** : player **2** : gambler

joufflu, -flue [ʒufly] *adj* : chubby-cheeked

joug [ʒu] *nm* : yoke

jouir [ʒwir] *vi* **~ de** : enjoy — **jouissance** [ʒwisɑ̃s] *nf* **1** : pleasure **2** : use, (legal) possession

jour [ʒur] *nm* **1** : day **2** : daylight, daytime **3** ASPECT : aspect, light **4 ~ de l'An** : New Year's Day **5 de nos ~s** : nowadays **6 donner le ~ à** : give birth to **7 mettre à ~** : update

journal [ʒurnal] *nm, pl* **-naux 1** : diary, journal **2** : newspaper **3 ~ télévisé** : television news

journalier, -lière [ʒurnalje, -ljɛr] *adj* : daily — **~** *n* : day worker, laborer

journaliste [ʒurnalist] *nmf* : journalist — **journalisme** [ʒurnalism] *nm* : journalism

journée [ʒurne] *nf* **1** : day **2 toute la ~** : all day long

jovial, -viale [ʒɔvjal] *adj, mpl* **-vials** *or* **-viaux** [-vjo] : jovial

joyau [ʒwajo] *nm, pl* **joyaux** : jewel, gem

joyeux, joyeuse [ʒwajø, -jøz] *adj* **1** : joyful, happy **2 Joyeux Noël!** : Merry Christmas!

jubiler [ʒybile] *vi* : rejoice, be jubilant — **jubilé** [ʒybile] *nm* : jubilee — **jubilation** [ʒybilasjɔ̃] *nf* : jubilation

jucher [ʒyʃe] *v* **se jucher** *vr* **~ sur** : perch on

judaïque [ʒydaik] *adj* : Judaic — **judaïsme** [ʒydaism] *nm* : Judaism

judiciaire [ʒydisjɛr] *adj* : judicial — **judicieux, -cieuse** [ʒydisjø, -sjøz] *adj* : judicious

judo [ʒydo] *nm* : judo

juger [ʒyʒe] {17} *vt* **1** ÉVALUER : judge **2** CONSIDÉRER : think, consider **3** : try (in law) **4 ~ de** : assess — **se juger** *vr* : consider oneself — **juge** [ʒyʒ] *nm* : judge — **jugement** [ʒyʒmɑ̃] *nm* **1** : judgment, opinion **2** VERDICT : verdict, sentence

juguler [ʒygyle] *vt* : stifle, suppress

juif, juive [ʒɥif, ʒɥiv] *adj* : Jewish

juillet [ʒɥijɛ] *nm* : July

juin [ʒɥɛ̃] *nm* : June

jumeau, -melle [ʒymo, -mɛl] *adj & n, mpl* **-meaux** : twin — **jumeler** [ʒymle] {8} *vt* : twin, couple — **jumelles** [ʒymɛl] *nfpl* : binoculars, field glasses

jument [ʒymɑ̃] *nf* : mare

jungle [ʒœ̃gl] *nf* : jungle

junior [ʒynjɔr] *adj & nmf* : junior

jupe [ʒyp] *nf* : skirt — **jupon** [ʒypɔ̃] *nm* : slip, petticoat

jurer [ʒyre] *vt* : swear, vow — *vi* **1** : swear, curse **2 ~ avec** : clash with **3 ~ de** : swear to — **juré, -rée** [ʒyre] *n* : juror

juridiction [ʒyridiksjɔ̃] *nf* : jurisdiction

juridique [ʒyridik] *adj* : legal

juriste [ʒyrist] *nmf* : legal expert, lawyer

juron [ʒyrɔ̃] *nm* : swearword

jury [ʒyri] *nm* : jury

jus [ʒy] *nms & pl* **1** : juice **2** : gravy

jusque [ʒyskə] (**jusqu'** [ʒysk] *before a vowel*) *prep* **1** : even **2** *or* **jusqu'à** : up to, as far as **3 jusqu'à** *or* **jusqu'en** : until **4 jusqu'à présent** : up to now **5 jusqu'où?** : how far?

justaucorps [ʒystokɔr] *nms & pl* : leotard

juste [ʒyst] *adj* **1** ÉQUITABLE : just, fair **2** EXACT : correct, accurate **3** SERRÉ : tight **4 au ~** : exactly, precisely — **~** *adv* **1** : just, exactly **2** : in tune **3** *or* **tout ~** : only just, barely — **justement** [ʒystəmɑ̃] *adv* **1** EXACTEMENT : exactly, precisely **2** ÉQUITABLEMENT : justly **3** : just now — **justesse** [ʒystɛs] *nf* **1** PRÉCISION : accuracy **2** : soundness (of reasoning, etc.) **3 de ~** : just barely

justice [ʒystis] *nf* **1** ÉQUITÉ : fairness **2** : law, justice

justifier [ʒystifje] {96} *vt* : justify — *vi* **~ de** : give proof of — **se justifier** *vr* : justify oneself — **justification** [ʒustifikasjɔ̃] *nf* : justification

juteux, -teuse [ʒytø, -tøz] *adj* : juicy

juvénile [ʒyvenil] *adj* : youthful, juvenile

juxtaposer [ʒykstapoze] *vt* : juxtapose

K

k [ka] *nm* : k, 11th letter of the alphabet

kaki [kaki] *adj* : khaki

kangourou [kɑ̃guru] *nm* : kangaroo

karaté [karate] *nm* : karate

kascher [kaʃɛr] *adj* : kosher

kayak *or* **kayac** [kajak] *nm* : kayak

kermesse [kɛrmɛs] *nf* : fair, bazaar

kérosène [kerozɛn] *nm* : kerosene

ketchup [kɛtʃœp] *nm* : ketchup

kidnapper [kidnape] *vt* : kidnap — **kidnappeur, -peuse** [kidnapœr, -pøz] *n* : kidnapper

kilo [kilo] *nm* : kilo — **kilogramme** [kilɔgram] *nm* : kilogram — **kilomètre** [kilɔmɛtr] *nm* : kilometer — **kilométrage** [kilɔmetraʒ] *nm* : distance in kilometers, mileage — **kilowatt** [kilɔwat] *nm* : kilowatt

kimono [kimɔno] *nm* : kimono

kinésithérapie [kineziterapi] *nf* : physical therapy

kiosque [kjɔsk] *nm* **1** : kiosk, stall **2 ~ à musique** : bandstand

kiwi [kiwi] *nm* : kiwi

klaxon [klaksɔn] *nm* : horn — **klaxonner** [klaksɔne] *vi* : honk

kyrielle [kirjɛl] *nf* **une ~ de** : a string of

kyste [kist] *nm* : cyst

L

l [ɛl] *nm* : l, 12th letter of the alphabet

l' *pron & art* → **le**

la *pron & art* → **le**

là [la] *adv* **1** (*indicating a place*) : there, here **2** : then **3** (*indicating a situation or a certain point*) : when **4 de ~** : hence **5 ~ où** : where **6 par ~** : over there, that way — **là–bas** [laba] *adv* : over there

label [labɛl] *nm* : label

labeur [labœr] *nm* : toil, labor

laboratoire [labɔratwar] *nm* : laboratory

laborieux, -rieuse [labɔrjø, -rjøz] *adj* **1** : laborious **2** INDUSTRIEUX : hardworking

labourer [labure] *vt* : plow — **labour** [labur] *nm* : plowing

labyrinthe [labirɛ̃t] *nm* : labyrinth, maze

lac [lak] *nm* : lake

lacer [lase] {6} *vt* : lace up

lacérer [lasere] {87} *vt* : tear up, shred

lacet [lasɛ] *nm* **1** : shoelace **2** : sharp bend (in a road)

lâcher [laʃe] *vt* **1** RELÂCHER : loosen **2** LIBÉRER : release **3** : let out (a word, etc.) **4** *fam* : drop (someone) — *vi* : give way — **lâche** [laʃ] *adj* **1** : loose, slack **2** POLTRON : cowardly — **~** *nmf* : coward — **lâcheté** [laʃte] *nf* : cowardice

laconique [lakɔnik] *adj* : laconic

lacrymogène [lakrimɔʒɛn] *adj* **gaz ~** : tear gas

lacune [lakyn] *nf* : gap

là–dedans [laddɑ̃] *adv* : in here, in there

là–dessous [ladsu] *adv* : under here, under there

là–dessus [ladsy] *adv* **1** : on here, on there **2 il n'y a aucun doute ~** : there's no doubt about it

ladite → **ledit**

lagune [lagyn] *nf* : lagoon

là–haut [lao] *adv* **1** : up there **2** : upstairs

laïc [laik] *nm* **les ~s** : the laity

laid, laide [lɛ, lɛd] *adj* **1** : ugly **2** : despicable (of an action) — **laideur** [lɛdœr] *nf* : ugliness

laine [lɛn] *nf* : wool — **lainage** [lɛnaʒ] *nm* **1** : woolen fabric **2** : woolen garment

laïque [laik] *adj* : lay, secular — **~** *nmf* : layman, laywoman

laisse [lɛs] *nf* : lead, leash

laisser [lɛse] *vt* : leave — *v aux* **1** : let, allow **2 ~ faire** : not interfere — **se laisser** *vr* **1** : allow oneself **2 ~ aller** : let oneself go — **laisser–aller** [lɛseale] *nms & pl* : carelessness — **laissez–passer** [lɛsepase] *nms & pl* : pass, permit

lait [lɛ] *nm* : milk — **laiterie** [lɛtri] *nf* **1** : dairy industry **2** : dairy — **laiteux, -teuse** [lɛtø, -tøz] *adj* : milky — **laitier, -tière** [lɛtje, -tjɛr] *adj* : dairy — **~** *n* **1** : milkman **2** : dairyman

laiton [lɛtɔ̃] *nm* : brass

laitue [lety] *nf* : lettuce

lambeau [lɑ̃bo] *nm, pl* **-beaux 1** : rag, scrap **2 en ~x** : in tatters

lambiner [lɑ̃bine] *vi fam* : dawdle

lambris [lɑ̃bri] *nms & pl* : paneling

lame [lam] *nf* **1** : strip, slat **2 ~ de razoir** : razor blade — **lamelle** [lamɛl] *nf* : thin strip

lamenter [lamɑ̃te] *v* **se lamenter** *vr* : lament — **lamentable** [lamɑ̃tabl] *adj* **1** : deplorable **2** PITOYABLE : pitiful, pathetic

lampe [lɑ̃p] *nf* **1** : lamp **2 ~ de poche** : flashlight — **lampadaire** [lɑ̃padɛr] *nm* **1** : floor lamp **2** : streetlight — **lampion** [lɑ̃pjɔ̃] *nm* : Chinese lantern

lance [lɑ̃s] *nf* **1** : spear, lance **2** *or* **~ à eau** : hose

lancée [lɑ̃se] *nf* **1** : momentum **2 continuer sur sa ~** : keep going

lancer [lɑ̃se] {6} *vt* **1** : throw, hurl **2** : launch **3** ÉMETTRE : issue, give out **4** : start up (a motor) — **se lancer** *vr* **~ dans** : launch into — **~** *nm* : throw, throwing — **lancement** [lɑ̃smɑ̃] *nm* **1** : throwing **2** : launching — **lance–pierres** [lɑ̃spjɛr] *nms & pl* : slingshot

lanciner [lɑ̃sine] *vi* : throb — *vt* : haunt, obsess — **lancinant, -nante** [lɑ̃sinɑ̃, -nɑ̃t] *adj* : shooting, throbbing

landau [lɑ̃do] *nm France* : baby carriage

lande [lɑ̃d] *nf* : moor, heath

langage [lɑ̃gaʒ] *nm* : language

lange [lɑ̃ʒ] *nm* : baby blanket

langouste [lɑ̃gust] *nf* : crayfish — **langoustine** [lɑ̃gustin] *nf* : prawn

langue [lɑ̃g] *nf* **1** : tongue **2** : language — **languette** [lɑ̃gɛt] *nf* **1** : tongue (of a shoe) **2** : strip

langueur [lɑ̃gœr] *nf* : languor, lethargy — **languir** [lɑ̃gir] *vi* **1** : languish, pine **2** : flag (of conversation, etc.) — **languissant, -sante** [lɑ̃gisɑ̃, -sɑ̃t] *adj* : languid, listless

lanière [lanjɛr] *nf* : strap, lash, thong

lanterne [lɑ̃tɛrn] *nf* **1** LAMPE : lantern **2** : parking light

laper [lape] *vt* : lap up

lapider [lapide] *vt* : stone

lapin, -pine [lapɛ̃, -pin] *n* **1** : rabbit **2 poser un ~ à qqn** : stand s.o. up

laps [laps] *nms & pl* : lapse (of time) — **lapsus** [lapsys] *nms & pl* : slip, error

laque [lak] *nf* **1** : lacquer **2** : hair spray

laquelle → **lequel**

larcin [larsɛ̃] *nm* : petty theft

lard [lar] *nm* **1** : fat, lard **2** : bacon

large [larʒ] *adj* **1** : wide, broad **2** CONSIDÉRABLE : extensive **3** AMPLE : loose-fitting **4** GÉNÉREUX : generous — **~** *nm* **1 de ~** : wide, in width **2 le ~** : the open sea — **~** *adv* : on a large scale, generously — **largement** [larʒəmɑ̃] *adv* **1** : widely **2** DE BEAUCOUP : greatly, by far **3** GÉNÉREUSEMENT : generously **4** AU MOINS : easily — **largesse** [larʒɛs] *nf* : generosity — **largeur** [larʒœr] *nf* **1** : width, breadth **2 ~ d'esprit** : broad-mindedness

larguer [large] *vt* **1** : release, drop **2** *fam* : ditch, get rid of

larme [larm] *nf* **1** : tear **2** *fam* : drop, small quantity — **larmoyant, -moyante** [larmwajɑ̃, -mwajɑ̃t] *adj* : tearful

larve [larv] *nf* : larva

larynx [larɛ̃ks] *nms & pl* : larynx — **laryngite** [larɛ̃ʒit] *nf* : laryngitis

las, lasse [la, las] *adj* : weary

lasagne [lazaɲ] *nf* : lasagna

laser [lazɛr] *nm* : laser

lasser [lase] *vt* **1** : weary, tire out **2** ENNUYER : bore — **se lasser** *vr* **~ de** : grow weary of — **lassitude** [lasityd] *nf* : weariness

latent, -tente [latɑ̃, -tɑ̃t] *adj* : latent

latéral, -rale [lateral] *adj, mpl* **-raux** [-ro] : side, lateral

latex [latɛks] *nms & pl* : latex

latin, -tine [latɛ̃, -tin] *adj* : Latin — **latin** *nm* : Latin (language)

latitude [latityd] *nf* : latitude

latte [lat] *nf* : lath, floorboard

lauréat, -réate [lɔrea, -reat] *n* : prizewinner

laurier [lɔrje] *nm* **1** : laurel **2 feuille de ~** : bay leaf

lavable [lavabl] *adj* : washable

lavabo [lavabo] *nm* **1** : (bathroom) sink **2 ~s** *nmpl France* : toilets

lavage [lavaʒ] *nm* **1** : wash, washing **2 ~ de cerveau** : brainwashing

lavande [lavɑ̃d] *nf* : lavender

lave [lav] *nf* : lava

laver [lave] *vt* : wash — **se laver** *vr* **1** : wash oneself **2 ~ les mains** : wash one's hands — **lave–linge** [lavlɛ̃ʒ] *nms & pl France* : washing machine — **laverie** [lavri] *nf* : self-service laundry — **lavette** [lavɛt] *nf* : dishcloth — **laveur, -veuse** [lavœr, -vøz] *n* : washer, cleaner — **lave–vaisselle** [lavvesɛl] *nms & pl* : dishwasher — **lavoir** [lavwar] *nm Can* : self-service laundry

laxatif [laksatif] *nm* : laxative

le, la [lə, la] (**l'** [l] *before a vowel or mute h*) *pron, pl* **les** [le] : him, her, it, them — *art* **1** : the **2** : a, an, per

lécher [leʃe] {87} *vt* : lick, lap — **se lécher** *vr* : lick (one's fingers, etc.) — **lèche–vitrines** [lɛʃvitrin] *nms & pl* **faire du ~** : window-shop

leçon [ləsɔ̃] *nf* : lesson

lecteur, -trice [lɛktœr, -tris] *n* : reader — **lecteur** *nm* **1 ~ de disquettes** : disk drive **2 ~ laser** : CD player — **lecture** [lɛktyr] *nf* : reading

ledit, ladite [lədi, ladit] *adj, pl* **lesdits, lesdites** [ledi, ledit] : the aforesaid

légal, -gale [legal] *adj, mpl* **-gaux** [lego] : legal, lawful — **légaliser** [legalize] *vt* : legalize — **légalité** [legalite] *nf* : lawfulness

légende [leʒɑ̃d] *nf* **1** : legend, tale **2** : caption (of an illustration) — **légendaire** [leʒɑ̃dɛr] *adj* : legendary

léger, -gère [leʒe, -ʒɛr] *adj* **1** : light **2** FAIBLE : slight, faint **3** IMPRUDENT : thoughtless **4 à la légère** : rashly — **légèrement** [leʒɛrmɑ̃] *adv* **1** : lightly **2** : slightly — **légèreté** [leʒɛrte] *nf* **1** : lightness **2** : thoughtlessness

légiférer [leʒifere] {87} *vi* : legislate

légion [leʒjɔ̃] *nf* : legion

législation [leʒislasjɔ̃] *nf* : legislation — **législateur, -trice** [leʒislatœr, -tris] *n* : legislator, lawmaker — **législatif, -tive** [leʒislatif, -tiv] *adj* : legislative — **législatif** *nm* : legislature — **législature** [leʒislatyr] *nf* : term (of office)

légitime [leʒitim] *adj* **1** LÉGAL : lawful **2** : rightful, legitimate **3 ~ défense** : self-defense

legs [lɛg] *nms & pl* : legacy — **léguer** [lege] {87} *vt* **1** : bequeath **2** TRANSMETTRE : pass on

légume [legym] *nm* : vegetable

lendemain [lɑ̃dmɛ̃] *nm* **1** : next day **2 au ~ de** : just after, following **3 du jour au ~** : in a very short time **4 le ~ matin** : the next morning

lent, lente [lɑ̃, lɑ̃t] *adj* : slow — **lenteur** [lɑ̃tœr] *nf* : slowness

lentille [lɑ̃tij] *nf* **1** : lentil **2** : (optical) lens

léopard [leɔpar] *nm* : leopard

lèpre [lɛpr] *nf* : leprosy

lequel, laquelle [ləkɛl, lakɛl] *pron, pl* **lesquels, lesquelles** [lekɛl] (*with* **à** *and* **de** *contracted to* **auquel, auxquels, auxquelles; duquel, desquels, desquelles**) **1** : which **2** : who, whom **3 lequel préférez-vous?** : which one do you prefer?

les → **le**

lesbienne [lɛsbjɛn] *nf* : lesbian

lesdits, lesdites → **ledit**

léser [leze] {87} *vt* **1** : wrong **2** BLESSER : injure

lésiner [lezine] *vi* **~ sur** : skimp on

lésion [lezjɔ̃] *nf* : lesion

lesquels, lesquelles → **lequel**

lessive [lɛsiv] *nf* **1** LAVAGE : washing, wash **2** : laundry detergent — **lessiver** [lɛsive] *vt* **1** : wash, scrub **2 être lessivé** *fam* : be exhausted

lest [lɛst] *nm* : ballast

leste [lɛst] *adj* : nimble

léthargie [letarʒi] *nf* : lethargy — **léthargique** [letarʒik] *adj* : lethargic

lettre [lɛtr] *nf* **1** : letter (of the alphabet) **2** CORRESPONDANCE : letter **3 ~s** *nfpl* : arts, humanities **4 à la ~** : exactly **5 en toutes ~s** : in full — **lettré, -trée** [lɛtre] *adj* : well-read

leucémie [løsemi] *nf* : leukemia

leur [lœr] *adj, pl* **leurs** : their — **~** *pron* **1** : (to) them **2 le ~, la ~, les ~s** : theirs

leurre [lœr] *nm* **1** : (fishing) lure **2** ILLUSION : illusion, deception — **leurrer** [lœre] *vt* : deceive, delude — **se leurrer** *vr* : delude oneself

levain [ləvɛ̃] *nm* **1** : leaven **2 sans ~** : unleavened

lever [ləve] {52} *vt* **1** : lift **2** : raise **3** : close (a meeting), lift (a ban) — *vi* **1** : come up (of plants) **2** : rise (in cooking) — **se lever** *vr* **1** : get up **2** : stand up **3** : rise (of the sun) **4 le jour se lève** : day is breaking — **~** *nm* **1** : rising, rise **2 ~ du soleil** : sunrise — **levée** [ləve] *nf* **1** SUPPRESSION : lifting **2** : collection (of mail, etc.)

levier [ləvje] *nm* **1** : lever **2 ~ de vitesse** : gearshift

lèvre [lɛvr] *nf* : lip

lévrier [levrije] *nm* : greyhound

levure [ləvyr] *nf* **1** : yeast **2 ~ chimique** : baking powder

lexique [lɛksik] *nm* **1** : glossary, lexicon **2** VOCABULAIRE : vocabulary

lézard [lezar] *nm* : lizard

lézarder [lezarde] *v* **se lézarder** *vr* : crack

liaison [ljɛzɔ̃] *nf* : liaison

liant, liante [ljɑ̃, ljɑ̃t] *adj* : sociable

liasse [ljas] *nf* : bundle, wad

libanais, -naise [libanɛ, -nɛz] *adj* : Lebanese

libeller [libele] *vt* : draw up (a document), make out (a check)
libellule [libelyl] *nf* : dragonfly
libéral, -rale [liberal] *adj & n, mpl* **-raux** [-ro] : liberal
libérer [libere] {87} *vt* : free, release, liberate — **se libérer** *vr* : free oneself — **libération** [liberasjɔ̃] *nf* : liberation, freeing — **libéré, -rée** [libere] *adj* **~ de** : free from
liberté [libɛrte] *nf* **1** : freedom, liberty **2 en ~ conditionnelle** : on probation **3 mettre en ~** : set free
libido [libido] *nf* : libido
libraire [librɛr] *nmf* : bookseller — **librairie** [librɛri] *nf* : bookstore
libre [libr] *adj* **1** : free **2** DISPONIBLE : available, unoccupied **3** DÉGAGÉ : clear, free **4 ~ arbitre** : free will — **libre-échange** [librəʃɑ̃ʒ] *nm, pl* **libres-échanges** [librəzeʃɑ̃ʒ] : free trade — **librement** [librəmɑ̃] *adv* : freely — **libre-service** [librəsɛrvis] *nm, pl* **libres-services** : self-service
licence [lisɑ̃s] *nf* **1** : (bachelor's) degree **2** : license, permit **3 prendre des ~s avec** : take liberties with — **licencié, -ciée** [lisɑ̃sje] *n* : (university) graduate
licencier [lisɑ̃sje] {96} *vt* : lay off, dismiss — **licenciement** [lisɑ̃simɑ̃] *nm* : layoff, dismissal
lichen [likɛn] *nm* : lichen
licite [lisit] *adj* : lawful
lie [li] *nf* : sediment, dregs
liège [ljɛʒ] *nm* : cork
lien [ljɛ̃] *nm* **1** ATTACHE : bond, strap **2** RAPPORT : link **3** RELATION : tie, relationship — **lier** [lje] {96} *vt* **1** : bind, tie up **2** RELIER : link up **3** : strike up (a friendship, etc.) **4** UNIR : unite — **se lier** *vr* **~ avec** : become friends with
lierre [ljɛr] *nm* : ivy
liesse [ljɛs] *nf* : jubilation
lieu [ljø] *nm, pl* **lieux 1** ENDROIT : place **2 au ~ de** : instead of **3 avoir ~** : take place **4 avoir ~ de** : have reason to **5 en premier ~** : in the first place **6 tenir ~ de** : serve as **7 ~x** *nmpl* : premises — **lieu-dit** *or* **lieudit** [ljødi] *nm, pl* **lieux-dits** *or* **lieudits** : locality
lieutenant [ljøtnɑ̃] *nm* : lieutenant
lièvre [ljɛvr] *nm* : hare
ligament [ligamɑ̃] *nm* : ligament
ligne [liɲ] *nf* **1** : line **2** PARCOURS : route **3 en ~** : online (in computers) **4 ~ droite** : beeline — **lignée** [liɲe] *nf* **1** : line, lineage **2** DESCENDANTS : descendants *pl*
ligoter [ligɔte] *vt* : tie up, bind
ligue [lig] *nf* : league, alliance — **liguer** [lige] *v* **se liguer** *vr* **1** : join forces **2 ~ contre** : conspire against
lilas [lila] *nms & pl* : lilac
limace [limas] *nf* : slug (mollusk)
lime [lim] *nf* **1** : file **2 ~ à ongles** : nail file — **limer** [lime] *vt* : file — **se limer** *vr* **~ les ongles** : file one's nails
limiter [limite] *vt* : limit — **limitation** [limitasjɔ̃] *nf* : limitation — **limite** [limit] *adj* **1 cas ~** : borderline case **2 date ~** : deadline **3 vitesse ~** : speed limit — **~** *nf* **1** : limit **2** : border, boundary
limitrophe [limitrɔf] *adj* : bordering, adjacent
limoger [limɔʒe] {17} *vt* : dismiss
limon [limɔ̃] *nm* : silt
limonade [limɔnad] *nf* : lemonade
limousine [limuzin] *nf* : limousine
limpide [lɛ̃pid] *adj* : (crystal) clear — **limpidité** [lɛ̃pidite] *nf* : clearness
lin [lɛ̃] *nm* **1** : flax **2** : linen
linceul [lɛ̃sœl] *nm* : shroud
linéaire [lineɛr] *adj* : linear
linge [lɛ̃ʒ] *nm* **1** : (household) linen **2** LESSIVE : wash, washing **3** CHIFFON : cloth **4** *or* **~ de corps** : underwear **5** *Can fam* : clothes *pl*, clothing — **lingerie** [lɛ̃ʒri] *nf* **1** : lingerie **2** *Can* : linen closet
lingot [lɛ̃go] *nm* : ingot
linguistique [lɛ̃gɥistik] *adj* : linguistic — **~** *nf* : linguistics — **linguiste** [lɛ̃gɥist] *nmf* : linguist
linoléum [linɔleɔm] *nm* : linoleum
lion, lionne [ljɔ̃, ljɔn] *n* : lion, lioness *f* — **lionceau** [ljɔ̃so] *nm, pl* **-ceaux** : lion cub
liqueur [likœr] *nf* **1** : liqueur **2** *Can* : soft drink
liquide [likid] *adj* : liquid — **~** *nm* **1** : liquid **2** ARGENT : cash — **liquidation** [likidasjɔ̃] *nf* **1** : liquidation **2** : clearance sale — **liquider** [likide] *vt* **1** : liquidate **2** : eliminate — **liquidités** [likidite] *nfpl* : liquid assets
lire [lir] {51} *vt* : read
lis *or* **lys** [lis] *nms & pl* : lily
lisible [lizibl] *adj* : legible — **lisibilité** [-zibilite] *nf* : legibility
lisière [lizjɛr] *nf* : edge, outskirts *pl*
lisse [lis] *adj* : smooth, sleek
liste [list] *nf* : list
lit [li] *nm* **1** : bed **2 ~ de camp** : cot — **literie** [litri] *nf* : bedding — **litière** [litjɛr] *nf* : litter
litige [litiʒ] *nm* : dispute
litre [litr] *nm* : liter
littérature [literatyr] *nf* : literature — **littéraire** [literɛr] *adj* : literary — **littéral, -rale** [literal] *adj, mpl* **-raux** [-ro] : literal
littoral [litɔral] *nm* : coast(line) — **~** *adj* : coastal
liturgie [lityrʒi] *nf* : liturgy — **liturgique** [lityrʒik] *adj* : liturgical
livide [livid] *adj* : pallid, pale
livraison [livrɛzɔ̃] *nf* : delivery
livre[1] [livr] *nm* **1** : book **2 ~ de poche** : paperback **3 ~ de recettes** : cookbook
livre[2] *nf* **1** : pound **2** *or* **~ sterling** : pound (monetary unit)
livrer [livre] *vt* **1** : deliver **2** REMETTRE : hand over — **se livrer** *vr* **1 ~ à** : devote oneself to **2 ~ à** : surrender to **3 ~ à** : confide in
livret [livrɛ] *nm* : booklet
livreur, -vreuse [livrœr, -vrøz] *n* : deliveryman *m*, delivery woman *f*
lobe [lɔb] *nm* : lobe
local, -cale [lɔkal] *adj, mpl* **-caux** [lɔko] : local — **local** *nm, pl* **-caux** : place, premises *pl* — **localiser** [lɔkalize] *vt* **1** SITUER : locate **2** LIMITER : localize — **localité** [lɔkalite] *nf* : locality
location [lɔkasjɔ̃] *nf* **1** : renting, leasing **2** : rented property — **locataire** [lɔkatɛr] *nmf* : tenant
locomotive [lɔkɔmɔtiv] *nf* : locomotive, engine
locution [lɔkysjɔ̃] *nf* : phrase, idiom
loge [lɔʒ] *nf* **1** : dressing room **2** : box (at the theater) **3** : lodge
loger [lɔʒe] {17} *vt* **1** : lodge **2** CONTENIR : accommodate — **se loger** *vr* **1** : find accommodations **2 ~ dans** : lodge itself in — **logement** [lɔʒmɑ̃] *nm* **1** : accommodation **2** : apartment **3** HABITAT : housing
logiciel [lɔʒisjɛl] *nm* : software
logique [lɔʒik] *adj* : logical — **~** *nf* : logic
logis [lɔʒi] *nms & pl* : dwelling, abode
logistique [lɔʒistik] *nf* : logistics
loi [lwa] *nf* : law
loin [lwɛ̃] *adv* **1** : far **2** : a long time ago **3 ~ de** : far from **4 plus ~** : further — **~** *nm* **1 au ~** : in the distance **2 de ~** : from a distance **3 de ~** : by far — **lointain, -taine** [lwɛ̃tɛ̃, -tɛn] *adj* : distant — **lointain** *nm* : distance
loisir [lwazir] *nm* **1** : leisure **2 ~s** *nmpl* : leisure activities
long, longue [lɔ̃, lɔ̃g] *adj* : long — **long** [lɔ̃] *adv* : much, a lot — **~** *nm* **1** : length **2 de ~** : long, in length **3 le ~ de** : along — **à la longue** *adv phr* : in the long run
longer [lɔ̃ʒe] {17} *vt* **1** : walk along, follow **2** LIMITER : border
longévité [lɔ̃ʒevite] *nf* : longevity
longitude [lɔ̃ʒityd] *nf* : longitude
longtemps [lɔ̃tɑ̃] *adv* **1** : a long time **2 avant ~** : before long
longue → **long** — **longuement** [lɔ̃gmɑ̃] *adv* **1** : for a long time **2** : at length — **longueur** [lɔ̃gœr] *nf* **1** : length **2 à ~ de journée** : all day long **3 ~ d'onde** : wavelength **4 ~s** *nfpl* : tedious parts (of a film, etc.) — **longue-vue** [lɔ̃gvy] *nf, pl* **longues-vues** : telescope
lopin [lɔpɛ̃] *nm* **~ de terre** : plot of land
loquace [lɔkas] *adj* : talkative
loque [lɔk] *nf* **1** : wreck (person) **2 ~s** *nfpl* : rags
loquet [lɔkɛ] *nm* : latch
lorgner [lɔrɲe] *vt* : eye, ogle
lors [lɔr] *adv* **~ de 1** : at the time of **2** : during
lorsque [lɔrskə] (**lorsqu'** [lɔrsk] *before a vowel or mute h*) *conj* : when
losange [lɔzɑ̃ʒ] *nm* **1** : lozenge, diamond shape **2** *Can* : (baseball) diamond
lot [lo] *nm* **1** SORT : fate, lot **2** PRIX : prize **3** PART : share
loterie [lɔtri] *nf* : lottery
lotion [lɔsjɔ̃] *nf* : lotion
lotissement [lɔtismɑ̃] *nm* : (housing) development
louange [lwɑ̃ʒ] *nf* : praise — **louable** [lwabl] *adj* : praiseworthy
louche[1] [luʃ] *nf* : ladle
louche[2] *adj* : shady, suspicious — **loucher** [luʃe] *vi* **1** : be cross-eyed **2** : squint
louer[1] [lwe] *vt* : praise — **se louer** *vr* **~ de** : be satisfied about
louer[2] *vt* : rent, lease — **se louer** *vr* : be for rent
loufoque [lufɔk] *adj fam* : crazy, zany
loup [lu] *nm* : wolf
loupe [lup] *nf* : magnifying glass
louper [lupe] *vt fam* **1** : bungle, mess up **2** : miss (a train, etc.)
lourd, lourde [lur, lurd] *adj* : heavy — **lourd** *adv* **peser ~** : be heavy — **lourdement** [lurdəmɑ̃] *adv* : heavily — **lourdeur** [lurdœr] *nf* : heaviness
loutre [lutr] *nf* : otter
louvoyer [luvwaje] {58} *vi* : hedge, equivocate
loyal, loyale [lwajal] *adj, mpl* **loyaux** [lwajo] **1** : loyal **2** HONNÊTE : fair — **loyauté** [lwajote] *nf* **1** : loyalty **2** : fairness
loyer [lwaje] *nm* : rent
lu [ly] *pp* → **lire**
lubie [lybi] *nf* : whim
lubrifier [lybrifje] {96} *vt* : lubricate — **lubrifiant** [lybrifjɑ̃] *nm* : lubricant
lucarne [lykarn] *nf* : skylight
lucide [lysid] *adj* : lucid — **lucidité** [lysidite] *nf* : lucidity
lucratif, -tive [lykratif, -tiv] *adj* : lucrative, profitable
ludique [lydik] *adj* : play, playing
lueur [lɥœr] *nf* **1** : faint light **2** : glimmer (of hope, etc.)
luge [lyʒ] *nf* : sled
lugubre [lygybr] *adj* : gloomy, dismal
lui [lɥi] *pron* **1** (*used as indirect object*) : (to) him, (to) her, (to) it **2** (*used as object of a preposition*) : him, it **3** (*used as subject or for emphasis*) : he **4** (*used as a reflexive pronoun*) : himself — **lui-même** [lɥimɛm] *pron* : himself, itself
luire [lɥir] {49} *vi* : shine, gleam — **luisant, -sante** [lɥizɑ̃, -zɑ̃t] *adj* : shining, gleaming
lumière [lymjɛr] *nf* : light — **luminaire** [lyminɛr] *nm* : lamp, light — **lumineux, -neuse** [lyminø, -nøz] *adj* **1** : luminous **2** RADIEUX : radiant, bright
lunaire [lynɛr] *adj* : lunar, moon
lunatique [lynatik] *adj* : whimsical
lunch [lœ̃ʃ] *nm, pl* **lunchs** *or* **lunches 1** BUFFET : buffet **2** *Can* : lunch
lundi [lœ̃di] *nm* : Monday
lune [lyn] *nf* **1** : moon **2 ~ de miel** : honeymoon
lunette [lynɛt] *nf* **1** : telescope **2 ~ arrière** : rear window (of an automobile) **3 ~s** *nfpl* : glasses **4 ~s bifocales** : bifocals
lurette [lyrɛt] *nf* **il y a belle ~** *fam* : ages ago
lustre [lystr] *nm* **1** : luster, sheen **2** : chandelier — **lustré, -trée** [lystre] *adj* : shiny, glossy
luth [lyt] *nm* : lute
lutin [lytɛ̃] *nm* : imp, goblin
lutrin [lytrɛ̃] *nm* : lectern
lutte [lyt] *nf* **1** : fight, struggle **2** : wrestling — **lutter** [lyte] *vi* **1** SE BATTRE : fight, struggle **2** : wrestle — **lutteur, -teuse** [lytœr, -tøz] *n* **1** : fighter **2** : wrestler
luxation [lyksasjɔ̃] *nf* : dislocation (of a joint)
luxe [lyks] *nm* : luxury
luxer [lykse] *v* **se luxer** *vr* : dislocate (one's shoulder, etc.)
luxueux, -xueuse [lyksɥø, -sɥøz] *adj* : luxurious
luxure [lyksyr] *nf* : lust — **luxurieux, -rieuse** [lyksyrjø, -rjøz] *adj* : lustful
luzerne [lyzɛrn] *nf* : alfalfa
lycée [lise] *nm France* : high school — **lycéen, -céenne** [liseɛ̃, -seɛn] *n France* : high school student
lynx [lɛ̃ks] *nm* : lynx
lyrique [lirik] *adj* : lyric(al)
lys → **lis**

M

m [ɛm] *nm* : m, 13th letter of the alphabet
ma → **mon**
macabre [makabr] *adj* : macabre
macaron [makarɔ̃] *nm* **1** : macaroon **2** INSIGNE : badge, sticker
macaronis [makarɔni] *nmpl* : macaroni
macédoine [masedwan] *nf* : mixture (of fruits or vegetables)
macérer [masere] {87} *v* : steep, soak
mâcher [maʃe] *vt* : chew
machin [maʃɛ̃] *nm fam* : thingamajig, thing
machine [maʃin] *nf* **1** : machine **2** : engine (of a ship, a train, etc.) **3 ~ à écrire** : typewriter **4 ~ à laver** : washing machine — **machiniste** [maʃinist] *nmf* : (bus) driver
mâchoire [maʃwar] *nf* : jaw
mâchonner [maʃɔne] *vt* : chew
maçon [masɔ̃] *nm* : bricklayer, mason — **maçonnerie** [masɔnri] *nf* : masonry
maculer [makyle] *vt* : stain
madame [madam] *nf, pl* **mesdames** [medam] **1** : Mrs., Ms., Madam **2** : lady — **mademoiselle** [madmwazɛl] *nf, pl* **mesdemoiselles** [medmwazɛl] **1** : Miss, Ms. **2** : young lady
mafia *or* **maffia** [mafja] *nf* : Mafia
magasin [magazɛ̃] *nm* **1** : shop, store **2** ENTREPÔT : warehouse **3** : magazine (of a gun or camera) **4 grand ~** : department store
magazine [magazin] *nm* REVUE : magazine
magie [maʒi] *nf* : magic — **magicien, -cienne** [maʒisjɛ̃, -sjɛn] *n* : magician — **magique** [maʒik] *adj* : magic(al)
magistral, -trale [maʒistral] *adj, mpl* **-traux** [-tro] **1** : brilliant, masterly **2 cours magistral** : lecture
magistrat [maʒistra] *nm* : magistrate
magnanime [maɲanim] *adj* : magnanimous
magnat [maɲa] *nm* : magnate, tycoon
magnétique [maɲetik] *adj* : magnetic — **magnétiser** [maɲetize] *vt* : magnetize — **magnétisme** [maɲetism] *nm* : magnetism
magnétophone [maɲetɔfɔn] *nm* : tape recorder
magnétoscope [maɲetɔskɔp] *nm* : videocassette recorder, VCR
magnifique [maɲifik] *adj* : magnificent
magnolia [maɲɔlja] *nm* : magnolia
mai [mɛ] *nm* : May
maigre [mɛgr] *adj* **1** MINCE : thin **2** INSUFFISANT : meager **3** : low-fat, lean (of meat) — **maigrir** [megrir] *vi* : lose weight, reduce
maille [maj] *nf* **1** : stitch (in knitting) **2** : mesh (of a net)
maillot [majo] *nm* **1** : jersey **2 ~ de bain** : bathing suit
main [mɛ̃] *nf* **1** : hand **2** SAVOIR-FAIRE : know-how, skill **3 de première ~** : firsthand **4 donner un coup de ~ à** : lend a helping hand to **5 ~ courante** : handrail — **main-d'œuvre** [mɛ̃dœvr] *nf, pl* **mains-d'œuvre** : manpower, workforce
maint, mainte [mɛ̃, mɛ̃t] *adj* : many a
maintenant [mɛ̃tnɑ̃] *adv* **1** : now **2** : nowadays
maintenir [mɛ̃tnir] {92} *vt* **1** : maintain **2** SOUTENIR : support — **se maintenir** *vr* : remain, persist — **maintien** [mɛ̃tjɛ̃] *nm* **1** : maintaining, maintenance **2** PORT : bearing, deportment
maire, mairesse [mɛr, mɛrɛs] *n* : mayor — **mairie** [meri] *nf* : town hall, city hall
mais [mɛ] *conj* **1** : but **2 ~ oui** : certainly, of course
maïs [mais] *nm* : corn, maize
maison [mɛzɔ̃] *nf* **1** : house, home **2** SOCIÉTÉ : firm — **~** *adj* **1** : homemade **2** : in-house (of an employee) — **maisonnée** [mɛzɔne] *nf* : household
maître, -tresse [mɛtr, -trɛs] *n* **1** : master, mistress **2 ~ d'école** : schoolteacher — **~** *adj* : main, key — **maître** [mɛtr] *nm* **1** : master (of a pet, etc.) **2** EXPERT : expert — **maîtrise** [metriz] *nf* **1** : skill, mastery **2** : master's degree **3 ~ de soi** : self-control — **maîtriser** [metrize] *vt* **1** : master **2** CONTENIR : control, restrain
majesté [maʒɛste] *nf* : majesty — **majestueux, -tueuse** [maʒɛstɥø, -tɥøz] *adj* : majestic
majeur, -jeure [maʒœr] *adj* **1** : major, main **2** : of age (in law) — **majeur** *nm* : middle finger — **majorité** [maʒɔrite] *nf* : majority
majuscule [maʒyskyl] *adj* : capital, uppercase — **~** *nf* : capital letter
mal [mal] *adv* **1** : poorly, badly **2** INCORRECTEMENT : wrongly **3 aller ~** : be unwell — **~** *adj* **1** : wrong **2** MAUVAIS : bad — **~** *nm, pl* **maux** [mo] **1** DOULEUR : pain **2** MALADIE : sickness **3** DOMMAGE : harm **4** : evil **5** PEINE : trouble, difficulty
malade [malad] *adj* : sick, ill — **~** *nmf* : sick person, patient — **maladie** [maladi] *nf* : illness, disease — **maladif, -dive** [maladif, -div] *adj* : sickly
maladresse [maladrɛs] *nf* **1** : clumsiness **2** BÉVUE : blunder — **maladroit, -droite** [maladrwa, -drwat] *adj* : clumsy, awkward
malaise [malɛz] *nm* **1** : dizziness **2** GÊNE : uneasiness, malaise
malaxer [malakse] *vt* **1** : knead **2** MÉLANGER : mix
malchance [malʃɑ̃s] *nf* : bad luck, misfortune — **malchanceux, -ceuse** [malʃɑ̃sø, -søz] *adj* : unfortunate
mâle [mal] *adj* **1** : male **2** : manly — **~** *nm* : male
malédiction [malediksjɔ̃] *nf* : curse
maléfique [malefik] *adj* : evil
malencontreux, -treuse [malɑ̃kɔ̃trø, -trøz] *adj* : unfortunate, untoward
malentendu [malɑ̃tɑ̃dy] *nm* : misunderstanding
malfaçon [malfasɔ̃] *nf* : fault, defect
malfaisant, -sante [malfəzɑ̃, -zɑ̃t] *adj* : evil, harmful — **malfaiteur** [malfɛtœr] *nm* : criminal
malgré [malgre] *prep* **1** : in spite of, despite **2 ~ tout** : nevertheless, even so
malheur [malœr] *nm* : misfortune — **malheureux, -reuse** [malœrø, -røz] *adj* **1** : unhappy **2** MALCHANCEUX : unfortunate — **~** *n* : unfortunate person — **malheureusement** [malœrøzmɑ̃] *adv* : unfortunately
malhonnête [malɔnɛt] *adj* : dishonest — **malhonnêteté** [malɔnɛtte] *nf* : dishonesty
malice [malis] *nf* : mischief, mischievousness — **malicieux, -cieuse** [malisjø, -sjøz] *adj* : mischievous
malin, -ligne [malɛ̃, -liɲ] *adj* **1** : clever **2** *fam* : difficult **3** MÉCHANT : malicious **4** : malignant (in medicine)
malle [mal] *nf* : trunk
malléable [maleabl] *adj* : malleable
mallette [malɛt] *nf* : small suitcase, valise
malnutrition [malnytrisjɔ̃] *nf* : malnutrition

malodorant, -rante [malɔdɔrɑ̃, -rɑ̃t] *adj* : foul-smelling, smelly

malpropre [malprɔpr] *adj* : dirty — **malpropreté** [malprɔprəte] *nf* : dirtiness

malsain, -saine [malsɛ̃, -sɛn] *adj* : unhealthy

malt [malt] *nm* : malt

maltraiter [maltrete] *vt* : mistreat

malveillance [malvɛjɑ̃s] *nf* : spite, malevolence — **malveillant, -lante** [malvɛjɑ̃, -jɑ̃t] *adj* : spiteful

maman [mamɑ̃] *nf* : mom, mommy

mamelle [mamɛl] *nf* **1** : teat **2** PIS : udder — **mamelon** [mamɛlɔ̃] *nm* : nipple

mammifère [mamifɛr] *nm* : mammal

mammouth [mamut] *nm* : mammoth

manche [mɑ̃ʃ] *nf* **1** : sleeve (of a shirt) **2** : round (in sports), set (in tennis) **3** *Can* : inning (in baseball) **4 la Manche** : the English Channel — ~ *nm* **1** : handle, neck, shaft **2** **~ à balai** : broomstick — **manchette** [mɑ̃ʃɛt] *nf* **1** : cuff **2** : headline (in the press)

manchot [mɑ̃ʃo] *nm* : penguin

mandarine [mɑ̃darin] *nf* : tangerine, mandarin orange

mandat [mɑ̃da] *nm* **1** : mandate **2** *or* **~ d'arrêt** : (arrest) warrant **3** *or* **~ postal** : money order — **mandataire** [mɑ̃datɛr] *nmf* **1** REPRÉSENTANT : representative, agent **2** : proxy (in politics)

manège [manɛʒ] *nm* **1** : riding school **2** : merry-go-round

manette [manɛt] *nf* : lever

manger [mɑ̃ʒe] {17} *vt* **1** : eat **2** DÉPENSER : consume, use up — *vi* : eat — ~ *nm* : food — **mangeable** [mɑ̃ʒabl] *adj* : edible — **mangeoire** [mɑ̃ʒwar] *nf* : feeding trough

mangue [mɑ̃g] *nf* : mango

maniable [manjabl] *adj* : easy to handle, manageable

maniaque [manjak] *adj* : fussy — ~ *nmf* **1** : fussy person **2** : fanatic — **manie** [mani] *nf* **1** HABITUDE : habit **2** : quirk, obsession

manier [manje] {96} *vt* **1** MANIPULER : handle **2** UTILISER : use — **maniement** [manimɑ̃] *nm* : handling, use, operation

manière [manjɛr] *nf* **1** : manner, way **2 de ~ à** : so as to **3 de toute ~** : in any case, anyway **4 ~s** *nfpl* : manners — **maniéré, -rée** [manjere] *adj* : affected, mannered

manifester [manifɛste] *vt* **1** : express **2** RÉVÉLER : reveal, show — *vi* : demonstrate — **se manifester** *vr* : appear — **manifestation** [manifɛstasjɔ̃] *nf* **1** : (political) demonstration **2** MARQUE : indication **3** : appearance (of an illness, etc.) — **manifestant, -tante** [manifɛstɑ̃, -tɑ̃t] *n* : demonstrator — **manifeste** [manifɛst] *adj* : obvious — ~ *nm* : manifesto

manigance [manigɑ̃s] *nf* : scheme, trick — **manigancer** [manigɑ̃se] {6} *vt* : plot

manipuler [manipyle] *vt* **1** MANIER : handle **2** : manipulate — **manipulation** [manipylasjɔ̃] *nf* **1** MANIEMENT : handling **2** : manipulation

manivelle [manivɛl] *nf* : crank

mannequin [mankɛ̃] *nm* **1** : dummy, mannequin **2** : (fashion) model

manœuvre [manœvr] *nf* : maneuver — **manœuvrer** [manœvre] *vt* **1** : maneuver **2** : operate (a machine, etc.) **3** MANIPULER : manipulate — *vi* : maneuver

manoir [manwar] *nm* : manor

manquer [mɑ̃ke] *vt* : miss (an opportunity, etc.) — *vi* **1** : lack, be missing **2** ÉCHOUER : fail **3** : be absent (of a student, etc.) **4 ~ de** : be short of — **manque** [mɑ̃k] *nm* **1** : lack **2** LACUNE : gap — **manqué, -quée** [mɑ̃ke] *adj* **1** : failed **2** : missed

mansarde [mɑ̃sard] *nf* : attic

manteau [mɑ̃to] *nm, pl* **-teaux** [-to] : coat

manucure [manykyr] *nf* : manicure — ~ *nmf* : manicurist

manuel, -elle [manɥɛl] *adj* : manual — **manuel** *nm* : manual, handbook

manufacture [manyfaktyr] *nf* : factory — **manufacturer** [manyfaktyre] *vt* : manufacture

manuscrit, -scrite [manyskri, -skrit] *adj* : handwritten — **manuscrit** *nm* : manuscript

manutention [manytɑ̃sjɔ̃] *nf* **1** : handling **2 frais de ~** : handling charges

maquereau [makro] *nm, pl* **-reaux** [-ro] : mackerel

maquette [makɛt] *nf* : (scale) model

maquiller [makije] *vt* : make up (one's face) — **se maquiller** *vr* : put on makeup — **maquillage** [makijaʒ] *nm* : makeup

maquis [maki] *nm France* : brush, undergrowth

marais [marɛ] *nm* : marsh, swamp

marasme [marasm] *nm* **1** : dejection, depression **2** : (economic) stagnation

marathon [maratɔ̃] *nm* : marathon

marauder [marode] *vi* VOLER : pilfer, thieve

marbre [marbr] *nm* **1** : marble **2** *Can* : home plate (in baseball)

marchand, -chande [marʃɑ̃, -ʃɑ̃d] *n* : storekeeper, merchant — ~ *adj* : market — **marchander** [marʃɑ̃de] *vt* : haggle over — *vi* : haggle, bargain — **marchandises** [marʃɑ̃diz] *nfpl* : goods, merchandise

marche [marʃ] *nf* **1** : step, stair **2** PROMENADE : walk, walking **3** RYTHME : pace **4** : march (in music) **5 ~ arrière** : reverse **6 en ~** : running, operating **7 mettre en ~** : start up

marché [marʃe] *nm* **1** : market **2** ACCORD : deal **3 bon ~** : cheap **4 ~ noir** : black market

marchepied [marʃəpje] *nm* : step, steps *pl*

marcher [marʃe] *vi* **1** : walk, march **2 ~ sur** : step on, tread on **3** FONCTIONNER : work, go, run — **marcheur, -cheuse** [marʃœr, -ʃøz] *n* : walker

mardi [mardi] *nm* **1** : Tuesday **2 ~ gras** : Mardi Gras

mare [mar] *nf* **1** : pond **2 ~ de** : pool of

marécage [marekaʒ] *nm* : marsh, swamp — **marécageux, -geuse** [marekaʒø, -ʒøz] *adj* : marshy, swampy

maréchal [mareʃal] *nm, pl* **-chaux** [-ʃo] : marshal

marée [mare] *nf* **1** : tide **2 ~ noire** : oil slick

marelle [marɛl] *nf* : hopscotch

margarine [margarin] *nf* : margarine

marge [marʒ] *nf* : margin — **marginal, -nale** [marʒinal] *adj, mpl* **-naux** [-no] : marginal

marguerite [margərit] *nf* : daisy

marier [marje] {96} *vt* **1** : marry **2** : blend (colors, etc.) — **se marier** *vr* : get married — **mari** [mari] *nm* : husband — **mariage** [marjaʒ] *nm* **1** : marriage **2** : wedding — **marié, -riée** [marje] *adj* : married — ~ *n* **1** : groom *m*, bride *f* **2 les mariés** : the newlyweds

marin, -rine [marɛ̃, -rin] *adj* : sea, marine — **marin** *nm* : sailor — **marine** *nf* : navy

mariner [marine] *v* : marinate

marionnette [marjɔnɛt] *nf* **1** : puppet **2 ~ à fils** : marionette

maritime [maritim] *adj* : maritime, coastal

marmelade [marməlad] *nf* **1** : stewed fruit **2** : marmalade

marmite [marmit] *nf* : cooking pot

marmonner [marmɔne] *v* : mutter, mumble

marmot [marmo] *nm fam* : kid, brat

marmotte [marmɔt] *nf* : woodchuck

marmotter [marmɔte] *v* : mutter, mumble

marocain, -caine [marɔkɛ̃, -kɛn] *adj* : Moroccan

marotte [marɔt] *nf* : craze, fad

marquer [marke] *vt* **1** : mark **2** INDIQUER : show, indicate **3** ÉCRIRE : note (down) **4** : score (in sports) — *vi* **1** : leave a mark **2** : stand out (of an event, etc.) — **marquant, -quante** [markɑ̃, -kɑ̃t] *adj* : memorable, outstanding — **marque** [mark] *nf* **1** : mark, trace **2** : brand, make **3** : score (in sports) **4 ~ déposée** : registered trademark — **marqué, -quée** [marke] *adj* : marked, distinct

marquise [markiz] *nf* : canopy, marquee

marraine [marɛn] *nf* : godmother

marrant, -rante [marɑ̃, -rɑ̃t] *adj fam* : amusing, funny

marre [mar] *adv* **en avoir ~** *fam* : be fed up

marron, -ronne [marɔ̃, -rɔn] *adj* : brown — **marron** *nm* **1** : chestnut **2** : brown — **marronnier** [marɔnje] *nm* : chestnut tree

mars [mars] *nm* : March

Mars *nf* : Mars (planet)

marsouin [marswɛ̃] *nm* : porpoise

marteau [marto] *nm, pl* **-teaux** [marto] **1** : hammer **2 ~ pneumatique** : pneumatic drill — **marteau–piqueur** [martopikœr] *nm, pl* **marteaux–piqueurs** : jackhammer — **marteler** [martəle] {20} *vt* : hammer

martial, -tiale [marsjal] *adj, mpl* **-tiaux** [-sjo] : martial

martyr, -tyre [martir] *n* : martyr — **martyriser** [martirize] *vt* : martyr

mascarade [maskarad] *nf* : masquerade

mascotte [maskɔt] *nf* : mascot

masculin, -line [maskylɛ̃, -lin] *adj* : male, masculine — **masculin** *nm* : masculine

masque [mask] *nm* : mask — **masquer** [maske] *vt* : mask, conceal

massacrer [masakre] *vt* : massacre — **massacre** [masakr] *nm* : massacre

massage [masaʒ] *nm* : massage

masse [mas] *nf* **1** : mass, body (of water, etc.) **2** : sledgehammer **3 les ~s** : the masses

masser [mase] *vt* **1** : massage **2** ASSEMBLER : gather — **masseur, -seuse** [masœr, -søz] *n* : masseur *m*, masseuse *f*

massif, -sive [masif, -siv] *adj* **1** : massive **2** : solid (of gold, silver, etc.) — **massif** *nm* : clump (of trees)

massue [masy] *nf* : club, bludgeon

mastic [mastik] *nm* : putty — **mastiquer** [mastike] *vt* : chew

masturber [mastyrbe] *v* **se masturber** *vr* : masturbate — **masturbation** [mastyrbasjɔ̃] *nf* : masturbation

mat, mate [mat] *adj* **1** : dull, matte (of a finish, etc.) **2** : checkmated (in chess)

mât [ma] *nm* **1** : mast **2** POTEAU : pole, post

match [matʃ] *nm* : match, game

matelas [matla] *nm* : mattress — **matelasser** [matlase] *vt* REMBOURRER : pad

matelot [matlo] *nm* : sailor, seaman

mater [mate] *vt* DOMPTER : subdue, curb

matériaux [materjo] *nmpl* : materials

matériel, -rielle [materjɛl] *adj* : material — **matériel** *nm* **1** : equipment, material(s) **2** : computer hardware — **matérialiser** [materjalize] *vt* : realize, make happen — **se matérialiser** *vr* : materialize — **matérialiste** [materjalist] *adj* : materialistic

maternel, -nelle [matɛrnɛl] *adj* : maternal, motherly — **maternelle** *nf or* **école ~** : nursery school — **maternité** [matɛrnite] *nf* **1** : maternity **2** GROSSESSE : pregnancy

mathématique [matematik] *adj* : mathematical — **mathématicien, -cienne** [matematisjɛ̃, -sjɛn] *n* : mathematician — **mathématiques** [matematik] *nfpl* : mathematics — **maths** *or* **math** [mat] *nfpl fam* : math

matière [matjɛr] *nf* **1** : matter, substance **2** SUJET : subject **3 ~s premières** : raw materials

matin [matɛ̃] *nm* : morning — **matinal, -nale** [matinal] *adj, mpl* **-naux** [-no] **1** : morning **2 être ~** : be up early — **matinée** [matine] *nf* **1** : morning **2** : matinee

matraque [matrak] *nf* : club — **matraquer** [matrake] *vt* **1** : club, bludgeon **2** : plug (a product)

matrice [matris] *nf* : matrix

matricule [matrikyl] *nf* : register, roll

matrimonial, -niale [matrimɔnjal] *adj, mpl* **-niaux** [-njo] : matrimonial

maturité [matyrite] *nf* : maturity

maudire [modir] *vt* : curse, damn — **maudit, -dite** [modi, -dit] *adj* : damned

maugréer [mogree] {89} *vi* GROGNER : grumble

maussade [mosad] *adj* **1** MOROSE : sullen **2 temps ~** : dismal weather

mauvais, -vaise [movɛ, -vɛz] *adj* **1** : bad (of a grade, etc.) **2** : wrong (of an answer, etc.) **3** DÉPLAISANT : nasty, unpleasant

mauve [mov] *adj & nm* : mauve

mauviette [movjɛt] *nf* : weakling

maux → **mal**

maxillaire [maksilɛr] *nm* : jawbone

maxime [maksim] *nf* ADAGE : maxim, proverb

maximum [maksimɔm] *adj & nm, pl* **-mums** [-mɔm] *or* **-ma** [-ma] : maximum

mayonnaise [majɔnɛz] *nf* : mayonnaise

mazout [mazut] *nm* : heating oil

me [mə] *pron* (**m'** [m] *before a vowel or mute h*) **1** : me, to me **2** : myself, to myself

mec [mɛk] *nm fam* : guy

mécanique [mekanik] *nf* **1** : mechanics **2** : mechanism — ~ *adj* : mechanical — **mécanicien, -cienne** [mekanisjɛ̃, -sjɛn] *n* **1** : mechanic **2** : (railway or flight) engineer — **mécanisme** [mekanism] *nm* : mechanism

méchant, -chante [meʃɑ̃, -ʃɑ̃t] *adj* **1** : nasty, malicious **2** : naughty, bad (of a child) **3** : vicious (of a dog) — ~ *n* **1** : villain (in a book or film) **2** : naughty child — **méchamment** [meʃamɑ̃] *adv* : nastily — **méchanceté** [meʃɑ̃ste] *nf* : nastiness

mèche [mɛʃ] *nf* **1** : wick (of a candle) **2** : lock (of hair) **3** : bit (of a drill)

méconnaissable [mekɔnɛsabl] *adj* : unrecognizable

mécontent, -tente [mekɔ̃tɑ̃, -tɑ̃t] *adj* : discontented, dissatisfied — **mécontentement** [mekɔ̃tɑ̃tmɑ̃] *nm* : discontent, dissatisfaction

médaille [medaj] *nf* : medal — **médaillé, -lée** [medaje] *n* : medalist — **médaillon** [medajɔ̃] *nm* **1** : medallion **2** : locket

médecin [medsɛ̃] *nm* : doctor, physician — **médecine** [medsin] *nf* : medicine

média [medja] *nm* **1** : medium **2 les ~s** : the media

médian, -diane [medjɑ̃, -djan] *adj* : median

médiation [medjasjɔ̃] *nf* : mediation, arbitration — **médiateur, -trice** [medjatœr, -tris] *n* : mediator, arbitrator

médical, -cale [medikal] *adj, mpl* **-caux** [-ko] : medical — **médicament** [medikamɑ̃] *nm* : medicine, drug — **médication** [medikasjɔ̃] *nf* : medication — **médicinal, -nale** [medisinal] *adj, mpl* **-naux** [-no] : medicinal

médiéval, -vale [medjeval] *adj, mpl* **-vaux** [-vo] : medieval

médiocre [medjɔkr] *adj* : mediocre — **médiocrité** [medjɔkrite] *nf* : mediocrity

méditer [medite] *vt* : reflect on, think over — *vi* : meditate — **méditation** [meditasjɔ̃] *nf* : meditation

médium [medjɔm] *nm* : medium, psychic

méduse [medyz] *nf* : jellyfish

meeting [mitiŋ] *nm* **1** : meeting **2** : meet (in sports)

méfait [mefɛ] *nm* **1** : misdeed, misdemeanour **2 ~s** *nmpl* : ravages

méfier [mefje] {96} *v* **se méfier** *vr* **1** : be careful, beware **2 ~ de** : distrust — **méfiance** [mefjɑ̃s] *nf* : distrust — **méfiant, -fiante** [mefjɑ̃, -fjɑ̃t] *adj* : distrustful

mégarde [megard] *nf* **par ~** : inadvertently

mégot [mego] *nm* : cigarette butt

meilleur, -leure [mɛjœr] *adj* **1** : better **2** : best — ~ *n* : best (one) — **meilleur** *adv* : better

mélancolie [melɑ̃kɔli] *nf* : melancholy — **mélancolique** [melɑ̃kɔlik] *adj* : melancholy

mélanger [melɑ̃ʒe] {17} *vt* **1** : mix, blend **2** CONFONDRE : mix up, confuse — **se mélanger** *vr* **1** : blend (with) **2** : get mixed up — **mélange** [melɑ̃ʒ] *nm* **1** : mixing, blending **2** : mixture, blend

mélasse [melas] *nf* : molasses

mêlée [mele] *nf* **~ générale** : free-for-all

mêler [mele] *vt* : mix — **se mêler** *vr* **1** : mix, mingle **2 mêlez-vous de vos affaires** : mind your own business

mélodie [melɔdi] *nf* : melody

mélomane [melɔman] *nmf* : music lover

melon [məlɔ̃] *nm* : melon

membrane [mɑ̃bran] *nf* : membrane

membre [mɑ̃br] *nm* **1** : limb **2** : member (of a group)

même [mɛm] *adj* **1** : same, identical **2** (*used as an intensifier*) : very, actual **3** → **elle–même, lui–même, eux–mêmes** — ~ *pron* **le ~, la ~, les ~s** : the same (one, ones) — ~ *adv* **1** : even **2 de ~** : likewise, the same

mémère [memɛr] *nf fam* **1** : grandma **2** *Can* : gossip

mémoire [memwar] *nf* : memory — ~ *nm* **1** : dissertation, thesis **2 ~s** *nmpl* : memoirs

mémorable [memɔrabl] *adj* : memorable

mémorandum [memɔrɑ̃dɔm] *nm* : memorandum

mémoriser [memɔrize] *vt* : memorize

menacer [mənase] {6} *v* : threaten — **menaçant, -çante** [mənasɑ̃, -sɑ̃t] *adj* : threatening — **menace** [mənas] *nf* : threat

ménage [menaʒ] *nm* **1** : household, family **2 faire le ~** : do the housework **3 un heureux ~** : a happy couple — **ménagement** [menaʒmɑ̃] *nm* : consideration, care — **ménager** [menaʒe] {17} *vt* **1** ÉPARGNER : save **2** : handle or treat with care — **se ménager** *vr* : take it easy — **ménager, -gère** [menaʒe, -ʒɛr] *adj* : household, domestic — **ménagère** [menaʒɛr] *nf* : housewife

mendier [mɑ̃dje] {96} *v* : beg — **mendiant, -diante** [mɑ̃djɑ̃, -djɑ̃t] *n* : beggar

menées [məne] *nfpl* : scheming, intrigues

mener [məne] {52} *vt* **1** : lead **2** DIRIGER : conduct, run **3 ~ qqch à terme** : see sth through — **meneur, -neuse** [mənœr, -nøz] *n* **1** : leader **2 meneuse de claque** *Can* : cheerleader

méningite [menɛ̃ʒit] *nf* : meningitis

ménopause [menɔpoz] *nf* : menopause

menottes [mənɔt] *nfpl* : handcuffs

mensonge [mɑ̃sɔ̃ʒ] *nm* **1** : lie **2 le ~** : lying — **mensonger, -gère** [mɑ̃sɔ̃ʒe, -ʒɛr] *adj* : false, misleading

menstruation [mɑ̃stryasjɔ̃] *nf* RÈGLES : menstruation — **menstruel, -struelle** [mɑ̃stryɛl] *adj* : menstrual

mensuel, -suelle [mɑ̃sɥɛl] *adj* : monthly — **mensuel** *nm* : monthly (magazine)

mensurations [mɑ̃syrasjɔ̃] *nfpl* : measurements

mental, -tale [mɑ̃tal] *adj, mpl* **-taux** [-to] : mental — **mentalité** [mɑ̃talite] *nf* : mentality

menteur, -teuse [mɑ̃tœr, -tøz] *adj* : untruthful, false — ~ *n* : liar

menthe [mɑ̃t] *nf* : mint

mention [mɑ̃sjɔ̃] *nf* **1** : mention **2** : (academic) distinction — **mentionner** [mɑ̃sjɔne] *vt* : mention

mentir [mɑ̃tir] {82} *vi* : lie

menton [mɑ̃tɔ̃] *nm* : chin

menu, -nue [məny] *adj* **1** PETIT : tiny **2** : minor, trifling — **menu** *adv* : finely — ~ *nm* : menu

menuiserie [mənɥizri] *nf* : woodworking, carpentry — **menuisier** [mənɥizje] *nm* : woodworker, carpenter

méprendre [meprɑ̃dr] {70} *v* **se méprendre** *vr* **~ sur** : be mistaken about

mépris [mepri] *nm* **1** DÉDAIN : contempt **2 au ~ de** : regardless of — **méprisable** [meprizabl] *adj* : despicable, contemptible — **méprisant, -sante** [meprizɑ̃, -zɑ̃t] *adj* : contemptuous, scornful — **mépriser** [meprize] *vt* : despise, scorn

mer [mɛr] *nf* **1** : sea **2** MARÉE : tide

mercenaire [mɛrsənɛr] *adj & nmf* : mercenary

mercerie [mɛrsəri] *nf* : notions *pl*

merci [mɛrsi] *interj* : thank you!, thanks! — ~ *nm* : thank-you — ~ *nf* : mercy

mercredi [mɛrkrədi] *nm* : Wednesday

mercure [mɛrkyr] *nm* : mercury

Mercure *nf* : Mercury (planet)

mère [mɛr] *nf* : mother

méridional, -nale [meridjɔnal] *adj, mpl* **-naux** [-no] : southern

meringue [mərɛ̃g] *nf* : meringue

mérite [merit] *nm* : merit, credit — **mériter** [merite] *vt* : deserve, merit — **méritoire** [meritwar] *adj* : commendable

merle [mɛrl] *nm* : blackbird

merveille [mɛrvɛj] *nf* **1** : wonder, marvel **2 à ~** : wonderfully — **merveilleux, -leuse** [mɛrvɛjø, -jøz] *adj* : wonderful, marvelous

mes → **mon**

mésaventure [mezavɑ̃tyr] *nf* : misfortune, mishap

mesdames → **madame**

mesdemoiselles → **mademoiselle**

mésentente [mezɑ̃tɑ̃t] *nf* DÉSACCORD : misunderstanding, disagreement

mesquin, -quine [mɛskɛ̃, -kin] *adj* **1** : mean, petty **2** : cheap, stingy — **mesquinerie** [mɛskinri] *nf* **1** : pettiness **2** AVARICE : stinginess

message [mɛsaʒ] *nm* : message — **messager, -gère** [mɛsaʒe, -ʒɛr] *n* : messenger — **messagerie** [mɛsaʒri] *nf* : parcel delivery service

messe [mɛs] *nf* : Mass

mesure [məzyr] *nf* **1** : measure, measurement **2** RETENUE : moderation **3 à la ~ de** : worthy of **4 à ~ que** : as **5 dans la ~ où** : insofar as — **mesuré, -rée** [məzyre] *adj* : measured, restrained — **mesurer** [məzyre] *vt* **1** : measure **2** ÉVALUER : assess

métabolisme [metabɔlism] *nm* : metabolism

métal [metal] *nm, pl* **-taux** [meto] : metal — **métallique** [metalik] *adj* : metallic

métamorphose [metamɔrfoz] *nf* : metamorphosis

métaphore [metafɔr] *nf* : metaphor

météo [meteo] *nf fam* : weather forecast

météore [meteɔr] *nm* : meteor

météorologie [meteɔrɔlɔʒi] *nf* : meteorology — **météorologique** [meteɔrɔlɔʒik] *adj* : meteorological, weather — **météorologiste** [meteɔrɔlɔʒist] *nmf* : meteorologist

méthode [metɔd] *nf* **1** : method, system **2** MANUEL : primer — **méthodique** [metɔdik] *adj* : methodical

méticuleux, -leuse [metikylø, -løz] *adj* : meticulous

métier [metje] *nm* **1** : job, profession **2** : experience, skill **3** *or* **~ à tisser** : loom

métis, -tisse [metis] *adj & n* : half-breed, half-caste

métrage [metraʒ] *nm* **1** : length (of an object) **2** : footage (of a film)

mètre [mɛtr] *nm* **1** : meter **2 ~ ruban** : tape measure — **métrique** [metrik] *adj* : metric

métro [metro] *nm* : subway

métropole [metrɔpɔl] *nf* : city, metropolis — **métropolitain, -taine** [metrɔpɔlitɛ̃, -tɛn] *adj* : metropolitan

mets [mɛ] *nm* PLAT : dish

metteur [mɛtœr] *nm* **~ en scène** : producer, director

mettre [mɛtr] {53} *vt* **1** PLACER : put, place **2** : put on, wear **3** AJOUTER : add (in), put in **4** DISPOSER : prepare, arrange **5 ~ au point** : develop, finalize **6 ~ en marche** : turn on, switch on — **se mettre** *vr* **1** : become, get **2** : put on, wear **3 ~ à faire** : start doing **4 ~ à table** : sit down at the table

meuble [mœbl] *nm* **1** : piece of furniture **2 ~s** *nmpl* : furniture — **meublé, -blée** [mœble] *adj* : furnished — **meubler** [mœble] *vt* : furnish

meugler [møgle] *vi* : moo, low — **meuglement** [møgləmɑ̃] *nm* : mooing, lowing

meule [møl] *nf* **1** : millstone **2 ~ de foin** : haystack

meurtre [mœrtr] *nm* : murder — **meurtrier, -trière** [mœrtrije, -trijɛr] *adj* : deadly — **~** *n* ASSASSIN : murderer

meurtrir [mœrtrir] *vt* : bruise — **meurtrissure** [mœrtrisyr] *nf* : bruise

meute [møt] *nf* : pack (of hounds)

mexicain, -caine [mɛksikɛ̃, -kɛn] *adj* : Mexican

miaou [mjau] *nm* : meow — **miauler** [mjole] *vi* : meow

mi–bas [miba] *nms & pl* : kneesock

miche [miʃ] *nf* : round loaf of bread

mi–chemin [miʃmɛ̃] **à ~** *adv phr* : halfway, midway

microbe [mikrɔb] *nm* : germ, microbe

microfilm [mikrɔfilm] *nm* : microfilm

micro–ondes [mikrɔɔ̃d] *nms & pl* : microwave oven

microphone [mikrɔfɔn] *nm* : microphone

microscope [mikrɔskɔp] *nm* : microscope — **microscopique** [mikrɔskɔpik] *adj* : microscopic

microsillon [mikrɔsijɔ̃] *nm* : long-playing record

midi [midi] *nm* **1** : midday, noon **2** : lunchtime **3** SUD : south

mie [mi] *nf* : inside, soft part (of a loaf of bread)

miel [mjɛl] *nm* : honey — **mielleux, -leuse** [mjɛlø, -løz] *adj* : sickly sweet

mien, mienne [mjɛ̃, mjɛn] *adj* : mine, my own — **~** *pron* **le mien, la mienne, les miens, les miennes** : mine

miette [mjɛt] *nf* **1** : crumb **2 en ~s** : in pieces

mieux [mjø] *adv & adj* **1** (*comparative of* **bien**) : better **2** (*superlative of* **bien**) **le ~, la ~, les ~** : the best — **~** *nm* **1** : best **2 il y a du ~** : there's some improvement

mignon, -gnonne [miɲɔ̃, -ɲɔn] *adj* **1** : sweet, cute **2** GENTIL : nice, kind

migraine [migrɛn] *nf* : headache, migraine

migration [migrasjɔ̃] *nf* : migration — **migrateur, -trice** [migratœr, -tris] *adj* : migratory

mijoter [miʒɔte] *vt* **1** : simmer **2** MANIGANCER : plot, cook up — *vi* : simmer, stew

mil [mil] → **mille**

mile [majl] *nm* : mile

milice [milis] *nf* : militia

milieu [miljø] *nm, pl* **-lieux** **1** CENTRE : middle **2** ENTOURAGE : environment **3 au ~ de** : among, in the midst of

militaire [militɛr] *adj* : military — **~** *nm* SOLDAT : soldier, serviceman

militant, -tante [militɑ̃, -tɑ̃t] *adj & n* : militant

millage [milaʒ] *nm Can* : mileage (of a motor vehicle)

mille [mil] *adj* : one thousand — **~** *nm or* **~ marin** : nautical mile

millénaire [milenɛr] *nm* : millennium

mille–pattes [milpat] *nms & pl* **1** : centipede **2** : millipede

millésime [milezim] *nm* **1** : year (of manufacture) **2** : vintage year

millet [mijɛ] *nm* : millet

milliard [miljar] *nm* : billion — **milliardaire** [miljardɛr] *nmf* : billionaire

millier [milje] *nm* : thousand

milligramme [miligram] *nm* : milligram

millimètre [milimɛtr] *nm* : millimeter

million [miljɔ̃] *nm* : million — **millionnaire** [miljɔnɛr] *nmf* : millionaire

mime [mim] *nmf* : mime — **mimer** [mime] *vt* : mimic

mimique [mimik] *nf* GRIMACE : face

minable [minabl] *adj* : shabby

mince [mɛ̃s] *adj* **1** : thin, slender **2** INSIGNIFIANT : meager, scanty — **minceur** [mɛ̃sœr] *nf* : thinness, slenderness

mine[1] [min] *nf* : appearance, look

mine[2] *nf* **1** : (coal) mine **2** : (pencil) lead — **miner** [mine] *vt* : undermine, weaken — **minerai** [minrɛ] *nm* : ore

minéral, -rale [mineral] *adj, mpl* **-raux** [-ro] : mineral — **minéral** *nm* : mineral

minet, -nette [minɛ, -nɛt] *n fam* : pussycat

mineur[1], **-neure** [minœr] *adj & nmf* : minor

mineur[2] *nm* : miner

miniature [minjatyr] *adj & nf* : miniature

minimal, -male [minimal] *adj, mpl* **-maux** [-mo] : minimal, minimum — **minime** [minim] *adj* : minimal, negligible — **minimiser** [minimize] *vt* : minimize — **minimum** [minimɔm] *adj & nm, pl* **-mums** [-mɔm] *or* **-ma** [-ma] : minimum

ministère [ministɛr] *nm* **1** : department, ministry **2** CABINET : government — **ministériel, -rielle** [ministerjɛl] *adj* : governmental — **ministre** [ministr] *nm* : minister, secretary

minorité [minɔrite] *nf* : minority — **minoritaire** [minɔritɛr] *adj* : minority

minou [minu] *nm fam* : pussycat

minuit [minɥi] *nm* : midnight

minuscule [minyskyl] *adj* : minute, tiny — **~** *nf* : small (lowercase) letter

minute [minyt] *nf* : minute — **minuter** [minyte] *vt* : time — **minuterie** [minytri] *nf* : timer

minutieux, -tieuse [minysjø, -sjøz] *adj* **1** MÉTICULEUX : meticulous **2** : detailed (of work, etc.) — **minutie** [minysi] *nf* : meticulousness

miracle [mirakl] *nm* : miracle — **miraculeux, -leuse** [mirakylø, -løz] *adj* : miraculous

mirage [miraʒ] *nm* : mirage

mire [mir] *nf* **point de ~** : target

miroir [mirwar] *nm* : mirror

miroiter [mirwate] *vi* BRILLER : sparkle, shimmer — **miroitement** [mirwatmɑ̃] *nm* : sparkling, shimmering

mis, mise [mi, miz] *adj* **1** : clad **2 bien ~** : well-dressed

mise [miz] *nf* **1** : putting, placing **2** : stake (in games of chance) **3** TENUE : dress, attire — **miser** [mize] *vt* : bet — *vi* **~ sur** : bet on, count on

misérable [mizerabl] *adj* **1** PITOYABLE : wretched, pitiful **2** INSIGNIFIANT : meager, paltry — **~** *nmf* **1** : wretch **2** : scoundrel — **misère** [mizɛr] *nf* **1** : poverty **2** : misery

miséricorde [mizerikɔrd] *nf* : mercy, forgiveness

missile [misil] *nm* : missile

mission [misjɔ̃] *nf* : mission — **missionnaire** [misjɔnɛr] *adj & nmf* : missionary

mitaine [mitɛn] *nf Can, Switz* : mitten

mite [mit] *nf* : clothes moth

mi–temps [mitɑ̃] *nms & pl* : part-time job — **~** *nfs & pl* : halftime (in sports)

miteux, -teuse [mitø, -tøz] *adj* : seedy, shabby

mitigé, -gée [mitiʒe] *adj* **1** : lukewarm, reserved **2 sentiments mitigés** : mixed feelings

mitoyen, -toyenne [mitwajɛ̃, -jɛn] *adj* : common, dividing

mitrailleuse [mitrajøz] *nf* : machine gun

mi–voix [mivwa] **à ~** *adv phr* : in a low voice

mixeur [miksœr] *or* **mixer** [miksɛr] *nm* : mixer, blender

mixte [mikst] *adj* **1** : mixed **2 école ~** : coeducational school

mobile [mɔbil] *adj* **1** : mobile, moving **2 feuilles ~s** : loose-leaf paper — **~** *nm* **1** : motive (of a crime) **2** : (paper) mobile — **mobilier** [mɔbilje] *nm* MEUBLES : furniture

mobiliser [mɔbilize] *vt* : mobilize

mobilité [mɔbilite] *nf* : mobility

mocassin [mɔkasɛ̃] *nm* : moccasin

moche [mɔʃ] *adj fam* **1** : ugly **2** MAUVAIS : lousy

modalité [mɔdalite] *nf* : form, mode

mode [mɔd] *nm* **1** : mode, method **2 ~ d'emploi** : directions for use — **~** *nf* : fashion

modèle [mɔdɛl] *nm* : model — **~** *adj* : model, exemplary — **modeler** [mɔdle] {20} *vt* : mold, shape

modem [mɔdɛm] *nm* : modem

modérer [mɔdere] {87} *vt* : moderate, restrain — **modérateur, -trice** [mɔderatœr, -tris] *adj* : moderating — **modération** [mɔderasjɔ̃] *nf* MESURE : moderation, restraint — **modéré, -rée** [mɔdere] *adj* : moderate

moderne [mɔdɛrn] *adj* : modern — **moderniser** [mɔdɛrnize] *vt* : modernize

modeste [mɔdɛst] *adj* : modest — **modestie** [mɔdɛsti] *nf* : modesty

modifier [mɔdifje] {96} *vt* : modify — **se modifier** *vr* : change — **modification** [mɔdifikasjɔ̃] *nf* : modification

modique [mɔdik] *adj* : modest, low

moduler [mɔdyle] *vt* : modulate, adjust

moelle [mwal] *nf* **1** : marrow **2 ~ épinière** : spinal cord — **moelleux, -leuse** [mwalø, -løz] *adj* **1** DOUX : soft **2** : moist (of a cake)

mœurs [mœr(s)] *nfpl* **1** : morals **2** USAGES : customs, habits

moi [mwa] *pron* **1** : I **2** : me **3 à ~** : mine — **~** *nm* **le ~** : the self, the ego — **moi–même** [mwamɛm] *pron* : myself

moindre [mwɛ̃dr] *adj* **1** : lesser, smaller, lower **2 le ~, la ~** : the least, the slightest

moine [mwan] *nm* : monk

moineau [mwano] *nm, pl* **-neaux** : sparrow

moins [mwɛ̃] *adv* **1** : less **2 le ~** : least, the least **3 ~ de** : less than, fewer **4 à ~ que** : unless **5 en ~** : missing — **~** *nm* **1** : minus (sign) **2 au ~** *or* **du ~** : at least **3 pour le ~** : at (the very) least — **~** *prep* **1** : minus **2** (*in expressions of time*) : to, of **3** (*in expressions of temperature*) : below

mois [mwa] *nm* : month

moisi, -sie [mwazi] *adj* : moldy — **moisi** *nm* : mold, mildew — **moisir** [mwazir] *vi* **1** : become moldy **2** *fam* : stagnate — **moisissure** [mwazisyr] *nf* : mold, mildew

moisson [mwasɔ̃] *nf* : harvest, crop — **moissonner** [mwasɔne] *vt* : harvest, reap — **moissonneuse** [mwasɔnøz] *nf* : harvester, reaper — **moissonneuse–batteuse** [mwasɔnøzbatøz] *nf, pl* **moissonneuses–batteuses** : combine (harvester)

moite [mwat] *adj* : damp, clammy

moitié [mwatje] *nf* **1** : half **2 à ~** : half, halfway — **moitié–moitié** *adv* : fifty-fifty

moka [mɔka] *nm* : mocha

mol → **mou**

molaire [mɔlɛr] *nf* : molar

molécule [mɔlekyl] *nf* : molecule

molle → **mou** — **mollesse** [mɔlɛs] *nf* **1** : softness **2** INDOLENCE : indolence, apathy — **mollement** [mɔlmɑ̃] *adv* **1** DOUCEMENT : softly, gently **2** : weakly, feebly

mollet [mɔlɛ] *nm* : calf (of the leg)

mollir [mɔlir] *vi* **1** : soften, go soft **2** FAIBLIR : weaken, slacken

mollusque [mɔlysk] *nm* : mollusk

môme [mom] *nmf France fam* : kid, youngster

moment [mɔmɑ̃] *nm* **1** : moment, while **2** INSTANT : minute, instant **3** OCCASION : time, occasion **4** : present (time) **5 du ~ que** : since — **momentané, -née** [mɔmɑ̃tane] *adj* : momentary, temporary — **momentanément** [-nemɑ̃] *adv* **1** : momentarily **2** : at the moment

momie [mɔmi] *nf* : mummy

mon [mɔ̃], **ma** [ma] *adj, pl* **mes** [mɛ] : my

monarchie [mɔnarʃi] *nf* : monarchy — **monarque** [mɔnark] *nm* : monarch

monastère [mɔnastɛr] *nm* : monastery

monceau [mɔ̃so] *nm, pl* **-ceaux** [mɔ̃so] : heap, pile

mondain, -daine [mɔ̃dɛ̃, -dɛn] *adj* **1** : society, social **2** RAFFINÉ : fashionable

monde [mɔ̃d] *nm* **1** : world **2** : society, people *pl* **3 tout le ~** : everyone — **mondial, -diale** [mɔ̃djal] *adj, mpl* **-diaux** [-djo] **1** : world **2** : worldwide, global — **mondialement** [mɔ̃djalmɑ̃] *adv* : throughout the world

monétaire [monetɛr] *adj* : monetary

moniteur, -trice [mɔnitœr, -tris] *n* : instructor, coach — **moniteur** *nm* : monitor, screen

monnaie [mɔnɛ] *nf* **1** : money, currency **2** PIÈCE : coin — **monnayer** [mɔnɛje] {11} *vt* **1** : convert into cash **2** : capitalize on (experience, etc.) — **monnayeur** [mɔnɛjœr] *nm* → **faux–monnayeur**

monocorde [mɔnɔkɔrd] *adj* : droning, monotonous

monogramme [mɔnɔgram] *nm* : monogram

monologue [mɔnɔlɔg] *nm* : monologue, soliloquy

monopole [mɔnɔpɔl] *nm* : monopoly — **monopoliser** [mɔnɔpɔlize] *vt* : monopolize

monotone [mɔnɔtɔn] *adj* : monotonous, dull — **monotonie** [mɔnɔtɔni] *nf* : monotony

monsieur [məsjø] *nm, pl* **messieurs** [mesjø] **1** : Mr., sir **2** : man, gentleman

monstre [mɔ̃str] *nm* : monster — **~** *adj* : huge, colossal — **monstrueux, -trueuse** [mɔ̃stryø, -tryøz] *adj* **1** : monstrous, huge **2** TERRIBLE : hideous — **monstruosité** [mɔ̃stryozite] *nf* : monstrosity

mont [mɔ̃] *nm* : mount, mountain

montage [mɔ̃taʒ] *nm* **1** : editing (of a film) **2 chaîne de ~** : assembly line

montagne [mɔ̃taɲ] *nf* **1** : mountain **2 la ~** : the mountains **3 ~s russes** : roller coaster — **montagneux, -gneuse** [mɔ̃taɲø, -ɲøz] *adj* : mountainous

montant, -tante [mɔ̃tɑ̃, -tɑ̃t] *adj* : uphill, rising — **montant** *nm* **1** : upright, post **2** SOMME : total, sum

mont–de–piété [mɔ̃dpjete] *nm, pl* **monts–de–piété** *France* : pawnshop

monte–charge [mɔ̃tʃarʒ] *nms & pl* : freight elevator

monter [mɔ̃te] *vi* **1** : go up, come up, climb (up) **2** : rise (of temperature, etc.) **3 ~ à** : ride (a bicycle, etc.) **4 ~ dans** : get into, board **5 ~ sur** : mount, get on (a horse) — *vt* (*with auxiliary verb* **avoir**) **1** : take up, bring up **2** : raise, turn up (volume, etc.) **3** : go up, climb (up) **4** : assemble, put together **5 ~ à cheval** : ride a horse — **se monter** *vr* **~ à** : amount to — **montée** [mɔ̃te] *nf* **1** : rise, rising **2** : ascent, climb **3** PENTE : slope

montre [mɔ̃tr] *nf* **1** : watch **2 faire ~ de** : show, display

montréalais, -laise [mɔrealɛ, -lɛz] *adj* : of or from Montreal

montre–bracelet [mɔ̃trəbraslɛ] *nf, pl* **montres–bracelets** : wristwatch

montrer [mɔ̃tre] *vt* **1** : show, reveal **2** INDIQUER : point out — **se montrer** *vr* **1** : show oneself **2** : prove to be

monture [mɔ̃tyr] *nf* **1** : mount, horse **2** : setting (for jewelry) **3** : frames *pl* (for eyeglasses)

monument [mɔnymɑ̃] *nm* : monument — **monumental, -tale** [mɔnymɑ̃tal] *adj, mpl* **-taux** [-to] : monumental

moquer [mɔke] *v* **se moquer** *vr* **1 ~ de** : make fun of, mock **2 je m'en moque** : I couldn't care less — **moquerie** [mɔkri] *nf* : mockery

moquette [mɔkɛt] *nf* : wall-to-wall carpeting

moqueur, -queuse [mɔkœr, -køz] *adj* : mocking

moral, -rale [mɔral] *adj, mpl* **-raux** [mɔro] : moral — **moral** *nm* : morale, spirits *pl* — **morale** *nf* **1** : morals *pl*, morality **2** : moral (of a story) — **moralisateur, -trice** [mɔralizatœr, -tris] *adj* : moralizing — **moralité** [mɔralite] *nf* : morality

morbide [mɔrbid] *adj* : morbid

morceau [mɔrso] *nm, pl* **-ceaux** : piece, bit — **morceler** [mɔrsəle] {8} *vt* : break up, divide

mordant, -dante [mɔrdɑ̃, -dɑ̃t] *adj* : biting, scathing — **mordant** *nm* : bite, punch

mordiller [mɔrdije] *vt* : nibble at

mordre [mɔrdr] {63} *v* : bite — **se mordre** *vr* **~ la langue** : bite one's tongue — **mordu, -due** *adj* : smitten (with love) — **~** *n fam* : fan, buff

morfondre [mɔrfɔ̃dr] {63} *v* **se morfondre** *vr* **1** : mope **2** *Can* : wear oneself out

morgue [mɔrg] *nf* **1** : morgue, mortuary **2** ARROGANCE : arrogance

morille [mɔrij] *nf* : type of mushroom

morne [mɔrn] *adj* **1** SOMBRE : gloomy, glum **2** MAUSSADE : dismal, dreary

morose [mɔroz] *adj* : morose, sullen

morphine [mɔrfin] *nf* : morphine

mors [mɔr] *nm* : bit (of a bridle)

morse [mɔrs] *nm* **1** : walrus **2** : Morse code

morsure [mɔrsyr] *nf* : bite

mort, morte [mɔr, mɔrt] *adj* : dead — **~** *n* **1** : dead person, corpse **2** VICTIME : fatality — **mort** *nf* : death — **mortalité** [mɔrtalite] *nf* : mortality — **mortel, -telle** [mɔrtɛl] *adj* **1** : mortal **2** FATAL : fatal — **~** *n* : mortal

mortier [mɔrtje] *nm* : mortar

mortifier [mɔrtifje] {96} *vt* : mortify

mortuaire [mɔrtɥɛr] *adj* **1** FUNÈBRE : funeral **2 salon ~** *Can* : funeral home

morue [mɔry] *nf* : cod

mosaïque [mɔzaik] *adj & nf* : mosaic

mosquée [mɔske] *nf* : mosque

mot [mo] *nm* **1** : word **2** : note, line **3** ~ **de passe** : password **4** ~**s croisés** : crossword puzzle

motel [mɔtɛl] *nm* : motel

moteur [mɔtœr] *nm* : engine, motor — **moteur, -trice** [mɔtœr, -tris] *adj* **1** : motor **2 force motrice** : driving force

motif [mɔtif] *nm* **1** RAISON : motive, grounds *pl* **2** DESSIN : pattern, design

motion [mɔsjɔ̃] *nf* : motion (in politics)

motiver [mɔtive] *vt* **1** : motivate **2** EXPLIQUER : justify, explain — **motivation** [mɔtivasjɔ̃] *nf* : motivation, incentive

moto [mɔto] *nf* : bike, motorbike — **motocyclette** [mɔtɔsiklɛt] *nf* : motorcycle

motoriser [mɔtɔrize] *vt* : motorize

motte [mɔt] *nf* : clod, lump (of earth, etc.)

mou [mu] (**mol** [mɔl] *before vowel or mute h*), **molle** [mɔl] *adj* **1** : soft **2** FLASQUE : flabby, limp **3** LÂCHE : slack **4 avoir les jambes molles** : be weak in the knees

mouchard, -charde [muʃar, -ʃard] *n fam* : informer, stool pigeon

mouche [muʃ] *nf* : fly

moucher [muʃe] *v* **se moucher** *vr* : blow one's nose

moucheron [muʃrɔ̃] *nm* : gnat

moucheté [muʃte] *adj* : speckled, flecked

mouchoir [muʃwar] *nm* : handkerchief

moudre [mudr] {54} *vt* : grind

moue [mu] *nf* **1** : pout **2 faire la** ~ : pout

mouette [mwɛt] *nf* : gull, seagull

mouffette *or* **moufette** [mufɛt] *nf* : skunk

moufle [mufl] *nf* : mitten

mouiller [muje] *vt* **1** : wet, moisten **2** ~ **l'ancre** : drop anchor — **se mouiller** *vr* **1** : get wet **2** *fam* : become involved — **mouillage** [mujaʒ] *nm* : anchorage, berth — **mouillé, -lée** [muje] *adj* : wet

moulage [mulaʒ] *nm* **1** : molding, casting **2 faire un** ~ **de** : take a cast of

moulant, -lante [mulɑ̃, -lɑ̃t] *adj* : tight-fitting (of clothes, etc.)

moule[1] [mul] *nf* : mussel

moule[2] *nm* **1** : mold, matrix **2** ~ **à gâteaux** : cake pan — **mouler** [mule] *vt* **1** : mold **2** : cast (a statue)

moulin [mulɛ̃] *nm* **1** : mill **2** ~ **à café** : coffee grinder **3** ~ **à paroles** *fam* : chatterbox — **moulinet** [mulinɛ] *nm* : reel, winch

moulu, -lue [muly] *adj* **1** : ground (of coffee, etc.) **2** *fam* : worn-out

moulure [mulyr] *nf* : molding

mourir [murir] {55} *vi* **1** : die **2** : die out (of a sound, etc.) **3** ~ **de faim** : be dying of hunger — **mourant, -rante** [murɑ̃, -rɑ̃t] *n* : dying person

mousquet [muskɛ] *nm* : musket — **mousquetaire** [muskətɛr] *nm* : musketeer

mousse [mus] *nf* **1** : moss (in botany) **2** : foam, lather **3** : mousse (in cooking) — **moussant, -sante** [musɑ̃, -sɑ̃t] *adj* : foaming — **mousser** [muse] *vi* : foam, froth, lather — **mousseux, -seuse** [musø, -søz] *adj* **1** : foaming, frothy **2 vin** ~ : sparkling wine

moustache [mustaʃ] *nf* **1** : mustache **2** ~**s** *nfpl* : whiskers (of an animal)

moustique [mustik] *nm* : mosquito — **moustiquaire** [mustikɛr] *nf* **1** : mosquito net **2** : screen (for a window, etc.)

moutarde [mutard] *nf* : mustard

mouton [mutɔ̃] *nm* **1** : sheep, sheepskin **2** : mutton (in cooking)

mouvement [muvmɑ̃] *nm* **1** : movement **2** ACTIVITÉ : activity, bustle **3** IMPULSION : impulse, reaction — **mouvementé, -tée** [muvmɑ̃te] *adj* **1** : eventful, hectic **2** ACCIDENTÉ : rough, uneven — **mouvoir** [muvwar] {56} *vt* : move, prompt

moyen, moyenne [mwajɛ̃, -jɛn] *adj* **1** : medium **2** : average **3 Moyen Âge** : Middle Ages *pl* — **moyen** *nm* **1** : way, means *pl* **2** : possibility **3** ~**s** *nmpl* : means, resources — **moyenne** *nf* : average — **moyennement** [mwajɛnmɑ̃] *adv* MODÉRÉMENT : fairly, moderately

moyeu [mwajø] *nm, pl* **moyeux** : hub (of a wheel)

muer [mɥe] *vi* **1** : molt, shed **2** : change, break (of the voice) — **mue** [my] *nf* : molting, shedding

muet, muette [mɥɛ, mɥɛt] *adj* **1** : dumb **2** SILENCIEUX : silent — ~ *n* : mute, dumb person

muffin [mɔfœn] *nm Can* : muffin

muguet [mygɛ] *nm* : lily of the valley

mule [myl] *nf* : female mule — **mulet** [mylɛ] *nm* : male mule

multicolore [myltikɔlɔr] *adj* : multicolored

multimédia [myltimedja] *adj* : multimedia

multinational, -nale [myltinasjɔnal] *adj, mpl* **-naux** [-no] : multinational

multiple [myltipl] *adj* **1** : multiple **2** DIVERS : many — ~ *nm* : multiple — **multiplication** [myltiplikasjɔ̃] *nf* : multiplication — **multiplier** [myltiplije] {96} *vt* : multiply — **se multiplier** *vr* : proliferate

multitude [myltityd] *nf* : multitude, mass

municipal, -pale [mynisipal] *adj, mpl* **-paux** [-po] : municipal, town — **municipalité** [mynisipalite] *nf* **1** : municipality, town **2** : town council

munir [mynir] *vt* : equip, provide — **se munir** *vr* ~ **de** : equip oneself with

munitions [mynisjɔ̃] *nfpl* : ammunition, munitions

mur [myr] *nm* : wall

mûr, mûre [myr] *adj* **1** : ripe (of a fruit) **2** : mature (of a person)

muraille [myraj] *nf* : (high) wall — **mural, -rale** [myral] *adj, mpl* **-raux** [myro] : wall, mural — **murale** [myral] *nf* : mural

mûre [myr] *nf* : blackberry

mûrir [myrir] *v* **1** : ripen **2** ÉVOLUER : mature, develop

murmure [myrmyr] *nm* : murmur — **murmurer** [myrmyre] *v* : murmur

muscade [myskad] *nf or* **noix** ~ : nutmeg

muscle [myskl] *nm* : muscle — **musclé, -clée** [myskle] *adj* : muscular, powerful — **musculaire** [myskylɛr] *adj* : muscular — **musculature** [myskylatyr] *nf* : muscles *pl*

muse [myz] *nf* : muse

museau [myzo] *nm, pl* **-seaux** : muzzle, snout

musée [myze] *nm* : museum

museler [myzle] {8} *vt* : muzzle — **muselière** [myzəljɛr] *nf* : muzzle

musique [myzik] *nf* : music — **musical, -cale** [myzikal] *adj* **-caux** [-ko] : musical — **musicien, -cienne** [myzisjɛ̃, -sjɛn] *n* : musician

musulman, -mane [myzylmɑ̃, -man] *adj & n* : Muslim

mutant, -tante [mytɑ̃, -tɑ̃t] *adj & n* : mutant — **mutation** [mytasjɔ̃] *nf* **1** : transformation **2** : transfer (of an employee) — **muter** [myte] *vt* : transfer (an employee)

mutiler [mytile] *vt* : mutilate

mutiner [mytine] *v* **se mutiner** *vr* : mutiny, rebel — **mutinerie** [mytinri] *nf* RÉBELLION : mutiny, rebellion

mutuel, -tuelle [mytɥɛl] *adj* : mutual

myope [mjɔp] *adj* : nearsighted — **myopie** [mjɔpi] *nf* : myopia, nearsightedness

myrtille [mirtil] *nf France* : blueberry

mystère [mistɛr] *nm* : mystery — **mystérieux, -rieuse** [misterjø, -rjøz] *adj* : mysterious

mystifier [mistifje] {96} *vt* DUPER : deceive, dupe

mystique [mistik] *adj* : mystic, mystical

mythe [mit] *nm* : myth — **mythique** [mitik] *adj* : mythic(al) — **mythologie** [mitɔlɔʒi] *nf* : mythology

N

n [ɛn] *nm* : n, 14th letter of the alphabet

nacre [nakr] *nf* : mother-of-pearl — **nacré, -crée** [nakre] *adj* : pearly

nager [naʒe] {17} *v* : swim — **nage** [naʒ] *nf* **1** : swimming **2** : stroke (in swimming) **3 en** ~ : dripping with sweat — **nageoire** [naʒwar] *nf* : fin, flipper — **nageur, -geuse** [naʒœr, -ʒøz] *n* : swimmer

naguère [nagɛr] *adv* **1** RÉCEMMENT : recently **2** AUTREFOIS : formerly

naïf, naïve [naif, naiv] *adj* **1** INGÉNU : naive **2** CRÉDULE : gullible

nain, naine [nɛ̃, nɛn] *n* : dwarf, midget

naître [nɛtr] {57} *vi* **1** : be born **2** : rise, originate — **naissance** [nɛsɑ̃s] *nf* **1** : birth **2 donner** ~ **à** : give rise to — **naissant, -sante** [nɛsɑ̃, -sɑ̃t] *adj* : incipient

naïveté [naivte] *nf* : naïveté

nantir [nɑ̃tir] *vt* ~ **de** : provide with — **nanti, -tie** [nɑ̃ti] *adj* : affluent, well-to-do — **nantissement** [nɑ̃tismɑ̃] *nm* : collateral

nappe [nap] *nf* **1** : tablecloth **2** : layer, sheet (of water, oil, etc.) — **napper** [nape] *vt* : coat, cover — **napperon** [naprɔ̃] *nm* : mat, doily

narcotique [narkɔtik] *nm* : narcotic

narguer [narge] *vt* : mock, taunt

narine [narin] *nf* : nostril

narquois, -quoise [narkwa, -kwaz] *adj* : sneering, derisive

narrer [nare] *vt* : narrate, tell — **narrateur, -trice** [naratœr, -tris] *n* : narrator — **narration** [narasjɔ̃] *nf* : narration, narrative

nasal, -sale [nazal] *adj, mpl* **-saux** [nazo] : nasal — **naseau** [nazo] *nm, pl* **-seaux** : nostril (of an animal) — **nasillard, -larde** [nazijar, -jard] *adj* : nasal (in tone)

natal, -tale [natal] *adj, mpl* **-tals** : native (of a country, etc.) — **natalité** [natalite] *nf* : birthrate

natation [natasjɔ̃] *nf* : swimming

natif[1], **-tive** [natif, -tiv] *adj* ~ **de** : be born in

natif[2], **-tive** *n* : native

nation [nasjɔ̃] *nf* : nation — **national, -nale** [nasjɔnal] *adj, mpl* **-naux** [-no] : national — **nationale** *nf France* : highway — **nationaliser** [nasjɔnalize] *vt* : nationalize — **nationalisme** [nasjɔnalism] *nm* : nationalism — **nationalité** [nasjɔnalite] *nf* : nationality

nativité [nativite] *nf* : nativity

natte [nat] *nf* **1** : (straw) mat **2** : braid (of hair) — **natter** [nate] *vt* : braid, plait

naturaliser [natyralize] *vt* : naturalize

nature [natyr] *nf* **1** : nature **2** ~ **morte** : still life — ~ *adj* : plain (of yogurt, etc.) — **naturel, -relle** [natyrɛl] *adj* : natural — **naturel** *nm* **1** : nature, disposition **2** AISANCE : naturalness — **naturellement** [natyrɛlmɑ̃] *adv* **1** : naturally **2** : of course

naufrage [nofraʒ] *nm* : shipwreck — **naufragé, -gée** [nofraʒe] *adj & n* : castaway

nausée [noze] *nf* : nausea — **nauséabond, -bonde** [nozeabɔ̃, -bɔnd] *adj* : nauseating, revolting

nautique [notik] *adj* : nautical

naval, -vale [naval] *adj, mpl* **-vals** : naval

navet [navɛ] *nm* **1** : turnip **2** *fam* : third-rate film, novel, etc.

navette [navɛt] *nf* **1** : shuttle **2 faire la** ~ : shuttle back and forth, commute

naviguer [navige] *vi* : sail, navigate — **navigable** [navigabl] *adj* : navigable — **navigateur, -trice** [navigatœr, -tris] *n* : navigator — **navigation** [navigasjɔ̃] *nf* : navigation

navire [navir] *nm* : ship, vessel

navrant, -vrante [navrɑ̃, -vrɑ̃t] *adj* **1** : upsetting, distressing **2** REGRETTABLE : unfortunate — **navré, -vrée** [navre] *adj* **être** ~ **de** : be sorry about

ne [nə] (**n'** *before a vowel or mute h*) *adv* **1** ~ **pas** : not **2** ~ **jamais** : never **3** ~ **plus** : no longer **4** ~ **que** : only

né, née [ne] *adj* : born

néanmoins [neɑ̃mwɛ̃] *adv* : nevertheless, yet

néant [neɑ̃] *nm* : emptiness, nothingness

nébuleux, -leuse [nebylø, -løz] *adj* **1** : cloudy (of the sky) **2** VAGUE : nebulous

nécessaire [nesesɛr] *adj* : necessary — ~ *nm* **1** : necessity, need **2** TROUSSE : bag, kit — **nécessairement** [nesesɛrmɑ̃] *adv* : necessarily — **nécessité** [nesesite] *nf* : necessity, need — **nécessiter** [nesesite] *vt* EXIGER : require, call for

nécrologie [nekrɔlɔʒi] *nf* : obituary

nectar [nɛktar] *nm* : nectar

nectarine [nɛktarin] *nf* : nectarine

nef [nɛf] *nf* : nave

néfaste [nefast] *adj* NUISIBLE : harmful

négatif, -tive [negatif, -tiv] *adj* : negative — **négatif** *nm* : negative (in photography) — **négative** *nf* **répondre par la** ~ : reply in the negative — **négation** [negasjɔ̃] *nf* : negative (in grammar)

négliger [negliʒe] {17} *vt* **1** : neglect **2** IGNORER : disregard — **négligé, -gée** [negliʒe] *adj* : untidy (of appearance, etc.) — **négligé** *nm* : negligee — **négligeable** [negliʒabl] *adj* : negligible — **négligence** [negliʒɑ̃s] *nf* : negligence, carelessness — **négligent, -gente** [negliʒɑ̃, -ʒɑ̃t] *adj* : negligent

négoce [negɔs] *nm* : business, trade — **négociant, -ciante** [negɔsjɑ̃, -sjɑ̃t] *n* : merchant

négocier [negɔsje] {96} *v* : negotiate — **négociable** [negɔsjabl] *adj* : negotiable — **négociateur, -trice** [negɔsjatœr, -tris] *n* : negotiator — **négociation** [negɔsjasjɔ̃] *nf* : negotiation

nègre, négresse [nɛgr, negrɛs] *adj & n* (*sometimes considered offensive*) : Negro

neige [nɛʒ] *nf* **1** : snow **2** ~ **fondue** : slush — **neiger** [neʒe] {17} *v impers* : snow — **neigeux, -geuse** [nɛʒø, -ʒøz] *adj* : snowy

nénuphar [nenyfar] *nm* : water lily

néon [neɔ̃] *nm* : neon

néophyte [neɔfit] *nmf* : novice, beginner

Neptune [nɛptyn] *nf* : Neptune (planet)

nerf [nɛr] *nm* **1** : nerve **2** VIGUEUR : vigor, spirit — **nerveux, -veuse** [nɛrvø, -vøz] *adj* : nervous, tense — **nervosité** [nɛrvozite] *nf* : nervousness

nervure [nɛrvyr] *nf* : vein (of a leaf)

n'est-ce pas [nɛspa] *adv* : no?, isn't that right?, isn't it?

net, nette [nɛt] *adj* **1** PROPRE : clean, tidy **2** CLAIR : clear, distinct — **net** *adv* : plainly, flatly — **nettement** [nɛtmɑ̃] *adv* **1** : clearly, distinctly **2** : definitely — **netteté** [nɛtte] *nf* **1** : cleanness **2** : clearness, sharpness

nettoyer [nɛtwaje] {58} *vt* **1** : clean (up) **2** ~ **à sec** : dry-clean — **nettoyage** [nɛtwajaʒ] *nm* : cleaning — **nettoyant** [nɛtwajɑ̃] *nm* : cleaning agent

neuf[1] [nœf] *adj* **1** : nine **2** : ninth (in dates) — ~ *nms & pl* : nine

neuf[2], **neuve** [nœf, nœv] *adj* : new — **neuf** *nm* **quoi de** ~? : what's new?

neurologie [nørɔlɔʒi] *nf* : neurology

neutre [nøtr] *adj* **1** : neuter (in grammar) **2** : neutral — **neutraliser** [nøtralize] *vt* : neutralize — **neutralité** [nøtralite] *nf* : neutrality

neutron [nøtrɔ̃] *nm* : neutron

neuvième [nœvjɛm] *adj & nmf & nm* : ninth

neveu [nəvø] *nm, pl* **-veux** : nephew

névrosé, -sée [nevroze] *adj & n* : neurotic — **névrotique** [nevrɔtik] *adj* : neurotic

nez [ne] *nm* : nose

ni [ni] *conj* **1** ~ . . . ~ : neither . . . nor **2** ~ **plus** ~ **moins** : no more, no less

niais, niaise [njɛ, njɛz] *adj* : simple, foolish — **niaiserie** [njɛzri] *nf* : foolishness

niche [niʃ] *nf* **1** : niche, recess **2** : kennel — **nicher** [niʃe] *vi* : nest

nickel [nikɛl] *nm* : nickel

nicotine [nikɔtin] *nf* : nicotine

nid [ni] *nm* **1** : nest **2** ~ **de brigands** : den of thieves

nièce [njɛs] *nf* : niece

nier [nje] {96} *vt* : deny

nigaud, -gaude [nigo, -god] *n* : simpleton, fool

niveau [nivo] *nm, pl* **-veaux** [nivo] **1** : level **2** ~ **de vie** : standard of living — **niveler** [nivle] {8} *vt* : level

noble [nɔbl] *adj* : noble — ~ *nmf* : noble, nobleman *m*, noblewoman *f* — **noblesse** [nɔblɛs] *nf* : nobility

noce [nɔs] *nf* **1** : wedding, wedding party **2** ~**s** *nfpl* : wedding

nocif, -cive [nɔsif, -siv] *adj* : noxious, harmful

nocturne [nɔktyrn] *adj* : nocturnal, night

Noël [nɔɛl] *nm* **1** : Christmas **2 père** ~ : Santa Claus

nœud [nø] *nm* **1** : knot, tie **2** : knot (nautical speed) **3** ~ **coulant** : noose **4** ~ **papillon** : bow tie

noir, noire [nwar] *adj* **1** : black **2** SALE : dirty, grimy **3** OBSCUR : dark — **noir** *nm* **1** : black **2 dans le** ~ : in the dark, in darkness — **Noir, Noire** *n* : black man, black woman — **noirceur** [nwarsœr] *nf* **1** : blackness **2** *Can* : darkness — **noircir** [nwarsir] *vi* : grow dark, darken — *vt* : blacken

noisette [nwazɛt] *nf* : hazelnut

noix [nwa] *nfs & pl* **1** : nut, walnut **2** : piece, lump (of butter, etc.) **3** ~ **de cajou** : cashew (nut)

nom [nɔ̃] *nm* **1** : name **2** : (proper) noun

nomade [nɔmad] *nmf* : nomad — ~ *adj* : nomadic

nombre [nɔ̃br] *nm* : number — **nombreux, -breuse** [nɔ̃brø, -brøz] *adj* : numerous

nombril [nɔ̃bril] *nm* : navel

nominal, -nale [nɔminal] *adj, mpl* **-naux** [-no] : nominal

nommer [nɔme] *vt* **1** : name, call **2** : appoint, nominate **3** CITER : mention — **se nommer** *vr* **1** S'APPELER : be named **2** : introduce oneself — **nommément** [nɔmemɑ̃] *adv* : by name, namely

non [nɔ̃] *adv* **1** : no **2 je pense que** ~ : I don't think so **3** ~ **plus** : neither, either — ~ *nm* : no

nonchalance [nɔ̃ʃalɑ̃s] *nf* : nonchalance — **nonchalant, -lante** [nɔ̃ʃalɑ̃, -lɑ̃t] *adj* : nonchalant

non-sens [nɔsɑ̃s] *nms & pl* ABSURDITÉ : nonsense, absurdity

nord [nɔr] *adj* : north, northern — ~ *nm* **1** : north **2 le Nord** : the North

nord-est [nɔrɛst] *adj s & pl* : northeast, northeastern — ~ *nm* : northeast

nord-ouest [nɔrwɛst] *adj s & pl* : northwest, northwestern — ~ *nm* : northwest

normal, -male [nɔrmal] *adj, mpl* **-maux** [nɔrmo] : normal — **normale** *nf* **1** : average **2** NORME : norm — **normalement** [nɔrmalmɑ̃] *adv* : normally, usually — **normaliser** [nɔrmalize] *vt* : normalize, standardize — **normalité** [nɔrmalite] *nf* : normality — **norme** [nɔrm] *nf* : norm, standard

nos → **notre**

nostalgie [nɔstalʒi] *nf* : nostalgia — **nostalgique** [nɔstalʒik] *adj* : nostalgic

notable [nɔtabl] *adj & nm* : notable

notaire [nɔtɛr] *nm* : notary public

notamment [nɔtamɑ̃] *adv* : especially, particularly

notation [nɔtasjɔ̃] *nf* : notation

note [nɔt] *nf* **1** : note **2** ADDITION : bill, check **3** : mark, grade (in school) — **noter** [nɔte] *vt* **1** REMARQUER : note, notice **2** MARQUER : mark, write (down) **3** : mark, grade (an exam)

notice [nɔtis] *nf* : instructions *pl*

notifier [nɔtifje] {96} *vt* : notify

notion [nosjɔ̃] *nf* : notion, idea

notoire [nɔtwar] *adj* **1** CONNU : well-known **2** : notorious (of a criminal) — **notoriété** [nɔtɔrjete] *nf* : notoriety

notre [nɔtr] *adj, pl* **nos** [no] : our

nôtre [notr] *pron* **le** ~, **la** ~, **les** ~**s** : ours

nouer [nwe] *vt* : tie, knot — **noueux, noueuse** [nwø, nwøz] *adj* : gnarled

nougat [nuga] *nm* : nougat

nouille [nuj] *nf* **1** *fam* : nitwit, idiot **2** ~**s** *nfpl* : noodles, pasta

nourrir [nurir] *vt* **1** ALIMENTER : feed, nourish **2** : provide for (a family, etc.) **3** : nurse, harbor (a grudge, etc.) — **se nourrir** *vr* : eat — **nourrice** [nuris] *nf* : wet nurse — **nourrissant, -sante** [nurisɑ̃, -sɑ̃t] *adj* : nourishing, nutritious — **nourrisson** [nurisɔ̃] *nm* : infant — **nourriture** [nurityr] *nf* : food

nous [nu] *pron* **1** : we **2** : us **3 ~-mêmes** : ourselves
nouveau [nuvo] (**-vel** [-vɛl] *before a vowel or mute h*), **-velle** [-vɛl] *adj, mpl* **-veaux** [nuvo] **1** : new **2 de ~** *or* **à ~** : again, once again **3 ~ venu** : newcomer — **nouveau** *nm* **1 du ~** : something new **2 le ~** : the new — **nouveau–né, -née** [nuvone] *adj & n, mpl* **nouveau–nés** : newborn — **nouveauté** [nuvote] *nf* **1** : newness, novelty **2** INNOVATION : innovation
nouvelle [nuvɛl] *nf* **1** : piece of news **2** : short story **3 ~s** *nfpl* : news — **nouvellement** [nuvɛlmɑ̃] *adv* : newly, recently
novateur, -trice [nɔvatœr, -tris] *adj* : innovative — **~** *n* : innovator
novembre [nɔvɑ̃br] *nm* : November
novice [nɔvis] *adj* : inexperienced — **~** *nmf* : novice, beginner
noyau [nwajo] *nm, pl* **noyaux** [nwajo] **1** : pit, stone (of a fruit) **2** : nucleus, core (in science)
noyauter [nwajote] *vt* : infiltrate
noyer[1] [nwaje] {58} *vt* **1** : drown **2** : flood (an engine) — **se noyer** *vr* : drown — **noyé, noyée** [nwaje] *n* : drowning victim
noyer[2] *nm* : walnut tree
nu, nue [ny] *adj* **1** : naked, nude **2** : plain, bare (of a wall) — **nu** *nm* **1** : nude **2 à ~** : bare, exposed
nuage [nɥaʒ] *nm* : cloud — **nuageux, -geuse** [nɥaʒø, -ʒøz] *adj* : cloudy
nuance [nɥɑ̃s] *nf* **1** TON : hue, shade **2** SUBTILITÉ : nuance — **nuancer** [nɥɑ̃se] {6} *vt* : qualify (opinions, etc.)
nucléaire [nykleɛr] *adj* : nuclear
nudité [nydite] *nf* : nudity, nakedness
nuée [nɥe] *nf* : horde, swarm
nuire [nɥir] {49} *vi* **~ à** : harm, injure — **nuisible** [nɥizibl] *adj* : harmful
nuit [nɥi] *nf* **1** : night, nighttime **2 faire ~** : be dark out
nul, nulle [nyl] *adj* **1** AUCUN : no **2** : null, invalid **3 être nul en maths** : be hopeless in math **5 nulle part** : nowhere — **nul** *pron* : no one, nobody — **nullement** [nylmɑ̃] *adv* : by no means
numéraire [nymerɛr] *nm* : cash
numéral, -rale [nymeral] *adj, mpl* **-raux** [-ro] : numeral — **numéral** *nm, pl* **-raux** : numeral — **numérique** [nymerik] *adj* **1** : numerical **2** : digital — **numéro** [nymero] *nm* **1** : number **2** : issue (of a periodical) — **numéroter** [nymerɔte] *vt* : number
nuptial, -tiale [nypsjal] *adj, mpl* **-tiaux** [-sjo] : nuptial, wedding
nuque [nyk] *nf* : nape of the neck
nutrition [nytrisjɔ̃] *nf* : nutrition — **nutritif, -tive** [nytritif, -tiv] *adj* **1** : nutritious **2** : nutritional
nylon [nilɔ̃] *nm* : nylon
nymphe [nɛ̃f] *nf* : nymph

O

o [o] *nm* : o, 15th letter of the alphabet
oasis [ɔazis] *nf* : oasis
obéir [ɔbeir] *vi* **~ à 1** : obey **2** : respond to — **obéissance** [ɔbeisɑ̃s] *nf* : obedience — **obéissant, -sante** [ɔbeisɑ̃, -sɑ̃t] *adj* : obedient
obélisque [ɔbelisk] *nm* : obelisk
obèse [ɔbɛz] *adj* : obese — **obésité** [ɔbezite] *nf* : obesity
objecter [ɔbʒɛkte] *vt* **1** : raise as an objection **2** PRÉTEXTER : plead (as an excuse) — **objectif, -tive** [ɔbʒɛktif, -tiv] *adj* : objective — **objectif** *nm* **1** BUT : objective, goal **2** : lens (of an optical instrument) — **objectivité** [ɔbʒɛktivite] *nf* : objectivity — **objection** [ɔbʒɛksjɔ̃] *nf* : objection — **objet** [ɔbʒɛ] *nm* **1** : object, thing **2** : subject, topic **3** BUT : aim, purpose **4 complément d'~** : object (in grammar)
obligation [ɔbligasjɔ̃] *nf* **1** : obligation **2** : (savings) bond — **obligatoire** [ɔbligatwar] *adj* : compulsory, obligatory — **obligatoirement** [ɔbligatwarmɑ̃] *adv* : necessarily
obliger [ɔbliʒe] {17} *vt* **1** : oblige **2** CONTRAINDRE : force, compel — **obligé, -gée** [ɔbliʒe] *adj* **1 c'est obligé** *fam* : it's bound to happen, it's inevitable **2 être obligé de** : have to — **obligeance** [ɔbliʒɑ̃s] *nf* AMABILITÉ : kindness — **obligeant, -geante** [ɔbliʒɑ̃, -ʒɑ̃t] *adj* : obliging, kind
oblique [ɔblik] *adj* **1** : oblique **2 en ~** : crosswise, diagonally — **obliquer** [ɔblike] *vi* : bear, turn (off)
oblitérer [ɔblitere] {87} *vt* : cancel (a stamp)
oblong, oblongue [ɔblɔ̃, ɔblɔ̃g] *adj* : oblong
obscène [ɔpsɛn] *adj* : obscene — **obscénité** [ɔpsenite] *nf* : obscenity
obscur, -cure [ɔpskyr] *adj* **1** SOMBRE : dark **2** VAGUE : obscure — **obscurcir** [ɔpskyrsir] *vt* **1** ASSOMBRIR : darken **2** : obscure, blur — **s'obscurcir** *vr* **1** : grow dark **2** : become obscure — **obscurité** [ɔpskyrite] *nf* **1** : darkness **2** : obscurity
obséder [ɔpsede] {87} *vt* : obsess — **obsédant, -dante** [ɔpsedɑ̃, -dɑ̃t] *adj* : haunting, obsessive — **obsédé, -dée** [ɔpsede] *n* : obsessive, fanatic
obsèques [ɔpsɛk] *nfpl* : funeral
observer [ɔpsɛrve] *vt* : observe — **observateur, -trice** [ɔpsɛrvatœr, -tris] *adj* : observant, perceptive — **~** *n* : observer — **observation** [ɔpsɛrvasjɔ̃] *nf* **1** : observance **2** : observation — **observatoire** [ɔpsɛrvatwar] *nm* **1** : observatory **2** : observation post
obsession [ɔpsesjɔ̃] *nf* : obsession — **obsessionnel, -nelle** [ɔpsesjɔnɛl] *adj* : obsessive
obsolète [ɔpsɔlɛt] *adj* : obsolete
obstacle [ɔpstakl] *nm* : obstacle
obstétrique [ɔpstetrik] *nf* : obstetrics
obstiner [ɔpstine] *v* **s'obstiner** *vr* **~ à** : persist in — **obstiné, -née** [ɔpstine] *adj* ENTÊTÉ : obstinate, stubborn
obstruction [ɔpstryksjɔ̃] *nf* : obstruction — **obstruer** [ɔpstrye] *vt* : obstruct
obtenir [ɔptənir] {92} *vt* : obtain, get — **obtention** [ɔptɑ̃sjɔ̃] *nf* : obtaining
obturer [ɔptyre] *vt* **1** : seal, stop up **2** : fill (a tooth)
obtus, -tuse [ɔpty, -tyz] *adj* : obtuse
obus [ɔby] *nm* **1** : (mortar) shell **2 éclats d'~** : shrapnel
occasion [ɔkazjɔ̃] *nf* **1** : opportunity **2** CIRCONSTANCE : occasion **3** : bargain **4 d'~** : secondhand — **occasionnel, -nelle** [ɔkazjɔnɛl] *adj* : occasional — **occasionnel, -nelle** *n Can* : temp, temporary employee — **occasionner** [ɔkazjɔne] *vt* CAUSER : cause
occident [ɔksidɑ̃] *nm* **1** : west **2 l'Occident** : the West — **occidental, -tale** [ɔksidɑ̃tal] *adj, mpl* **-taux** [-to] : western, Western
occulte [ɔkylt] *adj* : occult
occuper [ɔkype] *vt* **1** : occupy **2** REMPLIR : take up, fill **3 ~ un poste** : hold a job — **s'occuper** *vr* **1** : keep busy **2 ~ de** : handle, take care of — **occupant, -pante** [ɔkypɑ̃, -pɑ̃t] *n* : occupant — **occupation** [ɔkypasjɔ̃] *nf* **1** : occupation **2** : occupancy — **occupé, -pée** [ɔkype] *adj* **1** : busy **2 zone occupée** : occupied zone
occurrence [ɔkyrɑ̃s] *nf* **1** : instance, occurrence **2 en l'~** : in this case
océan [ɔseɑ̃] *nm* : ocean — **océanique** [ɔseanik] *adj* : oceanic, ocean
ocre [ɔkr] *nf* : ocher, ochre
octave [ɔktav] *nf* : octave
octet [ɔktɛ] *nm* : byte
octobre [ɔktɔbr] *nm* : October
octogone [ɔktɔgɔn] *nm* : octagon
octroyer [ɔktrwaje] {58} *vt* : grant, bestow
oculaire [ɔkylɛr] *adj* : ocular, eye — **oculiste** [ɔkylist] *nmf* : oculist
ode [ɔd] *nf* : ode
odeur [ɔdœr] *nf* : odor, smell
odieux, -dieuse [ɔdjø, -djøz] *adj* EXÉCRABLE : odious, hateful
odorant, -rante [ɔdɔrɑ̃, -rɑ̃t] *adj* PARFUMÉ : fragrant
odorat [ɔdɔra] *nm* : sense of smell
œil [œj] *nm, pl* **yeux** [jø] **1** : eye **2 coup d'~** : glance — **œillade** [œjad] *nf* : wink — **œillères** [œjɛr] *nfpl* : blinders — **œillet** [œjɛ] *nm* : carnation
œsophage [ezɔfaʒ] *nm* : esophagus
œstrogène [ɛstrɔʒɛn] *nm* : estrogen
œuf [œf] *nm, pl* **œufs** [ø] : egg
œuvre [œvr] *nm* : (body of) work — **~** *nf* **1** : work, undertaking, task **2 ~ d'art** : work of art — **œuvrer** [œvre] *vi* : work
offense [ɔfɑ̃s] *nf* : insult, offense — **offenser** [ɔfɑ̃se] *vt* : offend — **s'offenser** *vr* **~ de** : take offense at — **offensif, -sive** [ɔfɑ̃sif, -siv] *adj* : offensive, attacking — **offensive** *nf* : offensive
office [ɔfis] *nm* **1** : service (in religion) **2 faire ~ de** : act as
officiel, -cielle [ɔfisjɛl] *adj & n* : official — **officialiser** [ɔfisjalize] *vt* : make official — **officier** [ɔfisje] *nm* : officer (in the armed forces) — **officieux, -cieuse** [ɔfisjø, -sjøz] *adj* : unofficial, informal
offrande [ɔfrɑ̃d] *nf* : offering
offre [ɔfr] *nf* **1** : offer, bid **2 l'~ et la demande** : supply and demand
offrir [ɔfrir] {83} *vt* : offer, give — **s'offrir** *vr* **1** : treat oneself to **2** SE PRÉSENTER : present itself
offusquer [ɔfyske] *vt* : offend — **s'offusquer** *vr* : take offense
ogive [ɔʒiv] *nf* : warhead
ogre, ogresse [ɔgr, ɔgrɛs] *n* : ogre
oh [o] *interj* : oh — **ohé** [ɔe] *interj* : hey
oie [wa] *nf* : goose
oignon [ɔɲɔ̃] *nm* **1** : onion **2** : bulb (of a tulip, etc.) **3** : bunion (in medicine)
oindre [wɛ̃dr] {59} *vt* : anoint
oiseau [wazo] *nm, pl* **oiseaux** : bird
oisif, -sive [wazif, -ziv] *adj* : idle — **oisiveté** [wazivte] *nf* : idleness
oisillon [wazijɔ̃] *nm* : fledgling
oléoduc [ɔleɔdyk] *nm* : (oil) pipeline
olfactif, -tive [ɔlfaktif, -tiv] *adj* : olfactory
olive [ɔliv] *nf* : olive
olympique [ɔlɛ̃pik] *adj* : Olympic
ombilical, -cale [ɔ̃bilikal] *adj, mpl* **-caux** [-ko] : umbilical
ombrage [ɔ̃braʒ] *nm* **1** OMBRE : shade **2 porter ~ à** : offend — **ombragé, -gée** [ɔ̃braʒe] *adj* : shady, shaded — **ombre** [ɔ̃br] *nf* **1** : shadow **2** SOUPÇON : hint, trace **3 à l'~** : in the shade
omelette [ɔmlɛt] *nf* : omelet
omettre [ɔmɛtr] {53} *vt* : omit, leave out — **omission** [ɔmisjɔ̃] *nf* : omission
omnibus [ɔmnibys] *nm* : local train
omnipotent, -tente [ɔmnipɔtɑ̃, -tɑ̃t] *adj* : omnipotent
omoplate [ɔmɔplat] *nf* : shoulder blade
on [ɔ̃] *pron* **1** : one, we, you **2** : they, people **3** QUELQU'UN : someone
once [ɔ̃s] *nf* : ounce
oncle [ɔ̃kl] *nm* : uncle
onctueux, -tueuse [ɔ̃ktɥø, -tɥøz] *adj* : smooth, creamy
onde [ɔ̃d] *nf* : wave
on–dit [ɔ̃di] *nms & pl* : rumor
onduler [ɔ̃dyle] *vi* **1** : undulate, sway **2** : be wavy (of hair) — **ondulation** [ɔ̃dylasjɔ̃] *nf* : undulation, wave — **ondulé, -lée** [ɔ̃dyle] *adj* **1** : wavy **2 carton ondulé** : corrugated cardboard
onéreux, -reuse [ɔnerø, -røz] *adj* COÛTEUX : costly
ongle [ɔ̃gl] *nm* : nail, fingernail
onguent [ɔ̃gɑ̃] *nm* : ointment
onyx [ɔniks] *nm* : onyx
onze [ɔ̃z] *adj* **1** : eleven **2** : eleventh (in dates) — **~** *nms & pl* : eleven — **onzième** [ɔ̃zjɛm] *adj & nmf & nm* : eleventh
opale [ɔpal] *nf* : opal
opaque [ɔpak] *adj* : opaque
opéra [ɔpera] *nm* **1** : opera **2** : opera house
opération [ɔperasjɔ̃] *nf* **1** : operation **2** : transaction (in banking, etc.) — **opérateur, -trice** [ɔperatœr, -tris] *n* : operator — **opérationnel, -nelle** [ɔperasjɔnɛl] *adj* : operational — **opérer** [ɔpere] {87} *vt* : operate on (a patient) — *vi* **1** : take effect, work **2** INTERVENIR : act
opiner [ɔpine] *vi* **~ de la tête** : nod in agreement
opiniâtre [ɔpinjatr] *adj* OBSTINÉ : stubborn, persistent
opinion [ɔpinjɔ̃] *nf* : opinion, belief
opium [ɔpjɔm] *nm* : opium
opportun, -tune [ɔpɔrtœ̃, -tyn] *adj* : opportune, timely — **opportunisme** [ɔpɔrtynism] *nm* : opportunism — **opportuniste** [ɔpɔrtynist] *adj* : opportunist, opportunistic — **~** *nmf* : opportunist
opposer [ɔpoze] *vt* **1** : put up (an objection, etc.) **2** : contrast (ideas, etc.) **3** DIVISER : divide — **s'opposer** *vr* **1** : clash, conflict **2 ~ à** : be opposed to — **opposant, -sante** [ɔpozɑ̃, -zɑ̃t] *n* ADVERSAIRE : opponent — **opposé, -sée** [ɔpoze] *adj* **1** : opposing **2** : opposite **3 ~ à** : opposed to — **opposé** *nm* **1** : opposite **2 à l'~ de** : contrary to — **opposition** [ɔpozisjɔ̃] *nf* **1** : opposition **2** : objection (in law)
oppresser [ɔprese] *vt* : oppress, burden — **oppressif, -sive** [ɔpresif, -siv] *adj* : oppressive — **oppresseur** [ɔpresœr] *nm* : oppressor — **oppression** [ɔpresjɔ̃] *nf* : oppression
opprimer [ɔprime] *vt* : oppress
opter [ɔpte] *vi* **~ pour** : opt for, choose
opticien, -cienne [ɔptisjɛ̃, -sjɛn] *n* : optician
optimisme [ɔptimism] *nm* : optimism — **optimiste** [ɔptimist] *adj* : optimistic — **~** *nmf* : optimist
optimum [ɔptimɔm] *adj & nm* : optimum
option [ɔpsjɔ̃] *nf* : option, choice — **optionnel, -nelle** [ɔpsjɔnɛl] *adj* FACULTATIF : optional
optique [ɔptik] *adj* : optic(al) — **~** *nf* **1** : optics **2** PERSPECTIVE : viewpoint
opulent, -lente [ɔpylɑ̃, -lɑ̃t] *adj* : opulent — **opulence** [-lɑ̃s] *nf* : opulence
or[1] [ɔr] *nm* : gold
or[2] *conj* **1** : but, yet **2** : now
oracle [ɔrakl] *nm* : oracle
orage [ɔraʒ] *nm* : storm, thunderstorm — **orageux, -geuse** [ɔraʒø, -ʒøz] *adj* : stormy
oral, -rale [ɔral] *adj, mpl* **oraux** [ɔro] : oral
orange [ɔrɑ̃ʒ] *adj* : orange — **~** *nf* : orange (fruit) — **~** *nm* : orange (color) — **oranger** [ɔrɑ̃ʒe] *nm* : orange tree
orateur, -trice [ɔratœr, -tris] *n* : orator, speaker
orbite [ɔrbit] *nf* **1** : orbit **2** : eye socket
orchestre [ɔrkɛstr] *nm* : orchestra
orchidée [ɔrkide] *nf* : orchid
ordinaire [ɔrdinɛr] *adj* **1** : ordinary, common **2** HABITUEL : usual — **~** *nm* **1 l'~** : the ordinary **2 d'~** : usually, as a rule — **ordinairement** [-nɛrmɑ̃] *adv* : usually
ordinateur [ɔrdinatœr] *nm* : computer
ordonnance [ɔrdɔnɑ̃s] *nf* **1** : order **2** : (medical) prescription
ordonner [ɔrdɔne] *vt* **1** : put in order, arrange **2** COMMANDER : order **3** : ordain (in religion) — **ordonné, -née** [ɔrdɔne] *adj* : tidy, orderly
ordre [ɔrdr] *nm* **1** : order **2** PROPRETÉ : tidiness **3** NATURE : nature, sort **4 ~ du jour** : agenda
ordure [ɔrdyr] *nf* **1** : filth **2 ~s** *nfpl* : trash, garbage — **ordurier, -rière** [ɔrdyrje] *adj* : filthy
oreille [ɔrɛj] *nf* **1** : ear **2** OUÏE : hearing
oreiller [ɔrɛje] *nm* : pillow
oreillons [ɔrɛjɔ̃] *nmpl* : mumps
orfèvre [ɔrfɛvr] *nm* : goldsmith
organe [ɔrgan] *nm* : organ (of the body) — **organique** [ɔrganik] *adj* : organic
organiser [ɔrganize] *vt* : organize — **s'organiser** *vr* : get organized — **organisateur, -trice** [ɔrganizatœr, -tris] *n* : organizer — **organisation** [ɔrganizasjɔ̃] *nf* : organization
organisme [ɔrganism] *nm* **1** : organism (in biology) **2** : organization, body
organiste [ɔrganist] *nmf* : organist
orgasme [ɔrgasm] *nm* : orgasm
orge [ɔrʒ] *nf* : barley
orgelet [ɔrʒəlɛ] *nm* : sty (in medicine)
orgie [ɔrʒi] *nf* : orgy
orgue [ɔrg] *nm* : organ (musical instrument)
orgueil [ɔrgœj] *nm* : pride — **orgueilleux, -leuse** [ɔrgœjø, -jøz] *adj* : proud
orient [ɔrjɑ̃] *nm* **1** : east **2 l'Orient** : the Orient, the East — **oriental, -tale** [ɔrjɑ̃tal] *adj, mpl* **-taux** [-to] **1** : eastern **2** : oriental
orienter [ɔrjɑ̃te] *vt* **1** : position, orient **2** GUIDER : guide, direct — **s'orienter** *vr* : find one's bearings — **orientation** [ɔrjɑ̃tasjɔ̃] *nf* **1** : orientation, direction, aspect **2** : guidance, (career) counseling
orifice [ɔrifis] *nm* : orifice
originaire [ɔriʒinɛr] *adj* **être ~ de** : be a native of
original, -nale [ɔriʒinal, -nal] *adj, mpl* **-naux** [-no] **1** : original **2** EXCENTRIQUE : eccentric — **~** *n* : character, eccentric — **original** *nm, pl* **-naux** : original — **originalité** [ɔriʒinalite] *nf* **1** : originality **2** : eccentricity — **origine** [ɔriʒin] *nf* **1** : origin **2 à l'~** : originally — **originel, -nelle** [ɔriʒinɛl] *adj* : original, primary
orignal [ɔriɲal] *nm, pl* **-naux** [-ɲo] : moose
orme [ɔrm] *nm* : elm
orner [ɔrne] *vt* DÉCORER : decorate, adorn — **orné, -née** [ɔrne] *adj* : ornate, flowery — **ornement** [ɔrnəmɑ̃] *nm* : ornament, adornment — **ornemental, -tale** [ɔrnəmɑ̃tal] *adj, mpl* **-taux** [-to] : ornamental
ornière [ɔrnjɛr] *nf* : rut
ornithologie [ɔrnitɔlɔʒi] *nf* : ornithology
orphelin, -line [ɔrfəlɛ̃, -lin] *n* : orphan
orteil [ɔrtɛj] *nm* : toe
orthodoxe [ɔrtɔdɔks] *adj* : orthodox — **orthodoxie** [ɔrtɔdɔksi] *nf* : orthodoxy
orthographe [ɔrtɔgraf] *nf* : spelling, orthography — **orthographier** [ɔrtɔgrafje] {96} *vt* : spell
orthopédie [ɔrtɔpedi] *nf* : orthopedics — **orthopédique** [ɔrtɔpedik] *adj* : orthopedic
ortie [ɔrti] *nf* : nettle
os [ɔs] *nm* : bone
osciller [ɔsile] *vi* **1** : oscillate **2** HESITATE : vacillate, waver — **oscillation** [ɔsilasjɔ̃] *nf* : oscillation
oser [oze] *vt* **1** : dare **2 si j'ose dire** : if I may say so — **osé, -sée** [oze] *adj* : daring, bold
osier [ozje] *nm* **1** : willow (tree) **2** : wicker (furniture)
osmose [ɔsmoz] *nf* : osmosis
ossature [ɔsatyr] *nf* **1** : skeleton, bone structure **2** : frame(work) — **ossements** [ɔsmɑ̃] *nmpl* : remains, bones — **osseux, -seuse** [ɔsø, -søz] *adj* : bony
ostensible [ɔstɑ̃sibl] *adj* : conspicuous, obvious — **ostentation** [ɔstɑ̃tasjɔ̃] *nf* : ostentation
ostéopathe [ɔsteɔpat] *nmf* : osteopath
ostracisme [ɔstrasism] *nm* : ostracism
otage [ɔtaʒ] *nm* : hostage
ôter [ote] *vt* **1** RETIRER : remove, take away **2** SOUSTRAIRE : subtract
otite [ɔtit] *nf* : ear infection
ou [u] *conj* **1** : or **2 ou . . . ou . . .** : either . . . or . . .
où [u] *adv* **1** : where, wherever **2 d'~** : from which, from where — **~** *pron* : where, that, in which, on which, to which
ouate [wat] *nf* **1** : absorbent cotton **2** BOURRE : padding, wadding — **ouaté, -tée** [wate] *adj* : padded, quilted
oublier [ublije] {96} *vt* : forget — **s'oublier** *vr* **1** : be forgotten **2** : forget oneself — **oubli** [ubli] *nm* **1** : forgetfulness **2** : oversight — **oublieux, -blieuse** [ublijø, -blijøz] *adj* : forgetful
ouest [wɛst] *adj* : west, western — **~** *nm* **1** : west **2 l'Ouest** : the West
oui [wi] *adv & nms & pl* : yes
ouïe [wi] *nf* **1** : (sense of) hearing **2 ~s** *nfpl* : gills — **ouï–dire** [widir] *nms & pl* : hearsay
ouïr [wir] {60} *vt* : hear
ouragan [uragɑ̃] *nm* : hurricane

ourler [urle] *vt* : hem — **ourlet** [urlɛ] *nm* : hem
ours [urs] *nm* **1** : bear **2 ~ blanc** *or* **~ polaire** : polar bear — **ourse** [urs] *nf* : she-bear
outil [uti] *nm* : tool — **outillage** [utijaʒ] *nm* **1** : set of tools **2** : equipment — **outiller** [utije] *vt* ÉQUIPER : equip
outrager [utraʒe] {17} *vt* INSULTER : offend, insult — **outrage** [utraʒ] *nm* : insult
outrance [utrɑ̃s] *nf* : excess — **outrancier, -cière** [utrɑ̃sje, -sjɛr] *adj* : excessive, extreme
outre [utr] *adv* **1 en ~** : in addition, besides **2 ~ mesure** : overly, unduly **3 passer ~ à** : disregard — **~** *prep* : besides, in addition to — **outre–mer** [utrəmɛr] *adv* : overseas — **outrepasser** [utrəpase] *vt* : exceed, overstep
outrer [utre] *vt* **1** EXAGÉRER : exaggerate **2** INDIGNER : outrage
ouvert, -verte [uvɛr, -vɛrt] *adj* **1** : open **2** : on, running (of a light, a faucet, etc.) — **ouverture** [uvɛrtyr] *nf* **1** : opening **2** : overture (in music) **3 ~ d'esprit** : openmindedness
ouvrable [uvrabl] *adj* **1 jour ~** : weekday, working day **2 heures ~s** : business hours
ouvrage [uvraʒ] *nm* : work
ouvre–boîtes [uvrəbwat] *nms & pl* : can opener — **ouvre–bouteilles** [uvrəbutɛj] *nms & pl* : bottle opener
ouvreur, -vreuse [uvrœr, -vrøz] *n* : usher, usherette *f*
ouvrier, -vrière [uvrije, -vrijɛr] *n* : worker — **~** *adj* : working-class
ouvrir [uvrir] {83} *vt* **1** : open **2** : turn on (a light, a radio, etc.) — *vi* : open — **s'ouvrir** *vr* : open (up)
ovaire [ɔvɛr] *nm* : ovary
ovale [ɔval] *adj & nm* : oval
ovation [ɔvasjɔ̃] *nf* : ovation
overdose [ɔvœrdoz] *nf* : overdose
oxyde [ɔksid] *nm* **~ de carbone** : carbon monoxide — **oxyder** [ɔkside] *v* **s'oxyder** *vr* : rust
oxygène [ɔksiʒɛn] *nm* : oxygen
ozone [ozɔn] *nm* : ozone

P

p [pe] *nm* : p, 16th letter of the alphabet
pacifier [pasifje] {96} *vt* : pacify, calm — **pacifique** [pasifik] *adj* **1** : peaceful **2 l'océan Pacifique** : the Pacific Ocean — **pacifiste** [pasifist] *nmf* : pacifist
pacotille [pakɔtij] *nf* **1** : shoddy goods **2 de ~** : cheap
pacte [pakt] *nm* ACCORD : pact, agreement
pagaie [pagɛ] *nf* : paddle
pagaille *or* **pagaïe** [pagaj] *nf fam* **1** : mess, chaos **2 en ~** : in great quantities
pagayer [pagaje] {11} *vi* : paddle
page [paʒ] *nf* : page
paie [pɛ] *nf* : pay, wages *pl* — **paiement** [pɛmɑ̃] *nm* : payment
païen, païenne [pajɛ̃, pajɛn] *adj & n* : pagan, heathen
paillard, -larde [pajar, -jard] *adj* : bawdy
paillasson [pajasɔ̃] *nm* : doormat
paille [paj] *nf* **1** : (piece of) straw **2** : (drinking) straw
paillette [pajɛt] *nf* : sequin
pain [pɛ̃] *nm* **1** : bread **2** : loaf (of bread) **3** : cake, bar (of soap, etc.)
pair, paire [pɛr] *adj* : even — **pair** *nm* **1** : peer **2 aller de ~** : go hand in hand **3 hors ~** : without equal — **paire** [pɛr] *nf* : pair
paisible [pezibl] *adj* : peaceful, quiet
paître [pɛtr] {61} *vi* : graze
paix [pɛ] *nf* : peace
palace [palas] *nm* : luxury hotel
palais [palɛ] *nms & pl* **1** : palace **2** : palate **3 ~ de justice** : courts of law
palan [palɑ̃] *nm* : hoist
pale [pal] *nf* : blade (of a propeller, etc.)
pâle [pal] *adj* **1** BLÊME : pale **2** CLAIR : light, pale
palet [palɛ] *nm* : puck (in ice hockey)
paletot [palto] *nm* : short coat
palette [palɛt] *nf* **1** : palette **2** : shoulder (of pork, etc.)
pâleur [palœr] *nf* : paleness
palier [palje] *nm* **1** : landing, floor **2** NIVEAU : level, stage
pâlir [palir] *vi* : turn pale
palissade [palisad] *nf* : fence
pallier [palje] {96} *vt* : alleviate, compensate for
palmarès [palmarɛs] *nms & pl* : list of winners
palme [palm] *nf* **1** : palm leaf **2** NAGEOIRE : flipper **3 remporter la ~** : be victorious
palmé, -mée [palme] *adj* : webbed
palmier [palmje] *nm* : palm tree
palourde [palurd] *nf* : clam
palper [palpe] *vt* : feel, finger — **palpable** [palpabl] *adj* : tangible
palpiter [palpite] *vi* : palpitate, throb — **palpitant, -tante** [palpitɑ̃, -tɑ̃t] *adj* : thrilling, exciting
paludisme [palydism] *nm* : malaria
pâmer [pame] *v* **se pâmer** *vr* : be ecstatic, swoon
pamphlet [pɑ̃flɛ] *nm* : lampoon
pamplemousse [pɑ̃pləmus] *nmf* : grapefruit
pan [pɑ̃] *nm* **1** : section, piece **2** : tail (of a garment)
panacée [panase] *nf* : panacea
panais [panɛ] *nm* : parsnip
pancarte [pɑ̃kart] *nf* : sign, placard
pancréas [pɑ̃kreas] *nm* : pancreas
panda [pɑ̃da] *nm* : panda
paner [pane] *vt* : coat with breadcrumbs
panier [panje] *nm* : basket
panique [panik] *nf* : panic — **paniquer** [panike] *vi* : panic
panne [pan] *nf* **1** : breakdown **2 ~ d'électricité** : power failure, blackout
panneau [pano] *nm, pl* **-neaux 1** : panel **2** : sign, signpost **3 ~ de signalisation** : road sign **4 ~ publicitaire** : billboard
panoplie [panɔpli] *nf* **1** GAMME : array, range **2** DÉGUISEMENT : outfit, costume
panorama [panɔrama] *nm* : panorama — **panoramique** [panɔramik] *adj* : panoramic
panser [pɑ̃se] *vt* **1** : groom (a horse) **2** : dress, bandage (a wound) — **pansement** [pɑ̃smɑ̃] *nm* : dressing, bandage
pantalon [pɑ̃talɔ̃] *nm* : pants *pl*, trousers *pl*
panthère [pɑ̃tɛr] *nf* : panther
pantin [pɑ̃tɛ̃] *nm* FANTOCHE : puppet (person)
pantomime [pɑ̃tɔmim] *nf* : pantomime
pantoufle [pɑ̃tufl] *nf* : slipper
panure [panyr] *nf* : bread crumbs *pl*
paon [pɑ̃] *nm* : peacock
papa [papa] *nm fam* : dad, daddy
pape [pap] *nm* : pope
paperasse [papras] *nf* : papers *pl*, paperwork
papeterie [papɛtri] *nf* : stationery
papier [papje] *nm* **1** : paper **2** : document, paper **3 ~ d'aluminium** : aluminum foil, tinfoil **4 ~ hygiénique** : toilet paper **5 ~ mouchoir** *Can* : tissue **6 ~ peint** : wallpaper **7 ~s** *nmpl* : (identification) papers
papillon [papijɔ̃] *nm* **1** : butterfly **2 ~ de nuit** : moth
papoter [papɔte] *vi* : gab, chatter
Pâque [pak] *nf* : Passover
paquebot [pakbo] *nm* : liner, ship
pâquerette [pakrɛt] *nf* : daisy
Pâques [pak] *nm & nfpl* : Easter
paquet [pakɛ] *nm* **1** : package, parcel **2** : pack (of cigarettes, etc.) **3 un ~ de** : a heap of, a pile of
par [par] *prep* **1** : through **2** : by, by means of **3** : as, for **4** : at, during **5 ~ avion** : by airmail **6 ~ exemple** : for example **7 ~ ici** : around here **8 ~ moments** : at times **9 ~ personne** : per person **10 de ~** : throughout
parabole [parabɔl] *nf* : parable
parachever [paraʃve] {52} *vt* : complete, perfect
parachute [paraʃyt] *nm* : parachute — **parachutiste** [paraʃytist] *nmf* : paratrooper
parade [parad] *nf* : parade — **parader** [parade] *vi* : strut, show off
paradis [paradi] *nm* : paradise, heaven
paradoxe [paradɔks] *nm* : paradox — **paradoxal, -xale** [paradɔksal] *adj, mpl* **-xaux** [-kso] : paradoxical
paraffine [parafin] *nf* : paraffin (wax)
parages [paraʒ] *nmpl* **dans les ~** : in the vicinity
paragraphe [paragraf] *nm* : paragraph
paraître [parɛtr] {7} *vi* **1** : appear **2** : show, be visible **3** SEMBLER : seem, look **4 à ~** : forthcoming — *v impers* **il paraît que** : it seems that, apparently
parallèle [paralɛl] *adj* : parallel — **~** *nm* **1** : parallel **2 mettre en ~** : compare — **~** *nf* : parallel (line)
paralyser [paralyze] *vt* : paralyze — **paralysie** [paralizi] *nf* : paralysis
paramètre [paramɛtr] *nm* : parameter
paranoïa [paranɔja] *nf* : paranoia
parapet [parapɛ] *nm* : parapet
paraphe [paraf] *nm* **1** : initials *pl* **2** : signature — **parapher** [parafe] *vt* : initial
paraphrase [parafraz] *nf* : paraphrase
parapluie [paraplɥi] *nm* : umbrella
parascolaire [paraskɔlɛr] *adj* : extracurricular
parasite [parazit] *nm* **1** : parasite **2 ~s** *nmpl* : (radio) interference
parasol [parasɔl] *nm* : parasol, sunshade
paravent [paravɑ̃] *nm* : screen, partition
parc [park] *nm* **1** : park **2** : grounds *pl* **3** ENCLOS : pen, playpen **4** : fleet (of automobiles) **5 ~ d'attractions** : amusement park
parcelle [parsɛl] *nf* **1** : fragment **2** : plot (of land)
parce que [parskə] *conj* : because
parchemin [parʃəmɛ̃] *nm* : parchment
parcimonieux, -nieuse [parsimɔnjø, -njøz] *adj* : parsimonious
par–ci, par–là [parsiparla] *adv* : here and there
parcmètre [parkmɛtr] *nm France* : parking meter
parcomètre [parkɔmɛtr] *nm Can* : parking meter
parcourir [parkurir] {23} *vt* **1** : cover (a distance), travel through **2** : leaf through (a text)
parcours [parkur] *nm* **1** : course (of a river), route (of a bus, etc.) **2** : course (in sports)
par–delà *or* **par delà** [pardəla] *prep* : beyond
par–dessous [pardəsu] *adv & prep* : underneath
pardessus [pardəsy] *nms & pl* : overcoat
par–dessus [pardəsy] *adv* : over, above, on top — **~** *prep* **1** : over, above **2 ~ bord** : overboard **3 ~ tout** : above all
par–devant [pardəvɑ̃] *adv* : in front, at the front
pardonner [pardɔne] *vt* **1** : forgive, pardon **2 pardonnez-moi** : excuse me — **pardon** [pardɔ̃] *nm* **1** : forgiveness, pardon **2 ~?** : pardon?, what did you say? **3 ~** : pardon me, sorry
pare–balles [parbal] *adj s & pl* : bulletproof
pare–brise [parbriz] *nms & pl* : windshield
pare–chocs [parʃɔk] *nms & pl* : bumper
pareil, -reille [parɛj] *adj* **1** SEMBLABLE : similar, alike **2** TEL : such — **~** *n* **1** ÉGAL : equal, peer **2 sans pareil** : unequaled — **pareil** [parɛj] *adv fam* : in the same way
parent, -rente [parɑ̃, -rɑ̃t] *adj* : similar, related — **~** *n* **1** : relative, relation **2 parents** *nmpl* : parents — **parenté** [parɑ̃te] *nf* **1** : relationship **2** : family, relations *pl*
parenthèse [parɑ̃tɛz] *nf* : parenthesis, bracket
parer [pare] *vt* **1** : adorn, array **2** : ward off, parry — *vi* **~ à** : deal with
paresser [parɛse] *vi* : laze around — **paresse** [parɛs] *nf* : laziness, idleness — **paresseux, -seuse** [parɛsø, -søz] *adj* : lazy — **paresseux** *nm* : sloth (animal)
parfaire [parfɛr] {62} *vt* : perfect, refine — **parfait, -faite** [parfɛ, -fɛt] *adj* **1** : perfect **2** TOTAL : absolute, complete — **parfaitement** [-fɛtmɑ̃] *adv* **1** : perfectly **2** ABSOLUMENT : definitely
parfois [parfwa] *adv* : sometimes
parfumer [parfyme] *vt* **1** : scent, perfume **2** : flavor (ice cream, etc.) — **se parfumer** *vr* : wear perfume — **parfum** [parfœ̃] *nm* **1** : scent, fragrance **2** : perfume **3** GOÛT : flavor — **parfumé, -mée** [parfyme] *adj* **1** : fragrant, scented **2** : flavored — **parfumerie** [parfymri] *nf* : perfume shop
pari [pari] *nm* : bet, wager — **parier** [parje] {96} *vt* : bet, wager
paria [parja] *nm* : outcast
parisien, -sienne [parizjɛ̃, -zjɛn] *adj* : Parisian
parjurer [parʒyre] *v* **se parjurer** *vr* : perjure oneself
parking [parkiŋ] *nm* : parking lot
parlant, -lante [parlɑ̃, -lɑ̃t] *adj* : vivid, eloquent
parlement [parləmɑ̃] *nm* : parliament — **parlementaire** [parləmɑ̃tɛr] *adj* : parliamentary — **parlementer** [parləmɑ̃te] *vi* : negotiate
parler [parle] *vt* : talk, speak — *vi* **1** : talk, speak **2 ~ à** : talk to **3 ~ de** : mention, refer to — **se parler** *vr* **1** : speak to each other **2** : be spoken (of a language) — **~** *nm* : speech, way of speaking
parloir [parlwar] *nm* : parlor
parmi [parmi] *prep* : among
parodie [parɔdi] *nf* : parody — **parodier** [parɔdje] {96} *vt* : parody, mimic
paroi [parwa] *nf* **1** : partition **2** : wall (in anatomy, etc.) **3 ~ rocheuse** : rock face
paroisse [parwas] *nf* : parish — **paroissien, -sienne** [parwasjɛ̃, -sjɛn] *n* : parishioner
parole [parɔl] *nf* **1** : (spoken) word **2** PROMESSE : word, promise **3** : speech **4 ~s** *nfpl* : lyrics **5 prendre la ~** : speak
paroxysme [parɔksism] *nm* : height, climax
parquer [parke] *vt* **1** : pen (cattle, etc.) **2** GARER : park
parquet [parkɛ] *nm* : parquet (floor)
parrain [parɛ̃] *nm* **1** : godfather **2** : sponsor, patron — **parrainer** [parɛne] *vt* : sponsor
parsemer [parsəme] {52} *vt* **~ de** : scatter with, strew with
part [par] *nf* **1** : portion, piece **2** : part, share **3** : side, position **4 à ~** : apart from **5 de la ~ de** : on behalf of **6 de toutes ~s** : from all sides **7 d'une ~** : on (the) one hand **8 faire sa ~** : do one's share **9 prendre ~ à** : take part in
partager [partaʒe] {17} *vt* **1** : divide up **2** RÉPARTIR : share — **se partager** *vr* : share — **partage** [partaʒ] *nm* : sharing, dividing
partance [partɑ̃s] *nf* **1 en ~** : ready to depart **2 en ~ pour** : bound for — **partant, -tante** [partɑ̃, -tɑ̃t] *adj* : ready, willing
partenaire [partənɛr] *nmf* : partner
parterre [partɛr] *nm* **1** : flower bed **2** : orchestra section (in a theater)
parti [parti] *nm* **1** : group, camp **2** : (political) party **3 ~ pris** : bias **4 prendre ~** : take a stand **5 prendre son ~** : make up one's mind **6 tirer ~ de** : take advantage of — **parti, -tie** [parti] *adj fam* : intoxicated, high
partial, -tiale [parsjal] *adj, mpl* **-tiaux** [-sjo] : biased, partial
participe [partisip] *nm* : participle
participer [partisipe] *vi* **~ à 1** : participate in **2** : contribute to — **participant, -pante** [partisipɑ̃, -pɑ̃t] *n* : participant — **participation** [partisipasjɔ̃] *nf* **1** : participation **2** : contribution
particule [partikyl] *nf* : particle
particulier, -lière [partikylje, -ljɛr] *adj* **1** : particular, specific **2** SINGULIER : peculiar **3** PRIVÉ : private, personal **4 en ~** : especially, in particular — **particularité** [partikylarite] *nf* : idiosyncrasy — **particulier** [partikylje] *nm* : individual — **particulièrement** [partikyljɛrmɑ̃] *adv* : especially, particularly
partie [parti] *nf* **1** : part **2** : game, match **3** : party, participant **4** SORTIE : outing **5 en ~** : partly, in part **6 faire ~ de** : be a part of — **partiel, -tielle** [parsjɛl] *adj* : partial
partir [partir] {82} *vi* **1** : leave, depart **2** : start up, go off **3** COMMENCER : start **4** S'ENLEVER : come out (of a stain, etc.) **5 à ~ de** : from
partisan, -sane [partizɑ̃, -zan] *adj & n* : partisan
partition [partisjɔ̃] *nf* : score (in music)
partout [partu] *adv* **1** : everywhere **2** : all (in sports)
parure [paryr] *nf* **1** : finery **2** ENSEMBLE : set
parution [parysjɔ̃] *nf* : publication, launch
parvenir [parvənir] {92} *vi* **1 ~ à** : reach, arrive at **2 ~ à faire** : manage to do
parvis [parvi] *nm* : square (in front of a church)
pas[1] [pa] *adv* **1** → **ne 2** : not **3 ~ du tout** : not at all **4 ~ mal de** : quite a lot of
pas[2] *nms & pl* **1** : step, footstep **2** : footprint **3** : pace, gait **4** : step (in dancing) **5 de ce ~** : right away **6 ~ de la porte** : doorstep
passable [pasabl] *adj* : passable, fair — **passablement** [pasabləmɑ̃] **1** : quite, rather **2** : reasonably well
passage [pasaʒ] *nm* **1** : passing, crossing **2** SÉJOUR : stay, visit **3** CHEMIN : route, way **4** : passage (in a text) **5 ~ pour piétons** : pedestrian crossing **6 ~ interdit** : do not enter — **passager, -gère** [pasaʒe, -ʒɛr] *adj* : passing, temporary — **~** *n* **1** : passenger **2 ~ clandestin** : stowaway — **passant, -sante** [pasɑ̃, -sɑ̃t] *adj* : busy, crowded — **~** *n* : passerby
passe [pas] *nf* **1** : pass (in sports) **2 mauvaise ~** : difficult time
passé, -sée [pase] *adj* **1** : last, past **2** DÉCOLORÉ : faded — **passé** *nm* **1** : past **2** : past tense — **~** *prep* : after, beyond
passe–partout [paspartu] *nms & pl* : master key
passeport [paspɔr] *nm* : passport
passer [pase] *vt* **1** : cross, go over **2** : pass, go past **3** : hand over **4** : put through to (on the telephone) **5** : take (an exam, etc.) **6** : spend (time) **7** : skip, pass over **8** ENFILER : slip on **9** : show (a film), play (a cassette, etc.) — *vi* **1** : pass, go past, go by **2** : drop by **3** ALLER : go **4 en passant** : incidentally **5 laissez-moi passer** : let me through — **se passer** *vr* **1** : take place **2** SE DÉROULER : turn out **3** : pass, go by (of time) **4 ~ de** : dispense with, do without
passereau [pasro] *nm, pl* **-reaux** : sparrow
passerelle [pasrɛl] *nf* **1** : footbridge **2** : gangplank
passe–temps [pastɑ̃] *nms & pl* : hobby, pastime
passeur, -seuse [pasœr, -søz] *n* : smuggler
passible [pasibl] *adj* **~ de** : liable to
passif, -sive [pasif, -siv] *adj* : passive — **passif** *nm* **1** : passive voice **2** : liabilities *pl*
passionner [pasjɔne] *vt* : fascinate, captivate — **se passionner** *vr* **~ pour** : have a passion for — **passion** [pasjɔ̃] *nf* : passion — **passionnant, -nante** [pasjɔnɑ̃, -nɑ̃t] *adj* : exciting, fascinating — **passionné, -née** [pasjɔne] *adj* : passionate — **~** *n* : enthusiast
passoire [paswar] *nf* : sieve, colander
pastel [pastɛl] *adj & nm* : pastel
pastèque [pastɛk] *nf* : watermelon
pasteur [pastœr] *nm* : minister, pastor
pasteuriser [pastœrize] *vt* : pasteurize
pastille [pastij] *nf* : lozenge
patate [patat] *nf* **1** *fam* : potato **2** *or* **~ douce** : sweet potato
patauger [patoʒe] {17} *vi* : splash about, paddle
pâte [pat] *nf* **1** : dough, batter **2 ~ à mo-**

deler : modeling clay 3 ~ **dentifrice** : toothpaste 4 ~s *nfpl* : pasta

pâté [pate] *nm* 1 : pâté 2 *or* ~ **de maisons** : block (of houses)

patelin [patlɛ̃] *nm fam* : little village

patent, -tente [patɑ̃, -tɑ̃t] *adj* : obvious, patent

patère [patɛr] *nf* : peg, hook

paternel, -nelle [patɛrnɛl] *adj* : paternal, fatherly — **paternité** [patɛrnite] *nf* : fatherhood

pâteux, -teuse [patø, -tøz] *adj* 1 : pasty, doughy 2 **avoir la langue pâteuse** : have a coated tongue

pathologie [patɔlɔʒi] *nf* : pathology

patience [pasjɑ̃s] *nf* 1 : patience 2 **jeu de** ~ : solitaire — **patient, -tiente** [pasjɑ̃, -sjɑ̃t] *adj & n* : patient — **patiemment** [pasjamɑ̃] *adv* : patiently — **patienter** [pasjɑ̃te] *vi* : wait

patin [patɛ̃] *nm* 1 : skate 2 ~**s à glace** : ice skates 3 ~**s à roulettes** : roller skates — **patinage** [patinaʒ] *nm* : skating — **patiner** [patine] *vi* 1 : skate 2 : skid — **patineur, -neuse** [patinœr, -nøz] *n* : skater — **patinoire** [patinwar] *nf* : skating rink

pâtisserie [patisri] *nf* 1 : cake, pastry 2 : pastry shop, bakery

patrie [patri] *nf* : homeland

patrimoine [patrimwan] *nm* 1 : inheritance 2 HÉRITAGE : heritage

patriote [patrijɔt] *adj* : patriotic — ~ *nmf* : patriot — **patriotique** [patrijɔtik] *adj* : patriotic

patron, -tronne [patrɔ̃, -trɔn] *n* : boss, manager — **patron** *nm* : pattern (in sewing) — **patronner** [patrɔne] *vt* : support, sponsor

patrouille [patruj] *nf* : patrol — **patrouiller** [patruje] *vi* : patrol

patte [pat] *nf* 1 : paw, hoof, foot 2 *fam* : leg, foot (of a person) 3 : tab, flap

pâturage [patyraʒ] *nm* : pasture

paume [pom] *nf* : palm (of the hand)

paumer [pome] *v fam* : lose — **se paumer** *vr fam* : get lost

paupière [popjɛr] *nf* : eyelid

pause [poz] *nf* 1 : pause 2 : break (from work)

pauvre [povr] *adj* : poor — ~ *nmf* : poor man, poor woman — **pauvreté** [povrəte] *nf* : poverty

pavaner [pavane] *v* **se pavaner** *vr* : strut about

paver [pave] *vt* : pave — **pavé** [pave] *nm* 1 : pavement 2 : cobblestone

pavillon [pavijɔ̃] *nm* 1 : pavilion 2 *France* : (detached) house 3 : ward, wing (in a hospital) 4 : flag (on a ship)

pavoiser [pavwaze] *vi fam* : rejoice

pavot [pavo] *nm* : poppy

paye [pɛj] → **paie**

payement [pɛmɑ̃] → **paiement**

payer [peje] {11} *vt* : pay (for) — *vi* : pay — **se payer** *vr* : treat oneself

pays [pei] *nm* 1 : country 2 : region, area 3 **du** ~ : local — **paysage** [peizaʒ] *nm* : scenery, landscape — **paysan, -sanne** [peizɑ̃, -zan] *adj* 1 : agricultural, farming 2 : rural, rustic — ~ *n* 1 : small farmer 2 : peasant

péage [peaʒ] *nm* 1 : toll 2 : tollbooth

peau [po] *nf, pl* **peaux** 1 : (human) skin 2 : hide, pelt 3 : peel, skin (of a fruit) 4 **petites peaux** : cuticle

pêche [pɛʃ] *nf* 1 : peach 2 : fishing

péché [peʃe] *nm* : sin — **pécher** [peʃe] {87} *vi* : sin

pêcher[1] [peʃe] *vt* 1 : fish for 2 *fam* : get, dig up — *vi* : fish

pêcher[2] [peʃe] *nm* : peach tree

pécheur[1], **-cheresse** [peʃœr, -ʃrɛs] *n* : sinner

pêcheur[2], **-cheuse** [pɛʃœr, -ʃøz] *n* 1 : fisherman 2 **pêcheur à la ligne** : angler

pécule [pekyl] *nm* : savings *pl*

pécuniaire [pekynjɛr] *adj* : financial

pédagogie [pedagɔʒi] *nf* : education — **pédagogique** [pedagɔʒik] *adj* : educational

pédale [pedal] *nf* : pedal — **pédaler** [pedale] *vi* : pedal — **pédalo** [pedalo] *nm* : pedal boat

pédant, -dante [pedɑ̃, -dɑ̃t] *adj* : pedantic — ~ *n* : pedant

pédestre [pedɛstr] *adj* **randonnée** ~ : hike

pédiatre [pedjatr] *nmf* : pediatrician

pédicure [pedikyr] *nmf* : chiropodist

pègre [pɛgr] *nf* : (criminal) underworld

peigne [pɛɲ] *nm* : comb — **peigner** [peɲe] *vt* : comb — **se peigner** *vr* : comb one's hair — **peignoir** [pɛɲwar] *nm* : bathrobe

peindre [pɛ̃dr] {37} *vt* 1 : paint 2 DÉCRIRE : depict, portray

peine [pɛn] *nf* 1 : sorrow, sadness 2 EFFORT : trouble 3 : punishment 4 **à** ~ : hardly, barely — **peiner** [pene] *vt* ATTRISTER : sadden, distress — *vi* 1 : struggle 2 : labor (of an engine, etc.)

peintre [pɛ̃tr] *nm* : painter — **peinture** [pɛ̃tyr] *nf* 1 : paint 2 : painting

péjoratif, -tive [peʒɔratif, -tiv] *adj* : derogatory

pelage [pəlaʒ] *nm* : coat, fur (of an animal)

pêle-mêle [pɛlmɛl] *adv* : every which way

peler [pəle] {20} *v* : peel

pèlerin, -rine [pɛlrɛ̃] *n* : pilgrim — **pèlerinage** [pɛlrinaʒ] *nm* : pilgrimage — **pèlerine** [pɛlrin] *nf* : cape

pélican [pelikɑ̃] *nm* : pelican

pelle [pɛl] *nf* 1 : shovel 2 ~ **à poussière** : dustpan — **pelletée** [pɛlte] *nf* : shovelful — **pelleter** [pɛlte] {8} *vt* : shovel

pellicule [pelikyl] *nf* 1 : (photographic) film 2 : thin layer, film 3 ~**s** *nfpl* : dandruff

pelote [pəlɔt] *nf* : ball (of string, etc.) — **peloton** [plɔtɔ̃] *nm* 1 : pack, group 2 : squad, platoon 3 ~ **de tête** : front runners — **pelotonner** [pəlɔtɔne] *v* **se pelotonner** *vr* : curl up (into a ball)

pelouse [pəluz] *nf* 1 : lawn, grass 2 : field (in sports)

peluche [pəlyʃ] *nf* 1 : plush 2 ~**s** *nfpl* : fluff, lint 3 *or* **animal en** ~ : stuffed animal

pelure [pəlyr] *nf* : peel, skin

pénal, -nale [penal] *adj, mpl* **-naux** [peno] : penal — **pénaliser** [penalize] *vt* : penalize — **pénalité** [penalite] *nf* : penalty

penaud, -naude [pəno, -nod] *adj* : sheepish

penchant [pɑ̃ʃɑ̃] *nm* : tendency, inclination

pencher [pɑ̃ʃe] *vt* INCLINER : tilt, tip — *vi* 1 : slant, lean 2 ~ **pour** : favor — **se pencher** *vr* : hunch over

pendaison [pɑ̃dɛzɔ̃] *nf* 1 : hanging 2 ~ **de crémaillère** : housewarming

pendant, -dante [pɑ̃dɑ̃, -dɑ̃t] *adj* : hanging, dangling — **pendant** *nm* 1 *or* ~ **d'oreille** : drop earring 2 CONTREPARTIE : counterpart — ~ *prep* 1 : during, for 2 ~ **que** : while — **pendentif** [pɑ̃dɑ̃tif] *nm* : pendant

penderie [pɑ̃dri] *nf* : closet, wardrobe

pendre [pɑ̃dr] {63} *v* : hang — **se pendre** *vr* : hang oneself

pendule [pɑ̃dyl] *nm* : pendulum — ~ *nf* : clock

pêne [pɛn] *nm* : bolt (of a lock)

pénétrer [penetre] {87} *vt* : penetrate — *vi* ~ **dans** : enter

pénible [penibl] *adj* 1 : painful, distressing 2 ARDU : difficult — **péniblement** [penibləmɑ̃] *adv* : with difficulty

péniche [peniʃ] *nf* 1 : barge 2 ~ **aménagée** : houseboat

pénicilline [penisilin] *nf* : penicillin

péninsule [penɛ̃syl] *nf* : peninsula

pénis [penis] *nm* : penis

pénitent, -tente [penitɑ̃, -tɑ̃t] *adj* : repentant — **pénitencier** [penitɑ̃sje] *nm* : penitentiary

pénombre [penɔ̃br] *nf* : half-light

pensée [pɑ̃se] *nf* 1 IDÉE : thought 2 ESPRIT : mind 3 : pansy — **penser** [pɑ̃se] *vt* 1 : think 2 CROIRE : believe, suppose 3 ~ **faire** : plan on doing — *vi* ~ **à** : think about — **pensif, -sive** [pɑ̃sif, -siv] *adj* : pensive

pension [pɑ̃sjɔ̃] *nf* 1 : pension 2 : boardinghouse 3 : room and board 4 ~ **alimentaire** : alimony — **pensionnaire** [pɑ̃sjɔnɛr] *nmf* : boarder, roomer — **pensionnat** [pɑ̃sjɔna] *nm* : boarding school

pentagone [pɛ̃tagɔn] *nm* : pentagon

pente [pɑ̃t] *nf* 1 : slope 2 **en** ~ : sloping

pénurie [penyri] *nf* : shortage, scarcity

pépé [pepe] *nm France fam* : grandpa

pépier [pepje] {96} *vi* : chirp, tweet — **pépiement** [pepimɑ̃] *nm* : peep (of a bird)

pépin [pepɛ̃] *nm* 1 : seed (of a fruit) 2 *fam* : snag, hitch — **pépinière** [pepinjɛr] *nf* : (tree) nursery

pépite [pepit] *nf* : nugget

perçant, -çante [pɛrsɑ̃, -sɑ̃t] *adj* 1 : piercing 2 : sharp, keen (of vision)

percée [pɛrse] *nf* 1 : opening, gap 2 DÉCOUVERTE : breakthrough

percepteur [pɛrsɛptœr] *nm* : tax collector

perceptible [pɛrsɛptibl] *adj* : perceptible, noticeable

perception [pɛrsɛpsjɔ̃] *nf* 1 : perception 2 RECOUVREMENT : collection (of taxes)

percer [pɛrse] {6} *vt* 1 : pierce, puncture 2 PÉNÉTRER : penetrate 3 ~ **ses dents** : be teething — *vi* 1 : break through 2 : come through (of a tooth) — **perceuse** [pɛrsøz] *nf* : drill

percevoir [pɛrsəvwar] {26} *vt* 1 : perceive 2 : collect (taxes)

perche [pɛrʃ] *nf* 1 : pole, rod 2 : perch, bass (fish)

percher [pɛrʃe] *v* **se percher** *vr* : perch, roost — **perchoir** [pɛrʃwar] *nm* : perch, roost

percussion [pɛrkysjɔ̃] *nf* : percussion

percuter [pɛrkyte] *vt* : strike, crash into — **percutant, -tante** [pɛrkytɑ̃, -tɑ̃t] *adj* : forceful, striking

perdre [pɛrdr] {63} *vt* 1 : lose 2 GASPILLER : waste 3 MANQUER : miss 4 : ruin (one's reputation, etc.) — *vi* : lose — **se perdre** *vr* : get lost — **perdant, -dante** [pɛrdɑ̃, -dɑ̃t] *adj* : losing — ~ *n* : loser

perdrix [pɛrdri] *nfs & pl* : partridge

perdu, -due [pɛrdy] *adj* 1 : lost 2 **temps perdu** : wasted time

père [pɛr] *nm* 1 : father 2 ~**s** *nmpl* : ancestors

perfectionner [pɛrfɛksjɔne] *vt* : perfect, improve — **se perfectionner** *vr* : improve — **perfection** [pɛrfɛksjɔ̃] *nf* 1 : perfection 2 **à la** ~ : perfectly — **perfectionné, -née** [pɛrfɛksjɔne] *adj* : sophisticated — **perfectionnement** [pɛrfɛksjɔnmɑ̃] *nm* : improvement

perforer [pɛrfɔre] *vt* : perforate, pierce

performance [pɛrfɔrmɑ̃s] *nf* 1 : performance 2 RÉUSSITE : achievement — **performant, -mante** [pɛrfɔrmɑ̃, -mɑ̃t] *adj* : high-performance

péril [peril] *nm* : peril, danger — **périlleux, -leuse** [perijø, -jøz] *adj* : perilous

périmé, -mée [perime] *adj* : out-of-date, expired

périmètre [perimɛtr] *nm* : perimeter

période [perjɔd] *nf* 1 : period, time 2 **par** ~**s** : periodically — **périodique** [perjɔdik] *adj* : periodic, periodical — ~ *nm* : periodical

péripétie [peripesi] *nf* : incident, event

périphérie [periferi] *nf* 1 : periphery, circumference 2 : outskirts *pl* (of a city) — **périphérique** [periferik] *adj* 1 : peripheral 2 : outlying (areas)

périple [peripl] *nm* : journey

périr [perir] *vi* : perish

périssable [perisabl] *adj* : perishable

perle [pɛrl] *nf* 1 : pearl 2 : gem, treasure (of a person)

permanent, -nente [pɛrmanɑ̃, -nɑ̃t] *adj* : permanent — **permanente** *nf* : perm, permanent — **permanence** [pɛrmanɑ̃s] *nf* : permanence

permettre [pɛrmɛtr] {53} *vt* 1 : allow, permit 2 : enable, make possible — **se permettre** *vr* 1 : allow oneself 2 ~ **de** : take the liberty of — **permis** [pɛrmi] *nm* : license, permit — **permission** [pɛrmisjɔ̃] *nf* 1 : permission 2 : leave (in the military)

permuter [pɛrmyte] *vt* : switch around — *vi* : switch places

pernicieux, -cieuse [pɛrnisjø, -sjøz] *adj* : pernicious

peroxyde [pɛrɔksid] *nm* : peroxide

perpendiculaire [pɛrpɑ̃dikylɛr] *adj* : perpendicular

perpétrer [pɛrpetre] {87} *vt* : perpetrate, commit

perpétuer [pɛrpetɥe] *vt* : perpetuate — **perpétuel, -tuelle** [pɛrpetɥɛl] *adj* 1 : perpetual 2 : permanent — **perpétuité** [pɛrpetɥite] *nf* **à** ~ : for life

perplexe [pɛrplɛks] *adj* : perplexed, puzzled — **perplexité** [pɛrplɛksite] *nf* : perplexity

perquisition [pɛrkizisjɔ̃] *nf* : (police) search

perron [pɛrɔ̃] *nm* : (front) steps

perroquet [pɛrɔkɛ] *nm* : parrot

perruche [peryʃ] *nf* : parakeet

perruque [peryk] *nf* : wig

persécuter [pɛrsekyte] *vt* 1 : persecute 2 HARCELER : harass — **persécution** [pɛrsekysjɔ̃] *nf* : persecution

persévérer [pɛrsevere] {87} *vi* : persevere, persist — **persévérance** [pɛrseverɑ̃s] *nf* : perseverance

persienne [pɛrsjɛn] *nf* : shutter

persil [pɛrsi] *nm* : parsley

persister [pɛrsiste] *vi* : persist — **persistant, -tante** [pɛrsistɑ̃, -tɑ̃t] *adj* : persistent — **persistance** [-tɑ̃s] *nf* : persistence

personnage [pɛrsɔnaʒ] *nm* 1 : (fictional) character 2 : character, individual

personnalité [pɛrsɔnalite] *nf* 1 : personality 2 : celebrity

personne [pɛrsɔn] *nf* : person — ~ *pron* 1 : no one, nobody 2 : anyone, anybody — **personnel, -nelle** [pɛrsɔnɛl] *adj* : personal, private — **personnel** *nm* : personnel, staff

perspective [pɛrspɛktiv] *nf* 1 : perspective (in art) 2 : point of view 3 POSSIBILITÉ : outlook, prospect

perspicace [pɛrspikas] *adj* : insightful, shrewd — **perspicacité** [pɛrspikasite] *nf* : shrewdness

persuader [pɛrsɥade] *vt* : persuade, convince — **persuasion** [pɛrsɥazjɔ̃] *nf* : persuasion

perte [pɛrt] *nf* 1 : loss 2 GASPILLAGE : waste 3 **à** ~ **de vue** : as far as the eye can see

pertinent, -nente [pɛrtinɑ̃, -nɑ̃t] *adj* : pertinent — **pertinence** [pɛrtinɑ̃s] *nf* : pertinence

perturber [pɛrtyrbe] *vt* 1 INTERROMPRE : disrupt 2 DÉRANGER : disturb, upset — **perturbation** [pɛrtyrbasjɔ̃] *nf* : disruption

pervertir [pɛrvɛrtir] *vt* : pervert, corrupt — **pervers, -verse** [pɛrvɛr, -vɛrs] *adj* : perverse

peser [pəze] {52} *vt* 1 : weigh 2 EXAMINER : consider — *vi* 1 : weigh 2 INFLUER : carry weight 3 ~ **sur** : press, push — **pesamment** [pəzamɑ̃] *adv* : heavily — **pesant, -sante** [pəzɑ̃, -zɑ̃t] *adj* 1 : heavy 2 : burdensome — **pesanteur** [pəzɑ̃tœr] *nf* 1 : gravity (in physics) 2 LOURDEUR : heaviness, weight — **pesée** [pəze] *nf* : weighing

pèse-personne [pɛzpɛrsɔn] *nm, pl* **pèse-personnes** : (bathroom) scales

pessimiste [pesimist] *adj* : pessimistic — ~ *nmf* : pessimist — **pessimisme** [pesimism] *nm* : pessimism

peste [pɛst] *nf* 1 : plague 2 : pest (person)

pesticide [pɛstisid] *nm* : pesticide

pétale [petal] *nm* : petal

pétarader [petarade] *vi* : backfire — **pétard** [petar] *nm* : firecracker

péter [pete] {87} *vi fam* : go off, explode — *vt fam* : bust, break

pétiller [petije] *vi* 1 : sparkle 2 : bubble, fizz 3 : crackle (of fire) — **pétillant, -lante** [petijɑ̃, -jɑ̃t] *adj* 1 : sparkling 2 : bubbly

petit, -tite [p(ə)ti, -tit] *adj* 1 : small, little 2 COURT : short 3 : young (of an animal) 4 **ma petite sœur** : my little sister 5 **petit ami, petite amie** : boyfriend, girlfriend 6 **petit déjeuner** : breakfast — ~ *n* : little boy *m*, little girl *f* — **petit** *nm* : cub

petit-fils, petite-fille [p(ə)tifis, p(ə)titfij] *n* : grandson *m*, granddaughter *f*

pétition [petisjɔ̃] *nf* : petition

petits-enfants [p(ə)tizɑ̃fɑ̃] *nmpl* : grandchildren

pétrifier [petrifje] {96} *vt* : petrify

pétrin [petrɛ̃] *nm fam* : fix, jam

pétrir [petrir] *vt* : knead

pétrole [petrɔl] *nm* 1 : oil, petroleum 2 *or* ~ **lampant** : kerosene — **pétrolier, -lière** [petrɔlje, -ljɛr] *adj* : oil, petroleum — **pétrolier** *nm* 1 : oil tanker 2 : oilman

pétulant, -lante [petylɑ̃, -lɑ̃t] *adj* : vivacious

peu [pø] *adv* 1 : little, not much 2 : not very 3 ~ **après** : shortly after — ~ *nm* 1 ~ **à** ~ : little by little 2 **le** ~ **de** : the few, the little 3 **un** ~ : a little, a bit — ~ *pron* 1 : few (people) 2 ~ **de** : few

peupler [pœple] *vt* : populate, inhabit — **se peupler** *vr* : become populated — **peuple** [pœpl] *nm* : people *pl*

peuplier [pøplije] *nm* : poplar

peur [pœr] *nf* 1 : fear 2 **avoir** ~ **de** : be afraid of 3 **de** ~ **que** : lest 4 **faire** ~ **à** : frighten — **peureux, -reuse** [pœrø, -røz] *adj* : fearful, afraid

peut-être [pøtɛtr] *adv* : perhaps, maybe

pharaon [faraɔ̃] *nm* : pharaoh

phare [far] *nm* 1 : lighthouse 2 : headlight

pharmacie [farmasi] *nf* : pharmacy, drugstore — **pharmacien, -cienne** [farmasjɛ̃, -sjɛn] *n* : pharmacist

phase [faz] *nf* : phase, stage

phénomène [fenɔmɛn] *nm* : phenomenon

philanthrope [filɑ̃trɔp] *nmf* : philanthropist

philatélie [filateli] *nf* : stamp collecting

philosophe [filɔzɔf] *nmf* : philosopher — **philosophie** [filɔzɔfi] *nf* : philosophy

phobie [fɔbi] *nf* : phobia

phonétique [fɔnetik] *adj* : phonetic — ~ *nf* : phonetics

phoque [fɔk] *nm* : seal

phosphore [fɔsfɔr] *nm* : phosphorous

photo [fɔto] *nf* : photo

photocopie [fɔtɔkɔpi] *nf* : photocopy — **photocopier** [fɔtɔkɔpje] {96} *vt* : photocopy — **photocopieur** [fɔtɔkɔpjœr] *nm or* **photocopieuse** [fɔtɔkɔpjøz] *nf* : photocopier

photographie [fɔtɔgrafi] *nf* 1 : photography 2 : photograph — **photographe** [fɔtɔgraf] *nmf* : photographer — **photographier** [fɔtɔgrafje] {96} *vt* : photograph

phrase [fraz] *nf* : sentence

physicien, -cienne [fizisjɛ̃, -sjɛn] *n* : physicist

physiologie [fizjɔlɔʒi] *nf* : physiology

physionomie [fizjɔnɔmi] *nf* : face

physique [fizik] *adj* : physical — ~ *nm* : physique — ~ *nf* : physics

piailler [pjaje] *vi* : squawk

piano [pjano] *nm* 1 : piano 2 ~ **à queue** : grand piano — **pianiste** [pjanist] *nmf* : pianist

pic [pik] *nm* 1 : woodpecker 2 CIME : peak 3 : pick(ax)

pichet [piʃɛ] *nm* : pitcher, jug

pickpocket [pikpɔkɛt] *nm* : pickpocket

picorer [pikɔre] *v* : peck

picoter [pikɔte] *vi* : prickle, sting — **picotement** [pikɔtmɑ̃] *nm* : prickling, stinging

pie [pi] *nf* 1 : magpie 2 *fam* : chatterbox

pièce [pjɛs] *nf* 1 : piece, bit 2 : part, item 3 : room, bedroom 4 : piece (in music) 5 ~ **de théâtre** : play 6 *or* ~ **de monnaie** : coin 7 ~ **jointe** : enclosure (in correspondence)

pied [pje] *nm* 1 : foot 2 : base, bottom, leg (of a table, etc.) 3 : stalk, head (of lettuce) 4 **aux** ~**s nus** : barefoot 5 **coup de** ~ : kick 6 **mettre sur** ~ : set up, get off the ground — **piédestal** [pjedɛstal] *nm, pl* **-taux** [-to] : pedestal

piège [pjɛʒ] *nm* 1 : trap, snare 2 : pitfall 3 **prendre au** ~ : entrap — **piéger** [pjeʒe] {64} *vt* 1 : trap 2 : booby-trap

pierre [pjɛr] *nf* 1 : stone 2 ~ **de touche** : touchstone 3 ~ **tombale** : tombstone — **pierreries** [pjɛrri] *nfpl* : precious stones, gems — **pierreux, -reuse** [pjɛrø, -røz] *adj* : stony

piété [pjete] *nf* : piety
piétiner [pjetine] *vt* : trample on — *vi* 1 : stamp one's feet 2 STAGNER : make no headway
piéton, -tonne [pjetɔ̃, -tɔn] *n* : pedestrian — **piétonnier, -nière** [pjetɔnje, -njɛr] *adj* : pedestrian
piètre [pjɛtr] *adj* : poor, wretched
pieu [pjø] *nm, pl* **pieux** : post, stake
pieuvre [pjøvr] *nf* : octopus
pieux, pieuse [pjø, pjøz] *adj* : pious
pige [piʒ] *nf* **à la ~** : freelance
pigeon [piʒɔ̃] *nm* : pigeon
piger [piʒe] {17} *vt fam* 1 : understand 2 *Can* : to pick (a card, a number, etc.) 3 **tu piges?** : get it?
pigment [pigmɑ̃] *nm* : pigment
pignon [piɲɔ̃] *nm* 1 : gable 2 : cogwheel
pile [pil] *nf* 1 : pile, heap 2 : (storage) battery 3 **~ ou face?** : heads or tails? — **~** *adv fam* 1 : abruptly 2 JUSTE : exactly, right 3 **à l'heure ~** : on the dot
piler [pile] *vt* 1 : crush, pound 2 *Can* : mash (potatoes, etc.)
pilier [pilje] *nm* : pillar, column
piller [pije] *vt* : loot, pillage — **pillage** [pijaʒ] *nm* : looting — **pillard, -larde** [pijar, -jard] *n* : looter
pilon [pilɔ̃] *nm* 1 : pestle 2 : (chicken) drumstick — **pilonner** [pilɔne] *vt* 1 : crush, pound 2 : bombard, shell
pilote [pilɔt] *adj* : pilot, test — **~** *nm* 1 : pilot, driver 2 GUIDE : guide — **pilotage** [pilɔtaʒ] *nm* : piloting, flying — **piloter** [pilɔte] *vt* 1 : pilot, fly, drive 2 GUIDER : show around
pilule [pilyl] *nf* : pill
piment [pimɑ̃] *nm* 1 : pepper 2 **~ rouge** : hot pepper 3 **~ doux** : sweet pepper
pin [pɛ̃] *nm* : pine
pinard [pinar] *nm fam* : (cheap) wine
pince [pɛ̃s] *nf* 1 : pliers *pl* 2 : tongs *pl* 3 : pincer, claw 4 : dart, fold 5 **~ à épiler** : tweezers *pl* 6 **~ à linge** : clothespin
pinceau [pɛ̃so] *nm, pl* **-ceaux** : paintbrush
pincer [pɛ̃se] {6} *vt* 1 : pinch 2 : nip at, sting (of wind, etc.) 3 *fam* : nab — *vi* : be nippy (of weather) — **pincé, -cée** [pɛ̃se] *adj* : forced, stiff — **pincée** [pɛ̃se] *nf* : pinch, small amount — **pincement** [pɛ̃smɑ̃] *nm* 1 : pinch 2 : twinge — **pincettes** [pɛ̃sɛt] *nfpl* 1 : small tweezers 2 : (fire) tongs
pinède [pinɛd] *nf* : pine forest
pingouin [pɛ̃gwɛ̃] *nm* : auk
pingre [pɛ̃gr] *adj* : stingy
pintade [pɛ̃tad] *nf* : guinea fowl
pinte [pɛ̃t] *nf* : pint
pioche [pjɔʃ] *nf* : pickax, pick — **piocher** [pjɔʃe] *vt* : dig (up)
pion, pionne [pjɔ̃, pjɔn] *n France fam* : student monitor — **pion** *nm* 1 : pawn (in chess) 2 : piece (in checkers)
pionnier, -nière [pjɔnje, -njɛr] *n* : pioneer
pipe [pip] *nf* : pipe
pipeline [pajplajn] *nm* : pipeline
piquant, -quante [pikɑ̃, -kɑ̃t] *adj* 1 : prickly, bristly 2 ÉPICÉ : hot, spicy — **piquant** *nm* 1 : prickle, thorn 2 : spine, quill
pique [pik] *nm* : spade (in playing cards) — **~** *nf* : cutting remark
pique–assiette [pikasjɛt] *nmfs & pl* : freeloader
pique–nique [piknik] *nm, pl* **pique–niques** : picnic
piquer [pike] *vt* 1 : prick, puncture 2 : sting, bite 3 : stick (into) 4 ÉVEILLER : arouse (interest, etc.) 5 *fam* : pinch, swipe 6 *fam* : nab, catch — *vi* 1 : sting, burn 2 : dive, swoop down — **se piquer** *vr* **~ de** : pride oneself on — **piquet** [pikɛ] *nm* 1 : post, stake, peg 2 **~ de grève** : picket line — **piqûre** [pikyr] *nf* 1 : prick 2 : sting, bite 3 : injection, shot
pirate [pirat] *nm* 1 : pirate 2 **~ de l'air** : hijacker
pire [pir] *adj* 1 : worse 2 **le ~, la ~, les ~s** : the worst — **~** *nm* 1 **le ~** : the worst 2 **au ~** : at the worst
pis [pi] *adv* 1 : worse 2 **de mal en ~** : from bad to worse — **~** *adj* : worse — **~** *nms & pl* 1 : udder 2 **le ~** : the worst
pis–aller [pizale] *nms & pl* : last resort
piscine [pisin] *nf* : swimming pool
pissenlit [pisɑ̃li] *nm* : dandelion
pistache [pistaʃ] *nf* : pistachio
piste [pist] *nf* 1 TRACE : track, trail 2 : path, route 3 : (ski) slope 4 : racetrack 5 INDICE : lead, clue 6 *or* **~ d'atterrissage** : runway, airstrip
pistolet [pistɔlɛ] *nm* 1 : pistol, handgun 2 : spray gun
piston [pistɔ̃] *nm* : piston
pitié [pitje] *nf* : pity, mercy — **piteux, -teuse** [pitø, -tøz] *adj* : pitiful
piton [pitɔ̃] *nm* 1 : eye, hook 2 *Can fam* : button, switch
pitoyable [pitwajabl] *adj* : pitiful
pitre [pitr] *nm* : clown
pittoresque [pitɔrɛsk] *adj* : picturesque
pivot [pivo] *nm* : pivot — **pivoter** [pivɔte] *vi* : pivot, revolve
pizza [pidza] *nf* : pizza — **pizzeria** [pidzerja] *nf* : pizzeria
placage [plakaʒ] *nm* : veneer
placard [plakar] *nm* 1 : cupboard, closet 2 AFFICHE : poster — **placarder** [plakarde] *vt* : post, put up
placer [plase] {6} *vt* 1 : place, set, put 2 : seat (s.o.) 3 : put in, interject 4 : invest (money, etc.) — **se placer** *vr* 1 : position oneself 2 : get a job 3 **~ premier** : finish first — **place** [plas] *nf* 1 : place, spot 2 : room, space 3 : seat (at the theater) 4 : rank, position 5 : (public) square 6 EMPLOI : job, position 7 **à la ~ de** : instead of 8 **mettre en ~** : set up — **placement** [plasmɑ̃] *nm* 1 : investment 2 **bureau de ~** : placement agency
placide [plasid] *adj* : placid, calm
plafond [plafɔ̃] *nm* : ceiling — **plafonner** [plafɔne] *vi* : reach a maximum, peak
plage [plaʒ] *nf* 1 : beach, shore 2 : seaside resort
plagier [plaʒje] {96} *vt* : plagiarize — **plagiat** [plaʒja] *nm* : plagiarism
plaider [plede] *vi* : plead, litigate — *vt* : plead (a case)
plaie [plɛ] *nf* : wound, cut
plaignant, -gnante [plɛɲɑ̃, -ɲɑ̃t] *n* : plaintiff
plaindre [plɛ̃dr] {65} *vt* : pity — **se plaindre** *vr* 1 : moan 2 **~ de** : complain about — **plainte** [plɛ̃t] *nf* 1 : moan 2 : complaint
plaire [plɛr] {66} *vi* 1 : be pleasing 2 **~ à** : please, suit — *v impers* 1 : please 2 **s'il vous plaît** : please — **se plaire** *vr* **~ à** : like, enjoy — **plaisance** [plɛzɑ̃s] *nf or* **navigation de ~** : sailing, boating — **plaisant, -sante** [plɛzɑ̃, -zɑ̃t] *adj* 1 AGRÉABLE : pleasant 2 AMUSANT : amusing, funny — **plaisanter** [plɛzɑ̃te] *vi* : joke, jest — **plaisanterie** [plɛzɑ̃tri] *nf* 1 BLAGUE : joke, jest 2 FARCE : prank — **plaisantin** [plɛzɑ̃tɛ̃] *nm* : practical joker — **plaisir** [plezir] *nm* 1 : pleasure 2 **au ~** : see you soon 3 **avec ~!** : of course! 4 **faire ~ à** : please
plan, plane [plɑ̃, plan] *adj* : flat, level — **plan** *nm* 1 : plane (in geometry) 2 : plan, strategy 3 : map, diagram 4 **premier ~** : foreground
planche [plɑ̃ʃ] *nf* 1 : board, plank 2 **~ à repasser** : ironing board 3 **~ à roulettes** : skateboard — **plancher** [plɑ̃ʃe] *nm* : floor
planer [plane] *vi* 1 : glide, soar 2 **~ sur** : hover over
planète [planɛt] *nf* : planet — **planétaire** [planetɛr] *adj* : planetary
planeur [planœr] *nm* : glider
planifier [planifje] {96} *vt* : plan — **planification** [planifikasjɔ̃] *nf* : planning
planque [plɑ̃k] *nf fam* : hideout — **planquer** [plɑ̃ke] *vt fam* : hide away, stash
planter [plɑ̃te] *vt* 1 : plant 2 ENFONCER : drive in 3 INSTALLER : put up, set up 4 *fam* : ditch, drop — **se planter** *vr* 1 *fam* : stand, plant oneself 2 *fam* : get it wrong, mess up — **plant** [plɑ̃] *nm* : seedling, young plant — **plantation** [plɑ̃tasjɔ̃] *nf* 1 : planting 2 : plantation — **plante** [plɑ̃t] *nf* 1 : sole (of the foot) 2 : plant
plaquer [plake] *vt* 1 : veneer, plate 2 APLATIR : stick (down), flatten 3 : tackle (in football) 4 *fam* : ditch, get rid of — **plaque** [plak] *nf* 1 : plate, sheet 2 : plaque, nameplate 3 : patch (of ice, etc.) 4 **~ chauffante** : hotplate 5 **~ d'immatriculation** : license plate — **plaqué, -quée** [plake] *adj* : plated — **plaquette** [plakɛt] *nf* 1 : slab (of butter, etc.) 2 : pamphlet
plastique [plastik] *adj & nm* : plastic
plat, plate [pla, plat] *adj* 1 : flat, level 2 : dull, bland — **plat** *nm* 1 : plate, dish 2 : course (of a meal) 3 **à ~** : flat down 4 **à ~** : dead (of a battery) 5 **~ de résistance** : main course
platane [platan] *nm* : plane tree
plateau [plato] *nm, pl* **-teaux** 1 : tray, platter 2 : plateau (in geography) 3 : stage, set (in theater)
plate–bande [platbɑ̃d] *nf, pl* **plates–bandes** : flower bed
plate–forme [platfɔrm] *nf, pl* **plates–formes** : platform
platine[1] [platin] *nm* : platinum
platine[2] *nf* : turntable
platitude [platityd] *nf* : trite remark
platonique [platɔnik] *adj* : platonic
plâtre [platr] *nm* 1 : plaster 2 : plaster cast — **plâtrer** [platre] *vt* 1 : plaster 2 : put in a (plaster) cast
plausible [plozibl] *adj* : plausible, likely
plein, pleine [plɛ̃, plɛn] *adj* 1 REMPLI : full, filled (up) 2 : rounded, full 3 : pregnant (of an animal) 4 **en plein jour** : in broad daylight 5 **le plein air** : the outdoors — **plein** *nm* 1 **à ~** : fully, totally 2 **faire le ~** : fill up — **plénitude** [plenityd] *nf* : fullness
pleurer [plœre] *vt* 1 : weep for, mourn 2 : shed (tears) — *vi* 1 : cry, weep 2 : water (of eyes) 3 **~ sur** : bemoan — **pleurnicher** [plœrniʃe] *vi fam* : whine, snivel — **pleurs** [plœr] *nfpl* **en ~** : in tears
pleuvoir [pløvwar] {67} *v impers* 1 : rain 2 **il pleut** : it's raining — *vi* : rain down, pour down
plier [plije] {96} *vt* 1 : fold (up) 2 : bend — *vi* 1 : bend, sag 2 : yield, give in — **se plier** *vr* 1 : fold 2 **~ à** : submit to — **pli** [pli] *nm* 1 : fold, pleat, crease 2 HABITUDE : habit 3 **sous ce ~** : enclosed — **pliant, pliante** [plijɑ̃, plijɑ̃t] *adj* : folding, collapsible
plinthe [plɛ̃t] *nf* : baseboard
plisser [plise] *vt* 1 : pleat, fold, crease 2 FRONCER : wrinkle (one's brow), pucker (one's lips)
plomb [plɔ̃] *nm* 1 : lead 2 : (lead) pellet 3 FUSIBLE : fuse — **plombage** [plɔ̃baʒ] *nm* : filling (of a tooth) — **plomber** [plɔ̃be] *vt* 1 : weight with lead 2 : fill (a tooth) — **plomberie** [plɔ̃bri] *nf* : plumbing — **plombier** [plɔ̃bje] *nm* : plumber
plonger [plɔ̃ʒe] {17} *vt* : thrust, plunge — *vi* 1 : dive 2 **~ dans** : plunge into — **se plonger** *vr* **~ dans** : immerse oneself into — **plongeant, -geante** [plɔ̃ʒɑ̃, -ʒɑ̃t] *adj* 1 : plunging 2 **vue plongeante** : bird's-eye view — **plongée** [plɔ̃ʒe] *nf* 1 : diving 2 **~ sous–marine** : skin diving — **plongeoir** [plɔ̃ʒwar] *nm* : diving board — **plongeon** [plɔ̃ʒɔ̃] *nm* 1 : dive 2 : loon (bird) — **plongeur, -geuse** [plɔ̃ʒœr, -ʒøz] *n* 1 : diver 2 : dishwasher (person)
plouf [pluf] *nm* : splash
ployer [plwaje] {58} *v* : bow, bend
pluie [plɥi] *nf* 1 : rain, rainfall 2 **une ~ de** : a stream of
plume [plym] *nf* 1 : feather 2 : quill pen — **plumage** [plymaʒ] *nm* : feathers *pl* — **plumeau** [plymo] *nm, pl* **-meaux** [plymo] : feather duster — **plumer** [plyme] *vt* : pluck
plupart [plypar] *nf* 1 **la ~ des** : most, the majority of 2 **pour la ~** : for the most part, mostly
pluriel, -rielle [plyrjɛl] *adj & nm* : plural — **pluriel** *nm* : plural
plus [ply(s)] *adv* 1 : more 2 (*used with* **ne**) : no more, no longer 3 **~ de** : more (than) 4 **de ~** : in addition, furthermore 5 **de ~ en ~** : increasingly 6 **en ~** : as well 7 **le ~** : the most 8 **non ~** : neither, either — **~** *nm* 1 : plus (sign) 2 *fam* : plus, advantage — **~** *conj* : plus (in calculations)
plusieurs [plyzjœr] *adj & pron* : several
plutôt [plyto] *adv* 1 : rather, instead 2 **~ que** : rather than
pluvieux, -vieuse [plyvjø, -vjøz] *adj* : rainy, wet
pneu [pnø] *nm, pl* **pneus** : tire — **pneumatique** [pnømatik] *adj* : inflatable
pneumonie [pnømɔni] *nf* : pneumonia
poche [pɔʃ] *nf* 1 : pocket (in clothing) 2 **~s** *nfpl* CERNES : bags (under the eyes) — **pocher** [pɔʃe] *vt* : poach (in cooking) — **pochette** [pɔʃɛt] *nf* 1 : folder, case, sleeve 2 : book (of matches) 3 : pocket handkerchief
poêle [pwal] *nm* : stove — **~** *nf or* **~ à frire** : frying pan
poème [pɔɛm] *nm* : poem — **poésie** [pɔezi] *nf* 1 : poetry 2 : poem — **poète** [pɔɛt] *nmf* : poet — **poétique** [pɔetik] *adj* : poetic(al)
poids [pwa] *nms & pl* 1 : weight, heaviness 2 FARDEAU : burden 3 IMPORTANCE : meaning, influence 4 **~ et mesures** : weights and measures 5 **~ et haltères** : weight lifting
poignant, -gnante [pwaɲɑ̃, -ɲɑ̃t] *adj* : moving, poignant
poignard [pwaɲar] *nm* : dagger — **poignarder** [pwaɲarde] *vt* : stab
poigne [pwaɲ] *nf* 1 : grip, grasp 2 **à ~** : firm, forceful
poignée [pwaɲe] *nf* 1 : handful 2 : handle, knob 3 **~ de main** : handshake
poignet [pwaɲɛ] *nm* 1 : wrist 2 : cuff
poil [pwal] *nm* 1 : hair 2 : fur, coat 3 : bristle (of a brush) 4 **à ~** *fam* : stark naked — **poilu, -lue** [pwaly] *adj* : hairy
poinçon [pwɛ̃sɔ̃] *nm* 1 : awl, punch 2 MARQUE : hallmark, stamp — **poinçonner** [pwɛ̃sɔne] *vt* : punch, perforate
poing [pwɛ̃] *nm* 1 : fist 2 **coup de ~** : punch
point [pwɛ̃] *nm* 1 : point, position 2 DEGRÉ : degree, extent 3 : period (in punctuation) 4 QUESTION : matter 5 : point (in sports) 6 : stitch (in sewing) 7 **à ~** : just right, just in time 8 **mettre au ~** : adjust, perfect 9 **~ culminant** : highlight 10 **~ de vue** : point of view 11 **~ du jour** : daybreak 12 **~ mort** : neutral (gear) 13 **~s cardinaux** : points of the compass — **~** *adv* 1 (*used with* **ne**) : not 2 **~ du tout** : not at all
pointe [pwɛ̃t] *nf* 1 : point, tip 2 SOUPÇON : touch, hint 3 **de ~** : state-of-the-art 4 **heures de ~** : rush hour 5 **sur la ~ des pieds** : on tiptoe
pointer [pwɛ̃te] *vt* 1 COCHER : check, mark off 2 : aim (a rifle at), point (a finger at) — *vi* 1 : clock in 2 : break, dawn (of a new day) — **se pointer** *vr fam* : show up
pointillé [pwɛ̃tije] *nm* : dotted line
pointilleux, -leuse [pwɛ̃tijø, -jøz] *adj* : finicky, fussy
pointu, -tue [pwɛ̃ty] *adj* : pointed, sharp
pointure [pwɛ̃tyr] *nf* : size (of clothing)
point–virgule [pwɛ̃virgyl] *nm, pl* **points–virgules** : semicolon
poire [pwar] *nf* : pear
poireau [pwaro] *nm, pl* **-reaux** : leek — **poireauter** [pwarote] *vi fam* : hang around
poirier [pwarje] *nm* : pear tree
pois [pwa] *nms & pl* 1 : pea 2 **à ~** : spotted, polka-dot
poison [pwazɔ̃] *nm* : poison
poisse [pwas] *nf fam* : bad luck
poisseux, -seuse [pwasø, -søz] *adj* : sticky
poisson [pwasɔ̃] *nm* 1 : fish 2 **~ d'avril!** : April fool! — **poissonnerie** [pwasɔnri] *nf* : fish market — **poissonnier, -nière** [pwasɔnje, -njɛr] *n* : fish merchant
poitrine [pwatrin] *nf* 1 : chest 2 : breasts *pl*, bosom 3 : breast (in cooking)
poivre [pwavr] *nm* : pepper — **poivré, -vrée** [pwavre] *adj* : peppery — **poivrer** [pwavre] *vt* : pepper — **poivrier** [pwavrije] *nm or* **poivrière** [pwavrijɛr] *nf* : pepper shaker — **poivron** [pwavrɔ̃] *nm* : pepper (vegetable)
poker [pɔkɛr] *nm* : poker
pôle [pol] *nm* : pole — **polaire** [pɔlɛr] *adj* : polar
polémique [pɔlemik] *adj* : controversial — **~** *nf* : debate, controversy
poli, -lie [pɔli] *adj* 1 COURTOIS : polite 2 LISSE : polished, smooth
police [pɔlis] *nf* 1 : police, police force 2 **~ d'assurance** : insurance policy — **policier, -cière** [pɔlisje, -sjɛr] *adj* 1 : police 2 **roman policier** : detective novel — **policier** *nm* : police officer
poliomyélite [pɔljɔmjelit] *nf* : poliomyelitis
polir [pɔlir] *vt* : polish, shine
polisson, -sonne [pɔlisɔ̃, -sɔn] *n* : naughty child, rascal
politesse [pɔlitɛs] *nf* 1 : politeness 2 : polite remark
politique [pɔlitik] *adj* : political — **~** *nf* 1 : politics 2 : policy, procedure — **politicien, -cienne** [pɔlitisjɛ̃, -sjɛn] *n* : politician
pollen [pɔlɛn] *nm* : pollen
polluer [pɔlɥe] *vt* : pollute — **polluant** [pɔlɥɑ̃] *nm* : pollutant — **pollution** [pɔlysjɔ̃] *nf*
polo [pɔlo] *nm* 1 : polo 2 : polo shirt
poltron, -tronne [pɔltrɔ̃, -trɔn] *adj* : cowardly — **~** *n* : coward
polyester [pɔliɛstɛr] *nm* : polyester
polyvalent, -lente [pɔlivalɑ̃, -lɑ̃t] *adj* : versatile, multipurpose
pommade [pɔmad] *nf* : ointment
pomme [pɔm] *nf* 1 : apple 2 **~ d'Adam** : Adam's apple 3 **~ de pin** : pinecone 4 **~ de terre** : potato 5 **~s frites** : French fries — **pommeau** [pɔmo] *nm* : knob (of a cane) — **pommette** [pɔmɛt] *nf* : cheekbone — **pommier** [pɔmje] *nm* : apple tree
pompe [pɔ̃p] *nf* 1 : pump 2 APPARAT : pomp, ceremony 3 **~s funèbres** : funeral home — **pomper** [pɔ̃pe] *vt* : pump
pompette [pɔ̃pɛt] *adj fam* : tipsy
pompeux, -peuse [pɔ̃pø, -pøz] *adj* : pompous
pompier [pɔ̃pje] *nm* : firefighter, fireman
pompiste [pɔ̃pist] *nmf* : service station attendant
pompon [pɔ̃pɔ̃] *nm* : pompom
pomponner [pɔ̃pɔne] *v* **se pomponner** *vr* : get all dressed up
poncer [pɔ̃se] {6} *vt* : sand (down)
ponctualité [pɔ̃ktɥalite] *nf* : punctuality
ponctuation [pɔ̃ktɥasjɔ̃] *nf* : punctuation
ponctuel, -tuelle [pɔ̃ktɥɛl] *adj* 1 : prompt, punctual 2 : limited, selective
ponctuer [pɔ̃ktɥe] *vt* : punctuate
pondéré, -rée [pɔ̃dere] *adj* : levelheaded, sensible
pondre [pɔ̃dr] {63} *vt* : lay (eggs)
poney [pɔnɛ] *nm* : pony
pont [pɔ̃] *nm* 1 : bridge 2 : deck (of a ship)
ponte [pɔ̃t] *nf* : laying (of eggs)
pont–levis [pɔ̃ləvi] *nm, pl* **ponts–levis** : drawbridge
ponton [pɔ̃tɔ̃] *nm* : pontoon
pop [pɔp] *adj s & pl* : pop
pop–corn [pɔpkɔrn] *nms & pl* : popcorn
popote [pɔpɔt] *nf* 1 : mess (in the military) 2 *fam* : cooking
populaire [pɔpylɛr] *adj* 1 : popular 2 : working-class — **popularité** [pɔpylarite] *nf* : popularity
population [pɔpylasjɔ̃] *nf* : population — **populeux, -leuse** [pɔpylø, -løz] *adj* : densely populated
porc [pɔr] *nm* 1 : pig, hog 2 : pork (in cooking)
porcelaine [pɔrsəlɛn] *nf* 1 : porcelain 2 : china, chinaware
porc–épic [pɔrkepik] *nm, pl* **porcs–épics** : porcupine
porche [pɔrʃ] *nm* : porch
porcherie [pɔrʃəri] *nf* : pigpen, pigsty
pore [pɔr] *nm* : pore — **poreux, -reuse** [pɔrø, -røz] *adj* : porous
pornographie [pɔrnɔgrafi] *nf* : pornography — **pornographique** [-grafik] *adj* : pornographic
port [pɔr] *nm* 1 : port, harbor 2 : wearing,

carrying (of arms, etc.) 3 MAINTIEN : bearing 4 ~ **payé** : postpaid

portable [pɔrtabl] adj : portable

portail [pɔrtaj] nm : gate

portant, -tante [pɔrtɑ̃, -tɑ̃t] adj **bien portant** : in good health

portatif, -tive [pɔrtatif, -tiv] adj : portable

porte [pɔrt] nf 1 : door, doorway 2 : gate (at an airport, etc.) 3 ~ **de sortie** : exit, way out

porte–avions [pɔrtavjɔ̃] nms & pl : aircraft carrier

porte–bagages [pɔrtbagaʒ] nms & pl : luggage rack

porte–bonheur [pɔrtbɔnœr] nms & pl : lucky charm

porte–clés or **porte–clefs** [pɔrtəkle] nms & pl : key ring

porte–documents [pɔrtdɔkymɑ̃] nms & pl : briefcase

portée [pɔrte] nf 1 : range 2 : impact, significance 3 : litter (of kittens, etc.) 4 **à ~ de** : within reach of

portefeuille [pɔrtəfœj] nm 1 : wallet 2 : portfolio (in finance or politics)

portemanteau [pɔrtmɑ̃to] nm, pl **-teaux** [-to] : coat rack

porte–monnaie [pɔrtmɔnɛ] nms & pl : change purse

porte–parole [pɔrtparɔl] nms & pl : spokesperson

porter [pɔrte] vt 1 TRANSPORTER : carry 2 : wear, have on 3 APPORTER : bring 4 : bear (responsibility, etc.) 5 **être porté à** : be inclined to — vi 1 : carry (of a voice) 2 ~ **sur** CONCERNER : be about — **se porter** vr 1 : be worn 2 ~ **bien** : be (feel, go) well

porte–savon [pɔrtsavɔ̃] nms & pl : soap dish

porte–serviettes [pɔrtsɛrvjɛt] nms & pl : towel rack

porteur, -teuse [pɔrtœr, -tøz] n 1 : porter 2 : holder, bearer (of news, etc.) 3 : carrier (of disease)

porte–voix [pɔrtəvwa] nms & pl : megaphone

portier, -tière [pɔrtje, -tjɛr] n : doorman

portière nf : door (of an automobile)

portillon [pɔrtijɔ̃] nm : gate

portion [pɔrsjɔ̃] nf : portion

porto [pɔrto] nm : port (wine)

portrait [pɔrtrɛ] nm : portrait

portuaire [pɔrtɥɛr] adj : harbor, port

portugais, -gaise [pɔrtygɛ, -gɛz] adj : Portuguese — **portugais** nm : Portuguese (language)

poser [poze] vt 1 : put (down), place 2 INSTALLER : put up, install 3 : pose (a problem) 4 ~ **sa candidature** : apply (for a job) — vi : pose, sit — **se poser** vr 1 : land, alight 2 : arise, come up — **pose** [poz] nf 1 : installing 2 : pose, posture — **posé, -sée** [poze] adj : composed, calm

positif, -tive [pozitif, -tiv] adj : positive

position [pozisjɔ̃] nf 1 : position 2 **prendre ~** : take a stand — **positionner** [pozisjɔne] vt : position, place

posologie [pozɔlɔʒi] nf : dosage

posséder [pɔsede] {87} vt 1 AVOIR : possess, have 2 MAÎTRISER : know thoroughly — **possesseur** [pɔsesœr] nm : owner, possessor — **possessif, -sive** [pɔsesif, -siv] adj : possessive — **possession** [pɔsesjɔ̃] nf : ownership, possession

possible [pɔsibl] adj : possible — ~ nm 1 **dans la mesure du ~** : as far as possible 2 **faire son ~** : do one's utmost — **possibilité** [pɔsibilite] nf 1 : possibility 2 ~**s** nfpl : means, resources

poste [pɔst] nm 1 : job, position 2 : post, station 3 : (telephone) extension 4 ~ **d'essence** : gas station 5 ~ **de pilotage** : cockpit 6 ~ **de pompiers** Can : fire station 7 ~ **de télévision** : television set — ~ nf 1 : mail service 2 : post office — **postal, -tale** [pɔstal] adj, mpl **-taux** [pɔsto] : postal, mail — **poster** [pɔste] vt 1 : post, station 2 : mail

postérieur, -rieure [pɔsterjœr] adj 1 : later (of a date, etc.) 2 : rear, back — **postérieur** nm fam : bottom, buttocks pl

postérité [pɔsterite] nf : posterity

posthume [pɔstym] adj : posthumous

postiche [pɔstiʃ] adj : false, fake

postier, -tière [pɔstje, -tjɛr] n : postal worker

post–scriptum [pɔstskriptɔm] nms & pl : postscript

postuler [pɔstyle] vt : apply for (a position) — **postulant, -lante** [pɔstylɑ̃, -lɑ̃t] n : candidate, contestant

posture [pɔstyr] nf : posture

pot [po] nm 1 : pot, jar, container 2 fam : drink, glass 3 ~ **d'échappement** : muffler (of an automobile)

potable [pɔtabl] adj 1 : drinkable 2 fam : fair, passable

potage [pɔtaʒ] nm : soup — **potager** [pɔtaʒe] adj **jardin ~** : vegetable garden

pot–au–feu [pɔtofø] nms & pl : beef stew

pot–de–vin [podvɛ̃] nm, pl **pots–de–vin** : bribe

pote [pot] nm fam : pal, buddy

poteau [pɔto] nm, pl **-teaux** 1 : post, pole 2 ~ **indicateur** : signpost

potelé, -lée [pɔtle] adj : chubby, plump

potence [pɔtɑ̃s] nf : gallows

potentiel, -tielle [pɔtɑ̃sjɛl] adj & nm : potential

poterie [pɔtri] nf : pottery

potin [pɔtɛ̃] nm fam 1 France : noise, racket 2 ~**s** nmpl : gossip

potion [pɔsjɔ̃] nf : potion

potiron [pɔtirɔ̃] nm : large pumpkin

pot–pourri [popuri] nm, pl **pots–pourris** : potpourri

pou [pu] nm, pl **poux** : louse

poubelle [pubɛl] nf : garbage can

pouce [pus] nm 1 : thumb 2 : big toe 3 : inch (measurement) 4 **faire du ~** Can : hitchhike

poudre [pudr] nf : powder — **poudrer** [pudre] vt : powder — **poudrerie** [pudrəri] nf Can : (snow) flurries pl — **poudreux, -dreuse** [pudrø, -drøz] adj : powdery — **poudrier** [pudrije] nm : (powder) compact

pouffer [pufe] vi ~ **de rire** : burst out laughing

pouilleux, -leuse [pujø, -jøz] adj 1 : lousy, flea-ridden 2 : seedy (of a neighborhood)

poulailler [pulaje] nm : henhouse, chicken coop

poulain [pulɛ̃] nm 1 : colt, foal 2 PROTÉGÉ : protégé

poule [pul] nf 1 : hen 2 : fowl (in cooking) — **poulet** [pulɛ] nm : chicken

pouliche [puliʃ] nf : filly

poulie [puli] nf : pulley

pouls [pu] nm : pulse

poumon [pumɔ̃] nm : lung

poupe [pup] nf : stern

poupée [pupe] nf : doll

poupon [pupɔ̃] nm 1 : tiny baby 2 : baby doll — **pouponnière** [puponjɛr] nf : nursery (for babies)

pour [pur] prep 1 : for 2 : to, in order to 3 ~ **cent** : percent 4 ~ **que** : in order that, so that — ~ nm **le ~ et le contre** : the pros and cons

pourboire [purbwar] nm : tip

pourcentage [pursɑ̃taʒ] nm : percentage

pourchasser [purʃase] vt : pursue, hunt down

pourparlers [purparle] nmpl : talks, negotiations

pourquoi [purkwa] adv & conj : why — ~ nms & pl : reason, cause

pourrir [purir] v : rot, decay — **pourri, -rie** [puri] adj : rotten — **pourriture** [purityr] nf : rot, decay

poursuivre [pursɥivr] {88} vt 1 : pursue, chase 2 CONTINUER : carry on with 3 ~ **en justice** : sue, prosecute 4 HARCELER : hound — vi : continue — **poursuite** [pursɥit] nf 1 : pursuit 2 ~**s** nfpl : legal proceedings, lawsuit — **poursuivant, -vante** [pursɥivɑ̃, -vɑ̃t] n 1 : pursuer 2 : plaintiff

pourtant [purtɑ̃] adv : however, yet

pourtour [purtur] nm : perimeter

pourvoir [purvwar] {68} vt ~ **de** : provide with — vi ~ **à** : provide for — **pourvu** [purvy] conj ~ **que** 1 : provided that 2 : let's hope (that)

pousser [puse] vt 1 : push, shove 2 INCITER : encourage, urge 3 POURSUIVRE : pursue, continue (with) 4 : let out (a scream) — vi 1 : push 2 CROÎTRE : grow — **se pousser** vr : move over — **pousse** [pus] nf 1 : growth 2 BOURGEON : shoot, sprout — **poussé, -sée** [puse] adj : advanced, extensive — **poussée** [puse] nf 1 : pressure 2 IMPULSION : push 3 AUGMENTATION : upsurge 4 ACCÈS : attack, outbreak (in medicine) — **poussette** [pusɛt] nf : stroller

poussière [pusjɛr] nf : dust — **poussiéreux, -reuse** [pusjerø, -røz] adj : dusty

poussin [pusɛ̃] nm : chick

poutre [putr] nf : beam, girder

pouvoir [puvwar] {69} v aux 1 : be able to 2 : be permitted to — v impers : be possible — vt 1 : be able to do 2 **je n'en peux plus!** : I can't take anymore! — **se pouvoir** v impers : be possible — ~ nm : power

pragmatique [pragmatik] adj : pragmatic

prairie [preri] nf : meadow

pratiquer [pratike] vt 1 : practice 2 : play (a sport) 3 : use, apply 4 EFFECTUER : carry out — **praticable** [pratikabl] adj 1 : feasible 2 : passable (of a road, etc.) — **praticien, -cienne** [pratisjɛ̃, -sjɛn] n : practitioner — **pratiquant, -quante** [pratikɑ̃, -kɑ̃t] adj : practicing — ~ n : churchgoer, follower — **pratique** [pratik] adj : practical — ~ nf : practice

pré [pre] nm : meadow

préalable [prealabl] adj 1 : preliminary 2 **sans avis ~** : without prior notice — ~ nm 1 : prerequisite 2 **au ~** : beforehand

préambule [preɑ̃byl] nm 1 : preamble 2 **sans ~** : without warning

préau [preo] nm, pl **préaux** [preo] : (covered) playground, courtyard

préavis [preavi] nm : (prior) notice

précaire [prekɛr] adj : precarious

précaution [prekosjɔ̃] nf 1 : precaution 2 PRUDENCE : caution, care

précéder [presede] {87} vt : precede — **précédemment** [presedamɑ̃] adv : previously — **précédent, -dente** [presedɑ̃, -dɑ̃t] adj : previous, prior — **précédent** nm : precedent

prêcher [preʃe] v : preach

précieux, -cieuse [presjø, -sjøz] adj 1 : precious 2 UTILE : valuable

précipice [presipis] nm : abyss, chasm

précipiter [presipite] vt 1 : hurl, throw 2 HÂTER : hasten, speed up — **se précipiter** vr 1 : hasten, rush 2 ~ **sur** : throw oneself on — **précipitation** [presipitasjɔ̃] nf 1 : hurry, haste 2 ~**s** nfpl : precipitation (in meteorology) — **précipité, -tée** [presipite] adj 1 : rapid 2 HÂTIF : hasty, rash

préciser [presize] vt : specify, make clear — **se préciser** vr : become clearer — **précis, -cise** [presi, -siz] adj 1 : precise, accurate 2 : clear, specific — **précis** nms & pl 1 : summary 2 MANUEL : handbook — **précisément** [presizemɑ̃] adv : precisely, exactly — **précision** [presizjɔ̃] nf 1 : precision 2 : clarity

précoce [prekɔs] adj 1 : early 2 : precocious (of a child, etc.)

préconçu, -cue [prekɔ̃sy] adj : preconceived

préconiser [prekonize] vt : recommend, advocate

précurseur [prekyrsœr] nm : forerunner

prédateur [predatœr] nm : predator

prédécesseur [predesɛsœr] nm : predecessor

prédilection [predilɛksjɔ̃] nf 1 : partiality 2 **de ~** : favorite

prédire [predir] {29} vt : predict — **prédiction** [prediksjɔ̃] nf : prediction

prédisposer [predispoze] vt : predispose

prédominant, -nante [predɔminɑ̃, -nɑ̃t] adj : predominant

préfabriqué, -quée [prefabrike] adj : prefabricated

préface [prefas] nf : preface

préfecture [prefɛktyr] nf ~ **de police** France : police headquarters

préférer [prefere] {87} vt : prefer — **préférable** [preferabl] adj : preferable — **préféré, -rée** [prefere] adj & n : favorite — **préférence** [preferɑ̃s] nf : preference

préfet [prefɛ] nm ~ **de police** France : police commissioner

préfixe [prefiks] nm : prefix

préhistorique [preistɔrik] adj : prehistoric

préjudice [preʒydis] nm 1 : harm, damage 2 **porter ~ à** : cause harm to — **préjudiciable** [preʒydisjabl] adj : harmful, detrimental

préjugé [preʒyʒe] nm : prejudice

prélasser [prelase] v **se prélasser** vr : lounge (around)

prélever [prelәve] {52} vt 1 : withdraw, deduct 2 : take (a sample of) — **prélèvement** [prelɛvmɑ̃] nm 1 : withdrawal, deduction 2 : (blood) sample

préliminaire [preliminɛr] adj : preliminary

prélude [prelyd] nm : prelude

prématuré, -rée [prematyre] adj : premature

prémédité [premedite] adj : premeditated

premier, -mière [prәmje, -mjɛr] adj 1 : first 2 : top, leading 3 **premier ministre** : prime minister — ~ n : first (one) — **premier** nm : first (in dates) — **première** nf 1 : first class 2 : premiere (of a show) — **premièrement** [prәmjɛrmɑ̃] adv : in the first place, firstly

prémunir [premynir] v **se prémunir** vr ~ **contre** : protect oneself against

prendre [prɑ̃dr] {70} vt 1 : take 2 ACHETER : get, pick up 3 : take on (responsibility) 4 ATTRAPER : catch, capture 5 : put on, gain (weight) 6 : have (a meal) — vi 1 : set, thicken 2 : break out (of fire) 3 ~ **à droite** : bear right 4 ~ **sur soi** : take upon oneself — **se prendre** vr 1 : be taken 2 : get caught 3 ~ **les doigts dans** : catch one's fingers in 4 ~ **pour** : consider oneself 5 **s'en ~ à** : attack — **preneur, -neuse** [prәnœr, -nøz] n : buyer, taker

prénom [prenɔ̃] nm : given name, first name

préoccuper [preɔkype] vt : worry, preoccupy — **préoccupation** [preɔkypasjɔ̃] nf : worry, concern

préparer [prepare] vt 1 : prepare, make ready 2 ~ **qqn à** : prepare s.o. for — **se préparer** vr : prepare oneself, get ready — **préparatifs** [preparatif] nmpl : preparations — **préparation** [preparasjɔ̃] nf : preparation

prépondérant, -rante [prepɔ̃derɑ̃, -rɑ̃t] adj : predominant

préposer [prepoze] vt ~ **à** : put in charge of — **préposé, -sée** [prepoze] n 1 : employee, clerk 2 France : mailman

préposition [prepɔzisjɔ̃] nf : preposition

prérogative [prerɔgativ] nf : prerogative

près [prɛ] adv 1 : close, near(by) 2 : near, soon 3 **à . . . ~** : more or less, within about 4 **à peu ~** : almost, just about 5 **de ~** : closely 6 ~ **de** : near

présage [prezaʒ] nm : omen — **présager** [prezaʒe] {17} vt 1 : foresee 2 : portend, bode

presbyte [prɛsbit] adj : farsighted

presbytère [prɛsbitɛr] nm : rectory

prescrire [prɛskrir] {33} vt : prescribe — **prescription** [prɛskripsjɔ̃] nf : prescription

préséance [preseɑ̃s] nf : precedence

présent, -sente [prezɑ̃, -zɑ̃t] adj : present — ~ nm : present (time) — **présence** [prezɑ̃s] nf 1 : presence 2 **en ~** : face to face 3 ~ **d'esprit** : presence of mind — **présentement** [prezɑ̃tmɑ̃] adv : at the moment, now

présenter [prezɑ̃te] vt 1 MONTRER : present, show 2 : introduce (to) 3 : pay, offer (one's condolences) 4 : submit (a proposal, etc.) — **se présenter** vr 1 : go, come, appear 2 : introduce oneself 3 ~ **à** : run for (an office) — **présentateur, -trice** [prezɑ̃tatœr, -tris] n : newscaster, anchor — **présentation** [prezɑ̃tasjɔ̃] nf 1 : presentation 2 : introduction — **présentoir** [prezɑ̃twar] nm : display shelf

préserver [prezɛrve] vt 1 : protect 2 CONSERVER : preserve — **préservatif** [prezɛrvatif] nm : condom — **préservation** [prezɛrvasjɔ̃] nf : protection, preservation

présider [prezide] vt : preside over, chair — vi ~ **à** : rule over, govern — **président, -dente** [prezidɑ̃, -dɑ̃t] n 1 : president 2 : chairperson — **présidence** [prezidɑ̃s] nf 1 : presidency 2 : chairmanship — **présidentiel, -tielle** [prezidɑ̃sjɛl] adj : presidential

présomption [prezɔ̃psjɔ̃] nf : presumption — **présomptueux, -tueuse** [prezɔ̃ptɥø, -tɥøz] adj : presumptuous

presque [prɛsk] adv : almost, nearly

presqu'île [prɛskil] nf : peninsula

pressant, -sante [prɛsɑ̃, -sɑ̃t] adj : urgent, pressing

presse [prɛs] nf : press

pressé, -sée [prese] adj 1 : hurried 2 : urgent 3 : freshly squeezed

pressentir [presɑ̃tir] {82} vt : sense, have a premonition about — **pressentiment** [presɑ̃timɑ̃] nm : premonition

presse–papiers [prɛspapje] nms & pl : paperweight

presser [prese] vt 1 : press, squeeze 2 INCITER : urge 3 HÂTER : hurry, rush — vi : be pressing, be urgent — **se presser** vr 1 SE HÂTER : hurry up 2 ~ **contre** or ~ **sur** : snuggle up against — **pression** [presjɔ̃] nf : pressure

prestance [prɛstɑ̃s] nf : (imposing) presence

prestation [prɛstasjɔ̃] nf : benefit, allowance — **prestataire** [prɛstatɛr] nm : recipient

prestidigitateur, -trice [prɛstidiʒitatœr, -tris] n : magician, conjurer

prestige [prɛstiʒ] nm : prestige — **prestigieux, -gieuse** [prɛstiʒjø, -ʒjøz] adj : prestigious

présumer [prezyme] vt : presume, suppose — vi ~ **de** : overestimate, overrate

prêt[1]**, prête** [prɛ, prɛt] adj 1 : ready, prepared 2 DISPOSÉ : willing

prêt[2] nm : loan

prêt–à–porter [prɛtapɔrte] nm, pl **prêts–à–porter** : ready-to-wear (clothing)

prétendre [pretɑ̃dr] {63} vt 1 : claim, maintain 2 VOULOIR : intend — **prétendant, -dante** [pretɑ̃dɑ̃, -dɑ̃t] n : pretender (to a throne) — **prétendant** nm : suitor — **prétendu, -due** [pretɑ̃dy] adj : so-called, alleged

prétention [pretɑ̃sjɔ̃] nf : pretentiousness — **prétentieux, -tieuse** [pretɑ̃sjø, -sjøz] adj : pretentious

prêter [prete] vt 1 : lend 2 ~ **à** : attribute to 3 ~ **attention** : pay attention 4 ~ **l'oreille** : listen — vi ~ **à** : give rise to, cause — **se prêter** vr ~ **à** : lend itself to, suit — **prêteur, -teuse** [prɛtœr, -tøz] n **prêteur sur gages** : pawnbroker

prétexte [pretɛkst] nm : pretext, excuse — **prétexter** [pretɛkste] vt : use as an excuse

prêtre [prɛtr] nm : priest

preuve [prœv] nf 1 : proof, evidence 2 **faire ~ de** : show

prévaloir [prevalwar] {71} vi : prevail — **se prévaloir** vr 1 ~ **de** : take advantage of 2 ~ **de** : boast of

prévenant, -nante [prevnɑ̃, -nɑ̃t] adj : considerate, thoughtful

prévenir [prevnir] {92} vt 1 ÉVITER : prevent 2 AVISER : tell, inform 3 AVERTIR : warn 4 ANTICIPER : anticipate — **prévention** [prevɑ̃sjɔ̃] nf : prevention — **prévenu, -nue** [prevny] n : defendant, accused

prévoir [prevwar] {99} vt 1 : predict, anticipate 2 : plan (on), schedule 3 : provide for, allow (for) — **prévisible** [previzibl] adj : foreseeable — **prévision** [previzjɔ̃] nf 1 : prediction 2 ~**s** nfpl 1 : forecast — **prévoyant, -voyante** [prevwajɑ̃, -vwajɑ̃t] adj : provident, farsighted — **prévoyance** [prevwajɑ̃s] nf : foresight

prier [prije] {96} vi : pray — vt 1 ~ **de** : ask to, request to 2 **je vous en prie** : please 3 **je vous en prie** : don't mention it, you're welcome — **prière** [prijɛr] *nf* : prayer

primaire [primɛr] *adj* : primary, elementary

prime[1] [prim] *adj* 1 : early, first 2 **de ∼ abord** : at first

prime[2] *nf* 1 : premium, allowance 2 RÉCOMPENSE : bonus, gift

primer [prime] *vt* : prevail over — *vi* : be of primary importance

primeurs [primœr] *nfpl* : early produce

primevère [primvɛr] *nf* : primrose

primitif, -tive [primitif, -tiv] *adj* : primitive

primordial, -diale [primɔrdjal] *adj, mpl* **-diaux** [-djo] : essential, vital

prince [prɛ̃s] *nm* : prince — **princesse** [prɛ̃sɛs] *nf* : princess

principal, -pale [prɛ̃sipal] *adj, mpl* **-paux** [-po] : main, principal — **principal** *nm* ESSENTIEL : main thing — **principalement** [prɛ̃sipalmɑ̃] *adv* : primarily, mainly

principe [prɛ̃sip] *nm* : principle, rule

printemps [prɛ̃tɑ̃] *nm* : spring

priorité [prijɔrite] *nf* 1 : priority 2 : right-of-way 3 **en ∼** : first

pris[1] [pri] *pp* → **prendre**

pris[2], **prise** [pri, priz] *adj* 1 : taken, sold 2 OCCUPÉ : busy 3 **∼ de** : afflicted with

prise [priz] *nf* 1 : capture, catch 2 : hold, grip 3 *Can* : strike (in baseball) 4 **∼ de courant** : (electrical) outlet 5 **∼ de sang** : blood test

priser [prize] *vt* : prize, value

prison [prizɔ̃] *nf* : prison — **prisonnier, -nière** [prizɔnje, -njɛr] *adj* : captive — **∼** *n* : prisoner

priver [prive] *vt* : deprive — **se priver** *vr* **∼ de** : go without — **privé, -vée** [prive] *adj* : private — **privé** *nm* 1 : private sector 2 **en ∼** : in private

privilégier [privileʒje] {96} *vt* : privilege, favor — **privilège** [privilɛʒ] *nm* : privilege

prix [pri] *nms & pl* 1 : price, cost 2 : prize 3 **à tout ∼** : at all costs

probable [prɔbabl] *adj* : probable, likely — **probabilité** [prɔbabilite] *nf* : probability — **probablement** [prɔbabləmɑ̃] *adv* : probably

problème [prɔblɛm] *nm* : problem

procéder [prɔsede] {87} *vi* 1 : proceed 2 **∼ à** : carry out — **procédé** [prɔsede] *nm* : process, procedure — **procédure** [prɔsedyr] *nf* 1 : procedure 2 : proceedings *pl* (in law)

procès [prɔsɛ] *nm* 1 : lawsuit 2 : (criminal) trial

procession [prɔsesjɔ̃] *nf* : procession

processus [prɔsesys] *nms & pl* : process, system

procès–verbal [prɔsɛvɛrbal] *nm, pl* **procès–verbaux** [-vɛrbo] 1 : minutes *pl* (of a meeting) 2 *France* : (parking) ticket

prochain, -chaine [prɔʃɛ̃, -ʃɛn] *adj* 1 SUIVANT : next, following 2 PROCHE : imminent, forthcoming 3 **à la prochaine!** *fam* : see you!, until next time! — **prochain** *nm* : fellowman — **prochainement** [prɔʃɛnmɑ̃] *adv* : soon, shortly

proche [prɔʃ] *adj* 1 : near(by) 2 : imminent, near 3 **∼ de** : close to — **proches** [prɔʃ] *nmpl* : close relatives

proclamer [prɔklame] *vt* : proclaim, declare — **proclamation** [prɔklamasjɔ̃] *nf* : proclamation, declaration

procuration [prɔkyrasjɔ̃] *nf* : proxy (in an election)

procurer [prɔkyre] *vt* : provide, give — **se procurer** *vr* : get, obtain — **procureur** [prɔkyrœr] *nm or* **∼ général** : prosecutor

prodige [prɔdiʒ] *nm* : prodigy — **prodigieux, -gieuse** [prɔdiʒjø, -ʒjøz] *adj* : prodigious, extraordinary

prodigue [prɔdig] *adj* 1 : extravagant 2 GÉNÉREUX : lavish — **prodiguer** [prɔdige] *vt* : lavish

produire [prɔdɥir] {49} *vt* 1 : produce 2 CAUSER : bring about — **se produire** *vr* 1 : occur, happen 2 : perform (on stage) — **producteur**[prɔdyktœr] *nm* : producer — **production** [prɔdyksjɔ̃] *nf* : production — **produit** [prɔdɥi] *nm* : product

profaner [prɔfane] *vt* : defile, desecrate — **profane** [prɔfan] *adj* : secular — **∼** *nmf* : layperson

proférer [prɔfere] {87} *vt* : utter

professer [prɔfese] *vt* : profess

professeur [prɔfesœr] *nm* 1 : (school)-teacher 2 : professor

profession [prɔfesjɔ̃] *nf* : occupation, trade — **professionnel, -nelle** [prɔfɛsjɔnɛl] *adj & n* : professional

profil [prɔfil] *nm* : profile

profit [prɔfi] *nm* 1 : profit 2 AVANTAGE : benefit — **profiter** [prɔfite] *vi* 1 **∼ à** : be of benefit to 2 **∼ de** : take advantage of

profond, -fonde [prɔfɔ̃, -fɔ̃d] *adj* 1 : deep 2 : profound — **profondément** [prɔfɔ̃demɑ̃] *adv* : profoundly, deeply — **profondeur** [prɔfɔ̃dœr] *nf* : depth

profusion [prɔfyzjɔ̃] *nf* : profusion

progéniture [prɔʒenityr] *nf* : offspring

programme [prɔgram] *nm* 1 : program 2 : plan, schedule 3 : curriculum, syllabus (in academics) — **programmer** [prɔgrame] *vt* 1 : program (a computer) 2 : plan, schedule — **programmeur, -meuse** [prɔgramœr, -møz] *n* : (computer) programmer

progrès [prɔgrɛ] *nm* : progress — **progresser** [prɔgrese] *vi* : make progress — **progressif, -sive** [prɔgresif, -siv] *adj* : progressive — **progressivement** [-sivmɑ̃] *adv* : progressively, gradually

prohiber [prɔibe] *vt* : prohibit — **prohibition** [prɔibisjɔ] *nf* : prohibition

proie [prwa] *nf* : prey

projecteur [prɔʒɛktœr] *nm* 1 : projector 2 : spotlight — **projectile** [prɔʒɛktil] *nm* : missile, projectile — **projection** [prɔʒɛksjɔ̃] *nf* : projection, showing

projeter [prɔʃte] {8} *vt* 1 LANCER : throw 2 : project, show (a film, etc.) 3 : cast, project (light) 4 PRÉVOIR : plan — **projet** [prɔʒɛ] *nm* 1 : plan, project 2 ÉBAUCHE : draft, outline

proliférer [prɔlifere] {87} *vi* : proliferate — **prolifération** [-ferasjɔ̃] *nf* : proliferation — **prolifique** [prɔlifik] *adj* : prolific

prologue [prɔlɔg] *nm* : prologue

prolonger [prɔlɔ̃ʒe] {17} *vt* : prolong, extend — **se prolonger** *vr* : continue — **prolongation** [prɔlɔ̃gasjɔ̃] *nf* : extension (of time) — **prolongement** [prɔlɔ̃ʒmɑ̃] *nm* : extension (of a road, etc.)

promener [prɔmne] {52} *vt* : take for a walk — **se promener** *vr* : go for a walk — **promenade** [prɔmnad] *nf* 1 : walk, stroll 2 : trip, ride (in a car, etc.) 3 : walkway, promenade — **promeneur, -neuse** [prɔmnœr, -nøz] *n* : walker

promettre [prɔmɛtr] {53} *v* : promise — **se promettre** *vr* **∼ de** : resolve to — **promesse** [prɔmɛs] *nf* : promise — **prometteur, -teuse** [prɔmɛtœr, -tøz] *adj* : promising

promontoire [prɔmɔ̃twar] *nm* : headland

promouvoir [prɔmuvwar] {56} *vt* : promote — **promotion** [prɔmosjɔ̃] *nf* : promotion

prompt, prompte [prɔ̃, prɔ̃t] *adj* : prompt, quick

prôner [prone] *vt* : advocate

pronom [prɔnɔ̃] *nm* : pronoun

prononcer [prɔnɔ̃se] {6} *vt* : pronounce — *vi* : hand down a decision (in law) — **se prononcer** *vr* : give one's opinion — **prononciation** [prɔnɔ̃sjasjɔ̃] *nf* : pronunciation

pronostic [prɔnɔstik] *nm* 1 : prognosis 2 PRÉVISION : forecast

propagande [prɔpagɑ̃d] *nf* : propaganda

propager [prɔpaʒe] {17} *vt* : propagate, spread — **se propager** *vr* : spread — **propagation** [prɔpagasjɔ̃] *nf* : propagation

prophète [prɔfɛt] *nm* : prophet — **prophétie** [prɔfesi] *nf* : prophecy — **prophétique** [prɔfetik] *adj* : prophetic — **prophétiser** [prɔfetize] *vt* : prophesy

propice [prɔpis] *adj* : favorable

proportion [prɔpɔrsjɔ̃] *nf* 1 : proportion, ratio 2 **∼s** *nfpl* : dimensions, size — **proportionnel, -nelle** [prɔpɔrsjɔnɛl] *adj* : proportional

proposer [prɔpoze] *vt* 1 : suggest, propose 2 OFFRIR : offer 3 : nominate (for election) — **se proposer** *vr* **∼ de** : intend to — **propos** [prɔpo] *nms & pl* 1 : subject 2 BUT : intention, point 3 **∼** *nmpl* : comments, talk 4 **à ∼** : appropriate 5 **à ∼ de** : regarding, about — **proposition** [prɔpozisjɔ̃] *nf* 1 : suggestion 2 OFFRE : offer, proposal

propre [prɔpr] *adj* 1 : clean, neat 2 : proper, correct (of a word) 3 **∼ à** : characteristic of 4 **∼ à** : suitable for 5 **par sa ∼ faute** : through his own fault — **proprement** [prɔprəmɑ̃] *adv* **à ∼ parler** : strictly speaking — **propreté** [prɔprəte] *nf* : cleanliness, neatness

propriété [prɔprijete] *nf* 1 : property 2 : ownership — **propriétaire** [prɔprijetɛr] *nmf* 1 : owner 2 : landlord, landlady *f*

propulser [prɔpylse] *vt* : propel

prorata [prɔrata] *nms & pl* **au ∼ de** : in proportion to

proscrire [prɔskrir] {33} *vt* 1 INTERDIRE : ban, prohibit 2 BANNIR : banish — **proscrit, -scrite** [prɔskri, -skrit] *n* : outcast

prose [proz] *nf* : prose

prospectus [prɔspɛktys] *nms & pl* : leaflet

prospérer [prɔspere] {87} *vi* : flourish, thrive — **prospérité** [prɔsperite] *nf* : prosperity

prosterner [prɔstɛrne] *v* **se prosterner** *vr* : bow down

prostituée [prɔstitɥe] *nf* : prostitute — **prostitution** [prɔstitysjɔ̃] *nf* : prostitution

prostré, -trée [prɔstre] *adj* : prostrate

protagoniste [prɔtagɔnist] *nmf* : protagonist

protéger [prɔteʒe] {64} *vt* 1 : protect 2 PATRONNER : support — **se protéger** *vr* **∼ de** : protect oneself from — **protecteur, -trice** [prɔtɛktœr, -tris] *adj* : protective — **∼** *n* 1 : protector 2 : patron — **protection** [prɔtɛksjɔ̃] *nf* : protection

protéine [prɔtein] *nf* : protein

protestant, -tante [prɔtɛstɑ̃, -tɑ̃t] *adj & n* : Protestant

protester [prɔteste] *vi* : protest — **protestation** [prɔtɛstasjɔ̃] *nf* : protest

prothèse [prɔtɛz] *nf* 1 : prosthesis 2 **∼ dentaire** : denture

protocole [prɔtɔkɔl] *nm* : protocol

protubérant, -rante [prɔtyberɑ̃, -rɑ̃t] *adj* : protruding — **protubérance** [prɔtyberɑ̃s] *nf* : protuberance

proue [pru] *nf* : prow, bow (of a ship)

prouesse [pruɛs] *nf* : feat

prouver [pruve] *vt* 1 ÉTABLIR : prove 2 MONTRER : show, demonstrate

provenance [prɔvnɑ̃s] *nf* 1 : source, origin 2 **en ∼ de** : from

provenir [prɔvnir] {92} *vi* **∼ de** 1 : come from 2 : result from

proverbe [prɔvɛrb] *nm* : proverb

providence [prɔvidɑ̃s] *nf* : providence

province [prɔvɛ̃s] *nf* : province — **provincial, -ciale** [-vɛ̃sjal] *adj, mpl* **-ciaux** [-sjo] : provincial

proviseur [prɔvizœr] *nm France* : principal (of a school)

provision [prɔvizjɔ̃] *nf* 1 : stock, supply 2 **∼s** *nfpl* : provisions, food

provisoire [prɔvizwar] *adj* : temporary

provoquer [prɔvɔke] *vt* 1 : give rise to 2 DÉFIER : provoke — **provocant, -cante** [prɔvɔkɑ̃, -kɑ̃t] *adj* : provocative — **provocation** [prɔvɔkasjɔ̃] *nf* : provocation

proximité [prɔksimite] *nf* : closeness, proximity

prude [pryd] *nf* : prude

prudent, -dente [prydɑ̃, -dɑ̃t] *adj* : careful, cautious — **prudemment** [prydamɑ̃] *adv* : carefully, cautiously — **prudence** [prydɑ̃s] *nf* : care, caution

prune [pryn] *nf* : plum — **pruneau** [pryno] *nm, pl* **-neaux** : prune

prunelle [prynɛl] *nf* : pupil (of the eye)

psaume [psom] *nm* : psalm

pseudonyme [psødɔnim] *nm* : pseudonym

psychanalyser [psikanalize] *vt* : psychoanalyze — **psychanalyse** [psikanaliz] *nf* : psychoanalysis — **psychanalyste** [-list] *nmf* : psychoanalyst

psychiatrie [psikjatri] *nf* : psychiatry — **psychiatre** [psikjatr] *nmf* : psychiatrist — **psychiatrique** [psikjatrik] *adj* : psychiatric

psychologie [psikɔlɔʒi] *nf* : psychology — **psychologique** [psikɔlɔʒik] *adj* : psychological — **psychologue** [psikɔlɔg] *nmf* : psychologist

puant, puante [pɥɑ̃, -ɑ̃t] *adj* : foul, stinking — **puanteur** [pɥɑ̃tœr] *nf* : stink, stench

puberté [pybɛrte] *nf* : puberty

public, -blique [pyblik] *adj* : public — **public** *nm* 1 : public 2 : audience, spectators *pl*

publication [pyblikasjɔ̃] *nf* : publication

publicité [pyblisite] *nf* 1 : publicity 2 : (television) commercial — **publicitaire** [pyblisitɛr] *adj* : advertising

publier [pyblije] {96} *vt* : publish

puce [pys] *nf* 1 : flea 2 : computer chip

pudeur [pydœr] *nf* : modesty — **pudique** [pydik] *adj* : modest, decent

puer [pɥe] *vi* : smell, stink — *vt* : reek of

puéril, -rile [pɥeril] *adj* : childish

puis [pɥi] *adv* : then, afterwards

puiser [pɥize] *vt* **∼ dans** : draw from, dip into

puisque [pɥiskə] *conj* : since, as, because

puissant, -sante [pɥisɑ̃, -sɑ̃t] *adj* : powerful — **puissance** [pɥisɑ̃s] *nf* : power

puits [pɥi] *nm* 1 : well 2 : (mine) shaft

pull *or* **pull–over** [pyl, pylɔvɛr] *nm France* : pullover sweater

pulpe [pylp] *nf* : pulp

pulsation [pylsasjɔ̃] *nf* BATTEMENT : beat

pulsion [pylsjɔ̃] *nf* : drive, urge

pulvériser [pylverize] *vt* 1 : pulverize 2 VAPORISER : spray

punaise [pynɛz] *nf* 1 : (bed)bug 2 : thumbtack

punch [pɔ̃ʃ] *nm* : punch (drink)

punir [pynir] *vt* : punish — **punition** [pynisjɔ̃] *nf* : punishment

pupille[1] [pypij] *nmf* : ward (of the court)

pupille[2] *nf* : pupil (of the eye)

pupitre [pypitr] *nm* 1 : music stand 2 BUREAU : desk

pur, pure [pyr] *adj* : pure — **pureté** [pyrte] *nf* : purity

purée [pyre] *nf* 1 : puree 2 **∼ de pommes de terre** : mashed potatoes

purgatoire [pyrgatwar] *nm* : purgatory

purger [pyrʒe] {17} *vt* 1 : drain (a radiator, etc.) 2 : rid of, purge 3 : serve (a sentence) — **purge** [pyrʒ] *nf* : purge

purifier [pyrifje] {96} *vt* : purify — **purification** [pyrifikasjɔ̃] *nf* : purification

puritain, -taine [pyritɛ̃, -tɛn] *n* : puritan — **∼** *adj* : puritanical

pur–sang [pyrsɑ̃] *nms & pl* : Thoroughbred

pus [py] *nm* : pus

putride [pytrid] *adj* : rotten

puzzle [pœzl] *nm* : (jigsaw) puzzle

pyjama [piʒama] *nm* : pajamas *pl*

pylône [pilon] *nm* : pylon

pyramide [piramid] *nf* : pyramid

pyromane [pirɔman] *nmf* : arsonist

python [pitɔ̃] *nm* : python

Q

q [ky] *nm* : q, 17th letter of the alphabet

quadriller [kadrije] *vt* : surround, take control of — **quadrillage** [kadrijaʒ] *nm* : crisscross pattern, grid — **quadrillé, -lée** [kadrije] *adj* : squared

quadrupède [k(w)adrypɛd] *nm* : quadruped

quadruple [k(w)adrypl] *adj* : quadruple

quai [kɛ] *nm* 1 : quay, wharf 2 : platform (at a railway station)

qualifier [kalifje] {96} *vt* 1 : qualify 2 DÉCRIRE : describe — **qualification** [kalifikasjɔ̃] *nf* : qualification

qualité [kalite] *nf* 1 : quality, excellence 2 : quality, property 3 **en ∼ de** : in one's role as

quand [kɑ̃] *adv & conj* 1 : when 2 **∼ même** : all the same, even so

quant [kɑ̃] **∼ à** *prep phr* : as for, as to, regarding

quantité [kɑ̃tite] *nf* : quantity

quarantaine [karɑ̃tɛn] *nf* 1 : quarantine 2 **une ∼ de** : about forty

quarante [karɑ̃t] *adj & nms & pl* : forty — **quarantième** [karɑ̃tjɛm] *adj & nmf & nm* : fortieth

quart [kar] *nm* 1 : quarter, fourth 2 **un ∼ d'heure** : fifteen minutes

quartier [kartje] *nm* 1 : piece, segment, quarter 2 : area, district 3 **∼ général** : (military) headquarters

quartz [kwarts] *nm* : quartz

quasi [kazi] *adv* : nearly, almost

quatorze [katɔrz] *adj* 1 : fourteen 2 : fourteenth (in dates) — **∼** *nms & pl* : fourteen — **quatorzième** [katɔrzjɛm] *adj & nmf & nm* : fourteenth

quatre [katr] *adj* 1 : four 2 : fourth (in dates) — **∼** *nms & pl* : four

quatre–vingt–dix [katrəvɛ̃dis] *adj & nms & pl* : ninety

quatre–vingts [katrəvɛ̃] (**quatre-vingt** *with another numeral adjective*) *adj & nms & pl* : eighty

quatrième [katrijɛm] *adj & nmf* : fourth

quatuor [kwatɥɔr] *nm* : quartet

que [kə] *conj* 1 : that 2 **plus ∼ nécessaire** : more than necessary 3 **qu'il fasse soleil ou non** : whether it's sunny or not 4 → **ne** — **∼** *pron* 1 : who, whom, that 2 : which 3 **∼ faire?** : what should we do? — **∼** *adv* : how (much), how (many)

québécois, -coise [kebekwa, -kwaz] *adj* : Quebecer, Quebecois

quel, quelle [kɛl] *adj* 1 : what, which 2 : whatever, whichever, whoever — **∼** *pron* : who, which one

quelconque [kɛlkɔ̃k] *adj* 1 : some sort of, any 2 **un être ∼** : an ordinary person

quelque [kɛlk(ə)] *adj* 1 : a few, several, some 2 **∼ chose** : something 3 **∼ part** : somewhere 4 **∼ peu** : somewhat — **∼** *adv* : about, approximately

quelquefois [kɛlkəfwa] *adv* : sometimes

quelques–uns, quelques–unes [kɛlkəzœ̃, kɛlkəzyn] *pron* : some, a few

quelqu'un [kɛlkœ̃] *pron* 1 : someone, somebody 2 : anyone, anybody 3 **y a-t-il quelqu'un?** : is anybody there?

quémander [kemɑ̃de] *vt* : beg for

qu'en–dira–t–on [kɑ̃diratɔ̃] *nms & pl* : gossip

querelle [kərɛl] *nf* : quarrel — **quereller** [kərele] *v* **se quereller** *vr* : quarrel — **querelleur, -leuse** [kərɛlœr, -løz] *adj* : quarrelsome

question [kɛstjɔ̃] *nf* 1 : question 2 : matter, issue — **questionnaire** [kɛstjɔnɛr] *nm* : questionnaire — **questionner** [kɛstjɔne] *vt* : question

quête [kɛt] *nf* 1 : quest, search 2 : collection (of money) — **quêter** [kete] *vt* : look for, seek — *vi* : take a collection

queue [kø] *nf* 1 : tail 2 : tail end, rear, bottom 3 : handle (of a pot) 4 **∼ de billard** : cue (stick) 5 **∼ de cheval** : ponytail 6 **faire la ∼** : stand in line

qui [ki] *pron* 1 : who, whom 2 : which, that 3 **∼ que** : whoever, whomever

quiconque [kikɔ̃k] *pron* 1 : whoever, whomever 2 : anyone, anybody

quiétude [kjetyd] *nf* : quiet, tranquility

quille [kij] *nf* 1 : keel 2 **∼s** *nfpl* : ninepins

quincaillerie [kɛ̃kajri] *nf* 1 : hardware 2 : hardware store

quinte [kɛ̃t] *nf or* **∼ de toux** : coughing fit

quintuple [kɛ̃typl] *adj* : fivefold

quinzaine [kɛ̃zɛn] *nf* 1 **une ∼ de** : about fifteen 2 **une ∼ de jours** : two weeks

quinze [kɛ̃z] *adj* 1 : fifteen 2 : fifteenth (in dates) — **∼** *nms & pl* : fifteen — **quinzième** [kɛ̃zjɛm] *adj & nmf & nm* : fifteenth

quiproquo [kiprɔko] *nm* : misunderstanding

quittance [kitɑ̃s] *nf* : receipt

quitte [kit] *adj* 1 : even, quits 2 **∼ à** : even if, at the risk of

quitter [kite] *vt* 1 : leave, depart from 2 : take off (a hat, etc.) 3 **ne quittez pas**

: hold the (telephone) line — **se quitter** *vr* : part, separate
qui-vive [kiviv] *nms & pl* **être sur le ~** : be on the alert
quoi [kwa] *pron* **1** : what **2** (*after a pronoun*) : which **3 ~ que** : whatever
quoique [kwakə] *conj* : although, though
quota [kɔta] *nm* : quota
quotidien, -dienne [kɔtidjɛ̃, -djɛn] *adj* **1** : daily **2** : everyday, routine — **quotidien** *nm* **1** : daily (newspaper) **2 au ~** : on a daily basis — **quotidiennement** [kɔtidjɛnmɑ̃] *adv* : daily
quotient [kɔsjɑ̃] *nm* : quotient

R

r [ɛr] *nm* : r, 18th letter of the alphabet
rabâcher [rabaʃe] *vt* : repeat over and over
rabaisser [rabɛse] *vt* **1** : reduce **2** DÉPRÉCIER : belittle, degrade — **rabais** [rabɛ] *nms & pl* RÉDUCTION : reduction, discount
rabat [raba] *nm* : flap
rabat–joie [rabaʒwa] *nms & pl* : killjoy, spoilsport
rabattre [rabatr] {12} *vt* **1** : reduce, diminish **2** : bring down, pull down — **se rabattre** *vr* **1** : fold up, shut **2 ~ sur** : make do with
rabbin [rabɛ̃] *nm* : rabbi
rabot [rabo] *nm* : plane (tool) — **raboter** [rabɔte] *vt* : plane
raboteux, -teuse [rabɔtø, -tøz] *adj* INÉGAL : rough, uneven
rabougri, -grie [rabugri] *adj* **1** : stunted **2** : shriveled (up)
rabrouer [rabrue] *vt* : snub
raccommoder [rakɔmɔde] *vt* : mend, patch up
raccompagner [rakɔ̃paɲe] *vt* : take (someone) back, see home
raccorder [rakɔrde] *vt* : connect, link up — **raccord** [rakɔr] *nm* : link, connection — **raccordement** [rakɔrdəmɑ̃] *nm* : linking, connection
raccourcir [rakursir] *vt* : shorten — *vi* : become shorter, shrink — **raccourci** [rakursi] *nm* **1** : shortcut **2 en ~** : in short, briefly
raccrocher [rakrɔʃe] *vt* **~ le récepteur** : hang up (a telephone receiver) — *vi* : hang up (on s.o.) — **se raccrocher** *vr* **~ à** : hang on to
race [ras] *nf* **1** : (human) race **2** : breed (of animals) **3 de ~** : thoroughbred
racheter [raʃte] {20} *vt* **1** : buy back **2** : buy more of **3** : redeem (in religion) **4** COMPENSER : make up for — **rachat** [raʃa] *nm* : buying back
racial, -ciale [rasjal] *adj, mpl* **-ciaux** [rasjo] : racial
racine [rasin] *nf* : root
racisme [rasism] *nm* : racism — **raciste** [rasist] *adj & nmf* : racist
racler [rakle] *vt* : scrape (off) — **raclée** [rakle] *nf fam* : beating, thrashing
racoler [rakɔle] *vt* : solicit
raconter [rakɔ̃te] *vt* **1** CONTER : tell, relate **2** : say, talk about — **racontars** [rakɔ̃tar] *nmpl* : gossip — **raconteur, -teuse** [rakɔ̃tœr, -tøz] *n* : storyteller
radar [radar] *nm* : radar
rade [rad] *nf* **en ~** : stranded
radeau [rado] *nm, pl* **-deaux** : raft
radiateur [radjatœr] *nm* **1** : radiator **2** : heater
radical, -cale [radikal] *adj, mpl* **-caux** [-ko] : radical — **~** *n* : radical
radier [radje] {96} *vt* : cross off
radieux, -dieuse [radjø, -djøz] *adj* : radiant, dazzling
radin, -dine [radɛ̃] *adj fam* : stingy — **~** *n fam* : cheapskate
radio [radjo] *nf* **1** : radio **2** RADIOGRAPHIE : X ray
radioactif, -tive [radjɔaktif, -tiv] *adj* : radioactive
radiodiffuser [radjɔdifyze] *vt* : broadcast — **radiodiffusion** [radjɔdifyzjɔ̃] *nf* : broadcasting
radiographie [radjɔgrafi] *nf* : X ray — **radiographier** [radjɔgrafje] {96} *vt* : X-ray
radis [radi] *nm* : radish
radoter [radɔte] *vi* : ramble on
radoucir [radusir] *vt* : soften (up) — **se radoucir** *vr* : grow milder
rafale [rafal] *nf* **1** : gust (of wind, etc.) **2** : burst (of gunfire)
raffermir [rafɛrmir] *vt* : firm up, tone up
raffiner [rafine] *vt* : refine — **raffinage** [rafinaʒ] *nm* : refining — **raffiné, -née** [rafine] *adj* : refined — **raffinement** [rafinmɑ̃] *nm* : refinement — **raffinerie** [rafinri] *nf* : refinery
raffoler [rafɔle] *vi* **~ de** : adore, be crazy about
rafistoler [rafistɔle] *vt fam* : patch up, fix up
rafler [rafle] *vt fam* : swipe, steal — **rafle** [rafl] *nf* : (police) raid
rafraîchir [rafrɛʃir] *vt* : refresh, cool — **se rafraîchir** *vr* **1** : get cooler **2** : freshen up — **rafraîchissant, -sante** [rafrɛʃisɑ̃, -sɑ̃t] *adj* : refreshing — **rafraîchissement** [rafrɛʃismɑ̃] *nm* **1** : cooling **2 ~s** *nmpl* : cool drinks, refreshments
rage [raʒ] *nf* **1** : rabies **2** FUREUR : rage — **rager** [raʒe] {17} *vi* : rage, fume
ragot [rago] *nm fam* : gossip
ragoût [ragu] *nm* : ragout, stew
raide [rɛd] *adj* **1** : stiff (of muscles) **2** : tight, taut (of a rope) **3** : steep (of a hill) **4** : straight (of hair) — **~** *adv* : steeply — **raideur** [rɛdœr] *nf* **1** : stiffness **2** : steepness — **raidir** [redir] *vt* : stiffen, tighten — **se raidir** *vr* : tighten, tense up
raie [rɛ] *nf* **1** : stripe **2** : part (in hair)
raifort [rɛfɔr] *nm* : horseradish
rail [raj] *nm* : rail, track
railler [raje] *vt* : make fun of — **raillerie** [rajri] *nf* : mockery — **railleur, -leuse** [rajœr, -jøz] *adj* MOQUEUR : mocking
rainure [rɛnyr] *nf* : groove, slot
raisin [rɛzɛ̃] *nm* **1** : grape **2 ~ de Corinthe** : currant **3 ~ sec** : raisin
raison [rɛzɔ̃] *nf* **1** : reason **2 avoir ~** : be right **3 en ~ de** : because of **4 perdre la ~** : lose one's mind — **raisonnable** [rɛzɔnabl] *adj* : sensible, reasonable — **raisonnement** [rɛzɔnmɑ̃] *nm* **1** : reasoning **2** : argument — **raisonner** [rɛzɔne] *vi* : reason — *vt* : reason with
rajeunir [raʒœnir] *vt* : make look younger — *vi* : look younger
rajouter [raʒute] *vt* **1** : add **2 en ~** : exaggerate — **rajout** [raʒu] *nm* : addition
rajuster [raʒyste] *vt* : (re)adjust
râle [ral] *nm* : groan
ralentir [ralɑ̃tir] *v* : slow down — **ralenti, -tie** [ralɑ̃ti] *adj* : slow — **ralenti** *nm* **1** : slow motion **2** : idling speed (of a car) — **ralentissement** [ralɑ̃tismɑ̃] *nm* : slowing down
râler [rale] *vi* **1** : groan **2** *fam* : grumble
rallier [ralje] {96} *vt* : rally (troops) — **se rallier** *vr* : rally
rallonger [ralɔ̃ʒe] {17} *vt* : lengthen — *vi* : get longer — **rallonge** [ralɔ̃ʒ] *nf* : extension (cord)
rallumer [ralyme] *vt* **1** : turn back on **2** RANIMER : revive
ramasser [ramase] *vt* **1** : pick up, collect **2** CUEILLIR : pick, gather — **se ramasser** *vr* : crouch — **ramassage** [ramasaʒ] *nm* : picking up, collection
rambarde [rɑ̃bard] *nf* : guardrail
rame [ram] *nf* **1** AVIRON : oar **2** : (subway) train **3** : ream (of paper)
rameau [ramo] *nm, pl* **-meaux** : branch, bough
ramener [ramne] {52} *vt* **1** : bring back, take back **2** RÉDUIRE : reduce
ramer [rame] *vi* : row
ramification [ramifikasjɔ̃] *nf* : offshoot
ramollir [ramɔlir] *vt* : soften — **se ramollir** *vr* : soften
ramoner [ramɔne] *vt* : sweep (a chimney), clean out (pipes) — **ramoneur** [ramɔnœr] *nm* : chimney sweep
rampe [rɑ̃p] *nf* **1** : (access) ramp **2** : banister, handrail **3** : footlights *pl* **4 ~ de lancement** : launching pad
ramper [rɑ̃pe] *vi* **1** : crawl, creep **2** S'ABAISSER : grovel
rancart [rɑ̃kar] *nm* **mettre au ~** *fam* : discard, scrap
rance [rɑ̃s] *adj* : rancid — **rancir** [rɑ̃sir] *vi* : turn rancid
rancœur [rɑ̃kœr] *nf* RESSENTIMENT : rancor, resentment
rançon [rɑ̃sɔ̃] *nf* : ransom — **rançonner** [rɑ̃sɔne] *vt* : hold to ransom
rancune [rɑ̃kyn] *nf* **1** : rancor, resentment **2 garder ~ à** : hold a grudge against
randonnée [rɑ̃dɔne] *nf* **1** : ride, trip **2** : walk, hike — **randonneur, -neuse** [rɑ̃dɔnœr, -nøz] *n* : hiker
rang [rɑ̃] *nm* **1** RANGÉE : row **2** : rank (in a hierarchy) — **rangée** [rɑ̃ʒe] *nf* : row, line — **rangement** [rɑ̃ʒmɑ̃] *nm* **1** : tidying up **2** : storage space — **ranger** [rɑ̃ʒe] {17} *vt* **1** : tidy up **2** CLASSER : put in order **3** : put away (objects), park (a vehicle) — **se ranger** *vr* **1** : line up **2** SE GARER : park **3** S'ASSAGIR : settle down **4 ~ à** : go along with
ranimer [ranime] *vt* **1** : revive **2** : rekindle (a fire)
rapace [rapas] *adj* : rapacious — **~** *nm* : bird of prey
rapatrier [rapatrije] {96} *vt* : repatriate, send home
râper [rape] *vt* : grate (cheese, etc.) — **râpe** [rap] *nf* : grater
rapetisser [raptise] *vt* : shorten — *vi* : shrink — **se rapetisser** *vr* : shrink
râpeux, -peuse [rapø, -pøz] *adj* : rough
rapide [rapid] *adj* **1** : quick, rapid **2** : steep — **~** *nm* **1** : rapids *pl* **2** : express train — **rapidement** [rapidmɑ̃] *adv* : rapidly, swiftly — **rapidité** [rapidite] *nf* : rapidity, speed
rapiécer [rapjese] {6} *vt* : patch (up)
rappeler [raple] {8} *vt* **1** : remind **2** : call back — **se rappeler** *vr* : remember, recall — **rappel** [rapɛl] *nm* **1** : reminder **2** : recall
rapporter [rapɔrte] *vt* **1** : bring back, take back **2** : yield (in finance) **3** RELATER : tell, report — *vi* **1** : yield a profit **2** *fam* : tell tales — **se rapporter** *vr* **~ à** : relate to — **rapport** [rapɔr] *nm* **1** : report **2** LIEN : connection **3** RENDEMENT : return, yield **4** PROPORTION : ratio **5 ~s** *nmpl* : relations **6 ~s** *nmpl* : sexual intercourse — **rapporteur, -teuse** [rapɔrtœr, -tøz] *n* : tattletale
rapprocher [raprɔʃe] *vt* **1** : bring closer **2** COMPARER : compare — **se rapprocher** *vr* **1 ~ de** : approach, come closer to **2 ~ de** : resemble — **rapproché, -chée** [raprɔʃe] *adj* : close
raquette [rakɛt] *nf* **1** : (tennis) racket **2** : snowshoe
rare [rar] *adj* **1** : rare, uncommon **2** : infrequent **3** CLAIRSEMÉ : sparse — **rarement** [rarmɑ̃] *adv* : seldom, rarely — **rareté** [rarte] *nf* : rarity, scarcity
ras[ra] *adv* : short — **ras, rase** [ra, raz] *adj* : short (of hair)
raser [raze] {87} *vt* **1** : shave **2** DÉTRUIRE : raze **3** FRÔLER : graze, skim — **se raser** *vr* : shave — **rasage** [razaʒ] *nm* : shaving — **rasoir** [razwar] *nm* : razor
raseur, -seuse [razœr, -zøz] *n fam* : bore
rassasier [rasazje] {96} *vt* : satisfy — **se rassasier** *vr* : eat one's fill
rassembler [rasɑ̃ble] *vt* : gather, collect — **se rassembler** *vr* : gather, assemble — **rassemblement** [rasɑ̃bləmɑ̃] *nm* : gathering, assembly
rasseoir [raswar] {9} *v* **se rasseoir** *vr* : sit down again
rassir [rasir] {72} *vi* : go stale
rassis, -sise [rasi, -siz] *adj* : stale
rassurer [rasyre] *vt* : reassure — **rassurant, -rante** [rasyrɑ̃, -rɑ̃t] *adj* : reassuring
rat [ra] *nm* : rat
ratatiner [ratatine] *v* **se ratatiner** *vr* : shrivel up
rate [rat] *nf* : spleen
râteau [rato] *nm, pl* **-teaux** : rake
rater [rate] *vt* **1** MANQUER : miss **2** : fail (an exam, etc.) — *vi* ÉCHOUER : fail, go wrong
ratifier [ratifje] {96} *vt* : ratify — **ratification** [-tifikasjɔ̃] *nf* : ratification
ration [rasjɔ̃] *nf* : share, ration
rationaliser [rasjɔnalize] *vt* : rationalize — **rationnel, -nelle** [rasjɔnɛl] *adj* : rational
rationner [rasjɔne] *vt* : ration
ratisser [ratise] *vt* : rake
raton [ratɔ̃] *nm* **~ laveur** : raccoon
rattacher [rataʃe] *vt* **1** : tie up again **2** RELIER : link, connect
rattraper [ratrape] *vt* **1** : recapture **2** : catch up with (s.o.) **3 ~ le temps perdu** : make up for lost time
raturer [ratyre] *vt* BIFFER : delete — **rature** [ratyr] *nf* : deletion
rauque [rok] *adj* ENROUÉ : hoarse
ravager [ravaʒe] {17} *vt* : ravage, devastate — **ravages** [ravaʒ] *nmpl* **faire des ~** : wreak havoc
ravaler [ravale] *vt* **1** : restore (a building) **2** : stifle (one's anger)
ravi, -vie [ravi] *adj* ENCHANTÉ : delighted
ravin [ravɛ̃] *nm* : ravine
ravir [ravir] *vt* : delight
raviser [ravise] *v* **se raviser** *vr* : change one's mind
ravisseur, -seuse [ravisœr, -søz] *n* : kidnapper
ravitailler [ravitaje] *vt* **1** : supply (with food) **2** : refuel
raviver [ravive] *vt* : revive
ravoir [ravwar] {73} *vt* : get back
rayer [rɛje] {11} *vt* **1** ÉRAFLER : scratch **2** BARRER : cross out, erase — **rayé, rayée** [rɛje] *adj* : striped
rayon [rɛjɔ̃] *nm* **1** : ray **2** : radius (of a circle) **3** : range, scope **4** ÉTAGÈRE : shelf **5** : department (in a store) **6 ~ de miel** : honeycomb
rayonnant, -nante [rɛjɔnɑ̃, -nɑ̃t] *adj* : radiant
rayonne [rɛjɔn] *nf* : rayon
rayonner [rɛjɔne] *vi* **1** : radiate **2** BRILLER : shine **3** : tour around **4 ~ sur** : exert influence on — **rayonnement** [rɛjɔnmɑ̃] *nm* : radiation
rayure [rɛjyr] *nf* **1** : stripe **2** ÉRAFLURE : scratch
raz–de–marée [radmare] *nms & pl* : tidal wave
réagir [reaʒir] *vi* : react — **réacteur** [reaktœr] *nm* **1** : jet engine **2** : (nuclear) reactor — **réaction** [reaksjɔ̃] *nf* **1** : reaction **2 à ~** : jet-propelled — **réactionnaire** [reaksjɔnɛr] *adj & nmf* : reactionary
réaliser [realize] *vt* **1** : carry out, execute **2** ACCOMPLIR : achieve **3** : direct (a film) **4** : realize (a profit) — **se réaliser** *vr* : materialize, come true — **réalisateur, -trice** [realizatœr, -tris] *n* : director (in movies, television, etc.) — **réalisation** [realizasjɔ̃] *nf* **1** EXÉCUTION : execution, carrying out **2** : accomplishment **3** : production (of a film)
réaliste [realist] *adj* : realistic
réalité [realite] *nf* **1** : reality **2 en ~** : in fact, actually
réanimer [reanime] *vt* : resuscitate
réapparaître [reaparɛtr] {7} *vi* : reappear
rébarbatif, -tive [rebarbatif, -tiv] *adj* : forbidding, daunting
rebâtir [rəbatir] *vt* : rebuild
rebattu, -tue [rəbaty] *adj* : hackneyed
rebelle [rəbɛl] *nmf* : rebel — **~** *adj* : rebellious — **rebeller** [rəbɛle] *v* **se rebeller** *vr* : rebel — **rébellion** [rebɛljɔ̃] *nf* : rebellion
rebondir [rəbɔ̃dir] *vi* **1** : bounce, rebound **2** : start (up) again — **rebond** [rəbɔ̃] *nm* : bounce, rebound
rebord [rəbɔr] *nm* : edge, sill (of a window)
rebours [rəbur] **à ~** *adv phr* : the wrong way
rebrousse–poil [rəbruspwal] **à ~** *adv phr* : the wrong way
rebrousser [rəbruse] *vt* **1** : brush back **2 ~ chemin** : turn back
rebuffade [rəbyfad] *nf* : rebuff, snub
rebut [rəby] *nm* **1** : trash, scrap **2 mettre au ~** : discard — **rebutant, -tante** [rəbytɑ̃, -tɑ̃t] *adj* : repellent, disagreeable — **rebuter** [rəbyte] *vt* : put off, discourage
récalcitrant, -trante [rekalsitrɑ̃, -trɑ̃t] *adj* : stubborn
récapituler [rekapityle] *vt* RÉSUMER : recapitulate, sum up
recel [rəsɛl] *nm* : possession of stolen goods
récemment [resamɑ̃] *adv* DERNIÈREMENT : recently
recensement [rəsɑ̃smɑ̃] *nm* : census
récent, -cente [resɑ̃, -sɑ̃t] *adj* : recent
récépissé [resepise] *nm* : receipt
récepteur [resɛptœr] *nm* : receiver
réception [resɛpsjɔ̃] *nf* : reception — **réceptionniste** [resɛpsjɔnist] *nmf* : receptionist
récession [resesjɔ̃] *nf* : recession
recette [rəsɛt] *nf* **1** : recipe (in cooking) **2** : take, receipts *pl*
recevoir [rəsəvwar] {26} *vt* **1** : receive, get **2** ACCUEILLIR : welcome **3** : see (a client, etc.) **4** : accommodate, hold — **receveur, -veuse** [rəsəvœr, -vøz] *n* **1** *Can* : catcher (in sports) **2 ~ des contributions** : tax collector
rechange [rəʃɑ̃ʒ] *nm* **de ~ 1** : spare, extra **2** : alternative
réchapper [reʃape] *vi* **~ de** : come through, survive
recharger [rəʃarʒe] {17} *vt* **1** : refill **2** : recharge — **recharge** [rəʃarʒ] *nf* **1** : refill **2** : recharging
réchaud [reʃo] *nm* : (portable) stove
réchauffer [reʃofe] *vt* : reheat — **se réchauffer** *vr* : warm up, get warmer
rêche [rɛʃ] *adj* : rough, prickly
rechercher [rəʃɛrʃe] *vt* : search for, seek — **recherche** [rəʃɛrʃ] *nf* **1** : search **2** : (academic) research — **recherché, -chée** [rəʃɛrʃe] *adj* : sought-after, in demand
rechigner [rəʃiɲe] *vi* **1** : grumble **2 ~ à** : balk at
rechute [rəʃyt] *nf* : relapse
récif [resif] *nm* : reef
récipient [resipjɑ̃] *nm* : container
réciproque [resiprɔk] *adj* : reciprocal
réciter [resite] *vt* : recite — **récit** [resi] *nm* : account, story — **récital** [resital] *nm, pl* **-tals** : recital
réclamer [reklame] *vt* **1** : call for, demand **2** REVENDIQUER : claim — **réclamation** [reklamasjɔ̃] *nf* PLAINTE : complaint — **réclame** [reklam] *nf* **1** : advertisement **2** : advertising
reclus, -cluse [rəkly, -klyz] *n* : recluse
recoin [rəkwɛ̃] *nm* : nook, corner
récolte [rekɔlt] *nf* **1** : harvesting **2** : harvest, crop — **récolter** [rekɔlte] *vt* **1** : harvest **2** RAMASSER : gather, collect
recommander [rəkɔmɑ̃de] *vt* **1** : recommend **2** : register (a letter, etc.) — **recommandation** [rəkɔmɑ̃dasjɔ̃] *nf* : recommendation
recommencer [rəkɔmɑ̃se] {6} *v* : begin again
récompenser [rekɔ̃pɑ̃se] *vt* : reward — **récompense** [rekɔ̃pɑ̃s] *nf* : reward
réconcilier [rekɔ̃silje] {96} *vt* : reconcile — **réconciliation** [rekɔ̃siljasjɔ̃] *nf* : reconciliation
reconduire [rəkɔ̃dɥir] {49} *vt* RACCOMPAGNER : see home, accompany
réconforter [rekɔ̃fɔrte] *vt* : comfort — **réconfort** [rekɔ̃fɔr] *nm* : comfort — **réconfortant, -tante** [rekɔ̃fɔrtɑ̃, -tɑ̃t] *adj* : comforting, heartwarming
reconnaître [rəkɔnɛtr] {7} *vt* **1** : recognize **2** ADMETTRE : acknowledge — **reconnaissance** [rəkɔnɛsɑ̃s] *nf* **1** : recognition **2** GRATITUDE : gratitude — **reconnaissable** [rəkɔnɛsabl] *adj* : recognizable — **reconnaissant, -sante** [rəkɔnɛsɑ̃, -sɑ̃t] *adj* : grateful — **reconnu, -nue** [rəkɔny] *adj* : well-known
reconsidérer [rəkɔ̃sidere] {87} *vt* : reconsider

reconstituer [rəkɔ̃stitɥe] *vt* : recreate, reconstruct
reconstruire [rəkɔ̃strɥir] {49} *vt* : reconstruct, rebuild
record [rəkɔr] *nm* : record
recouper [rəkupe] *v* **se recouper** *vr* : tally, match up
recourbé, -bée [rəkurbe] *adj* : curved, hooked
recourir [rəkurir] {23} *vi* **~ à** : resort to — **recours** [rəkur] *nm* : recourse, resort
recouvrer [rəkuvre] *vt* : recover, regain
recouvrir [rəkuvrir] {83} *vt* : cover (up)
récréation [rekreasjɔ̃] *nf* **1** LOISIRS : recreation **2** : recess, break — **récréatif, -tive** [rekreatif, -tiv] *adj* : recreational
recréer [rəkree] {89} *vt* : re-create
récrier [rekrije] {96} *v* **se récrier** *vr* : exclaim
récrimination [rekriminasjɔ̃] *nf* : reproach
récrire [rekrir] {33} *vt* : rewrite
recroqueviller [rəkrɔkvije] *v* **se recroqueviller** *vr* **1** : curl up **2** : shrivel up
recruter [rəkryte] *vt* : recruit — **recrue** [rəkry] *nf* : recruit — **recrutement** [rəkrytmɑ̃] *nm* : recruitment
rectangle [rɛktɑ̃gl] *nm* : rectangle — **rectangulaire** [-tɑ̃gylɛr] *adj* : rectangular
rectifier [rɛktifje] {96} *vt* : rectify, correct — **rectification** [rɛktifikasjɔ̃] *nf* : correction
recto [rɛkto] *nm* : right side (of a page)
rectum [rɛktɔm] *nm* : rectum
reçu, -cue [rəsy] *adj* : accepted, approved — **reçu** *nm* : receipt
recueillir [rəkœjir] {3} *vt* **1** : collect, gather **2** : obtain (information) — **se recueillir** *vr* : meditate — **recueil** [rəkœj] *nm* : collection
reculer [rəkyle] *vt* **1** REPOUSSER : move back, push back **2** DIFFÉRER : postpone — *vi* **1** : move back, back up **2 ~ devant** : shrink from — **recul** [rəkyl] *nm* **1** : recoil (of a fire arm) **2 avec le ~** : with hindsight — **reculons** [rəkylɔ̃] **à ~** *adv phr* : backward
récupérer [rekypere] {87} *vt* **1** : recover, get back **2** : salvage **3** : make up (hours of work, etc.) — *vi* SE RÉTABLIR : recover, recuperate
récurer [rekyre] *vt* : scour
recycler [rəsikle] *vt* **1** : retrain (personnel) **2** : recycle — **se recycler** *vr* : retrain
rédacteur, -trice [redaktœr, -tris] *n* : editor — **rédaction** [redaksjɔ̃] *nf* **1** : writing, editing **2** : editorial staff
reddition [redisjɔ̃] *nf* : surrender
rédemption [redɑ̃psjɔ̃] *nf* : redemption
redevable [rədəvabl] *adj* **être ~ à** : be indebted to — **redevance** [rədəvɑ̃s] *nf* : dues *pl*, fees *pl*
rédiger [rediʒe] {17} *vt* : draw up, write
redire [rədir] {29} *vt* RÉPÉTER : repeat
redondant, -dante [rədɔ̃dɑ̃, -dɑ̃t] *adj* SUPERFLU : redundant
redonner [rədɔne] *vt* **1** RENDRE : give back **2** RÉTABLIR : restore (confidence)
redoubler [rəduble] *vt* **1** DOUBLER : double **2** : repeat (a year in school) **3 ~ ses efforts** : intensify one's efforts
redouter [rədute] *vt* : fear — **redoutable** [rədutabl] *adj* : formidable
redresser [rədrɛse] *vt* **1** : straighten (up) **2** : rectify, redress (wrongs, etc.) — **se redresser** *vr* : straighten up
réduction [redyksjɔ̃] *nf* : reduction
réduire [redɥir] {49} *vt* **1** : reduce **2 ~ en** : crush to — **réduit, -duite** [redɥi, -dɥit] *adj* **1** : reduced (of speed) **2** : small, limited — **réduit** *nm* : recess, nook
rééduquer [reedyke] *vt* : rehabilitate — **rééducation** [reedykasjɔ̃] *nf* : rehabilitation
réel, -elle [reɛl] *adj* : real — **réel** *nm* : reality — **réellement** [reɛlmɑ̃] *adv* : really
refaire [rəfɛr] {42} *vt* : do again, redo — **réfection** [refɛksjɔ̃] *nf* : repair
référence [referɑ̃s] *nf* : reference
référendum [referɛ̃dɔm] *nm* : referendum
référer [refere] {87} *v* **se référer** *vr* **~ à** : refer to
réfléchir [refleʃir] *vt* : reflect — *vi* PENSER : think — **réfléchi, -chie** [refleʃi] *adj* **1** : thoughtful **2** : reflexive (of a verb)
refléter [rəflete] {87} *vt* : reflect, mirror — **reflet** [rəflɛ] *nm* : reflection, image
réflexe [reflɛks] *adj & nm* : reflex
réflexion [reflɛksjɔ̃] *nf* **1** : reflection (of light, etc.) **2** PENSÉE : thought
refluer [rəflye] *vi* **1** : ebb, flow back **2** : surge back (of crowds, etc.) — **reflux** [rəflys] *nm* : ebb
réformer [refɔrme] *vt* : reform — **réformateur, -trice** [refɔrmatœr, -tris] *n* : reformer — **réforme** [refɔrm] *nf* : reform
refouler [rəfule] *vt* **1** : drive back (a crowd) **2 ~ ses larmes** : hold back tears
réfractaire [refraktɛr] *adj* **~ à** : resistant to
refrain [rəfrɛ̃] *nm* : refrain, chorus
refréner [rəfrene] *or* **réfréner** [refrene] {87} *vt* : curb, check
réfrigérer [refriʒere] {87} *vt* : refrigerate — **réfrigérateur** [refriʒeratœr] *nm* : refrigerator
refroidir [rəfrwadir] *v* : cool (down) — **refroidissement** [rəfrwadismɑ̃] *nm* **1** : cooling **2** RHUME : cold, chill
refuge [rəfyʒ] *nm* : refuge — **réfugié, -giée** [refyʒje] *n* : refugee — **réfugier** [refyʒje] {96} *v* **se réfugier** *vr* : take refuge
refuser [rəfyze] *vt* : refuse — **refus** [rəfy] *nm* : refusal
réfuter [refyte] *vt* : refute
regagner [rəgaɲe] *vt* **1** : win back **2 ~ son domicile** : return home
régal [regal] *nm, pl* **-gals** DÉLICE : delight, treat — **régaler** [regale] *vt* : treat — **se régaler** *vr* **1** : enjoy oneself **2 ~ de** : feast on
regard [rəgar] *nm* **1** : look **2 au ~ de** : in regard to — **regarder** [rəgarde] *vt* **1** : look at, watch **2** CONSIDÉRER : consider **3** CONCERNER : concern — *vi* : look — **se regarder** *vr* **1** : look at oneself **2** : look at each other
régénérer [reʒenere] {87} *vt* : regenerate
régie [reʒi] *nf* **1** *France* : public corporation **2** *Can* : provincial public-service agency
régime [reʒim] *nm* **1** : (political) regime **2** : system **3** : cluster, bunch (of bananas) **4 au ~** : on a diet
région [reʒjɔ̃] *nf* : region, area — **régional, -nale** [reʒjɔnal] *adj, mpl* **-naux** [-no] : regional
régir [reʒir] *vt* : govern
registre [rəʒistr] *nm* : register
réglable [reglabl] *adj* **1** : adjustable **2** : payable — **réglage** [reglaʒ] *nm* : adjustment
règle [rɛgl] *nf* **1** : ruler (instrument) **2** LOI : rule **3 ~s** *nfpl* : menstrual period **4 en ~** : in order, valid — **réglé, -glée** [regle] *adj* ORGANISÉ : orderly, organized — **règlement** [rɛgləmɑ̃] *nm* **1** : regulations *pl* **2** RÉSOLUTION : settlement — **réglementation** [rɛgləmɑ̃tasjɔ̃] *nf* : regulation — **régler** [regle] {87} *vt* **1** : adjust, regulate **2** : settle (a dispute)
réglisse [reglis] *nf* : licorice
régner [reɲe] {87} *vi* : reign — **règne** [rɛɲ] *nm* : reign, rule
regorger [rəgɔrʒe] {17} *vi* **~ de** : overflow with
regretter [rəgrɛte] *vt* **1** : regret, be sorry about **2** : miss (s.o.) — **regret** [rəgrɛ] *nm* : regret
régularité [regylarite] *nf* : regularity — **régulier, -lière** [regylje, -ljɛr] *adj* **1** : regular **2** CONSTANT : even, steady
réhabiliter [reabilite] *vt* **1** : rehabilitate **2** RÉNOVER : renovate — **réhabilitation** [reabilitasjɔ̃] *nf* : rehabilitation
rein [rɛ̃] *nm* **1** : kidney **2 ~s** *nmpl* DOS : back
reine [rɛn] *nf* : queen
réinsérer [reɛ̃sere] {87} *vt* : rehabilitate
réitérer [reitere] {87} *vt* : reiterate, repeat
rejeter [rəʒte] {8} *vt* **1** RENVOYER : throw back **2** REFUSER : reject — **rejet** [rəʒɛ] *nm* : rejection
rejoindre [rəʒwɛ̃dr] {50} *vt* **1** RENCONTRER : join, meet **2** RATTRAPER : catch up with **3** REGAGNER : return to — **se rejoindre** *vr* : meet
réjouir [reʒwir] *vt* : delight — **se réjouir** *vr* : rejoice, be delighted — **réjouissance** [reʒwisɑ̃s] *nf* **1** : rejoicing **2 ~s** *nfpl* : festivities — **réjouissant, -sante** [reʒwisɑ̃, -sɑ̃t] *adj* : cheering, delightful
relâcher [rəlaʃe] *vt* **1** DESSERRER : loosen (up), slacken **2** LIBÉRER : release — **se relâcher** *vr* **1** : loosen **2** : become lax — **relâche** [rəlaʃ] *nf* : respite
relais [rəlɛ] *nm* **1** : relay **2 ~ routier** : truck stop
relancer [rəlɑ̃se] {6} *vt* **1** : throw back **2** : revive, boost (the economy, etc.) — **relance** [rəlɑ̃s] *nf* : boost
relatif, -tive [rəlatif, -tiv] *adj* : relative — **relativité** [rəlativite] *nf* : relativity
relation [rəlasjɔ̃] *nf* **1** : connection, relation **2** : relationship **3** CONNAISSANCE : acquaintance **4 ~s** *nfpl* : relations
relaxer [rəlakse] *vt* : relax — **relaxation** [rəlaksasjɔ̃] *nf* : relaxation
relayer [rəleje] {11} *vt* : relieve — **se relayer** *vr* : take turns
reléguer [rəlege] {87} *vt* : relegate
relent [rəlɑ̃] *nm* : stench
relève [rəlɛv] *nf* **1** : relief **2 prendre la ~** : take over
relever [rəlve] {52} *vt* **1** : pick up, raise (up) **2** AUGMENTER : increase **3** RELAYER : relieve **4** : bring out, enhance — **se relever** *vr* : get up (again) — **relevé** [rəlve] *nm* **1** : (bank) statement **2** : reading (of a meter)
relief [rəljɛf] *nm* **1** : relief **2 mettre en ~** : highlight
relier [rəlje] {96} *vt* **1** : link, join **2** : bind (a book)
religion [rəliʒjɔ̃] *nf* : religion — **religieux, -gieuse** [rəliʒjø, -ʒjøz] *adj* : religious — **~** *n* : monk *m*, nun *f*
relique [rəlik] *nf* : relic
reliure [rəljyr] *nf* : binding
reluire [rəlɥir] {49} *vi* BRILLER : glisten, shine — **reluisant, -sante** [rəlɥizɑ̃, -zɑ̃t] *adj* : gleaming
remanier [rəmanje] {96} *vt* : revise, modify
remarquer [rəmarke] *vt* **1** : remark, observe **2** CONSTATER : notice — **remarquable** [rəmarkabl] *adj* : remarkable — **remarque** [rəmark] *nf* : remark
remblai [rɑ̃blɛ] *nm* : embankment
rembobiner [rɑ̃bɔbine] *vt* : rewind
rembourrer [rɑ̃bure] *vt* : pad
rembourser [rɑ̃burse] *vt* **1** : repay (a debt) **2** : refund, reimburse — **remboursement** [rɑ̃bursəmɑ̃] *nm* : refund, reimbursement
remède [rəmɛd] *nm* : remedy, cure — **remédier** [rəmedje] {96} *vi* **~ à** : remedy, cure
remercier [rəmɛrsje] {96} *vt* **1** : thank **2** CONGÉDIER : dismiss, fire — **remerciement** [rəmɛrsimɑ̃] *nm* **1** : thanking **2 ~s** *nmpl* : thanks
remettre [rəmɛtr] {53} *vt* **1** REMPLACER : replace **2** RAJOUTER : add **3** : put back (on) **4** DONNER : deliver, hand over **5** : postpone **6** RECONNAÎTRE : recognize, place — **se remettre** *vr* **1** : go back, get back **2** : put on again **3** : recover, get better **4 ~ à** : begin again **5 ~ de** : get over — **remise** [rəmiz] *nf* **1** : postponement **2** LIVRAISON : delivery **3** : remission (of a debt, etc.) **4** RABAIS : discount **5** : shed — **rémission** [remisjɔ̃] *nf* : remission
remonter [rəmɔ̃te] *vt* **1** : take back up, bring back up, raise up (again) **2** : go back up (the stairs, etc.) **3** : cheer up, invigorate — *vi* **1** : go back up, rise (again) **2 ~ à** : date back to — **remontée** [rəmɔ̃te] *nf* **1** : climb, ascent **2 ~ mécanique** : ski lift — **remonte–pente** [rəmɔ̃tpɑ̃t] *nm, pl* **remonte–pentes** : ski lift
remords [rəmɔr] *nm* : remorse
remorquer [rəmɔrke] *vt* : tow — **remorque** [rəmɔrk] *nf* : trailer — **remorqueuse** [rəmɔrkøz] *nf Can* : tow truck
remous [rəmu] *nm* : (back)wash
remplacer [rɑ̃plase] {6} *vt* : replace — **remplaçant, -çante** [rɑ̃plasɑ̃, -sɑ̃t] *n* : substitute — **remplacement** [rɑ̃plasmɑ̃] *nm* : replacement
remplir [rɑ̃plir] *vt* **1** : fill (up) **2** : fill out (a form, etc.) **3** : carry out, fulfill — **remplissage** [rɑ̃plisaʒ] *nm* : filling, filler
remporter [rɑ̃pɔrte] *vt* **1** REPRENDRE : take back **2** : win (a prize, etc.)
remue–ménage [rəmymenaʒ] *nms & pl* : commotion, fuss
remuer [rəmɥe] *vt* **1** MÉLANGER : stir, mix **2 ~ la queue** : wag its tail — *vi* : fidget, squirm
rémunérer [remynere] {87} *vt* : pay (for) — **rémunération** [remynerasjɔ̃] *nf* : payment
renâcler [rənakle] *vi* **1** : snort **2 ~ à** : balk at
renaître [rənɛtr] {57} *vi* : be reborn — **renaissance** [rənɛsɑ̃s] *nf* : rebirth, revival
renard [rənar] *nm* : fox
renchérir [rɑ̃ʃerir] *vi* **1** : become more expensive **2 ~ sur** : go (one step) further than
rencontrer [rɑ̃kɔ̃tre] *vt* **1** : meet **2** TROUVER : come across, encounter — **se rencontrer** *vr* **1** : meet **2** SE TROUVER : be found — **rencontre** [rɑ̃kɔ̃tr] *nf* **1** : meeting, encounter **2** : match, game
rendement [rɑ̃dmɑ̃] *nm* **1** : output **2** RAPPORT : yield
rendez–vous [rɑ̃devu] *nms & pl* **1** : appointment, meeting **2** : meeting place
rendre [rɑ̃dr] {63} *vt* **1** : give back, return **2** : pronounce (a verdict) **3** EXPRIMER : convey **4 ~ grâces** : give thanks — *vi* VOMIR : vomit — **se rendre** *vr* **1** : surrender **2 ~ à** : go to **3 ~ compte de** : realize, be aware of
rêne [rɛn] *nf* : rein
renfermer [rɑ̃fɛrme] *vt* : contain — **se renfermer** *vr* : withdraw (into oneself) — **renfermé** [rɑ̃fɛrme] *nm* : mustiness
renfler [rɑ̃fle] *v* **se renfler** *vr* : bulge, swell — **renflement** [rɑ̃fləmɑ̃] *nm* : bulge
renforcer [rɑ̃fɔrse] {6} *vt* : reinforce — **renfort** [rɑ̃fɔr] *nm* : reinforcement
renfrogné, -gnée [rɑ̃frɔɲe] *adj* : sullen, scowling
rengaine [rɑ̃gɛn] *nf* **la même ~** : the same old story
renier [rənje] {96} *vt* : deny, disown
renifler [rənifle] *v* : sniff
renne [rɛn] *nm* : reindeer
renom [rənɔ̃] *nm* : renown, fame — **renommé, -mée** [rənɔme] *adj* : renowned — **renommée** *nf* : fame, renown
renoncer [rənɔ̃se] {6} *vi* **~ à** : renounce, give up — **renonciation** [rənɔ̃sjasjɔ̃] *nf* : renunciation
renouer [rənwe] *vt* REPRENDRE : renew, resume
renouveau [rənuvo] *nm, pl* **-veaux** : revival
renouveler [rənuvle] {8} *vt* : renew — **renouvellement** [rənuvɛlmɑ̃] *nm* : renewal
rénover [renɔve] *vt* : renovate — **rénovation** [renɔvasjɔ̃] *nf* : renovation
renseigner [rɑ̃seɲe] *vt* : inform — **se renseigner** *vr* : ask, make inquiries — **renseignement** [rɑ̃sɛɲəmɑ̃] *nm* : information
rentable [rɑ̃tabl] *adj* : profitable
rente [rɑ̃t] *nf* **1** : (private) income **2 ~ viagère** : annuity
rentrer [rɑ̃tre] *vi* **1** : go in, get in **2** : go back in **3** RETOURNER : return — *vt* **1** : bring in, take in **2** : pull in (one's stomach) — **rentrée** [rɑ̃tre] *nf* **1** : return (to work, etc.) **2 ~ scolaire** : start of the new school year
renverser [rɑ̃vɛrse] *vt* **1** : knock down, overturn **2** RÉPANDRE : spill **3** : overthrow (a regime) **4** STUPÉFIER : astonish — **se renverser** *vr* : fall over, overturn — **renversement** [rɑ̃vɛrsəmɑ̃] *nm* : reversal
renvoyer [rɑ̃vwaje] {36} *vt* **1** : send back, throw back **2** CONGÉDIER : dismiss **3** REMETTRE : postpone **4 ~ à** : refer to **5** *Can fam* : throw up — **renvoi** [rɑ̃vwa] *nm* **1** : return (of a package) **2** LICENCIEMENT : dismissal **3** : cross-reference **4** REMISE : postponement **5** : belch, burp
réorganiser [reɔrganize] *vt* : reorganize
repaire [rəpɛr] *nm* : den, lair
répandre [repɑ̃dr] {63} *vt* **1** : spill **2** : shed (blood, tears, etc.) **3** : spread (the news) **4** : give off, emit — **se répandre** *vr* **1** : spill **2** SE PROPAGER : spread — **répandu, -due** [repɑ̃dy] *adj* : widespread
réparer [repare] *vt* **1** : repair **2** : make up for (an error) — **réparation** [reparasjɔ̃] *nf* : repair, repairing
repartir [rəpartir] {82} *vt* : retort — *vi* **1** : leave again **2** : start again
répartir [repartir] *vt* **1** : divide up, distribute **2** : spread (out) — **se répartir** *vr* : divide — **répartition** [repartisjɔ̃] *nf* : distribution
repas [rəpa] *nm* : meal
repasser [rəpase] *vt* **1** : pass again, take again, show again **2** : iron, press **3** : go (back) over — *vi* : pass by again, come again — **repassage** [rəpasaʒ] *nm* : ironing
repentir [rəpɑ̃tir] {82} *v* **se repentir** *vr* : repent — **~** *nm* : repentance
répercuter [repɛrkyte] *v* **se répercuter** *vr* **1** : echo **2 ~ sur** : have repercussions on — **répercussion** [repɛrkysjɔ̃] *nf* : repercussion
repère [rəpɛr] *nm* **1** : line, mark **2 point de ~** : landmark — **repérer** [rəpere] {87} *vt* **1** : mark **2** SITUER : locate — **se repérer** *vr* : find one's way
répertoire [repɛrtwar] *nm* **1** : list, index **2** : repertoire (in theater) **3 ~ d'adresses** : address book **4 ~ téléphonique** : telephone directory
répéter [repete] {87} *vt* **1** : repeat **2** : rehearse (in theater) — **répétitif, -tive** [repetitif, -tiv] *adj* : repetitive, repetitious — **répétition** [repetisjɔ̃] *nf* **1** : repetition **2** : rehearsal
répit [repi] *nm* : respite
replacer [rəplase] {6} *vt* : replace
replier [rəplije] {96} *vt* : fold up, fold over — **se replier** *vr* **1** : fold up **2 ~ sur soi–même** : withdraw into oneself
répliquer [replike] *vt* RÉPONDRE : reply — *vi* **1** : respond **2** RIPOSTER : retort — **réplique** [replik] *nf* **1** : reply **2** : line (in a play) **3** : replica (in art)
répondre [repɔ̃dr] {63} *v* : answer, reply — **répondeur** [repɔ̃dœr] *nm* : answering machine — **réponse** [repɔ̃s] *nf* : answer, response
report [rəpɔr] *nm* RENVOI : postponement
reportage [rəpɔrtaʒ] *nm* : report
reporter[1] [rəpɔrte] *vt* **1** : take back **2** REMETTRE : postpone **3** : carry forward (a calculation, etc.)
reporter[2] [rəpɔrtɛr] *nm* : reporter
reposer [rəpoze] *v* : rest — **se reposer** *vr* **1** : rest **2 ~ sur** : rely on — **repos** [rəpo] *nm* : rest — **reposant, -sante** [rəpozɑ̃, -zɑ̃t] *nm* : restful
repousser [rəpuse] *vi* : grow back — *vt* **1** : push back **2** DÉGOÛTER : disgust **3** : turn down (an offer) **4** REPORTER : postpone — **repoussant, -sante** [rəpusɑ̃, -sɑ̃t] *adj* DÉGOÛTANT : repulsive
reprendre [rəprɑ̃dr] {70} *vt* **1** : take (up) again **2** : take back, return **3** RETROUVER : regain **4** RECOMMENCER : resume **5** : repair, alter (a garment) — *vi* **1** : pick up, improve **2** : resume
représailles [rəprezaj] *nfpl* : reprisals
représenter [rəprezɑ̃te] *vt* **1** : represent **2** JOUER : perform — **représentant, -tante** [rəprezɑ̃tɑ̃, -tɑ̃t] *n* : representative — **représentatif, -tive** [rəprezɑ̃tatif, -tiv] *adj* : representative — **représentation** [rəprezɑ̃tasjɔ̃] *nf* **1** : representation **2** : performance (in theater)
réprimander [reprimɑ̃de] *vt* : reprimand — **réprimande** [reprimɑ̃d] *nf* : reprimand
réprimer [reprime] *vt* : repress, suppress
reprise [rəpriz] *nf* **1** : recapture **2** : resumption **3** : repeat, revival **4** : recovery **5** : trade-in (of goods) **6** : round (in sports) **7** : darn, mend — **repriser** [rəprize] *vt* : darn, mend
reprocher [rəprɔʃe] *vt* **~ à** : reproach — **reproche** [rəprɔʃ] *nm* : reproach
reproduire [rəprɔdɥir] {49} *vt* : reproduce — **se reproduire** *vr* **1** : reproduce **2** SE RÉPÉTER : recur — **reproduction** [rəprɔdyksjɔ̃] *nf* : reproduction

réprouver [repruve] *vt* : condemn

reptile [rɛptil] *nm* : reptile

repu, -pue [rəpy] *adj* : satiated, full

république [repyblik] *nf* : republic — **républicain, -caine** [repyblikɛ̃, -kɛn] *adj & n* : republican

répudier [repydje] {96} *vt* : repudiate

répugner [repyɲe] *vt* : disgust — *vi* ~ **à** : be averse to — **répugnance** [repyɲɑ̃s] *nf* **1** : repugnance **2** : reluctance — **répugnant, -gnante** [repyɲɑ̃, -ɲɑ̃t] *adj* : repugnant

réputation [repytasjɔ̃] *nf* : reputation — **réputé, -tée** [repyte] *adj* : renowned, famous

requérir [rəkerir] {21} *vt* : require

requête [rəkɛt] *nf* : request

requin [rəkɛ̃] *nm* : shark

requis, -quise [rəki, -kiz] *adj* : required

rescapé, -pée [rɛskape] *n* : survivor

rescousse [rɛskus] *nf* : rescue, aid

réseau [rezo] *nm, pl* **-seaux** : network

réserver [rezɛrve] *vt* : reserve — **réservation** [rezɛrvasjɔ̃] *nf* : reservation — **réserve** [rezɛrv] *nf* **1** PROVISION : stock **2** RETENUE : reserve **3** : (Indian) reservation **4** : (game) preserve **5 sous** ~ **de** : subject to — **réservé, -vée** [rezɛrve] *adj* : reserved

réservoir [rezɛrvwar] *nm* **1** : tank **2** : reservoir

résidence [rezidɑ̃s] *nf* : residence — **résident, -dente** [rezidɑ̃, -dɑ̃t] *n* : resident — **résidentiel, -tielle** [rezidɑ̃sjɛl] *adj* : residential — **résider** [rezide] *vi* : reside

résidu [rezidy] *nm* : residue

résigner [reziɲe] *vt* : resign — **se résigner** *vr* ~ **à** : resign oneself to — **résignation** [reziɲasjɔ̃] *nf* : resignation

résilier [rezilje] {96} *vt* : terminate

résine [rezin] *nf* : resin

résister [reziste] *vi* ~ **à** : resist — **résistance** [rezistɑ̃s] *nf* : resistance — **résistant, -tante** [rezistɑ̃, -tɑ̃t] *adj* : tough, durable

résolu, -lue [rezɔly] *adj* : resolute, resolved — **résolution** [rezɔlysjɔ̃] *nf* **1** : resolution **2** DÉTERMINATION : resolve

résonner [rezɔne] *vi* : resound — **résonance** [rezɔnɑ̃s] *nf* : resonance — **résonnant, -nante** [rezɔnɑ̃, -nɑ̃t] *adj* : resonant

résorber [rezɔrbe] *vt* : absorb, reduce

résoudre [rezudr] {74} *vt* : solve, resolve — **se résoudre** *vr* ~ **à** : decide to

respect [rɛspɛ] *nm* : respect — **respectable** [rɛspɛktabl] *adj* : respectable — **respecter** [rɛspɛkte] *vt* : respect

respectif, -tive [rɛspɛktif, -tiv] *adj* : respective

respectueux, -tueuse [rɛspɛktɥø, -tɥøz] *adj* : respectful

respirer [rɛspire] *v* : breathe — **respiration** [rɛspirasjɔ̃] *nf* : breathing

resplendir [rɛsplɑ̃dir] *vi* : shine — **resplendissant, -sante** [rɛsplɑ̃disɑ̃, -sɑ̃t] *adj* : radiant

responsable [rɛspɔ̃sabl] *adj* : responsible — **responsabilité** [rɛspɔ̃sabilite] *nf* **1** : responsibility **2** : liability

resquiller [rɛskije] *vi fam* **1** : sneak in (without paying) **2** : cut in line

ressaisir [rəsezir] *v* **se ressaisir** *vr* : pull oneself together

ressasser [rəsase] *vt* : keep going over

ressembler [rəsɑ̃ble] *vi* ~ **à** : resemble — **se ressembler** *vr* : resemble each other, look alike — **ressemblance** [rəsɑ̃blɑ̃s] *nf* **1** : resemblance, likeness **2** SIMILITUDE : similarity

ressentir [rəsɑ̃tir] {82} *vt* : feel — **se ressentir** *vr* : feel the effects of — **ressentiment** [rəsɑ̃timɑ̃] *nm* : resentment

resserrer [rəsere] *vt* : tighten (a knot, etc.) — **se resserrer** *vr* **1** : tighten (up) **2** : narrow

ressortir [rəsɔrtir] {82} *vt* : take out again, bring out again — *vi* **1** : go out again **2** : stand out — *v impers* : emerge, be evident — **ressort** [rəsɔr] *nm* **1** : spring (of a mattress, etc.) **2** : impulse, motivation **3 en dernier** ~ : as a last resort — **ressortissant, -sante** [rəsɔrtisɑ̃, -sɑ̃t] *n* : national

ressource [rəsurs] *nf* : resource

ressusciter [resysite] *vt* : resuscitate — *vi* : come back to life, revive

restant, -tante [rɛstɑ̃, -tɑ̃t] *adj* : remaining — **restant** *nm* : remainder

restaurant [rɛstɔrɑ̃] *nm* : restaurant

restaurer [rɛstɔre] *vt* : restore

rester [rɛste] *vi* **1** : stay, remain **2** : be left — *v impers* **il reste** : there remains — **reste** [rɛst] *nm* **1** : remainder, rest **2 au** ~ *or* **du** ~ : besides, moreover **3** ~**s** *nmpl* : leftovers **4** ~**s** *nmpl* : remains

restituer [rɛstitɥe] *vt* **1** : restore, return **2** : reproduce (sound, etc.)

restreindre [rɛstrɛ̃dr] {37} *vt* : restrict

restrictif, -tive [rɛstriktif, -tiv] *adj* : restrictive — **restriction** [rɛstriksjɔ̃] *nf* : restriction

résultat [rezylta] *nm* : result — **résulter** [rezylte] {75} *vi* ~ **de** : result from — *v impers* **il résulte** : it follows

résumer [rezyme] *vt* : summarize, sum up — **résumé** [rezyme] *nm* **1** : summary **2 en** ~ : in short

résurrection [rezyrɛksjɔ̃] *nf* : resurrection

rétablir [retablir] *vt* : restore — **se rétablir** *vr* **1** : be restored **2** GUÉRIR : recover — **rétablissement** [retablismɑ̃] *nm* **1** : restoration **2** GUÉRISON : recovery

retarder [rətarde] *vt* **1** : delay **2** REPORTER : postpone **3** : set back (a clock, etc.) — *vi* : be slow — **retard** [rətar] *nm* **1** : lateness, delay **2** : backwardness — **retardataire** [rətardatɛr] *nmf* : latecomer

retenir [rətənir] {92} *vt* **1** : hold back, stop **2** RETARDER : keep, detain **3** GARDER : retain **4** RÉSERVER : reserve, book **5** SE RAPPELER : remember **6** : carry (in mathematics) — **se retenir** *vr* **1** : restrain oneself **2** ~ **à** : hold on to

retentir [rətɑ̃tir] *vi* : ring, resound — **retentissant, -sante** [rətɑ̃tisɑ̃, -sɑ̃t] *adj* : resounding — **retentissement** [rətɑ̃tismɑ̃] *nm* : effect, impact

retenue [rətəny] *nf* **1** : deduction **2** : detention (in school) **3** RÉSERVE : reserve, restraint

réticent, -cente [retisɑ̃, -sɑ̃t] *adj* : reticent, reluctant — **réticence** [-tisɑ̃s] *nf* : reticence, reluctance

rétine [retin] *nf* : retina

retiré, -rée [rətire] *adj* : remote, secluded

retirer [rətire] *vt* **1** : take off (clothing, etc.) **2** : take away, remove **3** : withdraw (money, support, etc.) **4** : collect (baggage, etc.) **5** *Can* : retire, put out (in baseball) — **se retirer** *vr* : withdraw, retreat

retomber [rətɔ̃be] *vi* : fall again, fall back — **retombées** [rətɔ̃be] *nfpl* : repercussions, consequences

rétorquer [retɔrke] *vt* : retort

rétorsion [retɔrsjɔ̃] *nf* : retaliation

retoucher [rətuʃe] *vt* **1** : touch up **2** : alter (a dress, etc.) — **retouche** [rətuʃ] *nf* **1** : touching up **2** : alteration

retour [rətur] *nm* **1** : return **2 de** ~ : back

retourner [rəturne] *vt* **1** : turn over **2** : return (a compliment, etc.) — *vi* REVENIR : return — **se retourner** *vr* **1** : turn around **2** : overturn (of a boat, etc.) **3** ~ **contre** : turn against

retrait [rətrɛ] *nm* **1** : withdrawal **2 en** ~ : set back **3** *Can* : out (in baseball)

retraite [rətrɛt] *nf* **1** : retirement **2** : retreat (in religion, etc.) **3** PENSION : pension

retransmettre [rətrɑ̃smɛtr] {53} *vt* : broadcast — **retransmission** [rətrɑ̃smisjɔ̃] *nf* : broadcast

rétrécir [retresir] *vi* : shrink

rétribuer [retribɥe] *vt* : pay — **rétribution** [retribysjɔ̃] *nf* RÉMUNÉRATION : payment

rétroactif, -tive [retrɔaktif, -tiv] *adj* : retroactive

rétrograder [retrɔgrade] *vt* : demote — *vi* : downshift (of a gear)

retrousser [rətruse] *vt* : turn up, roll up

retrouvailles [rətruvaj] *nfpl* : reunion

retrouver [rətruve] *vt* **1** : find (again) **2** REVOIR : see again **3** SE RAPPELER : remember — **se retrouver** *vr* **1** : meet again **2** : find one's way

rétroviseur [retrɔvizœr] *nm* : rearview mirror

réunir [reynir] *vt* RASSEMBLER : gather, collect — **se réunir** *vr* : meet — **réunion** [reynjɔ̃] *nf* : meeting

réussir [reysir] *vi* : succeed — *vt* **1** : make a success of **2** : pass (an exam) — **réussi, -sie** [reysi] *adj* : successful — **réussite** [reysit] *nf* : success

revanche [rəvɑ̃ʃ] *nf* **1** : revenge **2 en** ~ : on the other hand

rêve [rɛv] *nm* : dream

réveiller [reveje] *vt* **1** : wake up **2** : awaken — **se réveiller** *vr* : wake up — **réveil** [revɛj] *nm* **1** : waking up, awakening **2** : alarm clock — **réveille–matin** [revɛjmatɛ̃] *nms & pl* : alarm clock

révéler [revele] {87} *vt* **1** : reveal **2** INDIQUER : show — **se révéler** *vr* : prove to be —**révélation** [revelasjɔ̃] *nf* : revelation

revendiquer [rəvɑ̃dike] *vt* **1** : claim **2** EXIGER : demand — **revendication** [rəvɑ̃dikasjɔ̃] *nf* : claim

revendre [rəvɑ̃dr] {63} *vt* : sell

revenir [rəvnir] {92} *vi* **1** : come back, return **2** ~ **à** : return to, go back to **3** ~ **à** : come down to, amount to **4** ~ **de** : get over

revente [rəvɑ̃t] *nf* : resale

revenu [rəvəny] *nm* : revenue, income

rêver [reve] *v* : dream

réverbère [revɛrbɛr] *nm* : streetlight

révérence [reverɑ̃s] *nf* **1** VÉNÉRATION : reverence **2** : bow, curtsy

révérend, -rende [reverɑ̃, -rɑ̃d] *adj* : reverend

rêverie [rɛvri] *nf* : daydreaming

revers [rəvɛr] *nm* **1** ENVERS : back, reverse **2** : lapel (of a jacket), cuff (of trousers) **3** : backhand (in tennis) **4** ÉCHEC : setback

réversible [reversibl] *adj* : reversible

revêtement [rəvɛtmɑ̃] *nm* **1** : facing (in construction) **2** : surface (of a road)

rêveur, -veuse [rɛvœr, -vøz] *adj* : dreamy — ~ *n* : dreamer

revirement [rəvirmɑ̃] *nm* : reversal, turnabout

réviser [revize] *vt* **1** : revise, review **2** : overhaul (a vehicle) — **révision** [revizjɔ̃] *nf* **1** : review, revision **2** : service (of a vehicle)

révocation [revɔkasjɔ̃] *nf* **1** : dismissal **2** : repeal

revoir [rəvwar] {99} *vt* **1** : see again **2** RÉVISER : review — **se revoir** *vr* : meet (each other) again — ~ *nm* **au** ~ : goodbye

révolter [revɔlte] *vt* : revolt, outrage — **se révolter** *vr* : rebel — **révolte** [revɔlt] *nf* : revolt

révolu, -lue [revɔly] *adj* : past

révolution [revɔlysjɔ̃] *nf* : revolution — **révolutionnaire** [revɔlysjɔnɛr] *adj & nmf* : revolutionary — **révolutionner** [revɔlysjɔne] *vt* : revolutionize

revolver [revɔlvɛr] *nm* : revolver

révoquer [revɔke] *vt* **1** : dismiss **2** : revoke (a privilege, etc.)

revue [rəvy] *nf* **1** : magazine **2 passer en** ~ : go over

rez–de–chaussée [redʃose] *nms & pl* : first floor, ground floor

rhabiller [rabije] *v* **se rhabiller** *vr* : get dressed again

rhétorique [retɔrik] *adj* : rhetorical — ~ *nf* : rhetoric

rhinocéros [rinɔserɔs] *nm* : rhinoceros

rhubarbe [rybarb] *nf* : rhubarb

rhum [rɔm] *nm* : rum

rhumatisme [rymatism] *nm* : rheumatism

rhume [rym] *nm* : cold

ricaner [rikane] *vi* : snicker, giggle

riche [riʃ] *adj* : rich — ~ *nmf* : rich person — **richesse** [riʃɛs] *nf* **1** : wealth **2** : richness

ricocher [rikɔʃe] *vi* : ricochet — **ricochet** [rikɔʃɛ] *nm* : ricochet

ride [rid] *nf* **1** : wrinkle **2** : ripple (on water)

rideau [rido] *nm, pl* **-deaux** : curtain

rider [ride] *vt* **1** : wrinkle **2** : ripple (water)

ridicule [ridikyl] *adj* ABSURDE : ridiculous — ~ *nm* : ridicule — **ridiculiser** [ridikylize] *vt* : ridicule

rien [rjɛ̃] *pron* **1** : nothing **2** : anything **3 de** ~ : don't mention it, you're welcome **4** ~ **que** : only, just — ~ *nm* : trifle

rigide [riʒid] *adj* **1** : rigid **2** RIGOUREUX : strict — **rigidité** [riʒidite] *nf* : rigidity

rigoler [rigɔle] *vi fam* **1** : have fun **2** PLAISANTER : laugh, joke — **rigolo, -lote** [rigɔlo, -lɔt] *adj fam* : funny, comical

rigueur [rigœr] *nf* **1** SÉVÉRITÉ : rigor, harshness **2** : precision **3 à la** ~ : if absolutely necessary **4 de** ~ : obligatory — **rigoureux, -reuse** [rigurø, -røz] *adj* **1** : rigorous **2** : harsh (of climate)

rimer [rime] *vi* : rhyme — **rime** [rim] *nf* : rhyme

rincer [rɛ̃se] {6} *vt* : rinse — **rinçage** [rɛ̃saʒ] *nm* : rinsing, rinse

riposte [ripɔst] *nf* **1** RÉPLIQUE : retort **2** CONTRE-ATTAQUE : counterattack — **riposter** [ripɔste] *vt* : retort — *vi* : counter, retaliate

rire [rir] {76} *vi* **1** : laugh **2** S'AMUSER : joke, have fun **3** ~ **de** : mock, make fun of — ~ *nm* : laugh, laughter

risque [risk] *nm* : risk — **risqué, -quée** [riske] *adj* : risky — **risquer** [riske] *vt* **1** : risk **2 ça risque d'arriver** : it may very well happen — **se risquer** *vr* : venture

rissoler [risɔle] *v* : brown (in cooking)

ristourne [risturn] *nf* REMISE : discount

rite [rit] *nm* : rite, ritual — **rituel, -tuelle** [ritɥɛl] *adj* : ritual — **rituel** *nm* : rite, ritual

rivage [rivaʒ] *nm* : shore

rival, -vale [rival] *adj & n, mpl* **-vaux** [rivo] : rival — **rivaliser** [rivalize] *vi* ~ **avec** : compete with, rival — **rivalité** [rivalite] *nf* : rivalry

rive [riv] *nf* : bank, shore

river [rive] *vt* : rivet

riverain, -raine [rivrɛ̃, -rɛn] *n* : resident (on a street)

rivet [rivɛ] *nm* : rivet

rivière [rivjɛr] *nf* : river

rixe [riks] *nf* BAGARRE : brawl, fight

riz [ri] *nm* : rice — **rizière** [rizjɛr] *nf* : (rice) paddy

robe [rɔb] *nf* **1** : dress **2** PELAGE : coat **3** ~ **de mariée** : wedding gown **4** ~ **de nuit** *Can* : nightgown

robinet [rɔbinɛ] *nm* : faucet

robot [rɔbo] *nm* : robot

robuste [rɔbyst] *adj* : robust

roc [rɔk] *nm* : rock — **roche** [rɔʃ] *nf* : rock — **rocher** [rɔʃe] *nm* : rock — **rocheux, -cheuse** [rɔʃø, -ʃøz] *adj* : rocky

roder [rɔde] *vt* **1** : break in (a vehicle) **2** *fam* : polish up (a performance, etc.)

rôder [rode] *vi* **1** : prowl **2** ERRER : wander about — **rôdeur, -deuse** [rodœr, -døz] *n* : prowler

rogne [rɔɲ] *nf fam* : anger

rognon [rɔɲɔ̃] *nm* : kidney (in cooking)

roi [rwa] *nm* : king

rôle [rol] *nm* : role, part

roman [rɔmɑ̃] *nm* : novel — **romancier, -cière** [rɔmɑ̃sje, -sjɛr] *n* : novelist

romantique [rɔmɑ̃tik] *adj* : romantic

rompre [rɔ̃pr] {77} *vt* : break (off) — *vi* : break up

ronce [rɔ̃s] *nf* : bramble

rond, ronde [rɔ̃, rɔ̃d] *adj* : round — **rond** *nm* **1** : circle, ring **2** : (round) slice **3** *Can* : burner (of a stove) — **ronde** *nf* : rounds *pl*, patrol

rondelet, -lette [rɔ̃dlɛ, -lɛt] *adj fam* : plump

rondelle [rɔ̃dɛl] *nf* **1** : washer **2** TRANCHE : slice **3** *Can* : (hockey) puck

rondeur [rɔ̃dœr] *nf* : roundness

rondin [rɔ̃dɛ̃] *nm* : log

rond–point [rɔ̃pwɛ̃] *nm, pl* **ronds–points** : traffic circle, rotary

ronfler [rɔ̃fle] *vi* : snore — **ronflement** [rɔ̃fləmɑ̃] *nm* : snore, snoring

ronger [rɔ̃ʒe] {17} *vt* **1** : gnaw, nibble **2** : eat away at — **se ronger** *vr* ~ **les ongles** : bite one's nails — **rongeur** [rɔ̃ʒœr] *nm* : rodent

ronronner [rɔ̃rɔne] *vi* **1** : purr **2** : hum (of an engine, etc.)

rosbif [rɔzbif] *nm* : roast beef

rose [roz] *nf* : rose — ~ *adj & nm* : rose, pink (color) — **rosé, -sée** [roze] *adj* : rosy, pinkish

roseau [rozo] *nm, pl* **-seaux** : reed

rosée [roze] *nf* : dew

rosier [rozje] *nm* : rosebush

rosser [rɔse] *vt* : beat, thrash

rossignol [rɔsiɲɔl] *nm* : nightingale

rotatif, -tive [rɔtatif, -tiv] *adj* : rotary — **rotation** [rɔtasjɔ̃] *nf* : rotation

roter [rɔte] *vi fam* : burp, belch

rôti [roti] *nm* : roast (meat)

rotin [rɔtɛ̃] *nm* : rattan

rôtir [rotir] *v* : roast — **rôtissoire** [rotiswar] *nf* : rotisserie

rotule [rɔtyl] *nf* : kneecap

rouage [rwaʒ] *nm* **1** : cogwheel **2** ~**s** *nmpl* : workings

roucouler [rukule] *vi* : coo

roue [ru] *nf* **1** : wheel **2 grande** ~ : Ferris wheel

rouer [rwe] *vt* ~ **de coups** : thrash, beat

rouet [rwɛ] *nm* : spinning wheel

rouge [ruʒ] *adj* : red — ~ *n* **1** : red **2** ~ **à lèvres** : lipstick — **rougeâtre** [ruʒatr] *adj* : reddish — **rougeaud, -geaude** [ruʒo, -ʒod] *adj* : ruddy

rouge–gorge [ruʒgɔrʒ] *nm, pl* **rouges–gorges** : robin

rougeole [ruʒɔl] *nf* : measles

rougeoyer [ruʒwaje] {58} *vi* : turn red, glow

rougeur [ruʒœr] *nf* **1** : redness **2** ~**s** *nfpl* : red blotches (on skin)

rougir [ruʒir] *vt* : make red — *vi* **1** : redden, turn red **2** : blush (with shame, etc.)

rouille [ruj] *nf* : rust — **rouillé, -lée** [ruje] *adj* : rusty — **rouiller** [ruje] *v* : rust

rouler [rule] *vt* : roll (up) — *vi* **1** : roll **2** : go, run (of a car) **3** CONDUIRE : drive — **roulant, -lante** [rulɑ̃, -lɑ̃t] *adj* : on wheels — **rouleau** [rulo] *nm, pl* **-leaux 1** : roller **2** : roll (of paper) — **roulement** [rulmɑ̃] *nm* **1** : roll, rolling **2** : rumble (of thunder) **3** : turnover (in finance) **4** ~ **à billes** : ball bearing **5** ~ **de tambour** : drum roll

roulette [rulɛt] *nf* : roulette

roulotte [rulɔt] *nf Can* : trailer, camper

rouspéter [ruspete] {87} *vi fam* RONCHONNER : grumble — **rouspéteur, -teuse** [ruspetœr, -tøz] *n* : grouch

roussir [rusir] *vt* : scorch, singe

route [rut] *nf* **1** : road **2** : route, highway **3** CHEMIN : way, path **4 bonne** ~ ! : have a good trip! **5 se mettre en** ~ : set out, get going

routier, -tière [rutje, -tjɛr] *adj* : road — **routier** *nm* **1** : truck driver **2** : truck stop

routine [rutin] *nf* : routine — **routinier, -nière** [rutinje, -njɛr] *adj* : routine

roux, rousse [ru, rus] *adj* : russet, red — ~ *n* : redhead

royal, royale [rwajal] *adj, mpl* **royaux** [rwajo] : royal, regal — **royaume** [rwajom] *nm* : kingdom, realm — **royauté** [rwajɔte] *nf* : royalty

ruban [rybɑ̃] *nm* **1** : ribbon **2** ~ **adhésif** : adhesive tape

rubéole [rybeɔl] *nf* : German measles

rubis [rybi] *nms & pl* : ruby

rubrique [rybrik] *nf* **1** : column (in a newspaper) **2** : heading

ruche [ryʃ] *nf* : hive, beehive

rude [ryd] *adj* **1** : rough (of a surface, etc.) **2** PÉNIBLE : hard, tough **3** : severe, harsh (of winter) — **rudement** [rydmɑ̃] *adv* **1** : roughly, harshly **2** *fam* DRÔLEMENT : awfully, terribly

rudimentaire [rydimɑ̃tɛr] *adj* : rudimentary — **rudiments** [rydimɑ̃] *nmpl* : rudiments

rue [ry] *nf* : street

ruée [rɥe] *nf* : rush

ruelle [rɥɛl] *nf* : alley(way)

ruer [rɥe] *vi* : buck (of a horse) — **se ruer** *vr* **1** ~ **sur** : fling oneself at **2** ~ **vers** : rush toward

rugir [ryʒir] *vt* : bellow out — *vi* : roar — **rugissement** [ryʒismɑ̃] *nm* **1** : roar **2** : howling

ruine [rɥin] *nf* **1** : ruin **2 tomber en** ~

: fall into ruin — **ruiner** [rɥine] *vt* 1 : ruin 2 DÉTRUIRE : wreck
ruisseau [rɥiso] *nm, pl* **-seaux** : stream, creek
ruisseler [rɥisle] {8} *vi* : stream, flood
rumeur [rymœr] *nf* : rumor
ruminer [rymine] *vt* : ponder — *vi* : brood
rupture [ryptyr] *nf* 1 : break, breaking 2 : breakup (of a relationship) 3 : breach (of contract)
rural, -rale [ryral] *adj, mpl* **-raux** [ryro] : rural
ruse [ryz] *nf* 1 : trick 2 : cunning — **rusé, -sée** [ryze] *adj* MALIN : cunning
russe [rys] *adj* : Russian — ~ *nm* : Russian (language)
rustique [rystik] *adj* : rustic
rythme [ritm] *nm* 1 : rhythm, beat 2 : rate, pace — **rythmique** [ritmik] *adj* : rhythmic, rhythmical

S

s [ɛs] *nm* : s, 19th letter of the alphabet
sa → **son**
sabbat [saba] *nm* : Sabbath
sable [sabl] *nm* 1 : sand 2 **~s mouvants** : quicksand — **sablé** [sable] *nm* : shortbread (cookie) — **sabler** [sable] *vt* : sand — **sablonneux, -neuse** [sablɔnø, -nøz] *adj* : sandy
saborder [sabɔrde] *vt* : scuttle (a ship)
sabot [sabo] *nm* 1 : clog, wooden shoe 2 : hoof
saboter [sabɔte] *vt* 1 : sabotage 2 : botch up — **sabotage** [sabɔtaʒ] *nm* : sabotage — **saboteur, -teuse** [sabɔtœr, -tøz] *n* : saboteur
sabre [sabr] *nm* : saber
sac [sak] *nm* 1 : sack, bag 2 **~ à dos** : backpack, knapsack 3 **~ à main** : handbag, purse
saccade [sakad] *nf* : jerk, jolt — **saccadé, -dée** [sakade] *adj* : jerky
saccager [sakaʒe] {17} *vt* 1 : sack 2 DÉVASTER : devastate, wreck
sacerdoce [sasɛrdɔs] *nm* 1 : priesthood 2 : vocation
sachet [saʃɛ] *nm* 1 : packet, small bag 2 : sachet
sacoche [sakɔʃ] *nf* : bag, satchel
sacrer [sakre] *vt* 1 : crown 2 : consecrate — **sacre** [sakr] *nm* 1 : coronation 2 : consecration — **sacré, -crée** [sakre] *adj* 1 : sacred, holy 2 *fam* : damned, heck of a — **sacrement** [sakrəmɑ̃] *nm* : sacrament
sacrifier [sakrifje] {96} *vt* : sacrifice — *vi* **~ à** : conform to — **se sacrifier** *vr* : sacrifice oneself — **sacrifice** [sakrifis] *nm* : sacrifice
sacrilège [sakrilɛʒ] *nm* : sacrilege — ~ *adj* : sacrilegious
sadique [sadik] *adj* : sadistic — **sadisme** [sadism] *nm* : sadism
safari [safari] *nm* : safari
sagace [sagas] *adj* : shrewd
sage [saʒ] *adj* 1 : wise 2 DOCILE : well-behaved — ~ *n* : wise person, sage — **sage-femme** [saʒfam] *nf, pl* **sages-femmes** : midwife — **sagesse** [saʒɛs] *nf* : wisdom
saigner [seɲe] *v* : bleed — **saignant, -gnante** [seɲɑ̃, -ɲɑ̃t] *adj* : rare, undercooked — **saignement** [seɲmɑ̃] *nm* : bleeding
saillir [sajir] {78} *vi* : project — **saillant, -lante** [sajɑ̃, -jɑ̃t] *adj* 1 : projecting 2 : salient — **saillie** [saji] *nf* 1 : projection 2 **faire ~** : project
sain, saine [sɛ̃, sɛn] *adj* 1 : healthy, sound 2 : wholesome
saindoux [sɛ̃du] *nm* : lard
saint, sainte [sɛ̃, sɛ̃t] *adj* : holy — ~ *n* : saint
saisir [sezir] *vt* 1 : seize, grab 2 COMPRENDRE : grasp 3 IMPRESSIONNER : strike, impress 4 : enter (data) — **se saisir** *vr* **~ de** : seize — **saisie** [sezi] *nf* : seizure (of property) — **saisissant, -sante** [sezisɑ̃, -sɑ̃t] *adj* : striking
saison [sɛzɔ̃] *nf* : season — **saisonnier, -nière** [sɛzɔnje, -njɛr] *adj* : seasonal
salade [salad] *nf* : salad — **saladier** [saladje] *nm* : salad bowl
salaire [salɛr] *nm* : salary, wages — **salarié, -riée** [salarje] *n* : salaried employee
salaud [salo] *nm usu vulgar* : bastard
sale [sal] *adj* : dirty — **saleté** [salte] *nf* 1 : dirt 2 : dirtiness 3 *fam* : dirty trick
saler [sale] *vt* : salt — **salé, -lée** [sale] *adj* 1 : salty 2 : salted 3 *fam* : steep — **salière** [saljɛr] *nf* : saltshaker
salir [salir] *vt* : soil — **se salir** *vr* : get dirty
salive [saliv] *nf* : saliva
salle [sal] *nf* 1 : room 2 : auditorium, hall 3 **~ à manger** : dining room 4 **~ de bains** : bathroom
salon [salɔ̃] *nm* 1 : living room 2 : (beauty) salon 3 EXPOSITION : exhibition, show
salopette [salɔpɛt] *nf* : overalls *pl*
salubre [salybr] *adj* : healthy
saluer [salɥe] *vt* 1 : greet 2 : say goodbye to 3 : salute — **salut** [saly] *nm* 1 : greeting 2 : salute 3 : safety 4 : salvation 5 **~!** : hello!, good-bye! — **salutation** [salytasjɔ̃] *nf* : greeting
samedi [samdi] *nm* : Saturday
sanction [sɑ̃ksjɔ̃] *nf* : sanction — **sanctionner** [sɑ̃ksjɔne] *vt* 1 : sanction 2 : punish
sanctuaire [sɑ̃ktɥɛr] *nm* : sanctuary
sandale [sɑ̃dal] *nf* : sandal
sandwich [sɑ̃dwitʃ] *nm, pl* **-wiches** *or* **-wichs** [-witʃ] : sandwich
sang [sɑ̃] *nm* : blood — **sang-froid** [sɑ̃frwa] *nms & pl* 1 : composure, calm 2 **de ~** : in cold blood — **sanglant, -glante** [sɑ̃glɑ̃, -glɑ̃t] *adj* 1 : bloody 2 : cruel
sangle [sɑ̃gl] *nf* : strap
sanglot [sɑ̃glo] *nm* : sob — **sangloter** [sɑ̃glɔte] *vi* : sob
sangsue [sɑ̃sy] *nf* : leech
sanguin, -guine [sɑ̃gɛ̃, -gin] *adj* 1 : blood 2 : sanguine
sanitaire [sanitɛr] *adj* 1 : sanitary 2 : health — **~s** *nmpl* : bathroom
sans [sɑ̃] *adv & prep* 1 : without 2 **~ que** : without
santé [sɑ̃te] *nf* 1 : health 2 **à votre ~ !** : to your health!, cheers!
saper [sape] *vt* MINER : undermine
sapeur-pompier [sapœrpɔ̃pje] *nm, pl* **sapeurs-pompiers** *France* : firefighter
saphir [safir] *nm* : sapphire
sapin [sapɛ̃] *nm* : fir
sarcastique [sarkastik] *adj* : sarcastic — **sarcasme** [sarkasm] *nm* : sarcasm
sarcler [sarkle] *vt* : weed
sardine [sardin] *nf* : sardine
satellite [satelit] *nm* : satellite
satin [satɛ̃] *nm* : satin
satire [satir] *nf* : satire — **satirique** [satirik] *adj* : satirical
satisfaire [satisfɛr] {42} *vt* : satisfy — *vi* **~ à** : satisfy — **se satisfaire** *vr* **~ de** : be content with — **satisfaction** [satisfaksjɔ̃] *nf* : satisfaction — **satisfaisant, -sante** [satisfəzɑ̃, -zɑ̃t] *adj* 1 : satisfactory 2 : satisfying — **satisfait, -faite** [satisfɛ, -fɛt] *adj* : satisfied
saturer [satyre] *vt* : saturate
Saturne [satyrn] *nf* : Saturn
sauce [sos] *nf* : sauce
saucisse [sosis] *nf* : sausage — **saucisson** [sosisɔ̃] *nm* : sausage, cold cut
sauf, sauve [sof, sov] *adj* : safe — **sauf** *prep* 1 : except (for), apart from 2 **~ si** : unless
sauge [soʒ] *nf* : sage (herb)
saugrenu, -nue [sogrəny] *adj* : preposterous
saule [sol] *nm* : willow
saumon [somɔ̃] *nm* : salmon
sauna [sona] *nm* : sauna
saupoudrer [sopudre] *vt* : sprinkle
saut [so] *nm* 1 : jump, leap 2 **faire un ~ chez qqn** : drop in on s.o. — **sauter** [sote] *vt* 1 : jump over 2 OMETTRE : skip — *vi* 1 BONDIR : jump, leap 2 EXPLOSER : blow up — **sauterelle** [sotrɛl] *nf* : grasshopper — **sauteur, -teuse** [sotœr, -tøz] *n* : jumper — **sautiller** [sotije] *vi* : hop
sauvage [sovaʒ] *adj* 1 CRUEL : savage 2 : wild 3 FAROUCHE : shy — ~ *nmf* : savage — **sauvagerie** [sovaʒri] *nf* 1 : savagery 2 : unsociability
sauvegarde [sovgard] *nf* 1 : safeguard 2 : backup (of a computer file) — **sauvegarder** [sovgarde] *vt* 1 : safeguard 2 : save (a computer file)
sauver [sove] *vt* : save, rescue — **se sauver** *vr* 1 : escape 2 *fam* : leave, rush off — **sauve-qui-peut** [sovkipø] *nms & pl* : stampede, panic — **sauvetage** [sovtaʒ] *nm* : rescue — **sauveteur** [sovtœr] *nm* : rescuer, lifesaver — **sauvette** [sovɛt] **à la ~** *adv phr* : hastily — **sauveur** [sovœr] *nm* : savior
savant, -vante [savɑ̃, -vɑ̃t] *adj* : learned, scholarly — ~ *n* : scholar — **savant** *nm* : scientist
saveur [savœr] *nf* : flavor, savor
savoir [savwar] {79} *vt* 1 : know 2 : be able to, know how to — ~ *nm* 1 : learning, knowledge 2 **à ~** : namely — **savoir-faire** [savwarfɛr] *nms & pl* : know-how, expertise
savon [savɔ̃] *nm* : soap — **savonner** [savɔne] *vt* : soap (up), lather — **savonnette** [savɔnɛt] *nf* : bar of soap — **savonneux, -neuse** [savɔnø, -nøz] *adj* : soapy
savourer [savure] *vt* : savor — **savoureux, -reuse** [savurø, -røz] *adj* : savory, tasty
saxophone [saksɔfɔn] *nm* : saxophone
scandale [skɑ̃dal] *nf* 1 : scandal 2 SCÈNE : scene, row — **scandaleux, -leuse** [skɑ̃dalø, -løz] *adj* : scandalous — **scandaliser** [skɑ̃dalize] *vt* : scandalize
scandinave [skɑ̃dinav] *adj* : Scandinavian
scarabée [skarabe] *nm* : beetle
scarlatine [skarlatin] *nf* : scarlet fever
sceau [so] *nm* 1 : seal 2 : hallmark, stamp
scélérat, -rate [selera, -rat] *n* : villain
sceller [sele] *vt* : seal — **scellé** [sele] *nm* : seal
scène [sɛn] *nf* 1 : scene 2 : stage (in theater) — **scénario** [senarjo] *nm* : scenario
sceptique [sɛptik] *adj* : skeptical — ~ *nmf* : skeptic
schéma [ʃema] *nm* : diagram — **schématique** [ʃematik] *adj* : schematic
schisme [ʃism] *nm* : schism
scie [si] *nf* : saw
sciemment [sjamɑ̃] *adv* : knowingly
science [sjɑ̃s] *nf* 1 : science 2 SAVOIR : learning, knowledge — **scientifique** [sjɑ̃tifik] *adj* : scientific — ~ *nmf* : scientist
scier [sje] {96} *vt* : saw — **scierie** [siri] *nf* : sawmill
scinder [sɛ̃de] *vt* : split, divide — **se scinder** *vr* : be divided, split up
scintiller [sɛ̃tije] *vi* : sparkle — **scintillement** [sɛ̃tijmɑ̃] *nm* : sparkling, twinkling
scission [sisjɔ̃] *nf* : split
scolaire [skɔlɛr] *adj* : school — **scolarité** [skɔlarite] *nf* : schooling
score [skɔr] *nm* : score
scotch [skɔtʃ] *nm* : Scotch whiskey
scrupule [skrypyl] *nm* : scruple — **scrupuleux, -leuse** [skrypylø, -løz] *adj* : scrupulous
scruter [skryte] *vt* : scrutinize — **scrutin** [skrytɛ̃] *nm* 1 : ballot 2 : polls *pl*
sculpter [skylte] *vt* : sculpt, sculpture — **sculpteur** [skyltœr] *nm* : sculptor — **sculpture** [skyltyr] *nf* : sculpture
se [sə] (**s'** *before a vowel or mute h*) *pron* 1 : oneself, himself, herself, themselves, itself 2 : each other, one another
séance [seɑ̃s] *nf* 1 : session, meeting 2 : performance
seau [so] *nm, pl* **seaux** : bucket, pail
sec, sèche [sɛk, sɛʃ] *adj* 1 : dry 2 : dried (of fruit) 3 DUR : harsh, sharp — **sec** [sɛk] *adv* BRUSQUEMENT : abruptly, hard — ~ *nm* 1 : dryness 2 **à ~** : dried up 3 **à ~** *fam* : broke — **sèche-cheveux** [sɛʃʃəvø] *nms & pl* : hairdryer — **sécher** [seʃe] {87} *vt* 1 : dry 2 *France fam* : skip (a class, etc.) — *vi* : dry (up), dry out — **sécheresse** [seʃrɛs] *nf* 1 : drought 2 : dryness — **séchoir** [seʃwar] *nm* : dryer
second, -conde [səgɔ̃, -gɔ̃d] *adj & nmf* : second — **second** *nm* 1 : assistant, helper 2 : third floor — **secondaire** [səgɔ̃dɛr] *adj* : secondary — **seconde** [səgɔ̃d] *nf* : second — **seconder** [səgɔ̃de] *vt* : assist
secouer [səkwe] *vt* 1 : shake (one's head, etc.) 2 : shake off
secourir [səkurir] {23} *vt* 1 : help, aid 2 : rescue — **secouriste** [səkurist] *nmf* : first aid worker — **secours** [səkur] *nms & pl* 1 : help, aid 2 **au ~!** : help! 3 **de ~** : (for) emergency 4 **premiers ~** : first aid 5 **secours** *nmpl* : rescuers
secousse [səkus] *nf* 1 SACCADE : jolt, jerk 2 CHOC : shock 3 : tremor
secret, -crète [səkrɛ, -krɛt] *adj* : secret — **secret** *nm* 1 : secret 2 : secrecy
secrétaire [səkretɛr] *nmf* : secretary — **secrétariat** [səkretarja] *nm* : secretary's office
sécréter [sekrete] {87} *vt* : secrete — **sécrétion** [-resjɔ̃] *nf* : secretion
secte [sɛkt] *nf* : sect
secteur [sɛktœr] *nm* : sector, area
section [sɛksjɔ̃] *nf* : section — **sectionner** [sɛksjɔne] *vt* 1 DIVISER : divide 2 : sever
séculaire [sekylɛr] *adj* : age-old
sécurité [sekyrite] *nf* 1 : security 2 : safety — **sécuriser** [sekyrize] *vt* : reassure
sédatif, -tive [sedatif, -tiv] *adj* : sedative — **sédatif** *nm* : sedative
sédentaire [sedɑ̃tɛr] *adj* : sedentary
sédiment [sedimɑ̃] *nm* : sediment
séduire [sedɥir] {49} *vt* 1 : seduce 2 : charm 3 : appeal to — **séducteur, -trice** [sedyktœr, -tris] *adj* : seductive — ~ *n* : seducer — **séduction** [sedyksjɔ̃] *nf* 1 : seduction 2 : charm, appeal — **séduisant, -sante** [sedɥizɑ̃, -zɑ̃t] *adj* : seductive, attractive
segment [sɛgmɑ̃] *nm* : segment
ségrégation [segregasjɔ̃] *nf* : segregation
seigle [sɛgl] *nm* : rye
seigneur [sɛɲœr] *nm* 1 : lord 2 **le Seigneur** : the Lord
sein [sɛ̃] *nm* 1 : breast, bosom 2 **au ~ de** : within
séisme [seism] *nm* : earthquake
seize [sɛz] *adj* 1 : sixteen 2 : sixteenth (in dates) — ~ *nms & pl* : sixteen — **seizième** [sɛzjɛm] *adj & nmf & nm* : sixteenth
séjour [seʒur] *nm* : stay — **séjourner** [seʒurne] *vi* : stay (at a hotel, etc.)
sel [sɛl] *nm* : salt
sélection [selɛksjɔ̃] *nf* : selection — **sélectionner** [selɛksjɔne] *vt* : select, choose
selle [sɛl] *nf* : saddle
sellette [selɛt] *nf* **être sur la ~** : be in the hot seat
selon [səlɔ̃] *prep* 1 : according to 2 **~ que** : depending on whether
semaine [səmɛn] *nf* : week
sémantique [semɑ̃tik] *adj* : semantic — ~ *nf* : semantics
sembler [sɑ̃ble] *vi* : seem — *v impers* **il semble que** : it seems that — **semblable** [sɑ̃blabl] *adj* 1 : similar, like 2 TEL : such — ~ *nmf* : fellow creature — **semblant** [sɑ̃blɑ̃] *nm* 1 : semblance, appearance 2 **faire ~** : pretend
semelle [səmɛl] *nf* : sole
semer [səme] {52} *vt* 1 : sow, seed 2 RÉPANDRE : scatter — **semence** [səmɑ̃s] *nf* : seed
semestre [səmɛstr] *nm* : semester — **semestriel, -trielle** [səmɛstrijɛl] *adj* : semiannual
séminaire [seminɛr] *nm* 1 : seminary 2 : seminar
semi-remorque [səmirəmɔrk] *nm, pl* **semi-remorques** : semitrailer
semis [səmi] *nm* 1 : seedling 2 : seedbed
semonce [səmɔ̃s] *nf* RÉPRIMANDE : reprimand
semoule [səmul] *nf* : semolina
sénat [sena] *nm* : senate — **sénateur** [senatœr] *nm* : senator
sénile [senil] *adj* : senile — **sénilité** [senilite] *nf* : senility
sens [sɑ̃s] *nms & pl* 1 : sense 2 SIGNIFICATION : meaning 3 DIRECTION : direction, way 4 **à mon ~** : in my opinion 5 **~ dessus dessous** : upside down
sensation [sɑ̃sasjɔ̃] *nf* : sensation — **sensationnel, -nelle** [sɑ̃sasjɔnɛl] *adj* : sensational
sensé, -sée [sɑ̃se] *adj* : sensible
sensibiliser [sɑ̃sibilize] *vt* **~ à** : make sensitive to — **sensibilité** [sɑ̃sibilite] *nf* : sensitivity — **sensible** [sɑ̃sibl] *adj* 1 : sensitive 2 APPRÉCIABLE : noticeable — **sensiblement** [sɑ̃sibləmɑ̃] *adv* 1 : noticeably 2 : approximately
sensoriel, -rielle [sɑ̃sɔrjɛl] *adj* : sensory
sensuel, -suelle [sɑ̃sɥɛl] *adj* : sensual, sensuous — **sensualité** [sɑ̃sɥalite] *nf* : sensuality
sentence [sɑ̃tɑ̃s] *nf* JUGEMENT : sentence
senteur [sɑ̃tœr] *nf* : scent
sentier [sɑ̃tje] *nm* : path
sentiment [sɑ̃timɑ̃] *nm* 1 : sentiment, feeling 2 **recevez l'expression de mes ~s respectueux** : yours truly — **sentimental, -tale** [sɑ̃timɑ̃tal] *adj, mpl* **-taux** [-to] : sentimental — **sentimentalité** [-talite] *nf* : sentimentality
sentinelle [sɑ̃tinɛl] *nf* : sentinel
sentir [sɑ̃tir] {82} *vt* 1 : smell, taste 2 : feel 3 : appreciate 4 PRESSENTIR : sense — *vi* : smell — **se sentir** *vr* : feel (tired, sick, etc.)
seoir [swar] {80} *vi* **~ à** : suit
séparer [separe] *vt* 1 DÉTACHER : separate 2 : divide — **se séparer** *vr* 1 : separate 2 **~ de** : part with, be without — **séparation** [separasjɔ̃] *nf* : separation — **séparé, -rée** [separe] *adj* 1 : separate 2 : separated — **séparément** [separemɑ̃] *adv* : separately
sept [sɛt] *adj* 1 : seven 2 : seventh (in dates) — ~ *nms & pl* : seven
septante [sɛptɑ̃t] *adj Bel, Switz* 1 : seventy 2 : seventieth — ~ *nms & pl Bel, Switz* : seventy
septembre [sɛptɑ̃br] *nm* : September
septième [sɛtjɛm] *adj & nmf & nm* : seventh
sépulture [sepyltyr] *nf* TOMBE : grave
séquelle [sekɛl] *nf* 1 : consequence 2 **~s** *nfpl* : aftereffects
séquence [sekɑ̃s] *nf* : sequence
séquestrer [sekɛstre] *nm* : confine, sequester
serein, -reine [sərɛ̃, -rɛn] *adj* CALME : serene, calm — **sérénité** [serenite] *nf* : serenity
sergent [sɛrʒɑ̃] *nm* : sergeant
série [seri] *nf* 1 : series 2 : set 3 **de ~** : mass-produced, standard 4 **fabrication en ~** : mass production
sérieux, -rieuse [serjø, -rjøz] *adj* : serious — **sérieux** *nm* 1 : seriousness 2 **prendre au ~** : take seriously — **sérieusement** [serjøzmɑ̃] *adv* : seriously
serin [sərɛ̃] *nm* : canary
seringue [sərɛ̃g] *nf* : syringe
serment [sɛrmɑ̃] *nm* 1 : oath 2 : vow, promise
sermon [sɛrmɔ̃] *nm* : sermon
serpent [sɛrpɑ̃] *nm* 1 : snake 2 **~ à sonnettes** : rattlesnake — **serpenter** [sɛrpɑ̃te] *vi* : meander — **serpentin** [sɛrpɑ̃tɛ̃] *nm* : streamer
serre [sɛr] *nf* 1 : greenhouse, hothouse 2 **~s** *nfpl* : claws
serré, -rée [sere] *adj* 1 : tight 2 : crowded, cramped, dense
serrer [sere] *vt* 1 : squeeze, grip 2 : clench (one's fists, etc.) 3 : tighten (a knot, etc.) 4 : stay close to 5 : push closer together — **se serrer** *vr* 1 : huddle up 2 : tighten (up) 3 **~ la main** : shake hands
serrure [sɛryr] *nf* : lock — **serrurier** [sɛryrje] *nm* : locksmith
sérum [serɔm] *nm* : serum
serveur, -veuse [sɛrvœr, -vøz] *n* : waiter *m*, waitress *f* — **serveur** *nm* : (computer) server
serviable [sɛrvjabl] *adj* : helpful, obliging

service [sɛrvis] *nm* **1** : service **2** FAVEUR : favor **3** : serving, course **4** : department **5** : (coffee) set **6** : serve (in sports) **7 hors ~** : out of order

serviette [sɛrvjɛt] *nf* **1** : napkin **2** : towel **3** : briefcase **4 ~ hygiénique** : sanitary napkin

servir [sɛrvir] {81} *vt* **1** : serve **2** : wait on, attend to — *vi* **1** : be useful, serve **2 ~ de** : serve as — **se servir** *vr* **1** : serve oneself, help oneself **2 ~ de** : make use of

serviteur [sɛrvitœr] *nm* : servant

ses → **son**

session [sesjɔ̃] *nf* : session

seuil [sœj] *nm* : threshold

seul, seule [sœl] *adj* **1** : alone **2** : lonely **3** UNIQUE : only, sole — **~** *pron* : only one, single one — **seulement** [sœlmɑ̃] *adv* **1** : only **2** MÊME : even — **~** *conj* : but, only

sève [sɛv] *nf* : sap

sévère [sevɛr] *adj* : severe — **sévérité** [severite] *nf* : severity

sévir [sevir] *vi* **1** : rage **2 ~ contre** : punish

sevrer [səvre] *vt* : wean

sexe [sɛks] *nm* **1** : sex **2** : sex organs, genitals — **sexisme** [sɛksism] *nm* : sexism — **sexiste** [sɛksist] *adj & nmf* : sexist — **sexualité** [sɛksɥalite] *nf* : sexuality — **sexuel, sexuelle** [sɛksɥɛl] *adj* : sexual

seyant, seyante [sɛjɑ̃, -jɑ̃t] *adj* : becoming, flattering

shampooing [ʃɑ̃pwɛ̃] *nm* : shampoo

shérif [ʃerif] *nm* : sheriff

short [ʃɔrt] *nm* : shorts *pl*

si[1] [si] *adv* **1** TELLEMENT : so, such, as **2** : yes **3 ~ bien que** : with the result that, so

si[2] *conj* : if, whether

sida [sida] *nm* : AIDS

sidérer [sidere] {87} *vt fam* : stagger, amaze

sidérurgie [sideryrʒi] *nf* : steel industry

siècle [sjɛkl] *nm* : century

siège [sjɛʒ] *nm* **1** : seat **2** : siege **3** *or* **~ social** : headquarters — **siéger** [sjeʒe] {64} *vi* **1** : sit (in an assembly) **2** : have its headquarters

sien, sienne [sjɛ̃, sjɛn] *adj* : his, hers, its, one's — **~** *pron* **le sien, la sienne, les siens, les siennes** : his, hers, its, one's, theirs

sieste [sjɛst] *nf* : siesta, nap

siffler [sifle] *vt* **1** : whistle **2** : whistle for, whistle at **3** : boo — *vi* **1** : whistle **2** : hiss **3** : wheeze — **sifflement** [sifləmɑ̃] *nm* : whistling — **sifflet** [siflɛ] *nm* **1** : whistle **2 ~s** *nmpl* : boos — **siffloter** [siflɔte] *v* : whistle

sigle [sigl] *nm* : acronym

signaler [siɲale] *vt* **1** : signal **2** : point out — **se signaler** *vr* : distinguish oneself — **signal** [siɲal] *nm, pl* **-gnaux** [-ɲo] : signal — **signalement** [siɲalmɑ̃] *nm* : description — **signalisation** [siɲalizasjɔ̃] *nf* : signals *pl*, signs *pl*

signature [siɲatyr] *nf* **1** : signature **2** : signing

signe [siɲ] *nm* **1** : sign **2** : (punctuation) mark — **signer** [siɲe] *vt* : sign — **se signer** *vr* : cross oneself

signifier [siɲifje] {96} *vt* : signify, mean — **significatif, -tive** [siɲifikatif, -tiv] *adj* : significant — **signification** [siɲifikasjɔ̃] *nf* : significance, meaning

silence [silɑ̃s] *nm* **1** : silence **2** : rest (in music) — **silencieux, -cieuse** [silɑ̃sjø, -sjøz] *adj* : silent, quiet — **silencieux** *nm* : muffler

silex [silɛks] *nm* : flint

silhouette [silwɛt] *nf* : silhouette, outline

silicium [silisjɔm] *nm* : silicon

sillage [sijaʒ] *nm* : wake (of a ship)

sillon [sijɔ̃] *nm* **1** : furrow **2** : groove (of a disc, etc.) — **sillonner** [sijɔne] *vt* **1** CREUSER : furrow **2** : crisscross

silo [silo] *nm* : silo

simagrée [simagre] *nf* **faire des ~s** : put on airs

similaire [similɛr] *adj* : similar — **similitude** [similityd] *nf* : similarity

simple [sɛ̃pl] *adj* **1** : simple **2** : mere **3 aller ~** : one-way ticket — **~** *nm* : singles (in tennis) — **simplement** [sɛ̃pləmɑ̃] *adv* : simply — **simplicité** [sɛ̃plisite] *nf* : simplicity — **simplifier** [sɛ̃plifje] {96} *vt* : simplify

simulacre [simylakr] *nm* : sham, pretense

simuler [simyle] *vt* : simulate — **simulation** [simylasjɔ̃] *nf* : simulation

simultané, -née [simyltane] *adj* : simultaneous

sincère [sɛ̃sɛr] *adj* : sincere — **sincèrement** [-sɛrmɑ̃] *adv* : sincerely — **sincérité** [sɛ̃serite] *nf* : sincerity

singe [sɛ̃ʒ] *nm* : monkey — **singer** [sɛ̃ʒe] {17} *vt* **1** IMITER : mimic **2** FEINDRE : feign — **singeries** [sɛ̃ʒri] *nfpl* : antics

singulariser [sɛ̃gylarize] *vt* : draw attention to — **se singulariser** *vr* : call attention to oneself

singularité [sɛ̃gylarite] *nf* : peculiarity

singulier, -lière [sɛ̃gylje, -ljɛr] *adj* : singular — **singulier** *nm* : singular (in grammar) — **singulièrement** [sɛ̃gyljɛrmɑ̃] *nm* **1** : strangely **2** NOTAMMENT : particularly

sinistre [sinistr] *adj* : sinister — **~** *nm* DÉSASTRE : disaster — **sinistré, -trée** [sinistre] *adj* : damaged, stricken — **~** *n* : disaster victim

sinon [sinɔ̃] *conj* **1** : or else **2** : if not **3 ~ que** : except that

sinueux, -nueuse [sinɥø, -nɥøz] *adj* : winding, meandering

siphon [sifɔ̃] *nm* : siphon

sirène [sirɛn] *nf* **1** : mermaid **2** : siren, alarm

sirop [siro] *nm* : syrup

siroter [sirɔte] *vt fam* : sip

sis, sise [si, siz] *adj* : located (in law)

site [sit] *nm* **1** : site **2** : setting

sitôt [sito] *adv* **1** : as soon as **2 ~ après** : immediately after

situer [sitɥe] *vt* : situate, locate — **situation** [sitɥasjɔ̃] *nf* **1** : situation **2 ~ de famille** : marital status

six [sis, *before consonant* si, *before vowel* siz] *adj* **1** : six **2** : sixth (in dates) — **~** *nms & pl* : six — **sixième** [sizjɛm] *adj & nmf & nm* : sixth

ski [ski] *nm* **1** : ski **2** : skiing **3 ~ nautique** : waterskiing — **skier** [skje] {96} *vi* : ski — **skieur, skieuse** [skjœr, skjøz] *n* : skier

slip [slip] *nm* **1** : briefs *pl* **2** : panties *pl*

smoking [smɔkiŋ] *nm* : tuxedo

snob [snɔb] *adj* : snobbish — **~** *nmf* : snob — **snober** [snɔbe] *vt* : snub — **snobisme** [snɔbism] *nm* : snobbery

sobre [sɔbr] *adj* : sober — **sobriété** [sɔbrijete] *nf* : sobriety

soccer [sɔkɛr] *nm Can* : soccer

sociable [sɔsjabl] *adj* : sociable

social, -ciale [sɔsjal] *adj, mpl* **-ciaux** [-sjo] : social — **socialisme** [sɔsjalism] *nm* : socialism — **socialiste** [-sjalist] *adj & nmf* : socialist — **société** [sɔsjete] *nf* **1** : society **2** COMPAGNIE : company, firm

sociologie [sɔsjɔlɔʒi] *nf* : sociology — **sociologique** [sɔsjɔlɔʒik] *adj* : sociological — **sociologue** [sɔsjɔlɔg] *nmf* : sociologist

socle [sɔkl] *nm* : base, pedestal

soda [sɔda] *nm* : soda, soft drink

sodium [sɔdjɔm] *nm* : sodium

sœur [sœr] *nf* **1** : sister **2** : nun

sofa [sɔfa] *nm* : sofa

soi [swa] *pron* : oneself, himself, herself, itself — **soi–disant** [swadizɑ̃] *adv* : supposedly — **~** *adj* : so-called

soie [swa] *nf* **1** : silk **2** : bristle

soif [swaf] *nf* **1** : thirst **2 avoir ~** : be thirsty

soigner [swaɲe] *vt* **1** : treat, nurse, look after **2** : do with care — **se soigner** *vr* : take care of oneself — **soigné, -gnée** [swaɲe] *adj* **1** : carefully done **2** : neat — **soigneux, -gneuse** [swaɲø, -ɲøz] *adj* **1** : careful **2** : neat, tidy

soi–même [swamɛm] *pron* : oneself

soin [swɛ̃] *nm* **1** : care **2 ~s** *nmpl* : care **3 premiers ~s** : first aid **4 prendre ~ de** : take care of

soir [swar] *nm* : evening, night — **soirée** [sware] *nf* **1** : evening **2** FÊTE : party

soit [swa] *adv* : so be it, very well — **~** *conj* **1** : that is, in other words **2 soit . . . soit . . .** : either . . . or . . .

soixante [swasɑ̃t] *adj & nms & pl* : sixty — **soixante–dix** [swasɑ̃tdis] *adj & nms & pl* : seventy — **soixante–dixième** [swasɑ̃tdizjɛm] *adj & nmf & nm* : seventieth — **soixantième** [swasɑ̃tjɛm] *adj & nmf & nm* : sixtieth

soja [sɔʒa] *nm* : soybean

sol [sɔl] *nm* **1** : ground, floor **2** PLANCHER : flooring **3** TERRE : soil

solaire [sɔlɛr] *adj* **1** : solar **2** : sun

soldat [sɔlda] *nm* : soldier

solde[1] [sɔld] *nf* : pay

solde[2] *nm* **1** : balance (in finance) **2** *or* **~s** *nmpl* : sale — **solder** [sɔlde] *vt* **1** : settle (an account, etc.) **2** : sell off, put on sale — **se solder** *vr* **~ par** : end in

sole [sɔl] *nf* : sole (fish)

soleil [sɔlɛj] *nm* **1** : sun **2** : sunshine, sunlight

solennel, -nelle [sɔlanɛl] *adj* **1** : solemn **2** : formal — **solennité** [sɔlanite] *nf* : solemnity

solidaire [sɔlidɛr] *adj* **1** : united **2** : interdependent — **solidarité** [sɔlidarite] *nf* : solidarity

solide [sɔlid] *adj* : solid — **~** *nm* : solid — **solidement** [sɔlidmɑ̃] *adv* : solidly — **solidifier** [sɔlidifje] {96} *v* **se solidifier** *vr* : solidify — **solidité** [sɔlidite] *nf* : solidity

solitaire [sɔlitɛr] *adj* : solitary — **~** *nmf* : loner, recluse — **~** *nm* : solitaire — **solitude** [sɔlityd] *nf* **1** : solitude **2** : loneliness

solliciter [sɔlisite] *vt* **1** : solicit, seek **2** : appeal to, approach — **sollicitude** [sɔlisityd] *nf* : solicitude, concern

solo [sɔlo] *nm, pl* **solos** *or* **soli** : solo

soluble [sɔlybl] *adj* : soluble — **solution** [sɔlysjɔ̃] *nf* : solution

solvable [sɔlvabl] *adj* : solvent

sombre [sɔ̃br] *adj* **1** OBSCUR : dark **2** TRISTE : gloomy

sombrer [sɔ̃bre] *vi* COULER : sink

sommaire [sɔmɛr] *adj* **1** : brief, concise **2** : summary — **~** *nm* : summary

somme[1] [sɔm] *nf* **1** : sum **2 en ~** : in short, all in all

somme[2] *nm* : short nap, catnap

sommeil [sɔmɛj] *nm* : sleep — **sommeiller** [sɔmeje] *vi* **1** : doze **2** : lie dormant

sommer [sɔme] *vt* : summon

sommet [sɔmɛ] *nm* : summit, top

sommier [sɔmje] *nm* : base (of a bed), bedsprings *pl*

somnambule [sɔmnɑ̃byl] *nmf* : sleepwalker

somnifère [sɔmnifɛr] *nm* : sleeping pill

somnolence [sɔmnɔlɑ̃s] *nf* : drowsiness — **somnolent, -lente** [sɔmnɔlɑ̃, -lɑ̃t] *adj* : drowsy — **somnoler** [sɔmnɔle] *vi* : doze

somptueux, -tueuse [sɔ̃ptɥø, -tɥøz] *adj* : sumptuous

son[1], **sa** [sɔ̃, sa] *adj, pl* **ses** [se] : his, her, its, one's

son[2] *nm* **1** : sound **2** : volume **3** : (wheat) bran

sonde [sɔ̃d] *nf* **1** : probe **2** : sounding line — **sondage** [sɔ̃daʒ] *nm* : poll, survey — **sonder** [sɔ̃de] *vt* **1** : survey, poll **2** : sound, probe

songe [sɔ̃ʒ] *nm* : dream — **songer** [sɔ̃ʒe] {17} *vt* : consider, imagine — *vi* **1** : dream **2 ~ à** : think about — **songeur, -geuse** [sɔ̃ʒœr, -ʒøz] *adj* : pensive

sonner [sɔne] *v* **1** : ring **2** : strike, sound — **sonnant, -nante** [sɔnɑ̃, -nɑ̃t] *adj* **à cinq heures sonnantes** : at five o'clock sharp — **sonné, -née** [sɔne] *adj* **1** *fam* : groggy **2** *fam* : crazy, nuts **3 il est minuit sonné** : it's past midnight — **sonnerie** [sɔnri] *nf* **1** : ringing, ring **2** : alarm (bell)

sonnet [sɔnɛ] *nm* : sonnet

sonnette [sɔnɛt] *nf* : bell, doorbell

sonore [sɔnɔr] *adj* **1** : resonant **2** : sound — **sonorisation** [sɔnɔrizasjɔ̃] *nf* : sound system — **sonorité** [sɔnɔrite] *nf* **1** : tone **2** : resonance, acoustics

sophistiqué, -quée [sɔfistike] *adj* : sophisticated

soporifique [sɔpɔrifik] *adj* : soporific

soprano [sɔprano] *nmf* : soprano

sorbet [sɔrbɛ] *nm* : sorbet

sorcier, -cière [sɔrsje, -sjɛr] *n* : sorcerer, witch — **sorcellerie** [sɔrsɛlri] *nf* : sorcery, witchcraft

sordide [sɔrdid] *adj* **1** : sordid **2** : squalid

sornettes [sɔrnɛt] *nfpl* : nonsense

sort [sɔr] *nm* **1** : fate, lot **2** : spell, hex

sortant, -tante [sɔrtɑ̃, -tɑ̃t] *adj* : outgoing, resigning

sorte [sɔrt] *nf* **1** ESPÈCE : sort, kind **2 de ~ que** : so that **3 en quelque ~** : in a way

sortie [sɔrti] *nf* **1** : exit **2** DÉPART : departure **3** : launch, release (of a book, etc.) **4** EXCURSION : outing

sortilège [sɔrtilɛʒ] *nm* : spell

sortir [sɔrtir] {82} *vt* **1** : take out, bring out **2** : launch, release — *vi* **1** : go out, come out **2** PARTIR : leave, exit **3 ~ de** : come from, come out of — **se sortir** *vr* **1 ~ de** : get out of **2 s'en sortir** : get by, pull through

sosie [sɔzi] *nm* : double

sot, sotte [so, sɔt] *adj* : foolish, silly — **~** *n* : fool — **sottise** [sɔtiz] *nf* **1** : foolishness **2** : foolish act or remark

sou [su] *nm* **être sans le ~** : be penniless

soubresaut [subrəso] *nm* : jolt, start

souche [suʃ] *nf* **1** : stump (of a tree) **2** : stock, descent

soucier [susje] {96} *v* **se soucier** *vr* : worry, be concerned — **souci** [susi] *nm* : worry, concern — **soucieux, -cieuse** [susjø, -sjøz] *adj* : anxious, concerned

soucoupe [sukup] *nf* **1** : saucer **2 ~ volante** : flying saucer

soudain, -daine [sudɛ̃, -dɛn] *adj* : sudden — **soudainement** [-dɛnmɑ̃] *adv* : suddenly

soude [sud] *nf* : soda

souder [sude] *vt* : weld, solder

soudoyer [sudwaje] {58} *vt* : bribe

soudure [sudyr] *nf* **1** : solder **2** : soldering

souffler [sufle] *vi* **1** : blow **2** ÉTEINDRE : blow out **3** CHUCHOTER : whisper — *vi* **1** : blow **2** HALETER : pant, puff — **souffle** [sufl] *nm* **1** : breath, breathing **2** : puff, gust — **soufflé** [sufle] *nm* : soufflé — **soufflet** [suflɛ] *nm* : bellows

souffrir [sufrir] {83} *vt* **1** SUPPORTER : tolerate **2** PERMETTRE : allow — *vi* : suffer — **souffrance** [sufrɑ̃s] *nf* **1** : suffering **2 en ~** : pending — **souffrant, -frante** [sufrɑ̃, -frɑ̃t] *adj* : unwell

soufre [sufr] *nm* : sulfur

souhait [swɛ] *nm* **1** : wish **2 à vos ~s!** : bless you! — **souhaitable** [swɛtabl] *adj* : desirable — **souhaiter** [swete] *vt* : wish, hope for

souiller [suje] *vt* : soil

soûl, soûle [su, sul] *adj* : drunk

soulager [sulaʒe] {17} *vt* : relieve — **soulagement** [sulaʒmɑ̃] *nm* : relief

soûler [sule] *vt* : make drunk, intoxicate — **se soûler** *vr* : get drunk

soulever [sulve] {52} *vt* **1** : lift, raise **2** PROVOQUER : stir up — **se soulever** *vr* **1** : rise up **2** : lift oneself up — **soulèvement** [sulɛvmɑ̃] *nm* : uprising

soulier [sulje] *nm* : shoe

souligner [suliɲe] *vt* **1** : underline **2** : emphasize

soumettre [sumɛtr] {53} *vt* **1** : subjugate **2** PRÉSENTER : submit **3 ~ à** : subject to — **se soumettre** *vr* : submit — **soumis, -mise** [sumi, -miz] *adj* : submissive — **soumission** [sumisjɔ̃] *nf* : submission

soupape [supap] *nf* : valve

soupçon [supsɔ̃] *nm* **1** : suspicion **2** : hint, touch — **soupçonner** [supsɔne] *vt* : suspect — **soupçonneux, -neuse** [supsɔnø, -nøz] *adj* : suspicious

soupe [sup] *nf* : soup

souper [supe] *vi Can* : have supper — **~** *nm Can* : supper

soupeser [supəze] {52} *vt* **1** : feel the weight of **2** PESER : weigh, consider

soupière [supjɛr] *nf* : tureen

soupirer [supire] *vi* : sigh — **soupir** [supir] *nm* : sigh

souple [supl] *adj* : supple, flexible — **souplesse** [suplɛs] *nf* : suppleness, flexibility

source [surs] *nf* **1** : source **2** : spring (of water)

sourcil [sursi] *nm* : eyebrow — **sourciller** [sursije] *vi* **sans ~** : without batting an eyelid — **sourcilleux, -leuse** [sursijø, -jøz] *adj* **1** : finicky **2** : supercilious

sourd, sourde [sur, surd] *adj* : deaf — **~** *nmf* : deaf person — **sourd–muet, sourde–muette** [surmɥɛ, surdmɥɛt] *n* : deaf-mute

sourdre [surdr] {84} *vi* MONTER : well up

sourire [surir] {76} *vi* : smile — **~** *nm* : smile — **souriant, -riante** [surjɑ̃, -rjɑ̃t] *adj* : smiling, cheerful

souris [suri] *nf* : mouse

sournois, -noise [surnwa, -nwaz] *adj* : sly, underhanded

sous [su] *prep* **1** : under, beneath **2** : during **3 ~ peu** : shortly

sous–alimenté, -tée [suzalimɑ̃te] *adj* : malnourished

sous–bois [subwa] *nms & pl* : undergrowth

souscrire [suskrir] {33} *vi* **~ à** : subscribe to — **souscription** [suskripsjɔ̃] *nf* : subscription

sous–développé, -pée [sudevlɔpe] *adj* : underdeveloped

sous–entendre [suzɑ̃tɑ̃dr] {63} *vt* : imply, infer — **sous–entendu** [suzɑ̃tɑ̃dy] *nm* : insinuation

sous–estimer [suzɛstime] *vt* : underestimate

sous–jacent, -cente [suʒasɑ̃, -sɑ̃t] *adj* : underlying

sous–louer [sulwe] *vt* : sublet

sous–marin, -rine [sumarɛ̃, -rin] *adj* : underwater — **sous–marin** *nm* : submarine

sous–officier [suzɔfisje] *nm* : noncommissioned officer

sous–produit [suprɔdɥi] *nm* : by-product

sous–sol [susɔl] *nm* : basement, cellar

sous–titre [sutitr] *nm* : subtitle

soustraire [sustrɛr] {40} *vt* **1** : subtract **2** : remove, take away — **se soustraire** *vr* **~ à** : escape from — **soustraction** [sustraksjɔ̃] *nf* : subtraction

sous–vêtement [suvɛtmɑ̃] *nm* **1** : undergarment **2 ~s** *nmpl* : underwear

soutane [sutan] *nf* : cassock

soute [sut] *nf* : hold (of a ship)

soutenir [sutnir] {92} *vt* **1** MAINTENIR : support, hold up **2** RÉSISTER : withstand **3** : sustain — **soutenu, -nue** [sutny] *adj* **1** : formal **2** : sustained

souterrain, -raine [sutɛrɛ̃, -rɛn] *adj* : underground — **souterrain** *nm* : underground passage

soutien [sutjɛ̃] *nm* : support

soutien–gorge [sutjɛ̃gɔrʒ] *nm, pl* **soutiens–gorge** : bra, brassiere

soutirer [sutire] *vt* **~ à** : extract from

souvenir [suvnir] {92} *v* **se souvenir** *vr* **1 ~ de** : remember **2 ~ que** : remember that — **~** *nm* **1** : memory **2** : souvenir **3 mes meilleurs ~s à** : my best regards to

souvent [suvɑ̃] *adv* : often

souverain, -raine [suvrɛ̃, -rɛn] *adj* **1** : supreme **2** : sovereign — **~** *n* : sovereign — **souveraineté** [suvrɛnte] *nf* : sovereignty

soviétique [sɔvjetik] *adj* : Soviet

soyeux, soyeuse [swajø, swajøz] *adj* : silky

spacieux, -cieuse [spasjø, -sjøz] *adj* : spacious

spaghetti [spagɛti] *nmpl* : spaghetti

sparadrap [sparadra] *nm* : adhesive tape

spasme [spasm] *nm* : spasm

spatial, -tiale [spasjal] *adj, mpl* **-tiaux 1** : spatial **2 vaisseau spatial** : spaceship

speaker, -kerine [spikœr, -krin] *n France* : announcer (on radio, TV, etc.)

spécial, -ciale [spesjal] *adj, mpl* **-ciaux** [-sjo] **1** : special **2** BIZARRE : odd, peculiar — **spécialement** [spesjalmɑ̃] *adv* **1** EXPRÈS : specially **2** : especially — **spécialiser** [spesjalize] *v* **se spécialiser** *vr* : specialize — **spécialiste** [spesjalist] *nmf* : specialist — **spécialité** [spesjalite] *nf* : specialty

spécifier [spesifje] {96} *vt* : specify — **spécifique** [spesifik] *adj* : specific

spécimen [spesimɛn] *nm* : specimen

spectacle [spɛktakl] *nm* **1** : spectacle, sight **2** : show — **spectaculaire** [spɛktakylɛr] *adj* : spectacular — **spectateur, -trice** [spɛktatœr, -tris] *n* **1** : spectator **2** : observer, onlooker

spectre [spɛktr] *nm* **1** : specter, ghost **2** : spectrum

spéculer [spekyle] *vi* : speculate — **spéculation** [spekylasjɔ̃] *nf* : speculation

sperme [spɛrm] *nm* : sperm

sphère [sfɛr] *nf* : sphere — **sphérique** [sferik] *adj* : spherical

spirale [spiral] *nf* : spiral

spirituel, -tuelle [spiritɥɛl] *adj* : spiritual — **spiritualité** [spiritɥalite] *nf* : spirituality

splendeur [splɑ̃dœr] *nf* : splendor — **splendide** [splɑ̃did] *adj* : splendid

spongieux, -gieuse [spɔ̃ʒjø, -ʒjøz] *adj* : spongy

spontané, -née [spɔ̃tane] *adj* : spontaneous — **spontanéité** [spɔ̃taneite] *nf* : spontaneity — **spontanément** [-nemɑ̃] *adv* : spontaneously

sporadique [spɔradik] *adj* : sporadic

sport [spɔr] *adj* : sport, sports — ~ *nm* **1** : sport **2 ~s d'équipes** : team sports — **sportif, -tive** [spɔrtif, -tiv] *adj* **1** : sport, sports **2** : sportsmanlike **3** : athletic — ~ *n* : sportsman *m*, sportswoman *f*

spot [spɔt] *nm* **1** : spotlight **2** PUBLICITÉ : commercial

sprint [sprint] *nm* : sprint

square [skwar] *nm France* : small public garden

squelette [skəlɛt] *nm* : skeleton

stabiliser [stabilize] *vt* : stabilize — **stabilité** [stabilite] *nf* : stability — **stable** [stabl] *adj* : stable, steady

stade [stad] *nm* **1** : stadium **2** ÉTAPE : stage, phase

stage [staʒ] *nm* **1** : internship **2** : (training) course — **stagiaire** [staʒjɛr] *nmf* : trainee, intern

stagner [stagne] *vi* : stagnate — **stagnant, -gnante** [stagnɑ̃, -gnɑ̃t] *adj* : stagnant

stalle [stal] *nf* : stall

stand [stɑ̃d] *nm* **1** : stand, stall, booth **2 ~ de tir** : shooting range

standard [stɑ̃dar] *adj* : standard — ~ *nm* **1** : standard **2** : (telephone) switchboard — **standardiste** [stɑ̃dardist] *nmf* : switchboard operator

standing [stɑ̃diŋ] *nm* : standing, status

star [star] *nf* VEDETTE : star

station [stasjɔ̃] *nf* **1** : station **2 ~ d'autobus** : bus stop **3 ~ balnéaire** : seaside resort — **stationnaire** [stasjɔnɛr] *adj* : stationary — **stationner** [stasjɔne] *vi* : park — **stationnement** [stasjɔnmɑ̃] *nm* : parking — **station–service** [stasjɔ̃sɛrvis] *nf, pl* **stations–service** : gas station, service station

statistique [statistik] *adj* : statistical — ~ *nf* **1** : statistic **2** : statistics

statue [staty] *nf* : statue

statuer [statɥe] *vi* : decree, ordain

stature [statyr] *nf* : stature

statut [staty] *nm* **1** : statute **2** : status — **statutaire** [statytɛr] *adj* : statutory

steak [stɛk] *nm* : steak

stéréo [stereo] *adj & nf* : stereo

stéréotype [stereɔtip] *nm* **1** : stereotype **2** : cliché

stérile [steril] *adj* : sterile — **stérilisation** [-lizasjɔ̃] *nf* : sterilization — **stériliser** [sterilize] *vt* : sterilize — **stérilité** [sterilite] *nf* : sterility

stéthoscope [stetɔskɔp] *nm* : stethoscope

stigmate [stigmat] *nm* : mark, stigma — **stigmatiser** [stigmatize] *vt* : stigmatize

stimuler [stimyle] *vt* : stimulate — **stimulation** [-mylasjɔ̃] *nf* : stimulation — **stimulant, -lante** [stimylɑ̃, -lɑ̃t] *adj* : stimulating — **stimulant** *nm* **1** : stimulant **2** : stimulus

stipuler [stipyle] *vt* : stipulate

stock [stɔk] *nm* : stock, goods — **stocker** [stɔke] *vt* : stock

stoïque [stɔik] *adj* : stoic, stoical — ~ *nmf* : stoic

stop [stɔp] *nm* **1** : stop sign **2** : brake light — ~ *interj* : stop — **stopper** [stɔpe] *vt* **1** : stop, halt **2** : mend — *vi* : stop

store [stɔr] *nm* **1** : awning **2** : blind, window shade

strapontin [strapɔ̃tɛ̃] *nm* : folding seat

stratagème [strataʒɛm] *nm* : stratagem — **stratégie** [strateʒi] *nf* : strategy — **stratégique** [strateʒik] *adj* : strategic

stress [strɛs] *nms & pl* : stress — **stressant, -sante** [strɛsɑ̃, -sɑ̃t] *adj* : stressful

strict, stricte [strikt] *adj* **1** : strict **2** : austere, plain

strident, -dente [stridɑ̃, -dɑ̃t] *adj* : strident, shrill

strier [strije] {96} *vt* : streak

strophe [strɔf] *nf* : stanza

structure [stryktyr] *nf* : structure — **structural, -rale** [stryktyral] *adj, mpl* **-raux** [-ro] : structural — **structurer** [stryktyre] *vt* : structure

studieux, -dieuse [stydjø, -djøz] *adj* : studious

studio [stydjo] *nm* **1** : studio **2** : studio apartment

stupéfier [stypefje] {96} *vt* : astonish, stun — **stupéfaction** [stypefaksjɔ̃] *nf* : astonishment — **stupéfait, -faite** [stypefɛ, -fɛt] *adj* : amazed, astounded — **stupéfiant, -fiante** [stypefjɑ̃, -fjɑ̃t] *adj* : amazing, astounding — **stupéfiant** *nm* : drug, narcotic

stupeur [stypœr] *nf* **1** : astonishment **2** : stupor

stupide [stypid] *adj* : stupid — **stupidité** [stypidite] *nf* : stupidity

style [stil] *nm* : style

stylo [stilo] *nm* **1** : pen **2 ~ à bille** : ballpoint (pen)

suave [sɥav] *adj* **1** : sweet **2** : smooth, suave

subalterne [sybaltɛrn] *adj & nmf* : subordinate

subconscient, -ciente [sybkɔ̃sjɑ̃, -sjɑ̃t] *adj & nm* : subconscious

subdiviser [sybdivize] *vt* : subdivide

subir [sybir] *vt* **1** : undergo **2** : suffer **3** SUPPORTER : put up with **4** : take (an exam)

subit, -bite [sybi, -bit] *adj* : sudden — **subitement** [-bitmɑ̃] *adv* : suddenly

subjectif, -tive [sybʒɛktif, -tiv] *adj* : subjective — **subjectivité** [sybʒɛktivite] *nf* : subjectivity

subjonctif [sybʒɔ̃ktif] *nm* : subjunctive

subjuguer [sybʒyge] *vt* : captivate

sublime [syblim] *adj* : sublime

submerger [sybmɛrʒe] {17} *vt* **1** : submerge, flood **2** : overwhelm

subordonner [sybɔrdɔne] *vt* : subordinate — **subordonné, -née** [sybɔrdɔne] *adj & n* : subordinate

subreptice [sybrɛptis] *adj* : surreptitious

subséquent, -quente [sybsekɑ̃, -kɑ̃t] *adj* : subsequent

subside [sypsid] *nm* : grant, subsidy

subsidiaire [sypsidjɛr] *adj* : subsidiary

subsister [sybziste] *vi* **1** SURVIVRE : subsist, survive (on) **2** DURER : remain

substance [sypstɑ̃s] *nf* : substance — **substantiel, -tielle** [sypstɑ̃sjɛl] *adj* : substantial

substantif [sypstɑ̃tif] *nm* : noun

substituer [sypstitɥe] *vt* : substitute — **se substituer** *vr* **~ à** : substitute for, replace — **substitut** [sypstity] *nm* : substitute — **substitution** [sypstitysjɔ̃] *nf* : substitution

subterfuge [syptɛrfyʒ] *nm* : ploy, subterfuge

subtil, -tile [syptil] *adj* : subtle — **subtilité** [syptilite] *nf* : subtlety

subvenir [sybvənir] {92} *vi* **~ à** : provide for, meet — **subvention** [sybvɑ̃sjɔ̃] *nf* : subsidy — **subventionner** [sybvɑ̃sjɔne] *vt* : subsidize

subversif, -sive [sybvɛrsif, -siv] *adj* : subversive — **subversion** [sybvɛrsjɔ̃] *nf* : subversion

suc [syk] *nm* **1** : juice **2** : sap

succédané [syksedane] *nm* : substitute

succéder [syksede] {87} *vi* **~ à** : succeed, follow — **se succéder** *vr* : follow one another

succès [syksɛ] *nm* : success

successeur [syksesœr] *nm* : successor — **successif, -sive** [syksesif, -siv] *adj* : successive — **succession** [syksesjɔ̃] *nf* : succession

succinct, -cincte [syksɛ̃, -sɛ̃t] *adj* : succinct

succion [syksjɔ̃, sysjɔ̃] *nf* : suction, sucking

succomber [sykɔ̃be] *vi* **1** : die **2 ~ à** : succumb to

succulent, -lente [sykylɑ̃, -lɑ̃t] *adj* : succulent

succursale [sykyrsal] *nf* : branch (of a bank, etc.)

sucer [syse] {6} *vt* : suck

sucette [sysɛt] *nf* **1** : lollipop **2** : pacifier

sucre [sykr] *nm* : sugar — **sucré, -crée** [sykre] *adj* : sweet, sweetened — **sucrer** [sykre] *vt* : sweeten, add sugar to

sud [syd] *adj* : south, southern, southerly — ~ *nm* **1** : south **2 le Sud** : the South

sud–africain, -caine [sydafrikɛ̃, -kɛn] *adj* : South African

sud–américain, -caine [sydamerikɛ̃, -kɛn] *adj* : South American

sud–est [sydɛst] *adj s & pl* : southeast, southeastern — ~ *nm* : southeast

sud–ouest [sydwɛst] *adj s & pl* : southwest, southwestern — ~ *nm* : southwest

suédois, -doise [sɥedwa, -dwaz] *adj* : Swedish — **suédois** *nm* : Swedish (language)

suer [sɥe] *vi* : sweat — *vt* : sweat, ooze — **sueur** [sɥœr] *nf* : sweat

suffire [syfir] {86} *vi* : suffice — **se suffire** *vr or* **~ à soi–même** : be self-sufficient — **suffisamment** [syfizamɑ̃] *adv* : sufficiently — **suffisance** [syfizɑ̃s] *nf* : self-importance — **suffisant, -sante** [syfizɑ̃, -zɑ̃t] *adj* **1** : sufficient **2** : conceited

suffixe [syfiks] *nm* : suffix

suffoquer [syfɔke] *v* : suffocate, choke

suffrage [syfraʒ] *nm* : suffrage, vote

suggérer [sygʒere] {86} *vt* : suggest — **suggestion** [sygʒɛstjɔ̃] *nf* : suggestion

suicide [sɥisid] *nm* : suicide — **suicider** [sɥiside] *v* **se suicider** *vr* : commit suicide

suie [sɥi] *nf* : soot

suinter [sɥɛ̃te] *vi* : ooze, seep

suisse [sɥis] *adj* : Swiss

suite [sɥit] *nf* **1** : suite **2** : continuation, sequel **3** SÉRIE : series, sequence **4** CONSÉQUENCE : result **5 par la ~** : later, afterwards **6 par ~ de** : due to, as a result of

suivre [sɥivr] {88} *vt* **1** : follow **2** : take (a course) **3** : keep up with — *vi* **1** : follow **2** : keep up **3 faire ~** : forward (mail) — **se suivre** *vr* : follow one another — **suivant, -vante** [sɥivɑ̃, -vɑ̃t] *adj* : following, next — ~ *n* : next one, following one — **suivant** *prep* : according to — **suivi, -vie** [sɥivi] *adj* **1** : regular, steady **2** : coherent

sujet, -jette [syʒɛ, -ʒɛt] *adj* **~ à** : subject to, prone to — ~ *n* : subject (of a state or country) — **sujet** *nm* **1** : subject, topic **2** RAISON : cause

summum [sɔmɔm] *nm* : height, peak

super [sypɛr] *adj s & pl fam* : great, super

superbe [sypɛrb] *adj* : superb

supercherie [sypɛrʃəri] *nf* TROMPERIE : deception

superficie [sypɛrfisi] *nf* : area, surface — **superficiel, -cielle** [sypɛrfisjɛl] *adj* : superficial

superflu, -flue [sypɛrfly] *adj* : superfluous

supérieur, -rieure [syperjœr] *adj* **1** : superior **2** : upper, top **3 ~ à** : higher than — ~ *n* : superior — **supériorité** [syperjɔrite] *nf* : superiority

superlative [sypɛrlatif] *nm* : superlative

supermarché [sypɛrmarʃe] *nm* : supermarket

superstitieux, -tieuse [sypɛrstisjø, -sjøz] *adj* : superstitious — **superstition** [sypɛrstisjɔ̃] *nf* : superstition

superviser [sypɛrvize] *vt* : supervise

supplanter [syplɑ̃te] *vt* : supplant

suppléer [syplee] {89} *vt* **1** REMPLACER : replace, fill in for **2** : supplement — *vi* **~ à** : make up for — **suppléant, -pléante** [sypleɑ̃, -pleɑ̃t] *adj & n* : substitute, replacement

supplément [syplemɑ̃] *nm* **1** : supplement **2** : extra charge — **supplémentaire** [syplemɑ̃tɛr] *adj* : additional, extra

supplication [syplikasjɔ̃] *nf* : plea

supplice [syplis] *nm* : torture — **supplicier** [syplisje] {96} *vt* TORTURER : torture

supplier [syplije] {96} *vt* : implore, beg

supporter[1] [sypɔrte] *vt* **1** SOUTENIR : support, hold up **2** ENDURER : tolerate, bear — **support** [sypɔr] *nm* : support, prop — **supportable** [sypɔrtabl] *adj* : bearable, tolerable

supporter[2] [sypɔrtɛr] *nm* : supporter, fan

supposer [sypoze] *vt* **1** : suppose, assume **2** IMPLIQUER : imply — **supposition** [sypozisjɔ̃] *nf* : supposition

suppositoire [sypozitwar] *nm* : suppository

supprimer [syprime] *vt* **1** : abolish **2** : take out, delete — **suppression** [syprɛsjɔ̃] *nf* **1** : removal, elimination **2** : deletion

suppurer [sypyre] *vi* : fester

suprême [syprɛm] *adj* : supreme — **suprématie** [sypremasi] *nf* : supremacy

sur[1] [syr] *prep* **1** : on, upon **2** : over, above **3** : about, on **4** PARMI : out of **5** : by (in measurements)

sur[2], **sure** [syr] *adj* : sour

sûr, sûre [syr] *adj* **1** CERTAIN : sure, certain **2** FIABLE : reliable **3** : safe, secure **4** : sound **5 ~ de soi** : self-confident

surabondance [syrabɔ̃dɑ̃s] *nf* : overabundance

suranné, -née [syrane] *adj* : outdated

surcharger [syrʃarʒe] {17} *vt* **1** : overload **2** : alter — **surcharge** [syrʃarʒ] *nf* : overload

surchauffer [syrʃofe] *vt* : overheat

surclasser [syrklase] *vt* : outclass

surcroît [syrkrwa] *nm* **1** : increase **2 de ~** : in addition

surdité [syrdite] *nf* : deafness

surélever [syrelve] {52} *vt* : raise, heighten

sûrement [syrmɑ̃] *adv* **1** : surely **2** : safely **3 ~ pas** : certainly not

surenchérir [syrɑ̃ʃerir] *vi* : bid higher

surestimer [syrɛstime] *vt* : overestimate, overrate

sûreté [syrte] *nf* **1** SÉCURITÉ : safety **2** : surety, guarantee (in law)

surexcité, -tée [syrɛksite] *adj* : overexcited

surf [sœrf] *nm* : surfing

surface [syrfas] *nf* : surface

surgelé [syrʒəle] *adj* : frozen (of food)

surgir [syrʒir] *vi* : appear suddenly, arise

surhumain, -maine [syrymɛ̃, -mɛn] *adj* : superhuman

sur–le–champ [syrləʃɑ̃] *adv* : immediately

surlendemain [syrlɑ̃dmɛ̃] *nm* **le ~** : two days later

surmener [syrməne] {52} *vt* : overwork — **surmenage** [syrmənaʒ] *nm* : overwork

surmonter [syrmɔ̃te] *vt* **1** : overcome **2** : surmount, top

surnager [syrnaʒe] {17} *vi* : float

surnaturel, -relle [syrnatyrɛl] *adj & nm* : supernatural

surnom [syrnɔ̃] *nm* : nickname

surnombre [syrnɔ̃br] *nm* **en ~** : excess, too many

surnommer [syrnɔme] *vt* : nickname

surpasser [syrpase] *vt* : surpass, outdo

surpeuplé, -plée [syrpœple] *adj* : overpopulated

surplomber [syrplɔ̃be] *v* : overhang

surplus [syrply] *nm* : surplus

surprendre [syrprɑ̃dr] {70} *vt* **1** ÉTONNER : surprise **2** : catch, take by surprise **3** : overhear — **surprenant, -nante** [syrprənɑ̃, -nɑ̃t] *adj* : surprising — **surprise** [syrpriz] *nf* : surprise

sursaut [syrso] *nm* : start, jump — **sursauter** [syrsote] *vi* : start, jump

surseoir [syrswar] {90} *vi* **~ à** : postpone, defer

sursis [syrsi] *nm* : reprieve

surtaxe [syrtaks] *nf* : surcharge

surtout [syrtu] *adv* **1** : above all **2** : especially, particularly

surveiller [syrvɛje] *vt* **1** : watch (over) **2** : supervise — **surveillance** [syrvɛjɑ̃s] *nf* **1** : supervision **2** : watch, surveillance — **surveillant, -lante** [syrvɛjɑ̃, -jɑ̃t] *n* **1** : supervisor, overseer **2 ~ de prison** : prison guard

survenir [syrvənir] {92} *vi* : occur, take place

survivre [syrvivr] {98} *vi* **1** : survive **2 ~ à** : outlive — **survie** [syrvi] *nf* : survival — **survivant, -vante** [syrvivɑ̃, -vɑ̃t] *n* : survivor

survoler [syrvɔle] *vi* **1** : fly over **2** : skim through

sus [sy(s)] *adv* **1 en ~** : extra **2 en ~ de** : in addition to

susceptible [sysɛptibl] *adj* **1** : sensitive, touchy **2 ~ de** : likely to — **susceptibilité** [sysɛptibilite] *nf* : susceptibility

susciter [sysite] *vt* : arouse, give rise to

suspect, -pecte [syspɛ, -pɛkt] *adj* : suspicious, suspect — ~ *n* : suspect — **suspecter** [syspɛkte] *vt* : suspect

suspendre [syspɑ̃dr] {63} *vt* **1** INTERROMPRE : suspend, interrupt **2** PENDRE : hang up — **se suspendre** *vr* **~ à** : hang from — **suspens** [syspɑ̃] *nm* **en ~** : unresolved, uncertain

suspense [syspɑ̃s] *nm* : suspense

suspicion [syspisjɔ̃] *nf* : suspicion

suture [sytyr] *nf* **1** : suture **2 point de ~** : stitch

svelte [zvɛlt] *adj* : slender, svelte

syllabe [silab] *nf* : syllable

symbole [sɛ̃bɔl] *nm* : symbol — **symbolique** [sɛ̃bɔlik] *adj* : symbolic — **symboliser** [sɛ̃bɔlize] *vt* : symbolize — **symbolisme** [sɛ̃bɔlism] *nm* : symbolism

symétrie [simetri] *nf* : symmetry — **symétrique** [simetrik] *adj* : symmetrical, symmetric

sympathie [sɛ̃pati] *nf* **1** : liking **2** CONDOLÉANCES : condolences — **sympathique** [sɛ̃patik] *adj* : nice, likeable — **sympathiser** [sɛ̃patize] *vi* **~ avec** : get along with

symphonie [sɛ̃fɔni] *nf* : symphony — **symphonique** [sɛ̃fɔnik] *adj* : symphonic

symptôme [sɛ̃ptom] *nm* : symptom

synagogue [sinagɔg] *nf* : synagogue

syndicat [sɛ̃dika] *nm* : union, labor union — **syndiquer** [sɛ̃dike] *vt* : unionize — **se syndiquer** *vr* : join a union

syndrome [sɛ̃drom] *nm* : syndrome

synonyme [sinɔnim] *nm* : synonym — ~ *adj* : synonymous

syntaxe [sɛ̃taks] *nf* : syntax

synthèse [sɛ̃tɛz] *nf* : synthesis — **synthétique** [sɛ̃tetik] *adj* : synthetic

système [sistɛm] *nm* : system — **systématique** [sistematik] *adj* : systematic

T

t [te] *nm* : t, 20th letter of the alphabet

tabac [taba] *nm* **1** : tobacco **2 ~ à priser** : snuff **3** *France* : tobacco shop

table [tabl] *nf* **1** : table **2 se mettre à ~** : sit down to eat **3 ~ de matières** : table of contents

tableau [tablo] *nm, pl* **-leaux** **1** PEINTURE : painting **2** : picture, scene **3** : table, chart **4 ~ d'affichage** : bulletin board **5 ~ de bord** : dashboard **6 ~ noir** : blackboard

tabler [table] *vt* **~ sur** : count on

tablette [tablɛt] *nf* **1** : shelf **2** : bar (of candy), stick (of gum)

tablier [tablije] *nm* : apron

tabou, -boue [tabu] *adj* : taboo — **tabou** *nm* : taboo

tabouret [taburɛ] *nm* : stool

tache [taʃ] *nf* **1** : stain, spot **2 ~ de rousseur** : freckle — **tacher** [taʃe] *vt* SALIR : stain, spot

tâche [taʃ] *nf* : task — **tâcher** [taʃe] *vi* **~ de** : try to

tacheté [taʃte] *adj* : speckled
tacite [tasit] *adj* : tacit
tact [takt] *nm* : tact
tactique [taktik] *adj* : tactical — ~ *nf* STRATÉGIE : tactics *pl*
taie [tɛ] *nf or* **~ d'oreiller** : pillowcase
tailler [taje] *vt* **1** : cut, prune, trim **2** : sharpen (a pencil) — **taille** [taj] *nf* **1** : cutting, pruning **2** : size (of clothing, etc.) **3** HAUTEUR : height **4** : waist — **tailleur** [tajœr] *nm* **1** : woman's suit **2** : tailor
taire [tɛr] {91} *vt* : hush up, keep secret — **se taire** *vr* **1** : be quiet **2** : fall silent
talc [talk] *nm* : talcum powder
talent [talɑ̃] *nm* : talent — **talentueux, -tueuse** [talɑ̃tɥø, -tɥøz] *adj* : talented
talon [talɔ̃] *nm* **1** : heel **2** : stub (of a check) — **talonner** [talɔne] *vt* **1** : follow closely **2** : harass
talus [taly] *nms & pl* : embankment, slope
tambour [tɑ̃bur] *nm* : drum — **tambouriner** [tɑ̃burine] *vt* : drum
tamia [tamja] *nm* : chipmunk
tamis [tami] *nms & pl* : sieve, sifter — **tamiser** [tamize] *vt* **1** : sift **2** : filter
tampon [tɑ̃pɔ̃] *nm* **1** BOUCHON : plug **2** : buffer (of a railway car) **3** : rubber stamp **4** **~ encreur** : ink pad **5** **~ hygiénique** : tampon — **tamponner** [tɑ̃pɔne] *vt* **1** : dab **2** HEURTER : crash into **3** : stamp (a document)
tandis [tɑ̃di] **~ que** *conj phr* **1** : while **2** : whereas
tangente [tɑ̃ʒɑ̃t] *nf* : tangent
tangible [tɑ̃ʒibl] *adj* : tangible
tango [tɑ̃go] *nm* : tango
tanguer [tɑ̃ge] *vi* : pitch (of a ship, etc.)
tanière [tanjɛr] *nf* : lair, den
tanner [tane] *vt* **1** : tan (leather, etc.) **2** *fam* : pester, annoy
tant [tɑ̃] *adv* **1** : so much, so many **2** **en ~ que** : as, in so far as **3** **~ mieux!** : so much the better! **4** **~ pis!** : too bad! **5** **~ que** : as much as, as long as
tante [tɑ̃t] *nf* : aunt
tantôt [tɑ̃to] *adv* **1** : sometimes **2** *Can* : later **3** *France* : this afternoon
tapage [tapaʒ] *nm* **1** : uproar, din **2** SCANDALE : scandal — **tapageur, -geuse** [tapaʒœr, -ʒøz] *adj* **1** : rowdy **2** TAPE-À-L'ŒIL : flashy
tape [tap] *nf* : slap — **tape-à-l'œil** [tapalœj] *adj* : flashy
taper [tape] *vt* **1** : hit, slap **2** : type — *vi* **1** : hit, bang **2** : beat down (of the sun)
tapir [tapir] *v* **se tapir** *vr* : crouch
tapis [tapi] *nms & pl* **1** : carpet **2** **~ roulant** : moving walkway, conveyor belt — **tapisser** [tapise] *vt* **1** : wallpaper **2** **~ de** : cover with — **tapisserie** [tapisri] *nf* **1** : tapestry **2** : wallpaper
tapoter [tapɔte] *vt* : tap, pat
taquiner [takine] *vt* : tease — **taquinerie** [takinri] *nf* : teasing
tarabiscoté, -tée [tarabiskɔte] *adj* : fussy, overelaborate
tard [tar] *adv* : late — **tarder** [tarde] *vi* : take a long time — **tardif, -dive** [tardif, -div] *adj* : late
tare [tar] *nf* DÉFAUT : defect
tarif [tarif] *nm* **1** : rate, fare **2** : price, schedule of prices **3** **~ douanier** : tariff, customs duty
tarir [tarir] *v* : dry up
tarte [tart] *nf* : tart, pie
tartine [tartin] *nf* : slice of bread (and butter) — **tartiner** [tartine] *vt* : spread (with butter, etc.)
tartre [tartr] *nm* : tartar
tas [ta] *nms & pl* **1** : heap, pile **2** **des ~ de** : a lot of, piles of
tasse [tas] *nf* : cup
tasser [tase] *vt* **1** : pack down **2** ENTASSER : cram, squeeze **3** *Can* : move over — **se tasser** *vr* **1** : shrink **2** : cram (into a car)
tâter [tate] *vt* **1** : feel **2** **~ le terrain** : check out the lay of the land — *vi* **~ de** : try one's hand at
tatillon, -lonne [tatijɔ̃, -jɔn] *adj* : fussy, finicky
tâtonner [tatɔne] *vi* : grope about — **tâtons** [tatɔ̃] **à ~** *adv phr* **avancer à ~** : feel one's way
tatouer [tatwe] *vt* : tattoo — **tatouage** [tatwaʒ] *nm* **1** : tattoo **2** : tattooing
taudis [todi] *nms & pl* : hovel, slum
taule [tol] *nf fam* : prison
taupe [top] *nf* : mole
taureau [tɔro] *nm, pl* **-reaux** : bull
taux [to] *nms & pl* **1** : rate **2** : level **3** **~ de change** : exchange rate **4** **~ de cholestérol** : cholesterol level
taverne [tavɛrn] *nf* : inn, tavern
taxe [taks] *nf* : tax — **taxer** [takse] *vt* : tax
taxi [taksi] *nm* : taxi, taxicab
te [tə] (**t'** *before a vowel or mute h*) *pron* **1** : you, to you **2** (*used as a reflexive pronoun*) : yourself
technique [tɛknik] *nf* : technique — ~ *adj* : technical — **technicien, -cienne** [tɛknisjɛ̃, -sjɛn] *n* : technician
technologie [tɛknɔlɔʒi] *nf* : technology — **technologique** [tɛknɔlɔʒik] *adj* : technological
tee-shirt [tiʃœrt] *nm, pl* **tee-shirts** : T-shirt
teindre [tɛ̃dr] {37} *vt* : dye — **teint** [tɛ̃] *nm* : complexion — **teinte** [tɛ̃t] *nf* **1** : shade, hue **2** **une ~ de** : a tinge of — **teinter** [tɛ̃te] *vt* : tint, stain — **teinture** [tɛ̃tyr] *nf* **1** : dye **2** : dyeing — **teinturerie** [tɛ̃tyrri] *nf* **1** : dyeing **2** : dry cleaner's — **teinturier, -rière** [tɛ̃tyrje, -rjɛ] *n* : dry cleaner
tel, telle [tɛl] *adj* **1** : such **2** : such and such, a certain **3** **~ que** : such as, like **4** **tel quel** : as (it) is — ~ *pron* **1** : a certain one, someone **2** **un tel, une telle** : so-and-so
télé [tele] *nf fam* : TV
télécommande [telekɔmɑ̃d] *nf* : remote control
télécommunication [telekɔmynikasjɔ̃] *nf* : telecommunication
télécopie [telekɔpi] *nf* : fax — **télécopieur** [telekɔpjœr] *nm* : fax machine
télégramme [telegram] *nm* : telegram
télégraphe [telegraf] *nm* : telegraph
téléphone [telefɔn] *nm* : telephone — **téléphoner** [telefɔne] *vt* : telephone, call — **téléphonique** [telefɔnik] *adj* : telephone
télescope [teleskɔp] *nm* : telescope — **télescoper** [teleskɔpe] *v* **se télescoper** *vr* **1** : collide **2** : overlap — **télescopique** [teleskɔpik] *adj* : telescopic
télésiège [telesjɛʒ] *nm* : chairlift
téléski [teleski] *nm* : ski lift
téléviser [televize] *vt* : televise — **téléviseur** [televizœr] *nm* : television set — **télévision** [televizjɔ̃] *nf* **1** : television **2** TÉLÉVISEUR : television set
tellement [tɛlmɑ̃] *adv* **1** : so, so much **2** **~ de** : so many, so much
téméraire [temerɛr] *adj* : rash, reckless — **témérité** [temerite] *nf* : rashness, recklessness
témoin [temwɛ̃] *nm* **1** : witness **2** : baton (in a relay race) — **témoignage** [temwaɲaʒ] *nm* **1** RÉCIT : account, story **2** : testimony (in court) **3** PREUVE : evidence — **témoigner** [temwaɲe] *vt* **1** : testify, attest **2** MONTRER : show — *vi* : testify
tempe [tɑ̃p] *nf* : temple
tempérament [tɑ̃peramɑ̃] *nm* CARACTÈRE : temperament
température [tɑ̃peratyr] *nf* : temperature
tempéré, -rée [tɑ̃pere] *adj* : temperate
tempête [tɑ̃pɛt] *nf* : storm
temple [tɑ̃pl] *nm* **1** : temple **2** : (protestant) church
temporaire [tɑ̃pɔrɛr] *adj* : temporary
temporel, -relle [tɑ̃pɔrɛl] *adj* : temporal, worldly
temps [tɑ̃] *nms & pl* **1** : time **2** : weather **3** : tense (in grammar) **4** **à plein ~** : full-time **5** **de ~ à autre** : from time to time **6** **quel ~ fait-il?** : what's the weather like?
tenace [tənas] *adj* : tenacious, stubborn — **tenacité** [tənasite] *nf* : tenacity
tenailles [tənaj] *nfpl* : pincers, tongs
tendance [tɑ̃dɑ̃s] *nf* **1** : tendency **2** COURANT : trend
tendon [tɑ̃dɔ̃] *nm* : tendon, sinew
tendre¹ [tɑ̃dr] {63} *vt* **1** : tense, tighten (a rope, etc.) **2** **~ la main** : hold out one's hand **3** **~ un piège à** : set a trap for — *vi* **1** **~ à** : tend to **2** **~ vers** : strive for — **se tendre** *vr* **1** : tighten **2** : become strained — **tendu, -due** [tɑ̃dy] *adj* **1** : tight, taut **2** : tense, strained **3** : outstretched (of a hand)
tendre² *adj* **1** : tender, soft **2** : gentle, loving — **tendresse** [tɑ̃drɛs] *nf* : tenderness, affection
ténèbres [tenɛbr] *nfpl* : darkness — **ténébreux, -breuse** [tenebrø, -brøz] *adj* OBSCUR : dark
teneur [tənœr] *nf* : content
tenir [tənir] {92} *vt* **1** : hold, keep **2** : have, catch **3** : run, manage (a hotel, store, etc.) **4** : take up (a space) **5** CONSIDÉRER : hold, regard — *vi* **1** : hold, stay in place **2** DURER : hold up, last **3** : fit (into a space) **4** **~ à** : be fond of **5** **~ à** : be anxious to **6** **~ de** : take after — *v impers* : depend — **se tenir** *vr* **1** : hold, hold up, hold onto **2** RESTER : remain **3** : behave (oneself) **4** **~ debout** : stand still
tennis [tenis] *nm* **1** : tennis **2** ~ *nmpl France* : sneakers
ténor [tenɔr] *nm* : tenor
tension [tɑ̃sjɔ̃] *nf* : tension
tentacule [tɑ̃takyl] *nm* : tentacle
tentation [tɑ̃tasjɔ̃] *nf* : temptation
tentative [tɑ̃tativ] *nf* : attempt
tente [tɑ̃t] *nf* : tent
tenter [tɑ̃te] *vt* **1** : tempt **2** ESSAYER : attempt
tenu, -nue [təny] *adj* **1** : obliged **2** **bien ~** : well-kept, tidy
ténu, -nue [teny] *adj* : tenuous
tenue *nf* **1** : conduct, manners *pl* **2** MAINTIEN : posture **3** : clothes *pl*, dress **4** **~ de livres** : bookkeeping
terme [tɛrm] *nm* **1** : term, word **2** ÉCHÉANCE : deadline **3** **mettre un ~ à** : put an end to
terminer [tɛrmine] *v* FINIR : finish — **se terminer** *vr* : end — **terminaison** [tɛrminɛzɔ̃] *nf* : ending — **terminal, -nale** [tɛrminal] *adj, mpl* **-naux** [-no] : final, terminal — **terminal** *nm, pl* **-naux** : terminal
terminologie [tɛrminɔlɔʒi] *nf* : terminology
terminus [tɛrminys] *nms & pl* : terminus
terne [tɛrn] *adj* **1** FADE : drab **2** ENNUYEUX : dull
ternir [tɛrnir] *vt* : tarnish
terrain [tɛrɛ̃] *nm* **1** : ground **2** PARCELLE : plot (of land) **3** : land, terrain **4** **~ d'aviation** : airfield **5** **~ de camping** : campsite
terrasse [tɛras] *nf* : terrace — **terrasser** [tɛrase] *vt* : knock down, floor
terre [tɛr] *nf* **1** TERRAIN : land **2** : dirt, soil **3** : earth, world **4** **aller à ~** : go ashore **5** **la Terre** : the Earth **6** **par ~** : on the ground, on the floor **7** **sous ~** : underground **8** **terre-à-terre** : down-to-earth, matter-of-fact
terrestre [tɛrɛstr] *adj* **1** : earth, terrestrial **2** : earthly, worldly
terreur [tɛrœr] *nf* : terror
terreux, -reuse [tɛrø, -røz] *adj* : earthy
terrible [tɛribl] *adj* **1** : terrible **2** *fam* FORMIDABLE : terrific, great
terrier [tɛrje] *nm* **1** : hole, burrow **2** CHIEN : terrier
terrifier [tɛrifje] {96} *vt* ÉPOUVANTER : terrify
territoire [tɛritwar] *nm* : territory — **territorial, -riale** [tɛritɔrjal] *adj, mpl* **-riaux** [-rjo] : territorial
terroriser [tɛrɔrize] *vt* : terrorize — **terrorisme** [tɛrɔrism] *nm* : terrorism — **terroriste** [-rɔrist] *adj & nmf* : terrorist
tes → **ton**¹
tesson [tɛsɔ̃] *nm* : fragment, shard
test [tɛst] *nm* : test
testament [tɛstamɑ̃] *nm* **1** : will, testament **2** **Ancien Testament** : Old Testament
tester [tɛste] *vt* : test
testicule [tɛstikyl] *nm* : testicle
tétanos [tetanos] *nms & pl* : tetanus
têtard [tɛtar] *nm* : tadpole
tête [tɛt] *nf* **1** : head **2** VISAGE : face **3** MENEUR : leader **4** : top (of a class, etc.) **5** ESPRIT : mind, brain **6** **faire la ~** : sulk **7** **tenir ~ à** : stand up to — **tête-à-queue** [tɛtakø] *nms & pl* : spin (of an automobile) — **tête-à-tête** [tɛtatɛt] *nms & pl* : tête-à-tête
téter [tete] {87} *vt* : suck (at) — *vi* : suckle, nurse — **tétine** [tetin] *nf* **1** : teat **2** : nipple (on a baby's bottle), pacifier
têtu, -tue [tety] *adj* : stubborn
texte [tɛkst] *nm* : text
textile [tɛkstil] *nm* : textile
texture [tɛkstyr] *nf* : texture
thé [te] *nm* : tea
théâtre [teatr] *nm* : theater — **théâtral, -trale** [teatral] *adj, mpl* **-traux** [-tro] : theatrical
théière [tejɛr] *nf* : teapot
thème [tɛm] *nm* : theme
théologie [teɔlɔʒi] *nf* : theology
théorie [teɔri] *nf* : theory — **théorique** [teɔrik] *adj* : theoretical
thérapie [terapi] *nf* : therapy — **thérapeute** [terapøt] *nmf* : therapist — **thérapeutique** [terapøtik] *adj* : therapeutic
thermal, -male [tɛrmal] *adj, mpl* **-maux** [tɛrmo] : thermal — **thermique** [tɛrmik] *adj* : thermal
thermomètre [tɛrmɔmɛtr] *nm* : thermometer
thermos [tɛrmos] *nmfs & pl* : thermos
thermostat [tɛrmɔsta] *nm* : thermostat
thèse [tɛz] *nf* : thesis
thon [tɔ̃] *nm* : tuna
thym [tɛ̃] *nm* : thyme
tibia [tibja] *nm* : shin(bone)
tic [tik] *nm* **1** : tic, twitch **2** HABITUDE : mannerism
ticket [tikɛ] *nm* BILLET : ticket
tiède [tjɛd] *adj* : lukewarm — **tiédir** [tjedir] *vi* : warm up, cool down
tien, tienne [tjɛ̃, tjɛn] *adj* : yours, of yours — ~ *pron* **le tien, la tienne, les tiens, les tiennes** : yours
tiers, tierce [tjɛr, tjɛrs] *adj* : third — **tiers** *nm* **1** : third **2** : third party
tige [tiʒ] *nf* **1** : stem, stalk **2** : (metal) rod
tigre [tigr] *nm* : tiger — **tigresse** [tigrɛs] *nf* : tigress
tilleul [tijœl] *nm* : linden (tree)
timbale [tɛ̃bal] *nf* : tumbler, cup
timbre [tɛ̃br] *nm* **1** : (postage) stamp **2** SONNETTE : bell **3** TON : timbre, tone — **timbrer** [tɛ̃bre] *vt* : stamp, postmark
timide [timid] *adj* : timid, shy — **timidité** [timidite] *nf* : shyness
tintamarre [tɛ̃tamar] *nm* : din, racket
tinter [tɛ̃te] *vt* : ring, toll — *vi* **1** : ring, chime **2** : jingle, tinkle — **tintement** [tɛ̃tmɑ̃] *nm* : ringing, chiming
tir [tir] *nm* : shooting, firing
tirage [tiraʒ] *nm* **1** : printing, printout **2** : circulation (of a newspaper, etc.) **3** : drawing (in a lottery)
tirailler [tiraje] *vt* : pull at, tug at
tiré, -rée [tire] *adj* : drawn, haggard
tire-bouchon [tirbuʃɔ̃] *nm, pl* **tire-bouchons** : corkscrew
tirelire [tirlir] *nf* : piggy bank
tirer [tire] *vt* **1** : pull, tug **2** : fire, shoot **3** **~ de** : pull out of, draw away from **4** **~ la langue** : stick out one's tongue **5** **~ une ligne** : draw a line — *vi* **1** : pull **2** : fire, shoot **3** **~ au sort** : draw lots — **se tirer** *vr* **1** **~ de** : get through, escape from **2** **s'en tirer** *fam* : cope, manage
tiret [tirɛ] *nm* : dash, hyphen
tireur, -reuse [tirœr, -røz] *n* : gunman
tiroir [tirwar] *nm* : drawer
tisane [tizan] *nf* : herbal tea
tisonnier [tizɔnje] *nm* : poker
tisser [tise] *vt* : weave — **tissage** [tisaʒ] *nm* **1** : weaving **2** : weave
tissu [tisy] *nm* **1** : material, fabric **2** : tissue (in biology)
titre [titr] *nm* **1** : title (of a book, etc.) **2** : rank, qualification **3** *or* **gros ~** : headline **4** : security, bond **5** **à ~ d'exemple** : as an example
tituber [titybe] *vi* : stagger
titulaire [titylɛr] *adj* : tenured, permanent — ~ *nmf* **1** : holder **2** : tenured professor
toast [tost] *nm* : toast
toboggan [tɔbɔgɑ̃] *nm* : toboggan, sleigh
toge [tɔʒ] *nf* : gown, robe (of a judge, etc.)
toi [twa] *pron* **1** : you **2** TOI-MÊME : yourself
toile [twal] *nf* **1** : cloth, fabric **2** TABLEAU : canvas, painting **3** **~ d'araignée** : spiderweb, cobweb
toilette [twalɛt] *nf* **1** : washing up **2** TENUE : clothing, outfit **3** *Can* : toilet, bathroom **4** **~s** *nfpl* : toilet, bathroom
toi-même [twamɛm] *pron* : yourself
toison [twazɔ̃] *nf* : fleece
toit [twa] *nm* : roof — **toiture** [twatyr] *nf* : roofing
tôle [tol] *nf* **1** : sheet metal **2** **~ ondulée** : corrugated iron
tolérer [tɔlere] {87} *vt* : tolerate — **tolérance** [tɔlerɑ̃s] *nf* : tolerance — **tolérant, -rante** [tɔlerɑ̃, -rɑ̃t] *adj* : tolerant
tollé [tɔle] *nm* : outcry
tomate [tɔmat] *nf* : tomato
tombant, -bante [tɔ̃bɑ̃, -bɑ̃t] *adj* : sloping, drooping
tombe [tɔ̃b] *nf* SÉPULTURE : grave, tomb — **tombeau** [tɔ̃bo] *nm, pl* **-beaux** : tomb, mausoleum
tomber [tɔ̃be] *vi* **1** : fall, drop **2** : die down, subside **3** : droop, sag **4** **~ amoureux** : fall in love **5** **~ malade** : fall ill **6** **~ sur** : run into, come across **7** **laisser ~** : give up — **tombée** [tɔ̃be] *nf* **à la ~ du jour** *or* **à la ~ de la nuit** : at nightfall, at the close of day
tome [tɔm] *nm* : volume (of a book)
ton¹ [tɔ̃] (*before a vowel or mute h*), **ta** [ta] *adj, pl* **tes** [te] : your
ton² *nm* **1** : tone, pitch **2** : hue, shade — **tonalité** [tɔnalite] *nf* **1** : tone **2** : tonality, key (in music) **3** : dial tone
tondre [tɔ̃dr] {63} *vt* **1** : mow (the lawn) **2** : shear, clip (hair) — **tondeuse** [tɔ̃døz] *nf* **1** *or* **~ à gazon** : lawn mower **2** : clippers *pl*, shears *pl*
tonifier [tɔnifje] {96} *vt* REVIGORER : tone up, invigorate — **tonique** [tɔnik] *nm* : tonic
tonne [tɔn] *nf* : ton
tonneau [tɔno] *nm, pl* **-neaux** **1** : barrel, cask **2** : rollover (of an automobile) — **tonnelet** [tɔnlɛ] *nm* : keg
tonner [tɔne] *vi* : thunder — **tonnerre** [tɔnɛr] *nm* : thunder
tonton [tɔ̃tɔ̃] *nm fam* : uncle
tonus [tɔnys] *nms & pl* **1** : (muscle) tone **2** : energy, vigor
toqué, -quée [tɔke] *adj fam* : crazy
torche [tɔrʃ] *nf* : torch
torchon [tɔrʃɔ̃] *nm* **1** CHIFFON : rag **2** **~ à vaisselle** : dishcloth — **torcher** [tɔrʃe] *vt fam* : wipe
tordre [tɔrdr] {63} *vt* : twist, wring — **se tordre** *vr* **1** : twist **2** : double up (with pain, laughter, etc.) — **tordu, -due** [tɔrdy] *adj* : twisted, warped
torero [tɔrero] *nm* : bullfighter
tornade [tɔrnad] *nf* : tornado
torpeur [tɔrpœr] *nf* : lethargy
torpille [tɔrpij] *nf* : torpedo
torrent [tɔrɑ̃] *nm* : torrent
torride [tɔrid] *adj* : torrid
torsade [tɔrsad] *nf* : twist, coil
torse [tɔrs] *nm* : torso, chest
tort [tɔr] *nm* **1** : wrong **2** **à ~** : wrongly **3** **avoir ~** : be wrong **4** **faire du ~ à** : harm
torticolis [tɔrtikɔli] *nms & pl* : stiff neck
tortiller [tɔrtije] *vt* : twist — **se tortiller** *vr* : wriggle, squirm
tortue [tɔrty] *nf* : turtle, tortoise
tortueux, -euse [tɔrtɥø, -øz] *adj* **1** : winding (of a road) **2** : convoluted, tortuous
torture [tɔrtyr] *nf* : torture — **torturer** [tɔrtyre] *vt* : torture
tôt [to] *adv* **1** : soon **2** : early **3** **~ ou tard** : sooner or later
total, -tale [tɔtal] *adj, mpl* **-taux** [tɔto] : total — **total** *nm, pl* **-taux** : total —

totaliser [tɔtalize] *vt* : total — **totalitaire** [tɔtalitɛr] *adj* : totalitarian — **totalité** [tɔtalite] *nf* **1 en ~** : completely **2 la ~ de** : all of

toucher [tuʃe] *vt* **1** : touch, handle **2** : hit, strike **3** CONCERNER : affect **4** ÉMOUVOIR : move, touch **5** : receive, earn (a salary) — *vi* **~ à 1** : touch upon, bring up **2** : relate to — **se toucher** *vr* : touch each other — **~** *nm* **1** : sense of touch **2** SENSATION : feel — **touchant, -chante** [tuʃɑ̃, -ʃɑ̃t] *adj* ÉMOUVANT : touching — **touche** [tuʃ] *nf* **1** : key (on a keyboard) **2** TRACE : trace, hint

touffe [tuf] *nf* : tuft, clump — **touffu, -fue** [tufy] *adj* : bushy

toujours [tuʒur] *adv* **1** : always, forever **2** ENCORE : still

toupet [tupɛ] *nm fam* : nerve, cheek

toupie [tupi] *nf* : top (toy)

tour[1] [tur] *nm* **1** : tour, circuit **2** : walk, ride **3 ~ de taille** : girth (of a person) **4 attendre son ~** : wait one's turn **5 jouer un ~ à qqn** : play a trick on s.o. **6** : lathe (in carpentry)

tour[2] *nf* **1** : tower **2** : castle (in chess)

tourbe [turb] *nf* : peat

tourbillon [turbijɔ̃] *nm* **1** : whirlwind, whirlpool **2** : whirl, bustle — **tourbillonner** [turbijɔne] *vi* : whirl, swirl

tourelle [turɛl] *nf* : turret

touriste [turist] *nmf* : tourist — **tourisme** [turism] *nm* : tourism — **touristique** [turistik] *adj* : tourist

tourment [turmɑ̃] *nm* : torment — **tourmenter** [turmɑ̃te] *vt* : torment — **se tourmenter** *vr* S'INQUIÉTER : worry

tourner [turne] *vt* **1** : turn, rotate **2** : stir (a sauce), toss (a salad) **3** : shoot, film — *vi* **1** : turn, revolve, spin **2** : run (of an engine, etc.) **3** : make a film **4** : go bad, sour (of milk) **5 bien ~** : turn out well — **se tourner** *vr* : turn around — **tournant, -nante** [turnɑ̃, -nɑ̃t] *adj* : turning, revolving — **tournant** *nm* **1** : bend **2** : turning point — **tournée** [turne] *nf* **1** : tour **2** *fam* : round (of drinks)

tournesol [turnəsɔl] *nm* : sunflower

tournevis [turnəvis] *nms & pl* : screwdriver

tourniquet [turnikɛ] *nm* : turnstile

tournoi [turnwa] *nm* : tournament

tournoyer [turnwaje] {58} *vi* : whirl, spin

tournure [turnyr] *nf* **1** : turn (of events) **2** : expression

tourterelle [turtərɛl] *nf* : turtledove

tousser [tuse] *vi* : cough

tout [tu] (**toute(s)** [tut] *before feminine adjectives beginning with a consonant or an aspirate h*) *adv* **1** COMPLÈTEMENT : completely **2** : quite, very, all **3 ~ à coup** : suddenly **4 ~ à fait** : completely, entirely **5 ~ de suite** : immediately — **tout, toute** *adj, pl* **tous, toutes 1** : all **2** : each, every **3 à tout âge** : at any age **4 à toute vitesse** : at full speed **5 tout le monde** : everyone, everybody — **tout** *nm* **1 le ~** : the whole **2 pas du ~** : not at all — **tout** *pron, pl* **tous, toutes 1** : all, everything **2** : anyone, everyone

toutefois [tutfwa] *adv* : however

toux [tu] *nfs & pl* : cough

toxicomane [tɔksikɔman] *nmf* : drug addict

toxique [tɔksik] *adj* : toxic, poisonous

trac [trak] *nm* : stage fright, jitters *pl*

tracasser [trakase] *vt* : worry, bother — **se tracasser** *vr* : worry, fret — **tracas** [traka] *nms & pl* **1** : worry **2 ~** *nmpl* ENNUIS : troubles, problems

tracer [trase] {6} *vt* **1** : trace **2** DESSINER : draw **3 ~ le chemin** : pave the way — **trace** [tras] *nf* **1** : track, trail **2** : trace, vestige **3 ~s de pas** : footprints **4 suivre les ~s de qqn** : follow in s.o.'s footsteps — **tracé** [trase] *nm* PLAN : plan, layout

trachée [traʃe] *nf* : trachea, windpipe

tract [trakt] *nm* : leaflet

tractations [traktasjɔ̃] *nfpl* : negotiations

tracteur [traktœr] *nm* : tractor

traction [traksjɔ̃] *nf* **1** : traction **2 ~ avant** : front-wheel drive

tradition [tradisjɔ̃] *nf* : tradition — **traditionnel, -nelle** [tradisjɔnɛl] *adj* : traditional

traduire [tradɥir] {49} *vt* : translate — **traducteur, -trice** [tradyktœr, -tris] *n* : translator — **traduction** [tradyksjɔ̃] *nf* : translation

trafic [trafik] *nm* **1** : traffic **2** : (drug) trafficking — **trafiquant, -quante** [trafikɑ̃, -kɑ̃t] *n* : dealer, trafficker — **trafiquer** [trafike] *vt* : doctor, tamper with — *vi* : traffic, trade

tragédie [traʒedi] *nf* : tragedy — **tragique** [traʒik] *adj* : tragic

trahir [trair] *vt* : betray — **trahison** [traizɔ̃] *nf* **1** : betrayal **2** : treason

train [trɛ̃] *nm* **1** : (passenger) train **2** : pace, rate **3** : set, series **4 en ~ de** : in the process of **5 ~ de vie** : lifestyle

traîner [trene] *vt* **1** : pull, drag **2 ~ les pieds** : drag one's feet — *vi* **1** : drag **2** : dawdle, lag behind **3** : be lying around (of clothes, etc.) — **se traîner** *vr* : drag oneself, crawl — **traîne** [trɛn] *nf* **1** : train (of a dress) **2** *Can* : toboggan, sled — **traîneau** [treno] *nm, pl* **-neaux** : sled, sleigh — **traînée** [trene] *nf* **1** : streak **2** TRACE : trail **3** : drag (of an airplane, etc.)

train–train [trɛ̃trɛ̃] *nms & pl* ROUTINE : routine

traire [trɛr] {40} *vt* : milk (an animal)

trait [trɛ] *nm* **1** : (character) trait **2** : stroke, line **3 avoir ~ à** : relate to **4 d'un ~** : in one gulp **5 ~ d'union** : hyphen **6 ~s** *nmpl* : features

traite [trɛt] *nf* **1** : milking **2 d'une ~** : in one go **3 ~ bancaire** : bank draft

traité [trete] *nm* **1** : treaty **2** : treatise

traiter [trete] *vt* **1** : treat **2** : process (data) **3 ~ qqn de menteur** : call s.o. a liar — *vi* **~ de** : deal with — **traitement** [trɛtmɑ̃] *nm* **1** : treatment **2 ~ de texte** : word processing

traiteur [trɛtœr] *nm* : caterer

traître, -tresse [trɛtr, -trɛs] *n* : traitor — **~** *adj* : treacherous

trajectoire [traʒɛktwar] *nf* : trajectory

trajet [traʒɛ] *nm* **1** PARCOURS : route **2** VOYAGE : journey

trancher [trɑ̃ʃe] *vt* **1** COUPER : cut **2** : resolve (an issue) — *vi* **1** : stand out **2** : come to a decision — **tranchant, -chante** [trɑ̃ʃɑ̃, -ʃɑ̃t] *adj* : sharp, cutting — **tranchant** *nm* : cutting edge — **tranche** [trɑ̃ʃ] *nf* **1** : slice (of bread) **2** PARTIE : portion, section **3** : edge (of a book) — **tranchée** *nf* : trench

tranquille [trɑ̃kil] *adj* **1** : calm, quiet **2 tiens-toi ~!** : sit still! — **tranquillisant** [trɑ̃kilizɑ̃] *nm* : tranquilizer — **tranquilliser** [trɑ̃kilize] *vt* RASSURER : reassure — **tranquillité** [trɑ̃kilite] *nf* CALME : peacefulness, tranquillity

transaction [trɑ̃zaksjɔ̃] *nf* : transaction

transcrire [trɑ̃skrir] {33} *vt* : transcribe — **transcription** [trɑ̃skripsjɔ̃] *nf* : transcription

transe [trɑ̃s] *nf* : trance

transférer [trɑ̃sfere] *vt* : transfer — **transfert** [trɑ̃sfɛr] *nm* : transfer

transformer [trɑ̃sfɔrme] *vt* : transform, change — **se transformer** *vr* **~ en** : turn into — **transformateur** [trɑ̃sfɔrmatœr] *nm* : transformer — **transformation** [trɑ̃sfɔrmasjɔ̃] *nf* : transformation

transfusion [trɑ̃sfyzjɔ̃] *nf* : transfusion

transgresser [trɑ̃sgrese] *vt* ENFREINDRE : infringe, violate

transir [trɑ̃zir] *vt* **1** : chill (to the bone) **2** : paralyse (with fear)

transistor [trɑ̃zistɔr] *nm* : transistor

transit [trɑ̃zit] *nm* : transit

transitif, -tive [trɑ̃zitif, -tiv] *adj* : transitive

transition [trɑ̃zisjɔ̃] *nf* : transition — **transitoire** [trɑ̃zitwar] *adj* : transitory, transient

translucide [trɑ̃slysid] *adj* : translucent

transmettre [trɑ̃smɛtr] {53} *vt* **1** : transmit (signals, data, etc.) **2** : pass on, convey **3** : broadcast (a show) — **transmission** [trɑ̃smisjɔ̃] *nf* **1** : transmission **2** : broadcasting

transparent, -rente [trɑ̃sparɑ̃, -rɑ̃t] *adj* : transparent — **transparence** [trɑ̃sparɑ̃s] *nf* : transparency

transpercer [trɑ̃spɛrse] {6} *vt* : pierce

transpirer [trɑ̃spire] *vt* : perspire — **transpiration** [trɑ̃spirasjɔ̃] *nf* : perspiration

transplanter [trɑ̃splɑ̃te] *vt* : transplant — **transplantation** [trɑ̃splɑ̃tasjɔ̃] *nm* : transplant

transporter [trɑ̃spɔrte] *vt* : transport, carry — **transport** [trɑ̃spɔr] *nm* : transport — **transporteur** [trɑ̃spɔrtœr] *nm* : carrier, transporter

transposer [trɑ̃spoze] *vt* : transpose

transversal, -sale [trɑ̃svɛrsal] *adj, mpl* **-saux** [-so] : cross (of a beam)

trapèze [trapɛz] *nm* **1** : trapezoid **2** : trapeze

trappe [trap] *nf* **1** PIÈGE : trap **2** : trapdoor

trapu, -pue [trapy] *adj* : stocky, squat

traquer [trake] *vt* POURSUIVRE : track down

traumatiser [tromatize] *vt* : traumatize — **traumatisant, -sante** [tromatizɑ̃, -zɑ̃t] *adj* : traumatic — **traumatisme** [tromatism] *nm* : trauma

travailler [travaje] *vt* **1** : work **2** PRATIQUER : work on **3** TRACASSER : worry — *vi* : work — **travail** [travaj] *nm, pl* **-vaux** [travo] **1** : work **2** TÂCHE : task, job **3** EMPLOI : work, employment **4 travaux** *nmpl* : works, work — **travailleur, -leuse** [travajœr, -jøz] *adj* : hardworking, industrious — **~** *n* : worker

travée [trave] *nf* **1** : row (of seats) **2** : span (of a bridge)

travers [travɛr] *nms & pl* **1 à ~** *or* **au ~** : through **2 de ~** : askew, wrongly **3 en ~** : across, sideways — **traverser** [travɛrse] *vt* **1** : cross (the road, etc.) **2** : run through, pass through — **traversée** [travɛrse] *nf* : crossing

trébucher [trebyʃe] *vi* : stumble

trèfle [trɛfl] *nm* **1** : clover, shamrock **2** : clubs *pl* (in playing cards)

treillis [trɛji] *nms & pl* : trellis, lattice

treize [trɛz] *adj* **1** : thirteen **2** : thirteenth (in dates) — **~** *nms & pl* : thirteen — **treizième** [trɛzjɛm] *adj & nmf & nm* : thirteenth

trembler [trɑ̃ble] *vi* **1** : shake, tremble **2** : quiver (of the voice) — **tremblement** [trɑ̃bləmɑ̃] *nm* **1** : trembling **2** FRISSON : shiver **3 ~ de terre** : earthquake — **trembloter** [trɑ̃blɔte] *vi* : quaver

trémousser [tremuse] *v* **se trémousser** *vr* : wriggle around

tremper [trɑ̃pe] *vt* **1** : soak **2** : dip, dunk — **trempe** [trɑ̃p] *nf* : caliber, quality — **trempé, -pée** [trɑ̃pe] *adj* : soaked

tremplin [trɑ̃plɛ̃] *nm* **1** : springboard **2** *or* **~ à ski** : ski jump

trente [trɑ̃t] *adj* **1** : thirty **2** : thirtieth (in dates) — **~** *nms & pl* : thirty — **trentième** [trɑ̃tjɛm] *adj & nmf & nm* : thirtieth

trépied [trepje] *nm* : tripod

trépigner [trepiɲe] *vi* : stamp one's feet

très [trɛ] *adv* : very

trésor [trezɔr] *nm* : treasure

tressaillir [tresajir] {93}*vi* **1** : start (with surprise, etc.), wince (with pain) **2** TREMBLER : quiver, tremble — **tressaillement** [tresajmɑ̃] *nm* : start, wince

tresse [trɛs] *nf* : braid, plait — **tresser** [trɛse] *vt* **1** : braid, plait **2** : weave (a basket, etc.)

treuil [trœj] *nm* : winch

trêve [trɛv] *nf* **1** : truce **2** : respite

tri [tri] *nm* : sorting (out)

triangle [trijɑ̃gl] *nm* : triangle — **triangulaire** [trijɑ̃gylɛr] *adj* : triangular

tribal, -bale [tribal] *adj, mpl* **-baux** [tribo] : tribal

tribord [tribɔr] *nm* : starboard

tribu [triby] *nf* : tribe

tribulations [tribylasjɔ̃] *nfpl* : tribulations

tribunal [tribynal] *nm, pl* **-naux** [-no] : court

tribune [tribyn] *nf* **1** : gallery, grandstand **2** : rostrum, platform **3** DÉBAT : forum

tribut [triby] *nm* : tribute

tributaire [tribytɛr] *adj* **être ~ de** : be dependent on

tricher [triʃe] *vi* : cheat — **tricherie** [triʃri] *nf* : cheating — **tricheur, -cheuse** [triʃœr, -ʃøz] *n* : cheat

tricoter [trikɔte] *v* : knit — **tricot** [triko] *nm* **1** : knitting **2** : knitted fabric **3** CHANDAIL : sweater

tricycle [trisikl] *nm* : tricycle

trier [trije] {96} *vt* **1** : sort (out) **2** CHOISIR : select

trimbaler *or* **trimballer** [trɛ̃bale] *vt fam* : cart around

trimestre [trimɛstr] *nm* **1** : quarter (in economics, etc.) **2** : term (in school) — **trimestriel, -trielle** [trimɛstrijɛl] *adj* : quarterly

tringle [trɛ̃gl] *nf* : rod

trinité [trinite] *nf* : trinity

trinquer [trɛ̃ke] *vi* : clink glasses, drink (a toast)

trio [trijo] *nm* : trio

triomphe [trijɔ̃f] *nm* : triumph — **triompher** [trijɔ̃fe] *vi* : triumph

tripes [trip] *nfpl* **1** : tripe **2** *fam* : guts

triple [tripl] *adj & nm* : triple, treble — **tripler** [triple] *v* : triple — **triplés, -plées** [triple] *npl* : triplets

tripoter [tripɔte] *vt* : fiddle with

trique [trik] *nf* : cudgel

triste [trist] *adj* **1** : sad **2** : dismal **3** LAMENTABLE : deplorable, sorry — **tristesse** [tristɛs] *nf* : sadness, gloominess

triton [tritɔ̃] *nm* : newt

troc [trɔk] *nm* : swap

trognon [trɔɲɔ̃] *nm* : core (of an apple, etc.)

trois [trwa] *adj* **1** : three **2** : third (in dates) — **~** *nms & pl* : three — **troisième** [trwazjɛm] *adj & nmf* : third

trombe [trɔ̃b] *nf* **1** : waterspout **2 ~s d'eau** : downpour

trombone [trɔ̃bɔn] *nm* **1** : trombone **2** : paper clip

trompe [trɔ̃p] *nf* **1** : horn **2** : trunk (of an elephant)

tromper [trɔ̃pe] *vt* **1** DUPER : deceive **2** : be unfaithful to (one's spouse) — **se tromper** *vr* : make a mistake — **tromperie** [trɔ̃pri] *nf* : deception, deceit

trompette [trɔ̃pɛt] *nf* : trumpet

trompeur, -peuse [trɔ̃pœr, -pøz] *adj* **1** : deceitful **2** : misleading

tronc [trɔ̃] *nm* **1** : trunk (of a tree) **2** TORSE : torso

tronçon [trɔ̃sɔ̃] *nm* : section — **tronçonneuse** [trɔ̃sɔnøz] *nf* : chain saw

trône [tron] *nm* : throne

tronquer [trɔ̃ke] *vt* : truncate

trop [tro] *adv* **1** : too **2 ~ de** : too many, too much **3 de ~** *or* **en ~** : too many, extra

trophée [trɔfe] *nm* : trophy

tropique [trɔpik] *nm* **1** : tropic **2 ~s** *nmpl* : tropics — **tropical, -cale** [trɔpikal] *adj, mpl* **-caux** [-ko] : tropical

trop–plein [trɔplɛ̃] *nm, pl* **trop–pleins 1** : overflow **2** SURPLUS : excess, surplus

troquer [trɔke] *vt* : trade, barter

trotter [trɔte] *vi* : trot

trotteuse [trɔtøz] *nf* : second hand (of a watch)

trottiner [trɔtine] *vi* : scurry along

trottinette [trɔtinɛt] *nf* : scooter

trottoir [trɔtwar] *nm* : sidewalk

trou [tru] *nm* **1** : hole **2** : gap (of time) **3 ~ de mémoire** : memory lapse **4 ~ de (la) serrure** : keyhole

troubler [truble] *vt* **1** : disturb **2** BROUILLER : blur, cloud **3** INQUIÉTER : trouble — **trouble** [trubl] *adj* **1** : cloudy **2** FLOU : blurred, unclear — **~** *nm* **1** : confusion **2** : trouble **3 ~s** *nmpl* : disorder (in medicine) **4 ~s** *nmpl* : unrest

trouer [true] *vt* : make a hole in, pierce — **trouée** [true] *nf* : gap

trouille [truj] *nf fam* : fear, fright

troupe [trup] *nf* **1** : troop **2 ~ de théâtre** : theater company

troupeau [trupo] *nm, pl* **-peaux** : herd, flock

trousse [trus] *nf* **1** : kit, case **2 aux ~s de** : on the heels of

trousseau [truso] *nm, pl* **-seaux 1** : trousseau **2 ~ de clefs** : bunch of keys

trouver [truve] *vt* **1** : find **2** ESTIMER : think — **se trouver** *vr* **1** : be (found) **2** : find oneself **3** SE SENTIR : feel — *v impers* **il se trouve que** : it turns out that — **trouvaille** [truvaj] *nf* DÉCOUVERTE : find

truand [tryɑ̃] *nm* : gangster, crook

truc [tryk] *nm* **1** : trick **2** *fam* MACHIN : thing, thingamajig

truelle [tryɛl] *nf* : trowel

truffe [tryf] *nf* : truffle

truite [trɥit] *nf* : trout

truquer [tryke] *vt* : fix, rig

trust [trœst] *nm* : trust, cartel

tsar [tsar, dzar] *nm* : czar

t–shirt [tiʃœrt] *nm* → **tee–shirt**

tu [ty] *pron* : you

tuba [tyba] *nm* **1** : tuba **2** : snorkel

tube [tyb] *nm* **1** : tube **2** *fam* : hit (song)

tuberculose [tybɛrkyloz] *nf* : tuberculosis

tuer [tɥe] *vt* **1** : kill **2** ÉPUISER : exhaust — **se tuer** *vr* **1** : be killed, die **2** : kill oneself — **tuerie** [tyri] *nf* CARNAGE : slaughter — **tueur, tueuse** [tɥœr, tɥøz] *n* : killer

tue–tête [tytɛt] **à ~** *adv phr* : at the top of one's lungs

tuile [tɥil] *nf* **1** : tile **2** *fam* : bad luck

tulipe [tylip] *nf* : tulip

tumeur [tymœr] *nf* : tumor

tumulte [tymylt] *nm* : tumult, commotion — **tumultueux, -tueuse** [tymyltɥø, -tɥøz] *adj* : stormy, turbulent

tunique [tynik] *nf* : tunic

tunnel [tynɛl] *nm* : tunnel

tuque [tyk] *nf Can* : stocking cap

turban [tyrbɑ̃] *nm* : turban

turbine [tyrbin] *nf* : turbine

turbulence [tyrbylɑ̃s] *nf* : turbulence — **turbulent, -lente** [tyrbylɑ̃, -lɑ̃t] *adj* **1** : unruly **2** : turbulent

turc, turque [tyrk] *adj* : Turkish — **turc** *nm* : Turkish (language)

turquoise [tyrkwaz] *adj* : turquoise

tutelle [tytɛl] *nf* **1** : guardianship **2** : care, protection

tuteur, -trice [tytœr, -tris] *n* **1** : guardian **2** : tutor — **tuteur** *nm* : stake

tutoyer [tytwaje] {58} *vt* : address someone as *tu*

tuyau [tɥijo] *nm, pl* **tuyaux 1** : pipe, tube **2** *fam* : tip, advice — **tuyauterie** [tɥijotri] *nf* : pipes *pl*, plumbing

tympan [tɛ̃pɑ̃] *nm* : eardrum

type [tip] *nm* **1** : type, kind **2** : example, model **3** : (physical) type **4** *fam* : guy, fellow

typhon [tifɔ̃] *nm* : typhoon

typique [tipik] *adj* : typical

tyran [tirɑ̃] *nm* : tyrant — **tyrannie** [tirani] *nf* : tyranny

U

u [y] *nm* : u, 21st letter of the alphabet

ulcère [ylsɛr] *nm* : ulcer

ultérieur, -rieure [ylterjœr] *adj* : later, subsequent — **ultérieurement** [ylterjœrmɑ̃] *adv* : subsequently

ultimatum [yltimatɔm] *nm* : ultimatum — **ultime** [yltim] *adj* : ultimate, final

ultraviolet, -lette [yltravjɔlɛ, -lɛt] *adj* : ultraviolet

un, une [œ̃ (œn *before a vowel or mute* h), yn] *adj* : a, an, one — **~** *n & pron* **1** : one **2 une par une** : one by one — **~** *art, pl* **des 1** (*used in the singular*) : a, an **2** (*used in the plural*) : some — **un** *nm* : (number) one

unanime [ynanim] *adj* : unanimous — **unanimité** [ynanimite] *nf* : unanimity

uni, -nie [yni] *adj* **1** : united **2** LISSE : smooth **3** : solid (of a color) **4** : close-knit (of a family)

unifier [ynifje] {96} *vt* : unite, unify — **unification** [ynifikasjɔ̃] *nf* : unification

uniforme [ynifɔrm] *adj* : uniform, even — ~ *nm* : uniform — **uniformiser** *vt* : make uniform, standardize — **uniformité** [ynifɔrmite] *nf* : uniformity

unilatéral, -rale [ynilateral] *adj, pl* **-raux** [-ro] : unilateral

union [ynjɔ̃] *nf* : union

unique [ynik] *adj* **1** : unique **2 enfant ~** : only child **3 sens ~** : one-way — **uniquement** [ynikmɑ̃] *adv* : only, solely

unir [ynir] *vt* **1** : unite, connect **2** COMBINER : combine — **s'unir** *vr* : unite

unisson [ynisɔ̃] *nm* : unison

unité [ynite] *nf* **1** : unity **2** : unit

univers [ynivɛr] *nm* : universe — **universel, -selle** [ynivɛrsɛl] *vt* : universal

universitaire [ynivɛrsitɛr] *adj* : university, academic — **université** [ynivɛrsite] *nf* : university

uranium [yranjɔm] *nm* : uranium

Uranus [yranys] *nm* : Uranus

urbain, -baine [yrbɛ̃, -bɛn] *adj* : urban, city — **urbanisme** [yrbanism] *nm* : city planning

urgence [yrʒɑ̃s] *nf* **1** : urgency **2** : emergency **3 d'~** : urgently, immediately — **urgent, -gente** [yrʒɑ̃, -ʒɑ̃t] *adj* : urgent

urine [yrin] *nf* : urine — **uriner** [yrine] *vi* : urinate — **urinoir** [yrinwar] *nm* : urinal

urne [yrn] *nf* **1** : urn **2** : ballot box

urticaire [yrtikɛr] *nf* : hives

usage [yzaʒ] *nm* **1** : use **2** : usage (of a word) **3** COUTUME : habit, custom — **usagé, -gée** [yzaʒe] *adj* **1** : worn **2** : used, secondhand — **usager** [yzaʒe] *nm* : user

user [yze] *vt* **1** CONSOMMER : use **2** : wear out, to use up — *vi* **1 ~ de** : exercise (one's rights, etc.) **2 ~ de** : make use of — **usé, -sée** [yze] *adj* **1** : worn-out **2** : hackneyed, trite

usine [yzin] *nf* : factory

usité, -tée [yzite] *adj* : commonly used

ustensile [ystɑ̃sil] *nm* : utensil

usuel, -suelle [yzɥɛl] *adj* : common, usual — **usuellement** [yzɥɛlmɑ̃] *adv* : usually, ordinarily

usure [yzyr] *nm* : wear (and tear)

usurper [yzyrpe] *vt* : usurp

utérus [yterys] *nms & pl* : uterus

utile [ytil] *adj* : useful — **utilisable** [ytilizabl] *adj* : usable — **utiliser** [ytilize] *vt* : use — **utilisateur, -trice** [ytilizatœr, -tris] *n* : user — **utilisation** [ytilizasjɔ̃] *nf* : use — **utilité** [ytilite] *nf* : usefulness

utopie [ytɔpi] *nf* : utopia — **utopique** [ytɔpik] *adj* : utopian

V

v [ve] *nm* : v, 22d letter of the alphabet

va [va], *etc.* → **aller**

vacances [vakɑ̃s] *nfpl* : vacation — **vacancier, -cière** [vakɑ̃sje, -sjɛr] *n* : vacationer — **vacant, -cante** [vakɑ̃, -kɑ̃t] *adj* : vacant

vacarme [vakarm] *nm* : racket, din

vaccin [vaksɛ̃] *nm* : vaccine — **vacciner** [vaksine] *vt* : vaccinate — **vaccination** [vaksinasjɔ̃] *nf* : vaccination

vache [vaʃ] *nf* : cow — ~ *adj fam* : mean, nasty — **vachement** [vaʃmɑ̃] *adv fam* : really, very — **vacherie** [vaʃri] *nf fam* **1** : nastiness **2** : dirty trick

vaciller [vasije] *vi* **1** : stagger, sway **2** : flicker (of a light) **3** : falter, fail — **vacillant, -lante** [vasijɑ̃, -jɑ̃t] *adj* **1** : unsteady, shaky **2** : wavering, faltering — **vacillement** [vasijmɑ̃] *nm* **1** : flicker **2** : faltering

va–et–vient [vaevjɛ̃] *nms & pl* **1** : comings and goings **2** : to-and-fro motion

vagabond, -bonde [vagabɔ̃, -bɔ̃d] *n* : vagrant, tramp — **vagabonder** [vagabɔ̃de] *vi* : roam, wander

vagin [vaʒɛ̃] *nm* : vagina

vague[1] [vag] *adj* : vague, indistinct — ~ *nm* : vagueness — **vaguement** [vagmɑ̃] *adv* : vaguely, slightly

vague[2] *nf* : wave

vaillant, -lante [vajɑ̃, -jɑ̃t] *adj* **1** : valiant, brave **2** : healthy, robust — **vaillamment** [vajamɑ̃] *adv* : courageously

vain, vaine [vɛ̃, vɛn] *adj* **1** : vain, futile **2 en ~** : in vain

vaincre [vɛ̃kr] {94} *vt* **1** BATTRE : defeat **2** SURMONTER : overcome — **vaincu, -cue** [vɛ̃ky] *adj* : defeated — **vainqueur** [vɛ̃kœr] *nm* : victor, winner

vaisseau [vɛso] *nm, pl* **-seaux 1** : (blood) vessel **2** : vessel, ship **3 ~ spatial** : spaceship

vaisselle [vɛsɛl] *nf* : crockery, dishes *pl*

valable [valabl] *adj* **1** VALIDE : valid **2** BON : good, worthwhile

valet [valɛ] *nm* **1** : servant **2** : jack (in playing cards)

valeur [valœr] *nf* **1** : value **2** MÉRITE : merit, worth **3 objets de ~** : valuables **4 ~s** *nfpl* : stocks, securities

valide [valid] *adj* : valid — **valider** [valide] *vt* : validate — **validité** [validite] *nf* : validity

valise [valiz] *nf* : suitcase

vallée [vale] *nf* : valley — **vallon** [valɔ̃] *nm* : small valley — **vallonné, -née** [valɔne] *adj* : hilly

valoir [valwar] {95} *vi* **1** : have a (certain) cost **2** : be worth **3** : apply, be valid **4 ça vaut combien?** : how much is it worth? **5 faire ~** : point out, assert — *vt* **1** PROCURER : earn, bring (to) **2 ~ la peine** : be worth the trouble — *v impers* **il vaut mieux** : it's better (to) — **se valoir** *vr* : be equivalent

valoriser [valɔrize] *vt* : increase the value of

valse [vals] *nf* : waltz — **valser** [valse] *vi* : waltz

valve [valv] *nf* : valve

vampire [vɑ̃pir] *nm* : vampire

vandale [vɑ̃dal] *nmf* : vandal — **vandalisme** [vɑ̃dalism] *nm* : vandalism

vanille [vanij] *nf* : vanilla

vanité [vanite] *nf* : vanity — **vaniteux, -teuse** [vanitø, -tøz] *adj* : conceited, vain

vanne [van] *nf* **1** : floodgate **2** *fam* : dig, gibe

vanter [vɑ̃te] *vt* : vaunt, praise — **se vanter** *vr* **1** : boast **2 ~ de** : pride oneself on — **vantard, -tarde** [vɑ̃tar, -tard] *adj* : boastful — ~ *n* : braggart — **vantardise** [vɑ̃tardiz] *nf* : boast

va–nu–pieds [vanypje] *nmfs & pl* : beggar

vapeur [vapœr] *nf* **1** : steam **2 ~s** *nfpl* : fumes

vaporiser [vapɔrize] *vt* : spray — **vaporisateur** [vapɔrizatœr] *nm* : spray, atomizer

vaquer [vake] *vi* **~ à** : attend to, see to

varappe [varap] *nf* : rock climbing

variable [varjabl] *adj* : variable, changeable — **variante** [varjɑ̃t] *nf* : variant — **variation** [varjasjɔ̃] *nf* : variation

varice [varis] *nf* : varicose vein

varicelle [varisɛl] *nf* : chicken pox

varier [varje] {96} *v* : vary — **varié, -riée** [varje] *adj* **1** : varied, varying **2** : various, diverse — **variété** [varjete] *nf* : variety

variole [varjɔl] *nf* : smallpox

vase[1] [vaz] *nm* : vase

vase[2] *nf* BOUE : mud, silt — **vaseux, -seuse** [vazø, -zøz] *adj* BOUEUX : muddy

vaste [vast] *adj* : vast, immense

vaurien, -rienne [vorjɛ̃, -rjɛn] *n* : good-for-nothing

vautour [votur] *nm* : vulture

vautrer [votre] *v* **se vautrer** *vr* **~ dans** : wallow in

veau [vo] *nm, pl* **veaux 1** : calf **2** : veal

vécu [veky] *pp* → **vivre** — **vécu, -cue** [veky] *adj* : real, true

vedette [vədɛt] *nf* **1** : star, celebrity **2 mettre en ~** : put in the spotlight, feature

végétal, -tale [veʒetal] *adj, mpl* **-taux** : vegetable, plant — **végétal** *nm* : vegetable, plant — **végétarien, -rienne** [veʒetarjɛ̃, -rjɛn] *adj & n* : vegetarian — **végéter** [veʒete] {87} *vi* : vegetate — **végétation** [veʒetasjɔ̃] *nf* : vegetation

véhément, -mente [veemɑ̃, -mɑ̃t] *adj* : vehement — **véhémence** [veemɑ̃s] *nf* : vehemence

véhicule [veikyl] *nm* : vehicle

veiller [veje] *vt* : sit up with, watch over — *vi* **1** : stay awake **2** : keep watch **3** : be vigilant **4 ~ à** : see to — **veille** [vɛj] *nf* **1** : day before, eve **2** : watch, vigil — **veillée** [veje] *nf* **1** SOIRÉE : evening **2 ~ funèbre** : wake — **veilleur, -leuse** [vejœr, -jøz] *n* **1** : lookout, sentry **2 ~ de nuit** : night watchman — **veilleuse** *nf* **1** : night-light **2** : pilot light

veine [vɛn] *nf* **1** : vein **2** *fam* : luck

vélo [velo] *nm* : bike, bicycle

vélomoteur [velɔmɔtœr] *nm* : moped

velours [vəlur] *nm* **1** : velvet, velour **2 ~ côtelé** : corduroy — **velouté, -tée** [vəlute] *adj* : velvety, smooth

velu, -lue [vəly] *adj* : hairy

venaison [vənɛzɔ̃] *nf* : venison

vendange [vɑ̃dɑ̃ʒ] *nf* : grape harvest

vendre [vɑ̃dr] {63} *vt* **1** : sell **2 à ~** : for sale — **se vendre** : sell — **vendeur, -deuse** [vɑ̃dœr, -døz] *n* : salesperson

vendredi [vɑ̃drədi] *nm* : Friday

vénéneux, -neuse [venenø, -nøz] *adj* : poisonous

vénérer [venere] {87} *vt* : venerate — **vénérable** [venerabl] *adj* : venerable

vénérien, -rienne [venerjɛ̃, -rjɛn] *adj* : venereal

venger [vɑ̃ʒe] {17} *vt* : avenge — **se venger** *vr* : take revenge — **vengeance** [vɑ̃ʒɑ̃s] *nf* : vengeance, revenge — **vengeur, -geresse** [vɑ̃ʒœr, -ʒrɛs] *adj* : vengeful — ~ *n* : avenger

venin [vənɛ̃] *nm* : venom, poison — **venimeux, -meuse** [vənimø, -møz] *adj* : poisonous

venir [vənir] {92} *vi* **1** : come **2 ~ de** : come from **3 en ~ à** : come to (a conclusion, etc.) **4 faire ~** : send for — *v aux* **1** : come and, come to **2 ~ de** : have just

vent [vɑ̃] *nm* **1** : wind **2 il y a du ~** *or* **il fait du ~** : it's windy — **venteux, -teuse** [vɑ̃tø, -tøz] *adj* : windy

vente [vɑ̃t] *nf* **1** : sale, selling **2 en ~** : for sale

ventiler [vɑ̃tile] *vt* : ventilate — **ventilateur** [vɑ̃tilatœr] *nm* : (electric) fan, ventilator — **ventilation** [vɑ̃tilasjɔ̃] *nf* : ventilation

ventouse [vɑ̃tuz] *nf* **1** : suction cup **2** : plunger

ventre [vɑ̃tr] *nm* **1** : stomach, belly **2** : womb **3 avoir mal au ~** : have a stomachache

ventriloque [vɑ̃trilɔk] *nmf* : ventriloquist

venu [vəny] *pp* → **venir** — **venu, -nue** [vəny] *adj* **1 bien venu** : timely **2 mal venu** : ill-advised, unwelcome — **venue** *nf* : coming, arrival

Vénus [venys] *nf* : Venus (planet)

ver [vɛr] *nm* **1** : worm **2 ~ de terre** : earthworm

véranda [verɑ̃da] *nf* : veranda, porch

verbe [vɛrb] *nm* : verb — **verbal, -bale** [vɛrbal] *adj, mpl* **-baux** [-bo] : verbal

verdeur [vɛrdœr] *nf* : vigor, vitality

verdict [vɛrdikt] *nm* : verdict

verdir [vɛrdir] *v* : turn green — **verdoyant, -doyante** [vɛrdwajɑ̃, -dwajɑ̃t] *adj* : green, verdant — **verdure** [vɛrdyr] *nf* : greenery

verge [vɛrʒ] *nf* : rod, stick

verger [vɛrʒe] *nm* : orchard

verglacé, -cée [vɛrglase] *adj* : icy — **verglas** [vɛrgla] *nm* : black ice

vergogne [vɛrgɔɲ] *nf* **sans ~** : shamelessly

véridique [veridik] *adj* : truthful

vérifier [verifje] {96} *vt* : verify, check — **vérification** [verifikasjɔ̃] *nf* : verification, check

vérité [verite] *nf* **1** : truth **2 en ~** : in fact — **véritable** [veritabl] *adj* **1** RÉEL : true, actual **2** AUTHENTIQUE : genuine **3** (*used as an intensive*) : real — **véritablement** [-tabləmɑ̃] *adv* : actually, really

vermine [vɛrmin] *nf* : vermin

vernis [vɛrni] *nms & pl* **1** : varnish **2** : glaze (on pottery) **3** : veneer, facade **4 ~ à ongles** : nail polish — **vernir** [vɛrnir] *vt* : varnish — **vernissage** [vɛrnisaʒ] *nm* **1** : varnishing **2** : opening (of an art exhibition) — **vernisser** [vɛrnise] *vt* : glaze (ceramics)

verre [vɛr] *nm* **1** : glass **2** : (drinking) glass **3 ~s** *nmpl* : eyeglasses, lenses **4 prendre un ~** : have a drink — **verrerie** [vɛrri] *nf* : glassware — **verrière** [vɛrjɛr] *nf* **1** : glass roof **2** : glass wall

verrou [vɛru] *nm* : bolt — **verrouiller** [vɛruje] *vt* : bolt, lock

verrue [vɛry] *nf* : wart

vers[1] [vɛr] *nms & pl* : line, verse (of poetry)

vers[2] *prep* **1** : toward, towards **2** : about, around, near

versant [vɛrsɑ̃] *nm* : slope, side (of a hill, etc.)

versatile [vɛrsatil] *adj* : fickle

verser [vɛrse] *vt* **1** : pour, serve **2** PAYER : pay **3** RÉPANDRE : shed (tears, etc.) — *vi* **1** : overturn **2 ~ dans** : lapse into — **verse** [vɛrs] *nf* **pleuvoir à ~** : pour (rain) — **versé, -sée** [vɛrse] *adj* **~ dans** : (well-)versed in — **versement** [vɛrsəmɑ̃] *nm* **1** : payment **2** : installment

verset [vɛrsɛ] *nm* : verse

version [vɛrsjɔ̃] *nf* : version

verso [vɛrso] *nm* : back (of a page)

vert, verte [vɛr, vɛrt] *adj* **1** : green **2** : unripe **3** GAILLARD : sprightly, vigorous — **vert** *nm* : green

vertèbre [vɛrtɛbr] *nf* : vertebra — **vertébral, -brale** [vɛrtebral] *adj, mpl* **-braux** [-bro] : vertebral

vertement [vɛrtəmɑ̃] *adv* : sharply, severely

vertical, -cale [vɛrtikal] *adj, mpl* **-caux** [-ko] : vertical — **verticale** *nf* **à la ~** : vertically — **verticalement** [-kalmɑ̃] *adv* : vertically

vertige [vɛrtiʒ] *nm* : dizziness — **vertigineux, -neuse** [vɛrtiʒinø, -nøz] *adj* **1** : dizzy **2** : breathtaking

vertu [vɛrty] *nf* **1** : virtue **2 en ~ de** : by virtue of — **vertueux, -tueuse** [vɛrtɥø, -tɥøz] *adj* : virtuous

verve [vɛrv] *nf* : humor, wit

vésicule [vezikyl] *nf* **~ biliaire** : gallbladder

vessie [vesi] *nf* : bladder

veste [vɛst] *nf* **1** : jacket **2** *Can* : vest

vestiaire [vɛstjɛr] *nm* : locker room

vestibule [vɛstibyl] *nm* : hall

vestige [vɛstiʒ] *nm* **1** : vestige **2** : relic, remains

veston [vɛstɔ̃] *nm* : (man's) jacket

vêtement [vɛtmɑ̃] *nm* **1** : garment, article of clothing **2 ~s** *nmpl* : clothes, clothing

vétéran [veterɑ̃] *nm* : veteran

vétérinaire [veterinɛr] *nmf* : veterinarian

vêtir [vetir] {97} *vt* HABILLER : dress — **se vêtir** *vr* : get dressed — **vêtu, -tue** [vety] *adj* : dressed

veto [veto] *nms & pl* : veto

veuf, veuve [vœf, vœv] *adj* : widowed — ~ *n* : widower *m*, widow *f*

vexer [vɛkse] *vt* : vex, upset — **se vexer** *vr* : take offense — **vexant, -xante** [vɛksɑ̃, -ksɑ̃t] *adj* : hurtful

via [vja] *prep* : via

viable [vjabl] *adj* : viable

viaduc [vjadyk] *nm* : viaduct

viande [vjɑ̃d] *nf* **1** : meat **2 ~ hachée** : hamburger

vibrer [vibre] *vi* : vibrate — **vibrant, -brante** [vibrɑ̃, -brɑ̃t] *adj* : vibrant — **vibration** [vibrasjɔ̃] *nf* : vibration

vicaire [vikɛr] *nm* : vicar, curate

vice [vis] *nm* **1** DÉBAUCHE : vice **2** DÉFAUT : defect

vice–président, -dente [visprezidɑ̃, -dɑ̃t] *n* : vice president

vice versa *or* **vice–versa** [viseversa] *adv* : vice versa

vicier [visje] {96} *vt* : pollute, taint

vicieux, -cieuse [visjø, -sjøz] *adj* : perverse, depraved

victime [viktim] *nf* : victim

victoire [viktwar] *nf* : victory — **victorieux, -rieuse** [viktɔrjø, -rjøz] *adj* : victorious

vidange [vidɑ̃ʒ] *nf* **1** : emptying, draining **2** : oil change — **vidanger** [vidɑ̃ʒe] {17} *vt* : empty, drain

vide [vid] *adj* : empty — ~ *nm* **1** : emptiness, void **2** LACUNE : gap

vidéo [video] *adj s & pl* : video — ~ *nf* : video

vidéocassette [videɔkasɛt] *nf* : videocassette, videotape

vider [vide] *vt* **1** : empty **2** : vacate (the premises) **3** : clean (a fowl), gut (a fish) — **videur** [vidœr] *nm* : bouncer

vie [vi] *nf* **1** : life **2** : lifetime **3** : livelihood, living **4 à ~** : for life **5 être en ~** : be alive **6 jamais de la ~!** : never!

vieil → **vieux**

viellard [vjɛjar] *nm* : old man

vieille → **vieux**

vieillir [vjejir] *vt* : make (someone) old, age — *vi* **1** : grow old, age **2** : become outdated — **vieillesse** [vjɛjɛs] *nf* : old age

vierge [vjɛrʒ] *adj* **1** : virgin **2** : empty, blank (of a tape, etc.) — ~ *nf* : virgin

vieux [vjø] (**vieil** [vjɛj] *before a vowel or mute h*), **vieille** [vjɛj] *adj, mpl* **vieux 1** : old **2 vieille fille** : old maid **3 vieux jeu** : old-fashioned — ~ *n* : old man *m*, old woman *f*

vif, vive [vif, viv] *adj* **1** : lively, animated **2** AIGU : sharp, keen **3** : vivid (of a color) **4** : brisk, bracing (of the wind) — **vif** *nm* **1 à ~** : open, exposed **2 le ~ du sujet** : the heart of the matter **3 sur le ~** : on the spot, from life

vigilant, -lante [viʒilɑ̃, -lɑ̃t] *adj* : vigilant — **vigilance** [viʒilɑ̃s] *nf* : vigilance

vigne [viɲ] *nf* **1** : grapevine **2** : vineyard — **vigneron, -ronne** [viɲrɔ̃, -rɔn] *n* : winegrower

vignette [viɲɛt] *nf* : label, sticker

vignoble [viɲɔbl] *nm* : vineyard

vigueur [vigœr] *nf* **1** : vigor **2 en ~** : in force — **vigoureux, -reuse** [vigurø, -røz] *adj* **1** : vigorous, sturdy **2** : forceful, energetic

VIH [veiaʃ] *nm* (*V*irus de l'*I*mmunodéficience *H*umaine) : HIV

vil, vile [vil] *adj* : vile, base

vilain, -laine [vilɛ̃, -lɛn] *adj* **1** LAID : ugly **2** MÉCHANT : naughty

villa [vila] *nf* : villa

village [vilaʒ] *nm* : village — **villageois, -geoise** [vilaʒwa, -ʒwaz] *n* : villager

ville [vil] *nf* **1** : city, town **2 en ~** : downtown

villégiature [vileʒjatyr] *nf* **1** : vacation **2** *or* **lieu de ~** : resort

vin [vɛ̃] *nm* : wine

vinaigre [vinɛgr] *nm* : vinegar — **vinaigrette** [vinɛgrɛt] *nf* : vinaigrette

vindicatif, -tive [vɛ̃dikatif, -tiv] *adj* : vindictive

vingt [vɛ̃ (vɛ̃t *before a vowel, mute h, and the numbers 22-29*)] *adj* **1** : twenty **2** : twentieth (in dates) — ~ *nms & pl* : twenty — **vingtaine** [vɛ̃tɛn] *nf* : about twenty — **vingtième** [vɛ̃tjɛm] *adj & nmf & nm* : twentieth

vinicole [vinikɔl] *adj* : wine, wine-growing

vinyle [vinil] *nm* : vinyl

viol [vjɔl] *nm* : rape — **violation** [vjɔlasjɔ̃] *nf* : violation

violent, -lente [vjɔlɑ̃, -lɑ̃t] *adj* : violent — **violemment** [vjɔlamɑ̃] *adv* : violently — **violence** [vjɔlɑ̃s] *nf* : violence

violer [vjɔle] *vt* **1** : rape **2** : violate, break (a law, etc.)

violet, -lette [vjɔlɛ, -lɛt] *adj* : purple, violet — **violet** *nm* : purple, violet — **violette** *nf* : violet (flower)

violon [vjɔlɔ̃] *nm* : violin — **violoncelle** [vjɔlɔ̃sɛl] *nm* : cello — **violoniste** [vjɔlɔnist] *nmf* : violinist

vipère [vipɛr] *nf* : adder, viper

virer [vire] *vt* **1** : transfer (funds) **2** *fam* : fire, expel — *vi* **1** : veer, turn **2** : change color — **virage** [viraʒ] *nm* **1** COURBE : bend, turn **2** : change, shift (in direction)

— **virée** [vire] *nf fam* : outing, trip — **virement** [virmɑ̃] *nm* : (bank) transfer
virevolter [virvɔlte] *vi* : twirl
virginité [virʒinite] *nf* : virginity
virgule [virgyl] *nf* **1** : comma **2** : (decimal) point
viril, -rile [viril] *adj* : virile, manly — **virilité** [virilite] *nf* : virility
virtuel, -tuelle [virtɥɛl] *adj* : virtual
virtuose [virtɥoz] *nmf* : virtuoso
virulent, -lente [virylɑ̃, -lɑ̃t] *adj* : virulent
virus [virys] *nms & pl* : virus
vis [vi] *nfs & pl* : screw
visa [viza] *nm* : visa
visage [vizaʒ] *nm* : face
vis–à–vis [vizavi] *adv* ~ **de 1** : opposite, facing **2** : towards, with respect to — ~ *nms & pl* **en** ~ : facing each other
viscères [visɛr] *nmpl* : innards
viser [vize] *vt* : aim for, aim at — *vi* **1** : aim **2** ~ **à** : aim at, intend to — **visée** [vize] *nf* : aim, design
visible [vizibl] *adj* **1** : visible **2** : obvious — **visibilité** [vizibilite] *nf* : visibility
visière [vizjɛr] *nf* : visor (of a cap, etc.)
vision [vizjɔ̃] *nf* : vision — **visionnaire** [vizjɔnɛr] *adj & nmf* : visionary — **visionner** [vizjɔne] *vt* : view
visite [vizit] *nf* **1** : visit **2** VISITEUR : visitor **3** : examination, inspection **4 rendre** ~ **à qqn** : visit s.o. — **visiter** [vizite] *vt* **1** : visit **2** EXAMINER : examine, inspect — **visiteur, -teuse** [vizitœr, -tøz] *n* : visitor
vison [vizɔ̃] *nm* : mink
visqueux, -queuse [viskø, -køz] *adj* : viscous
visser [vise] *vt* : screw (on)
visuel, -suelle [vizɥɛl] *adj* : visual — **visualiser** [vizɥalize] *vt* : visualize
vital, -tale [vital] *adj, mpl* **-taux** [vito] : vital — **vitalité** [vitalite] *nf* : vitality
vitamine [vitamin] *nf* : vitamin
vite [vit] *adv* **1** RAPIDEMENT : fast, quickly **2** TÔT : soon — **vitesse** [vitɛs] *nf* **1** : speed **2** : gear (of a car)
viticole [vitikɔl] *adj* : wine, wine-growing — **viticulture** [vitikyltyr] *nf* : wine growing
vitre [vitr] *nf* **1** : pane, windowpane **2** : window (of a car, train, etc.) — **vitrail** [vitraj] *nm, pl* **-traux** [vitro] : stained-glass window — **vitré, -trée** [vitre] *adj* : glass, glazed — **vitrer** [vitre] *vt* : glaze — **vitreux, -treuse** [vitrø, -trøz] *adj* : glassy — **vitrine** [vitrin] *nf* **1** : shop window **2** : display case
vivable [vivabl] *adj* : bearable
vivacité [vivasite] *nf* **1** : vivacity, liveliness **2** AGILITÉ : quickness **3** : sharpness, vividness
vivant, -vante [vivɑ̃, -vɑ̃t] *adj* **1** : alive, living **2** ANIMÉ : lively — **vivant** *nm* **1 du** ~ **de** : during the lifetime of **2 les** ~**s** : the living
vivats [viva] *nmpl* : cheers
vive ù vif — ~ [viv] *interj* : long live, three cheers for — **vivement** [vivmɑ̃] *adv* **1** : quickly **2** : greatly
vivier [vivje] *nm* : fishpond
vivifier [vivifje] {96} *vt* : invigorate — **vivifiant, -fiante** [vivifjɑ̃, -fjɑ̃t] *adj* : invigorating
vivre [vivr] {98} *vt* : live through, experience — *vi* **1** : live **2** ~ **de** : live on, live by — **vivres** [vivr] *nmpl* : provisions, food
vocabulaire [vɔkabylɛr] *nm* : vocabulary
vocation [vɔkasjɔ̃] *nf* : vocation, calling
vociférer [vɔsifere] {87} *v* : shout, scream
vodka [vɔdka] *nf* : vodka
vœu [vø] *nm, pl* **vœux 1** SOUHAIT : wish **2** SERMENT : vow **3 meilleurs** ~**x** : best wishes
vogue [vɔg] *nf* : vogue, fashion
voici [vwasi] *prep* **1** : here is, here are **2** : this is, these are **3 me** ~ : here I am **4** ~ **trois jours** : three days ago
voie [vwa] *nf* **1** : road, route, way **2** : lane (of a highway) **3** : way, course **4** *or* ~ **ferrée** : railroad track, railroad **5 en** ~ **de** : in the process of **6 la Voie lactée** : the Milky Way
voilà [vwala] *prep* **1** : there is, there are **2** : that is, those are **3** VOICI : here is, here are **4** ~ **tout!** : that's all! **5** ~ **un an** : a year ago
voile [vwal] *nm* : veil — ~ *nf* **1** : sail **2** : sailing — **voiler** [vwale] *vt* **1** : veil **2** DISSIMULER : conceal — **se voiler** *vr* : warp (of wood) — **voilier** [vwalje] *nm* : sailboat — **voilure** [vwalyr] *nf* : sails *pl*
voir [vwar] {99} *vt* **1** : see **2 faire** ~ *or* **laisser** ~ : show — *vi* **1** : see **2** ~ **à** : see to, make sure that **3 voyons** : let's see — **se voir** *vr* **1** : see oneself **2** : see each other **3 ça se voit** : that's obvious, it shows
voire [vwar] *adv* : indeed, or even
voirie [vwari] *nf* : highway department
voisin, -sine [vwazɛ̃, -zin] *adj* **1** : neighboring, adjoining **2** ~ **de** : similar to — ~ *n* : neighbor — **voisinage** [vwazinaʒ] *nm* **1** : neighborhood **2** ENVIRONS : vicinity
voiture [vwatyr] *nf* **1** AUTOMOBILE : car, automobile **2** WAGON : (railroad) car, coach **3** ~ **d'enfant** : baby carriage
voix [vwa] *nfs & pl* **1** : voice **2** VOTE : vote **3 à haute** ~ : out loud
vol [vɔl] *nm* **1** : (plane) flight **2** : flock (of birds) **3** : theft, robbery
volage [vɔlaʒ] *adj* : fickle, flighty
volaille [vɔlaj] *nf* **1** : poultry **2** : fowl
volant [vɔlɑ̃] *nm* **1** : steering wheel **2** : shuttlecock **3** : flounce (of a skirt)
volcan [vɔlkɑ̃] *nm* : volcano — **volcanique** [vɔlkanik] *adj* : volcanic
volée [vɔle] *nf* **1** : volley **2** VOL : flock, flight
voler[1] [vɔle] *vt* **1** : steal **2** : rob **3** ~ **à l'étalage** : shoplift
voler[2] *vi* : fly — **volet** [vɔlɛ] *nm* **1** : shutter, flap **2** : (detachable) section — **voleter** [vɔlte] {8} *vi* : flutter, flit
voleur, -leuse [vɔlœr, -løz] *adj* : dishonest — ~ *n* : thief, robber
volière [vɔljɛr] *nf* : aviary
volley [vɔlɛ] *or* **volley–ball** [vɔlɛbol] *nm* : volleyball
volontaire [vɔlɔ̃tɛr] *adj* **1** : voluntary **2** : deliberate **3** DÉTERMINÉ : willful — ~ *nmf* : volunteer — **volontairement** [vɔlɔ̃tɛrmɑ̃] *adv* **1** : voluntarily **2** : deliberately — **volonté** [vɔlɔ̃te] *nf* **1** : will **2** : willpower **3 à** ~ : at will **4 bonne** ~ : goodwill — **volontiers** [vɔlɔ̃tje] *adv* : willingly, gladly
volt [vɔlt] *nm* : volt — **voltage** [vɔltaʒ] *nm* : voltage
volte–face [vɔltəfas] *nfs & pl* : about-face
voltiger [vɔltiʒe] {17} *vi* : flutter about — **voltige** [vɔltiʒ] *nf* : acrobatics
volubile [vɔlybil] *adj* : voluble
volume [vɔlym] *nm* : volume — **volumineux, -neuse** [vɔlyminø, -nøz] *adj* : bulky
volupté [vɔlypte] *nf* : sensual pleasure — **voluptueux, -tueuse** [vɔlyptɥø, -tɥøz] *adj* : voluptuous
volute [vɔlyt] *nf* : coil (of smoke, etc.)
vomir [vɔmir] *vt* : vomit — *vi* : vomit
vorace [vɔras] *adj* : voracious
vote [vɔt] *nm* **1** : vote **2** : voting — **voter** [vɔte] *vi* : vote — *vt* : vote for
votre [vɔtr] *adj, pl* **vos** [vo] : your
vôtre [votr] *pron* **le** ~, **la** ~, **les** ~**s** : yours, your own
vouer [vwe] *vt* **1** PROMETTRE : vow, pledge **2** CONSACRER : dedicate, devote **3 voué à** : doomed to
vouloir [vulwar] {100} *vt* **1** : want, wish for **2** CONSENTIR À : agree to, be willing to **3** ~ **dire** : mean **4 en** ~ **à** : bear a grudge against **5 veuillez patienter** : please wait — **voulu, -lue** [vuly] *adj* **1** DÉLIBÉRÉ : intentional **2** REQUIS : required
vous [vu] *pron* **1** (*as subject or direct object*) : you **2** (*as indirect object*) : you, to you **3** : yourself **4 à** ~ : yours — **vous–même** [vumɛm] *pron, pl* **vous–mêmes** : yourself
voûte [vut] *nf* : vault, arch — **voûté, -tée** [vute] *adj* **1** : arched **2** : stooped, bent over
vouvoyer [vuvwaje] {58} *vt* : address as *vous*
voyage [vwajaʒ] *nm* **1** : trip, voyage **2 avoir son** ~ *Can fam* : to be fed up — **voyager** [vwajaʒe] {17} *vi* : travel — **voyageur, -geuse** [vwajaʒœr, -ʒøz] *n* **1** : traveler **2** : passenger
voyance [vwajɑ̃s] *nf* : clairvoyance — **voyant, voyante** [vwajɑ̃, vwajɑ̃t] *adj* : loud, gaudy — ~ *n* : clairvoyant — **voyant** *nm* : warning light
voyelle [vwajɛl] *nf* : vowel
voyou [vwaju] *nm* : thug, hoodlum
vrac [vrak] *adv* **1 en** ~ : loose, in bulk **2 en** ~ : haphazardly
vrai, vraie [vrɛ] *adj* **1** : true **2** : real **3 à vrai dire** : to tell the truth — **vraiment** [vrɛmɑ̃] *adv* : really
vraisemblable [vrɛsɑ̃blabl] *adj* : likely, probable — **vraisemblance** [vrɛsɑ̃blɑ̃s] *nf* : likelihood, probability
vrombir [vrɔ̃bir] *vi* **1** : hum, buzz **2** : roar (of an engine) — **vrombissement** [vrɔ̃bismɑ̃] *nm* : humming, buzzing, roaring
vu [vy] *pp* **ù voir** — ~ *prep* : in view of, considering — **vu, vue** [vy] *adj* **1** : seen, regarded **2 bien vu** : well thought of — **vue** *nf* **1** : sight, eyesight **2** : view, vista **3** IDÉE : opinion, view — **vu que** *conj phr* : seeing that, inasmuch as
vulgaire [vylgɛr] *adj* **1** GROSSIER : vulgar **2** ORDINAIRE : common — **vulgariser** [vylgarize] *vt* : popularize — **vulgarité** [vylgarite] *nf* : vulgarity
vulnérable [vylnerabl] *adj* : vulnerable — **vulnérabilité** [vylnerabilite] *nf* : vulnerability

w [dublәve] *nm* : w, 23d letter of the alphabet
wagon [vagɔ̃] *nm* : car (of a train)
wagon–lit [vagɔ̃li] *nm, pl* **wagons–lits** : sleeping car
wagon–restaurant [vagɔ̃rɛstɔrɑ̃] *nm, pl* **wagons–restaurants** : dining car
wallon, -lonne [walɔ̃, -lɔn] *adj* : Walloon
watt [wat] *nm* : watt
w-c [vese] *nmpl* : toilet
week–end [wikɛnd] *nm, pl* **week–ends** : weekend
western [wɛstɛrn] *nm* : western
whisky [wiski] *nm, pl* **-kies** : whiskey

x [iks] *nm* : x, 24th letter of the alphabet
xénophobie [gzenɔfɔbi] *nf* : xenophobia
xérès [gzerɛs, kserɛs] *nm* : sherry
xylophone [ksilɔfɔn] *nm* : xylophone

Y

y [igrɛk] *nm* : y, 25th letter of the alphabet
y [i] *adv* **1** : there **2 ça** ~ **est !** : finally! **3 il** ~ **a** : there is, there are — ~ *pron* **1** : it, about it, on it, in it **2** : them, about them, on them, in them **3 j'y suis!** : I've got it!
yacht [jot] *nm* : yacht
yaourt [jaurt] *nm* : yogurt
yeux [jø] → **œil**
yoga [jɔga] *nm* : yoga
yogourt *or* **yoghourt** [jɔgurt] → **yaourt**
yo–yo *or* **yoyo** [jojo] *nm* : yo-yo

Z

z [zɛd] *nm* : z, 26th letter of the alphabet
zèbre [zɛbr] *nm* : zebra — **zébrure** [zebryr] *nf* **1** : stripe **2** : welt
zèle [zɛl] *nm* : zeal — **zélé, -lée** [zele] *adj* : zealous
zénith [zenit] *nm* : zenith
zéro [zero] *adj* **1** : zero **2** : nil, worthless — ~ *nm* : zero, naught
zézayer [zezeje] *vi* : lisp
zigzag [zigzag] *nm* : zigzag — **zigzaguer** [zigzage] *vi* : zigzag
zinc [zɛ̃g] *nm* : zinc
zizanie [zizani] *nf* : discord, conflict
zodiaque [zɔdjak] *nm* : zodiac
zona [zona] *nm* : shingles
zone [zon] *nf* : zone, area — **zonage** [zonaʒ] *nm* : zoning
zoo [zo(o)] *nm* : zoo — **zoologie** [zɔɔlɔʒi] *nf* : zoology
zoom [zum] *nm* **1** : zoom lens **2 faire un** ~ : zoom in
zut [zyt] *interj fam* : darn!, damn it!

English-French

A

a[1] ['eɪ] *n, pl* **a's** *or* **as** ['eɪz] : a *m*, première lettre de l'alphabet
a[2] [ə, 'eɪ] *art* (**an** [ən, 'æn] *before a vowel or silent h*) **1** : un *m*, une *f* **2** PER : par
aback [ə'bæk] *adv* **taken ~** : déconcerté
abandon [ə'bændən] *vt* : abandonner — **~** *n* : abandon *m*
abashed [ə'bæʃt] *adj* : décontenancé
abate [ə'beɪt] *vi* **abated; abating** : s'apaiser, se calmer
abbey ['æbi] *n, pl* **-beys** : abbaye *f* — **abbot** ['æbət] *n* : abbé *m*
abbreviate [ə'bri:vi,eɪt] *vt* **-ated; -ating** : abréger — **abbreviation** [ə,bri:vi'eɪʃən] *n* : abréviation *f*
abdicate ['æbdɪ,keɪt] *v* **-cated; -cating** : abdiquer
abdomen ['æbdəmən, æb'do:mən] *n* : abdomen *m* — **abdominal** [æb'dɑmənəl] *adj* : abdominal
abduct [æb'dʌkt] *vt* : enlever — **abduction** [æb'dʌkʃən] *n* : enlèvement *m*
aberration [,æbə'reɪʃən] *n* : aberration *f*
abhor [əb'hɔr, æb-] *vt* **-horred; -horring** : abhorrer, détester
abide [ə'baɪd] *v* **abode** [ə'bo:d] *or* **abided; abiding** *vt* : supporter — *vi* **~ by** : respecter, se conformer à
ability [ə'bɪləṭi] *n, pl* **-ties 1** : aptitude *f* **2** SKILL : habileté *f*, talent *m*
ablaze [ə'bleɪz] *adj* : en feu
able ['eɪbəl] *adj* **abler; ablest 1** CAPABLE : capable **2** SKILLED : habile — **ably** ['eɪbəli] *adv* : habilement
abnormal [æb'nɔrmel] *adj* : anormal — **abnormality** [,æbnər'mæləṭi, -nɔr-] *n, pl* **-ties** : anormalité *f*, anomalie *f*
aboard [ə'bord] *adv* : à bord — **~** *prep* : à bord de, dans
abode [ə'bo:d] *n* : demeure *f*, domicile *m*
abolish [ə'bɑlɪʃ] *vt* : abolir — **abolition** [,æbə'lɪʃən] *n* : abolition *f*
abominable [ə'bɑmənəbəl] *adj* : abominable
aborigine [,æbə'rɪʤəni] *n* : aborigène *mf*
abort [ə'bɔrt] *vt* : faire avorter — **abortion** [ə'bɔrʃən] *n* : avortement *m*
abound [ə'baʊnd] *vi* **~ in** : abonder en
about [ə'baʊt] *adv* **1** APPROXIMATELY : vers, environ **2** AROUND : autour **3** NEARBY : près **4 be ~ to** : être sur le point de — **~** *prep* **1** AROUND : autour de **2** CONCERNING : sur, de
above [ə'bʌv] *adv* **1** OVERHEAD : au-dessus, en haut **2** PREVIOUSLY : ci-dessus — **~** *prep* **1** OVER : au-dessus de **2** EXCEEDING : plus de **3 ~ all** : surtout
abrasive [ə'breɪsɪv] *adj* : abrasif
abreast [ə'brɛst] *adv* **1** : de front, côte à côte **2 ~ of** : au courant de
abridge [ə'brɪʤ] *vt* **abridged; abridging** : abréger
abroad [ə'brɔd] *adv* **1** : à l'étranger **2** WIDELY : de tous côtés
abrupt [ə'brʌpt] *adj* **1** SUDDEN : brusque **2** STEEP : abrupt
abscess ['æb,sɛs] *n* : abcès *m*
absence ['æbsənts] *n* **1** : absence *f* **2** LACK : manque *m* — **absent** ['æbsənt] *adj* : absent — **absentee** [,æbsən'ti:] *n* : absent *m*, -sente *f* — **absentminded** [,æbsənt'maɪndəd] *adj* : distrait
absolute ['æbsə,lu:t, ,æbsə'lu:t] *adj* : absolu — **absolutely** ['æbsə,lu:tli, ,æbsə'lu:tli] *adv* : absolument
absolve [əb'zɑlv, æb-, -'sɑlv] *vt* **-solved; -solving** : absoudre
absorb [əb'zɔrb, æb-, -'sɔrb] *vt* : absorber — **absorbent** [əb'zɔrbənt, æb-, -'sɔr-] *adj* : absorbant — **absorption** [əb'zɔrpʃən, æb-, -'sɔrp-] *n* : absorption *f*
abstain [əb'steɪn, æb-] *vi* **~ from** : s'abstenir de — **abstinence** ['æbstənənts] *n* : abstinence *f*
abstract [æb'strækt, 'æb,-] *adj* : abstrait — **~** *n* SUMMARY : résumé *m*
absurd [əb'sərd, -'zərd] *adj* : absurde — **absurdity** [əb'sərdəṭi, -'zər-] *n, pl* **-ties** : absurdité *f*
abundant [ə'bʌndənt] *adj* : abondant — **abundance** [ə'bʌndənts] *n* : abondance *f*
abuse [ə'bju:z] *vt* **abused; abusing 1** MISUSE : abuser de **2** MISTREAT : maltraiter **3** INSULT : injurier — **~** [ə'bju:s] *n* **1** MISUSE : abus *m* **2** MISTREATMENT : mauvais traitement *m* **3** INSULTS : insultes *fpl*, injures *fpl* — **abusive** [ə'bju:sɪv] *adj* : injurieux
abut [ə'bʌt] *vi* **abutted; abutting ~ on** : être contigu à
abyss [ə'bɪs, 'æbɪs] *n* : abîme *m*
academy [ə'kædəmi] *n, pl* **-mies 1** SCHOOL : école *f*, collège *m* **2** SOCIETY : académie *f* — **academic** [,ækə'dɛmɪk] *adj* **1** : universitaire **2** THEORETICAL : théorique
accelerate [ɪk'sɛlə,reɪt, æk-] *v* **-ated; -ating** : accélérer — **acceleration** [ɪk,sɛlə'reɪʃən, æk-] *n* : accélération *f*
accent ['æk,sɛnt, æk'sɛnt] *vt* : accentuer — **~** ['æk,sɛnt, -sənt] *n* : accent *m* — **accentuate** [ɪk'sɛnʧʊ,eɪt, æk-] *vt* **-ated; -ating** : accentuer
accept [ɪk'sɛpt, æk-] *vt* : accepter — **acceptable** [ɪk'sɛptəbəl, æk-] *adj* : acceptable — **acceptance** [ɪk'sɛptənts, æk-] *n* **1** : acceptation *f* **2** APPROVAL : approbation *f*
access ['æk,sɛs] *n* : accès *m* — **accessible** [ɪk'sɛsəbəl, æk-] *adj* : accessible
accessory [ɪk'sɛsəri, æk-] *n, pl* **-ries 1** : accessoire *m* **2** ACCOMPLICE : complice *mf*
accident ['æksədənt] *n* **1** : accident *m* **2 by ~** : par hasard — **accidental** [,æksə'dɛntəl] *adj* : accidentel — **accidentally** [,æksə'dɛntəli, -'dɛntli] *adv* : accidentellement, par hasard
acclaim [ə'kleɪm] *vt* : acclamer — **~** *n* : acclamation *f*
acclimate ['æklə,meɪt, ə'klaɪmət] *vt* **-mated; -mating** : acclimater
accommodate [ə'kɑmə,deɪt] *vt* **-dated; -dating 1** ADAPT : accommoder **2** SATISFY : satisfaire **3** LODGE : loger **4** HOLD : contenir — **accommodation** [ə,kɑmə'deɪʃən] *n* **1** : accommodation *f* **2 ~s** *npl* LODGING : logement *m*
accompany [ə'kʌmpəni, -'kɑm-] *vt* **-nied; -nying** : accompagner
accomplice [ə'kɑmpləs, -'kʌm-] *n* : complice *mf*
accomplish [ə'kɑmplɪʃ, -'kʌm-] *vt* **1** : accomplir **2** REALIZE : réaliser — **accomplishment** [ə'kɑmplɪʃmənt, -'kʌm-] *n* : accomplissement *m*
accord [ə'kɔrd] *n* **1** AGREEMENT : accord *m* **2 of one's own ~** : de son plein gré — **accordance** [ə'kɔrdənts] *n* **in ~ with** : conformément à — **accordingly** [ə'kɔrdɪŋli] *adv* : en conséquence — **according to** [ə'kɔrdɪŋ] *prep* : selon, d'après
accordion [ə'kɔrdiən] *n* : accordéon *m*
account [ə'kaʊnt] *n* **1** : compte *m* **2** REPORT : compte *m* rendu **3** WORTH : importance *f* **4 on ~ of** : à cause de **5 on no ~** : en aucun cas **6 take into ~** : tenir compte de — **~** *vi* **~ for** : expliquer — **accountable** [ə'kaʊntəbəl] *adj* : responsable — **accountant** [ə'kaʊntənt] *n* : comptable *mf* — **accounting** [ə'kaʊntɪŋ] *n* : comptabilité *f*
accrue [ə'kru:] *vi* **-crued; -cruing** : s'accumuler
accumulate [ə'kju:mjə,leɪt] *v* **-lated; -lating** *vt* : accumuler — *vi* s'accumuler — **accumulation** [ə,kju:mjə'leɪʃən] *n* : accumulation *f*
accurate ['ækjərət] *adj* : exact, précis — **accurately** *adv* : exactement, avec précision — **accuracy** ['ækjərəsi] *n, pl* **-cies** : exactitude *f*, précision *f*
accuse [ə'kju:z] *vt* **-cused; -cusing** : accuser — **accusation** [akyzasjɔ̃] *n* : accusation *f*
accustom [ə'kʌstəm] *vt* : accoutumer — **accustomed** [ə'kʌstəmd] *adj* **1** CUSTOMARY : habituel **2 become ~ to** : s'habituer à
ace ['eɪs] *n* : as *m*
ache [eɪk] *vi* **ached; aching** : faire mal — **~** *n* : douleur *f*
achieve [ə'ʧi:v] *vt* **achieved; achieving** : accomplir, atteindre — **achievement** [ə'ʧi:vmənt] *n* : accomplissement *m*, réussite *f*
acid ['æsəd] *adj* : acide — **~** *n* : acide *m*
acknowledge [ɪk'nɑlɪʤ, æk-] *vt* **-edged; -edging 1** ADMIT : admettre **2** RECOGNIZE : reconnaître **3 ~ receipt of** : accuser réception de — **acknowledgment** [ɪk'nɑlɪʤmənt, æk-] *n* **1** : reconnaissance *f* **2 ~ of receipt** : accusé *m* de réception
acne ['ækni] *n* : acné *f*
acorn ['eɪ,kɔrn, -kərn] *n* : gland *m*
acoustic [ə'ku:stɪk] *or* **acoustical** [ə'ku:stɪkəl] *adj* : acoustique — **acoustics** [ə'ku:stɪks] *ns & pl* : acoustique *f*
acquaint [ə'kweɪnt] *vt* **1 ~ s.o. with** : mettre qqn au courant de **2 be ~ed with** : connaître (une personne) — **acquaintance** [ə'kweɪntənts] *n* : connaissance *f*
acquire [ə'kwaɪr] *vt* **-quired; -quiring** : acquérir — **acquisition** [,ækwə'zɪʃən] *n* : acquisition *f*
acquit [ə'kwɪt] *vt* **-quitted; -quitting** : acquitter
acre ['eɪkər] *n* : acre *f* — **acreage** ['eɪkərɪʤ] *n* : superficie *f*
acrid ['ækrəd] *adj* : âcre
acrobat ['ækrə,bæt] *n* : acrobate *mf* — **acrobatic** [,ækrə'bæṭɪk] *adj* : acrobatique — **acrobatics** [,ækrə'bæṭɪks] *ns & pl* : acrobatie *f*
across [ə'krɔs] *adv* **1** : de large, d'un côté à l'autre **2 ~ from** : en face de **3 go ~** : traverser — **~** *prep* **1 ~ the street** : de l'autre côté de la rue **2 lie ~ sth** : être en travers de qqch
acrylic [ə'krɪlɪk] *n* : acrylique *m*
act ['ækt] *vi* **1** : agir **2** PERFORM : jouer, faire du théâtre **3 ~ as** : servir de — *vt* : jouer (un rôle) — **~** *n* **1** ACTION : acte *m* **2** DECREE : loi *f* **3** : acte *m* (d'une pièce de théâtre), numéro *m* (de variétés) **4 put on an ~** : jouer la comédie — **acting** *adj* : intérimaire
action ['ækʃən] *n* **1** : action *f* **2** DEED : acte *m* **2** LAWSUIT : procès *m*, action *f*
activate ['æktə,veɪt] *vt* **-vated; -vating** : activer
active ['æktɪv] *adj* : actif — **activity** [æk'tɪvəṭi] *n, pl* **-ties** : activité *f*
actor ['æktər] *n* : acteur *m*, -trice *f* — **actress** ['æktrəs] *n* : actrice *f*
actual ['ækʧʊəl] *adj* **1** : réel, véritable **2** VERY : même — **actually** ['ækʧʊəli, -ʧəli] *adv* **1** REALLY : vraiment **2** IN FACT : en fait
acupuncture ['ækjʊ,pʌŋkʧər] *n* : acupuncture *f*
acute [ə'kju:t] *adj* **acuter; acutest 1** : aigu **2** KEEN : fin
ad ['æd] *n* → **advertisement**
adamant ['ædəmənt, -,mænt] *adj* : inflexible
adapt [ə'dæpt] *vt* : adapter — *vi* : s'adapter — **adaptable** [ə,dæptəbəl] *adj* : adaptable — **adaptation** [,æ,dæp'teɪʃən, -dəp-] *n* : adaptation *f* — **adapter** [ə'dæptər] *n* : adapteur *m*
add ['æd] *vt* **1** : ajouter **2 ~ up** : additionner — *vi* : additionner
addict ['ædɪkt] *n or* **drug ~** : toxicomane *mf*; drogué *m*, -guée *f* — **addiction** [ə'dɪkʃən] *n* **1** : dépendance *f* **2 drug ~** : toxicomanie *f*
addition [ə'dɪʃən] *n* **1** : addition *f* **2 in ~** : en plus — **additional** [ə'dɪʃənəl] *adj* : additionnel, supplémentaire — **additive** ['ædəṭɪv] *n* : additif *m*
address [ə'drɛs] *vt* **1** : adresser (une lettre, etc.) **2** : s'adresser à (une personne), aborder (un problème) — **~** [ə'drɛs, 'æ,drɛs] *n* **1** : adresse *f* **2** SPEECH : discours *m*
adept [ə'dɛpt] *adj* : habile
adequate ['ædɪkwət] *adj* : adéquat, suffisant — **adequately** ['ædɪkwətli] *adv* : suffisamment
adhere [æd'hir, əd-] *vi* **-hered; -hering 1** STICK : adhérer **2 ~ to** KEEP : adhérer à, observer — **adherence** [æd'hɪrənts, əd-] *n* : adhésion *f* — **adhesion** [æd'hiʒən, əd-] *n* : adhésion *f*, adhérence *f* — **adhesive** [æd'hi:sɪv, əd-, -zɪv] *adj* : adhésif — **~** *n* : adhésif *m*
adjacent [ə'ʤeɪsənt] *adj* : adjacent, contigu
adjective ['æʤɪktɪv] *n* : adjectif *m*
adjoining [ə'ʤɔɪnɪŋ] *adj* : contigu
adjourn [ə'ʤərn] *vt* : ajourner — *vi* : suspendre la séance
adjust [ə'ʤʌst] *vt* : ajuster — *vi* ADAPT : s'adapter — **adjustable** [ə'ʤʌstəbəl] *adj* : réglable, ajustable — **adjustment** [ə'ʤʌstmənt] *n* **1** : ajustement *m* **2** ADAPTATION : adaptation *f*
ad–lib ['æd'lɪb] *vt* **ad–libbed; ad–libbing** : improviser
administer [æd'mɪnəstər, əd-] *vt* : administrer — **administration** [æd,mɪnə'streɪʃən, əd-] *n* : administration *f* — **administrative** [æd'mɪnə,streɪṭɪv, əd-] *adj* : administratif — **administrator** [æd'mɪnə,streɪṭər, əd-] *n* : administrateur *m*, -trice *f*
admirable ['ædmərəbəl] *adj* : admirable
admiral ['ædmərəl] *n* : amiral *m*
admire [æd'maɪr] *vt* **-mired; -miring** : admirer — **admiration** [,ædmə'reɪʃən] *n* : admiration *f* — **admirer** [æd'maɪrər] *n* : admirateur *m*, -trice *f* — **admiring** [æd'maɪrɪŋ] *adj* : admiratif
admit [æd'mɪt, əd-] *vt* **-mitted; -mitting 1** : admettre **2** ACKNOWLEDGE : reconnaître **3** CONFESS : avouer — **admission** [æd'mɪʃən] *n* **1** ADMITTANCE : admission *f* **2** FEE : entrée *f* **3** CONFESSION : aveu *m* — **admittance** [æd'mɪtənts, əd-] *n* : entrée *f*
admonish [æd'mɑnɪʃ, əd-] *vt* : réprimander
ado [ə'du:] *n* **1** : agitation *f* **2 without further ~** : sans plus de cérémonie
adolescent [,ædəl'ɛsənt] *n* : adolescent *m*, -cente *f* — **adolescence** [,ædəl'ɛsənts] *n* : adolescence *f*
adopt [ə'dɑpt] *vt* : adopter — **adoption** [ə'dɑpʃən] *n* : adoption *f*
adore [ə'dor] *vt* **adored; adoring** : adorer — **adorable** [ə'dorəbəl] *adj* : adorable — **adoration** [,ædə'reɪʃən] *n* : adoration *f*
adorn [ə'dɔrn] *vt* : orner
adrift [ə'drɪft] *adv & adj* : à la dérive
adroit [ə'drɔɪt] *adj* : adroit, habile
adult [ə'dʌlt, 'æ,dʌlt] *adj* : adulte — **~** *n* : adulte *mf*
adultery [ə'dʌltəri] *n, pl* **-teries** : adultère *m*
advance [æd'vænts, əd-] *v* **-vanced; -vancing** *vt* : avancer — *vi* **1** : avancer **2** IMPROVE : progresser — **~** *n* **1** : avance *f* **2 in ~** : à l'avance, d'avance — **advancement** [æd'væntsmənt, əd-] *n* : avancement *m*
advantage [əd'væntɪʤ, æd-] *n* **1** : avantage *m* **2 take ~ of** : profiter de — **advantageous** [,æd,væn'teɪʤəs, -vən-] *adj* : avantageux
advent ['æd,vɛnt] *n* **1** : avènement *m* **2 Advent** : Avent *m*
adventure [æd'vɛnʧər, əd-] *n* : aventure *f* — **adventurous** [æd'vɛnʧərəs, əd-] *adj* : aventureux
adverb ['æd,vərb] *n* : adverbe *m*
adversary ['ædvər,sɛri] *n, pl* **-saries** : adversaire *mf*
adverse [æd'vɛrs, 'æd,-] *adj* : défavorable — **adversity** [æd'vərsəṭi, əd-] *n, pl* **-ties** : adversité *f*
advertise ['ædvər,taɪz] *v* **-tised; -tising** *vt* : faire de la publicité pour — *vi* : passer une annonce (dans un journal) — **advertisement** ['ædvər,taɪzmənt, æd'vərṭəzmənt] *n* : publicité *f*, annonce *f* — **advertiser** ['ædvər,taɪzər] *n* : annonceur *m* — **advertising** ['ædvər,taɪzɪŋ] *n* : publicité *f*
advice [æd'vaɪs] *n* : conseils *mpl*
advise [æd'vaɪz, əd-] *vt* **-vised; -vising 1** : conseiller **2** RECOMMEND : recommander **3** INFORM : aviser — **advisable** [æd'vaɪzəbəl, əd-] *adj* : recommandé, prudent — **adviser** [æd'vaɪzər, əd-] *n* : conseiller *m*, -lère *f* — **advisory** [æd'vaɪzəri, əd-] *adj* : consultatif
advocate ['ædvə,keɪt] *vt* **-cated; -cating** : préconiser — **~** ['ædvəkət] *n* **1** SUPPORTER : défenseur *m* **2** LAWYER : avocat *m*, -cate *f*
aerial ['æriəl] *adj* : aérien — **~** *n* : antenne *f*
aerobics [,ær'o:bɪks] *ns & pl* : aérobic *m*
aerodynamic [,æro:daɪ'næmɪk] *adj* : aérodynamique
aerosol ['ærə,sɔl] *n* : aérosol *m*
aesthetic [ɛs'θɛṭɪk] *adj* : esthétique
afar [ə'fɑr] *adv* **from ~** : de loin
affable ['æfəbəl] *adj* : affable
affair [ə'fær] *n* **1** : affaire *f* **2** *or* **love ~** : liaison *f*, affaire *f* de cœur
affect [ə'fɛkt, æ-] *vt* : affecter — **affection** [ə'fɛkʃən] *n* : affection *f* — **affectionate** [ə'fɛkʃənət] *adj* : affectueux
affirm [ə'fərm] *vt* : affirmer — **affirmative** [ə'fərməṭɪv] *adj* : affirmatif
affix [ə'fɪks] *vt* : apposer (une signature), coller (un timbre)

afflict [ə'flɪkt] *vt* : affliger — **affliction** [ə'flɪkʃən] *n* : affliction *f*
affluent ['æ,flu:ənt; æ'flu:-, ə-] *adj* : riche
afford [ə'ford] *vt* **1** : avoir les moyens d'acheter **2 ~ to do** : se permettre de faire
affront [ə'frʌnt] *n* : affront *m*
afloat [ə'flo:t] *adj & adv* : à flot
afoot [ə'fʊt] *adv & adj* : en train, en cours
afraid [ə'freɪd] *adj* **1 be ~ of** : avoir peur de, craindre **2 be ~ that** : regretter que **3 I'm ~ not** : hélas, non
African ['æfrɪkən] *adj* : africain
after ['æftər] *adv* **1** AFTERWARD : après **2** BEHIND : en arrière — **~** *conj* : après que — **~** *prep* **1** : après **2 ~ all** : après tout **3 it's ten ~ five** : il est cinq heures dix
aftereffect ['æftərɪ,fɛkt] *n* : répercussion *f*
aftermath ['æftər,mæθ] *n* : suites *fpl*
afternoon [,æftər'nu:n] *n* : après-midi *mf*
afterward ['æftərwərd] *or* **afterwards** [-wərdz] *adv* : après, ensuite
again [ə'gɛn, -'gɪn] *adv* **1** : encore (une fois), de nouveau **2 ~ and ~** : maintes et maintes fois **3 then ~** : d'autre part
against [ə'gɛntst, -'gɪntst] *prep* **1** : contre **2 go ~** : aller à l'encontre
age ['eɪʤ] *n* **1** : âge *m* **2** ERA : ère *f*, époque *f* **3 come of ~** : atteindre la majorité **4 for ~s** : depuis longtemps **5 old ~** : vieillesse *f* — **~** *v* **age; aging** : vieillir — **aged** ['eɪʤəd, 'eɪʤd] *adj* **1** : âgé de **2** ['eɪʤd] OLD : vieux, âgé
agency ['eɪʤəntsi] *n, pl* **-cies** : agence *f*
agenda [ə'ʤɛndə] *n* : ordre *m* du jour, programme *m*
agent ['eɪʤənt] *n* : agent *m*
aggravate ['ægrə,veɪt] *vt* **-vated; -vating** **1** WORSEN : aggraver **2** ANNOY : agacer, énerver
aggregate ['ægrɪgət] *adj* : total, global — **~** *n* : ensemble *m*, total *m*
aggression [ə'grɛʃən] *n* : agression *f* — **aggressive** [ə'grɛsɪv] *adj* : agressif — **aggressor** [ə'grɛsər] *n* : agresseur *m*
aghast [ə'gæst] *adj* : horrifié
agile ['æʤəl] *adj* : agile — **agility** [ə'ʤɪləṭi] *n, pl* **-ties** : agilité *f*
agitate ['æʤə,teɪt] *vt* **-tated; -tating** **1** SHAKE : agiter **2** TROUBLE : inquiéter — **agitation** [,æʤə'teɪʃən] *n* : agitation *f*
ago [ə'go:] *adv* **1** : il y a **2 long ~** : il y a longtemps
agony ['ægəni] *n, pl* **-nies** : angoisse *f*, souffrance *f* — **agonize** ['ægə,naɪz] *vi* **-nized; -nizing** : se tourmenter — **agonizing** ['ægə,naɪzɪŋ] *adj* : déchirant
agree [ə'gri:] *v* **agreed; agreeing** *vt* **1** ADMIT : convenir **2 ~ that** : reconnaître que — *vi* **1** : être d'accord **2** CORRESPOND : concorder **3 ~ to** : consentir à — **agreeable** [ə'gri:əbəl] *adj* **1** PLEASING : agréable **2** WILLING : consentant — **agreement** [ə'gri:mənt] *n* : accord *m*
agriculture ['ægrɪ,kʌltʃər] *n* : agriculture *f* — **agricultural** [,ægrɪ'kʌltʃərəl] *adj* : agricole
aground [ə'graʊnd] *adv* **run ~** : s'échouer
ahead [ə'hɛd] *adv* **1** IN FRONT : en avant, devant **2** BEFOREHAND : à l'avance **3** LEADING : en avance **4 go ~!** : allez-y! — **ahead of** *prep* **1** IN FRONT OF : devant **2 ~ time** : avant l'heure
aid ['eɪd] *vt* : aider — **~** *n* : aide *f*, secours *m*
AIDS ['eɪdz] *n* (*a*cquired *i*mmuno*d*eficiency *s*yndrome) : sida *m*
ail ['eɪl] *vi* : être souffrant — **ailment** ['eɪlmənt] *n* : maladie *f*
aim ['eɪm] *vt* : braquer (une arme à feu), diriger (une remarque, etc.) — *vi* **1 ~ to** : avoir l'intention de **2 ~ at** *or* **~ for** : viser — **~** *n* : but *m* — **aimless** ['eɪmləs] *adj* : sans but
air ['ær] *vt* **1** : aérer **2** EXPRESS : exprimer **3** BROADCAST : diffuser — **~** *n* **1** : air *m* **2 on the ~** : à l'antenne — **air–conditioned** [,ærkən'dɪʃənd] *adj* : climatisé — **air–conditioning** [,ærkən'dɪʃənɪŋ] *n* : climatisation *f* — **aircraft** ['ær,kræft] *ns & pl* : avion *m* — **air force** *n* : armée *f* de l'air — **airline** ['ær,laɪn] *n* : compagnie *f* aérienne — **airmail** ['ær,meɪl] *n* **1** : poste *f* aérienne **2 by ~** : par avion — **airplane** ['ær,pleɪn] *n* : avion *m* — **airport** ['ær,port] *n* : aéroport *m* — **airstrip** ['ær,strɪp] *n* : piste *f* d'atterrissage — **airtight** ['ær'taɪt] *adj* : hermétique — **airy** ['æri] *adj* **airier; -est** : aéré
aisle ['aɪl] *n* : allée *f* (d'un théâtre, etc.), couloir *m* (d'un avion)
ajar [ə'ʤɑr] *adj & adv* : entrouvert
akin [ə'kɪn] *adj* **~ to** : semblable à
alarm [ə'lɑrm] *n* **1** : alarme *f* **2** ANXIETY : inquiétude *f* — **~** *vt* : alarmer — **alarm clock** *n* : réveille-matin *m*
alas [ə'læs] *interj* : hélas!
album ['ælbəm] *n* : album *m*
alcohol ['ælkə,hɔl] *n* : alcool *m* — **alcoholic** [,ælkə'hɔlɪk] *adj* : alcoolisé, alcoolique — **~** *n* : alcoolique *mf* — **alcoholism** ['ælkəhɔ,lɪzəm] *n* : alcoolisme *m*
alcove ['æl,ko:v] *n* : alcôve *f*
ale ['eɪl] *n* : bière *f*
alert [ə'lərt] *adj* **1** WATCHFUL : vigilant **2** LIVELY : alerte, éveillé — **~** *n* : alerte *f* — **~** *vt* : alerter — **alertness** [ə'lərtnəs] *n* **1** : vigilance *f* **2** : vivacité *f*
alfalfa [æl'fælfə] *n* : luzerne *f*
alga ['ælgə] *n, pl* **-gae** ['æl,ʤi:] : algue *f*
algebra ['ælʤəbrə] *n* : algèbre *f*
Algerian [æl'ʤɪriən] *adj* : algérien
alias ['eɪliəs] *adv* : alias — **~** *n* : nom *m* d'emprunt, faux nom *m*
alibi ['ælə,baɪ] *n* : alibi *m*
alien ['eɪliən] *adj* : étranger — **~** *n* **1** FOREIGNER : étranger *m*, -gère *f* **2** EXTRATERRESTRIAL : extraterrestre *mf* — **alienate** ['eɪliə,neɪt] *vt* **-ated; -ating** : aliéner — **alienation** [,eɪliə'neɪʃən] *n* : aliénation *f*
alight [ə'laɪt] *vi* : descendre, se poser
align [ə'laɪn] *vt* : aligner — **alignment** [ə'laɪnmənt] *n* : alignement *m*
alike [ə'laɪk] *adv* : de la même façon — **~** *adj* **1** : semblable **2 be ~** : se ressembler
alimony ['ælə,mo:ni] *n, pl* **-nies** : pension *f* alimentaire
alive [ə'laɪv] *adj* **1** LIVING : vivant, en vie **2** LIVELY : vif, animé
all ['ɔl] *adv* **1** COMPLETELY : tout, complètement **2 ~ at once** : tout d'un coup **3 ~ the better** : tant mieux — **~** *adj* : tout — **~** *pron* **1** EVERYTHING : tout **2** EVERYONE : tous, toutes **3 ~ in ~** : tout compte fait — **all–around** [,ɔlə'raʊnd] *adj* VERSATILE : complet
allay [ə'leɪ] *vt* : calmer, apaiser
allege [ə'lɛʤ] *vt* **-leged; -leging** : alléguer, prétendre — **allegation** [,ælɪ'geɪʃən] *n* : allégation *f* — **alleged** [ə'lɛʤd, ə'lɛʤəd] *adj* : présumé, prétendu — **allegedly** [ə'lɛʤədli] *adv* : prétendument
allegiance [ə'li:ʤənts] *n* : allégeance *f*
allergy ['ælərʤi] *n, pl* **-gies** : allergie *f* — **allergic** [ə'lərʤɪk] *adj* : allergique
alleviate [ə'li:vi,eɪt] *vt* **-ated; -ating** : soulager, alléger
alley ['æli] *n, pl* **-leys** : ruelle *f*, allée *f*
alliance [ə'laɪənts] *n* : alliance *f*
alligator ['ælə,geɪṭər] *n* : alligator *m*
allocate ['ælə,keɪt] *vt* **-cated; -cating** : allouer, assigner
allot [ə'lɑt] *vt* **allotted; allotting** **1** ASSIGN : attribuer **2** DISTRIBUTE : répartir — **allotment** [ə'lɑtmənt] *n* : allocation *f*
allow [ə'laʊ] *vt* **1** PERMIT : permettre **2** CONCEDE : admettre **3** GRANT : accorder — *vi* **~ for** : tenir compte de — **allowance** [ə'laʊənts] *n* **1** : allocation *f* **2** : argent *m* de poche (pour les enfants) **3 make ~s for** : tenir compte de
alloy ['æ,lɔɪ] *n* : alliage *m*
all right *adv* **1** YES : d'accord **2** WELL : bien **3** CERTAINLY : bien, sans doute — **~** *adj* : pas mal, bien
allude [ə'lu:d] *vi* **-luded; -luding ~ to** : faire allusion à
allure [ə'lʊr] *vt* **-lured; -luring** : attirer
allusion [ə'lu:ʒən] *n* : allusion *f*
ally [ə'laɪ, 'æ,laɪ] *vt* **-lied; -lying** **1** : allier **2 ~ oneself with** : s'allier avec — **~** ['æ,laɪ, ə'laɪ] *n, pl* **allies** : allié *m*, -liée *f*
almanac ['ɔlmə,næk, 'æl-] *n* : almanach *m*
almighty [ɔl'maɪṭi] *adj* : tout puissant, formidable
almond ['ɑmənd, 'ɑl-, 'æ-, 'æl-] *n* : amande *f*
almost ['ɔl,mo:st, ɔl'mo:st] *adv* : presque
alms ['ɑmz, 'ɑlmz, 'ælmz] *ns & pl* : aumône *f*
alone [ə'lo:n] *adv* **1** : seul **2 leave ~** : laisser tranquille — **~** *adj* : seul
along [ə'lɔŋ] *adv* **1 all ~** : tout le temps **2 ~ with** : avec, accompagné de — **~** *prep* **1** : le long de **2** ON : sur — **alongside** [ə,lɔŋ'saɪd] *adv* : à côté — **~** *or* **~ of** *prep* : à côté de
aloof [ə'lu:f] *adj* : distant
aloud [ə'laʊd] *adv* : à haute voix
alphabet ['ælfə,bɛt] *n* : alphabet *m* — **alphabetic** [,ælfə'bɛtɪk] *or* **alphabetical** [-tɪkəl] *adj* : alphabétique
already [ɔl'rɛdi] *adv* : déjà
also ['ɔl,so:] *adv* : aussi
altar ['ɔltər] *n* : autel *m*
alter ['ɔltər] *vt* **1** : changer, modifier **2** : retoucher (un vêtement) — **alteration** [,ɔltə'reɪʃən] *n* **1** : changement *m*, modification *f* **2 ~s** *npl* : retouches *fpl*
alternate ['ɔltərnət] *adj* : alternatif — **~** ['ɔltər,neɪt] *v* **-nated; -nating** *vt* : faire alterner — *vi* : alterner — **alternating current** ['ɔltər,neɪṭɪŋ] *n* : courant *m* alternatif — **alternative** [ɔl'tərnəṭɪv] *adj* : alternatif — **~** *n* : alternative *f*
although [ɔl'ðo:] *conj* : bien que, quoique
altitude ['æltə,tu:d, -,tju:d] *n* : altitude *f*
altogether [,ɔltə'gɛðər] *adv* **1** COMPLETELY : entièrement, tout à fait **2** ON THE WHOLE : dans l'ensemble **3 how much ~?** : combien en tout?
aluminum [ə'lu:mənəm] *n* : aluminium *m*
always ['ɔlwiz, -,weɪz] *adv* **1** : toujours **2** FOREVER : pour toujours
am → **be**
amass [ə'mæs] *vt* : amasser
amateur ['æmətʃər, -tər, -,tʊr, -,tjʊr] *adj* : amateur — **~** *n* : amateur *m*
amaze [ə'meɪz] *vt* **amazed; amazing** : étonner, stupéfier — **amazement** [ə'meɪzmənt] *n* : stupéfaction *f* — **amazing** [ə'meɪzɪŋ] *adj* : étonnant
ambassador [æm'bæsə,dər] *n* : ambassadeur *m*, -drice *f*
amber ['æmbər] *n* : ambre *m*
ambiguous [æm'bɪgjuəs] *adj* : ambigu — **ambiguity** [,æmbə'gju:əṭi] *n, pl* **-ties** : ambiguïté *f*
ambition [æm'bɪʃən] *n* : ambition *f* — **ambitious** [æm'bɪʃəs] *adj* : ambitieux
ambivalence [æm'bɪvələnts] *n* : ambivalence *f* — **ambivalent** [æm'bɪvələnt] *adj* : ambivalent
amble ['æmbəl] *vi* **-bled; -bling** : déambuler
ambulance ['æmbjələnts] *n* : ambulance *f*
ambush ['æmbʊʃ] *vt* : tendre une embuscade à — **~** *n* : embuscade *f*
amenable [ə'mi:nəbəl, -'mɛ-] *adj* **1** : accommodant **2 ~ to** : disposé à
amend [ə'mɛnd] *vt* : amender, modifier — **amendment** [ə'mɛndmənt] *n* : amendement *m* — **amends** [ə'mɛndz] *ns & pl* **make ~** : réparer ses torts
amenities [ə'mɛnəṭiz, -'mi:-] *npl* : équipements *mpl*, aménagements *mpl*
American [ə'mɛrɪkən] *adj* : américain
amiable ['eɪmiəbəl] *adj* : aimable
amicable ['æmɪkəbəl] *adj* : amical
amid [ə'mɪd] *or* **amidst** [ə'mɪdst] *prep* : au milieu de, parmi
amiss [ə'mɪs] *adv* **1** : mal **2 take sth ~** : prendre qqch de travers — **~** *adj* **something is ~** : quelque chose ne va pas
ammonia [ə'mo:njə] *n* : ammoniaque *f*
ammunition [,æmjə'nɪʃən] *n* : munitions *fpl*
amnesia [æm'ni:ʒə] *n* : amnésie *f*
amnesty ['æmnəsti] *n, pl* **-ties** : amnistie *f*
amoeba [ə'mi:bə] *n, pl* **-bas** *or* **-bae** [-bi:] : amibe *f*
among [ə'mʌŋ] *prep* : parmi, entre
amount [ə'maʊnt] *vi* **1 ~ to** TOTAL : s'élever à **2 that ~s to the same thing** : cela revient au même — **~** *n* **1** : quantité *f* **2** SUM : somme *f*, montant *m*
amphibian [æm'fɪbiən] *n* : amphibien *m* — **amphibious** [æm'fɪbiəs] *adj* : amphibie
amphitheater ['æmfə,θi:əṭər] *n* : amphithéâtre *m*
ample ['æmpəl] *adj* **-pler; -plest** **1** SPACIOUS : ample **2** PLENTIFUL : abondant
amplify ['æmplə,faɪ] *vt* **-fied; -fying** : amplifier — **amplifier** ['æmplə,faɪər] *n* : amplificateur *m*
amputate ['æmpjə,teɪt] *v* **-tated; -tating** : amputer — **amputation** [,æmpjə'teɪʃən] *n* : amputation *f*
amuse [ə'mju:z] *vt* **amused; amusing** : amuser — **amusement** [ə'mju:zmənt] *n* **1** ENJOYMENT : amusement *m* **2** DIVERSION : divertissement *m*
an → **a**[2]
analgesic [,ænəl'ʤi:zɪk, -sɪk] *n* : analgésique *m*
analogy [ə'næləʤi] *n, pl* **-gies** : analogie *f* — **analogous** [ə'næləgəs] *adj* : analogue
analysis [ə'næləsəs] *n, pl* **-yses** [-,si:z] : analyse *f* — **analytic** [,ænə'lɪtɪk] *or* **analytical** [-ṭɪkəl] *adj* : analytique — **analyze** *or Brit* **analyse** ['ænə,laɪz] *vt* **-lyzed** *or Brit* **-lysed; -lyzing** *or Brit* **-lysing** : analyser
anarchy ['ænərki, -,nɑr-] *n* : anarchie *f*
anatomy [ə'næṭəmi] *n, pl* **-mies** : anatomie *f* — **anatomic** [,ænə'tɑmɪk] *or* **anatomical** [-mɪkəl] *adj* : anatomique
ancestor ['æn,sɛstər] *n* : ancêtre *mf* — **ancestral** [æn'sɛstrəl] *adj* : ancestral — **ancestry** ['æn,sɛstri] *n* **1** LINEAGE : ascendance *f* **2** ANCESTORS : ancêtres *mpl*
anchor ['æŋkər] *n* **1** : ancre *f* **2** : présentateur *m*, -trice *f* (à la télévision) — **~** *vt* : ancrer — *vi* : jeter l'ancre
anchovy ['æn,ʧo:vi, æn'ʧo:-] *n, pl* **-vies** *or* **-vy** : anchois *m*
ancient ['eɪnʃənt] *adj* : ancien
and ['ænd] *conj* **1** : et **2 come ~ see** : venez voir **3 more ~ more** : de plus en plus **4 try ~ finish it soon** : tâchez de l'achever bientôt
anecdote ['ænɪk,do:t] *n* : anecdote *f*
anemia [ə'ni:miə] *n* : anémie *f* — **anemic** [ə'ni:mɪk] *adj* : anémique
anesthesia [,ænəs'θi:ʒə] *n* : anesthésie *f* — **anesthetic** [,ænəs'θɛṭɪk] *adj* : anesthésique — **~** *n* : anesthésique *m*
anew [ə'nu:, -'nju:] *adv* : encore, de nouveau
angel ['eɪnʤəl] *n* : ange *m* — **angelic** [æn'ʤɛlɪk] *or* **angelical** [-lɪkəl] *adj* : angélique
anger ['æŋgər] *vt* : fâcher, mettre en colère — **~** *n* : colère *f*
angle ['æŋgəl] *n* **1** : angle *m* **2 at an ~** : de biais — **angler** ['æŋglər] *n* : pêcheur *m*, -cheuse *f* à la ligne
Anglo–Saxon [,æŋglo'sæksən] *adj* : anglo-saxon
angry ['æŋgri] *adj* **-grier; -est** : fâché, en colère — **angrily** ['æŋgrəli] *adv* : avec colère
anguish ['æŋgwɪʃ] *n* : angoisse *f*
angular ['æŋgjələr] *adj* : anguleux
animal ['ænəməl] *n* : animal *m*
animate ['ænə,meɪt] *vt* **-mated; -mating** : animer, stimuler — **~** ['ænəmət] *adj* ALIVE : vivant — **animated** ['ænə,meɪṭəd] *adj* **1** : animé **2 ~ cartoon** : dessin *m* animé — **animation** [,ænə'meɪʃən] *n* : animation *f*
animosity [,ænə'mɑsəṭi] *n, pl* **-ties** : animosité *f*
anise ['ænəs] *n* : anis *m*
ankle ['æŋkəl] *n* : cheville *f*
annex [ə'nɛks, 'æ,nɛks] *vt* : annexer — **~** ['æ,nɛks, -nɪks] *n* : annexe *f*
annihilate [ə'naɪə,leɪt] *vt* **-lated; -lating** : anéantir, annihiler — **annihilation** [ə,naɪə'leɪʃən] *n* : anéantissement *m*
anniversary [,ænə'vərsəri] *n, pl* **-ries** : anniversaire *m*
annotate ['ænə,teɪt] *vt* **-tated; -tating** : annoter
announce [ə'naʊnts] *vt* **-nounced; -nouncing** : annoncer — **announcement** [ə'naʊntsmənt] *n* **1** : annonce *f* **2** NOTIFICATION : avis *m* **3** : faire-part *m* (de mariage, etc.) — **announcer** [ə'naʊntsər] *n* : présentateur *m*, -trice *f*; speaker *m*, -kerine *f France*
annoy [ə'nɔɪ] *vt* : agacer, ennuyer — **annoyance** [ə'nɔɪənts] *n* : contrariété *f* — **annoying** [ə'nɔɪɪŋ] *adj* : agaçant
annual ['ænjʊəl] *adj* : annuel
annuity [ə'nu:əṭi] *n, pl* **-ties** : rente *f* (viagère)
annul [ə'nʌl] *vt* **annulled; annulling** : annuler — **annulment** [ə'nʌlmənt] *n* : annulation *f*
anoint [ə'nɔɪnt] *vt* : oindre
anomaly [ə'nɑməli] *n, pl* **-lies** : anomalie *f*
anonymous [ə'nɑnəməs] *adj* : anonyme — **anonymity** [,ænə'nɪməṭi] *n* : anonymat *m*
another [ə'nʌðər] *adj* **1** : un(e) autre **2 ~ beer** : encore une bière **3 in ~ year** : dans un an — **~** *pron* **1** : un autre *m*, une autre *f* **2 one after ~** : l'un après l'autre
answer ['æntsər] *n* **1** REPLY : réponse *f* **2** SOLUTION : solution *f* — **~** *vt* **1** : répondre à **2 ~ the door** : aller ouvrir la porte — *vi* : répondre
ant ['ænt] *n* : fourmi *f*
antagonize [æn'tægə,naɪz] *vt* **-nized; -nizing** : éveiller l'hostilité de, contrarier — **antagonistic** [æn,tægə'nɪstɪk] *adj* : antagoniste
antarctic [ænt'ɑrktɪk, -'ɑrṭɪk] *adj* : antarctique
antelope ['æntəl,o:p] *n, pl* **-lope** *or* **-lopes** : antilope *f*
antenna [æn'tɛnə] *n, pl* **-nae** *or* **-nas** : antenne *f*
anthem ['ænθəm] *n* : hymne *m*
anthology [æn'θɑləʤi] *n, pl* **-gies** : anthologie *f*
anthropology [,ænθrə'pɑləʤi] *n* : anthropologie *f*
antibiotic [,æntibaɪ'ɑṭɪk, ,æn,taɪ-, -bi-] *adj* : antibiotique — **~** *n* : antibiotique *m*
antibody ['ænti,bɑdi] *n, pl* **-bodies** : anticorps *m*
anticipate [æn'tɪsə,peɪt] *vt* **-pated; -pating** **1** FORESEE : anticiper **2** EXPECT : s'attendre à — **anticipation** [æn,tɪsə'peɪʃən] *n* : anticipation *f*
antics ['æntɪks] *npl* : singeries *fpl*
antidote ['æntɪ,do:t] *n* : antidote *m*
antifreeze ['æntɪ,fri:z] *n* : antigel *m*
antipathy [æn'tɪpəθi] *n, pl* **-thies** : antipathie *f*
antiquated ['æntə,kweɪṭəd] *adj* : dépassé
antique [æn'ti:k] *adj* : ancien, antique — **~** *n* : antiquité *f* — **antiquity** [æn'tɪkwəṭi] *n, pl* **-ties** : antiquité *f*
anti–Semitic [,æntisə'mɪṭɪk, ,æn,taɪ-] *adj* : antisémite
antiseptic [,æntə'sɛptɪk] *adj* : antiseptique — **~** *n* : antiseptique *m*
antisocial [,ænti'so:ʃəl, ,æn,taɪ-] *adj* UNSOCIABLE : peu sociable
antlers ['æntlərz] *npl* : bois *mpl*, ramure *f*
antonym ['æntə,nɪm] *n* : antonyme *m*
anus ['eɪnəs] *n* : anus *m*
anvil ['ænvəl, -vɪl] *n* : enclume *f*
anxiety [æŋk'zaɪəṭi] *n, pl* **-ties** **1** APPREHENSION : anxiété *f* **2** EAGERNESS : impatience *f* — **anxious** ['æŋkʃəs] *adj* **1** WORRIED : inquiet, anxieux **2** EAGER : impatient — **anxiously** ['æŋkʃəsli] *adv* **1** : anxieusement **2** : avec impatience
any ['ɛni] *adv* **1** SOMEWHAT : un peu **2** AT ALL : du tout **3 do you want ~ more tea?** : voulez-vous encore du thé? **4 she doesn't smoke ~ longer** : elle ne fume plus — **~** *adj* **1** : de, de la, du, des **2** WHICHEVER : quelconque, n'importe quel **3 at ~ moment** : à tout moment **4 we don't have ~ money** : nous n'avons pas d'argent — **~** *pron* **1** WHICHEVER : n'importe lequel **2 do you have ~** : est-ce que vous en avez?
anybody ['ɛni,bʌdi, -,bɑ-] → **anyone**
anyhow ['ɛni,haʊ] *adv* **1** : de toute façon, en tout cas **2** HAPHAZARDLY : n'importe comment
anymore [,ɛni'mor] *adv* **not ~** : ne plus
anyone ['ɛni,wʌn] *pron* **1** SOMEONE : quelqu'un **2** (*in negative constructions*)

: personne 3 ∼ can play : tout le monde peut jouer, n'importe qui peut jouer

anyplace ['ɛni,pleɪs] → anywhere

anything ['ɛni,θɪŋ] pron 1 WHATEVER : n'importe quoi 2 SOMETHING : quelque chose 3 (in negative constructions) : rien 4 ∼ but : tout sauf 5 hardly ∼ : presque rien

anytime ['ɛni,taɪm] adv : n'importe quand

anyway ['ɛni,weɪ] → anyhow

anywhere ['ɛni,hwɛr] adv 1 : n'importe où 2 SOMEWHERE : quelque part 3 (in negative constructions) : nulle part 4 ∼ else : partout ailleurs

apart [ə'pɑrt] adv 1 ASIDE : à part, à l'écart 2 SEPARATED : éloigné 3 ∼ from : en dehors de 4 five minutes ∼ : à cinq minutes d'intervalle 5 take ∼ : démonter 6 tell ∼ : distinguer

apartment [ə'pɑrtmənt] n : appartement m

apathy ['æpəθi] n : apathie f — **apathetic** [,æpə'θɛtɪk] adj : apathique

ape ['eɪp] n : grand singe m

aperture ['æpərtʃər, -,tʃʊr] n : ouverture f

apex ['eɪ,pɛks] n, pl apexes or apices ['eɪpə,si:z, 'æ-] : sommet m

apiece [ə'pi:s] adv 1 : chacun 2 two dollars ∼ : deux dollars la pièce

aplomb [ə'plɑm, -'plʌm] n : aplomb m

apology [ə'pɑlədʒi] n, pl -gies : excuses fpl — **apologetic** [ə,pɑlə'dʒɛtɪk] adj 1 : d'excuse 2 be ∼ : s'excuser — **apologize** [ə'pɑlə,dʒaɪz] vi -gized; -gizing : s'excuser, faire des excuses

apostle [ə'pɑsəl] n : apôtre m

apostrophe [ə'pɑstrə,fi:] n : apostrophe f

appall or Brit **appal** [ə'pɔl] vt -palled; -palling : épouvanter — **appalling** [ə'pɔlɪŋ] adj : épouvantable

apparatus [,æpə'rætəs, -'reɪ-] n, pl -tuses or -tus : appareil m

apparel [ə'pærəl] n : habillement m

apparent [ə'pærənt] adj 1 OBVIOUS : évident 2 SEEMING : apparent — **apparently** [ə'pærəntli] adv : apparemment

apparition [,æpə'rɪʃən] n : apparition f

appeal [ə'pi:l] vt : faire appel contre (un jugement) — vi 1 ∼ for : lancer un appel à 2 ∼ to ATTRACT : plaire à 3 ∼ to INVOKE : faire appel à — ∼ n 1 REQUEST : appel m 2 ATTRACTION : attrait m — **appealing** [ə'pi:lɪŋ] adj : attrayant, séduisant

appear [ə'pɪr] vi 1 : apparaître 2 SEEM : paraître, sembler 3 COME OUT : paraître, sortir — **appearance** [ə'pɪrənts] n 1 LOOK : apparence f 2 ARRIVAL : apparition f 3 ∼s npl : apparences fpl

appease [ə'pi:z] vt -peased; -peasing : apaiser

appendix [ə'pɛndɪks] n, pl -dixes or -dices [-də,si:z] : appendice m — **appendicitis** [ə,pɛndə'saɪtəs] n : appendicite f

appetite ['æpə,taɪt] n : appétit m — **appetizer** ['æpə,taɪzər] n : amuse-gueule m — **appetizing** ['æpə,taɪzɪŋ] adj : appétissant

applaud [ə'plɔd] v : applaudir — **applause** [ə'plɔz] n : applaudissements mpl

apple ['æpəl] n : pomme f

appliance [ə'plaɪənts] n : appareil m

apply [ə'plaɪ] v -plied; -plying vt 1 : appliquer 2 EXERT : exercer 3 ∼ oneself : s'appliquer — vi 1 : s'appliquer 2 ∼ for : poser sa candidature pour — **applicant** ['æplɪkənt] n : candidat m, -date f — **application** [,æplə'keɪʃən] n 1 USE : application f 2 : demande f (d'emploi)

appoint [ə'pɔɪnt] vt 1 SET : fixer 2 NAME : nommer — **appointment** [ə'pɔɪntmənt] n 1 : nomination f 2 MEETING : rendez-vous m

apportion [ə'porʃən] vt : répartir

appraise [ə'preɪz] vt -praised; -praising : évaluer — **appraisal** [ə'preɪzəl] n : évaluation f

appreciate [ə'pri:ʃi,eɪt, -'prɪ-] vt -ated; -ating 1 VALUE : apprécier 2 REALIZE : comprendre, se rendre compte de 3 I ∼ your help : je vous suis reconnaissant de m'avoir aidé — **appreciation** [ə,pri:ʃi'eɪʃən, -,prɪ-] n 1 EVALUATION : appréciation f 2 GRATITUDE : reconnaissance f — **appreciative** [ə'pri:ʃətɪv, -'prɪ-; ə'pri:ʃi,eɪ-] adj : reconnaissant

apprehend [,æprɪ'hɛnd] vt 1 ARREST : appréhender 2 UNDERSTAND : comprendre 3 DREAD : appréhender — **apprehension** [,æprɪ'hɛntʃən] n : appréhension f — **apprehensive** [,æprɪ'hɛntsɪv] adj : inquiet

apprentice [ə'prɛntɪs] n : apprenti m, -tie f — **apprenticeship** [ə'prɛntɪs,ʃɪp] n : apprentissage m

approach [ə'pro:tʃ] vt 1 NEAR : s'approcher de 2 : s'adresser à (quelqu'un), aborder (un problème, etc.) — vi : s'approcher — ∼ n : approche f — **approachable** [ə'pro:tʃəbəl] adj : abordable, accessible

appropriate [ə'pro:pri,eɪt] vt -ated; -ating 1 SEIZE : s'approprier 2 ALLOCATE : affecter — ∼ [ə'pro:priət] adj : approprié

approve [ə'pru:v] vt -proved; -proving or ∼ of : approuver — **approval** [ə'pru:vəl] n : approbation f

approximate [ə'prɑksəmət] adj : approximatif — ∼ [ə'prɑksə,meɪt] vt -mated; -mating : se rapprocher de — **approximately** [ə'prɑksəmətli] adv : à peu près, environ

apricot ['æprə,kɑt, 'eɪ-] n : abricot m

April ['eɪprəl] n : avril m

apron ['eɪprən] n : tablier m

apt ['æpt] adj 1 : approprié 2 be ∼ to : avoir tendance à — **aptitude** ['æptə,tu:d, -,tju:d] n : aptitude f

aquarium [ə'kwæriəm] n, pl -iums or -ia [-iə] : aquarium m

aquatic [ə'kwɑtɪk, -'kwæ-] adj 1 : aquatique 2 : nautique (se dit des sports)

aqueduct ['ækwə,dʌkt] n : aqueduc m

Arab ['ærəb] or **Arabic** ['ærəbɪk] adj : arabe — **Arabic** n : arabe m (langue)

arbitrary ['ɑrbə,trɛri] adj : arbitraire

arbitrate ['ɑrbə,treɪt] v -trated; -trating : arbitrer — **arbitration** [,ɑrbə'treɪʃən] n : arbitrage m

arc ['ɑrk] n : arc m

arcade [ɑr'keɪd] n 1 : arcade f 2 shopping ∼ : galerie f marchande

arch ['ɑrtʃ] n : voûte f, arc m — ∼ vt : arquer, courber

archaeology or **archeology** [,ɑr-ki'ɑlədʒi] n : archéologie f — **archaeological** [,ɑrkiə'lɑdʒɪkəl] adj : archéologique — **archaeologist** [,ɑrki'ɑlədʒɪst] n : archéologue mf

archaic [ɑr'keɪɪk] adj : archaïque

archbishop [ɑrtʃ'bɪʃəp] n : archevêque m

archery ['ɑrtʃəri] n : tir m à l'arc

archipelago [,ɑrkə'pɛlə,go:, ,ɑrtʃə-] n, pl -goes or -gos [-go:z] : archipel m

architecture ['ɑrkə,tɛktʃər] n : architecture f — **architect** ['ɑrkə,tɛkt] n : architecte mf — **architectural** [,ɑrkə'tɛktʃərəl] adj : architectural

archives ['ɑr,kaɪvz] npl : archives fpl

archway ['ɑrtʃ,weɪ] n : voûte f, arcade f

arctic ['ɑrktɪk, 'ɑrt-] adj : arctique

ardent ['ɑrdənt] adj : ardent — **ardently** ['ɑrdəntli] adv : ardemment — **ardor** ['ɑrdər] n : ardeur f

arduous ['ɑrdʒʊəs] adj : ardu

are → be

area ['æriə] n 1 REGION : région f 2 SURFACE : aire f 3 FIELD : domaine m 4 ∼ code : indicatif m de zone, indicatif m régional Can

arena [ə'ri:nə] n : arène f, aréna m Can

aren't ['ɑrnt, 'ɑrənt] (contraction of are not) → be

argue ['ɑr,gju:] v -gued; -guing vi 1 QUARREL : se disputer 2 DEBATE : argumenter — vt DEBATE : discuter — **argument** ['ɑrgjəmənt] n 1 QUARREL : dispute f 2 DEBATE : discussion f 3 REASONING : argument m

arid ['ærəd] adj : aride

arise [ə'raɪz] vi arose [ə'ro:z]; arisen [ə'rɪzən]; arising 1 : se présenter 2 ∼ from : résulter de

aristocracy [,ærə'stɑkrəsi] n, pl -cies : aristocratie f — **aristocrat** [ə'rɪstə,kræt] n : aristocrate mf — **aristocratic** [ə,rɪstə'krætɪk] adj : aristocratique

arithmetic [ə'rɪθmə,tɪk] n : arithmétique f

ark ['ɑrk] n : arche f

arm ['ɑrm] n 1 : bras m 2 WEAPON : arme f — ∼ vt : armer — **armament** ['ɑrməmənt] n : armement m — **armchair** ['ɑrm,tʃɛr] n : fauteuil m — **armed** ['ɑrmd] adj 1 : armé 2 ∼ forces : forces fpl armées 3 ∼ robbery : vol m à main armée

armistice ['ɑrməstɪs] n : armistice m

armor or Brit **armour** ['ɑrmər] n 1 : armure f 2 or ∼ plating : blindage m — **armored** or Brit **armoured** ['ɑrmərd] adj : blindé — **armory** or Brit **armoury** ['ɑrməri] n, pl -ries : arsenal m

armpit ['ɑrm,pɪt] n : aisselle f

army ['ɑrmi] n, pl -mies : armée f

aroma [ə'ro:mə] n : arôme m — **aromatic** [,ærə'mætɪk] adj : aromatique

around [ə'raʊnd] adv 1 : de circonférence 2 NEARBY : là, dans les parages 3 APPROXIMATELY : environ, à peu près 4 all ∼ : tout autour — ∼ prep 1 SURROUNDING : autour de 2 THROUGHOUT : partout dans 3 ∼ here : par ici 4 ∼ noon : vers midi

arouse [ə'raʊz] vt aroused; arousing 1 AWAKE : réveiller 2 STIMULATE : éveiller

arrange [ə'reɪndʒ] v -ranged; -ranging vt : arranger — vi ∼ for : prendre des dispositions pour — **arrangement** [ə'reɪndʒmənt] n 1 ORDER : arrangement m 2 ∼s npl : dispositions fpl

array [ə'reɪ] n : sélection f

arrears [ə'rɪrz] npl 1 : arriéré m 2 be in ∼ : avoir du retard

arrest [ə'rɛst] vt : arrêter — ∼ n : arrestation f

arrive [ə'raɪv] vi -rived; -riving 1 : arriver 2 ∼ at : parvenir à, atteindre — **arrival** [ə'raɪvəl] n : arrivée f

arrogance ['ærəgənts] n : arrogance f — **arrogant** ['ærəgənt] adj : arrogant

arrow ['æro] n : flèche f

arsenal ['ɑrsənəl] n : arsenal m

arsenic ['ɑrsənɪk] n : arsenic m

arson ['ɑrsən] n : incendie m criminel

art ['ɑrt] n : art m

artefact Brit → artifact

artery ['ɑrtəri] n, pl -teries : artère f

artful ['ɑrtfəl] adj : rusé, astucieux

arthritis [ɑr'θraɪtəs] n, pl -thritides [-'θrɪtə,di:z] : arthrite f — **arthritic** [ɑr'θrɪtɪk] adj : arthritique

artichoke ['ɑrtə,tʃo:k] n : artichaut m

article ['ɑrtɪkəl] n : article m

articulate [ɑr'tɪkjə,leɪt] vt -lated; -lating : articuler — ∼ [ɑr'tɪkjələt] adj be ∼ : s'exprimer bien

artifact or Brit **artefact** ['ɑrtə,fækt] n : objet m fabriqué

artificial [,ɑrtə'fɪʃəl] adj : artificiel

artillery [ɑr'tɪləri] n, pl -leries : artillerie f

artist ['ɑrtɪst] n : artiste mf — **artistic** [ɑr'tɪstɪk] adj : artistique

as ['æz] adv 1 ∼ much : autant 2 ∼ tall ∼ : aussi grand que 3 ∼ well : aussi — ∼ conj 1 LIKE : comme 2 WHILE : tandis que, alors que 3 SINCE : puisque, comme 4 ∼ is : tel quel — ∼ prep : en tant que, comme — ∼ pron 1 : que 2 ∼ you know : comme vous savez

asbestos [æz'bɛstəs, æs-] n : amiante m

ascend [ə'sɛnd] vt : monter (à), gravir — vi : monter — **ascent** [ə'sɛnt] n : ascension f

ascertain [,æsər'teɪn] vt : établir

ascribe [ə'skraɪb] vt -cribed; -cribing ∼ to: attribuer à

as for prep : quant à

ash[1] ['æʃ] n : cendre f

ash[2] n : frêne m (arbre)

ashamed [ə'ʃeɪmd] adj 1 : honteux 2 be ∼ : avoir honte

ashore [ə'ʃor] adv : à terre

ashtray ['æʃ,treɪ] n : cendrier m

Asian ['eɪʒən, -ʃən] adj : asiatique

aside [ə'saɪd] adv : de côté, à part — **aside from** prep 1 BESIDES : à part 2 EXCEPT : sauf

as if conj : comme si

ask ['æsk] vt 1 : demander 2 INVITE : inviter 3 ∼ a question : poser une question 4 ∼ s.o. : demandez à qqn — vi : demander

askance [ə'skænts] adv look ∼ : regarder du coin de l'œil

askew [ə'skju:] adv & adj : de travers

asleep [ə'sli:p] adj 1 : endormi 2 fall ∼ : s'endormir

as of prep : dès, à partir de

asparagus [ə'spærəgəs] ns & pl : asperges fpl

aspect ['æ,spɛkt] n : aspect m

asphalt ['æs,fɔlt] n : asphalte m

asphyxiate [æ'sfɪksi,eɪt] vt -ated; -ating : asphyxier — **asphyxiation** [æ,sfɪksi'eɪʃən] n : asphyxie f

aspire [ə'spaɪr] vi -pired; -piring ∼ to : aspirer à — **aspiration** [,æspə'reɪʃən] n : aspiration f

aspirin ['æsprən, 'æspə-] n, pl aspirin or aspirins : aspirine f

ass ['æs] n 1 : âne m 2 FOOL : idiot m, -diote f

assail [ə'seɪl] vt : assaillir — **assailant** [ə'seɪlənt] n : assaillant m, -lante f

assassin [ə'sæsən] n : assassin m — **assassinate** [ə'sæsən,eɪt] vt -nated; -nating : assassiner — **assassination** [ə,sæsən'eɪʃən] n : assassinat m

assault [ə'sɔlt] vt : agresser — ∼ n : agression f, assaut m (militaire)

assemble [ə'sɛmbəl] v -bled; -bling vt 1 CONSTRUCT : assembler 2 GATHER : rassembler — vi CONVENE : se rassembler — **assembly** [ə'sɛmbli] n, pl -blies 1 MEETING : assemblée f, réunion f 2 ∼ line : chaîne f de montage

assent [ə'sɛnt] vi : consentir — ∼ n : assentiment m

assert [ə'sərt] vt 1 : affirmer 2 ∼ oneself : s'imposer — **assertion** [ə'sərʃən] n : assertion f — **assertive** [ə'sərtɪv] adj : assuré

assess [ə'sɛs] vt : évaluer — **assessment** [ə'sɛsmənt] n : évaluation f

asset ['æ,sɛt] n 1 : avantage m, atout m 2 ∼s npl : biens mpl, actif m

assiduous [ə'sɪdʒʊəs] adj : assidu

assign [ə'saɪn] vt 1 ALLOT : assigner 2 APPOINT : nommer — **assignment** [ə'saɪnmənt] n 1 TASK : mission f 2 HOMEWORK : devoir m

assimilate [ə'sɪmə,leɪt] vt -lated; -lating : assimiler

assist [ə'sɪst] vt : aider, assister — **assistance** [ə'sɪstənts] n : aide f, assistance f — **assistant** [ə'sɪstənt] n : assistant m, -tante f; adjoint m, -jointe f

associate [ə'so:ʃi,eɪt, -si-] v -ated; -ating vt : associer — vi ∼ with : fréquenter — ∼ [ə'so:ʃiət, -siət] n : associé m, -ciée f — **association** [ə,so:ʃi'eɪʃən, -si-] n : association f

as soon as conj : aussitôt que

assorted [ə'sɔrtəd] adj : assorti — **assortment** [ə'sɔrtmənt] n : assortiment m

assume [ə'su:m] vt -sumed; -suming 1 : assumer 2 SUPPOSE : supposer, présumer — **assumption** [ə'sʌmpʃən] n : supposition f

assure [ə'ʃʊr] vt -sured; -suring : assurer — **assurance** [ə'ʃʊrənts] n : assurance f

asterisk ['æstə,rɪsk] n : astérisque m

asthma ['æzmə] n : asthme m

as though → as if

as to prep : sur, concernant

astonish [ə'stɑnɪʃ] vt : étonner — **astonishing** [ə'stɑnɪʃɪŋ] adj : étonnant — **astonishment** [ə'stɑnɪʃmənt] n : étonnement m

astound [ə'staʊnd] vt : stupéfier — **astounding** [ə'staʊndɪŋ] adj : stupéfiant

astray [ə'streɪ] adv 1 go ∼ : s'égarer 2 lead ∼ : égarer

astrology [ə'strɑlədʒi] n : astrologie f

astronaut ['æstrə,nɔt] n : astronaute mf

astronomy [ə'strɑnəmi] n, pl -mies : astronomie f — **astronomer** [ə'strɑnəmər] n : astronome mf — **astronomical** [,æstrə'nɑmɪkəl] adj : astronomique

astute [ə'stu:t, -'stju:t] adj : astucieux — **astuteness** [ə'stu:tnəs, -'stju:t-] n : astuce f

as well as conj : en plus de — ∼ prep : ainsi que, à part

asylum [ə'saɪləm] n : asile m

at ['æt] prep 1 : à 2 ∼ the dentist's : chez le dentiste 3 ∼ three o'clock : à trois heures 4 ∼ war : en guerre 5 be angry ∼ : être fâché contre 6 laugh ∼ : rire de 7 shoot ∼ : tirer sur — **at all** adv : du tout

ate ['eɪt] → eat

atheist ['eɪθiɪst] n : athée mf — **atheism** ['eɪθi,ɪzəm] n : athéisme m

athlete ['æθ,li:t] n : athlète mf — **athletic** [æθ'lɛtɪk] adj : athlétique — **athletics** [æθ'lɛtɪks] ns & pl : athlétisme m

atlas ['ætləs] n : atlas m

atmosphere ['ætmə,sfɪr] n : atmosphère f — **atmospheric** [,ætmə'sfɪrɪk, -'sfɛr-] adj : atmosphérique

atom ['ætəm] n : atome m — **atomic** [ə'tɑmɪk] adj : atomique

atomizer ['ætə,maɪzər] n : atomiseur m

atone [ə'to:n] vi atoned; atoning ∼ for : expier — **atonement** [ə'to:nmənt] n : expiation f

atrocious [ə'tro:ʃəs] adj : atroce — **atrocity** [ə'trɑsəti] n, pl -ties : atrocité f

atrophy ['ætrəfi] vi -phied; phying : s'atrophier

attach [ə'tætʃ] vt 1 : attacher 2 become ∼ed to : s'attacher à — vi ADHERE : s'attacher —**attachment** [ə'tætʃmənt] n 1 AFFECTION : attachement m 2 ACCESSORY : accessoire m

attack [ə'tæk] v : attaquer — ∼ n 1 : attaque f 2 heart ∼ : crise f cardiaque — **attacker** [ə'tækər] n : agresseur m

attain [ə'teɪn] vt : atteindre — **attainment** [ə'teɪnmənt] n : réalisation f

attempt [ə'tɛmpt] vt : tenter — ∼ n : tentative f

attend [ə'tɛnd] vt 1 : assister à 2 ∼ church : aller à l'église — vi 1 ∼ to : s'occuper de 2 ∼ to HEED : prêter attention à — **attendance** [ə'tɛndənts] n 1 : présence f 2 TURNOUT : assistance f — **attendant** [ə'tɛndənt] n 1 : gardien m, -dienne f 2 service station ∼ : pompiste mf

attention [ə'tɛntʃən] n 1 : attention f 2 pay ∼ to : prêter attention à — **attentive** [ə'tɛntɪv] adj : attentif

attest [ə'tɛst] vt : attester — vi ∼ to : témoigner de

attic ['ætɪk] n : grenier m

attitude ['ætə,tu:d, -,tju:d] n : attitude f

attorney [ə'tərni] n, pl -neys : avocat m, -cate f

attract [ə'trækt] vt : attirer — **attraction** [ə'trækʃən] n 1 : attrait f 2 : attraction f (en science) — **attractive** [ə'træktɪv] adj : attirant, attrayant

attribute ['ætrə,bju:t] n : attribut m — ∼ [ə'trɪ,bju:t] vt -uted; -uting : attribuer

auburn ['ɔbərn] adj : auburn

auction ['ɔkʃən] vt : vendre aux enchères — ∼ n : vente f aux enchères

audacious [ɔ'deɪʃəs] adj : audacieux — **audacity** [ɔ'dæsəti] n, pl -ties : audace f

audible ['ɔdəbəl] adj : audible

audience ['ɔdiənts] n : assistance f, public m

audio ['ɔdi,o:] adj : audio — **audiovisual** [,ɔdio'vɪʒʊəl] adj : audiovisuel

audition [ɔ'dɪʃən] n : audition f — ∼ v : auditionner

auditor ['ɔdətər] n : auditeur m, -trice f

auditorium [,ɔdə'toriəm] n, pl -riums or -ria [-riə] : salle f

augment [ɔg'mɛnt] vt : augmenter

augur ['ɔgər] vi ∼ well : être de bon augure

August ['ɔgəst] n : août m

aunt ['ænt, 'ɑnt] n : tante f

aura ['ɔrə] n : aura f, atmosphère f

auspices ['ɔspəsəz, -,si:z] npl : auspices mpl

auspicious [ɔ'spɪʃəs] adj : favorable

austere [ɔ'stɪr] adj : austère — **austerity** [ɔ'stɛrəti] n, pl -ties : austérité f

Australian [ɔ'streɪljən] adj : australien

authentic [ə'θɛntɪk, ɔ-] adj : authentique

author ['ɔθər] n : auteur m

authority [ə'θɔrəti, ɔ-] n, pl -ties : autorité f — **authoritarian** [ə,θɔrə'tɛriən, ɔ-] adj : autoritaire — **authoritative** [ə'θɔrə-

ˌteɪt̬ɪv, ɔ-] *adj* 1 DICTATORIAL : autoritaire 2 DEFINITIVE : qui fait autorité — **authorization** [ˌɔθərəˈzeɪʃən] *n* : autorisation *f* — **authorize** [ˈɔθəˌraɪz] *vt* **-rized; -rizing** : autoriser

autobiography [ˌɔt̬oˌbaɪˈɑgrəfi] *n, pl* **-phies** : autobiographie *f* — **autobiographical** [ˌɔt̬obaɪəˈgræfɪkəl] *adj* : autobiographique

autograph [ˈɔt̬əˌgræf] *n* : autographe *m*

automate [ˈɔt̬əˌmeɪt] *v* **-mated; -mating** : automatiser — **automatic** [ˌɔt̬əˈmæt̬ɪk] *adj* : automatique — **automation** [ˌɔt̬əˈmeɪʃən] *n* : automatisation *f*

automobile [ˌɔt̬əmoˈbi:l, -ˈmo:ˌbi:l] *n* : automobile *f,* voiture *f*

autonomy [ɔˈtɑnəmi] *n, pl* **-mies** : autonomie *f* — **autonomous** [ɔˈtɑnəməs] *adj* : autonome

autopsy [ˈɔˌtɑpsi, -təp-] *n, pl* **-sies** : autopsie *f*

autumn [ˈɔt̬əm] *n* : automne *m*

auxiliary [ɔgˈzɪljəri, -ˈzɪləri] *adj* : auxiliaire — ~ *n, pl* **-ries** : auxiliaire *mf*

avail [əˈveɪl] *vt* ~ **oneself of** : profiter de — ~ *n* **to no** ~ : en vain, sans résultat

available [əˈveɪləbəl] *adj* : disponible — **availability** [əˌveɪləˈbɪlət̬i] *n, pl* **-ties** : disponibilité *f*

avalanche [ˈævəˌlænʧ] *n* : avalanche *f*

avarice [ˈævərəs] *n* : avarice *f*

avenge [əˈvɛnʤ] *vt* **avenged; avenging** : venger

avenue [ˈævəˌnu:, -ˌnju:] *n* : avenue *f*

average [ˈævrɪʤ, ˈævə-] *vt* **-aged; -aging** : faire en moyenne — ~ *adj* : moyen — ~ *n* : moyenne *f*

averse [əˈvərs] *adj* **be** ~ **to** : répugner à — **aversion** [əˈvərʒən] *n* : aversion *f*

avert [əˈvərt] *vt* 1 AVOID : éviter 2 ~ **one's eyes** : détourner les yeux

aviation [ˌeɪviˈeɪʃən] *n* : aviation *f*

avid [ˈævɪd] *adj* 1 **be** ~ **for** : être avide de 2 ENTHUSIASTIC : passionné — **avidly** [ˈævɪdli] *adv* : avidement

avocado [ˌævəˈkɑdo, ˌɑvə-] *n, pl* **-dos** : avocat *m*

avoid [əˈvɔɪd] *vt* : éviter

await [əˈweɪt] *vt* : attendre

awake [əˈweɪk] *v* **awoke** [əˈwo:k]; **awoken** [əˈwo:kən] *or* **awaked** [əˈweɪkt]; **awaking** *vt* : réveiller, éveiller — *vi* WAKE UP : se réveiller — ~ *adj* : éveillé, réveillé — **awaken** [əˈweɪkən] → **awake**

award [əˈwərd] *vt* 1 GRANT : accorder 2 CONFER : décerner — ~ *n* : prix *m*

aware [əˈwær] *adj* 1 : au courant 2 **be** ~ **of** : être conscient de — **awareness** [əˈwærnəs] *n* : conscience *f*

awash [əˈwɔʃ] *adj* ~ **with** : inondé de

away [əˈweɪ] *adv* 1 **chatter** ~ : bavarder sans arrêt 2 **give** ~ : donner 3 **go** ~! : allez-vous en! 4 **take** ~ : enlever 5 **ten kilometers** ~ : à dix kilomètres d'ici 6 **turn** ~ : se détourner — ~ *adj* 1 ABSENT : absent 2 ~ **game** : match *m* à l'extérieur

awe [ˈɔ] *n* : crainte *f* mêlée de respect — **awesome** [ˈɔsəm] *adj* : impressionnant

awful [ˈɔfəl] *adj* 1 : affreux 2 **an** ~ **lot of** : énormément de — **awfully** [ˈɔfəli] *adv* : extrêmement

awhile [əˈhwaɪl] *adv* : un moment

awkward [ˈɔkwərd] *adj* 1 : gauche, maladroit 2 EMBARRASSING : gênant 3 DIFFICULT : difficile — **awkwardly** [ˈɔkwərdli] *adv* : maladroitement

awning [ˈɔnɪŋ] *n* : auvent *m*

awoke, awoken → **awake**

awry [əˈraɪ] *adv* **go** ~ : mal tourner

ax *or* **axe** [ˈæks] *n* : hache *f*

axiom [ˈæksiəm] *n* : axiome *m*

axis [ˈæksɪs] *n, pl* **axes** [-si:z] : axe *m*

axle [ˈæksəl] *n* : essieu *m*

B

b [ˈbi:] *n, pl* **b's** *or* **bs** [ˈbi:z] : b *m,* deuxième lettre de l'alphabet

babble [ˈbæbəl] *vi* **-bled; -bling** 1 : babiller, gazouiller 2 MURMUR : murmurer — ~ *n* : babillage *m*

baboon [bæˈbu:n] *n* : babouin *m*

baby [ˈbeɪbi] *n, pl* **-bies** : bébé *m* — ~ *vt* **-bied; -bying** : dorloter — **baby carriage** *n* : voiture *f* d'enfant, landau *m France* — **babyish** [ˈbeɪbiɪʃ] *adj* : enfantin — **baby-sit** [ˈbeɪbiˌsɪt] *vi* **-sat** [-ˌsæt]; **-sitting** : garder des enfants, faire du baby-sitting *France* — **baby-sitter** [ˈbeɪbiˌsɪt̬ər] *n* : gardienne *f* d'enfants, baby-sitter *mf France*

bachelor [ˈbæʧələr] *n* 1 : célibataire *m* 2 GRADUATE : licencié *m,* -ciée *f*

back [ˈbæk] *n* 1 : dos *m* 2 REVERSE : revers *m,* dos *m* 3 REAR : derrière *m,* arrière *m,* fond *m* 4 : arrière *m* (aux sports) — ~ *adv* 1 : en arrière, vers l'arrière 2 **be** ~ : être de retour 3 **go** ~ : retourner 4 **two years** ~ : il y a deux ans — ~ *adj* 1 REAR : arrière, de derrière 2 OVERDUE : arriéré — ~ *vt* 1 SUPPORT : soutenir, appuyer 2 *or* ~ **up** : mettre en marche arrière (un véhicule) — *vi* 1 ~ **down** : céder 2 ~ **up** : reculer — **backache** [ˈbækˌeɪk] *n* : mal *m* de dos — **backbone** [ˈbækˌbo:n] *n* : colonne *f* vertébrale — **backfire** [ˈbækˌfaɪr] *vi* **-fired; -firing** : pétarader — **background** [ˈbækˌgraʊnd] *n* 1 : arrière-plan *m,* fond *m* (d'un tableau) 2 EXPERIENCE : formation *f* — **backhand** [ˈbækˌhænd] *adj* : de revers — **backhanded** [ˈbækˌhændəd] *adj* : équivoque — **backing** [ˈbækɪŋ] *n* : soutien *m,* appui *m* — **backlash** [ˈbækˌlæʃ] *n* : contrecoup *m,* répercussion *f* — **backlog** [ˈbækˌlɔg] *n* : accumulation *f* (de travail, etc.) — **backpack** [ˈbækˌpæk] *n* : sac *m* à dos — **backstage** [ˌbækˈsteɪʤ, ˈbækˌ-] *adv* : dans les coulisses — **backtrack** [ˈbækˌtræk] *vi* : revenir sur ses pas — **backup** [ˈbækˌʌp] *n* 1 SUPPORT : soutien *m,* appui *m* 2 : sauvegarde *f* (en informatique) — **backward** [ˈbækwərd] *or* **backwards** [-wərdz] *adv* 1 : en arrière 2 **bend over** ~**s** : faire tout son possible 3 **do it** ~ : fais-le à l'envers 4 **fall** ~ : tomber à la renverse — **backward** *adj* : en arrière

bacon [beɪkən] *n* : lard *m,* bacon *m*

bacteria [bækˈtɪriə] *npl* : bactéries *fpl*

bad [ˈbæd] *adj* **worse** [ˈwərs]; **worst** [ˈwərst] 1 : mauvais 2 ROTTEN : pourri 3 SEVERE : grave, aigu 4 **from** ~ **to worse** : de mal en pis 5 **too** ~! : quel dommage! — ~ *adv* → **badly**

badge [ˈbæʤ] *n* : insigne *m,* plaque *f*

badger [ˈbæʤər] *n* : blaireau *m* — ~ *vt* : harceler

badly [ˈbædli] *adv* 1 : mal 2 SEVERELY : gravement 3 **need** ~ : avoir grand besoin de

baffle [ˈbæfəl] *vt* **-fled; -fling** : déconcerter

bag [ˈbæg] *n* 1 : sac *m* 2 HANDBAG : sac *m* à main 3 SUITCASE : valise *f* — ~ *vt* **bagged; bagging** : mettre en sac

baggage [ˈbægɪʤ] *n* : bagages *mpl*

baggy [ˈbægi] *adj* **-gier; -est** : ample, trop grand

bagpipes [ˈbægˌpaɪps] *npl* : cornemuse *f*

bail [ˌbeɪl] *n* : caution *f* — ~ *vt* 1 *or* ~ **out** : vider, écoper (un bateau) 2 *or* ~ **out** RELEASE : mettre en liberté sous caution 3 ~ **out** EXTRICATE : tirer d'affaire

bailiff [ˈbeɪlɪf] *n* : huissier *m*

bait [ˈbeɪt] *vt* 1 : appâter 2 HARASS : tourmenter — ~ *n* : appât *m*

bake [ˈbeɪk] *v* **baked; baking** *vt* : faire cuire au four — *vi* : cuire (au four) — **baker** [ˈbeɪkər] *n* : boulanger *m,* -gère *f* — **bakery** [ˈbeɪkəri] *n, pl* **-ries** : boulangerie *f* — **baking soda** *n* : bicarbonate *m* de soude

balance [ˈbælənts] *n* 1 SCALES : balance *f* 2 COUNTERBALANCE : contrepoids *m* 3 EQUILIBRIUM : équilibre *m* 4 REMAINDER : reste *m* 5 *or* **bank** ~ : solde *m* — ~ *v* **-anced; -ancing** *vt* 1 : faire ses comptes 2 EQUALIZE : équilibrer 3 WEIGH : peser — *vi* : être en équilibre

balcony [ˈbælkəni] *n, pl* **-nies** : balcon *m*

bald [ˈbɔld] *adj* 1 : chauve 2 WORN : usé

balk [ˈbɔk] *vi* ~ **at** : reculer devant

ball [ˈbɔl] *n* 1 : balle *f,* ballon *m,* boule *f* 2 DANCE : bal *m* 3 ~ **of string** : pelote *f* de ficelle

ballad [ˈbæləd] *n* : ballade *f*

ballast [ˈbæləst] *n* : lest *m,* ballast *m*

ballerina [ˌbæləˈri:nə] *n* : ballerine *f*

ballet [bæˈleɪ, ˈbæˌleɪ] *n* : ballet *m*

ballistic [bəˈlɪstɪk] *adj* : balistique

balloon [bəˈlu:n] *n* : ballon *m,* balloune *f Can*

ballot [ˈbælət] *n* 1 : bulletin *m* de vote 2 VOTING : scrutin *m*

ballpoint pen [ˈbɔlˌpɔɪnt] *n* : stylo *m* à bille

ballroom [ˈbɔlˌru:m, -ˌrʊm] *n* : salle *f* de danse, salle *f* de bal

balm [ˈbɑm, ˈbɑlm] *n* : baume *m* — **balmy** [ˈbɑmi, ˈbɑl-] *adj* **balmier; -est** : doux, agréable

baloney [bəˈlo:ni] *n* NONSENSE : balivernes *fpl*

bamboo [bæmˈbu:] *n* : bambou *m*

bamboozle [bæmˈbu:zəl] *vt* **-zled; -zling** : embobiner *fam*

ban [ˈbæn] *vt* **banned; banning** : interdire — ~ *n* : interdiction *f*

banana [bəˈnænə] *n* : banane *f*

band [ˈbænd] *n* 1 STRIP : bande *f* 2 GROUP : groupe *m,* orchestre *m* — ~ *vi* ~ **together** : se réunir, se grouper

bandage [ˈbændɪʤ] *n* : pansement *m,* bandage *m* — ~ *vt* : bander, panser

bandy [ˈbændi] *vt* **-died; -dying** ~ **about** : faire circuler

bang [ˈbæŋ] *vt* 1 STRIKE : frapper 2 SLAM : claquer — *vi* ~ **on** : cogner sur — ~ *n* 1 BLOW : coup *m* 2 EXPLOSION : détonation *f* 3 SLAM : claquement *m*

bangs [ˈbæŋz] *npl* : frange *f*

banish [ˈbænɪʃ] *vt* : bannir

banister [ˈbænəstər] *n* : rampe *f*

bank [ˈbæŋk] *n* 1 : banque *f* 2 : talus *m,* rive *f* (d'un fleuve) 3 EMBANKMENT : terre-plein *m* — ~ *vt* : déposer — *vi* 1 : avoir un compte en banque 2 ~ **on** : compter sur — **banker** [ˈbæŋkər] *n* : banquier *m* — **banking** [ˈbæŋkɪŋ] *n* : opérations *fpl* bancaires

bankrupt [ˈbæŋˌkrʌpt] *adj* : en faillite — **bankruptcy** [ˈbæŋˌkrʌptsi] *n, pl* **-cies** : faillite *f*

banner [ˈbænər] *n* : bannière *f*

banquet [ˈbæŋkwət] *n* : banquet *m*

banter [ˈbæntər] *n* : plaisanteries *fpl* — ~ *vi* : plaisanter

baptize [bæpˈtaɪz, ˈbæpˌtaɪz] *vt* **-tized; -tizing** : baptiser — **baptism** [ˈbæpˌtɪzəm] *n* : baptême *m*

bar [ˈbɑr] *n* 1 : barre *f* (de métal), barreau *m* (d'une fenêtre) 2 BARRIER : obstacle *m,* barrière *f* 3 TAVERN : bar *m* 4 **behind** ~**s** : sous les verrous 5 ~ **of soap** : pain *m* de savon — ~ *vt* **barred; barring** 1 OBSTRUCT : barrer, bloquer 2 EXCLUDE : exclure 3 PROHIBIT : interdire — ~ *prep* 1 : sauf 2 ~ **none** : sans exception

barbarian [bɑrˈbæriən] *n* : barbare *mf* — **barbaric** [bɑrˈbærɪk] *adj* : barbare

barbecue [ˈbɑrbɪˌkju:] *vt* **-cued; -cuing** : griller au charbon de bois — ~ *n* : barbecue *m*

barbed wire [ˈbɑrbdˈwaɪr] *n* : fil *m* de fer barbelé

barber [ˈbɑrbər] *n* : coiffeur *m,* -feuse *f;* barbier *m Can*

bare [ˈbær] *adj* **barer; barest** 1 : dénudé 2 EMPTY : vide 3 MINIMUM : essentiel — **barefaced** [ˈbærˌfeɪst] *adj* : éhonté — **barefoot** [ˈbærˌfʊt] *or* **barefooted** [-ˌfʊt̬əd] *adv* : pieds nus — ~ *adj* **be** ~ : être nu-pieds — **barely** [ˈbærli] *adv* : à peine, tout juste

bargain [ˈbɑrgən] *n* 1 AGREEMENT : marché *m* 2 BUY : aubaine *f* — ~ *vi* 1 : négocier, marchander 2 ~ **for** : s'attendre à

barge [ˈbɑrʤ] *n* : chaland *m* — ~ *vi* **barged; barging** ~ **in** : interrompre

baritone [ˈbærəˌto:n] *n* : baryton *m*

bark[1] [ˈbɑrk] *vi* : aboyer — ~ *n* : aboiement *m* (d'un chien)

bark[2] *n* : écorce *f* (d'un arbre)

barley [ˈbɑrli] *n* : orge *f*

barn [ˈbɑrn] *n* : grange *f*

barometer [bəˈrɑmət̬ər] *n* : baromètre *m*

baron [ˈbærən] *n* : baron *m* — **baroness** [ˈbærənɪs, -nəs, -ˈnɛs] *n* : baronne *f*

barracks [ˈbærəks] *npl* : caserne *f*

barrage [bəˈrɑʒ, -ˈrɑʤ] *n* 1 : tir *m* de barrage 2 : déluge *m* (de questions, etc.)

barrel [ˈbærəl] *n* 1 : tonneau *m,* fût *m,* baril *m* 2 : canon *m* (d'une arme à feu)

barren [ˈbærən] *adj* : stérile

barricade *vt* [ˈbærəˌkeɪd, ˌbærəˈ-] **-caded; -cading** : barricader — ~ *n* : barricade *f*

barrier [ˈbæriər] *n* : barrière *f*

barring [ˈbɑrɪŋ] *prep* : excepté, sauf

bartender [ˈbɑrˌtɛndər] *n* : barman *m*

barter [ˈbɑrt̬ər] *vt* : échanger, troquer — ~ *n* : échange *m,* troc *m*

base [ˈbeɪs] *n, pl* **bases** : base *f* — ~ *vt* **based; basing** : baser, fonder — ~ *adj* **baser; basest** : bas, vil

baseball [ˈbeɪsˌbɔl] *n* : baseball *m,* baseball *m*

basement [ˈbeɪsmənt] *n* : sous-sol *m*

bash [ˈbæʃ] *vt* : cogner, frapper — ~ *n* 1 BLOW : coup *m* 2 PARTY : fête *f*

bashful [ˈbæʃfəl] *adj* : timide, gêné *Can*

basic [ˈbeɪsɪk] *adj* : fondamental, de base — **basically** [ˈbeɪsɪkli] *adv* : au fond, fondamentalement

basil [ˈbeɪzəl, ˈbæzəl] *n* : basilic *m*

basin [ˈbeɪsən] *n* : bassin *m* (d'un fleuve)

basis [ˈbeɪsəs] *n, pl* **bases** [-ˌsi:z] : base *f*

bask [ˈbæsk] *vi* ~ **in the sun** : se chauffer au soleil

basket [ˈbæskət] *n* : corbeille *f,* panier *m* — **basketball** [ˈbæskətˌbɔl] *n* : basket *m,* basket-ball *m,* ballon-panier *m Can*

bass[1] [ˈbæs] *n, pl* **bass** *or* **basses** : perche *f,* bar *m* (poisson)

bass[2] [ˈbeɪs] *n* : basse *f* (voix, instrument)

bassoon [bəˈsu:n, bæ-] *n* : basson *m*

bastard [ˈbæstərd] *n* : bâtard *m,* -tarde *f*

baste [ˈbeɪst] *vt* **basted; basting** 1 STITCH : faufiler, bâtir 2 : arroser (un rôti, etc.)

bat[1] [ˈbæt] *n* : chauve-souris *f* (animal)

bat[2] *n* : batte *f,* bâton *m Can* — ~ *vt* **batted; batting** : frapper

batch [ˈbæʧ] *n* : liasse *f* (de papiers, etc.), lot *m* (de marchandises), fournée *f* (de pain, etc.)

bath [ˈbæθ] *n, pl* **baths** [ˈbæðz, ˈbæθs] 1 : bain *m* 2 BATHROOM : salle *f* de bains 3 **take a** ~ : prendre un bain — **bathe** [ˈbeɪð] *v* **bathed; bathing** *vt* : baigner — *vi* : se baigner, prendre un bain — **bathrobe** [ˈbæθˌro:b] *n* : peignoir *m* (de bain), robe *f* de chambre — **bathroom** [ˈbæθˌru:m, -ˌrʊm] *n* : salle *f* de bains — **bathtub** [ˈbæθˌtʌb] *n* : baignoire *f*

baton [bəˈtɑn] *n* : bâton *m*

battalion [bəˈtæljən] *n* : bataillon *m*

batter [ˈbæt̬ər] *vt* 1 BEAT : battre 2 MISTREAT : maltraiter — ~ *n* 1 : pâte *f* (à cuire) 2 HITTER : batteur *m* (au baseball)

battery [ˈbæt̬əri] *n, pl* **-teries** : batterie *f,* pile *f* (d'une radio, etc.)

battle [ˈbæt̬əl] *n* 1 : bataille *f* 2 STRUGGLE : lutte *f* — ~ *vi* **-tled; -tling** : lutter — **battlefield** [ˈbæt̬əlˌfi:ld] *n* : champ *m* de bataille — **battleship** [ˈbæt̬əlˌʃɪp] *n* : cuirassé *m*

bawdy [ˈbɔdi] *adj* **bawdier; -est** : paillard, grivois

bawl [ˈbɔl] *vi* : brailler *fam*

bay[1] [ˈbeɪ] *n* INLET : baie *f*

bay[2] *n or* ~ **leaf** : laurier *m*

bay[3] *vi* : aboyer — ~ *n* : aboiement *m*

bayonet [ˌbeɪəˈnɛt, ˈbeɪəˌnɛt] *n* : baïonnette *f*

bay window *n* : fenêtre *f* en saillie

bazaar [bəˈzɑr] *n* 1 : bazar *m* 2 SALE : vente *f* (de charité)

be [ˈbi:] *v* **was** [ˈwəz, ˈwɑz]; **were** [ˈwər]; **been** [ˈbɪn]; **being; am** [ˈæm]; **is** [ˈɪz]; **are** [ˈɑr] *vi* 1 : être 2 (*expressing a state*) : être, avoir 3 (*expressing age*) : avoir 4 (*expressing equality*) : faire, égaler 5 (*expressing health or well-being*) : aller, se porter — *v aux* 1 : être en train de 2 (*indicating obligation*) : devoir 3 (*used in passive constructions*) : être — *v impers* 1 (*indicating weather*) : faire 2 (*indicating time*) : être

beach [ˈbi:ʧ] *n* : plage *f*

beacon [ˈbi:kən] *n* : phare *m,* signal *m* lumineux

bead [ˈbi:d] *n* 1 : perle *f* 2 DROP : goutte *f* 3 ~**s** *npl* NECKLACE : collier *m*

beak [ˈbi:k] *n* : bec *m*

beaker [ˈbi:kər] *n* : gobelet *m*

beam [ˈbi:m] *n* 1 : poutre *f* (de bois) 2 RAY : rayon *m* — ~ *vi* SHINE : rayonner — ~ *vt* BROADCAST : diffuser, transmettre

bean [ˈbi:n] *n* 1 : haricot *m* 2 *or* **coffee** ~ : grain *m* (de café)

bear[1] [ˈbær] *n, pl* **bears** *or* **bear** : ours *m,* ourse *f*

bear[2] *v* **bore** [ˈbor]; **borne** [ˈbɔrn]; **bearing** *vt* 1 CARRY : porter 2 ENDURE : supporter — *vi* 1 ~ **in mind** : tenir compte de 2 ~ **left/right** : prendre à gauche, à droite — **bearable** [ˈbærəbəl] *adj* : supportable

beard [ˈbɪrd] *n* : barbe *f*

bearer [ˈbærər] *n* : porteur *m,* -teuse *f*

bearing [ˈbærɪŋ] *n* 1 MANNER : maintien *m* 2 SIGNIFICANCE : rapport *m* 3 **get one's** ~**s** : s'orienter

beast [ˈbi:st] *n* : bête *f*

beat [ˈbi:t] *v* **beat; beaten** [ˈbi:tən] *or* **beat; beating** : battre — ~ *n* 1 : battement *m* 2 RHYTHM : rythme *m,* temps *m* — **beating** [ˈbitɪŋ] *n* 1 : raclée *f fam* 2 DEFEAT : défaite *f*

beauty [ˈbju:t̬i] *n, pl* **-ties** : beauté *f* — **beautician** [bju:ˈtɪʃən] *n* : esthéticien *m,* -cienne *f* — **beautiful** [ˈbju:t̬ɪfəl] *adj* 1 : beau 2 WONDERFUL : merveilleux — **beautifully** [ˈbju:t̬ɪfəli] *adv* WONDERFULLY : merveilleusement — **beautify** [ˈbju:t̬ɪˌfaɪ] *vt* **-fied; -fying** : embellir

beaver [ˈbi:vər] *n* : castor *m*

because [bɪˈkʌz, -ˈkɔz] *conj* : parce que — **because of** *prep* : à cause de

beckon [ˈbɛkən] *vt* : faire signe à, attirer — *vi* : faire signe

become [bɪˈkʌm] *v* **-came** [-ˈkeɪm]; **-come; -coming** *vi* : devenir — *vt* SUIT : aller à, convenir à — **becoming** [bɪˈkʌmɪŋ] *adj* 1 SUITABLE : convenable 2 FLATTERING : seyant

bed [ˈbɛd] *n* 1 : lit *m* 2 BOTTOM : fond *m* (de la mer) 3 **go to** ~ : se coucher — **bedclothes** [ˈbɛdˌklo:z, -ˌklo:ðz] *npl* : draps *mpl* et couvertures *fpl*

bedridden [ˈbɛdˌrɪdən] *adj* : alité

bedroom [ˈbɛdˌru:m, -ˌrʊm] *n* : chambre *f* (à coucher)

bedspread [ˈbɛdˌsprɛd] *n* : couvre-lit *m*

bedtime [ˈbɛdˌtaɪm] *n* : heure *f* du coucher

bee [ˈbi:] *n* : abeille *f*

beech [ˈbi:ʧ] *n, pl* **beeches** *or* **beech** : hêtre *m*

beef [ˈbi:f] *n* : bœuf *m* — **beefsteak** [ˈbifˌsteɪk] *n* : bifteck *m*

beehive [ˈbi:ˌhaɪv] *n* : ruche *f*

beeline [ˈbi:ˌlaɪn] *n* **make a** ~ **for** : se diriger droit vers

been → **be**

beep [ˈbi:p] *n* : coup *m* de klaxon, bip *m* — ~ *vi* : klaxonner, faire bip — **beeper** [ˈbi:pər] *n* : récepteur *m* de radiomessagerie

beer [ˈbɪr] *n* : bière *f*

beet [ˈbi:t] *n* : betterave *f*

beetle [ˈbi:t̬əl] *n* : scarabée *m*

before [bɪˈfor] *adv* 1 : avant, auparavant 2 **the month** ~ : le mois dernier — ~ *prep* 1 (*in space*) : devant 2 (*in time*) : avant 3 ~ **my eyes** : sous mes yeux — ~ *conj* : avant de, avant que — **beforehand** [bɪˈforˌhænd] *adv* : à l'avance

befriend [bɪˈfrɛnd] *vt* : offrir son amitié à

beg [ˈbɛg] *v* **begged; begging** *vt* 1 : mendier 2 ENTREAT : supplier, prier — *vi* : mendier — **beggar** [ˈbɛgər] *n* : mendiant *m,* -diante *f*

begin [bɪˈgɪn] *v* **-gan** [-ˈgæn]; **-gun** [-ˈgʌn]; **-ginning** : commencer — **beginner** [bɪˈgɪnər] *n* : débutant *m,* -tante *f* —

beginning [bɪˈgɪnɪŋ] *n* : début *m*, commencement *m*
begrudge [bɪˈgrʌʤ] *vt* **-grudged; -grudging 1** : accorder à regret **2** ENVY : envier
behalf [bɪˈhæf, -ˈhaf] *n* **on ~ of** : de la part de, au nom de
behave [bɪˈheɪv] *vi* **-haved; -having** : se conduire, se comporter — **behavior** *or Brit* **behaviour** [bɪˈheɪvjər] *n* : conduite *f*, comportement *m*
behind [bɪˈhaɪnd] *adv* **1** : derrière, en arrière **2 fall ~** : prendre du retard — ~ *prep* **1** : derrière, en arrière de **2** : en retard sur (l'horaire, etc.) **3 her friends are ~ her** : elle a l'appui de ses amis
behold [bɪˈho:ld] *vt* **-held; -holding** : contempler
beige [ˈbeɪʒ] *adj & nm* : beige
being [ˈbi:ɪŋ] *n* **1** : être *m*, créature *f* **2 come into ~** : prendre naissance
belated [bɪˈleɪtəd] *adj* : tardif
belch [ˈbɛlʧ] *vi* : roter *fam* — ~ *n* : renvoi *m*
belfry [ˈbɛlfri] *n, pl* **-fries** : beffroi *m*, clocher *m*
Belgian [ˈbɛlʤən] *adj* : belge
belie [bɪˈlaɪ] *vt* **-lied; -lying** : démentir, contredire
belief [bəˈli:f] *n* **1** TRUST : confiance *f* **2** CONVICTION : croyance *f* **3** FAITH : foi *f* — **believable** [bəˈli:vəbəl] *adj* : croyable — **believe** [bəˈli:v] *v* **-lieved; -lieving** : croire — **believer** [bəˈli:vər] *n* : croyant *m*, croyante *f*
belittle [bɪˈlɪtəl] *vt* **-tled; -tling** : rabaisser
bell [ˈbɛl] *n* **1** : cloche *f*, clochette *f* **2** : sonnette *f* (d'une porte, etc.)
belligerent [bəˈlɪʤərənt] *adj* : belligérant
bellow [ˈbɛˌlo:] *vi* **1** : beugler **2** HOWL : brailler *fam*, hurler
belly [ˈbɛli] *n, pl* **-lies** : ventre *m*
belong [bɪˈlɔŋ] *vi* **1 ~ to** : appartenir à, être à **2 ~ to** : être membre de (un club, etc.) **3 where does it ~?** : où va-t-il? — **belongings** [bɪˈlɔŋɪŋz] *npl* : affaires *fpl*, effets *mpl* personnels
beloved [bɪˈlʌvəd, -ˈlʌvd] *adj* : bien-aimé — ~ *n* : bien-aimé *m*, -mée *f*
below [bɪˈlo:] *adv* : en dessous, en bas — ~ *prep* : sous, au-dessous de, en dessous de
belt [ˈbɛlt] *n* **1** : ceinture *f* **2** STRAP : courroie *f* (d'une machine) **3** AREA : zone *f*, région *f* — ~ *vt* THRASH : donner un coup à
bench [ˈbɛnʧ] *n* **1** : banc *m* **2** WORKBENCH : établi *m* **3** COURT : cour *f*, tribunal *m*
bend [ˈbɛnd] *v* **bent** [ˈbɛnt]; **bending** *vt* : plier, courber — *vi* **1** : se plier, se courber **2** *or* **~ over** : se pencher — ~ *n* : virage *m*, coude *m*
beneath [bɪˈni:θ] *adv* : au-dessous, en bas — ~ *prep* : sous, en dessous de
benediction [ˌbɛnəˈdɪkʃən] *n* : bénédiction *f*
benefactor [ˈbɛnəˌfæktər] *n* : bienfaiteur *m*, -trice *f*
benefit [ˈbɛnəfɪt] *n* **1** : avantage *m*, bénéfice *m* **2** AID : allocation *f*, prestation *f* — ~ *vt* : profiter à, bénéficier à — *vi* : profiter, tirer avantage — **beneficial** [ˌbɛnəˈfɪʃəl] *adj* : avantageux — **beneficiary** [ˌbɛnəˈfɪʃiˌɛri, -ˈfɪʃəri] *n, pl* **-ries** : bénéficiaire *mf*
benevolent [bəˈnɛvələnt] *adj* : bienveillant
benign [bɪˈnaɪn] *adj* **1** KIND : bienveillant, aimable **2** : bénin (en médecine)
bent [ˈbɛnt] *adj* **1** : tordu, courbé **2 be ~ on doing** : être décidé à faire — ~ *n* : aptitude *f*, penchant *m*
bequeath [bɪˈkwi:θ, -kwi:ð] *vt* : léguer — **bequest** [bɪˈkwɛst] *n* : legs *m*
berate [bɪˈreɪt] *vt* **-rated; -rating** : réprimander
bereaved [bɪˈri:vd] *adj* : endeuillé, attristé — **bereavement** [bɪˈri:vmənt] *n* : deuil *m*
beret [bəˈreɪ] *n* : béret *m*
berry [ˈbɛri] *n, pl* **-ries** : baie *f*
berserk [bərˈsərk, -ˈzərk] *adj* **1** : fou, enragé **2 go ~** : devenir fou furieux
berth [ˈbərθ] *n* **1** MOORING : mouillage *m* **2** BUNK : couchette *f*
beset [bɪˈsɛt] *vt* **-set; -setting 1** HARASS : assaillir **2** SURROUND : encercler
beside [bɪˈsaɪd] *prep* **1** : à côté de, près de **2 be ~ oneself** : être hors de soi — **besides** [bɪˈsaɪdz] *adv* : en plus — ~ *prep* **1** : en plus de **2** EXCEPT : sauf
besiege [bɪˈsi:ʤ] *vt* **-sieged; -sieging** : assiéger
best [ˈbɛst] *adj* (*superlative of* **good**) **1** : meilleur **2** : plus beau — ~ *adv* (*superlative of* **well**) : le mieux, le plus — ~ *n* **1 at ~** : au mieux **2 do one's ~** : faire de son mieux **3 the ~** : le meilleur — **best man** *n* : garçon *m* d'honneur, témoin *n*
bestow [bɪˈsto:] *vt* : accorder, concéder
bet [ˈbɛt] *n* : pari *m*, gageure *f Can* — ~ *v* **bet; betting** *vt* : parier, gager *Can* — *vi* **~ on sth** : parier sur qqch
betray [bɪˈtreɪ] *vt* : trahir — **betrayal** [bɪˈtreɪəl] *n* : trahison *f*
better [ˈbɛtər] *adj* (*comparative of* **good**) **1** : meilleur **2 get ~** : s'améliorer — ~ *adv* (*comparative of* **well**) **1** : mieux **2 all the ~** : tant mieux — ~ *n* **1 the ~** : le meilleur, la meilleure **2 get the ~ of** : l'emporter sur — ~ *vt* **1** IMPROVE : améliorer **2** SURPASS : surpasser, faire mieux que
between [bɪˈtwi:n] *prep* : entre — ~ *adv* *or* **in ~** : au milieu
beverage [ˈbɛvrɪʤ, ˈbɛvə-] *n* : boisson *f*
beware [bɪˈwær] *vi* **~ of** : prendre garde à, se méfier de
bewilder [bɪˈwɪldər] *vt* : rendre perplexe, déconcerter — **bewilderment** [bɪˈwɪldərmənt] *n* : perplexité *f*, confusion *f*
bewitch [bɪˈwɪʧ] *vt* : enchanter
beyond [biˈjɑnd] *adv* : au-delà, plus loin — ~ *prep* : au-delà de
bias [ˈbaɪəs] *n* **1** PREJUDICE : préjugé *m* **2** TENDENCY : penchant *m* — **biased** [ˈbaɪəst] *adj* : partial
bib [ˈbɪb] *n* : bavoir *m* (d'un bébé)
Bible [ˈbaɪbəl] *n* : Bible *f* — **biblical** [ˈbɪblɪkəl] *adj* : biblique
bibliography [ˌbɪbliˈɑgrəfi] *n, pl* **-phies** : bibliographie *f*
biceps [ˈbaɪˌsɛps] *ns & pl* : biceps *m*
bicker [ˈbɪkər] *vi* : se chamailler
bicycle [ˈbaɪsɪkəl, -ˌsɪ-] *n* : bicyclette *f*, vélo *m* — ~ *vi* **-cled; -cling** : faire de la bicyclette, faire du vélo
bid [ˈbɪd] *vt* **bade** [ˈbæd, ˈbeɪd] *or* **bid; bidden** [ˈbɪdən] *or* **bid; bidding 1** OFFER : offrir **2 ~ farewell** : dire adieu — ~ *n* **1** OFFER : offre *f*, enchère *f* **2** ATTEMPT : tentative *f*
bide [ˈbaɪd] *vt* **bode** [ˈbo:d] *or* **bided; bided; biding ~ one's time** : attendre le bon moment
bifocals [baɪˌfo:kəlz] *npl* : lunettes *fpl* bifocales
big [ˈbɪg] *adj* **bigger; biggest** : grand, gros
bigot [ˈbɪgət] *n* : fanatique *mf* — **bigotry** [ˈbɪgətri] *n, pl* **-tries** : fanatisme *m*
bike [ˈbaɪk] *n* **1** BICYCLE : vélo *m* **2** MOTORCYCLE : moto *f*
bikini [bəˈki:ni] *n* : bikini *m*
bile [ˈbaɪl] *n* : bile *f*
bilingual [baɪˈlɪŋgwəl] *adj* : bilingue
bill [ˈbɪl] *n* **1** BEAK : bec *m* (d'un oiseau) **2** INVOICE : facture *f*, compte *m*, addition *f* (au restaurant) **3** LAW : projet *m* de loi **4** BANKNOTE : billet *m* (de banque) — ~ *vt* : facturer, envoyer la facture à
billiards [ˈbɪljərdz] *n* : billard *m*
billion [ˈbɪljən] *n, pl* **billions** *or* **billion** : milliard *m*
billow [ˈbɪlo] *vi* : onduler (se dit d'un drapeau)
bin [ˈbɪn] *n* : coffre *m*, boîte *f*
binary [ˈbaɪnəri, -ˌnɛri] *adj* : binaire
bind [ˈbaɪnd] *vt* **bound** [ˈbaʊnd]; **binding 1** TIE : lier **2** OBLIGE : obliger **3** UNITE : unir **4** : relier (un livre) — **binder** [ˈbaɪndər] *n* FOLDER : classeur *m* — **binding** [ˈbaɪndɪŋ] *n* : reliure *f* (d'un livre)
binge [ˈbɪnʤ] *n* : bringue *f fam*
bingo [ˈbɪŋˌgo:] *n, pl* **-gos** : bingo *m*
binoculars [bəˈnɑkjələrz, baɪ-] *npl* : jumelles *fpl*
biochemistry [ˌbaɪoˈkɛməstri] *n* : biochimie *f*
biography [baɪˈɑgrəfi, bi:-] *n, pl* **-phies** : biographie *f* — **biographer** [baɪˈɑgrəfər] *n* : biographe *mf* — **biographical** [ˌbaɪəˈgræfɪkəl] *adj* : biographique
biology [baɪˈɑləʤi] *n* : biologie *f* — **biological** [-ˈʤɪkəl] *adj* : biologique — **biologist** [baɪˈɑləʤɪst] *n* : biologiste *mf*
birch [ˈbərʧ] *n* : bouleau *m*
bird [ˈbərd] *n* : oiseau *m*
birth [ˈbərθ] *n* **1** : naissance *f* **2 give ~ to** : accoucher de — **birthday** [ˈbərθˌdeɪ] *n* : anniversaire *m* — **birthmark** [ˈbərθˌmark] *n* : tache *f* de vin — **birthplace** [ˈbərθˌpleɪs] *n* : lieu *m* de naissance — **birthrate** [ˈbərθˌreɪt] *n* : natalité *f*
biscuit [ˈbɪskət] *n* : petit pain *m* au lait
bisexual [ˌbaɪˈsɛkʃəwəl, -ˈsɛkʃəl] *adj* : bisexuel
bishop [ˈbɪʃəp] *n* **1** : évêque *m* **2** : fou *m* (aux échecs)
bison [ˈbaɪzən, -sən] *ns & pl* : bison *m*
bit[1] [ˈbɪt] *n* : mors *m* (d'une bride)
bit[2] *n* **1** : morceau *m*, bout *m* **2** : bit *m* (en informatique) **3 a ~** : un peu
bitch [ˈbɪʧ] *n* : chienne *f* — ~ *vi* COMPLAIN : râler *fam*
bite [ˈbaɪt] *v* **bit** [ˈbɪt]; **bitten** [ˈbɪtən]; **biting** *vt* **1** : mordre **2** STING : piquer — *vi* : mordre — ~ *n* **1** : piqûre *f* (d'insecte), morsure *f* (de chien, etc.) **2** MOUTHFUL : bouchée *f* — **biting** *adj* **1** PENETRATING : pénétrant **2** SCATHING : mordant
bitter [ˈbɪtər] *adj* **1** : amer **2 it's ~ cold** : il fait un froid glacial — **bitterness** [ˈbɪtərnəs] *n* : amertume *f*
bizarre [bəˈzɑr] *adj* : bizarre
black [ˈblæk] *adj* : noir — ~ *n* **1** : noir *m* (couleur) **2** : Noir *m*, Noire *f* (personne) — **black–and–blue** [ˌblækənˈblu:] *adj* : couvert de bleus — **blackberry** [ˈblækˌbɛri] *n, pl* **-ries** : mûre *f* — **blackboard** [ˈblækˌbord] *n* : tableau *m* (noir) — **blacken** [ˈblækən] *vt* : noircir — **blackmail** [ˈblækˌmeɪl] *n* : chantage *m* — ~ *vi* : faire chanter — **black market** *n* : marché *m* noir — **blackout** [ˈblækˌaʊt] *n* **1** : panne *f* d'électricité **2** FAINT : évanouissement *m* — **blacksmith** [ˈblækˌsmɪθ] *n* : forgeron *m* — **blacktop** [ˈblækˌtɑp] *n* : asphalte *m*
bladder [ˈblædər] *n* : vessie *f*
blade [ˈbleɪd] *n* **1** : lame *f* (de couteau) **2** : pale *f* (d'hélice, de rame, etc.) **3 ~ of grass** : brin *m* d'herbe
blame [ˈbleɪm] *vt* **blamed; blaming** : blâmer, reprocher — ~ *n* : faute *f*, responsabilité *f* — **blameless** [ˈbleɪmləs] *adj* : irréprochable
bland [ˈblænd] *adj* : fade, insipide
blank [ˈblæŋk] *adj* **1** : blanc (se dit d'une page, etc.) **2** EMPTY : vide — ~ *n* : blanc *m*, vide *m*
blanket [ˈblæŋkət] *n* **1** : couverture *f* (d'un lit) **2 ~ of snow** : couche *f* de neige — ~ *vt* : recouvrir
blare [ˈblær] *vi* **blared; blaring** : beugler
blasé [blɑˈzeɪ] *adj* : blasé
blasphemy [ˈblæsfəmi] *n, pl* **-mies** : blasphème *m*
blast [ˈblæst] *n* **1** GUST : rafale *f*, souffle *m* **2** EXPLOSION : explosion *f* **3 at full ~** : à plein volume — ~ *vt* BLOW UP : faire sauter — **blast–off** [ˈblæstˌɔf] *n* : lancement *m*
blatant [ˈbleɪtənt] *adj* : flagrant
blaze [ˈbleɪz] *n* **1** FIRE : incendie *f* **2** BRIGHTNESS : éclat *m* — ~ *v* **blazed; blazing** : flamber
blazer [ˈbleɪzər] *n* : blazer *m*
bleach [ˈbli:ʧ] *vt* : blanchir, décolorer — ~ *n* : décolorant *m*, eau *f* de Javel
bleachers [ˈbli:ʧərz] *npl* : gradins *mpl*
bleak [ˈbli:k] *adj* **1** DESOLATE : désolé **2** GLOOMY : triste, sombre
bleat [ˈbli:t] *vi* : bêler — ~ *n* : bêlement *m*
bleed [ˈbli:d] *v* **bled** [ˈblɛd]; **bleeding** : saigner
blemish [ˈblɛmɪʃ] *vt* : tacher, ternir — ~ *n* : tache *f*, défaut *m*
blend [ˈblɛnd] *vt* : mélanger — ~ *n* : mélange *m*, combinaison *f* — **blender** [ˈblɛndər] *n* : mixer *m*
bless [ˈblɛs] *vt* **blessed** [ˈblɛst]; **blessing** : bénir — **blessed** [ˈblɛsəd] *or* **blest** [ˈblɛst] *adj* : bénit, saint — **blessing** [ˈblɛsɪŋ] *n* : bénédiction *f*
blew → **blow**
blind [ˈblaɪnd] *adj* : aveugle — ~ *vt* **1** : aveugler **2** DAZZLE : éblouir — ~ *n* **1** : store *m* (d'une fenêtre) **2 the ~** : les non-voyants *mpl* — **blindfold** [ˈblaɪndˌfo:ld] *vt* : bander les yeux à — ~ *n* : bandeau *m* — **blindly** [ˈblaɪndli] *adv* : aveuglément — **blindness** [ˈblaɪndnəs] *n* : cécité *f*
blink [ˈblɪŋk] *vi* **1** : cligner des yeux **2** FLICKER : clignoter — ~ *n* : battement *m* des paupières — **blinker** [ˈblɪŋkər] *n* : clignotant *m*
bliss [ˈblɪs] *n* : félicité *f* — **blissful** [ˈblɪsfəl] *adj* : bienheureux
blister [ˈblɪstər] *n* **1** : ampoule *f*, cloque *f* (sur la peau) **2** : boursouflure *f* (sur une surface peinte) — ~ *vi* **1** : se couvrir d'ampoules *fpl* (se dit de la peau) **2** : se boursoufler (se dit de la peinture, etc.)
blitz [ˈblɪts] *n* : bombardement *m*
blizzard [ˈblɪzərd] *n* : tempête *f* de neige
bloated [ˈblo:təd] *adj* : boursouflé, gonflé
blob [ˈblɑb] *n* **1** DROP : goutte *f* **2** SPOT : tache *f*
block [ˈblɑk] *n* **1** : bloc *m* **2** OBSTRUCTION : obstruction *f* **3** : pâté *m* de maisons, bloc *m Can* **4** *or* **building ~** : cube *m* — ~ *vt* : bloquer, boucher — **blockade** [blɑˈkeɪd] *n* : blocus *m* — **blockage** [ˈblɑkɪʤ] *n* : obstruction *f*
blond *or* **blonde** [ˈblɑnd] *adj* : blond — ~ *n* : blond *m*, blonde *f*
blood [ˈblʌd] *n* : sang *m* — **blood pressure** *n* : tension *f* artérielle — **bloodshed** [ˈblʌdˌʃɛd] *n* : carnage *m* — **bloodshot** [ˈblʌdˌʃɑt] *adj* : injecté de sang — **bloodstained** [ˈblʌdˌsteɪnd] *adj* : taché de sang — **bloodstream** [ˈblʌdˌstri:m] *n* : sang *m*, système *m* sanguin — **bloodthirsty** [ˈblʌdˌθərsti] *adj* : sanguinaire — **bloody** [ˈblʌdi] *adj* **bloodier; -est** : ensanglanté
bloom [ˈblu:m] *n* **1** : fleur *f* **2 in full ~** : en pleine floraison — ~ *vi* : fleurir, éclore
blossom [ˈblɑsəm] *n* : fleur *f* — ~ *vi* **1** : fleurir **2** MATURE : s'épanouir
blot [ˈblɑt] *n* : tache *f* (d'encre, etc.) — ~ *vt* **blotted; blotting 1** : tacher **2** DRY : sécher
blotch [ˈblɑʧ] *n* : tache *f* — **blotchy** [ˈblɑʧi] *adj* **blotchier; -est** : tacheté
blouse [ˈblaʊs, ˈblaʊz] *n* : chemisier *m*
blow [ˈblo:] *v* **blew** [ˈblu:]; **blown** [ˈblo:n]; **blowing** *vi* **1** : souffler **2** SOUND : sonner **3** *or* **~ out** : éclater (se dit d'un pneu), s'éteindre (se dit d'une bougie) — *vt* **1** : souffler **2** SOUND : jouer de (la trompette, etc.) **3** BUNGLE : rater **4 ~ one's nose** : se moucher — ~ *n* : coup *m* — **blowout** [ˈblo:ˌaʊt] *n* : éclatement *m* — **blow up** *vi* : exploser, sauter — *vt* **1** EXPLODE : faire sauter **2** INFLATE : gonfler
blubber [ˈblʌbər] *n* : graisse *f* de baleine
bludgeon [ˈblʌʤən] *n* : matraque *f* — ~ *vt* : matraquer
blue [ˈblu:] *adj* **bluer; bluest 1** : bleu **2** MELANCHOLY : triste — ~ *n* : bleu *m* — **blueberry** [ˈblu:ˌbɛri] *n, pl* **-ries** : myrtille *f France*, bleuet *m Can* — **bluebird** [ˈblu:ˌbərd] *n* : oiseau *m* bleu — **blue cheese** *n* : (fromage *m*) bleu *m* — **blueprint** [ˈblu:ˌprɪnt] *n* : plan *m* (de travail) — **blues** [ˈblu:z] *ns & pl* **1** : cafard *m* **2** : blues *m* (musique)
bluff [ˈblʌf] *v* : bluffer — ~ *n* **1** : falaise *f*, escarpement *m* **2** DECEPTION : bluff *m* — **blunder** [ˈblʌndər] *vi* : faire une gaffe — ~ *n* : gaffe *f fam*
blunt [ˈblʌnt] *adj* **1** DULL : émoussé **2** DIRECT : brusque, franc — ~ *vt* : émousser
blur [ˈblər] *n* : image *f* floue — ~ *vt* **blurred; blurring** : brouiller, rendre flou
blurb [ˈblərb] *n* : notice *f* publicitaire
blurt [ˈblərt] *vt or* **~ out** : laisser échapper
blush [ˈblʌʃ] *n* : rougeur *f* — ~ *vi* : rougir
blustery [ˈblʌstəri] *adj* : venteux, orageux
boar [ˈbor] *n* : sanglier *m*
board [ˈbord] *n* **1** PLANK : planche *f* **2** COMMITTEE : conseil *m* **3** : tableau *m* (d'un jeu) **4 room and ~** : pension *f* complète — ~ *vt* **1** : monter à bord de (un avion, un navire), monter dans (un train) **2** LODGE : prendre en pension **3 ~ up** : couvrir de planches — **boarder** [ˈbordər] *n* : pensionnaire *mf*
boast [ˈbo:st] *n* : vantardise *f* — ~ *vi* : se vanter — **boastful** [ˈbo:stfəl] *adj* : vantard
boat [ˈbo:t] *n* : bateau *m*, barque *f*
bob [ˈbɑb] *vi* **bobbed; bobbing** *or* **~ up and down** : monter et descendre
bobbin [ˈbɑbən] *n* : bobine *f*
body [ˈbɑdi] *n, pl* **bodies 1** : corps *m* **2** CORPSE : cadavre *m* **3** : carrosserie *f* (d'une voiture) **4 ~ of water** : masse *f* d'eau — **bodily** [ˈbɑdəli] *adj* : physique, corporel —**bodyguard** [ˈbɑdiˌgɑrd] *n* : garde *m* du corps
bog [ˈbɑg, ˈbɔg] *n* : marais *m*, marécage *m* — ~ *vi* **bogged; bogging** *or* **~ down** : s'embourber
bogus [ˈbo:gəs] *adj* : faux
bohemian [bo:ˈhi:miən] *adj* : bohème
boil [ˈbɔɪl] *vt* : faire bouillir — *vi* : bouillir — ~ *n* **1** : ébullition *f* **2** : furoncle *m* (en médecine) — **boiler** [ˈbɔɪlər] *n* : chaudière *f*
boisterous [ˈbɔɪstərəs] *adj* : bruyant, tapageur
bold [ˈbo:ld] *adj* **1** DARING : hardi, audacieux **2** IMPUDENT : effronté — **boldness** [ˈbo:ldnəs] *n* : hardiesse *f*, audace *f*
bologna [bəˈlo:ni] *n* : gros *m* saucisson
bolster [ˈbo:lstər] *n* : traversin *m* — ~ *vt* **-stered; -stering** *or* **~ up** : soutenir
bolt [ˈbo:lt] *n* **1** LOCK : verrou *m* **2** SCREW : boulon *m* **3 ~ of lightning** : éclair *m*, coup *m* de foudre — ~ *vt* LOCK : verrouiller — *vi* FLEE : se sauver
bomb [ˈbɑm] *n* : bombe *f* — ~ *vt* : bombarder — **bombard** [bɑmˈbɑrd, bəm-] *vt* : bombarder — **bombardment** [bɑmˈbɑrdmənt] *n* : bombardement *m* — **bomber** [ˈbɑmər] *n* : bombardier *m*
bond [ˈbɑnd] *n* **1** TIE : lien *m* **2** SECURITY : bon *m* — ~ *vi* **~ with** : s'attacher à
bondage [ˈbɑndɪʤ] *n* : esclavage *m*
bone [ˈbo:n] *n* : os *m*, arête *f* — ~ *vt* **boned; boning** : désosser
bonfire [ˈbɑnˌfaɪr] *n* : feu *m* de joie
bonus [ˈbo:nəs] *n* : gratification *f*, prime *f*
bony [ˈbo:ni] *adj* **bonier; -est** : plein d'os, plein d'arêtes
boo [ˈbu:] *n, pl* **boos** : huée *f* — ~ *vt* : huer, siffler
book [ˈbʊk] *n* **1** : livre *m* **2** NOTEBOOK : cahier *m* — ~ *vt* : réserver — **bookcase** [ˈbʊkˌkeɪs] *n* : bibliothèque *f* — **bookkeeping** [ˈbʊkˌki:pɪŋ] *n* : comptabilité *f* — **booklet** [ˈbʊklət] *n* : brochure *f* — **bookmark** [ˈbʊkˌmɑrk] *n* : signet *m* — **bookseller** [ˈbʊkˌsɛlər] *n* : libraire *mf* — **bookshelf** [ˈbʊkˌʃɛlf] *n, pl* **-shelves** : rayon *m*, étagère *f* (à livres) — **bookstore** [ˈbʊkˌstor] *n* : librairie *f*
boom [ˈbu:m] *vi* **1** : gronder, retentir **2** PROSPER : prospérer — ~ *n* **1** : grondement *m* **2** : boom *m* (économique)
boon [ˈbu:n] *n* : bienfait *m*
boost [ˈbu:st] *vt* **1** LIFT : soulever **2** INCREASE : augmenter — ~ *n* **1** INCREASE : augmentation *f* **2** ENCOURAGEMENT : encouragement *m*
boot [ˈbu:t] *n* : botte *f* — ~ *vt* **1** : donner un coup de pied à **2** *or* **~ up** : amorcer (en informatique)
booth [ˈbu:θ] *n, pl* **booths** [ˈbu:ðz, ˈbu:θs] : baraque *f* (d'un marché), cabine *f* (téléphonique)
booze [ˈbu:z] *n* : alcool *m*, boissons *fpl* alcoolisées
border [ˈbɔrˌdər] *n* **1** EDGE : bord *m* **2** BOUNDARY : frontière *f* **3** : bordure *f* (d'un vêtement, etc.)
bore[1] [ˈbor] *vt* **bored; boring** DRILL : percer, forer
bore[2] *vt* TIRE : ennuyer — ~ *n* : raseur *m*, -seuse *f fam* — **boredom** [ˈbordəm] *n* : ennui *m* — **boring** [ˈborɪŋ] *adj* : ennuyeux, ennuyant *Can*
born [ˈbɔrn] *adj* **1** : né **2 be ~** : naître
borough [ˈbəro] *n* : arrondissement *m* urbain

borrow [ˈbɑro] *vt* : emprunter
bosom [ˈbʊzəm, ˈbu:-] *n* BREAST : poitrine *f* — ~ *adj* **~ friend** : ami intime
boss [ˈbɔs] *n* : patron *m*, -tronne *f*; chef *m* — ~ *vt* SUPERVISE : diriger — **bossy** [ˈbɔsi] *adj* **bossier; -est** : autoritaire
botany [ˈbɑtəni] *n* : botanique *f* — **botanical** [bəˈtænɪkəl] *adj* : botanique
botch [ˈbɑʧ] *vt or* **~ up** : bousiller *fam*, saboter
both [ˈbo:θ] *adj* : les deux — ~ *conj* : à la fois — ~ *pron* : tous les deux, l'un et l'autre
bother [ˈbɑðər] *vt* **1** TROUBLE : préoccuper **2** PESTER : harceler — *vi* **~ to** : se donner la peine de — ~ *n* : ennui *m*
bottle [ˈbɑtəl] *n* **1** : bouteille *f* **2** *or* **baby ~** : biberon *m* — ~ *vt* **-tled; -tling** : mettre en bouteille — **bottleneck** [ˈbɑtəlˌnɛk] *n* : embouteillage *m*
bottom [ˈbɑṭəm] *n* **1** : bas *m* (d'une page, etc.), fond *m* (d'une bouteille, d'un lac, etc.), pied *m* (d'un escalier) **2** BUTTOCKS : derrière *m fam* — ~ *adj* : du bas, inférieur — **bottomless** [ˈbɑṭəmləs] *adj* : insondable
bough [ˈbaʊ] *n* : rameau *m*
bought → **buy**
boulder [ˈbo:ldər] *n* : rocher *m*
boulevard [ˈbʊləˌvɑrd, ˈbu:-] *n* : boulevard *m*
bounce [ˈbaʊnts] *v* **bounced; bouncing** *vt* : faire rebondir — *vi* : rebondir — ~ *n* : bond *m*, rebond *m*
bound[1] [ˈbaʊnd] *adj* **~ for** : à destination de
bound[2] *adj* **1** OBLIGED : obligé **2 be ~ to** : être certain de
bound[3] *n* **out of ~s** : interdit — **boundary** [ˈbaʊndri, -dəri] *n, pl* **-aries** : limite *f*, frontière *f* — **boundless** [ˈbaʊndləs] *adj* : sans bornes
bouquet [bo:ˈkeɪ, bu:-] *n* : bouquet *m*
bourbon [ˈbərbən, ˈbʊr-] *n* : bourbon *m*
bourgeois [ˈbʊrʒˌwɑ, bʊrʒˈwɑ] *adj* : bourgeois
bout [ˈbaʊt] *n* **1** : combat *m* (aux sports) **2** : accès *m* (de fièvre)
bow[1] [ˈbaʊ] *vi* : s'incliner — *vt* **1** : incliner **2 ~ one's head** : baisser la tête — ~ [ˈbaʊ:] *n* : révérence *f*, salut *m*
bow[2] [ˈbo:] *n* **1** : arc *m* **2 tie a ~** : faire un nœud
bow[3] [ˈbaʊ] *n* : proue *f* (d'un bateau)
bowels [ˈbaʊəlz] *npl* **1** : intestins *mpl* **2** DEPTHS : entrailles *fpl*
bowl[1] [ˈbo:l] *n* : bol *m*, cuvette *f*
bowl[2] *vi* : jouer au bowling — **bowling** [ˈbo:lɪŋ] *n* : bowling *m*
box[1] [ˈbɑks] *vi* FIGHT : boxer, faire de la boxe — **boxer** [ˈbɑksər] *n* : boxeur *m* — **boxing** [ˈbɑksɪŋ] *n* : boxe *f*
box[2] *n* **1** : boîte *f*, caisse *f*, coffre *m* **2** : loge *f* (au théâtre) — ~ *vt* : mettre en boîte — **box office** *n* : guichet *m*, billetterie *f*
boy [ˈbɔɪ] *n* : garçon *m*
boycott [ˈbɔɪˌkɑt] *vt* : boycotter — ~ *n* : boycott *m*, boycottage *m*
boyfriend [ˈbɔɪˌfrɛnd] *n* : petit ami *m*
bra [ˈbrɑ] → **brassiere**
brace [ˈbreɪs] *n* **1** SUPPORT : support *m* **2 ~s** *npl* : appareil *m* orthodontique — ~ *vi* **~ oneself for** : se préparer pour
bracelet [ˈbreɪslət] *n* : bracelet *m*
bracket [ˈbrækət] *n* **1** SUPPORT : support *m* **2** : parenthèse *f*, crochet *m* (signe de ponctuation) **3** CATEGORY : catégorie *f* — ~ *vt* : mettre entre parenthèses, mettre entre crochets
brag [ˈbræg] *vi* **bragged; bragging** : se vanter
braid [ˈbreɪd] *vt* : tresser — ~ *n* : tresse *f* (de cheveux)
braille [ˈbreɪl] *n* : braille *m*
brain [ˈbreɪn] *n* **1** : cerveau *m* **2** *or* **~s** *npl* : intelligence *f* — **brainstorm** [ˈbreɪnˌstɔrm] *n* : idée *f* géniale — **brainwash** [ˈbreɪnˌwɔʃ, -ˌwɑʃ] *vt* : faire un lavage de cerveau à — **brainy** [ˈbreɪni] *adj* **brainier; -est** : intelligent, calé *fam*
brake [ˈbreɪk] *n* : frein *m* — ~ *vi* **braked; braking** : freiner
bramble [ˈbræmbəl] *n* : ronce *f*
bran [ˈbræn] *n* : son *m*
branch [ˈbrænʧ] *n* **1** : branche *f* (d'un arbre) **2** DIVISION : succursale *f* — ~ *vi or* **~ off** : bifurquer
brand [ˈbrænd] *n* **1** : marque *f* (sur un animal) **2** *or* **~ name** : marque *f* déposée — ~ *vt* **1** : marquer (au fer rouge) **2** LABEL : étiqueter
brandish [ˈbrændɪʃ] *vt* : brandir
brand-new [ˈbrændˈnu:, -ˈnju:] *adj* : tout neuf
brandy [ˈbrændi] *n, pl* **-dies** : cognac *m*, eau-de-vie *f*
brash [ˈbræʃ] *adj* : impertinent
brass [ˈbræs] *n* **1** : cuivre *m* (jaune), laiton *m* **2** : cuivres *mpl* (d'un orchestre)
brassiere [brəˈzɪr, brɑ-] *n* : soutien-gorge *m*, brassière *f Can*
brat [ˈbræt] *n* : môme *mf France fam;* gosse *mf France fam*
bravado [brəˈvɑˌdo] *n, pl* **-does** *or* **-dos** : bravade *f*
brave [ˈbreɪv] *adj* **braver; bravest** : courageux, brave — ~ *vt* **braved; braving** : braver, défier — **bravery** [ˈbreɪvəri] *n, pl* **-eries** : courage *m*
brawl [ˈbrɔl] *n* : bagarre *f*
brawn [ˈbrɔn] *n* : muscles *mpl* — **brawny** [ˈbrɔni] *adj* **brawnier; -est** : musclé
bray [ˈbreɪ] *vi* : braire
brazen [ˈbreɪzən] *adj* : effronté
Brazilian [brəˈzɪljən] *adj* : brésilien
breach [bri:ʧ] *n* **1** VIOLATION : infraction *f* **2** GAP : brèche *f*
bread [ˈbrɛd] *n* **1** : pain *m* **2 ~ crumbs** : chapelure *f*
breadth [ˈbrɛtθ] *n* : largeur *f*
break [ˈbreɪk] *v* **broke** [ˈbro:k]; **broken** [ˈbro:kən]; **breaking** *vt* **1** : casser, briser **2** VIOLATE : violer (la loi) **3** INTERRUPT : interrompre **4** SURPASS : battre (un record, etc.) **5 ~ a habit** : se défaire d'une habitude **6 ~ the news** : annoncer la nouvelle — *vi* **1** : se casser, se briser **2 ~ away** : s'évader **3 ~ down** : tomber en panne (se dit d'une voiture) **4 ~ into** : entrer par effraction **5 ~ up** SEPARATE : rompre, se quitter — ~ *n* **1** : cassure *f*, rupture *f* **2** GAP : trouée *f*, brèche *f* **3** REST : pause *f*, break *m Can* **4 a lucky ~** : un coup de veine — **breakable** [ˈbreɪkəb'l] *adj* : cassable — **breakdown** [ˈbreɪkˌdaʊn] *n* **1** : panne *f* (d'une machine), rupture *f* (des négociations) **2** *or* **nervous ~** : dépression *f* nerveuse
breakfast [ˈbrɛkfəst] *n* : petit déjeuner *m France*, déjeuner *Can*
breast [ˈbrɛst] *n* **1** : sein *m* (d'une femme) **2** CHEST : poitrine *f* — **breast-feed** [ˈbrɛstˌfi:d] *vt* **-fed** [-ˌfɛd]; **-feeding** : allaiter
breath [ˈbrɛθ] *n* : souffle *m*, haleine *f*, respiration *f* — **breathe** [ˈbri:ð] *v* **breathed; breathing** : respirer — **breathless** [ˈbrɛθləs] *adj* : à bout de souffle, hors d'haleine — **breathtaking** [ˈbrɛθˌteɪkɪŋ] *adj* : à couper le souffle
breed [ˈbri:d] *v* **bred** [ˈbrɛd]; **breeding** *vt* **1** : élever (du bétail) **2** CAUSE : engendrer — *vi* : se reproduire — ~ *n* **1** : race *f* **2** CLASS : espèce *f*, sorte *f*
breeze [ˈbri:z] *n* : brise *f* — **breezy** [ˈbri:zi] *adj* **breezier; -est 1** WINDY : venteux **2** NONCHALANT : désinvolte
brevity [ˈbrɛvəṭi] *n, pl* **-ties** : brièveté *f*
brew [ˈbru:] *vt* : brasser (de la bière), faire infuser (du thé) — *vi* : fermenter (se dit de la bière), infuser (se dit du thé, etc.) — **brewery** [ˈbru:əri, ˈbrʊri] *n, pl* **-eries** : brasserie *f*
bribe [ˈbraɪb] *n* : pot-de-vin *m* — ~ *vt* **bribed; bribing** : soudoyer — **bribery** [ˈbraɪbəri] *n, pl* **-eries** : corruption *f*
brick [ˈbrɪk] *n* : brique *f* — **bricklayer** [ˈbrɪkˌleɪər] *n* : maçon *m*
bride [ˈbraɪd] *n* : mariée *f* — **bridal** [ˈbraɪdəl] *adj* : nuptial — **bridegroom** [ˈbraɪdˌgru:m] *n* : marié *m* — **bridesmaid** [ˈbraɪdzˌmeɪd] *n* : demoiselle *f* d'honneur
bridge [ˈbrɪʤ] *n* **1** : pont *m* **2** : arête *f* (du nez) **3** : bridge *m* (jeu de cartes) — ~ *vt* **bridged; bridging 1** : construire un pont sur **2 ~ the gap** : combler une lacune
bridle [ˈbraɪdəl] *n* : bride *f* — ~ *vt* **-dled; -dling** : brider
brief [ˈbri:f] *adj* : bref — ~ *n* **1** : résumé *m* **2 ~s** *npl* UNDERPANTS : slip *m* — ~ *vt* : donner des instructions à — **briefcase** [ˈbri:fˌkeɪs] *n* : serviette *f*, porte-documents *m* — **briefly** [ˈbri:fli] *adv* : brièvement
brigade [brɪˈgeɪd] *n* : brigade *f*
bright [ˈbraɪt] *adj* **1** : brillant, éclatant **2** CHEERFUL : joyeux **3** INTELLIGENT : intelligent — **brighten** [ˈbraɪtən] *vi* **1** : s'éclaircir (se dit du temps) **2** *or* **~ up** : s'animer — *vt* ENLIVEN : égayer
brilliant [ˈbrɪljənt] *adj* : brillant — **brilliance** [ˈbrɪljənts] *n* **1** BRIGHTNESS : éclat *m* **2** INTELLIGENCE : intelligence *f*
brim [ˈbrɪm] *n* : bord *m* (d'un chapeau, etc.) — ~ *vi* **brimmed; brimming** *or* **~ over** : être plein jusqu'à déborder
brine [ˈbraɪn] *n* : saumure *f*
bring [ˈbrɪŋ] *vt* **brought** [ˈbrɔt]; **bringing 1** : amener (une personne ou un animal), apporter (une chose) **2 ~ about** : occasionner **3 ~ around** PERSUADE : convaincre **4 ~ back** : rapporter **5 ~ down** : faire tomber **6 ~ on** CAUSE : provoquer **7 ~ out** : sortir **8 ~ to an end** : mettre fin à **9 ~ up** REAR : élever **10 ~ up** MENTION : mentionner
brink [ˈbrɪŋk] *n* **1** EDGE : bord *m* **2 on the ~ of** : au bord de
brisk [ˈbrɪsk] *adj* **1** FAST : rapide **2** LIVELY : vif
bristle [ˈbrɪsəl] *n* **1** : soie *f* (d'un animal) **2** : poil *m* (d'une brosse) — ~ *vi* **-tled; -tling** : se hérisser
British [ˈbrɪṭɪʃ] *adj* : britannique
brittle [ˈbrɪṭəl] *adj* **-tler; -tlest** : fragile
broach [ˈbro:ʧ] *vt* : entamer
broad [ˈbrɔd] *adj* **1** WIDE : large **2** GENERAL : grand **3 in ~ daylight** : en plein jour
broadcast [ˈbrɔdˌkæst] *v* **-cast; -casting** *vt* : diffuser, téléviser — *vi* : émettre — ~ *n* : émission *f*
broaden [ˈbrɔdən] *vt* : élargir — *vi* : s'élargir — **broadly** [ˈbrɔdli] *adv* : en général — **broad-minded** [ˈbrɔdˈmaɪndəd] *adj* : large d'esprit, tolérant
broccoli [ˈbrɑkəli] *n* : brocoli *m*
brochure [broˈʃʊr] *n* : brochure *f*, dépliant *m*
broil [ˈbrɔɪl] *v* : griller
broke [ˈbro:k] → **break** — ~ *adj* : fauché *fam*, cassé *Can fam* — **broken** [ˈbro:kən] *adj* : cassé, brisé — **brokenhearted** [ˌbro:kənˈhɑrṭəd] *adj* : au cœur brisé
broker [ˈbro:kər] *n* : courtier *m*, -tière *f*
bronchitis [brɑnˈkaɪṭəs, brɑŋ-] *n* : bronchite *f*
bronze [ˈbrɑnz] *n* : bronze *m*
brooch [ˈbro:ʧ, ˈbru:ʧ] *n* : broche *f*
brood [ˈbru:d] *n* : couvée *f* (d'oiseaux) — ~ *vi* **1** INCUBATE : couver **2 ~ about** : ressasser, ruminer
brook [ˈbrʊk] *n* : ruisseau *m*
broom [ˈbru:m, ˈbrʊm] *n* : balai *m* — **broomstick** [ˈbru:mˌstɪk, ˈbrʊm-] *n* : manche *m* à balai
broth [ˈbrɔθ] *n, pl* **broths** [ˈbrɔθs, ˈbrɔðz] : bouillon *m*
brothel [ˈbrɑθəl, ˈbrɔ-] *n* : bordel *m fam*
brother [ˈbrʌðər] *n* : frère *m* — **brotherhood** [ˈbrʌðərˌhʊd] *n* : fraternité *f* — **brother-in-law** [ˈbrʌðərɪnˌlɔ] *n, pl* **brothers-in-law** : beau-frère *m* — **brotherly** [ˈbrʌðərli] *adj* : fraternel
brought → **bring**
brow [ˈbraʊ] *n* **1** EYEBROW : sourcil *m* **2** FOREHEAD : front *m* **3** : sommet *m* (d'une colline)
brown [ˈbraʊn] *adj* : brun, marron — ~ *n* : brun *m*, marron *m* — ~ *vt* : faire dorer (en cuisine)
browse [ˈbraʊz] *vi* **browsed; browsing** : regarder, jeter un coup d'œil
browser [ˈbraʊzər] *n* : navigateur *m* (en informatique)
bruise [ˈbru:z] *vt* **bruised; bruising 1** : faire un bleu à, contusionner **2** : taler (un fruit) — ~ *n* : bleu *m*, contusion *f*, prune *f Can*
brunch [ˈbrʌnʧ] *n* : brunch *m*
brunet *or* **brunette** [bru:ˈnɛt] *n* : brun *m*, brune *f*
brunt [ˈbrʌnt] *n* **bear the ~ of** : subir le plus gros de
brush [ˈbrʌʃ] *n* **1** : brosse *f* (à cheveux), pinceau *m* (de peintre) **2** UNDERGROWTH : brousses *fpl* — ~ *vt* **1** : brosser **2** GRAZE : effleurer **3 ~ off** DISREGARD : écarter — *vi* **~ up on** : réviser — **brush-off** [ˈbrʌʃˌɔf] *n* **give s.o. the ~** : envoyer promener qqn
brusque [ˈbrʌsk] *adj* : brusque
brutal [ˈbru:ṭəl] *adj* : brutal — **brutality** [bru:ˈtæləṭi] *n, pl* **-ties** : brutalité *f*
brute [ˈbru:t] *adj* : brutal — ~ *n* : brute *f*
bubble [ˈbʌbəl] *n* : bulle *f* — ~ *vi* **-bled; -bling** : bouillonner
buck [ˈbʌk] *n, pl* **bucks 1** *or pl* **buck** : mâle *m* (animal) **2** DOLLAR : dollar *m* — ~ *vi* **1** : ruer (se dit d'un cheval) **2 ~ up** : ne pas se laisser abattre — *vt* OPPOSE : résister
bucket [ˈbʌkət] *n* : seau *m*
buckle [ˈbʌkəl] *n* : boucle *f* — ~ *v* **-led; -ling** *vt* **1** FASTEN : boucler **2** WARP : gauchir — *vi* BEND : se courber, se voiler
bud [ˈbʌd] *n* : bourgeon *m* (d'une feuille), bouton *m* (d'une fleur) — ~ *vi* **budded; budding** : bourgeonner
Buddhism [ˈbu:ˌdɪzəm, ˈbʊ-] *n* : bouddhisme *m* — **Buddhist** [ˈbu:ˌdɪst, ˈbʊ-] *adj* : bouddhiste — ~ *n* : bouddhiste *mf*
buddy [ˈbʌdi] *n, pl* **-dies** : copain *m*, -pine *f*
budge [ˈbʌʤ] *vi* **budged; budging 1** MOVE : bouger **2** YIELD : céder
budget [ˈbʌʤət] *n* : budget *m* — ~ *vt* : budgétiser — *vi* : dresser un budget — **budgetary** [ˈbʌʤəˌtɛri] *adj* : budgétaire
buff [ˈbʌf] *n* **1** : chamois *m* (couleur) **2** ENTHUSIAST : mordu *m*, -due *f fam;* fanatique *mf* — ~ *adj* : chamois, beige — ~ *vt* POLISH : polir
buffalo [ˈbʌfəˌlo:] *n, pl* **-lo** *or* **-loes** : buffle *m*, bison *m* (d'Amérique)
buffer [ˈbʌfər] *n* : tampon *m*
buffet [ˌbʌˈfeɪ, ˌbu:-] *n* : buffet *m* (repas ou meuble)
buffoon [ˌbʌˈfu:n] *n* : bouffon *m*
bug [ˈbʌg] *n* **1** INSECT : insecte *m*, bestiole *f* **2** FLAW : défaut *m* **3** GERM : microbe *m* **4** : bogue *m* (en informatique) — ~ *vt* **bugged; bugging 1** : installer un microphone dans (une maison, etc.) **2** PESTER : embêter
buggy [ˈbʌgi] *n, pl* **-gies 1** CARRIAGE : calèche *f* **2** *or* **baby ~** : voiture *f* d'enfant, landau *m France*
bugle [ˈbju:gəl] *n* : clairon *m*
build [ˈbɪld] *v* **built** [ˈbɪlt]; **building** *vt* **1** : construire, bâtir **2** DEVELOP : établir — *vi* **1** *or* **~ up** INTENSIFY : augmenter, intensifier **2** *or* **~ up** ACCUMULATE : s'accumuler — ~ *n* PHYSIQUE : carrure *f*, charpente *f* — **builder** [ˈbɪldər] *n* : entrepreneur *m* — **building** [ˈbɪldɪŋ] *n* **1** : bâtiment *m*, immeuble *m* **2** CONSTRUCTION : construction *f* — **built-in** [ˈbɪltˈɪn] *adj* : encastré
bulb [ˈbʌlb] *n* **1** : bulbe *m* **2** LIGHTBULB : ampoule *f*
bulge [ˈbʌlʤ] *vi* **bulged; bulging** : être gonflé, se renfler — ~ *n* : renflement *m*
bulk [ˈbʌlk] *n* **1** : masse *f*, volume *m* **2 in ~** : en gros — **bulky** [ˈbʌlki] *adj* **bulkier; -est** : volumineux
bull [ˈbʊl] *n* **1** : taureau *m* **2** MALE : mâle *m*
bulldog [ˈbʊlˌdɔg] *n* : bouledogue *m*
bulldozer [ˈbʊlˌdo:zər] *n* : bulldozer *m*
bullet [ˈbʊlət] *n* : balle *f* (d'un fusil)
bulletin [ˈbʊlətən, -ləṭən] *n* : bulletin *m* — **bulletin board** *n* : tableau *m* d'affichage, babillard *m Can*
bulletproof [ˈbʊlətˌpru:f] *adj* : pare-balles
bullfight [ˈbʊlˌfaɪt] *n* : corrida *f* — **bullfighter** [ˈbʊlˌfaɪṭər] *n* : torero *m*
bull's-eye [ˈbʊlzˌaɪ] *n, pl* **bull's-eyes** : centre *m* (de la cible)
bully [ˈbʊli] *n, pl* **-lies** : tyran *m* — ~ *vt* **-lied; -lying** : malmener, maltraiter
bum [ˈbʌm] *n* : clochard *m*, -charde *f*
bumblebee [ˈbʌmbəlˌbi:] *n* : bourdon *m*
bump [ˈbʌmp] *n* **1** BULGE : bosse *f*, protubérance *f* **2** IMPACT : coup *m*, choc *m* **3** JOLT : secousse *f* — ~ *vt* : heurter, cogner — *vi* **~ into** MEET : tomber sur — **bumper** [ˈbʌmpər] *n* : pare-chocs *m* — ~ *adj* : exceptionnel — **bumpy** [ˈbʌmpi] *adj* **bumpier; -est 1** : cahoteux (se dit d'un chemin) **2 a ~ flight** : un vol agité
bun [ˈbʌn] *n* : petit pain *m* (au lait)
bunch [ˈbʌnʧ] *n* **1** : bouquet *m* (de fleurs), grappe *f* (de raisins), botte *f* (de légumes, etc.) **2** GROUP : groupe *m* — ~ *vt* **~ together** : mettre ensemble — *vi* **~ up** : s'entasser
bundle [ˈbʌndəl] *n* **1** : liasse *f* (de papiers, etc.) **2** PARCEL : paquet *m* — ~ *vi* **-dled; -dling ~ up** : s'emmitoufler
bungalow [ˈbʌŋgəˌlo:] *n* : maison *f* sans étage
bungle [ˈbʌŋgəl] *vt* **-gled; -gling** : gâcher
bunion [ˈbʌnjən] *n* : oignon *m*
bunk [ˈbʌŋk] *n* **1** : couchette *f* **2 ~ bed** : lits *mpl* superposés
bunny [ˈbʌni] *n, pl* **-nies** : lapin *m*
buoy [ˈbu:i, ˈbɔɪ] *n* : bouée *f* — ~ *vt or* **~ up** : revigorer — **buoyant** [ˈbɔɪənt, ˈbu:jənt] *adj* **1** : qui flotte **2** LIGHTHEARTED : allègre, optimiste
burden [ˈbərdən] *n* : fardeau *m* — ~ *vt* **~ sth with** : accabler qqn de — **burdensome** [ˈbərdənsəm] *adj* : lourd
bureau [ˈbjʊro] *n* **1** : commode *f* (meuble) **2** : service *m* (gouvernemental) **3** AGENCY : agence *f* — **bureaucracy** [bjʊˈrɑkrəsi] *n, pl* **-cies** : bureaucratie *f* — **bureaucrat** [ˈbjʊrəˌkræt] *n* : bureaucrate *mf* — **bureaucratic** [ˌbjʊrəˈkræṭɪk] *adj* : bureaucratique
burglar [ˈbərglər] *n* : cambrioleur *m*, -leuse *f* — **burglarize** [ˈbərgləˌraɪz] *vt* **-ized; -izing** : cambrioler — **burglary** [ˈbərgləri] *n, pl* **-glaries** : cambriolage *m*
Burgundy [ˈbərgəndi] *n, pl* **-dies** : bourgogne *m* (vin)
burial [ˈbɛriəl] *n* : enterrement *m*
burly [ˈbərli] *adj* **-lier; -est** : costaud *fam*
burn [ˈbərn] *v* **burned** [ˈbərnd, ˈbərnt] *or* **burnt** [ˈbərnt]; **burning** : brûler — ~ *n* : brûlure *f* — **burner** [ˈbərnər] *n* : brûleur *m* (d'une cuisinière), rond *m Can*
burnish [ˈbərnɪʃ] *vt* : polir
burp [ˈbərp] *vi* : avoir des renvois, roter *fam* — ~ *n* : renvoi *m*
burrow [ˈbəro] *n* : terrier *m* — ~ *vt* : creuser — *vi* **~ into** : fouiller dans
burst [ˈbərst] *v* **burst** *or* **bursted; bursting** *vi* **1** : crever, éclater **2 ~ into tears** : fondre en larmes **3 ~ out laughing** : éclater de rire — ~ *vt* : crever, faire éclater — ~ *n* **1** EXPLOSION : explosion *f* **2** OUTBURST : élan *m* (d'enthousiasme), éclat *m* (de rire)
bury [ˈbɛri] *vt* **buried; burying 1** : enterrer **2** HIDE : enfouir, cacher
bus [ˈbʌs] *n, pl* **buses** *or* **busses** : bus *m*, autobus *m* — ~ *v* **bused** *or* **bussed** [ˈbʌst]; **busing** *or* **bussing** [ˈbʌsɪŋ] *vt* : transporter en autobus — *vi* : voyager en autobus
bush [ˈbʊʃ] *n* SHRUB : buisson *m*
bushel [ˈbʊʃəl] *n* : boisseau *m*
bushy [ˈbʊʃi] *adj* **bushier; -est** : touffu
busily [ˈbɪzəli] *adv* : activement
business [ˈbɪznəs, -nəz] *n* **1** COMMERCE : affaires *fpl* **2** COMPANY : entreprise *f* **3 it's none of your ~** : ce n'est pas de vos affaires — **businessman** [ˈbɪznəsˌmæn, -nəz-] *n, pl* **-men** : homme *m* d'affaires — **businesswoman** [ˈbɪznəsˌwʊmən, -nəz-] *n, pl* **-women** : femme *f* d'affaires
bust[1] [ˈbʌst] *vt* BREAK : briser
bust[2] *n* **1** : buste *m* (en sculpture) **2** BREASTS : seins *fpl*, poitrine *f*
bustle [ˈbʌsəl] *vi* **-tled; -tling** *or* **~ about** : s'affairer — ~ *n or* **hustle and ~** : agitation *f*, activité *f*
busy [ˈbɪzi] *adj* **busier; -est 1** : occupé **2** BUSTLING : animé
but [ˈbʌt] *conj* : mais — ~ *prep* : sauf, excepté

butcher [ˈbʊtʃər] *n* : boucher *m*, -chère *f* — ~ *vt* **1** : abattre **2** BOTCH : bousiller *fam*
butler [ˈbʌtlər] *n* : maître *m* d'hôtel
butt [ˈbʌt] *vi* — ~ **in** : interrompre — ~ *n* **1** : crosse *f* (d'un fusil) **2** : mégot *m fam* (de cigarette)
butter [ˈbʌtər] *n* : beurre *m* — ~ *vt* : beurrer
butterfly [ˈbʌtərˌflaɪ] *n, pl* **-flies** : papillon *m*
buttermilk [ˈbʌtərˌmɪlk] *n* : babeurre *m*
buttocks [ˈbʌtəks, -ˌtɑks] *npl* : fesses *fpl*
button [ˈbʌtən] *n* : bouton *m* — ~ *vt* : boutonner — *vi or* ~ **up** : se boutonner — **buttonhole** [ˈbʌtənˌho:l] *n* : boutonnière *f*
buttress [ˈbʌtrəs] *n* : contrefort *m*
buy [ˈbaɪ] *vt* **bought** [ˈbɔt]; **buying** : acheter — ~ *n* : achat *m* — **buyer** [ˈbaɪər] *n* : acheteur *m*, -teuse *f*
buzz [ˈbʌz] *vi* : bourdonner — ~ *n* : bourdonnement *m*
buzzer [ˈbʌzər] *n* : sonnette *f*
by [ˈbaɪ] *prep* **1** NEAR : près de, à côté de **2** VIA : par, en **3** PAST : devant, à côté de **4** DURING : pendant **5** (*in expressions of time*) : avant **6** (*indicating cause or agent*) : par — ~ *adv* **1** ~ **and** ~ : bientôt **2** ~ **and large** : en général **3 go** ~ : passer **4 stop** ~ : arrêter
bygone [ˈbaɪˌgɔn] *adj* **1** : passé, d'autrefois **2 let** ~**s be** ~**s** : enterrer le passé
bypass [ˈbaɪˌpæs] *n* : route *f* de contournement — ~ *vt* : contourner
by–product [ˈbaɪˌprɑdəkt] *n* : sous-produit *m*, dérivé *m*
bystander [ˈbaɪˌstændər] *n* : spectateur *m*, -trice *f*
byte [ˈbaɪt] *n* : octet *m*

C

c [ˈsi:] *n, pl* **c's** *or* **cs** : c *m*, troisième lettre de l'alphabet
cab [ˈkæb] *n* **1** : taxi *m* **2** : cabine *f* (d'un camion, etc.)
cabbage [ˈkæbɪdʒ] *n* : chou *m*
cabin [ˈkæbən] *n* **1** : cabane *f* **2** : cabine *f* (d'un navire, d'un avion, etc.)
cabinet [ˈkæbnət] *n* **1** CUPBOARD : armoire *f* **2** : cabinet *m* (en politique) **3** *or* **medicine** ~ : pharmacie *f*
cable [ˈkeɪbəl] *n* : câble *m* — **cable television** *n* : câble *m*
cackle [ˈkækəl] *vi* **-led; -ling** : caqueter, glousser
cactus [ˈkæktəs] *n, pl* **cacti** [-ˌtaɪ] *or* **-tuses** : cactus *m*
cadence [ˈkeɪdənts] *n* : cadence *f*, rythme *m*
cadet [kəˈdɛt] *n* : élève *mf* officier
café [kæˈfeɪ, kə-] *n* : café *m*, bistrot *m* — **cafeteria** [ˌkæfəˈtɪriə] *n* : cafétéria *f*
caffeine [kæˈfi:n] *n* : caféine *f*
cage [ˈkeɪdʒ] *n* : cage *f*
cajole [kəˈdʒo:l] *vt* **-joled; -joling** : cajoler, enjôler
Cajun [ˈkeɪdʒən] *adj* : acadien, cajun
cake [ˈkeɪk] *n* **1** : gâteau *m* **2** BAR : pain *m* (de savon) — **caked** [ˈkeɪkt] *adj* ~ **with** : couvert de
calamity [kəˈlæməṭi] *n, pl* **-ties** : calamité *f*
calcium [ˈkælsiəm] *n* : calcium *m*
calculate [ˈkælkjəˌleɪt] *v* **-lated; -lating** : calculer — **calculating** [ˈkælkjəˌleɪṭɪŋ] *adj* : calculateur — **calculation** [ˌkælkjəˈleɪʃən] *n* : calcul *m* — **calculator** [ˈkælkjəˌleɪṭər] *n* : calculatrice *f*
calendar [ˈkæləndər] *n* : calendrier *m*
calf[1] [ˈkæf] *n, pl* **calves** [ˈkævz] : veau *m* (de bovin)
calf[2] *n, pl* **calves** : mollet *m* (de la jambe)
caliber *or* **calibre** [ˈkæləbər] *n* : calibre *m*
call [ˈkɔl] *vi* **1** : appeler **2** VISIT : passer, faire une visite **3** ~ **for** : demander — *vt* **1** : appeler **2** ~ **back** : rappeler **3** ~ **off** : annuler — ~ *n* **1** : appel *m* **2** SHOUT : cri *m* **3** VISIT : visite *f* **4** NEED : demande *f* — **calling** [ˈkɔlɪŋ] *n* : vocation *f*
callous [ˈkæləs] *adj* : dur, sans cœur
calm [ˈkɑm, ˈkɑlm] *n* : calme *m*, tranquillité *f* — ~ *vt* : calmer, apaiser — *vi or* ~ **down** : se calmer — ~ *adj* : calme, tranquille
calorie [ˈkæləri] *n* : calorie *f*
came → **come**
camel [ˈkæməl] *n* : chameau *m*
camera [ˈkæmrə, ˈkæmərə] *n* : appareil *m* photo, caméra *f*
camouflage [ˈkæməˌflɑʒ, -ˌflɑdʒ] *n* : camouflage *m* — ~ *vt* **-flaged; -flaging** : camoufler
camp [ˈkæmp] *n* **1** : camp *m* **2** FACTION : parti *m* — ~ *vi* : camper, faire du camping
campaign [kæmˈpeɪn] *n* : campagne *f* — ~ *vi* : faire campagne
camping [ˈkæmpɪŋ] *n* : camping *m*
campus [ˈkæmpəs] *n* : campus *m*, cité *f* universitaire *Can*
can[1] [ˈkæn] *v aux, past* **could** [ˈkʊd]; *present s & pl* **can 1** (*expressing possibility or permission*) : pouvoir **2** (*expressing knowledge or ability*) : savoir **3 that cannot be** : cela n'est pas possible
can[2] *n* : boîte *f* (d'aliments), canette *f* (de boisson gazeuse), bidon *m* (d'essence, etc.) — ~ *vt* **canned; canning** : mettre en boîte
Canadian [kəˈneɪdiən] *adj* : canadien
canal [kəˈnæl] *n* : canal *m*
canary [kəˈnɛri] *n, pl* **-naries** : canari *m*, serin *m*
cancel [ˈkæntsəl] *vt* **-celed** *or* **-celled; -celing** *or* **-celling** : annuler — **cancellation** [ˌkæntsəˈleɪʃən] *n* : annulation *f*
cancer [ˈkæntsər] *n* : cancer *m* — **cancerous** [ˈkæntsərəs] *adj* : cancéreux
candid [ˈkændɪd] *adj* : franc, sincère
candidate [ˈkændəˌdeɪt, -dət] *n* : candidat *m*, -date *f* — **candidacy** [ˈkændədəsi] *n, pl* **-cies** : candidature *f*
candle [ˈkændəl] *n* : bougie *f*, chandelle *f* — **candlestick** [ˈkændəlˌstɪk] *n* : chandelier *m*, bougeoir *m*
candor *or Brit* **candour** [ˈkændər] *n* : franchise *f*
candy [ˈkændi] *n, pl* **-dies 1** : bonbon *m* **2** ~ **store** : confiserie *f*
cane [ˈkeɪn] *n* : canne *f* — ~ *vt* **caned; caning** FLOG : fouetter
canine [ˈkeɪˌnaɪn] *n or* ~ **tooth** : canine *f* — ~ *adj* : canin
canister [ˈkænəstər] *n* : boîte *f*
cannibal [ˈkænəbəl] *n* : cannibale *mf*
cannon [ˈkænən] *n, pl* **-nons** *or* **-non** : canon *m*
cannot (**can not**) [ˈkænˌɑt, kəˈnɑt] → **can**[1]
canoe [kəˈnu:] *n* : canoë *m*, canot *m Can*
canon [ˈkænən] *n* : canon *m*, règle *f*
can opener *n* : ouvre-boîtes *m*
canopy [ˈkænəpi] *n, pl* **-pies** : auvent *m*, baldaquin *m*
can't [ˈkænt, ˈkɑnt] (*contraction of* **can not**) → **can**[1]
cantaloupe [ˈkæntəlˌo:p] *n* : cantaloup *m*
cantankerous [kænˈtæŋkərəs] *adj* : acariâtre
canteen [kænˈti:n] *n* CAFETERIA : cantine *f*
canter [ˈkæntər] *vi* : aller au petit galop — ~ *n* : petit galop *m*
canvas [ˈkænvəs] *n* : toile *f*
canvass [ˈkænvəs] *vt* : solliciter les voix de (les électeurs) — ~ *n* : démarchage *m* électoral
canyon [ˈkænjən] *n* : canyon *m*
cap [ˈkæp] *n* **1** : casquette *f* **2** : capsule *f* (d'une bouteille), capuchon *m* (d'un stylo, etc.) — ~ *vt* **capped; capping** COVER : couvrir
capable [ˈkeɪpəbəl] *adj* : capable — **capability** [ˌkeɪpəˈbɪləṭi] *n, pl* **-ties** : aptitude *f*, capacité *f*
capacity [kəˈpæsəṭi] *n, pl* **-ties 1** : capacité *f* **2** ROLE : qualité *f*
cape[1] [ˈkeɪp] *n* : cap *m* (en géographie)
cape[2] *n* CLOAK : cape *f*, pèlerine *f*
caper [ˈkeɪpər] *n* : câpre *f*
capital [ˈkæpəṭəl] *adj* **1** : capital, principal **2** : majuscule (se dit d'une lettre) — ~ *n* **1** *or* ~ **city** : capitale *f* **2** WEALTH : capital *m*, fonds *mpl* **3** *or* ~ **letter** : majuscule *f* — **capitalism** [ˈkæpəṭəlˌɪzəm] *n* : capitalisme *m* — **capitalist** [ˈkæpəṭəlɪst] *or* **capitalistic** [ˌkæpəṭəlˈɪstɪk] *adj* : capitaliste — **capitalize** [ˈkæpəṭəlˌaɪz] *v* **-ized; -izing** *vt* : écrire avec une majuscule — *vi* ~ **on** : tirer profit de
capitol [ˈkæpəṭˈl] *n* : capitole *m*
capsize [ˈkæpˌsaɪz, kæpˈsaɪz] *v* **-sized; -sizing** *vt* : faire chavirer — *vi* : chavirer
capsule [ˈkæpsəl, -ˌsu:l] *n* : capsule *f*
captain [ˈkæptən] *n* : capitaine *m*
caption [ˈkæpʃən] *n* **1** : légende *f* (d'une illustration) **2** SUBTITLE : sous-titre *m*
captivate [ˈkæptəˌveɪt] *vt* **-vated; -vating** : captiver, fasciner
captive [ˈkæptɪv] *adj* : captif — ~ *n* : captif *m*, -tive *f* — **captivity** [kæpˈtɪvəṭi] *n* : captivité *f*
capture [ˈkæpʃər] *n* : capture *f*, prise *f* — ~ *vt* **-tured; -turing 1** SEIZE : capturer **2** : captiver (l'imagination), capter (l'attention)
car [ˈkɑr] *n* **1** : voiture *f*, automobile *f* **2** *or* **railroad** ~ : wagon *m*
carafe [kəˈræf, -ˈrɑf] *n* : carafe *f*
caramel [ˈkɑrməl; ˈkærəməl, -ˌmɛl] *n* : caramel *m*
carat [ˈkærət] *n* : carat *m*
caravan [ˈkærəˌvæn] *n* : caravane *f*
carbohydrate [ˌkɑrboˈhaɪˌdreɪt, -drət] *n* : hydrate *m* de carbone
carbon [ˈkɑrbən] *n* : carbone *m*
carburetor [ˈkɑrbəˌreɪṭər, -bjə-] *n* : carburateur *m*
carcass [ˈkɑrkəs] *n* : carcasse *f*
card [ˈkɑrd] *n* : carte *f* — **cardboard** [ˈkɑrdˌbord] *n* : carton *m*
cardiac [ˈkɑrdiˌæk] *adj* : cardiaque
cardigan [ˈkɑrdɪgən] *n* : cardigan *m*
cardinal [ˈkɑrdənəl] *n* : cardinal *m* — ~ *adj* : cardinal, essentiel
care [ˈkær] *n* **1** : soin *m* **2** WORRY : préoccupation *f* — ~ *vi* **cared; caring 1** : se préoccuper, se soucier **2** ~ **for** TEND : prendre soin de **3** ~ **for** LIKE : aimer **4 I don't** ~ : ça m'est égal
career [kəˈrɪr] *n* : carrière *f*, profession *f*
carefree [ˈkærˌfri:, ˌkærˈ-] *adj* : insouciant
careful [ˈkærfəl] *adj* **1** : prudent **2 be** ~! : fais attention! — **carefully** [ˈkærfəli] *adv* : prudemment, avec soin — **careless** [ˈkærləs] *adj* : négligent — **carelessness** [ˈkærləsnəs] *n* : négligence *f*
caress [kəˈrɛs] *n* : caresse *f* — ~ *vt* : caresser
cargo [ˈkɑrˌgo:] *n, pl* **-goes** *or* **-gos** : chargement *m*, cargaison *f*
Caribbean [ˌkærəˈbi:ən, kəˈrɪbiən] *adj* : des Caraïbes
caricature [ˈkærɪkəˌtʃʊr] *n* : caricature *f*
caring [ˈkærɪŋ] *adj* : aimant, affectueux
carnage [ˈkɑrnɪdʒ] *n* : carnage *m*
carnation [kɑrˈneɪʃən] *n* : œillet *m*
carnival [ˈkɑrnəvəl] *n* : carnaval *m*
carol [ˈkærəl] *n* : chant *m* de Noël
carpenter [ˈkɑrpəntər] *n* : charpentier *m*, menuisier *m* — **carpentry** [ˈkɑrpəntri] *n* : charpenterie *f*, menuiserie *f*
carpet [ˈkɑrpət] *n* : tapis *m*
carriage [ˈkærɪdʒ] *n* **1** : transport *m* (de marchandises) **2** BEARING : maintien *m* **3** → **baby carriage 4** *or* **horse-drawn** ~ : calèche *f*, carrosse *m*
carrier [ˈkæriər] *n* **1** : transporteur *m* **2** : porteur *m*, -teuse *f* (d'une maladie)
carrot [ˈkærət] *n* : carotte *f*
carry [ˈkæri] *v* **-ried; -rying** *vt* **1** : porter **2** TRANSPORT : transporter **3** STOCK : vendre **4** ENTAIL : comporter **5** ~ **oneself** : se présenter — *vi* : porter (se dit de la voix) — **carry away** *vt* **get carried away** : s'emballer — **carry on** *vt* CONDUCT : réaliser — *vi* **1** : mal se comporter **2** CONTINUE : continuer — **carry out** *vt* **1** : réaliser, effectuer **2** FULFILL : accomplir
cart [ˈkɑrt] *n* : charette *f* — ~ *vt or* ~ **around** : trimbaler *fam*
carton [ˈkɑrtən] *n* : boîte *f* de carton
cartoon [kɑrˈtu:n] *n* **1** : dessin *m* humoristique **2** COMIC STRIP : bande *f* dessinée **3** *or* **animated** ~ : dessin *m* animé
cartridge [ˈkɑrtrɪdʒ] *n* : cartouche *f*
carve [ˈkɑrv] *vt* **carved; carving 1** : tailler (le bois, etc.) **2** : découper (de la viande)
case [ˈkeɪs] *n* **1** : boîte *f*, caisse *f* **2 in any** ~ : en tout cas **3 in** ~ **of** : au cas de **4 just in** ~ : au cas où
cash [ˈkæʃ] *n* : espèces *fpl*, argent *m* liquide — ~ *vt* : encaisser
cashew [ˈkæˌʃu:, kəˈʃu:] *n* : noix *f* de cajou
cashier [kæˈʃɪr] *n* : caissier *m*, -sière *f*
cashmere [ˈkæʒˌmɪr, ˈkæʃ-] *n* : cachemire *m*
cash register *n* : caisse *f* enregistreuse
casino [kəˈsi:ˌno:] *n, pl* **-nos** : casino *m*
cask [ˈkæsk] *n* : fût *m*, tonneau *f*
casket [ˈkæskət] *n* : cercueil *m*
casserole [ˈkæsəˌro:l] *n* : ragoût *m*
cassette [kəˈsɛt, kæ-] *n* : cassette *f*
cast [ˈkæst] *vt* **cast; casting 1** THROW : jeter, lancer **2** : donner un rôle à (au cinéma, etc.) **3** MOLD : couler (du métal) **4** ~ **one's vote** : voter — ~ *n* **1** : distribution *f* (d'acteurs) **2** *or* **plaster** ~ : plâtre *m*
cast iron *n* : fonte *f*
castle [ˈkæsəl] *n* : château *m*
castrate [ˈkæsˌtreɪt] *vt* **-trated; -trating** : châtrer
casual [ˈkæʒʊəl] *adj* **1** : nonchalant **2** INFORMAL : décontracté — **casually** [ˈkæʒʊəli, ˈkæʒəli] *adv* **1** : nonchalamment **2** ~ **dressed** : habillé simplement
casualty [ˈkæʒʊəlti, ˈkæʒəl-] *n, pl* **-ties 1** : accident *m* grave, désastre *m* **2** VICTIM : blessé *m*, -sée *f*; accidenté *m*, -tée *f*; mort *m*, morte *f*
cat [ˈkæt] *n* : chat *m*, chatte *f*
catalog *or* **catalogue** [ˈkæṭəˌlɔg] *n* : catalogue *m*
cataract [ˈkæṭəˌrækt] *n* : cataracte *f*
catastrophe [kəˈtæstrəˌfi:] *n* : catastrophe *f*
catch [ˈkætʃ, ˈkɛtʃ] *v* **caught** [ˈkɔt]; **catching** *vt* **1** CAPTURE, TRAP : attraper **2** SURPRISE : surprendre **3** GRASP : saisir **4** SNAG : accrocher **5** : prendre (le train, etc.) **6** ~ **one's breath** : reprendre son souffle — *vi* **1** SNAG : s'accrocher **2** ~ **fire** : prendre feu — ~ *n* **1** : prise *f*, capture *f* **2** PITFALL : piège *f* — **catching** [ˈkætʃɪŋ, ˈkɛ-] *adj* : contagieux — **catchy** [ˈkætʃi, ˈkɛ-] *adj* **catchier; -est** : entraînant
category [ˈkæṭəˌgori] *n, pl* **-ries** : catégorie *f*, classe *f* — **categorical** [ˌkæṭəˈgɔrɪkəl] *adj* : catégorique
cater [ˈkeɪṭər] *vi* **1** : fournir des repas **2** ~ **to** : pourvoir à — **caterer** [ˈkeɪṭərər] *n* : traiteur *m*
caterpillar [ˈkæṭərˌpɪlər] *n* : chenille *f*
cathedral [kəˈθi:drəl] *n* : cathédrale *f*
catholic [ˈkæθəlɪk] *adj* **1** : universel **2 Catholic** : catholique — **catholicism** [kəˈθɑləˌsɪzəm] *n* : catholicisme *m*
cattle [ˈkæṭəl] *npl* : bétail *m*, bovins *mpl*
caught → **catch**
cauldron [ˈkɔldrən] *n* : chaudron *m*
cauliflower [ˈkɑlɪˌflauər, ˈkɔ-] *n* : chou-fleur *m*
cause [ˈkɔz] *n* **1** : cause *f* **2** REASON : raison *f*, motif *m* — ~ *vt* **caused; causing** : causer, occasionner
caution [ˈkɔʃən] *n* **1** WARNING : avertissement *m* **2** CARE : prudence *f* — ~ *vt* : avertir, mettre en garde — **cautious** [ˈkɔʃəs] *adj* : prudent, avisé — **cautiously** [ˈkɔʃəsli] *adv* : prudemment
cavalier [ˌkævəˈlɪr] *adj* : cavalier, désinvolte
cavalry [ˈkævəlri] *n, pl* **-ries** : cavalerie *f*
cave [ˈkeɪv] *n* : grotte *f*, caverne *f* — ~ *vi* **caved; caving** *or* ~ **in** : s'affaisser, s'effondrer
cavern [ˈkævərn] *n* : caverne *f*
caviar *or* **caviare** [ˈkæviˌɑr, ˈkɑ-] *n* : caviar *m*
cavity [ˈkævəṭi] *n, pl* **-ties 1** : cavité *f* **2** : carie *f* (dentaire)
CD [ˌsi:ˈdi:] *n* : CD *m*, disque *m* compact
cease [ˈsi:s] *v* **ceased; ceasing** : cesser — **cease-fire** [ˈsi:sˈfaɪr] *n* : cessez-le-feu *m* — **ceaseless** [ˈsi:sləs] *adj* : incessant, continuel
cedar [ˈsi:dər] *n* : cèdre *m*
cedilla [sɪˈdɪlə] *n* : cédille *nf*
ceiling [ˈsi:lɪŋ] *n* : plafond *m*
celebrate [ˈsɛləˌbreɪt] *v* **-brated; -brating** *vt* : fêter, célébrer — *vi* : faire la fête — **celebrated** [ˈsɛləˌbreɪṭəd] *adj* : célèbre — **celebration** [ˌsɛləˈbreɪʃən] *n* **1** : célébration *f* **2** FESTIVITY : fête *f* — **celebrity** [səˈlɛbrəṭi] *n, pl* **-ties** : célébrité *f*
celery [ˈsɛləri] *n, pl* **-eries** : céleri *m*
cell [ˈsɛl] *n* : cellule *f*
cellar [ˈsɛlər] *n* : cave *f*
cello [ˈtʃɛˌlo:] *n, pl* **-los** : violoncelle *m*
cellular [ˈsɛljələr] *adj* : cellulaire
cement [sɪˈmɛnt] *n* : ciment *m*
cemetery [ˈsɛməˌtɛri] *n, pl* **-teries** : cimetière *m*
censor [ˈsɛntsər] *vt* : censurer — **censorship** [ˈsɛntsərˌʃɪp] *n* : censure *f* — **censure** [ˈsɛntʃər] *n* : censure *f*, blâme *m* — ~ *vt* **-sured; -suring** : critiquer, blâmer
census [ˈsɛntsəs] *n* : recensement *m*
cent [ˈsɛnt] *n* : cent *m*
centennial [sɛnˈtɛniəl] *n* : centenaire *m*
center *or Brit* **centre** [ˈsɛntər] *n* : centre *m* — ~ *v* **centered** *or Brit* **centred; centering** *or Brit* **centring** *vt* : centrer — *vi* ~ **on** : se concentrer sur
centigrade [ˈsɛntəˌgreɪd, ˈsɑn-] *adj* : centigrade
centimeter [ˈsɛntəˌmi:ṭər, ˈsɑn-] *n* : centimètre *m*
centipede [ˈsɛntəˌpi:d] *n* : mille-pattes *m*
central [ˈsɛntrəl] *adj* : central — **centralize** [ˈsɛntrəˌlaɪz] *vt* **-ized; -izing** : centraliser
centre → **center**
century [ˈsɛntʃəri] *n, pl* **-ries** : siècle *m*
ceramics [səˈræmɪks] *n* : céramique *f*
cereal [ˈsɪriəl] *n* : céréale *f*
ceremony [ˈsɛrəˌmo:ni] *n, pl* **-nies** : cérémonie *f*
certain [ˈsərtən] *adj* **1** : certain **2 be** ~ **of** : être assuré de **3 for** ~ : au juste — **certainly** [ˈsərtənli] *adv* : certainement, bien sûr — **certainty** [ˈsərtənti] *n, pl* **-ties** : certitude *f*
certify [ˈsərṭəˌfaɪ] *vt* **-fied; -fying** : certifier — **certificate** [sərˈtɪfɪkət] *n* : certificat *m*
chafe [ˈtʃeɪf] *vi* **chafed; chafing 1** RUB : frotter **2** ~ **at** : s'irriter de
chain [ˈtʃeɪn] *n* **1** : chaîne *f* **2** ~ **of events** : série *f* d'événements — ~ *vt* : enchaîner
chair [ˈtʃɛr] *n* **1** : chaise *f* **2** : chaire *f* (d'une université) — ~ *vt* : présider — **chairman** [ˈtʃɛrmən] *n, pl* **-men** [-mən, -ˌmɛn] : président *m* — **chairperson** [ˈtʃɛrˌpərsən] *n* : presidente *m*, -dente *f*
chalk [ˈtʃɔk] *n* : craie *f*
challenge [ˈtʃælɪndʒ] *vt* **-lenged; -lenging 1** DISPUTE : contester **2** DARE : défier — ~ *n* : défi *m* — **challenging** [ˈtʃælɪndʒɪŋ] *adj* : stimulant
chamber [ˈtʃeɪmbər] *n* : chambre *f* (de commerce, etc.)
champagne [ʃæmˈpeɪn] *n* : champagne *m*
champion [ˈtʃæmpiən] *n* : champion *m*, -pionne *f* — **championship** [ˈtʃæmpiənˌʃɪp] *n* : championnat *m*
chance [ˈtʃænts] *n* **1** LUCK : hasard *m* **2** OPPORTUNITY : occasion *f* **3** LIKELIHOOD : chances *fpl* **4 by** ~ : par hasard **5 take a** ~ : prendre un risque — ~ *vt* **chanced; chancing** : hasarder, risquer — ~ *adj* : fortuit
chandelier [ˌʃændəˈlɪr] *n* : lustre *m*
change [ˈtʃeɪndʒ] *v* **changed; changing** *vt* **1** : changer **2** SWITCH : changer de — *vi* **1** : changer **2** *or* ~ **clothes** : se changer — ~ *n* **1** : changement *m* **2** COINS : monnaie *f* — **changeable** [ˈtʃeɪndʒəbəl] *adj* : changeant
channel [ˈtʃænəl] *n* **1** : canal *m* **2** : chenal *m* (dans un fleuve, etc.) **3** : chaîne *f* (de télévision)
chant [ˈtʃænt] *n* : chant *m*
chaos [ˈkeɪˌɑs] *n* : chaos *m* — **chaotic** [keɪˈɑṭɪk] *adj* : chaotique
chap[1] [ˈtʃæp] *vi* **chapped; chapping** : se gercer

chap² n : type m fam, bonhomme m fam

chapel ['ʧæpəl] n : chapelle f

chaperon or **chaperone** ['ʃæpəˌro:n] n : chaperon m

chaplain ['ʧæplɪn] n : aumônier m

chapter ['ʧæptər] n : chapitre m

char ['ʧɑr] vt **charred; charring** : carboniser

character ['kærɪktər] n 1 : caractère m 2 : personnage m (d'un roman, etc.) — **characteristic** [ˌkærɪktə'rɪstɪk] adj : caractéristique — ~ n : caractéristique f — **characterize** ['kærɪktəˌraɪz] vt **-ized; -izing** : caractériser

charcoal ['ʧɑrˌko:l] n : charbon m de bois

charge ['ʧɑrʤ] n 1 : charge f (électrique) 2 COST : prix m, frais mpl 3 ACCUSATION : inculpation f 4 **be in ~** : être responsable — ~ v **charged; charging** vt 1 : charger (une batterie) 2 ENTRUST : charger, confier 3 ACCUSE : inculper 4 : payer par carte de crédit — vi 1 : se précipiter, foncer 2 **~ too much** : demander trop (d'argent)

charisma [kə'rɪzmə] n : charisme m — **charismatic** [ˌkærəz'mætɪk] adj : charismatique

charity ['ʧærəṭi] n, pl **-ties** 1 : organisation f caritative 2 GOODWILL : charité f

charlatan ['ʃɑrlətən] n : charlatan m

charm ['ʧɑrm] n : charme m — ~ vt : charmer, captiver — **charming** ['ʧɑrmɪŋ] adj : charmant

chart ['ʧɑrt] n : graphique m, tableau m

charter ['ʧɑrṭər] n : charte f — ~ vt : affréter (un vol, etc.)

chase ['ʧeɪs] n : poursuite f — ~ vt **chased; chasing** 1 : poursuivre, courir après 2 or **~ away** : chasser

chasm ['kæzəm] n : gouffre m, abîme m

chaste ['ʧeɪst] adj **chaster; chastest** : chaste — **chastity** ['ʧæstəṭi] n : chasteté f

chat ['ʧæt] vi **chatted; chatting** : bavarder, causer — ~ n : causerie f — **chatter** ['ʧæṭər] vi 1 : bavarder 2 : claquer (se dit des dents) — ~ n : bavardage m — **chatterbox** ['ʧæṭərˌbɑks] n : moulin m à paroles fam — **chatty** ['ʧæṭi] adj **chattier; -est** : bavard

chauffeur ['ʃo:fər, ʃo'fər] n : chauffeur m

chauvinist ['ʃo:vənɪst] or **chauvinistic** [ˌʃo:və'nɪstɪk] adj : chauvin

cheap ['ʧi:p] adj 1 INEXPENSIVE : bon marché 2 SHODDY : de mauvaise qualité — ~ adv : à bon marché

cheat ['ʧi:t] vt : frauder, tromper — vi 1 : tricher 2 **~ on s.o.** : tromper qqn — ~ or **cheater** ['ʧi:ṭər] n : tricheur m, -cheuse f

check ['ʧɛk] n 1 HALT : arrêt m 2 RESTRAINT : limite f, frein m 3 INSPECTION : contrôle m 4 or Brit **cheque** DRAFT : chèque m 5 BILL : addition f — ~ vt 1 HALT : freiner, arrêter 2 RESTRAIN : retenir, contenir 3 VERIFY : vérifier 4 **~ in** : se présenter à la réception (à l'hôtel) 5 or **~ off** MARK : cocher 6 **~ out** : quitter (l'hôtel) 7 **~ out** VERIFY : vérifier — **checkbook** ['ʧɛkˌbʊk] n : carnet m de chèques

checkers ['ʧɛkərz] n : jeu m de dames

checkmate ['ʧɛkˌmeɪt] n : échec m et mat

checkpoint ['ʧɛkˌpɔɪnt] n : poste m de contrôle

checkup ['ʧɛkˌʌp] n : examen m médical

cheek ['ʧik] n : joue f

cheer ['ʧɪr] n 1 : gaieté f 2 APPLAUSE : acclamation f 3 **~s!** : à votre santé! — ~ vt 1 COMFORT : encourager 2 APPLAUD : acclamer — **cheerful** ['ʧɪrfəl] adj : de bonne humeur

cheese ['ʧi:z] n : fromage m

cheetah ['ʧi:ṭə] n : guépard m

chef ['ʃɛf] n : cuisinier m, -nière f; chef m (cuisinier)

chemical ['kɛmɪkəl] adj : chimique — ~ n : produit m chimique — **chemist** ['kɛmɪst] n : chimiste mf — **chemistry** ['kɛmɪstri] n, pl **-tries** : chimie f

cheque Brit → **check**

cherish ['ʧɛrɪʃ] vt 1 : chérir, aimer 2 HARBOR : caresser, nourrir (un espoir, etc.)

cherry ['ʧɛri] n, pl **-ries** : cerise f

chess ['ʧɛs] n : échecs mpl

chest ['ʧɛst] n 1 BOX : coffre m 2 : poitrine f (du corps) 3 or **~ of drawers** : commode f

chestnut ['ʧɛstˌnʌt] n : marron m, châtaigne f

chew ['ʧu:] vt : mastiquer, mâcher — **chewing gum** n : chewing-gum m France, gomme f à mâcher

chick ['ʧɪk] n : poussin m — **chicken** ['ʧɪkən] n : poulet m — **chicken pox** n : varicelle f

chicory ['ʧɪkəri] n, pl **-ries** 1 : endive f 2 : chicorée f

chief ['ʧi:f] adj : principal, en chef — ~ n : chef m — **chiefly** ['ʧi:fli] adv : principalement, surtout

child ['ʧaɪld] n, pl **children** ['ʧɪldrən] 1 : enfant mf 2 OFFSPRING : fils m, fille f — **childbirth** ['ʧaɪldˌbərθ] n : accouchement m — **childhood** ['ʧaɪldˌhʊd] n : enfance f — **childish** ['ʧaɪldɪʃ] adj : puéril, enfantin — **childlike** ['ʧaɪldˌlaɪk] adj : innocent, d'enfant — **childproof** ['ʧlaɪdˌpru:f] adj : de sécurité pour enfants

chili or **chile** or **chilli** ['ʧɪli] n, pl **chilies** or **chiles** or **chillies** 1 or **~ pepper** : piment m fort 2 : chili m con carne

chill ['ʧɪl] n 1 : froid m 2 **catch a ~** : attraper un coup de froid 3 **there's a ~ in the air** : il fait un peu froid — ~ vt : refroidir, réfrigérer — **chilly** ['ʧɪli] adj **chillier; -est** : frais, froid

chime ['ʧaɪm] v **chimed; chiming** : carillonner — ~ n : carillon m

chimney ['ʧɪmni] n, pl **-neys** : cheminée f

chimpanzee [ˌʧɪmˌpæn'zi:, ˌʃɪm-; ʧɪm'pænzi, ʃɪm-] n : chimpanzé m

chin ['ʧɪn] n : menton m

china ['ʧaɪnə] n : porcelaine f

Chinese ['ʧaɪ'ni:z, -ni:s] adj : chinois — ~ n : chinois m (langue)

chip ['ʧɪp] n 1 : éclat m (de verre), copeau m (de bois) 2 : jeton m (de poker, etc.) 3 NICK : ébréchure f 4 or **computer ~** : puce f — ~ v **chipped; chipping** vt : ébrécher (de la vaisselle, etc.), écailler (de la peinture) — vi **~ in** : contribuer

chipmunk ['ʧɪpˌmʌŋk] n : tamia m

chiropodist [kə'rɑpədɪst, ʃə-] n : pédicure mf

chiropractor ['kaɪrəˌpræktər] n : chiropracteur m

chirp ['ʧərp] vi : pépier

chisel ['ʧɪzəl] n : ciseau m — ~ vt **-eled** or **-elled; -eling** or **-elling** : ciseler

chitchat ['ʧɪtˌʧæt] n : bavardage m

chivalry ['ʃɪvəlri] n, pl **-ries** : chevalerie f

chive ['ʧaɪv] n : ciboulette f

chlorine ['klorˌi:n] n : chlore m

chock–full ['ʧɑk'fʊl, 'ʧʌk-] adj : bondé, plein à craquer

chocolate ['ʧɑkələt, 'ʧɔk-] n : chocolat m

choice ['ʧɔɪs] n : choix m — ~ adj **choicer; choicest** : de choix, de première qualité

choir ['kwaɪr] n : chœur m

choke ['ʧo:k] v **choked; choking** vt 1 : étrangler, étouffer 2 BLOCK : boucher — vi : s'étouffer (en mangeant) — ~ n : starter m (d'une voiture)

cholesterol [kə'lɛstəˌrɔl] n : cholestérol m

choose ['ʧu:z] v **chose** ['ʧo:z]; **chosen** ['ʧo:zən]; **choosing** vt 1 SELECT : choisir 2 DECIDE : décider — vi : choisir — **choosy** or **choosey** ['ʧu:zi] adj **choosier; -est** : exigeant

chop ['ʧɑp] vt **chopped; chopping** 1 : couper (du bois), hacher (des légumes, etc.) 2 **~ down** : abattre — ~ n : côtelette f (de porc, etc.) — **choppy** ['ʧɑpi] adj **-pier; -est** : agité (se dit de la mer)

chopsticks ['ʧɑpˌstɪks] npl : baguettes fpl

chord ['kɔrd] n : accord m (en musique)

chore ['ʧor] n 1 : corvée f 2 **household ~s** : travaux mpl ménagers

choreography [ˌkori'ɑgrəfi] n, pl **-phies** : chorégraphie f

chorus ['korəs] n 1 : chœur m (de chanteurs) 2 REFRAIN : refrain m

chose, chosen → **choose**

christen ['krɪsən] vt : baptiser — **christening** ['krɪsənɪŋ] n : baptême m

Christian ['krɪsʧən] adj : chrétien — ~ n : chrétien m, -tienne f — **Christianity** [ˌkrɪsʧi'ænəṭi, ˌkrɪs'ʧæ-] n : christianisme m

Christmas ['krɪsməs] n : Noël m

chrome ['kro:m] n : chrome m — **chromium** ['kro:miəm] n : chrome m

chronic ['krɑnɪk] adj : chronique

chronicle ['krɑnɪkəl] n : chronique f

chronology [krə'nɑləʤi] n, pl **-gies** : chronologie f — **chronological** [ˌkrɑnəl'ɑʤɪkəl] adj : chronologique

chrysanthemum [krɪ'sæntθəməm] n : chrysanthème m

chubby ['ʧʌbi] adj **-bier; -est** : potelé, dodu

chuck ['ʧʌk] vt : tirer, lancer

chuckle ['ʧʌkəl] vi **-led; -ling** : glousser, rire tout bas — ~ n : petit rire m

chum ['ʧʌm] n : copain m, -pine f; camarade mf

chunk ['ʧʌŋk] n : (gros) morceau m

church ['ʧərʧ] n : église f

churn ['ʧərn] vt 1 : battre (du beurre) 2 STIR : agiter, remuer 3 **~ out** : produire en série

cider ['saɪdər] n : cidre m

cigar [sɪ'gɑr] n : cigare m — **cigarette** [ˌsɪgə'rɛt, 'sɪgəˌrɛt] n : cigarette f

cinch ['sɪnʧ] n **it's a ~** : c'est du gateau

cinema ['sɪnəmə] n : cinéma m

cinnamon ['sɪnəmən] n : cannelle f

cipher ['saɪfər] n 1 ZERO : zéro m 2 CODE : chiffre m

circa ['sərkə] prep : environ, vers

circle ['sərkəl] n : cercle m — ~ vt **-cled; -cling** 1 : faire le tour de 2 SURROUND : entourer, encercler

circuit ['sərkət] n : circuit m — **circuitous** [ˌsər'kju:əṭəs] adj : détourné, indirect

circular ['sərkjələr] adj : circulaire — ~ n LEAFLET : circulaire f

circulate ['sərkjəˌleɪt] v **-lated; -lating** : circuler — **circulation** [ˌsərkjə'leɪʃən] n 1 FLOW : circulation f 2 : tirage m (d'un journal)

circumcise ['sərkəmˌsaɪz] vt **-cised; -cising** : circoncire — **circumcision** [ˌsərkəm'sɪʒən, 'sərkəmˌ-] n : circoncision f

circumference [sər'kʌmpfrənts] n : circonférence f

circumflex ['sərkəmˌflɛks] n : accent m circonflexe

circumspect ['sərkəmˌspɛkt] adj : circonspect, prudent

circumstance ['sərkəmˌstænts] n 1 : circonstance f 2 **under no ~s** : en aucun cas

circus ['sərkəs] n : cirque m

cistern ['sɪstərn] n TANK : citerne f

cite ['saɪt] vt **cited; citing** : citer — **citation** [saɪ'teɪʃən] n : citation f

citizen ['sɪṭəzən] n : citoyen m, -toyenne f — **citizenship** ['sɪṭəzənˌʃɪp] n : citoyenneté f

citrus ['sɪtrəs] n, pl **-rus** or **-ruses** or **~ fruit** : agrumes mpl

city ['sɪṭi] n, pl **-ties** : ville f — **city hall** n : hôtel m de ville

civic ['sɪvɪk] adj : civique — **civics** ['sɪvɪks] ns & pl : instruction f civique

civil ['sɪvəl] adj 1 : civil 2 **~ rights** : droits mpl civiques 3 **~ service** : fonction f publique — **civilian** [sə'vɪljən] n : civil m, -vile f — **civility** [sə'vɪləṭi] n, pl **-ties** : civilité f, courtoisie f — **civilization** [ˌsɪvələ'zeɪʃən] n : civilisation f — **civilize** ['sɪvəˌlaɪz] vt **-lized; -lizing** : civiliser

clad ['klæd] adj **~ in** : vêtu de, habillé de

claim ['kleɪm] vt 1 DEMAND : revendiquer, réclamer 2 MAINTAIN : prétendre — ~ n 1 : revendication f 2 ASSERTION : affirmation f

clam ['klæm] n : palourde f

clamber ['klæmbər] vi : grimper (avec difficulté)

clammy ['klæmi] adj **-mier; -est** : moite

clamor or Brit **clamour** ['klæmər] n : clameur f, cris mpl — ~ vi : vociférer

clamp ['klæmp] n : crampon m — ~ vt : attacher, fixer

clan ['klæn] n : clan m

clandestine [klæn'dɛstɪn] adj : clandestin, secret

clang ['klæŋ] n : bruit m métallique

clap ['klæp] v **clapped; clapping** : applaudir — ~ n : applaudissement m

clarify ['klærəˌfaɪ] vt **-fied; -fying** : clarifier, éclaircir — **clarification** [ˌklærəfə'keɪʃən] n : clarification f

clarinet [ˌklærə'nɛt] n : clarinette f

clarity ['klærəṭi] n : clarté f

clash ['klæʃ] vi : s'opposer, se heurter — ~ n : conflit m

clasp ['klæsp] n : fermoir m, boucle f — ~ vt 1 FASTEN : attacher 2 HOLD : serrer

class ['klæs] n 1 : classe f 2 COURSE : cours m — ~ vt : classer, classifier

classic ['klæsɪk] or **classical** ['klæsɪkəl] adj : classique — **classic** n : classique m

classify ['klæsəˌfaɪ] vt **-fied; -fying** : classer, classifier — **classification** [ˌklæsəfə'keɪʃən] n : classification f — **classified** ['klæsəˌfaɪd] adj 1 : confidentiel 2 **~ ads** : petites annonces fpl

classmate ['klæsˌmeɪt] n : compagnon m, compagne f de classe

classroom ['klæsˌru:m] n : salle f de classe

clatter ['klæṭər] vi : cliqueter — ~ n : bruit m, cliquetis m

clause ['klɔz] n : clause f

claustrophobia [ˌklɔstrə'fo:biə] n : claustrophobie f

claw ['klɔ] n : griffe f (d'un chat, etc.), pince f (d'un crustacé)

clay ['kleɪ] n : argile f

clean ['kli:n] adj 1 : propre 2 UNADULTERATED : pur — ~ vt : nettoyer, laver — **cleanliness** ['klɛnlinəs] n : propreté f — **cleanse** ['klɛnz] vt **cleansed; cleansing** : nettoyer, purifier

clear ['klɪr] adj 1 : clair 2 TRANSPARENT : transparent 3 OPEN : libre, dégagé — ~ vt 1 : débarrasser (un espace, etc.), dégager (une voie) 2 **~ a check** : encaisser un chèque 3 **~ up** RESOLVE : résoudre — vi 1 **~ up** BRIGHTEN : s'éclaircir (se dit du temps, etc.) 2 **~ up** VANISH : disparaître (se dit d'un symptôme, etc.) — ~ adv 1 **hear loud and ~** : entendre très clairement 2 **make oneself ~** : s'expliquer — **clearance** ['klɪrənts] n 1 SPACE : espace m libre 2 AUTHORIZATION : autorisation f 3 **~ sale** : liquidation f — **clearing** ['klɪrɪŋ] n : clairière f — **clearly** ['klɪrli] adv 1 DISTINCTLY : clairement 2 OBVIOUSLY : évidemment

cleaver ['kli:vər] n : couperet m

clef ['klɛf] n : clé f (en musique)

clement ['klɛmənt] adj : doux, clément — **clemency** ['klɛməntsi] n, pl **-cies** : clémence f

clench ['klɛnʧ] vt : serrer

clergy ['klərʤi] n, pl **-gies** : clergé m — **clergyman** ['klərʤimən] n, pl **-men** [-mən, -ˌmɛn] : ecclésiastique m — **clerical** ['klɛrɪkəl] adj 1 : clérical, du clergé 2 **~ work** : travail m de bureau

clerk ['klərk, Brit 'klɑrk] n 1 : employé m, -ployée f de bureau 2 SALESPERSON : vendeur m, -deuse f

clever ['klɛvər] adj 1 SKILLFUL : habile, adroit 2 SMART : astucieux — **cleverly** ['klɛvərli] adv 1 : habilement 2 : astucieusement — **cleverness** ['klɛvərnəs] n 1 SKILL : habileté f 2 INTELLIGENCE : intelligence f

cliché [kli'ʃeɪ] n : cliché m

click ['klɪk] vt : faire claquer — vi 1 : faire un déclic 2 : cliquer (en informatique) — ~ n : déclic m

client ['klaɪənt] n : client m, cliente f — **clientele** [ˌklaɪən'tɛl, ˌkli:-] n : clientèle f

cliff ['klɪf] n : falaise f

climate ['klaɪmət] n : climat m

climax ['klaɪˌmæks] n : point m culminant, apogée m

climb ['klaɪm] vt : monter, gravir — vi RISE : monter, augmenter — ~ n : montée f, ascension f

cling ['klɪŋ] vi **clung** ['klʌŋ]; **clinging ~ to** : s'accrocher à

clinic ['klɪnɪk] n : clinique f — **clinical** ['klɪnɪkəl] adj : clinique

clink ['klɪŋk] vi : cliqueter

clip ['klɪp] vt **clipped; clipping** 1 : couper, tailler 2 FASTEN : attacher (avec un trombone) — ~ n FASTENER : attache f, pince f — **clippers** ['klɪpərz] npl 1 or **nail ~** : coupe-ongles m 2 SHEARS : tondeuse f

cloak ['klo:k] vt : cape f

clock ['klɑk] n 1 : horloge f, pendule f 2 **around the ~** : d'affilée — **clockwise** ['klɑkˌwaɪz] adv & adj : dans le sens des aiguilles d'une montre

clog ['klɑg] n : sabot m — ~ v **clogged; clogging** vt : boucher, bloquer — vi or **~ up** : se boucher

cloister ['klɔɪstər] n : cloître m

close¹ ['klo:z] v **closed; closing** vt : fermer — vi 1 : fermer, se fermer 2 TERMINATE : prendre fin, se terminer 3 **~ in** : se rapprocher — ~ n : fin f, conclusion f

close² ['klo:s] adj **closer; closest** 1 NEAR : proche 2 INTIMATE : intime 3 STRICT : rigoureux, étroit 4 **a ~ game** : une partie serrée — ~ adv : près — **closely** ['klo:sli] adv : de près — **closeness** ['klo:snəs] n 1 : proximité f 2 INTIMACY : intimité f

closet ['klɑzət] n : placard m, garde-robe f

closure ['klo:ʒər] n : fermeture f, clôture f

clot ['klɑt] n : caillot m — ~ vi **clotted; clotting** : cailler, (se) coaguler

cloth ['klɔθ] n, pl **cloths** ['klɔðz, 'klɔθs] : tissu m

clothe ['klo:ð] vt **clothed** or **clad** ['klæd]; **clothing** : habiller, vêtir — **clothes** ['klo:z, 'klo:ðz] npl 1 : vêtements mpl 2 **put on one's ~** : s'habiller — **clothespin** ['klo:zˌpɪn] n : pince f (à linge) — **clothing** ['klo:ðɪŋ] n : vêtements mpl

cloud ['klaʊd] n : nuage m — ~ vi or **~ over** : se couvrir de nuages — **cloudy** ['klaʊdi] adj **cloudier; -est** : nuageux, couvert

clout ['klaʊt] n : influence m, poids m

clove ['klo:v] n 1 : clou m de girofle 2 or **garlic ~** : gousse f d'ail

clover ['klo:vər] n : trèfle m

clown ['klaʊn] n : clown m — ~ vi or **~ around** : faire le clown

cloying ['klɔɪɪŋ] adj : mièvre

club ['klʌb] n 1 : massue f, matraque f 2 ASSOCIATION : club m, groupe m 3 **~s** npl : trèfle m (aux cartes) — ~ vt **clubbed; clubbing** : matraquer

cluck ['klʌk] vi : glousser

clue ['klu:] n 1 : indice m 2 **I haven't got a ~** : je n'ai aucune idée

clump ['klʌmp] n : massif m (d'arbres), touffe f (d'herbe)

clumsy ['klʌmzi] adj **-sier; -est** : maladroit, gauche

cluster ['klʌstər] n : groupe m (de personnes), grappe f (de raisins, etc.) — vi : se rassembler, se grouper

clutch ['klʌʧ] vt : saisir, étreindre — vi **~ at** : s'agripper à — ~ n : embrayage m (d'une voiture)

clutter ['klʌṭər] vt : encombrer — ~ n : désordre m, fouillis m

coach ['ko:ʧ] n 1 CARRIAGE : carrosse m 2 : voiture f, wagon m (d'un train) 3 BUS : autocar m 4 : billet m d'avion de deuxième classe 5 TRAINER : entraîneur m, -neuse f — ~ vt 1 : entraîner (une équipe sportive) 2 TUTOR : donner des leçons à

coagulate [ko'ægjəˌleɪt] v **-lated; -lating** vt : coaguler — vi : se coaguler

coal ['ko:l] n : charbon m

coalition [ˌko:ə'lɪʃən] n : coalition f

coarse ['kors] adj **coarser; coarsest** 1 : gros (se dit du sable, du sel, etc.) 2 CRUDE : grossier, vulgaire — **coarseness** ['korsnəs] n 1 ROUGHNESS : rudesse f 2 CRUDENESS : grossièreté f

coast ['ko:st] n : côte f — **coastal** ['ko:stəl] adj : côtier, littoral

coaster ['ko:stər] n : dessous-de-verre m

coast guard n : gendarmerie f maritime France, garde f côtière Can

coastline ['ko:stˌlaɪn] n : littoral m

coat ['ko:t] n 1 : manteau m 2 : pelage m

(d'un animal) 3 : couche f (de peinture) — ~ vt ~ **with** : couvrir de, recouvrir de — **coat hanger** n : cintre m — **coating** ['ko:t̬ɪŋ] n : couche f, revêtement m — **coat of arms** n : blason m, armoiries fpl

coax ['ko:ks] vt : amadouer, cajoler

cob ['kɑb] → **corncob**

cobblestone ['kɑbəl,sto:n] n : pavé m

cobweb ['kɑb,wɛb] n : toile f d'araignée

cocaine [ko:'keɪn, 'ko:,keɪn] n : cocaïne f

cock ['kɑk] n ROOSTER : coq m — ~ vt 1 : armer (un fusil) 2 TILT : pencher (la tête, etc.) — **cockeyed** ['kɑk,aɪd] adj 1 ASKEW : de travers 2 ABSURD : insensé

cockpit ['kɑk,pɪt] n : poste m de pilotage

cockroach ['kɑk,ro:tʃ] n : cafard m

cocktail ['kɑk,teɪl] n : cocktail m

cocoa ['ko:,ko:] n : cacao m

coconut ['ko:kə,nʌt] n : noix f de coco

cocoon [kə'ku:n] n : cocon m

cod ['kɑd] ns & pl : morue f

coddle ['kɑdəl] vt **-dled; -dling** : dorloter

code ['ko:d] n : code m — ~ vt : coder

coeducational [,ko:,ɛʤə'keɪʃənəl] adj : mixte

coerce [ko'ərs] vt **-erced; -ercing** : contraindre — **coercion** [ko'ərʒən, -ʃən] n : contrainte f

coffee ['kɔfi] n : café m — **coffeepot** ['kɔfi,pɑt] n : cafetière f

coffer ['kɔfər] n : coffre m, caisse f

coffin ['kɔfən] n : cercueil m, bière f

cog ['kɑg] n : dent f (d'une roue)

cogent ['ko:ʤənt] adj : convaincant, persuasif

cognac ['ko:n,jæk] n : cognac m

cogwheel ['kɑg,hwi:l] n : pignon m

coherent [ko'hɪrənt] adj : cohérent

coil ['kɔɪl] vt : enrouler — vi : s'enrouler — ~ n 1 : rouleau m 2 : volute f (de fumée)

coin ['kɔɪn] n : pièce f de monnaie

coincide [,ko:ɪn'saɪd, 'ko:ɪn,saɪd] vi **-cided; -ciding** : coïncider — **coincidence** [ko'ɪntsədənts] n : coïncidence f

colander ['kɑləndər, 'kʌ-] n : passoire f

cold ['ko:ld] adj 1 : froid 2 **be ~** : avoir froid 3 **it's ~ today** : il fait froid aujourd'hui — ~ n 1 : froid m 2 : rhume m (en médecine) 3 **catch a ~** : s'enrhumer

coleslaw ['ko:l,slɔ] n : salade f de chou cru

colic ['kɑlɪk] n : coliques fpl

collaborate [kə'læbə,reɪt] vi **-rated; -rating** : collaborer, coopérer — **collaboration** [kə,læbə'reɪʃən] n : collaboration f

collapse [kə'læps] vi **-lapsed; -lapsing** : s'effondrer, s'écrouler — ~ n : effondrement m, écroulement m — **collapsible** [kə'læpsəbəl] adj : pliant

collar ['kɑlər] n : col m — **collarbone** ['kɑlər,bo:n] n : clavicule f

collateral [kə'læt̬ərəl] n : nantissement m

colleague ['kɑ,li:g] n : collègue mf

collect [kə'lɛkt] vt 1 GATHER : ramasser, recueillir 2 : percevoir (des impôts), encaisser (une somme d'argent) 3 : collectionner (des objets) — vi 1 ASSEMBLE : se rassembler, se réunir 2 ACCUMULATE : s'accumuler — ~ adv **call ~** : téléphoner en PCV *France*, téléphoner à frais virés *Can* — **collection** [kə'lɛkʃən] n 1 : collection f (de livres, etc.) 2 : quête f (à l'église) — **collective** [kə'lɛktɪv] adj : collectif

college ['kɑlɪʤ] n : établissement m d'enseignement supérieur

collide [kə'laɪd] vi **-lided; -liding** : se heurter, entrer en collision — **collision** [kə'lɪʒən] n : collision f

colloquial [kə'lo:kwiəl] adj : familier

cologne [kə'lo:n] n : eau f de Cologne

colon[1] ['ko:lən] n, pl **colons** or **cola** [-lə] : côlon m (en anatomie)

colon[2] n, pl **colons** : deux-points m

colonel ['kərnəl] n : colonel m

colony ['kɑləni] n, pl **-nies** : colonie f — **colonial** [kə'lo:niəl] adj : colonial — **colonize** ['kɑlə,naɪz] vt **-nized; -nizing** : coloniser

color or *Brit* **colour** ['kʌlər] n : couleur f — ~ vt : colorer — **color–blind** or *Brit* **colour–blind** ['kʌlər,blaɪnd] adj : daltonien — **colored** or *Brit* **coloured** ['kʌlərd] adj : coloré — **colorful** or *Brit* **colourful** ['kʌlərfəl] adj : coloré — **colorless** or *Brit* **colourless** ['kʌlərləs] adj : incolore

colossal [kə'lɑsəl] adj : colossal

colt ['ko:lt] n : poulain m

column ['kɑləm] n 1 : colonne f 2 : rubrique f (dans la presse) — **columnist** ['kɑləmnɪst, -ləmɪst] n : chroniqueur m, -queuse f

coma ['ko:mə] n : coma m

comb ['ko:m] n 1 : peigne m 2 : crête f (d'un coq) — ~ vt : (se) peigner

combat ['kɑm,bæt] n : combat m — ~ [kəm'bæt, 'kɑm,bæt] vt **-bated** or **-batted; -bating** or **-batting** : combattre — **combatant** [kəm'bætənt] n : combattant m, -tante f

combine [kəm'baɪn] vt **-bined; -bining** : combiner — ~ ['kɑm,baɪn] n HARVESTER : moissonneuse-batteuse f — **combination** [,kɑmbə'neɪʃən] n : combinaison f

combustion [kəm'bʌstʃən] n : combustion f

come ['kʌm] vi **came** ['keɪm]; **come; coming** 1 : venir 2 ARRIVE : arriver 3 **~ about** : se produire 4 **~ back** : revenir 5 **~ from** : provenir de 6 **~ in** : entrer 7 **~ out** : sortir 8 **~ to** REVIVE : revenir à soi 9 **~ on!** : allez! 10 **~ up** OCCUR : se présenter 11 **how ~?** : comment ça se fait? — **comeback** ['kʌm,bæk] n 1 RETURN : rentrée f 2 RETORT : réplique f

comedy ['kɑmədi] n, pl **-dies** : comédie f — **comedian** [kə'mi:diən] n : comique mf

comet ['kɑmət] n : comète f

comfort ['kʌmpfərt] vt : consoler, réconforter — ~ n 1 : confort m 2 SOLACE : consolation f, réconfort m — **comfortable** ['kʌmpfərt̬əbəl, 'kʌmpftə-] adj : confortable

comic ['kɑmɪk] or **comical** ['kɑmɪkəl] adj : comique — ~ n : comique mf — **comic strip** n : bande f dessinée

coming ['kʌmɪŋ] adj : à venir

comma ['kɑmə] n : virgule f

command [kə'mænd] vt 1 ORDER : ordonner, commander 2 **~ respect** : inspirer le respect — vi : donner des ordres — ~ n 1 ORDER : ordre m 2 MASTERY : maîtrise f — **commander** [kə'mændər] n : commandant m — **commandment** [kə'mændmənt] n : commandement m (en religion)

commemorate [kə'mɛmə,reɪt] vt **-rated; -rating** : commémorer — **commemoration** [kə,mɛmə'reɪʃən] n : commémoration f

commence [kə'mɛnts] v **-menced; -mencing** : commencer — **commencement** [kə'mɛntsmənt] n : remise f des diplômes

commend [kə'mɛnd] vt : louer — **commendable** [kə'mɛndəbəl] adj : louable

comment ['kɑ,mɛnt] n : commentaire m, remarque f — ~ vi : faire des commentaires — **commentary** ['kɑmən,tɛri] n, pl **-taries** : commentaire m — **commentator** ['kɑmən,teɪt̬ər] n : commentateur m, -trice f

commerce ['kɑmərs] n : commerce m — **commercial** [kə'mərʃəl] adj : commercial — ~ n : annonce f publicitaire — **commercialize** [kə'mərʃə,laɪz] vt **-ized; -izing** : commercialiser

commiserate [kə'mɪzə,reɪt] vi **-ated; -ating** : compatir

commission [kə'mɪʃən] n : commission f, comité m — ~ vt : commander (une œuvre d'art) — **commissioner** [kə'mɪʃənər] n : commissaire m

commit [kə'mɪt] vt **-mitted; -mitting** 1 ENGAGE : confier 2 : commettre (un crime, etc.) 3 **~ oneself** : s'engager — **commitment** [kə'mɪtmənt] n 1 PROMISE : engagement m 2 OBLIGATION : obligation f

committee [kə'mɪt̬i] n : comité m

commodity [kə'mɑdət̬i] n, pl **-ties** : marchandise f, denrée f

common ['kɑmən] adj 1 : commun 2 WIDESPREAD : universel — ~ n **in ~** : en commun — **commonly** ['kɑmənli] adv : communément — **commonplace** ['kɑmən,pleɪs] adj : commun, banal — **common sense** n : bon sens m

commotion [kə'mo:ʃən] n : vacarme m, brouhaha m

commune ['kɑ,mju:n, kə'mju:n] n : communauté f — **communal** [kə'mju:nəl] adj : communautaire

communicate [kə'mju:nə,keɪt] v **-cated; -cating** : communiquer — **communication** [kə,mju:nə'keɪʃən] n : communication f

communion [kə'mju:njən] n : communion f

Communism ['kɑmjə,nɪzəm] n : communisme m — **Communist** ['kɑmjə,nɪst] adj : communiste

community [kə'mju:nət̬i] n, pl **-ties** : communauté f

commute [kə'mju:t] vi **-muted; -muting** : faire la navette, faire un trajet journalier

compact [kəm'pækt, 'kɑm,pækt] adj : compact — ~ ['kɑm,pækt] n 1 or **~ car** : voiture f compacte 2 or **powder ~** : poudrier m — **compact disc** ['kɑm,pækt'dɪsk] n : disque m compact, compact m

companion [kəm'pænjən] n : compagnon m, compagne f — **companionship** [kəm'pænjən,ʃɪp] n : compagnie f

company ['kʌmpəni] n, pl **-nies** 1 : compagnie f, société f 2 : troupe f (de théâtre) 3 GUESTS : invités mpl

compare [kəm'pær] v **-pared; -paring** vt : comparer — vi **~ with** : être comparable à — **comparative** [kəm'pærət̬ɪv] adj : comparatif, relatif — **comparison** [kəm'pærəsən] n : comparaison f

compartment [kəm'pɑrtmənt] n : compartiment m

compass ['kʌmpəs, 'kɑm-] n 1 : boussole f 2 **points of the ~** : points mpl cardinaux

compassion [kəm'pæʃən] n : compassion f — **compassionate** [kəm'pæʃənət] adj : compatissant

compatible [kəm'pæt̬əbəl] adj : compatible — **compatibility** [kəm,pæt̬ə'bɪlət̬i] n : compatibilité f

compel [kəm'pɛl] vt **-pelled; -pelling** : contraindre, obliger — **compelling** [kəm'pɛlɪŋ] adj : irrésistible

compensate ['kɑmpən,seɪt] v **-sated; -sating** vi **~ for** : compenser — vt : indemniser — **compensation** [,kɑmpən'seɪʃən] n : compensation f

compete [kəm'pi:t] vi **-peted; -peting** : faire concurrence, rivaliser — **competent** ['kɑmpət̬ənt] adj : compétent — **competition** [,kɑmpə'tɪʃən] n 1 : concurrence f 2 CONTEST : compétition f — **competitor** [kəm'pɛt̬ət̬ər] n : concurrent m, -rente f

compile [kəm'paɪl] vt **-piled; -piling** : dresser (une liste, etc.)

complacency [kəm'pleɪsəntsi] n : satisfaction f de soi, suffisance f — **complacent** [kəm'pleɪsənt] adj : content de soi

complain [kəm'pleɪn] vi : se plaindre — **complaint** [kəm'pleɪnt] n : plainte f

complement ['kɑmpləmənt] n : complément m — ~ ['kɑmplə,mɛnt] vt : aller bien avec — **complementary** [,kɑmplə'mɛntəri] adj : complémentaire

complete [kəm'pli:t] adj **-pleter; -est** 1 WHOLE : complet, intégral 2 FINISHED : achevé 3 TOTAL : complet, absolu — ~ vt **-pleted; -pleting** 1 : compléter (un puzzle, etc.), remplir (un questionnaire) 2 FINISH : achever — **completely** [kəm'pli:tli] adv : complètement — **completion** [kəm'pli:ʃən] n : achèvement m

complex [kɑm'plɛks, kəm-; 'kɑm,plɛks] adj : complexe — ~ ['kɑm,plɛks] n : complexe m

complexion [kəm'plɛkʃən] n : teint m

complexity [kəm'plɛksət̬i, kɑm-] n, pl **-ties** : complexité f

compliance [kəm'plaɪənts] n 1 : conformité f 2 **in ~ with** : conformément à — **compliant** [kəm'plaɪənt] adj : soumis

complicate ['kɑmplə,keɪt] vt **-cated; -cating** : compliquer — **complicated** ['kɑmplə,keɪt̬əd] adj : compliqué — **complication** [,kɑmplə'keɪʃən] n : complication f

compliment ['kɑmpləmənt] n : compliment m — ~ ['kɑmplə,mɛnt] vt : complimenter — **complimentary** [,kɑmplə'mɛntəri] adj 1 FLATTERING : flatteur 2 FREE : gratuit

comply [kəm'plaɪ] vi **-plied; -plying ~ with** : se conformer à, respecter

component [kəm'po:nənt, 'kɑm,po:-] n : composant m, élément m

compose [kəm'po:z] vt **-posed; -posing** 1 : composer 2 **~ oneself** : retrouver son calme — **composer** [kəm'po:zər] n : compositeur m, -trice f — **composition** [,kɑmpə'zɪʃən] n : composition f — **composure** [kəm'po:ʒər] n : calme m, sang-froid m

compound[1] [kɑm'paʊnd, kəm-; 'kɑm,paʊnd] adj : composé — ~ ['kɑm,paʊnd] n : composé m (en chimie)

compound[2] ['kɑm,paʊnd] n ENCLOSURE : enceinte f, enclos m

comprehend [,kɑmprɪ'hɛnd] vt : comprendre — **comprehension** [,kɑmprɪ'hɛntʃən] n : compréhension f — **comprehensive** [,kɑmprɪ'hɛntsɪv] adj : complet, détaillé

compress [kəm'prɛs] vt : comprimer — **compression** [kəm'prɛʃən] n : compression f

comprise [kəm'praɪz] vt **-prised; -prising** : comprendre

compromise ['kɑmprə,maɪz] n : compromis m — ~ v **-mised; -mising** vi : faire un compromis — vt : compromettre

compulsion [kəm'pʌlʃən] n URGE : envie f — **compulsory** [kəm'pʌlsəri] adj : obligatoire

compute [kəm'pju:t] vt **-puted; -puting** : calculer — **computer** [kəm'pju:t̬ər] n 1 : ordinateur m 2 **~ science** : informatique f — **computerize** [kəm'pju:t̬ə,raɪz] vt **-ized; -izing** : informatiser

con ['kɑn] vt **conned; conning** : duper, escroquer — ~ n **the pros and ~s** : le pour et le contre

concave [kɑn'keɪv, 'kɑn,keɪv] adj : concave

conceal [kən'si:l] vt : dissimuler, cacher

concede [kən'si:d] vt **-ceded; -ceding** : accorder, concéder

conceit [kən'si:t] n : suffisance f, vanité f — **conceited** [kən'si:təd] adj : suffisant, vaniteux

conceive [kən'si:v] v **-ceived; -ceiving** vt : concevoir — vi **~ of** : concevoir

concentrate ['kɑntsən,treɪt] v **-trated; -trating** vt : concentrer — vi : se concentrer — **concentration** [,kɑntsən'treɪʃən] n : concentration f

concept ['kɑn,sɛpt] n : concept m — **conception** [kən'sɛpʃən] n : conception f

concern [kən'sərn] vt 1 : concerner 2 **~ oneself about** : s'inquiéter de — ~ n 1 BUSINESS : affaire f 2 WORRY : inquiétude f — **concerned** [kən'sərnd] adj 1 ANXIOUS : inquiet 2 **as far as I'm ~** : en ce qui me concerne — **concerning** [kən'sərnɪŋ] prep : concernant

concert ['kɑn,sərt] n : concert m — **concerted** [kən'sərt̬əd] adj : concerté

concession [kən'sɛʃən] n : concession f

concise [kən'saɪs] adj : concis

conclude [kən'klu:d] v **-cluded; -cluding** vt : conclure — vi : s'achever, se terminer — **conclusion** [kən'klu:ʒən] n : conclusion f — **conclusive** [kən'klu:sɪv] adj : concluant

concoct [kən'kɑkt, kɑn-] vt 1 PREPARE : confectionner 2 DEVISE : fabriquer — **concoction** [kən'kɑkʃən] n : mélange m

concrete [kɑn'kri:t, 'kɑn,kri:t] adj 1 : de béton 2 REAL : concret, réel — ~ ['kɑn,kri:t, kɑn'kri:t] n : béton m

concur [kən'kər] vi **-curred, -curring** : être d'accord

concussion [kən'kʌʃən] n : commotion f cérébrale

condemn [kən'dɛm] vt : condamner — **condemnation** [,kɑn,dɛm'neɪʃən] n : condamnation f

condense [kən'dɛnts] vt **-densed; -densing** : condenser — **condensation** [,kɑn,dɛn'seɪʃən, -dən-] n : condensation f

condescending [,kɑndɪ'sɛndɪŋ] adj : condescendant

condiment ['kɑndəmənt] n : condiment m

condition [kən'dɪʃən] n 1 : condition f 2 **in good ~** : en bon état — **conditional** [kən'dɪʃənəl] adj : conditionnel

condolences [kən'do:ləntsəz] npl : condoléances fpl

condom ['kɑndəm] n : préservatif m

condominium [,kɑndə'mɪniəm] n, pl **-ums** : immeuble m en copropriété

condone [kən'do:n] vt **-doned; -doning** : excuser

conducive [kən'du:sɪv, -'dju:-] adj : propice, favorable

conduct ['kɑn,dʌkt] n : comportement m, conduite f — ~ [kən'dʌkt] vt 1 : conduire, diriger 2 **~ oneself** : se comporter — **conductor** [kən'dʌktər] n 1 : conducteur m (d'électricité) 2 : chef m d'orchestre 3 : contrôleur m (de train, etc.)

cone ['ko:n] n 1 : cône m 2 or **ice-cream ~** : cornet m (de crème glacée)

confection [kən'fɛkʃən] n : confiserie f, bonbon m

confederation [kən,fɛdə'reɪʃən] n : confédération f

confer [kən'fər] v **-ferred; -ferring** vt : conférer — vi **~ with** : conférer avec, s'entretenir avec — **conference** ['kɑnfrənts, -fərənts] n : conférence f

confess [kən'fɛs] vt : confesser, avouer — vi **~ to** : admettre — **confession** [kən'fɛʃən] n : confession f

confetti [kən'fɛt̬i] n : confettis mpl

confide [kən'faɪd] v **-fided; -fiding** vt : confier — vi **~ in** : se confier à — **confidence** ['kɑnfədənts] n 1 TRUST : confiance f 2 SELF-ASSURANCE : confiance f en soi, assurance f 3 SECRET : confidence f — **confident** ['kɑnfədənt] adj 1 SURE : confiant, sûr 2 SELF-ASSURED : sûr de soi — **confidential** [,kɑnfə'dɛntʃəl] adj : confidentiel

confine [kən'faɪn] vt **-fined; -fining** 1 LIMIT : confiner, limiter 2 IMPRISON : enfermer — **confines** ['kɑn,faɪnz] npl : confins mpl, limites fpl

confirm [kən'fərm] vt : confirmer — **confirmation** [,kɑnfər'meɪʃən] n : confirmation f

confiscate ['kɑnfə,skeɪt] vt **-cated; -cating** : confisquer

conflict ['kɑn,flɪkt] n : conflit m — ~ [kən'flɪkt] vi : être en conflit, s'opposer

conform [kən'fɔrm] vi **~ with** : se conformer à, être conforme à — **conformity** [kən'fɔrmət̬i] n, pl **-ties** : conformité f

confound [kən'faʊnd, kɑn-] vt : confondre, déconcerter

confront [kən'frʌnt] vt : affronter, faire face à — **confrontation** [,kɑnfrən'teɪʃən] n : confrontation f

confuse [kən'fju:z] vt **-fused; -fusing** : troubler, déconcerter — **confusing** [kən'fju:zɪŋ] adj : déroutant — **confusion** [kən'fju:ʒən] n : confusion f

congenial [kən'ʤi:niəl] adj : sympathique

congested [kən'ʤɛstəd] adj 1 : congestionné (en médecine) 2 OBSTRUCTED : encombré — **congestion** [kən'ʤɛstʃən] n : congestion f

Congolese [,kɑŋgə'li:z, -'li:s] adj : congolais

congratulate [kən'grædʒə,leɪt, -'grætʃə-] vt **-lated; -lating** : féliciter — **congratulations** [kən,grædʒə'leɪʃənz, -,grætʃə-] npl : félicitations fpl

congregate ['kɑŋgrɪ,geɪt] vi **-gated; -gating** : se rassembler, se réunir — **congregation** [,kɑŋgrɪ'geɪʃən] n : assemblée f (de fidèles)

congress ['kɑŋgrəs] n : congrès m — **congressman** ['kɑŋgrəsmən] n, pl **-men** [-mən, -,mɛn] : membre m d'un congrès

conjecture [kən'ʤɛktʃər] n : conjecture f, supposition f — ~ vt **-tured; -turing** : conjecturer, présumer

conjugate ['kɑnʤə,geɪt] vt **-gated; -gat-**

ing : conjuguer — **conjugation** [ˌkɑndʒəˈgeɪʃən] *n* : conjugaison *f*
conjunction [kənˈdʒʌŋkʃən] *n* : conjonction *f* (en grammaire)
conjure [ˈkɑndʒər, ˈkʌn-] *vt* **-jured; -juring ~ up** : invoquer, évoquer
connect [kəˈnɛkt] *vi* : assurer la correspondance (avec un train, etc.) — *vt* **1** JOIN : relier **2** ASSOCIATE : associer **3** : brancher (en électricité) — **connection** [kəˈnɛkʃən] *n* **1** : lien *m*, rapport *m* **2** : correspondance *f* (de train, etc.) **3 ~s** *npl* : relations *fpl* (sociales)
connote [kəˈno:t] *vt* **-noted; -noting** : évoquer, indiquer
conquer [ˈkɑŋkər] *vt* : conquérir, vaincre — **conqueror** [ˈkɑŋkərər] *n* : conquérant *m*, -rante *f* — **conquest** [ˈkɑnˌkwɛst, ˈkɑŋ-] *n* : conquête *f*
conscience [ˈkɑntʃənts] *n* : conscience *f* — **conscientious** [ˌkɑntʃiˈɛntʃəs] *adj* : consciencieux
conscious [ˈkɑntʃəs] *adj* **1** AWARE : conscient **2** INTENTIONAL : délibéré — **consciously** [ˈkɑntʃəsli] *adv* : consciemment — **consciousness** [ˈkɑntʃəsnəs] *n* **1** AWARENESS : conscience *f* **2 lose ~** : perdre connaissance
consecrate [ˈkɑntsəˌkreɪt] *vt* **-crated; -crating** : consacrer
consecutive [kənˈsɛkjət̬ɪv] *adj* : consécutif
consensus [kənˈsɛntsəs] *n* : consensus *m*
consent [kənˈsɛnt] *vi* : consentir — **~** *n* : consentement *m*, accord *m*
consequence [ˈkɑntsəˌkwɛnts, -kwənts] *n* **1** : conséquence *f* **2 of no ~** : sans importance — **consequently** [ˈkɑntsəkwəntli, -ˌkwɛnt-] *adv* : par conséquent
conserve [kənˈsərv] *vt* **-served; -serving** : conserver, préserver — **conservation** [ˌkɑntsərˈveɪʃən] *n* : conservation *f* — **conservative** [kənˈsərvət̬ɪv] *adj* **1** : conservateur **2** CAUTIOUS : modéré, prudent — **~** *n* : conservateur *m*, -trice *f* — **conservatory** [kənˈsərvəˌtori] *n, pl* **-ries** : conservatoire *m*
consider [kənˈsɪdər] *vt* : considérer — **considerable** [kənˈsɪdərəbəl] *adj* : considérable — **considerate** [kənˈsɪdərət] *adj* : attentionné, prévenant — **consideration** [kənˌsɪdəˈreɪʃən] *n* : considération *f* — **considering** [kənˈsɪdərɪŋ] *prep* : étant donné, vu
consign [kənˈsaɪn] *vt* SEND : expédier, envoyer — **consignment** [kənˈsaɪnmənt] *n* : envoi *m*
consist [kənˈsɪst] *vi* **1 ~ in** : consister à **2 ~ of** : se composer de, consister en — **consistency** [kənˈsɪstəntsi] *n, pl* **-cies 1** TEXTURE : consistance *f* **2** COHERENCE : cohérence *f* — **consistent** [kənˈsɪstənt] *adj* **1** : constant, régulier **2 ~ with** : en accord avec
console [kənˈso:l] *vt* **-soled; -soling** : consoler, réconforter — **consolation** [ˌkɑntsəˈleɪʃən] *n* : consolation *f*
consolidate [kənˈsɑləˌdeɪt] *vt* **-dated; -dating** : consolider — **consolidation** [kənˌsɑləˈdeɪʃən] *n* : consolidation *f*
consonant [ˈkɑntsənənt] *n* : consonne *f*
conspicuous [kənˈspɪkjuəs] *adj* **1** OBVIOUS : évident, visible **2** STRIKING : voyant
conspire [kənˈspaɪr] *vi* **-spired; -spiring** : conspirer, comploter — **conspiracy** [kənˈspɪrəsi] *n, pl* **-cies** : conspiration *f*
constant [ˈkɑntstənt] *adj* : constant — **constantly** [ˈkɑntstəntli] *adv* : constamment
constellation [ˌkɑntstəˈleɪʃən] *n* : constellation *f*
constipated [ˈkɑntstəˌpeɪtəd] *adj* : constipé — **constipation** [ˌkɑntstəˈpeɪʃən] *n* : constipation *f*
constituent [kənˈstɪtʃuənt] *n* **1** COMPONENT : composant *m* **2** VOTER : électeur *m*, -trice *f*
constitute [ˈkɑntstəˌtu:t, -tju:t] *vt* **-tuted; -tuting** : constituer — **constitution** [ˌkɑntstəˈtu:ʃən, -ˈtju:-] *n* : constitution *f* — **constitutional** [ˌkɑntstəˈtu:ʃənəl, -ˈtju:-] *adj* : constitutionnel
constraint [kənˈstreɪnt] *n* : contrainte *f*
construct [kənˈstrʌkt] *vt* : construire, bâtir — **construction** [kənˈstrʌkʃən] *n* : construction *f* — **constructive** [kənˈstrʌktɪv] *adj* : constructif
construe [kənˈstru:] *vt* **-strued; -struing** : interpréter
consulate [ˈkɑntsələt] *n* : consulat *m*
consult [kənˈsʌlt] *vt* : consulter — **consultant** [kənˈsʌltənt] *n* : consultant *m*, -tante *f* — **consultation** [ˌkɑntsəlˈteɪʃən] *n* : consultation *f*
consume [kənˈsu:m] *vt* **-sumed; -suming** : consommer — **consumer** [kənˈsu:mər] *n* : consommateur *m*, -trice *f* — **consumption** [kənˈsʌmpʃən] *n* : consommation *f*
contact [ˈkɑnˌtækt] *n* **1** TOUCHING : contact *m* **2 be in ~ with** : être en rapport avec **3 business ~** : relation *f* de travail — **~** [ˈkɑnˌtækt, kənˈ-] *vt* : contacter — **contact lens** [ˈkɑnˌtæktˈlɛnz] *n* : lentille *f* (de contact), verre *m* de contact
contagious [kənˈteɪdʒəs] *adj* : contagieux
contain [kənˈteɪn] *vt* **1** : contenir **2 ~ oneself** : se contenir, se maîtriser — **container** [kənˈteɪnər] *n* : récipient *m*
contaminate [kənˈtæməˌneɪt] *vt* **-nated; -nating** : contaminer — **contamination** [kənˌtæməˈneɪʃən] *n* : contamination *f*
contemplate [ˈkɑntəmˌpleɪt] *v* **-plated; -plating** *vt* **1** : contempler **2** CONSIDER : envisager, considérer — *vi* : réfléchir — **contemplation** [ˌkɑntəmˈpleɪʃən] *n* : contemplation *f*, réflexion *f*
contemporary [kənˈtɛmpəˌrɛri] *adj* : contemporain — **~** *n, pl* **-raries** : contemporain *m*, -raine *f*
contempt [kənˈtɛmpt] *n* : mépris *m*, dédain *m* — **contemptible** [kənˈtɛmptəbəl] *adj* : méprisable — **contemptuous** [kənˈtɛmptʃuəs] *adj* : méprisant
contend [kənˈtɛnd] *vi* **1** COMPETE : rivaliser **2 ~ with** : faire face à — *vt* : soutenir, maintenir — **contender** [kənˈtɛndər] *n* : concurrent *m*, -rente *f*
content[1] [ˈkɑnˌtɛnt] *n* **1** : contenu *m* **2 table of ~s** : table *f* des matières
content[2] [kənˈtɛnt] *adj* : content — **~** *vt* **~ oneself with** : se contenter de, être satisfait de — **contented** [kənˈtɛntəd] *adj* : content, satisfait
contention [kənˈtɛntʃən] *n* **1** ARGUMENT : dispute *f*, discussion *f* **2** OPINION : affirmation *f*, assertion *f*
contentment [kənˈtɛntmənt] *n* : contentement *m*
contest [kənˈtɛst] *vt* : contester, disputer — **~** [ˈkɑnˌtɛst] *n* **1** STRUGGLE : lutte *f* **2** COMPETITION : concours *m*, compétition *f* — **contestant** [kənˈtɛstənt] *n* : concurrent *m*, -rente *f*
context [ˈkɑnˌtɛkst] *n* : contexte *m*
continent [ˈkɑntənənt] *n* : continent *m* — **continental** [ˌkɑntənˈɛntəl] *adj* : continental
contingency [kənˈtɪndʒəntsi] *n, pl* **-cies** : éventualité *f*
continue [kənˈtɪnju:] *v* **-ued; -uing** *vt* **1** KEEP UP : continuer (à) **2** RESUME : reprendre — *vi* : continuer — **continual** [kənˈtɪnjuəl] *adj* : continuel — **continuation** [kənˌtɪnjuˈeɪʃən] *n* : continuation *f* — **continuity** [ˌkɑntənˈu:ət̬i, -ˈju:-] *n, pl* **-ties** : continuité *f* — **continuous** [kənˈtɪnjuəs] *adj* : continu
contort [kənˈtɔrt] *vt* : tordre — **contortion** [kənˈtɔrʃən] *n* : contorsion *f*
contour [ˈkɑnˌtʊr] *n* : contour *m*
contraband [ˈkɑntrəˌbænd] *n* : contrebande *f*
contraception [ˌkɑntrəˈsɛpʃən] *n* : contraception *f* — **contraceptive** [ˌkɑntrəˈsɛptɪv] *adj* : contraceptif — **~** *n* : contraceptif *m*
contract [ˈkɑnˌtrækt] *n* : contrat *m* — **~** [kənˈtrækt] *vt* : contracter — *vi* : se contracter — **contraction** [kənˈtrækʃən] *n* : contraction *f* — **contractor** [ˈkɑnˌtræktər, kənˈtræk-] *n* : entrepreneur *m*, -neuse *f*
contradiction [ˌkɑntrəˈdɪkʃən] *n* : contradiction *f* — **contradict** [ˌkɑntrəˈdɪkt] *vt* : contredire — **contradictory** [ˌkɑntrəˈdɪktəri] *adj* : contradictoire
contraption [kənˈtræpʃən] *n* : truc *m fam*, machin *m fam*
contrary [ˈkɑnˌtrɛri] *n, pl* **-traries 1** : contraire *m* **2 on the ~** : au contraire — **~** *adj* **1** : contraire, opposé **2 ~ to** : contrairement à
contrast [kənˈtræst] *vi* : contraster — **~** [ˈkɑnˌtræst] *n* : contraste *m*
contribute [kənˈtrɪbjət] *v* **-uted; -uting** *vi* : contribuer — *vt* : apporter, donner — **contribution** [ˌkɑntrəˈbju:ʃən] *n* : contribution *f* — **contributor** [kənˈtrɪbjət̬ər] *n* : collaborateur *m*, -trice *f*
contrite [ˈkɑnˌtraɪt, kənˈtraɪt] *adj* : contrit
contrive [kənˈtraɪv] *vt* **-trived; -triving 1** DEVISE : inventer, imaginer **2 ~ to** : parvenir à, réussir à
control [kənˈtro:l] *vt* **-trolled; -trolling 1** RULE, RUN : diriger **2** REGULATE : contrôler, régler **3** RESTRAIN : maîtriser — **~** *n* **1** : contrôle *m*, régulation *f* **2** RESTRAINT : maîtrise *f* **3 remote ~** : commande *f* à distance
controversy [ˈkɑntrəˌvərsi] *n, pl* **-sies** : controverse *f* — **controversial** [ˌkɑntrəˈvərʃəl, -siəl] *adj* : controversé
convalescence [ˌkɑnvəˈlɛsənts] *n* : convalescence *f*
convene [kənˈvi:n] *v* **-vened; -vening** *vt* : convoquer — *vi* : se réunir
convenience [kənˈvi:njənts] *n* **1** : commodité *f*, confort *m* **2 at your ~** : quand cela vous conviendra — **convenient** [kənˈvi:njənt] *adj* : commode
convent [ˈkɑnvənt, -ˌvɛnt] *n* : couvent *m*
convention [kənˈvɛntʃən] *n* **1** : convention *f* **2** CUSTOM : usage *m* — **conventional** [kənˈvɛntʃənəl] *adj* : conventionnel
converge [kənˈvərdʒ] *vi* **-verged; -verging** : converger
converse[1] [kənˈvərs] *vi* **-versed; -versing ~ with** : s'entretenir avec — **conversation** [ˌkɑnvərˈseɪʃən] *n* : conversation *f*
converse[2] [kənˈvɛrs, ˈkɑnˌvɛrs] *n* : contraire *m*, inverse *m* — **conversely** [kənˈvərsli, ˈkɑnˌvərs-] *adv* : inversement
conversion [kənˈvərʒən] *n* : conversion *f* — **convert** [kənˈvərt] *vt* : convertir — **convertible** [kənˈvərt̬əbəl] *n* : décapotable *f*
convex [kɑnˈvɛks, ˈkɑnˌ-, kənˈ-] *adj* : convexe
convey [kənˈveɪ] *vt* **-veyed; -veying** : transmettre, exprimer
convict [kənˈvɪkt] *vt* : déclarer coupable — **~** [ˈkɑnˌvɪkt] *n* : détenu *m*, -nue *f* — **conviction** [kənˈvɪkʃən] *n* **1** : condamnation *f* **2** BELIEF : conviction *f*
convince [kənˈvɪnts] *vt* **-vinced; -vincing** : convaincre, persuader — **convincing** [kənˈvɪntsɪŋ] *adj* : convaincant
convoluted [ˈkɑnvəˌlu:t̬əd] *adj* : compliqué
convulsion [kənˈvʌlʃən] *n* : convulsion *f*
cook [ˈkʊk] *n* : cuisinier *m*, -nière *f* — **~** *vi* : cuisiner, faire la cuisine — *vt* : préparer (de la nourriture) — **cookbook** [ˈkʊkˌbʊk] *n* : livre *m* de recettes
cookie *or* **cooky** [ˈkʊki] *n, pl* **-ies** : biscuit *m*, gâteau *m* sec
cooking [ˈkʊkɪŋ] *n* : cuisine *f*
cool [ˈku:l] *adj* **1** : frais **2** CALM : calme **3** UNFRIENDLY : indifférent, froid — **~** *vt* : refroidir — *vi or* **~ down** : se refroidir — **~** *n* **1** : fraîcheur *m* **2 lose one's ~** : perdre son sang-froid — **cooler** [ˈku:lər] *n* : glacière *f* — **coolness** [ˈku:lnəs] *n* : fraîcheur *f*
coop [ˈku:p, ˈkʊp] *n or* **chicken ~** : poulailler *m* — **~** *vt or* **~ up** : enfermer
cooperate [koˈɑpəˌreɪt] *vi* **-ated; -ating** : coopérer — **cooperation** [koˌɑpəˈreɪʃən] *n* : coopération *f* — **cooperative** [koˈɑpərət̬ɪv, -ˈɑpəˌreɪt̬ɪv] *adj* : coopératif
coordinate [koˈɔrdənˌeɪt] *vt* **-nated; -nating** : coordonner — **coordination** [koˌɔrdənˈeɪʃən] *n* : coordination *f*
cop [ˈkɑp] *n* **1** : flic *m fam* **2 the ~s** : la police *fam*
cope [ˈko:p] *vi* **coped; coping 1** : se débrouiller **2 ~ with** : faire face à
copious [ˈko:piəs] *adj* : copieux
copper [ˈkɑpər] *n* : cuivre *m*
copy [ˈkɑpi] *n, pl* **copies 1** : copie *f*, reproduction *f* **2** : exemplaire *m* (d'un livre, etc.) — **~** *vt* **copied; copying 1** : faire une copie de **2** IMITATE : copier — **copyright** [ˈkɑpiˌraɪt] *n* : droits *mpl* d'auteur
coral [ˈkɔrəl] *n* : corail *m*
cord [ˈkɔrd] *n* : corde *f*, cordon *m*
cordial [ˈkɔrdʒəl] *adj* : cordial, amical
corduroy [ˈkɔrdəˌrɔɪ] *n* : velours *m* côtelé
core [ˈkor] *n* **1** : trognon *m* (d'un fruit) **2** CENTER : cœur *m*, centre *m*
cork [ˈkɔrk] *n* **1** : liège *m* **2** : bouchon *m* (d'une bouteille) — **corkscrew** [ˈkɔrkˌskru:] *n* : tire-bouchon *m*
corn [ˈkɔrn] *n* **1** : grain *m* (de blé, etc.) **2** *or* **Indian ~** : maïs *m* **3** : cor *m* (sur le pied) — **corncob** [ˈkɔrnˌkɑb] *n* : épi *m* de maïs
corner [ˈkɔrnər] *n* **1** : coin *m*, angle *m* **2 around the ~** : à deux pas d'ici — **cornerstone** [ˈkɔrnərˌsto:n] *n* : pierre *f* angulaire
cornmeal [ˈkɔrnˌmi:l] *n* : farine *f* de maïs — **cornstarch** [ˈkɔrnˌstɑrtʃ] *n* : fécule *f* de maïs
corny [ˈkɔrni] *adj* **cornier; -est** : banal, à l'eau de rose
coronary [ˈkɔrəˌnɛri] *n, pl* **-naries** : infarctus *m*
coronation [ˌkɔrəˈneɪʃən] *n* : couronnement *m*
corporal [ˈkɔrpərəl] *n* : caporal-chef *m*
corporation [ˌkɔrpəˈreɪʃən] *n* : compagnie *f* commerciale, société *f* — **corporate** [ˈkɔrpərət] *adj* : d'entreprise
corps [ˈkor] *n, pl* **corps** [ˈkorz] : corps *m*
corpse [ˈkɔrps] *n* : cadavre *m*
corpulent [ˈkɔrpjələnt] *adj* : corpulent, gras
corral [kəˈræl] *n* : corral *m*
correct [kəˈrɛkt] *vt* : corriger — **~** *adj* **1** : juste, correct **2 that's ~** : c'est exact — **correction** [kəˈrɛkʃən] *n* : correction *f*
correlation [ˌkɔrəˈleɪʃən] *n* : corrélation *f*
correspond [ˌkɔrəˈspɑnd] *vi* : correspondre — **correspondence** [ˌkɔrəˈspɑndənts] *n* : correspondance *f* — **correspondent** [ˌkɔrəˈspɑndənt] *n* **1** : correspondant *m*, -dante *f* **2** REPORTER : journaliste *mf*
corridor [ˈkɔrədər, -ˌdɔr] *n* : corridor *m*
corroborate [kəˈrɑbəˌreɪt] *vt* **-rated; -rating** : corroborer
corrode [kəˈro:d] *vt* **-roded; -roding** : corroder — **corrosion** [kəˈroːʒən] *n* : corrosion *f*
corrugated [ˈkɔrəˌgeɪt̬əd] *adj* : ondulé
corrupt [kəˈrʌpt] *vt* : corrompre — **~** *adj* : corrompu — **corruption** [kəˈrʌpʃən] *n* : corruption *f*
cosmetic [kɑzˈmɛt̬ɪk] *n* : cosmétique *f* — **~** *adj* : cosmétique
cosmic [ˈkɑzmɪk] *adj* : cosmique
cosmopolitan [ˌkɑzməˈpɑlət̬ən] *adj* : cosmopolite
cosmos [ˈkɑzməs, -ˌmo:s, -ˌmɑs] *n* : cosmos *m*, univers *m*
cost [ˈkɔst] *n* : coût *m*, prix *m* — **~** *vi* **cost; costing 1** : coûter **2 how much does it ~?** : combien ça coûte? — **costly** [ˈkɔstli] *adj* **-lier; -est** : coûteux, cher
costume [ˈkɑsˌtu:m, -ˌtju:m] *n* : costume *m*
cot [ˈkɑt] *n* : lit *m* de camp
cottage [ˈkɑt̬ɪdʒ] *n* : petite maison *f* — **cottage cheese** *n* : fromage *m* blanc
cotton [ˈkɑtən] *n* : coton *m*
couch [ˈkaʊtʃ] *n* : canapé *m*, sofa *m*
cough [ˈkɔf] *vi* : tousser — **~** *n* : toux *f*
could [ˈkʊd] → **can**[1]
council [ˈkaʊntsəl] *n* : conseil *m*, assemblée *f* — **councillor** *or* **councilor** [ˈkaʊntsələr] *n* : conseiller *m*, -lère *f*
counsel [ˈkaʊntsəl] *n* **1** ADVICE : conseil *m* **2** LAWYER : avocat *m*, -cate *f* — **~** *vt* **-seled** *or* **-selled; -seling** *or* **-selling** : conseiller, guider — **counselor** *or* **counsellor** [ˈkaʊntsələr] *n* **1** : conseiller *m*, -lère *f* **2** *or* **camp ~** : moniteur *m*, -trice *f*
count[1] [ˈkaʊnt] *vt* : compter, énumérer — *vi* **1** : compter **2 ~ on** : compter sur — **~** *n* : compte *m*, décompte *m*
count[2] *n* : comte *m* (noble)
counter[1] [ˈkaʊntər] *n* **1** : comptoir *m* **2** TOKEN : jeton *m*
counter[2] *vt* : s'opposer à, contrecarrer — *vi* : riposter — **~** *adv* **~ to** : à l'encontre de — **counteract** [ˌkaʊntərˈækt] *vt* : neutraliser — **counterattack** [ˈkaʊntərəˌtæk] *n* : contre-attaque *f* — **counterbalance** [ˌkaʊntərˈbælənts] *n* : contrepoids *m* — **counterclockwise** [ˌkaʊntərˈklɑkˌwaɪz] *adv & adj* : dans le sens contraire des aiguilles d'une montre — **counterfeit** [ˈkaʊntərˌfɪt] *vt* : contrefaire — **~** *adj* : faux — **counterpart** [ˈkaʊntərˌpɑrt] *n* : homologue *mf* (d'une personne), équivalent *m* (d'une chose)
countess [ˈkaʊntɪs] *n* : comtesse *f*
countless [ˈkaʊntləs] *adj* : innombrable, incalculable
country [ˈkʌntri] *n, pl* **-tries 1** NATION : pays *m*, patrie *f* **2** COUNTRYSIDE : campagne *f* — **~** *adj* : champêtre, rural — **countryside** [ˈkʌntriˌsaɪd] *n* : campagne *f*
county [ˈkaʊnti] *n, pl* **-ties** : comté *m*
coup [ˈku:] *n, pl* **coups** [ˈku:z] *or* **~ d'état** : coup *m* d'état
couple [ˈkʌpəl] *n* **1** : couple *m* **2 a ~ of** : deux ou trois — **~** *v* **-pled; -pling** *vt* : accoupler — *vi* : s'accoupler
coupon [ˈku:ˌpɑn, ˈkju:-] *n* : coupon *m*
courage [ˈkərɪdʒ] *n* : courage *m* — **courageous** [kəˈreɪdʒəs] *adj* : courageux
courier [ˈkʊriər, ˈkəriər] *n* : messager *m*, -gère *f*
course [ˈkors] *n* **1** : cours *m* **2** : service *m*, plat *m* (au restaurant) **3 ~ of action** : ligne *f* de conduite **4 golf ~** : terrain *m* de golf **5 in the ~ of** : au cours de **6 of ~** : bien sûr
court [ˈkort] *n* **1** : cour *f* (d'un souverain, etc.) **2** : court *m*, terrain *m* (de sports) **3** TRIBUNAL : cour *f*, tribunal *m* — **~** *vt* : courtiser, faire la cour à
courteous [ˈkərt̬iəs] *adj* : courtois, poli — **courtesy** [ˈkərt̬əsi] *n, pl* **-sies** : courtoisie *f*
courthouse [ˈkortˌhaʊs] *n* : palais *m* de justice — **courtroom** [ˈkortˌru:m] *n* : salle *f* de tribunal
courtship [ˈkortˌʃɪp] *n* : cour *f*
courtyard [ˈkortˌjɑrd] *n* : cour *f*, patio *m*
cousin [ˈkʌzən] *n* : cousin *m*, -sine *f*
cove [ˈko:v] *n* : anse *f*
covenant [ˈkʌvənənt] *n* : contrat *m*, convention *f*
cover [ˈkʌvər] *vt* **1** : couvrir, recouvrir **2** *or* **~ up** : cacher **3** DEAL WITH : traiter **4** : parcourir (une distance) **5** INSURE : assurer — **~** *n* **1** LID : couvercle *m* **2** SHELTER : abri *m*, refuge *m* **3** : couverture *f* (d'un livre) **4 ~s** *npl* BEDCLOTHES : couvertures *fpl* — **coverage** [ˈkʌvərɪdʒ] *n* : reportage *m*, couverture *f* — **covert** [ˈko:ˌvərt, ˈkʌvərt] *adj* : voilé, secret — **cover–up** [ˈkʌvərˌʌp] *n* : opération *f* de camouflage
covet [ˈkʌvət] *vt* : convoiter — **covetous** [ˈkʌvət̬əs] *adj* : avide, cupide
cow [ˈkaʊ] *n* : vache *f*
coward [ˈkaʊərd] *n* : lâche *mf;* poltron *m*, -tronne *f* — **cowardice** [ˈkaʊərdɪs] *n* : lâcheté *f* — **cowardly** [ˈkaʊərdli] *adj* : lâche
cowboy [ˈkaʊˌbɔɪ] *n* : cow-boy *m*
cower [ˈkaʊər] *vi* : se recroqueviller
coy [ˈkɔɪ] *adj* : faussement timide
coyote [kaɪˈo:t̬i, ˈkaɪˌo:t] *n, pl* **coyotes** *or* **coyote** : coyote *m*
cozy [ˈko:zi] *adj* **-zier; -est** : douillet, confortable
crab [ˈkræb] *n* : crabe *m*
crack [ˈkræk] *vt* **1** SPLIT : fêler, fendre **2** : casser (un œuf, etc.) **3** : faire claquer (un fouet) **4 ~ down on** : sévir contre — *vi* **1** SPLIT : se fêler, se fendre **2** BREAK : se casser, muer (se dit de la voix) — **~** *n* **1** : craquement *m*, bruit *m* sec **2** CREVICE : crevasse *f*, fissure *f*
cracker [ˈkrækər] *n* : biscuit *m* salé

crackle ['krækəl] *vi* -led; -ling : crépiter, pétiller — ~ *n* : crépitement *m*
cradle ['kreɪdəl] *n* : berceau *m* — ~ *vt* -dled; -dling : bercer (un enfant)
craft ['kræft] *n* 1 TRADE : métier *m*, art *m* 2 CUNNING : ruse *f* 3 *pl usu* craft BOAT : embarcation *f* — craftsman ['kræftsmən] *n, pl* -men [-mən, -ˌmɛn] : artisan *m*, -sane *f* — craftsmanship ['kræftsmənˌʃɪp] *n* : artisanat *m* — crafty ['kræfti] *adj* craftier; -est : astucieux, rusé
cram ['kræm] *v* crammed; cramming *vt* : fourrer, entasser — *vi* : étudier à la dernière minute
cramp ['kræmp] *n* : crampe *f*
cranberry ['krænˌbɛri] *n, pl* -ries : canneberge *f*
crane ['kreɪn] *n* : grue *f* — ~ *vt* craned; craning : tendre (le cou, etc.)
crank ['kræŋk] *n* 1 : manivelle *f* 2 ECCENTRIC : excentrique *mf* — cranky ['kræŋki] *adj* crankier; -est : irritable
crash ['kræʃ] *vi* 1 : se fracasser, s'écraser 2 : faire faillite (se dit d'une banque), s'effondrer (se dit du marché) — *vt* ~ one's car : avoir un accident de voiture — ~ *n* 1 : fracas *m*, bruit *m* sourd 2 COLLISION : accident *m*
crass ['kræs] *adj* : grossier
crate ['kreɪt] *n* : cageot *m*, caisse *f*
crater ['kreɪtər] *n* : cratère *m*
crave ['kreɪv] *vt* craved; craving : désirer, avoir très envie de — craving ['kreɪvɪŋ] *n* : envie *f* (incontrôlable), soif *f*
crawl ['krɔl] *vi* : ramper, marcher à quatre pattes — ~ *n* at a ~ : à un pas de tortue
crayon ['kreɪˌɑn, -ən] *n* : crayon *m* de cire
craze ['kreɪz] *n* : mode *f* passagère
crazy ['kreɪzi] *adj* -zier; -est 1 : fou 2 go ~ : devenir fou — craziness ['kreɪzinəs] *n* : folie *f*
creak ['kri:k] *vi* : grincer, craquer — ~ *n* : grincement *m*
cream ['kri:m] *n* : crème *f* — creamy ['kri:mi] *adj* creamier; -est : crémeux
crease ['kri:s] *n* : (faux) pli *m* — ~ *v* creased; creasing *vt* : froisser — *vi* : se froisser
create [kri'eɪt] *vt* -ated; -ating : créer — creation [kri'eɪʃən] *n* : création *f* — creative [kri'eɪtɪv] *adj* : créateur — creator [kri'eɪtər] *n* : créateur *m*, -trice *f*
creature ['kri:tʃər] *n* : créature *f*
credence ['kri:dənts] *n* give ~ to : accorder du crédit à
credentials [krɪ'dɛntʃəlz] *npl* : références *fpl*
credible ['krɛdəbəl] *adj* : crédible — credibility [ˌkrɛdə'bɪləti] *n* : crédibilité *f*
credit ['krɛdɪt] *n* 1 : crédit *m* 2 RECOGNITION : mérite *m* 3 to his ~ : à son honneur — ~ *vt* 1 : créditer (un compte de banque) 2 ~ with : attribuer à — credit card *n* : carte *f* de crédit — creditor ['krɛdɪtər] *n* : créancier *m*, -cière *f*
credulous ['krɛdʒələs] *adj* : crédule
creed ['kri:d] *n* : credo *m*
creek ['kri:k, 'krɪk] *n* : ruisseau *m*
creep ['kri:p] *vi* crept ['krɛpt]; creeping 1 CRAWL : ramper 2 : avancer sans un bruit — ~ *n* 1 ~s *npl* : frissons *mpl*, chair *f* de poule 2 move at a ~ : avancer au ralenti
cremate ['kri:ˌmeɪt] *vt* -mated; -mating : incinérer
crescent ['krɛsənt] *n* : croissant *m*
cress ['krɛs] *n* : cresson *m*
crest ['krɛst] *n* : crête *f*
crevice ['krɛvɪs] *n* : fissure *f*, fente *f*
crew ['kru:] *n* 1 : équipage *m* (d'un navire) 2 TEAM : équipe *f*
crib ['krɪb] *n* : lit *m* d'enfant
cricket ['krɪkət] *n* 1 : grillon *m* (insecte) 2 : cricket *m* (jeu)
crime ['kraɪm] *n* : crime *m*, délit *m* — criminal ['krɪmənəl] *adj* : criminel — ~ *n* : criminel *m*, -nelle *f*
cringe ['krɪndʒ] *vi* cringed; cringing : reculer (devant)
crinkle ['krɪŋkəl] *vt* -kled; -kling : froisser, chiffonner
cripple ['krɪpəl] *vt* -pled; -pling 1 DISABLE : estropier 2 INCAPACITATE : paralyser
crisis ['kraɪsɪs] *n, pl* -ses [-ˌsi:z] : crise *f*
crisp ['krɪsp] *adj* : croustillant, croquant — crispy ['krɪspi] *adj* crispier; -est : croustillant, croquant
crisscross ['krɪsˌkrɔs] *vt* : entrecroiser
criterion [kraɪ'tɪriən] *n, pl* -ria [-riə] : critère *m*
critic ['krɪtɪk] *n* : critique *mf* — critical ['krɪtɪkəl] *adj* : critique — criticism ['krɪtəˌsɪzəm] *n* : critique *f* — criticize ['krɪtəˌsaɪz] *vt* -cized; -cizing : critiquer
croak ['kro:k] *vi* : coasser
crockery ['krɑkəri] *n* : faïence *f*
crocodile ['krɑkəˌdaɪl] *n* : crocodile *m*
crony ['kro:ni] *n, pl* -nies : copain *m*, -pine *f*
crook ['krʊk] *n* 1 STAFF : houlette *f* (d'un berger) 2 THIEF : escroc *m* 3 BEND : courbe *f* — crooked ['krʊkəd] *adj* 1 BENT : crochu, courbé 2 DISHONEST : malhonnête
crop ['krɑp] *n* 1 HARVEST : récolte *f*, moisson *f* 2 PRODUCE : culture *f* — ~ *v* cropped; cropping *vt* TRIM : tailler — *vi* ~ up : surgir, se présenter
cross ['krɔs] *n* : croix *f* — ~ *vt* 1 : traverser (la rue, etc.) 2 CROSSBREED : croiser 3 OPPOSE : contrarier 4 : croiser (les bras, etc.) 5 ~ out : rayer — ~ *adj* 1 ANGRY : fâché, contrarié 2 ~ street : rue *f* transversale — crossbreed ['krɔsˌbri:d] *vt* -bred [-brɛd]; -breeding : croiser (deux espèces) — cross–eyed ['krɔsˌaɪd] *adj* : qui louche — cross fire *n* : feux *mpl* croisés — crossing ['krɔsɪŋ] *n* 1 : croisement *m* 2 → crosswalk — cross–reference [ˌkrɔs'rɛfrənts, -'rɛfərənts] *n* : renvoi *m* — crossroads ['krɔsˌro:dz] *n* : carrefour *m* — cross section *n* 1 : coupe *f* transversale 2 SAMPLE : échantillon *m* — crosswalk ['krɔsˌwɔk] *n* : passage *m* pour piétons — crossword puzzle ['krɔsˌwərd] *n* : mots *mpl* croisés
crotch ['krɑtʃ] *n* : entre-jambes *m*
crouch ['kraʊtʃ] *vi* : s'accroupir
crow ['kro:] *n* : corbeau *m* — ~ *vi* crowed *or Brit* crew; crowing : chanter (se dit du coq)
crowbar ['kro:ˌbɑr] *n* : (pince à) levier *m*
crowd ['kraʊd] *vi* : se presser, s'entasser — *vt* : serrer, entasser — ~ *n* : foule *f*
crown ['kraʊn] *n* : couronne *f* — ~ *vt* : couronner
crucial ['kru:ʃəl] *adj* : crucial
crucify ['kru:səˌfaɪ] *vt* -fied; -fying : crucifier — crucifix ['kru:səˌfɪks] *n* : crucifix *m* — crucifixion [ˌkru:sə'fɪkʃən] *n* : crucifixion *f*
crude ['kru:d] *adj* cruder; crudest 1 RAW : brut 2 VULGAR : grossier 3 ROUGH : rudimentaire
cruel ['kru:əl] *adj* -eler *or* -eller; -elest *or* -ellest : cruel — cruelty ['kru:əlti] *n, pl* -ties : cruauté *f*
cruet ['kru:ɪt] *n* : huilier *m*, vinaigrier *m*
cruise ['kru:z] *vi* cruised; cruising : rouler à sa vitesse de croisière — ~ *n* : croisière *f* — cruiser ['kru:zər] *n* 1 WARSHIP : croiseur *m* 2 *or* police ~ : véhicule *m* de police
crumb ['krʌm] *n* : miette *f*
crumble ['krʌmbəl] *v* -bled; -bling *vt* : émietter — *vi* : s'émietter, s'effriter
crumple ['krʌmpəl] *vt* -pled; -pling : froisser, chiffonner
crunch ['krʌntʃ] *vt* : croquer — crunchy ['krʌntʃi] *adj* crunchier; -est : croquant
crusade [kru:'seɪd] *n* : croisade *f*, campagne *f*
crush ['krʌʃ] *vt* : écraser, aplatir — ~ *n* have a ~ on s.o. : avoir le béguin pour qqn
crust ['krʌst] *n* : croûte *f*
crutch ['krʌtʃ] *n* : béquille *f*
crux ['krʌks, krʊks] *n* : point *m* crucial, cœur *m*
cry ['kraɪ] *vi* cried; crying 1 SHOUT : crier, pousser un cri 2 WEEP : pleurer — ~ *n, pl* cries : cri *m*
crypt ['krɪpt] *n* : crypte *f*
crystal ['krɪstəl] *n* : cristal *m*
cub ['kʌb] *n* : petit *m* (d'un animal)
cube ['kju:b] *n* : cube *m* — cubic ['kju:bɪk] *adj* : cube, cubique
cubicle ['kju:bɪkəl] *n* : box *m*
cuckoo ['ku:ˌku:, 'kʊ-] *n, pl* -oos : coucou *m* (oiseau)
cucumber ['kju:ˌkʌmbər] *n* : concombre *m*
cuddle ['kʌdəl] *v* -dled; -dling *vt* : caresser, câliner — *vi* : se câliner
cudgel ['kʌdʒəl] *n* : gourdin *m*, trique *f*
cue[1] ['kju:] *n* SIGNAL : signal *m*
cue[2] *n or* ~ stick : queue *f* de billard
cuff ['kʌf] *n* : poignet *m* (de chemise), revers *m* (de pantalon)
cuisine [kwɪ'zi:n] *n* : cuisine *f*
culinary ['kʌləˌnɛri, 'kju:lə-] *adj* : culinaire
cull ['kʌl] *vt* : choisir, sélectionner
culminate ['kʌlməˌneɪt] *vi* -nated; -nating : culminer — culmination [ˌkʌlmə'neɪʃən] *n* : point *m* culminant
culprit ['kʌlprɪt] *n* : coupable *mf*
cult ['kʌlt] *n* : culte *m*
cultivate ['kʌltəˌveɪt] *vt* -vated; -vating : cultiver — cultivation [ˌkʌltə'veɪʃən] *n* : culture *f* (de la terre)
culture ['kʌltʃər] *n* : culture *f* — cultural ['kʌltʃərəl] *adj* : culturel — cultured ['kʌltʃərd] *adj* : cultivé
cumbersome ['kʌmbərsəm] *adj* : encombrant
cumulative ['kju:mjələtɪv, -ˌleɪtɪv] *adj* : cumulatif
cunning ['kʌnɪŋ] *adj* : astucieux — ~ *n* : ruse *f*, astuce *f*
cup ['kʌp] *n* 1 : tasse *f* 2 TROPHY : coupe *f*
cupboard ['kʌbərd] *n* : placard *m*, armoire *f*
curator ['kjʊrˌeɪtər, kjʊ'reɪtər] *n* : conservateur *m*, -trice *f*
curb ['kərb] *n* 1 RESTRAINT : contrainte *f*, frein *m* 2 : bord *m* du trottoir — ~ *vt* : mettre un frein à
curdle ['kərdəl] *vi* -dled; -dling : (se) cailler
cure ['kjʊr] *n* : remède *m* — ~ *vt* cured; curing : guérir
curfew ['kərˌfju:] *n* : couvre-feu *m*
curious ['kjʊriəs] *adj* : curieux — curiosity [ˌkjʊri'ɑsəti] *n, pl* -ties : curiosité *f*
curl ['kərl] *vt* 1 : friser, boucler 2 COIL : enrouler — *vi* 1 : boucler (se dit des cheveux) 2 ~ up : se pelotonner — ~ *n* : boucle *f* (de cheveux) — curler ['kərlər] *n* : bigoudi *m* — curly ['kərli] *adj* curlier; -est : bouclé, frisé
currant ['kərənt] *n* 1 BERRY : groseille *f* 2 RAISIN : raisin *m* de Corinthe
currency ['kərəntsi] *n, pl* -cies 1 : monnaie *f*, devise *f* 2 gain ~ : se répandre
current ['kərənt] *adj* 1 PRESENT : en cours 2 PREVALENT : courant, commun — ~ *n* : courant *m*
curriculum [kə'rɪkjələm] *n, pl* -la [-lə] : programme *m* (scolaire)
curry ['kəri] *n, pl* -ries : curry *m*
curse ['kərs] *n* : malédiction *f* — ~ *v* cursed; cursing *vt* : maudire — *vi* SWEAR : sacrer, jurer
cursor ['kərsər] *n* : curseur *m*
cursory ['kərsəri] *adj* : superficiel, hâtif
curt ['kərt] *adj* : brusque
curtail [kər'teɪl] *vt* : écourter
curtain ['kərtən] *n* : rideau *m*
curtsy ['kərtsi] *vi* -sied; *or* -seyed; *or* -sying *or* -seying : faire la révérence — ~ *n* : révérence *f*
curve ['kərv] *v* curved; curving *vt* : courber — *vi* : se courber, faire une courbe — ~ *n* : courbe *f*
cushion ['kʊʃən] *n* : coussin *m* — ~ *vt* : amortir
custard ['kʌstərd] *n* : flan *m*
custody ['kʌstədi] *n, pl* -dies 1 CARE : garde *f* 2 be in ~ : être en détention
custom ['kʌstəm] *n* : coutume *f*, tradition *f* — ~ *adj* : fait sur commande — customary ['kʌstəˌmɛri] *adj* : habituel, coutumier — customer ['kʌstəmər] *n* : client *m*, cliente *f* — customs ['kʌst'mz] *npl* : douane *f*
cut ['kʌt] *v* cut; cutting *vt* 1 : couper 2 REDUCE : réduire 3 ~ oneself : se couper (le doigt, etc.) 4 *or* ~ up : découper — *vi* 1 : couper 2 ~ in : interrompre — ~ *n* 1 : coupure *f* 2 REDUCTION : réduction *f*
cute ['kju:t] *adj* cuter; cutest : mignon, joli
cutlery ['kʌtləri] *n* : couverts *mpl*
cutlet ['kʌtlət] *n* : escalope *f*
cutting ['kʌtɪŋ] *adj* 1 : cinglant (se dit du vent) 2 CURT : mordant, tranchant
cyanide ['saɪəˌnaɪd, -nɪd] *n* : cyanure *m*
cycle ['saɪkəl] *n* : cycle *m* — ~ *vi* -cled; -cling : faire de la bicyclette — cyclic ['saɪklɪk, 'sɪ-] *or* cyclical [-klɪkəl] *adj* : cyclique — cyclist ['saɪklɪst] *n* : cycliste *mf*
cyclone ['saɪˌklo:n] *n* : cyclone *m*
cylinder ['sɪləndər] *n* : cylindre *m* — cylindrical [sə'lɪndrɪkəl] *adj* : cylindrique
cymbal ['sɪmbəl] *n* : cymbale *f*
cynic ['sɪnɪk] *n* : cynique *mf* — cynical ['sɪnɪkəl] *adj* : cynique — cynicism ['sɪnəˌsɪzəm] *n* : cynisme *m*
cypress ['saɪprəs] *n* : cyprès *m*
cyst ['sɪst] *n* : kyste *m*
czar ['zɑr, 'sɑr] *n* : tsar *m*

D

d ['di:] *n, pl* d's *or* ds ['di:z] : d *m*, quatrième lettre de l'alphabet
dab ['dæb] *n* : touche *f*, petite quantité *f* — ~ *vt* dabbed; dabbing : appliquer délicatement
dabble ['dæbəl] *vi* -bled; -bling ~ in : s'intéresser superficiellement à
dad ['dæd] *n* : papa *m fam* — daddy ['dædi] *n, pl* -dies : papa *m fam*
daffodil ['dæfəˌdɪl] *n* : jonquille *f*
dagger ['dægər] *n* : poignard *m*
daily ['deɪli] *adj* : quotidien — ~ *adv* : quotidiennement
dainty ['deɪnti] *adj* -tier; -est : délicat
dairy ['dæri] *n, pl* dairies : laiterie *f*, crémerie *f France*
daisy ['deɪzi] *n, pl* -sies : marguerite *f*
dam ['dæm] *n* : barrage *m*
damage ['dæmɪdʒ] *n* 1 : dégâts *mpl* 2 ~s *npl* : dommages *mpl* et intérêts *mpl* — ~ *vt* -aged; -aging : endommager (des objets), abîmer (sa santé)
damn ['dæm] *vt* 1 CONDEMN : condamner 2 CURSE : maudire — ~ *n* not give a ~ : s'en ficher *fam* — ~ *or* damned ['dæmd] *adj* : fichu *fam*, sacré *fam*
damp ['dæmp] *adj* : humide, moite — dampen ['dæmpən] *vt* 1 MOISTEN : humecter 2 DISCOURAGE : décourager — dampness ['dæmpnəs] *n* : humidité *f*
dance ['dænts] *v* danced; dancing *vt* : danser — ~ *n* : danse *f* — dancer ['dæntsər] *n* : danseur *m*, -seuse *f*
dandelion ['dænd'lˌaɪən] *n* : pissenlit *m*
dandruff ['dændrəf] *n* : pellicules *fpl*
danger ['deɪndʒər] *n* : danger *m* — dangerous ['deɪndʒərəs] *adj* : dangereux
dangle ['dæŋgəl] *v* -gled; -gling *vi* HANG : pendre — *vt* : balancer, laisser pendre
dank ['dæŋk] *adj* : froid et humide
dare ['dær] *v* dared; daring *vt* : défier — *vi* : oser — ~ *n* : défi *m* — daring ['dærɪŋ] *adj* : audacieux, hardi
dark ['dɑrk] *adj* 1 : noir 2 : foncé (se dit des cheveux, etc.) 3 GLOOMY : sombre 4 get ~ : faire nuit — darken ['dɑrkən] *vt* : obscurcir — *vi* : s'obscurcir — darkness ['dɑrknəs] *n* : obscurité *f*, noirceur *f Can*
darling ['dɑrlɪŋ] *n* BELOVED : chéri *m*, -rie *f* — ~ *adj* : chéri
darn ['dɑrn] *vt* : repriser (en couture) — ~ *adj* : sacré
dart ['dɑrt] *n* 1 : fléchette *f*, dard *m Can* 2 ~s *npl* : fléchettes *fpl* (jeu) — ~ *vi* : se précipiter, s'élancer
dash ['dæʃ] *vt* ~ off : terminer à la hâte — *vi* : se précipiter — ~ *n* 1 : tiret *m* (signe de ponctuation) 2 PINCH : pincée *f*, soupçon *m* 3 RUSH : course *f* folle — dashboard ['dæʃˌbord] *n* : tableau *m* de bord — dashing ['dæʃɪŋ] *adj* : fringant, élégant
data ['deɪtə, 'dæ-, 'dɑ-] *ns & pl* : données *fpl* — database ['deɪtəˌbeɪs, 'dæ-, 'dɑ-] *n* : base *f* de données
date[1] ['deɪt] *n* : datte *f* (fruit)
date[2] *n* 1 : date *f* 2 APPOINTMENT : rendez-vous *m* — ~ *v* dated; dating *vt* 1 : dater (un chèque, etc.) 2 : sortir avec (qqn) — *vi* ~ from : dater de, remonter à — dated ['deɪtəd] *adj* : démodé
daughter ['dɔtər] *n* : fille *f* — daughter–in–law ['dɔtərɪnˌlɔ] *n, pl* daughters–in–law : belle-fille *f*, bru *f*
daunt ['dɔnt] *vt* : décourager
dawdle ['dɔdəl] *vi* -dled; -dling : lambiner *fam*, traîner
dawn ['dɔn] *vi* 1 : se lever (se dit du jour) 2 it ~ed on him that : il s'est rendu compte que — ~ *n* : aube *f*
day ['deɪ] *n* 1 : jour *m* 2 *or* working ~ : journée *f* (de travail) 3 the ~ before : la veille 4 the ~ before yesterday : avant-hier 5 the ~ after : le lendemain 6 the ~ after tomorrow : après-demain — daybreak ['deɪˌbreɪk] *n* : aube *f* — daydream ['deɪˌdri:m] *n* : rêve *m*, rêverie *f* — ~ *vi* : rêver — daylight ['deɪˌlaɪt] *n* : lumière *f* du jour — daytime ['deɪˌtaɪm] *n* : jour *m*, journée *f*
daze ['deɪz] *vt* dazed; dazing : abasourdir — ~ *n* in a ~ : hébété
dazzle ['dæzəl] *vt* -zled; -zling : éblouir
dead ['dɛd] *adj* : mort — ~ *n* the ~ : les morts — ~ *adv* COMPLETELY : complètement — deaden ['dɛdən] *vt* 1 : calmer (une douleur) 2 MUFFLE : assourdir — dead end ['dɛd'ɛnd] *n* : cul-de-sac *m*, impasse *f* — deadline ['dɛdˌlaɪn] *n* : date *f* limite — deadly ['dɛdli] *adj* -lier; -est : mortel — dealings ['di:lɪŋz] *npl* : transactions *fpl*, affaires *fpl*
deaf ['dɛf] *adj* : sourd — deafen ['dɛfən] *vt* : assourdir — deafness ['dɛfnəs] *n* : surdité *f*
deal ['di:l] *n* 1 TRANSACTION : affaire *f*, marché *m* 2 : donne *f* (aux cartes) — ~ *v* dealt; dealing *vt* 1 : donner 2 : distribuer (des cartes) 3 ~ a blow : assener un coup — *vi* ~ with CONCERN : traiter de — dealer ['di:lər] *n* : marchand *m*, -chande *f*; négociant *m*, -ciante *f*
dean ['di:n] *n* : doyen *m*, doyenne *f*
dear ['dɪr] *adj* : cher — ~ *n* : chéri *m*, -rie *f* — dearly ['dɪrli] *adv* : beaucoup
death ['dɛθ] *n* : mort *f*
debate [di'beɪt] *n* : débat *m*, discussion *f* — ~ *v* -bated; -bating : discuter
debit ['dɛbɪt] *vt* : débiter — ~ *n* : débit *m*
debris [də'bri:, deɪ-; 'deɪˌbri:] *n, pl* -bris [-'bri:z, -ˌbri:z] : décombres *mpl*
debt ['dɛt] *n* : dette *f*
debug [ˌdi:'bʌg] *vt* : déboguer
debut [deɪ'bju:, 'deɪˌbju:] *n* : débuts *mpl* — ~ *vi* : débuter
decade ['dɛˌkeɪd, dɛ'keɪd] *n* : décennie *f*
decadence ['dɛkədənts] *n* : décadence *f* — decadent ['dɛkədənt] *adj* : décadent
decanter [di'kæntər] *n* : carafe *f*
decay [di'keɪ] *vi* 1 DECOMPOSE : se décomposer, pourrir 2 : se carier (se dit d'une dent) — ~ *n* 1 : pourriture *f* 2 *or* tooth ~ : carie *f* (dentaire)
deceased [di'si:st] *adj* : décédé, défunt — ~ *n* the ~ : le défunt, la défunte
deceive [di'si:v] *vt* -ceived; -ceiving : tromper *m* deceit [di'si:t] *n* : tromperie *f* — deceitful [di'si:tfəl] *adj* : trompeur
December [di'sɛmbər] *n* : décembre *m*
decent ['di:sənt] *adj* 1 : décent, convenable 2 KIND : bien, aimable — decency ['di:səntsi] *n, pl* -cies : décence *f*
deception [di'sɛpʃən] *n* : tromperie *f* — deceptive [di'sɛptɪv] *adj* : trompeur
decide [di'saɪd] *v* -cided; -ciding *vt* : décider — *vi* : se décider — decided [di'saɪdəd] *adj* RESOLUTE : décidé
decimal ['dɛsəməl] *adj* : décimal — ~ *n* : décimale *f* — decimal point *n* : virgule *f*
decipher [di'saɪfər] *vt* : déchiffrer

decision [dɪˈsɪʒən] *n* : décision *f* — **decisive** [dɪˈsaɪsɪv] *adj* **1** RESOLUTE : décidé **2** CONCLUSIVE : décisif

deck [ˈdɛk] *n* **1** : pont *m* (d'un navire) **2** *or* **~ of cards** : jeu *m* de cartes

declare [diˈklær] *vt* **-clared; -claring** : déclarer — **declaration** [ˌdɛkləˈreɪʃən] *n* : déclaration *f*

decline [diˈklaɪn] *v* **-clined; -clining** : décliner — **~** *n* **1** DETERIORATION : déclin *m* **2** DECREASE : baisse *f*

decompose [ˌdi:kəmˈpo:z] *vt* **-posed; -posing** : décomposer — *vi* : se décomposer

decongestant [ˌdi:kənˈʤɛstənt] *n* : décongestif *m*

decorate [ˈdɛkəˌreɪt] *vt* **-rated; -rating** : décorer — **decor** *or* **décor** [deɪˈkɔr, ˈdeɪˌkɔr] *n* : décor *m* — **decoration** [ˌdɛkəˈreɪʃən] *n* : décoration *f* — **decorative** [ˈdɛkərət̬ɪv, -ˌreɪ-] *adj* : décoratif — **decorator** [ˈdɛkəˌreɪt̬ər] *n* : décorateur *m*, -trice *f*

decoy [ˈdiˌkɔɪ, diˈ-] *n* : appeau *m*

decrease [diˈkri:s] *v* **-creased; -creasing** : diminuer — **~** [ˈdi:ˌkri:s] *n* : diminution *f*

decree [diˈkri:] *n* : décret *m* — **~** *vt* **-creed; -creeing** : décréter

decrepit [diˈkrɛpɪt] *adj* **1** FEEBLE : décrépit **2** DILAPIDATED : délabré

dedicate [ˈdɛdɪˌkeɪt] *vt* **-cated; -cating 1** : dédier **2 ~ oneself to** : se consacrer à — **dedication** [dɛdɪˈkeɪʃən] *n* **1** DEVOTION : dévouement *m* **2** INSCRIPTION : dédicace *f*

deduce [diˈdu:s, -ˈdju:s] *vt* **-duced; -ducing** : déduire — **deduct** [diˈdʌkt] *vt* : déduire — **deduction** [diˈdʌkʃən] *n* : déduction *f*

deed [ˈdi:d] *n* : action *f*, acte *m*

deem [ˈdi:m] *vt* : juger, considérer

deep [ˈdi:p] *adj* : profond — **~** *adv* **1** DEEPLY : profondément **2 ~ down** : au fond — **deepen** [ˈdi:pən] *vt* : approfondir — *vi* : devenir plus profond — **deeply** [ˈdi:pli] *adv* : profondément

deer [ˈdɪr] *ns & pl* : cerf *m*

default [diˈfɔlt, ˈdi:ˌfɔlt] *n* **by ~** : par défaut — **~** *vi* **1** : ne pas s'acquitter (d'une dette) **2** : déclarer forfait (aux sports)

defeat [diˈfi:t] *vt* : battre, vaincre — **~** *n* : défaite *f*

defect [ˈdi:ˌfɛkt, diˈfɛkt] *n* : défaut *m* — **defective** [diˈfɛktɪv] *adj* : défectueux

defence *Brit* → **defense**

defend [diˈfɛnd] *vt* : défendre — **defendant** [diˈfɛndənt] *n* : défendeur *m*, -deresse *f*; accusé *m*, -sée *f* — **defense** *or Brit* **defence** [diˈfɛnts, ˈdi:ˌfɛnts] *n* : défense *f* — **defensive** [diˈfɛntsɪv] *adj* : défensif — **~** *n* **on the ~** : sur la défensive

defer [diˈfər] *v* **-ferred; -ferring** *vt* : différer — *vi* **~ to** : s'en remettre à

defiance [diˈfaɪənts] *n* **1** : défi *m* **2 in ~ of** : au mépris de — **defiant** [diˈfaɪənt] *adj* : de défi

deficient [diˈfɪʃənt] *adj* **1** INADEQUATE : insuffisant **2** FAULTY : défectueux — **deficiency** [diˈfɪʃəntsi] *n, pl* **-cies 1** LACK : carence *f* **2** FLAW : défaut *m*

deficit [ˈdɛfəsɪt] *n* : déficit *m*

defile [diˈfaɪl] *vt* **-filed; -filing** DESECRATE : profaner

define [diˈfaɪn] *vt* **-fined; -fining** : définir — **definite** [ˈdɛfənɪt] *adj* **1** : défini, précis **2** CERTAIN : certain, sûr — **definitely** [ˈdɛfənɪtli] *adv* : certainement — **definition** [ˌdɛfəˈnɪʃən] *n* : définition *f* — **definitive** [dəˈfɪnət̬ɪv] *adj* : définitif

deflate [diˈfleɪt] *v* **-flated; -flating** *vt* : dégonfler (un pneu, etc.) — *vi* : se dégonfler

deflect [diˈflɛkt] *vt* : faire dévier — *vi* : dévier

deform [diˈfɔrm] *vt* : déformer — **deformity** [diˈfɔrmət̬i] *n, pl* **-ties** : difformité *f*

defraud [diˈfrɔd] *vt* : frauder, escroquer

defrost [diˈfrɔst] *vt* THAW : décongeler

defy [diˈfaɪ] *vt* **-fied; -fying 1** CHALLENGE : défier **2** RESIST : résister à

degenerate [diˈʤɛnəˌreɪt] *vi* **-ated; -ating** : dégénérer

degrade [diˈgreɪd] *vt* **-graded; -grading** : dégrader — **degrading** *adj* : dégradant

degree [diˈgri:] *n* **1** : degré *m* **2** *or* **academic ~** : diplôme *m*

dehydrate [diˈhaɪˌdreɪt] *vt* **-drated; -drating** : déshydrater

deign [ˈdeɪn] *vi* **~ to** : daigner

deity [ˈdi:ət̬i, ˈdeɪ-] *n, pl* **-ties** : dieu *m*, déesse *f*

dejected [diˈʤɛktəd] *adj* : abattu — **dejection** [diˈʤɛkʃən] *n* : abattement *m*

delay [diˈleɪ] *n* : retard *m*, délai *m* — **~** *vt* **1** POSTPONE : différer **2** HOLD UP : retarder

delectable [diˈlɛktəbəl] *adj* : délicieux

delegate [ˈdɛlɪgət, -ˌgeɪt] *n* : délégué *m*, -guée *f* — **~** [ˈdɛlɪˌgeɪt] *v* **-gated; -gating** : déléguer — **delegation** [ˌdɛlɪˈgeɪʃən] *n* : délégation *f*

delete [diˈli:t] *vt* **-leted; -leting** : supprimer, effacer

deliberate [dɪˈlɪbəˌreɪt] *v* **-ated; -ating** *vt* : délibérer sur — *vi* : délibérer — **~** [dɪˈlɪbərət] *adj* : délibéré — **deliberately** [dɪˈlɪbərətli] *adv* : exprès

delicacy [ˈdɛlɪkəsi] *n, pl* **-cies 1** : délicatesse *f* **2** FOOD : mets *m* fin — **delicate** [ˈdɛlɪkət] *adj* : délicat

delicatessen [ˌdɛlɪkəˈtɛsən] *n* : charcuterie *f*

delicious [diˈlɪʃəs] *adj* : délicieux

delight [diˈlaɪt] *n* : plaisir *m*, joie *f* — **~** *vt* : réjouir — *vi* **~ in** : prendre plaisir à — **delightful** [diˈlaɪtfəl] *adj* : charmant, ravissant

delinquent [diˈlɪŋkwənt] *adj* : délinquant — **~** *n* : délinquant *m*, -quante *f*

delirious [diˈlɪriəs] *adj* : délirant, en délire — **delirium** [diˈlɪriəm] *n* : délire *m*

deliver [diˈlɪvər] *vt* **1** DISTRIBUTE : livrer **2** FREE : libérer **3** : mettre au monde (un enfant) **4** : prononcer (un discours, etc.) **5** DEAL : asséner (un coup, etc.) — **delivery** [diˈlɪvəri] *n, pl* **-eries 1** DISTRIBUTION : livraison *f*, distribution *f* **2** LIBERATION : délivrance *f* **3** CHILDBIRTH : accouchement *m*

delude [diˈlu:d] *vt* **-luded; -luding 1** : tromper **2 ~ oneself** : se faire des illusions

deluge [ˈdɛlˌju:ʤ, -ju:ʒ] *n* : déluge *m*

delusion [diˈlu:ʒən] *n* : illusion *f*

deluxe [diˈlʌks, -ˈlʊks] *adj* : de luxe

delve [ˈdɛlv] *vi* **delved; delving 1** : creuser **2 ~ into** PROBE : fouiller dans

demand [diˈmænd] *n* **1** REQUEST : demande *f* **2** CLAIM : réclamation *f* **3** → **supply** — **~** *vt* : exiger — **demanding** [diˈmændɪŋ] *adj* : exigeant

demean [diˈmi:n] *vt* **~ oneself** : s'abaisser

demeanor *or Brit* **demeanour** [diˈmi:nər] *n* : comportement *m*

demented [diˈmɛntəd] *adj* : dément, fou

democracy [diˈmɑkrəsi] *n, pl* **-cies** : démocratie *f* — **democrat** [ˈdɛməˌkræt] *n* : démocrate *mf* — **democratic** [ˌdɛməˈkrætɪk] *adj* : démocratique

demolish [diˈmɑlɪʃ] *vt* : démolir — **demolition** [ˌdɛməˈlɪʃən, ˌdi:-] *n* : démolition *f*

demon [ˈdi:mən] *n* : démon *m*

demonstrate [ˈdɛmənˌstreɪt] *v* **-strated; -strating** *vt* : démontrer — *vi* RALLY : manifester — **demonstration** [dɛmənˈstreɪʃən] *n* **1** : démonstration *f* **2** RALLY : manifestation *f* — **demonstrative** [diˈmɑntstrət̬ɪv] *adj* : démonstratif — **demonstrator** [ˈdɛmənˌstreɪt̬ər] *n* PROTESTOR : manifestant *m*, -tante *f*

demoralize [diˈmɔrəˌlaɪz] *vt* **-ized; -izing** : démoraliser

demote [diˈmo:t] *vt* **-moted; -moting** : rétrograder

demure [diˈmjʊr] *adj* : modeste, réservé

den [ˈdɛn] *n* LAIR : antre *m*, tanière *f*

denial [diˈnaɪəl] *n* **1** : démenti *m*, dénégation *f* **2** REFUSAL : refus *m*

denim [ˈdɛnəm] *n* : jean *m*

denomination [dɪˌnɑməˈneɪʃən] *n* **1** : confession *f* (religieuse) **2** : valeur *f* (monétaire)

denote [diˈno:t] *vt* **-noted; -noting** : dénoter

denounce [diˈnaʊnts] *vt* **-nounced; -nouncing** : dénoncer

dense [ˈdɛnts] *adj* **denser; -est 1** THICK : dense **2** STUPID : bête, obtus — **density** [ˈdɛntsət̬i] *n, pl* **-ties** : densité *f*

dent [ˈdɛnt] *vt* : cabosser — **~** *n* : bosse *f*

dental [ˈdɛntəl] *adj* : dentaire — **dental floss** *n* : fil *m* dentaire — **dentist** [ˈdɛntɪst] *n* : dentiste *mf* — **dentures** [ˈdɛntʃərz] *npl* : dentier *m*

denunciation [diˌnʌntsiˈeɪʃən] *n* : dénonciation *f*

deny [diˈnaɪ] *vt* **-nied; -nying 1** : nier **2** REFUSE : refuser

deodorant [diˈo:dərənt] *n* : déodorant *m*

depart [diˈpɑrt] *vi* **1** : partir **2 ~ from** : s'écarter de

department [diˈpɑrtmənt] *n* : ministère *m* (gouvernemental), service *m* (d'un hôpital, etc.), rayon *m* (d'un magasin) — **department store** *n* : grand magasin *m*

departure [diˈpɑrtʃər] *n* **1** : départ *m* **2** DEVIATION : écart *m*

depend [diˈpɛnd] *vi* **1 ~ on** : dépendre de, compter sur **2 ~ on s.o.** : compter sur qqn **3 that ~s** : tout dépend — **dependable** [diˈpɛndəbəl] *adj* : digne de confiance — **dependence** [diˈpɛndənts] *n* : dépendance *f* — **dependent** [diˈpɛndənt] *adj* : dépendant

depict [diˈpɪkt] *vt* **1** PORTRAY : représenter **2** DESCRIBE : dépeindre

deplete [diˈpli:t] *vt* **-pleted; -pleting** : épuiser, réduire

deplore [diˈplor] *vt* **-plored; -ploring** : déplorer — **deplorable** [diˈplorəbəl] *adj* : déplorable

deploy [diˈplɔɪ] *vt* : déployer

deport [diˈport] *vt* : expulser (d'un pays) — **deportation** [ˌdiˌporˈteɪʃən] *n* : expulsion *f*

deposit [diˈpɑzət] *vt* **-ited; -iting** : déposer — **~** *n* **1** : dépôt *m* **2** DOWN PAYMENT : acompte *m*, arrhes *fpl France*

depreciate [diˈpri:ʃiˌeɪt] *vi* **-ated; -ating** : se déprécier — **depreciation** [diˌpri:ʃiˈeɪʃən] *n* : dépréciation *f*

depress [diˈprɛs] *vt* **1** PRESS : appuyer sur **2** SADDEN : déprimer — **depressed** [diˈprɛst] *adj* : déprimé — **depressing** [diˈprɛsɪŋ] *adj* : déprimant — **depression** [diˈprɛʃən] *n* : dépression *f*

deprive [diˈpraɪv] *vt* **-prived; -priving** : priver

depth [ˈdɛpθ] *n, pl* **depths** : profondeur *f*

deputy [ˈdɛpjət̬i] *n, pl* **-ties** : adjoint *m*, -jointe *f*

derail [diˈreɪl] *vi* : dérailler — **derailment** [diˈreɪlmənt] *n* : déraillement *m*

deride [diˈraɪd] *vt* **-rided; -riding** : railler — **derision** [diˈrɪʒən] *n* : dérision *f*

derive [diˈraɪv] *vi* **-rived; -riving ~ from** : provenir de

derogatory [diˈrɑgəˌtori] *adj* : désobligeant

descend [diˈsɛnd] *v* : descendre — **descendant** [diˈsɛndənt] *n* : descendant *m*, -dante *f* — **descent** [diˈsɛnt] *n* **1** : descente *f* **2** LINEAGE : descendance *f*

describe [diˈskraɪb] *vt* **-scribed; -scribing** : décrire — **description** [diˈskrɪpʃən] *n* : description *f* — **descriptive** [diˈskrɪptɪv] *adj* : descriptif

desecrate [ˈdɛsɪˌkreɪt] *vt* **-crated; -crating** : profaner

desert [ˈdɛzərt] *n* : désert *m* — **~** *adj* **~ island** : île *f* déserte — **~** [diˈzərt] *vt* : abandonner — *vi* : déserter — **deserter** [diˈzərt̬ər] *n* : déserteur *m*

deserve [diˈzərv] *vt* **-served; -serving** : mériter

design [diˈzaɪn] *vt* **1** DEVISE : concevoir **2** DRAW : dessiner — **~** *n* **1** : conception *f* **2** PLAN : plan *m* **3** SKETCH : dessin *m* **4** PATTERN : motif *m*

designate [ˈdɛzɪgˌneɪt] *vt* **-nated; -nating** : désigner

designer [diˈzaɪnər] *n* : dessinateur *m*, -trice *f*

desire [diˈzaɪr] *vt* **-sired; -siring** : désirer — **~** *n* : désir *m*

desk [ˈdɛsk] *n* : bureau *m*, pupitre *m* (d'un élève)

desolate [ˈdɛsələt, -zə-] *adj* : désolé

despair [diˈspær] *vi* : désespérer — **~** *n* : désespoir *m*

desperate [ˈdɛspərət] *adj* : désespéré — **desperation** [ˌdɛspəˈreɪʃən] *n* : désespoir *m*

despise [diˈspaɪz] *vt* **-spised; -spising** : mépriser — **despicable** [diˈspɪkəbəl, ˈdɛspɪ-] *adj* : méprisable

despite [dəˈspaɪt] *prep* : malgré

dessert [diˈzərt] *n* : dessert *m*

destination [ˌdɛstɪˈneɪʃən] *n* : destination *f* — **destined** [ˈdɛstənd] *adj* **1** : destiné **2 ~ for** : à destination de — **destiny** [ˈdɛstəni] *n, pl* **-nies** : destin *m*, destinée *f*

destitute [ˈdɛstəˌtu:t, -ˌtju:t] *adj* : indigent

destroy [diˈstrɔɪ] *vt* : détruire — **destruction** [diˈstrʌkʃən] *n* : destruction *f* — **destructive** [diˈstrʌktɪv] *adj* : destructeur

detach [diˈtætʃ] *vt* : détacher — **detached** [diˈtætʃt] *adj* : détaché

detail [diˈteɪl, ˈdi:ˌteɪl] *n* : détail *m* — **~** *vt* : détailler — **detailed** [diˈteɪld, ˈdi:ˌteɪld] *adj* : détaillé

detain [diˈteɪn] *vt* **1** : détenir (un prisonnier) **2** DELAY : retenir

detect [diˈtɛkt] *vt* : détecter, déceler — **detection** [diˈtɛkʃən] *n* : détection *f* — **detective** [diˈtɛktɪv] *n* : détective *m*

detention [diˈtɛntʃən] *n* : détention *f*

deter [diˈtər] *vt* **-terred; -terring** : dissuader

detergent [diˈtərʤənt] *n* : détergent *m*

deteriorate [diˈtɪriəˌreɪt] *vi* **-rated; -rating** : se détériorer — **deterioration** [diˌtɪriəˈreɪʃən] *n* : détérioration *f*

determine [diˈtərmən] *vt* **-mined; -mining 1** : déterminer **2** RESOLVE : décider — **determined** [diˈtərmənd] *adj* RESOLUTE : déterminé — **determination** [diˌtərməˈneɪʃən] *n* : détermination *f*

detest [diˈtɛst] *vt* : détester

detour [ˈdi:ˌtʊr, diˈtʊr] *n* : détour *m* — **~** *vi* : faire un détour

devastate [ˈdɛvəˌsteɪt] *vt* **-tated; -tating** : dévaster — **devastating** [ˈdɛvəˌsteɪtɪŋ] *adj* : accablant — **devastation** [ˌdɛvəˈsteɪʃən] *n* : dévastation *f*

develop [diˈvɛləp] *vt* **1** : développer **2 ~ an illness** : contracter une maladie — *vi* **1** GROW : se développer **2** HAPPEN : se manifester — **developing** [diˈvɛləpɪŋ] *adj* **1** : en expansion **2 ~ country** : pays en voie de développement — **development** [diˈvɛləpmənt] *n* : développement *m*

deviate [ˈdi:viˌeɪt] *vi* **-ated; -ating** : dévier, s'écarter

device [diˈvaɪs] *n* : appareil *m*, mécanisme *m*

devil [ˈdɛvəl] *n* : diable *m* — **devilish** [ˈdɛvəlɪʃ] *adj* : diabolique

devious [ˈdi:viəs] *adj* CRAFTY : sournois

devise [diˈvaɪz] *vt* **-vised; -vising** : inventer, concevoir

devoid [diˈvɔɪd] *adj* **~ of** : dépourvu de

devote [diˈvo:t] *vt* **-voted; -voting** : consacrer, dédier — **devoted** [diˈvo:t̬əd] *adj* : dévoué — **devotion** [diˈvo:ʃən] *n* **1** DEDICATION : dévouement *m* **2** PIETY : dévotion *f*

devour [diˈvaʊər] *vt* : dévorer

devout [diˈvaʊt] *adj* **1** PIOUS : dévot **2** EARNEST : fervent

dew [ˈdu:, ˈdju:] *n* : rosée *f*

dexterity [dɛkˈstɛrət̬i] *n, pl* **-ties** : dextérité *f*

diabetes [ˌdaɪəˈbi:t̬iz] *n* : diabète *m* — **diabetic** [ˌdaɪəˈbɛt̬ɪk] *adj* : diabétique — **~** *n* : diabétique *mf*

diabolic [ˌdaɪəˈbɑlɪk] *or* **diabolical** [-lɪkəl] *adj* : diabolique

diagnosis [ˌdaɪɪgˈno:sɪs] *n, pl* **-ses** [-ˈno:ˌsi:z] : diagnostic *m* — **diagnose** [ˈdaɪɪgˌno:s, ˌdaɪɪgˈno:s] *vt* **-nosed; -nosing** : diagnostiquer

diagonal [daɪˈægənəl] *adj* : diagonal — **diagonally** [daɪˈægənəli] *adv* : en diagonale

diagram [ˈdaɪəˌgræm] *n* : diagramme *m*

dial [ˈdaɪl] *n* : cadran *m* (d'une horloge), bouton *m* (d'une radio) — **~** *vt* **-aled** *or* **-alled; -aling** *or* **-alling** : faire, composer (un numéro de téléphone)

dialect [ˈdaɪəˌlɛkt] *n* : dialecte *m*

dialogue [ˈdaɪəˌlɔg] *n* : dialogue *m*

diameter [daɪˈæmət̬ər] *n* : diamètre *m*

diamond [ˈdaɪmənd, ˈdaɪə-] *n* **1** : diamant *m* **2** : losange *m* (forme géométrique) **3** : carreau *m* (aux cartes) **4** *or* **baseball ~** : terrain *m* de baseball, losange *m Can*

diaper [ˈdaɪpər, ˈdaɪə-] *n* : couche *f* (de bébé)

diaphragm [ˈdaɪəˌfræm] *n* : diaphragme *m*

diarrhea *or Brit* **diarrhoea** [ˌdaɪəˈri:ə] *n* : diarrhée *f*

diary [ˈdaɪəri:] *n, pl* **-ries** : journal *m* intime

dice [ˈdaɪs] *ns & pl* : dé *m* (à jouer)

dictate [ˈdɪkˌteɪt, dɪkˈteɪt] *vt* **-tated; -tating** : dicter — **dictation** [dɪkˈteɪʃən] *n* : dictée *f* — **dictator** [ˈdɪkˌteɪt̬ər] *n* : dictateur *m*

dictionary [ˈdɪkʃəˌnɛri] *n, pl* **-naries** : dictionnaire *m*

did → **do**

die[1] [ˈdaɪ] *vi* **died** [ˈdaɪd]; **dying** [ˈdaɪɪŋ] **1** : mourir, décéder **2** *or* **~ down** SUBSIDE : diminuer **3 be dying to** : mourir d'envie de

die[2] [ˈdaɪ] *n, pl* **dice** [ˈdaɪs] : dé *m* (à jouer)

diesel [ˈdi:zəl, -səl] *n* : diesel *m*

diet [ˈdaɪət] *n* **1** FOOD : alimentation *f* **2 go on a ~** : être au régime — **~** *vi* : suivre un régime

differ [ˈdɪfər] *vi* **-ferred; -ferring** : différer — **difference** [ˈdɪfrənts, ˈdɪfərənts] *n* : différence *f* — **different** [ˈdɪfrənt, ˈdɪfərənt] *adj* : différent — **differentiate** [dɪfəˈrɛntʃiˌeɪt] *v* **-ated; -ating** *vt* : différencier — *vi* **~ between** : faire la différence entre — **differently** [ˈdɪfrəntli, ˈdɪfərəntli] *adv* : différemment

difficult [ˈdɪfɪˌkʌlt] *adj* : difficile — **difficulty** [ˈdɪfɪˌkʌlti] *n, pl* **-ties** : difficulté *f*

dig [ˈdɪg] *vt* **dug** [ˈdʌg]; **digging 1** : creuser **2 ~ up** : déterrer

digest [ˈdaɪˌʤɛst] *n* : résumé *m* — **~** [ˈdaɪˌʤɛst] *vt* **1** : digérer **2** SUMMARIZE : résumer — **digestion** [daɪˈʤɛstʃən, dɪ-] *n* : digestion *f* — **digestive** [daɪˈʤɛstɪv, dɪ-] *adj* : digestif

digit [ˈdɪʤət] *n* NUMERAL : chiffre *m* — **digital** [ˈdɪʤət̬əl] *adj* : digital

dignity [ˈdɪgnət̬i] *n, pl* **-ties** : dignité *f* — **dignified** [ˈdɪgnəˌfaɪd] *adj* : digne

digress [daɪˈgrɛs, də-] *vi* : s'écarter (du sujet)

dike [ˈdaɪk] *n* : digue *f*

dilapidated [dəˈlæpəˌdeɪt̬əd] *adj* : délabré

dilate [daɪˈleɪt, ˈdaɪˌleɪt] *v* **-lated; -lating** *vt* : dilater — *vi* : se dilater

dilemma [diˈlɛmə] *n* : dilemme *m*

diligence [ˈdɪləʤənts] *n* : assiduité *f* — **diligent** [ˈdɪləʤənt] *adj* : assidu, appliqué

dilute [daɪˈlu:t, də-] *vt* **-luted; -luting** : diluer

dim [ˈdɪm] *v* **dimmed; dimming** *vt* : baisser — *vi* : baisser, s'affaiblir — **~** *adj* **dimmer; dimmest 1** DARK : sombre **2** FAINT : faible, vague

dime [ˈdaɪm] *n* : pièce *f* de dix cents

dimension [dəˈmɛntʃən, daɪ-] *n* : dimension *f*

diminish [dəˈmɪnɪʃ] *v* : diminuer

diminutive [dəˈmɪnjət̬ɪv] *adj* : minuscule

dimple [ˈdɪmpəl] *n* : fossette *f*

din [ˈdɪn] *n* : vacarme *m*, tapage *m*

dine [ˈdaɪn] *vi* **dined; dining** : dîner — **diner** [ˈdaɪnər] *n* **1** : dîneur *m*, -neuse *f* **2** : petit restaurant *m* — **dining room** *n* : salle *f* à manger — **dinner** [ˈdɪnər] *n* : dîner *m*

dinosaur [ˈdaɪnəˌsɔr] *n* : dinosaure *m*

dip [ˈdɪp] *v* **dipped; dipping** *vt* : plonger, tremper — *vi* : baisser, descendre — **~** *n* **1** DROP : déclivité *f* **2** SWIM : petite baignade *f* **3** SAUCE : sauce *f*

diploma [dəˈplo:mə] *n* : diplôme *m*

diplomacy [dəˈplo:məsi] *n* : diplomatie *f* — **diplomat** [ˈdɪpləˌmæt] *n* : diplomate *mf* — **diplomatic** [ˌdɪpləˈmæt̬ɪk] *adj* **1** : diplomatique **2** TACTFUL : diplomate

dire [ˈdaɪr] *adj* **direr; direst 1** : grave, terrible **2** EXTREME : extrême

direct [dəˈrɛkt, daɪ-] *vt* **1** : diriger **2** ORDER : ordonner — **~** *adj* **1** STRAIGHT : direct **2** FRANK : franc — **~** *adv* : directement — **direct current** *n* : courant *m* continu — **direction** [də'rɛkʃən, daɪ-] *n* 1 : direction *f* 2 **ask for ~s** : demander des indications — **directly** [də'rɛktli, daɪ-] *adv* 1 STRAIGHT : directement 2 IMMEDIATELY : tout de suite — **director** [də'rɛktər, daɪ-] *n* 1 : directeur *m*, -trice *f* 2 **board of ~s** : conseil *m* d'administration — **directory** [də'rɛktəri, daɪ-] *n, pl* **-ries** : annuaire *m* (téléphonique)

dirt ['dərt] *n* 1 : saleté *f* 2 SOIL : terre *f* — **dirty** ['dərṭi] *adj* **dirtier; -est** 1 : sale 2 INDECENT : obscène, cochon *fam* — **~** *vt* **dirtied; dirtying** : salir

disability [ˌdɪsə'bɪləṭi] *n, pl* **-ties** : infirmité *f* — **disable** [dɪs'eɪbəl] *vt* **-abled; -abling** : rendre infirme — **disabled** [dɪs'eɪbəld] *adj* : handicapé, infirme

disadvantage [ˌdɪsəd'væntɪʤ] *n* : désavantage *m*

disagree [ˌdɪsə'gri:] *vi* 1 : ne pas être d'accord (avec qqn) 2 CONFLICT : ne pas convenir — **disagreeable** [ˌdɪsə'gri:əbəl] *adj* : désagréable — **disagreement** [ˌdɪsə'gri:mənt] *n* 1 : désaccord *m* 2 ARGUMENT : différend *m*

disappear [ˌdɪsə'pɪr] *vi* : disparaître — **disappearance** [ˌdɪsə'pi:rənts] *n* : disparition *f*

disappoint [ˌdɪsə'pɔɪnt] *vt* : décevoir — **disappointment** [ˌdɪsə'pɔɪntmənt] *n* : déception *f*

disapprove [ˌdɪsə'pru:v] *vi* **-proved; -proving ~ of** : désapprouver — **disapproval** [ˌdɪsə'pru:vəl] *n* : désapprobation *f*

disarm [dɪs'ɑrm] *v* : désarmer — **disarmament** [dɪs'ɑrməmənt] *n* : désarmement *m*

disarray [dɪsə'reɪ] *n* : désordre *m*

disaster [dɪ'zæstər] *n* : désastre *m* — **disastrous** [dɪ'zæstrəs] *adj* : désastreux

disbelief [ˌdɪsbɪ'li:f] *n* : incrédulité *f*

disc → **disk**

discard [dɪs'kɑrd, 'dɪsˌkɑrd] *vt* : se débarrasser de

discern [dɪ'sərn, -'zərn] *vt* : discerner — **discernible** [dɪ'sərnəbəl, -'zər-] *adj* : perceptible

discharge [dɪs'ʧɑrʤ, 'dɪsˌ-] *vt* **-charged; -charging** 1 UNLOAD : décharger 2 DISMISS : renvoyer 3 RELEASE : libérer — **~** ['dɪsˌʧɑrʤ, dɪs'-] *n* 1 : décharge *f* (électrique) 2 FLOW : écoulement *m* 3 DISMISSAL : renvoi *m* 4 RELEASE : libération *f*

disciple [dɪ'saɪpəl] *n* : disciple *mf*

discipline ['dɪsəplən] *n* : discipline *f* — **~** *vt* **-plined; -plining** 1 PUNISH : punir 2 CONTROL : discipliner

disclose [dɪs'klo:z] *vt* **-closed; -closing** : révéler

discomfort [dɪs'kʌmfərt] *n* 1 : malaise *m* 2 UNEASINESS : gêne *f*

disconcert [ˌdɪskən'sərt] *vt* : déconcerter

disconnect [ˌdɪskə'nɛkt] *vt* : débrancher (un appareil électrique), couper (l'électricité, etc.)

discontinue [ˌdɪskən'tɪnˌju:] *vt* **-ued; -uing** : cesser, interrompre

discord ['dɪsˌkɔrd] *n* STRIFE : discorde *m*

discount ['dɪsˌkaʊnt, dɪs'-] *n* : rabais *m*, remise *f* — **~** *vt* : faire une remise de

discourage [dɪs'kərɪʤ] *vt* **-aged; -aging** : décourager — **discouragement** [dɪs'kərɪʤmənt] *n* : découragement *m*

discover [dɪs'kʌvər] *vt* : découvrir — **discovery** [dɪs'kʌvəri] *n, pl* **-eries** : découverte *f*

discredit [dɪs'krɛdət] *vt* : discréditer

discreet [dɪ'skri:t] *adj* : discret

discrepancy [dɪs'krɛpəntsi] *n, pl* **-cies** : divergence *f*

discretion [dɪs'krɛʃən] *n* : discrétion *f*

discriminate [dɪs'krɪməˌneɪt] *vi* **-nated; -nating** 1 **~ against** : être l'objet de discriminations 2 **~ between** : distinguer entre — **discrimination** [dɪsˌkrɪmə'neɪʃən] *n* discrimination *f*, préjugés *mpl*

discuss [dɪs'kʌs] *vt* : discuter de, parler de — **discussion** [dɪs'kʌʃən] *n* : discussion *f*

disdain [dɪs'deɪn] *n* : dédain *m* — **~** *vt* : dédaigner

disease [dɪ'zi:z] *n* : maladie *f*

disembark [ˌdɪsɪm'bɑrk] *vi* : débarquer

disengage [ˌdɪsɪn'geɪʤ] *vt* **-gaged; -gaging** 1 RELEASE : dégager 2 **~ the clutch** : débrayer

disentangle [ˌdɪsɪn'tæŋgəl] *vt* **-gled; -gling** : démêler

disfigure [dɪs'fɪgjər] *vt* **-ured; -uring** : défigurer

disgrace [dɪ'skreɪs] *vt* **-graced; -gracing** : déshonorer — **~** *n* 1 DISHONOR : disgrâce *f* 2 SHAME : honte *f* — **disgraceful** [dɪ'skreɪsfəl] *adj* : honteux

disgruntled [dɪs'grʌntəld] *adj* : mécontent

disguise [dɪ'skaɪz] *vt* **-guised; -guising** : déguiser — **~** *n* : déguisement *m*

disgust [dɪ'skʌst] *n* : dégoût *m* — **~** *vt* : dégoûter — **disgusting** [dɪ'skʌstɪŋ] *adj* : écœurant, dégoûtant

dish ['dɪʃ] *n* 1 : assiette *f* 2 *or* **serving ~** : plat *m* de service 3 **~es** *npl* : vaisselle *f* — **~** *vt or* **~ out** : servir — **dishcloth** ['dɪʃˌklɔθ] *n* : torchon *m* (à vaisselle), lavette *f*

dishearten [dɪs'hɑrṭən] *vt* : décourager

disheveled *or* **dishevelled** [dɪ'ʃɛvəld] *adj* : en désordre (se dit des vêtements, etc.)

dishonest [dɪ'sɑnəst] *adj* : malhonnête — **dishonesty** [dɪ'sɑnəsti] *n, pl* **-ties** : malhonnêteté *f*

dishonor [dɪ'sɑnər] *n* : déshonneur *m* — **~** *vt* : déshonorer — **dishonorable** [dɪ'sɑnərəbəl] *adj* : déshonorant

dishwasher ['dɪʃˌwɔʃər] *n* : lave-vaisselle *m*

disillusion [dɪsə'lu:ʒən] *vt* : désillusionner — **disillusionment** [ˌdɪsə'lu:ʒənmənt] *n* : désillusion *f*

disinfect [ˌdɪsɪn'fɛkt] *vt* : désinfecter — **disinfectant** [ˌdɪsɪn'fɛktənt] *n* : désinfectant *m*

disintegrate [dɪs'ɪntəˌgreɪt] *vi* **-grated; -grating** : se désagréger, se désintégrer

disinterested [dɪs'ɪntərəstəd, -ˌrɛs-] *adj* : désintéressé

disjointed [dɪs'ʤɔɪntəd] *adj* : décousu, incohérent

disk *or* **disc** ['dɪsk] *n* : disque *m*

dislike [dɪs'laɪk] *n* : aversion *f*, antipathie *f* — **~** *vt* **-liked; -liking** : ne pas aimer

dislocate ['dɪsloˌkeɪt, dɪs'lo:-] *vt* **-cated; -cating** : se démettre, se luxer

dislodge [dɪs'lɑʤ] *vt* **-lodged; -lodging** : déplacer, déloger

disloyal [dɪs'lɔɪəl] *adj* : déloyal — **disloyalty** [dɪs'lɔɪəlti] *n, pl* **-ties** : déloyauté *f*

dismal ['dɪzməl] *adj* : sombre, triste

dismantle [dɪs'mæntəl] *vt* **-tled; -tling** : démonter

dismay [dɪs'meɪ] *vt* : consterner — **~** *n* : consternation *f*

dismiss [dɪs'mɪs] *vt* 1 DISCHARGE : renvoyer, congédier 2 REJECT : ne pas tenir compte de — **dismissal** [dɪs'mɪsəl] *n* : renvoi *m*, licenciement *m*

disobey [ˌdɪsə'beɪ] *vt* : désobéir à — *vi* : désobéir — **disobedience** [ˌdɪsə'bi:diənts] *n* : désobéissance *f* — **disobedient** [-ənt] *adj* : désobéissant

disorder [dɪs'ɔrdər] *n* 1 : désordre *m* 2 AILMENT : troubles *mpl*, maladie *f* — **disorderly** [dɪs'ɔrdərli] *adj* : désordonné

disorganize [dɪs'ɔrgəˌnaɪz] *vt* **-nized; -nizing** : désorganiser

disown [dɪs'o:n] *vt* : renier

disparage [dɪs'pærɪʤ] *vt* **-aged; -aging** : dénigrer

disparity [dɪs'pærəṭi] *n, pl* **-ties** : disparité *f*

dispatch [dɪs'pæʧ] *vt* : envoyer, expédier

dispel [dɪs'pɛl] *vt* **-pelled; -pelling** : dissiper

dispense [dɪs'pɛnts] *v* **-pensed; -pensing** *vt* : distribuer — *vi* **~ with** : se passer de

disperse [dɪs'pərs] *v* **-persed; -persing** *vt* : disperser — *vi* : se disperser

display [dɪs'pleɪ] *vt* PRESENT : exposer — **~** *n* : exposition *f*, étalage *m*

dispose [dɪs'po:z] *v* **-posed; -posing** *vt* : disposer — *vi* **~ of** : se débarrasser de — **disposable** [dɪs'po:zəbəl] *adj* : jetable — **disposal** [dɪs'po:zəl] *n* 1 : élimination *f* (de déchets) 2 **have at one's ~** : avoir à sa disposition — **disposition** [ˌdɪspə'zɪʃən] *n* : TEMPERAMENT : caractère *m*

dispute [dɪs'pju:t] *vt* **-puted; -puting** : contester — **~** *n* : dispute *f*, conflit *m*

disqualify [dɪs'kwɑləˌfaɪ] *vt* **-fied; -fying** : disqualifier

disregard [ˌdɪsrɪ'gɑrd] *vt* : ne pas tenir compte de — **~** *n* : indifférence *f*

disreputable [dɪs'rɛpjuṭəbəl] *adj* : mal famé

disrespect [ˌdɪsrɪ'spɛkt] *n* : manque *m* de respect — **disrespectful** [ˌdɪsrɪ'spɛktfəl] *adj* : irrespectueux

disrupt [dɪs'rʌpt] *vt* : perturber, déranger — **disruption** [dɪs'rʌpʃən] *n* : perturbation *f*

dissatisfied [dɪs'sæṭəsˌfaɪd] *adj* : mécontent

disseminate [dɪ'sɛməˌneɪt] *vt* **-nated; -nating** : disséminer

dissent [dɪ'sɛnt] *vi* : différer, être en désaccord — **~** *n* : dissentiment *m*

dissertation [ˌdɪsər'teɪʃən] *n* THESIS : thèse *f*

dissipate ['dɪsəˌpeɪt] *v* **-pated; -pating** *vt* DISPERSE : dissiper — *vi* : se dissiper

dissolve [dɪ'zɑlv] *v* **-solved; -solving** *vt* : dissoudre — *vi* : se dissoudre

dissuade [dɪ'sweɪd] *vt* **-suaded; -suading** : dissuader

distance ['dɪstənts] *n* 1 : distance *f* 2 **in the ~** : au loin — **distant** ['dɪstənt] *adj* : distant

distaste [dɪs'teɪst] *n* : dégoût *m* — **distasteful** [dɪs'teɪstfəl] *adj* : déplaisant, répugnant

distill *or Brit* **distil** [dɪ'stɪl] *vt* **-tilled; -tilling** : distiller

distinct [dɪ'stɪŋkt] *adj* 1 CLEAR : distinct 2 DEFINITE : net — **distinction** [dɪ'stɪŋkʃən] *n* : distinction *f* — **distinctive** [dɪ'stɪŋktɪv] *adj* : distinctif

distinguish [dɪ'stɪŋgwɪʃ] *vt* : distinguer — **distinguished** [dɪ'stɪŋgwɪʃt] *adj* : distingué

distort [dɪ'stɔrt] *vt* : déformer — **distortion** [dɪ'stɔrʃən] *n* : déformation *f*

distract [dɪ'strækt] *vt* : distraire — **distraction** [dɪ'strækʃən] *n* : distraction *f*

distraught [dɪ'strɔt] *adj* : éperdu

distress [dɪ'strɛs] *n* 1 : angoisse *f*, affliction *f* 2 **in ~** : en détresse *f* — **~** *vt* : affliger — **distressing** [dɪ'strɛsɪŋ] *adj* : pénible

distribute [dɪ'strɪˌbju:t, -bjut] *vt* **-uted; -uting** : distribuer, répartir — **distribution** [ˌdɪstrə'bju:ʃən] *n* : distribution *f* — **distributor** [dɪ'strɪbjuṭər] *n* : distributeur *m*

district ['dɪsˌtrɪkt] *n* 1 AREA : région *f* 2 : quartier *m* (d'une ville) 3 : district *m* (administratif)

distrust [dɪs'trʌst] *n* : méfiance *f* — **~** *vt* : se méfier de

disturb [dɪ'stərb] *vt* 1 BOTHER : déranger 2 WORRY : troubler, inquiéter

disturbance [dɪ'stərbənts] *n* **to cause a ~** : faire du tapage

disuse [dɪs'ju:s] *n* **fall into ~** : tomber en désuétude

ditch ['dɪʧ] *n* : fossé *m*

dive ['daɪv] *vi* **dived** *or* **dove** ['do:v]; **dived; diving** : plonger — **~** *n* 1 : plongeon *m* 2 DESCENT : piqué *m* — **diver** ['daɪvər] *n* : plongeur *m*, -geuse *f*

diverge [də'vərʤ, daɪ-] *vi* **-verged; -verging** : diverger

diverse [daɪ'vərs, də-, 'daɪˌvərs] *adj* : divers — **diversify** [daɪ'vərsəˌfaɪ, də-] *vt* **-fied; -fying** : diversifier

diversion [daɪ'vərʒən, də-] *n* 1 DEVIATION : déviation *f* 2 AMUSEMENT : divertissement *m*

diversity [daɪ'vərsəṭi, də-] *n, pl* **-ties** : diversité *f*

divert [də'vərt, daɪ-] *vt* 1 DEFLECT : détourner 2 AMUSE : divertir

divide [də'vaɪd] *v* **-vided; -viding** *vt* : diviser — *vi* : se diviser

dividend ['dɪvɪˌdɛnd, -dənd] *n* : dividende *m*

divine [də'vaɪn] *adj* **diviner; -est** : divin — **divinity** [də'vɪnəṭi] *n, pl* **-ties** : divinité *f*

division [dɪ'vɪʒən] *n* : division *f*

divorce [də'vors] *n* : divorce *m* — **~** *vi* **-vorced; -vorcing** : divorcer

divulge [də'vʌlʤ, daɪ-] *vt* **-vulged; -vulging** : divulguer

dizzy ['dɪzi] *adj* **dizzier; -est** : vertigineux — **dizziness** ['dɪzinəs] *n* : vertige *m*, étourdissement *m*

DNA [ˌdi:ˌɛn'eɪ] *n* (deoxyribonucleic acid) : ADN *m*

do ['du:] *v* **did** ['dɪd]; **done** ['dʌn]; **doing; does** ['dʌz] *vt* 1 : faire 2 PREPARE : préparer 3 **~ one's hair** : se coiffer — *vi* 1 BEHAVE : faire 2 MANAGE : s'en sortir 3 SUFFICE : suffire 4 **~ away with** : éliminer 5 **how are you doing?** : comment vas-tu? — *v aux* 1 **does he work?** : travaille-t-il? 2 **I don't know** : je ne sais pas 3 **~ be careful** : fais attention, je t'en prie 4 **he reads more than I ~** : il lit plus que moi 5 **you know him, don't you?** : vous le connaissez, n'est-ce pas?

dock ['dɑk] *n* : dock *m* — **~** *vi* : se mettre à quai

doctor ['dɑktər] *n* 1 : docteur *m* (de droit, etc.) 2 PHYSICIAN : médecin *m*, docteur *m*

doctrine ['dɑktrɪn] *n* : doctrine *f*

document ['dɑkjumənt] *n* : document *m* — **documentary** [ˌdɑkju'mɛntəri] *n, pl* **-ries** : documentaire *m*

dodge ['dɑʤ] *n* : ruse *f*, truc *m* — **~** *vt* **dodged; dodging** : esquiver

doe ['do:] *n, pl* **does** *or* **doe** : biche *f*

does → **do**

doesn't ['dʌzɪnt] (*contraction of* **do not**) → **do**

dog ['dɔg, 'dɑg] *n* : chien *m* — **~** *vt* **dogged; dogging** : poursuivre — **dogged** ['dɔgəd] *adj* : tenace

dogma ['dɔgmə] *n* : dogme *m*

doldrums ['do:ldrəmz, 'dɑl-] *npl* **be in the ~** : être dans le marasme

doll ['dɑl, 'dɔl] *n* : poupée *f*

dollar ['dɑlər] *n* : dollar *m*

dolphin ['dɑlfən, 'dɔl-] *n* : dauphin *m*

domain [do'meɪn, də-] *n* : domaine *m*

dome ['do:m] *n* : dôme *m*

domestic [də'mɛstɪk] *adj* 1 FAMILY : familial 2 HOUSEHOLD : ménager, domestique 3 INTERNAL : intérieur, du pays — **~** *n* SERVANT : domestique *mf* — **domesticate** [də'mɛstɪˌkeɪt] *vt* **-cated; -cating** : domestiquer

dominant ['dɑmənənt] *adj* : dominant — **dominate** ['dɑməˌneɪt] *v* **-nated; -nating** : dominer — **domineer** [ˌdɑmə'nɪr] *vi* : se montrer autoritaire

donate ['do:ˌneɪt, do:'-] *vt* **-nated; -nating** : faire (un) don de — **donation** [do:'neɪʃən] *n* : don *m*, donation *f*

done ['dʌn] → **do** — **~** *adj* 1 FINISHED : fini, terminé 2 COOKED : cuit

donkey ['dɑŋki, 'dʌŋ] *n, pl* **-keys** : âne *m*

donor ['do:nər] *n* 1 : donateur *m*, -trice *f* 2 **blood ~** : donneur *m*, -neuse *f* de sang

don't ['do:nt] (*contraction of* **do not**) → **do**

doodle ['du:dəl] *v* **-dled; -dling** : gribouiller

doom ['du:m] *n* : perte *f*, ruine *f* — **~** *vt* : vouer, condamner

door ['dor] *n* 1 : porte *f* 2 : portière *f* (d'une voiture) 3 ENTRANCE : entrée *f* — **doorbell** ['dorˌbɛl] *n* : sonnette *f* — **doorknob** ['dorˌnɑb] *n* : bouton *m* de porte — **doormat** ['dorˌmæt] *n* : paillasson *m* — **doorstep** ['dorˌstɛp] *n* : pas *m* de la porte — **doorway** ['dorˌweɪ] *n* : porte *f*, embrasure *f* (de la porte)

dope ['do:p] *n* 1 DRUG : drogue *f* 2 IDIOT : imbécile *mf*

dormitory ['dɔrməˌtori] *n, pl* **-ries** : dortoir *m*

dose ['do:s] *n* : dose *f* — **dosage** ['do:sɪʤ] *n* : posologie *f*

dot ['dɑt] *n* 1 POINT : point *m* 2 **on the ~** : pile *fam*

dote ['do:t] *vi* **doted; doting ~ on** : adorer

double ['dʌbəl] *adj* : double — **~** *v* **-bled; -bling** *vt* 1 : doubler 2 FOLD : plier (en deux) — *vi* : doubler — **~** *adv* 1 : deux fois 2 **see ~** : voir double — **~** *n* : double *m* — **double bass** *n* : contrebasse *f* — **doubly** ['dʌbli] *adv* : doublement, deux fois plus

doubt ['daʊt] *vt* 1 : douter 2 DISTRUST : douter de — **~** *n* : doute *m* — **doubtful** ['daʊtfəl] *adj* : douteux

dough ['do:] *n* : pâte *f* (en cuisine) — **doughnut** ['do:ˌnʌt] *n* : beignet *m*, beigne *m Can*

douse ['daʊs, 'daʊz] *vt* **doused; dousing** 1 DRENCH : tremper 2 EXTINGUISH : éteindre

dove[1] ['do:v] → **dive**

dove[2] ['dʌv] *n* : colombe *f*

down ['daʊn] *adv* 1 DOWNWARD : en bas, vers le bas 2 **fall ~** : tomber 3 **go ~** : descendre — **~** *prep* 1 : en bas de 2 ALONG : le long de — **~** *adj* 1 : qui descend 2 DOWNCAST : déprimé, abattu — **~** *n* : duvet *m* — **downcast** ['daʊnˌkæst] *adj* : abattu — **downfall** ['daʊnˌfɔl] *n* : chute *f* — **downhearted** ['daʊnˌhɑrṭəd] *adj* : découragé — **downhill** ['daʊn'hɪl] *adv* **go ~** : descendre — **download** ['daʊnˌlo:d] *vt* : télécharger (en informatique) — **down payment** *n* : acompte *m* — **downpour** ['daʊnˌpor] *n* : averse *f* — **downright** ['daʊnˌraɪt] *adv* : carrément — **~** *adj* : véritable, catégorique — **downstairs** [*adv* 'daʊn'stærz, *adj* 'daʊnˌstærz] *adv & adj* : en bas — **downstream** ['daʊn'stri:m] *adv* : en aval — **down-to-earth** [ˌdaʊntu'ərθ] *adj* : terre à terre — **downtown** [ˌdaʊn'taʊn, 'daʊnˌtaʊn] *n* : centre-ville *m* — **~** [ˌdaʊn'taʊn] *adv* : en ville — **downward** ['daʊnwərd] *or* **downwards** [-wərdz] *adv* : en bas, vers le bas — **downward** *adj* : vers le bas

doze ['do:z] *vi* **dozed; dozing** : sommeiller, somnoler

dozen ['dʌzən] *n, pl* **-ens** *or* **-en** : douzaine *f*

drab ['dræb] *adj* **drabber; drabbest** : terne

draft ['dræft, 'drɑft] *n* 1 : courant *m* d'air 2 *or* **rough ~** : brouillon *m* 3 : conscription *f* (militaire) 4 *or* **bank ~** : traite *f* bancaire 5 *or* **~ beer** : bière *f* pression — **~** *vt* 1 OUTLINE : faire le brouillon de 2 : appeler (des soldats) sous les drapeaux — **drafty** ['dræfti] *adj* **draftier; -est** : plein de courants d'air

drag ['dræg] *v* **dragged; dragging** *vt* 1 HAUL : tirer 2 : traîner (les pieds, etc.) 3 : glisser (en informatique) — *vi* TRAIL : traîner — **~** *n* 1 RESISTANCE : résistance *f* (aérodynamique) 2 **what a ~!** : quelle barbe!

dragon ['drægən] *n* : dragon *m* — **dragonfly** ['drægənˌflaɪ] *n, pl* **-flies** : libellule *f*

drain ['dreɪn] *vt* 1 EMPTY : vider, drainer 2 EXHAUST : épuiser — *vi* : s'écouler, s'égoutter (se dit de la vaisselle) — **~** *n* 1 : tuyau *m* d'écoulement 2 SEWER : égout *m* 3 DEPLETION : épuisement *m* — **drainage** ['dreɪnɪʤ] *n* : drainage *m* — **drainpipe** ['dreɪnˌpaɪp] *n* : tuyau *m* d'écoulement

drama ['drɑmə, 'dræ-] *n* : drame *m* — **dramatic** [drə'mæṭɪk] *adj* : dramatique — **dramatize** ['dræməˌtaɪz, 'drɑ-] *vt* **-tized; -tizing** : dramatiser

drank → **drink**

drape ['dreɪp] *vt* **draped; draping** : draper — **drapes** *npl* CURTAINS : rideaux *mpl*

drastic ['dræstɪk] *adj* : sévère, énergique

draught ['dræft, 'drɑft] → **draft**

draw ['drɔ] *v* **drew** ['dru:]; **drawn** ['drɔn]; **drawing** ['drɔɪŋ] *vt* 1 PULL : tirer 2 ATTRACT : attirer 3 SKETCH : dessiner 4 MAKE : faire (une distinction, etc.) 5 *or* **~ up** FORMULATE : rédiger — *vi* 1 SKETCH : dessiner 2 **~ near** : approcher — **~** *n* 1 DRAWING : tirage *m* (au sort) 2 TIE : match *m* nul 3 ATTRACTION : attraction *f* — **drawback** ['drɔˌbæk] *n* : inconvénient *m* — **drawer** ['drɔr, 'drɔər] *n* : tiroir *m* — **drawing** ['drɔɪŋ] *n* 1 SKETCH : dessin *m* 2 LOTTERY : tirage *m* (au sort)

drawl ['drɔl] *n* : voix *f* traînante

dread ['drɛd] *vt* : redouter, craindre — **~** *n* : crainte *f*, terreur *f* — **dreadful** ['drɛdfəl] *adj* : affreux, épouvantable

dream ['dri:m] *n* : rêve *m* — **~** *v* **dreamed** ['dri:md] *or* **dreamt** ['drɛmpt]; **dreaming** : rêver — **dreamer** ['dri:mər] *n* : rêveur *m*, -veuse *f* — **dreamy** ['dri:mi] *adj* **dreamier; -est** : rêveur

dreary ['drɪri] *adj* **drearier; -est** : morne, sombre
dredge ['drɛʤ] *vt* **dredged; dredging** : draguer
dregs ['drɛgz] *npl* : lie *f*
drench ['drɛnʧ] *vt* : tremper
dress ['drɛs] *vt* **1** CLOTHE : habiller, vêtir **2** : assaisonner (une salade) **3** BANDAGE : panser (une blessure) — *vi* **1** : s'habiller **2** *or* ~ **up** : se mettre en grande toilette **3** ~ **up as** : se déguiser en — ~ *n* **1** CLOTHING : tenue *f* **2** : robe *f* (de femme) — **dresser** ['drɛsər] *n* : commode *f* à miroir — **dressing** ['drɛsɪŋ] *n* **1** SAUCE : sauce *f*, vinaigrette *f* **2** BANDAGE : pansement *m* — **dressmaker** ['drɛs,meɪkər] *n* : couturière *f* — **dressy** ['drɛsi] *adj* **dressier; -est** : habillé, élégant
drew → **draw**
dribble ['drɪbəl] *vi* **-bled; -bling 1** TRICKLE : tomber goutte à goutte **2** DROOL : baver **3** : dribbler (aux sports) — ~ *n* **1** TRICKLE : filet *m* **2** DROOL : bave *f*
drier, driest → **dry**
drift ['drɪft] *n* **1** MOVEMENT : mouvement *m* **2** HEAP : banc *m* (de neige) *Can* — ~ *vi* **1** : dériver (sur l'eau), être emporté (par le vent) **2** ACCUMULATE : s'amonceler
drill ['drɪl] *n* **1** : perceuse *f* (outil) **2** EXERCISE : exercice *m* — ~ *vt* **1** : percer, forer **2** TRAIN : entraîner
drink ['drɪŋk] *v* **drank** ['dræŋk]; **drunk** ['drʌŋk] *or* **drank; drinking** : boire — ~ *n* : boisson *f*
drip ['drɪp] *vi* **dripped; dripping** : tomber goutte à goutte, dégoutter — ~ *n* DROP : goutte *f*
drive ['draɪv] *v* **drove** ['dro:v]; **driven** ['drɪvən]; **driving** *vt* **1** : conduire **2** COMPEL : inciter — *vi* : conduire, rouler — ~ *n* **1** : promenade *f* (en voiture) **2** CAMPAIGN : campagne *f* **3** VIGOR : énergie *f* **4** NEED : besoin *m* fondamental
driver ['draɪvər] *n* **1** : conducteur *m*, -trice *f* **2** CHAUFFEUR : chauffeur *m*
driveway ['draɪv,weɪ] *n* : allée *f*, entrée *f* (de garage)
drizzle ['drɪzəl] *n* : bruine *f* — ~ *vi* **-zled; -zling** : bruiner
drone ['dro:n] *n* **1** BEE : abeille *f* mâle **2** HUM : bourdonnement *m* — ~ *vi* **droned; droning 1** BUZZ : bourdonner **2** *or* ~ **on** : parler d'un ton monotone
drool ['dru:l] *vi* : baver — ~ *n* : bave *f*
droop ['dru:p] *vi* : pencher, tomber
drop ['drɑp] *n* **1** : goutte *f* (de liquide) **2** DECLINE, FALL : baisse *f* **3** DESCENT : chute *f* — ~ *v* **dropped; dropping** *vt* **1** : laisser tomber **2** LOWER : baisser **3** ABANDON : abandonner **4** ~ **off** LEAVE : déposer — *vi* **1** FALL : tomber **2** DECREASE : baisser **3** ~ **by** : passer
drought ['draʊt] *n* : sécheresse *f*
drove ['dro:v] → **drive**
droves ['dro:vz] *npl* **in** ~ : en masse
drown ['draʊn] *vt* : noyer — *vi* : se noyer
drowsy ['draʊzi] *adj* **drowsier; -est** : somnolent — **drowsiness** ['draʊzinəs] *n* : somnolence *f*
drudgery ['drʌʤəri] *n, pl* **-eries** : corvée *f*
drug ['drʌg] *n* **1** MEDICATION : médicament *m* **2** NARCOTIC : drogue *f*, stupéfiant *m* — ~ *vt* **drugged; drugging** : droguer — **drugstore** ['drʌg,stor] *n* : pharmacie *f*
drum ['drʌm] *n* **1** : tambour *m* **2** *or* **oil** ~ : bidon *m* — ~ *v* **drummed; drumming** *vi* : jouer du tambour — *vt* : tambouriner — **drumstick** ['drʌm,stɪk] *n* **1** : baguette *f* de tambour **2** : pilon *m* (de poulet)
drunk ['drʌŋk] → **drink** — ~ *adj* : ivre — ~ *or* **drunkard** ['drʌŋkərd] *n* : ivrogne *m*, ivrognesse *f* — **drunken** ['drʌŋkən] *adj* : ivre
dry ['draɪ] *adj* **drier; driest** : sec — ~ *v* **dried; drying** *vt* **1** : sécher **2** WIPE : essuyer — *vi* : sécher — **dry–clean** ['draɪ,kli:n] *vt* : nettoyer à sec — **dry cleaner** *n* : teinturerie *f* — **dryer** ['draɪər] *n* : séchoir *m* — **dryness** ['draɪnəs] *n* : sécheresse *f*
dual ['du:əl, 'dju:-] *adj* : double
dub ['dʌb] *vt* **dubbed; dubbing** : doubler (un film, etc.)
dubious ['du:biəs, 'dju:-] *adj* **1** DOUBTFUL : douteux **2** QUESTIONABLE : suspect
duck ['dʌk] *n, pl* **ducks** *or* **duck** : canard *m* — ~ *vt* **1** PLUNGE : plonger **2** LOWER : baisser **3** AVOID, DODGE : éviter, esquiver — **duckling** ['dʌklɪŋ] *n* : caneton *m*
duct ['dʌkt] *n* : conduit *m*
due ['du:, 'dju:] *adj* **1** PAYABLE : dû, payable **2** APPROPRIATE : qui convient **3** EXPECTED : attendu **4** ~ **to** : en raison de — ~ *n* **1** : dû *m* **2** ~**s** *npl* FEE : cotisation *f* — ~ *adv* : plein, droit vers
duel ['du:əl, 'dju:-] *n* : duel *m*
duet [du:'ɛt, dju:-] *n* : duo *m*
dug → **dig**
duke ['du:k, 'dju:k] *n* : duc *m*
dull ['dʌl] *adj* **1** STUPID : stupide **2** BLUNT : émoussé **3** BORING : ennuyeux **4** LACKLUSTER : terne — ~ *vt* **1** BLUNT : émousser **2** DIM, TARNISH : ternir
duly ['du:li] *adv* **1** PROPERLY : dûment **2** EXPECTEDLY : comme prévu
dumb ['dʌm] *adj* **1** MUTE : muet **2** STUPID : bête
dumbfound *or* **dumfound** [,dʌm'faʊnd] *vt* : abasourdir
dummy ['dʌmi] *n, pl* **-mies 1** FOOL : imbécile *mf* **2** MANNEQUIN : mannequin *m* — ~ *adj* : faux
dump ['dʌmp] *vt* : déposer, jeter — ~ *n* **1** : décharge *f* (publique) **2 down in the** ~**s** : déprimé
dune ['du:n, 'dju:n] *n* : dune *f*
dung ['dʌŋ] *n* : fumier *m*
dungeon ['dʌnʤən] *n* : cachot *m*
dunk ['dʌŋk] *vt* : tremper
duo ['du:o:, 'dju:-] *n, pl* **duos** : duo *m*
dupe ['du:p, 'dju:p] *n* : dupe *f* — ~ *vt* **duped; duping** : duper
duplex ['du:,plɛks, 'dju:-] *n* : duplex *m*, maison *f* jumelée
duplicate ['du:plɪkət, 'dju:-] *adj* : en double — ~ ['du:plɪ,keɪt, 'dju:-] *vt* **-cated; -cating** : faire un double de, copier — ~ ['du:plɪkət, 'dju:-] *n* : double *m*
durable ['dʊrəbəl, 'djʊr-] *adj* : durable, résistant
duration [dʊ'reɪʃən, djʊ-] *n* : durée *f*
during ['dʊrɪŋ, 'djʊr-] *prep* : pendant
dusk ['dʌsk] *n* : crépuscule *m*
dust ['dʌst] *n* : poussière *f* — ~ *vt* **1** : épousseter **2** SPRINKLE : saupoudrer — **dustpan** ['dʌst,pæn] *n* : pelle *f* à poussière — **dusty** ['dʌsti] *adj* **dustier; -est** : poussiéreux
duty ['du:ti, 'dju:-] *n, pl* **-ties 1** TASK : fonction *f* **2** OBLIGATION : devoir *m* **3** TAX : taxe *f*, droit *m* — **dutiful** ['du:tɪfəl, 'dju:-] *adj* : obéissant
dwarf ['dwɔrf] *n* : nain *m*, naine *f*
dwell ['dwɛl] *vi* **dwelled** *or* **dwelt** ['dwɛlt]; **dwelling 1** RESIDE : demeurer **2** ~ **on** : penser sans cesse à — **dweller** ['dwɛlər] *n* : habitant *m*, -tante *f* — **dwelling** ['dwɛlɪŋ] *n* : habitation *f*
dwindle ['dwɪndəl] *vi* **-dled; -dling** : diminuer
dye ['daɪ] *n* : teinture *f* — ~ *vt* **dyed; dyeing** : teindre
dying → **die**[1]
dynamic [daɪ'næmɪk] *adj* : dynamique
dynamite ['daɪnə,maɪt] *n* : dynamite *f* — ~ *vt* **-mited; -miting** : dynamiter
dynasty ['daɪnəsti, -næs-] *n, pl* **-ties** : dynastie *f*

E

e ['i:] *n, pl* **e's** *or* **es** ['i:z] : e *m*, cinquième lettre de l'alphabet
each ['i:ʧ] *adj* : chaque — ~ *pron* **1** : chacun *m*, -cune *f* **2** ~ **other** : l'un l'autre **3 they love** ~ **other** : ils s'aiment — ~ *adv* : chacun, par personne
eager ['i:gər] *adj* **1** ENTHUSIASTIC : avide **2** IMPATIENT : impatient — **eagerness** ['i:gərnəs] *n* : enthousiasme *m*, empressement *m*
eagle ['i:gəl] *n* : aigle *m*
ear ['ɪr] *n* **1** : oreille *f* **2** ~ **of corn** : épi *m* de maïs — **eardrum** ['ɪr,drʌm] *n* : tympan *m*
earl ['ərl] *n* : comte *m*
earlobe ['ɪr,lo:b] *n* : lobe *m* de l'oreille
early ['ərli] *adv* **-lier; -est 1** : tôt, de bonne heure **2 as** ~ **as possible** : le plus tôt possible **3 ten minutes** ~ : en avance de dix minutes — ~ *adj* **-lier; -est 1** FIRST : premier **2** ANCIENT : ancien **3 in the** ~ **afternoon** : au début de l'après-midi
earmark ['ɪr,mark] *vt* : réserver, désigner
earn ['ərn] *vt* **1** : gagner **2** DESERVE : mériter
earnest ['ərnəst] *adj* : sérieux — ~ *n* **in** ~ : sérieusement
earnings ['ərnɪŋz] *npl* **1** WAGES : salaire *m* **2** PROFITS : gains *mpl*
earphone ['ɪr,fo:n] *n* : écouteur *m*
earring ['ɪr,rɪŋ] *n* : boucle *f* d'oreille
earshot ['ɪr,ʃat] *n* **within** ~ : à portée de voix
earth ['ərθ] *n* **1** GROUND : terre *f*, sol *m* **2 the Earth** : la terre — **earthly** ['ərθli] *adj* : terrestre — **earthquake** ['ərθ,kweɪk] *n* : tremblement *m* de terre — **earthworm** ['ərθ,wərm] *n* : ver *m* de terre — **earthy** ['ərθi] *adj* **earthier; earthiest** : terreux
ease ['i:z] *n* **1** FACILITY : facilité *f* **2** COMFORT : bien-être *m* **3 feel at** ~ : être à l'aise — ~ *v* **eased; easing** *vt* **1** FACILITATE : faciliter **2** ALLEVIATE : soulager, réduire — *vi* ~ **up** : s'atténuer
easel ['i:zəl] *n* : chevalet *m*
easily ['i:zəli] *adv* **1** : facilement **2** UNQUESTIONABLY : de loin
east ['i:st] *adv* : vers l'est, à l'est — ~ *adj* : est — ~ *n* **1** : est *m* **2 the East** : l'Est *m*, l'Orient *m*
Easter ['i:stər] *n* : Pâques *m*, Pâques *fpl*
easterly ['i:stərli] *adv* : vers l'est — ~ *adj* : d'est, de l'est
eastern ['i:stərn] *adj* **1** : est, de l'est **2 Eastern** : de l'Est, oriental
easy ['i:zi] *adj* **easier; easiest 1** : facile, aisé **2** RELAXED : décontracté — **easygoing** [,i:zi'go:ɪŋ] *adj* : accommodant
eat ['i:t] *v* **ate** ['eɪt]; **eaten** ['i:tən]; **eating** : manger
eaves ['i:vz] *npl* : avant-toit *m* — **eavesdrop** ['i:vz,drɑp] *vi* **-dropped; -dropping** : écouter aux portes
ebb ['ɛb] *n* : reflux *m* — ~ *vi* **1** : refluer **2** DECLINE : décliner
ebony ['ɛbəni] *n, pl* **-nies** : ébène *f*
eccentric [ɪk'sɛntrɪk] *adj* : excentrique — ~ *n* : excentrique *mf* — **eccentricity** [,ɛk,sɛn'trɪsəti] *n, pl* **-ties** : excentricité *f*
echo ['ɛ,ko:] *n, pl* **echoes** : écho *m* — ~ *v* **echoed; echoing** *vt* : répéter — *vi* : se répercuter, résonner
eclipse [ɪ'klɪps] *n* : éclipse *f*
ecology [i'kɑləʤi, ɛ-] *n, pl* **-gies** : écologie *f* — **ecological** [,i:kə'lɑʤɪkəl, ,ɛkə-] *adj* : écologique
economy [i'kɑnəmi] *n, pl* **-mies** : économie *f* — **economic** [,i:kə'nɑmɪk, ,ɛkə-] *adj* : économique — **economical** [,i:kə'nɑmɪkəl, ,ɛkə-] *adj* THRIFTY : économe — **economics** [,i:kə'nɑmɪks, ,ɛkə-] *ns & pl* : sciences *fpl* économiques, économie *f* — **economist** [i'kɑnəmɪst] *n* : économiste *mf* — **economize** [i'kɑnə,maɪz] *v* **-mized; -mizing** : économiser
ecstasy ['ɛkstəsi] *n, pl* **-sies** : extase *f* — **ecstatic** [ɛk'stætɪk, ɪk-] *adj* : extatique
edge ['ɛʤ] *n* **1** BORDER : bord *m* **2** : tranchant *m* (d'un couteau, etc.) **3** ADVANTAGE : avantage *m* — ~ *vi* **edged; edging** : avancer lentement — **edgewise** ['ɛʤ,waɪz] *adv* : de côté — **edgy** ['ɛʤi] *adj* **edgier; edgiest** : énervé
edible ['ɛdəbəl] *adj* : comestible
edit ['ɛdɪt] *vt* **1** : réviser, corriger **2** ~ **out** : couper — **edition** [ɪ'dɪʃən] *n* : édition *f* — **editor** ['ɛdɪtər] *n* : rédacteur *m*, -trice *f* (d'un journal); éditeur *m*, -trice *f* (d'un livre) — **editorial** [,ɛdɪ'toriəl] *n* : éditorial *m*
educate ['ɛʤə,keɪt] *vt* **-cated; -cating** : instruire, éduquer — **education** [,ɛʤə'keɪʃən] *n* **1** : éducation *f*, études *fpl* **2** TEACHING : enseignement *m*, instruction *f* — **educational** [,ɛʤə'keɪʃənəl] *adj* **1** : éducatif **2** TEACHING : pédagogique — **educator** ['ɛʤə,keɪtər] *n* : éducateur *m*, -trice *f*
eel ['i:l] *n* : anguille *f*
eerie ['ɪri] *adj* **eerier; -est** : étrange
effect [ɪ'fɛkt] *n* **1** : effet *m* **2 go into** ~ : entrer en vigueur — ~ *vt* : effectuer, réaliser — **effective** [ɪ'fɛktɪv] *adj* **1** : efficace **2 become** ~ : entrer en vigueur — **effectiveness** [ɪ'fɛktɪvnəs] *n* : efficacité *f*
effeminate [ə'fɛmənət] *adj* : efféminé
efficient [ɪ'fɪʃənt] *adj* : efficace — **efficiency** [ɪ'fɪʃəntsi] *n pl* **-cies** : efficacité *f*
effort ['ɛfərt] *n* **1** : effort *m* **2 it's not worth the** ~ : ça ne vaut pas la peine — **effortless** ['ɛfərtləs] *adj* : facile
egg ['ɛg] *n* : œuf *m* — **eggplant** ['ɛg,plænt] *n* : aubergine *f* — **eggshell** ['ɛg,ʃɛl] *n* : coquille *f* d'œuf
ego ['i:,go:] *n, pl* **egos 1** SELF : moi *m* **2** SELF-ESTEEM : amour-propre *m* — **egotism** ['i:gə,tɪzəm] *n* : égotisme *m* — **egotistic** [,i:gə'tɪstɪk] *or* **egotistical** [-'tɪstɪkəl] *adj* : égocentrique
Egyptian [i'ʤɪpʃən] *adj* : égyptien
eight ['eɪt] *n* : huit *m* — ~ *adj* : huit — **eighteen** [eɪt'ti:n] *n* : dix-huit *m* — ~ *adj* : dix-huit — **eighteenth** [eɪt'ti:nθ] *n* **1** : dix-huitième *mf* **2 October** ~ : le dix-huit octobre — ~ *adj* : dix-huitième — **eighth** ['eɪtθ] *n* **1** : huitième *mf* **2 February** ~ : le huit février — ~ *adj* : huitième — **eight hundred** *adj* : huit cents — **eightieth** ['eɪtiəθ] *n* : quatre-vingtième *mf* — ~ *adj* : quatre-vingtième — **eighty** ['eɪti] *n, pl* **eighties** : quatre-vingts *m* — ~ *adj* : quatre-vingts
either ['i:ðər, 'aɪ-] *adj* **1** : l'un ou l'autre **2** EACH : chaque — ~ *pron* : l'un ou l'autre, n'importe lequel — ~ *conj* **1** : ou, soit **2** (*in negative constructions*) : ni
eject [i'ʤɛkt] *vt* : éjecter, expulser
elaborate [i'læbərət] *adj* **1** DETAILED : détaillé **2** COMPLEX : compliqué — ~ [i'læbə,reɪt] *v* **-rated; -rating** *vt* : élaborer — *vi* ~ **on** : donner des détails sur
elapse [i'læps] *vi* **elapsed; elapsing** : s'écouler
elastic [i'læstɪk] *adj* : élastique — ~ *n* : élastique *m* — **elasticity** [i,læs'tɪsəti, ,i:,læs-] *n, pl* **-ties** : élasticité *f*
elated [i'leɪtəd] *adj* : fou de joie — **elation** [i'leɪʃən] *n* : allégresse *f*, joie *f*
elbow ['ɛl,bo:] *n* : coude *m*
elder ['ɛldər] *adj* : aîné, plus âgé — ~ *n* : aîné *m*, aînée *f* — **elderly** ['ɛldərli] *adj* : âgé
elect [i'lɛkt] *vt* : élire — ~ *adj* : élu, futur — **election** [i'lɛkʃən] *n* : élection *f* — **electoral** [i'lɛktərəl] *adj* : électoral — **electorate** [i'lɛktərət] *n* : électorat *m*
electricity [i,lɛk'trɪsəti] *n, pl* **-ties** : électricité *f* — **electric** [i'lɛktrɪk] *or* **electrical** [-trɪkəl] *adj* : électrique — **electrician** [i,lɛk'trɪʃən] *n* : électricien *m*, -cienne *f* — **electrocute** [i'lɛktrə,kju:t] *vt* **-cuted; -cuting** : électrocuter
electron [i'lɛk,trɑn] *n* : électron *m* — **electronic** [i,lɛk'trɑnɪk] *adj* : électronique — **electronic mail** *n* : courrier *m* électronique — **electronics** [i,lɛk'trɑnɪks] *n* : électronique *f*
elegant ['ɛlɪgənt] *adj* : élégant — **elegance** ['ɛlɪgənts] *n* : élégance *f*
element ['ɛləmənt] *n* **1** : élément *m* **2** ~**s** *npl* BASICS : rudiments *mpl* — **elementary** [,ɛlə'mɛntri] *adj* : élémentaire — **elementary school** *n* : école *f* primaire
elephant ['ɛləfənt] *n* : éléphant *m*
elevate ['ɛlə,veɪt] *vt* **-vated; -vating** : élever — **elevator** ['ɛlə,veɪtər] *n* : ascenseur *m*
eleven [ɪ'lɛvən] *n* : onze *m* — ~ *adj* : onze — **eleventh** [ɪ'lɛvənθ] *n* **1** : onzième *mf* **2 March** ~ : le onze mars — ~ *adj* : onzième
elf ['ɛlf] *n, pl* **elves** ['ɛlvz] : lutin *m*
elicit [ɪ'lɪsət] *vt* : provoquer
eligible ['ɛləʤəbəl] *adj* : éligible, admissible
eliminate [ɪ'lɪmə,neɪt] *vt* **-nated; -nating** : éliminer — **elimination** [ɪ,lɪmə'neɪʃən] *n* : élimination *f*
elite [eɪ'li:t, i-] *n* : élite *f*
elk ['ɛlk] *n* : élan *m* (d'Europe), wapiti *m* (d'Amérique)
elm ['ɛlm] *n* : orme *m*
elongate [i'lɔŋ,geɪt] *vt* **-gated; -gating** : allonger
elope [i'lo:p] *vi* **eloped; eloping** : s'enfuir (pour se marier) — **elopement** [i'lo:pmənt] *n* : fugue *f* amoureuse
eloquence ['ɛlə,kwənts] *n* : éloquence *f* — **eloquent** ['ɛlə,kwənt] *adj* : éloquent
else ['ɛls] *adv* **or** ~ : sinon, autrement — ~ *adj* **1 everyone** ~ : tous les autres **2 what** ~ : quoi d'autre — **elsewhere** ['ɛls,hwɛr] *adv* : ailleurs
elude [i'lu:d] *vt* **eluded; eluding** : échapper à, éluder — **elusive** [i'lu:sɪv] *adj* : insaisissable
elves → **elf**
e-mail ['i:,meɪl] *n* : courriel *m*, e-mail *m* *France*
emanate ['ɛmə,neɪt] *vi* **-nated; -nating** : émaner
emancipate [i'mæntsə,peɪt] *vt* **-pated; -pating** : émanciper
embalm [ɪm'bɑm, ɛm-, -'bɑlm] *vt* : embaumer
embankment [ɪm'bæŋkmənt, ɛm-] *n* : digue *f* (d'une rivière), remblai *m* (d'une route)
embargo [ɪm'bɑrgo, ɛm-] *n, pl* **-goes** : embargo *m*
embark [ɪm'bɑrk, ɛm-] *vt* : embarquer — *vi* ~ **on** : entreprendre
embarrass [ɪm'bærəs, ɛm-] *vt* : gêner, embarrasser — **embarrassing** [ɪm'bærəsɪŋ, ɛm-] *adj* : embarrassant — **embarrassment** [ɪm'bærəsmənt, ɛm-] *n* : gêne *f*, embarras *m*
embassy ['ɛmbəsi] *n, pl* **-sies** : ambassade *f*
embed [ɪm'bɛd, ɛm-] *vt* **-bedded; -bedding** : enfoncer
embellish [ɪm'bɛlɪʃ, ɛm-] *vt* : embellir — **embellishment** [ɪm'bɛlɪʃmənt, ɛm-] *n* : ornement *m*
embers ['ɛmbərz] *npl* : braise *f*
embezzle [ɪm'bɛzəl, ɛm-] *vt* **-zled; -zling** : détourner — **embezzlement** [ɪm'bɛzəlmənt, ɛm-] *n* : détournement *m* de fonds
emblem ['ɛmbləm] *n* : emblème *m*
embody [ɪm'bɑdi, ɛm-] *vt* **-bodied; -bodying** : incarner
embrace [ɪm'breɪs, ɛm-] *v* **-braced; -bracing** *vt* : embrasser — *vi* : s'embrasser — ~ *n* : étreinte *f*
embroider [ɪm'brɔɪdər, ɛm-] *vt* : broder — **embroidery** [ɪm'brɔɪdəri, ɛm-] *n, pl* **-deries** : broderie *f*
embryo ['ɛmbri,o:] *n* : embryon *m*
emerald ['ɛmrəld, 'ɛmə-] *n* : émeraude *f*
emerge [i'mərʤ] *vi* **emerged; emerging 1** APPEAR : apparaître **2** ~ **from** : émerger de — **emergence** [i'mərʤənts] *n* : apparition *f*
emergency [i'mərʤəntsi] *n, pl* **-cies 1** : urgence *f* **2** ~ **exit** : sortie *f* de secours **3** ~ **room** : salle *f* des urgences
emery ['ɛməri] *n, pl* **-eries 1** : émeri *m* **2** ~ **board** : lime *f* à ongles
emigrant ['ɛmɪgrənt] *n* : émigrant *m*, -grante *f* — **emigrate** ['ɛmə,greɪt] *vi* **-grated; -grating** : émigrer
eminence ['ɛmənənts] *n* : éminence *f* — **eminent** ['ɛmənənt] *adj* : éminent
emission [i'mɪʃən] *n* : émission *f* — **emit** [i'mɪt] *vt* **emitted; emitting** : émettre
emotion [i'mo:ʃən] *n* : émotion *f* — **emotional** [i'mo:ʃənəl] *adj* **1** : émotif **2** MOVING : émouvant
emperor ['ɛmpərər] *n* : empereur *m*
emphasis ['ɛmfəsɪs] *n, pl* **-ses** [-,si:z] : ac-

cent *m* — **emphasize** ['ɛmfəˌsaɪz] *vt* **-sized; -sizing** : insister sur — **emphatic** [ɪm'fætɪk, ɛm-] *adj* : énergique, catégorique
empire ['ɛmˌpaɪr] *n* : empire *m*
employ [ɪm'plɔɪ, ɛm-] *vt* : employer — **employee** [ɪmˌplɔɪ'i:, ɛm-, -'plɔɪˌi:] *n* : employé *m*, -ployée *f* — **employer** [ɪm'plɔɪər, ɛm-] *n* : employeur *m*, -ployeuse *f* — **employment** [ɪm'plɔɪmənt, ɛm-] *n* : emploi *m*, travail *m*
empower [ɪm'paʊər, ɛm-] *vt* : autoriser
empress ['ɛmprəs] *n* : impératrice *f*
empty ['ɛmpti] *adj* **-tier; -est 1** : vide **2** MEANINGLESS : vain — **~** *v* **-tied; -tying** *vt* : vider — *vi* : se vider — **emptiness** ['ɛmptinəs] *n* : vide *m*
emulate ['ɛmjəˌleɪt] *vt* **-lated; -lating** : imiter
enable [ɪ'neɪbəl, ɛ-] *vt* **-abled; -abling** : permettre
enact [ɪ'nækt, ɛ-] *vt* : promulguer (une loi, etc.)
enamel [ɪ'næməl] *n* : émail *m*
enchant [ɪn'ʧænt, ɛn-] *vt* : enchanter — **enchanting** [ɪn'ʧæntɪŋ, ɛn-] *adj* : enchanteur
encircle [ɪn'sərkəl, ɛn-] *vt* **-cled; -cling** : entourer, encercler
enclose [ɪn'klo:z, ɛn-] *vt* **-closed; -closing 1** SURROUND : entourer **2** INCLUDE : joindre (à une lettre) — **enclosure** [ɪn'klo:ʒər, ɛn-] *n* **1** : enceinte *f* **2** : pièce *f* jointe (à une lettre)
encompass [ɪn'kʌmpəs, ɛn-, -'kɑm-] *vt* **1** ENCIRCLE : entourer **2** INCLUDE : inclure
encore ['ɑnˌkor] *n* : bis *m*
encounter [ɪn'kaʊntər, ɛn-] *vt* : rencontrer — **~** *n* : rencontre *f*
encourage [ɪn'kərɪʤ, ɛn-] *vt* **-aged; -aging** : encourager — **encouragement** [ɪn'kərɪʤmənt, ɛn-] *n* : encouragement *m*
encroach [ɪn'kro:ʧ, ɛn-] *vi* **~ on** : empiéter sur
encyclopedia [ɪnˌsaɪklə'pi:diə, ɛn-] *n* : encyclopédie *f*
end ['ɛnd] *n* **1** : fin *f* **2** EXTREMITY : bout *m* **3 come to an ~** : prendre fin **4 in the ~** : finalement— **~** *vt* : terminer, mettre fin à — *vi* : se terminer
endanger [ɪn'deɪnʤər, ɛn-] *vt* : mettre en danger
endearing [ɪn'dɪrɪŋ, ɛn-] *adj* : attachant
endeavor *or Brit* **endeavour** [ɪn'dɛvər, ɛn-] *vt* **~ to** : s'efforcer de — **~** *n* : effort *m*
ending ['ɛndɪŋ] *n* : fin *f*, dénouement *m*
endive ['ɛnˌdaɪv, ˌɑn'di:v] *n* : endive *f*
endless ['ɛndləs] *adj* **1** INTERMINABLE : interminable **2** INNUMERABLE : innombrable **3 ~ possibilities** : possibilités *fpl* infinies
endorse [ɪn'dɔrs, ɛn-] *vt* **-dorsed; -dorsing 1** SIGN : endosser **2** APPROVE : approuver — **endorsement** [ɪn'dɔrsmənt, ɛn-] *n* APPROVAL : approbation *f*
endow [ɪn'daʊ, ɛn-] *vt* : doter
endure [ɪn'dʊr, ɛn-, -'djʊr-] *v* **-dured; -during** *vt* : supporter, endurer — *vi* LAST : durer — **endurance** [ɪn'dʊrənts, ɛn-, -'djʊr-] *n* : endurance *f*
enemy ['ɛnəmi] *n, pl* **-mies** : ennemi *m*, -mie *f*
energy ['ɛnərʤi] *n, pl* **-gies** : énergie *f* — **energetic** [ˌɛnər'ʤɛṭɪk] *adj* : énergique
enforce [ɪn'fors, ɛn-] *vt* **-forced; -forcing 1** : faire respecter (une loi) **2** IMPOSE : imposer — **enforcement** [ɪn'forsmənt, ɛn-] *n* : exécution *f*, application *f*
engage [ɪn'geɪʤ, ɛn-] *v* **-gaged; -gaging** *vt* **1** : engager (une conversation) **2 ~ the clutch** : embrayer — *vi* **~ in** : prendre part à, s'occuper de — **engaged** [ɪn'geɪʤd, ɛn-] *adj* **get ~ to** : se fiancer à — **engagement** [ɪn'geɪʤmənt, ɛn-] *n* **1** : fiançailles *fpl* **2** APPOINTMENT : rendez-vous *m* — **engaging** [ɪn'geɪʤɪŋ, ɛn-] *adj* : engageant, attirant
engine ['ɛnʤən] *n* **1** : moteur *m* **2** LOCOMOTIVE : locomotive *f* — **engineer** [ˌɛnʤə'nɪr] *n* : ingénieur *m*, -nieure *f* — **engineering** [ˌɛnʤə'nɪrɪŋ] *n* : ingénierie *f*
English ['ɪŋglɪʃ, 'ɪŋlɪʃ] *adj* : anglais — **~** *n* : anglais *m* (langue) — **Englishman** ['ɪŋglɪʃmən, 'ɪŋlɪʃ-] *n* : Anglais *m* — **Englishwoman** ['ɪŋglɪʃˌwʊmən, 'ɪŋlɪʃ-] *n* : Anglaise *f*
engrave [ɪn'greɪv, ɛn-] *vt* **-graved; -graving** : graver — **engraving** [ɪn'greɪvɪŋ, ɛn-] *n* : gravure *f*
engross [ɪn'gro:s, ɛn-] *vt* : absorber, occuper
engulf [ɪn'gʌlf, ɛn-] *vt* : engloutir
enhance [ɪn'hænts, ɛn-] *vt* **-hanced; -hancing** : améliorer, rehausser
enjoy [ɪn'ʤɔɪ, ɛn-] *vt* **1** LIKE : aimer **2** POSSESS : jouir de **3 ~ oneself** : s'amuser — **enjoyable** [ɪn'ʤɔɪəbəl, ɛn-] *adj* : agréable — **enjoyment** [ɪn'ʤɔɪmənt, ɛn-] *n* : plaisir *m*
enlarge [ɪn'lɑrʤ, ɛn-] *vt* **-larged; -larging** : agrandir — **enlargement** [ɪn'lɑrʤmənt, ɛn-] *n* : agrandissement *m*
enlighten [ɪn'laɪtən, ɛn-] *vt* : éclairer
enlist [ɪn'lɪst, ɛn-] *vt* **1** ENROLL : enrôler **2** OBTAIN : obtenir — *vi* : s'engager, s'enrôler
enliven [ɪn'laɪvən, ɛn-] *vt* : animer
enormous [ɪ'nɔrməs] *adj* : énorme
enough [i'nʌf] *adj* : assez de — **~** *adv* : assez — **~** *pron* **have ~ of** : en avoir assez de
enquire [ɪn'kwaɪr, ɛn-], **enquiry** ['ɪnˌkwaɪri, 'ɛn-, -kwəri; ɪn'kwaɪri, ɛn'-] → **inquire, inquiry**
enrage [ɪn'reɪʤ, ɛn-] *vt* **-raged; -raging** : rendre furieux
enrich [ɪn'rɪʧ, ɛn-] *vt* : enrichir
enroll *or* **enrol** [ɪn'ro:l, ɛn-] *v* **-rolled; -rolling** *vt* **1** : inscrire (à l'école, etc.) **2** ENLIST : enrôler — *vi* : s'inscrire
ensue [ɪn'su:, ɛn-] *vi* **-sued; -suing** : s'ensuivre
ensure [ɪn'ʃʊr, ɛn-] *vt* **-sured; -suring** : assurer
entail [ɪn'teɪl, ɛn-] *vt* : entraîner, comporter
entangle [ɪn'tæŋgəl, ɛn-] *vt* **-gled; -gling** : emmêler
enter ['ɛntər] *vt* **1** : entrer dans **2** RECORD : inscrire — *vi* **1** : entrer **2 ~ into** : entamer
enterprise ['ɛntərˌpraɪz] *n* **1** : entreprise *f* **2** INITIATIVE : initiative *f* — **enterprising** ['ɛntərˌpraɪzɪŋ] *adj* : entreprenant
entertain [ˌɛntər'teɪn] *vt* **1** AMUSE : amuser, divertir **2** CONSIDER : considérer **3** : recevoir (des invités) — **entertainment** [ˌɛntər'teɪnmənt] *n* : divertissement *m*
enthrall *or* **enthral** [ɪn'θrɔl, ɛn-] *vt* **-thralled; -thralling** : captiver
enthusiasm [ɪn'θu:ziˌæzəm, ɛn-, -'θju:-] *n* : enthousiasme *m* — **enthusiast** [ɪn'θu:ziˌæst, ɛn-, -'θju:-, -əst] *n* : enthousiaste *mf*; passionné *m*, -née *f* — **enthusiastic** [ɪnˌθu:zi'æstɪk, ɛn-, -'θju:-] *adj* : enthousiaste
entice [ɪn'taɪs, ɛn-] *vt* **-ticed; -ticing** : attirer, entraîner
entire [ɪn'taɪr, ɛn-] *adj* : entier, complet — **entirely** [ɪn'taɪrli, ɛn-] *adv* : entièrement — **entirety** [ɪn'taɪrṭi, ɛn-, -taɪrəṭi] *n, pl* **-ties 1** : totalité *f* **2 in its ~** : dans son ensemble
entitle [ɪn'taɪṭəl, ɛn-] *vt* **-tled; -tling 1** NAME : intituler **2** AUTHORIZE : autoriser, donner droit à — **entitlement** [ɪn'taɪṭəlmənt, ɛn-] *n* : droit *m*
entity ['ɛntəṭi] *n, pl* **-ties** : entité *f*
entrails ['ɛnˌtreɪlz, -trəlz] *npl* : entrailles *fpl*
entrance[1] [ɪn'trænts, ɛn-] *vt* **-tranced; -trancing** : transporter, ravir
entrance[2] ['ɛntrənts] *n* : entrée *f*
entreat [ɪn'tri:t, ɛn-] *vt* : supplier
entrée *or* **entree** ['ɑnˌtreɪ, ˌɑn'-] *n* : entrée *f*, plat *m* principal
entrust [ɪn'trʌst, ɛn-] *vt* : confier
entry ['ɛntri] *n, pl* **-tries** ENTRANCE : entrée *f*
enumerate [ɪ'nu:məˌreɪt, ɛ-, -'nju:-] *vt* **-ated; -ating** : énumérer
enunciate [i'nʌntsiˌeɪt, ɛ-] *vt* **-ated; -ating 1** STATE : énoncer **2** PRONOUNCE : articuler
envelop [ɪn'vɛləp, ɛn-] *vt* : envelopper — **envelope** ['ɛnvəˌlo:p, 'ɑn-] *n* : enveloppe *f*
envious ['ɛnviəs] *adj* : envieux, jaloux — **enviously** ['ɛnviəsli] *adv* : avec envie
environment [ɪn'vaɪrənmənt, ɛn-, -'vaɪərn-] *n* : environnement *m*, milieu *m* — **environmental** [ɪnˌvaɪrən'mɛntəl, ɛn-, -ˌvaɪərn-] *adj* : de l'environnement — **environmentalist** [ɪnˌvaɪrən'mɛntəlɪst, ɛn-, -ˌvaɪərn] *n* : écologiste *mf*
envision [ɪn'vɪʒən, ɛn-] *vt* : envisager
envoy ['ɛnˌvɔɪ, 'ɑn-] *n* : envoyé *m*, -voyée *f*
envy ['ɛnvi] *n* : envie *f*, jalousie *f* — **~** *vt* **-vied; -vying** : envier
enzyme ['ɛnˌzaɪm] *n* : enzyme *f*
epic ['ɛpɪk] *adj* : épique — **~** *n* : épopée *f*
epidemic [ˌɛpə'dɛmɪk] *n* : épidémie *f* — **~** *adj* : épidémique
epilepsy ['ɛpəˌlɛpsi] *n, pl* **-sies** : épilepsie *f* — **epileptic** [ˌɛpə'lɛptɪk] *adj* : épileptique — **~** *n* : épileptique *mf*
episode ['ɛpəˌso:d] *n* : épisode *m*
epitaph ['ɛpəˌtæf] *n* : épitaphe *f*
epitome [ɪ'pɪṭəmi] *n* : exemple *m* même, modèle *m* — **epitomize** [ɪ'pɪṭəˌmaɪz] *vt* **-mized; -mizing** : incarner
equal ['i:kwəl] *adj* **1** SAME : égal **2 be ~ to** : être à la hauteur de — **~** *n* : égal *m*, -gale *f* — **~** *vt* **equaled** *or* **equalled; equaling** *or* **equalling** : égaler — **equality** [ɪ'kwɑləṭi] *n, pl* **-ties** : égalité *f* — **equalize** ['i:kwəˌlaɪz] *vt* **-ized; -izing** : égaliser — **equally** ['i:kwəli] *adv* **1** : également **2 ~ important** : tout aussi important
equate [ɪ'kweɪt] *vt* **equated; equating ~ with** : assimiler à — **equation** [ɪ'kweɪʒən] *n* : équation *f*
equator [ɪ'kweɪṭər] *n* : équateur *m*
equilibrium [ˌi:kwə'lɪbriəm, ˌɛ-] *n, pl* **-riums** *or* **-ria** : équilibre *m*
equinox ['i:kwəˌnɑks, 'ɛ-] *n* : équinoxe *m*
equip [ɪ'kwɪp] *vt* **equipped; equipping** : équiper — **equipment** [ɪ'kwɪpmənt] *n* : équipement *m*, matériel *m*
equity ['ɛkwəṭi] *n, pl* **-ties 1** FAIRNESS : équité *f* **2 equities** *npl* STOCKS : actions *fpl* ordinaires
equivalent [ɪ'kwɪvələnt] *adj* : équivalent — **~** *n* : équivalent *m*
era ['ɪrə, 'ɛrə, 'i:rə] *n* : ère *f*, époque *f*
eradicate [ɪ'rædəˌkeɪt] *vt* **-cated; -cating** : éradiquer
erase [ɪ'reɪs] *vt* **erased; erasing** : effacer — **eraser** [ɪ'reɪsər] *n* : gomme *f*, efface *f Can*
erect [ɪ'rɛkt] *adj* : droit — **~** *vt* **1** BUILD : construire **2** RAISE : ériger — **erection** [ɪ'rɛkʃən] *n* **1** BUILDING : construction *f* **2** : érection *f* (en physiologie)
erode [ɪ'ro:d] *vt* **eroded; eroding** : éroder, ronger — **erosion** [ɪ'ro:ʒən] *n* : érosion *f*
erotic [ɪ'rɑṭɪk] *adj* : érotique
err ['ɛr, 'ər] *vi* : se tromper
errand ['ɛrənd] *n* : course *f*, commission *f*
erratic [ɪ'ræṭɪk] *adj* : irrégulier
error ['ɛrər] *n* : erreur *f* — **erroneous** [ɪ'ro:niəs, ɛ-] *adj* : erroné
erupt [ɪ'rʌpt] *vi* **1** : entrer en éruption (se dit d'un volcan) **2** : éclater (se dit de la guerre, etc.) — **eruption** [ɪ'rʌpʃən] *n* : éruption *f*
escalate ['ɛskəˌleɪt] *vi* **-lated; -lating 1** : s'intensifier **2** : monter en flèche (se dit des prix, etc.)
escalator ['ɛskəˌleɪṭər] *n* : escalier *m* mécanique
escape [ɪ'skeɪp, ɛ-] *v* **-caped; -caping** *vt* : échapper à, éviter — *vi* : s'échapper, s'évader — **~** *n* : fuite *f*, évasion *f*
escort ['ɛsˌkɔrt] *n* GUARD : escorte *f* — **~** [ɪ'skɔrt, ɛ-] *vt* : escorter
Eskimo ['ɛskəˌmo:] *adj* : esquimau
especially [ɪ'spɛʃəli] *adv* : particulièrement
espionage ['ɛspiəˌnɑʒ, -ˌnɑʤ] *n* : espionnage *m*
espresso [ɛ'sprɛˌso:] *n, pl* **-sos** : express *m*, café *m* express
essay ['ɛˌseɪ] *n* : essai *m* (littéraire), dissertation *f* (académique)
essence ['ɛsənts] *n* : essence *f* — **essential** [ɪ'sɛnʧəl] *adj* : essentiel — **~** *n* **1** : objet *m* essentiel **2 the ~s** : l'essentiel *m*
establish [ɪ'stæblɪʃ, ɛ-] *vt* : établir — **establishment** [ɪ'stæblɪʃmənt, ɛ-] *n* : établissement *m*
estate [ɪ'steɪt, ɛ-] *n* **1** POSSESSIONS : biens *mpl* **2** LAND, PROPERTY : propriété *f*, domaine *m*
esteem [ɪ'sti:m, ɛ-] *n* : estime *f* — **~** *vt* : estimer
esthetic [ɛs'θɛṭɪk] → **aesthetic**
estimate ['ɛstəˌmeɪt] *vt* **-mated; -mating** : estimer — **~** ['ɛstəmət] *n* : estimation *f* — **estimation** [ˌɛstə'meɪʃən] *n* **1** JUDGMENT : jugement *m* **2** ESTEEM : estime *f*
estuary ['ɛsʧʊˌwɛri] *n, pl* **-aries** : estuaire *m*
eternal [ɪ'tərnəl, i:-] *adj* : éternel — **eternity** [ɪ'tərnəṭi, i:-] *n, pl* **-ties** : éternité *f*
ether ['i:θər] *n* : éther *m*
ethical ['ɛθɪkəl] *adj* : éthique, moral — **ethics** ['ɛθɪks] *ns & pl* : éthique *f*, morale *f*
ethnic ['ɛθnɪk] *adj* : ethnique
etiquette ['ɛṭɪkət, -ˌkɛt] *n* : étiquette *f*, convenances *fpl*
Eucharist ['ju:kərɪst] *n* : Eucharistie *f*
eulogy ['ju:ləʤi] *n, pl* **-gies** : éloge *m*
euphemism ['ju:fəˌmɪzəm] *n* : euphémisme *m*
euphoria [jʊ'foriə] *n* : euphorie *f*
European [ˌjʊrə'pi:ən, -pi:n] *adj* : européen
evacuate [ɪ'vækjʊˌeɪt] *vt* **-ated; -ating** : évacuer — **evacuation** [ɪˌvækjʊ'eɪʃən] *n* : évacuation *f*
evade [ɪ'veɪd] *vt* **evaded; evading** : éviter, esquiver
evaluate [ɪ'væljʊˌeɪt] *vt* **-ated; -ating** : évaluer
evaporate [ɪ'væpəˌreɪt] *vi* **-rated; -rating** : s'évaporer
evasion [ɪ'veɪʒən] *n* : évasion *f* — **evasive** [ɪ'veɪsɪv] *adj* : évasif
eve ['i:v] *n* : veille *f*
even ['i:vən] *adj* **1** REGULAR, STEADY : régulier **2** LEVEL : uni, plat **3** EQUAL : égal **4 ~ number** : nombre *m* pair **5 get ~ with** : se venger de — **~** *adv* **1** : même **2 ~ better** : encore mieux **3 ~ so** : quand même — **~** *vt* : égaliser — *vi or* **~ out** : s'égaliser
evening ['i:vnɪŋ] *n* : soir *m*, soirée *f*
event [ɪ'vɛnt] *n* **1** : événement *m* **2** : épreuve *f* (aux sports) **3 in the ~ of** : en cas de — **eventful** [ɪ'vɛntfəl] *adj* : mouvementé
eventual [ɪ'vɛnʧʊəl] *adj* : final — **eventuality** [ɪˌvɛnʧʊ'æləṭi] *n, pl* **-ties** : éventualité *f* — **eventually** [ɪ'vɛnʧʊəli] *adv* : finalement, en fin de compte
ever ['ɛvər] *adv* **1** ALWAYS : toujours **2 ~ since** : depuis **3 hardly ~** : presque jamais
evergreen ['ɛvərˌgri:n] *n* : plante *f* à feuilles persistantes
everlasting [ˌɛvər'læstɪŋ] *adj* : éternel
every ['ɛvri] *adj* **1** EACH : chaque **2 ~ month** : tous les mois — **everybody** ['ɛvriˌbʌdi, -ˌbɑ-] *pron* : tout le monde — **everyday** [ˌɛvri'deɪ, 'ɛvriˌ-] *adj* : quotidien, de tous les jours — **everyone** ['ɛvriˌwʌn] → **everybody** — **everything** ['ɛvriˌθɪŋ] *pron* : tout — **everywhere** ['ɛvriˌhwɛr] *adv* : partout
evict [ɪ'vɪkt] *vt* : expulser — **eviction** [ɪ'vɪkʃən] *n* : expulsion *f*
evidence ['ɛvədənts] *n* **1** PROOF : preuve *f* **2** TESTIMONY : témoignage *m* — **evident** ['ɛvɪdənt] *adj* : évident — **evidently** ['ɛvɪdəntli, ˌɛvɪ'dɛntli] *adv* **1** OBVIOUSLY : évidemment, manifestement **2** APPARENTLY : apparemment
evil ['i:vəl, -vɪl] *adj* **eviler** *or* **eviller; evilest** *or* **evillest** : mauvais, méchant — **~** *n* : mal *m*
evoke [i'vo:k] *vt* **evoked; evoking** : évoquer
evolution [ˌɛvə'lu:ʃən, ˌi:-] *n* : évolution *f* — **evolve** [i'vɑlv] *vi* **evolved; evolving** : évoluer, se développer
exact [ɪg'zækt, ɛg-] *adj* : exact, précis — **~** *vt* : exiger — **exacting** [ɪg'zæktɪŋ, ɛg-] *adj* : exigeant — **exactly** [ɪg'zæktli, ɛg-] *adv* : exactement
exaggerate [ɪg'zæʤəˌreɪt, ɛg-] *v* **-ated; -ating** : exagérer — **exaggeration** [ɪgˌzæʤə'reɪʃən, ɛg-] *n* : exagération *f*
examine [ɪg'zæmən, ɛg-] *vt* **-ined; -ining 1** : examiner **2** QUESTION : interroger — **exam** [ɪg'zæm, ɛg-] *n* : examen *m* — **examination** [ɪgˌzæmə'neɪʃən, ɛg-] *n* : examen *m*
example [ɪg'zæmpəl, ɛg-] *n* : exemple *m*
exasperate [ɪg'zæspəˌreɪt, ɛg-] *vt* **-ated; -ating** : exaspérer — **exasperation** [ɪgˌzæspə'reɪʃən, ɛg-] *n* : exaspération *f*
excavate ['ɛkskəˌveɪt] *vt* **-vated; -vating** : creuser, excaver
exceed [ɪk'si:d, ɛk-] *vt* : dépasser — **exceedingly** [ɪk'si:dɪŋli, ɛk-] *adv* : extrêmement
excel [ɪk'sɛl, ɛk-] *vi* **-celled; -celling** : exceller — **excellence** ['ɛksələnts] *n* : excellence *f* — **excellent** ['ɛksələnt] *adj* : excellent
except [ɪk'sɛpt] *prep* **1** : sauf, excepté **2 ~ for** : à part — **~** *vt* : excepter — **exception** [ɪk'sɛpʃən] *n* : exception *f* — **exceptional** [ɪk'sɛpʃənəl] *adj* : exceptionnel
excerpt [ɛk'sərpt, 'ɛgˌzərpt] *n* : extrait *m*
excess [ɪk'sɛs, 'ɛkˌsɛs] *n* : excès *m* — **~** ['ɛkˌsɛs, ɪk'sɛs] *adj* : excédentaire, en trop — **excessive** [ɪk'sɛsɪv, ɛk-] *adj* : excessif
exchange [ɪks'ʧeɪnʤ, ɛks-; 'ɛksˌʧeɪnʤ] *n* **1** : échange *m* **2** : change *m* (en finances) — **~** *vt* **-changed; -changing** : échanger
excise ['ɛkˌsaɪz, ɛk-] *n or* **~ tax** : contribution *f* indirecte
excite [ɪk'saɪt, ɛk-] *vt* **-cited; -citing** : exciter — **excited** [ɪk'saɪṭəd, ɛk-] *adj* : excité, enthousiaste — **excitement** [ɪk'saɪtmənt, ɛk-] *n* : enthousiasme *m* — **exciting** [ɪk'saɪtɪŋ, ɛk-] *adj* : passionnant
exclaim [ɪks'kleɪm, ɛk-] *vi* : s'exclamer — **exclamation** [ˌɛksklə'meɪʃən] *n* : exclamation *f* — **exclamation point** *n* : point *m* d'exclamation
exclude [ɪks'klu:d, ɛks-] *vt* **-cluded; -cluding** : exclure — **excluding** [ɪks'klu:dɪŋ, ɛks-] *prep* : à part, à l'exclusion de — **exclusion** [ɪks'klu:ʒən, ɛks-] *n* : exclusion *f* — **exclusive** [ɪks'klu:sɪv, ɛks-] *adj* : exclusif
excrement ['ɛkskrəmənt] *n* : excréments *mpl*
excruciating [ɪk'skru:ʃiˌeɪṭɪŋ, ɛk-] *adj* : atroce, insupportable
excursion [ɪk'skərʒən, ɛk-] *n* : excursion *f*
excuse [ɪk'skju:z, ɛk-] *vt* **-cused; -cusing 1** : excuser **2 ~ me** : excusez-moi, pardon — **~** [ɪk'skju:s, ɛk-] *n* : excuse *f*
execute ['ɛksɪˌkju:t] *vt* **-cuted; -cuting** : exécuter — **execution** [ˌɛksɪ'kju:ʃən] *n* : exécution *f* — **executioner** [ˌɛksɪ'kju:ʃənər] *n* : bourreau *m*
executive [ɪg'zɛkjəṭɪv, ɛg-] *adj* : exécutif — **~** *n* **1** MANAGER : cadre *m* **2** *or* **~ branch** : executif *m*, pouvoir *m* exécutif
exemplify [ɪg'zɛmpləˌfaɪ, ɛg-] *vt* **-fied; -fying** : illustrer — **exemplary** [ɪg'zɛmpləri, ɛg-] *adj* : exemplaire
exempt [ɪg'zɛmpt, ɛg-] *adj* : exempt — **~** *vt* : exempter — **exemption** [ɪg'zɛmpʃən, ɛg-] *n* : exemption *f*
exercise ['ɛksərˌsaɪz] *n* : exercice *m* — **~** *v* **-cised; -cising** *vt* : exercer — *vi* : faire de l'exercice
exert [ɪg'zərt, ɛg-] *vt* **1** : exercer **2 ~ oneself** : se donner de la peine — **exertion** [ɪg'zərʃən, ɛg-] *n* : effort *m*
exhale [ɛks'heɪl] *v* **-haled; -haling** : expirer
exhaust [ɪg'zɔst, ɛg-] *vt* : épuiser — **~** *n* **1** *or* **~ fumes** : gaz *m* d'échappement **2** *or* **~ pipe** : tuyau *m* d'échappement — **exhaustion** [ɪg'zɔsʧən, ɛg-] *n* : épuisement *m* — **exhaustive** [ɪg'zɔstɪv, ɛg-] *adj* : exhaustif
exhibit [ɪg'zɪbət, ɛg-] *vt* **1** DISPLAY : exposer **2** SHOW : montrer — **~** *n* **1** : objet *m* exposé **2** EXHIBITION : exposition *f* — **exhibition** [ˌɛksə'bɪʃən] *n* : exposition *f*
exhilarate [ɪg'zɪləˌreɪt, ɛg-] *vt* **-rated; -rating** : animer — **exhilaration** [ɪgˌzɪlə'reɪʃən, ɛg-] *n* : joie *f*
exile ['ɛgˌzaɪl, 'ɛkˌsaɪl] *n* **1** : exil *m* **2** OUTCAST : exilé *m*, -lée *f* — **~** *vt* **exiled; exiling** : exiler

exist [ɪg'zɪst, ɛg-] *vi* : exister — **existence** [ɪg'zɪstənts, ɛg-] *n* : existence *f*

exit ['ɛgzət, 'ɛksət] *n* : sortie *f* — ~ *vi* : sortir

exodus ['ɛksədəs] *n* : exode *m*

exonerate [ɪg'zɑnəˌreɪt, ɛg-] *vt* **-ated; -ating** : disculper

exorbitant [ɪg'zɔrbətənt, ɛg-] *adj* : exorbitant, excessif

exotic [ɪg'zɑtɪk, ɛg-] *adj* : exotique

expand [ɪk'spænd, ɛk-] *vt* : étendre, élargir — *vi* : s'étendre, s'agrandir — **expanse** [ɪk'spænts, ɛk-] *n* : étendue *f* — **expansion** [ɪk'spæntʃən, ɛk-] *n* : expansion *f*

expatriate [ɛks'peɪtriət, -ˌeɪt] *n* : expatrié *m*, -triée *f* — ~ *adj* : expatrié

expect [ɪk'spɛkt, ɛk-] *vt* **1** ANTICIPATE : s'attendre à **2** AWAIT : attendre **3** REQUIRE : exiger, demander — *vi* **be expecting** : attendre un bébé, être enceinte — **expectancy** [ɪk'spɛktəntsi, ɛk-] *n, pl* **-cies** : attente *f*, espérance *f* — **expectant** [ɪk'spɛktənt, ɛk-] *adj* **1** : qui attend **2** ~ **mother** : future mère *f* — **expectation** [ˌɛkˌspɛk'teɪʃən] *n* : attente *f*

expedient [ɪk'spi:diənt, ɛk-] *adj* : opportun — ~ *n* : expédient *m*

expedition [ˌɛkspə'dɪʃən] *n* : expédition *f*

expel [ɪk'spɛl, ɛk-] *vt* **-pelled; -pelling** : expulser, renvoyer (un élève)

expend [ɪk'spɛnd, ɛk-] *vt* : dépenser — **expendable** [ɪk'spɛndəbəl, ɛk-] *adj* : remplaçable — **expenditure** [ɪk'spɛndɪtʃər, ɛk-, -ˌtʃʊr] *n* : dépense *f* — **expense** [ɪk'spɛnts, ɛk-] *n* **1** : dépense *f* **2** ~**s** *npl* : frais *mpl* **3 at the ~ of** : aux dépens de — **expensive** [ɪk'spɛntsɪv, ɛk-] *adj* : cher, coûteux

experience [ɪk'spɪriənts, ɛk-] *n* : expérience *f* — ~ *vt* **-enced; -encing** : éprouver, connaître — **experienced** [ɪk'spɪriəntst, ɛk-] *adj* : expérimenté — **experiment** [ɪk'spɛrəmənt, ɛk-, -'spɪr-] *n* : expérience *f* — ~ *vi* : expérimenter — **experimental** [ɪkˌspɛrə'mɛntəl, ɛk-, -ˌspɪr-] *adj* : expérimental

expert ['ɛkˌspərt, ɪk'spərt] *adj* : expert — ~ ['ɛkˌspərt] *n* : expert *m*, -perte *f* — **expertise** [ˌɛkspər'ti:z] *n* : compétence *f*

expire [ɪk'spaɪr, ɛk-] *vi* **-pired; -piring** : expirer — **expiration** [ˌɛkspə'reɪʃən] *n* : expiration *f*

explain [ɪk'spleɪn, ɛk-] *vt* **1** : expliquer **2** ~ **oneself** : s'expliquer — **explanation** [ˌɛksplə'neɪʃən] *n* : explication *f* — **explanatory** [ɪk'splænəˌtori, ɛk-] *adj* : explicatif

explicit [ɪk'splɪsət, ɛk-] *adj* : explicite

explode [ɪk'splo:d, ɛk-] *v* **-ploded; -ploding** *vt* : faire exploser — *vi* : exploser

exploit ['ɛkˌsplɔɪt] *n* : exploit *m* — ~ [ɪk'splɔɪt, ɛk-] *vt* : exploiter — **exploitation** [ˌɛkˌsplɔɪ'teɪʃən] *n* : exploitation *f*

exploration [ˌɛksplə'reɪʃən] *n* : exploration *f* — **explore** [ɪk'splor, ɛk-] *v* **-plored; -ploring** : explorer — **explorer** [ɪk'splorər, ɛk-] *n* : explorateur *m*, -trice *f*

explosion [ɪk'splo:ʒən, ɛk-] *n* : explosion *f* — **explosive** [ɪk'splo:sɪv, ɛk-] *adj* : explosif — ~ *n* : explosif *m*

export [ɛk'sport, 'ɛkˌsport] *vt* : exporter — ~ ['ɛkˌsport] *n* : exportation *f*

expose [ɪk'spo:z, ɛk-] *vt* **-posed; -posing 1** : exposer **2** REVEAL : révéler — **exposure** [ɪk'spo:ʒər, ɛk-] *n* : exposition *f*

express [ɪk'sprɛs, ɛk-] *adj* **1** SPECIFIC : exprès, formel **2** FAST : express — ~ *adv* **send ~** : envoyer en exprès — ~ *n or* ~ **train** : rapide *m*, express *m* — ~ *vt* : exprimer — **expression** [ɪk'sprɛʃən, ɛk-] *n* : expression *f* — **expressive** [ɪk'sprɛsɪv, ɛk-] *adj* : expressif — **expressly** [ɪk'sprɛsli, ɛk-] *adv* : expressément — **expressway** [ɪk'sprɛsˌweɪ, ɛk-] *n* : autoroute *f*

expulsion [ɪk'spʌlʃən, ɛk-] *n* : expulsion *f*, renvoi *m* (d'un élève)

exquisite [ɛk'skwɪzət, 'ɛkˌskwɪ-] *adj* : exquis

extend [ɪk'stɛnd, ɛk-] *vt* **1** STRETCH : étendre **2** LENGTHEN : prolonger **3** ENLARGE : agrandir **4** ~ **one's hand** : tendre la main — *vi* : s'étendre — **extension** [ɪk'stɛntʃən, ɛk-] *n* **1** : extension *f* **2** LENGTHENING : prolongation *f* **3** ANNEX : annexe *f* **4** : poste *m* (de téléphone) **5** ~ **cord** : rallonge *f* — **extensive** [ɪk'stɛntsɪv, ɛk-] *adj* : étendu, vaste — **extent** [ɪk'stɛnt, ɛk-] *n* **1** : étendue *f*, ampleur *f* **2** DEGREE : mesure *f*, degré *m*

exterior [ɛk'stɪriər] *adj* : extérieur — ~ *n* : extérieur *m*

exterminate [ɪk'stərməˌneɪt, ɛk-] *vt* **-nated; -nating** : exterminer — **extermination** [ɪkˌstərmə'neɪʃən, ɛk-] *n* : extermination *f*

external [ɪk'stərnəl, ɛk-] *adj* : externe — **externally** [ɪk'stərnəli, ɛk-] *adv* : extérieurement

extinct [ɪk'stɪŋkt, ɛk-] *adj* : disparu — **extinction** [ɪk'stɪŋkʃən, ɛk-] *n* : extinction *f*

extinguish [ɪk'stɪŋgwɪʃ, ɛk-] *vt* : éteindre — **extinguisher** [ɪk'stɪŋgwɪʃər, ɛk-] *n* : extincteur *m*

extol [ɪk'sto:l, ɛk-] *vt* **-tolled; -tolling** : louer

extort [ɪk'stɔrt, ɛk-] *vt* : extorquer — **extortion** [ɪk'stɔrʃən, ɛk-] *n* : extorsion *f*

extra ['ɛkstrə] *adj* : supplémentaire, de plus — ~ *n* : supplément *m* — ~ *adv* **1** : plus (que d'habitude) **2 cost ~** : coûter plus cher

extract [ɪk'strækt, ɛk-] *vt* : extraire, arracher — ~ ['ɛkˌstrækt] *n* : extrait *m* — **extraction** [ɪk'strækʃən, ɛk-] *n* : extraction *f*

extracurricular [ˌɛkstrəkə'rɪkjələr] *adj* : parascolaire

extraordinary [ɪk'strɔrdənˌɛri, ˌɛkstrə'ɔrd-] *adj* : extraordinaire

extraterrestrial [ˌɛkstrətə'rɛstriəl] *adj* : extraterrestre — ~ *n* : extraterrestre *mf*

extravagant [ɪk'strævɪgənt, ɛk-] *adj* **1** : extravagant **2** WASTEFUL : prodigue — **extravagance** [ɪk'strævɪgənts, ɛk-] *n* **1** : extravagance *f* **2** WASTEFULNESS : prodigalité *f*

extreme [ɪk'stri:m, ɛk-] *adj* : extrême — ~ *n* : extrême *m* — **extremity** [ɪk'strɛməṭi, ɛk-] *n, pl* **-ties** : extrémité *f*

extricate ['ɛkstrəˌkeɪt] *vt* **-cated; -cating 1** : dégager **2** ~ **oneself from** : s'extirper de

extrovert ['ɛkstrəˌvərt] *n* : extraverti *m*, -tie *f* — **extroverted** ['ɛkstrəˌvərṭəd] *adj* : extraverti

exuberant [ɪg'zu:bərənt, ɛg-] *adj* : exubérant — **exuberance** [ɪg'zu:bərənts, ɛg-] *n* : exubérance *f*

exult [ɪg'zʌlt, ɛg-] *vi* : exulter

eye ['aɪ] *n* **1** : œil *m* **2** VISION : vision *f* **3** GLANCE : regard *m* **4** ~ **of a needle** : chas *m* — ~ *vt* **eyed; eyeing** *or* **eying** : regarder — **eyeball** ['aɪˌbɔl] *n* : globe *m* oculaire — **eyebrow** ['aɪˌbraʊ] *n* : sourcil *m* — **eyeglasses** ['aɪˌglæsəz] *npl* : lunettes *fpl* — **eyelash** ['aɪˌlæʃ] *n* : cil *m* — **eyelid** [aɪˌlɪd] *n* : paupière *f* — **eyesight** ['aɪˌsaɪt] *n* : vue *f*, vision *f* — **eyewitness** ['aɪ'wɪtnəs] *n* : témoin *m* oculaire

F

f ['ɛf] *n, pl* **f's** *or* **fs** ['ɛfs] : f *m*, sixième lettre de l'alphabet

fable ['feɪbəl] *n* : fable *f*

fabric ['fæbrɪk] *n* : tissu *m*, étoffe *f*

fabulous ['fæbjələs] *adj* : fabuleux

facade [fə'sɑd] *n* : façade *f*

face ['feɪs] *n* **1** : visage *m*, figure *f* **2** EXPRESSION : mine *f* **3** SURFACE : face *f* (d'une monnaie), façade *f* (d'un bâtiment) **4** ~ **value** : valeur *f* nominale **5 in the ~ of** DESPITE : en dépit de **6 lose ~** : perdre la face **7 make a ~** : faire la grimace — ~ *vt* **faced; facing 1** CONFRONT : faire face à **2** OVERLOOK : être en face de, donner sur — **faceless** ['feɪsləs] *adj* : anonyme

facet ['fæsət] *n* : facette *f*

face–to–face *adv* : face à face

facial ['feɪʃəl] *adj* : du visage

facetious [fə'si:ʃəs] *adj* : facétieux

facility [fə'sɪləṭi] *n, pl* **-ties 1** : facilité *f* **2 facilities** *npl* : installations *fpl* — **facilitate** [fə'sɪləˌteɪt] *vt* **-tated; -tating** : faciliter

facsimile [fæk'sɪməli] *n* : fac-similé *m*

fact ['fækt] *n* **1** : fait *m* **2 in ~** : en fait

faction ['fækʃən] *n* : faction *f*

factor ['fæktər] *n* : facteur *m*

factory ['fæktəri] *n, pl* **-ries** : usine *f*, fabrique *f*

factual ['fæktʃʊəl] *adj* : factuel, basé sur les faits

faculty ['fækəlti] *n, pl* **-ties** : faculté *f*

fad ['fæd] *n* : mode *f* passagère, manie *f*

fade ['feɪd] *v* **faded; fading** *vi* **1** WITHER : se flétrir, se faner **2** DISCOLOR : se décolorer **3** DIM : s'affaiblir, diminuer **4** VANISH : disparaître — *vt* : décolorer

fail ['feɪl] *vi* **1** : échouer **2** WEAKEN : faiblir, baisser **3** BREAK DOWN : tomber en panne **4** ~ **in** : manquer à — *vt* **1** DISAPPOINT : décevoir **2** NEGLECT : manquer, négliger **3** : échouer à (un examen) — ~ *n* **without ~** : à coup sûr — **failing** ['feɪlɪŋ] *n* : défaut *m* — **failure** ['feɪljər] *n* **1** : échec *m* **2** BREAKDOWN : panne *f*

faint ['feɪnt] *adj* **1** WEAK : faible **2** INDISTINCT : vague **3 feel ~** : se sentir mal — ~ *vi* : s'évanouir — **fainthearted** ['feɪnt'hɑrṭəd] *adj* : timide — **faintly** ['feɪntli] *adv* **1** WEAKLY : faiblement **2** SLIGHTLY : légèrement

fair¹ ['fær] *n* : foire *f*

fair² *adj* **1** BEAUTIFUL : beau **2** : blond (se dit des cheveux), clair (se dit de la peau) **3** JUST : juste, équitable **4** ADEQUATE : passable **5** LARGE : grand — **fairly** ['færli] *adv* **1** HONESTLY : équitablement **2** QUITE : assez — **fairness** ['færnəs] *n* : équité *f*

fairy ['færi] *n, pl* **fairies 1** : fée *f* **2** ~ **tale** *n* : conte *m* de fées

faith ['feɪθ] *n, pl* **faiths** ['feɪθs, 'feɪðz] : foi *f* — **faithful** ['feɪθfəl] *adj* : fidèle — **faithfully** *adv* : fidèlement — **faithfulness** ['feɪθfəlnəs] *n* : fidélité *f*

fake ['feɪk] *v* **faked; faking** *vt* **1** FALSIFY : falsifier **2** FEIGN : simuler — *vi* PRETEND : faire semblant — ~ *adj* : faux — ~ *n* **1** IMITATION : faux *m* **2** IMPOSTER : imposteur *m*

falcon ['fælkən, 'fɔl-] *n* : faucon *m*

fall ['fɔl] *vi* **fell** ['fɛl]; **fallen** ['fɔlən]; **falling 1** : tomber **2** ~ **asleep** : s'endormir **3** ~ **back** : se retirer **4** ~ **back on** : avoir recours à **5** ~ **behind** : prendre du retard **6** ~ **in love** : tomber amoureux **7** ~ **out** QUARREL : se disputer — ~ *n* **1** : chute *f* **2** AUTUMN : automne *m* **3** ~**s** *npl* WATERFALL : chute *f* (d'eau), cascade *f*

fallacy ['fæləsi] *n, pl* **-cies** : erreur *f*

fallible ['fæləbəl] *adj* : faillible

fallow ['fælo] *adj* : en jachère

false ['fɔls] *adj* **falser; falsest 1** : faux **2** ~ **alarm** : fausse alerte *f* **3** ~ **teeth** : dentier *m* — **falsehood** ['fɔlsˌhʊd] *n* : mensonge *m* — **falsely** ['fɔlsli] *adv* : faussement — **falseness** ['fɔlsnəs] *n* : fausseté *f* — **falsify** ['fɔlsəˌfaɪ] *vt* **-fied; -fying** : falsifier

falter ['fɔltər] *vi* **1** STUMBLE : chanceler **2** WAVER : hésiter

fame ['feɪm] *n* : renommée *f*

familiar [fə'mɪljər] *adj* **1** : familier **2 be ~ with** : bien connaître — **familiarity** [fəˌmɪli'ærəṭi, -ˌmɪl'jær-] *n, pl* **-ties** : familiarité *f* — **familiarize** [fə'mɪljəˌraɪz] *vt* **-ized; -izing** ~ **oneself** : se familiariser

family ['fæmli, 'fæmə-] *n, pl* **-lies** : famille *f*

famine ['fæmən] *n* : famine *f*

famished ['fæmɪʃt] *adj* : affamé

famous ['feɪməs] *adj* : célèbre

fan ['fæn] *n* **1** : éventail *m*, ventilateur *m* (électrique) **2** ENTHUSIAST : enthousiaste *mf* — ~ *vt* **fanned; fanning 1** : attiser (un feu) **2** ~ **oneself** : s'éventer (le visage)

fanatic [fə'næṭɪk] *n* : fanatique *mf* — ~ *or* **fanatical** [-ṭɪkəl] *adj* : fanatique — **fanaticism** [fə'næṭəˌsɪzəm] *n* : fanatisme *m*

fancy ['fæntsi] *vt* **-cied; -cying 1** LIKE : aimer **2** WANT : avoir envie de **3** IMAGINE : s'imaginer — ~ *adj* **fancier; -est 1** ELABORATE : recherché **2** LUXURIOUS : fin, de luxe — ~ *n, pl* **-cies 1** LIKING : goût *m* **2** WHIM : fantaisie *f* **3 take a ~ to** : se prendre d'affection pour — **fanciful** ['fæntsɪfəl] *adj* : fantaisiste

fanfare ['fænˌfær] *n* : fanfare *f*

fang ['fæŋ] *n* : croc *m*, crochet *m* (d'un serpent)

fantasy ['fæntəsi] *n, pl* **-sies 1** DREAM : fantasme *m* **2** IMAGINATION : fantaisie *f* — **fantasize** ['fæntəˌsaɪz] *vi* **-sized; -sizing** : fantasmer — **fantastic** [fæn'tæstɪk] *adj* : fantastique

far ['fɑr] *adv* **farther** ['fɑrðər] *or* **further** ['fər-]; **farthest** *or* **furthest** [-ðəst] **1** : loin **2 as ~ as** : jusqu'à **3 as ~ as possible** : autant que possible **4 by ~** : de loin **5** ~ **away** : au loin **6** ~ **from it!** : pas du tout! **7** ~ **worse** : bien pire **8 so ~** : jusqu'ici — ~ *adj* **farther** *or* **further; farthest** *or* **furthest 1** : lointain **2 the ~ right** : l'extrême droite **3 the ~ side** : l'autre côté — **faraway** ['fɑrəˌweɪ] *adj* : éloigné, lointain

farce ['fɑrs] *n* : farce *f*

fare ['fær] *vi* **fared; faring** : aller — ~ *n* **1** : tarif *m*, prix *m* **2** FOOD : nourriture *f*

farewell [fær'wɛl] *n* : adieu *m* — ~ *adj* : d'adieu

far–fetched ['fɑr'fɛtʃt] *adj* : improbable, bizarre

farm ['fɑrm] *n* : ferme *f* — ~ *vt* : cultiver — *vi* : être fermier — **farmer** ['fɑrmər] *n* : fermier *m*, -mière *f* — **farmhand** ['fɑrmˌhænd] *n* : ouvrier *m*, -vrière *f* agricole — **farmhouse** ['fɑrmˌhaʊs] *n* : ferme *f* — **farming** ['fɑrmɪŋ] *n* : agriculture *f*, élevage (des animaux) — **farmyard** ['fɑrmˌjɑrd] *n* : cour *f* de ferme

far–off ['fɑrˌɔf, -'ɔf] *adj* : lointain

far–reaching ['fɑr'ri:tʃɪŋ] *adj* : d'une grande portée

farsighted ['fɑrˌsaɪṭəd] *adj* **1** : presbyte **2** SHREWD : prévoyant

farther ['fɑrðər] *adv* **1** : plus loin **2** MORE : de plus — ~ *adj* : plus éloigné, plus lointain — **farthest** ['fɑrðəst] *adv* : le plus loin — ~ *adj* : le plus éloigné

fascinate ['fæsənˌeɪt] *vt* **-nated; -nating** : fasciner — **fascination** [ˌfæsən'eɪʃən] *n* : fascination *f*

fascism ['fæʃˌɪzəm] *n* : fascisme *m* — **fascist** ['fæʃɪst] *adj* : fasciste — ~ *n* : fasciste *mf*

fashion ['fæʃən] *n* **1** MANNER : façon *f* **2** STYLE : mode *f* **3 out of ~** : démodé — **fashionable** ['fæʃənəbəl] *adj* : à la mode

fast¹ ['fæst] *vi* : jeûner — ~ *n* : jeûne *m*

fast² *adj* **1** SWIFT : rapide **2** SECURE : ferme **3 my watch is ~** : ma montre avance — ~ *adv* **1** SECURELY : solidement, ferme **2** SWIFTLY : rapidement, vite **3** ~ **asleep** : profondément endormi

fasten ['fæsən] *vt* : attacher, fermer — *vi* : s'attacher, se fermer — **fastener** ['fæsənər] *n* : attache *f*, fermeture *f*

fastidious [fæs'tɪdiəs] *adj* : méticuleux

fat ['fæt] *adj* **fatter; fattest 1** : gros, gras **2** THICK : épais — ~ *n* : gras *m* (de la viande), graisse *f* (du corps)

fatal ['feɪṭəl] *adj* **1** DEADLY : mortel **2** FATEFUL : fatal — **fatality** [feɪ'tæləṭi, fə-] *n, pl* **-ties** : mort *m*

fate ['feɪt] *n* **1** DESTINY : destin *m* **2** LOT : sort *m* — **fateful** ['feɪtfəl] *adj* : fatidique

father ['fɑðər] *n* : père *m* — **fatherhood** ['fɑðərˌhʊd] *n* : paternité *f* — **father–in–law** ['fɑðərɪnˌlɔ] *n, pl* **fathers–in–law** : beau-père *m* — **fatherly** ['fɑðərli] *adj* : paternel

fathom ['fæðəm] *vt* : comprendre

fatigue [fə'ti:g] *n* : fatigue *f* — ~ *vt* **-tigued; -tiguing** : fatiguer

fatten ['fætən] *vt* : engraisser — **fattening** ['fætənɪŋ] *n* : qui fait grossir

fatty ['fæti] *adj* **fattier; -est** : gras

faucet ['fɔsət] *n* : robinet *m*

fault ['fɔlt] *n* **1** FLAW : défaut *m* **2** RESPONSIBILITY : faute *f* **3** : faille *f* (géologique) — ~ *vt* : trouver des défauts à, critiquer — **faultless** ['fɔltləs] *adj* : irréprochable — **faulty** ['fɔlti] *adj* **faultier; -est** : fautif, défectueux

fauna ['fɔnə] *n* : faune *f*

favor *or Brit* **favour** ['feɪvər] *n* **1** APPROVAL : faveur *f* **2 do s.o. a ~** : rendre un service à qqn **3 in ~ of** : en faveur de, pour — ~ *vt* **1** : favoriser **2** PREFER : préférer — **favorable** *or Brit* **favourable** ['feɪvərəbəl] *adj* : favorable — **favorite** *or Brit* **favourite** ['feɪvərət] *adj* : favori, préféré — ~ *n* : favori *m*, -rite *f*; préféré *m*, -rée *f* — **favoritism** *or Brit* **favouritism** ['feɪvərəˌtɪzəm] *n* : favoritisme *m*

fawn¹ ['fɔn] *vi* ~ **upon** : flatter servilement

fawn² *n* : faon *m*

fax ['fæks] *n* : fax *m*, télécopie *f* — ~ *vt* : faxer, envoyer par télécopie

fear ['fɪr] *vt* : craindre, avoir peur de — *vi* ~ **for** : craindre pour — ~ *n* : crainte *f*, peur *f* — **fearful** ['fɪrfəl] *adj* **1** FRIGHTENING : effrayant **2** AFRAID : craintif, peureux

feasible [ˌfi:zəbəl] *adj* : faisable

feast ['fi:st] *n* : banquet *m*, festin *m* — ~ *vi* ~ **on** : se régaler de

feat ['fi:t] *n* : exploit *m*, prouesse *f*

feather ['fɛðər] *n* : plume *f*

feature ['fi:tʃər] *n* **1** : trait *m* (du visage) **2** CHARACTERISTIC : caractéristique *f* — ~ *vt* : mettre en vedette — *vi* : figurer

February ['fɛbjuˌɛri, 'fɛbu-, 'fɛbru-] *n* : février *m*

feces ['fi:ˌsi:z] *npl* : fèces *fpl*

federal ['fɛdrəl, -dərəl] *adj* : fédéral — **federation** [ˌfɛdə'reɪʃən] *n* : fédération *f*

fed up ['fɛd] *adj* **be ~** : en avoir assez, en avoir marre *fam*

fee ['fi:] *n* **1** : frais *mpl* (de scolarité), honoraires *mpl* (médicaux) **2** *or* **entrance ~** : droit *m* d'entrée

feeble ['fi:bəl] *adj* **-bler; -blest 1** : faible **2 a ~ excuse** : une piètre excuse

feed ['fi:d] *v* **fed** ['fɛd]; **feeding** *vt* **1** : nourrir, donner à manger à **2** SUPPLY : alimenter — *vi* EAT : manger, se nourrir — ~ *n* : fourrage *m*

feel ['fi:l] *v* **felt** ['fɛlt]; **feeling** *vt* **1** : sentir **2** TOUCH : toucher **3** EXPERIENCE : ressentir (un sentiment) **4** BELIEVE : croire — *vi* **1** : se sentir **2** SEEM : sembler **3** ~ **cold/thirsty** : avoir froid, soif **4** ~ **like** WANT : avoir envie de — ~ *n* : toucher *m*, sensation *f* — **feeling** ['fi:lɪŋ] *n* **1** SENSATION : sensation *f* **2** EMOTION : sentiment *m* **3** OPINION : avis *m* **4** ~**s** *npl* : sentiments *mpl*

feet → **foot**

feign ['feɪn] *vt* : feindre

feline ['fi:ˌlaɪn] *adj* : félin — ~ *n* : félin *m*

fell¹ → **fall**

fell² ['fɛl] *vt* : abattre (un arbre)

fellow ['fɛˌlo:] *n* **1** COMPANION : compagnon *m* **2** MAN : gars *m fam*, type *m fam* — **fellowship** ['fɛloˌʃɪp] *n* **1** COMPANIONSHIP : camaraderie *f* **2** GRANT : bourse *f* universitaire

felon ['fɛlən] *n* : criminel *m*, -nelle *f* — **felony** ['fɛləni] *n, pl* **-nies** : crime *m*

felt¹ → **feel**

felt² ['fɛlt] *n* : feutre *m*

female ['fi:ˌmeɪl] *adj* : femelle (se dit des animaux), féminin (se dit des personnes) — ~ *n* **1** : femelle *f* (animal) **2** WOMAN : femme *f*

feminine ['fɛmənən] *adj* : féminin — **femininity** [ˌfɛmə'nɪnəṭi] *n* : féminité *f* — **feminism** ['fɛməˌnɪzəm] *n* : féminisme *m* — **feminist** ['fɛmənɪst] *adj* : féministe — ~ *n* : féministe *mf*

fence ['fɛnts] *n* : clôture *f*, barrière *f* — ~ *v* **fenced; fencing** *vt* : clôturer — *vi* : faire de l'escrime — **fencing** ['fɛntsɪŋ] *n* : escrime *f*

fend ['fɛnd] *vt or* ~ **off** : parer (un coup) — *vi* ~ **for oneself** : se débrouiller tout seul

fender ['fɛndər] *n* : aile *f* (d'une voiture)

fennel ['fɛnəl] *n* : fenouil *m*

ferment [fɛr'mɛnt] *vi* : fermenter — **fermentation** [ˌfɑrmən'teɪʃən, -ˌmɛn-] *n* : fermentation *f*

fern ['fərn] *n* : fougère *f*

ferocious [fə'ro:ʃəs] *adj* : féroce — **ferocity** [fə'rɑsət̬i] *n* : férocité *f*

ferret ['fɛrət] *n* : furet *m* — ~ *vt* ~ **out** : dénicher

Ferris wheel ['fɛrɪs] *n* : grande roue *f*

ferry ['fɛri] *vt* **-ried; -rying** : transporter — ~ *n, pl* **-ries** : ferry-boat *m*

fertile ['fərt̬əl] *adj* : fertile — **fertility** [fər'tɪlət̬i] *n* : fertilité *f*, fécondité *f* — **fertilize** ['fərt̬əlˌaɪz] *vt* **-ized; -izing** : fertiliser (une terre), féconder (un œuf, etc.) — **fertilizer** ['fərt̬əlˌaɪzər] *n* : engrais *m*

fervent ['fərvənt] *adj* : fervent — **fervor** *or Brit* **fervour** ['fərvər] *n* : ferveur *f*

fester ['fɛstər] *vi* : suppurer

festival ['fɛstəvəl] *n* : festival *m* — **festive** ['fɛstɪv] *adj* : joyeux, de fête — **festivities** [fɛs'tɪvət̬iz] *npl* : réjouissances *fpl*

fetch ['fɛtʃ] *vt* 1 BRING : aller chercher 2 REALIZE : rapporter (de l'argent)

fetid ['fɛt̬əd] *adj* : fétide

fetish ['fɛt̬ɪʃ] *n* : fétiche *m*

fetter ['fɛt̬ər] *vt* : enchaîner — **fetters** ['fɛt̬ərz] *npl* : fers *mpl*, chaînes *fpl*

fetus ['fi:t̬əs] *n* : fœtus *m*

feud ['fju:d] *n* : querelle *f* — ~ *vi* : se quereller

feudal ['fju:dəl] *adj* : féodal

fever ['fi:vər] *n* : fièvre *f* — **feverish** ['fi:vərɪʃ] *adj* : fiévreux

few ['fju:] *adj* 1 : peu de 2 **a** ~ : quelques — ~ *pron* 1 : peu, quelques-uns, quelques-unes 2 **quite a** ~ : un assez grand nombre de — **fewer** ['fju:ər] *adj* : moins de — ~ *pron* : moins

fiancé, fiancée [ˌfi:ˌɑn'seɪ, ˌfi:'ɑnˌseɪ] *n* : fiancé *m*, -cée *f*

fiasco [fi'æsˌko:] *n, pl* **-coes** : fiasco *m*

fib ['fɪb] *n* : petit mensonge *m* — ~ *vi* **fibbed; fibbing** : raconter des histoires

fiber *or* **fibre** ['faɪbər] *n* : fibre *f* — **fiberglass** ['faɪbərˌglæs] *n* : fibre *f* de verre — **fibrous** ['faɪbrəs] *adj* : fibreux

fickle ['fɪkəl] *adj* : volage, inconstant

fiction ['fɪkʃən] *n* : fiction *f* — **fictional** ['fɪkʃənəl] *or* **fictitious** [fɪk'tɪʃəs] *adj* : fictif

fiddle ['fɪdəl] *n* : violon *m* — ~ *vi* **-dled; -dling** ~ **with** : tripoter

fidelity [fə'dɛlət̬i, faɪ-] *n, pl* **-ties** : fidélité *f*

fidget ['fɪdʒət] *vi* : remuer — **fidgety** ['fɪdʒət̬i] *adj* : agité

field ['fi:ld] *n* 1 : champ *m* 2 : terrain *m* (de sport) 3 SPECIALTY : domaine *m* — **field glasses** *npl* : jumelles *fpl* — **field trip** : sortie *f* éducative

fiend ['fi:nd] *n* 1 : diable *m* 2 FANATIC : mordu *m* — **fiendish** ['fi:ndɪʃ] *adj* : diabolique

fierce ['fɪrs] *adj* **fiercer; -est** 1 FEROCIOUS : féroce 2 INTENSE : violent — **fierceness** ['fɪrsnəs] *n* : férocité *f*

fiery ['faɪəri] *adj* **fierier; -est** 1 BURNING : brûlant 2 SPIRITED : ardent

fifteen [fɪf'ti:n] *n* : quinze *m* — ~ *adj* : quinze — **fifteenth** [fɪf'ti:nθ] *n* 1 : quinzième *mf* 2 **November** ~ : le 15 novembre — ~ *adj* : quinzième

fifth ['fɪfθ] *n* 1 : cinquième *mf* 2 **June** ~ : le cinq juin — ~ *adj* : cinquième

fiftieth ['fɪftiəθ] *n* : cinquantième *mf* — ~ *adj* : cinquantième

fifty ['fɪfti] *n, pl* **-ties** : cinquante *m* — ~ *adj* : cinquante — **fifty–fifty** [ˌfɪfti'fɪfti] *adv* : moitié-moitié — ~ *adj* **a** ~ **chance** : une chance sur deux

fig ['fɪg] *n* : figue *f*

fight ['faɪt] *v* **fought** ['fɔt]; **fighting** *vi* 1 BATTLE : se battre 2 QUARREL : se disputer 3 STRUGGLE : lutter — *vt* : se battre contre, combattre — ~ *n* 1 BATTLE : combat *m* 2 BRAWL : bagarre *f* 3 QUARREL : dispute *f* 4 STRUGGLE : lutte *f* — **fighter** ['faɪt̬ər] *n* 1 : combattant *m*, -tante *f* 2 *or* ~ **plane** : avion *m* de chasse

figment ['fɪgmənt] *n* ~ **of the imagination** : produit *m* de l'imagination

figurative ['fɪgjərət̬ɪv, -gə-] *adj* : figuré

figure ['fɪgjər, -gər] *n* 1 : figure *f* 2 NUMBER : chiffre *m* 3 SHAPE : forme *f* 4 ~ **of speech** : façon *f* de parler 5 **watch one's** ~ : surveiller sa ligne — ~ *v* **-ured; -uring** *vt* : penser, supposer — *vi* 1 APPEAR : figurer 2 **that** ~**s!** : ça se comprend! — **figurehead** ['fɪgjərˌhɛd, -gər-] *n* 1 : figure *f* de proue (d'un navire) 2 : homme *m* de paille — **figure out** *vt* : comprendre

file[1] ['faɪl] *n* : lime *f* (outil) — ~ *vt* **filed; filing** : limer

file[2] *v* **filed; filing** *vt* 1 CLASSIFY : classer 2 ~ **charges** : déposer une plainte — ~ *n* 1 : dossier *m* 2 *or* **computer** ~ : fichier *m*

file[3] ROW : file *f* — ~ *vi* ~ **past** : défiler devant

fill ['fɪl] *vt* 1 : remplir 2 PLUG : boucher (un trou) 3 : plomber (une dent) 4 ~ **in** INFORM : mettre au courant — *vi* 1 *or* ~ **up** : se remplir 2 ~ **in for** : remplacer — ~ *n* 1 **eat one's** ~ : se rassasier 2 **have had one's** ~ **of** : en avoir assez de

fillet [fɪ'leɪ, 'fɪˌleɪ, 'fɪlət] *n* : filet *m*

filling ['fɪlɪŋ] *n* 1 : garniture *f* (d'une tarte, etc.) 2 : plombage *m* (d'une dent) 3 ~ **station** → **service station**

filly ['fɪli] *n, pl* **-lies** : pouliche *f*

film ['fɪlm] *n* 1 : pellicule *f* 2 MOVIE : film *m* — ~ *vt* : filmer

filter ['fɪltər] *n* : filtre *m* — ~ *v* : filtrer

filth ['fɪlθ] *n* : saleté *f* — **filthiness** ['fɪlθinəs] *n* : saleté *f* — **filthy** ['fɪlθi] *adj* **filthier; -est** : sale, dégoûtant

fin ['fɪn] *n* : nageoire *f*

final ['faɪnəl] *adj* 1 LAST : dernier 2 CONCLUSIVE : définitif 3 ULTIMATE : final — ~ *n* 1 *or* ~**s** : finale *f* (d'une compétition) 2 ~**s** *npl* : examens *mpl* de fin de semestre — **finalist** ['faɪnəlɪst] *n* : finaliste *mf* — **finalize** ['faɪnəlˌaɪz] *vt* **-ized; -izing** : mettre au point — **finally** ['faɪnəli] *adv* : enfin, finalement

finance [fə'nænts, 'faɪˌnænts] *n* 1 : finance *f* 2 ~**s** *npl* RESOURCES : finances *fpl* — ~ *vt* **-nanced; -nancing** : financer — **financial** [fə'næntʃəl, faɪ-] *adj* : financier

find ['faɪnd] *vt* **found** ['faʊnd]; **finding** 1 LOCATE : trouver 2 REALIZE : s'apercevoir 3 ~ **out** : découvrir 4 ~ **guilty** : prononcer coupable — ~ *n* : trouvaille *f* — **finding** ['faɪndɪŋ] *n* 1 FIND : découverte *f* 2 ~**s** *npl* : conclusions *fpl*

fine[1] ['faɪn] *n* : amende *f* — ~ *vt* **fined; fining** : condamner à une amende

fine[2] *adj* **finer; -est** 1 DELICATE : fin 2 SUBTLE : subtil 3 EXCELLENT : excellent 4 : beau (se dit du temps) 5 **be** ~ : aller bien 6 **that's** ~ **with me** : ça me va — ~ *adv* OK : très bien — **fine arts** *npl* : beaux-arts *mpl* — **finely** ['faɪnli] *adv* 1 EXCELLENTLY : exceptionellement 2 PRECISELY : délicatement 3 MINUTELY : finement

finesse [fə'nɛs] *n* : finesse *f*

finger ['fɪŋgər] *n* : doigt *m* — ~ *vt* : toucher, palper — **fingernail** ['fɪŋgərˌneɪl] *n* : ongle *m* — **fingerprint** ['fɪŋgərˌprɪnt] *n* : empreinte *f* digitale — **fingertip** ['fɪŋgərˌtɪp] *n* : bout *m* du doigt

finicky ['fɪnɪki] *adj* : pointilleux

finish ['fɪnɪʃ] *vt* : finir, terminer — *vi* : finir, se terminer — ~ *n* 1 END : fin *f* 2 *or* ~ **line** : arrivée *f* 3 SURFACE : finition *f*, fini *m Can*

finite ['faɪˌnaɪt] *adj* : fini

fir ['fər] *n* : sapin *m*

fire ['faɪr] *n* 1 : feu *m* 2 BLAZE : incendie *m* 3 **catch** ~ : prendre feu 4 **on** ~ : en feu 5 **open** ~ **on** : ouvrir le feu sur — ~ *vt* **fired; firing** 1 IGNITE : incendier 2 DISMISS : renvoyer, virer 3 SHOOT : tirer — **fire alarm** *n* : avertisseur *m* d'incendie — **firearm** ['faɪrˌɑrm] *n* : arme *f* à feu — **firecracker** ['faɪrˌkrækər] *n* : pétard *m* — **fire engine** : pompe *f* à incendie — **fire escape** *n* : escalier *m* de secours — **fire extinguisher** *n* : extincteur *m* — **firefighter** ['faɪrˌfaɪt̬ər] *n* : pompier *m*, sapeur-pompier *m France* — **fireman** ['faɪrmən] *n, pl* **-men** [-mən, -ˌmɛn] → **firefighter** — **fireplace** ['faɪrˌpleɪs] *n* : cheminée *f*, foyer *m* — **fireproof** ['faɪrˌpru:f] *adj* : ignifuge — **fireside** ['faɪrˌsaɪd] *n* : coin *m* du feu — **fire station** *n* : caserne *f* de pompiers *France*, poste *m* de pompiers *Can* — **firewood** ['faɪrˌwʊd] *n* : bois *m* de chauffage — **fireworks** ['faɪrˌwərks] *npl* : feux *mpl* d'artifice

firm[1] ['fərm] *n* : entreprise *f*, firme *f*

firm[2] *adj* 1 : ferme 2 STEADY : solide 3 **stand** ~ : tenir bon — **firmly** ['fərmli] *adv* : fermement — **firmness** ['fərmnəs] *n* : fermeté *f*

first ['fərst] *adj* 1 : premier 2 **at** ~ **sight** : à première vue — ~ *adv* 1 : d'abord 2 **for the** ~ **time** : pour la première fois 3 ~ **of all** : tout d'abord — ~ *n* 1 : premier *m*, -mière *f* 2 *or* ~ **gear** : première *f* 3 **at** ~ : au début — **first aid** *n* : premiers secours *mpl* — **first–class** ['fərst'klæs] *adv* : en première — ~ *adj* : de première qualité, de première classe — **firstly** ['fərstli] *adv* : premièrement

fiscal ['fɪskəl] *adj* : fiscal

fish ['fɪʃ] *n, pl* **fish** *or* **fishes** : poisson *m* — ~ *vi* 1 : pêcher 2 ~ **for** SEEK : chercher 3 **go** ~**ing** : aller à la pêche — **fisherman** ['fɪʃərmən] *n, pl* **-men** [-mən, -mɛn] : pêcheur *m*, -cheuse *f* — **fishhook** ['fɪʃˌhʊk] *n* : hameçon *m* — **fishing** ['fɪʃɪŋ] *n* : pêche *f* — **fishing pole** *n* : canne *f* à la pêche — **fishy** ['fɪʃi] *adj* **fishier; -est** 1 : de poisson 2 SUSPICIOUS : louche

fist ['fɪst] *n* : poing *m*

fit[1] ['fɪt] *n* : crise *f* (épileptique), accès *m* (de colère, etc.)

fit[2] *adj* **fitter; fittest** 1 APPROPRIATE : convenable 2 HEALTHY : en forme 3 **see** ~ **to** : trouver bon de — ~ *v* **fitted; fitting** *vt* 1 (*relating to clothing*) : aller à 2 MATCH : correspondre à 3 INSTALL : poser, insérer 4 EQUIP : équiper — *vi* 1 : être de la bonne taille 2 *or* ~ **in** BELONG : s'intégrer — ~ *n* : coupe *f* (d'un vêtement) — **fitful** ['fɪtfəl] *adj* 1 : intermittent 2 : agité (se dit du sommeil) — **fitness** ['fɪtnəs] *n* 1 HEALTH : forme *f* physique 2 SUITABILITY : aptitude *f* — **fitting** ['fɪt̬ɪŋ] *adj* : approprié, convenable

five ['faɪv] *n* : cinq *m* — ~ *adj* : cinq — **five hundred** *adj* : cinq cents

fix ['fɪks] *vt* 1 ATTACH : fixer 2 REPAIR : réparer 3 PREPARE : préparer 4 RIG : truquer — ~ *n* **be in a** ~ : être dans le pétrin *m* — **fixed** ['fɪkst] *adj* : fixe — **fixture** ['fɪkstʃər] *n* : installation *f*

fizz ['fɪz] *vi* : pétiller — ~ *n* : pétillement *m*

fizzle ['fɪzəl] *vi* ~ **out** : s'éteindre

flabbergasted ['flæbərˌgæstəd] *adj* : sidéré

flabby ['flæbi] *adj* **flabbier; -est** : mou

flaccid ['flæksəd, 'flæsəd] *adj* : flasque

flag[1] ['flæg] *vi* WEAKEN : faiblir

flag[2] *n* : drapeau *m* — ~ *vt* **flagged; flagging** : faire signe à (un taxi, etc.) — **flagpole** [ˌflægˌpo:l] *n* : mât *m*

flagrant ['fleɪgrənt] *adj* : flagrant

flair ['flær] *n* 1 TALENT : don *m* 2 STYLE : style *m*

flake ['fleɪk] *n* : flocon *m* (de neige), écaille *f* (de peinture) — ~ *vi* **flaked; flaking** *or* ~ **off** : s'écailler

flamboyant [flæm'bɔɪənt] *adj* : extravagant

flame ['fleɪm] *n* 1 : flamme *f* 2 **burst into** ~**s** : s'embraser, s'enflammer

flamingo [flə'mɪŋgo] *n, pl* **-gos** : flamant *m*

flammable ['flæməbəl] *adj* : inflammable

flank ['flæŋk] *n* : flanc *m* — ~ *vt* : flanquer

flannel ['flænəl] *n* : flanelle *f*

flap ['flæp] *n* : rabat *m* — ~ *v* **flapped; flapping** *vt* : battre (des ailes) — *vi* ~ **in the wind** : claquer au vent

flare ['flær] *vi* **flared; flaring** ~ **up** 1 BLAZE : s'embraser 2 ERUPT : s'emporter (se dit d'une personne), éclater (se dit d'une dispute, etc.) — ~ *n* : fusée *f* éclairante

flash ['flæʃ] *vi* 1 SPARKLE : briller 2 BLINK : clignoter 3 ~ **past** : passer comme un éclair — *vt* 1 PROJECT : projeter 2 SHOW : montrer 3 ~ **a smile** : lancer un sourire — ~ *n* 1 éclat *m* 2 : flash *m* (d'un appareil photographique) 3 ~ **of lightning** : éclair *m* 4 **in a** ~ : dans un instant — **flashlight** ['flæʃˌlaɪt] *n* : lampe *f* de poche — **flashy** ['flæʃi] *adj* **flashier; -est** : tape-à-l'œil, tapageur

flask ['flæsk] *n* : flacon *m*

flat ['flæt] *adj* **flatter; flattest** 1 LEVEL : plat 2 DOWNRIGHT : catégorique 3 FIXED : fixe 4 MONOTONOUS : monotone 5 : éventé (se dit d'une boisson) 6 : bémol (en musique) 7 ~ **tire** : crevé, à plat — ~ *n* 1 : bémol *m* (en musique) 2 *Brit* APARTMENT : appartement *m* 3 *or* ~ **tire** : crevaison *f* — ~ *adv* 1 : à plat 2 ~ **broke** : complètement fauché 3 **in one hour** ~ : dans une heure pile *fam* — **flatly** ['flætli] *adv* : catégoriquement — **flatten** ['flætən] *vt* : aplatir — *vi or* ~ **out** : s'aplanir

flatter ['flæt̬ər] *vt* : flatter — **flatterer** ['flæt̬ərər] *n* : flatteur *m*, -teuse *f* — **flattering** ['flæt̬ərɪŋ] *adj* : flatteur — **flattery** ['flæt̬əri] *n, pl* **-ries** : flatterie *f*

flaunt ['flɔnt] *vt* : faire étalage de

flavor *or Brit* **flavour** ['fleɪvər] *n* 1 : goût *m* 2 FLAVORING : parfum *m* — ~ *vt* : parfumer — **flavorful** *or Brit* **flavourful** ['fleɪvərfəl] *adj* : savoureux — **flavoring** *or Brit* **flavouring** ['fleɪvərɪŋ] *n* : parfum *m*

flaw ['flɔ] *n* : défaut *m* — **flawless** ['flɔləs] *adj* : sans défaut, parfait

flax ['flæks] *n* : lin *m*

flea ['fli:] *n* : puce *f*

fleck ['flɛk] *n* : petite tache *f*, moucheture *f*

flee ['fli:] *v* **fled** ['flɛd]; **fleeing** : fuir

fleece ['fli:s] *n* : toison *f* — ~ *vt* **fleeced; fleecing** : escroquer

fleet ['fli:t] *n* : flotte *f*

fleeting ['fli:t̬ɪŋ] *adj* : bref

Flemish ['flɛmɪʃ] *adj* : flamand

flesh ['flɛʃ] *n* : chair *f* — **fleshy** ['flɛʃi] *adj* **fleshier; -est** : charnu

flew → **fly**[1]

flex ['flɛks] *vt* : fléchir — **flexible** ['flɛksəbəl] *adj* : flexible — **flexibility** [ˌflɛksə'bɪlət̬i] *n* : flexibilité *f*

flick ['flɪk] *n* : petit coup *m* — ~ *vt* ~ **a switch** : appuyer sur un bouton — *vi* ~ **through** : feuilleter

flicker ['flɪkər] *vi* : vaciller — ~ *n* 1 : vacillement *m* 2 **a** ~ **of hope** : une lueur d'espoir

flier ['flaɪər] *n* 1 PILOT : aviateur *m*, -trice *f* 2 *or* **flyer** LEAFLET : prospectus *m*

flight[1] ['flaɪt] *n* 1 FLYING : vol *m* 2 ~ **of stairs** : escalier *m*

flight[2] *n* ESCAPE : fuite *f*

flimsy ['flɪmzi] *adj* **flimsier; -est** 1 LIGHT : léger 2 SHAKY : peu solide 3 **a** ~ **excuse** : une pauvre excuse

flinch ['flɪntʃ] *vi* 1 WINCE : tressaillir 2 ~ **from** : reculer devant

fling ['flɪŋ] *vt* **flung** ['flʌŋ]; **flinging** 1 THROW : lancer 2 ~ **open** : ouvrir brusquement — ~ *n* 1 AFFAIR : affaire *f*, aventure *f* 2 **have a** ~ **at** : essayer de faire

flint ['flɪnt] *n* : silex *m*

flip ['flɪp] *v* **flipped; flipping** *vt* 1 *or* ~ **over** : faire sauter 2 ~ **a coin** : jouer à pile ou face — *vi* 1 *or* ~ **over** : se retourner 2 ~ **through** : feuilleter — ~ *n* : saut *m* périlleux

flippant ['flɪpənt] *adj* : désinvolte

flipper ['flɪpər] *n* : nageoire *f*

flirt ['flərt] *vi* : flirter — ~ *n* : flirteur *m*, -teuse *f* — **flirtatious** [ˌflər'teɪʃəs] *adj* : charmeur

flit ['flɪt] *vi* **flitted; flitting** : voleter

float ['flo:t] *n* 1 RAFT : radeau *m* 2 CORK : flotteur *m* 3 : char *m* (de carnaval) — ~ *vi* : flotter — *vt* : faire flotter

flock ['flɑk] *n* 1 : volée *f* (d'oiseaux), troupeau *m* (de moutons) 2 CROWD : foule *f* — ~ *vi* : affluer, venir en foule

flog ['flɑg] *vt* **flogged; flogging** : flageller

flood ['flʌd] *n* 1 : inondation *f* 2 : déluge *m* (de paroles, de larmes, etc.) — ~ *vt* : inonder — *vi* : déborder (se dit d'une rivière) — **floodlight** ['flʌdˌlaɪt] *n* : projecteur *m*

floor ['flor] *n* 1 : plancher *m* 2 GROUND : sol *m* 3 STORY : étage *m* 4 **dance** ~ : piste *f* de danse 5 **ground** ~ : rez-de-chaussée *m* — ~ *vt* 1 KNOCK DOWN : terrasser 2 ASTOUND : stupéfier — **floorboard** ['florˌbord] *n* : planche *f*

flop ['flɑp] *vi* **flopped; flopping** 1 : s'agiter mollement 2 *or* ~ **down** COLLAPSE : s'affaler 3 FAIL : échouer — ~ *n* : fiasco *m* — **floppy** ['flɑpi] *adj* **floppier; -est** : mou — **floppy disk** *n* : disquette *f*

flora ['florə] *n* : flore *f* — **floral** ['florəl] *adj* : floral — **florid** ['florɪd] *adj* 1 FLOWERY : fleuri 2 RUDDY : rougeaud — **florist** ['florɪst] *n* : fleuriste *mf*

floss ['flɔs] → **dental floss**

flounder[1] ['flaʊndər] *n, pl* **flounder** *or* **flounders** : flet *m*

flounder[2] *vi* 1 *or* ~ **about** : patauger 2 FALTER : bredouiller

flour ['flaʊər] *n* : farine *f*

flourish ['flərɪʃ] *vi* 1 PROSPER : prospérer 2 THRIVE : s'épanouir — *vt* BRANDISH : brandir — ~ *n* : grand geste *m* — **flourishing** ['flərɪʃɪŋ] *adj* : florissant

flout ['flaʊt] *vt* : bafouer

flow ['flo:] *vi* 1 : couler 2 MOVE : s'écouler 3 CIRCULATE : circuler 4 BILLOW : flotter — ~ *n* 1 : écoulement *m* (d'un liquide) 2 MOVEMENT : circulation *f* 3 : flux *m* (de la marée)

flower ['flaʊər] *n* : fleur *f* — ~ *vi* : fleurir — **flowering** ['flaʊərɪŋ] *n* : floraison *f* — **flowerpot** ['flaʊərˌpɑt] *n* : pot *m* de fleurs — **flowery** ['flaʊəri] *adj* : fleuri

flown → **fly**[1]

flu ['flu:] *n* : grippe *f*

fluctuate ['flʌktʃʊˌeɪt] *vi* **-ated; -ating** : fluctuer — **fluctuation** [ˌflʌktʃʊ'eɪʃən] *n* : fluctuation *f*

fluency ['flu:əntsi] *n* : aisance *f* — **fluent** ['flu:ənt] *adj* 1 : coulant, aisé 2 **be** ~ **in** : parler couramment — **fluently** ['flu:əntli] *adv* : couramment

fluff ['flʌf] *n* 1 DOWN : duvet *m* 2 FUZZ : peluches *fpl* — **fluffy** ['flʌfi] *adj* **fluffier; -est** : duveteux

fluid ['flu:ɪd] *adj* : fluide — ~ *n* : fluide *m*

flunk ['flʌŋk] *vt* FAIL : rater

fluorescent [ˌflʊr'ɛsənt, ˌflɔr-] *adj* : fluorescent

flurry ['fləri] *n, pl* **-ries** 1 GUST : rafale *f* 2 *or* **snow** ~ : poudrerie *f Can* 3 : tourbillon *m* (d'activité)

flush ['flʌʃ] *vi* BLUSH : rougir — *vt* ~ **the toilet** : tirer la chasse d'eau — ~ *n* 1 : chasse *f* (d'eau) 2 BLUSH : rougeur *f* — ~ *adj* : au même niveau — ~ *adv* : de niveau

fluster ['flʌstər] *vt* : troubler

flute ['flu:t] *n* : flûte *f*

flutter ['flʌt̬ər] *vi* 1 FLAP : battre (se dit des ailes) 2 FLIT : voleter 3 ~ **about** : s'agiter — ~ *n* 1 : battement *m* (d'ailes) 2 STIR : agitation *f*, émoi *m*

flux ['flʌks] *n* **in a state of** ~ : dans un état de perpétuel changement

fly[1] ['flaɪ] *v* **flew** ['flu:]; **flown** ['flo:n]; **flying** *vi* 1 : voler 2 TRAVEL : prendre l'avion 3 : flotter (se dit d'un drapeau) 4 RUSH : filer 5 FLEE : s'enfuir — *vt* : faire voler — ~ *n, pl* **flies** : braguette *f* (d'un pantalon)

fly[2] *n, pl* **flies** : mouche *f* (insecte)

flyer → **flier**

flying saucer *n* : soucoupe *f* volante

foal ['fo:l] *n* : poulain *m*

foam ['fo:m] *n* : mousse *f*, écume *f* — ~ *vi* : mousser, écumer — **foamy** ['fo:mi] *adj* **foamier; -est** : mousseux, écumeux (se dit de la mer)

focus ['fo:kəs] *n, pl* **foci** ['fo:ˌsaɪ, -ˌkaɪ] 1 : foyer *m* 2 **be in** ~ : être au point 3 ~ **of attention** : centre *m* d'attention — ~ *v* **-cused** *or* **-cussed; -cusing** *or* **-cussing** *vt* 1 : mettre au point (un instrument) 2 : fixer (les yeux) — *vi* ~ **on** : se concentrer sur

fodder ['fɑdər] *n* : fourrage *m*

foe ['fo:] *n* : ennemi *m*, -mie *f*

fog ['fɔg, 'fɑg] *n* : brouillard *m* — ~ *vi* **fogged; fogging** *or* ~ **up** : s'embuer — **foggy** ['fɔgi, 'fɑ-] *adj* **foggier; -est** : brumeux — **foghorn** ['fɔgˌhɔrn, 'fɑg-] *n* : corne *f* de brume

foil[1] [ˈfɔɪl] *vt* : déjouer
foil[2] *n* : feuille *f* (d'aluminium, etc.)
fold[1] [ˈfo:ld] *n* **1** : parc *m* à moutons **2 return to the ~** : rentrer au bercail
fold[2] *vt* **1** : plier **2 ~ one's arms** : croiser les bras — *vi* **1** *or* **~ up** : se plier **2** FAIL : échouer — **~** *n* CREASE : pli *m* — **folder** [ˈfo:ldər] *n* **1** FILE : chemise *f* **2** PAMPHLET : dépliant *m*
foliage [ˈfo:liɪʤ, -lɪʤ] *n* : feuillage *m*
folk [ˈfo:k] *n, pl* **folk** *or* **folks 1** PEOPLE : gens *mfpl* **2 ~s** *npl* PARENTS : famille *f*, parents *mpl* — **~** *adj* : populaire, folklorique — **folklore** [ˈfo:kˌlor] *n* : folklore *m*
follow [ˈfɑlo] *vt* **1** : suivre **2** PURSUE : poursuivre **3 ~ up** : donner suite à — *vi* **1** : suivre **2** ENSUE : s'ensuivre — **follower** [ˈfɑloər] *n* : partisan *m*, -sane *f* — **following** [ˈfɑloɪŋ] *adj* : suivant — **~** *n* : partisans *mpl* — **~** *prep* : après
folly [ˈfɑli] *n, pl* **-lies** : folie *f*
fond [ˈfɑnd] *adj* **1** : affectueux **2 be ~ of** : aimer beaucoup
fondle [ˈfɑndəl] *vt* **-dled; -dling** : caresser
fondness [ˈfɑndnəs] *n* **1** : affection *f* **2 have a ~ for** : avoir une prédilection pour
food [ˈfu:d] *n* : nourriture *f* — **foodstuffs** [ˈfu:dˌstʌfs] *npl* : denrées *fpl* alimentaires
fool [ˈfu:l] *n* **1** : idiot *m*, -diote *f* **2** JESTER : fou *m* — **~** *vt* DECEIVE : duper — *vi* **1** JOKE : plaisanter **2 ~ around** : perdre son temps — **foolhardy** [ˈfu:lˌhɑrdi] *adj* : téméraire — **foolish** [ˈfu:lɪʃ] *adj* : bête, idiot — **foolishness** [ˈfu:lɪʃnəs] *n* : bêtise *f*, sottise *f* — **foolproof** [ˈfu:lˌpru:f] *adj* : infaillible
foot [ˈfʊt] *n, pl* **feet** [ˈfi:t] : pied *m* — **footage** [ˈfʊtɪʤ] *n* : métrage *m* — **football** [ˈfʊtˌbɔl] *n* : football *m* américain, football *m Can* — **footbridge** [ˈfʊtˌbrɪʤ] *n* : passerelle *f* — **foothills** [ˈfʊtˌhɪlz] *npl* : contreforts *mpl* — **foothold** [ˈfʊtˌho:ld] *n* : prise *f* de pied — **footing** [ˈfʊtɪŋ] *n* **1** → **foothold 2** STATUS : position *f* **3 on equal ~** : sur pied d'égalité — **footlights** [ˈfʊtˌlaɪts] *npl* : rampe *f* — **footnote** [ˈfʊtˌno:t] *n* : note *f* (en bas de la page) — **footpath** [ˈfʊtˌpæθ] *n* : sentier *m* — **footprint** [ˈfʊtˌprɪnt] *n* : empreinte *f* (de pied) — **footstep** [ˈfʊtˌstɛp] *n* : pas *m* — **footwear** [ˈfʊtˌwær] *n* : chaussures *fpl*
for [ˈfɔr] *prep* **1** : pour **2** BECAUSE OF : de, à cause de **3** (*indicating duration*) : pour, pendant **4** (*indicating destination*) : pour, à destination de **5 a cure ~ cancer** : un remède contre le cancer **6 ~ sale** : à vendre — **~** *conj* BECAUSE : car
forage [ˈfɔrɪʤ] *vi* **-aged; -aging** : fourrager
foray [ˈfɔrˌeɪ] *n* : incursion *f*
forbid [fərˈbɪd] *vt* **-bade** [-ˈbæd, -ˈbeɪd] *or* **-bad** [-ˈbæd]; **-bidden** [-ˈbɪdən]; **-bidding** : interdire, défendre — **forbidding** [fərˈbɪdɪŋ] *adj* : menaçant
force [ˈfors] *n* **1** : force *f* **2** *or* **~s** *npl* : forces *fpl* **3 by ~** : de force **4 in ~** : en vigueur — **~** *vt* **forced; forcing 1** : forcer **2** IMPOSE : imposer — **forceful** [ˈforsfəl] *adj* : vigoureux
forceps [ˈfɔrsəps, -ˌsɛps] *ns & pl* : forceps *m*
forcibly [ˈforsəbli] *adv* : de force
ford [ˈford] *n* : gué *m* — **~** *vt* : passer à gué
fore [ˈfor] *n* **1** : avant *m* (d'un navire) **2 come to the ~** : se mettre en évidence
forearm [ˈforˌɑrm] *n* : avant-bras *m*
foreboding [forˈbo:dɪŋ] *n* : pressentiment *m*
forecast [ˈforˌkæst] *vt* **-cast; -casting** : prévoir — **~** *n or* **weather ~** : prévisions *fpl* météorologiques, météo *f fam*
forefathers [ˈforˌfɑðərz] *npl* : ancêtres *mfpl*, aïeux *mpl*
forefinger [ˈforˌfɪŋgər] *n* : index *m*
forefront [ˈforˌfrʌnt] *n* : premier rang *m*
forego [forˈgo:] → **forgo**
foregone [forˈgɔn] *adj* **it's a ~ conclusion** : c'est gagné d'avance
foreground [ˈforˌgraʊnd] *n* : premier plan *m*
forehead [ˈfɔrəd, ˈforˌhɛd] *n* : front *m*
foreign [ˈfɔrən] *adj* **1** : étranger (se dit d'une langue, etc.) **2 ~ trade** : commerce *m* extérieur — **foreigner** [ˈfɔrənər] *n* : étranger *m*, -gère *f*
foreman [ˈformən] *n, pl* **-men** [-mən, -ˌmɛn] : contremaître *m*
foremost [ˈforˌmo:st] *adj* : principal — **~** *adv* **first and ~** : tout d'abord
forensic [fəˈrɛnsɪk] *adj* : médico-légal
forerunner [ˈforˌrʌnər] *n* : précurseur *m*
foresee [forˈsi:] *vt* **-saw; -seen; -seeing** : prévoir — **foreseeable** [forˈsi:əbəl] *adj* : prévisible
foreshadow [forˈʃædo:] *vt* : présager
foresight [ˈforˌsaɪt] *n* : prévoyance *f*
forest [ˈfɔrəst] *n* : forêt *f* — **forestry** [ˈfɔrəstri] *n* : sylviculture *f*
foretaste [ˈforˌteɪst] *n* : avant-goût *m*
foretell [forˈtɛl] *vt* **-told; -telling** : prédire
forethought [ˈforˌθɔt] *n* : prévoyance *f*
forever [fərˈɛvər] *adv* **1** ETERNALLY : toujours **2** CONTINUALLY : sans cesse
forewarn [forˈwɔrn] *vt* : avertir, prévenir
foreword [ˈforwərd] *n* : avant-propos *m*
forfeit [ˈfɔrfət] *n* **1** PENALTY : peine *f* **2 pay a ~** : avoir un gage — **~** *vt* : perdre
forge [ˈforʤ] *n* : forge *f* — **~** *v* **forged; forging** *vt* **1** : forger (un métal, etc.) **2** COUNTERFEIT : contrefaire, falsifier — *vi* **~ ahead** : prendre de l'avance — **forger** [ˈforʤər] *n* : faussaire *mf*, faux-monnayeur *m* — **forgery** [ˈforʤəri] *n, pl* **-eries** : faux *m*, contrefaçon *f*
forget [fərˈgɛt] *v* **-got** [-ˈgɑt]; **-gotten** [-ˈgɑtən] *or* **-got; -getting** : oublier — **forgetful** [fərˈgɛtfəl] *adj* : distrait
forgive [fərˈgɪv] *vt* **-gave** [-ˈgeɪv]; **-given** [-ˈgɪvən]; **-giving** : pardonner — **forgiveness** [fərˈgɪvnəs] *n* : pardon *m*
forgo *or* **forego** [forˈgo:] *vt* **-went; -gone; -going** : renoncer à, se priver de
fork [ˈfɔrk] *n* **1** : fourchette *f* **2** PITCHFORK : fourche *f* **3** JUNCTION : bifurcation *f* (d'une route) — **~** *vt or* **~ over** : allonger *fam* — *vi* : bifurquer
forlorn [forˈlɔrn] *adj* : triste
form [ˈfɔrm] *n* **1** : forme *f* **2** DOCUMENT : formulaire *m* — **~** *vt* : former — *vi* : se former, prendre forme
formal [ˈfɔrməl] *adj* **1** : officiel, solennel **2** : soigné, soutenu (se dit du langage) — **~** *n* **1** *or* **~ dance** : bal *m* **2** *or* **~ dress** : tenue *f* de soirée — **formality** [fɔrˈmæləti] *n, pl* **-ties** : formalité *f*
format [ˈfɔrˌmæt] *n* : format *m* — **~** *vt* **-matted; -matting** : formater (une diskette, etc.)
formation [fɔrˈmeɪʃən] *n* : formation *f*
former [ˈfɔrmər] *adj* **1** PREVIOUS : ancien **2** FIRST : premier — **formerly** [ˈfɔrmərli] *adv* : autrefois
formidable [ˈfɔrmədəbəl, fɔrˈmɪdə-] *adj* : redoutable
formula [ˈfɔrmjələ] *n, pl* **-las** or **-lae** [-ˌli:, -ˌlaɪ] **1** : formule *f* **2** *or* **baby ~** : lait *m* reconstitué — **formulate** [ˈfɔrmjəˌleɪt] *vt* **-lated; -lating** : formuler
forsake [fərˈseɪk] *vt* **-sook** [-ˈsʊk]; **-saken** [-ˈseɪkən]; **-saking** : abandonner
fort [ˈfort] *n* : fort *m*
forth [ˈforθ] *adv* **1 and so ~** : et ainsi de suite **2 from this day ~** : dorénavant **3 go back and ~** : aller et venir — **forthcoming** [forθˈkʌmɪŋ, ˈforθ-] *adj* **1** COMING : prochain, à venir **2** OPEN : communicatif — **forthright** [ˈforθˌraɪt] *adj* : franc, direct
fortieth [ˈfɔrtiəθ] *n* : quarantième *mf* — **~** *adj* : quarantième
fortify [ˈfɔrtəˌfaɪ] *vt* **-fied; -fying** : fortifier — **fortification** [ˌfɔrtəfəˈkeɪʃən] *n* : fortification *f*
fortitude [ˈfɔrtəˌtu:d, -ˌtju:d] *n* : force *f* d'âme
fortnight [ˈfortˌnaɪt] *n* : quinzaine *f*, quinze jours *mpl*
fortress [ˈfɔrtrəs] *n* : forteresse *f*
fortunate [ˈfɔrʧənət] *adj* : heureux — **fortunately** [ˈfɔrʧənətli] *adv* : heureusement — **fortune** [ˈfɔrʧən] *n* **1** : fortune *f* **2** LUCK : chance *f* — **fortune–teller** [ˈfɔrʧənˌtɛlər] *n* : diseuse *f* de bonne aventure
forty [ˈfɔrti] *n, pl* **forties** : quarante *m* — **~** *adj* : quarante
forum [ˈforəm] *n, pl* **-rums** : forum *m*
forward [ˈforwərd] *adj* **1** : avant, en avant **2** BRASH : effronté — **~** *adv* : en avant, vers l'avant — **~** *n* : avant *m* (aux sports) — **~** *vt* : expédier (des marchandises), faire suivre (du courrier) — **forwards** [ˈforwərdz] *adv* → **forward**
fossil [ˈfɑsəl] *n* : fossile *m*
foster [ˈfɔstər] *adj* : adoptif, d'accueil — **~** *vt* **1** NURTURE : nourrir **2** ENCOURAGE : encourager
fought → **fight**
foul [ˈfaʊl] *adj* **1** : infect (se dit d'une odeur, etc.) **2 ~ language** : langage *m* ordurier **3 ~ play** : jeu *m* irrégulier **4 ~ weather** : sale temps *m* — **~** *n* : faute *f* (aux sports) — **~** *vt* : salir, souiller
found[1] [ˈfaʊnd] → **find**
found[2] *vt* : fonder, établir — **foundation** [faʊnˈdeɪʃən] *n* **1** : fondation *f* **2** BASIS : base *f*, fondement *m*
founder[1] [ˈfaʊndər] *n* : fondateur *m*, -trice *f*
founder[2] *vi* **1** SINK : sombrer **2** COLLAPSE : s'effondrer
fountain [ˈfaʊntən] *n* : fontaine *f*
four [ˈfor] *n* : quatre *m* — **~** *adj* : quatre — **fourfold** [ˈforˌfo:ld, -ˈfo:ld] *adj* : quadruple — **four hundred** *adj* : quatre cents
fourteen [forˈti:n] *n* : quatorze *m* — **~** *adj* : quatorze — **fourteenth** [forˈti:nθ] *n* **1** : quatorzième *mf* **2 June ~** : le quatorze juin — **~** *adj* : quatorzième
fourth [ˈforθ] *n* **1** : quatrième *mf* (dans une série) **2** : quart *m* (en mathématiques) **3 August ~** : le quatre août — **~** *adj* : quatrième
fowl [ˈfaʊl] *n, pl* **fowl** *or* **fowls** : volaille *f*
fox [ˈfɑks] *n, pl* **foxes** : renard *m* — **~** *vt* TRICK : tromper, berner — **foxy** [ˈfɑksi] *adj* **foxier; -est** SHREWD : rusé
foyer [ˈfɔɪər, ˈfɔɪˌjeɪ] *n* : vestibule *m*, foyer *m* (d'un théâtre)
fraction [ˈfrækʃən] *n* : fraction *f*
fracture [ˈfrækʧər] *n* : fracture *f* — **~** *vt* **-tured; -turing** : fracturer
fragile [ˈfræʤəl, -ˌʤaɪl] *adj* : fragile — **fragility** [frəˈʤɪləti] *n* : fragilité *f*
fragment [ˈfrægmənt] *n* : fragment *m*
fragrance [ˈfreɪgrənts] *n* : parfum *m* — **fragrant** [ˈfreɪgrənt] *adj* : parfumé
frail [ˈfreɪl] *adj* : frêle, fragile
frame [ˈfreɪm] *vt* **framed; framing 1** ENCLOSE : encadrer **2** DEVISE : élaborer **3** FORMULATE : formuler **4** INCRIMINATE : monter un coup contre — **~** *n* **1** : cadre *m* (d'un tableau, etc.) **2** : charpente *f* (d'un édifice, etc.) **3 ~s** *npl* : monture *f* (de lunettes) **4 ~ of mind** : état *m* d'esprit — **framework** [ˈfreɪmˌwərk] *n* : structure *f*, cadre *m*
franchise [ˈfrænˌʧaɪz] *n* **1** : franchise *f* (en commerce) **2** SUFFRAGE : droit *m* de vote
frank [ˈfræŋk] *adj* : franc — **frankly** [ˈfræŋkli] *adv* : franchement — **frankness** [ˈfræŋknəs] *n* : franchise *f*
frantic [ˈfræntɪk] *adj* : frénétique
fraternal [frəˈtərnəl] *adj* : fraternel — **fraternity** [frəˈtərnəti] *n, pl* **-ties** : fraternité *f* — **fraternize** [ˈfrætərˌnaɪz] *vi* **-nized; -nizing** : fraterniser
fraud [ˈfrɔd] *n* **1** DECEIT : fraude *f* **2** IMPOSTOR : imposteur *m* — **fraudulent** [ˈfrɔʤələnt] *adj* : frauduleux
fraught [ˈfrɔt] *adj* **~ with** : chargé de
fray[1] [ˈfreɪ] *n* : bagarre *f*
fray[2] *vt* : mettre (les nerfs) à vif — *vi* : s'effilocher
freak [ˈfri:k] *n* **1** ODDITY : phénomène *m* **2** ENTHUSIAST : fana *mf fam* — **~** *adj* : anormal — **freakish** [ˈfri:kɪʃ] *adj* : anormal, bizarre
freckle [ˈfrɛkəl] *n* : tache *f* de rousseur
free [ˈfri:] *adj* **freer; freest 1** : libre **2** *or* **~ of charge** : gratuit **3 ~ from** : dépourvu de — **~** *vt* **freed; freeing 1** RELEASE : libérer **2** DISENGAGE : dégager — **~** *adv* **1** : librement **2 for ~** : gratuitement — **freedom** [ˈfri:dəm] *n* : liberté *f* — **freelance** [ˈfri:ˌlænts] *adv* : à la pige — **freely** [ˈfri:li] *adv* **1** : librement **2** LAVISHLY : largement — **freeway** [ˈfri:ˌweɪ] *n* : autoroute *f* — **free will** [ˈfri:ˌwɪl] *n* **1** : libre arbitre *m* **2 of one's own ~** : de sa propre volonté
freeze [ˈfri:z] *v* **froze** [ˈfro:z]; **frozen** [ˈfro:zən]; **freezing** *vi* **1** : geler (de l'eau), congeler (des aliments, etc.) **2** FIX : bloquer — *vi* : geler — **~** *n* **1** : gel *m* **2** : blocage *m* (des prix, etc.) — **freeze–dry** [ˈfri:zˈdraɪ] *vt* **-dried; -drying** : lyophiliser — **freezer** [ˈfri:zər] *n* : congélateur *m* — **freezing** [ˈfri:zɪŋ] *adj* **1** : glacial **2 it's ~** : on gèle
freight [ˈfreɪt] *n* **1** SHIPPING : transport *m* **2** GOODS : fret *m*, marchandises *fpl*
French [ˈfrɛnʧ] *adj* : français — **~** *n* **1** : français *m* (langue) **2 the ~** : les Français
French Canadian *adj* : canadien français — **~** *n* : Canadien *m* français, Canadienne *f* française
french fries [ˈfrɛnʧˌfraɪz] *npl* : frites *fpl*
Frenchman [ˈfrɛnʧmən] *n, pl* **-men** [-mən, -ˌmɛn] : Français *m* — **Frenchwoman** [ˈfrɛnʧˌwʊmən] *n, pl* **-women** [-ˌwɪmən] : Française *f*
frenzy [ˈfrɛnzi] *n, pl* **-zies** : frénésie *f* — **frenzied** [ˈfrɛnzid] *adj* : frénétique
frequency [ˈfri:kwəntsi] *n, pl* **-cies** : fréquence *f* — **frequent** [friˈkwɛnt, ˈfri:kwənt] *vt* : fréquenter — **~** [ˈfri:kwənt] *adj* : fréquent — **frequently** [ˈfri:kwəntli] *adv* : fréquemment
fresco [ˈfrɛsˌko:] *n, pl* **-coes** : fresque *f*
fresh [ˈfrɛʃ] *adj* **1** : frais **2** NEW : nouveau **3** IMPUDENT : insolent **4 ~ water** : eau *f* douce — **freshen** [ˈfrɛʃən] *vt* : rafraîchir — *vi* **~ up** : se rafraîchir — **freshly** [ˈfrɛʃli] *adv* : récemment — **freshman** [ˈfrɛʃmən] *n, pl* **-men** [-mən, -ˌmɛn] : étudiant *m*, -diante *f* de première année — **freshness** [ˈfrɛʃnəs] *n* : fraîcheur *f*
fret [ˈfrɛt] *vi* **fretted; fretting** : s'inquiéter — **fretful** [ˈfrɛtfəl] *adj* : irritable
friar [ˈfraɪər] *n* : frère *m*
friction [ˈfrɪkʃən] *n* : friction *f*
Friday [ˈfraɪˌdeɪ, -di] *n* : vendredi *m*
friend [ˈfrɛnd] *n* : ami *m*, amie *f* — **friendliness** [ˈfrɛndlinəs] *n* : gentillesse *f* — **friendly** [ˈfrɛndli] *adj* **friendlier; -est** : gentil, amical — **friendship** [ˈfrɛndˌʃɪp] *n* : amitié *f*
frigate [ˈfrɪgət] *n* : frégate *f*
fright [ˈfraɪt] *n* : peur *f*, frayeur *f* — **frighten** [ˈfraɪtən] *vt* : faire peur à, effrayer — **frightened** [ˈfraitˈnd] *adj* : apeuré, effrayé — **frightening** [ˈfraitˈnɪŋ] *adj* : effrayant — **frightful** [ˈfraɪtfəl] *adj* : terrible, affreux
frigid [ˈfrɪʤɪd] *adj* : glacial
frill [ˈfrɪl] *n* **1** RUFFLE : volant *m* (d'une jupe), jabot *m* (d'une chemise) **2** LUXURY : luxe *m*
fringe [ˈfrɪnʤ] *n* **1** : frange *f* **2** EDGE : bordure *f* **3 ~ benefits** : avantages *mpl* sociaux
frisk [ˈfrɪsk] *vt* SEARCH : fouiller — **frisky** [ˈfrɪski] *adj* **friskier; -est** : vif, folâtre
fritter [ˈfrɪtər] *n* : beignet *m* — **~** *vt or* **~ away** : gaspiller
frivolous [ˈfrɪvələs] *adj* : frivole — **frivolity** [frɪˈvɑləti] *n, pl* **-ties** : frivolité *f*
frizzy [ˈfrɪzi] *adj* **frizzier; -est** : crépu
fro [ˈfro:] *adv* → **to**
frock [ˈfrɑk] *n* : robe *f*
frog [ˈfrɔg, ˈfrɑg] *n* **1** : grenouille *f* **2 have a ~ in one's throat** : avoir un chat dans la gorge — **frogman** [ˈfrɔgˌmæn, ˈfrɑg-, -mən] *n, pl* **-men** [-mən, -ˌmɛn] : homme-grenouille *m*
frolic [ˈfrɑlɪk] *vi* **-icked; -icking** : folâtrer
from [ˈfrʌm, ˈfrɑm] *prep* **1** (*indicating a starting point*) : de, à partir de **2** (*indicating a source or cause*) : de, par, à **3 ~ now on** : à partir de maintenant **4 protection ~ the sun** : protection contre le soleil **5 drink ~ a glass** : boire dans un verre
front [ˈfrʌnt] *n* **1** : avant *m*, devant *m* **2** APPEARANCE : air *m*, contenance *f* **3** : front *m* (militaire) **4** : façade *f* (d'un bâtiment) **5 in ~** : à l'avant **6 in ~ of** : devant — **~** *vi* **~ on** : donner sur — **~** *adj* **1** : de devant, (en) avant **2 ~ row** : premier rang *m*
frontier [ˌfrʌnˈtɪr] *n* : frontière *f*
frost [ˈfrɔst] *n* **1** : givre *m* **2** FREEZING : gel *m*, gelée *f* — **~** *vt* : glacer (un gâteau) — **frostbite** [ˈfrɔstˌbaɪt] *n* : gelure *f* — **frosting** [ˈfrɔstɪŋ] *n* ICING : glaçage *m* — **frosty** [ˈfrɔsti] *adj* **frostier; -est 1** : couvert de givre **2** FRIGID : glacial
froth [ˈfrɔθ] *n, pl* **froths** [ˈfrɔθs, ˈfrɔðz] : écume *f*, mousse *f* — **frothy** [ˈfrɔθi, -ði] *adj* **frothier; -est** : écumeux, mousseux
frown [ˈfraʊn] *vi* : froncer les sourcils — **~** *n* : froncement *m* de sourcils
froze, frozen → **freeze**
frugal [ˈfru:gəl] *adj* : économe
fruit [ˈfru:t] *n* : fruit *m* — **fruitcake** [ˈfru:tˌkeɪk] *n* : cake *m* — **fruitful** [ˈfru:tfəl] *adj* : fructueux — **fruition** [fru:ˈɪʃən] *n* **come to ~** : se réaliser — **fruity** [ˈfru:ti] *adj* **fruitier; -est** : fruité
frustrate [ˈfrʌsˌtreɪt] *vt* **-trated; -trating** : frustrer — **frustrating** [ˈfrʌsˌtreɪtɪŋ] *adj* : frustrant — **frustration** [ˌfrʌsˈtreɪʃən] *n* : frustration *f*
fry [ˈfraɪ] *v* **fried; frying** : frire — **~** *n, pl* **fries 1** *or* **small ~** : menu fretin *m* **2 fries** → **french fries** — **frying pan** *n* : poêle *f*
fudge [ˈfʌʤ] *n* : caramel *m* mou — **~** *vt* FALSIFY : truquer
fuel [ˈfju:əl] *n* : combustible *m*, carburant *m* — **~** *vt* **-eled** *or* **-elled; -eling** *or* **-elling 1** : alimenter en combustible **2** STIMULATE : aviver
fugitive [ˈfju:ʤətɪv] *n* : fugitif *m*, -tive *f*
fulfill *or* **fulfil** [fʊlˈfɪl] *vt* **-filled; -filling 1** EXECUTE : accomplir, réaliser **2** FILL, MEET : remplir — **fulfillment** [fʊlˈfɪlmənt] *n* **1** ACCOMPLISHMENT : réalisation *f* **2** SATISFACTION : contentement *m*
full [ˈfʊl, ˈfʌl] *adj* **1** FILLED : plein **2** COMPLETE : entier, total **3** : ample (se dit d'une jupe), rond (se dit d'un visage) **4** : complet (se dit d'un hotel, etc.) — **~** *adv* **1** DIRECTLY : carrément **2 know ~ well** : savoir très bien — **~** *n* **in ~** : entièrement — **full–fledged** [ˈfʊlˈflɛʤd] *adj* : à part entière — **fully** [ˈfʊli] *adv* : complètement
fumble [ˈfʌmbəl] *vi* **-bled; -bling** : tâtonner, fouiller
fume [ˈfju:m] *vi* **fumed; fuming** RAGE : rager, fulminer — **fumes** [ˈfju:mz] *npl* : vapeurs *fpl*
fumigate [ˈfju:məˌgeɪt] *vt* **-gated; -gating** : désinfecter par fumigation
fun [ˈfʌn] *n* **1** : amusement *m* **2 have ~** : s'amuser **3 for ~** : pour rire **4 make ~ of** : se moquer de
function [ˈfʌŋkʃən] *n* **1** : fonction *f* **2** GATHERING : réception *f*, cérémonie *f* — **~** *vi* **1** : fonctionner **2 ~ as** : servir de — **functional** [ˈfʌŋkʃənəl] *adj* : fonctionnel
fund [ˈfʌnd] *n* **1** : fonds *m* **2 ~s** *npl* RESOURCES : fonds *mpl* — **~** *vt* : financer
fundamental [ˌfʌndəˈmɛntəl] *adj* : fondamental — **fundamentals** *npl* : principes *mpl* de base
funeral [ˈfju:nərəl] *n* : enterrement *m*, funérailles *fpl* — **~** *adj* : funèbre — **funeral home** *or* **funeral parlor** *n* : entreprise *f* de pompes funèbres
fungus [ˈfʌŋgəs] *n, pl* **fungi** [ˈfʌnˌʤaɪ, ˈfʌŋˌgaɪ] **1** MUSHROOM : champignon *m* **2** MOLD : moisissure *f*
funnel [ˈfʌnəl] *n* **1** : entonnoir *m* **2** SMOKESTACK : cheminée *f*
funny [ˈfʌni] *adj* **funnier; -est 1** : drôle, amusant **2** PECULIAR : bizarre — **funnies** [ˈfʌniz] *npl* : bandes *fpl* dessinées
fur [ˈfər] *n* : fourrure *f* — **~** *adj* : de fourrure
furious [ˈfjʊriəs] *adj* : furieux
furnace [ˈfərnəs] *n* : fourneau *m*
furnish [ˈfərnɪʃ] *vt* **1** SUPPLY : fournir **2** : meubler (un appartement, etc.) — **furnishings** [ˈfərnɪʃɪŋz] *npl* : ameublement *m*, meubles *mpl* — **furniture** [ˈfərnɪʧər] *n* : meubles *mpl*
furrow [ˈfəro:] *n* : sillon *m*
furry [ˈfəri] *adj* **furrier; -est** : au poil touffu

(se dit d'un animal), en peluche (se dit d'un jouet, etc.)

further ['fərðər] *adv* 1 FARTHER : plus loin 2 MORE : davantage, plus 3 MOREOVER : de plus — ~ *adj* 1 FARTHER : plus éloigné 2 ADDITIONAL : supplémentaire 3 **until ~ notice** : jusqu'à nouvel ordre — **furthermore** ['fərðər,mor] *adv* : en outre, de plus — **furthest** ['fərðəst] *adv & adj* → **farthest**

furtive ['fərṭɪv] *adj* : furtif

fury ['fjʊri] *n, pl* **-ries** : fureur *f*

fuse[1] *or* **fuze** ['fju:z] *n* : amorce *f*, détonateur *m* (d'une bombe, etc.)

fuse[2] *v* **fused; fusing** *vt* 1 MELT : fondre 2 UNITE : fusionner — ~ *n* 1 : fusible *m*, plomb *m* (en électricité) 2 **blow a ~** : faire sauter un plomb — **fusion** ['fju:ʒən] *n* : fusion *f*

fuss ['fʌs] *n* 1 : agitation *f*, remue-ménage *m* 2 **make a ~** : faire des histoires — ~ *vi* 1 : s'agiter 2 WORRY : s'inquiéter — **fussy** ['fʌsi] *adj* **fussier; -est** 1 FINICKY : tatillon, pointilleux 2 ELABORATE : tarabiscoté

futile ['fju:ṭəl, 'fju:,taɪl] *adj* : futile, vain — **futility** [fju:'tɪləṭi] *n* : futilité *f*

future ['fju:ʧər] *adj* : futur — ~ *n* : avenir *m*, futur *m*

fuze *n* → **fuse**[1]

fuzz ['fʌz] *n* FLUFF : peluches *fpl* — **fuzzy** ['fʌzi] *adj* **fuzzier; -est** 1 FURRY : duveteux 2 INDISTINCT : flou 3 VAGUE : confus

G

g ['ʤi:] *n, pl* **g's** *or* **gs** ['ʤi:z] : g *m*, septième lettre de l'alphabet

gab ['gæb] *vi* **gabbed; gabbing** : bavarder — ~ *n* CHATTER : bavardage *m*

gable ['geɪbəl] *n* : pignon *m*

gadget ['gæʤət] *n* : gadget *m*

gag ['gæg] *v* **gagged; gagging** *vt* : bâillonner — *vi* CHOKE : avoir des haut-le-cœur — ~ *n* 1 : bâillon *m* 2 JOKE : blague *f*

gage → **gauge**

gaiety ['geɪəṭi] *n, pl* **-eties** : gaieté *f*

gain ['geɪn] *n* 1 PROFIT : profit *m* 2 INCREASE : augmentation *f* — ~ *vt* 1 OBTAIN : gagner 2 **~ weight** : prendre du poids — *vi* 1 PROFIT : gagner 2 : avancer (se dit d'une horloge) — **gainful** ['geɪnfəl] *adj* : rémunéré

gait ['geɪt] *n* : démarche *f*

gala ['geɪlə, 'gæ-, 'gɑ-] *n* : gala *m*

galaxy ['gæləksi] *n, pl* **-axies** : galaxie *f*

gale ['geɪl] *n* : coup *m* de vent

gall ['gɔl] *n* **have the ~ to** : avoir le culot de

gallant ['gælənt] *adj* : galant

gallbladder ['gɔl,blædər] *n* : vesicule *f* biliaire

gallery ['gæləri] *n, pl* **-leries** : galerie *f*

gallon ['gælən] *n* : gallon *m*

gallop ['gæləp] *vi* : galoper — ~ *n* : galop *m*

gallows ['gæ,lo:z] *n, pl* **-lows** *or* **-lowses** [-,lo:zəz] : gibet *m*, potence *f*

gallstone ['gɔl,sto:n] *n* : calcul *m* biliaire

galore [gə'lor] *adv* : en abondance

galoshes [gə'lɑʃəz] *npl* : caoutchoucs *mpl*, claques *fpl Can*

galvanize ['gælvən,aɪz] *vt* **-nized; -nizing** : galvaniser

gamble ['gæmbəl] *v* **-bled; -bling** *vi* : jouer — *vt* WAGER : parier — ~ *n* 1 BET : pari *m* 2 RISK : entreprise *f* risquée — **gambler** ['gæmbələr] *n* : joueur *m*, joueuse *f*

game ['geɪm] *n* 1 : jeu *m* 2 MATCH : match *m*, partie *f* 3 *or* **~ animals** : gibier *m* — ~ *adj* READY : partant, prêt

gamut ['gæmət] *n* : gamme *f*

gang ['gæŋ] *n* : bande *f* — ~ *vi* **~ up on** : se liguer contre

gangplank ['gæŋ,plæŋk] *n* : passerelle *f*

gangrene ['gæŋ,gri:n, 'gæn-; gæŋ'-, gæn'-] *n* : gangrène *f*

gangster ['gæŋstər] *n* : gangster *m*

gangway ['gæŋ,weɪ] → **gangplank**

gap ['gæp] *n* 1 OPENING : trou *m* 2 INTERVAL : intervalle *m* 3 DIFFERENCE : écart *m* 4 DEFICIENCY : lacune *f*

gape ['geɪp] *vi* **gaped; gaping** 1 OPEN : bâiller 2 STARE : rester bouche bée

garage [gə'rɑʒ, -'rɑʤ] *n* : garage *m*

garb ['gɑrb] *n* : costume *m*, mise *f*

garbage ['gɑrbɪʤ] *n* : ordures *fpl* — **garbage can** *n* : poubelle *f*

garble ['gɑrbəl] *vt* **-bled; -bling** : embrouiller — **garbled** ['gɑrbəld] *adj* : confus

garden ['gɑrdən] *n* : jardin *m* — ~ *vi* : jardiner — **gardener** ['gɑrdənər] *n* : jardinier *m*, -nière *f*

gargle ['gɑrgəl] *vi* **-gled; -gling** : se gargariser

garish ['gærɪʃ] *adj* : criard, voyant

garland ['gɑrlənd] *n* : guirlande *f*

garlic ['gɑrlɪk] *n* : ail *m*

garment ['gɑrmənt] *n* : vêtement *m*

garnish ['gɑrnɪʃ] *vt* : garnir — ~ *n* : garniture *f*

garret ['gærət] *n* : mansarde *f*

garrison ['gærəsən] *n* : garnison *f*

garter ['gɑrṭər] *n* : jarretière *f*

gas ['gæs] *n, pl* **gases** 1 : gaz *m* 2 GASOLINE : essence *f* — ~ *v* **gassed; gassing** *vt* : asphyxier au gaz — *vi* **~ up** : faire le plein d'essence — **gas station** *n* : station-service *f*

gash ['gæʃ] *n* : entaille *f* — ~ *vt* : entailler

gasket ['gæskət] *n* : joint *m* (d'étanchéité)

gasoline ['gæsə,li:n, ,gæsə'-] *n* : essence *f*

gasp ['gæsp] *vi* 1 : avoir le souffle coupé 2 PANT : haleter — ~ *n* : halètement *m*

gastric ['gæstrɪk] *adj* : gastrique

gastronomy [gæs'trɑnəmi] *n* : gastronomie *f*

gate ['geɪt] *n* 1 DOOR : porte *f* 2 BARRIER : barrière *f*, grille *f* — **gateway** ['geɪt,weɪ] *n* : porte *f*, entrée *f*

gather ['gæðər] *vt* 1 ASSEMBLE : rassembler 2 COLLECT : ramasser 3 CONCLUDE : déduire — *vi* ASSEMBLE : se rassembler — **gathering** ['gæðərɪŋ] *n* : rassemblement *m*

gaudy ['gɔdi] *adj* **-dier; -est** : criard, tape-à-l'œil

gauge ['geɪʤ] *n* 1 INDICATOR : jauge *f*, indicateur *m* 2 CALIBER : calibre *m* — ~ *vt* **gauged; gauging** 1 MEASURE : jauger 2 ESTIMATE : évaluer

gaunt ['gɔnt] *adj* : décharné, émacié

gauze ['gɔz] *n* : gaze *f*

gave → **give**

gawky ['gɔki] *adj* **gawkier; gawkiest** : gauche, maladroit

gay ['geɪ] *adj* 1 : gai 2 HOMOSEXUAL : gay

gaze ['geɪz] *vi* **gazed; gazing** : regarder (fixement) — ~ *n* : regard *m*

gazette [gə'zɛt] *n* : journal *m* officiel

gear ['gɪr] *n* 1 EQUIPMENT : équipement *m* 2 POSSESSIONS : effets *mpl* personnels 3 SPEED : vitesse *f* 4 *or* **~ wheel** : roue *f* dentée — ~ *vt* : adapter — *vi* **~ up** : se préparer — **gearshift** ['gɪr,ʃɪft] *n* : levier *m* de vitesse

geese → **goose**

gelatin ['ʤɛlətən] *n* : gélatine *f*

gem ['ʤɛm] *n* : pierre *f* précieuse, gemme *f* — **gemstone** ['ʤɛm,sto:n] *n* : pierre *f* précieuse

gender ['ʤɛndər] *n* 1 SEX : sexe *m* 2 : genre *m* (en grammaire)

gene ['ʤi:n] *n* : gène *m*

genealogy [,ʤi:ni'ɑləʤi, ,ʤɛ-, -'æ-] *n, pl* **-gies** : généalogie *f*

general ['ʤɛnrəl, 'ʤɛnə-] *adj* : général — ~ *n* 1 : général *m* (militaire) 2 **in ~** : en général — **generalize** ['ʤɛnrə,laɪz, 'ʤɛnərə-] *v* **-ized; -izing** : généraliser — **generally** ['ʤɛnrəli, 'ʤɛnərə-] *adv* : généralement, en général — **general practitioner** *n* : généraliste *mf*

generate ['ʤɛnə,reɪt] *vt* **-ated; -ating** : générer — **generation** [,ʤɛnə'reɪʃən] *n* : génération *f* — **generator** ['ʤɛnə,reɪṭər] *n* 1 : générateur *m* 2 : génératrice *f* (d'énergie électrique)

generous ['ʤɛnərəs] *adj* 1 : généreux 2 AMPLE : copieux — **generosity** [,ʤɛnə'rɑsəṭi] *n, pl* **-ties** : générosité *f*

genetic [ʤə'nɛṭɪk] *adj* : génétique — **genetics** [ʤə'nɛṭɪks] *n* : génétique *f*

genial ['ʤi:niəl] *adj* : affable

genital ['ʤɛnəṭəl] *adj* : génital — **genitals** ['ʤɛnəṭəlz] *npl* : organes *mpl* génitaux

genius ['ʤi:njəs] *n* : génie *m*

genocide ['ʤɛnə,saɪd] *n* : génocide *m*

genteel [ʤɛn'ti:l] *adj* : distingué

gentle ['ʤɛntəl] *adj* **-tler; -tlest** 1 MILD : doux 2 LIGHT : léger — **gentleman** ['ʤɛntəlmən] *n, pl* **-men** [-mən, -,mɛn] 1 MAN : monsieur *m* 2 **act like a ~** : agir en gentleman — **gentleness** ['ʤɛntəlnəs] *n* : douceur *f*

genuine ['ʤɛnjʊwən] *adj* 1 AUTHENTIC : authentique, véritable 2 SINCERE : sincère

geography [ʤi'ɑgrəfi] *n, pl* **-phies** : géographie *f* — **geographic** [,ʤi:ə'græfɪk] *or* **geographical** [-fɪkəl] *adj* : géographique

geology [ʤi'ɑləʤi] *n* : géologie *f* — **geologic** [,ʤi:ə'lɑʤɪk] *or* **geological** [-ʤɪkəl] *adj* : géologique

geometry [ʤi'ɑmətri] *n, pl* **-tries** : géométrie *f* — **geometric** [,ʤi:ə'mɛtrɪk] *or* **geometrical** [-trɪkəl] *adj* : géométrique

geranium [ʤə'reɪniəm] *n* : géranium *m*

geriatric [,ʤɛri'ætrɪk] *adj* : gériatrique — **geriatrics** [,ʤɛri'ætrɪks] *n* : gériatrie *f*

germ ['ʤərm] *n* 1 : germe *m* 2 MICROBE : microbe *m*

German ['ʤərmən] *adj* : allemand — ~ *n* : allemand *m* (langue)

germinate ['ʤərmə,neɪt] *v* **-nated; -nating** *vi* : germer — *vt* : faire germer

gestation [ʤɛ'steɪʃən] *n* : gestation *f*

gesture ['ʤɛsʧər] *n* : geste *m* — ~ *vi* **-tured; -turing** 1 : faire des gestes 2 **~ to** : faire signe à

get ['gɛt] *v* **got** ['gɑt]; **got** *or* **gotten** ['gɑtən]; **getting** *vt* 1 OBTAIN : obtenir, trouver 2 RECEIVE : recevoir, avoir 3 EARN : gagner 4 FETCH : aller chercher 5 CATCH : attraper (une maladie) 6 UNDERSTAND : comprendre 7 PREPARE : préparer 8 **~ one's hair cut** : se faire couper les cheveux 9 **have got to** : devoir — *vi* 1 BECOME : devenir 2 GO, MOVE : aller, arriver 3 PROGRESS : avancer 4 **~ ahead** : progresser 5 **~ at** MEAN : vouloir dire 6 **~ away** : s'échapper 7 **~ back at** : se venger de 8 **~ by** : s'en sortir 9 **~ out** : sortir 10 **~ over** : se remettre de 11 **~ together** MEET : se réunir 12 **~ up** : se lever — **get along** *vi* 1 MANAGE : aller 2 **get along with** : bien s'entendre avec — **getaway** ['gɛṭə,weɪ] *n* : fuite *f* — **get–together** ['gɛttə,gɛðər] *n* : réunion *f*

geyser ['gaɪzər] *n* : geyser *m*

ghastly ['gæstli] *adj* **-lier; -est** : épouvantable

ghetto ['gɛṭo:] *n, pl* **-tos** *or* **-toes** : ghetto *m*

ghost ['go:st] *n* : fantôme *m*, spectre *m* — **ghostly** ['go:stli] *adj* **-lier; -est** : spectral

giant ['ʤaɪənt] *n* : géant *m*, géante *f* — ~ *adj* : géant, gigantesque

gibberish ['ʤɪbərɪʃ] *n* : baragouin *m*, charabia *m fam*

gibe ['ʤaɪb] *vi* **gibed; gibing ~ at** : se moquer de — ~ *n* : moquerie *f*

giblets ['ʤɪbləts] *npl* : abats *mpl* (de volaille)

giddy ['gɪdi] *adj* **-dier; -est** : vertigineux — **giddiness** ['gɪdinəs] *n* : vertige *m*

gift ['gɪft] *n* 1 PRESENT : cadeau *m* 2 TALENT : don *m* — **gifted** ['gɪftəd] *adj* : doué

gigantic [ʤaɪ'gæntɪk] *adj* : gigantesque

giggle ['gɪgəl] *vi* **-gled; -gling** : rire bêtement — ~ *n* : petit rire *m*

gild ['gɪld] *vt* **gilded** ['gɪldəd] *or* **gilt** ['gɪlt]; **gilding** : dorer

gill ['gɪl] *n* : branchie *f*, ouïe *f*

gilt ['gɪlt] *adj* : doré

gimmick ['gɪmɪk] *n* : truc *m*, gadget *m*

gin ['ʤɪn] *n* : gin *m*

ginger ['ʤɪnʤər] *n* : gingembre *m* — **ginger ale** *n* : boisson *f* gazeuse au gingembre — **gingerbread** ['ʤɪnʤər,brɛd] *n* : pain *m* d'épice — **gingerly** ['ʤɪnʤərli] *adv* : avec précaution

giraffe [ʤə'ræf] *n* : girafe *f*

girdle ['gərdəl] *n* : gaine *f*

girl ['gərl] *n* : fille *f*, jeune fille *f* — **girlfriend** ['gərl,frɛnd] *n* : copine *f*, petite amie *f*

girth ['gərθ] *n* : circonférence *f*

gist ['ʤɪst] *n* **the ~** : l'essentiel *m*

give ['gɪv] *v* **gave** ['geɪv]; **given** ['gɪvən]; **giving** *vt* 1 : donner 2 **~ out** DISTRIBUTE : distribuer 3 **~ up smoking** : arrêter de fumer — *vi* 1 YIELD : céder 2 **~ in** *or* **~ up** : se rendre — ~ *n* : élasticité *f*, souplesse *f* — **given** ['gɪvən] *adj* 1 SPECIFIED : donné 2 INCLINED : enclin — **given name** *n* : prénom *m*

glacier ['gleɪʃər] *n* : glacier *m*

glad ['glæd] *adj* **gladder; gladdest** 1 : content 2 **be ~ to** : être heureux de 3 **~ to meet you** : enchanté — **gladden** ['glædən] *vt* : réjouir — **gladly** ['glædli] *adv* : avec plaisir, volontiers

glade ['gleɪd] *n* : clairière *f*

glamour *or* **glamor** ['glæmər] *n* : charme *m* — **glamorous** ['glæmərəs] *adj* : séduisant

glance ['glænts] *vi* **glanced; glancing ~ at** : jeter un coup d'œil à — ~ *n* : coup *m* d'œil

gland ['glænd] *n* : glande *f*

glare ['glær] *vi* **glared; glaring** 1 : briller d'un éclat éblouissant 2 **~ at** : lancer un regard furieux à — ~ *n* 1 : lumière *f* éblouissante 2 STARE : regard *m* furieux — **glaring** ['glærɪŋ] *adj* 1 BRIGHT : éblouissant 2 FLAGRANT : flagrant

glass ['glæs] *n* 1 : verre *m* 2 **~es** *npl* SPECTACLES : lunettes *fpl* — ~ *adj* : en verre — **glassware** ['glæs,wær] *n* : verrerie *f* — **glassy** ['glæsi] *adj* **glassier; glassiest** : vitreux

glaze ['gleɪz] *vt* **glazed; glazing** : vernisser (des céramiques) — ~ *n* 1 : vernis *m* 2 FROSTING : glaçage *m*

gleam ['gli:m] *n* : lueur *f* — ~ *vi* : luire, reluire

glee ['gli:] *n* : joie *f* — **gleeful** ['gli:fəl] *adj* : joyeux

glib ['glɪb] *adj* **glibber; glibbest** : désinvolte

glide ['glaɪd] *vi* **glided; gliding** : glisser (sur une surface), planer (en l'air) — **glider** ['glaɪdər] *n* : planeur *m*

glimmer ['glɪmər] *vi* : jeter une faible lueur — ~ *n* : lueur *f*

glimpse ['glɪmps] *vt* **glimpsed; glimpsing** : entrevoir — ~ *n* 1 : aperçu *m* 2 **catch a ~ of** : entrevoir

glint ['glɪnt] *vi* : étinceler — ~ *n* : reflet *m*

glisten ['glɪsən] *vi* : briller

glitter ['glɪṭər] *vi* : scintiller, étinceler — ~ *n* : scintillement *m*

gloat ['glo:t] *vi* : jubiler

globe ['glo:b] *n* : globe *m* — **global** ['glo:bəl] *adj* : mondial

gloom ['glu:m] *n* 1 DARKNESS : obscurité *f* 2 SADNESS : tristesse *f* — **gloomy** ['glu:mi] *adj* **gloomier; gloomiest** 1 DARK : sombre 2 DISMAL : lugubre

glory ['glori] *n, pl* **-ries** : gloire *f* — **glorify** ['glorə,faɪ] *vt* **-fied; -fying** : glorifier — **glorious** ['gloriəs] *adj* : glorieux

gloss ['glɔs, 'glɑs] *n* : brillant *m*, lustre *m*

glossary ['glɔsəri, 'glɑ-] *n, pl* **-ries** : glossaire *m*

glossy ['glɔsi, 'glɑ-] *adj* **glossier; glossiest** : brillant

glove ['glʌv] *n* : gant *m*

glow ['glo:] *vi* 1 : luire 2 **~ with health** : rayonner de santé — ~ *n* : lueur *f*

glue ['glu:] *n* : colle *f* — ~ *vt* **glued; gluing** *or* **glueing** : coller

glum ['glʌm] *adj* **glummer; glummest** : morne, triste

glut ['glʌt] *n* : surabondance *f*

glutton ['glʌtən] *n* : glouton *m*, -tonne *f* — **gluttonous** ['glʌtənəs] *adj* : glouton — **gluttony** ['glʌtəni] *n, pl* **-tonies** : gloutonnerie *f*

gnarled ['nɑrld] *adj* : noueux

gnash ['næʃ] *vt* **~ one's teeth** : grincer des dents

gnat ['næt] *n* : moucheron *m*

gnaw ['nɔ] *vt* : ronger

go ['go:] *v* **went** ['wɛnt]; **gone** ['gɔn, 'gɑn]; **going; goes** ['go:z] *vi* 1 : aller 2 LEAVE : partir, s'en aller 3 EXTEND : s'étendre 4 SELL : se vendre 5 FUNCTION : marcher 6 DISAPPEAR : disparaître 7 **~ back on** : revenir sur 8 **~ for** FAVOR : aimer 9 **~ off** EXPLODE : exploser 10 **~ out** : sortir 11 **~ with** MATCH : aller avec 12 **~ without** : se passer de — *v aux* **be going to do** : aller faire — ~ *n, pl* **goes** 1 ATTEMPT : essai *m*, tentative *f* 2 **be on the ~** : ne jamais s'arrêter

goad ['go:d] *vt* : aiguillonner (un animal), provoquer (une personne)

goal ['go:l] *n* : but *m* — **goalie** ['go:li] → **goalkeeper** — **goalkeeper** ['go:l,ki:pər] *n* : gardien *m* de but

goat ['go:t] *n* : chèvre *f*

goatee [go:'ti:] *n* : barbiche *f*

gobble ['gɑbəl] *vt* **-bled; -bling** *or* **~ up** : engloutir

goblet ['gɑblət] *n* : verre *m* à pied

goblin ['gɑblən] *n* : lutin *m*

god ['gɑd, 'gɔd] *n* 1 : dieu *m* 2 **God** : Dieu *m* — **goddess** ['gɑdəs, 'gɔ-] *n* : déesse *f* — **godchild** ['gɑd,ʧaɪld, 'gɔd-] *n, pl* **-children** : filleul *m*, -leule *f* — **godfather** ['gɑd,fɑðər, 'gɔd-] *n* : parrain *m* — **godmother** ['gɑd,mʌðər, 'gɔd-] *n* : marraine *f*

goes → **go**

goggles ['gɑgəlz] *npl* : lunettes *fpl* (protectrices)

gold ['go:ld] *n* : or *m* — **golden** ['go:ldən] *adj* 1 : en or, d'or 2 : doré, couleur *f* d'or — **goldfish** ['go:ld,fɪʃ] *n* : poisson *m* rouge — **goldsmith** ['go:ld,smɪθ] *n* : orfèvre *m*

golf ['gɑlf, 'gɔlf] *n* : golf *m* — ~ *vi* : jouer au golf — **golf ball** *n* : balle *f* de golfe — **golf course** *n* : terrain *m* de golf — **golfer** ['gɑlfər, 'gɔl-] *n* : joueur *m*, joueuse *f* de golf

gone ['gɔn] *adj* 1 PAST : passé 2 DEPARTED : parti

good ['gʊd] *adj* **better** ['bɛṭər]; **best** ['bɛst] 1 : bon 2 OBEDIENT : sage 3 **be ~ at** : être bon en 4 **feel ~** : se sentir bien 5 **~ evening** : bonsoir 6 **~ morning** : bonjour 7 **~ night** : bonsoir, bonne nuit 8 **have a ~ time** : s'amuser — ~ *n* 1 : bien *m* 2 GOODNESS : bonté *f* 3 **~s** *npl* PROPERTY : biens *mpl* 4 **~s** *npl* WARES : marchandises *fpl* 5 **for ~** : pour de bon — ~ *adv* : bien — **good–bye** *or* **good–by** [gʊd'baɪ] *n* : au revoir *m* — **good–looking** ['gʊd'lʊkɪŋ] *adj* : beau — **goodness** ['gʊdnəs] *n* 1 : bonté *f* 2 **thank ~!** : Dieu merci! — **goodwill** [,gʊd'wɪl] *n* : bienveillance *f* — **goody** ['gʊdi] *n, pl* **goodies** 1 **~!** : chouette! *fam* 2 **goodies** *npl* : friandises *fpl*

goof ['gu:f] *n* : gaffe *f fam* — ~ *vi* 1 *or* **~ up** : gaffer *fam* 2 **~ around** : faire l'imbécile

goose ['gu:s] *n, pl* **geese** ['gi:s] : oie *f* — **goose bumps** *npl* : chair *f* de poule

gopher ['go:fər] *n* : gaufre *m*

gore ['gor] *n* BLOOD : sang *m*

gorge ['gorʤ] *n* RAVINE : gorge *f*, défilé *m* — ~ *vt* **gorged; gorging ~ oneself** : se gorger

gorgeous ['gorʤəs] *adj* : magnifique, splendide

gorilla [gə'rɪlə] *n* : gorille *m*

gory ['gori] *adj* **gorier; goriest** : sanglant

gospel ['gɑspəl] *n* 1 : évangile *m* 2 **the Gospel** : l'Évangile

gossip ['gɑsɪp] *n* : commérages *mpl fam*, ragots *mpl fam* — ~ *vi* : bavarder — **gossipy** ['gɑsɪpi] *adj* : bavard

got → **get**

Gothic ['gɑθɪk] *adj* : gothique

gotten → **get**

gourmet ['gʊr,meɪ, gʊr'meɪ] *n* : gourmet *m*

govern ['gʌvərn] *v* : gouverner — **gov-**

erness ['gʌvərnəs] n : gouvernante f — government ['gʌvərmənt] n : gouvernement m — governor ['gʌvənər, 'gʌvərnər] n : gouverneur m

gown ['gaʊn] n 1 : robe f 2 : toge f (de juge, etc.)

grab ['græb] vt grabbed; grabbing : saisir

grace ['greɪs] n : grâce f — ~ vt graced; gracing 1 HONOR : honorer 2 ADORN : orner — graceful ['greɪsfəl] adj : gracieux — gracious ['greɪʃəs] adj : courtois, gracieux

grade ['greɪd] n 1 QUALITY : catégorie f, qualité f 2 RANK : grade m, rang m (militaire) 3 YEAR : classe f (à l'école) 4 MARK : note f 5 SLOPE : pente f — ~ vt graded; grading 1 CLASSIFY : classer 2 MARK : noter (un examen, etc.) — grade school → elementary school

gradual ['grædʒʊəl] adj : graduel, progressif — gradually ['grædʒʊəli, 'grædʒəli] adv : petit à petit

graduate ['grædʒʊət] n : diplômé m, -mée f — ~ ['grædʒʊ,eɪt] vi -ated; -ating : recevoir son diplôme — graduation [,grædʒʊ'eɪʃən] n : remise f des diplômes

graffiti [grə'fi:ti, græ-] npl : graffiti mpl

graft ['græft] n : greffe f — ~ vt : greffer

grain ['greɪn] n 1 : grain m 2 CEREAL : céréales fpl

gram ['græm] n : gramme m

grammar ['græmər] n : grammaire f — grammar school → elementary school

grand ['grænd] adj 1 : grand, magnifique 2 FABULOUS : formidable fam — grandchild ['grænd,tʃaɪld] n, pl -children [-,tʃɪldrən] : petit-fils m, petite-fille f — granddaughter ['grænd,dɔtər] n : petite-fille f — grandeur ['grændʒər] n : grandeur f — grandfather ['grænd,fɑðər] n : grand-père m — grandiose ['grændi,o:s, ,grændi'-] adj : grandiose — grandmother ['grænd,mʌðər] n : grand-mère f — grandparents ['grænd,pærənts] npl : grands-parents mpl — grandson ['grænd,sʌn] n : petit-fils m — grandstand ['grænd,stænd] n : tribune f

granite ['grænɪt] n : granit m, granite m

grant ['grænt] vt 1 : accorder 2 ADMIT : admettre 3 take for granted : prendre pour acquis — ~ n 1 SUBSIDY : subvention f 2 SCHOLARSHIP : bourse f

grape ['greɪp] n : raisin m

grapefruit ['greɪp,fru:t] n : pamplemousse mf

grapevine ['greɪp,vaɪn] n : vigne f

graph ['græf] n : graphique m — graphic ['græfɪk] adj : graphique

grapnel ['græpnəl] n : grappin m

grapple ['græpəl] vi -pled; -pling ~ with : lutter avec

grasp ['græsp] vt 1 : saisir 2 UNDERSTAND : comprendre — ~ n 1 : prise f 2 UNDERSTANDING : compréhension f 3 within s.o.'s ~ : à la portée de qqn

grass ['græs] n 1 : herbe f 2 LAWN : gazon m, pelouse f — grasshopper ['græs,hɑpər] n : sauterelle f

grate[1] ['greɪt] v grated; grating vt : râper (du fromage, etc.) — vi : grincer

grate[2] n : grille f

grateful ['greɪtfəl] adj : reconnaissant — gratefully ['greɪtfəli] adv : avec reconnaissance — gratefulness ['greɪtfəlnəs] n : gratitude f, reconnaissance f

grater ['greɪtər] n : râpe f

gratify ['grætə,faɪ] vt -fied; -fying 1 PLEASE : faire plaisir à 2 SATISFY : satisfaire

grating ['greɪtɪŋ] n : grille f

gratitude ['grætə,tu:d, -,tju:d] n : gratitude f

gratuitous [grə'tu:ətəs] adj : gratuit

gratuity [grə'tu:əti] n, pl -ities TIP : pourboire m

grave[1] ['greɪv] n : tombe f

grave[2] adj graver; gravest : grave, sérieux

gravel ['grævəl] n : gravier m

gravestone ['greɪv,sto:n] n : pierre f tombale — graveyard ['greɪv,jɑrd] n : cimetière m

gravity ['grævəti] n, pl -ties 1 SERIOUSNESS : gravité f 2 : pesanteur f (en physique)

gravy ['greɪvi] n, pl -vies : sauce f (au jus de viande)

gray ['greɪ] adj 1 : gris 2 GLOOMY : morne — ~ n : gris m — ~ vi or turn ~ : grisonner

graze[1] ['greɪz] vi grazed; grazing : paître

graze[2] vt 1 TOUCH : frôler 2 SCRATCH : écorcher

grease ['gri:s] n : graisse f — ~ ['gri:s, 'gri:z] vt greased; greasing : graisser — greasy ['gri:si, -zi] adj greasier; greasiest 1 : graisseux 2 OILY : huileux

great ['greɪt] adj 1 : grand 2 FANTASTIC : génial fam, formidable fam — great-grandchild [,greɪt'grænd,tʃaɪld] n, pl -children [-,tʃɪldrən] : arrière-petit-enfant m, arrière-petite-enfant f — great-grandfather [,greɪt'grænd,fɑðər] n : arrière-grand-père m — great-grandmother [,greɪt'grænd,mʌðər] n : arrière-grand-mère f — greatly ['greɪtli] adv 1 MUCH : beaucoup 2 VERY : énormément — greatness ['greɪtnəs] n : grandeur f

greed ['gri:d] n 1 : avarice f, avidité f 2 GLUTTONY : gloutonnerie f — greedily ['gri:dəli] adv : avidement — greedy ['gri:di] adj greedier; greediest 1 : avare, avide 2 GLUTTONOUS : glouton

Greek ['gri:k] adj : grec — ~ n : grec m (langue)

green ['gri:n] adj 1 : vert 2 INEXPERIENCED : inexpérimenté — ~ n 1 : vert m (couleur) 2 ~s npl : légumes mpl verts — greenery ['gri:nəri] n, pl -eries : verdure f — greenhouse ['gri:n,haʊs] n : serre f

greet ['gri:t] vt 1 : saluer 2 WELCOME : accueillir — greeting ['gri:tɪŋ] n 1 : salutation f 2 ~s npl REGARDS : salutations fpl 3 birthday ~s : vœux mpl d'anniversaire

grenade [grə'neɪd] n : grenade f

grew → grow

grey → gray

greyhound ['greɪ,haʊnd] n : lévrier m

grid ['grɪd] n 1 GRATING : grille f 2 : quadrillage m (d'une carte, etc.)

griddle ['grɪdəl] n : plaque f chauffante

grief ['gri:f] n : chagrin m, douleur f — grievance ['gri:vənts] n : grief m — grieve ['gri:v] v grieved; grieving vt DISTRESS : peiner, chagriner — vi ~ for : pleurer — grievous ['gri:vəs] adj : grave, sérieux

grill ['grɪl] vt 1 : griller (en cuisine) 2 INTERROGATE : cuisiner fam — ~ n : gril m (de cuisine) — grille or grill ['grɪl] n GRATING : grille f

grim ['grɪm] adj grimmer; grimmest 1 STERN : sévère 2 GLOOMY : sinistre

grimace ['grɪməs, grɪ'meɪs] n : grimace f — ~ vi -maced; -macing : grimacer

grime ['graɪm] n : saleté f, crasse f — grimy ['graɪmi] adj grimier; grimiest : sale, crasseux

grin ['grɪn] vi grinned; grinning : sourire — ~ n : (grand) sourire m

grind ['graɪnd] v ground ['graʊnd]; grinding vt 1 : moudre (du café, etc.) 2 SHARPEN : aiguiser 3 ~ one's teeth : grincer des dents — vi : grincer — ~ n the daily ~ : le train-train quotidien — grinder ['graɪndər] n : moulin m

grip ['grɪp] vt gripped; gripping 1 : serrer, empoigner 2 CAPTIVATE : captiver — ~ n 1 : prise f, étreinte f 2 TRACTION : adhérence f 3 come to ~s with : en venir aux prises avec

gripe ['graɪp] vi griped; griping : rouspéter fam, ronchonner fam — ~ n : plainte f

grisly ['grɪzli] adj -lier; -est : horrible, macabre

gristle ['grɪsəl] n : cartilage m

grit ['grɪt] n 1 : sable m, gravillon m 2 ~s npl : gruau m de maïs — ~ vt gritted; gritting ~ one's teeth : serrer les dents

groan ['gro:n] vi : gémir — ~ n : gémissement m

grocery ['gro:səri, -ʃəri] n, pl -ceries 1 or ~ store : épicerie f 2 groceries npl : épiceries fpl, provisions fpl — grocer ['gro:sər] n : épicier m, -cière f

groggy ['grɑgi] adj -gier; -est : chancelant, sonné fam

groin ['grɔɪn] n : aine f

groom ['gru:m, 'grʊm] n BRIDEGROOM : marié m — ~ vt : panser (un animal)

groove ['gru:v] n : rainure f, sillon m

grope ['gro:p] vi groped; groping 1 : tâtonner 2 ~ for : chercher à tâtons

gross ['gro:s] adj 1 SERIOUS : flagrant 2 TOTAL : brut 3 VULGAR : grossier — ~ n ~ income : recettes fpl brutes — grossly ['gro:sli] adv : extrêmement

grotesque [gro:'tesk] adj : grotesque

grouch ['graʊtʃ] n : rouspéteur m, -teuse f fam — grouchy ['graʊtʃi] adj grouchier; grouchiest : grognon

ground[1] ['graʊnd] → grind

ground[2] n 1 : sol m, terre f 2 or ~s LAND : terrain m 3 ~s npl REASON : raison f — ~ vt BASE : baser, fonder — groundhog ['graʊnd,hɔg] n : marmotte f d'Amérique — groundwork ['graʊnd,wərk] n : travail m préparatoire

group ['gru:p] n : groupe m — ~ vt : grouper, réunir — vi or ~ together : se grouper

grove ['gro:v] n : bosquet m

grovel ['grɑvəl, 'grʌ-] vi -eled or -elled; -eling or -elling : ramper

grow ['gro:] v grew ['gru:]; grown ['gro:n]; growing vi 1 : pousser (se dit des plantes), grandir (se dit des personnes) 2 INCREASE : croître 3 BECOME : devenir — vt 1 CULTIVATE : cultiver 2 : laisser pousser (la barbe, etc.) — grower ['gro:ər] n : cultivateur m, -trice f

growl ['graʊl] vi : grogner, gronder — ~ n : grognement m, grondement m

grown-up ['gro:n,əp] adj : adulte — ~ n : adulte mf

growth ['gro:θ] n 1 : croissance f 2 INCREASE : augmentation f 3 TUMOR : tumeur f

grub ['grʌb] n FOOD : bouffe f fam

grubby ['grʌbi] adj -bier; -est : sale

grudge ['grʌdʒ] n 1 : rancune f 2 hold a ~ : en vouloir à

grueling or **gruelling** ['gru:lɪŋ, gru:ə-] adj : exténuant, épuisant

gruesome ['gru:səm] adj : horrible

gruff ['grʌf] adj : bourru, brusque

grumble ['grʌmbəl] vi -bled; -bling : ronchonner fam

grumpy ['grʌmpi] adj grumpier; grumpiest : grincheux, grognon

grunt ['grʌnt] vi : grogner — ~ n : grognement m

guarantee [,gærən'ti:] n : garantie f — ~ vt -teed; -teeing : garantir

guarantor [,gærən'tɔr] n : garant m, -rante f

guard ['gɑrd] n 1 : garde m (personne) 2 be on one's ~ : être sur ses gardes — ~ vt : garder, surveiller — vi ~ against : se garder de — guardian ['gɑrdiən] n 1 : tuteur m, -trice f (d'un mineur) 2 PROTECTOR : gardien m, -dienne f

guerrilla or **guerilla** [gə'rɪlə] n 1 : guérillero m 2 ~ warfare : guérilla f

guess ['gɛs] vt 1 : deviner 2 SUPPOSE : penser — vi : deviner — ~ n : conjecture f

guest ['gɛst] n 1 VISITOR : invité m, -tée f 2 : client m, cliente f (d'un hôtel)

guide ['gaɪd] n 1 : guide mf (personne) 2 : guide m (livre, etc.) — ~ vt guided; guiding : guider — guidance ['gaɪdənts] n : conseils mpl, direction f — guidebook ['gaɪd,bʊk] n : guide m — guideline ['gaɪd,laɪn] n : ligne f directrice

guild ['gɪld] n : association f

guile ['gaɪl] n : ruse f

guilt ['gɪlt] n : culpabilité f — guilty ['gɪlti] adj guiltier; guiltiest : coupable

guinea pig ['gɪni-] n : cobaye m

guise ['gaɪz] n : apparence f

guitar [gə'tɑr, gɪ-] n : guitare f

gulf ['gʌlf] n : golfe m

gull ['gʌl] n : mouette f

gullible ['gʌlɪbəl] adj : crédule

gully ['gʌli] n, pl -lies : ravin m

gulp ['gʌlp] vt or ~ down : avaler — ~ n : gorgée f, bouchée f

gum[1] ['gʌm] n : gencive f

gum[2] n CHEWING GUM : chewing-gum m France, gomme f à mâcher

gun ['gʌn] n 1 FIREARM : arme f à feu, fusil m 2 or spray ~ : pistolet m — ~ vt gunned; gunning or ~ down : abattre — gunfire ['gʌn,faɪr] n : fusillade f, coups mpl de feu — gunman ['gʌnmən] n, pl -men [-mən, -,mɛn] : personne f armée — gunpowder ['gʌn,paʊdər] n : poudre f (à canon) — gunshot ['gʌn,ʃɑt] n : coup m de feu

gurgle ['gərgəl] vi -gled; -gling 1 : gargouiller 2 : gazouiller (se dit d'un bébé)

gush ['gʌʃ] vi 1 SPOUT : jaillir 2 ~ over : s'extasier devant

gust ['gʌst] n : rafale f

gusto ['gʌs,to:] n, pl -toes : enthousiasme m

gut ['gʌt] n 1 : intestin m 2 ~s npl INNARDS : entrailles fpl 3 ~s npl COURAGE : cran m fam — ~ vt gutted; gutting : détruire l'intérieur de (un édifice)

gutter ['gʌtər] n 1 : gouttière f (d'un toit) 2 : caniveau m (d'une rue)

guy ['gaɪ] n : type m fam

guzzle ['gʌzəl] vt -zled; -zling : bâfrer fam, engloutir

gym ['dʒɪm] or **gymnasium** [dʒɪm'neɪziəm, -ʒəm] n, pl -siums or -sia [-zi:ə, -ʒə] : gymnase m — gymnast ['dʒɪmnəst, -,næst] n : gymnaste mf — gymnastics [dʒɪm'næstɪks] n : gymnastique f

gynecology [,gaɪnə'kɑlədʒi] n : gynécologie f — gynecologist [,gaɪnə'kɑlədʒɪst] n : gynécologue mf

Gypsy ['dʒɪpsi] n, pl -sies : gitan m, -tane f

H

h ['eɪtʃ] n, pl h's or hs ['eɪtʃəz] : h m, huitième lettre de l'alphabet

habit ['hæbɪt] n 1 CUSTOM : habitude f, coutume f 2 : habit m (religieux)

habitat ['hæbɪ,tæt] n : habitat m

habitual [hə'bɪtʃʊəl] adj 1 CUSTOMARY : habituel 2 INVETERATE : invétéré

hack[1] ['hæk] n 1 : cheval m de louage 2 or ~ writer : écrivaillon m

hack[2] vt CUT : tailler — vi ~ into : entrer dans (en informatique)

hackneyed ['hæknid] adj : rebattu

hacksaw ['hæk,sɔ] n : scie f à métaux

had → have

haddock ['hædək] ns & pl : églefin m

hadn't ['hædənt] (contraction of had not) → have

hag ['hæg] n : vieille sorcière f

haggard ['hægərd] adj : hâve, exténué

haggle ['hægəl] vi -gled; -gling : marchander

hail[1] ['heɪl] vt 1 ACCLAIM : acclamer 2 : héler (un taxi)

hail[2] ['heɪl] n : grêle f (en météorologie) — ~ vi : grêler — hailstone ['heɪl,sto:n] n : grêlon m

hair ['hær] n 1 : cheveux mpl (sur la tête) 2 : poil m (de chien, sur les jambes, etc.) — hairbrush ['hær,brʌʃ] n : brosse f à cheveux — haircut ['hær,kʌt] n : coupe f de cheveux — hairdo ['hær,du:] n, pl -dos : coiffure f — hairdresser ['hær,drɛsər] n : coiffeur m, -feuse f — hairless ['hærləs] adj : sans cheveux, glabre — hairpin ['hær,pɪn] n : épingle f à cheveux — hair-raising ['hær,reɪzɪŋ] adj : à vous faire dresser les cheveux sur la tête — hair spray n : laque f — hairy ['hæri] adj hairier; -est : poilu, velu

Haitian ['heɪʃən, 'heɪtiən] adj : haïtien

half ['hæf] n, pl halves ['hævz] 1 : moitié f, demi m, -mie f 2 in ~ : en deux 3 or halftime : mi-temps f (aux sports) — ~ adj 1 : demi 2 ~ an hour : une demi-heure 3 in ~ : en deux — ~ adv : à demi, à moitié — halfhearted ['hæf'hɑrtəd] adj : sans enthousiasme — halfway ['hæf'weɪ] adv & adj : à mi-chemin

halibut ['hælɪbət] ns & pl : flétan m

hall ['hɔl] n 1 HALLWAY : couloir m 2 AUDITORIUM : salle f 3 LOBBY : entrée f, vestibule m 4 DORMITORY : résidence f universitaire

hallmark ['hɔl,mɑrk] n : marque f, sceau m

Halloween [,hælə'wi:n, ,hɑ-] n : Halloween f

hallucination [hə,lu:sən'eɪʃən] n : hallucination f

hallway ['hɔl,weɪ] n 1 ENTRANCE : entrée f, vestibule m 2 CORRIDOR : couloir m

halo ['heɪ,lo:] n, pl -los or -loes : auréole f

halt ['hɔlt] n 1 : halte f 2 come to a ~ : s'arrêter — ~ vi : s'arrêter — vt : arrêter

halve ['hæv] vt halved; halving 1 DIVIDE : couper en deux 2 REDUCE : réduire de moitié — halves → half

ham ['hæm] n : jambon m

hamburger ['hæm,bərgər] or **hamburg** [-,bərg] n 1 : viande f hachée (crue) 2 : hamburger m (cuit)

hammer ['hæmər] n : marteau m — ~ vt : marteler, enfoncer (à coups de marteau)

hammock ['hæmək] n : hamac m

hamper[1] ['hæmpər] vt : gêner

hamper[2] n : panier m (à linge)

hamster ['hæmpstər] n : hamster m

hand ['hænd] n 1 : main f 2 : aiguille f (d'une montre, etc.) 3 HANDWRITING : écriture f 4 : main f, jeu m (aux cartes) 5 WORKER : ouvrier m, -vrière f 6 by ~ : à la main 7 give s.o. a ~ : donner un coup de main à qqn 8 on ~ : disponible 9 on the other ~ : d'autre part — ~ vt 1 : donner, passer 2 ~ out : distribuer — handbag ['hænd,bæg] n : sac m à main — handbook ['hænd,bʊk] n : manuel m, guide m — handcuffs ['hænd,kʌfs] npl : menottes fpl — handful ['hænd,fʊl] n : poignée f — handgun ['hænd,gʌn] n : pistolet m, revolver m

handicap ['hændi,kæp] n : handicap m — ~ vt -capped; -capping : handicaper — handicapped ['hændi,kæpt] adj : handicapé

handicrafts ['hændi,kræfts] npl : objets mpl artisanaux

handiwork ['hændi,wərk] n : ouvrage m

handkerchief ['hæŋkərtʃəf, -,tʃi:f] n, pl -chiefs : mouchoir m

handle ['hændəl] n : manche m (d'un ustensile), poignée f (de porte), anse f (d'un panier, etc.) — ~ vt -dled; -dling 1 TOUCH : toucher à, manipuler 2 MANAGE : s'occuper de — handlebars ['hændəl,bɑrz] npl : guidon m

handmade ['hænd,meɪd] adj : fait à la main

handout ['hænd,aʊt] n 1 ALMS : aumône f 2 LEAFLET : prospectus m

handrail ['hænd,reɪl] n : rampe f

handshake ['hænd,ʃeɪk] n : poignée f de main

handsome ['hæntsəm] adj handsomer; -est 1 ATTRACTIVE : beau 2 GENEROUS : généreux 3 LARGE : considérable

handwriting ['hænd,raɪtɪŋ] n : écriture f — handwritten ['hænd,rɪtən] adj : écrit à la main

handy ['hændi] adj handier; -est 1 NEARBY : à portée de la main, proche 2 USEFUL : commode, pratique 3 CLEVER : adroit — handyman ['hændimən] n, pl -men [-mən, -,mɛn] : bricoleur m

hang ['hæŋ] v hung ['hʌŋ]; hanging vt 1 : suspendre, accrocher 2 (past tense often hanged) EXECUTE : pendre 3 ~ one's head : baisser la tête — vi 1 : être accroché, pendre 2 ~ up : raccrocher — ~ n get the ~ of : piger fam

hangar ['hæŋər, 'hæŋgər] n : hangar m

hanger ['hæŋər] n or coat ~ : cintre m

hangover ['hæŋ,o:vər] n : gueule f de bois

hanker ['hæŋkər] vi ~ for : désirer, avoir

envie de — hankering ['hæŋkərɪŋ] n : désir m, envie f
haphazard [hæp'hæzərd] adj : fait au hasard
happen ['hæpən] vi 1 OCCUR : arriver, se passer 2 CHANCE : arriver par hasard 3 it so happens that ... : il se trouve que ... — happening ['hæpənɪŋ] n : événement m
happy ['hæpi] adj happier; -est 1 : heureux 2 be ~ with : être satisfait de — happily ['hæpəli] adv : heureusement — happiness ['hæpinəs] n : bonheur m — happy-go-lucky ['hæpigo:'lʌki] adj : insouciant
harass [hə'ræs, 'hærəs] vt : harceler — harassment [hə'ræsmənt, 'hærəsmənt] n : harcèlement m
harbor or Brit harbour ['hɑrbər] n : port m — ~ vt 1 SHELTER : héberger 2 ~ a grudge against : garder rancune à
hard ['hɑrd] adj 1 : dur 2 DIFFICULT : difficile 3 ~ water : eau f calcaire — ~ adv 1 : dur 2 FORCEFULLY : fort 3 take sth ~ : mal prendre qqch — harden ['hɑrdən] vt : durcir, endurcir — vi : s'endurcir — hardheaded ['hɑrd'hɛdəd] adj : têtu, entêté — hard-hearted ['hɑrd'hɑrtəd] adj : dur, insensible — hardly ['hɑrdli] adv 1 BARELY : à peine, ne . . . guère 2 it's ~ surprising : ce n'est pas surprenant — hardness ['hɑrdnəs] n : dureté f — hardship ['hɑrd,ʃɪp] n : épreuves fpl — hardware ['hɑrd,wær] n 1 : quincaillerie f 2 : matériel m (en informatique) — hard-working ['hɑrd'wərkɪŋ] adj : travailleur, travaillant Can
hardy ['hɑrdi] adj hardier; -est 1 BOLD : hardi, intrépide 2 ROBUST : résistant
hare ['hær] n, pl hare or hares : lièvre m
harm ['hɑrm] n 1 INJURY : mal m 2 DAMAGE : dommage m 3 WRONG : tort m — ~ vt : faire du mal à, nuire à — harmful ['hɑrmfəl] adj : nuisible — harmless ['hɑrmləs] adj : inoffensif
harmonica [hɑr'mɑnɪkə] n : harmonica m
harmony ['hɑrməni] n, pl -nies : harmonie f — harmonious [hɑr'mo:niəs] adj : harmonieux — harmonize ['hɑrmə,naɪz] v -nized; -nizing vt : harmoniser — vi : s'harmoniser
harness ['hɑrnəs] n : harnais m — ~ vt 1 : harnacher 2 UTILIZE : exploiter
harp ['hɑrp] n : harpe f — ~ vi ~ on : rabâcher
harpoon [hɑr'pu:n] n : harpon m
harpsichord ['hɑrpsɪ,kɔrd] n : clavecin m
harsh ['hɑrʃ] adj 1 ROUGH : rude 2 SEVERE : dur, sévère 3 : cru (se dit des couleurs), rude (se dit des sons) — harshness ['hɑrʃnəs] n : sévérité f
harvest ['hɑrvəst] n : moisson f, récolte f — ~ vt : moissonner, récolter
has → have
hash ['hæʃ] vt 1 CHOP : hacher 2 ~ over DISCUSS : parler de, discuter — ~ n 1 : hachis m 2 JUMBLE : gâchis m
hasn't ['hæzənt] (contraction of has not) → have
hassle ['hæsəl] n : embêtements mpl, ennuis mpl — ~ vt : tracasser
haste ['heɪst] n : hâte f, précipitation f — hasten ['heɪsən] vt : hâter, précipiter — vi : se hâter, se dépêcher — hastily ['heɪstəli] adv : à la hâte — hasty ['heɪsti] adj hastier; -est : précipité
hat ['hæt] n : chapeau m
hatch ['hætʃ] n : écoutille f (d'un navire) — ~ vt 1 : couver, faire éclore 2 CONCOCT : tramer (un complot) — vi : éclore
hatchet ['hætʃət] n : hachette f
hate ['heɪt] n : haine f — ~ vt hated; hating : haïr — hateful ['heɪtfəl] adj : odieux — hatred ['heɪtrəd] n : haine f
haughty ['hɔti] adj haughtier; -est : hautain
haul ['hɔl] vt : tirer, traîner — ~ n 1 CATCH : prise f 2 LOOT : butin m 3 it's a long ~ : la route est longue
haunch ['hɔntʃ] n : hanche f (d'une personne), derrière m (d'un animal)
haunt ['hɔnt] vt : hanter
have ['hæv, in sense 2 as an auxiliary verb usu 'hæf] v had ['hæd]; having; has ['hæz,] vt 1 : avoir 2 WANT : vouloir, prendre 3 RECEIVE : recevoir 4 ALLOW : permettre, tolérer 5 HOLD : tenir 6 ~ a sandwich : manger un sandwich — v aux 1 : avoir, être 2 ~ to : devoir 3 you've finished, haven't you? : tu as fini, n'est-ce pas?
haven ['heɪvən] n : refuge m, havre m
havoc ['hævək] n : ravages mpl, dégâts mpl
hawk[1] ['hɔk] n : faucon m (oiseau)
hawk[2] vt : colporter
hay ['heɪ] n : foin m — hay fever n : rhume m des foins — haystack ['heɪ,stæk] n : meule f de foin — haywire ['heɪ,wær] adj go ~ : se détraquer
hazard ['hæzərd] n 1 PERIL : risque m 2 CHANCE : hasard m — ~ vt : hasarder, risquer — hazardous ['hæzərdəs] adj : dangereux
haze ['heɪz] n : brume f
hazel ['heɪzəl] n : noisette f (couleur) — hazelnut ['heɪzəl,nʌt] n : noisette f
hazy ['heɪzi] adj hazier; -est 1 : brumeux 2 VAGUE : vague, flou
he ['hi:] pron 1 : il 2 (used for emphasis or contrast) : lui
head ['hɛd] n 1 : tête f 2 END, TOP : bout m (d'une table), chevet m (d'un lit) 3 LEADER : chef m 4 ~s or tails : pile ou face 5 per ~ : par personne — ~ adj MAIN : principal — ~ vt 1 LEAD : être en tête de 2 DIRECT : diriger — vi : se diriger, aller — headache ['hɛd,eɪk] n : mal m de tête — headband ['hɛd,bænd] n : bandeau m — headdress ['hɛd,drɛs] n : coiffe f — headfirst ['hɛd'fərst] adv : la tête la première — heading ['hɛdɪŋ] n : titre m, rubrique f — headland ['hɛdlənd, -,lænd] n : promontoire m, cap m — headlight ['hɛd,laɪt] n : phare m — headline ['hɛd,laɪn] n : (gros) titre m — headlong ['hɛd'lɔŋ] adv : à toute allure — headmaster ['hɛd,mæstər] n : directeur m (d'école) — headmistress ['hɛd,mɪstrəs, -'mɪs-] n : directrice f (d'école) — head-on ['hɛd'ɑn, -'ɔn] adv & adj : de plein fouet — headphones ['hɛd,fo:nz] npl : casque m — headquarters ['hɛd,kwɔrtərz] ns & pl : siège m (d'une compagnie), quartier m général (militaire) — headstrong ['hɛd,strɔŋ] adj : têtu, obstiné — headwaiter ['hɛd'weɪtər] n : maître m d'hôtel — headway ['hɛd,weɪ] n 1 : progrès m 2 make ~ : avancer, progresser — heady ['hɛdi] adj headier; -est 1 : capiteux (se dit du vin) 2 EXCITING : grisant
heal ['hi:l] v : guérir
health ['hɛlθ] n : santé f — healthy ['hɛlθi] adj healthier; -est : sain, en bonne santé
heap ['hi:p] n : tas m — ~ vt : entasser
hear ['hɪr] v heard ['hərd]; hearing vt 1 : entendre 2 or ~ about : apprendre — vi 1 : entendre 2 ~ from : avoir des nouvelles de — hearing ['hɪrɪŋ] n 1 : ouïe f, audition f 2 : audience f (d'un tribunal) — hearing aid n : appareil m auditif — hearsay ['hɪr,seɪ] n : ouï-dire m
hearse ['hərs] n : corbillard m
heart ['hɑrt] n 1 : cœur m 2 at ~ : au fond 3 by ~ : par cœur 4 lose ~ : perdre courage — heartache ['hɑrt,eɪk] n : chagrin m, peine f — heart attack n : crise f cardiaque — heartbeat ['hɑrt,bi:t] n : battement m de cœur — heartbroken ['hɑrt,bro:kən] adj be ~ : avoir le cœur brisé — heartburn ['hɑrt,bərn] n : brûlures fpl d'estomac
hearth ['hɑrθ] n : foyer m
heartily ['hɑrtəli] adv 1 eat ~ : manger avec appétit 2 laugh ~ : rire de bon cœur
heartless ['hɑrtləs] adj : sans cœur, cruel
hearty ['hɑrti] adj heartier; -est 1 : cordial, chaleureux 2 : copieux (se dit d'un repas)
heat ['hi:t] v : chauffer — ~ n 1 : chaleur f 2 HEATING : chauffage m 3 PASSION : feu m, ardeur f — heated ['hi:təd] adj : animé, passionné — heater ['hi:tər] n : radiateur m, appareil m de chauffage
heath ['hi:θ] n : lande f
heathen [hi:ðən] adj : païen — ~ n, pl -thens or -then : païen m, païenne f
heather ['hɛðər] n : bruyère f
heave ['hi:v] v heaved or hove ['ho:v]; heaving vt 1 LIFT : lever, soulever (avec effort) 2 HURL : lancer 3 ~ a sigh : pousser un soupir — vi : se soulever — ~ n : effort m
heaven ['hɛvən] n : ciel m — heavenly ['hɛvənli] adj : céleste, divin
heavy ['hɛvi] adj heavier; -est 1 : lourd, pesant 2 : gros (se dit du corps, du cœur, etc.) 3 ~ sleep : sommeil m profond 4 ~ smoker : grand fumeur m 5 ~ traffic : circulation f dense — heavily ['hɛvəli] adv : lourdement, pesamment — heaviness ['hɛvinəs] n : lourdeur f, pesanteur f — heavyweight ['hɛvi,weɪt] n : poids m lourd
Hebrew ['hi:,bru:] adj : hébreu — ~ n : hébreu m (langue)
heckle ['hɛkəl] vt -led; -ling : interrompre bruyamment
hectic ['hɛktɪk] adj : mouvementé, agité
he'd ['hi:d] (contraction of he had or he would) → have, would
hedge ['hɛdʒ] n : haie f — ~ v hedged; hedging vt ~ one's bets : se couvrir — vi : éviter de s'engager — hedgehog ['hɛdʒ,hɔg, -,hɑg] n : hérisson m
heed ['hi:d] vt : faire attention à, écouter — ~ n take ~ of : tenir compte de — heedless ['hi:dləs] adj : insouciant
heel ['hi:l] n : talon m
hefty ['hɛfti] adj heftier; -est : gros, lourd
heifer ['hɛfər] n : génisse f
height ['haɪt] n 1 TALLNESS : taille f (d'une personne), hauteur f (d'un objet) 2 ALTITUDE : élévation f 3 the ~ of folly : le comble de la folie 4 what is your ~? : combien mesures-tu? — heighten ['haɪtən] vt : augmenter, intensifier
heir ['ær] n : héritier m, -tière f — heiress ['ærəs] n : héritière f — heirloom ['ær,lu:m] n : objet m de famille
held → hold
helicopter ['hɛlə,kɑptər] n : hélicoptère m
hell ['hɛl] n : enfer m — hellish ['hɛlɪʃ] adj : infernal
he'll ['hi:l] (contraction of he shall or he will) → shall, will
hello [hə'lo:, hɛ-] or Brit hullo [hʌ'leʊ] interj : bonjour!, allô! (au téléphone)
helm ['hɛlm] n : barre f
helmet ['hɛlmət] n : casque m
help ['hɛlp] vt 1 : aider, venir à l'aide de 2 PREVENT : empêcher 3 ~ yourself : servez-vous — ~ n 1 : aide f, secours m 2 STAFF : employés mpl, -ployées fpl 3 ~! : au secours! — helper ['hɛlpər] n : aide mf; assistant m, -tante f — helpful ['hɛlpfəl] adj : utile, serviable — helping ['hɛlpɪŋ] n SERVING : portion f — helpless ['hɛlpləs] adj : impuissant
hem ['hɛm] n : ourlet m — ~ vt hemmed; hemming : ourler
hemisphere ['hɛmə,sfɪr] n : hémisphère m
hemorrhage ['hɛmərɪdʒ] n : hémorragie f
hemorrhoids ['hɛmə,rɔɪdz, 'hɛm,rɔɪdz] npl : hémorroïdes fpl
hemp ['hɛmp] n : chanvre m
hen ['hɛn] n : poule f
hence ['hɛnts] adv 1 : d'où, donc 2 ten years ~ : d'ici dix ans — henceforth ['hɛnts,forθ, ,hɛnts'-] adv : dorénavant, désormais
henpeck ['hɛn,pɛk] vt : mener par le bout du nez
hepatitis [,hɛpə'taɪtəs] n, pl -titides [-'tɪtə,di:z] : hépatite f
her ['hər] adj : son, sa, ses — ~ ['hər, ər] pron 1 (used as a direct object) : la, l' 2 (used as an indirect object) : lui 3 (used as object of a preposition) : elle
herald ['hɛrəld] vt : annoncer
herb ['ərb, 'hərb] n : herbe f
herd ['hərd] n : troupeau m — ~ vt : mener, conduire — vi or ~ together : s'assembler
here ['hɪr] adv 1 : ici, là 2 NOW : alors 3 ~ is, ~ are : voici, voilà — hereabouts ['hɪrə,baʊts] or hereabout [-,baʊt] adv : par ici — hereafter [hɪr'æftər] adv : ci-après —hereby [hɪr'baɪ] adv : par la présente
hereditary [hə'rɛdə,tɛri] adj : héréditaire — heredity [hə'rɛdəti] n : hérédité f
heresy ['hɛrəsi] n, pl -sies : hérésie f
herewith [hɪr'wɪθ] adv : ci-joint
heritage ['hɛrətɪdʒ] n : héritage m, patrimoine m
hermit ['hərmət] n : ermite m
hernia ['hərniə] n, pl -nias or -niae [-ni,i:, -ni,aɪ] : hernie f
hero ['hi:,ro:, 'hɪr,o:] n, pl -roes : héros m — heroic [hɪ'ro:ɪk] adj : héroïque — heroine ['hɛroən] n : héroïne f — heroism ['hɛro,ɪzəm] n : héroïsme m
heron ['hɛrən] n : héron m
herring ['hɛrɪŋ] n, pl -ring or -rings : hareng m
hers ['hərz] pron 1 : le sien, la sienne, les siens, les siennes 2 some friends of ~ : des amis à elle — herself [hər'sɛlf] pron 1 (used reflexively) : se, s' 2 (used for emphasis) : elle-même 3 (used after a preposition) : elle, elle-même
he's ['hi:z] (contraction of he is or he has) → be, have
hesitant ['hɛzətənt] adj : hésitant, indécis — hesitate ['hɛzə,teɪt] vi -tated; -tating : hésiter — hesitation [,hɛzə'teɪʃən] n : hésitation f
heterogeneous [,hɛtərə'dʒi:niəs, -njəs] adj : hétérogène
heterosexual [,hɛtəro'sɛkʃʊəl] adj : hétérosexuel — ~ n : hétérosexuel m, -sexuelle f
hexagon ['hɛksə,gɑn] n : hexagone m
hey ['heɪ] interj : hé!, ohé!
heyday ['heɪ,deɪ] n : beaux jours mpl, apogée f
hi ['haɪ] interj : salut!
hibernate ['haɪbər,neɪt] vi -nated; -nating : hiberner
hiccup ['hɪkəp] vi -cuped; -cuping : hoqueter — ~ n have the ~s : avoir le hoquet
hide[1] ['haɪd] n : peau f (d'animal)
hide[2] v hid ['hɪd]; hidden ['hɪdən] or hid; hiding vt : cacher — vi : se cacher — hide-and-seek ['haɪdənd'si:k] n : cache-cache m
hideous ['hɪdiəs] adj : hideux, affreux
hideout ['haɪd,aʊt] n : cachette f
hierarchy ['haɪə,rɑrki] n, pl -chies : hiérarchie f — hierarchical [,haɪə'rɑrkɪkəl] adj : hiérarchique
high ['haɪ] adj 1 : haut 2 : élevé (se dit des prix, etc.) 3 INTOXICATED : parti fam, drogué 4 ~ speed : grande vitesse f 5 a ~ voice : une voix aiguë — ~ adv : haut — ~ n : record m, niveau m élevé — higher ['haɪər] adj 1 : plus haut 2 ~ education : études fpl supérieures — highlight ['haɪ,laɪt] n : point m culminant — ~ vt EMPHASIZE : souligner — highly ['haɪli] adv 1 VERY : très, extrêmement 2 think ~ of : penser du bien de — highness ['haɪnəs] n His/Her Highness : son Altesse — high school n : lycée m France, école f secondaire Can — high-strung ['haɪ'strʌŋ] adj : nerveux, très tendu — highway ['haɪ,weɪ] n 1 : autoroute f 2 → interstate
hijack ['haɪ,dʒæk] vt : détourner (un avion) — hijacker ['haɪ,dʒækər] n : pirate m de l'air — hijacking ['haɪ,dʒækɪŋ] n : détournement m
hike ['haɪk] v hiked; hiking vi : faire une randonnée — vt or ~ up RAISE : augmenter — ~ n : randonnée f — hiker ['haɪkər] n : randonneur m, -neuse f
hilarious [hɪ'læriəs, haɪ-] adj : désopilant, hilarant — hilarity [hɪ'lærəti, haɪ-] n : hilarité f
hill ['hɪl] n : colline f — hillside ['hɪl,saɪd] n : coteau m — hilly ['hɪli] adj hillier; -est : vallonné, côteux Can
hilt ['hɪlt] n : poignée f (d'une épée)
him ['hɪm, əm] pron 1 (used as a direct object) : le, l' 2 (used as an indirect object or as object of a preposition) : lui — himself [hɪm'sɛlf] pron 1 (used reflexively) : se, s' 2 (used for emphasis) : lui-même 3 (used after a preposition) : lui, lui-même
hind ['haɪnd] adj : de derrière
hinder ['hɪndər] vt : empêcher, entraver — hindrance ['hɪndrənts] n : entrave f
hindsight ['haɪnd,saɪt] n in ~ : avec du recul
Hindu ['hɪn,du:] adj : hindou
hinge ['hɪndʒ] n : charnière f, gond m — ~ vi hinged; hinging ~ on : dépendre de
hint ['hɪnt] n 1 INSINUATION : allusion f 2 TRACE : soupçon m 3 TIP : conseil m — ~ vt : insinuer — vi ~ at : faire une allusion à
hip ['hɪp] n : hanche f
hippie or hippy ['hɪpi] n, pl hippies : hippie mf, hippy mf
hippopotamus [,hɪpə'pɑtəməs] n, pl -muses or -mi [-,maɪ] : hippopotame m
hire ['haɪr] vt hired; hiring 1 : engager, embaucher 2 RENT : louer — ~ n 1 WAGES : gages mpl 2 for ~ : à louer
his ['hɪz, ɪz] adj 1 : son, sa, ses 2 it's ~ : c'est à lui — ~ pron 1 : le sien, la sienne, les siens, les siennes 2 a friend of ~ : un ami à lui
Hispanic [hɪ'spænɪk] adj : hispanique
hiss ['hɪs] vi : siffler — ~ n : sifflement m
history ['hɪstəri] n, pl -ries 1 : histoire f 2 : antécédents mpl (médicaux, etc.) — historian [hɪ'stɔriən] n : historien m, -rienne f — historic [hɪ'stɔrɪk] or historical [-ɪkəl] adj : historique
hit ['hɪt] v hit; hitting vt 1 : frapper (une balle, etc.) 2 STRIKE : heurter 3 AFFECT : toucher 4 REACH : atteindre — vi 1 : frapper 2 OCCUR : arriver — ~ n 1 : coup m (aux sports, etc.) 2 SUCCESS : succès m
hitch ['hɪtʃ] vt 1 : accrocher 2 or ~ up RAISE : remonter 3 ~ a ride : faire de l'auto-stop — ~ n PROBLEM : problème m — hitchhike ['hɪtʃ,haɪk] vi -hiked; -hiking : faire de l'auto-stop — hitchhiker ['hɪtʃ,haɪkər] n : auto-stoppeur m, -peuse f
hitherto ['hɪðər,tu:, ,hɪðər'-] adv : jusqu'à présent
HIV [,eɪtʃ,aɪ'vi:] n (human immunodeficiency virus) : VIH m
hive ['haɪv] n : ruche f
hives ['haɪvz] ns & pl : urticaire f
hoard ['hord] n : réserve f, provisions fpl — ~ vt : accumuler, amasser
hoarse ['hors] adj hoarser; -est : rauque, enroué
hoax ['ho:ks] n : canular m
hobble ['hɑbəl] vi -bled; -bling : boitiller
hobby ['hɑbi] n, pl -bies : passe-temps m
hobo ['ho:,bo:] n, pl -boes : vagabond m, -bonde f
hockey ['hɑki] n : hockey m
hoe ['ho:] n : houe f, binette f — ~ vi hoed; hoeing : biner
hog ['hɔg, 'hɑg] n : porc m, cochon m — ~ vt hogged; hogging : monopoliser
hoist ['hɔɪst] vt : hisser — ~ n : palan m
hold[1] ['ho:ld] v held ['hɛld]; holding vt 1 : tenir 2 POSSESS : posséder 3 CONTAIN : contenir 4 or ~ up SUPPORT : soutenir 5 : détenir (un prisonnier, etc.) 6 ~ the line : ne quittez pas 7 ~ s.o.'s attention : retenir l'attention de qqn — vi 1 LAST : durer, continuer 2 APPLY : tenir — ~ n 1 GRIP : prise f, étreinte f 2 get ~ of : trouver — holder ['ho:ldər] n : détenteur m, -trice f; titulaire mf — holdup ['ho:ld,ʌp] n 1 : vol m à main armée 2 DELAY : retard m — hold up vt DELAY : retarder
hold[2] n : cale f (d'un navire ou d'un avion)
hole ['ho:l] n : trou m
holiday ['hɑlə,deɪ] n 1 : jour m férié 2 Brit VACATION : vacances fpl
holiness ['ho:linəs] n : sainteté f
holler ['hɑlər] vi : gueuler fam, hurler — ~ n : hurlement m
hollow ['hɑ,lo:] n : creux m — ~ adj hollower; -est 1 : creux 2 FALSE : faux — ~ vt or ~ out : creuser
holly ['hɑli] n, pl -lies : houx m
holocaust ['hɑlə,kɔst, 'ho:-, 'hɔ-] n : holocauste m
holster ['ho:lstər] n : étui m de revolver
holy ['ho:li] adj holier; -est 1 : saint 2 ~ water : eau f bénite

homage ['ɑmɪʤ, 'hɑ-] *n* : hommage *m*
home ['ho:m] *n* **1** RESIDENCE : maison *f* **2** FAMILY : foyer *m*, chez-soi *m* **3** → **funeral home, nursing home** — ~ *adv* **go** ~ : rentrer à la maison, rentrer chez soi — **homeland** ['ho:m,lænd] *n* : patrie *f* — **homeless** ['ho:mləs] *n* **the** ~ : les sans-abri — **homely** ['ho:mli] *adj* **homelier; -est 1** SIMPLE : simple, ordinaire **2** UGLY : laid — **homemade** ['ho:m'meɪd] *adj* : fait à la maison — **homemaker** ['ho:m,meɪkər] *n* : femme *f* au foyer — **home page** *n* : page *f* d'accueil — **home run** *n* : coup *m* de circuit *Can* — **homesick** ['ho:m,sɪk] *adj* **be** ~ : avoir le mal du pays — **homeward** ['ho:mwərd] *or* **homewards** [-wərdz] *adv* : vers la maison — **homeward** *adj* : de retour — **homework** ['ho:m,wərk] *n* : devoirs *mpl* — **homey** ['ho:mi] *adj* **homier; -est** COZY, INVITING : accueillant
homicide ['hɑmə,saɪd, 'ho:-] *n* : homicide *m*
homogeneous [,ho:mə'ʤi:niəs, -njəs] *adj* : homogène
homosexual [,ho:mə'sɛkʃuəl] *adj* : homosexuel — ~ *n* : homosexuel *m*, -sexuelle *f* — **homosexuality** [,ho:mə,sɛkʃu'æləṭi] *n* : homosexualité *f*
honest ['ɑnəst] *adj* : honnête — **honestly** ['ɑnəstli] *adv* : honnêtement — **honesty** ['ɑnəsti] *n* : honnêteté *f*
honey ['hʌni] *n, pl* **-eys** : miel *m* — **honeycomb** ['hʌni,ko:m] *n* : rayon *m* de miel — **honeymoon** ['hʌni,mu:n] *n* : lune *f* de miel
honk ['hɑŋk, 'hɔŋk] *vi* : klaxonner — ~ *n* : coup *m* de klaxon
honor *or Brit* **honour** ['ɑnər] *n* : honneur *m* — ~ *vt* : honorer — **honorable** *or Brit* **honourable** ['ɑnərəbəl] *adj* : honorable — **honorary** ['ɑnə,rɛri] *adj* : honoraire, honorifique
hood ['hʊd] *n* **1** : capuchon *m* (d'un vêtement) **2** : capot *m* (d'une voiture)
hoodlum ['hʊdləm, 'hu:d-] *n* : voyou *m*
hoodwink ['hʊd,wɪŋk] *vt* : tromper
hoof ['hʊf, 'hu:f] *n, pl* **hooves** ['hʊvz, 'hu:vz] *or* **hoofs** : sabot *m* (d'un animal)
hook ['hʊk] *n* **1** : crochet *m* **2** FASTENER : agrafe *f* **3** → **fishhook** — ~ *vt* : accrocher — *vi* : s'accrocher
hoop ['hu:p] *n* : cerceau *m*
hoorah [hʊ'ra], **hooray** [hʊ'reɪ] → **hurrah**
hoot ['hu:t] *vi* **1** : hululer (se dit d'un hibou) **2** ~ **with laughter** : pouffer de rire — ~ *n* **1** : hululement *m* **2 I don't give a** ~ : je m'en fiche
hop [hɑp] *v* **hopped; hopping** *vi* : sauter, sautiller — *vt or* ~ **over** : sauter — ~ *n* : saut *m*
hope ['ho:p] *v* **hoped; hoping** : espérer — ~ *n* : espoir *m* — **hopeful** ['ho:pfəl] *adj* **1** OPTIMISTIC : plein d'espoir **2** PROMISING : encourageant — **hopefully** ['ho:pfəli] *adv* **1** : avec espoir **2** ~ **it will work** : on espère que cela marche — **hopeless** ['ho:pləs] *adj* : désespéré — **hopelessly** ['ho:pləsli] *adv* **1** : complètement **2** ~ **in love** : éperdument amoureux
hops [hɑps] *nmpl* : houblon *m*
horde ['hord] *n* : horde *f*, foule *f*
horizon [hə'raɪzən] *n* : horizon *m* — **horizontal** [,hɔrə'zɑntəl] *adj* : horizontal
hormone ['hɔr,mo:n] *n* : hormone *f*
horn ['hɔrn] *n* **1** : corne *f* (d'un animal) **2** : cor *m* (instrument de musique) **3** : klaxon *m* (d'un véhicule)
hornet ['hɔrnət] *n* : frelon *m*
horoscope ['hɔrə,sko:p] *n* : horoscope *m*
horrendous [hə'rɛndəs] *adj* : épouvantable — **horrible** ['hɔrəbəl] *adj* : horrible, affreux — **horrid** ['hɔrɪd] *adj* : horrible, hideux — **horrify** ['hɔrə,faɪ] *vt* **-fied; -fying** : horrifier — **horror** ['hɔrər] *n* : horreur *f*
hors d'oeuvre [ɔr'dərv] *n, pl* **hors d'oeuvres** [-'dərvz] : hors-d'œuvre *m*
horse ['hɔrs] *n* : cheval *m* — **horseback** ['hɔrs,bæk] *n* **on** ~ : à cheval — **horsefly** ['hɔrs,flaɪ] *n, pl* **-flies** : taon *m* — **horseman** ['hɔrsmən] *n, pl* **-men** [-mən, -,mɛn] : cavalier *m* — **horsepower** ['hɔrs,paʊər] *n* : cheval-vapeur *m* — **horseradish** ['hɔrs,rædɪʃ] *n* : raifort *m* — **horseshoe** ['hɔrs,ʃu:] *n* : fer *m* à cheval — **horsewoman** ['hɔrs,wʊmən] *n, pl* **-women** [-,wɪmən] : cavalière *f*
horticulture ['hɔrṭə,kʌlʧər] *n* : horticulture *f*
hose ['ho:z] *n* **1** *pl* **hoses** : tuyau *m* (d'arrosage, etc.) **2** *pl* **hose** STOCKINGS : bas *mpl* — ~ *vt* **hosed; hosing** : arroser — **hosiery** ['ho:ʒəri, 'ho:zə-] *n* : bonneterie *f*
hospice ['hɑspəs] *n* : hospice *m*
hospital ['hɑs,pɪṭəl] *n* : hôpital *m* — **hospitable** [hɑs'pɪṭəbəl, 'hɑ,spɪ-] *adj* : hospitalier — **hospitality** [,hɑspə'tæləṭi] *n, pl* **-ties** : hospitalité *f* — **hospitalize** ['hɑs,pɪṭə,laɪz] *vt* **-ized; -izing** : hospitaliser
host[1] ['ho:st] *n* **a** ~ **of** : une foule de
host[2] *n* **1** : hôte *mf* **2** : animateur *m*, -trice *f* (de radio, etc.) — ~ *vt* : animer (une émission de télévision, etc.)
host[3] *n* EUCHARIST : hostie *f*
hostage ['hɑstɪʤ] *n* : otage *m*
hostel ['hɑstəl] *n* : auberge *f*
hostess ['ho:stəs] *n* : hôtesse *f*
hostile ['hɑstəl, -,taɪl] *adj* : hostile — **hostility** [hɑs'tɪləṭi] *n, pl* **-ties** : hostilité *f*
hot ['hɑt] *adj* **hotter; hottest 1** : chaud **2** SPICY : épicé **3** ~ **news** : les dernières nouvelles **4 have a** ~ **temper** : s'emporter facilement **5 it's** ~ **today** : il fait chaud aujourd'hui
hot dog *n* : hot-dog *m*
hotel [ho:'tɛl] *n* : hôtel *m*
hotheaded ['hɑt'hɛdəd] *adj* : impétueux
hound ['haʊnd] *n* : chien *m* courant — ~ *vt* : traquer, poursuivre
hour ['aʊər] *n* : heure *f* — **hourglass** ['aʊər,glæs] *n* : sablier *m* — **hourly** ['aʊərli] *adv & adj* : toutes les heures
house ['haʊs] *n, pl* **houses** ['haʊzəz, -səz] **1** HOME : maison *f* **2** : chambre *f* (en politique) **3 publishing** ~ : maison *f* d'édition — ~ ['haʊz] *vt* **housed; housing** : loger, héberger — **houseboat** ['haʊs,bo:t] *n* : péniche *f* aménagée — **housefly** ['haʊs,flaɪ] *n, pl* **-flies** : mouche *f* — **household** ['haʊs,ho:ld] *adj* **1** : ménager **2** ~ **name** : nom *m* connu de tous — ~ *n* : ménage *m*, maison *f* — **housekeeper** ['haʊs,ki:pər] *n* : gouvernante *f* — **housekeeping** ['haʊs,ki:pɪŋ] *n* HOUSEWORK : ménage *m* — **housewarming** ['haʊs,wɔrmɪŋ] *n* : pendaison *f* de crémaillère — **housewife** ['haʊs,waɪf] *n, pl* **-wives** : femme *f* au foyer, ménagère *f* — **housework** ['haʊs,wərk] *n* : travaux *mpl* ménagers, ménage *m* — **housing** ['haʊzɪŋ] *n* : logement *m*
hovel ['hʌvəl, 'hɑ-] *n* : taudis *m*
hover ['hʌvər] *vi* **1** : planer **2** *or* ~ **about** : rôder — **hovercraft** ['hʌvər,kræft] *n* : aéroglisseur *m*
how ['haʊ] *adv* **1** : comment **2** (*used in exclamations*) : comme, que **3** ~ **about . . . ?** : que dirais-tu de . . . ? **4** ~ **come** WHY : comment, pourquoi **5** ~ **much** : combien **6** ~ **do you do?** : comment allez-vous? **7** ~ **old are you?** : quel âge as-tu? — ~ *conj* : comment
however [haʊ'ɛvər] *conj* **1** : de quelque manière que **2** ~ **you like** : comme vous voulez — ~ *adv* **1** NEVERTHELESS : cependant, toutefois **2** ~ **important it is** : si important que ce soit **3** ~ **you want** : comme tu veux
howl ['haʊl] *vi* : hurler — ~ *n* : hurlement *m*
hub ['hʌb] *n* **1** CENTER : centre *m* **2** : moyeu *m* (d'une roue)
hubbub ['hʌ,bʌb] *n* : vacarme *m*, brouhaha *m*
hubcap ['hʌb,kæp] *n* : enjoliveur *m*
huddle ['hʌdəl] *vi* **-dled; -dling** *or* ~ **together** : se blottir
hue ['hju:] *n* : couleur *f*, teinte *f*
huff ['hʌf] *n* **be in a** ~ : être fâché, être vexé
hug ['hʌg] *vt* **hugged; hugging 1** : serrer dans ses bras, étreindre **2** : serrer, longer (un mur, etc.) — ~ *n* : étreinte *f*
huge ['hju:ʤ] *adj* **huger; hugest** : énorme, immense
hull ['hʌl] *n* : coque *f* (d'un navire)
hullo *Brit* → **hello**
hum ['hʌm] *v* **hummed; humming** *vi* : bourdonner — *vt* : fredonner, chantonner — ~ *n* : bourdonnement *m*
human ['hju:mən, 'ju:-] *adj* **1** : humain **2** ~ **rights** : droits *mpl* de l'homme, droits *mpl* de la personne *Can* — ~ *n* : humain *m*, être *m* humain — **humane** [hju:'meɪn, ju:-] *adj* : humain — **humanitarian** [hju:,mænə'tɛriən, ju:-] *adj* : humanitaire — **humanity** [hju:'mænəṭi, ju:-] *n, pl* **-ties** : humanité *f*
humble ['hʌmbəl] *adj* **humbler; -blest** : humble, modeste — ~ *vt* **-bled; -bling 1** : humilier **2** ~ **oneself** : s'humilier
humdrum ['hʌm,drʌm] *adj* : monotone, banal
humid ['hju:məd, 'ju:-] *adj* : humide — **humidity** [hju:'mɪdəṭi, ju:-] *n, pl* **-ties** : humidité *f*
humiliate [hju:'mɪli,eɪt, ju:-] *vt* **-ated; -ating** : humilier — **humiliating** [hju:'mɪli,eɪṭɪŋ, ju:-] *adj* : humiliant — **humiliation** [hju:,mɪli'eɪʃən, ju:-] *n* : humiliation *f* — **humility** [hju:'mɪləṭi, ju:-] *n* : humilité *f*
humor *or Brit* **humour** ['hju:mər, 'ju:-] *n* **1** WIT : humour *m* **2** MOOD : humeur *f* — ~ *vt* : faire plaisir à, ménager — **humorist** ['hju:mərɪst, 'ju:-] *n* : humoriste *mf* — **humorous** ['hju:mərəs, 'ju:-] *adj* : plein d'humour, drôle
hump ['hʌmp] *n* : bosse *f*
hunch ['hʌnʧ] *vi or* ~ **over** : se pencher — ~ *n* : intuition *f*, petite idée *f*
hundred ['hʌndrəd] *n, pl* **-dreds** *or* **-dred** : cent *m* — ~ *adj* : cent — **hundredth** ['hʌndrədθ] *n* **1** : centième *mf* (dans une série) **2** : centième *m* (en mathématiques) — ~ *adj* : centième
hung → **hang**
hunger ['hʌŋgər] *n* : faim *f* — ~ *vi* ~ **for** : avoir envie de — **hungry** ['hʌŋgri] *adj* **hungrier; -est be** ~ : avoir faim
hunk ['hʌŋk] *n* : gros morceau *m*
hunt ['hʌnt] *vt* **1** : chasser **2** *or* ~ **for** : chercher — ~ *n* **1** : chasse *f* (sport) **2** SEARCH : recherche *f* — **hunter** ['hʌntər] *n* : chasseur *m*, -seuse *f* — **hunting** ['hʌntɪŋ] *n* : chasse *f*
hurdle ['hərdəl] *n* **1** : haie *f* (aux sports) **2** OBSTACLE : obstacle *m*
hurl ['hərl] *vt* : lancer, jeter
hurrah [hʊ'rɑ, -'rɔ] *interj* : hourra!
hurricane ['hərə,keɪn] *n* : ouragan *m*
hurry ['həri] *n* : hâte *f*, empressement *m* — ~ *v* **-ried; -rying** *vt* : presser, bousculer — *vi* **1** : se presser, se hâter **2** ~ **up!** : dépêche-toi! — **hurried** ['hərəd] *adj* : précipité — **hurriedly** ['hərədli] *adv* : à la hâte
hurt ['hərt] *v* **hurt; hurting** *vt* **1** INJURE : faire mal à, blesser **2** OFFEND : blesser — *vi* **1** : faire mal **2 my throat** ~**s** : j'ai mal à la gorge — ~ *adj* : blessé — ~ *n* **1** INJURY : blessure *f* **2** PAIN : douleur *f* — **hurtful** ['hərtfəl] *adj* : blessant
hurtle ['hərṭəl] *vi* **-tled; -tling** : aller à toute vitesse
husband ['hʌzbənd] *n* : mari *m*
hush ['hʌʃ] *vt or* ~ **up** : faire taire — *vi* **1** : se taire **2** ~! : chut! — ~ *n* : silence *m*
husk ['hʌsk] *n* : enveloppe *f*
husky[1] ['hʌski] *adj* **huskier; -est** HOARSE : rauque
husky[2] *n, pl* **-kies** : chien *m* esquimau
husky[3] *n* BURLY : costaud
hustle ['həsəl] *v* **-tled; -tling** *vt* : presser, pousser — *vi* : se dépêcher — ~ *n* ~ **and bustle** : agitation *f*, grande activité *f*
hut ['hʌt] *n* : hutte *f*, cabane *f*
hutch ['hʌʧ] *n* : clapier *m*
hyacinth ['haɪə,sɪnθ] *n* : jacinthe *f*
hybrid ['haɪbrɪd] *n* : hybride *m* — ~ *adj* : hybride
hydrant ['haɪdrənt] *n or* **fire** ~ : bouche *f* d'incendie
hydraulic [haɪ'drɔlɪk] *adj* : hydraulique
hydroelectric [,haɪdroɪ'lɛktrɪk] *adj* : hydroélectrique
hydrogen ['haɪdrəʤən] *n* : hydrogène *m*
hyena [haɪ'i:nə] *n* : hyène *f*
hygiene ['haɪ,ʤi:n] *n* : hygiène *f* — **hygienic** [haɪ'ʤɛnɪk, -'ʤi:-; ,haɪʤi:'ɛnɪk] *adj* : hygiénique
hymn ['hɪm] *n* : hymne *m*
hyperactive [,haɪpər'æktɪv] *adj* : hyperactif
hyphen ['haɪfən] *n* : trait *m* d'union
hypnosis [hɪp'no:sɪs] *n, pl* **-noses** [-,si:z] : hypnose *f* — **hypnotic** [hɪp'nɑṭɪk] *adj* : hypnotique — **hypnotism** ['hɪpnə,tɪzəm] *n* : hypnotisme *m* — **hypnotize** ['hɪpnə,taɪz] *vt* **-tized; -tizing** : hypnotiser
hypochondriac [,haɪpə'kɑndri,æk] *n* : hypocondriaque *mf*
hypocrisy [hɪ'pɑkrəsi] *n, pl* **-sies** : hypocrisie *f* — **hypocrite** ['hɪpə,krɪt] *n* : hypocrite *mf* — **hypocritical** [,hɪpə'krɪṭɪkəl] *adj* : hypocrite
hypothesis [haɪ'pɑθəsɪs] *n, pl* **-eses** [-,si:z] : hypothèse *f* — **hypothetical** [,haɪpə'θɛṭɪkəl] *adj* : hypothétique
hysteria [hɪs'tɛriə, -'tɪr-] *n* : hystérie *f* — **hysterical** [hɪs'tɛrɪkəl] *adj* : hystérique

I

i ['aɪ] *n, pl* **i's** *or* **is** ['aɪz] : i *m*, neuvième lettre de l'alphabet
I ['aɪ] *pron* : je
ice ['aɪs] *n* **1** : glace *f* **2** ~ **cube** : glaçon *m* — ~ *v* **iced; icing** *vt* : glacer — *vi or* ~ **up** : se givrer — **iceberg** ['aɪs,bərg] *n* : iceberg *m* — **icebox** ['aɪs,bɑks] → **refrigerator** — **ice–cold** ['aɪs'ko:ld] *adj* : glacé — **ice cream** *n* : glace *f France*, crème *f* glacée *Can* — **ice–skate** *vi* **-skated; -skating** : patiner — **ice skate** ['aɪs,skeɪt] *n* : patin *m* (à glace) — **icicle** ['aɪ,sɪkəl] *n* : glaçon *m* — **icing** ['aɪsɪŋ] *n* : glaçage *m*
icon ['aɪ,kɑn, -kən] *n* : icône *f* (en informatique)
icy ['aɪsi] *adj* **icier; -est 1** : verglacé (se dit d'une route) **2** FREEZING : glacial, glacé
I'd ['aɪd] (*contraction of* **I should** *or* **I would**) → **should, would**
idea [aɪ'di:ə] *n* : idée *f*
ideal [aɪ'di:əl] *adj* : idéal — ~ *n* : idéal *m* — **idealist** [aɪ'di:əlɪst] *n* : idéaliste *mf* — **idealistic** [aɪ,di:ə'lɪstɪk] *adj* : idéaliste — **idealize** [aɪ'di:ə,laɪz] *vt* **-ized; -izing** : idéaliser
identity [aɪ'dɛntəṭi] *n, pl* **-ties** : identité *f* — **identical** [aɪ'dɛntɪkəl] *adj* : identique — **identify** [aɪ'dɛntə,faɪ] *v* **-fied; -fying** *vt* : identifier — *vi* ~ **with** : s'identifier à — **identification** [aɪ,dɛntəfə'keɪʃən] *n* **1** : identification *f* **2** *or* ~ **card** : carte *f* d'identité
ideology [,aɪdi'ɑləʤi, ,ɪ-] *n, pl* **-gies** : idéologie *f* — **ideological** [,aɪdiə'lɑʤɪkəl, ,ɪ-] *adj* : idéologique
idiocy ['ɪdiəsi] *n, pl* **-cies** : idiotie *f*
idiom ['ɪdiəm] *n* **1** : expression *f* idiomatique **2** LANGUAGE : idiome *m* — **idiomatic** [,ɪdiə'mæṭɪk] *adj* : idiomatique
idiosyncrasy [,ɪdio'sɪŋkrəsi] *n, pl* **-sies** : particularité *f*
idiot ['ɪdiət] *n* : idiot *m*, -diote *f* — **idiotic** [,ɪdi'ɑṭɪk] *adj* : idiot
idle ['aɪdəl] *adj* **idler; idlest 1** UNOCCUPIED : désœuvré, oisif **2** LAZY : paresseux **3** VAIN : vain **4 out of** ~ **curiosity** : par pure curiosité **5 stand** ~ : être à l'arrêt — ~ *v* **idled; idling** *vi* : tourner au ralenti (se dit d'un moteur) — *vt or* ~ **away** : gaspiller (son temps) — **idleness** ['aɪdəlnəs] *n* : oisiveté *f*
idol ['aɪdəl] *n* : idole *f* — **idolize** ['aɪdəl,aɪz] *vt* **-ized; izing** : idolâtrer
idyllic [aɪ'dɪlɪk] *adj* : idyllique
if ['ɪf] *conj* **1** : si **2** THOUGH : bien que **3** ~ **so** : dans ce cas-là **4** ~ **not** : sinon
igloo ['ɪ,glu:] *n, pl* **-loos** : igloo *m*
ignite [ɪg'naɪt] *v* **-nited; -niting** *vt* : enflammer — *vi* : prendre feu, s'enflammer — **ignition** [ɪg'nɪʃən] *n* **1** : allumage *m* **2** *or* ~ **switch** : contact *m*
ignorance ['ɪgnərənts] *n* : ignorance *f* — **ignorant** ['ɪgnərənt] *adj* : ignorant — **ignore** [ɪg'nor] *vt* **-nored; -noring** : ignorer
ilk ['ɪlk] *n* : espèce *f*
ill ['ɪl] *adj* **worse; worst 1** SICK : malade **2** BAD : mauvais — ~ *adv* **worse** ['wərs]; **worst** ['wərst] : mal — ~ *n* : mal *m* — **ill–advised** [,ɪləd'vaɪzd, -əd-] *adj* : peu judicieux — **ill at ease** *adj* : mal à l'aise
I'll ['aɪl] (*contraction of* **I shall** *or* **I will**) → **shall, will**
illegal [ɪl'li:gəl] *adj* : illégal
illegible [ɪl'lɛʤəbəl] *adj* : illisible
illegitimate [,ɪlɪ'ʤɪṭəmət] *adj* : illégitime — **illegitimacy** [,ɪlɪ'ʤɪṭəməsi] *n* : illégitimité *f*
illicit [ɪl'lɪsət] *adj* : illicite
illiterate [ɪl'lɪṭərət] *adj* : analphabète, illettré — **illiteracy** [ɪl'lɪṭərəsi] *n, pl* **-cies** : analphabétisme *m*
ill–mannered [,ɪl'mænərd] *adj* : impoli
ill–natured [,ɪl'neɪʧərd] *adj* : désagréable
illness ['ɪlnəs] *n* : maladie *f*
illogical [ɪl'lɑʤɪkəl] *adj* : illogique
ill–treat [,ɪl'tri:t] *vt* : maltraiter
illuminate [ɪ'lu:mə,neɪt] *vt* **-nated; -nating** : éclairer — **illumination** [ɪ,lu:mə'neɪʃən] *n* : éclairage *m*
illusion [ɪ'lu:ʒən] *n* : illusion *f* — **illusory** [ɪ'lu:səri, -zəri] *adj* : illusoire
illustrate ['ɪləs,treɪt] *v* **-trated; -trating** : illustrer — **illustration** [,ɪləs'treɪʃən] *n* : illustration *f* — **illustrative** [ɪ'lʌstrəṭɪv, 'ɪlə,streɪṭɪv] *adj* : explicatif
illustrious [ɪ'lʌstriəs] *adj* : illustre
ill will *n* : malveillance *f*
I'm ['aɪm] (*contraction of* **I am**) → **be**
image ['ɪmɪʤ] *n* : image *f* — **imagination** [ɪ,mæʤə'neɪʃən] *n* : imagination *f* — **imaginary** [ɪ'mæʤə,nɛri] *adj* : imaginaire — **imaginative** [ɪ'mæʤɪnəṭɪv] *adj* : imaginatif — **imagine** [ɪ'mæʤən] *vt* **-ined; -ining** : imaginer, s'imaginer
imbalance [ɪm'bælənts] *n* : déséquilibre *m*
imbecile ['ɪmbəsəl, -,sɪl] *n* : imbécile *mf*
imbue [ɪm'bju:] *vt* **-bued; -buing** : imprégner
imitation [,ɪmə'teɪʃən] *n* : imitation *f* — ~ *adj* : artificiel, faux — **imitate** ['ɪmə,teɪt] *vt* **-tated; -tating** : imiter — **imitator** ['ɪmə,teɪṭər] *n* : imitateur *m*, -trice *f*
immaculate [ɪ'mækjələt] *adj* : impeccable
immaterial [,ɪmə'tɪriəl] *adj* : sans importance
immature [,ɪmə'ʧʊr, -'tjʊr, -'tʊr] *adj* : immature — **immaturity** [,ɪmə'ʧʊrəṭi, -'tjʊr-, -'tʊr-] *n, pl* **-ties** : immaturité *f*
immediate [ɪ'mi:diət] *adj* : immédiat — **immediately** [ɪ'mi:diətli] *adv* **1** : immédiatement **2** ~ **before** : juste avant
immense [ɪ'mɛnts] *adj* : immense — **immensity** [ɪ'mɛntsəṭi] *n, pl* **-ties** : immensité *f*
immerse [ɪ'mərs] *vt* **-mersed; -mersing** : plonger, immerger — **immersion** [ɪ'mərʒən] *n* : immersion *f*
immigrate ['ɪmə,greɪt] *vi* **-grated; -grating** : immigrer — **immigrant** ['ɪmɪgrənt] *n* : immigrant *m*, -grante *f*; immigré *m*, -grée *f* — **immigration** [,ɪmə'greɪʃən] *n* : immigration *f*
imminent ['ɪmənənt] *adj* : imminent — **imminence** ['ɪmənənts] *n* : imminence *f*
immobile [ɪ'mo:bəl] *adj* **1** FIXED : fixe **2** MOTIONLESS : immobile — **immobilize** [ɪ'mo:bə,laɪz] *vt* **-ized; -izing** : immobiliser
immoral [ɪ'mɔrəl] *adj* : immoral — **immorality** [,ɪmɔ'ræləṭi, ,ɪmə-] *n* : immoralité *f*
immortal [ɪ'mɔrṭəl] *adj* : immortel — **immortality** [,ɪ,mɔr'tæləṭi] *n* : immortalité *f*
immune [ɪ'mju:n] *adj* : immunisé — **immunity** [ɪ'mju:nəṭi] *n, pl* **-ties** : immunité *f* — **immunization** [,ɪmjʊnə'zeɪʃən] *n* : immunisation *f* — **immunize** ['ɪmjʊ,naɪz] *vt* **-nized; -nizing** : immuniser

imp ['ɪmp] *n* 1 : lutin *m* 2 RASCAL : polisson *m*, -sonne *f*
impact ['ɪm,pækt] *n* : impact *m*
impair [ɪm'pær] *vt* 1 WEAKEN : affaiblir 2 DAMAGE : détériorer
impart [ɪm'part] *vt* : communiquer
impartial [ɪm'parʃəl] *adj* : impartial — **impartiality** [ɪm,parʃi'æləṭi] *n* : impartialité *f*
impassable [ɪm'pæsəbəl] *adj* : impraticable
impasse ['ɪm,pæs] *n* : impasse *f*
impassive [ɪm'pæsɪv] *adj* : impassible
impatience [ɪm'peɪʃənts] *n* : impatience *f* — **impatient** [ɪm'peɪʃənt] *adj* : impatient — **impatiently** [ɪm'peɪʃəntli] *adv* : impatiemment
impeccable [ɪm'pɛkəbəl] *adj* : impeccable
impede [ɪm'pi:d] *vt* **-peded; -peding** : entraver, gêner — **impediment** [ɪm'pɛdəmənt] *n* : entrave *f*, obstacle *m*
impel [ɪm'pɛl] *vt* **-pelled; -pelling** 1 : inciter 2 PROPEL : pousser
impending [ɪm'pɛndɪŋ] *adj* : imminent
impenetrable [ɪm'pɛnətrəbəl] *adj* : impénétrable
imperative [ɪm'pɛrəṭɪv] *adj* 1 COMMANDING : impérieux 2 NECESSARY : impératif — ~ *n* : impératif *m* (en grammaire)
imperceptible [,ɪmpər'sɛptəbəl] *adj* : imperceptible
imperfection [ɪm,pər'fɛkʃən] *n* : imperfection *f* — **imperfect** [ɪm'pərfɪkt] *adj* : imparfait — ~ *n or* ~ **tense** : imparfait *m*
imperial [ɪm'pɪriəl] *adj* : impérial — **imperialism** [ɪm'pɪriə,lɪzəm] *n* : impérialisme *m* — **imperious** [ɪm'pɪriəs] *adj* : impérieux
impersonal [ɪm'pərsənəl] *adj* : impersonnel
impersonate [ɪm'pərsən,eɪt] *vt* **-ated; -ating** : se faire passer pour — **impersonation** [ɪm,pərsən'eɪʃən] *n* : imitation *f* — **impersonator** [ɪm'pərsən,eɪṭər] *n* : imitateur *m*, -trice *f*
impertinent [ɪm'pərtənənt] *adj* : impertinent — **impertinence** [ɪm'pərtənənts] *n* : impertinence *f*
impervious [ɪm'pərviəs] *adj* ~ **to** : imperméable à
impetuous [ɪm'pɛtʃuəs] *adj* : impétueux
impetus ['ɪmpəṭəs] *n* : impulsion *f*
impinge [ɪm'pɪndʒ] *vi* **-pinged; -pinging** 1 ~ **on** : affecter 2 ~ **on s.o.'s rights** : empiéter sur les droits de qqn
impish ['ɪmpɪʃ] *adj* : espiègle
implant [ɪm'plænt] *vt* : implanter — ~ ['ɪm,plænt] *n* : implant *m*
implausible [ɪm'plɔzəbəl] *adj* : invraisemblable
implement ['ɪmpləmənt] *n* : outil *m*, instrument *m* — ~ ['ɪmplə,mɛnt] *vt* : mettre en œuvre, appliquer
implicate ['ɪmplə,keɪt] *vt* **-cated; -cating** : impliquer — **implication** [,ɪmplə'keɪʃən] *n* : implication *f*
implicit [ɪm'plɪsət] *adj* 1 : implicite 2 UNQUESTIONING : absolu, total
implode [ɪm'plo:d] *vi* **-ploded; -ploding** : imploser
implore [ɪm'plor] *vt* **-plored; -ploring** : implorer
imply [ɪm'plaɪ] *vt* **-plied; -plying** : impliquer
impolite [,ɪmpə'laɪt] *adj* : impoli
import [ɪm'port] *vt* : importer (des marchandises) — ~ ['ɪm,port] *n* 1 IMPORTANCE : signification *f* 2 IMPORTATION : importation *f* — **importance** [ɪm'portənts] *n* : importance *f* — **important** [ɪm'portənt] *adj* : important — **importation** [,ɪm,por'teɪʃən] *n* : importation *f* — **importer** [ɪm'porṭər] *n* : importateur *m*, -trice *f*
impose [ɪm'po:z] *v* **-posed; -posing** *vt* : imposer — *vi* 1 : s'imposer 2 ~ **on** : déranger — **imposing** [ɪm'po:zɪŋ] *adj* : imposant — **imposition** [,ɪmpə'zɪʃən] *n* : imposition *f*
impossible [ɪm'pasəbəl] *adj* : impossible — **impossibility** [ɪm,pasə'bɪləṭi] *n, pl* **-ties** : impossibilité *f*
impostor *or* **imposter** [ɪm'pastər] *n* : imposteur *m*
impotent ['ɪmpəṭənt] *adj* : impuissant — **impotence** ['ɪmpəṭənts] *n* : impuissance *f*
impound [ɪm'paʊnd] *vt* : saisir, confisquer
impoverished [ɪm'pavərɪʃt] *adj* : appauvri
impracticable [ɪm'præktɪkəbəl] *adj* : impraticable
impractical [ɪm'præktɪkəl] *adj* : peu pratique
imprecise [,ɪmprɪ'saɪs] *adj* : imprécis
impregnable [ɪm'prɛgnəbəl] *adj* : imprenable
impregnate [ɪm'prɛg,neɪt] *vt* **-nated; -nating** 1 FERTILIZE : féconder 2 SATURATE : imprégner
impress [ɪm'prɛs] *vt* 1 IMPRINT : imprimer 2 AFFECT : impressionner 3 ~ **upon s.o.** : faire bien comprendre à qqn — **impression** [ɪm'prɛʃən] *n* : impression *f* — **impressionable** [ɪm'prɛʃənəbəl] *adj* : impressionnable — **impressive** [ɪm'prɛsɪv] *adj* : impressionnant
imprint [ɪm'prɪnt, 'ɪm,-] *vt* : imprimer — ~ ['ɪm,prɪnt] *n* MARK : empreinte *f*, marque *f*
imprison [ɪm'prɪzən] *vt* : emprisonner — **imprisonment** [ɪm'prɪzənmənt] *n* : emprisonnement *m*
improbable [ɪm'prabəbəl] *adj* : improbable — **improbability** [ɪm,prabə'bɪləṭi] *n, pl* **-ties** : improbabilité *f*
impromptu [ɪm'pramp,tu:, -,tju:] *adj* : impromptu
improper [ɪm'prapər] *adj* 1 UNSEEMLY : peu convenable 2 INCORRECT : incorrect 3 INDECENT : indécent — **impropriety** [,ɪmprə'praɪəṭi] *n, pl* **-ties** : inconvenance *f*
improve [ɪm'pru:v] *v* **-proved; -proving** *vt* : améliorer — *vi* : s'améliorer, faire des progrès — **improvement** [ɪm'pru:vmənt] *n* : amélioration *f*
improvise ['ɪmprə,vaɪz] *v* **-vised; -vising** : improviser — **improvisation** [ɪm,pravə'zeɪʃən, ,ɪmprəvə-] *n* : improvisation *f*
impudent ['ɪmpjədənt] *adj* : impudent — **impudence** ['ɪmpjədənts] *n* : impudence *f*
impulse ['ɪm,pʌls] *n* : impulsion *f* — **impulsive** [ɪm'pʌlsɪv] *adj* : impulsif — **impulsiveness** [ɪm'pʌlsɪvnəs] *n* : impulsivité *f*
impunity [ɪm'pju:nəṭi] *n* : impunité *f*
impure [ɪm'pjʊr] *adj* : impur — **impurity** [ɪm'pjʊrəṭi] *n, pl* **-ties** : impureté *f*
impute [ɪm'pju:t] *vt* **-puted; -puting** : imputer
in ['ɪn] *prep* 1 : dans, en, à 2 ~ **1938** : en 1938 3 ~ **an hour** : dans une heure 4 ~ **Canada** : au Canada 5 ~ **leather** : en cuir 6 ~ **my house** : chez moi 7 ~ **the hospital** : à l'hôpital 8 ~ **the sun** : au soleil 9 ~ **this way** : de cette manière 10 **be** ~ **a hurry** : être pressé 11 **be** ~ **luck** : avoir de la chance — ~ *adv* 1 INSIDE : dedans, à l'intérieur 2 **be** ~ : être là, être chez soi 3 **come** ~ : entrer 4 **she's** ~ **for a surprise** : elle va être surprise 5 ~ **power** : au pouvoir — ~ *adj* : à la mode
inability [,ɪnə'bɪləṭi] *n, pl* **-ties** : incapacité *f*
inaccessible [,ɪnɪk'sɛsəbəl] *adj* : inaccessible
inaccurate [ɪn'ækjərət] *adj* : inexact
inactive [ɪn'æktɪv] *adj* : inactif — **inactivity** [,ɪn,æk'tɪvəṭi] *n, pl* **-ties** : inactivité *f*
inadequate [ɪ'nædɪkwət] *adj* : insuffisant
inadvertently [,ɪnəd'vərtəntli] *adv* : par inadvertance
inadvisable [,ɪnæd'vaɪzəbəl] *adj* : déconseillé
inane [ɪ'neɪn] *adj* **inaner; -est** : inepte, stupide
inanimate [ɪ'nænəmət] *adj* : inanimé
inapplicable [ɪ'næplɪkəbəl, ,ɪnə'plɪkəbəl] *adj* : inapplicable
inappropriate [,ɪnə'pro:priət] *adj* : inopportun, peu approprié
inarticulate [,ɪnar'tɪkjələt] *adj* 1 : indistinct (se dit des mots, des sons, etc.) 2 **be** ~ : ne pas savoir s'exprimer
inasmuch as [,ɪnæz'mʌtʃæz] *conj* : vu que
inaudible [ɪn'ɔdəbəl] *adj* : inaudible
inauguration [ɪ,nɔgjə'reɪʃən, -gə-] *n* : inauguration *f* — **inaugural** [ɪ'nɔgjərəl, -gərəl] *adj* : inaugural — **inaugurate** [ɪ'nɔgjə,reɪt, -gə-] *vt* **-rated; -rating** : inaugurer
inborn ['ɪn,bɔrn] *adj* : inné
inbred ['ɪn,brɛd] *adj* INNATE : inné
incalculable [ɪn'kælkjələbəl] *adj* : incalculable
incapable [ɪn'keɪpəbəl] *adj* : incapable — **incapacitate** [,ɪnkə'pæsə,teɪt] *vt* **-tated; -tating** : rendre incapable — **incapacity** [,ɪnkə'pæsəṭi] *n, pl* **-ties** : incapacité *f*
incarcerate [ɪn'karsə,reɪt] *vt* **-ated; -ating** : incarcérer
incarnation [,ɪn,kar'neɪʃən] *n* : incarnation *f*
incense[1] ['ɪnsɛnts] *n* : encens *m*
incense[2] [ɪn'sɛnts] *vt* **-censed; -censing** : mettre en fureur
incentive [ɪn'sɛntɪv] *n* : motivation *f*
inception [ɪn'sɛpʃən] *n* : commencement *m*
incessant [ɪn'sɛsənt] *adj* : incessant — **incessantly** [ɪn'sɛsəntli] *adv* : sans cesse
incest ['ɪn,sɛst] *n* : inceste *m* — **incestuous** [ɪn'sɛstʃuəs] *adj* : incestueux
inch ['ɪntʃ] *n* : pouce *m* — ~ *v* : avancer petit à petit
incident ['ɪntsədənt] *n* : incident *m* — **incidental** [,ɪntsə'dɛntəl] *adj* : accessoire — **incidentally** [,ɪntsə'dɛntəli, -'dɛntli] *adv* : à propos
incinerate [ɪn'sɪnə,reɪt] *vt* **-ated; -ating** : incinérer — **incinerator** [ɪn'sɪnə,reɪṭər] *n* : incinérateur *m*
incision [ɪn'sɪʒən] *n* : incision *f*
incite [ɪn'saɪt] *vt* **-cited; -citing** : inciter
incline [ɪn'klaɪn] *v* **-clined; -clining** *vt* 1 BEND : incliner 2 **be** ~**d to** : avoir tendance à — *vi* 1 LEAN : s'incliner 2 ~ **towards** : tendre vers — ~ ['ɪn,klaɪn] *n* : inclinaison *f* — **inclination** [,ɪnklə'neɪʃən] *n* : penchant *m*, inclination *f*
include [ɪn'klu:d] *vt* **-cluded; -cluding** : inclure, comprendre — **inclusion** [ɪn'klu:ʒən] *n* : inclusion *f* — **inclusive** [ɪn'klu:sɪv] *adj* : inclus, compris
incognito [,ɪn,kag'ni:ṭo, ɪn'kagnə,to:] *adv & adj* : incognito
incoherence [,ɪnko'hɪrənts, -'hɛr-] *n* : incohérence *f* — **incoherent** [,ɪnko'hɪrənt, -'hɛr-] *adj* : incohérent
income ['ɪn,kʌm] *n* : revenu *m* — **income tax** *n* : impôt *m* sur le revenu
incomparable [ɪn'kampərəbəl] *adj* : incomparable
incompatible [,ɪnkəm'pæṭəbəl] *adj* : incompatible — **incompatibility** [,ɪnkəm,pæṭə'bɪləṭi] *n* : incompatibilité *f*
incompetent [ɪn'kampəṭənt] *adj* : incompétent — **incompetence** [ɪn'kampəṭənts] *n* : incompétence *f*
incomplete [,ɪnkəm'pli:t] *adj* : incomplet, inachevé
incomprehensible [,ɪn,kampri'hɛntsəbəl] *adj* : incompréhensible
inconceivable [,ɪnkən'si:vəbəl] *adj* : inconcevable
inconclusive [,ɪnkən'klu:sɪv] *adj* : peu concluant
incongruous [ɪn'kaŋgruəs] *adj* : incongru
inconsiderate [,ɪnkən'sɪdərət] *adj* 1 THOUGHTLESS : inconsidéré 2 **be** ~ **toward** : manquer d'égards envers
inconsistent [,ɪnkən'sɪstənt] *adj* 1 ERRATIC : changeant 2 CONTRADICTORY : contradictoire — **inconsistency** [,ɪnkən'sɪstəntsi] *n, pl* **-cies** : incohérence *f*, contradiction *f*
inconspicuous [,ɪnkən'spɪkjuəs] *adj* : qui passe inaperçu
inconvenience [,ɪnkən'vi:njənts] *n* 1 BOTHER : dérangement *m* 2 DISADVANTAGE : inconvénient *m* — ~ *vt* **-nienced; -niencing** : déranger — **inconvenient** [,ɪnkən'vi:njənt] *adj* : incommode
incorporate [ɪn'kɔrpə,reɪt] *vt* **-rated; -rating** : incorporer
incorrect [,ɪnkə'rɛkt] *adj* : incorrect
increase ['ɪn,kri:s, ɪn'kri:s] *n* : augmentation *f* — ~ [ɪn'kri:s, 'ɪn,kri:s] *v* **-creased; -creasing** : augmenter — **increasingly** [ɪn'kri:sɪŋli] *adv* : de plus en plus
incredible [ɪn'krɛdəbəl] *adj* : incroyable
incredulous [ɪn'krɛdʒələs] *adj* : incrédule
incriminate [ɪn'krɪmə,neɪt] *vt* **-nated; -nating** : incriminer
incubator ['ɪŋkju'beɪṭər, -'ɪn-] *n* : incubateur *m*, couveuse *f*
incumbent [ɪn'kʌmbənt] *n* : titulaire *mf*
incur [ɪn'kər] *vt* **-curred; -curring** : encourir (une pénalité, etc.), contracter (une dette)
incurable [ɪn'kjʊrəbəl] *adj* : incurable
indebted [ɪn'dɛṭəd] *adj* ~ **to** : redevable à
indecent [ɪn'di:sənt] *adj* : indécent — **indecency** [ɪn'di:səntsi] *n, pl* **-cies** : indécence *f*
indecisive [,ɪndɪ'saɪsɪv] *adj* : indécis
indeed [ɪn'di:d] *adv* : vraiment, en effet
indefinite [ɪn'dɛfənət] *adj* 1 : indéfini 2 VAGUE : imprécis — **indefinitely** [ɪn'dɛfənətli] *adv* : indéfiniment
indelible [ɪn'dɛləbəl] *adj* : indélébile
indent [ɪn'dɛnt] *vt* : mettre en alinéa — **indentation** [,ɪn,dɛn'teɪʃən] *n* DENT, NOTCH : creux *m*, bosse *f*
independent [,ɪndə'pɛndənt] *adj* : indépendant — **independence** [,ɪndə'pɛndənts] *n* : indépendance *f* — **independently** [,ɪndə'pɛndəntli] *adv* : de façon indépendante
indescribable [,ɪndɪ'skraɪbəbəl] *adj* : indescriptible
indestructible [,ɪndɪ'strʌktəbəl] *adj* : indestructible
index ['ɪn,dɛks] *n, pl* **-dexes** *or* **-dices** ['ɪndə,si:z] 1 : index *m* (d'un livre, etc.) 2 INDICATOR : indice *m* 3 *or* ~ **finger** : index *m* — ~ *vt* : classer
Indian ['ɪndiən] *adj* : indien
indication [,ɪndə'keɪʃən] *n* : indication *f* — **indicate** ['ɪndə,keɪt] *vt* **-cated; -cating** : indiquer — **indicative** [ɪn'dɪkəṭɪv] *adj* : indicatif — **indicator** ['ɪndə,keɪṭər] *n* : indicateur *m*
indict [ɪn'daɪt] *vt* : inculper — **indictment** [ɪn'daɪtmənt] *n* : inculpation *f*
indifferent [ɪn'dɪfrənt, -'dɪfə-] *adj* 1 UNCONCERNED : indifférent 2 MEDIOCRE : médiocre — **indifference** [ɪn'dɪfrənts, -'dɪfə-] *n* : indifférence *f*
indigenous [ɪn'dɪdʒənəs] *adj* : indigène
indigestion [,ɪndaɪ'dʒɛstʃən, -dɪ-] *n* : indigestion *f* — **indigestible** [,ɪndaɪ'dʒɛstəbəl, -dɪ-] *adj* : indigeste
indignation [,ɪndɪg'neɪʃən] *n* : indignation *f* — **indignant** [ɪn'dɪgnənt] *adj* : indigné — **indignity** [ɪn'dɪgnəṭi] *n, pl* **-ties** : indignité *f*
indigo ['ɪndɪ,go:] *n, pl* **-gos** *or* **-goes** : indigo *m*
indirect [,ɪndə'rɛkt, -daɪ-] *adj* : indirect
indiscreet [,ɪndɪ'skri:t] *adj* : indiscret — **indiscretion** [,ɪndɪ'skrɛʃən] *n* : indiscrétion *f*
indiscriminate [,ɪndɪ'skrɪmənət] *adj* 1 : sans discernement 2 RANDOM : fait au hasard
indispensable [,ɪndɪ'spɛntsəbəl] *adj* : indispensable
indisputable [,ɪndɪ'spju:ṭəbəl] *adj* : incontestable
indistinct [,ɪndɪ'stɪŋkt] *adj* : indistinct
individual [,ɪndə'vɪdʒuəl] *adj* 1 : individuel 2 SPECIFIC : particulier — ~ *n* : individu *m* — **individuality** [,ɪndə,vɪdʒu'æləṭi] *n, pl* **-ties** : individualité *f* — **individually** [,ɪndə'vɪdʒuəli, -dʒəli] *adv* : individuellement
indoctrinate [ɪn'daktrə,neɪt] *vt* **-nated; -nating** : endoctriner — **indoctrination** [ɪn,daktrə'neɪʃən] *n* : endoctrinement *m*
Indonesian [,ɪndo'ni:ʒən, -ʃən] *adj* : indonésien — ~ *n* : indonésien *m* (langue)
indoor ['ɪn'dor] *adj* 1 : d'intérieur 2 ~ **pool** : piscine *f* couverte 3 ~ **sports** : sports *mpl* pratiqués en salle — **indoors** ['ɪn'dorz] *adv* : à l'intérieur
induce [ɪn'du:s, -'dju:s] *vt* **-duced; -ducing** 1 PERSUADE : induire 2 CAUSE : provoquer — **inducement** [ɪn'du:smənt, -'dju:s-] *n* : encouragement *m*
indulge [ɪn'dʌldʒ] *v* **-dulged; -dulging** *vt* 1 GRATIFY : céder à 2 PAMPER : gâter — *vi* ~ **in** : se permettre — **indulgence** [ɪn'dʌldʒənts] *n* : indulgence *f* — **indulgent** [ɪn'dʌldʒənt] *adj* : indulgent
industrial [ɪn'dʌstriəl] *adj* : industriel — **industrialize** [ɪn'dʌstriə,laɪz] *vt* **-ized; -izing** : industrialiser — **industrious** [ɪn'dʌstriəs] *adj* : industrieux, travailleur — **industry** ['ɪndəstri] *n, pl* **-tries** : industrie *f*
inebriated [ɪ'ni:bri,eɪṭəd] *adj* : ivre
inedible [ɪ'nɛdəbəl] *adj* : immangeable
ineffective [,ɪnɪ'fɛktɪv] *adj* : inefficace — **ineffectual** [,ɪnɪ'fɛktʃuəl] *adj* : inefficace
inefficient [,ɪnɪ'fɪʃənt] *adj* 1 : inefficace 2 INCOMPETENT : incompétent — **inefficiency** [,ɪnɪ'fɪʃəntsi] *n, pl* **-cies** : inefficacité *f*
ineligible [ɪn'ɛlədʒəbəl] *adj* : inéligible
inept [ɪ'nɛpt] *adj* : inepte
inequality [,ɪnɪ'kwaləṭi] *n, pl* **-ties** : inégalité *f*
inert [ɪ'nərt] *adj* : inerte — **inertia** [ɪ'nərʃə] *n* : inertie *f*
inescapable [,ɪnɪ'skeɪpəbəl] *adj* : inéluctable
inevitable [ɪn'ɛvəṭəbəl] *adj* : inévitable — **inevitably** [-bli] *adv* : inévitablement
inexcusable [,ɪnɪk'skju:zəbəl] *adj* : inexcusable
inexpensive [,ɪnɪk'spɛntsɪv] *adj* : pas cher, bon marché
inexperienced [,ɪnɪk'spɪriəntst] *adj* : inexpérimenté
inexplicable [,ɪnɪk'splɪkəbəl] *adj* : inexplicable
infallible [ɪn'fæləbəl] *adj* : infaillible
infamous ['ɪnfəməs] *adj* : infâme, notoire
infancy ['ɪnfəntsi] *n, pl* **-cies** : petite enfance *f* — **infant** ['ɪnfənt] *n* : petit enfant *m*, petite enfant *f*; nourrisson *m* — **infantile** ['ɪnfən,taɪl, -təl, -,ti:l] *adj* : infantile
infantry ['ɪnfəntri] *n, pl* **-tries** : infanterie *f*
infatuated [ɪn'fætʃu,eɪṭəd] *adj* **be** ~ **with** : être épris de — **infatuation** [ɪn,fætʃu'eɪʃən] *n* : engouement *m*
infect [ɪn'fɛkt] *vt* : infecter — **infection** [ɪn'fɛkʃən] *n* : infection *f* — **infectious** [ɪn'fɛkʃəs] *adj* : infectieux, contagieux
infer [ɪn'fər] *vt* **-ferred; -ferring** : déduire — **inference** ['ɪnfərənts] *n* : déduction *f*
inferior [ɪn'fɪriər] *adj* : inférieur — ~ *n* : inférieur *m*, -rieure *f* — **inferiority** [ɪn,fɪri'ɔrəṭi] *n, pl* **-ties** : infériorité *f*
infernal [ɪn'fərnəl] *adj* : infernal — **inferno** [ɪn'fər,no:] *n, pl* **-nos** : brasier *m*
infertile [ɪn'fərṭəl, -,taɪl] *adj* 1 : infertile 2 STERILE : stérile — **infertility** [,ɪnfər'tɪləṭi] *n* : infertilité *f*
infest [ɪn'fɛst] *vt* : infester
infidelity [,ɪnfə'dɛləṭi, -faɪ-] *n, pl* **-ties** : infidélité *f*
infiltrate [ɪn'fɪl,treɪt, 'ɪnfɪl-] *v* **-trated; -trating** *vt* : infiltrer — *vi* : s'infiltrer
infinite ['ɪnfənət] *adj* : infini — **infinitive** [ɪn'fɪnəṭɪv] *n* : infinitif *m* — **infinity** [ɪn'fɪnəṭi] *n, pl* **-ties** : infinité *f*
infirm [ɪn'fərm] *adj* : infirme — **infirmary** [ɪn'fərməri] *n, pl* **-ries** : infirmerie *f* — **infirmity** [ɪn'fərməṭi] *n, pl* **-ties** : infirmité *f*
inflame [ɪn'fleɪm] *v* **-flamed; -flaming** *vt* : enflammer — *vi* : s'enflammer — **inflammable** [ɪn'flæməbəl] *adj* : (in)flammable — **inflammation** [,ɪnflə'meɪʃən] *n* : inflammation *f* — **inflammatory** [ɪn'flæmə,tori] *adj* : incendiaire
inflate [ɪn'fleɪt] *v* **-flated; -flating** *vt* : gonfler — *vi* : se gonfler — **inflatable** [ɪn'fleɪṭəbəl] *adj* : gonflable — **inflation** [ɪn'fleɪʃən] *n* : inflation *f* — **inflationary** [ɪn'fleɪʃə,nɛri] *adj* : inflationniste
inflexible [ɪn'flɛksɪbəl] *adj* : inflexible
inflict [ɪn'flɪkt] *vt* : infliger
influence ['ɪn,flu:ənts, ɪn'flu:ənts] *n* 1 : influence *f* 2 **under the** ~ **of** : sous l'effet de — ~ *vt* **-enced; -encing** : influencer, influer sur — **influential** [,ɪnflu'ɛntʃəl] *adj* : influent
influenza [,ɪnflu'ɛnzə] *n* : grippe *f*
influx ['ɪn,flʌks] *n* : afflux *m*
inform [ɪn'fɔrm] *vt* : informer, renseigner — *vi* ~ **on** : dénoncer

informal [ɪnˈfɔrməl] *adj* **1** : simple **2** CASUAL : familier, décontracté **3** UNOFFICIAL : officieux — **informally** [ɪnˈfɔrməli] *adv* : sans cérémonie, simplement

information [ˌɪnfərˈmeɪʃən] *n* : renseignements *mpl*, information *f* — **informative** [ɪnˈfɔrmət̬ɪv] *adj* : informatif — **informer** [ɪnˈfɔrmər] *n* : indicateur *m*, -trice *f*

infrared [ˌɪnfrəˈrɛd] *adj* : infrarouge

infrastructure [ˈɪnfrəˌstrʌkʧər] *n* : infrastructure *f*

infrequent [ɪnˈfri:kwənt] *adj* : rare, peu fréquent — **infrequently** [ɪnˈfri:kwəntli] *adv* : rarement

infringe [ɪnˈfrɪnʤ] *v* **-fringed; -fringing** *vt* : enfreindre — *vi* ~ **on** : empiéter sur — **infringement** [ɪnˈfrɪnʤmənt] *n* : infraction *f* (à la loi)

infuriate [ɪnˈfjʊriˌeɪt] *vt* **-ated; -ating** : rendre furieux — **infuriating** [ɪnˈfjʊriˌeɪt̬ɪŋ] *adj* : exaspérant

infuse [ɪnˈfju:z] *vt* **-fused; -fusing** : infuser — **infusion** [ɪnˈfju:ʒən] *n* : infusion *f*

ingenious [ɪnˈʤi:njəs] *adj* : ingénieux — **ingenuity** [ˌɪnʤəˈnu:ət̬i, -ˈnju:-] *n, pl* **-ties** : ingéniosité *f*

ingenuous [ɪnˈʤɛnjʊəs] *adj* : ingénu, naïf

ingot [ˈɪŋgət] *n* : lingot *m*

ingrained [ɪnˈgreɪnd] *adj* : enraciné

ingratiate [ɪnˈgreɪʃiˌeɪt] *vt* **-ated; -ating** ~ **oneself with** : gagner les bonnes grâces de

ingratitude [ɪnˈgræt̬əˌtu:d, -ˌtju:d] *n* : ingratitude *f*

ingredient [ɪnˈgri:diənt] *n* : ingrédient *m*

inhabit [ɪnˈhæbət] *vt* : habiter — **inhabitant** [ɪnˈhæbət̬ənt] *n* : habitant *m*, -tante *f*

inhale [ɪnˈheɪl] *v* **-haled; -haling** *vt* : inhaler, respirer — *vi* : inspirer

inherent [ɪnˈhɪrənt, -ˈhɛr-] *adj* : inhérent — **inherently** [ɪnˈhɪrəntli, -ˈhɛr-] *adv* : fondamentalement

inherit [ɪnˈhɛrət] *vt* : hériter de — **inheritance** [ɪnˈhɛrət̬ənts] *n* : héritage *m*

inhibit [ɪnˈhɪbət] *vt* IMPEDE : entraver, gêner — **inhibition** [ˌɪnhəˈbɪʃən, ˌɪnə-] *n* : inhibition *f*

inhuman [ɪnˈhju:mən, -ˈju:-] *adj* : inhumain — **inhumane** [ˌɪnhjuˈmeɪn, -ju-] *adj* : cruel — **inhumanity** [ˌɪnhjuˈmænət̬i, -ju-] *n, pl* **-ties** : inhumanité *f*

initial [ɪˈnɪʃəl] *adj* : initial, premier — ~ *n* : initiale *f* — ~ *vt* **-tialed** *or* **-tialled; -tialing** *or* **-tialling** : parapher — **initially** [ɪˈnɪʃəli] *adv* : au départ

initiate [ɪˈnɪʃiˌeɪt] *vt* **-ated; -ating** **1** BEGIN : amorcer, entreprendre **2** ~ **into** : initier à — **initiation** [ɪˌnɪʃiˈeɪʃən] *n* : initiation *f* — **initiative** [ɪˈnɪʃət̬ɪv] *n* : initiative *f*

inject [ɪnˈʤɛkt] *vt* : injecter — **injection** [ɪnˈʤɛkʃən] *n* : injection *f*

injure [ˈɪnʤər] *vt* **-jured; -juring** **1** WOUND : blesser **2** HARM : nuire à **3** ~ **oneself** : se blesser — **injury** [ˈɪnʤəri] *n, pl* **-ries** **1** WOUND : blessure *f* **2** WRONG : tort *m*

injustice [ɪnˈʤʌstəs] *n* : injustice *f*

ink [ˈɪŋk] *n* : encre *f* — **inkwell** [ˈɪŋkˌwɛl] *n* : encrier *m*

inland [ˈɪnˌlænd, -lənd] *adj* : intérieur — ~ *adv* : à l'intérieur, vers l'intérieur

in–laws [ˈɪnˌlɔz] *npl* : beaux-parents *mpl*

inlet [ˈɪnˌlɛt, -lət] *n* : bras *m* de mer

inmate [ˈɪnˌmeɪt] *n* **1** PRISONER : détenu *m*, -nue *f* **2** PATIENT : interné *m*, -née *f*

inn [ˈɪn] *n* : auberge *f*

innards [ˈɪnərdz] *npl* : entrailles *fpl*

innate [ɪˈneɪt] *adj* : inné

inner [ˈɪnər] *adj* : intérieur, interne — **innermost** [ˈɪnərˌmo:st] *adj* : le plus profond

inning [ˈɪnɪŋ] *n* : tour *m* de batte, manche *f* *Can* (au baseball)

innocence [ˈɪnəsənts] *n* : innocence *f* — **innocent** [ˈɪnəsənt] *adj* : innocent — ~ *n* : innocent *m*, -cente *f*

innocuous [ɪˈnɑkjəwəs] *adj* : inoffensif

innovate [ˈɪnəˌveɪt] *v* **-vated; -vating** : innover — **innovation** [ˌɪnəˈveɪʃən] *n* : innovation *f* — **innovative** [ˈɪnəˌveɪt̬ɪv] *adj* : innovateur — **innovator** [ˈɪnəˌveɪt̬ər] *n* : innovateur *m*, -trice *f*

innumerable [ɪˈnu:mərəbəl, -ˈnju:-] *adj* : innombrable

inoculate [ɪˈnɑkjəˌleɪt] *vt* **-lated; -lating** : inoculer — **inoculation** [ɪˌnɑkjəˈleɪʃən] *n* : inoculation *f*

inoffensive [ˌɪnəˈfɛnsɪv] *adj* : inoffensif

inpatient [ˈɪnˌpeɪʃənt] *n* : malade *m* hospitalisé, malade *f* hospitalisée

input [ˈɪnˌpʊt] *n* **1** : contribution *f* **2** : entrée *f* (de données) — ~ *vt* **-putted** *or* **-put; -putting** : entrer (des données)

inquire [ɪnˈkwaɪr] *v* **-quired; -quiring** *vt* : demander — *vi* **1** ~ **about** : se renseigner sur **2** ~ **into** : enquêter sur — **inquiry** [ɪnˈkwaɪri, ˈɪnˌkwaɪri; ˈɪnkwəri, ˈɪŋ-] *n, pl* **-ries** **1** QUESTION : demande *f* **2** INVESTIGATION : enquête *f* — **inquisition** [ˌɪnkwəˈzɪʃən, ˌɪŋ-] *n* : inquisition *f* — **inquisitive** [ɪnˈkwɪzət̬ɪv] *adj* : curieux

insane [ɪnˈseɪn] *adj* : fou — **insanity** [ɪnˈsænət̬i] *n, pl* **-ties** : folie *f*

insatiable [ɪnˈseɪʃəbəl] *adj* : insatiable

inscribe [ɪnˈskraɪb] *vt* **-scribed; -scribing** **1** : inscrire **2** DEDICATE : dédicacer — **inscription** [ɪnˈskrɪpʃən] *n* : inscription *f*

inscrutable [ɪnˈskru:t̬əbəl] *adj* : impénétrable

insect [ˈɪnˌsɛkt] *n* : insecte *m* — **insecticide** [ɪnˈsɛktəˌsaɪd] *n* : insecticide *m*

insecure [ˌɪnsɪˈkjʊr] *adj* **1** UNSAFE : peu sûr **2** FEARFUL : anxieux — **insecurity** [ˌɪnsɪˈkjʊrət̬i] *n, pl* **-ties** : insécurité *f*

insensitive [ɪnˈsɛntsət̬ɪv] *adj* : insensible — **insensitivity** [ɪnˌsɛntsəˈtɪvət̬i] *n* : insensibilité *f*

inseparable [ɪnˈsɛpərəbəl] *adj* : inséparable

insert [ɪnˈsɛrt] *vt* : insérer, introduire

inside [ɪnˈsaɪd, ˈɪnˌsaɪd] *n* **1** : intérieur *m* **2** ~**s** *npl* GUTS : entrailles *fpl* — ~ *adv* **1** : à l'intérieur **2** ~ **out** : à l'envers — ~ *adj* : intérieur — ~ *prep* : à l'intérieur de

insidious [ɪnˈsɪdiəs] *adj* : insidieux

insight [ˈɪnˌsaɪt] *n* : perspicacité *f* — **insightful** [ɪnˈsaɪtfəl] *adj* : perspicace

insignia [ɪnˈsɪgniə] *or* **insigne** [-ˌni:] *n, pl* **-nia** *or* **-nias** : insigne(s) *m(pl)*

insignificant [ˌɪnsɪgˈnɪfɪkənt] *adj* : insignifiant

insincere [ˌɪnsɪnˈsɪr] *adj* : pas sincère

insinuate [ɪnˈsɪnjʊˌeɪt] *vt* **-ated; -ating** : insinuer — **insinuation** [ɪnˌsɪnjʊˈeɪʃən] *n* : insinuation *f*

insipid [ɪnˈsɪpəd] *adj* : insipide

insist [ɪnˈsɪst] *v* : insister — **insistent** [ɪnˈsɪstənt] *adj* : insistant

insofar as [ˌɪnsoˈfɑræz] *conj* : dans la mesure où

insole [ˈɪnˌso:l] *n* : semelle *f* (intérieure)

insolence [ˈɪntsələnts] *n* : insolence *f* — **insolent** [ˈɪntsələnt] *adj* : insolent

insolvent [ɪnˈsɑlvənt] *adj* : insolvable

insomnia [ɪnˈsɑmniə] *n* : insomnie *f*

inspect [ɪnˈspɛkt] *vt* : examiner, inspecter — **inspection** [ɪnˈspɛkʃən] *n* : inspection *f* — **inspector** [ɪnˈspɛktər] *n* : inspecteur *m*, -trice *f*

inspire [ɪnˈspaɪr] *vt* **-spired; -spiring** : inspirer — **inspiration** [ˌɪntspəˈreɪʃən] *n* : inspiration *f* — **inspirational** [ˌɪntspəˈreɪʃənəl] *adj* : inspirant

instability [ˌɪntstəˈbɪlət̬i] *n* : instabilité *f*

install [ɪnˈstɔl] *vt* **-stalled; -stalling** : installer — **installation** [ˌɪntstəˈleɪʃən] *n* : installation *f* — **installment** [ɪnˈstɔlmənt] *n* **1** PAYMENT : versement *m*, acompte *m* **2** : épisode *m* (d'un feuilleton)

instance [ˈɪntstənts] *n* **1** : cas *m*, exemple *m* **2 for** ~ : par exemple

instant [ˈɪntstənt] *n* : instant *m*, moment *m* — ~ *adj* **1** IMMEDIATE : immédiat, instantané **2** ~ **coffee** : café *m* instantané — **instantaneous** [ˌɪntstənˈteɪniəs] *adj* : instantané — **instantly** [ˈɪntstəntli] *adv* : immédiatement, sur-le-champ

instead [ɪnˈstɛd] *adv* **1** : plutôt **2 I went** ~ : j'y suis allé à sa place — **instead of** *prep* : au lieu de, à la place de

instep [ˈɪnˌstɛp] *n* : cou-de-pied *m*

instigate [ˈɪntstəˌgeɪt] *vt* **-gated; -gating** : engager, provoquer — **instigation** [ˌɪntstəˈgeɪʃən] *n* : instigation *f* — **instigator** [ˈɪntstəˌgeɪt̬ər] *n* : instigateur *m*, -trice *f*

instill *or Brit* **instil** [ɪnˈstɪl] *vt* **-stilled; -stilling** : inculquer

instinct [ˈɪnˌstɪŋkt] *n* : instinct *m* — **instinctive** [ɪnˈstɪŋktɪv] *or* **instinctual** [ɪnˈstɪŋkʧʊəl] *adj* : instinctif

institute [ˈɪntstəˌtu:t, -ˌtju:t] *vt* **-tuted; -tuting** : instituer — ~ *n* : institut *m* — **institution** [ˌɪntstəˈtu:ʃən, -ˈtju:-] *n* : institution *f*

instruct [ɪnˈstrʌkt] *vt* **1** TEACH : instruire **2** DIRECT : charger — **instruction** [ɪnˈstrʌkʃən] *n* : instruction *f* — **instructor** [ɪnˈstrʌktər] *n* : moniteur *m*, -trice *f*

instrument [ˈɪntstrəmənt] *n* : instrument *m* — **instrumental** [ˌɪntstrəˈmɛntəl] *adj* **1** : instrumental **2 be** ~ **in** : contribuer à

insufferable [ɪnˈsʌfərəbəl] *adj* : insupportable

insufficient [ˌɪnsəˈfɪʃənt] *adj* : insuffisant

insular [ˈɪntsʊlər, -sjʊ-] *adj* **1** : insulaire **2** NARROW-MINDED : borné

insulate [ˈɪntsəˌleɪt] *vt* **-lated; -lating** : isoler — **insulation** [ˌɪntsəˈleɪʃən] *n* : isolation *f*

insulin [ˈɪntsələn] *n* : insuline *f*

insult [ɪnˈsʌlt] *vt* : insulter — ~ [ˈɪnˌsʌlt] *n* : insulte *f*, injure *f*

insure [ɪnˈʃʊr] *vt* **-sured; -suring** : assurer — **insurance** [ɪnˈʃʊrənts] *n* : assurance *f*

insurmountable [ˌɪnsərˈmaʊntəbəl] *adj* : insurmontable

intact [ɪnˈtækt] *adj* : intact

intake [ˈɪnˌteɪk] *n* **1** : consommation *f* (de nourriture) **2** ADMISSION : admission *f*

intangible [ɪnˈtænʤəbəl] *adj* : intangible

integral [ˈɪntɪgrəl] *adj* **1** : intégral **2 be an** ~ **part of** : faire partie intégrante de

integrate [ˈɪntəˌgreɪt] *v* **-grated; -grating** *vt* : intégrer — *vi* : s'intégrer

integrity [ɪnˈtɛgrət̬i] *n* : intégrité *f*

intellect [ˈɪntəlˌɛkt] *n* : intelligence *f* — **intellectual** [ˌɪntəˈlɛkʧʊəl] *adj* : intellectuel — ~ *n* : intellectuel *m*, -tuelle *f* — **intelligence** [ɪnˈtɛləʤənts] *n* : intelligence *f* — **intelligent** [ɪnˈtɛləʤənt] *adj* : intelligent — **intelligible** [ɪnˈtɛləʤəbəl] *adj* : intelligible

intend [ɪnˈtɛnd] *vt* **1 be** ~**ed for** : être destiné à **2** ~ **to** : avoir l'intention de — **intended** [ɪnˈtɛndəd] *adj* **1** PLANNED : voulu **2** INTENTIONAL : intentionnel

intense [ɪnˈtɛnts] *adj* : intense — **intensely** [ɪnˈtɛntsli] *adv* **1** : intensément **2** EXTREMELY : extrêmement — **intensify** [ɪnˈtɛntsəˌfaɪ] *v* **-fied; -fying** *vt* : intensifier — *vi* : s'intensifier — **intensity** [ɪnˈtɛntsət̬i] *n, pl* **-ties** : intensité *f* — **intensive** [ɪnˈtɛntsɪv] *adj* : intensif

intent [ɪnˈtɛnt] *n* : intention *f* — ~ *adj* **1** : absorbé, attentif **2** ~ **on doing** : résolu à faire — **intention** [ɪnˈtɛnʧən] *n* : intention *f* — **intentional** [ɪnˈtɛnʧənəl] *adj* : intentionnel — **intently** [ɪnˈtɛntli] *adv* : attentivement

interact [ˌɪntərˈækt] *vi* **1** : agir l'un sur l'autre **2** ~ **with** : communiquer avec — **interaction** [ˌɪntərˈækʃən] *n* : interaction *f*

intercede [ˌɪntərˈsi:d] *vi* **-ceded; -ceding** : intercéder

intercept [ˌɪntərˈsɛpt] *vt* : intercepter

interchange [ˌɪntərˈʧeɪnʤ] *vt* **-changed; -changing** EXCHANGE : échanger — ~ *n* [ˈɪntərˌʧeɪnʤ] **1** EXCHANGE : échange *m* **2** JUNCTION : échangeur *m* — **interchangeable** [ˌɪntərˈʧeɪnʤəbəl] *adj* : interchangeable

intercourse [ˈɪntərˌkors] *n* : rapports *mpl* (sexuels)

interest [ˈɪntrəst, -təˌrɛst] *n* : intérêt *m* — ~ *vt* : intéresser — **interesting** [ˈɪntrəstɪŋ, -təˌrɛstɪŋ] *adj* : intéressant

interface [ˈɪntərˌfeɪs] *n* : interface *f*

interfere [ˌɪntərˈfɪr] *vi* **-fered; -fering** **1** INTERVENE : intervenir **2** ~ **in** : s'immiscer dans — **interference** [ˌɪntərˈfɪrənts] *n* **1** : ingérence *f* **2** : interférence *f*, parasites *mpl* (à la radio, etc.)

interim [ˈɪntərəm] *n* **1** : intérim *m* **2 in the** ~ : entre-temps — ~ *adj* : provisoire

interior [ɪnˈtɪriər] *adj* : intérieur — ~ *n* : intérieur *m*

interjection [ˌɪntərˈʤɛkʃən] *n* : interjection *f*

interlock [ˌɪntərˈlɑk] *vi* : s'enclencher

intermediate [ˌɪntərˈmi:diət] *adj* : intermédiaire — **intermediary** [ˌɪntərˈmi:diˌɛri] *n, pl* **-aries** : intermédiaire *mf*

interminable [ɪnˈtərmənəbəl] *adj* : interminable

intermission [ˌɪntərˈmɪʃən] *n* **1** : pause *f* **2** : entracte *m* (au théâtre)

intermittent [ˌɪntərˈmɪtənt] *adj* : intermittent

intern[1] [ˈɪnˌtərn, ɪnˈtərn] *vt* CONFINE : interner

intern[2] [ˈɪnˌtərn] *n* : stagiaire *mf*

internal [ɪnˈtərnəl] *adj* : interne — **internally** [ɪnˈtərnəli] *adv* : intérieurement

international [ˌɪntərˈnæʃənəl] *adj* : international

Internet [ˈɪntərˌnɛt] *n* : Internet *m*

interpret [ɪnˈtərprət] *vt* : interpréter — **interpretation** [ɪnˌtərprəˈteɪʃən] *n* : interprétation *f* — **interpreter** [ɪnˈtərprət̬ər] *n* : interprète *mf*

interrogate [ɪnˈtɛrəˌgeɪt] *vt* **-gated; -gating** : interroger — **interrogation** [ɪnˌtɛrəˈgeɪʃən] *n* QUESTIONING : interrogatoire *m* — **interrogative** [ˌɪntəˈrɑgət̬ɪv] *adj* : interrogatif

interrupt [ˌɪntəˈrʌpt] *v* : interrompre — **interruption** [ˌɪntəˈrʌpʃən] *n* : interruption *f*

intersect [ˌɪntərˈsɛkt] *vt* : croiser, couper — *vi* : se croiser, se couper — **intersection** [ˌɪntərˈsɛkʃən] *n* JUNCTION : croisement *m*, carrefour *m*

intersperse [ˌɪntərˈspərs] *vt* **-spersed; -spersing** ~ **with** : parsemer de

interstate [ˈɪntərˌsteɪt] *n or* ~ **highway** : autoroute *f*

intertwine [ˌɪntərˈtwaɪn] *vi* **-twined; -twining** : s'entrelacer

interval [ˈɪntərvəl] *n* : intervalle *m*

intervene [ˌɪntərˈvi:n] *vi* **-vened; -vening** **1** : intervenir **2** HAPPEN : survenir — **intervention** [ˌɪntərˈvɛnʧən] *n* : intervention *f*

interview [ˈɪntərˌvju:] *n* **1** : entretien *m*, entrevue *f* **2** : interview *f* (à la télévision, etc.) — ~ *vt* **1** : faire passer une entrevue (pour un emploi) **2** : interviewer (à la télévision, etc.)

intestine [ɪnˈtɛstən] *n* : intestin *m* — **intestinal** [ɪnˈtɛstənəl] *adj* : intestinal

intimate[1] [ˈɪntəˌmeɪt] *vt* **-mated; -mating** : laisser entendre

intimate[2] [ˈɪntəmət] *adj* : intime — **intimacy** [ˈɪntəməsi] *n, pl* **-cies** : intimité *f*

intimidate [ɪnˈtɪməˌdeɪt] *vt* **-dated; -dating** : intimider — **intimidation** [ɪnˌtɪməˈdeɪʃən] *n* : intimidation *f*

into [ˈɪnˌtu:] *prep* **1** : en, dans **2 bump** ~ : se cogner contre **3** (*used in mathematics*) **4** ~ **12 is 3** : 12 divisé par 4 fait 3

intolerable [ɪnˈtɑlərəbəl] *adj* : intolérable — **intolerance** [ɪnˈtɑlərənts] *n* : intolérance *f* — **intolerant** [ɪnˈtɑlərənt] *adj* : intolérant

intoxicate [ɪnˈtɑksəˌkeɪt] *vt* **-cated; -cating** : enivrer — **intoxicated** [ɪnˈtɑksəˌkeɪt̬əd] *adj* : ivre

intransitive [ɪnˈtræntsət̬ɪv, -ˈtrænzə-] *adj* : intransitif

intravenous [ˌɪntrəˈvi:nəs] *adj* : intraveineux

intrepid [ɪnˈtrɛpəd] *adj* : intrépide

intricate [ˈɪntrɪkət] *adj* : compliqué — **intricacy** [ˈɪntrɪkəsi] *n, pl* **-cies** : complexité *f*

intrigue [ˈɪnˌtri:g, ɪnˈtri:g] *n* : intrigue *f* — ~ [ɪnˈtri:g] *v* **-trigued; -triguing** : intriguer — **intriguing** [ɪnˈtri:gɪŋ] *adj* : fascinant

intrinsic [ɪnˈtrɪnzɪk, -ˈtrɪntsɪk] *adj* : intrinsèque

introduce [ˌɪntrəˈdu:s, -ˈdju:s] *vt* **-duced; -ducing** **1** : introduire **2** PRESENT : présenter — **introduction** [ˌɪntrəˈdʌkʃən] *n* **1** : introduction *f* **2** PRESENTATION : présentation *f* — **introductory** [ˌɪntrəˈdʌktəri] *adj* : d'introduction, préliminaire

introvert [ˈɪntrəˌvərt] *n* : introverti *m*, -tie *f* — **introverted** [ˈɪntrəˌvərt̬əd] *adj* : introverti

intrude [ɪnˈtru:d] *vi* **-truded; -truding** : déranger, s'imposer — **intruder** [ɪnˈtru:dər] *n* : intrus *m*, -truse *f* — **intrusion** [ɪnˈtru:ʒən] *n* : intrusion *f* — **intrusive** [ɪnˈtru:sɪv] *adj* : importun, gênant

intuition [ˌɪntʊˈɪʃən, -tjʊ-] *n* : intuition *f* — **intuitive** [ɪnˈtu:ət̬ɪv, -ˈtju:-] *adj* : intuitif

inundate [ˈɪnənˌdeɪt] *vt* **-dated; -dating** : inonder

invade [ɪnˈveɪd] *vt* **-vaded; -vading** : envahir

invalid[1] [ɪnˈvæləd] *adj* : non valide, non valable

invalid[2] [ˈɪnvələd] *n* : infirme *mf*, invalide *mf*

invaluable [ɪnˈvæljəbəl, -ˈvæljʊə-] *adj* : inestimable, précieux

invariable [ɪnˈværiəbəl] *adj* : invariable

invasion [ɪnˈveɪʒən] *n* : invasion *f*

invent [ɪnˈvɛnt] *vt* : inventer — **invention** [ɪnˈvɛnʧən] *n* : invention *f* — **inventive** [ɪnˈvɛntɪv] *adj* : inventif — **inventor** [ɪnˈvɛntər] *n* : inventeur *m*, -trice *f*

inventory [ˈɪnvənˌtori] *n, pl* **-ries** : inventaire *m*

invert [ɪnˈvərt] *vt* : inverser, renverser

invertebrate [ɪnˈvərt̬əbrət, -ˌbreɪt] *adj* : invertébré — ~ *n* : invertébré *m*

invest [ɪnˈvɛst] *v* : investir

investigate [ɪnˈvɛstəˌgeɪt] *vt* **-gated; -gating** : enquêter sur, faire une enquête sur — **investigation** [ɪnˌvɛstəˈgeɪʃən] *n* : investigation *f*, enquête *f*

investment [ɪnˈvɛstmənt] *n* : investissement *m* — **investor** [ɪnˈvɛstər] *n* : investisseur *m*, -seuse *f*

inveterate [ɪnˈvɛt̬ərət] *adj* : invétéré

invigorating [ɪnˈvɪgəˌreɪt̬ɪŋ] *adj* : vivifiant, revigorant

invincible [ɪnˈvɪntsəbəl] *adj* : invincible

invisible [ɪnˈvɪzəbəl] *adj* : invisible

invitation [ˌɪnvəˈteɪʃən] *n* : invitation *f* — **invite** [ɪnˈvaɪt] *vt* **-vited; -viting** : inviter — **inviting** [ɪnˈvaɪt̬ɪŋ] *adj* : attrayant, engageant

invoice [ˈɪnˌvɔɪs] *n* : facture *f*

invoke [ɪnˈvo:k] *vt* **-voked; -voking** : invoquer

involuntary [ɪnˈvɑlənˌtɛri] *adj* : involontaire

involve [ɪnˈvɑlv] *vt* **-volved; -volving** **1** ENTAIL : entraîner **2** CONCERN : concerner, toucher — **involved** [ɪnˈvɑlvd] *adj* INTRICATE : complexe — **involvement** [ɪnˈvɑlvmənt] *n* : participation *f*

invulnerable [ɪnˈvʌlnərəbəl] *adj* : invulnérable

inward [ˈɪnwərd] *adj* : intérieur — ~ *or* **inwards** [ˈɪnwərdz] *adv* : vers l'intérieur

iodine [ˈaɪəˌdaɪn] *n* : iode *m*, teinture *f* d'iode

ion [ˈaɪən, ˈaɪˌɑn] *n* : ion *m*

iota [aɪˈo:t̬ə] *n* : brin *m*

IOU [ˌaɪˌoˈju:] *n* : reconnaissance *f* de dette

Iranian [ɪˈreɪniən, -ˈræ-, -ˈrɑ-; aɪˈ-] *adj* : iranien

Iraqi [ɪˈrɑki, -ˈræ-] *adj* : irakien

irate [aɪˈreɪt] *adj* : furieux

iris [ˈaɪrəs] *n, pl* **irises** *or* **irides** [ˈaɪrəˌdi:z, ˈɪr-] : iris *m*

Irish [ˈaɪrɪʃ] *adj* : irlandais

irksome [ˈərksəm] *adj* : irritant, agaçant

iron [ˈaɪərn] *n* **1** : fer *m* (métal) **2** : fer *m* à repasser — ~ *vt* PRESS : repasser — **ironing** [ˈaɪərnɪŋ] *n* : repassage *m*

irony [ˈaɪrəni] *n, pl* **-nies** : ironie *f* — **ironic** [aɪˈrɑnɪk] *or* **ironical** [-nɪkəl] *adj* : ironique

irrational [ɪˈræʃənəl] *adj* : irrationnel

irreconcilable [ɪˌrɛkənˈsaɪləbəl] *adj* : irréconciliable, inconciliable

irrefutable [ˌɪrɪˈfju:t̬əbəl, ɪrˈrɛfjə-] *adj* : irréfutable

irregular [ɪˈrɛgjələr] *adj* : irrégulier — **irregularity** [ɪˌrɛgjəˈlærət̬i] *n, pl* **-ties** : irrégularité *f*

irrelevant [ɪˈrɛləvənt] *adj* : sans rapport, non pertinent

irreparable [ɪˈrɛpərəbəl] *adj* : irréparable

irreplaceable [ˌɪrɪˈpleɪsəbəl] *adj* : irremplaçable

irreproachable [ˌɪrɪˈpro:ʧəbəl] *adj* : irréprochable

irresistible [ˌɪrɪˈzɪstəbəl] *adj* : irrésistible

irresolute [ɪˈrɛzəˌlu:t] *adj* : irrésolu, indécis

irrespective of [ˌɪrɪˈspɛktɪvəv] *prep* : sans tenir compte de

irresponsible [ˌɪrɪˈspɑntsəbəl] *adj* : irresponsable — **irresponsibility** [ˌɪrɪˌspɑntsəˈbɪləṭi] *n* : irresponsabilité *f*

irreverent [ɪˈrɛvərənt] *adj* : irrévérencieux

irrigate [ˈɪrəˌgeɪt] *vt* **-gated; -gating** : irriguer — **irrigation** [ˌɪrəˈgeɪʃən] *n* : irrigation *f*

irritate [ˈɪrəˌteɪt] *vt* **-tated; -tating** : irriter — **irritable** [ˈɪrəṭəbəl] *adj* : irritable — **irritating** [ˈɪrəˌteɪṭɪŋ] *adj* : irritant, agaçant — **irritation** [ˌɪrəˈteɪʃən] *n* : irritation *f*

is → **be**

Islam [ɪsˈlɑm, ɪz-, -ˈlæm; ˈɪsˌlɑm, ˈɪz-] *n* : islam *m* — **Islamic** [-mɪk] *adj* : islamique

island [ˈaɪlənd] *n* : île *f* — **isle** [ˈaɪl] *n* : île *f*, îlot *m*

isolate [ˈaɪsəˌleɪt] *vt* **-lated; -lating** : isoler — **isolation** [ˌaɪsəˈleɪʃən] *n* : isolement *m*

Israeli [ɪzˈreɪli] *adj* : israélien

issue [ˈɪˌʃu:] *n* **1** MATTER : question *f*, problème *m* **2** : publication *f* (d'un livre), émission *f* (de timbres, etc.) **3** : numéro *m* (d'une revue, etc.) **4 make an ~ of** : faire des histoires de — **~** *v* **-sued; -suing** *vt* **1** : émettre (un chèque, etc.), distribuer (des provisions, etc.), donner (un ordre) **2** PUBLISH : publier, sortir — *vi* **~ from** : provenir de

isthmus [ˈɪsməs] *n* : isthme *m*

it [ˈɪt] *pron* **1** (*as subject*) : il, elle **2** (*as direct object*) : le, la, l' **3** (*as indirect object*) : lui **4** (*as a nonspecific subject*) : ce, cela, ça **5 it's snowing** : il neige **6 that's ~** : c'est ça **7 who is ~?** : qui c'est?

Italian [ɪˈtæliən, aɪ-] *adj* : italien — **~** *n* : italien *m* (langue)

italics [ɪˈtælɪks] *npl* : italique *m*

itch [ˈɪʧ] *n* : démangeaison *f* — **~** *vi* : avoir des démangeaisons — **itchy** [ˈɪʧi] *adj* **itchier; -est** : qui démange

it'd [ˈɪṭəd] (*contraction of* **it had** *or* **it would**) → **have, would**

item [ˈaɪṭəm] *n* **1** : article *m*, chose *f* **2** : point *m* (d'un ordre du jour) **3 news ~** : nouvelle *f* — **itemize** [ˈaɪṭəˌmaɪz] *vt* **-ized; -izing** : détailler

itinerant [aɪˈtɪnərənt] *adj* : itinérant, ambulant

itinerary [aɪˈtɪnəˌrɛri] *n, pl* **-aries** : itinéraire *m*

it'll [ˈɪṭ'l] (*contraction of* **it shall** *or* **it will**) → **shall, will**

its [ˈɪts] *adj* : son, sa, ses

it's [ˈɪts] *contraction of* **it is** *or* **it has** → **be, have**

itself [ɪtˈsɛlf] *pron* **1** (*used reflexively*) : se **2** (*for emphasis*) : lui-même, elle-même, soi-même

I've [ˈaɪv] (*contraction of* **I have**) → **have**

Ivorian [ˈaɪvəriən] *adj* : ivoirien

ivory [ˈaɪvəri] *n, pl* **-ries** : ivoire *m*

ivy [ˈaɪvi] *n, pl* **ivies** : lierre *m*

J

j [ˈʤeɪ] *n, pl* **j's** *or* **js** [ˈʤeɪz] : j *m*, dixième lettre de l'alphabet

jab [ˈʤæb] *vt* **jabbed; jabbing 1** PIERCE : piquer **2** POKE : enfoncer — **~** *n* POKE : (petit) coup *m*

jabber [ˈʤæbər] *vi* : jacasser, bavarder

jack [ˈʤæk] *n* **1** : cric *m* (mécanisme) **2** : valet *m* (aux cartes) — **~** *vt or* **~ up** : soulever avec un cric

jackass [ˈʤækˌæs] *n* : âne *m*

jacket [ˈʤækət] *n* **1** : veste *f* **2** : jaquette *f* (d'un livre)

jackhammer [ˈʤækˌhæmər] *n* : marteau-piqueur *m*

jackknife [ˈʤækˌnaɪf] *n, pl* **-knives** : couteau *m* de poche

jackpot [ˈʤækˌpɑt] *n* : gros lot *m*

jaded [ˈʤeɪdəd] *adj* : blasé

jagged [ˈʤægəd] *adj* : dentelé

jail [ˈʤeɪl] *n* : prison *f* — **~** *vt* : emprisonner, mettre en prison — **jailer** *or* **jailor** [ˈʤeɪlər] *n* : geôlier *m*, -lière *f*

jam[1] [ˈʤæm] *v* **jammed; jamming** *vt* **1** CRAM : entasser **2** OBSTRUCT : bloquer — *vi* : se bloquer, se coincer — **~** *n* **1** *or* **traffic ~** : embouteillage *m* **2** FIX : pétrin *m fam*

jam[2] *n* PRESERVES : confiture *f*

janitor [ˈʤænəṭər] *n* : concierge *mf*

January [ˈʤænjuˌɛri] *n* : janvier *m*

Japanese [ˌʤæpəˈni:z, -ˈni:s] *adj* : japonais — **~** *n* : japonais *m* (langue)

jar[1] [ˈʤɑr] *v* **jarred; jarring** *vi* **1** : rendre un son discordant **2 ~ on** : agacer (qqn) — *vt* JOLT : secouer — **~** *n* : secousse *f*

jar[2] *n* : bocal *m*, pot *m*

jargon [ˈʤɑrgən] *n* : jargon *m*

jaundice [ˈʤɔndɪs] *n* : jaunisse *f*

jaunt [ˈʤɔnt] *n* : balade *f*

jaunty [ˈʤɔnti] *adj* **-tier; -est** : allègre, insouciant

jaw [ˈʤɔ] *n* : mâchoire *f* — **jawbone** [ˈʤɔˌbo:n] *n* : maxillaire *m*

jay [ˈʤeɪ] *n* : geai *m*

jazz [ˈʤæz] *n* : jazz *m* — **~** *vt or* **~ up** : animer — **jazzy** [ˈʤæzi] *adj* **jazzier; jazziest** FLASHY : voyant, tapageur

jealous [ˈʤɛləs] *adj* : jaloux — **jealousy** [ˈʤɛləsi] *n, pl* **-sies** : jalousie *f*

jeans [ˈʤi:nz] *npl* : jean *m*, blue-jean *m*

jeer [ˈʤɪr] *vt* BOO : huer — *vi* **~ at** : se moquer de — **~** *n* : raillerie *f*

jelly [ˈʤɛli] *n, pl* **-lies** : gelée *f* — **jellyfish** [ˈʤɛliˌfɪʃ] *n* : méduse *f*

jeopardy [ˈʤɛpərdi] *n* : danger *m*, péril *m* — **jeopardize** [ˈʤɛpərˌdaɪz] *vt* **-dized; -dizing** : mettre en danger, compromettre

jerk [ˈʤərk] *n* **1** JOLT : saccade *f*, secousse *f* **2** FOOL : idiot *m*, -diote *f* — **~** *vt* **1** YANK : tirer brusquement **2** JOLT : secouer

jersey [ˈʤərzi] *n, pl* **-seys** : jersey *m* (tissu)

jest [ˈʤɛst] *n* : plaisanterie *f* — **~** *vi* : plaisanter — **jester** [ˈʤɛstər] *n* : bouffon *m*

Jesus [ˈʤi:zəs, -zəz] *n* : Jésus *m*

jet [ˈʤɛt] *n* **1** STREAM : jet *m* **2** *or* **airplane** : jet *m*, avion *m* à réaction — **jet–propelled** *adj* : à réaction

jettison [ˈʤɛṭəsən] *vt* **1** : jeter par-dessus bord **2** DISCARD : se débarrasser de

jetty [ˈʤɛṭi] *n, pl* **-ties** : jetée *f*

jewel [ˈʤu:əl] *n* : bijou *m* — **jeweler** *or* **jeweller** [ˈʤu:ələr] *n* : bijoutier *m*, -tière *f*; joaillier *m*, -lière *f* — **jewelry** *or Brit* **jewellery** [ˈʤu:əlri] *n* : bijoux *mpl*

Jewish [ˈʤu:ɪʃ] *adj* : juif

jibe [ˈʤaɪb] *vi* **jibed; jibing** AGREE : concorder

jiffy [ˈʤɪfi] *n, pl* **-fies** : instant *m*

jig [ˈʤɪg] *n* : gigue *f* (danse)

jiggle [ˈʤɪgəl] *vt* **-gled; -gling** : secouer, agiter — **~** *n* : secousse *f*

jigsaw [ˈʤɪgˌsɔ] *n or* **~ puzzle** : puzzle *m*

jilt [ˈʤɪlt] *vt* : laisser tomber

jingle [ˈʤɪŋgəl] *v* **-gled; -gling** *vi* : tinter — **~** *vt* : faire tinter — **~** *n* : tintement *m*

jinx [ˈʤɪŋks] *n* : mauvais sort *m*

jitters [ˈʤɪṭərz] *npl* **have the ~** : être nerveux — **jittery** [ˈʤɪṭəri] *adj* : nerveux

job [ˈʤɑb] *n* **1** EMPLOYMENT : emploi *m* **2** TASK : travail *m*, tâche *f*

jockey [ˈʤɑki] *n, pl* **-eys** : jockey *m*

jog [ˈʤɑg] *vi* **jogged; jogging** : faire du jogging — **jogging** [ˈʤɑgɪŋ] *n* : jogging *m*

join [ˈʤɔɪn] *vt* **1** UNITE : joindre, unir **2** MEET : rejoindre **3** : devenir membre de (un club, etc.) — *vi or* **~ together** : s'unir, se joindre

joint [ˈʤɔɪnt] *n* **1** : articulation *f* (en anatomie) **2** : joint *m* (en menuiserie) — **~** *adj* : commun

joke [ˈʤo:k] *n* : plaisanterie *f*, blague *f* — **~** *vi* **joked; joking** : plaisanter — **joker** [ˈʤo:kər] *n* **1** : blagueur *m*, -gueuse *f* **2** : joker *m* (aux cartes)

jolly [ˈʤɑli] *adj* **-lier; -est** : jovial, gai

jolt [ˈʤo:lt] *vt* : secouer — **~** *n* **1** : secousse *f*, coup *m* **2** SHOCK : choc *m*

jostle [ˈʤɑsəl] *v* **-tled; -tling** *vt* : bousculer — *vi* : se bousculer

jot [ˈʤɑt] *vt* **jotted; jotting** *or* **~ down** : prendre note de

journal [ˈʤərnəl] *n* **1** DIARY : journal *m* (intime) **2** PERIODICAL : revue *f* — **journalism** [ˈʤərnəlˌɪzəm] *n* : journalisme *m* — **journalist** [ˈʤərnəlɪst] *n* : journaliste *mf*

journey [ˈʤərni] *n, pl* **-neys** : voyage *m*

jovial [ˈʤo:viəl] *adj* : jovial

joy [ˈʤɔɪ] *n* : joie *f* — **joyful** [ˈʤɔɪfəl] *adj* : joyeux — **joyous** [ˈʤɔɪəs] *adj* : joyeux

jubilant [ˈʤu:bələnt] *adj* : débordant de joie — **jubilee** [ˈʤu:bəˌli:] *n* : jubilé *m*

Judaism [ˈʤu:dəˌɪzəm, ˈʤu:di-, ˈʤu:ˌdeɪ-] *n* : judaïsme *m*

judge [ˈʤʌʤ] *vt* **judged; judging** : juger — **~** *n* : juge *m* — **judgment** *or* **judgement** [ˈʤʌʤmənt] *n* : jugement *m*

judicial [ʤʊˈdɪʃəl] *adj* : judiciaire — **judicious** [ʤʊˈdɪʃəs] *adj* : judicieux

jug [ˈʤʌg] *n* : cruche *f*, pichet *m*

juggle [ˈʤʌgəl] *vi* **-gled; -gling** : jongler — **juggler** [ˈʤʌgələr] *n* : jongleur *m*, -gleuse *f*

juice [ˈʤu:s] *n* : jus *m* — **juicy** [ˈʤu:si] *adj* **juicier; juiciest** : juteux

July [ʤʊˈlaɪ] *n* : juillet *m*

jumble [ˈʤʌmbəl] *vt* **-bled; -bling** : mélanger — **~** *n* : fouillis *m*, désordre *m*

jumbo [ˈʤʌmˌbo:] *adj* : géant

jump [ˈʤʌmp] *vi* **1** LEAP : sauter **2** START : sursauter **3** RISE : faire un bond **4 ~ at** : saisir (une occasion, etc.) — *vt or* **~ over** : sauter — **~** *n* **1** LEAP : saut *m* **2** INCREASE : hausse *f* — **jumper** [ˈʤʌmpər] *n* **1** : sauteur *m*, -teuse *f* (aux sports) **2** : robe-chasuble *f* (vêtement) — **jumpy** [ˈʤʌmpi] *adj* **jumpier; jumpiest** : nerveux

junction [ˈʤʌŋkʃən] *n* **1** : jonction *f* **2** : carrefour *m*, embranchement *m* (de deux routes) — **juncture** [ˈʤʌŋkʧər] *n* : conjoncture *f*

June [ˈʤu:n] *n* : juin *m*

jungle [ˈʤʌŋgəl] *n* : jungle *f*

junior [ˈʤu:njər] *adj* **1** YOUNGER : cadet, plus jeune **2** SUBORDINATE : subalterne — **~** *n* **1** : cadet *m*, -dette *f* **2** : étudiant *m*, -diante *f* de troisième année

junk [ˈʤʌŋk] *n* : camelote *f fam*

Jupiter [ˈʤu:pəṭər] *n* : Jupiter *f*

jurisdiction [ˌʤʊrəsˈdɪkʃən] *n* : juridiction *f*

jury [ˈʤʊri] *n, pl* **-ries** : jury *m* — **juror** [ˈʤʊrər] *n* : juré *m*, -rée *f*

just [ˈʤʌst] *adj* : juste — **~** *adv* **1** BARELY : à peine **2** EXACTLY : exactement **3** ONLY : seulement **4 he has ~ arrived** : il vient d'arriver **5 it's ~ perfect** : c'est parfait

justice [ˈʤʌstɪs] *n* **1** : justice *f* **2** JUDGE : juge *m*

justify [ˈʤʌstəˌfaɪ] *vt* **-fied; -fying** : justifier — **justification** [ˌʤʌstəfəˈkeɪʃən] *n* : justification *f*

jut [ˈʤʌt] *vi* **jutted; jutting** *or* **~ out** : dépasser, faire saillie

juvenile [ˈʤu:vəˌnaɪl, -vənəl] *adj* **1** YOUNG : jeune **2** CHILDISH : puéril — **~** *n* : jeune *mf*

juxtapose [ˈʤʌkstəˌpo:z] *vt* **-posed; -posing** : juxtaposer

K

k [ˈkeɪ] *n, pl* **k's** *or* **ks** [ˈkeɪz] : k *m*, onzième lettre de l'alphabet

kangaroo [ˌkæŋgəˈru:] *n, pl* **-roos** : kangourou *m*

karat [ˈkærət] *n* : carat *m*

karate [kəˈrɑṭi] *n* : karaté *m*

keel [ˈki:l] *n* : quille *f* — **~** *vi or* **~ over** : chavirer (se dit d'un bateau), s'écrouler (se dit d'une personne)

keen [ˈki:n] *adj* **1** PENETRATING : vif, pénétrant **2** ENTHUSIASTIC : enthousiaste

keep [ˈki:p] *v* **kept** [ˈkɛpt]; **keeping** *vt* **1** : garder **2** : tenir (une promesse, etc.) **3** DETAIN : retenir **4** PREVENT : empêcher **5 ~ up** : maintenir — *vi* **1** STAY : se tenir, rester **2** LAST : se conserver, se garder **3** *or* **~ on** CONTINUE : continuer — **~** *n* **for ~s** : pour de bon — **keeper** [ˈki:pər] *n* : gardien *m*, -dienne *f* — **keeping** [ˈki:pɪŋ] *n* **1** CARE : garde *f* **2 in ~ with** : en accord avec — **keepsake** [ˈki:pˌseɪk] *n* : souvenir *m*

keg [ˈkɛg] *n* : baril *m*, tonnelet *m*

kennel [ˈkɛnəl] *n* : niche *f*

kept → **keep**

kerchief [ˈkərʧəf, -ˌʧi:f] *n* : fichu *m*

kernel [ˈkərnəl] *n* **1** : amande *f* **2** CORE : noyau *m*, cœur *m*

kerosene *or* **kerosine** [ˈkɛrəˌsi:n, ˌkɛrəˈ-] *n* : kérosène *m*, pétrole *m* lampant

ketchup [ˈkɛʧəp, ˈkæ-] *n* : ketchup *m*

kettle [ˈkɛṭəl] *n* : bouilloire *f*

key [ˈki:] *n* **1** : clé *f* **2** : touche *f* (d'un clavier) — **~** *adj* : clé — **keyboard** [ˈki:ˌbord] *n* : clavier *m* — **keyhole** [ˈki:ˌho:l] *n* : trou *m* de serrure

khaki [ˈkæki, ˈkɑ-] *adj* : kaki

kick [ˈkɪk] *vt* : donner un coup de pied à — *vi* : donner un coup de pied — **~** *n* **1** : coup *m* de pied **2** PLEASURE, THRILL : plaisir *m*

kid [ˈkɪd] *n* **1** GOAT : chevreau *m* **2** CHILD : gosse *mf France fam*; flot *m Can* — **~** *v* **kidded; kidding** *vi or* **~ around** : blaguer, plaisanter — *vt* TEASE : taquiner — **kidnap** [ˈkɪdˌnæp] *vt* **-napped** *or* **-naped** [-ˌnæpt]; **-napping** *or* **-naping** [-ˌnæpɪŋ] : kidnapper, enlever

kidney [ˈkɪdˌni] *n, pl* **-neys** : rein *m*

kill [ˈkɪl] *v* : tuer — **~** *n* **1** KILLING : mise *f* à mort **2** PREY : proie *f* — **killer** [ˈkɪlər] *n* : meurtrier *m*, -trière *f*; tueur *m*, tueuse *f* — **killing** [ˈkɪlɪŋ] *n* : meurtre *m*

kiln [ˈkɪl, ˈkɪln] *n* : four *m*

kilo [ˈki:ˌlo:] *n, pl* **-los** : kilo *m* — **kilogram** [ˈkɪləˌgræm, ˈki:-] *n* : kilogramme *m* — **kilometer** [kɪˈlɑməṭər, ˈkɪləˌmi:-] *n* : kilomètre *m* — **kilowatt** [ˈkɪləˌwɑt] *n* : kilowatt *m*

kin [ˈkɪn] *n* : parents *mpl*, famille *f*

kind [ˈkaɪnd] *n* : espèce *f*, genre *m*, sorte *f* — **~** *adj* : gentil, bienveillant

kindergarten [ˈkɪndərˌgɑrtən, -dən] *n* : jardin *m* d'enfants *France*, école *f* maternelle *Can*

kindhearted [ˈkaɪndˈhɑrṭəd] *adj* : bon, qui a bon cœur

kindle [ˈkɪndəl] *v* **-dled; -dling** *vt* : allumer — *vi* : s'enflammer

kindly [ˈkaɪndli] *adj* **-lier; -est** : bienveillant — **~** *adv* **1** : avec gentillesse **2** OBLIGINGLY : gentiment — **kindness** [ˈkaɪndnəs] *n* : gentillesse *f*, bonté *f* — **kind of** *adv* SOMEWHAT : quelque peu

kindred [ˈkɪndrəd] *adj* **1** : apparenté **2 ~ spirit** : âme *f* sœur

king [ˈkɪŋ] *n* : roi *m* — **kingdom** [ˈkɪŋdəm] *n* : royaume *m*

kink [ˈkɪŋk] *n* **1** TWIST : nœud *m* **2** FLAW : défaut *m*, problème *m*

kinship [ˈkɪnˌʃɪp] *n* : parenté *f*

kiss [ˈkɪs] *vt* : embrasser, donner un baiser à — *vi* : s'embrasser — **~** *n* : baiser *m*

kit [ˈkɪt] *n* : trousse *f*

kitchen [ˈkɪʧən] *n* : cuisine *f*

kite [ˈkaɪt] *n* : cerf-volant *m*

kitten [ˈkɪtən] *n* : chaton *m* — **kitty** [ˈkɪṭi] *n, pl* **-ties** FUND : cagnotte *f*

knack [ˈnæk] *n* TALENT : don *m*

knapsack [ˈnæpˌsæk] *n* : sac *m* à dos

knead [ˈni:d] *vt* : pétrir

knee [ˈni:] *n* : genou *m* — **kneecap** [ˈni:ˌkæp] *n* : rotule *f*

kneel [ˈni:l] *vi* **knelt** [ˈnɛlt] *or* **kneeled** [ˈni:ld]; **kneeling** : s'agenouiller

knew → **know**

knife [naɪf] *n, pl* **knives** [ˈnaɪvz] : couteau *m* — **~** *vt* **knifed** [naɪft]; **knifing** : donner un coup de couteau à

knight [ˈnaɪt] *n* **1** : chevalier *m* **2** : cavalier *m* (aux échecs) — **knighthood** [ˈnaɪtˌhʊd] *n* : titre *m* de chevalier

knit [ˈnɪt] *v* **knit** *or* **knitted** [ˈnɪṭəd]; **knitting** : tricoter — **knitting** [ˈnɪtɪŋ] *n* : tricot *m*

knob [ˈnɑb] *n* : poignée *f*, bouton *m*

knock [ˈnɑk] *vt* **1** HIT : cogner, frapper **2** CRITICIZE : critiquer **3 ~ down** *or* **~ over** : renverser **4 ~ out** : assommer — *vi* **1** : frapper (à la porte) **2** : cogner (se dit d'un moteur) **3 ~ into** : heurter

knot [ˈnɑt] *n* : nœud *m* — **~** *vt* **knotted; knotting** : nouer, faire un nœud à — **knotty** [ˈnɑṭi] *adj* **-tier; -est** : épineux (se dit d'un problème)

know [ˈno:] *v* **knew** [ˈnu:, ˈnju:]; **known** [ˈno:n]; **knowing** *vt* **1** : savoir **2** : connaître (une personne, un lieu) **3** UNDERSTAND : comprendre — *vi* **1** : savoir **2 ~ about** : être au courant de, s'y connaître en (un sujet) — **knowing** [ˈno:ɪŋ] *adj* : entendu — **knowingly** [ˈno:ɪŋli] *adv* INTENTIONALLY : sciemment — **knowledge** [ˈnɑlɪʤ] *n* **1** : connaissance *f* **2** LEARNING : connaissances *fpl*, savoir *m* — **knowledgeable** [ˈnɑlɪʤəbəl] *adj* : bien informé

knuckle [ˈnʌkəl] *n* : jointure *f* du doigt, articulation *f* du doigt

Koran [kəˈrɑn, -ˈræn] *n* **the ~** : le Coran

Korean [kəˈri:ən] *adj* : coréen — **~** *n* : coréen *m* (langue)

kosher [ˈko:ʃər] *adj* : kascher, casher

L

l [ˈɛl] *n, pl* **l's** *or* **ls** [ˈɛlz] : l *m*, douzième lettre de l'alphabet

lab [ˈlæb] → **laboratory**

label [ˈleɪbəl] *n* **1** TAG : étiquette *f* **2** BRAND : marque *f* — **~** *vt* **-beled** *or* **-belled; -beling** *or* **-belling** : étiqueter

labor *or Brit* **labour** [ˈleɪbər] *n* **1** : travail *m* **2** WORKERS : main-d'œuvre *f* **3 in ~** : en train d'accoucher — **~** *vi* **1** : travailler **2** STRUGGLE : avancer péniblement — *vt* : insister sur (un point)

laboratory [ˈlæbrəˌtori, ləˈbɔrə-] *n, pl* **-ries** : laboratoire *m*

laborer *or Brit* **labourer** [ˈleɪbərər] *n* : ouvrier *m*, -vrière *f*

laborious [ləˈboriəs] *adj* : laborieux

lace [ˈleɪs] *n* **1** : dentelle *f* **2** SHOELACE : lacet *m* — **~** *vt* **laced; lacing 1** TIE : lacer **2 be laced with** : être mêlé de (se dit d'une boisson)

lacerate [ˈlæsəˌreɪt] *vt* **-ated; -ating** : lacérer

lack [ˈlæk] *vt* : manquer de, ne pas avoir — *vi or* **be lacking** : manquer — **~** *n* : manque *m*, carence *f*

lackadaisical [ˌlækəˈdeɪzɪkəl] *adj* : apathique, indolent

lackluster [ˈlækˌlʌstər] *adj* : terne, fade

lacquer [ˈlækər] *n* : laque *m*

lacrosse [ləˈkrɔs] *n* : crosse *f*

lacy [ˈleɪsi] *adj* **lacier; -est** : de dentelle

lad [ˈlæd] *n* : gars *m*, garçon *m*

ladder [ˈlædər] *n* : échelle *f*

laden [ˈleɪdən] *adj* : chargé

ladle [ˈleɪdəl] *n* : louche *f* — **~** *vt* **-dled; -dling** : servir à la louche

lady [ˈleɪdi] *n, pl* **-dies** : dame *f*, madame *f* — **ladybug** [ˈleɪdiˌbʌg] *n* : coccinelle *f* — **ladylike** [ˈleɪdiˌlaɪk] *adj* : élégant, de dame

lag [ˈlæg] *n* **1** DELAY : retard *m* **2** INTERVAL : décalage *m* — **~** *vi* **lagged; lagging** : traîner, être en retard

lager [ˈlɑgər] *n* : bière *f* blonde

lagoon [ləˈgu:n] *n* : lagune *f*

laid *pp* → **lay**[1]

lain *pp* → **lie**[1]

lair [ˈlær] *n* : tanière *f*

lake [ˈleɪk] *n* : lac *m*

lamb [ˈlæm] *n* : agneau *m*

lame ['leɪm] adj lamer; lamest 1 : boiteux 2 a ~ excuse : une excuse peu convaincante

lament [lə'mɛnt] vt 1 MOURN : pleurer 2 DEPLORE : déplorer — ~ n : lamentation f — lamentable ['læməntəbəl, lə'mɛntə-] adj : lamentable

laminate ['læmə,neɪt] vt -nated; -nating : laminer

lamp ['læmp] n : lampe f — lamppost ['læmp,post] n : réverbère m — lampshade ['læmp,ʃeɪd] n : abat-jour m

lance ['lænts] n : lance f — ~ vt lanced; lancing : percer (en médecine)

land ['lænd] n 1 : terre f 2 COUNTRY : pays m 3 or plot of ~ : terrain m — ~ vt 1 : faire un atterrissage, débarquer (des passagers) 2 CATCH : attraper (un poisson) 3 SECURE : décrocher (un emploi, etc.) — vi 1 : atterrir (se dit d'un avion) 2 FALL : tomber — landing ['lændɪŋ] n 1 : atterrissage m (d'un avion) 2 : débarquement m (d'un navire) 3 : palier m (d'un escalier) — landlady ['lænd,leɪdi] n, pl -dies : propriétaire f — landlord ['lænd,lɔrd] n : propriétaire m — landmark ['lænd,mɑrk] n 1 : point m de repère 2 MONUMENT : monument m historique — landowner ['lænd,o:nər] n : propriétaire m foncier, propriétaire f foncière — landscape ['lænd,skeɪp] n : paysage m — ~ vt -scaped; -scaping : aménager — landslide ['lænd,slaɪd] n 1 : glissement m de terrain 2 or ~ victory : victoire f écrasante

lane ['leɪn] n 1 : voie f (d'une autoroute) 2 PATH, ROAD : chemin m

language ['læŋgwɪʤ] n 1 : langue f 2 SPEECH : langage m

languid ['læŋgwɪd] adj : languissant — languish ['læŋgwɪʃ] vi : languir

lanky ['læŋki] adj lankier; -est : grand et maigre, dégingandé

lantern ['læntərn] n : lanterne f

lap ['læp] n 1 : genoux mpl 2 : tour m de piste (aux sports) — ~ v lapped; lapping vt or ~ up : boire à petites gorgées — vi ~ against : clapoter

lapel [lə'pɛl] n : revers m

lapse ['læps] n 1 : trou m (de mémoire, etc.) 2 INTERVAL : laps m, intervalle m — ~ vi lapsed; lapsing 1 EXPIRE : expirer 2 ELAPSE : passer 3 ~ into : tomber dans

laptop ['læp,tɑp] adj : portable

larceny ['lɑrsəni] n, pl -nies : vol m

lard ['lɑrd] n : saindoux m

large ['lɑrʤ] adj larger; largest 1 : grand 2 at ~ : en liberté 3 by and ~ : en général — largely ['lɑrʤli] adv : en grande partie

lark ['lɑrk] n 1 : alouette f (oiseau) 2 for a ~ : comme divertissement

larva ['lɑrvə] n, pl -vae [-,vi:, -,vaɪ] : larve f

larynx ['lærɪŋks] n, pl -rynges [lə'rɪn,ʤi:z] or -ynxes ['lærɪŋksəz] : larynx m — laryngitis [,lærən'ʤaɪtəs] n : laryngite f

lasagna [lə'zɑnjə] n : lasagnes fpl

laser ['leɪzər] n : laser m

lash ['læʃ] vt 1 WHIP : fouetter 2 BIND : attacher — vi ~ out at : invectiver contre — ~ n 1 BLOW : coup m de fouet 2 EYELASH : cil m

lass ['læs] or lassie ['læsi] n : fille f

lasso ['læ,so:, læ'su:] n, pl -sos or -soes : lasso m

last ['læst] vi : durer — ~ n 1 : dernier m, -nière f 2 at ~ : enfin, finalement — ~ adv 1 : pour la dernière fois, en dernière place 2 arrive ~ : arriver dernier — ~ adj 1 : dernier 2 ~ year : l'an passé — lastly ['læstli] adv : enfin, finalement

latch ['lætʃ] n : loquet m, serrure f

late ['leɪt] adj later; latest 1 : en retard 2 : avancé (se dit de l'heure) 3 DECEASED : défunt 4 RECENT : récent — ~ adv later; latest : en retard — lately ['leɪtli] adv : récemment, dernièrement — lateness ['leɪtnəs] n 1 : retard m 2 : heure f avancée

latent ['leɪtənt] adj : latent

lateral ['lætərəl] adj : latéral

latest ['leɪtəst] n at the ~ : au plus tard

lathe ['leɪð] n : tour m

lather ['læðər] n : mousse f — ~ vt : savonner — vi : faire mousser

Latin ['lætən] adj : latin — ~ n : latin m (langue)

latitude ['lætə,tu:d, -,tju:d] n : latitude f

latter ['lætər] adj 1 : dernier 2 SECOND : second — ~ pron the ~ : ce dernier, cette dernière, ces derniers

lattice ['lætəs] n : treillis m, treillage m

laugh ['læf] vi : rire — ~ n : rire m — laughable ['læfəbəl] adj : risible, ridicule — laughter ['læftər] n : rire m, rires mpl

launch ['lɔntʃ] vt : lancer — ~ n : lancement m

launder ['lɔndər] vt 1 : laver et repasser (du linge) 2 : blanchir (de l'argent) — laundry ['lɔndri] n, pl -dries 1 : linge m sale 2 : blanchisserie f (service) 3 do the ~ : faire la lessive

lava ['lɑvə, 'læ-] n : lave f

lavatory ['lævə,tori] n, pl -ries BATHROOM : toilettes fpl

lavender ['lævəndər] n : lavande f

lavish ['lævɪʃ] adj 1 EXTRAVAGANT : prodigue 2 ABUNDANT : abondant 3 LUXURIOUS : luxueux — ~ vt : prodiguer

law ['lɔ] n 1 : loi f 2 : droit m (profession, etc.) 3 practice ~ : exercer le droit — lawful ['lɔfəl] adj : légal, légitime

lawn ['lɔn] n : pelouse f — lawn mower n : tondeuse f

lawsuit ['lɔ,su:t] n : procès m

lawyer ['lɔɪər, 'lɔjər] n : avocat m, -cate f

lax ['læks] adj : peu strict, relâché

laxative ['læksətɪv] n : laxatif m

lay[1] ['leɪ] vt laid ['leɪd]; laying 1 PLACE, PUT : mettre, placer 2 ~ eggs : pondre des œufs 3 ~ off : licencier (un employé) 4 ~ out PRESENT : présenter, exposer 5 ~ out DESIGN : concevoir (un plan)

lay[2] → lie[1]

lay[3] adj 1 SECULAR : laïc 2 NONPROFESSIONAL : profane

layer ['leɪər] n : couche f

layman ['leɪmən] n, pl -men [-mən, -,mɛn] : profane mf, laïque mf (en religion)

layoff ['leɪ,ɔf] n : licenciement m, renvoi m

layout ['leɪ,aʊt] n ARRANGEMENT : disposition f

lazy ['leɪzi] adj -zier; -est : paresseux — laziness ['leɪzinəs] n : paresse f

lead[1] ['li:d] v led ['lɛd]; leading vt 1 GUIDE : conduire 2 DIRECT : diriger 3 HEAD : être à la tête de, aller au devant de — vi : mener, conduire (à) — ~ n 1 : devant m 2 follow s.o.'s ~ : suivre l'exemple de qqn

lead[2] ['lɛd] n 1 : plomb m (métal) 2 : mine f (d'un crayon) — leaden ['lɛdən] adj 1 : de plomb 2 HEAVY : lourd

leader ['li:dər] n : chef m; dirigeant m, -geante f — leadership ['li:dər,ʃɪp] n : direction f, dirigeants mpl

leaf ['li:f] n, pl leaves ['li:vz] 1 : feuille f 2 turn over a new ~ : tourner la page — ~ vi ~ through : feuilleter (se dit d'un livre, etc.) — leaflet ['li:flət] n : dépliant m, prospectus m

league ['li:g] n 1 : lieue f 2 be in ~ with : être de mèche avec

leak ['li:k] vt 1 : faire couler (un liquide ou un gaz) 2 : divulguer (un secret) — vi 1 : fuir, s'échapper (se dit d'un liquide ou d'un gaz) 2 : être divulgué (se dit de l'information) — ~ n : fuite f — leaky ['li:ki] adj leakier; -est : qui prend l'eau

lean[1] ['li:n] v leaned or Brit leant ['lɛnt]; leaning ['li:nɪŋ] vi 1 BEND : se pencher 2 ~ against : s'appuyer contre — vt : appuyer

lean[2] adj : mince (se dit d'une personne), maigre (se dit de la viande)

leaning ['li:nɪŋ] n : tendance f

leanness ['li:nnəs] n : minceur f (d'une personne), maigreur f (de la viande)

leap ['li:p] vi leaped or leapt ['li:pt, 'lɛpt]; leaping : sauter, bondir — ~ n : saut m, bond m — leap year n : année f bissextile

learn ['lərn] v learned ['lərnd, 'lərnt] or Brit learnt ['lərnt]; learning : apprendre — learned ['lərnəd] adj : savant, érudit — learner ['lərnər] n : débutant m, -tante f; étudiant m, -diante f — learning ['lərnɪŋ] n : savoir m, érudition f

lease ['li:s] n : bail m — ~ vt leased; leasing : louer à bail

leash ['li:ʃ] n : laisse f

least ['li:st] adj 1 : moins 2 SLIGHTEST : moindre — ~ n 1 at ~ : au moins 2 the ~ : le moins — ~ adv : moins

leather ['lɛðər] n : cuir m

leave ['li:v] v left ['lɛft]; leaving vt 1 : quitter 2 : sortir de (un endroit) 3 ~ out : omettre — vi DEPART : partir — ~ n or ~ of absence : congé m

leaves → leaf

lecture ['lɛktʃər] n 1 TALK : conférence f 2 REPRIMAND : sermon m, réprimande f — ~ v -tured; -turing vt : sermonner — vi : donner un cours, donner une conférence

led → lead[1]

ledge ['lɛʤ] n : rebord m (d'une fenêtre, etc.), saillie f (d'une montagne)

leech ['li:tʃ] n : sangsue f

leek ['li:k] n : poireau m

leer ['lɪr] vi : jeter un regard lascif — ~ n : regard m lascif

leery ['lɪri] adj : méfiant

leeway ['li:,weɪ] n : liberté f d'action, marge f de manœuvre

left[1] → leave

left[2] ['lɛft] adj : gauche — ~ adv : à gauche — ~ n : gauche f — left–handed ['lɛft'hændəd] adj : gaucher

leftovers ['lɛft,o:vərz] npl : restes mpl

leg ['lɛg] n 1 : patte f (d'un animal), jambe f (d'une personne ou d'un pantalon), pied m (d'une table, etc.) 2 : étape f (d'un voyage)

legacy ['lɛgəsi] n, pl -cies : legs m

legal ['li:gəl] adj 1 LAWFUL : légitime, légal 2 JUDICIAL : juridique — legality [li'gæləṭi] n, pl -ties : légalité f — legalize ['li:gə,laɪz] vt -ized; -izing : légaliser

legend ['lɛʤənd] n : légende f — legendary ['lɛʤən,dɛri] adj : légendaire

legible ['lɛʤəbəl] adj : lisible

legion ['li:ʤən] n : légion f

legislate ['lɛʤəs,leɪt] vi -lated; -lating : légiférer — legislation [,lɛʤəs'leɪʃən] n : législation f — legislative ['lɛʤəs,leɪtɪv] adj : législatif — legislature ['lɛʤəs,leɪtʃər] n : corps m législatif

legitimate [lɪ'ʤɪṭəmət] adj : légitime — legitimacy [lɪ'ʤɪṭəməsi] n : légitimité f

leisure ['li:ʒər, 'lɛ-] n 1 : loisir m, temps m libre 2 at your ~ : à votre convenance — leisurely ['li:ʒərli, 'lɛ-] adv : lentement, sans se presser — ~ adj : lent

lemon ['lɛmən] n : citron m — lemonade [,lɛmə'neɪd] n : limonade f

lend ['lɛnd] vt lent ['lɛnt]; lending : prêter

length ['lɛŋkθ] n 1 : longueur f 2 DURATION : durée f 3 at ~ FINALLY : finalement 4 at ~ EXTENSIVELY : longuement 5 go to any ~s : faire tout son possible — lengthen ['lɛŋkθən] vt 1 : rallonger 2 PROLONG : prolonger — vi : s'allonger — lengthways ['lɛŋkθ,weɪz] or lengthwise ['lɛŋkθ,waɪz] adv : dans le sens de la longueur — lengthy ['lɛŋkθi] adj lengthier; -est : long

lenient ['li:niənt] adj : indulgent — leniency ['li:niəntsi] n : indulgence f

lens ['lɛnz] n 1 : lentille f (d'un instrument) 2 → contact lens

Lent ['lɛnt] n : carême m

lentil ['lɛntəl] n : lentille f

leopard ['lɛpərd] n : léopard m

leotard ['li:ə,tɑrd] n : justaucorps m

lesbian ['lɛzbiən] n : lesbienne f

less ['lɛs] adv & adj (comparative of little) : moins — ~ pron : moins — ~ prep MINUS : moins — lessen ['lɛsən] v : diminuer — lesser ['lɛsər] adj : moindre

lesson ['lɛsən] n 1 CLASS : classe f, cours m 2 learn one's ~ : servir de leçon

lest ['lɛst] conj ~ we forget : de peur que nous n'oublions

let ['lɛt] vt let; letting 1 ALLOW : laisser, permettre 2 RENT : louer 3 ~'s go! : allons-y! 4 ~ down DISAPPOINT : décevoir 5 ~ in : laisser entrer 6 ~ off FORGIVE : pardonner 7 ~ up ABATE : diminuer, arrêter

letdown ['lɛt,daʊn] n : déception f

lethal ['li:θəl] adj : mortel

lethargic [lɪ'θɑrʤɪk] adj : léthargique

let's ['lɛts] (contraction of let us) → let

letter ['lɛṭər] n : lettre f

lettuce ['lɛṭəs] n : laitue f

letup ['lɛt,əp] n : pause f, répit m

leukemia [lu:'ki:miə] n : leucémie f

level ['lɛvəl] n 1 : niveau m 2 be on the ~ : être franc — ~ vt -eled or -elled; -eling or -elling 1 : niveler 2 AIM : diriger 3 RAZE : raser — ~ adj 1 FLAT : plat, plan 2 ~ with : au même niveau que — levelheaded ['lɛvəl'hɛdəd] adj : sensé, équilibré

lever ['lɛvər, 'li:-] n : levier m — leverage ['lɛvərɪʤ, 'li:-] n 1 : force f de levier (en physique) 2 INFLUENCE : influence f

levity ['lɛvəṭi] n : légèreté f

levy ['lɛvi] n, pl levies : impôt m — ~ vt levied; levying : imposer, prélever (une taxe)

lewd ['lu:d] adj : lascif

lexicon ['lɛksɪ,kɑn] n, pl -ica [-kə] or -icons : lexique m

liable ['laɪəbəl] adj 1 : responsable 2 LIKELY : probable 3 SUSCEPTIBLE : sujet — liability [,laɪə'bɪləṭi] n, pl -ties 1 RESPONSIBILITY : responsabilité f 2 DRAWBACK : désavantage m 3 liabilities npl DEBTS : dettes fpl, passif m

liaison ['li:ə,zɑn, li'eɪ-] n : liaison f

liar ['laɪər] n : menteur m, -teuse f

libel ['laɪbəl] n : diffamation f — ~ vt -beled or -belled; -beling or -belling : diffamer

liberal ['lɪbrəl, 'lɪbərəl] adj : libéral — ~ n : libéral m, -rale f

liberate ['lɪbə,reɪt] vt -ated; -ating : libérer — liberation [,lɪbə'reɪʃən] n : libération f

liberty ['lɪbərṭi] n, pl -ties : liberté f

library ['laɪ,brɛri] n, pl -braries : bibliothèque f — librarian [laɪ'brɛriən] n : bibliothécaire mf

lice → louse

license or licence n 1 PERMIT : permis m 2 FREEDOM : licence f 3 AUTHORIZATION : permission f — ~ ['laɪsənts] vt -censed; -censing : autoriser

lick ['lɪk] vt 1 : lécher 2 DEFEAT : battre (à plate couture) — ~ n : coup m de langue

licorice or Brit liquorice ['lɪkərɪʃ, -rəs] n : réglisse f

lid ['lɪd] n 1 : couvercle m 2 EYELID : paupière f

lie[1] ['laɪ] vi lay ['leɪ]; lain ['leɪn]; lying ['laɪɪŋ] 1 or ~ down : se coucher, s'allonger 2 BE : être, se trouver

lie[2] vi lied; lying ['laɪɪŋ] : mentir — ~ n : mensonge m

lieutenant [lu:'tɛnənt] n : lieutenant m

life ['laɪf] n, pl lives ['laɪvz] : vie f — lifeboat ['laɪf,bo:t] n : canot m de sauvetage — lifeguard ['laɪf,gɑrd] n : sauveteur m — lifeless ['laɪfləs] adj : sans vie — lifelike ['laɪf,laɪk] adj : naturel, réaliste — lifelong ['laɪf'lɔŋ] adj : de toute une vie — life preserver n : gilet m de sauvetage — lifestyle ['laɪf,staɪl] n : mode m de vie — lifetime ['laɪf,taɪm] n : vie f

lift ['lɪft] vt 1 RAISE : lever 2 STEAL : voler — vi 1 CLEAR UP : se dissiper 2 or ~ off : décoller (se dit d'un avion, etc.) — ~ n 1 LIFTING : soulèvement m 2 give s.o. a ~ : emmener qqn en voiture — liftoff ['lɪft,ɔf] n : lancement m

light[1] ['laɪt] n 1 : lumière f 2 LAMP : lampe f 3 HEADLIGHT : phare m 4 do you have a ~? : avez-vous du feu? — ~ adj 1 BRIGHT : bien illuminé 2 : clair (se dit des couleurs), blond (se dit des cheveux) — ~ v lit ['lɪt] or lighted; lighting vt 1 : allumer (un feu) 2 ILLUMINATE : éclairer — vi or ~ up : s'illuminer — lightbulb ['laɪt,bʌlb] n : ampoule f — lighten ['laɪtən] vt BRIGHTEN : éclairer — lighter ['laɪtər] n : briquet m — lighthouse ['laɪt,haʊs] n : phare m — lighting ['laɪṭɪŋ] n : éclairage m — lightning ['laɪtnɪŋ] n : éclairs mpl, foudre f — light–year ['laɪt,jɪr] n : année-lumière f

light[2] adj : léger — lighten ['laɪtən] vt : alléger — lightly ['laɪtli] adv 1 : légèrement 2 let off ~ : traiter avec indulgence — lightness ['laɪtnəs] n : légèreté f — lightweight ['laɪt,weɪt] adj : léger

like[1] ['laɪk] v liked; liking vt 1 : aimer (qqn) 2 WANT : vouloir — vi if you ~ : si vous voulez — likes npl : préférences fpl, goûts mpl — likable or likeable ['laɪkəbəl] adj : sympathique

like[2] adj SIMILAR : pareil — ~ prep : comme — ~ conj 1 AS : comme 2 AS IF : comme si — likelihood ['laɪkli,hʊd] n : probabilité f — likely ['laɪkli] adj -lier; -est : probable — liken ['laɪkən] vt : comparer — likeness ['laɪknəs] n : ressemblance f — likewise ['laɪk,waɪz] adv 1 : de même 2 ALSO : aussi

liking ['laɪkɪŋ] n : goût m (pour une chose), affection f (pour une personne)

lilac ['laɪlək, -læk, -lɑk] n : lilas m

lily ['lɪli] n, pl lilies : lis m — lily of the valley n : muguet m

lima bean ['laɪmə] n : haricot m de Lima

limb ['lɪm] n 1 : membre m (en anatomie) 2 : branche f (d'un arbre)

limber ['lɪmbər] vi ~ up : s'échauffer, faire des exercices d'assouplissement

limbo ['lɪm,bo:] n, pl -bos : limbes mpl

lime ['laɪm] n : lime f, citron m vert

limelight ['laɪm,laɪt] n be in the ~ : être en vedette

limerick ['lɪmərɪk] n : poème m humoristique en cinq vers

limestone ['laɪm,sto:n] n : pierre f à chaux, calcaire m

limit ['lɪmət] n : limite f — ~ vt : limiter, restreindre — limitation [,lɪmə'teɪʃən] n : limitation f, restriction f — limited ['lɪmətəd] adj : limité

limousine ['lɪmə,zi:n, ,lɪmə'-] n : limousine f

limp[1] ['lɪmp] vi : boiter — ~ n have a ~ : boiter

limp[2] adj : mou, flasque

line ['laɪn] n 1 : ligne f 2 ROPE : corde f 3 ROW : rangée f 4 QUEUE : file f 5 WRINKLE : ride f 6 drop s.o. a ~ : écrire un mot à qqn — ~ v lined; lining vt 1 : doubler (un vêtement, etc.), tapisser (un mur, etc.) 2 MARK : rayer, ligner 3 BORDER : border — vi ~ up : se mettre en ligne, faire la queue

lineage ['lɪniɪʤ] n : lignée f

linear ['lɪniər] adj : linéaire

linen ['lɪnən] n : lin m

liner ['laɪnər] n 1 LINING : doublure f 2 SHIP : paquebot m

lineup ['laɪn,əp] n 1 or police ~ : rangée f de suspects 2 : équipe f (aux sports)

linger ['lɪŋgər] vi 1 : s'attarder, flâner 2 PERSIST : persister

lingerie [,lɑnʤə'reɪ] n : vêtement m intime féminin, lingerie f

lingo ['lɪŋgo] n, pl -goes JARGON : jargon m

linguistics [lɪŋ'gwɪstɪks] n : linguistique f — linguist ['lɪŋgwɪst] n : linguiste mf — linguistic [lɪŋ'gwɪstɪk] adj : linguistique

lining ['laɪnɪŋ] n : doublure f

link ['lɪŋk] n 1 : maillon m (d'une chaîne) 2 BOND : lien m 3 CONNECTION : liaison f — ~ vt : relier, lier — vi or ~ up : se rejoindre, se relier

linoleum [lə'no:liəm] n : linoléum m, prélart m Can

lint ['lɪnt] n : peluches fpl

lion ['laɪən] n : lion m — lioness ['laɪənɪs] n : lionne f

lip ['lɪp] n 1 : lèvre f 2 EDGE : rebord m — lipstick ['lɪp,stɪk] n : rouge m à lèvres

liqueur [lɪ'kər, -'kʊr, -'kjʊr] n : liqueur f

liquid ['lɪkwəd] adj : liquide — ~ n : liquide m — liquidate ['lɪkwə,deɪt] vt -dated; -dating : liquider — liquidation [,lɪkwə'deɪʃən] n : liquidation f

liquor ['lɪkər] n : boissons fpl alcoolisées

lisp ['lɪsp] vi : zézayer — ~ n : zézaiement m

list[1] ['lɪst] n : liste f — ~ vt 1 ENUMERATE : faire une liste de, énumérer 2 INCLUDE : mettre (sur une liste)

list[2] vi : gîter (se dit d'un bateau)

listen ['lɪsən] *vi* **1** : écouter **2 ~ to reason** : entendre raison — **listener** ['lɪsənər] *n* : auditeur *m*, -trice *f*

listless ['lɪstləs] *adj* : apathique

lit ['lɪt] *pp* → **light**[1]

litany ['lɪtəni] *n, pl* **-nies** : litanie *f*

liter ['li:t̬ər] *n* : litre *m*

literacy ['lɪt̬ərəsi] *n* : alphabétisation *f*

literal ['lɪt̬ərəl] *adj* : littéral — **literally** ['lɪt̬ərəli] *adv* : littéralement, au pied de la lettre

literate ['lɪt̬ərət] *adj* : qui sait lire et écrire

literature ['lɪt̬ərə,ʧʊr, -ʧər] *n* : littérature *f* — **literary** ['lɪt̬ə,rɛri] *adj* : littéraire

lithe ['laɪð, 'laɪθ] *adj* : agile et gracieux

litigation [,lɪt̬ə'geɪʃən] *n* : litige *m*

litre → **liter**

litter ['lɪt̬ər] *n* **1** RUBBISH : ordures *fpl* **2** : portée *f* (se dit d'un animal) **3** *or* **kitty ~** : litière *f* (de chat) — **~** *vt* : mettre du désordre dans — *vi* : jeter des déchets

little ['lɪt̬əl] *adj* **littler** *or* **less** ['lɛs] *or* **lesser** ['lɛsər]; **littlest** *or* **least** ['li:st] **1** SMALL : petit **2 a ~** SOME : un peu de **3 he speaks ~ English** : il ne parle presque pas l'anglais — **~** *adv* **less** ['lɛs]; **least** ['li:st] : peu — **~** *pron* **1** : peu *m* **2 ~ by ~** : peu à peu

liturgy ['lɪt̬ərʤi] *n, pl* **-gies** : liturgie *f* — **liturgical** [lə'tərʤɪkəl] *adj* : liturgique

live ['lɪv] *v* **lived; living** *vi* **1** : vivre **2** RESIDE : habiter **3 ~ on** : vivre de — *vt* : vivre, mener — **~** ['laɪv] *adj* **1** : vivant **2** : sous tension (se dit d'un câble électrique) **3** : en direct (se dit d'un programme de télévision, etc.) — **livelihood** ['laɪvli,hʊd] *n* : subsistance *f*, gagne-pain *m* — **lively** ['laɪvli] *adj* **-lier; -est** : animé, vivant — **liven** ['laɪvən] *vt or* **~ up** : animer, égayer — *vi* : s'animer

liver ['lɪvər] *n* : foie *m*

livestock ['laɪv,stɑk] *n* : bétail *m*

livid ['lɪvəd] *adj* **1** : livide **2** ENRAGED : furieux

living ['lɪvɪŋ] *adj* : vivant — **~** *n* **make a ~** : gagner sa vie — **living room** *n* : salle *f* de séjour, salon *m*

lizard ['lɪzərd] *n* : lézard *m*

llama ['lɑmə, 'ja-] *n* : lama *m*

load ['lo:d] *n* **1** CARGO : chargement *m* **2** BURDEN : charge *f*, poids *m* **3 ~s of** : beaucoup de — **~** *vt* : charger

loaf[1] ['lo:f] *n, pl* **loaves** ['lo:vz] : pain *m*

loaf[2] *vi* : fainéanter, paresser — **loafer** ['lo:fər] *n* **1** : fainéant *m*, fainéante *f* **2** : mocassin *m* (soulier)

loan ['lo:n] *n* : emprunt *m*, prêt *m* — **~** *vt* : prêter

loathe ['lo:ð] *vt* **loathed; loathing** : détester — **loathsome** ['lo:θsəm, 'lo:ð-] *adj* : odieux

lobby ['lɑbi] *n, pl* **-bies** **1** : vestibule *m* **2** *or* **political ~** : groupe *m* de pression, lobby *m* — **~** *vt* **-bied; -bying** : faire pression sur

lobe ['lo:b] *n* : lobe *m*

lobster ['lɑbstər] *n* : homard *m*

local ['lo:kəl] *adj* : local — **~** *n* **the ~s** *npl* : les gens du coin — **locale** [lo'kæl] *n* : lieu *m* — **locality** [lo'kælət̬i] *n, pl* **-ties** : localité *f*

locate ['lo:,keɪt] *vt* **-cated; -cating** **1** SITUATE : situer, établir **2** FIND : trouver — **location** [lo'keɪʃən] *n* : emplacement *m*, endroit *m*

lock[1] ['lɑk] *n* : mèche *f* (de cheveux)

lock[2] *n* **1** : serrure *f* (d'une porte, etc.) **2** : écluse *f* (d'un canal) — **~** *vt* **1** : fermer (à clé) **2** *or* **~ up** CONFINE : enfermer — *vi* **1** : se fermer à clé **2** : se bloquer (se dit d'une roue, etc.) — **locker** ['lɑkər] *n* : vestiaire *m* — **locket** ['lɑkət] *n* : médaillon *m* — **locksmith** ['lɑk,smɪθ] *n* : serrurier *m*

locomotive [,lo:kə'mo:t̬ɪv] *n* : locomotive *f*

locust ['lo:kəst] *n* : criquet *m*, sauterelle *f*

lodge ['lɑʤ] *v* **lodged; lodging** *vt* **1** HOUSE : loger, héberger **2** FILE : déposer — *vi* : se loger — **~** *n* : pavillon *m* — **lodger** ['lɑʤər] *n* : locataire *mf*, pensionnaire *mf* — **lodging** ['lɑʤɪŋ] *n* **1** : hébergement *m* **2 ~s** *npl* : logement *m*

loft ['lɔft] *n* : grenier *m* (d'une maison, à foin, etc.) — **lofty** ['lɔfti] *adj* **loftier; -est** **1** : noble, élevé **2** HAUGHTY : hautain

log ['lɔg, 'lɑg] *n* **1** : bûche *f*, rondin *m* **2** RECORD : registre *m* de bord — **~** *vi* **logged; logging** **1** : tronçonner (des arbres) **2** RECORD : enregistrer, noter **3 ~ on** : entrer (dans le système) **4 ~ off** : sortir (du système) — **logger** ['lɔgər, 'lɑ-] *n* : bûcheron *m*, -ronne *f*

logic ['lɑʤɪk] *n* : logique *f* — **logical** ['lɑʤɪkəl] *adj* : logique — **logistics** [lə'ʤɪstɪks, lo-] *ns & pl* : logistique *f*

logo ['lo:,go:] *n, pl* **logos** [-,go:z] : logo *m*

loin ['lɔɪn] *n* : filet *m*

loiter ['lɔɪt̬ər] *vi* : traîner, flâner

lollipop *or* **lollypop** ['lɑli,pɑp] *n* : sucette *f France*, suçon *m Can*

lone ['lo:n] *adj* : solitaire — **loneliness** ['lo:nlinəs] *n* : solitude *f* — **lonely** ['lo:nli] *adj* **-lier; -est** : solitaire, seul — **loner** ['lo:nər] *n* : solitaire *mf* — **lonesome** ['lo:nsəm] *adj* : seul, solitaire

long[1] ['lɔŋ] *adj* **longer** ['lɔŋgər]; **longest** ['lɔŋgəst] : long — **~** *adv* **1** : longtemps **2 all day ~** : toute la journée **3 as ~ as** : tant que **4 no ~er** : ne…plus **5 so ~!** : à bientôt! — **~** *n* **1 before ~** : dans peu de temps **2 the ~ and short of it** : l'essentiel *m*

long[2] *vi* **~ for** : avoir envie de, désirer

longevity [lɑn'ʤɛvət̬i] *n* : longévité *f*

longing ['lɔŋɪŋ] *n* : envie *f*

longitude ['lɑnʤə,tu:d, -,tju:d] *n* : longitude *f*

look ['lʊk] *vi* **1** : regarder **2** SEEM : sembler **3 ~ after** : prendre soin (de) **4 ~ for** EXPECT : attendre **5 ~ for** SEEK : chercher **6 ~ into** : enquêter **7 ~ out** : faire attention **8 ~ over** EXAMINE : examiner **9 ~ up to** : respecter — *vt* : regarder — **~** *n* **1** : coup *m* d'œil, regard *m* **2** APPEARANCE : aspect *m*, air *m* — **lookout** ['lʊk,aʊt] *n* **1** : poste *m* d'observation **2** WATCHMAN : guetteur *m* **3 be on the ~** : faire le guet

loom[1] ['lu:m] *n* : métier *m* à tisser

loom[2] *vi* **1** APPEAR : surgir **2** APPROACH : être imminent

loop ['lu:p] *n* : boucle *f* — **~** *vt* : faire une boucle avec — **loophole** ['lu:p,ho:l] *n* : échappatoire *m*

loose ['lu:s] *adj* **looser; -est** **1** MOVABLE : desserré **2** SLACK : lâche **3** ROOMY : ample **4** APPROXIMATE : approximatif **5** FREE : libre **6** IMMORAL : dissolu — **loosely** ['lu:sli] *adv* **1** : sans serrer **2** ROUGHLY : approximativement — **loosen** ['lu:sən] *vt* : desserrer

loot ['lu:t] *n* : butin *m* — **~** *vt* : piller, saccager — **looter** ['lu:t̬ər] *n* : pillard *m*, -larde *f* — **looting** ['lu:t̬ɪŋ] *n* : pillage *m*

lop ['lɑp] *vt* **lopped; lopping** : couper, élaguer

lopsided ['lɑp,saɪdəd] *adj* : de travers, croche *Can*

lord ['lɔrd] *n* **1** : seigneur *m*, noble *m* **2 the Lord** : le Seigneur

lore ['lor] *n* : savoir *m* populaire, tradition *f*

lose ['lu:z] *v* **lost** ['lɔst]; **losing** ['lu:zɪŋ] *vt* **1** : perdre **2 ~ one's way** : se perdre **3 ~ time** : retarder (se dit d'une horloge) — *vi* : perdre — **loser** ['lu:zər] *n* : perdant *m*, -dante *f* — **loss** ['lɔs] *n* **1** : perte *f* **2** DEFEAT : défaite *f* **3 be at a ~ for words** : ne pas savoir quoi dire — **lost** ['lɔst] *adj* **1** : perdu **2 get ~** : se perdre

lot ['lɑt] *n* **1** FATE : sort *m* **2** PLOT : parcelle *f* **3 a ~ of** *or* **~s of** : beaucoup, une montagne de

lotion ['lo:ʃən] *n* : lotion *f*

lottery ['lɑt̬əri] *n, pl* **-teries** : loterie *f*

loud ['laʊd] *adj* **1** : grand, fort **2** NOISY : bruyant **3** FLASHY : criard — **~** *adv* **1** : fort **2 out ~** : à voix haute — **loudly** ['laʊdli] *adv* : à voix haute — **loudspeaker** ['laʊd,spi:kər] *n* : haut-parleur *m*

lounge ['laʊnʤ] *vi* **lounged; lounging** **1** : se vautrer **2 ~ about** : flâner — **~** *n* : salon *m*

louse ['laʊs] *n, pl* **lice** ['laɪs] : pou *m* — **lousy** ['laʊzi] *adj* **lousier; -est** **1** : pouilleux **2** BAD : piètre, très mauvais

love ['lʌv] *n* **1** : amour *m* **2 fall in ~** : tomber amoureux — **~** *v* **loved; loving** : aimer — **lovable** ['lʌvəbəl] *adj* : adorable — **lovely** ['lʌvli] *adj* **-lier; -est** : beau, joli — **lover** ['lʌvər] *n* : amant *m*, -mante *f* — **loving** ['lʌvɪŋ] *adj* : affectueux

low ['lo:] *adj* **lower** ['lo:ər]; **lowest** **1** : bas **2** SCARCE : limité **3** DEPRESSED : déprimé — **~** *adv* **1** : bas **2 turn the lights ~** : baisser les lumières — **~** *n* **1** : point *m* bas **2** *or* **~ gear** : première *f* — **lower** ['lo:ər] *adj* : inférieur, plus bas — **~** *vt* : baisser — **lowly** ['lo:li] *adj* **-lier; -est** : humble

loyal ['lɔɪəl] *adj* : loyal, fidèle — **loyalty** ['lɔɪəlti] *n, pl* **-ties** : loyauté *f*

lozenge ['lɑzənʤ] *n* : pastille *f*

lubricate ['lu:brə,keɪt] *vt* **-cated; -cating** : lubrifier — **lubricant** ['lu:brɪkənt] *n* : lubrifiant *m* — **lubrication** [,lu:brə'keɪʃən] *n* : lubrification *f*

lucid ['lu:səd] *adj* : lucide — **lucidity** [lu:'sɪdət̬i] *n* : lucidité *f*

luck ['lʌk] *n* **1** : chance *f* **2 good ~!** : bonne chance! — **luckily** ['lʌkəli] *adv* : heureusement — **lucky** ['lʌki] *adj* **luckier; -est** **1** : chanceux **2 ~ charm** : porte-bonheur *m*

lucrative ['lu:krət̬ɪv] *adj* : lucratif

ludicrous ['lu:dəkrəs] *adj* : ridicule, absurde

lug ['lʌg] *vt* **lugged; lugging** : traîner

luggage ['lʌgɪʤ] *n* : bagages *mpl*

lukewarm ['lu:k'wɔrm] *adj* : tiède

lull ['lʌl] *vt* **1** CALM : calmer **2 ~ to sleep** : endormir — **~** *n* : période *f* de calme, pause *f*

lullaby ['lʌlə,baɪ] *n, pl* **-bies** : berceuse *f*

lumber ['lʌmbər] *n* : bois *m* — **lumberjack** ['lʌmbər,ʤæk] *n* : bûcheron *m*, -ronne *f*

luminous ['lu:mənəs] *adj* : lumineux

lump ['lʌmp] *n* **1** CHUNK, PIECE : morceau *m*, motte *f* **2** SWELLING : bosse *f* **3** : grumeau *m* (dans une sauce) — **~** *vt or* **~ together** : réunir, regrouper — **lumpy** ['lʌmpi] *adj* **lumpier; -est** : grumeleux (se dit d'une sauce), bosselé (se dit d'un matelas)

lunacy ['lu:nəsi] *n, pl* **-cies** : folie *f*

lunar ['lu:nər] *adj* : lunaire

lunatic ['lu:nə,tɪk] *n* : fou *m*

lunch ['lʌnʧ] *n* : déjeuner *m*, dîner *m Can*, lunch *m Can* — **~** *vi* : déjeuner, dîner *Can* — **luncheon** ['lʌnʧən] *n* : déjeuner *m*

lung ['lʌŋ] *n* : poumon *m*

lunge ['lʌnʤ] *vi* **lunged; lunging** **1** : se précipiter **2 ~ at** : foncer sur

lurch[1] ['lərʧ] *vi* **1** STAGGER : tituber **2** : faire une embardée (se dit d'une voiture)

lurch[2] *n* **leave in a ~** : laisser en plan

lure ['lʊr] *n* **1** BAIT : leurre *m* **2** ATTRACTION : attrait *m* — **~** *vt* **lured; luring** : attirer

lurid ['lʊrəd] *adj* **1** GRUESOME : épouvantable **2** SENSATIONAL : à sensation **3** GAUDY : criard

lurk ['lərk] *vi* : être tapi

luscious ['lʌʃəs] *adj* : délicieux, exquis

lush ['lʌʃ] *adj* : luxuriant, somptueux

lust ['lʌst] *n* **1** : luxure *f* **2** CRAVING : envie *f*, désir *m* — **~** *vi* **~ after** : désirer (une personne), convoiter (des richesses, etc.)

luster *or* **lustre** ['lʌstər] *n* : lustre *m*

lusty ['lʌsti] *adj* **lustier; -est** : robuste, vigoureux

luxurious [,lʌg'ʒʊriəs, ,lʌk'ʃʊr-] *adj* : luxueux — **luxury** ['lʌkʃəri, 'lʌgʒə-] *n, pl* **-ries** : luxe *m*

lye ['laɪ] *n* : lessive *f*

lying → **lie**

lynch ['lɪnʧ] *vt* : lyncher

lynx ['lɪŋks] *n* : lynx *m*

lyric ['lɪrɪk] *or* **lyrical** ['lɪrɪkəl] *adj* : lyrique — **lyrics** *npl* : paroles *fpl* (d'une chanson)

M

m ['ɛm] *n, pl* **m's** *or* **ms** ['ɛmz] : m *m*, treizième lettre de l'alphabet

ma'am ['mæm] → **madam**

macabre [mə'kɑb, -'kɑbər, -'kɑbrə] *adj* : macabre

macaroni [,mækə'ro:ni] *n* : macaronis *mpl*

mace ['meɪs] *n* **1** : masse *f* (arme ou symbole) **2** : macis *m* (épice)

machete [mə'ʃɛt̬i] *n* : machette *f*

machine [mə'ʃi:n] *n* : machine *f* — **machine gun** *n* : mitrailleuse *f* — **machinery** [mə'ʃi:nəri] *n, pl* **-eries** **1** : machinerie *f* **2** WORKS : mécanisme *m*

mad ['mæd] *adj* **madder; maddest** **1** INSANE : fou **2** FOOLISH : insensé **3** ANGRY : furieux

madam ['mædəm] *n, pl* **mesdames** [meɪ'dɑm] : madame *f*

madden ['mædən] *vt* : exaspérer

made → **make**

madly ['mædli] *adv* : comme un fou, follement — **madman** ['mæd,mæn, -mən] *n, pl* **-men** [-mən, -,mɛn] : fou *m* — **madness** ['mædnəs] *n* : folie *f*

Mafia ['mɑfiə] *n* : mafia *f*

magazine ['mægə,zi:n] *n* **1** PERIODICAL : revue *f* **2** : magasin *m* (d'une arme à feu)

maggot ['mægət] *n* : asticot *m*

magic ['mæʤɪk] *n* : magie *f* — **~** *or* **magical** ['mæʤɪkəl] *adj* : magique — **magician** [mə'ʤɪʃən] *n* : magicien *m*, -cienne *f*

magistrate ['mæʤə,streɪt] *n* : magistrat *m*

magnanimous [mæg'nænəməs] *adj* : magnanime

magnate ['mæg,neɪt, -nət] *n* : magnat *m*

magnet ['mægnət] *n* : aimant *m* — **magnetic** [mæg'nɛt̬ɪk] *adj* : magnétique — **magnetism** ['mægnə,tɪzəm] *n* : magnétisme *m* — **magnetize** ['mægnə,taɪz] *vt* **-tized; -tizing** : magnétiser

magnificent [mæg'nɪfəsənt] *adj* : magnifique — **magnificence** [mæg'nɪfəsənts] *n* : splendeur *f*

magnify ['mægnə,faɪ] *vt* **-fied; -fying** **1** ENLARGE : amplifier **2** EXAGGERATE : exagérer — **magnifying glass** *n* : loupe *f*

magnitude ['mægnə,tu:d, -,tju:d] *n* : ampleur *f*

magnolia [mæg'no:ljə] *n* : magnolia *m*

mahogany [mə'hɑgəni] *n, pl* **-nies** : acajou *m*

maid ['meɪd] *n* : servante *f*, bonne *f*, domestique *f* — **maiden name** *n* : nom *m* de jeune fille

mail ['meɪl] *n* **1** : poste *f* **2** LETTERS : correspondence *f* — **~** *vt* : envoyer par la poste — **mailbox** ['meɪl,bɑks] *n* : boîte *f* aux lettres — **mailman** ['meɪl,mæn, -mən] *n, pl* **-men** [-mən, -,mɛn] : facteur *m*

maim ['meɪm] *vt* : mutiler

main ['meɪn] *n* : canalisation *f* principale (d'eau ou de gaz) — **~** *adj* : principal — **mainframe** ['meɪn,freɪm] *n* : ordinateur *m* central — **mainland** ['meɪn,lænd, -lənd] *n* : continent *m* — **mainly** ['meɪnli] *adv* : principalement — **mainstay** ['meɪn,steɪ] *n* : soutien *m* prinicpal — **mainstream** ['meɪn,stri:m] *n* : courant *m* dominant — **~** *adj* : dominant, conventionnel

maintain [meɪn'teɪn] *vt* : entretenir, maintenir — **maintenance** ['meɪntənənts] *n* : entretien *m*, maintien *m*

maize ['meɪz] *n* : maïs *m*

majestic [mə'ʤɛstɪk] *adj* : majestueux — **majesty** ['mæʤəsti] *n, pl* **-ties** : majesté *f*

major ['meɪʤər] *adj* **1** : très important, principal **2** : majeur (en musique) — **~** *n* **1** : commandant *m* (des forces armées) **2** : spécialité *f* (à l'université) — **~** *vi* **-jored; -joring** : se spécialiser — **majority** [mə'ʤɔrət̬i] *n, pl* **-ties** : majorité *f*

make ['meɪk] *v* **made** ['meɪd]; **making** *vt* **1** : faire **2** MANUFACTURE : fabriquer **3** CONSTITUTE : constituer **4** PREPARE : préparer **5** RENDER : rendre **6** COMPEL : obliger **7 ~ a decision** : prendre une décision **8 ~ a living** : gagner sa vie — *vi* **1 ~ do** : se débrouiller **2 ~ for** : se diriger vers **3 ~ good** SUCCEED : réussir — **~** *n* BRAND : marque *f* — **make–believe** [,meɪkbə'li:v] *n* : fantaisie *f* — **~** *adj* : imaginaire — **make out** *vt* **1** : faire (un chèque, etc.) **2** DISCERN : distinguer **3** UNDERSTAND : comprendre — *vi* **how did you ~?** : comment ça s'est passé? — **maker** ['meɪkər] *n* MANUFACTURER : fabricant *m*, -cante *f* — **makeshift** ['meɪk,ʃɪft] *adj* : improvisé — **makeup** ['meɪk,ʌp] *n* **1** COMPOSITION : composition *f* **2** COSMETICS : maquillage *m* — **make up** *vt* **1** PREPARE : préparer **2** INVENT : inventer **3** CONSTITUTE : former — *vi* RECONCILE : faire la paix

maladjusted [,mælə'ʤʌstəd] *adj* : inadapté

malaria [mə'lɛriə] *n* : paludisme *m*

male ['meɪl] *n* : mâle *m*, homme *m* — **~** *adj* **1** : mâle **2** MASCULINE : masculin

malevolent [mə'lɛvələnt] *adj* : malveillant

malfunction [mæl'fʌŋkʃən] *vi* : mal fonctionner — **~** *n* : mauvais fonctionnement *m*

malice ['mælɪs] *n* : mauvaise intention *f*, rancœur *f* — **malicious** [mə'lɪʃəs] *adj* : malveillant

malign [mə'laɪn] *adj* : pernicieux — **~** *vt* : calomnier

malignant [mə'lɪgnənt] *adj* : malveillant

mall ['mɔl] *n or* **shopping ~** : centre *m* commercial

malleable ['mæliəbəl] *adj* : malléable

mallet ['mælət] *n* : maillet *m*

malnutrition [,mælnʊ'trɪʃən, -njʊ-] *n* : malnutrition *f*

malpractice [,mæl'præktəs] *n* : négligence *f*

malt ['mɔlt] *n* : malt *m*

mama *or* **mamma** ['mɑmə] *n* : maman *f*

mammal ['mæməl] *n* : mammifère *m*

mammogram ['mæmə,græm] *n* : mammographie *f*

mammoth ['mæməθ] *adj* : gigantesque

man ['mæn] *n, pl* **men** ['mɛn] : homme *m* — **~** *vt* **manned; manning** : équiper en personnel

manage ['mænɪʤ] *v* **-aged; -aging** *vt* **1** HANDLE : manier **2** DIRECT : gérer, diriger — *vi* COPE : se débrouiller — **manageable** ['mænɪʤəbəl] *adj* : maniable — **management** ['mænɪʤmənt] *n* : gestion *f*, direction *f* — **manager** ['mænɪʤər] *n* : directeur *m*, -trice *f*; gérant *m*, -rante *f*; manager *m* (aux sports) — **managerial** [,mænə'ʤɪriəl] *adj* : de gestion

mandarin ['mændərən] *n or* **~ orange** : mandarine *f*

mandate ['mæn,deɪt] *n* : mandat *m*

mandatory ['mændə,tori] *adj* : obligatoire

mane ['meɪn] *n* : crinière *f*

maneuver *or Brit* **manoeuvre** [mə'nu:vər, -'nju:-] *n* : manœuvre *f* — **~** *v* **-vered** *or Brit* **-vred; -vering** *or Brit* **-vring** : manœuvrer

mangle ['mæŋgəl] *vt* **-gled; -gling** : mutiler

mango ['mæŋ,go:] *n, pl* **-goes** : mangue *f*

mangy ['meɪnʤi] *adj* **mangier; -est** : galeux

manhandle ['mæn,hændəl] *vt* **-dled; -dling** : malmener

manhole ['mæn,ho:l] *n* : bouche *f* d'égout

manhood ['mæn,hʊd] *n* **1** : âge *m* d'homme **2** : virilité *f*

mania ['meɪniə, -njə] *n* : manie *f* — **maniac** ['meɪni,æk] *n* : maniaque *mf*

manicure ['mænə,kjʊr] *n* : manucure *f* — **~** *vt* **-cured; -curing** : faire les ongles de

manifest ['mænə,fɛst] *adj* : manifeste, patent — **~** *vt* : manifester — **manifesto** [,mænə'fɛs,to:] *n, pl* **-tos** *or* **-toes** : manifeste *m*

manipulate [mə'nɪpjə,leɪt] *vt* **-lated; -lating** : manipuler — **manipulation** [mə,nɪpjə'leɪʃən] *n* : manipulation *f*

mankind ['mæn'kaɪnd, -,kaɪnd] *n* : le genre humain, humanité *f*

manly ['mænli] *adj* **-lier; -est** : viril — **manliness** ['mænlinəs] *n* : virilité *f*

mannequin ['mænɪkən] *n* : mannequin *m*

manner ['mænər] *n* **1** : manière *f* **2** KIND

: sorte f 3 ~s npl ETIQUETTE : manières fpl, éducation f — **mannerism** ['mænə,rɪzəm] n : particularité f
manoeuvre Brit → **maneuver**
manor ['mænər] n : manoir m
manpower ['mæn,paʊər] n : main-d'œuvre f
mansion ['mæntʃən] n : château m
manslaughter ['mæn,slɔt̬ər] n : homicide m involontaire
mantel ['mæntəl] or **mantelpiece** ['mæntəl,pi:s] n : cheminée f
manual ['mænjuəl] adj : manuel — ~ n : manuel m
manufacture [,mænjə'fæktʃər] n : fabrication f — ~ vt **-tured; -turing** : fabriquer — **manufacturer** [,mænjə'fæktʃərər] n : fabricant m, -cante f
manure [mə'nʊr, -'njʊr] n : fumier m
manuscript ['mænjə,skrɪpt] n : manuscrit m
many ['mɛni] adj **more** ['mor]; **most** ['mo:st] 1 : beaucoup de 2 **as ~** : autant de 3 **how ~** : combien 4 **too ~** : trop de — ~ pron : beaucoup
map ['mæp] n : carte f, plan m — ~ vt **mapped; mapping** 1 : faire la carte de 2 or **~ out** : élaborer
maple ['meɪpəl] n 1 : érable m 2 **~ syrup** : sirop m d'érable
mar ['mɑr] vt **marred; marring** : estropier
marathon ['mærə,θɑn] n : marathon m
marble ['mɑrbəl] n 1 : marbre m 2 : billes fpl (à jouer)
march ['mɑrtʃ] n : marche f — ~ vi : marcher, défiler
March ['mɑrtʃ] n : mars m
mare ['mær] n : jument f
margarine ['mɑrdʒərən] n : margarine f
margin ['mɑrdʒən] n : marge f — **marginal** ['mɑrdʒənəl] adj : marginal
marigold ['mærə,go:ld] n : souci m
marijuana [,mærə'hwɑnə] n : marijuana f
marinate ['mærə,neɪt] v **-nated; -nating** : mariner
marine [mə'ri:n] adj : marin — ~ n : fusilier m marin
marital ['mærət̬əl] adj 1 : conjugal 2 **~ status** : état m civil
maritime ['mærə,taɪm] adj : maritime
mark ['mɑrk] n 1 : marque f 2 STAIN : tache 3 IMPRINT : trace f 4 TARGET : cible f 5 GRADE : note f — ~ vt 1 : marquer 2 STAIN : tacher 3 POINT OUT : signaler 4 : corriger (un examen, etc.) 5 COMMEMORATE : commémorer 6 CHARACTERIZE : caractériser 7 **~ off** : délimiter — **marked** ['mɑrkt] adj : marqué, notable — **markedly** ['mɑrkədli] adv : sensiblement — **marker** ['mɑrkər] n 1 : repère m 2 PEN : marqueur m
market ['mɑrkət] n : marché m — ~ vt : vendre, commercialiser — **marketable** ['mɑrkət̬əbəl] adj : vendable — **marketplace** ['mɑrkət,pleɪs] n : marché m
marksman ['mɑrksmən] n, pl **-men** [-mən, -,mɛn] : tireur m, -reuse f d'élite — **marksmanship** ['mɑrksmən,ʃɪp] n : adresse f au tir
marmalade ['mɑrmə,leɪd] n : marmelade f
maroon[1] [mə'ru:n] vt : abandonner
maroon[2] n : rouge m foncé
marquee [mɑr'ki:] n CANOPY : marquise f
marriage ['mærɪdʒ] n 1 : mariage m 2 WEDDING : noces fpl — **married** ['mærid] adj 1 : marié 2 **get ~** : se marier
marrow ['mæro:] n : moelle f
marry ['mæri] v **-ried; -rying** vt 1 : marier 2 WED : se marier avec, épouser — vi : se marier
Mars ['mɑrz] n : Mars f
marsh ['mɑrʃ] n 1 : marécage m 2 or **salt ~** : marais m salant
marshal ['mɑrʃəl] n : maréchal m (militaire), commissaire m (de police) — ~ vt **-shaled** or **-shalled; -shaling** or **-shalling** : rassembler
marshmallow ['mɑrʃ,mɛlo:, -,mælo:] n : guimauve f
marshy ['mɑrʃi] adj **marshier; -est** : marécageux
mart ['mɑrt] n : marché m
martial ['mɑrʃəl] adj : martial
martyr ['mɑrt̬ər] n : martyr m, -tyre f — ~ vt : martyriser
marvel ['mɑrvəl] n : merveille f — ~ vi **-veled** or **-velled; -veling** or **-velling** : s'émerveiller — **marvelous** ['mɑrvələs] or **marvellous** adj : merveilleux
mascara [mæs'kærə] n : mascara m
mascot ['mæs,kɑt, -kət] n : mascotte f
masculine ['mæskjələn] adj : masculin — **masculinity** [,mæskjə'lɪnət̬i] n : masculinité f
mash ['mæʃ] vt 1 CRUSH : écraser, aplatir 2 PUREE : faire une purée de, piler Can — **mashed potatoes** npl : purée f de pommes de terre, patates fpl Can
mask ['mæsk] n : masque m — ~ vt : masquer
masochism ['mæsə,kɪzəm, 'mæzə-] n : masochisme m — **masochist** ['mæsə,kɪst, 'mæzə-] n : masochiste mf — **masochistic** [,mæsə'kɪstɪk] adj : masochiste
mason ['meɪsən] n : maçon m — **masonry** ['meɪsənri] n, pl **-ries** : maçonnerie f
masquerade [,mæskə'reɪd] n : mascarade f — ~ vi **-aded; -ading ~ as** : se déguiser en, se faire passer pour
mass ['mæs] n 1 : masse f 2 MULTITUDE : quantité f 3 **the ~es** : les masses
Mass n : messe f
massacre ['mæsɪkər] n : massacre m — ~ vt **-cred; -cring** : massacrer
massage [mə'sɑʒ, -'sɑdʒ] n : massage m — ~ vt **-saged; -saging** : donner un massage à, masser — **masseur** [mæ'sər] n : masseur m — **masseuse** [mæ'søz, -'su:z] n : masseuse f
massive ['mæsɪv] adj 1 BULKY : massif 2 HUGE : énorme
mast ['mæst] n : mât m
master ['mæstər] n 1 : maître m 2 **~'s degree** : maîtrise f — ~ vt : maîtriser — **masterful** ['mæstərfəl] adj : magistral — **masterpiece** ['mæstər,pi:s] n : chef m d'œuvre — **mastery** ['mæstəri] n : maîtrise f
masturbate ['mæstər,beɪt] vi **-bated; -bating** : se masturber — **masturbation** [,mæstər'beɪʃən] n : masturbation f
mat ['mæt] n 1 DOORMAT : paillasson m 2 RUG : tapis m
match ['mætʃ] n 1 : allumette f 2 EQUAL : égal m, égale f 3 GAME : match m, combat m (de boxe) 4 **be a good ~** : être un bon parti — ~ vt 1 or **~ up** : appareiller 2 EQUAL : égaler 3 : s'accorder avec, aller ensemble (vêtements, couleurs, etc.) — vi : correspondre
mate ['meɪt] n 1 COMPANION : compagnon m, -pagne f 2 : mâle m, femelle f (d'un animal) — ~ vi **mated; mating** : s'accoupler
material [mə'tɪriəl] adj 1 : matériel 2 IMPORTANT : important — ~ n 1 : matière f 2 FABRIC : tissu m, étoffe f — **materialistic** [mə,tɪriə'lɪstɪk] adj : matérialiste — **materialize** [mə'tɪriə,laɪz] vi **-ized; -izing** : se matérialiser
maternal [mə'tərnəl] adj : maternel — **maternity** [mə'tərnət̬i] n, pl **-ties** : maternité f — ~ adj : de maternité
math ['mæθ] → **mathematics**
mathematics [,mæθə'mæt̬ɪks] ns & pl : mathématiques fpl — **mathematical** [,mæθə'mæt̬ɪkəl] adj : mathématique — **mathematician** [,mæθəmə'tɪʃən] n : mathématicien m, -cienne f
matinee or **matinée** [,mætən'eɪ] n : matinée f (au cinéma)
matrimony ['mætrə,mo:ni] n : mariage m — **matrimonial** [,mætrə'mo:niəl] adj : matrimonial
matrix ['meɪtrɪks] n, pl **-trices** ['meɪtrə,si:z, 'mæ-] or **-trixes** ['meɪtrɪksəz] : matrice f
matte ['mæt] adj : mat
matter ['mæt̬ər] n 1 SUBSTANCE : matière f 2 QUESTION : affaire f, question f 3 **as a ~ of fact** : en fait, en réalité 4 **for that ~** : d'ailleurs 5 **to make ~s worse** : pour ne rien arranger 6 **what's the ~?** : qu'est-ce qu'il y a? — ~ vi : importer
mattress ['mætrəs] n : matelas m
mature [mə'tʊr, -'tjʊr, -'tʃʊr] adj **-turer; -est** : mûr — ~ vi **-tured; -turing** : mûrir — **maturity** [mə'tʊrət̬i, -'tjʊr-, -'tʃʊr-] n : maturité f
maul ['mɔl] vt : mutiler
mauve ['mo:v, 'mɔv] n : mauve m
maxim ['mæksəm] n : maxime f
maximum ['mæksəməm] n, pl **-ma** ['mæksəmə] or **-mums** : maximum m — ~ adj : maximum — **maximize** ['mæksə,maɪz] vt **-mized; -mizing** : porter au maximum
may ['meɪ] v aux, past **might** ['maɪt]; present s & pl **may** 1 : pouvoir 2 **come what ~** : quoiqu'il arrive 3 **it ~ rain** : il se peut qu'il pleuve, il va peut-être pleuvoir 4 **~ the best man win** : que le meilleur gagne
May ['meɪ] n : mai m
maybe ['meɪbi] adv : peut-être
mayhem ['meɪ,hɛm, 'meɪəm] n : pagaille f
mayonnaise ['meɪə,neɪz] n : mayonnaise f
mayor ['meɪər, 'mɛr] n : maire m, mairesse f
maze ['meɪz] n : labyrinthe m
me ['mi:] pron 1 : moi 2 : me, m' 3 **give it to ~** : donne-le moi 4 **will she come with ~?** : m'accompagnera-t-elle?
meadow ['mɛdo:] n : pré m, prairie f
meager or **meagre** ['mi:gər] adj : maigre
meal ['mi:l] n 1 : repas m 2 : farine f (de maïs, etc.) — **mealtime** ['mi:l,taɪm] n : l'heure f du repas
mean[1] ['mi:n] vt **meant** ['mɛnt]; **meaning** 1 SIGNIFY : vouloir dire 2 INTEND : avoir l'intention de 3 **be meant for** : être destiné à 4 **he didn't ~ it** : il ne l'a pas fait exprès
mean[2] adj 1 UNKIND : méchant 2 STINGY : mesquin
mean[3] adj AVERAGE : moyen — ~ n : moyenne f
meander [mi'ændər] vi 1 WIND : serpenter 2 WANDER : errer
meaning ['mi:nɪŋ] n : sens m, signification f — **meaningful** ['mi:nɪŋfəl] adj : significatif — **meaningless** ['mi:nɪŋləs] adj : sans signification
meanness ['mi:nnəs] n : méchanceté f
means ['mi:nz] n 1 : moyens mpl 2 **by all ~** : certainement 3 **by ~ of** : au moyen de 4 **by no ~** : d'aucune façon
meantime ['mi:n,taɪm] n 1 : intervalle m 2 **in the ~** : en attendant — ~ adv → **meanwhile**
meanwhile ['mi:n,hwaɪl] adv : entre-temps — ~ n → **meantime**
measles ['mi:zəlz] npl : rougeole f
measly ['mi:zli] adj **-slier; -est** : misérable, minable fam
measure ['mɛʒər, 'meɪ-] n : mesure f — ~ v **-sured; -suring** : mesurer — **measurable** ['mɛʒərəbəl, 'meɪ-] adj : mesurable — **measurement** ['mɛʒərmənt, 'meɪ-] n : mesure f — **measure up** vi **~ to** : être à la hauteur de
meat ['mi:t] n : viande f — **meatball** ['mi:t,bɔl] n : boulette f de viande — **meaty** ['mi:t̬i] adj **meatier; -est** 1 : de viande 2 SUBSTANTIAL : substantiel
mechanic [mɪ'kænɪk] n : mécanicien m, -cienne f — **mechanical** [mɪ'kænɪkəl] adj : mécanique — **mechanics** [mɪ'kænɪks] ns & pl 1 : mécanique f 2 WORKINGS : mécanisme m — **mechanism** ['mɛkə,nɪzəm] n : mécanisme m — **mechanize** ['mɛkə,naɪz] vt **-nized; -nizing** : mécaniser
medal ['mɛdəl] n : médaille f — **medallion** [mə'dæljən] n : médaillon m
meddle ['mɛdəl] vi **-dled; -dling** : se mêler
media ['mi:diə] or **mass ~** npl : les médias
median ['mi:diən] adj : médian
mediate ['mi:di,eɪt] vi **-ated; -ating** : servir de médiateur — **mediation** [,mi:di'eɪʃən] n : médiation f — **mediator** ['mi:di,eɪt̬ər] n : médiateur m, -trice f
medical ['mɛdɪkəl] adj : médical — **medicated** ['mɛdə,keɪt̬əd] adj : médical, traitant — **medication** [,mɛdə'keɪʃən] n : médicaments mpl — **medicinal** [mə'dɪsənəl] adj : médicinal — **medicine** ['mɛdəsən] n 1 : médecine f 2 MEDICATION : médicament m
medieval or **mediaeval** [mɪ'di:vəl, ,mi:-, ,mɛ-, -di'i:vəl] adj : médiéval
mediocre [,mi:di'o:kər] adj : médiocre — **mediocrity** [,mi:di'ɑkrət̬i] n, pl **-ties** : médiocrité f
meditate ['mɛdə,teɪt] vi **-tated; -tating** : méditer — **meditation** [,mɛdə'teɪʃən] n : méditation f
Mediterranean [,mɛdətə'reɪniən] adj : méditerranéen
medium ['mi:diəm] n, pl **-diums** or **-dia** ['mi:diə] 1 MEANS : moyen m 2 MEAN : milieu m 3 → **media** — ~ adj : moyen
medley ['mɛdli] n, pl **-leys** 1 : mélange m 2 : pot-pourri m (de chansons)
meek ['mi:k] adj : docile
meet ['mi:t] v **met** ['mɛt]; **meeting** vt 1 ENCOUNTER : rencontrer 2 SATISFY : satisfaire 3 **pleased to ~ you** : enchanté de faire votre connaissance — vi 1 : se rencontrer 2 ASSEMBLE : se réunir 3 : faire connaissance — ~ n : rencontre f (aux sports) — **meeting** ['mi:tɪŋ] n : réunion f
megabyte ['mɛgə,baɪt] n : mégaoctet m
megaphone ['mɛgə,fo:n] n : porte-voix m, mégaphone m
melancholy ['mɛlən,kɑli] n, pl **-cholies** : mélancolie f — ~ adj : mélancolique, triste
mellow ['mɛlo:] adj 1 : doux, moelleux 2 CALM : paisible — ~ vt : adoucir — vi : s'adoucir
melody ['mɛlədi] n, pl **-dies** : mélodie f
melon ['mɛlən] n : melon m
melt ['mɛlt] vi : fondre — vt : faire fondre
member ['mɛmbər] n : membre m — **membership** ['mɛmbər,ʃɪp] n 1 : adhésion f 2 MEMBERS : membres mpl
membrane ['mɛm,breɪn] n : membrane f
memory ['mɛmri, 'mɛmə-] n, pl **-ries** 1 : mémoire f 2 RECOLLECTION : souvenir m — **memento** [mɪ'mɛn,to:] n, pl **-tos** or **-toes** : souvenir m — **memo** ['mɛmo:] n, pl **memos** or **memorandum** [,mɛmə'rændəm] n, pl **-dums** or **-da** [-də] : mémorandum m — **memoirs** ['mɛm,wɑrz] npl : mémoires mpl — **memorable** ['mɛmərəbəl] adj : mémorable — **memorial** [mə'moriəl] adj : commémoratif — ~ n : monument m (commémoratif) — **memorize** ['mɛmə,raɪz] vt **-rized; -rizing** : apprendre par cœur
men → **man**
menace ['mɛnəs] n : menace f — ~ vt **-aced; -acing** : menacer — **menacing** ['mɛnəsɪŋ] adj : menaçant
mend ['mɛnd] vt 1 : réparer, arranger 2 DARN : raccommoder — vi HEAL : guérir
menial ['mi:niəl] adj : servile, bas
meningitis [,mɛnən'dʒaɪt̬əs] n, pl **-gitides** [-'dʒɪt̬ə,di:z] : méningite f
menopause ['mɛnə,pɔz] n : ménopause f
menstruate ['mɛnstru,eɪt] vi **-ated; -ating** : avoir ses règles — **menstruation** [,mɛnstru'eɪʃən] n : menstruation f, règles fpl
mental ['mɛntəl] adj : mental — **mentality** [mɛn'tælət̬i] n, pl **-ties** : mentalité f
mention ['mɛntʃən] n : mention f — ~ vt 1 : mentionner 2 **don't ~ it** : il n'y a pas de quoi
menu ['mɛn,ju:] n : menu m
meow [mi:'aʊ] n : miaulement m, miaou m — ~ vi : miauler
mercenary ['mərsən,ɛri] n, pl **-naries** : mercenaire mf
merchant ['mərtʃənt] n : marchand m, -chande f; commerçant m, -çante f — **merchandise** ['mərtʃən,daɪz, -,daɪs] n : marchandises fpl
merciful ['mərsɪfəl] adj : miséricordieux, compatissant — **merciless** ['mərsɪləs] adj : impitoyable
mercury ['mərkjəri] n : mercure m
Mercury ['mərkjəri] n : Mercure f
mercy ['mərsi] n, pl **-cies** 1 : miséricorde f, compassion f 2 **at the ~ of** : à la merci de
mere ['mɪr] adj, superlative **merest** : simple — **merely** ['mɪrli] adv : simplement
merge ['mərdʒ] v **merged; merging** vi : fusionner (se dit d'une compagnie), confluer (se dit d'une rivière, etc.) — vt : unir, fusionner — **merger** ['mərdʒər] n : union f, fusion f
merit ['mɛrət] n : mérite m — ~ vt : mériter
mermaid ['mər,meɪd] n : sirène f
merry ['mɛri] adj **-rier; -est** : allègre — **merry-go-round** ['mɛrigo,raʊnd] n : manège m
mesh ['mɛʃ] n : maille f
mesmerize ['mɛzmə,raɪz] vt **-ized; -izing** : hypnotiser
mess ['mɛs] n 1 : désordre m 2 MUDDLE : gâchis m 3 : cantine f (ambulante) — ~ vt 1 **~ up** : mettre en désordre 2 or **~ up** SOIL : salir 3 **~ up** BUNGLE : gâcher — vi 1 **~ around** PUTTER : bricoler 2 **~ with** PROVOKE : embêter
message ['mɛsɪdʒ] n : message m — **messenger** ['mɛsəndʒər] n : messager m, -gère f
messy ['mɛsi] adj **messier; -est** : désordonné
met → **meet**
metabolism [mə'tæbə,lɪzəm] n : métabolisme m
metal ['mɛt̬əl] n : métal m — **metallic** [mə'tælɪk] adj : métallique
metamorphosis [,mɛt̬ə'mɔrfəsɪs] n, pl **-phoses** [-,si:z] : métamorphose f
metaphor ['mɛt̬ə,fɔr, -fər] n : métaphore f
meteor ['mi:t̬iər, -t̬i,ɔr] n : météore m — **meteorological** [,mi:t̬i,ɔrə'lɑdʒɪkəl] adj : météorologique — **meteorologist** [,mi:t̬iə'rɑlədʒɪst] n : météorologue mf — **meteorology** [,mi:t̬iə'rɑlədʒi] n : météorologie f
meter or Brit **metre** ['mi:t̬ər] n 1 : mètre m 2 : compteur m (d'électricité, etc.)
method ['mɛθəd] n : méthode f — **methodical** [mə'θɑdɪkəl] adj : méthodique
meticulous [mə'tɪkjələs] adj : méticuleux
metric ['mɛtrɪk] or **metrical** [-trɪkəl] adj : métrique
metropolis [mə'trɑpələs] n : métropole f — **metropolitan** [,mɛtrə'pɑlət̬ən] adj : métropolitain
Mexican ['mɛksɪkən] adj : mexicain
mice → **mouse**
microbe ['maɪ,kro:b] n : microbe m
microfilm ['maɪkro,fɪlm] n : microfilm m
microphone ['maɪkrə,fo:n] n : microphone m
microscope ['maɪkrə,sko:p] n : microscope m — **microscopic** [,maɪkrə'skɑpɪk] adj : microscopique
microwave ['maɪkrə,weɪv] n or **~ oven** : (four m à) micro-ondes m
mid ['mɪd] adj 1 **~-morning** : au milieu de la matinée 2 **in ~-June** : à la mi-juin 3 **she is in her ~ thirties** : elle est dans la trentaine — **midair** ['mɪd'ær] n **in ~** : en plein ciel — **midday** ['mɪd'deɪ] n : midi m
middle ['mɪdəl] adj : du milieu, au milieu — ~ n 1 : milieu m, centre m 2 **in the ~ of** : au milieu de (un espace), en train de (faire une activité) — **middle-aged** adj : d'un certain age — **Middle Ages** npl : Moyen Âge m — **middle class** n : classe f moyenne — **Middle Eastern** adj : moyen-oriental — **middleman** ['mɪdəl,mæn] n, pl **-men** [-mən, -,mɛn] : intermédiaire mf
midget ['mɪdʒət] n : nain m, naine f
midnight ['mɪd,naɪt] n : minuit m
midriff ['mɪd,rɪf] n : diaphragme m
midst ['mɪdst] n 1 **in the ~ of** : au milieu de 2 **in our ~** : parmi nous
midsummer ['mɪd'sʌmər, -,sʌ-] n : milieu m de l'été
midway ['mɪd,weɪ] adv : à mi-chemin
midwife ['mɪd,waɪf] n, pl **-wives** [-,waɪvz] : sage-femme f
midwinter ['mɪd'wɪntər, -,wɪn-] n : milieu m de l'hiver
miff ['mɪf] vt : vexer
might[1] ['maɪt] (used to express permission or possibility or as a polite alternative to **may**) → **may**
might[2] n : force f, pouvoir m — **mighty**

['maɪt̬i] adj **mightier; -est** 1 : fort, puissant 2 GREAT : énorme — ~ adv : très, rudement fam

migraine ['maɪˌgreɪn] n : migraine f

migrate ['maɪˌgreɪt] vi **-grated; -grating** : émigrer — **migrant** ['maɪgrənt] n : travailleur m saisonnier

mild ['maɪld] adj 1 GENTLE : doux 2 LIGHT : léger

mildew ['mɪlˌdu:, -ˌdju:] n : moisissure f

mildly ['maɪldli] adv : doucement, légèrement — **mildness** ['maɪldnəs] n : douceur f

mile ['maɪl] n : mille m — **mileage** ['maɪlɪʤ] n : distance f parcourue (en milles), kilométrage m — **milestone** ['maɪlˌsto:n] n : jalon m

military ['mɪləˌtɛri] adj : militaire — ~ n **the ~** : les forces armées — **militant** ['mɪlətənt] adj : militant — ~ n : militant m, -tante f — **militia** [mə'lɪʃə] n : milice f

milk ['mɪlk] n : lait m — ~ vt : traire (une vache, etc.) — **milky** ['mɪlki] adj **milkier; -est** : laiteux — **Milky Way** n **the ~** : la Voie lactée

mill ['mɪl] n 1 : moulin m 2 FACTORY : usine f — ~ vt : moudre — vi or **~ about** : grouiller

millennium [mə'lɛniəm] n, pl **-nia** [-niə] or **-niums** : millénaire m

miller ['mɪlər] n : meunier m, -nière f

milligram ['mɪləˌgræm] n : milligramme m — **millimeter** or Brit **millimetre** ['mɪləˌmi:t̬ər] n : millimètre m

million ['mɪljən] n, pl **millions** or **million** : million m — ~ adj **a ~** : un million de — **millionaire** [ˌmɪljə'nær, 'mɪljəˌnær] n : millionnaire mf — **millionth** ['mɪljənθ] adj : millionième

mime ['maɪm] n 1 : mime mf 2 PANTOMIME : pantomime f — ~ v **mimed; miming** vt : imiter — vi : faire des mimiques — **mimic** vt **-icked; -icking** : imiter, singer

mince ['mɪnts] vt **minced; mincing** 1 : hacher 2 **not to ~ one's words** : ne pas mâcher ses mots

mind ['maɪnd] n 1 : esprit m 2 INTELLECT : capacité f intellectuelle 3 OPINION : opinion f 4 REASON : raison f 5 **have a ~ to** : avoir l'intention de — ~ vt 1 TEND : s'occuper de 2 OBEY : obéir à 3 WATCH : faire attention à 4 **I don't ~ the heat** : la chaleur ne m'incommode pas — vi 1 OBEY : obéir 2 **I don't ~** : ça m'est égal — **mindful** ['maɪndfəl] adj : attentif — **mindless** ['maɪndləs] adj 1 SENSELESS : stupide 2 DULL : ennuyeux

mine1 ['maɪn] pron 1 : le mien, la mienne, les miens, les miennes 2 **a friend of ~** : un ami à moi

mine2 n : mine f — ~ vt **mined; mining** 1 : extraire (de l'or, etc.) 2 : miner (avec des explosifs) — **minefield** ['maɪnˌfi:ld] n : champ m de mines — **miner** ['maɪnər] n : mineur m

mineral ['mɪnərəl] n : minéral m

mingle ['mɪŋgəl] v **-gled; -gling** vt : mêler, mélanger — vi : se mêler (à, avec)

miniature ['mɪniəˌʧʊr, 'mɪnɪˌʧʊr, -ʧər] n : miniature f — ~ adj : en miniature

minimal ['mɪnəməl] adj : minimal — **minimize** ['mɪnəˌmaɪz] vt **-mized; -mizing** : minimiser — **minimum** ['mɪnəməm] adj : minimum — ~ n, pl **-ma** ['mɪnəme] or **-mums** : minimum m

minister ['mɪnəstər] n 1 : pasteur m (d'une église) 2 : ministre m (en politique) — ~ vi **~ to** : pourvoir à, donner des soins à — **ministerial** [ˌmɪnə'stɪriəl] adj : ministériel — **ministry** ['mɪnəstri] n, pl **-tries** : ministère m (gouvernemental), sacerdoce m (religieux)

mink ['mɪŋk] n, pl **mink** or **minks** : vison m

minor ['maɪnər] adj 1 : mineur 2 INSIGNIFICANT : sans importance — ~ n 1 : mineur m, -neure f 2 : matière f secondaire (à l'université) — **minority** [mə'nɔrət̬i, maɪ-] n, pl **-ties** : minorité f

mint1 ['mɪnt] n 1 : menthe f (plante) 2 : bonbon m à la menthe

mint2 n 1 **the Mint** : l'Hôtel m de la Monnaie 2 **worth a ~** : valoir une fortune — ~ vt : frapper (la monnaie) — ~ adj **in ~ condition** : comme neuf

minus ['maɪnəs] prep 1 : moins 2 WITHOUT : sans — ~ n or **~ sign** : moins m

minuscule or **miniscule** ['mɪnəsˌkju:l] adj : minuscule

minute1 ['mɪnət] n 1 : minute f 2 MOMENT : moment m 3 **~s** npl : procès-verbal m

minute2 [maɪ'nu:t, mɪ-, -'nju:t] adj **-nuter; -est** 1 TINY : minuscule 2 DETAILED : minutieux

miracle ['mɪrɪkəl] n : miracle m — **miraculous** [mə'rækjələs] adj : miraculeux

mirage [mɪ'rɑʒ, chiefly Brit 'mɪrˌɑʒ] n : mirage m

mire ['maɪr] n : boue f, fange f

mirror ['mɪrər] n : miroir m, glace f — ~ vt : refléter, réfléchir

mirth ['mərθ] n : allégresse f, gaieté f

misapprehension [ˌmɪsˌæprə'hɛnʧən] n : malentendu m

misbehave [ˌmɪsbi'heɪv] vi **-haved; -having** : se conduire mal — **misbehavior** [ˌmɪsbi'heɪvjər] n : mauvaise conduite f

miscalculate [mɪs'kælkjəˌleɪt] v **-lated; -lating** : mal calculer

miscarriage [ˌmɪs'kærɪʤ, 'mɪsˌkærɪʤ] n 1 : fausse couche f 2 **~ of justice** : erreur f judiciaire

miscellaneous [ˌmɪsə'leɪniəs] adj : divers, varié

mischief ['mɪsʧəf] n : espièglerie f — **mischievous** ['mɪsʧəvəs] adj : espiègle

misconception [ˌmɪskən'sɛpʃən] n : concept m erroné

misconduct [mɪs'kɑndəkt] n : mauvaise conduite f

misdeed [mɪs'di:d] n : méfait m

misdemeanor [ˌmɪsdɪ'mi:nər] n : délit m judiciaire

miser ['maɪzər] n : avare m

miserable ['mɪzərəbəl] adj 1 UNHAPPY : malheureux 2 WRETCHED : misérable 3 **~ weather** : temps m maussade

miserly ['maɪzərli] adj : avare

misery ['mɪzəri] n, pl **-eries** 1 : souffrance f 2 WRETCHEDNESS : misère f

misfire [mɪs'faɪr] vi **-fired; -firing** : échouer

misfit ['mɪsˌfɪt] n : inadapté m, -tée f

misfortune [mɪs'fɔrʧən] n : malheur f, infortune f

misgiving [mɪs'gɪvɪŋ] n : doute m

misguided [mɪs'gaɪdəd] adj : malencontreux, peu judicieux

mishap ['mɪsˌhæp] n : contretemps m

misinform [ˌmɪsɪn'fɔrm] vt : mal renseigner

misinterpret [ˌmɪsɪn'tərprət] vt : mal interpréter

misjudge [mɪs'ʤʌʤ] vt **-judged; -judging** : mal juger

mislay [mɪs'leɪ] vt **-laid** [-'leɪd]; **-laying** : égarer

mislead [mɪs'li:d] vt **-led** [-'lɛd]; **-leading** : tromper — **misleading** [mɪs'li:dɪŋ] adj : trompeur

misnomer [mɪs'no:mər] n : terme m impropre

misplace [mɪs'pleɪs] vt **-placed; -placing** : égarer, perdre

misprint ['mɪsˌprɪnt, mɪs'-] n : faute f typographique, coquille f

miss ['mɪs] vt 1 : rater, manquer (une occasion, un vol, etc.) 2 OVERLOOK : laisser passer 3 AVOID : éviter 4 OMIT : sauter 5 **I ~ you** : tu me manques — ~ n 1 : coup m manqué 2 FAILURE : échec m

Miss ['mɪs] n : mademoiselle f

missile ['mɪsəl] n 1 : missile m 2 PROJECTILE : projectile m

missing ['mɪsɪŋ] adj : perdu, disparu

mission ['mɪʃən] n : mission f — **missionary** ['mɪʃəˌnɛri] n, pl **-aries** : missionnaire mf

misspell [mɪs'spɛl] vt : mal orthographier, mal écrire

mist ['mɪst] n : brume f

mistake [mɪ'steɪk] vt **-took** [-'stʊk]; **-taken** [-'steɪkən]; **-taking** 1 MISINTERPRET : mal comprendre 2 CONFUSE : confondre — ~ n 1 : faute f, erreur f 2 **make a ~** : se tromper — **mistaken** [mɪ'steɪkən] adj : erroné

mister ['mɪstər] n : monsieur m

mistletoe ['mɪsəlˌto:] n : gui m

mistreat [mɪs'tri:t] vt : maltraiter

mistress ['mɪstrəs] n 1 : maîtresse f (de classe) 2 LOVER : amante f

mistrust [mɪs'trʌst] n : méfiance f — ~ vt : se méfier de

misty ['mɪsti] adj **mistier; -est** : brumeux

misunderstand [ˌmɪsˌʌndər'stænd] vt **-stood** [-'stʊd]; **-standing** : mal comprendre — **misunderstanding** [ˌmɪsˌʌndər'stændɪŋ] n : malentendu m

misuse [mɪs'ju:z] vt **-used; -using** 1 : mal employer 2 MISTREAT : maltraiter — ~ [mɪs'ju:s] n : mauvais emploi m, abus m

mitigate ['mɪt̬əˌgeɪt] vt **-gated; -gating** : atténuer

mitt ['mɪt] n : gant m (de baseball) — **mitten** ['mɪtən] n : moufle f, mitaine f Can

mix ['mɪks] vt 1 : mélanger 2 **~ up** : confondre — vi : se mélanger — ~ n : mélange m — **mixture** ['mɪksʧər] n : mélange m — **mix–up** ['mɪksˌʌp] n : confusion f

moan ['mo:n] n : gémissement m — ~ vi : gémir

mob ['mɑb] n : foule f — ~ vt **mobbed; mobbing** : assaillir

mobile ['mo:bəl, -ˌbi:l, -ˌbaɪl] adj : mobile — ~ ['mo:ˌbi:l] n : mobile m — **mobile home** n : auto-caravane f — **mobility** [mo:'bɪlət̬i] n : mobilité f — **mobilize** ['mo:bəˌlaɪz] vt **-lized; -lizing** : mobiliser

moccasin ['mɑkəsən] n : mocassin m

mock ['mɑk, 'mɔk] vt : se moquer de — ~ adj : faux — **mockery** ['mɑkəri, 'mɔ-] n, pl **-eries** : moquerie f

mode ['mo:d] n : mode m

model ['mɑdəl] n 1 : modèle m 2 MOCK-UP : maquette f 3 : mannequin m (personne) — ~ v **-eled** or **-elled; -eling** or **-elling** vt 1 SHAPE : modeler 2 WEAR : porter — vi : travailler comme mannequin — ~ adj : modèle

modem ['mo:dəm, -ˌdɛm] n : modem m

moderate ['mɑdərət] adj : modéré — ~ n : modéré m, -rée f — ~ ['mɑdəˌreɪt] v **-ated; -ating** vt : modérer — vi : se modérer — **moderation** [ˌmɑdə'reɪʃən] n : modération f — **moderator** ['mɑdəˌreɪt̬ər] n : animateur m, -trice f

modern ['mɑdərn] adj : moderne — **modernize** ['mɑdərˌnaɪz] vt **-nized; -nizing** : moderniser

modest ['mɑdəst] adj : modeste — **modesty** ['mɑdəsti] n : modestie f

modify ['mɑdəˌfaɪ] vt **-fied; -fying** : modifier

moist ['mɔɪst] adj : humide — **moisten** ['mɔɪsən] vt : humecter — **moisture** ['mɔɪsʧər] n : humidité f — **moisturizer** ['mɔɪsʧəˌraɪzər] n : crème f hydratante

molar ['mo:lər] n : molaire f

molasses [mə'læsəz] n : mélasse f

mold1 ['mo:ld] n FORM : moule m — ~ vt : mouler, former

mold2 n : moisissure f — **moldy** ['mo:ldi] adj **moldier; -est** : moisi

mole1 ['mo:l] n : grain m de beauté (sur la peau)

mole2 n : taupe f (animal)

molecule ['mɑlɪˌkju:l] n : molécule f

molest [mə'lɛst] vt 1 HARASS : importuner 2 : abuser (sexuellement)

molt ['mo:lt] vi : muer

molten ['mo:ltən] adj : en fusion

mom ['mɑm] n : maman f

moment ['mo:mənt] n : instant m, moment m — **momentarily** [ˌmo:mən'tɛrəli] adv 1 : momentanément 2 SOON : dans un instant, immédiatement — **momentary** ['mo:mənˌtɛri] adj : momentané

momentous [mo'mɛntəs] adj : très important

momentum [mo'mɛntəm] n, pl **-ta** [-tə] or **-tums** 1 : moment m (en physique) 2 IMPETUS : élan m

monarch ['mɑˌnɑrk, -nərk] n : monarque m — **monarchy** ['mɑˌnɑrki, -nər-] n, pl **-chies** : monarchie f

monastery ['mɑnəˌstɛri] n, pl **-teries** : monastère m

Monday ['mʌnˌdeɪ, -di] n : lundi m

money ['mʌni] n, pl **-eys** or **-ies** [-iz] : argent m — **monetary** ['mɑnəˌtɛri, 'mʌnə-] adj : monétaire — **money order** n : mandat-poste m

mongrel ['mɑŋgrəl, 'mʌŋ-] n : chien m métisse

monitor ['mɑnət̬ər] n : moniteur m (d'un ordinateur, etc.) — ~ vt : surveiller

monk ['mʌŋk] n : moine m

monkey ['mʌŋki] n, pl **-keys** : singe m — **monkey wrench** n : clé f à molette

monogram ['mɑnəˌgræm] n : monogramme m

monologue ['mɑnəˌlɔg] n : monologue m

monopoly [mə'nɑpəli] n, pl **-lies** : monopole m — **monopolize** [mə'nɑpəˌlaɪz] vt **-lized; -lizing** : monopoliser

monotonous [mə'nɑtənəs] adj : monotone — **monotony** [mə'nɑtəni] n : monotonie f

monster ['mɑntstər] n : monstre m — **monstrosity** [mɑn'strɑsət̬i] n, pl **-ties** : monstruosité f — **monstrous** ['mɑntstrəs] adj 1 : monstrueux 2 HUGE : gigantesque

month ['mʌnθ] n : mois m — **monthly** ['mʌnθli] adv : mensuellement — ~ adj : mensuel

monument ['mɑnjəmənt] n : monument m — **monumental** [ˌmɑnjə'mɛntəl] adj : monumental

moo ['mu:] vi : meugler — ~ n : meuglement m

mood ['mu:d] n : humeur f — **moody** ['mu:di] adj **moodier; -est** 1 GLOOMY : mélancolique, déprimé 2 IRRITABLE : de mauvaise humeur 3 TEMPERAMENTAL : d'humeur changeante

moon ['mu:n] n : lune f — **moonlight** ['mu:nˌlaɪt] n : clair m de lune

moor1 ['mʊr] n : lande f

moor2 vt : amarrer — **mooring** ['mʊrɪŋ] n : mouillage m

moose ['mu:s] ns & pl : orignal m

moot ['mu:t] adj : discutable

mop ['mɑp] n 1 : balai m à franges 2 or **~ of hair** : tignasse f — ~ vt **mopped; mopping** : laver (le plancher, etc.)

mope ['mo:p] vi **moped; moping** : être déprimé

moped ['mo:ˌpɛd] n : cyclomoteur m, vélomoteur m

moral ['mɔrəl] adj : moral — ~ n 1 : morale f (d'une histoire, etc.) 2 **~s** npl : mœurs fpl — **morale** [mə'ræl] n : moral m — **morality** [mə'ræləti] n, pl **-ties** : moralité f

morbid ['mɔrbɪd] adj : morbide

more ['mor] adj : plus de — ~ adv 1 : plus, davantage 2 **~ and ~** : de plus en plus 3 **~ or less** : plus ou moins 4 **once ~** : encore une fois — ~ n **the ~** : le plus — ~ pron : plus — **moreover** [mor'o:vər] adv : de plus

morgue ['mɔrg] n : morgue f

morning ['mɔrnɪŋ] n 1 : matin m, avant-midi f Can 2 **good ~** : bonjour 3 **in the ~** : pendant la matinée

Moroccan [mə'rɑkən] adj : marocain

moron ['morˌɑn] n : imbécile mf

morose [mə'ro:s] adj : morose

morphine ['mɔrˌfi:n] n : morphine f

morsel ['mɔrsəl] n 1 BITE : bouchée f 2 FRAGMENT : morceau m

mortal ['mɔrt̬əl] adj : mortel — ~ n : mortel m, -telle f — **mortality** [mɔr'tælət̬i] n : mortalité f

mortar ['mɔrt̬ər] n : mortier m

mortgage ['mɔrgɪʤ] n : hypothèque f — ~ vt **-gaged; -gaging** : hypothéquer

mortify ['mɔrt̬əˌfaɪ] vt **-fied; -fying** : mortifier

mosaic [mo'zeɪɪk] n : mosaïque f

Moslem ['mɑzləm] → **Muslim**

mosque ['mɑsk] n : mosquée f

mosquito [mə'ski:t̬o] n, pl **-toes** : moustique m, maringouin m Can

moss ['mɔs] n : mousse f

most ['mo:st] adj 1 : la plupart de 2 **(the) ~** : le plus — ~ adv : plus — ~ n : plus m — ~ pron : la plupart — **mostly** ['mo:stli] adv 1 MAINLY : principalement, surtout 2 USUALLY : normalement

motel [mo'tɛl] n : motel m

moth ['mɔθ] n : papillon m de nuit, mite f

mother ['mʌðər] n : mère f — ~ vt 1 : s'occuper de 2 SPOIL : dorloter — **motherhood** ['mʌðərˌhʊd] n : maternité f — **mother–in–law** ['mʌðərɪnˌlɔ] n, pl **mothers–in–law** : belle-mère f — **motherly** ['mʌðərli] adj : maternel — **mother–of–pearl** [ˌmʌðərəv'pərl] n : nacre f

motif [mo'ti:f] n : motif m

motion ['mo:ʃən] n 1 : mouvement m 2 PROPOSAL : motion f 3 **set in ~** : mettre en marche — ~ vi **~ to** : faire signe à — **motionless** ['mo:ʃənləs] adj : immobile — **motion picture** n : film m

motive ['mo:t̬ɪv] n : motif m — **motivate** ['mo:t̬əˌveɪt] vt **-vated; -vating** : motiver — **motivation** [ˌmo:t̬ə'veɪʃən] n : motivation f

motor ['mo:t̬ər] n : moteur m — **motorbike** ['mo:t̬ərˌbaɪk] n : moto f — **motorboat** ['mo:t̬ərˌbo:t] n : canot m à moteur — **motorcycle** ['mo:t̬ərˌsaɪkəl] n : motocyclette f, moto f — **motorcyclist** ['mo:t̬ərˌsaɪkəlɪst] n : motocycliste mf — **motorist** ['mo:t̬ərɪst] n : automobiliste mf

motto ['mɑt̬o:] n, pl **-toes** : devise f

mould ['mo:ld] → **mold**

mound ['maʊnd] n 1 PILE : tas m 2 HILL : monticule m

mount1 ['maʊnt] n 1 HORSE : monture f 2 SUPPORT : support m — ~ vt : monter sur (un cheval, etc.)

mount2 n HILL : mont m — **mountain** ['maʊntən] n : montagne f — **mountainous** ['maʊnt'nəs] adj : montagneux

mourn ['morn] vt **~ for s.o.** : pleurer qqn — vi : porter le deuil — **mournful** ['mornfəl] adj : triste — **mourning** ['mornɪŋ] n : deuil m

mouse ['maʊs] n, pl **mice** ['maɪs] : souris f — **mousetrap** ['maʊsˌtræp] n : souricière f

moustache ['mʌˌstæʃ, mə'stæʃ] → **mustache**

mouth ['maʊθ] n : bouche f (d'une personne, etc.), gueule f (d'un animal) — **mouthful** ['maʊθˌfʊl] n : bouchée f — **mouthpiece** ['maʊθˌpi:s] n : bec m, embouchure f (d'un instrument de musique)

move ['mu:v] v **moved; moving** vi 1 GO : aller 2 RELOCATE : déménager 3 STIR : bouger 4 ACT : agir — vt 1 : déplacer 2 AFFECT : émouvoir 3 TRANSPORT : transporter 4 PROPOSE : proposer — ~ n 1 MOVEMENT : mouvement m 2 RELOCATION : déménagement m 3 STEP : pas m, étape m — **movable** or **moveable** ['mu:vəbəl] adj : mobile — **movement** ['mu:vmənt] n : mouvement m

movie ['mu:vi] n 1 : film m 2 **~s** npl : cinéma m

mow ['mo:] vt **mowed; mowed** or **mown** ['mo:n]; **mowing** : tondre — **mower** ['mo:ər] → **lawn mower**

Mr. ['mɪstər] n, pl **Messrs.** ['mɛsərz] : Monsieur m

Mrs. ['mɪsəz, -səs, esp South 'mɪzəz, -zəs] n, pl **Mesdames** [meɪ'dɑm, -'dæm] : Madame f

Ms. ['mɪz] n : Madame f, Mademoiselle f

much ['mʌʧ] adj **more; most** : beaucoup de — ~ adv **more** ['mor]; **most** ['mo:st] 1 : beaucoup 2 **as ~** : autant 3 **how ~?** : combien? 4 **too ~** : trop — ~ pron : beaucoup

muck ['mʌk] n : saleté f

mucus ['mju:kəs] n : mucus m

mud ['mʌd] n : boue f, bouette f Can fam

muddle ['mʌdəl] v **-dled; -dling** vt 1 CONFUSE : confondre 2 JUMBLE : embrouiller — vi **~ through** : se tirer d'affaire — ~ n : désordre m, fouillis m

muddy ['mʌdi] adj **-dier; -est** : boueux

muffin ['mʌfən] n : muffin m Can

muffle ['mʌfəl] vt **muffled; muffling** : étouffer (des sons) — **muffler** ['mʌflər] n : silencieux m (d'un véhicule)

mug ['mʌg] n CUP : tasse f — ~ vt

mugged; mugging : agresser, attaquer — **mugger** ['mʌgər] *n* : agresseur *m*

muggy ['mʌgi] *adj* **-gier; -est** : lourd et humide

mule ['mju:l] *n* : mule *f*, mulet *m*

mull ['mʌl] *vt or* ~ **over** : réfléchir sur

multicolored ['mʌlti,kʌlərd, 'mʌl,taɪ-] *adj* : multicolore

multimedia [,mʌlti'mi:diə, ,mʌl,taɪ-] *adj* : multimédia

multinational [,mʌlti'næʃənəl, ,mʌl,taɪ-] *adj* : multinational

multiple ['mʌltəpəl] *adj* : multiple — ~ *n* : multiple *m* — **multiplication** [,mʌltəplə'keɪʃən] *n* : multiplication *f* — **multiply** ['mʌltə,plaɪ] *v* **-plied; -plying** *vt* : multiplier — *vi* : se multiplier

multitude ['mʌltə,tu:d, -,tju:d] *n* : multitude *f*

mum ['mʌm] *adj* **keep** ~ : garder le silence

mumble ['mʌmbəl] *vi* **-bled; -bling** : marmonner

mummy ['mʌmi] *n, pl* **-mies** : momie *f*

mumps ['mʌmps] *ns & pl* : oreillons *mpl*

munch ['mʌntʃ] *v* : mâcher, mastiquer

mundane [,mʌn'deɪn, 'mʌn,-] *adj* : routinier, ordinaire

municipal [mjʊ'nɪsəpəl] *adj* : municipal — **municipality** [mjʊ,nɪsə'pæləti] *n, pl* **-ties** : municipalité *f*

munitions [mjʊ'nɪʃənz] *npl* : munitions *fpl*

mural ['mjʊrəl] *n* : peinture *f* murale

murder ['mərdər] *n* : meurtre *m* — ~ *vt* : assassiner — **murderer** ['mərdərər] *n* : meurtrier *m*, -trière *f*; assassin *m* — **murderous** ['mərdərəs] *adj* : meurtrier

murky ['mərki] *adj* **murkier; -est** : obscur, sombre

murmur ['mərmər] *n* : murmure *m* — ~ *v* : murmurer

muscle ['mʌsəl] *n* : muscle *m* — ~ *vi* **-cled; -cling** *or* ~ **in** : s'ingérer avec force dans — **muscular** ['mʌskjələr] *adj* **1** : musculaire **2** STRONG : musclé

muse[1] ['mju:z] *n* : muse *f*

muse[2] *vi* **mused; musing** : méditer

museum [mjʊ'zi:əm] *n* : musée *m*

mushroom ['mʌʃ,ru:m, -,rʊm] *n* : champignon *m* — ~ *vi* : proliférer, se multiplier

mushy ['mʌʃi] *adj* **mushier; -est** **1** SOFT : mou **2** SENTIMENTAL : mièvre

music ['mju:zɪk] *n* : musique *f* — **musical** ['mju:zɪkəl] *adj* : musical — ~ *n* : comédie *f* musicale — **musician** [mjʊ'zɪʃən] *n* : musicien *m*, -cienne *f*

musket ['mʌskət] *n* : mousquet *m*

Muslim ['mʌzləm, 'mʊs-, 'mʊz-] *adj* : musulman — ~ *n* : musulman *m*, -mane *f*

muslin ['mʌzlən] *n* : mousseline *f*

mussel ['mʌsəl] *n* : moule *f*

must ['mʌst] *v aux* **1** : devoir **2 she ~ try** : elle doit essayer **3 you ~ decide** : il faut que tu te décides — ~ *n* : nécessité *f*

mustache ['mʌs,tæʃ, mʌ'stæʃ] *n* : moustache *f*

mustard ['mʌstərd] *n* : moutarde *f*

muster ['mʌstər] *vt* : rassembler, réunir

musty ['mʌsti] *adj* **mustier; -est** : qui sent le renfermé

mute ['mju:t] *adj* **muter; mutest** : muet — ~ *n* : muet *m*, muette *f*

mutilate ['mju:tə,leɪt] *vt* **-lated; -lating** : mutiler

mutiny ['mju:təni] *n, pl* **-nies** : mutinerie *f* — ~ *vi* **-nied; -nying** : se mutiner

mutter ['mʌtər] *vi* : marmonner

mutton ['mʌtən] *n* : viande *f* de mouton

mutual ['mju:tʃʊəl] *adj* **1** : mutuel **2** COMMON : commun — **mutually** ['mju:tʃʊəli, -tʃəli] *adv* : mutuellement

muzzle ['mʌzəl] *n* **1** SNOUT : museau *m* **2** : muselière *f* (pour un chien, etc.) **3** : gueule *f* (d'une arme à feu) — ~ *vt* **-zled; -zling** : museler

my ['maɪ] *adj* : mon, ma, mes

myopia [maɪ'o:piə] *n* : myopie *f* — **myopic** [maɪ'o:pɪk, -'ɑ-] *adj* : myope

myself [maɪ'sɛlf] *pron* **1** (*reflexive*) : me **2** (*emphatic*) : moi aussi **3 by ~** : tout seul

mystery ['mɪstəri] *n, pl* **-teries** : mystère *m* — **mysterious** [mɪ'stɪriəs] *adj* : mystérieux

mystic ['mɪstɪk] *adj or* **mystical** ['mɪstɪkəl] : mystique

mystify ['mɪstə,faɪ] *vt* **-fied; -fying** : rendre perplexe

myth ['mɪθ] *n* : mythe *m* — **mythical** ['mɪθɪkəl] *adj* : mythique

N

n ['ɛn] *n, pl* **n's** *or* **ns** ['ɛnz] : n *m*, quatorzième lettre de l'alphabet

nab ['næb] *vt* **nabbed; nabbing** : pincer *fam*

nag ['næg] *v* **nagged; nagging** *vi* COMPLAIN : se plaindre — *vt* : harceler — **nagging** ['nægɪŋ] *adj* : persistant

nail ['neɪl] *n* **1** : clou *m* **2** FINGERNAIL : ongle *m* — ~ *vt or* ~ **down** : clouer — **nail file** *n* : lime *f* à ongles — **nail polish** *n* : vernis *m* à ongles

naive *or* **naïve** [nɑ'i:v] *adj* **-iver; -est** : naïf

naked ['neɪkəd] *adj* : nu — **nakedness** ['neɪkədnəs] *n* : nudité *f*

name ['neɪm] *n* **1** : nom *m* **2** REPUTATION : réputation *f* **3 what is your ~ ?** : comment vous appelez-vous? — ~ *vt* **named; naming 1** : nommer **2** : fixer (une date, un prix, etc.) — **nameless** ['neɪmləs] *adj* : sans nom, anonyme — **namely** ['neɪmli] *adv* : c'est-à-dire, savoir — **namesake** ['neɪm,seɪk] *n* : homonyme *m*

nap ['næp] *vi* **napped; napping** : faire un somme — ~ *n* : somme *m*, sieste *f*

nape ['neɪp, 'næp] *n* : nuque *f*

napkin ['næpkən] *n* **1** : serviette *f* **2** → **sanitary napkin**

narcotic [nɑr'kɑtɪk] *n* **1** : narcotique *m* (en pharmacie) **2** DRUG : stupéfiant *m*

narrate ['nær,eɪt] *vt* **narrated; narrating** : raconter, narrer — **narration** [næ'reɪʃən] *n* : narration *f* — **narrative** ['nærətɪv] *n* : récit *m* — **narrator** ['nær,eɪtər] *n* : narrateur *m*, -trice *f*

narrow ['nær,o:] *adj* **1** : étroit **2 by a ~ margin** : de justesse — ~ *vt* : limiter, réduire — *vi* : se rétrécir — **narrowly** ['næroli] *adv* : de justesse, de peu — **narrow–minded** [,næro'maɪndəd] *adj* : étroit d'esprit

nasal ['neɪzəl] *adj* : nasal

nasty ['næsti] *adj* **-tier; -est 1** MEAN : mauvais, méchant **2** UNPLEASANT : désagréable, sale **3** SERIOUS : grave — **nastiness** ['næstinəs] *n* : méchanceté *f*

nation ['neɪʃən] *n* : pays *m*, nation *f* — **national** ['næʃənəl] *adj* : national — **nationalism** ['næʃənə,lɪzəm] *n* : nationalisme *m* — **nationality** [,næʃə'næləti] *n, pl* **-ties** : nationalité *f* — **nationalize** ['næʃənə,laɪz] *vt* **-ized; -izing** : nationaliser — **nationwide** ['neɪʃən'waɪd] *adj* : dans tout le pays

native ['neɪtɪv] *adj* **1** : natal (se dit d'un pays, etc.) **2** INNATE : inné **3 ~ language** : langue *f* maternelle — ~ *n* **1** : natif *m*, -tive *f* **2 be a ~ of** : être originaire de — **Native American** *adj* : amérindien *m* — **nativity** [nə'tɪvəti, neɪ-] *n, pl* **-ties** : nativité *f*

natural ['nætʃərəl] *adj* **1** : naturel **2** INBORN : né, inné — **naturalize** ['nætʃərə,laɪz] *vt* **-ized; -izing** : naturaliser — **naturally** ['nætʃərəli] *adv* **1** : naturellement **2** OF COURSE : bien sûr — **nature** ['neɪtʃər] *n* : nature *f*

naught ['nɔt] *n* **1** NOTHING : rien *m* **2** ZERO : zéro *m*

naughty ['nɔti] *adj* **-tier; -est** : méchant, vilain

nausea ['nɔziə, 'nɔʃə] *n* : nausée *f* — **nauseating** ['nɔzi,eɪtɪŋ] *adj* : écœurant, nauséabond — **nauseous** ['nɔʃəs, -ziəs] *adj* : écœuré

nautical ['nɔtɪkəl] *adj* : nautique

naval ['neɪvəl] *adj* : naval

nave ['neɪv] *n* : nef *f* (d'une église)

navel ['neɪvəl] *n* : nombril *m*

navigate ['nævə,geɪt] *v* **-gated; -gating** *vi* : naviguer — *vt* : naviguer sur (la mer, etc.), piloter (un avion), gouverner (un bateau) — **navigable** ['nævɪgəbəl] *adj* : navigable — **navigation** [,nævə'geɪʃən] *n* : navigation *f* — **navigator** ['nævə,geɪtər] *n* : navigateur *m*, -trice *f*

navy ['neɪvi] *n, pl* **-vies** : marine *f* — **navy blue** *adj* : bleu marine

near ['nɪr] *adv* **1** : près **2 nowhere ~ enough** : loin d'être suffisant — ~ *prep* : près de — ~ *adj* : proche — ~ *vt* : approcher de — **nearby** [nɪr'baɪ, 'nɪr,baɪ] *adv* : tout près — ~ *adj* : voisin, proche — **nearly** ['nɪrli] *adv* : presque — **nearsighted** ['nɪr,saɪtəd] *adj* : myope

neat ['ni:t] *adj* **1** TIDY : soigné, net **2** ORDERLY : bien rangé (se dit d'une chambre, etc.) **3** SKILLFUL : habile — **neatly** ['ni:tli] *adv* **1** : soigneusement **2** SKILLFULLY : habilement — **neatness** ['ni:tnəs] *n* : ordre *m*, propreté *f*

nebulous ['nɛbjələs] *adj* : nébuleux

necessary ['nɛsə,sɛri] *adj* : nécessaire — **necessarily** [,nɛsə'sɛrəli] *adv* : nécessairement, forcément — **necessitate** [nɪ'sɛsə,teɪt] *vt* **-tated; -tating** : nécessiter, exiger — **necessity** [nɪ'sɛsəti] *n, pl* **-ties 1** : nécessité *f* **2 necessities** *npl* : choses *fpl* essentielles

neck ['nɛk] *n* **1** : cou *m* **2** COLLAR : col *m*, encolure *f* **3** : col *m*, goulot *m* (d'une bouteille) — **necklace** ['nɛkləs] *n* : collier *m* — **necktie** ['nɛk,taɪ] *n* : cravate *f*

nectar ['nɛktər] *n* : nectar *m*

nectarine [,nɛktə'ri:n] *n* : nectarine *f*

need ['ni:d] *n* **1** : besoin *m* **2 if ~ be** : si nécessaire, s'il le faut — ~ *vt* **1** : avoir besoin de **2 ~ to** : devoir — *v aux* **not ~ to** : ne pas être obligé de

needle ['ni:dəl] *n* : aiguille *f* — ~ *vt* **-dled; -dling** : agacer

needless ['ni:dləs] *adj* **1** : inutile **2 ~ to say** : il va sans dire

needlework ['ni:dəl,wərk] *n* : travaux *mpl* d'aiguille

needy ['ni:di:] *adj* **needier; -est** : dans le besoin

negative ['nɛgətɪv] *adj* : négatif — ~ *n* **1** : négatif *m* (en photographie) **2** : négation *f* (en grammaire)

neglect [nɪ'glɛkt] *vt* : négliger — ~ *n* : négligence *f*

negligee [,nɛglə'ʒeɪ] *n* : négligé *m*

negligence ['nɛglɪdʒənts] *n* : négligence *f* — **negligent** ['nɛglɪdʒənt] *adj* : négligent

negligible ['nɛglɪdʒəbəl] *adj* : négligeable

negotiate [nɪ'go:ʃi,eɪt] *v* **-ated; -ating** : négocier — **negotiable** [nɪ'go:ʃəbəl, -ʃiə-] *adj* : négociable — **negotiation** [nɪ,goʃi'eɪʃən, -si'eɪ-] *n* : négociation *f* — **negotiator** [nɪ'go:ʃi,eɪtər, -si,eɪ-] *n* : négociateur *m*, -trice *f*

Negro ['ni:,gro:] *n, pl* **-groes** *sometimes considered offensive* : nègre *m*, négresse *f*

neigh ['neɪ] *vi* : hennir — ~ *n* : hennissment *m*

neighbor *or Brit* **neighbour** ['neɪbər] *n* : voisin *m*, -sine *f* — ~ *vt* : avoisiner — *vi* **~ on** : être voisin de — **neighborhood** *or Brit* **neighbourhood** ['neɪbər,hʊd] *n* **1** : quartier *m*, voisinage *m* **2 in the ~ of** : environ — **neighborly** *or Brit* **neighbourly** ['neɪbərli] *adj* : amical

neither ['ni:ðər, 'naɪ-] *conj* **1 ~ . . . nor** : ni . . . ni **2 ~ do I** : moi non plus — ~ *pron* : aucun — ~ *adj* : aucun (des deux)

neon ['ni:,ɑn] *n* : néon *m*

nephew ['nɛ,fju:, *chiefly Brit* 'nɛ,vju:] *n* : neveu *m*

Neptune ['nɛp,tu:n, -,tju:n] *n* : Neptune *f*

nerve ['nərv] *n* **1** : nerf *m* **2** COURAGE : courage *m* **3** GALL : culot *m fam*, toupet *m fam* **4 ~s** *npl* JITTERS : nerfs *mpl* — **nervous** ['nərvəs] *adj* : nerveux — **nervousness** ['nərvəsnəs] *n* : nervosité *f* — **nervy** ['nərvi] *adj* **nervier; -est** : effronté

nest ['nɛst] *n* : nid *m* — ~ *vi* : nicher

nestle ['nɛsəl] *vi* **-tled; -tling** : se blottir

net[1] ['nɛt] *n* : filet *m* — ~ *vt* **netted; netting** : prendre au filet (des poissons)

net[2] *adj* : net — ~ *vt* **netted; netting** YIELD : rapporter

nettle ['nɛtəl] *n* : ortie *f*

network ['nɛt,wərk] *n* : réseau *m*

neurology [nʊ'rɑlədʒi, njʊ-] *n* : neurologie *f*

neurosis [nʊ'ro:sɪs, njʊ-] *n, pl* **-roses** [-,si:z] : névrose *f* — **neurotic** [nʊ'rɑtɪk, njʊ-] *adj* : névrosé

neuter ['nu:tər, 'nju:-] *adj* : neutre — ~ *vt* : châtrer

neutral ['nu:trəl, 'nju:-] *adj* : neutre — ~ *n* : point *m* mort, neutre *m Can* — **neutralize** ['nu:trə,laɪz, 'nju:-] *vt* **-ized; -izing** : neutraliser — **neutrality** [nu:'træləti, nju:-] *n* : neutralité *f*

neutron ['nu:,trɑn, 'nju:-] *n* : neutron *m*

never ['nɛvər] *adv* **1** : jamais **2 I ~ said a word** : je n'ai rien dit — **nevermore** [,nɛvər'mor] *adv* : plus jamais, jamais plus — **nevertheless** [,nɛvərðə'lɛs] *adv* : néanmoins

new ['nu:, 'nju:] *adj* : neuf, nouveau — **newborn** ['nu:,bɔrn, 'nju:-] *adj* : nouveau-né — **newcomer** ['nu:,kʌmər, 'nju:-] *n* : nouveau venu *m*, nouvelle venue *f* — **newly** ['nu:li, 'nju:-] *adv* : récemment — **newlywed** ['nu:li,wɛd, 'nju:-] *n* : nouveau marié *m*, nouvelle mariée *f* — **news** ['nu:z, 'nju:z] *n* : nouvelles *fpl* — **newscast** ['nu:z,kæst, 'nju:z-] *n* : journal *m* télévisé — **newscaster** ['nu:z,kæstər, 'nju:z-] *n* : présentateur *m*, -trice *f* — **newsgroup** ['nu:z,gru:p, 'nju:z-] *n* : forum *m* (en informatique) — **newsletter** ['nu:z,lɛtər, 'nju:z-] *n* : bulletin *m* — **newspaper** ['nu:z,peɪpər, 'nju:z-] *n* : journal *m* — **newsstand** ['nu:z,stænd, 'nju:z-] *n* : kiosque *m* à journaux

newt ['nu:t, 'nju:t] *n* : triton *m*

New Year's Day *n* : jour *m* de l'An

next ['nɛkst] *adj* **1** : prochain **2** FOLLOWING : suivant — ~ *adv* **1** : la prochaine fois **2** AFTERWARD : ensuite **3** NOW : maintenant — **next door** ['nɛkst'dor] *adv* : à côté — **next–door** *adj* : voisin, d'à côté — **next to** *prep* **1** BESIDE : à côté de **2 ~ nothing** : presque rien

nib ['nɪb] *n* : bec *m* (d'un stylo)

nibble ['nɪbəl] *vt* **-bled; -bling** : grignoter

nice ['naɪs] *adj* **nicer; nicest 1** PLEASANT : bon, agréable **2** KIND : gentil, aimable — **nicely** ['naɪsli] *adv* **1** WELL : bien **2** KINDLY : gentiment — **niceness** ['naɪsnəs] *n* : gentillesse *f* — **niceties** ['naɪsətiz] *npl* : subtilités *fpl*

niche ['nɪtʃ] *n* **1** : niche *f* **2 find one's ~** : trouver sa voie

nick ['nɪk] *n* **1** NOTCH : entaille *f*, encoche *f* **2 in the ~ of time** : juste à temps — ~ *vt* : faire une entaille dans

nickel ['nɪkəl] *n* **1** : nickel *m* (métal) **2** : pièce *f* de cinq cents

nickname ['nɪk,neɪm] *n* : surnom *m* — ~ *vt* : surnommer

nicotine ['nɪkə,ti:n] *n* : nicotine *f*

niece ['ni:s] *n* : nièce *f*

niggling ['nɪgəlɪŋ] *adj* **1** PETTY : insignifiant **2** NAGGING : persistant

night ['naɪt] *n* **1** : nuit *f*, soir *m* **2 at ~** : le soir **3 tomorrow ~** : demain soir — ~ *adj* : de nuit — **nightclub** ['naɪt,klʌb] *n* : boîte *f* de nuit — **nightfall** ['naɪt,fɔl] *n* : tombée *f* de la nuit — **nightgown** ['naɪt,gaʊn] *n* : chemise *f* de nuit, robe *f* de nuit *Can* — **nightingale** ['naɪtən,geɪl, 'naɪtɪŋ-] *n* : rossignol *m* — **nightly** ['naɪtli] *adv & adj* : (de) tous les soirs — **nightmare** ['naɪt,mær] *n* : cauchemar *m* — **nighttime** ['naɪt,taɪm] *n* : nuit *f*

nil ['nɪl] *n* NOTHING : zéro *m* — ~ *adj* : nul

nimble ['nɪmbəl] *adj* **-bler; -blest** : agile

nine ['naɪn] *n* : neuf *m* — ~ *adj* : neuf — **nine hundred** *adj* : neuf cents — **nineteen** [naɪn'ti:n] *n* : dix-neuf *m* — ~ *adj* : dix-neuf — **nineteenth** [naɪn'ti:nθ] *n* **1** : dix-neuvième *mf* **2 January ~** : le dix-neuf janvier — ~ *adj* : dix-neuvième — **ninetieth** ['naɪntiəθ] *n* : quatre-vingt-dixième *mf* — ~ *adj* : quatre-vingt-dixième — **ninety** ['naɪnti] *n, pl* **-ties** : quatre-vingt-dix *m* — **ninth** ['naɪnθ] *n* **1** : neuvième *mf* **2 March ~** : le neuf mars — ~ *adj* : neuvième

nip ['nɪp] *vt* **nipped; nipping 1** BITE : mordre **2** PINCH : pincer — ~ *n* **1** BITE : morsure *f* **2** PINCH : pincement *m* **3 there's a ~ in the air** : il fait frisquet — **nippy** ['nɪpi] *adj* **-pier; -est** : frisquet

nipple ['nɪpəl] *n* **1** : mamelon *m* (d'une femme) **2** : tétine *f* (d'un biberon)

nitrogen ['naɪtrədʒən] *n* : azote *m*

nitwit ['nɪt,wɪt] *n* : imbécile *mf*

no ['no:] *adv* **1** : non **2 ~ better** : pas mieux **3 ~ bigger** : pas plus grand **4 ~ longer** : ne … plus — ~ *adj* **1** : pas de, aucun **2 ~ parking** : stationnement interdit **3 ~ smoking** : défense de fumer — ~ *n, pl* **noes** *or* **nos** ['no:z] : non *m*

noble ['nobəl] *adj* **-bler; -blest** : noble — ~ *n* : noble *mf* — **nobility** [no'bɪləti] *n* : noblesse *f*

nobody ['no:bədi, -,bɑdi] *pron* : personne

nocturnal [nɑk'tərnəl] *adj* : nocturne

nod ['nɑd] *v* **nodded; nodding** *vi* **1** : faire un signe de la tête **2** *or* **~ off** : s'endormir — *vt* **~ one's head** : faire un signe de la tête — ~ *n* : signe *m* de la tête

noise ['nɔɪz] *n* : bruit *m* — **noisily** ['nɔɪzəli] *adv* : bruyamment — **noisy** ['nɔɪzi] *adj* **noisier; -est** : bruyant

nomad ['no:,mæd] *n* : nomade *mf* — **nomadic** [no'mædɪk] *adj* : nomade

nominal ['nɑmənəl] *adj* : nominal

nominate ['nɑmə,neɪt] *vt* **-nated; -nating 1** PROPOSE : proposer **2** APPOINT : nommer — **nomination** [,nɑmə'neɪʃən] *n* : nomination *f*

nonalcoholic [,nɑn,ælkə'hɔlɪk] *adj* : non alcoolisé

nonchalant [,nɑnʃə'lɑnt] *adj* : nonchalant — **nonchalance** [,nɑnʃə'lɑnts] *n* : nonchalance *f*

noncommissioned officer [,nɑnkə'mɪʃənd] *n* : sous-officier *m*

noncommittal [,nɑnkə'mɪtəl] *adj* : évasif

nondescript [,nɑndɪ'skrɪpt] *adj* : quelconque

none ['nʌn] *pron* : aucun, aucune — ~ *adv* **1 ~ too** : pas tellement **2 ~ the worse** : pas plus mal

nonentity [,nɑn'ɛntəti] *n, pl* **-ties** : être *m* insignifiant

nonetheless [,nʌnðə'lɛs] *adv* : néanmoins

nonexistent [,nɑnɪg'zɪstənt] *adj* : inexistant

nonfat [,nɑn'fæt] *adj* : sans matière grasse

nonfiction [,nɑn'fɪkʃən] *n* : œuvres *fpl* non romanesques

nonprofit [,nɑn'prɑfət] *adj* : à but non lucratif

nonsense ['nɑn,sɛnts, -sənts] *n* : absurdités *fpl*, sottises *fpl* — **nonsensical** [nɑn'sɛntsɪkəl] *adj* : absurde

nonstop [,nɑn'stɑp] *adj* **1** : sans arrêt **2 ~ flight** : vol *m* direct

noodle ['nu:dəl] *n* : nouille *f*

nook ['nʊk] *n* : coin *m*, recoin *m*

noon ['nu:n] *n* : midi *m* — ~ *adj* : de midi

no one *pron* : personne *f*

noose ['nu:s] *n* : nœud *m* coulant

nor ['nɔr] *conj* **1** : ni **2 ~ can I** : moi non plus

norm ['nɔrm] *n* : norme *f* — **normal** ['nɔrməl] *adj* : normal — **normality** [nɔr'mæləti] *n* : normalité *f* — **normally** ['nɔrməli] *adv* : normalement

north ['nɔrθ] *adv* : au nord, vers le nord — ~ *adj* : nord, du nord — ~ *n* **1** : nord *m* **2 the North** : le Nord — **North American** *adj* : nord-américain — ~ *n* : Nord-Américain *m*, -caine *f* — **northeast** [nɔrθ'i:st] *adv* : au nord-est, vers le nord-est — ~ *adj* : nord-est, du nord-est — ~ *n* : nord-est *m* — **northeastern** [nɔrθ'i:stərn] *adj* : nord-est, du nord-est — **northerly** ['nɔrðərli] *adj* : du nord — **northern** ['nɔrðərn] *adj* : nord, du nord — **northwest** [nɔrθ'wɛst] *adv* : au nord-ouest, vers le nord-ouest — ~ *adj* : nord-ouest, du nord-ouest — ~ *n* : nord-ouest m — **northwestern** [nɔr'θwɛstərn] *adj* : nord-ouest, du nord-ouest

Norwegian [nɔr'wi:ʤən] *adj* : norvégien

nose ['no:z] *n* 1 : nez *m* 2 **blow one's ~** : se moucher — **~** *vi* **nosed; nosing** *or* **~ around** : fouiner *fam* — **nosebleed** ['no:z,bli:d] *n* : saignement *m* de nez — **nosedive** ['no:z,daɪv] *n* : piqué *m*

nostalgia [nɑ'stælʤə, nə-] *n* : nostalgie *f* — **nostalgic** [-ʤɪk] *adj* : nostalgique

nostril ['nɑstrəl] *n* : narine *f* (d'une personne), naseau *m* (d'un animal)

nosy *or* **nosey** ['no:zi] *adj* **nosier; -est** : curieux, fureteur

not ['nɑt] *adv* 1 (*used to form a negative*) : ne...pas 2 (*used to replace a negative clause*) : non, pas 3 **~ at all** : pas du tout 4 **I hope ~** : j'espère que non

notable ['no:t̬əbəl] *adj* : notable — **~** *n* : notable *m* — **notably** ['no:t̬əbli] *adv* : notamment

notary public ['no:t̬əri] *n, pl* **notaries public** *or* **notary publics** : notaire *m*

notation [no'teɪʃən] *n* : notation *f*

notch ['nɑʧ] *n* : entaille *f*, encoche *f*

note ['no:t] *vt* **noted; noting** 1 NOTICE : remarquer 2 *or* **~ down** : noter — **~** *n* 1 : note *f* 2 LETTER : mot *m* 3 **an artist of ~** : un artiste de renom — **notebook** ['no:t,bʊk] *n* : carnet *m* — **noted** ['no:t̬əd] *adj* : éminent, célèbre — **noteworthy** ['no:t,wərði] *adj* : notable, remarquable

nothing ['nʌθɪŋ] *pron* : rien — **~** *adv* **~ like** : pas du tout comme — **~** *n* 1 TRIFLE : rien *m* 2 ZERO : zéro *m*

notice ['no:t̬ɪs] *n* 1 : avis *m*, annonce *f* 2 **be given one's ~** : recevoir son congé 3 **take ~ of** : faire attention à — **~** *vt* **-ticed; -ticing** : s'apercevoir de, remarquer — **noticeable** ['no:t̬ɪsəbəl] *adj* : visible

notify ['no:t̬ə,faɪ] *vt* **-fied; -fying** : aviser, notifier — **notification** [,no:t̬əfə'keɪʃən] *n* : avis *m*

notion ['no:ʃən] *n* 1 : notion *f*, idée *f* 2 **~s** *npl* : mercerie *f*

notorious [no'to:riəs] *adj* : notoire — **notoriety** [,no:t̬ə'raɪət̬i] *n, pl* **-ties** : notoriété *f*

notwithstanding [,nɑtwɪθ'stændɪŋ, -wɪð-] *adv* : néanmoins — **~** *prep* : malgré

nougat ['nu:gət] *n* : nougat *m*

nought ['nɔt, 'nɑt] → **naught**

noun ['naʊn] *n* : nom *m*, substantif *m*

nourish ['nərɪʃ] *vt* : nourrir — **nourishing** ['nərɪʃɪŋ] *adj* : nourrissant — **nourishment** ['nərɪʃmənt] *n* : nourriture *f*, alimentation *f*

novel ['nɑvəl] *adj* : nouveau, original — **~** *n* : roman *m* — **novelist** ['nɑvəlɪst] *n* : romancier *m*, -cière *f* — **novelty** ['nɑvəlti] *n, pl* **-ties** : nouveauté *f*

November [no'vɛmbər] *n* : novembre *m*

novice ['nɑvɪs] *n* : novice *mf*; débutant *m*, -tante *f*

now ['naʊ] *adv* 1 : maintenant 2 **~ and then** : de temps à autre — **~** *conj* **~ that** : maintenant que — **~** *n* 1 **by ~** : déjà 2 **for ~** : pour le moment 3 **up until ~** : jusqu'à maintenant — **nowadays** ['naʊə,deɪz] *adv* : de nos jours

nowhere ['no:,hwɛr] *adv* 1 : nulle part 2 **~ near** : loin de

noxious ['nɑkʃəs] *adj* : nocif

nozzle ['nɑzəl] *n* : ajutage *m*

nuance ['nu:,ɑnts, 'nju:-] *n* : nuance *f*

nucleus ['nu:kliəs, 'nju:-] *n, pl* **-clei** [-kli,aɪ] : noyau *m* — **nuclear** ['nu:kliər, 'nju:-] *adj* : nucléaire

nude ['nu:d, 'nju:d] *adj* **nuder; nudest** : nu — **~** *n* : nu *m*

nudge ['nʌʤ] *vt* **nudged; nudging** : donner un coup de coude à — **~** *n* : coup *m* de coude

nudity ['nu:dət̬i, 'nju:-] *n* : nudité *f*

nugget ['nʌgət] *n* : pépite *f*

nuisance ['nu:sənts, 'nju:-] *n* 1 ANNOYANCE : ennui *m* 2 PEST : peste *f*

null ['nʌl] *adj* **~ and void** : nul et non avenu

numb ['nʌm] *adj* 1 : engourdi 2 **~ with fear** : paralysé par la peur — **~** *vt* : engourdir

number ['nʌmbər] *n* 1 : nombre *m*, numéro *m* 2 NUMERAL : chiffre *m* 3 **a ~ of** : un certain nombre de — **~** *vt* 1 : numéroter 2 INCLUDE : compter — **numeral** ['nu:mərəl, 'nju:-] *n* : chiffre *m* — **numerical** [nʊ'mɛrɪkəl, nyʊ-] *adj* : numérique — **numerous** ['nu:mərəs, 'nju:-] *adj* : nombreux

nun ['nʌn] *n* : religieuse *f*

nuptial ['nʌpʃəl] *adj* : nuptial

nurse ['nərs] *n* : infirmier *m*, -mière *f* — **~** *v* **nursed; nursing** *vt* 1 : soigner (un malade) 2 BREAST-FEED : allaiter — *vi* SUCKLE : téter — **nursery** ['nərsəri] *n, pl* **-eries** 1 : crèche *f France*, garderie *f Can* 2 : pépinière *f* (pour les plantes) — **nursing home** *n* : maison *f* de retraite, centre *m* d'accueil *Can*

nurture ['nərʧər] *vt* **-tured; -turing** 1 : élever 2 : nourrir (des espoirs, etc.)

nut ['nʌt] *n* 1 : noix *f* 2 LUNATIC : fou *m*, folle *f* 3 ENTHUSIAST : mordu *m*, -due *f fam* 4 **~s and bolts** : des écrous et des boulons — **nutcracker** ['nʌt,krækər] *n* : casse-noix *m* — **nutmeg** ['nʌt,mɛg] *n* : muscade *f*

nutrient ['nu:triənt, 'nju:-] *n* : substance *f* nutritive — **nutrition** [nʊ'trɪʃən, njʊ-] *n* : nutrition *f*, alimentation *f* — **nutritional** [nʊ'trɪʃənəl, njʊ-] *adj* : nutritif — **nutritious** [nʊ'trɪʃəs, njʊ-] *adj* : nourrissant, nutritif

nuts ['nʌts] *adj* : fou, cinglé *fam*

nutshell ['nʌt,ʃɛl] *n* 1 : coquille *f* de noix 2 **in a ~** : en un mot

nuzzle ['nʌzəl] *v* **-zled; -zling** *vt* : frotter son nez contre — *vi* : se blottir

nylon ['naɪ,lɑn] *n* 1 : nylon *m* 2 **~s** *npl* : bas *mpl* de nylon

nymph ['nɪmpf] *n* : nymphe *f*

O

o ['o:] *n, pl* **o's** *or* **os** ['o:z] 1 : o *m*, quinzième lettre de l'alphabet 2 ZERO : zéro *m*

O ['o:] → **oh**

oak ['o:k] *n, pl* **oaks** *or* **oak** : chêne *m*

oar ['or] *n* : rame *f*, aviron *m*

oasis [o'eɪsɪs] *n, pl* **oases** [-,si:z] : oasis *f*

oath ['o:θ] *n, pl* **oaths** ['o:ðz, 'o:θs] 1 : serment *m* 2 SWEARWORD : juron *m*

oats ['o:ts] *npl* : avoine *f* — **oatmeal** ['o:t,mi:l] *n* : farine *f* d'avoine

obedient [o'bi:diənt] *adj* : obéissant — **obedience** [o'bi:diənts] *n* : obéissance *f* — **obediently** [o'bi:diəntli] *adv* : docilement

obese [o'bi:s] *adj* : obèse — **obesity** [o'bi:sət̬i] *n* : obésité *f*

obey [o'beɪ] *v* **obeyed; obeying** *vt* : obéir à — *vi* : obéir

obituary [ə'bɪʧʊ,ɛri] *n, pl* **-aries** : nécrologie *f*

object ['ɑbʤɪkt] *n* 1 : objet *m* 2 AIM : objectif *m*, but *m* 3 : complément *m* d'objet (en grammaire) — **~** [əb'ʤɛkt] *vi* : protester, s'opposer — *vt* : objecter — **objection** [əb'ʤɛkʃən] *n* : objection *f* — **objectionable** [əb'ʤɛkʃənəbəl] *adj* : désagréable — **objective** [əb'ʤɛktɪv] *adj* : objectif — **~** *n* : objectif *m*

oblige [ə'blaɪʤ] *vt* **obliged; obliging** 1 : obliger 2 **be much ~d** : être très reconnaissant 3 **~ s.o.** : rendre service à qqn — **obligation** [,ɑblə'geɪʃən] *n* : obligation *f* — **obligatory** [ə'blɪgə,tori] *adj* : obligatoire — **obliging** [ə'blaɪʤɪŋ] *adj* : obligeant, aimable

oblique [o'bli:k] *adj* : oblique

obliterate [ə'blɪt̬ə,reɪt] *vt* **-ated; -ating** : effacer, détruire

oblivion [ə'blɪviən] *n* : oubli *m* — **oblivious** [ə'blɪviəs] *adj* : inconscient

oblong ['ɑ,blɔŋ] *adj* : oblong

obnoxious [ɑb'nɑkʃəs, əb-] *adj* : odieux

oboe ['o:,bo:] *n* : hautbois *m*

obscene [ɑb'si:n, əb-] *adj* : obscène — **obscenity** [ɑb'sɛnət̬i, əb-] *n, pl* **-ties** : obscénité *f*

obscure [ɑb'skjʊr, əb-] *vt* **-scured; -scuring** 1 DARKEN : obscurcir 2 HIDE : cacher — **~** *adj* : obscur — **obscurity** [əb'skjʊrət̬i, əb-] *n, pl* **-ties** : obscurité *f*

observe [əb'zərv] *vt* **-served; -serving** : observer — **observant** [əb'zərvənt] *adj* : observateur — **observation** [,ɑbsər'veɪʃən, -zər-] *n* : observation *f* — **observatory** [əb'zərvə,tori] *n, pl* **-ries** : observatoire *m* — **observer** [əb'zərvər] *n* : observateur *m*, -trice *f*

obsess [əb'sɛs] *vt* : obséder — **obsession** [ɑb'sɛʃən, əb-] *n* : obsession *f* — **obsessive** [ɑb'sɛsɪv, əb-] *adj* : obsessionnel, obsédant

obsolete [,ɑbsə'li:t, 'ɑbsə,-] *adj* : obsolète, démodé

obstacle ['ɑbstɪkəl] *n* : obstacle *m*

obstetrics [əb'stɛtrɪks] *ns & pl* : obstétrique *f*

obstinate ['ɑbstənət] *adj* : obstiné

obstruct [əb'strʌkt] *vt* 1 BLOCK : obstruer 2 HINDER : entraver — **obstruction** [əb'strʌkʃən] *n* : obstruction *f*

obtain [əb'teɪn] *vt* : obtenir

obtrusive [əb'tru:sɪv] *adj* : trop voyant (se dit des choses), importun (se dit des personnes)

obtuse [ɑb'tu:s, əb-, -'tju:s] *adj* : obtus

obvious ['ɑbviəs] *adj* : évident — **obviously** ['ɑbviəsli] *adv* 1 CLEARLY : manifestement 2 OF COURSE : évidemment, bien sûr

occasion [ə'keɪʒən] *n* 1 : occasion *f* 2 EVENT : événement *m* — **~** *vt* : occasionner, provoquer — **occasional** [ə'keɪʒənəl] *adj* : occasionnel — **occasionally** [ə'keɪʒənəli] *adv* : de temps en temps

occult [ə'kʌlt, 'ɑ,kʌlt] *adj* : occulte

occupy ['ɑkjə,paɪ] *vt* **-pied; -pying** 1 : occuper 2 **~ oneself with** : s'occuper de — **occupancy** ['ɑkjəpəntsi] *n, pl* **-cies** : occupation *f* — **occupant** ['ɑkjəpənt] *n* : occupant *m*, -pante *f* — **occupation** [,ɑkjə'peɪʃən] *n* 1 : occupation *f* 2 JOB : profession *f*, métier *m* — **occupational** [,ɑkjə'peɪʃənəl] *adj* 1 : professionnel 2 **~ hazard** : risque *m* du métier

occur [ə'kər] *vi* **occurred; occurring** 1 HAPPEN : avoir lieu, se produire, arriver 2 APPEAR : se trouver 3 **~ to s.o.** : venir à l'esprit de qqn — **occurrence** [ə'kərənts] *n* 1 EVENT : événement *m* 2 INSTANCE : cas *m*, apparition *f*

ocean ['o:ʃən] *n* : océan *m* — **oceanic** [,o:ʃi'ænɪk] *adj* : océanique

ocher *or* **ochre** ['o:kər] *n* : ocre *mf*

o'clock [ə'klɑk] *adv* 1 **at six ~** : à six heures 2 **it's ten ~** : il est dix heures

octagon ['ɑktə,gɑn] *n* : octogone *m*

octave ['ɑktɪv] *n* : octave *f*

October [ɑk'to:bər] *n* : octobre *m*

octopus ['ɑktə,pʊs, -pəs] *n, pl* **-puses** *or* **-pi** [-,paɪ] : pieuvre *f*

ocular ['ɑkjələr] *adj* : oculaire — **oculist** ['ɑkjəlɪst] *n* : oculiste *mf*

odd ['ɑd] *adj* 1 STRANGE : étrange, bizarre 2 : dépareillé (se dit d'une chaussette, etc.) 3 **~ jobs** : travaux *mpl* divers 4 **~ number** : nombre *m* impair 5 **a hundred ~ dollars** : cent dollars et quelques — **oddity** ['ɑdət̬i] *n, pl* **-ties** : étrangeté *f* — **oddly** ['ɑdli] *adv* : étrangement — **odds** ['ɑdz] *npl* 1 RATIO : cote *f* 2 CHANCES : chances *fpl* 3 **at ~s** : en conflit — **odds and ends** *npl* : objets *mpl* divers

ode ['o:d] *n* : ode *f*

odious ['o:diəs] *adj* : odieux

odor *or Brit* **odour** ['o:dər] *n* : odeur *f* — **odorless** *or Brit* **odourless** ['o:dərləs] *adj* : inodore

of ['ʌv, 'ɑv] *prep* 1 : de 2 **five minutes ~ ten** : dix heures moins cinq 3 **made ~ wood** : en bois 4 **the eighth ~ April** : le huit avril

off ['ɔf] *adv* 1 **be ~** LEAVE : s'en aller 2 **come ~** : se détacher 3 **cut ~** : couper 4 **day ~** : jour *m* de congé 5 **far ~** : éloigné 6 **~ and on** : par périodes 7 **take ~** REMOVE : enlever 8 **ten miles ~** : à dix milles d'ici 9 **three weeks ~** : en trois semaines — **~** *prep* 1 : de 2 **be ~ duty** : être libre 3 **be ~ the point** : ne pas être la question 4 **~ center** : mal centré — **~** *adj* 1 OUT : éteint, fermé 2 CANCELED : annulé 3 **on the ~ chance** : au cas où

offend [ə'fɛnd] *vt* : offenser — **offender** [ə'fɛndər] *n* : délinquant *m*, -quante *f*; coupable *mf* — **offense** *or* **offence** [ə'fɛnts, 'ɔ,fɛnts] *n* 1 INSULT : offense *f* 2 CRIME : délit *m* 3 : attaque *f* (aux sports) 4 **take ~** : s'offenser — **offensive** [ə'fɛntsɪv, 'ɔ,fɛnt-] *adj* : offensif — **~** *n* : offensive *f*

offer ['ɔfər] *vt* : offrir, présenter — **~** *n* : proposition *f*, offre *f* — **offering** ['ɔfərɪŋ] *n* : offre *f*, offrande *f* (en religion)

offhand ['ɔf'hænd] *adv* : spontanément, au pied levé — **~** *adj* : désinvolte

office ['ɔfəs] *n* 1 : bureau *m* 2 POSITION : fonction *f*, poste *m* — **officer** ['ɔfəsər] *n* 1 *or* **police ~** : policier *m*, agent *m* (de police) 2 OFFICIAL : fonctionnaire *mf* 3 : officier *m* (dans l'armée) — **official** [ə'fɪʃəl] *adj* : officiel — **~** *n* : officiel *m*, -cielle *f*

offing ['ɔfɪŋ] *n* **in the ~** : en perspective, imminent

offset ['ɔf,sɛt] *vt* **-set; -setting** : compenser

offshore ['ɔf'ʃor] *adv* : en mer — **~** *adj* : côtier, marin

offspring ['ɔf,sprɪŋ] *ns & pl* : progéniture *f*

often ['ɔfən, 'ɔftən] *adv* 1 : souvent, fréquemment 2 **every so ~** : de temps en temps

ogle ['o:gəl] *vt* **ogled; ogling** : lorgner

ogre ['o:gər] *n* : ogre *m*, ogresse *f*

oh ['o:] *interj* 1 : oh 2 **~ really?** : vraiment?

oil ['ɔɪl] *n* 1 : huile *f* (d'olive, etc.) 2 PETROLEUM : pétrole *m* 3 *or* **heating ~** : mazout *m* — **~** *vt* : huiler, lubrifier — **oilskin** ['ɔɪl,skɪn] *n* : ciré *m* — **oily** ['ɔɪli] *adj* **oilier; -est** : huileux

ointment ['ɔɪntmənt] *n* : pommade *f*

OK *or* **okay** [,o:'keɪ] *adv* 1 WELL : bien 2 YES : oui — **~** *adj* 1 ALL RIGHT : bien 2 **are you ~?** : ça va? — **~** *vt* **OK'd** *or* **okayed; OK'ing** *or* **okaying** : approuver — **~** *n* 1 APPROVAL : accord *m* 2 **give the ~** : donner le feu vert

okra ['o:krə, *south also* -kri] *n* : gombo *m*

old ['o:ld] *adj* 1 : vieux 2 FORMER : ancien 3 **any ~** : n'importe quel 4 **be ten years ~** : avoir dix ans 5 **~ age** : vieillesse *f* 6 **~ man** : vieux *m* 7 **~ woman** : vieille *f* — **~** *n* **the ~** : les vieux, les personnes âgées — **old-fashioned** ['o:ld'fæʃənd] *adj* : démodé

olive ['ɑlɪv, -ləv] *n* 1 : olive *f* (fruit) 2 *or* **~ green** : vert *m* olive

Olympic [o'lɪmpɪk] *adj* : olympique — **Olympic Games** [o'lɪmpɪk] *or* **Olympics** [-pɪks] *npl* : jeux *mpl* Olympiques

omelet *or* **omelette** ['ɑmlət, 'ɑmə-] *n* : omelette *f*

omen ['o:mən] *n* : augure *m*, présage *m*

omit [o'mɪt] *vt* **omitted; omitting** : omettre — **omission** [o'mɪʃən] *n* : omission *f*

omnipotent [ɑm'nɪpət̬ənt] *adj* : omnipotent

on ['ɑn, 'ɔn] *prep* 1 : sur 2 **~ fire** : en feu 3 **~ foot** : à pied 4 **~ Friday** : vendredi 5 **~ the plane** : dans l'avion 6 **~ the right** : à droite — **~** *adv* 1 **from that moment ~** : à partir de ce moment-là 2 **later ~** : plus tard 3 **put ~** : mettre — **~** *adj* 1 : allumé (se dit d'une lumière), en marche (se dit d'un moteur), ouvert (se dit d'un robinet) 2 **be ~** : avoir lieu (se dit d'un événement)

once ['wʌnts] *adv* 1 : une fois 2 FORMERLY : autrefois — **~** *n* 1 : une seule fois 2 **at ~** SIMULTANEOUSLY : en même temps 3 **at ~** IMMEDIATELY : tout de suite — **~** *conj* : dès que, une fois que

oncoming ['ɑn,kʌmɪŋ, 'ɔn-] *adj* : qui approche

one ['wʌn] *n* 1 : un *m* (numéro) 2 **~ o'clock** : une heure — **~** *adj* 1 : un, une 2 ONLY : seul, unique 3 SAME : même — **~** *pron* 1 : un, une 2 **~ another** : l'un l'autre 3 **~ never knows** : on ne sait jamais 4 **this ~** : celui-ci, celle-ci 5 **that ~** : celui-là, celle-là 6 **which ~?** : lequel?, laquelle? — **oneself** [,wʌn'sɛlf] *pron* 1 (*used reflexively*) : se 2 (*used for emphasis*) : soi-même 3 (*used after prepositions*) : soi 4 **by ~** : seul — **one-sided** ['wʌn'saɪdəd] *adj* 1 UNEQUAL : inégal 2 BIASED : partial — **one-way** ['wʌn'weɪ] *adj* 1 : à sens unique (se dit d'une route) 2 **~ ticket** : aller *m* simple

ongoing ['ɑn,go:ɪŋ] *adj* : continu, en cours

onion ['ʌnjən] *n* : oignon *m*

online ['ɑn,laɪn, 'ɔn-] *adj or adv* : en ligne

only ['o:nli] *adj* : seul, unique — **~** *adv* 1 : seulement, ne...que 2 **if ~** : si, si seulement 3 **~ too well** : trop bien — **~** *conj* BUT : mais

onset ['ɑn,sɛt] *n* : début *m*

onslaught ['ɑn,slɔt, 'ɔn-] *n* : attaque *f*

onto ['ɑn,tu:, 'ɔn-] *prep* : sur

onus ['o:nəs] *n* : responsabilité *f*, charge *f*

onward ['ɑnwərd, 'ɔn-] *adv & adj* 1 : en avant 2 **from today ~** : à partir d'aujourd'hui

onyx ['ɑnɪks] *n* : onyx *m*

ooze ['u:z] *vi* **oozed; oozing** : suinter

opal ['o:pəl] *n* : opale *f*

opaque [o'peɪk] *adj* : opaque

open ['o:pən] *adj* 1 : ouvert 2 FRANK : franc, sincère 3 CLEAR : dégagé 4 PUBLIC : public 5 UNCOVERED : découvert — **~** *vt* 1 : ouvrir 2 START : commencer — *vi* 1 : s'ouvrir 2 BEGIN : commencer 3 **~ onto** : donner sur — **~** *n* 1 **in the ~** OUTDOORS : au grand air, dehors 2 **in the ~** KNOWN : connu — **open-air** ['o:pən'ær] *adj* : en plein air — **opener** ['o:pənər] *n or* **can ~** : ouvre-boîtes — **opening** ['o:pənɪŋ] *n* 1 : ouverture *f* 2 START : début *m* 3 OPPORTUNITY : occasion *f* — **~** *adj* : premier, préliminaire — **openly** ['o:pənli] *adv* : ouvertement, franchement

opera ['ɑprə, 'ɑpərə] *n* : opéra *m*

operate ['ɑpə,reɪt] *v* **-ated; -ating** *vi* 1 FUNCTION : fonctionner, marcher 2 **~ on s.o.** : opérer qqn — *vt* 1 : faire fonctionner (une machine) 2 MANAGE : diriger, gérer — **operation** [,ɑpə'reɪʃən] *n* 1 : opération *f* 2 **in ~** : en marche, en service — **operational** [,ɑpə'reɪʃənəl] *adj* : opérationnel — **operative** ['ɑpərət̬ɪv, -,reɪ-] *adj* : en vigueur — **operator** ['ɑpə,reɪt̬ər] *n* 1 : opérateur *m*, -trice *f* 2 *or* **telephone ~** : standardiste *mf*

opinion [ə'pɪnjən] *n* : opinion *f*, avis *m* — **opinionated** [ə'pɪnjə,neɪt̬əd] *adj* : opiniâtre

opium ['o:piəm] *n* : opium *m*

opossum [ə'pɑsəm] *n* : opossum *m*

opponent [ə'po:nənt] *n* : adversaire *mf*

opportunity [,ɑpər'tu:nət̬i, -'tju:-] *n, pl* **-ties** : occasion *f* — **opportune** [,ɑpər'tu:n, -'tju:n] *adj* : opportun — **opportunism** [,ɑpər'tu:,nɪzəm, -'tju:-] *n* : opportunisme *m* — **opportunist** [,ɑpər'tu:nɪst, -'tju:-] *n* : opportuniste *mf* — **opportunistic** [,ɑpərtu:'nɪstɪk, -tju:-] *adj* : opportuniste

oppose [ə'po:z] *vt* **-posed; -posing** : s'opposer à — **opposed** [ə'po:zd] *adj* **~ to** : opposé à

opposite ['ɑpəzət] *adj* 1 FACING : d'en face 2 CONTRARY : opposé, inverse — **~** *n* : contraire *m* — **~** *adv* : en face — **~** *prep* : en face de — **opposition** [,ɑpə'zɪʃən] *n* : opposition *f*

oppress [ə'prɛs] *vt* 1 PERSECUTE : opprimer 2 BURDEN : oppresser — **oppression** [ə'prɛʃən] *n* : oppression *f* — **oppressive** [ə'prɛsɪv] *adj* : oppressif — **oppressor** [ə'prɛsər] *n* : oppresseur *m*

opt ['ɑpt] *vi* : opter

optic ['ɑptɪk] *or* **optical** ['ɑptɪkəl] *adj* : optique — **optician** [ɑp'tɪʃən] *n* : opticien *m*, -cienne *f*

optimism ['ɑptə,mɪzəm] *n* : optimisme *m* — **optimist** ['ɑptəmɪst] *n* : optimiste *mf* — **optimistic** [,ɑptə'mɪstɪk] *adj* : optimiste

optimum ['ɑptəməm] *adj* : optimum — ~ *n, pl* **-ma** ['ɑptəmə] : optimum *m*
option ['ɑpʃən] *n* : option *f* — **optional** ['ɑpʃənəl] *adj* : facultatif, optionnel
opulence ['ɑpjələnts] *n* : opulence *f* — **opulent** [-lənt] *adj* : opulent
or ['ɔr] *conj* **1** (*indicating an alternative*) : ou **2** (*following a negative*) : ni **3** ~ **else** OTHERWISE : sinon
oracle ['ɔrəkəl] *n* : oracle *m*
oral ['orəl] *adj* : oral
orange ['ɔrɪnʤ] *n* **1** : orange *f* (fruit) **2** : orange *m* (couleur)
orator ['ɔrəṭər] *n* : orateur *m*, -trice *f*
orbit ['ɔrbət] *n* : orbite *f* — ~ *vt* : graviter autour de
orchard ['ɔrʧərd] *n* : verger *m*
orchestra ['ɔrkəstrə] *n* : orchestre *m*
orchid ['ɔrkɪd] *n* : orchidée *f*
ordain [ɔr'deɪn] *vt* **1** DECREE : décréter **2** : ordonner (en religion)
ordeal [ɔr'di:l, 'ɔr,di:l] *n* : épreuve *f*
order ['ɔrdər] *vt* **1** COMMAND : ordonner **2** REQUEST : commander (un repas, etc.) **3** ORGANIZE : organiser — ~ *n* **1** : ordre *m* **2** COMMAND, REQUEST : commande *f* **3 in good** ~ : en bon état **4 in** ~ **to** : afin de **5 out of** ~ : en panne — **orderly** ['ɔrdərli] *adj* **1** TIDY : en ordre, ordonné **2** DISCIPLINED : discipliné
ordinary ['ɔrdən,ɛri] *adj* **1** USUAL : normal, habituel **2** AVERAGE : ordinaire, moyen — **ordinarily** [,ɔrdən'ɛrəli] *adv* : d'ordinaire, d'habitude
ore ['or] *n* : minerai *m*
oregano [ə'rɛgə,no:] *n* : origan *m*
organ ['ɔrgən] *n* **1** : orgue *m* (instrument de musique) **2** : organe *m* (du corps) — **organic** [ɔr'gænɪk] *adj* **1** : organique **2** NATUREL : biologique — **organism** ['ɔrgə,nɪzəm] *n* : organisme *m* — **organist** ['ɔrgənɪst] *n* : organiste *mf* — **organize** ['ɔrgə,naɪz] *vt* **-nized; -nizing 1** : organiser **2 get organized** : s'organiser — **organization** [,ɔrgənə'zeɪʃən] *n* : organisation *f* — **organizer** ['ɔrgə,naɪzər] *n* : organisateur *m*, -trice *f*
orgasm ['ɔr,gæzəm] *n* : orgasme *m*
orgy ['ɔrʤi] *n, pl* **-gies** : orgie *f*
Orient ['ori,ɛnt] *n* **the** ~ : l'Orient *m* — **orient** *vt* : orienter — **oriental** [,ori'ɛntəl] *adj* : oriental, d'Orient — **orientation** [,oriən'teɪʃən] *n* : orientation *f*
orifice ['ɔrəfəs] *n* : orifice *m*
origin ['ɔrəʤən] *n* : origine *f* — **original** [ə'rɪʤənəl] *adj* **1** : original **2** FIRST : premier — ~ *n* : original *m* — **originality** [ə,rɪʤə'næləṭi] *n* : originalité *f* — **originally** [ə'rɪʤənəli] *adv* : à l'origine — **originate** [ə'rɪʤə,neɪt] *v* **-nated; -nating** *vt* : donner naissance à — *vi* : provenir, prendre naissance
ornament ['ɔrnəmənt] *n* : ornement *m* — **ornamental** [,ɔrnə'mɛntəl] *adj* : ornemental — **ornate** [ɔr'neɪt] *adj* : orné
ornithology [,ɔrnə'θɑləʤi] *n, pl* **-gies** : ornithologie *f*
orphan ['ɔrfən] *n* : orphelin *m*, -line *f*
orthodox ['ɔrθə,dɑks] *adj* : orthodoxe — **orthodoxy** ['ɔrθə,dɑksi] *n, pl* **-doxies** : orthodoxie *f*
orthopedic [,ɔrθə'pi:dɪk] *adj* : orthopédique — **orthopedics** [,ɔrθə'pi:dɪks] *ns & pl* : orthopédie *f*
oscillate ['ɑsə,leɪt] *vi* **-lated; -lating** : osciller — **oscillation** [,ɑsə'leɪʃən] *n* : oscillation *f*
ostensible [ɑ'stɛntsəbəl] *adj* : apparent — **ostentation** [,ɑstən'teɪʃən] *n* : ostentation *f*
osteopath ['ɑstiə,pæθ] *n* : ostéopathe *mf*
ostracism ['ɑstrə,sɪzəm] *n* : ostracisme *m* — **ostracize** ['ɑstrə,saɪz] *vt* **-cized; -cizing** : mettre au ban de la société
ostrich ['ɑstrɪʧ, 'ɔs-] *n* : autruche *f*
other ['ʌðər] *adj* **1** : autre **2 every** ~ **day** : tous les deux jours **3 on the** ~ **hand** : d'autre part — ~ *pron* **1** : autre **2 the** ~**s** : les autres **3 someone or** ~ : quelqu'un — **other than** *prep* : autrement que, à part — **otherwise** ['ʌðər,waɪz] *adv* **1** : autrement **2** OR ELSE : sinon — ~ *adj* : autre
otter ['ɑṭər] *n* : loutre *f*
ought ['ɔt] *v aux* **1** : devoir **2 you** ~ **to have done it** : tu aurais dû le faire
ounce ['aʊnts] *n* : once *f*
our ['ɑr, 'aʊr] *adj* : notre, nos — **ours** ['aʊrz, 'ɑrz] *pron* **1** : le nôtre, la nôtre **2 a friend of** ~ : un de nos amis **3 that's** ~ : c'est à nous — **ourselves** [ɑr'sɛlvz, aʊr-] *pron* **1** (*used reflexively*) : nous **2** (*used for emphasis*) : nous-mêmes
oust ['aʊst] *vt* : évincer
out ['aʊt] *adv* **1** OUTSIDE : dehors **2 cry** ~ : crier **3 eat** ~ : aller au restaurant **4 go** ~ : sortir **5 turn** ~ : éteindre — ~ *prep* → **out of** — ~ *adj* **1** ABSENT : absent, sorti **2** RELEASED : sorti **3** UNFASHIONABLE : démodé **4** EXTINGUISHED : éteint **5 the sun is** ~ : il fait soleil
outboard motor ['aʊt,bɔrd] *n* : hors-bord *m*
outbreak ['aʊt,breɪk] *n* : éruption *f* (d'une maladie, etc.), déclenchement *m* (des hostilités, etc.)
outburst ['aʊt,bərst] *n* : explosion *f*, accès *m*
outcast ['aʊt,kæst] *n* : paria *m*
outcome ['aʊt,kʌm] *n* : résultat *m*
outcry ['aʊt,kraɪ] *n, pl* **-cries** : tollé *m*
outdated [,aʊt'deɪṭəd] *adj* : démodé
outdo [,aʊt'du:] *vt* **-did** [-'dɪd]; **-done** [-'dʌn]; **-doing** [-'du:ɪŋ]; **-does** [-'dʌz] : surpasser
outdoor ['aʊt'dor] *adj* : en plein air, de plein air — **outdoors** ['aʊt'dorz] *adv* : dehors
outer ['aʊṭər] *adj* : extérieur — **outer space** *n* : espace *m* cosmique
outfit ['aʊt,fɪt] *n* **1** EQUIPMENT : équipement *m* **2** COSTUME : tenue *f* **3** GROUP : équipe *f* — ~ *vt* **-fitted; -fitting** : équiper
outgoing ['aʊt,go:ɪŋ] *adj* **1** LEAVING : en partance (se dit d'un train, etc.), sortant (se dit d'une personne) **2** EXTROVERTED : ouvert **3** ~ **mail** : courrier *m* à expédier
outgrow [,aʊt'gro:] *vt* **-grew** [-'gru:]; **-grown** [-'gro:n]; **-growing** : devenir trop grand pour
outing ['aʊṭɪŋ] *n* : excursion *f*, sortie *f*
outlandish [aʊt'lændɪʃ] *adj* : bizarre
outlast [,aʊt'læst] *vt* : durer plus longtemps que
outlaw ['aʊt,lɔ] *n* : hors-la-loi *m* — ~ *vt* : proscrire
outlay ['aʊt,leɪ] *n* : dépenses *fpl*
outlet ['aʊt,lɛt, -lət] *n* **1** EXIT : sortie *f*, issue *f* **2** MARKET : débouché *m* **3** RELEASE : exutoire *m* **4** *or* **electrical** ~ : prise *f* de courant **5** *or* **retail** ~ : point *m* de vente
outline ['aʊt,laɪn] *n* **1** CONTOUR : contour *m* **2** SKETCH : esquisse *f* — ~ *vt* **-lined; -lining 1** : souligner le contour de **2** SUMMARIZE : exposer dans ses grandes lignes
outlive [,aʊt'lɪv] *vt* **-lived; -living** : survivre à
outlook ['aʊt,lʊk] *n* : perspective *f*
outlying ['aʊt,laɪɪŋ] *adj* : écarté, périphérique
outmoded [,aʊt'mo:dəd] *adj* : démodé
outnumber [,aʊt'nʌmbər] *vt* : surpasser en nombre
out of *prep* **1** OUTSIDE : en dehors de **2** FROM : de **3 four** ~ **five** : quatre sur cinq **4 made** ~ **plastic** : fait en plastique **5** ~ **control** : hors de contrôle **6** ~ **money** : sans argent **7** ~ **spite** : par dépit — **out–of–date** [,aʊṭəv'deɪt] *adj* **1** OLD-FASHIONED : démodé **2** EXPIRED : périmé — **out–of–doors** [aʊṭəv'dorz] → **outdoors**
outpost ['aʊt,po:st] *n* : avant-poste *m*
output ['aʊt,pʊt] *n* : rendement *m*, production *f*
outrage ['aʊt,reɪʤ] *n* **1** AFFRONT : outrage *m*, affront *m* **2** ANGER : indignation *f* — ~ *vt* **-raged; -raging** : outrager — **outrageous** [,aʊt'reɪʤəs] *adj* **1** DISGRACEFUL : scandaleux **2** EXCESSIVE : outrancier
outright ['aʊt,raɪt] *adv* **1** COMPLETELY : complètement **2** INSTANTLY : sur le coup **3** FRANKLY : carrément — ~ *adj* : total, absolu
outset ['aʊt,sɛt] *n* : début *m*, commencement *m*
outside [,aʊt'saɪd, 'aʊt,-] *n* : extérieur *m* — ~ *adj* : extérieur — ~ *adv* : à l'extérieur, dehors — ~ *prep or* ~ **of** : en dehors de, à part — **outsider** [,aʊt'saɪdər] *n* : étranger *m*, -gère *f*
outskirts ['aʊt,skɔrts] *npl* : banlieue *f*, périphérie *f*
outspoken [,aʊt'spo:kən] *adj* : franc, direct
outstanding [,aʊt'stændɪŋ] *adj* **1** UNPAID : impayé **2** UNRESOLVED : en suspens **3** NOTABLE : exceptionnel
outstretched [,aʊt'strɛʧt] *adj* : tendu
outstrip [,aʊt'strɪp] *vt* **-stripped; -stripping** : devancer
outward ['aʊtwərd] *or* **outwards** [-wərdz] *adv* **1** : vers l'extérieur **2** ~ **bound** : en partance — ~ *adj* : extérieur — **outwardly** ['aʊtwərdli] *adv* : en apparence
outweigh [,aʊt'weɪ] *vt* : l'emporter sur
outwit [,aʊt'wɪt] *vt* **-witted; -witting** : se montrer plus malin que
oval ['o:vəl] *adj* : ovale — ~ *n* : ovale *m*
ovary ['o:vəri] *n, pl* **-ries** : ovaire *m*
ovation [o'veɪʃən] *n* : ovation *f*
oven ['ʌvən] *n* : four *m*
over ['o:vər] *adv* **1** ABOVE : au-dessus **2** MORE : de trop **3** AGAIN : encore **4 all** ~ : partout **5 ask** ~ : inviter **6 four times** ~ : quatre fois de suite **7** ~ **here** : ici **8** ~ **there** : là-bas **9 start** ~ : recommencer — ~ *prep* **1** ABOVE : au-dessus de, par-dessus **2** MORE THAN : plus de **3** ACROSS : de l'autre côté de **4** DURING : pendant, au cours de **5** CONCERNING : au sujet de — ~ *adj* : fini, terminé
overall [,o:vər'ɔl] *adv* GENERALLY : en général — ~ *adj* : d'ensemble, total — **overalls** ['o:vər,ɔlz] *npl* : salopette *f*
overbearing [,o:vər'bærɪŋ] *adj* : impérieux, autoritaire
overboard ['o:vər,bord] *adv* : par-dessus bord
overburden [,o:vər'bərdən] *vt* : surcharger
overcast ['o:vər,kæst] *adj* : couvert
overcharge [,o:vər'ʧɑrʤ] *vt* **-charged; -charging** : faire payer trop cher à
overcoat ['o:vər,ko:t] *n* : pardessus *m*
overcome [,o:vər'kʌm] *vt* **-came** [-'keɪm]; **-come; -coming 1** CONQUER : vaincre, surmonter **2** OVERWHELM : accabler
overcook [,o:vər'kʊk] *vt* : faire trop cuire
overcrowded [,o:vər'kraʊdəd] *adj* : bondé
overdo [,o:vər'du:] *vt* **-did** [-'dɪd]; **-done** [-'dʌn]; **-doing; -does** [-'dʌz] **1** : exagérer **2** → **overcook**
overdose ['o:vər,do:s] *n* : overdose *f*
overdraw [,o:vər'drɔ] *vt* **-drew** [-'dru:]; **-drawn** [-'drɔn]; **-drawing** : mettre à découvert — **overdraft** ['o:vər,dræft] *n* : découvert *m*
overdue [,o:vər'du:] *adj* **1** UNPAID : arriéré **2** LATE : en retard
overestimate [,o:vər'ɛstə,meɪt] *vt* **-mated; -mating** : surestimer
overflow [,o:vər'flo:] *v* : déborder — ~ ['o:vər,flo:] *n* : trop-plein *m*, débordement *m*
overgrown [,o:vər'gro:n] *adj* : envahi par la végétation
overhand ['o:vər,hænd] *adv* : par-dessus la tête
overhang [,o:vər'hæŋ] *vt* **-hung** [-'hʌŋ]; **-hanging** : surplomber
overhaul [,o:vər'hɔl] *vt* : réviser (un moteur, etc.), remanier (un système, etc.)
overhead [,o:vər'hɛd] *adv* : au-dessus — ~ *adj* : aérien — ~ *n* : frais *mpl* généraux
overhear [,o:vər'hɪr] *vt* **-heard** [-'hərd]; **-hearing** : entendre par hasard
overheat [,o:vər'hi:t] *vt* : surchauffer
overjoyed [,o:vər'ʤɔɪd] *adj* : ravi
overland ['o:vər,lænd, -lənd] *adv & adj* : par voie de terre
overlap [,o:vər'læp] *v* **-lapped; -lapping** *vt* : chevaucher — *vi* : se chevaucher
overload [,o:vər'lo:d] *vt* : surcharger
overlook [,o:vər'lʊk] *vt* **1** : donner sur (un jardin, la mer, etc.) **2** IGNORE : négliger, laisser passer
overly ['o:vərli] *adv* : trop
overnight [,o:vər'naɪt] *adv* **1** : (pendant) la nuit **2** SUDDENLY : du jour au lendemain — ~ ['o:vər,naɪt] *adj* **1** : de nuit, d'une nuit **2** SUDDEN : soudain
overpass ['o:vər,pæs] *n* : voie *f* surélevée *Can*, pont *m* autoroutier
overpopulated [,o:vər'pɑpjə,leɪṭəd] *adj* : surpeuplé
overpower [,o:vər'paʊər] *vt* **1** CONQUER : vaincre **2** OVERWHELM : accabler
overrate [,o:vər'reɪt] *vt* **-rated; -rating** : surestimer
override [,o:vər'raɪd] *vt* **-rode** [-'ro:d]; **-ridden** [-'rɪdən]; **-riding 1** : passer outre à **2** ANNUL : annuler — **overriding** [o:vər'raɪdɪŋ] *adj* : primordial
overrule [,o:vər'ru:l] *vt* **-ruled; -ruling** : rejeter
overrun [,o:vər'rʌn] *vt* **-ran** [-'ræn]; **-running 1** INVADE : envahir **2** EXCEED : dépasser
overseas [,o:vər'si:z] *adv* : à l'étranger, outre-mer — ~ ['o:vər,si:z] *adj* : à l'étranger, extérieur
oversee [,o:vər'si:] *vt* **-saw** [-'sɔ]; **-seen** [-'si:n]; **-seeing** : surveiller
overshadow [,o:vər'ʃæ,do:] *vt* : éclipser
oversight ['o:vər,saɪt] *n* : oubli *m*, omission *f*
oversleep [,o:vər'sli:p] *vi* **-slept** [-'slɛpt]; **-sleeping** : se réveiller trop tard
overstep [,o:vər'stɛp] *vt* **-stepped; -stepping** : outrepasser
overt [o'vərt, 'o:,vərt] *adj* : manifeste
overtake [,o:vər'teɪk] *vt* **-took** [-'tʊk]; **-taken** [-'teɪkən]; **-taking** : dépasser
overthrow [,o:vər'θro:] *vt* **-threw** [-'θru:]; **-thrown** [-'θro:n]; **-throwing** : renverser
overtime ['o:vər,taɪm] *n* **1** : heures *fpl* supplémentaires **2** : prolongations *fpl* (aux sports)
overtone ['o:vər,to:n] *n* : nuance *f*, sous-entendu *m*
overture ['o:vər,ʧʊr, -ʧər] *n* : ouverture *f* (en musique)
overturn [,o:vər'tərn] *vt* : renverser — *vi* : se renverser
overweight [,o:vər'weɪt] *adj* : trop gros, obèse
overwhelm [,o:vər'hwɛlm] *vt* **1** : submerger, accabler **2** DEFEAT : écraser — **overwhelming** [,o:vər'hwɛlmɪŋ] *adj* : accablant, écrasant
overwork [,o:vər'wərk] *vt* : surmener — ~ *n* : surmenage *m*
overwrought [,o:vər'rɔt] *adj* : à bout de nerfs
owe ['o:] *vt* **owed; owing** : devoir — **owing to** *prep* : à cause de
owl ['aʊl] *n* : hibou *m*
own ['o:n] *adj* : propre — ~ *vt* : posséder, avoir — *vi* ~ **up** : avouer — ~ *pron* **1 my (your, his/her, our, their)** ~ : le mien, la mienne; le tien, la tienne; le vôtre, la vôtre; le sien, la sienne; le nôtre, la nôtre; le leur, la leur **2 on one's** ~ : tout seul **3 to each his** ~ : chacun son goût — **owner** ['o:nər] *n* : propriétaire *mf* — **ownership** ['o:nər,ʃɪp] *n* : possession *f*
ox ['ɑks] *n, pl* **oxen** ['ɑksən] : bœuf *m*
oxygen ['ɑksɪʤən] *n* : oxygène *m*
oyster ['ɔɪstər] *n* : huître *f*
ozone ['o:,zo:n] *n* : ozone *m*

P

p ['pi:] *n, pl* **p's** *or* **ps** ['pi:z] : p *m*, seizième lettre de l'alphabet
pace ['peɪs] *n* **1** STEP : pas *m* **2** SPEED : allure *f* **3 keep** ~ **with** : suivre — ~ *v* **paced; pacing** *vt* : arpenter — *vi* ~ **to and fro** : faire les cent pas
pacify ['pæsə,faɪ] *vt* **-fied; -fying** : pacifier, apaiser — **pacifier** ['pæsə,faɪər] *n* : tétine *f*, sucette *f* — **pacifist** ['pæsəfɪst] *n* : pacifiste *mf*
pack ['pæk] *n* **1** PACKAGE : paquet *m* **2** BAG : sac *m* **3** GROUP : bande *f*, meute *f* (de chiens) **4** : jeu *m* (de cartes) — ~ *vt* **1** PACKAGE : emballer **2** FILL : remplir **3** : faire (ses bagages) — **package** ['pækɪʤ] *vt* **-aged; -aging** : empaqueter — ~ *n* : paquet *m*, colis *m* — **packet** ['pækət] *n* : paquet *m*
pact ['pækt] *n* : pacte *m*
pad ['pæd] *n* **1** CUSHION : coussin *m* **2** TABLET : bloc *m* (de papier) **3 ink** ~ : tampon *m* encreur **4 launching** ~ : rampe *m* de lancement **5** : protection *f* (aux sports) — ~ *vt* **padded; padding** : rembourrer — **padding** ['pædɪŋ] *n* STUFFING : rembourrage *m*
paddle ['pædəl] *n* **1** : pagaie *f*, aviron *m Can* **2** : raquette *f* (aux sports) — ~ *vt* **-dled; -dling** : pagayer
padlock ['pæd,lɑk] *n* : cadenas *m* — ~ *vt* : cadenasser
pagan ['peɪgən] *n* : païen *m*, païenne *f* — ~ *adj* : païen
page[1] ['peɪʤ] **paged; paging** *vt* : appeler
page[2] *n* : page *f* (d'un livre)
pageant ['pæʤənt] *n* : spectacle *m* — **pageantry** ['pæʤəntri] *n* : apparat *m*
paid → **pay**
pail ['peɪl] *n* : seau *m*
pain ['peɪn] *n* **1** : douleur *f* **2 take** ~**s** *npl* : se donner de la peine — ~ *vt* : peiner, faire souffrir — **painful** ['peɪnfəl] *adj* : douloureux — **painkiller** ['peɪn,kɪlər] *n* : analgésique *m* — **painless** ['peɪnləs] *adj* : indolore, sans douleur — **painstaking** ['peɪn,steɪkɪŋ] *adj* : soigneux, méticuleux
paint ['peɪnt] *v* : peindre, peinturer *Can* — ~ *n* : peinture *f* — **paintbrush** ['peɪnt,brʌʃ] *n* : pinceau *m* (d'un artiste), brosse *f* — **painter** ['peɪntər] *n* : peintre *m* — **painting** ['peɪntɪŋ] *n* : peinture *f*
pair ['pær] *n* **1** : paire *f* **2** COUPLE : couple *m* — ~ *vi* : accoupler
pajamas *or Brit* **pyjamas** [pə'ʤɑməz, -'ʤæ-] *npl* : pyjama *m*
pal ['pæl] *n* : copain *m*, -pine *f*
palace ['pæləs] *n* : palais *m*
palate ['pælət] *n* : palais *m* — **palatable** ['pæləṭəbəl] *adj* : savoureux
pale ['peɪl] *adj* **paler; palest** : pâle — ~ *vi* **paled; paling** : pâlir — **paleness** ['peɪlnəs] *n* : pâleur *f*
palette ['pælət] *n* : palette *f*
pallid ['pæləd] *adj* : pâle
palm[1] ['pɑm, 'pɑlm] *n* : paume *f* (de la main)
palm[2] *or* ~ **tree** : palmier *m* — **Palm Sunday** *n* : dimanche *m* des Rameaux
palpitate ['pælpə,teɪt] *vi* **-tated; -tating** : palpiter — **palpitation** [,pælpə'teɪʃən] *n* : palpitation *f*
paltry ['pɔltri] *adj* **-trier; -est** : dérisoire
pamper ['pæmpər] *vt* : dorloter
pamphlet ['pæmpflət] *n* : dépliant *m*, brochure *f*
pan ['pæn] *n* **1** SAUCEPAN : casserole *f* **2** FRYING PAN : poêle *f*
pancake ['pæn,keɪk] *n* : crêpe *f*
pancreas ['pæŋkriəs, 'pæn-] *n* : pancréas *m*
panda ['pændə] *n* : panda *m*
pandemonium [,pændə'mo:niəm] *n* : tumulte *m*
pander ['pændər] *vi* : flatter (bassement)
pane ['peɪn] *n* : vitre *f*, carreau *m*
panel ['pænəl] *n* **1** : panneau *m* **2** COMMITTEE : comité *m* **3** *or* **control** ~ : tableau *m* (de bord) — **paneling** ['pænəlɪŋ] *n* : lambris *m*
pang ['pæŋ] *n* : tiraillement *m*
panic ['pænɪk] *n* : panique *f* — ~ *v* **-icked; -icking** : paniquer
panorama [,pænə'ræmə, -'rɑ-] *n* : panorama *m* — **panoramic** [,pænə'ræmɪk, -'rɑ-] *adj* : panoramique
pansy ['pænzi] *n, pl* **-sies** : pensée *f*
pant ['pænt] *vi* : haleter
panther ['pænθər] *n* : panthère *f*

panties [ˈpæntiz] npl : (petite) culotte f, slip m France

pantomime [ˈpæntəˌmaɪm] n : pantomime f

pantry [ˈpæntri] n, pl **-tries** : garde-manger m

pants [ˈpænts] npl : pantalon m

panty hose [ˈpæntiˌhoːz] npl : collant m

papaya [pəˈpaɪə] n : papaye f

paper [ˈpeɪpər] n **1** : papier m **2** DOCUMENT : document m **3** NEWSPAPER : journal m **4** : devoir m (scolaire) — ~ vt WALLPAPER : tapisser — ~ adj : de papier, en papier — **paperback** [ˈpeɪpərˌbæk] n : livre m de poche — **paper clip** n : trombone m —**paperwork** [ˈpeɪpərˌwərk] n : paperasserie f

par [ˈpɑr] n **1** EQUALITY : égalité f **2 on a ~ with** : de pair avec

parable [ˈpærəbəl] n : parabole f

parachute [ˈpærəˌʃuːt] n : parachute m

parade [pəˈreɪd] n **1** : défilé m, parade f (militaire) **2** DISPLAY : étalage m — ~ v **-raded; -rading** vi MARCH : défiler — vt DISPLAY : faire étalage de

paradise [ˈpærəˌdaɪs, -ˌdaɪz] n : paradis m

paradox [ˈpærəˌdɑks] n : paradoxe m — **paradoxical** [ˌpærəˈdɑksɪkəl] adj : paradoxal

paragraph [ˈpærəˌgræf] n : paragraphe m

parakeet [ˈpærəˌkiːt] n : perruche f

parallel [ˈpærəˌlɛl, -ləl] adj : parallèle — ~ n **1** : parallèle f (en géometrie) **2** SIMILARITY : parallèle m — ~ vt MATCH : égaler

paralysis [pəˈræləsɪs] n, pl **-yses** [-ˌsiːz] : paralysie f — **paralyze** or Brit **paralyse** [ˈpærəˌlaɪz] vt **-lyzed** or Brit **-lysed; -lyzing** or Brit **-lysing** : paralyser

parameter [pəˈræmət̬ər] n : paramètre m

paramount [ˈpærəˌmaʊnt] adj : suprême

paranoia [ˌpærəˈnɔɪə] n : paranoïa f — **paranoid** [ˈpærəˌnɔɪd] adj : paranoïaque

parapet [ˈpærəpət, -ˌpɛt] n : parapet m

paraphernalia [ˌpærəfəˈneɪljə, -fər-] ns & pl : attirail m

paraphrase [ˈpærəˌfreɪz] n : paraphrase f — ~ vt **-phrased; -phrasing** : paraphraser

paraplegic [ˌpærəˈpliːdʒɪk] n : paraplégique mf

parasite [ˈpærəˌsaɪt] n : parasite m

parasol [ˈpærəˌsɔl] n : parasol m

paratrooper [ˈpærəˌtruːpər] n : parachutiste m (militaire)

parcel [ˈpɑrsəl] n : paquet m

parch [ˈpɑrtʃ] vt : dessécher

parchment [ˈpɑrtʃmənt] n : parchemin m

pardon [ˈpɑrdən] n **1** FORGIVENESS : pardon m **2** : grâce f (en droit) — ~ vt **1** FORGIVE : pardonner **2** ABSOLVE : gracier

parent [ˈpærənt] n **1** : mère f, père m **2 ~s** npl : parents mpl — **parental** [pəˈrɛntəl] adj : parental

parenthesis [pəˈrɛnθəsəs] n, pl **-ses** [-ˌsiːz] : parenthèse f

parish [ˈpærɪʃ] n : paroisse f — **parishioner** [pəˈrɪʃənər] n : paroissien m, -sienne f

Parisian [pəˈrɪʒən, -ˈri-] adj : parisien

parity [ˈpærət̬i] n, pl **-ties** : parité f

park [ˈpɑrk] n : parc m — ~ vt : garer — vi : se garer, stationner

parka [ˈpɑrkə] n : parka m

parliament [ˈpɑrləmənt] n : parlement m — **parliamentary** [ˌpɑrləˈmɛntəri] adj : parlementaire

parlor or Brit **parlour** [ˈpɑrlər] n : salon m

parochial [pəˈroːkiəl] adj **1** : paroissial **2** PROVINCIAL : de clocher, provincial

parody [ˈpærədi] n, pl **-dies** : parodie f — ~ vt **-died; -dying** : parodier

parole [pəˈroːl] n : liberté f conditionnelle

parquet [pɑrˌkeɪ, pɑrˈkeɪ] n : parquet m

parrot [ˈpærət] n : perroquet m

parry [ˈpæri] vt **-ried; -rying 1** : parer (un coup) **2** EVADE : éluder (une question)

parsley [ˈpɑrsli] n : persil m

parsnip [ˈpɑrsnɪp] n : panais m

part [ˈpɑrt] n **1** : partie f **2** PIECE : pièce f **3** ROLE : rôle m **4** SHARE : part f **5** SIDE : parti m **6** : raie f (entre les cheveux) — ~ vi **1** or **~ company** : se séparer **2 ~ with** : se défaire de — vt SEPARATE : séparer

partake [pɑrˈteɪk, pər-] vi **-took** [-ˈtʊk]; **-taken** [-ˈteɪkən]; **-taking ~ in** : participer à

partial [ˈpɑrʃəl] adj **1** INCOMPLETE : partiel **2** BIASED : partial

participate [pərˈtɪsəˌpeɪt, pɑr-] vi **-pated; -pating** : participer — **participant** [pərˈtɪsəpənt, pɑr-] n : participant m, -pante f

participle [ˈpɑrt̬əˌsɪpəl] n : participe m

particle [ˈpɑrt̬ɪkəl] n : particule f

particular [pərˈtɪkjələr] adj **1** : particulier **2** FUSSY : exigeant — ~ n **1 in ~** : en particulier **2 ~s** npl DETAILS : détails mpl — **particularly** [pərˈtɪkjələrli] adv : particulièrement

partisan [ˈpɑrt̬əzən, -sən] n : partisan m, -sane f

partition [pərˈtɪʃən, pɑr-] n **1** DISTRIBUTION : division f **2** DIVIDER : cloison f — ~ vt **1** : diviser **2** : cloisonner (une pièce)

partly [ˈpɑrtli] adv : en partie

partner [ˈpɑrtnər] n **1** ASSOCIATE : associé m, -ciée f **2** : partenaire mf (aux sports, en danse) — **partnership** [ˈpɑrtnərˌʃɪp] n : association f

party [ˈpɑrti] n, pl **-ties 1** : parti m (politique) **2** PARTICIPANT : partie f **3** GATHERING : fête f **4** GROUP : groupe m

pass [ˈpæs] vi **1** MOVE : passer **2 come to ~** : se passer, advenir **3** or **~ away** DIE : mourir **4 ~ out** FAINT : s'évanouir — vt **1** : passer **2** OVERTAKE : dépasser **3** : réussir (un examen) **4 ~ up** : laisser passer — ~ n **1** PERMIT : permis m, laissez-passer m **2** : passe f (aux sports) **3** or **mountain ~** : col m de montagne — **passable** [ˈpæsəbəl] adj ACCEPTABLE : passable — **passage** [ˈpæsɪdʒ] n **1** : passage m **2** CORRIDOR : couloir m — **passageway** [ˈpæsɪdʒˌweɪ] n : passage m, couloir m

passenger [ˈpæsəndʒər] n : passager m, -gère f

passerby [ˌpæsərˈbaɪ, ˈpæsərˌ-] n, pl **passersby** : passant m, -sante f

passing [ˈpæsɪŋ] adj : passager

passion [ˈpæʃən] n : passion f — **passionate** [ˈpæʃənət] adj : passionné

passive [ˈpæsɪv] adj : passif

Passover [ˈpæsˌoːvər] n : Pâque f (juive)

passport [ˈpæsˌport] n : passeport m

password [ˈpæsˌwərd] n : mot m de passe

past [ˈpæst] adj **1** : dernier, passé **2** FORMER : ancien — ~ prep **1** BEYOND : au-delà de **2** IN FRONT OF : devant **3 half ~ one** : une heure et demie — ~ n : passé m — ~ adv : devant

pasta [ˈpɑstə, ˈpæs-] n : pâtes fpl

paste [ˈpeɪst] n **1** GLUE : colle f **2** DOUGH : pâte f — ~ vt **pasted; pasting** : coller

pastel [pæˈstɛl] n : pastel m — ~ adj : pastel

pasteurize [ˈpæstʃəˌraɪz, ˈpæstjə-] vt **-ized; -izing** : pasteuriser

pastime [ˈpæsˌtaɪm] n : passe-temps m

pastor [ˈpæstər] n : pasteur m

pastry [ˈpeɪstri] n, pl **-tries** : pâtisserie f

pasture [ˈpæstʃər] n : pâturage m

pasty [ˈpeɪsti] adj **-tier; -est 1** DOUGHY : pâteux **2** PALLID : terreux

pat [ˈpæt] n **1** TAP : (petite) tape f **2** : noix f (de beurre, etc.) — ~ vt **patted; patting** : tapoter — ~ adv **have down ~** : connaître par cœur

patch [ˈpætʃ] n **1** : pièce f (d'étoffe) **2** : plaque f (de glace) — ~ vt **1** REPAIR : rapiécer **2 ~ up** : réparer — **patchy** [ˈpætʃi] adj **patchier; patchiest** : inégal, irrégulier

patent [ˈpætənt] adj **1** or **patented** [-təd] : breveté **2** [ˈpætənt, ˈpeɪt-] OBVIOUS : patent, évident — ~ [ˈpætənt] n : brevet m — ~ [ˈpætənt] vt : breveter

paternal [pəˈtərnəl] adj : paternel — **paternity** [pəˈtərnət̬i] n : paternité f

path [ˈpæθ, ˈpɑθ] n **1** : allée f (dans un parc) **2** TRAIL : chemin m, sentier m **3** COURSE : trajectoire f

pathetic [pəˈθɛt̬ɪk] adj : pitoyable

pathology [pəˈθɑlədʒi] n, pl **-gies** : pathologie f

pathway [ˈpæθˌweɪ] n : chemin m, sentier m

patience [ˈpeɪʃənts] n : patience f — **patient** [ˈpeɪʃənt] adj : patient — ~ n : patient m, -tiente f; malade mf — **patiently** [ˈpeɪʃəntli] adv : patiemment

patio [ˈpæt̬iˌoː, ˈpɑt-] n, pl **-tios** : patio m

patriot [ˈpeɪtriət, -ˌɑt] n : patriote mf — **patriotic** [ˌpeɪtriˈɑt̬ɪk] adj : patriote

patrol [pəˈtroːl] n : patrouille f — ~ vi **-trolled; -trolling** : patrouiller

patron [ˈpeɪtrən] n **1** SPONSOR : mécène m **2** CUSTOMER : client m, cliente f — **patronage** [ˈpeɪtrənɪdʒ, ˈpæ-] n **1** SPONSORSHIP : patronage m **2** CLIENTELE : clientèle f — **patronize** [ˈpeɪtrəˌnaɪz, ˈpæ-] vt **-ized; -izing 1** SUPPORT : patronner, parrainer **2** : traiter avec condescendance

patter [ˈpæt̬ər] n : crépitement m

pattern [ˈpæt̬ərn] n **1** MODEL : modèle m **2** DESIGN : dessin m, motif m **3** NORM : mode m, norme f — ~ vt : modeler

paunch [ˈpɔntʃ] n : bedaine f

pause [ˈpɔz] n : pause f — ~ vi **paused; pausing** : faire une pause

pave [ˈpeɪv] vt **paved; paving** : paver — **pavement** [ˈpeɪvmənt] n : chaussée f

pavilion [pəˈvɪljən] n : pavillon m

paw [ˈpɔ] n : patte f — ~ vt : tripoter

pawn[1] [ˈpɔn] n : gage m

pawn[2] vt : mettre en gage — **pawnbroker** [ˈpɔnˌbroːkər] n : prêteur m, -teuse f sur gages — **pawnshop** [ˈpɔnˌʃɑp] n : mont-de-piété m France

pay [ˈpeɪ] v **paid** [ˈpeɪd]; **paying** vt **1** : payer **2 ~ attention to** : prêter attention à **3 ~ back** : rembourser **4 ~ one's respects** : présenter ses respects **5 ~ s.o. a visit** : rendre visite à qqn — vi : payer — ~ n : paie f, salaire m — **payable** [ˈpeɪəbəl] adj : payable — **paycheck** [ˈpeɪˌtʃɛk] n : chèque m de paie — **payment** [ˈpeɪmənt] n : paiement m

PC [ˌpiːˈsiː] n, pl **PCs** or **PC's** COMPUTER : PC m, micro-ordinateur m

pea [ˈpiː] n : pois m

peace [ˈpiːs] n : paix f — **peaceful** [ˈpiːsfəl] adj : paisible

peach [ˈpiːtʃ] n : pêche f

peacock [ˈpiːˌkɑk] n : paon m

peak [ˈpiːk] n **1** SUMMIT : sommet m, pic m **2** APEX : apogée f — ~ adj : maximal — ~ vi : atteindre un sommet

peanut [ˈpiːˌnʌt] n : cacahouète f

pear [ˈpær] n : poire f

pearl [ˈpərl] n : perle f

peasant [ˈpɛzənt] n : paysan m, -sanne f

peat [ˈpiːt] n : tourbe f

pebble [ˈpɛbəl] n : caillou m

pecan [pɪˈkɑn, -ˈkæn, ˈpiːˌkæn] n : noix f de pécan France, noix f de pacane Can

peck [ˈpɛk] vt : picorer — ~ n **1** : coup m de bec **2** KISS : bécot m

peculiar [pɪˈkjuːljər] adj **1** DISTINCTIVE : particulier **2** STRANGE : bizarre — **peculiarity** [pɪˌkjuːlˈjærət̬i, -ˌkjuːliˈær-] n, pl **-ties 1** DISTINCTIVENESS : particularité f **2** STRANGENESS : bizarrerie f

pedal [ˈpɛdəl] n : pédale f — ~ vt **-aled** or **-alled; -aling** or **-alling** : pédaler

pedantic [pɪˈdæntɪk] adj : pédant

peddle [ˈpɛdəl] vt **-dled; -dling** : colporter — **peddler** [ˈpɛdlər] n : colporteur m, -teuse f

pedestal [ˈpɛdəstəl] n : piédestal m

pedestrian [pəˈdɛstriən] n : piéton m — ~ adj **~ crossing** : passage m pour piétons

pediatrics [ˌpiːdiˈætrɪks] ns & pl : pédiatrie f — **pediatrician** [ˌpiːdiəˈtrɪʃən] n : pédiatre mf

pedigree [ˈpɛdəˌgriː] n : pedigree m (d'un animal)

peek [ˈpiːk] vi GLANCE : jeter un coup d'œil — ~ n : coup m d'œil furtif

peel [ˈpiːl] vt : peler (un fruit), éplucher (un oignon, etc.) — vi **1** : peler (se dit de la peau) **2** : s'écailler (se dit de la peinture) — ~ n : pelure f (de pomme), écorce f (d'orange), épluchure f (de pomme de terre)

peep[1] [ˈpiːp] vi : pépier (se dit d'un oiseau) — ~ n : pépiement m (d'un oiseau)

peep[2] vi PEEK : jeter un coup d'œil — ~ n GLANCE : coup m d'œil

peer[1] [ˈpɪr] n : pair m

peer[2] vi : regarder attentivement

peeve [ˈpiːv] vt **peeved; peeving** : irriter — **peevish** [ˈpiːvɪʃ] adj : grincheux

peg [ˈpɛg] n **1** HOOK : patère f **2** STAKE : piquet m

pelican [ˈpɛlɪkən] n : pélican m

pellet [ˈpɛlət] n **1** BALL : boulette f **2** SHOT : plomb m

pelt[1] [ˈpɛlt] n : peau f (d'un animal)

pelt[2] vt THROW : bombarder

pelvis [ˈpɛlvɪs] n, pl **-vises** [-vɪsəz] or **-ves** [-ˌviːz] : bassin m

pen[1] [ˈpɛn] vt **penned; penning** ENCLOSE : enfermer — ~ n : parc m, enclos m

pen[2] n : stylo m

penal [ˈpiːnəl] adj : pénal — **penalize** [ˈpiːnəlˌaɪz, ˈpɛn-] vt **-ized; -izing** : pénaliser — **penalty** [ˈpɛnəlti] n, pl **-ties 1** : peine f (en droit) **2** : pénalité f (aux sports)

penance [ˈpɛnənts] n : pénitence f

pencil [ˈpɛntsəl] n : crayon m

pending [ˈpɛndɪŋ] adj **1** UNDECIDED : en instance **2** IMMINENT : imminent — ~ prep **1** DURING : pendant **2** AWAITING : en attendant

penetrate [ˈpɛnəˌtreɪt] v **-trated; -trating** : pénétrer — **penetration** [ˌpɛnəˈtreɪʃən] n : pénétration f

penguin [ˈpɛŋgwɪn, ˈpɛn-] n : manchot m

penicillin [ˌpɛnəˈsɪlən] n : pénicilline f

peninsula [pəˈnɪntsələ, -ˈnɪntʃʊlə] n : péninsule f

penis [ˈpiːnəs] n, pl **-nes** [-ˌniːz] or **-nises** : pénis m

penitentiary [ˌpɛnəˈtɛntʃəri] n, pl **-ries** : pénitencier m, prison f

pen name n : nom m de plume

penny [ˈpɛni] n, pl **-nies** : centime m, cent m, sou m — **penniless** [ˈpɛnɪləs] adj : sans le sou

pension [ˈpɛntʃən] n : pension f, retraite f

pensive [ˈpɛntsɪv] adj : pensif

pentagon [ˈpɛntəˌgɑn] n : pentagone m

people [ˈpiːpəl] ns & pl **1 people** npl : personnes fpl, gens mfpl **2** pl **~s** : peuple m — ~ vt **-pled; -pling** : peupler

pep [ˈpɛp] n : entrain m

pepper [ˈpɛpər] n **1** : poivre m (condiment) **2** : poivron m (légume) — **peppermint** [ˈpɛpərˌmɪnt] n : menthe f poivrée

per [ˈpər] prep **1** : par **2** ACCORDING TO : selon **3 ten miles ~ hour** : dix miles à l'heure

perceive [pərˈsiːv] vt **-ceived; -ceiving** : percevoir

percent [pərˈsɛnt] adv : pour cent — **percentage** [pərˈsɛntɪdʒ] n : pourcentage m

perceptible [pərˈsɛptəbəl] adj : perceptible

perception [pərˈsɛpʃən] n : perception f — **perceptive** [pərˈsɛptɪv] adj : perspicace

perch[1] [ˈpərtʃ] n : perchoir m — ~ vi : se percher

perch[2] n : perche f (poisson)

percolate [ˈpərkəˌleɪt] v **-lated; -lating** vi SEEP : filtrer — vt : passer (du café) — **percolator** [ˈpərkəˌleɪt̬ər] n : cafetière f à pression

percussion [pərˈkʌʃən] n : percussion f

perennial [pəˈrɛniəl] adj **1** RECURRING : perpétuel **2 ~ flowers** : fleurs fpl vivaces

perfect [ˈpərfɪkt] adj : parfait — ~ [pərˈfɛkt] vt : perfectionner — **perfection** [pərˈfɛkʃən] n : perfection f — **perfectionist** [pərˈfɛkʃənɪst] n : perfectionniste mf

perforate [ˈpərfəˌreɪt] vt **-rated; -rating** : perforer

perform [pərˈfɔrm] vt **1** CARRY OUT : exécuter, faire **2** PRESENT : jouer — vi **1** ACT : jouer **2** FUNCTION : fonctionner — **performance** [pərˈfɔrˌmənts] n **1** EXECUTION : exécution f **2** : interprétation f (d'un acteur), performance f (d'un athlète) **3** PRESENTATION : représentation f — **performer** [pərˈfɔrmər] n : interprète mf

perfume [ˈpərˌfjuːm, pərˈ-] n : parfum m

perhaps [pərˈhæps] adv : peut-être

peril [ˈpɛrəl] n : péril m — **perilous** [ˈpɛrələs] adj : périlleux

perimeter [pəˈrɪmət̬ər] n : périmètre m

period [ˈpɪriəd] n **1** : point m (signe de ponctuation) **2** TIME : période f **3** ERA : époque f **4** or **menstrual ~** : règles fpl — **periodic** [ˌpɪriˈɑdɪk] adj : périodique — **periodical** [ˌpɪriˈɑdɪkəl] n : périodique m

peripheral [pəˈrɪfərəl] adj : périphérique

perish [ˈpɛrɪʃ] vi : périr — **perishable** [ˈpɛrɪʃəbəl] adj : périssable — **perishables** [ˈpɛrɪʃəbəlz] npl : denrées fpl périssables

perjury [ˈpərdʒəri] n : faux témoignage m

perk [ˈpərk] vi **~ up** : se ragaillardir — ~ n : avantage m — **perky** [ˈpərki] adj **perkier; perkiest** : guilleret

permanence [ˈpərmənənts] n : permanence f — **permanent** [ˈpərmənənt] adj : permanent — ~ n : permanente f

permeate [ˈpərmiˌeɪt] vt **-ated; -ating** : pénétrer

permission [pərˈmɪʃən] n : permission f — **permissible** [pərˈmɪsəbəl] adj : permis, admissible — **permissive** [pərˈmɪsɪv] adj : permissif — **permit** [pərˈmɪt] v **-mitted; -mitting** : permettre — ~ [ˈpərˌmɪt, pərˈ-] n : permis m

peroxide [pəˈrɑkˌsaɪd] n : peroxyde m

perpendicular [ˌpərpənˈdɪkjələr] adj : perpendiculaire

perpetrate [ˈpərpəˌtreɪt] vt **-trated; -trating** : perpétrer — **perpetrator** [ˈpərpəˌtreɪt̬ər] n : auteur m (d'un délit)

perpetual [pərˈpɛtʃʊəl] adj : perpétuel

perplex [pərˈplɛks] vt : laisser perplexe — **perplexity** [pərˈplɛksət̬i] n, pl **-ties** : perplexité f

persecute [ˈpərsɪˌkjuːt] vt **-cuted; -cuting** : persécuter — **persecution** [ˌpərsɪˈkjuːʃən] n : persécution f

persevere [ˌpərsəˈvɪr] vi **-vered; -vering** : persévérer — **perseverance** [ˌpərsəˈvɪrənts] n : persévérance f

persist [pərˈsɪst] vi : persister — **persistence** [pərˈsɪstənts] n : persistance f — **persistent** [pərˈsɪstənt] adj : persistant

person [ˈpərsən] n : personne f — **personal** [ˈpərsənəl] adj : personnel — **personality** [ˌpərsənˈælət̬i] n, pl **-ties** : personnalité f — **personally** [ˈpərsənəli] adv : personnellement — **personnel** [ˌpərsəˈnɛl] n : personnel m

perspective [pərˈspɛktɪv] n : perspective f

perspiration [ˌpərspəˈreɪʃən] n : transpiration f — **perspire** [pərˈspaɪr] vi **-spired; -spiring** : transpirer

persuade [pərˈsweɪd] vt **-suaded; -suading** : persuader — **persuasion** [pərˈsweɪʒən] n **1** : persuasion f **2** BELIEF : conviction f

pertain [pərˈteɪn] vi **~ to** : avoir rapport à — **pertinent** [ˈpərtənənt] adj : pertinent

perturb [pərˈtərb] vt : troubler

pervade [pərˈveɪd] vt **-vaded; -vading** : se répandre dans — **pervasive** [pərˈveɪsɪv, -zɪv] adj : envahissant

perverse [pərˈvərs] adj **1** CORRUPT : pervers **2** STUBBORN : obstiné — **pervert** [ˈpərˌvərt] n : pervers m, -verse f

pessimism [ˈpɛsəˌmɪzəm] n : pessimisme m — **pessimist** [ˈpɛsəmɪst] n : pessimiste mf — **pessimistic** [ˌpɛsəˈmɪstɪk] adj : pessimiste

pest [ˈpɛst] n **1** : plante f ou animal m nuisible **2** NUISANCE : peste f

pester [ˈpɛstər] vt **-tered; -tering** : importuner, harceler

pesticide [ˈpɛstəˌsaɪd] n : pesticide m

pet [ˈpɛt] n **1** : animal m domestique **2** FAVORITE : chouchou m fam — ~ vt **petted; petting** : caresser

petal [ˈpɛtəl] n : pétale m

petition [pəˈtɪʃən] n : pétition f — ~ vt : adresser une pétition à

petrify [ˈpɛtrəˌfaɪ] vt **-fied; -fying** : pétrifier

petroleum [pəˈtroːliəm] n : pétrole m

petty [ˈpɛt̬i] adj **-tier; -est 1** INSIGNIFICANT : insignifiant **2** MEAN : mesquin

petulant [ˈpɛtʃələnt] adj : irritable

pew [ˈpjuː] n : banc m d'église

pewter [ˈpjuːt̬ər] *n* : étain *m*

pharmacy [ˈfɑrməsi] *n, pl* **-cies** : pharmacie *f* — **pharmacist** [ˌfɑrməsɪst] *n* : pharmacien *m*, -cienne *f*

phase [ˈfeɪz] *n* : phase *f* — ~ *vt* **phased; phasing 1** ~ **in** : introduire graduellement **2** ~ **out** : discontinuer progressivement

phenomenon [fɪˈnɑməˌnɑn, -nən] *n, pl* **-na** [-nə] *or* **-nons** : phénomène *m* — **phenomenal** [fɪˈnɑmənəl] *adj* : phénoménal

philanthropy [fəˈlænʔθrəpi] *n, pl* **-pies** : philanthropie *f* — **philanthropist** [fəˈlænʔθrəpɪst] *n* : philanthrope *mf*

philosophy [fəˈlɑsəfi] *n, pl* **-phies** : philosophie *f* — **philosopher** [fəˈlɑsəfər] *n* : philosophe *mf*

phlegm [ˈflɛm] *n* : mucosité *f*

phobia [ˈfoːbiə] *n* : phobie *f*

phone [ˈfoːn] → **telephone**

phonetic [fəˈnɛt̬ɪk] *adj* : phonétique

phony *or* **phoney** [ˈfoːni] *adj* **-nier; -est** : faux — ~ *n, pl* **-nies** : charlatan *m*

phosphorus [ˈfɑsfərəs] *n* : phosphore *m*

photo [ˈfoːt̬o] *n, pl* **-tos** : photo *f* — **photocopier** [ˈfoːt̬oˌkɑpiər] *n* : photocopieur *m*, photocopieuse *f* — **photocopy** [ˈfoːt̬oˌkɑpi] *n, pl* **-pies** : photocopie *f* — ~ *vt* **-copied; -copying** : photocopier — **photograph** [ˈfoːt̬əˌgræf] *n* : photographie *f*, photo *f* — ~ *vt* : photographier — **photographer** [fəˈtɑgrəfər] *n* : photographe *mf* — **photographic** [ˌfoːt̬əˈgræfɪk] *adj* : photographique — **photography** [fəˈtɑgrəfi] *n* : photographie *f*

phrase [ˈfreɪz] *n* : expression *f* — ~ *vt* **phrased; phrasing** : formuler, exprimer

physical [ˈfɪzɪkəl] *adj* : physique — ~ *n* : examen *m* médical

physician [fəˈzɪʃən] *n* : médecin *mf*

physics [ˈfɪzɪks] *ns & pl* : physique *f* — **physicist** [ˈfɪzəsɪst] *n* : physicien *m*, -cienne *f*

physiology [ˌfɪziˈɑləʤi] *n* : physiologie *f*

physique [fəˈziːk] *n* : physique *m*

piano [piˈænoː] *n, pl* **-anos** : piano *m* — **pianist** [piˈænɪst, ˈpiːənɪst] *n* : pianiste *mf*

pick [ˈpɪk] *vt* **1** CHOOSE : choisir **2** GATHER : cueillir **3** REMOVE : enlever **4** ~ **a fight** : chercher la bagarre — *vi* **1** CHOOSE : choisir **2** ~ **on** : harceler — ~ *n* **1** CHOICE : choix *m* **2** BEST : meilleur *m* **3** *or* **pickax** [ˈpɪkˌæks] : pic *m*

picket [ˈpɪkət] *n* **1** STAKE : piquet *m* **2** *or* ~ **line** : piquet *m* de grève — ~ *vi* : faire un piquet de grève

pickle [ˈpɪkəl] *n* **1** : cornichon *m* **2** JAM : pétrin *m fam* — ~ *vt* **-led; -ling** : conserver dans la saumure

pickpocket [ˈpɪkˌpɑkət] *n* : voleur *m*, -leuse *f* à la tire

pickup [ˈpɪkˌəp] *n or* ~ **truck** : camionnette *f* — **pick up** *vt* **1** LIFT : ramasser **2** LEARN : apprendre **3** RESUME : reprendre **4** TIDY : mettre en ordre **5** COLLECT : prendre — *vi* IMPROVE : s'améliorer

picnic [ˈpɪkˌnɪk] *n* : pique-nique *m* — ~ *vi* **-nicked; -nicking** : pique-niquer

picture [ˈpɪkʧər] *n* **1** PAINTING : tableau *m* **2** DRAWING : dessin *m* **3** PHOTO : photo *f*, photographie *f* **4** IMAGE : image *f* **5** MOVIE : film *m* — ~ *vt* **-tured; -turing 1** DEPICT : dépeindre **2** IMAGINE : s'imaginer — **picturesque** [ˌpɪkʧəˈrɛsk] *adj* : pittoresque

pie [ˈpaɪ] *n* **1** : tarte *f* (dessert) **2** : pâté *m*, tourte *f*

piece [ˈpiːs] *n* **1** : pièce *f* **2** FRAGMENT : morceau *m* — ~ *vt* **pieced; piecing** *or* ~ **together** : rassembler — **piecemeal** [ˈpiːsˌmiːl] *adv* : graduellement — ~ *adj* : fragmentaire

pier [ˈpɪr] *n* : jetée *f*

pierce [ˈpɪrs] *vt* **pierced; piercing** : percer — **piercing** [ˈpɪrsɪŋ] *adj* : perçant

piety [ˈpaɪət̬i] *n, pl* **-eties** : piété *f*

pig [ˈpɪg] *n* : porc *m*, cochon *m*

pigeon [ˈpɪʤən] *n* : pigeon *m* — **pigeonhole** [ˈpɪʤənˌhoːl] *n* : casier *m*

piggyback [ˈpɪgiˌbæk] *adv & adj* : sur le dos

pigment [ˈpɪgmənt] *n* : pigment *m*

pigpen [ˈpɪgˌpɛn] *n* : porcherie *f*

pigtail [ˈpɪgˌteɪl] *n* : natte *f*

pile[1] [ˈpaɪl] *n* HEAP : pile *f*, tas *m* — ~ *v* **piled; piling** *vt* **1** STACK : empiler **2** LOAD : remplir — *vi* **1** *or* ~ **up** : s'accumuler **2** CROWD : s'empiler

pile[2] *n* NAP : poil *m* (d'un tapis, etc.)

pilfer [ˈpɪlfər] *vt* : chaparder *fam*

pilgrim [ˈpɪlgrəm] *n* : pèlerin *m*, -rine *f* — **pilgrimage** [ˈpɪlgrəmɪʤ] *n* : pèlerinage *m*

pill [ˈpɪl] *n* : pilule *f*, cachet *m*

pillage [ˈpɪlɪʤ] *n* : pillage *m* — ~ *vt* **-laged; -laging** : piller

pillar [ˈpɪlər] *n* : pilier *m*

pillow [ˈpɪˌloː] *n* : oreiller *m* — **pillowcase** [ˈpɪloˌkeɪs] *n* : taie *f* d'oreiller

pilot [ˈpaɪlət] *n* : pilote *m* — ~ *vt* : piloter — **pilot light** *n* : veilleuse *f*

pimple [ˈpɪmpəl] *n* : bouton *m*

pin [ˈpɪn] *n* **1** : épingle *f* **2** BROOCH : broche *f* **3** *or* **bowling** ~ : quille *f* — ~ *vt* **pinned; pinning 1** FASTEN : épingler **2** *or* ~ **down** : fixer

pincers [ˈpɪnʔsərz] *npl* : tenailles *fpl*

pinch [ˈpɪnʧ] *vt* **1** : pincer **2** STEAL : piquer — *vi* : serrer — ~ *n* **1** SQUEEZE : pincement *m* **2** LITTLE : pincée *f* **3 in a** ~ : à la rigueur

pine[1] [ˈpaɪn] *n* : pin *m*

pine[2] *vi* **pined; pining 1** LANGUISH : languir **2** ~ **for** : désirer ardemment

pineapple [ˈpaɪnˌæpəl] *n* : ananas *m*

pink [ˈpɪŋk] *adj* : rose — ~ *n* : rose *m*

pinnacle [ˈpɪnɪkəl] *n* : pinacle *m*

pinpoint [ˈpɪnˌpɔɪnt] *vt* : préciser

pint [ˈpaɪnt] *n* : pinte *f*

pioneer [ˌpaɪəˈnɪr] *n* : pionnier *m*, -nière *f*

pious [ˈpaɪəs] *adj* : pieux

pipe [ˈpaɪp] *n* **1** : tuyau *m* **2** : pipe *f* (pour fumer du tabac) — **pipeline** [ˈpaɪpˌlaɪn] *n* : pipeline *m*

piquant [ˈpiːkənt, ˈpɪkwənt] *adj* : piquant

pirate [ˈpaɪrət] *n* : pirate *m*

pistachio [pəˈstæʃiˌoː, -ˈstɑ-] *n, pl* **-chios** : pistache *f*

pistol [ˈpɪstəl] *n* : pistolet *m*

piston [ˈpɪstən] *n* : piston *m*

pit [ˈpɪt] *n* **1** HOLE : trou *m*, fosse *f* **2** MINE : mine *f* **3** : creux *m* (de l'estomac) **4** : noyau *m* (d'un fruit) — ~ *vt* **pitted; pitting 1** MARK : marquer **2** : dénoyauter (un fruit) **3** ~ **against** : opposer à

pitch [ˈpɪʧ] *vt* **1** : dresser (une tente, etc.) **2** THROW : lancer — *vi* LURCH : tanguer (se dit d'un navire, etc.) — ~ *n* **1** DEGREE, LEVEL : degré *m*, niveau *m* **2** TONE : ton *m* **3** THROW : lancement *m* **4** *or* **sales** ~ : boniment *m* de vente — **pitcher** [ˈpɪʧər] *n* **1** JUG : cruche *f* **2** : artilleur *m Can* (au baseball) — **pitchfork** [ˈpɪʧˌfɔrk] *n* : fourche *f*

pitfall [ˈpɪtˌfɔl] *n* : piège *m*

pith [ˈpɪθ] *n* : moelle *f* — **pithy** [ˈpɪθi] *adj* **pithier; pithiest** : concis

pity [ˈpɪt̬i] *n, pl* **pities 1** : pitié *f* **2 what a** ~! : quel dommage! — ~ *vt* **pitied; pitying** : avoir pitié de — **pitiful** [ˈpɪt̬ɪfəl] *adj* : pitoyable — **pitiless** [ˈpɪt̬ɪləs] *adj* : impitoyable

pivot [ˈpɪvət] *n* : pivot *m* — ~ *vi* : pivoter

pizza [ˈpiːtsə] *n* : pizza *f*

placard [ˈplækərd, -ˌkɑrd] *n* POSTER : affiche *f*

placate [ˈpleɪˌkeɪt, ˈplæ-] *vt* **-cated; -cating** : calmer

place [ˈpleɪs] *n* **1** : place *f* **2** LOCATION : endroit *m*, lieu *m* **3 in the first** ~ : tout d'abord **4 take** ~ : avoir lieu — ~ *vt* **placed; placing 1** PUT, SET : placer, mettre **2** RECOGNIZE : remettre **3** ~ **an order** : passer une commande — **placement** [ˈpleɪsmənt] *n* : placement *m*

placid [ˈplæsəd] *adj* : placide

plagiarism [ˈpleɪʤəˌrɪzəm] *n* : plagiat *m* — **plagiarize** [ˈpleɪʤəˌraɪz] *vt* **-rized; -rizing** : plagier

plague [ˈpleɪg] *n* **1** : peste *f* **2** CALAMITY : fléau *m*

plaid [ˈplæd] *n* : tissu *m* écossais — ~ *adj* : écossais

plain [ˈpleɪn] *adj* **1** SIMPLE : simple **2** CLEAR : clair, évident **3** FRANK : franc **4** HOMELY : ordinaire — ~ *n* : plaine *f* — **plainly** [ˈpleɪnli] *adv* **1** SIMPLY : simplement **2** CLEARLY : clairement **3** FRANKLY : franchement

plaintiff [ˈpleɪntɪf] *n* : demandeur *m*, -deresse *f*; plaignant *m*, -gnante *f*

plan [ˈplæn] *n* **1** DIAGRAM : plan *m* **2** IDEA : projet *m* — ~ *v* **planned; planning** *vt* **1** INTEND : projeter **2** PREPARE : organiser — *vi* : faire des projets

plane[1] [ˈpleɪn] *n* **1** SURFACE : plan *m* **2** AIRPLANE : avion *m*

plane[2] *n or* **carpenter's** ~ : rabot *m*

planet [ˈplænət] *n* : planète *f*

plank [ˈplæŋk] *n* : planche *f*

planning [ˈplænɪŋ] *n* : organisation *f*, planification *f*

plant [ˈplænt] *vt* : planter — ~ *n* **1** : plante *f* **2** FACTORY : usine *f*

plaque [ˈplæk] *n* : plaque *f*

plaster [ˈplæstər] *n* : plâtre *m* — ~ *vt* **1** : plâtrer **2** COVER : couvrir

plastic [ˈplæstɪk] *adj* **1** : de plastique, en plastique **2** ~ **surgery** : chirurgie *f* esthétique — ~ *n* : plastique *m*

plate [ˈpleɪt] *n* **1** SHEET : plaque *f* **2** DISH : assiette *f* **3** ILLUSTRATION : planche *f* — ~ *vt* **plated; plating** : plaquer (avec un métal)

plateau [plæˈtoː] *n, pl* **-teaus** *or* **-teaux** [-ˈtoːz] : plateau *m*

platform [ˈplætˌfɔrm] *n* **1** STAGE : tribune *f*, estrade *f* **2** : quai *m* (d'une gare) **3** *or* **political** ~ : plate-forme *f* (électorale)

platinum [ˈplætənəm] *n* : platine *m*

platoon [pləˈtuːn] *n* : section *f* (dans l'armée)

platter [ˈplæt̬ər] *n* : plat *m*

plausible [ˈplɔzəbəl] *adj* : plausible

play [ˈpleɪ] *n* **1** : jeu *m* **2** DRAMA : pièce *f* de théâtre — ~ *vi* : jouer — *vt* **1** : jouer à (un jeu, un sport) **2** : jouer de (un instrument de musique) **3** PERFORM : jouer **4** ~ **down** : minimiser **5** ~ **up** EMPHASIZE : souligner — **player** [ˈpleɪər] *n* : joueur *m*, joueuse *f* — **playful** [ˈpleɪfəl] *adj* : enjoué — **playground** [ˈpleɪˌgraʊnd] *n* : cour *f* de récréation — **playing card** *n* : carte *f* à jouer — **playmate** [ˈpleɪˌmeɪt] *n* : camarade *mf* de jeu — **play–off** [ˈpleɪˌɔf] *n* : match *m* crucial — **playpen** [ˈpleɪˌpɛn] *n* : parc *m* (pour bébés) — **plaything** [ˈpleɪˌθɪŋ] *n* : jouet *m* — **playwright** [ˈpleɪˌraɪt] *n* : dramaturge *mf*, auteur *m* dramatique

plea [ˈpliː] *n* **1** : défense *f* (en droit) **2** REQUEST : appel *m*, requête *f* — **plead** [ˈpliːd] *v* **pleaded** *or* **pled** [ˈplɛd]; **pleading** : plaider

pleasant [ˈplɛzənt] *adj* : agréable — **please** [ˈpliːz] *v* **pleased; pleasing** *vt* **1** GRATIFY : plaire à, faire plaisir à **2** SATISFY : contenter — *vi* : plaire, faire plaisir — ~ *adv* : s'il vous plaît — **pleasing** [ˈpliːzɪŋ] *adj* : agréable — **pleasure** [ˈplɛʒər] *n* : plaisir *m*

pleat [ˈpliːt] *n* : pli *m*

pledge [ˈplɛʤ] *n* **1** SECURITY : gage *m* **2** PROMISE : promesse *f* — ~ *vt* **pledged; pledging 1** PAWN : mettre en gage **2** PROMISE : promettre

plenty [ˈplɛnti] *n* **1** ABUNDANCE : abondance *f* **2** ~ **of** : beaucoup de — **plentiful** [ˈplɛntɪfəl] *adj* : abondant

pliable [ˈplaɪəbəl] *adj* : flexible, malléable

pliers [ˈplaɪərz] *npl* : pinces *fpl*

plight [ˈplaɪt] *n* : situation *f* difficile

plod [ˈplɑd] *vi* **plodded; plodding 1** : marcher lourdement **2** LABOR : peiner

plot [ˈplɑt] *n* **1** LOT : lopin *m*, parcelle *f* (de terre) **2** STORY : intrigue *f* **3** CONSPIRACY : complot *m* — ~ *v* **plotted; plotting** *vt* : faire un plan de — *vi* CONSPIRE : comploter

plow *or* **plough** [ˈplaʊ] *n* **1** : charrue *f* **2** → **snowplow** — ~ *vt* **1** : labourer (la terre) **2** : déneiger

ploy [ˈplɔɪ] *n* : stratagème *m*

pluck [ˈplʌk] *vt* **1** : cueillir (une fleur) **2** : plumer (un oiseau) **3** : pincer (une corde) **4** ~ **one's eyebrows** : s'épiler les sourcis

plug [ˈplʌg] *n* **1** STOPPER : bouchon *m*, tampon *m* **2** : prise *f* (électrique) — ~ *vt* **plugged; plugging 1** BLOCK : boucher **2** ADVERTISE : faire de la publicité pour **3** ~ **in** : brancher

plum [ˈplʌm] *n* : prune *f*, pruneau *m Can*

plumb [ˈplʌm] *adj* : vertical, droit — **plumber** [ˈplʌmər] *n* : plombier *m* — **plumbing** [ˈplʌmɪŋ] *n* **1** : plomberie *f* **2** PIPES : tuyauterie *f*

plummet [ˈplʌmət] *vi* : tomber

plump [ˈplʌmp] *adj* : grassouillet, dodu

plunder [ˈplʌndər] *vt* : piller — ~ *n* : pillage *m*

plunge [ˈplʌnʤ] *v* **plunged; plunging** *vt* : plonger — *vi* **1** DIVE : plonger **2** DROP : chuter — ~ *n* **1** DIVE : plongeon *m* **2** DROP : chute *f* — **plunger** [ˈplʌnʤər] *n* : ventouse *f*

plural [ˈplʊrəl] *adj* : pluriel — ~ *n* : pluriel *m*

plus [ˈplʌs] *adj* : positif — ~ *n* **1** *or* ~ **sign** : plus *m* **2** ADVANTAGE : plus *m*, avantage *m* — ~ *prep* : plus — ~ *conj* AND : et

plush [ˈplʌʃ] *n* : peluche *f* — ~ *adj* : somptueux

Pluto [ˈpluːt̬oː] *n* : Pluton *f*

plutonium [pluːˈtoːniəm] *n* : plutonium *m*

ply [ˈplaɪ] *vt* **plied; plying 1** USE : manier (un outil) **2** PRACTICE : exercer

plywood [ˈplaɪˌwʊd] *n* : contre-plaqué *m*

pneumatic [nʊˈmæt̬ɪk, njʊ-] *adj* : pneumatique

pneumonia [nʊˈmoːnjə, njʊ-] *n* : pneumonie *f*

poach[1] [ˈpoːʧ] *vt* : pocher (des œufs)

poach[2] *vt or* ~ **game** : braconner le gibier — **poacher** [ˈpoːʧər] *n* : braconnier *m*, -nière *f*

pocket [ˈpɑkət] *n* : poche *f* — ~ *vt* : empocher — **pocketbook** [ˈpɑkətˌbʊk] *n* PURSE : sac *m* à main, sacoche *f Can* — **pocketknife** [ˈpɑkətˌnaɪf] *n, pl* **-knives** : canif *m*

pod [ˈpɑd] *n* : cosse *f*

poem [ˈpoːəm] *n* : poème *m* — **poet** [ˈpoːət] *n* : poète *mf* — **poetic** [poˈɛt̬ɪk] *or* **poetical** [-t̬ɪkəl] *adj* : poétique — **poetry** [ˈpoːətri] *n* : poésie *f*

poignant [ˈpɔɪnjənt] *adj* : poignant

point [ˈpɔɪnt] *n* **1** : point *m* **2** PURPOSE : utilité *f*, but *m* **3** TIP : pointe *f* **4** FEATURE : qualité *f* **5 at one** ~ : à un moment donné — ~ *vt* **1** AIM : braquer **2** *or* ~ **out** INDICATE : indiquer — **point–blank** [ˈpɔɪntˈblæŋk] *adv* : à bout portant — **pointer** [ˈpɔɪntər] *n* **1** ROD : baguette *f* **2** TIP : conseil *m* — **pointless** [ˈpɔɪntləs] *adj* : inutile — **point of view** *n* : point *m* de vue

poise [ˈpɔɪz] *n* **1** EQUILIBRIUM : équilibre *m* **2** COMPOSURE : assurance *f*

poison [ˈpɔɪzən] *n* : poison *m* — ~ *vt* : empoisonner — **poisonous** [ˈpɔɪzənəs] *adj* : vénéneux (se dit d'une plante), vénimeux (se dit d'un animal), toxique (se dit d'une substance)

poke [ˈpoːk] *v* **poked; poking** *vt* **1** JAB : pousser **2** THRUST : fourrer *fam* — ~ *n* JAB : coup *m*

poker[1] [ˈpoːkər] *n* : tisonnier *m* (pour le feu)

poker[2] *n* : poker *m* (jeu de cartes)

polar [ˈpoːlər] *adj* : polaire — **polar bear** *n* : ours *m* polaire, ours *m* blanc — **polarize** [ˈpoːləˌraɪz] *vt* **-ized; -izing** : polariser

pole[1] [ˈpoːl] *n* ROD : perche *f*

pole[2] *n* : pôle *m* (en géographie)

police [pəˈliːs] *vt* **-liced; -licing** : surveiller — ~ *ns & pl* **the** ~ : la police — **policeman** [pəˈliːsmən] *n, pl* **-men** [-mən, -ˌmɛn] : policier *m* — **police officer** *n* : agent *m* de police — **policewoman** [pəˈliːsˌwʊmən] *n, pl* **-women** [-ˌwɪmən] : femme *f* policier

policy [ˈpɑləsi] *n, pl* **-cies 1** : politique *f* **2** *or* **insurance** ~ : police *f* d'assurance

polio [ˈpoːliˌoː] *or* **poliomyelitis** [ˌpoːliˌoːˌmaɪəˈlaɪt̬əs] *n* : polio *f*, poliomyélite *f*

polish [ˈpɑlɪʃ] *vt* **1** : polir **2** : cirer (se dit des chaussures, etc) — ~ *n* **1** LUSTER : poli *m*, éclat *m* **2** WAX : cire *f* (pour les meubles, etc.), cirage *m* (pour les chaussures) **3 nail** ~ : vernis *m* à ongles

polite [pəˈlaɪt] *adj* **-liter; -est** : poli — **politeness** [pəˈlaɪtnəs] *n* : politesse *f*

political [pəˈlɪt̬ɪkəl] *adj* : politique — **politician** [ˌpɑləˈtɪʃən] *n* : politicien *m*, -cienne *f* — **politics** [ˈpɑləˌtɪks] *ns & pl* : politique *f*

polka [ˈpoːlkə, ˈpoːkə] *n* : polka *f* — **polka dot** *n* : pois *m*, picot *m Can*

poll [ˈpoːl] *n* **1** SURVEY : sondage *m* **2** ~**s** *npl* : urnes *fpl* — ~ *vt* **1** : obtenir (des voix) **2** CANVASS : sonder

pollen [ˈpɑlən] *n* : pollen *m*

pollute [pəˈluːt] *vt* **-luted; -luting** : polluer — **pollution** [pəˈluːʃən] *n* : pollution *f*

polyester [ˈpɑliˌɛstər, ˌpɑliˈ-] *n* : polyester *m*

polymer [ˈpɑləmər] *n* : polymère *m*

pomegranate [ˈpɑməˌgrænət, ˈpɑmˌgræ-] *n* : grenade *f* (fruit)

pomp [ˈpɑmp] *n* : pompe *f* — **pompous** [ˈpɑmpəs] *adj* : pompeux

pond [ˈpɑnd] *n* : étang *m*, mare *f*

ponder [ˈpɑndər] *vt* : considérer — *vi* ~ **over** : réfléchir à, méditer sur

pontoon [pɑnˈtuːn] *n* : ponton *m*

pony [ˈpoːni] *n, pl* **-nies** : poney *m* — **ponytail** [ˈpoːniˌteɪl] *n* : queue *f* de cheval

poodle [ˈpuːdəl] *n* : caniche *m*

pool [ˈpuːl] *n* **1** PUDDLE : flaque *f* (d'eau), mare *f* (de sang) **2** RESERVE : fonds *m* commun **3** BILLIARDS : billard *m* américain **4** *or* **swimming** ~ : piscine *f* — ~ *vt* : mettre en commun

poor [ˈpʊr, ˈpor] *adj* **1** : pauvre **2** INFERIOR : mauvais — **poorly** [ˈpʊrli, ˈpor-] *adv* BADLY : mal

pop[1] [ˈpɑp] *v* **popped; popping** *vt* **1** BURST : faire éclater **2** PUT : mettre — *vi* **1** BURST : éclater, exploser **2** ~ **in** : faire une petite visite **3** *or* ~ **out** : sortir **4** ~ **up** APPEAR : surgir — ~ *n* **1** : bruit *m* sec **2** SODA : boisson *f* gazeuse — ~ *adj* : pop

pop[2] *n or* ~ **music** : musique *f* pop

popcorn [ˈpɑpˌkorn] *n* : pop-corn *m*

pope [ˈpoːp] *n* : pape *m*

poplar [ˈpɑplər] *n* : peuplier *m*

poppy [ˈpɑpi] *n, pl* **-pies** : coquelicot *m*

popular [ˈpɑpjələr] *adj* : populaire — **popularity** [ˌpɑpjəˈlærət̬i] *n* : popularité *f* — **popularize** [ˈpɑpjələˌraɪz] *vt* **-ized; -izing** : populariser

populate [ˈpɑpjəˌleɪt] *vt* **-lated; -lating** : peupler — **population** [ˌpɑpjəˈleɪʃən] *n* : population *f*

porcelain [ˈporsələn] *n* : porcelaine *f*

porch [ˈporʧ] *n* : porche *m*

porcupine [ˈporkjəˌpaɪn] *n* : porc-épic *m*

pore[1] [ˈpor] *vi* **pored; poring** ~ **over** : étudier de près

pore[2] *n* : pore *m*

pork [ˈpork] *n* : porc *m*

pornography [porˈnɑgrəfi] *n* : pornographie *f* — **pornographic** [ˌpornəˈgræfɪk] *adj* : pornographique

porous [ˈporəs] *adj* : poreux

porpoise [ˈporpəs] *n* : marsouin *m*

porridge [ˈporɪʤ] *n* : porridge *m France*, gruau *m Can*

port[1] [ˈport] *n* HARBOR : port *m*

port[2] *n or* ~ **side** : bâbord *m*

port[3] *n or* ~ **wine** : porto *m*

portable [ˈport̬əbəl] *adj* : portatif

porter [ˈport̬ər] *n* : porteur *m*, -teuse *f*

portfolio [portˈfoːliˌo] *n, pl* **-lios** : portefeuille *m*

porthole [ˈportˌhoːl] *n* : hublot *m*

portion [ˈporʃən] *n* : portion *f*

portrait [ˈportrət, -ˌtreɪt] *n* : portrait *m*

portray [porˈtreɪ] *vt* DEPICT : représenter

Portuguese [ˌporʧəˈgiːz, -ˈgiːs] *adj* : portugais — ~ *n* : portugais *m* (langue)

pose [ˈpoːz] *v* **posed; posing** *vt* : poser — *vi* **1** : poser **2** ~ **as** : se faire passer pour — ~ *n* : pose *f*

posh [ˈpɑʃ] *adj* : chic

position [pəˈzɪʃən] *n* **1** : position *f* **2** JOB : poste *m* — ~ *vt* **1** PLACE : placer **2** ORIENT : positionner

positive [ˈpɑzət̬ɪv] *adj* **1** : positif **2** SURE : sûr, certain

possess [pəˈzɛs] *vt* : posséder — **possession** [pəˈzɛʃən] *n* **1** : possession *f* **2** ~**s** *npl* BELONGINGS : biens *mpl* — **possessive** [pəˈzɛsɪv] *adj* : possessif

possible ['pɑsəbəl] *adj* : possible — **possibility** [ˌpɑsə'bɪləṭi] *n, pl* **-ties** : possibilité *f* — **possibly** ['pɑsəbli] *adv* : peut-être, possiblement *Can*

post[1] ['po:st] *n* POLE : poteau *m*

post[2] *n* POSITION : poste *m*

post[3] *n* MAIL : poste *f,* courrier *m* — ~ *vt* **1** MAIL : poster **2 keep ~ed** : tenir au courant — **postage** ['po:stɪʤ] *n* : affranchissement *m* — **postal** ['po:stəl] *adj* : postal — **postcard** ['po:stˌkɑrd] *n* : carte *f* postale

poster ['po:stər] *n* : poster *m,* affiche *f*

posterity [pɑ'stɛrəṭi] *n* : postérité *f*

posthumous ['pɑsʧəməs] *adj* : posthume

postman ['po:stmən, -ˌmæn] *n, pl* **-men** [-mən, -ˌmɛn] → **mailman** — **post office** *n* : bureau *m* de poste

postpone [ˌpo:st'po:n] *vt* **-poned; -poning** : remettre, reporter — **postponement** [ˌpo:st'po:nmənt] *n* : renvoi *m,* remise *f*

postscript ['po:stˌskrɪpt] *n* : post-scriptum *m*

posture ['pɑsʧər] *n* : posture *f*

postwar [ˌpo:st'wɔr] *adj* : d'après-guerre

pot ['pɑt] *n* **1** SAUCEPAN : marmite *f,* casserole *f* **2** CONTAINER : pot *m*

potassium [pə'tæsiəm] *n* : potassium *m*

potato [pə'teɪṭo] *n, pl* **-toes** : pomme *f* de terre, patate *f fam*

potent ['po:tənt] *adj* **1** POWERFUL : puissant **2** EFFECTIVE : efficace

potential [pə'tɛnʧəl] *adj* : potentiel — ~ *n* : potentiel *m*

pothole ['pɑtˌho:l] *n* : nid-de-poule *m*

potion ['po:ʃən] *n* : potion *f*

pottery ['pɑṭəri] *n, pl* **-teries** : poterie *f*

pouch ['paʊʧ] *n* **1** BAG : petit sac *m* **2** : poche *f* (des marsupiaux)

poultry ['po:ltri] *n* : volaille *f*

pounce ['paʊnts] *vi* **pounced; pouncing** : bondir

pound[1] ['paʊnd] *n* **1** : livre *f* (unité de mesure) **2** : livre *f* sterling

pound[2] *n* SHELTER : fourrière *f*

pound[3] *vt* **1** CRUSH : piler **2** HAMMER : marteler **3** BEAT : battre — *vi* BEAT : battre

pour ['por] *vt* : verser — *vi* **1** FLOW : couler **2** RAIN : pleuvoir à verse

pout ['paʊt] *vi* : faire la moue — ~ *n* : moue *f*

poverty ['pɑvərṭi] *n* : pauvreté *f*

powder ['paʊdər] *vt* **1** : poudrer **2** CRUSH : pulvériser — ~ *n* : poudre *f* — **powdery** ['paʊdəri] *adj* : poudreux

power ['paʊər] *n* **1** AUTHORITY : pouvoir *m* **2** ABILITY : capacité *f* **3** STRENGTH : puissance *f* **4** CURRENT : courant *m* — ~ *vt* : faire fonctionner, faire marcher — **powerful** ['paʊərfəl] *adj* : puissant — **powerless** ['paʊərləs] *adj* : impuissant

practical ['præktɪkəl] *adj* : pratique — **practically** ['præktɪkli] *adv* : pratiquement

practice *or* **practise** ['præktəs] *v* **-ticed** *or* **-tised; -ticing** *or* **-tising** *vt* **1** : pratiquer **2** : exercer (une profession) — *vi* **1** : s'exercer **2** TRAIN : s'entraîner — ~ *n* **1** : pratique *f* **2** : exercice *m* (d'une profession) **3** TRAINING : entraînement *m* — **practitioner** [præk'tɪʃənər] *n* : praticien *m,* -cienne *f*

pragmatic [præg'mæṭɪk] *adj* : pragmatique

prairie ['prɛri] *n* : prairie *f*

praise ['preɪz] *vt* **praised; praising** : louer — ~ *n* : louange *f* — **praiseworthy** ['preɪzˌwərði] *adj* : louable, digne d'éloges

prance ['prænts] *vt* **pranced; prancing** : caracoler (se dit d'un cheval), cabrioler (se dit d'une personne)

prank ['præŋk] *n* : farce *f*

prawn ['prɔn] *n* : crevette *f* (rose)

pray ['preɪ] *vi* : prier — **prayer** ['prɛr] *n* : prière *f*

preach ['pri:ʧ] *v* : prêcher — **preacher** ['pri:ʧər] *n* : pasteur *m*

precarious [prɪ'kæriəs] *adj* : précaire

precaution [prɪ'kɔʃən] *n* : précaution *f*

precede [prɪ'si:d] *vt* **-ceded; -ceding** : précéder — **precedence** ['prɛsədənts, prɪ'si:dənts] *n* **1** : préséance *f* **2** PRIORITY : priorité *f* — **precedent** ['prɛsədənt] *n* : précédent *m*

precinct ['pri:ˌsɪŋkt] *n* **1** DISTRICT : arrondissement *m* (en France), circonscription *f* (au Canada) **2 ~s** *npl* : environs *mpl*

precious ['prɛʃəs] *adj* : précieux

precipice ['prɛsəpəs] *n* : précipice *m*

precipitate [pri'sɪpəˌteɪt] *v* **-tated; -tating** : précipiter — **precipitation** [priˌsɪpə'teɪʃən] *n* **1** HASTE : précipitation *f,* hâte *f* **2** : précipitations *fpl* (en météorologie)

precise [pri'saɪs] *adj* : précis — **precisely** [pri'saɪsli] *adv* : précisément — **precision** [pri'sɪʒən] *n* : précision *f*

preclude [pri'klu:d] *vt* **-cluded; -cluding** : empêcher

precocious [pri'ko:ʃəs] *adj* : précoce

preconceived [ˌpri:kən'si:vd] *adj* : préconçu

predator ['prɛdəṭər] *n* : prédateur *m*

predecessor ['prɛdəˌsɛsər, 'pri:-] *n* : prédécesseur *m*

predicament [pri'dɪkəmənt] *n* : situation *f* difficile

predict [pri'dɪkt] *vt* : prédire — **predictable** [pri'dɪktəbəl] *adj* : prévisible — **prediction** [pri'dɪkʃən] *n* : prédiction *f*

predispose [ˌpri:dɪ'spo:z] *vt* : prédisposer

predominant [pri'dɑmənənt] *adj* : prédominant

preen ['pri:n] *vt* : lisser (ses plumes)

prefabricated [ˌpri:'fæbrəˌkeɪṭəd] *adj* : préfabriqué

preface ['prɛfəs] *n* : préface *f*

prefer [pri'fər] *vt* **-ferred; -ferring** : préférer — **preferable** ['prɛfərəbəl] *adj* : préférable — **preference** ['prɛfrənts, 'prɛfər-] *n* : préférence *f* — **preferential** [ˌprɛfə'rɛnʧəl] *adj* : préférentiel

prefix ['pri:ˌfɪks] *n* : préfixe *m*

pregnancy ['prɛgnəntsi] *n, pl* **-cies** : grossesse *f* — **pregnant** ['prɛgnənt] *adj* : enceinte

prehistoric [ˌpri:hɪs'tɔrɪk] *or* **prehistorical** [-ɪkəl] *adj* : préhistorique

prejudice ['prɛʤədəs] *n* **1** HARM : préjudice *m* **2** BIAS : préjugés *mpl* — ~ *vt* **-diced; -dicing 1** : porter préjudice à (en droit) **2 be ~d** : avoir des préjugés

preliminary [pri'lɪməˌnɛri] *adj* : préliminaire

prelude ['prɛˌlu:d, 'prɛlˌju:d; 'preɪˌlu:d, 'pri:-] *n* : prélude *m*

premature [ˌpri:mə'tʊr, -'tjʊr, -'ʧʊr] *adj* : prématuré

premeditated [pri'mɛdəˌteɪṭəd] *adj* : prémédité

premier [pri'mɪr, -'mjɪr; 'pri:miər] *adj* : premier — ~ *n* → **prime minister**

premiere [prɪ'mjɛr, -'mɪr] *n* : première *f* (d'un spectacle)

premise ['prɛmɪs] *n* **1** : prémisse *f* (d'un raisonnement) **2 ~s** *npl* : lieux *mpl*

premium ['pri:miəm] *n* : prime *f*

preoccupied [pri'ɑkjəˌpaɪd] *adj* : préoccupé

prepare [prɪ'pær] *v* **-pared; -paring** *vt* : préparer — *vi* : se préparer — **preparation** [ˌprɛpə'reɪʃən] *n* **1** PREPARING : préparation *f* **2 ~s** *npl* ARRANGEMENTS : préparatifs *mpl* — **preparatory** [pri'pærəˌtori] *adj* : préparatoire

prepay [ˌpri:'peɪ] *vt* **-paid; -paying** : payer d'avance

preposition [ˌprɛpə'zɪʃən] *n* : préposition *f*

preposterous [pri'pɑstərəs] *adj* : absurde, insensé

prerequisite [pri'rɛkwəzət] *n* : préalable *m*

prerogative [prɪ'rɑgəṭɪv] *n* : prérogative *f*

prescribe [pri'skraɪb] *vt* **-scribed; -scribing** : prescrire — **prescription** [pri'skrɪpʃən] *n* : prescription *f*

presence ['prɛzənts] *n* : présence *f*

present[1] ['prɛzənt] *adj* **1** CURRENT : actuel **2** ATTENDING : présent — ~ *n or* **~ time** : présent *m*

present[2] ['prɛzənt] *n* GIFT : cadeau *m* — ~ [pri'zɛnt] *vt* : présenter — **presentation** [ˌpri:ˌzɛn'teɪʃən, ˌprɛzən-] *n* : présentation *f*

presently ['prɛzəntli] *adv* **1** SOON : bientôt **2** NOW : actuellement, en ce moment

preserve [pri'zərv] *vt* **-served; -serving 1** PROTECT : préserver **2** MAINTAIN : conserver — ~ *n* **1** *or* **game ~** : réserve *f* **2 ~s** *npl* : confitures *fpl* — **preservation** [ˌprɛzər'veɪʃən] *n* : préservation *f,* maintien *m* — **preservative** [pri'zərvəṭɪv] *n* : agent *m* de conservation

president ['prɛzədənt] *n* : président *m* — **presidency** ['prɛzədəntsi] *n, pl* **-cies** : présidence *f* — **presidential** [ˌprɛzə'dɛnʧəl] *adj* : présidentiel

press ['prɛs] *n* : presse *f* — ~ *vt* **1** PUSH : presser, appuyer sur **2** IRON : repasser — *vi* **1** PUSH : appuyer **2** CROWD : se presser — **pressing** ['prɛsɪŋ] *adj* : urgent — **pressure** ['prɛʃər] *n* : pression *f* — ~ *vt* **-sured; -suring** : pousser, faire pression sur

prestige [prɛ'sti:ʒ, -'sti:ʤ] *n* : prestige *m* — **prestigious** [prɛ'stɪʤəs, -'sti-, prə-] *adj* : prestigieux

presume [pri'zu:m] *vt* **-sumed; -suming** : présumer — **presumably** [pri'zu:məbli] *adv* : vraisemblablement — **presumption** [prɪ'zʌmpʃən] *n* : présomption *f* — **presumptuous** [prɪ'zʌmpʧʊəs] *adj* : présomptueux

pretend [pri'tɛnd] *vt* **1** PROFESS : prétendre **2** FEIGN : faire semblant de — *vi* : faire semblant — **pretense** *or* **pretence** ['pri:ˌtɛnts, pri'tɛnts] *n* **1** CLAIM : prétention *f* **2** PRETEXT : prétexte *m* — **pretentious** [pri'tɛnʧəs] *adj* : prétentieux

pretext ['pri:ˌtɛkst] *n* : prétexte *m*

pretty ['prɪṭi] *adj* **-tier; -est** : joli, beau — ~ *adv* FAIRLY : assez

pretzel ['prɛtsəl] *n* : bretzel *m*

prevail [pri'veɪl] *vi* : prévaloir — **prevalent** ['prɛvələnt] *adj* : répandu

prevent [pri'vɛnt] *vt* : empêcher — **prevention** [pri'vɛnʧən] *n* : prévention *f* — **preventive** [pri'vɛntɪv] *adj* : préventif

preview ['pri:ˌvju] *n* : avant-première *f*

previous ['pri:viəs] *adj* : antérieur, précédent — **previously** ['pri:viəsli] *adv* : antérieurement, auparavant

prey ['preɪ] *ns & pl* : proie *f* — **prey on** *vt* : faire sa proie de

price ['praɪs] *n* : prix *m* — ~ *vt* **priced; pricing** : fixer un prix sur — **priceless** ['praɪsləs] *adj* : inestimable

prick ['prɪk] *n* : piqûre *f* — ~ *vt* **1** : piquer **2 ~ up one's ears** : dresser l'oreille — **prickly** ['prɪkəli] *adj* **-lier; -est** : épineux

pride ['praɪd] *n* : fierté *f,* orgueil *m* — ~ *vt* **prided; priding ~ oneself on** : être fier de

priest ['pri:st] *n* : prêtre *m* — **priesthood** ['pri:stˌhʊd] *n* : prêtrise *f*

prim ['prɪm] *adj* **primmer; primmest** : guindé

primary ['praɪˌmɛri, 'praɪməri] *adj* **1** FIRST : primaire **2** PRINCIPAL : principal — **primarily** [praɪ'mɛrəli] *adv* : principalement

prime[1] ['praɪm] *vt* **primed; priming 1** LOAD : charger **2** PREPARE : apprêter **3** COACH : préparer

prime[2] *n* **the ~ of life** : la force de l'âge — ~ *adj* **1** MAIN : principal **2** EXCELLENT : excellent — **prime minister** *n* : Premier ministre *m*

primer[1] ['praɪmər] *n* : apprêt *m*

primer[2] ['prɪmər] *n* : premier livre *m* de lecture

primitive ['prɪməṭɪv] *adj* : primitif

primrose ['prɪmˌro:z] *n* : primevère *f*

prince ['prɪnts] *n* : prince *m* — **princess** ['prɪntsəs, 'prɪnˌsɛs] *n* : princesse *f*

principal ['prɪntsəpəl] *adj* : principal — ~ *n* **1** DIRECTOR : directeur *m,* -trice *f* **2** : principal *m* (d'une dette), capital *m* (d'une somme)

principle ['prɪntsəpəl] *n* : principe *m*

print ['prɪnt] *n* **1** MARK : empreinte *f* **2** LETTER : caractère *m* **3** ENGRAVING : gravure *f* **4** : imprimé *m* (d'un tissu) **5** : épreuve *f* (en photographie) **6 in ~** : disponible — ~ *vt* : imprimer (un texte, etc.) — *vi* : écrire en lettres moulées — **printer** ['prɪntər] *n* **1** : imprimeur *m* (personne) **2** : imprimante *f* (machine) — **printing** ['prɪntɪŋ] *n* **1** : imprimerie *f* (technique) **2** IMPRESSION : impression *f* **3** LETTERING : écriture *f* en lettres moulées

prior ['praɪər] *adj* **1** : antérieur, précédent **2 ~ to** : avant — **priority** [praɪ'ɔrəṭi] *n, pl* **-ties** : priorité *f*

prison ['prɪzən] *n* : prison *f* — **prisoner** ['prɪzənər] *n* : prisonnier *m,* -nière *f*

privacy ['praɪvəsi] *n, pl* **-cies** : intimité *f* — **private** ['praɪvət] *adj* **1** : privé **2** PERSONAL : personnel — ~ *n* : (simple) soldat *m* — **privately** ['praɪvətli] *adv* : en privé

privilege ['prɪvlɪʤ, 'prɪvə-] *n* : privilège *m* — **privileged** ['prɪvlɪʤd, 'prɪvə-] *adj* : privilégié

prize ['praɪz] *n* : prix *m* — ~ *adj* : primé — ~ *vt* **prized; prizing** : priser — **prizewinning** ['praɪzˌwɪnɪŋ] *adj* : primé, gagnant

pro ['pro:] *n* **1** → **professional 2 the ~s and cons** : le pour et le contre

probability [ˌprɑbə'bɪləṭi] *n, pl* **-ties** : probabilité *f* — **probable** ['prɑbəbəl] *adj* : probable — **probably** [-bli] *adv* : probablement

probation [pro'beɪʃən] *n* : période *f* d'essai (d'un employé)

probe ['pro:b] *n* **1** : sonde *f* (en médecine) **2** INVESTIGATION : enquête *f* — ~ *vt* **probed; probing** : sonder

problem ['prɑbləm] *n* : problème *m*

procedure [prə'si:ʤər] *n* : procédure *f*

proceed [pro'si:d] *vi* **1** ACT : procéder **2** CONTINUE : continuer **3** ADVANCE : avancer, aller — **proceedings** [pro'si:dɪŋz] *npl* **1** EVENTS : événements *mpl* **2** *or* **legal ~** : poursuites *fpl* — **proceeds** ['pro:ˌsi:dz] *npl* : recette *f*

process ['prɑˌsɛs, 'pro:-] *n, pl* **-cesses** ['prɑˌsɛsəz, 'pro:-, -səsəz, -səˌsi:z] **1** : processus *m* **2** METHOD : procédé *m* **3 in the ~ of** : en train de — ~ *vt* : traiter — **procession** [prə'sɛʃən] *n* : procession *f*

proclaim [pro'kleɪm] *vt* : proclamer — **proclamation** [ˌprɑklə'meɪʃən] *n* : proclamation *f*

procrastinate [prə'kræstəˌneɪt] *vi* **-nated; -nating** : remettre à plus tard

procure [prə'kjʊr] *vt* **-cured; -curing** : obtenir

prod ['prɑd] *vt* **prodded; prodding** : pousser

prodigal ['prɑdɪgəl] *adj* : prodigue

prodigious [prə'dɪʤəs] *adj* : prodigieux

prodigy ['prɑdəʤi] *n, pl* **-gies** : prodige *m*

produce [prə'du:s, -'dju:s] *vt* **-duced; -ducing 1** : produire **2** SHOW : présenter **3** CAUSE : causer — ~ ['prɑˌdu:s, 'pro:-, -ˌdju:s] *n* : produits *mpl* agricoles — **producer** [prə'du:sər, -'dju:-] *n* : producteur *m,* -trice *f* — **product** ['prɑˌdʌkt] *n* : produit *m* — **productive** [prə'dʌktɪv] *adj* : productif

profane [pro'feɪn] *adj* **1** SECULAR : profane **2** IRREVERENT : sacrilège — **profanity** [pro'fænəṭi] *n, pl* **-ties** : juron *m*

profess [prə'fɛs] *vt* : professer — **profession** [prə'fɛʃən] *n* : profession *f* — **professional** [prə'fɛʃənəl] *adj* : professionnel — ~ *n* : professionnel *m,* -nelle *f* — **professor** [prə'fɛsər] *n* : professeur *m*

proficiency [prə'fɪʃəntsi] *n, pl* **-cies** : compétence *f* — **proficient** [prə'fɪʃənt] *adj* : compétent

profile ['pro:ˌfaɪl] *n* : profil *m*

profit ['prɑfət] *n* : profit *m,* bénéfice *m* — ~ *vi* **~ from** : tirer profit de — *vt* BENEFIT : profiter à — **profitable** ['prɑfətəbəl] *adj* : profitable

profound [prə'faʊnd] *adj* : profond

profuse [prə'fju:s] *adj* **1** ABUNDANT : abondant **2** LAVISH : prodigue — **profusion** [prə'fju:ʒən] *n* : profusion *f*

prognosis [prɑg'no:sɪs] *n, pl* **-ses** [-ˌsi:z] : pronostic *m*

program *or Brit* **programme** ['pro:ˌgræm, -grəm] *n* **1** : programme *m* **2 television ~** : émission *f* de télévision — ~ *vt* **-grammed** *or* **-gramed; -gramming** *or* **-graming** : programmer

progress ['prɑgrəs, -ˌgrɛs] *n* **1** : progrès *m* **2 in ~** : en cours — ~ [prə'grɛs] *vi* : progresser — **progressive** [prɑ'grɛsɪv] *adj* **1** : progressiste (en politique, etc.) **2** : progressif

prohibit [pro'hɪbət] *vt* : interdire — **prohibition** [ˌpro:ə'bɪʃən, ˌpro:hə-] *n* : prohibition *f*

project ['prɑˌʤɛkt, -ʤɪkt] *n* : projet *m* — ~ [prə'ʤɛkt] *vt* : projeter — *vi* PROTRUDE : faire saillie — **projectile** [prə'ʤɛktəl, -ˌtaɪl] *n* : projectile *m* — **projection** [prə'ʤɛkʃən] *n* **1** : projection *f* **2** BULGE : saillie *f* — **projector** [prə'ʤɛktər] *n* : projecteur *m*

proliferate [prə'lɪfəˌreɪt] *vi* **-ated; -ating** : proliférer — **proliferation** [prəˌlɪfə'reɪʃən] *n* : prolifération *f* — **prolific** [prə'lɪfɪk] *adj* : prolifique

prologue ['pro:ˌlɔg, -ˌlɑg] *n* : prologue *m*

prolong [prə'lɔŋ] *vt* : prolonger

prom ['prɑm] *n* : bal *m* d'étudiants

prominent ['prɑmənənt] *adj* **1** : proéminent **2** IMPORTANT : important — **prominence** ['prɑmənənts] *n* **1** : proéminence *f* **2** IMPORTANCE : importance *f*

promiscuous [prə'mɪskjʊəs] *adj* : de mœurs légères

promise ['prɑməs] *n* : promesse *f* — ~ *v* **-mised; -mising** : promettre — **promising** ['prɑməsɪŋ] *adj* : prometteur

promote [prə'mo:t] *vt* **-moted; -moting** : promouvoir — **promoter** [prə'mo:ṭər] *n* : promoteur *m,* -trice *f* — **promotion** [prə'mo:ʃən] *n* : promotion *f*

prompt ['prɑmpt] *vt* **1** INCITE : inciter **2** CAUSE : provoquer — ~ *adj* **1** QUICK : prompt **2** PUNCTUAL : ponctuel

prone ['pro:n] *adj* **1** APT : sujet, enclin **2** FLAT : à plat ventre

prong ['prɔŋ] *n* : dent *f*

pronoun ['pro:ˌnaʊn] *n* : pronom *m*

pronounce [prə'naʊnts] *vt* **-nounced; -nouncing** : prononcer — **pronouncement** [prə'naʊntsmənt] *n* : déclaration *f* — **pronunciation** [prəˌnʌntsi'eɪʃən] *n* : prononciation *f*

proof ['pru:f] *n* **1** EVIDENCE : preuve *f* **2** PRINT : épreuve *f* — **proofread** ['pru:fˌri:d] *vt* **-read** [-ˌrɛd]; **-reading** : corriger les épreuves de

prop ['prɑp] *n* **1** SUPPORT : étai *m* **2 ~s** *npl* : accessoires *mpl* — ~ *vt* **propped; propping 1** LEAN : appuyer **2 ~ up** SUPPORT : étayer

propaganda [ˌprɑpə'gændə, ˌpro:-] *n* : propagande *f*

propagate ['prɑpəˌgeɪt] *v* **-gated; -gating** *vt* : propager — *vi* : se propager

propel [prə'pɛl] *vt* **-pelled; -pelling** : propulser — **propeller** [prə'pɛlər] *n* : hélice *f*

propensity [prə'pɛntsəṭi] *n, pl* **-ties** : propension *f*

proper ['prɑpər] *adj* **1** SUITABLE : convenable **2** REAL : vrai **3** CORRECT : correct **4 ~ name** : nom propre — **properly** ['prɑpərli] *adv* : correctement

property ['prɑpərṭi] *n, pl* **-ties 1** POSSESSIONS : biens *mpl,* propriété *f* **2** REAL ESTATE : biens *mpl* immobiliers **3** QUALITY : propriété *f*

prophet ['prɑfət] *n* : prophète *m* — **prophecy** ['prɑfəsi] *n, pl* **-cies** : prophétie *f* — **prophesy** ['prɑfəˌsaɪ] *vt* **-sied; -sying** : prophétiser — **prophetic** [prə'fɛṭɪk] *adj* : prophétique

proponent [prə'po:nənt] *n* : partisan *m,* -sane *f*

proportion [prə'porʃən] *n* **1** : proportion *f* **2** SHARE : part *f* — **proportional** [prə'porʃənəl] *adj* : proportionnel — **proportionate** [prə'porʃənət] *adj* : proportionnel

proposal [prə'po:zəl] *n* : proposition *f*

propose [prə'po:z] *v* **-posed; -posing** *vt* : proposer — *vi* : faire une demande en mariage — **proposition** [ˌprɑpə'zɪʃən] *n* : proposition *f*

proprietor [prə'praɪəṭər] *n* : propriétaire *mf*

propriety [prə'praɪəṭi] *n, pl* **-ties** : convenance *f*

propulsion [prə'pʌlʃən] *n* : propulsion *f*

prose ['pro:z] *n* : prose *f*

prosecute ['prɑsɪˌkju:t] *vt* **-cuted; -cuting** : poursuivre — **prosecution** [ˌprɑsɪ'kju:ʃən] *n* : poursuites *fpl* judiciaires — **prosecutor** ['prɑsɪˌkju:t̬ər] *n* : procureur *m*

prospect ['prɑˌspɛkt] *n* **1** VIEW : vue *f* **2** POSSIBILITY : perspective *f* **3** **~s** : espérances *fpl* — **prospective** [prə'spɛktɪv, 'prɑˌspɛk-] *adj* : éventuel

prosper ['prɑspər] *vt* : prospérer — **prosperity** [prɑ'spɛrət̬i] *n* : prospérité *f* — **prosperous** ['prɑspərəs] *adj* : prospère

prostitute ['prɑstəˌtu:t, -ˌtju:t] *n* : prostituée *f* — **prostitution** [ˌprɑstə'tu:ʃən, -'tju:-] *n* : prostitution *f*

prostrate ['prɑˌstreɪt] *adj* **1** : allongé à plat ventre **2** STRICKEN : prostré

protagonist [pro'tægənɪst] *n* : protagoniste *mf*

protect [prə'tɛkt] *vt* : protéger — **protection** [prə'tɛkʃən] *n* : protection *f* — **protective** [prə'tɛktɪv] *adj* : protecteur — **protector** [prə'tɛktər] *n* : protecteur *m*, -trice *f*

protein ['pro:ˌti:n] *n* : protéine *f*

protest ['pro:ˌtɛst] *n* **1** DEMONSTRATION : manifestation *f* **2** OBJECTION : protestation *f* — **~** [pro'tɛst] *v* : protester — **Protestant** ['prɑt̬əstənt] *n* : protestant *m*, -tante *f* — **protester** *or* **protestor** ['pro:ˌtɛstər, prə'-] *n* : manifestant *m*, -tante *f*

protocol ['pro:t̬əˌkɔl] *n* : protocole *m*

protrude [pro'tru:d] *vi* **-truded; -truding** : dépasser

proud ['praʊd] *adj* **1** : fier **2** ARROGANT : orgueilleux

prove ['pru:v] *v* **proved; proved** *or* **proven** ['pru:vən]; **proving** *vt* : prouver — *vi* : s'avérer, se montrer

proverb ['prɑˌvərb] *n* : proverbe *m*

provide [prə'vaɪd] *v* **-vided; -viding** *vt* : fournir — *vi* **~ for** SUPPORT : subvenir aux besoins de — **provided** [prə'vaɪdəd] *or* **~ that** *conj* : à condition que — **providence** ['prɑvədənts] *n* : providence *f*

province ['prɑvɪnts] *n* **1** : province *f* **2** SPHERE : domaine *m* — **provincial** [prə'vɪntʃəl] *adj* : provincial

provision [prə'vɪʒən] *n* **1** SUPPLYING : approvisionnement *m* **2** STIPULATION : stipulation *f* **3** **~s** *npl* : provisions *fpl* — **provisional** [prə'vɪʒənəl] *adj* : provisoire

provoke [prə'vo:k] *vt* **-voked; -voking** : provoquer — **provocative** [prə'vɑkət̬ɪv] *adj* : provocant, provocateur

prow ['praʊ] *n* : proue *f*

prowess ['praʊəs] *n* : prouesse *f*

prowl ['praʊl] *vi* : rôder — **~** *n* **be on the ~** : rôder — **prowler** ['praʊlər] *n* : rôdeur *m*, -deuse *f*

proximity [prɑk'sɪmət̬i] *n* : proximité *f* — **proxy** ['prɑksi] *n*, *pl* **proxies** : procuration *f*

prude ['pru:d] *n* : prude *f*

prudence ['pru:dənts] *n* : prudence *f* — **prudent** ['pru:dənt] *adj* : prudent

prune[1] ['pru:n] *n* : pruneau *m*

prune[2] *vt* **pruned; pruning** : élaguer, tailler

pry ['praɪ] *v* **pried; prying** *vi* **~ into** : mettre son nez dans — *vt or* **~ open** : forcer avec un levier

psalm ['sɑm, 'sɑlm] *n* : psaume *m*

pseudonym ['su:dənɪm] *n* : pseudonyme *m*

psychiatry [sə'kaɪətri, saɪ-] *n* : psychiatrie *f* — **psychiatric** [ˌsaɪki'ætrɪk] *adj* : psychiatrique — **psychiatrist** [sə'kaɪətrɪst, saɪ-] *n* : psychiatre *mf*

psychic ['saɪkɪk] *adj* : psychique

psychoanalysis [ˌsaɪkoə'næləsɪs] *n* : psychanalyse *f* — **psychoanalyst** [ˌsaɪko'ænəlɪst] *n* : psychanalyste *mf* — **psychoanalyze** [ˌsaɪko'ænəˌlaɪz] *vt* **-lyzed; -lyzing** : psychanalyser

psychology [saɪ'kɑləʤi] *n*, *pl* **-gies** : psychologie *f* — **psychological** [ˌsaɪkə'lɑʤɪkəl] *adj* : psychologique — **psychologist** [saɪ'kɑləʤɪst] *n* : psychologue *mf*

psychotherapy [ˌsaɪko'θɛrəpi] *n* : psychothérapie *f*

puberty ['pju:bərt̬i] *n* : puberté *f*

public ['pʌblɪk] *adj* : public — **~** *n* : public *m* — **publication** [ˌpʌblə'keɪʃən] *n* : publication *f* — **publicity** [pə'blɪsət̬i] *n* : publicité *f* — **publicize** ['pʌbləˌsaɪz] *vt* **-cized; -cizing** : rendre public, faire connaître

publish ['pʌblɪʃ] *vt* : publier — **publisher** ['pʌblɪʃər] *n* **1** : éditeur *m*, -trice *f* **2** : maison *f* d'édition (entreprise)

puck ['pʌk] *n* : palet *m*, rondelle *f Can* (au hockey)

pucker ['pʌkər] *vt* : plisser — *vi* : se plisser

pudding ['pʊdɪŋ] *n* : pudding *m*, pouding *m*

puddle ['pʌdəl] *n* : flaque *f* (d'eau)

puff ['pʌf] *vi* **1** BLOW : souffler **2** PANT : haleter **3** **~ up** SWELL : enfler — *vt or* **~ out** : gonfler — **~** *n* **1** : bouffée *f* **2** **cream ~** : chou *m* à la crème **3** *or* **powder ~** : houppette *f* — **puffy** ['pʌfi] *adj* **puffier; puffiest** : enflé, bouffi

pull ['pʊl, 'pʌl] *vt* **1** : tirer **2** STRAIN : se froisser **3** EXTRACT : arracher **4** DRAW : sortir **5** **~ off** : enlever **6** **~ oneself together** : se ressaisir **7** **~ up** RAISE : remonter — *vi* **1** **~ away** : se retirer **2** **~ out of** : quitter **3** **~ through** RECOVER : s'en tirer **4** **~ together** COOPERATE : agir en concert **5** **~ up** STOP : s'arrêter — **~** *n* **1** TUG : coup *m* **2** INFLUENCE : influence *f* — **pulley** ['pʊli] *n*, *pl* **-leys** : poulie *f* — **pullover** ['pʊlˌo:vər] *n* : chandail *m*, pull-over *m France*

pulmonary ['pʊlməˌnɛri, 'pʌl-] *adj* : pulmonaire

pulp ['pʌlp] *n* : pulpe *f*

pulpit ['pʊlˌpɪt] *n* : chaire *f*

pulsate ['pʌlˌseɪt] *vi* **-sated; -sating** **1** BEAT : palpiter **2** VIBRATE : vibrer — **pulse** ['pʌls] *n* : pouls *m*

pummel ['pʌməl] *vt* **-meled; -meling** : bourer de coups

pump[1] ['pʌmp] *n* : pompe *f* — **~** *vt* **1** : pomper (de l'eau) **2** **~ up** : gonfler

pump[2] *n* SHOE : escarpin *m*

pumpernickel ['pʌmpərˌnɪkəl] *n* : pain *m* noir

pumpkin ['pʌmpkɪn, 'pʌŋkən] *n* : citrouille *f*, potiron *m France*

pun ['pʌn] *n* : jeu *m* de mots

punch[1] ['pʌntʃ] *vt* **1** : donner un coup de poing à **2** PERFORATE : poinçonner — **~** *n* BLOW : coup *m* de poing

punch[2] *n* : punch *m* (boisson)

punctual ['pʌŋktʃʊəl] *adj* : ponctuel — **punctuality** [ˌpʌŋktʃʊ'ælət̬i] *n* : ponctualité *f*

punctuate ['pʌŋktʃʊˌeɪt] *vt* **-ated; -ating** : ponctuer — **punctuation** [ˌpʌŋktʃʊ'eɪʃən] *n* : ponctuation *f*

puncture ['pʌŋktʃər] *n* **1** HOLE : perforation *f* **2** PRICK : piqûre *f* — **~** *vt* **-tured; -turing** **1** PIERCE : perforer **2** : crever (un ballon, un pneu, etc.)

pungent ['pʌnʤənt] *adj* : âcre

punish ['pʌnɪʃ] *vt* : punir — **punishment** ['pʌnɪʃmənt] *n* : punition *f* — **punitive** ['pju:nət̬ɪv] *adj* : punitif

puny ['pju:ni] *adj* **-nier; -est** : chétif

pup ['pʌp] *n* : chiot *m*, jeune animal *m*

pupil[1] ['pju:pəl] *n* STUDENT : élève *mf*

pupil[2] *n* : pupille *f* (de l'œil)

puppet ['pʌpət] *n* : marionnette *f*

puppy ['pʌpi] *n*, *pl* **-pies** : chiot *m*

purchase ['pərtʃəs] *vt* **-chased; -chasing** : acheter — **~** *n* : achat *m*

pure ['pjʊr] *adj* **purer; purest** : pur

puree [pjʊ'reɪ, -'ri:] *n* : purée *f*

purely ['pjʊrli] *adv* : purement

purgatory ['pərgəˌtori] *n*, *pl* **-ries** : purgatoire *m* — **purge** ['pərʤ] *vt* **purged; purging** : purger — **~** *n* : purge *f*

purify ['pjʊrəˌfaɪ] *vt* **-fied; -fying** : purifier — **purifier** ['pjʊrəˌfaɪər] *n* : purificateur *m*

puritan ['pju:rətən] *n* : puritain *m*, -taine *f* — **puritanical** [ˌpju:rə'tænɪkəl] *adj* : puritain

purity ['pjʊrət̬i] *n* : pureté *f*

purple ['pərpəl] *adj* : violet, pourpre — **~** *n* : violet *m*, pourpre *m*

purpose ['pərpəs] *n* **1** AIM : intention *f*, but *m* **2** DETERMINATION : résolution *f* **3** **on ~** : exprès — **purposeful** ['pərpəsfəl] *adj* **1** MEANINGFUL : significatif **2** INTENTIONAL : réfléchi **3** DETERMINED : résolu — **purposely** ['pərpəsli] *adv* : exprès

purr ['pər] *n* : ronronnement *m* — **~** *vi* : ronronner

purse ['pərs] *n* **1** *or* **change ~** : porte-monnaie *m* **2** HANDBAG : sac *m* à main, sacoche *f Can*

pursue [pər'su:] *vt* **-sued; -suing** : poursuivre — **pursuer** [pər'su:ər] *n* : poursuivant *m*, -vante *f* — **pursuit** [pər'su:t] *n* **1** : poursuite *f* **2** OCCUPATION : activité *f*

pus ['pʌs] *n* : pus *m*

push ['pʊʃ] *vt* **1** : pousser **2** PRESS : appuyer sur **3** THRUST : enfoncer **4** **~ away** : repousser — *vi* **1** : pousser **2** **~ on** : continuer **3** **~ (oneself)** : s'exercer — **~** *n* **1** SHOVE : poussée *f* **2** EFFORT : effort *m* — **pushy** ['pʊʃi] *adj* **pushier; pushiest** : arriviste

pussycat ['pʊsiˌkæt] *n* : minet *m*, minou *m fam*

put ['pʊt] *v* **put; putting** *vt* **1** : mettre **2** PLACE : placer, poser **3** EXPRESS : dire **4** **~ forward** PROPOSE : avancer, proposer — *vi* **~ up with** TOLERATE : supporter — **put away** *vt* **1** STORE : ranger **2** *or* **~ aside** : mettre de côté — **put down** *vt* **1** : poser, déposer **2** WRITE : mettre (par écrit) — **put off** *vt* POSTPONE : remettre à plus tard, retarder — **put on** *vt* **1** ASSUME : prendre **2** PRESENT : monter (un spectacle, etc.) **3** WEAR : mettre — **put out** *vt* **1** EXTINGUISH, TURN OFF : éteindre **2** INCONVENIENCE : déranger — **put up** *vt* **1** BUILD : ériger **2** LODGE : loger **3** HANG : accrocher

putrefy ['pju:trəˌfaɪ] *v* **-fied; -fying** *vt* : putréfier — *vi* : se putréfier

putty ['pʌt̬i] *n*, *pl* **-ties** : mastic *m*

puzzle ['pʌzəl] *vt* **-zled; -zling** CONFUSE : intriguer, laisser perplexe — **~** *n* **1** : casse-tête *m* **2** *or* **jigsaw ~** : puzzle *m* **3** MYSTERY : énigme *f*, mystère *m*

pyjamas *Brit* → **pajamas**

pylon ['paɪˌlɑn, -lən] *n* : pylône *m*

pyramid ['pɪrəˌmɪd] *n* : pyramide *f*

python ['paɪˌθɑn, -θən] *n* : python *m*

Q

q ['kju:] *n*, *pl* **q's** *or* **qs** ['kju:z] : q *m*, dix-septième lettre de l'alphabet

quack[1] ['kwæk] *vi* : faire des coin-coin

quack[2] *n* CHARLATAN : charlatan *m*

quadruped ['kwɑdrəˌpɛd] *n* : quadrupède *m*

quadruple [kwɑ'dru:pəl, -'drʌ-; 'kwɑdrə-] *v* **-pled; -pling** : quadrupler — **~** *adj* : quadruple

quagmire ['kwægˌmaɪr, 'kwɑg-] *n* : bourbier *m*

quail ['kweɪl] *n*, *pl* **quail** *or* **quails** : caille *f*

quaint ['kweɪnt] *adj* **1** ODD : bizarre **2** PICTURESQUE : pittoresque

quake ['kweɪk] *vi* **quaked; quaking** : trembler

qualify ['kwɑləˌfaɪ] *v* **-fied; -fying** *vt* **1** LIMIT : poser des conditions sur **2** AUTHORIZE : qualifier, autoriser **3** MODERATE : mitiger — *vi* : se qualifier — **qualification** [ˌkwɑləfə'keɪʃən] *n* **1** : qualification *f* **2** LIMITATION : réserve *f* **3** ABILITY : compétence *f* — **qualified** ['kwɑləˌfaɪd] *adj* : qualifié, compétent

quality ['kwɑlət̬i] *n*, *pl* **-ties** : qualité *f*

qualm ['kwɑm, 'kwɑlm, 'kwɔm] *n* : scrupule *m*

quandary ['kwɑndri] *n*, *pl* **-ries** : dilemme *m*

quantity ['kwɑntət̬i] *n*, *pl* **-ties** : quantité *f*

quarantine ['kwɔrənˌti:n] *n* : quarantaine *f* — **~** *vt* **-tined; -tining** : mettre en quarantaine

quarrel ['kwɔrəl] *n* : dispute *f*, querelle *f* — **~** *vi* **-reled** *or* **-relled; -reling** *or* **-relling** : se quereller, se disputer — **quarrelsome** ['kwɔrəlsəm] *adj* : querelleur

quarry ['kwɔri] *n*, *pl* **-ries** EXCAVATION : carrière *f*

quart ['kwɔrt] *n* : quart *m* de gallon

quarter ['kwɔrt̬ər] *n* **1** : quart *m* **2** : (pièce de) vingt-cinq cents *m* **3** DISTRICT : quartier *m* **4** : trimestre *m* (de l'année fiscale) **5** **~ after three** : trois heures et quart **6** **~s** *npl* LODGINGS : logement *m* — **~** *vt* : diviser en quatre — **quarterly** ['kwɔrt̬ərli] *adv* : tous les trois mois, trimestriellement — **~** *adj* : trimestriel — **~** *n*, *pl* **-lies** : publication *f* trimestrielle

quartet [kwɔr'tɛt] *n* : quatuor *m*

quartz ['kwɔrts] *n* : quartz *m*

quash ['kwɑʃ, 'kwɔʃ] *vt* : étouffer, réprimer

quaver ['kweɪvər] *vi* : trembloter

quay ['ki:, 'keɪ, 'kweɪ] *n* WHARF : quai *m*

queasy ['kwi:zi] *adj* **-sier; -est** : nauséeux

Quebecer [kwɪ'bɛkər] *adj* : québécois

Quebecois *or* **Québécois** [kebe'kwɑ:] *adj* : québécois

queen ['kwi:n] *n* : reine *f*

queer ['kwɪr] *adj* ODD : étrange, bizarre

quell ['kwɛl] *vt* SUPPRESS : réprimer

quench ['kwɛntʃ] *vt* **1** EXTINGUISH : éteindre **2** **~ one's thirst** : étancher la soif

query ['kwɪri, 'kwɛr-] *n*, *pl* **-ries** : question *f* — **~** *vt* **-ried; -rying** ASK : poser une question à

quest ['kwɛst] *n* : quête *f*

question ['kwɛstʃən] *n* : question *f* — **~** *vt* **1** ASK : poser une question à **2** INTERROGATE : questionner **3** DOUBT : mettre en doute — **questionable** ['kwɛstʃənəbəl] *adj* : discutable — **question mark** *n* : point *m* d'interrogation — **questionnaire** [ˌkwɛstʃə'nær] *n* : questionnaire *m*

queue ['kju:] *n* LINE : queue *f*, file *f* — **~** *vi* **queued; queuing** *or* **queueing** : faire la queue

quibble ['kwɪbəl] *vi* **-bled; -bling** : chicaner — **~** *n* : chicane *f*

quick ['kwɪk] *adj* : rapide — **~** *adv* : rapidement, vite — **quicken** ['kwɪkən] *vt* : accélérer — **~** *vi* : s'accélérer — **quickly** ['kwɪkli] *adv* : rapidement, vite — **quickness** ['kwɪknəs] *n* : rapidité *f*, vitesse *f* — **quicksand** ['kwɪkˌsænd] *n* : sables *mpl* mouvants

quiet ['kwaɪət] *n* **1** : silence *m* **2** CALM : calme *m* — **~** *adj* **1** SILENT : silencieux **2** CALM : tranquille — **~** *vt* **1** SILENCE : faire taire **2** CALM : calmer — *vi or* **~ down** : se calmer — **quietly** ['kwaɪətli] *adv* **1** SILENTLY : sans bruit, doucement **2** CALMLY : tranquillement

quilt ['kwɪlt] *n* : édredon *m*

quintet [kwɪn'tɛt] *n* : quintette *m* — **quintuple** [kwɪn'tu:pəl, -'tju:-, -'tʌ-; 'kwɪntə-] *adj* : quintuple

quip ['kwɪp] *n* : raillerie *f*

quirk ['kwərk] *n* : bizarrerie *f* — **quirky** ['kwərki] *adj* **quirkier; quirkiest** : excentrique

quit ['kwɪt] *v* **quit; quitting** *vt* **1** LEAVE : quitter **2** STOP : arrêter — *vi* **1** GIVE UP : abandonner **2** RESIGN : démissionner

quite ['kwaɪt] *adv* **1** COMPLETELY : tout à fait **2** RATHER : assez **3** POSITIVELY : vraiment

quits ['kwɪts] *adj* **1** : quitte **2** **we called it ~** : nous y avons renoncé

quiver ['kwɪvər] *vi* : trembler

quiz ['kwɪz] *n*, *pl* **quizzes** TEST : interrogation *f* — **~** *vt* **quizzed; quizzing** : questionner, interroger

quota ['kwo:t̬ə] *n* : quota *m*

quotation [kwo'teɪʃən] *n* **1** CITATION : citation *f* **2** ESTIMATE : devis *m* — **quotation marks** *npl* : guillemets *mpl* — **quote** ['kwo:t] *vt* **quoted; quoting** **1** CITE : citer **2** STATE : indiquer (un prix) **3** : coter (un prix à la Bourse) — **~** *n* **1** → **quotation** **2** **~s** *npl* → **quotation marks**

quotient ['kwo:ʃənt] *n* : quotient *m*

R

r ['ɑr] *n*, *pl* **r's** *or* **rs** ['ɑrz] : r *m*, dix-huitième lettre de l'alphabet

rabbi ['ræˌbaɪ] *n* : rabbin *m*

rabbit ['ræbət] *n*, *pl* **-bit** *or* **-bits** : lapin *m*, -pine *f*

rabies ['reɪbi:z] *ns & pl* : rage *f* — **rabid** ['ræbɪd] *adj* **1** : enragé (se dit d'un chien) **2** FURIOUS : furieux

raccoon [ræ'ku:n] *n*, *pl* **-coon** *or* **-coons** : raton *m* laveur

race[1] ['reɪs] *n* **1** : race *f* **2** **human ~** : genre *m* humain

race[2] *n* : course *f* (à pied, etc.) — **~** *vi* **raced; racing** : courir — **racehorse** ['reɪsˌhɔrs] *n* : cheval *m* de course — **racetrack** ['reɪsˌtræk] *n* : hippodrome *m*

racial ['reɪʃəl] *adj* : racial — **racism** ['reɪˌsɪzəm] *n* : racisme *m* — **racist** ['reɪsɪst] *n* : raciste *mf*

rack ['ræk] *n* **1** SHELF : étagère *f* **2** **luggage ~** : porte-bagages *m* — **~** *vt* **1** **~ed with** : tourmenté par **2** **~ one's brains** : se creuser les méninges

racket[1] ['rækət] *n* : raquette *f* (de tennis, etc.)

racket[2] *n* **1** DIN : vacarme *m* **2** SWINDLE : escroquerie *f*

racy ['reɪsi] *adj* **racier; -est** : osé, risqué

radar ['reɪˌdɑr] *n* : radar *m*

radiant ['reɪdiənt] *adj* : radieux — **radiance** ['reɪdiənts] *n* : éclat *m* — **radiate** ['reɪdiˌeɪt] *v* **-ated; -ating** *vt* : irradier — *vi* : rayonner — **radiation** [ˌreɪdi'eɪʃən] *n* : rayonnement *m* — **radiator** ['reɪdiˌeɪt̬ər] *n* : radiateur *m*

radical ['rædɪkəl] *adj* : radical — **~** *n* : radical *m*, -cale *f*

radii → **radius**

radio ['reɪdiˌo:] *n*, *pl* **-dios** : radio *f* — **~** *vt* : transmettre par radio — **radioactive** [ˌreɪdio'æktɪv] *adj* : radioactif

radish ['rædɪʃ] *n* : radis *m*

radius ['reɪdiəs] *n*, *pl* **radii** [-diˌaɪ] : rayon *m*

raffle ['ræfəl] *vt* **-fled; -fling** : mettre en tombola — **~** *n* : tombola *f*

raft ['ræft] *n* : radeau *m*

rafter ['ræftər] *n* : chevron *m*

rag ['ræg] *n* **1** : chiffon *m*, guenille *f Can* **2** **in ~s** : en haillons

rage ['reɪʤ] *n* **1** : colère *f*, rage *f* **2** **be all the ~** : faire fureur — **~** *vi* **raged; raging** **1** : être furieux **2** : hurler (se dit du vent, etc.)

ragged ['rægəd] *adj* **1** UNEVEN : inégal **2** TATTERED : en loques

raid ['reɪd] *n* **1** : invasion *f*, raid *m* **2** *or* **police ~** : descente *f*, rafle *f* — **~** *vt* INVADE : envahir

rail[1] ['reɪl] *vi* **~ at** : invectiver contre

rail[2] *n* **1** BAR : barre *f* **2** HANDRAIL : balustrade *f* **3** TRACK : rail *m* **4** **by ~** : par train — **railing** ['reɪlɪŋ] *n* **1** : rampe *f* (d'un escalier), balustrade *f* (d'un balcon) **2** RAILS : grille *f* — **railroad** ['reɪlˌro:d] *n* : chemin *m* de fer — **railway** ['reɪlˌweɪ] → **railroad**

rain ['reɪn] *n* : pluie *f* — **~** *vi* : pleuvoir — **rainbow** ['reɪnˌbo:] *n* : arc-en-ciel *m* — **raincoat** ['reɪnˌko:t] *n* : imperméable *m* — **rainfall** ['reɪnˌfɔl] *n* : précipitations *fpl* — **rainy** ['reɪni] *adj* **rainier; -est** : pluvieux

raise ['reɪz] *vt* **raised; raising** **1** : lever **2** REAR : élever **3** GROW : cultiver **4** INCREASE : augmenter **5** : soulever (des objections) **6** **~ money** : collecter des fonds — **~** *n* : augmentation *f*

raisin ['reɪzən] *n* : raisin *m* sec

rake ['reɪk] *n* : râteau *m* — **~** *vt* **raked; raking** : ratisser

rally ['ræli] *v* **-lied; -lying** *vi* : se rallier, se rassembler — *vt* : rallier, rassembler — **~** *n*, *pl* **-lies** : ralliement *m*, rassemblement *m*

ram ['ræm] *n* : bélier *m* (mouton) — **~** *vt* **rammed; ramming** **1** CRAM : fourrer **2** *or* **~ into** : percuter

RAM ['ræm] *n* (*random-access memory*) : RAM *f*

ramble ['ræmbəl] *vi* **-bled; -ling** **1** WANDER : se balader **2** *or* **~ on** : divaguer — **~** *n* : randonnée *f*, excursion *f*

ramp ['ræmp] *n* **1** : rampe *f* **2** : passerelle *f* (pour accéder à un avion)

rampage ['ræm,peɪʤ] *vi* **-paged; -paging** : se déchaîner

rampant ['ræmpənt] *adj* : déchaîné

ramshackle ['ræm,ʃækəl] *adj* : délabré

ran → **run**

ranch ['ræntʃ] *n* : ranch *m*

rancid ['ræntsɪd] *adj* : rance

rancor *or Brit* **rancour** ['ræŋkər] *n* : rancœur *f*, rancune *f*

random ['rændəm] *adj* **1** : aléatoire **2 at ~** : au hasard

rang → **ring**

range ['reɪnʤ] *n* **1** : chaîne *f* (de montagnes) **2** STOVE : cuisinière *f* **3** VARIETY : gamme *f* **4** SCOPE : portée *f* — ~ *vi* **ranged; ranging 1** EXTEND : s'étendre **2 ~ from ... to ...** : varier entre ... et ... — **ranger** ['reɪnʤər] *n or* **forest ~** : garde *m* forestier

rank[1] ['ræŋk] *adj* : fétide

rank[2] *n* **1** ROW : rang *m* **2** : grade *m* (militaire) **3 ~s** : simples soldats *mpl* **4 the ~ and file** : la base — ~ *vt* RATE : classer, ranger — *vi* : se classer, compter

rankle ['ræŋkəl] *vi* **-kled; -kling** : rester sur le cœur

ransack ['ræn,sæk] *vt* **1** SEARCH : fouiller **2** LOOT : saccager

ransom ['ræntsəm] *n* : rançon *f* — ~ *vt* : payer une rançon pour

rant ['rænt] *vi or* **~ and rave** : fulminer

rap[1] ['ræp] *n* KNOCK : coup *m* sec — ~ *v* **rapped; rapping** : cogner

rap[2] *n or* **~ music** : rap *m*

rapacious [rə'peɪʃəs] *adj* : rapace

rape ['reɪp] *vt* **raped; raping** : violer — ~ *n* : viol *m*

rapid ['ræpɪd] *adj* : rapide — **rapids** ['ræpɪdz] *npl* : rapides *mpl*

rapture ['ræptʃər] *n* : extase *f*

rare ['rær] *adj* **rarer; rarest 1** FINE : exceptionnel **2** UNCOMMON : rare **3** : saignant (se dit de la viande) — **rarely** ['rærli] *adv* : rarement — **rarity** ['rærəṭi] *n, pl* **-ties** : rareté *f*

rascal ['ræskəl] *n* : polisson *m*, -sonne *f*

rash[1] ['ræʃ] *adj* : irréfléchi

rash[2] *n* : rougeurs *fpl*

raspberry ['ræz,bɛri] *n, pl* **-ries** : framboise *f*

rat ['ræt] *n* : rat *m*

rate ['reɪt] *n* **1** PACE : vitesse *f*, rythme *m* **2** : taux *m* (d'intérêt, etc.) **3** PRICE : tarif *m* **4 at any ~** : de toute manière — ~ *vt* **rated; rating 1** REGARD : considérer **2** RANK : classer

rather ['ræðər, 'rʌ-, 'rɑ-] *adv* **1** FAIRLY : assez, plutôt **2 I'd ~ decide** : je préférerais décider

ratify ['ræṭə,faɪ] *vt* **-fied; -fying** : ratifier — **ratification** [,ræṭəfə'keɪʃən] *n* : ratification *f*

rating ['reɪtɪŋ] *n* **1** : classement *m*, cote *f* **2 ~s** *npl* : indice *m* d'écoute

ratio ['reɪʃio] *n, pl* **-tios** : rapport *m*, proportion *f*

ration ['ræʃən, 'reɪʃən] *n* **1** : ration *f* **2 ~s** *npl* : vivres *mpl* — ~ *vt* **rationed; rationing** : rationner

rational ['ræʃənəl] *adj* : rationnel — **rationale** [,ræʃə'næl] *n* : logique *f*, raisons *fpl* — **rationalize** ['ræʃənə,laɪz] *vt* **-ized; -izing** : rationaliser

rattle ['ræṭəl] *v* **-tled; -tling** *vi* : faire du bruit — *vt* **1** SHAKE : agiter **2** UPSET : déconcerter **3 ~ off** : débiter à toute vitesse — ~ *n* **1** : succession *f* de bruits secs **2** *or* **baby's ~** : hochet *m* — **rattlesnake** ['ræṭəl,sneɪk] *n* : serpent *m* à sonnettes

ravage ['rævɪʤ] *vt* **-aged; -aging** : ravager — **ravages** ['rævɪʤəz] *npl* : ravages *mpl*

rave ['reɪv] *vi* **raved; raving 1** : délirer **2 ~ about** : parler avec enthousiasme de

raven ['reɪvən] *n* : grand corbeau *m*

ravenous ['rævənəs] *adj* **1** HUNGRY : affamé **2** VORACIOUS : vorace

ravine [rə'vi:n] *n* : ravin *m*

ravishing ['rævɪʃɪŋ] *adj* : ravissant

raw ['rɔ] *adj* **rawer; rawest 1** UNCOOKED : cru **2** INEXPERIENCED : novice **3** CHAFED : à vif (se dit d'une plaie) **4** : cru et humide (se dit de la température) **5 ~ materials** : matières *fpl* premières

ray ['reɪ] *n* : rayon *m* (de lumière), lueur *f* (d'espoir, etc.)

rayon ['reɪ,ɑn] *n* : rayonne *f*

raze ['reɪz] *vt* **razed; razing** : raser, détruire

razor ['reɪzər] *n* : rasoir *m* — **razor blade** *n* : lame *f* de rasoir

reach ['ri:tʃ] *vt* **1** : atteindre **2** *or* **~ out** : tendre **3** : parvenir à (une entente, etc.) **4** CONTACT : rejoindre — *vi* EXTEND : s'étendre — ~ *n* **1** : portée *f*, proximité *f* **2 within ~** : à portée de la main

react [ri'ækt] *vi* : réagir — **reaction** [ri'ækʃən] *n* : réaction *f* — **reactionary** [ri'ækʃə,nɛri] *adj* : réactionnaire — ~ *n, pl* **-ries** : réactionnaire *mf* — **reactor** [ri'æktər] *n* : réacteur *m*

read ['ri:d] *v* **read** ['rɛd]; **reading** *vt* **1** : lire **2** INTERPRET : interpréter **3** SAY : dire **4** INDICATE : indiquer — *vi* : se lire — **readable** ['ri:dəbəl] *adj* : lisible — **reader** ['ri:dər] *n* : lecteur *m*, -trice *f*

readily ['rɛdəli] *adv* **1** WILLINGLY : volontiers **2** EASILY : facilement

reading ['ri:dɪŋ] *n* : lecture *f*

readjust [,ri:ə'ʤʌst] *vt* : réajuster — *vi* : se réadapter

ready ['rɛdi] *adj* **readier; -est 1** : prêt, disposé **2** AVAILABLE : disponible **3 get ~** : se préparer — ~ *vt* **readied; readying** : préparer

real ['ri:l] *adj* **1** : véritable, réel **2** GENUINE : authentique — ~ *adv* VERY : très — **real estate** *n* : biens *mpl* immobiliers — **realistic** [,ri:ə'lɪstɪk] *adj* : réaliste — **reality** [ri'æləṭi] *n, pl* **-ties** : réalité *f*

realize ['ri:ə,laɪz] *vt* **-ized; -izing 1** : se rendre compte de **2** ACHIEVE : réaliser

really ['rɪli, 'rɪ:-] *adv* : vraiment

realm ['rɛlm] *n* **1** KINGDOM : royaume *m* **2** SPHERE : domaine *m*

reap ['ri:p] *vt* : moissonner, récolter

reappear [,ri:ə'pɪr] *vi* : réapparaître

rear[1] ['rɪr] *vt* : élever (des enfants, etc.)

rear[2] *n* : arrière *m*, derrière *m* — ~ *adj* : postérieur

rearrange [,ri:ə'reɪnʤ] *vt* **-ranged; -ranging** : réarranger

reason ['ri:zən] *n* : raison *f* — ~ *vi* : raisonner — **reasonable** ['ri:zənəbəl] *adj* : raisonnable — **reasoning** ['ri:zənɪŋ] *n* : raisonnement *m*

reassure [,ri:ə'ʃʊr] *vt* **-sured; -suring** : rassurer — **reassurance** [,ri:ə'ʃʊrənts] *n* : réconfort *m*

rebate ['ri:,beɪt] *n* : ristourne *f*

rebel ['rɛbəl] *n* : rebelle *mf* — ~ [rɪ'bɛl] *vi* **-belled; -belling** : se rebeller — **rebellion** [rɪ'bɛljən] *n* : rébellion *f* — **rebellious** [rɪ'bɛljəs] *adj* : rebelle

rebirth [,ri:'bərθ] *n* : renaissance *f*

reboot [,ri:'bu:t] *vt* : réamorcer, redémarrer (en informatique)

rebound ['ri:,baʊnd, rɪ:'baʊnd] *vi* : rebondir — ~ ['ri:,baʊnd] *n* : rebond *m*

rebuff [rɪ'bʌf] *vt* : rabrouer — ~ *n* : rebuffade *f*

rebuild [,ri:'bɪld] *vt* **-built** [-'bɪlt]; **-building** : reconstruire

rebuke [rɪ'bju:k] *vt* **-buked; -buking** : reprocher — ~ *n* : réprimande *f*

rebut [rɪ'bʌt] *vt* **-butted; -butting** : réfuter — **rebuttal** [ri'bʌṭəl] *n* : réfutation *f*

recall [rɪ'kɔl] *vt* **1** : rappeler (au devoir, etc.) **2** REMEMBER : se rappeler **3** REVOKE : annuler — ~ [rɪ'kɔl, 'ri:,kɔl] *n* : rappel *m*

recapitulate [,ri:kə'pɪtʃə,leɪt] *v* **-lated; -lating** : récapituler

recapture [,ri:'kæptʃər] *vt* **-tured; -turing 1** : reprendre **2** RELIVE : revivre

recede [rɪ'si:d] *vi* **-ceded; -ceding** : se retirer

receipt [rɪ'si:t] *n* **1** : reçu *m* **2 ~s** *npl* : recettes *fpl*

receive [rɪ'si:v] *vt* **-ceived; -ceiving** : recevoir — **receiver** [rɪ'si:vər] *n* : récepteur *m*, combiné *m*

recent ['ri:sənt] *adj* : récent — **recently** [-li] *adv* : récemment

receptacle [rɪ'sɛptɪkəl] *n* : récipient *m*

reception [rɪ'sɛpʃən] *n* : réception *f* — **receptionist** [rɪ'sɛpʃənɪst] *n* : réceptionniste *mf* — **receptive** [rɪ'sɛptɪv] *adj* : réceptif

recess ['ri:,sɛs, rɪ'sɛs] *n* **1** ALCOVE : recoin *m* **2** BREAK : récréation *f* (scolaire) — **recession** [rɪ'sɛʃən] *n* : récession *f*

recharge [,ri:'tʃɑrʤ] *vt* **-charged; -charging** : recharger — **rechargeable** [,ri:'tʃɑrʤəbəl] *adj* : rechargeable

recipe ['rɛsə,pi:] *n* : recette *f*

recipient [rɪ'sɪpiənt] *n* : récipiendaire *mf*

reciprocal [rɪ'sɪprəkəl] *adj* : réciproque

recite [rɪ'saɪt] *vt* **-cited; -citing 1** : réciter (un poème, etc.) **2** LIST : énumérer — **recital** [rɪ'saɪṭəl] *n* : récital *m*

reckless ['rɛkləs] *adj* : imprudent — **recklessness** ['rɛkləsnəs] *n* : imprudence *f*

reckon ['rɛkən] *vt* : estimer, penser — **reckoning** ['rɛkənɪŋ] *n* : calculs *mpl*

reclaim [rɪ'kleɪm] *vt* : récupérer

recline [rɪ'klaɪn] *vi* **-clined; -clining** : s'allonger — **reclining** [rɪ'klaɪnɪŋ] *adj* : réglable (se dit d'un siège)

recluse ['rɛ,klu:s, rɪ'klu:s] *n* : reclus *m*, -cluse *f*

recognition [,rɛkɪg'nɪʃən] *n* : reconnaissance *f* — **recognizable** ['rɛkəg,naɪzəbəl] *adj* : reconnaissable — **recognize** ['rɛkɪg,naɪz] *vt* **-nized; -nizing** : reconnaître

recoil [rɪ'kɔɪl] *vi* : reculer — ~ ['ri:,kɔɪl, rɪ'-] *n* : recul *m* (d'une arme à feu)

recollect [,rɛkə'lɛkt] *v* : se souvenir — **recollection** [,rɛkə'lɛkʃən] *n* : souvenir *m*

recommend [,rɛkə'mɛnd] *vt* : recommander — **recommendation** [,rɛkəmən'deɪʃən] *n* : recommandation *f*

reconcile ['rɛkən,saɪl] *v* **-ciled; -ciling** *vt* **1** : réconcilier (des personnes), concilier (des dates, etc.) **2 ~ oneself to** : se résigner à — *vi* MAKE UP : se réconcilier — **reconciliation** [,rɛkən,sɪli'eɪʃən] *n* : réconciliation *f*

reconsider [,ri:kən'sɪdər] *vt* : reconsidérer

reconstruct [,ri:kən'strʌkt] *vt* : reconstruire

record [rɪ'kɔrd] *vt* **1** : enregistrer **2** WRITE DOWN : noter — ~ ['rɛkərd] *n* **1** DOCUMENT : dossier *m* **2** REGISTER : registre *m* **3** HISTORY : passé *m* **4** : disque *m* (de musique) **5** *or* **police ~** : casier *m* judiciaire **6 world ~** : record *m* mondial — **recorder** [rɪ'kɔrdər] *n* **1** : flûte *f* à bec **2** *or* **tape ~** : magnétophone *m* — **recording** [rɪ'kɔrdɪŋ] *n* : enregistrement *m*

recount[1] [rɪ'kaʊnt] *vt* NARRATE : raconter

recount[2] ['ri:,kaʊnt, ,ri'-] *vt* : recompter (des votes, etc.) — ~ *n* : décompte *m*

recourse ['ri:,kors, rɪ'-] *n* **1** : recours *m* **2 have ~ to** : recourir à

recover [rɪ'kʌvər] *vt* : récupérer — *vi* RECUPERATE : se remettre, se rétablir — **recovery** [rɪ'kʌvəri] *n, pl* **-ries** : rétablissement *m*

recreation [,rɛkri'eɪʃən] *n* : loisirs *mpl*, récréation *f* — **recreational** [,rɛkri'eɪʃənəl] *adj* : récréatif

recruit [rɪ'kru:t] *vt* : recruter — ~ *n* : recrue *f* — **recruitment** [rɪ'kru:tmənt] *n* : recrutement *m*

rectangle ['rɛk,tæŋgəl] *n* : rectangle *m* — **rectangular** [rɛk'tæŋgjələr] *adj* : rectangulaire

rectify ['rɛktə,faɪ] *vt* **-fied; -fying** : rectifier

rector ['rɛktər] *n* : pasteur *m* — **rectory** ['rɛktəri] *n, pl* **-ries** : presbytère *m*

rectum ['rɛktəm] *n, pl* **-tums** *or* **-ta** [-tə] : rectum *m*

recuperate [rɪ'ku:pə,reɪt, -'kju:-] *v* **-ated; -ating** *vt* : récupérer — *vi* : se rétablir

recur [rɪ'kər] *vi* **-curred; -curring** : réapparaître — **recurrence** [rɪ'kərənts] *n* : répétition *f* — **recurrent** [rɪ'kərənt] *adj* : qui se répète

recycle [ri'saɪkəl] *vt* **-cled; -cling** : recycler

red ['rɛd] *adj* : rouge — ~ *n* : rouge *m* — **redden** ['rɛdən] *v* : rougir — **reddish** ['rɛdɪʃ] *adj* : rougeâtre

redecorate [,ri:'dɛkə,reɪt] *vt* **-rated; -rating** : repeindre

redeem [rɪ'di:m] *vt* : racheter, sauver — **redemption** [rɪ'dɛmpʃən] *n* : rédemption *f*

red–handed ['rɛd'hændəd] *adv & adj* : la main dans le sac

redhead ['rɛd,hɛd] *n* : roux *m*, rousse *f*

red–hot ['rɛd'hɑt] *adj* : brûlant

redness ['rɛdnəs] *n* : rougeur *f*

redo [,ri:'du:] *vt* **-did** [-dɪd]; **-done** [-'dʌn]; **-doing** : refaire

red tape *n* : paperasserie *f*

reduce [rɪ'du:s, -'dju:s] *vt* **-duced; -ducing** : réduire — **reduction** [rɪ'dʌkʃən] *n* : réduction *f*

redundant [rɪ'dʌndənt] *adj* : superflu

reed ['ri:d] *n* : roseau *m*

reef ['ri:f] *n* : récif *m*

reek ['ri:k] *vi* : empester

reel ['ri:l] *n* : bobine *f* (de fil, etc.) — ~ *vt* **~ in** : enrouler (une ligne de pêche), ramener (un poisson) — *vi* **1** STAGGER : tituber **2** SPIN : tournoyer

reestablish [,ri:ɪ'stæblɪʃ] *vt* : rétablir

refer [ri'fər] *v* **-ferred; -ferring** *vt* DIRECT : renvoyer — *vi* **~ to 1** : faire allusion à **2** CONSULT : consulter

referee [,rɛfə'ri:] *n* : arbitre *m* — ~ *v* **-eed; -eeing** : arbitrer

reference ['rɛfrənts, 'rɛfə-] *n* **1** : référence *f* **2 in ~ to** : en ce qui concerne

refill [,ri:'fɪl] *vt* : remplir à nouveau — ~ ['ri:,fɪl] *n* : recharge *f*, cartouche *f* (d'encre)

refine [rɪ'faɪn] *vt* **-fined; -fining** : raffiner — **refined** [rɪ'faɪnd] *adj* : raffiné — **refinement** [rɪ'faɪnmənt] *n* : raffinement *m* — **refinery** [rɪ'faɪnəri] *n, pl* **-eries** : raffinerie *f*

reflect [rɪ'flɛkt] *vt* : réfléchir (la lumière), refléter (une image, etc.) — *vi* **1** PONDER : réfléchir **2 ~ badly on** : faire du tort à — **reflection** [rɪ'flɛkʃən] *n* **1** : réflexion *f* **2** IMAGE : reflet *m*

reflex ['ri:,flɛks] *n* : réflexe *m*

reflexive [rɪ'flɛksɪv] *adj* : réfléchi

reform [rɪ'fɔrm] *vt* : réformer — ~ *n* : réforme *f* — **reformer** [rɪ'fɔrmər] *n* : réformateur *m*, -trice *f*

refrain[1] [rɪ'freɪn] *vi* **~ from** : se retenir de

refrain[2] *n* : refrain *m* (en musique)

refresh [rɪ'frɛʃ] *vt* : rafraîchir — **refreshments** [rɪ'frɛʃmənts] *npl* : rafraîchissements *mpl*

refrigerate [rɪ'frɪʤə,reɪt] *vt* **-ated; -ating** : réfrigérer — **refrigeration** [rɪ,frɪʤə'reɪʃən] *n* : réfrigération *f* — **refrigerator** [rɪ'frɪʤə,reɪṭər] *n* : réfrigérateur *m*

refuel [ri:'fju:əl] *v* **-eled** *or* **-elled; -eling** *or* **-elling** *vt* : ravitailler en carburant — *vi* : se ravitailler

refuge ['rɛ,fju:ʤ] *n* : refuge *m*, abri *m* — **refugee** [,rɛfjʊ'ʤi:] *n* : réfugié *m*, -giée *f*

refund [rɪ'fʌnd, 'ri:,fʌnd] *vt* : rembourser — ~ ['ri:,fʌnd] *n* : remboursement *m*

refurbish [rɪ'fərbɪʃ] *vt* : remettre à neuf

refuse[1] [rɪ'fju:z] *vt* **-fused; -fusing 1** : refuser **2 ~ to do sth** : se refuser à faire qqch — **refusal** [rɪ'fju:zəl] *n* : refus *m*

refuse[2] ['rɛ,fju:s, -,fju:z] *n* : ordures *fpl*, déchets *mpl*

refute [rɪ'fju:t] *vt* **-futed; -futing** : réfuter

regain [ri:'geɪn] *vt* : retrouver

regal ['ri:gəl] *adj* : royal, majestueux — **regalia** [rɪ'geɪljə] *npl* : insignes *mpl*, vêtements *mpl* de cérémonie

regard [rɪ'gɑrd] *n* **1** : égard *m*, considération *f* **2** ESTEEM : estime *f* **3 ~s** *npl* : amitiés *fpl* **4 with ~ to** : en ce qui concerne — ~ *vt* **1** HEED : tenir compte de **2** ESTEEM : estimer **3 as ~s** : en ce qui concerne **4 ~ as** : considérer — **regarding** [rɪ'gɑrdɪŋ] *prep* : concernant — **regardless** [rɪ'gɑrdləs] *adv* : malgré tout — **regardless of** *prep* **1** : sans tenir compte de **2** IN SPITE OF : malgré

regime [reɪ'ʒi:m, rɪ-] *n* : régime *m* — **regimen** ['rɛʤəmən] *n* : régimen *m*

regiment ['rɛʤəmənt] *n* : régiment *m*

region ['ri:ʤən] *n* : région *f* — **regional** ['ri:ʤənəl] *adj* : régional

register ['rɛʤəstər] *n* : registre *m* — ~ *vt* **1** : inscrire, enregistrer **2** SHOW : exprimer **3** RECORD : indiquer (la température, etc.) **4** : immatriculer (un véhicule) — *vi* ENROLL : s'inscrire — **registration** [,rɛʤə'streɪʃən] *n* **1** : inscription *f*, enregistrement *m* **2 ~ number** : numéro *m* d'immatriculation — **registry** ['rɛʤəstri] *n, pl* **-tries** : registre *m*

regret [rɪ'grɛt] *vt* **-gretted; -gretting** : regretter — ~ *n* **1** REMORSE : remords *m* **2** SORROW : regret *m* — **regrettable** [rɪ'grɛṭəbəl] *adj* : lamentable

regular ['rɛgjələr] *adj* **1** : régulier **2** CUSTOMARY : habituel — ~ *n* : habitué *m*, -tuée *f* — **regularity** [,rɛgjə'lærəṭi] *n, pl* **-ties** : régularité *f* — **regularly** ['rɛgjələrli] *adv* : régulièrement — **regulate** ['rɛgjə,leɪt] *vt* **-lated; -lating** : régler — **regulation** [,rɛgjə'leɪʃən] *n* **1** RULE : règlement *m*, règle *f* **2** CONTROL : réglementation *f*

rehabilitate [,ri:hə'bɪlə,teɪt, ,ri:ə-] *vt* **-tated; -tating** : réhabiliter — **rehabilitation** [,ri:hə,bɪlə'teɪʃən, ,ri:ə-] *n* : réhabilitation *f*

rehearse [rɪ'hərs] *vt* **-hearsed; -hearsing** : répéter — **rehearsal** [rɪ'hərsəl] *n* : répétition *f*

reign ['reɪn] *n* : règne *m* — ~ *vi* : régner

reimburse [,ri:əm'bərs] *vt* **-bursed; -bursing** : rembourser — **reimbursement** [,ri:əm'bərsmənt] *n* : remboursement *m*

rein ['reɪn] *n* : rêne *f*

reindeer ['reɪn,dɪr] *n* : renne *m*

reinforce [,ri:ən'fors] *vt* **-forced; -forcing** : renforcer — **reinforcement** [,ri:ən'forsmənt] *n* : renfort *m*

reinstate [,ri:ən'steɪt] *vt* **-stated; -stating** : rétablir (dans ses fonctions)

reiterate [ri'ɪṭə,reɪt] *vt* **-ated; -ating** : réitérer

reject [rɪ'ʤɛkt] *vt* : rejeter — **rejection** [rɪ'ʤɛkʃən] *n* : rejet *m*

rejoice [rɪ'ʤɔɪs] *vi* **-joiced; -joicing** : se réjouir

rejuvenate [rɪ'ʤu:və,neɪt] *vt* **-nated; -nating** : rajeunir

rekindle [,ri:'kɪndəl] *vt* **-dled; -dling** : raviver, ranimer

relapse ['ri:,læps, ri'læps] *n* : rechute *f* — ~ [ri'læps] *vi* **-lapsed; -lapsing** : rechuter

relate [rɪ'leɪt] *v* **-lated; -lating** *vt* **1** TELL : raconter **2** ASSOCIATE : relier — *vi* **1 ~ to** : se rapporter à **2 ~ to** : s'entendre (avec) **3 ~ to** : apprécier, comprendre — **related** [rɪ'leɪṭəd] *adj* **~ to** : apparenté à — **relation** [rɪ'leɪʃən] *n* **1** : rapport *m*, lien *m* **2** RELATIVE : parent *m*, -rente *f* **3 in ~ to** : par rapport à **4 ~s** *npl* : rapports *mpl*, relations *fpl* — **relationship** [rɪ'leɪʃən,ʃɪp] *n* **1** : rapport *m*, relations *fpl* **2** KINSHIP : liens *mpl* de parenté — **relative** ['rɛləṭɪv] *n* : parent *m*, -rente *f* — ~ *adj* : relatif — **relatively** ['rɛləṭɪvli] *adv* : relativement

relax [rɪ'læks] *vt* : détendre — *vi* : se détendre — **relaxation** [,ri:,læk'seɪʃən] *n* : détente *f*, relaxation *f*

relay ['ri:,leɪ] *n* **1** : relève *m* **2** *or* **~ race** : course *f* de relais — ~ ['ri:,leɪ, ri'leɪ] *vt* **-layed; -laying** : relayer, transmettre

release [ri'li:s] *vt* **-leased; -leasing 1** FREE : libérer, mettre en liberté **2** : relâcher (une bride, etc.) **3** EMIT : émettre **4** : publier (un livre), sortir (un nouveau film) — ~ *n* **1** : libération *f* **2** : sortie *f* (d'un film), parution *f* (d'un livre)

relegate ['rɛlə,geɪt] *vt* **-gated; -gating** : reléguer

relent [rɪ'lɛnt] *vi* **1** GIVE IN : céder **2** ABATE : se calmer — **relentless** [rɪ'lɛntləs] *adj* : implacable

relevant ['rɛləvənt] *adj* : pertinent — **relevance** ['rɛləvənts] *n* : pertinence *f*

reliable [rɪ'laɪəbəl] *adj* : fiable, sûr — **reliability** [rɪ,laɪə'bɪləṭi] *n, pl* **-ties** : fiabilité *f* — **reliance** [rɪ'laɪənts] *n* **1** : dépendance *f* **2** TRUST : confiance *f*

relic ['rɛlɪk] *n* : relique *f*

relief [rɪ'li:f] *n* **1** : soulagement *m* **2** AID : aide *f*, secours *m* **3** : relief *m* (d'une carte géographique) **4** REPLACEMENT : relève *f* — **relieve** [rɪ'li:v] *vt* **-lieved; -lieving 1**

: soulager 2 REPLACE : relayer (qqn) 3 ~ **s.o. of** : libérer qqn de

religion [rɪˈlɪʤən] *n* : religion *f* — **religious** [rɪˈlɪʤəs] *adj* : religieux

relinquish [rɪˈlɪŋkwɪʃ, -ˈlɪn-] *vt* : renoncer à

relish [ˈrɛlɪʃ] *n* **1** : condiment *m* à base de cornichons **2 with** ~ : avec un plaisir évident — ~ *vt* : savourer

relocate [ˌriːˈloːˌkeɪt, ˌriːloˈkeɪt] *v* **-cated; -cating** *vt* : transférer — *vi* : déménager, s'établir ailleurs — **relocation** [ˌriːloˈkeɪʃən] *n* : déménagement *m*

reluctance [rɪˈlʌktənts] *n* : réticence *f* — **reluctant** [rɪˈlʌktənt] *adj* : réticent — **reluctantly** [rɪˈlʌktəntli] *adv* : à contrecœur

rely [rɪˈlaɪ] *vi* **-lied; -lying** ~ **on 1** : dépendre de **2** TRUST : se fier à

remain [rɪˈmeɪn] *vi* : rester — **remainder** [rɪˈmeɪndər] *n* : reste *m*, restant *m* — **remains** [rɪˈmeɪnz] *npl* : restes *mpl*

remark [rɪˈmɑrk] *n* : remarque *f*, observation *f* — ~ *vt* **1** : remarquer **2** SAY : mentionner — *vi* ~ **on** : observer que — **remarkable** [rɪˈmɑrkəbəl] *adj* : remarquable

remedy [ˈrɛmədi] *n, pl* **-dies** : remède *m* — ~ *vt* **-died; -dying** : remédier à — **remedial** [rɪˈmiːdiəl] *adj* : de rattrapage

remember [rɪˈmɛmbər] *vt* **1** : se rappeler, se souvenir de **2** ~ **to** : ne pas oublier de — *vi* : se rappeler, se souvenir — **remembrance** [rɪˈmɛmbrənts] *n* : souvenir *m*

remind [rɪˈmaɪnd] *vt* ~ **s.o. of sth** : rappeler qqch à qqn — **reminder** [rɪˈmaɪndər] *n* : rappel *m*

reminisce [ˌrɛməˈnɪs] *vi* **-nisced; -niscing** : se rappeler le bon vieux temps — **reminiscent** [ˌrɛməˈnɪsənt] *adj* ~ **of** : qui rappelle, qui fait penser à

remission [rɪˈmɪʃən] *n* : rémission *f*

remit [rɪˈmɪt] *vt* **-mitted; -mitting** : envoyer (de l'argent)

remnant [ˈrɛmnənt] *n* **1** : reste *m*, restant *m* **2** TRACE : vestige *m*

remorse [rɪˈmɔrs] *n* : remords *m* — **remorseful** [rɪˈmɔrsfəl] *adj* : plein de remords

remote [rɪˈmoːt] *adj* **-moter; -est 1** : lointain, éloigné **2** ALOOF : distant — **remote control** *n* : télécommande *f*

remove [rɪˈmuːv] *vt* **-moved; -moving 1** : enlever, ôter **2** DISMISS : renvoyer **3** ELIMINATE : supprimer, dissiper — **removable** [rɪˈmuːvəbəl] *adj* : amovible — **removal** [rɪˈmuːvəl] *n* : élimination *f*

remunerate [rɪˈmjuːnəˌreɪt] *vt* **-ated; -ating** : rémunérer

render [ˈrɛndər] *vt* : rendre

rendition [rɛnˈdɪʃən] *n* : interprétation *f*

renegade [ˈrɛnɪˌgeɪd] *n* : renégat *m*, -gate *f*

renew [rɪˈnuː, -ˈnjuː] *vt* **1** : renouveler **2** RESUME : reprendre — **renewal** [rɪˈnuːəl, -ˈnjuː-] *n* : renouvellement *m*

renounce [rɪˈnaʊnts] *vt* **-nounced; -nouncing** : renoncer à

renovate [ˈrɛnəˌveɪt] *vt* **-vated; -vating** : rénover — **renovation** [ˌrɛnəˈveɪʃən] *n* : rénovation *f*

renown [rɪˈnaʊn] *n* : renommée *f*, renom *m* — **renowned** [rɪˈnaʊnd] *adj* : renommé, célèbre

rent [ˈrɛnt] *n* **1** : loyer *m* (somme d'argent) **2 for** ~ : à louer — ~ *vt* : louer — **rental** [ˈrɛntəl] *n* : location *f* — ~ *adj* : de location — **renter** [ˈrɛntər] *n* : locataire *mf*

renunciation [rɪˌnʌntsiˈeɪʃən] *n* : renonciation *f*

reorganize [ˌriːˈɔrgəˌnaɪz] *vt* **-nized; -nizing** : réorganiser — **reorganization** [ˌriːˌɔrgənəˈzeɪʃən] *n* : réorganisation *f*

repair [rɪˈpær] *vt* : réparer — ~ *n* **1** : réparation *f* **2 in bad** ~ : en mauvais état

repay [rɪˈpeɪ] *vt* **-paid; -paying** : rembourser (un emprunt), rendre (une faveur, etc.)

repeal [rɪˈpiːl] *vt* : abroger, révoquer — ~ *n* : abrogation *f*, révocation *f*

repeat [rɪˈpiːt] *vt* : répéter — ~ *n* **1** : répétition *f* **2** : rediffusion *f* (se dit d'une émission) — **repeatedly** [rɪˈpiːtədli] *adv* : à plusieurs reprises

repel [rɪˈpɛl] *vt* **-pelled; -pelling** : repousser — **repellent** [rɪˈpɛlənt] *adj* : repoussant

repent [rɪˈpɛnt] *vi* : se repentir — **repentance** [rɪˈpɛntənts] *n* : repentir *m*

repercussion [ˌriːpərˈkʌʃən, ˌrɛpər-] *n* : répercussion *f*

repertoire [ˈrɛpərˌtwɑr] *n* : répertoire *m*

repetition [ˌrɛpəˈtɪʃən] *n* : répétition *f* — **repetitious** [ˌrɛpəˈtɪʃəs] *adj* : répétitif — **repetitive** [rɪˈpɛtətɪv] *adj* : répétitif

replace [rɪˈpleɪs] *vt* **-placed; -placing 1** : remettre (à sa place) **2** SUBSTITUTE : remplacer **3** EXCHANGE : échanger — **replacement** [rɪˈpleɪsmənt] *n* **1** : remplacement *m* **2** SUBSTITUTE : remplaçant *m*, -çante *f* **3** ~ **part** : pièce *f* de rechange

replenish [rɪˈplɛnɪʃ] *vt* **1** : réapprovisionner **2** : remplir (de nouveau)

replica [ˈrɛplɪkə] *n* : réplique *f*

reply [rɪˈplaɪ] *vi* **-plied; -plying** : répondre, répliquer — ~ *n, pl* **-plies** : réponse *f*, réplique *f*

report [rɪˈport] *n* **1** : rapport *m*, compte rendu *m* **2** *or* **news** ~ : reportage *m* **3 weather** ~ : bulletin *m* (météorologique) — ~ *vt* **1** RELATE : raconter **2** ~ **an accident** : signaler un accident — *vi* ~ **to s.o.** : se présenter à qqn — **report card** *n* : bulletin *m* scolaire — **reporter** [rɪˈportər] *n* : journaliste *mf*, reporter *m*

reprehensible [ˌrɛprɪˈhɛntsəbəl] *adj* : répréhensible

represent [ˌrɛprɪˈzɛnt] *vt* : représenter — **representation** [ˌrɛprɪˌzɛnˈteɪʃən, -zən-] *n* : représentation *f* — **representative** [ˌrɛprɪˈzɛntətɪv] *adj* : représentatif — ~ *n* : représentant *m*, -tante *f*

repress [rɪˈprɛs] *vt* : réprimer — **repression** [rɪˈprɛʃən] *n* : répression *f*

reprieve [rɪˈpriːv] *n* : sursis *m*

reprimand [ˈrɛprəˌmænd] *n* : réprimande *f* — ~ *vt* : réprimander

reprint [rɪˈprɪnt] *vt* : réimprimer — ~ [ˈriːˌprɪnt, riˈprɪnt] *n* : réimpression *f*

reprisal [rɪˈpraɪzəl] *n* : représailles *fpl*

reproach [rɪˈproːʧ] *n* **1** : reproche *m* **2 beyond** ~ : irréprochable — ~ *vt* : reprocher à — **reproachful** [rɪˈproːʧfəl] *adj* : de reproche

reproduce [ˌriːprəˈduːs, -ˈdjuːs] *v* **-duced; -ducing** *vt* : reproduire — *vi* : se reproduire — **reproduction** [ˌriːprəˈdʌkʃən] *n* : reproduction *f*

reptile [ˈrɛpˌtaɪl] *n* : reptile *m*

republic [rɪˈpʌblɪk] *n* : république *f* — **republican** [rɪˈpʌblɪkən] *n* : républicain *m*, -caine *f* — ~ *adj* : républicain

repudiate [rɪˈpjuːdiˌeɪt] *vt* **-ated; -ating** : répudier

repugnant [rɪˈpʌgnənt] *adj* : répugnant — **repugnance** [rɪˈpʌgnənts] *n* : répugnance *f*

repulse [rɪˈpʌls] *vt* **-pulsed; -pulsing** : repousser — **repulsive** [rɪˈpʌlsɪv] *adj* : repoussant

reputation [ˌrɛpjəˈteɪʃən] *n* : réputation *f* — **reputable** [ˈrɛpjətəbəl] *adj* : de bonne réputation — **reputed** [rɪˈpjuːtəd] *adj* : réputé

request [rɪˈkwɛst] *n* : demande *f* — ~ *vt* : demander

require [rɪˈkwaɪr] *vt* **-quired; -quiring 1** CALL FOR : requérir **2** NEED : avoir besoin de — **requirement** [rɪˈkwaɪrmənt] *n* **1** NEED : besoin *m* **2** DEMAND : exigence *f* — **requisite** [ˈrɛkwəzɪt] *adj* : nécessaire

resale [ˈriːˌseɪl, ˌriːˈseɪl] *n* : revente *f*

rescind [rɪˈsɪnd] *vt* : annuler, abroger

rescue [ˈrɛsˌkjuː] *vt* **-cued; -cuing** : sauver, secourir — ~ *n* : sauvetage *m* — **rescuer** [ˈrɛsˌkjuːər] *n* : sauveteur *m*, secouriste *mf*

research [rɪˈsərʧ, ˈriːˌsərʧ] *n* : recherches *fpl* — ~ *vt* : faire des recherches sur — **researcher** [rɪˈsərʧər, ˈriːˌ-] *n* : chercheur *m*, -cheuse *f*

resemble [rɪˈzɛmbəl] *vt* **-bled; -bling** : ressembler à — **resemblance** [rɪˈzɛmbləns] *n* : ressemblance *f*

resent [rɪˈzɛnt] *vt* : en vouloir à, s'offenser de — **resentful** [rɪˈzɛntfəl] *adj* : éprouver du ressentiment — **resentment** [rɪˈzɛntmənt] *n* : ressentiment *m*

reserve [rɪˈzərv] *vt* **-served; -serving** : réserver — ~ *n* : réserve *f* — **reservation** [ˌrɛzərˈveɪʃən] *n* **1** : réserve *f* (indienne) **2** RESERVING : réservation *f* — **reserved** [rɪˈzərvd] *adj* : réservé, discret — **reservoir** [ˈrɛzərˌvwɑr, -ˌvwɔr, -ˌvɔr] *n* : réservoir *m*

reset [ˌriːˈsɛt] *vt* **-set; -setting** : remettre à l'heure (une montre), remettre à zéro (un compteur)

residence [ˈrɛzədənts] *n* : résidence *f* — **reside** [rɪˈzaɪd] *vi* **-sided; -siding** : résider — **resident** [ˈrɛzədənt] *adj* : résidant — ~ *n* : résident *m*, -dente *f* — **residential** [ˌrɛzəˈdɛnʧəl] *adj* : résidentiel

residue [ˈrɛzəˌduː, -ˌdjuː] *n* : résidu *m*

resign [rɪˈzaɪn] *vt* **1** QUIT : démissionner **2** ~ **oneself to** : se résigner à — **resignation** [ˌrɛzɪgˈneɪʃən] *n* **1** : démission *f* **2** ACCEPTANCE : résignation *f*

resilient [rɪˈzɪljənt] *adj* **1** : résistant **2** ELASTIC : élastique — **resilience** [rɪˈzɪljənts] *n* **1** : résistance *f* **2** ELASTICITY : élasticité *f*

resin [ˈrɛzən] *n* : résine *f*

resist [rɪˈzɪst] *vt* : résister à — **resistance** [rɪˈzɪstənts] *n* : résistance *f* — **resistant** [rɪˈzɪstənt] *adj* : résistant

resolve [rɪˈzɑlv] *vt* **-solved; -solving 1** : résoudre **2** ~ **to do** : décider de faire — ~ *n* : résolution *f*, détermination *f* — **resolution** [ˌrɛzəˈluːʃən] *n* : résolution *f* — **resolute** [ˈrɛzəˌluːt] *adj* : résolu

resonance [ˈrɛzənənts] *n* : résonance *f* — **resonant** [ˈrɛzənənt] *adj* : résonant

resort [rɪˈzɔrt] *n* **1** : recours *m* **2** : centre *m* touristique, station *f* (de ski, etc.) — ~ *vi* ~ **to** : recourir à, avoir recours à

resound [rɪˈzaʊnd] *vi* : résonner, retentir — **resounding** [rɪˈzaʊndɪŋ] *adj* : retentissant

resource [ˈriːˌsors, rɪˈsors] *n* : ressource *f* — **resourceful** [rɪˈsorsfəl, -ˈzors-] *adj* : ingénieux, débrouillard

respect [rɪˈspɛkt] *n* **1** : respect *m* **2** ~**s** *npl* : respects *mpl*, hommages *mpl* **3 in** ~ **to** : en ce qui concerne **4 in some** ~**s** : à certains égards — ~ *vt* : respecter — **respectable** [rɪˈspɛktəbəl] *adj* : respectable — **respectful** [rɪˈspɛktfəl] *adj* : respectueux — **respective** [rɪˈspɛktɪv] *adj* : respectif — **respectively** [rɪˈspɛktɪvli] *adv* : respectivement

respiratory [ˈrɛspərəˌtori, rɪˈspaɪrə-] *adj* : respiratoire

respite [ˈrɛspɪt, rɪˈspaɪt] *n* : répit *m*, sursis *m*

response [rɪˈspɑnts] *n* : réponse *f* — **respond** [rɪˈspɑnd] *vi* : répondre — **responsibility** [rɪˌspɑntsəˈbɪləti] *n, pl* **-ties** : responsabilité *f* — **responsible** [rɪˈspɑntsəbəl] *adj* : responsable — **responsive** [rɪˈspɑntsɪv] *adj* : réceptif

rest[1] [ˈrɛst] *n* **1** : repos *m* **2** SUPPORT : appui *m* **3** : silence *m* (en musique) **4** ~ **area** : aire *f* de repos, halte *f* routière *Can* — ~ *vi* **1** : se reposer **2** LEAN : s'appuyer **3** ~ **on** DEPEND : dépendre de — *vt* **1** : reposer **2** LEAN : appuyer

rest[2] *n* REMAINDER : reste *m*

restaurant [ˈrɛstəˌrɑnt, -rənt] *n* : restaurant *m*

restful [ˈrɛstfəl] *adj* : reposant, paisible

restless [ˈrɛstləs] *adj* : inquiet, agité

restore [rɪˈstor] *vt* **-stored; -storing 1** RETURN : retourner **2** REESTABLISH : rétablir **3** REPAIR : restaurer — **restoration** [ˌrɛstəˈreɪʃən] *n* **1** : rétablissement *m* **2** REPAIR : restauration *f*

restrain [rɪˈstreɪn] *vt* **1** : retenir **2** ~ **oneself** : se retenir — **restrained** [rɪˈstreɪnd] *adj* : contenu, maîtrisé — **restraint** [rɪˈstreɪnt] *n* **1** : restriction *f*, contrainte *f* **2** SELF-CONTROL : retenue *f*, maîtrise *f* de soi

restrict [rɪˈstrɪkt] *vt* : restreindre — **restriction** [rɪˈstrɪkʃən] *n* : restriction *f* — **restrictive** [rɪˈstrɪktɪv] *adj* : restrictif

result [rɪˈzʌlt] *vi* **1** ~ **from** : résulter de **2** ~ **in** : avoir pour résultat — ~ *n* **1** : résultat *m* **2 as a** ~ **of** : à la suite de

resume [rɪˈzuːm] *v* **-sumed; -suming** : reprendre

résumé *or* **resume** *or* **resumé** [ˈrɛzəˌmeɪ, ˌrɛzəˈ-] *n* : curriculum *m* vitæ

resumption [rɪˈzʌmpʃən] *n* : reprise *f*

resurgence [rɪˈsərʤənts] *n* : réapparition *f*

resurrection [ˌrɛzəˈrɛkʃən] *n* : résurrection *f* — **resurrect** [ˌrɛzəˈrɛkt] *vt* : ressusciter

resuscitate [rɪˈsʌsəˌteɪt] *vt* **-tated; -tating** : réanimer

retail [ˈriːˌteɪl] *vt* : vendre au détail — ~ *n* : vente *f* au détail — ~ *adj* : de détail — ~ *adv* : au détail — **retailer** [ˈriːˌteɪlər] *n* : détaillant *m*, -lante *f*

retain [rɪˈteɪn] *vt* : retenir

retaliate [rɪˈtæliˌeɪt] *vi* **-ated; -ating** : riposter — **retaliation** [rɪˌtæliˈeɪʃən] *n* : riposte *f*, représailles *fpl*

retarded [rɪˈtɑrdəd] *adj* : arriéré

retention [rɪˈtɛnʧən] *n* : rétention

reticence [ˈrɛtəsənts] *n* : réticence *f* — **reticent** [ˈrɛtəsənt] *adj* : réticent, hésitant

retina [ˈrɛtənə] *n, pl* **-nas** *or* **-nae** [-ənˌiː, -ənˌaɪ] : rétine *f*

retire [rɪˈtaɪr] *vi* **-tired; -tiring 1** WITHDRAW : se retirer **2** : prendre sa retraite **3** : aller se coucher — **retirement** [rɪˈtaɪrmənt] *n* : retraite *f*

retort [rɪˈtɔrt] *vt* : rétorquer, riposter — ~ *n* : riposte *f*

retrace [ˌriːˈtreɪs] *vt* **-traced; -tracing** ~ **one's steps** : revenir sur ses pas

retract [rɪˈtrækt] *vt* **1** WITHDRAW : retirer **2** : rentrer (ses griffes, etc.) — **retractable** [rɪˈtræktəbəl] *adj* : escamotable

retrain [ˌriːˈtreɪn] *vt* : recycler

retreat [rɪˈtriːt] *n* **1** : retraite *f* **2** REFUGE : refuge *m* — ~ *vi* : se retirer, reculer

retribution [ˌrɛtrəˈbjuːʃən] *n* : châtiment *m*

retrieve [rɪˈtriːv] *vt* **-trieved; -trieving** : retrouver, récupérer — **retrieval** [rɪˈtriːvəl] *n* : récupération *f*

retroactive [ˌrɛtroˈæktɪv] *adj* : rétroactif

retrospect [ˈrɛtrəˌspɛkt] *n* **in** ~ : avec le recul — **retrospective** [ˌrɛtrəˈspɛktɪv] *adj* : rétrospectif

return [rɪˈtərn] *vi* **1** : retourner, revenir **2** REAPPEAR : réapparaître — *vt* **1** : rapporter, rendre **2** YIELD : produire — ~ *n* **1** : retour *m* **2** YIELD : rapport *m*, rendement *m* **3 in** ~ **for** : en échange de **4** *or* **tax** ~ : déclaration *f* d'impôts — ~ *adj* : de retour

reunite [ˌriːjʊˈnaɪt] *vt* **-nited; -niting** : réunir — **reunion** [riˈjuːnjən] *n* : réunion *f*

revamp [ˌriːˈvæmp] *vt* : retaper (une maison), réviser (un texte)

reveal [rɪˈviːl] *vt* **1** : révéler **2** SHOW : laisser voir

revel [ˈrɛvəl] *vi* **-eled** *or* **-elled; -eling** *or* **-elling** ~ **in** : se délecter de

revelation [ˌrɛvəˈleɪʃən] *n* : révélation *f*

revelry [ˈrɛvəlri] *n, pl* **-ries** : festivités *fpl*, réjouissances *fpl*

revenge [rɪˈvɛnʤ] *vt* **-venged; -venging** : venger — ~ *n* **1** : vengeance *f* **2 take** ~ **on** : se venger sur

revenue [ˈrɛvəˌnuː, -ˌnjuː] *n* : revenu *m*

reverberate [rɪˈvərbəˌreɪt] *vi* **-ated; -ating** : retentir, résonner

reverence [ˈrɛvərənts] *n* : révérence *f*, vénération *f* — **revere** [rɪˈvɪr] *vt* **-vered; -vering** : révérer, vénérer — **reverend** [ˈrɛvərənd] *adj* : révérend — **reverent** [ˈrɛvərənt] *adj* : respectueux

reverse [rɪˈvərs] *adj* : inverse, contraire — ~ *v* **-versed; -versing** *vt* **1** : inverser **2** CHANGE : renverser, annuler — *vi* : faire marche arrière (se dit d'une voiture) — ~ *n* **1** BACK : dos *m*, envers *m* **2** *or* ~ **gear** : marche *f* arrière **3 the** ~ : le contraire — **reversal** [rɪˈvərsəl] *n* **1** : renversement *m* **2** CHANGE : revirement *m* **3** SETBACK : revers *m* — **reversible** [rɪˈvərsəbəl] *adj* : réversible — **revert** [rɪˈvərt] *vi* ~ **to** : revenir à

review [rɪˈvjuː] *n* **1** : révision *f* **2** OVERVIEW : résumé *m* **3** : critique *f* **4** : revue *f* (militaire) — ~ *vt* **1** EXAMINE : examiner **2** : repasser (une leçon) **3** : faire la critique de (un roman, etc.) — **reviewer** [rɪˈvjuːər] *n* : critique *mf*

revile [rɪˈvaɪl] *vt* **-viled; -viling** : injurier

revise [rɪˈvaɪz] *vt* **-vised; -vising 1** : réviser, corriger **2** : modifier (une politique) — **revision** [rɪˈvɪʒən] *n* : révision *f*

revive [rɪˈvaɪv] *v* **-vived; -viving** *vt* **1** : ranimer, raviver **2** : réanimer (une personne) **3** RESTORE : rétablir — *vi* COME TO : reprendre connaissance — **revival** [rɪˈvaɪvəl] *n* : renouveau *m*, renaissance *f*

revoke [rɪˈvoːk] *vt* **-voked; -voking** : révoquer

revolt [rɪˈvoːlt] *vt* : révolter, dégoûter — *vi* ~ **against** : se révolter contre — ~ *n* : révolte *f*, insurrection *f* — **revolting** [rɪˈvoːltɪŋ] *adj* : révoltant, dégoûtant

revolution [ˌrɛvəˈluːʃən] *n* : révolution *f* — **revolutionary** [ˌrɛvəˈluːʃənˌɛri] *adj* : révolutionnaire — ~ *n, pl* **-aries** : révolutionnaire *mf* — **revolutionize** [ˌrɛvəˈluːʃəˌnaɪz] *vt* **-ized; -izing** : révolutionner

revolve [rɪˈvɑlv] *v* **-volved; -volving** *vt* : faire tourner — *vi* : tourner

revolver [rɪˈvɑlvər] *n* : revolver *m*

revulsion [rɪˈvʌlʃən] *n* : répugnance *f*

reward [rɪˈword] *vt* : récompenser — ~ *n* : récompense *f*

rewrite [ˌriːˈraɪt] *vt* **-wrote** [-ˈroːt]; **-written** [-ˈrɪtən]; **-writing** : récrire

rhetoric [ˈrɛtərɪk] *n* : rhétorique *f* — **rhetorical** [rɪˈtɔrɪkəl] *adj* : rhétorique

rheumatism [ˈruːməˌtɪzəm, ˈrʊ-] *n* : rhumatisme *m*

rhino [ˈraɪˌnoː] *n, pl* **-no** *or* **-nos** → **rhinoceros** — **rhinoceros** [raɪˈnɑsərəs] *n, pl* **-noceroses** *or* **-noceros** *or* **-noceri** [-ˌraɪ] : rhinocéros *m*

rhubarb [ˈruːˌbɑrb] *n* : rhubarbe *f*

rhyme [ˈraɪm] *n* **1** : rime *f* **2** VERSE : vers *m* — ~ *vi* **rhymed; rhyming** : rimer

rhythm [ˈrɪðəm] *n* : rythme *m* — **rhythmic** [ˈrɪðmɪk] *or* **rhythmical** [-mɪkəl] *adj* : rythmique

rib [ˈrɪb] *n* : côte *f* (en anatomie) — ~ *vt* **ribbed; ribbing** : taquiner

ribbon [ˈrɪbən] *n* : ruban *m*

rice [ˈraɪs] *n* : riz *m*

rich [ˈrɪʧ] *adj* **1** : riche **2** ~ **meal** : repas *m* lourd — **riches** [ˈrɪʧəz] *npl* : richesses *fpl* — **richness** [ˈrɪʧnəs] *n* : richesse *f*

rickety [ˈrɪkəti] *adj* : branlant

ricochet [ˈrɪkəˌʃeɪ] *n* : ricochet *m* — ~ *vi* **-cheted** [-ˌʃeɪd] *or* **-chetted** [-ˌʃɛtəd]; **-cheting** [-ˌʃeɪɪŋ] *or* **-chetting** [-ˌʃɛtɪŋ] : ricocher

rid [ˈrɪd] *vt* **rid; ridding 1** : débarrasser **2** ~ **oneself of** : se débarrasser de — **riddance** [ˈrɪdənts] *n* **good** ~! : bon débarras!

riddle[1] [ˈrɪdəl] *n* : énigme *f*, devinette *f*

riddle[2] *vt* **-dled; -dling 1** : cribler **2** ~ **with** : plein de

ride [ˈraɪd] *v* **rode** [ˈroːd]; **ridden** [ˈrɪdən]; **riding** *vt* **1** : monter (à cheval, à bicyclette), prendre (le bus, etc.) **2** TRAVEL : parcourir — *vi* **1** *or* ~ **horseback** : monter à cheval **2** : aller (en auto, etc.) — ~ *n* **1** : tour *m*, promenade *f* **2** : manège *m* (à la foire) **3 give s.o. a** ~ : conduire qqn en voiture — **rider** [ˈraɪdər] *n* **1** : cavalier *m*, -lière *f* **2** CYCLIST : cycliste *mf*, motocycliste *mf*

ridge [ˈrɪʤ] *n* : chaîne *f* (de montagnes)

ridiculous [rəˈdɪkjələs] *adj* : ridicule — **ridicule** [ˈrɪdəˌkjuːl] *n* : ridicule *m*, dérision *f* — ~ *vt* **-culed; -culing** : ridiculiser

rife [ˈraɪf] *adj* **be** ~ **with** : être abondant en

rifle[1] [ˈraɪfəl] *vi* **-fled; -fling** ~ **through** : fouiller dans

rifle[2] *n* : carabine *f*, fusil *m*

rift [ˈrɪft] *n* **1** : fente *f*, fissure *f* **2** BREACH : désaccord *m*

rig[1] [ˈrɪg] *vt* : truquer (une élection)

rig[2] *vt* **rigged; rigging 1** : gréer (un navire) **2** EQUIP : équiper **3** *or* ~ **out** DRESS : habiller **4** *or* ~ **up** : bricoler — ~ *n* **1** : gréement *m* **2** *or* **oil** ~ : plateforme *f* pétrolière — **rigging** [ˈrɪgɪŋ, -gən] *n* : gréement *m*

right [ˈraɪt] *adj* **1** JUST : bien, juste **2** CORRECT : exact **3** APPROPRIATE : convenable **4** STRAIGHT : droit **5 be** ~ : avoir raison **6** → **right–hand** — ~ *n* **1** GOOD : bien *m* **2** ENTITLEMENT : droit *m* **3 on the** ~ : à droite **4** *or* ~ **side** : droite *f* — ~ *adv* **1** WELL : bien, comme il faut **2** EXACTLY

: précisément 3 DIRECTLY : droit 4 IMMEDIATELY : tout de suite 5 COMPLETELY : tout à fait 6 *or* **to the ~** : à la droite — ~ *vt* 1 RESTORE : redresser 2 **~ a wrong** : réparer un tort — **right angle** *n* : angle *m* droit — **righteous** ['raɪtʃəs] *adj* : juste, droit — **rightful** ['raɪtfəl] *adj* : légitime — **right–hand** ['raɪt'hænd] *adj* 1 : du côté droit 2 **~ man** : bras *m* droit — **right–handed** ['raɪt'hændəd] *adj* : droitier — **rightly** ['raɪtli] 1 : à juste titre 2 CORRECTLY : correctement — **right–of–way** [ˌraɪtə'weɪ, -əv-] *n, pl* **rights–of–way** : priorité *f* (sur la route) — **right–wing** ['raɪt'wɪŋ] *adj* : de droite (en politique)

rigid ['rɪʤɪd] *adj* : rigide

rigor *or Brit* **rigour** ['rɪgər] *n* : rigueur *f* — **rigorous** ['rɪgərəs] *adj* : rigoureux

rim ['rɪm] *n* 1 EDGE : bord *m* 2 : jante *f* (d'une roue)

rind ['raɪnd] *n* : écorce *f* (de citron, etc.)

ring[1] ['rɪŋ] *v* **rang** ['ræŋ]; **rung** ['rʌŋ]; **ringing** *vi* 1 : sonner 2 RESOUND : résonner — *vt* : sonner (une cloche, etc.) — ~ *n* 1 : son *m*, tintement *m* 2 CALL : coup *m* de téléphone

ring[2] *n* 1 : bague *f*, anneau *m* 2 CIRCLE : cercle *m* 3 *or* **boxing ~** : ring *m* (de boxe) 4 NETWORK : réseau *m* (clandestin) — ~ *vt* **ringed; ringing** : encercler — **ringleader** ['rɪŋˌli:dər] *n* : meneur *m*, -neuse *f*

rink ['rɪŋk] *n* : piste *f*, patinoire *f*

rinse ['rɪnts] *vt* **rinsed; rinsing** : rincer — ~ *n* : rinçage *m*

riot ['raɪət] *n* : émeute *f* — ~ *vi* : faire une émeute — **rioter** ['raɪət̬ər] *n* : émeutier *m*, -tière *f*

rip ['rɪp] *v* **ripped; ripping** *vt* 1 : déchirer 2 **~ off** : arracher — *vi* : se déchirer — ~ *n* : déchirure *f*

ripe ['raɪp] *adj* **riper; ripest** : mûr, prêt — **ripen** ['raɪpən] *v* : mûrir

ripple ['rɪpəl] *v* **-pled; -pling** *vi* : onduler (se dit de l'eau) — *vt* : rider — ~ *n* : ondulation *f*, ride *f*

rise ['raɪz] *vi* **rose** ['ro:z]; **risen** ['rɪzən]; **rising** 1 : se lever (se dit d'une personne, du soleil, etc.) 2 INCREASE : augmenter, monter 3 **~ up** REBEL : se soulever (contre) — ~ *n* 1 ASCENT : montée *f* 2 INCREASE : augmentation *f* 3 INCLINE : pente *f* — **riser** ['raɪzər] *n* 1 **early ~** : lève-tôt *mf* 2 **late ~** : lève-tard *mf*

risk ['rɪsk] *n* : risque *m* — ~ *vt* : risquer — **risky** ['rɪski] *adj* **riskier; -est** : risqué, hasardeux

rite ['raɪt] *n* : rite *m* — **ritual** ['rɪtʃʊəl] *adj* : rituel — ~ *n* : rituel *m*

rival ['raɪvəl] *n* : rival *m*, -vale *f* — ~ *adj* : rival — ~ *vt* **-valed** *or* **-valled; -valing** *or* **-valling** : rivaliser avec — **rivalry** ['raɪvəlri] *n, pl* **-ries** : rivalité *f*

river ['rɪvər] *n* : rivière *f*, fleuve *m* — ~ *adj* : fluvial

rivet ['rɪvət] *n* : rivet *m* — ~ *vt* 1 : river, fixer 2 **be ~ed by** : être fasciné par

road ['ro:d] *n* 1 : route *f* 2 STREET : rue *f* 3 PATH : chemin *m* — **roadblock** ['ro:dˌblɑk] *n* : barrage *m* routier — **roadside** ['ro:dˌsaɪd] *n* : bord *m* de la route — **roadway** ['ro:dˌweɪ] *n* : chaussée *f*

roam ['ro:m] *vi* : errer

roar ['ror] *vi* 1 : rugir 2 **~ with laughter** : éclater de rire — *vt* : hurler — ~ *n* 1 : rugissement *m* 2 : grondement *m* (d'un avion, etc.)

roast ['ro:st] *vt* : rôtir (de la viande, etc.), griller (des noix, etc.) — ~ *n* : rôti *m* — **roast beef** *n* : rosbif *m*

rob ['rɑb] *vt* **robbed; robbing** 1 : dévaliser (une banque), cambrioler (une maison) 2 STEAL : voler — **robber** ['rɑbər] *n* : voleur *m*, -leuse *f* — **robbery** ['rɑbəri] *n, pl* **-beries** : vol *m*

robe ['ro:b] *n* 1 : toge *f* (d'un juge) 2 → **bathrobe**

robin ['rɑbən] *n* : rouge-gorge *m*

robot ['ro:ˌbɑt, -bət] *n* : robot *m*

robust [ro'bʌst, 'ro:ˌbʌst] *adj* : robuste

rock[1] ['rɑk] *vt* 1 : bercer (un enfant), balancer (un berceau) 2 SHAKE : secouer — *vi* : se balancer — ~ *n or* **~ music** : musique *f* rock

rock[2] *n* 1 : roche *f*, roc *m* 2 BOULDER : rocher *m* 3 STONE : pierre *f*

rocket ['rɑkət] *n* : fusée *f*

rocking chair *n* : fauteuil *m* à bascule

rocky ['rɑki] *adj* **rockier; -est** 1 : rocheux 2 SHAKY : précaire

rod ['rɑd] *n* 1 : baguette *f* (de bois), tige *f* (de métal) 2 *or* **fishing ~** : canne *f* à pêche

rode → **ride**

rodent ['ro:dənt] *n* : rongeur *m*

rodeo ['ro:diˌo:, ro'deɪˌo:] *n, pl* **-deos** : rodéo *m*

roe ['ro:] *n* : œufs *mpl* de poisson

roe deer *n* : chevreuil *m*

role ['ro:l] *n* : rôle *m*

roll ['ro:l] *n* 1 : rouleau *m* 2 LIST : liste *f* 3 BUN : petit pain *m* 4 : roulement *m* (de tambour) — ~ *vt* 1 : rouler 2 **~ down** : baisser 3 **~ out** : dérouler 4 **~ up** : retrousser (ses manches) — *vi* 1 : (se) rouler 2 **~ over** : se retourner — **roller** ['ro:lər] *n* : rouleau *m* — **roller coaster** ['ro:lərˌko:stər] *n* : montagnes *fpl* russes — **roller–skate** ['ro:lərˌskeɪt] *vi* **-skated; -skating** : faire du patin à roulettes — **roller skates** *npl* : patins *mpl* à roulettes

Roman ['ro:mən] *adj* : romain — **Roman Catholic** *adj* : catholique

romance [ro'mænts, 'ro:ˌmænts] *n* 1 : roman *m* d'amour 2 AFFAIR : liaison *f* amoureuse

romantic [ro'mæntɪk] *adj* : romantique

roof ['ru:f, 'rʊf] *n, pl* **roofs** ['ru:fs, 'rʊfs; 'ru:vz, 'rʊvz] 1 : toit *m* 2 **~ of the mouth** : palais *m* — **roofing** ['ru:fɪŋ, 'rʊfɪŋ] *n* : toiture *f* — **rooftop** ['ru:fˌtɑp, 'rʊf-] *n* → **roof**

rook ['rʊk] *n* : tour *f* (aux échecs)

rookie ['rʊki] *n* : novice *mf*

room ['ru:m, 'rʊm] *n* 1 : chambre *f* (à coucher), salle *f* (de conférence) 2 SPACE : espace *m* 3 OPPORTUNITY : possibilité *f* — **roommate** ['ru:mˌmeɪt, 'rʊm-] *n* : camarade *mf* de chambre — **roomy** ['ru:mi, 'rʊmi] *adj* **roomier; -est** : spacieux

roost ['ru:st] *n* : perchoir *m* — ~ *vi* : se percher — **rooster** ['ru:stər, 'rʊs-] *n* : coq *m*

root[1] ['ru:t, 'rʊt] *n* 1 : racine *f* 2 SOURCE : origine *f* 3 CORE : fond *m*, cœur *m* — *vt* **~ out** : extirper

root[2] *vi* **~ for** SUPPORT : encourager

rope ['ro:p] *n* : corde *f* — ~ *vt* **roped; roping** 1 : attacher (avec une corde) 2 **~ off** : interdire l'accès à

rosary ['ro:zəri] *n, pl* **-ries** : chapelet *m*

rose[1] → **rise**

rose[2] ['ro:z] *n* : rose *f* (fleur), rose *m* (couleur) — **rosebush** ['ro:zˌbʊʃ] *n* : rosier *m*

rosemary ['ro:zˌmɛri] *n, pl* **-maries** : romarin *m*

Rosh Hashanah [ˌrɑʃhɑ'ʃɑnə, ˌro:ʃ-] *n* : le Nouvel An juif

rostrum ['rɑstrəm] *n, pl* **-tra** [-trə] *or* **-trums** : tribune *f*

rosy ['ro:zi] *adj* **rosier; -est** 1 : rose, rosé 2 PROMISING : prometteur

rot ['rɑt] *v* **rotted; rotting** : pourrir — ~ *n* : pourriture *f*

rotary ['ro:t̬əri] *adj* : rotatif — ~ *n* : rond-point *m*

rotate ['ro:ˌteɪt] *v* **-tated; -tating** *vi* : tourner — *vt* 1 : tourner 2 ALTERNATE : faire à tour de rôle — **rotation** [ro'teɪʃən] *n* : rotation *f*

rote ['ro:t] *n* **by ~** : par cœur

rotten ['rɑtən] *adj* 1 : pourri 2 BAD : mauvais

rouge ['ru:ʒ] *n* : rouge *m* à joues

rough ['rʌf] *adj* 1 COARSE : rugueux 2 RUGGED : accidenté 3 CHOPPY : agité 4 DIFFICULT : difficile 5 FORCEFUL : brusque 6 APPROXIMATE : approximatif 7 **~ draft** : brouillon *m* — ~ *vt* 1 → **roughen** 2 **~ up** BEAT : tabasser *fam* — **roughage** ['rʌfɪʤ] *n* : fibres *mpl* alimentaires — **roughen** ['rʌfən] *vt* : rendre rugueux — **roughly** ['rʌfli] *adv* 1 : rudement 2 ABOUT : environ — **roughness** ['rʌfnəs] *n* : rugosité *f*

roulette [ˌru:'lɛt] *n* : roulette *f*

round ['raʊnd] *adj* : rond — ~ *adv* → **around** — ~ *n* 1 : série *f* (de négociations, etc.) 2 : manche *f* (d'un match) 3 **~ of applause** : salve *f* d'applaudissements 4 **~s** *npl* : visites *fpl* (d'un médecin, etc.), rondes *fpl* (d'un policier, etc.) — ~ *vt* 1 TURN : tourner 2 **~ off** : arrondir 3 **~ off** *or* **~ out** COMPLETE : compléter 4 **~ up** GATHER : rassembler — ~ *prep* → **around** — **roundabout** ['raʊndəˌbaʊt] *adj* : indirect — **round–trip** ['raʊndˌtrɪp] *n* : voyage *m* aller et retour — **roundup** ['raʊndˌʌp] *n* : rassemblement *m*

rouse ['raʊz] *vt* **roused; rousing** 1 AWAKEN : réveiller 2 EXCITE : susciter

rout ['raʊt] *n* : déroute *f* — ~ *vt* : mettre en déroute

route ['ru:t, 'raʊt] *n* 1 : route *f* 2 *or* **delivery ~** : tournée *f* de livraison

routine [ru:'ti:n] *n* : routine *f* — ~ *adj* : routinier

row[1] ['ro:] *vi* : ramer

row[2] ['ro:] *n* 1 : file *f* (de gens), rangée *f* (de maisons, etc.) 2 **in a ~** SUCCESSIVELY : de suite

row[3] ['raʊ] *n* 1 RACKET : vacarme *m* 2 QUARREL : dispute *f*

rowboat ['ro:ˌbo:t] *n* : bateau *m* à rames

rowdy ['raʊdi] *adj* **-dier; -est** : tapageur

royal ['rɔɪəl] *adj* : royal — **royalty** ['rɔɪəlti] *n, pl* **-ties** 1 : royauté *f* 2 **royalties** *npl* : droits *mpl* d'auteur

rub ['rʌb] *v* **rubbed; rubbing** *vt* 1 : frotter 2 **~ in** : faire pénétrer — *vi* 1 **~ against** : frotter contre 2 **~ off** : enlever (en frottant) — ~ *n* : friction *f*, massage *m*

rubber ['rʌbər] *n* : caoutchouc *m* — **rubber band** *n* : élastique *m* — **rubber stamp** *n* : tampon *m* (de caoutchouc) — **rubbery** ['rʌbəri] *adj* : caoutchouteux

rubbish ['rʌbɪʃ] *n* 1 : ordures *fpl*, déchets *mpl* 2 NONSENSE : bêtises *fpl*

rubble ['rʌbəl] *n* : décombres *mpl*

ruby ['ru:bi] *n, pl* **-bies** : rubis *m*

rudder ['rʌdər] *n* : gouvernail *m*

ruddy ['rʌdi] *adj* **-dier; -est** : rougeaud

rude ['ru:d] *adj* **ruder; rudest** 1 IMPOLITE : grossier 2 ABRUPT : brusque — **rudely** ['ru:dli] *adv* : grossièrement — **rudeness** ['ru:dnəs] *n* : manque *m* d'éducation

rudiment ['ru:dəmənt] *n* : rudiment *m* — **rudimentary** [ˌru:də'mɛntəri] *adj* : rudimentaire

ruffle ['rʌfəl] *vt* **-fled; -fling** 1 : ébouriffer (ses cheveux), hérisser (ses plumes) 2 VEX : contrarier — ~ *n* : volant *m* (d'une jupe, etc.)

rug ['rʌg] *n* : tapis *m*, carpette *f*

rugged ['rʌgəd] *adj* 1 : accidenté (se dit d'un terrain), escarpé (se dit d'une montagne) 2 STURDY : robuste

ruin ['ru:ən] *n* : ruine *f* — ~ *vt* : ruiner

rule ['ru:l] *n* 1 : règle *f*, règlement *m* 2 CONTROL : autorité *f* 3 **as a ~** : en général — ~ *v* **ruled; ruling** *vt* 1 GOVERN : gouverner 2 : juger, décider (d'un juge) 3 **~ out** : écarter — *vi* : gouverner, régner — **ruler** ['ru:lər] *n* 1 : dirigeant *m*, -geante *f*; souverain *m*, -raine *f* 2 : règle *f* (pour mesurer) — **ruling** ['ru:lɪŋ] *n* VERDICT : décision *f*

rum ['rʌm] *n* : rhum *m*

rumble ['rʌmbəl] *vi* **-bled; -bling** 1 : gronder 2 : gargouiller (se dit de l'estomac) — ~ *n* : grondement *m*

rummage ['rʌmɪʤ] *vi* **-maged; -maging** **~ in** : fouiller dans

rumor *or Brit* **rumour** ['ru:mər] *n* : rumeur *f* — ~ *vt* **be ~ed that** : il paraît que

rump ['rʌmp] *n* 1 : croupe *f* (d'un animal) 2 *or* **~ steak** : romsteck *m*

run ['rʌn] *v* **ran** ['ræn]; **run; running** *vi* 1 : courir 2 FUNCTION : marcher 3 LAST : durer 4 : déteindre (se dit des couleurs) 5 EXTEND : passer (se dit d'un câble) 6 : se présenter (comme candidat) 7 **~ away** : s'enfuir 8 **~ into** ENCOUNTER : rencontrer 9 **~ into** HIT : heurter 10 **~ late** : être en retard 11 **~ out of** : manquer de 12 **~ over** : écraser — *vt* 1 : courir 2 OPERATE : faire marcher 3 : faire couler (de l'eau) 4 MANAGE : diriger 5 **~ a fever** : faire de la température — ~ *n* 1 : course *f* 2 TRIP : tour *m*, excursion *f* 3 SERIES : série *f* 4 **in the long ~** : à la longue — **runaway** ['rʌnəˌweɪ] *n* : fugitif *m*, -tive *f* — ~ *adj* : fugueur — **rundown** ['rʌnˌdaʊn] *n* : résumé *m* — **run–down** ['rʌn'daʊn] *adj* 1 : délabré 2 EXHAUSTED : fatigué

rung[1] → **ring**[1]

rung[2] ['rʌŋ] *n* : barreau *m* (d'une échelle, etc.)

runner ['rʌnər] *n* : coureur *m*, -reuse *f* — **runner–up** [ˌrʌnər'ʌp] *n, pl* **runners–up** : second *m*, -conde *f* — **running** ['rʌnɪŋ] *adj* 1 FLOWING : courant 2 CONTINUOUS : continuel 3 CONSECUTIVE : de suite

runway ['rʌnˌweɪ] *n* : piste *f* (d'envol ou d'atterrissage)

rupture ['rʌptʃər] *n* : rupture *f* — ~ *v* **-tured; -turing** *vt* : rompre — *vi* : se rompre

rural ['rʊrəl] *adj* : rural

ruse ['ru:s, 'ru:z] *n* : ruse *f*, stratagème *m*

rush[1] ['rʌʃ] *n* 1 : jonc *m* (plante) 2 **in a ~** : pressé

rush[2] *vi* : se précipiter — *vt* 1 : presser, bousculer 2 ATTACK : prendre d'assaut 3 : transporter d'urgence (à l'hôpital, etc.) — ~ *n* 1 : hâte *f*, empressement *m* 2 : bouffée *f* (d'air), torrent *m* (d'eau) — **rush hour** *n* : heure *f* de pointe

russet ['rʌsət] *adj* : roux

Russian ['rʌʃən] *adj* : russe — ~ *n* : russe (langue)

rust ['rʌst] *n* : rouille *f* — ~ *vi* : se rouiller — *vt* : rouiller

rustic ['rʌstɪk] *adj* : rustique, champêtre

rustle ['rʌsəl] *vi* **-tled; -tling** bruire — ~ *n* : bruissement *m*

rusty ['rʌsti] *adj* **rustier; -est** : rouillé

rut ['rʌt] *n* 1 : ornière *f* 2 **be in a ~** : s'enliser dans une routine

ruthless ['ru:θləs] *adj* : impitoyable, cruel

rye ['raɪ] *n* : seigle *m*

S

s ['ɛs] *n, pl* **s's** *or* **ss** ['ɛsəz] : s *m*, dix-neuvième lettre de l'alphabet

Sabbath ['sæbəθ] *n* 1 : sabbat *m* (judaïsme) 2 : dimanche *m* (christianisme)

sabotage ['sæbəˌtɑʒ] *n* : sabotage *m* — ~ *vt* **-taged; -taging** : saboter

sack ['sæk] *n* : sac *m* — ~ *vt* 1 FIRE : virer *fam* 2 PLUNDER : saccager

sacred ['seɪkrəd] *adj* : sacré

sacrifice ['sækrəˌfaɪs] *n* : sacrifice *m* — ~ *vt* **-ficed; -ficing** : sacrifier

sad ['sæd] *adj* **sadder; saddest** : triste — **sadden** ['sædən] *vt* : attrister

saddle ['sædəl] *n* : selle *f* — ~ *vt* **-dled; -dling** : seller

sadistic [sə'dɪstɪk] *adj* : sadique

sadness ['sædnəs] *n* : tristesse *f*

safari [sə'fɑri, -'fær-] *n* : safari *m*

safe ['seɪf] *adj* **safer; safest** 1 : sûr 2 UNHARMED : en sécurité 3 CAREFUL : prudent 4 **~ and sound** : sain et sauf — ~ *n* : coffre-fort *m* — **safeguard** ['seɪfˌgɑrd] *n* : sauvegarde *f* — ~ *vt* : sauvegarder — **safely** ['seɪfli] *adv* 1 : sûrement 2 **arrive ~** : bien arriver — **safety** ['seɪfti] *n, pl* **-ties** : sécurité *f* — **safety belt** *n* : ceinture *f* de sécurité — **safety pin** *n* : épingle *f* de sûreté

sag ['sæg] *vi* **sagged; sagging** : s'affaisser

sage[1] ['seɪʤ] *n* : sauge *f* (plante)

sage[2] *n* : sage *m*

said → **say**

sail ['seɪl] *n* 1 : voile *f* (d'un bateau) 2 **go for a ~** : faire un tour en bateau 3 **set ~** : prendre la mer — ~ *vi* : naviguer — *vt* 1 : manœuvrer (un bateau) 2 **~ the seas** : parcourir les mers — **sailboat** ['seɪlˌbo:t] *n* : voilier *m* — **sailor** ['seɪlər] *n* : marin *m*, matelot *m*

saint ['seɪnt, *before a name* ˌseɪnt *or* sənt] *n* : saint *m*, sainte *f*

sake ['seɪk] *n* 1 **for goodness' ~!** : pour l'amour de Dieu! 2 **for the ~ of** : pour le bien de

salad ['sæləd] *n* : salade *f*

salary ['sæləri] *n, pl* **-ries** : salaire *m*

sale ['seɪl] *n* 1 : vente *f* 2 **for ~** : à vendre 3 **on ~** : en solde — **salesman** ['seɪlzmən] *n, pl* **-men** [-mən, -ˌmɛn] : vendeur *m*, représentant *m* — **saleswoman** ['seɪlzˌwʊmən] *n, pl* **-women** [-ˌwɪmən] : vendeuse *f*, représentante *f*

salient ['seɪljənt] *adj* : saillant

saliva [sə'laɪvə] *n* : salive *f*

salmon ['sæmən] *ns & pl* : saumon *m*

salon [sə'lɑn, 'sæˌlɑn] *n* : salon *m*

saloon [sə'lu:n] *n* : bar *m*

salt ['sɔlt] *n* : sel *m* — ~ *vt* : saler — **saltwater** ['sɔltˌwɔt̬ər, -ˌwɑ-] *adj* : de mer — **salty** ['sɔlti] *adj* **saltier; -est** : salé

salute [sə'lu:t] *vt* **-luted; -luting** : saluer — ~ *n* : salut *m*

salvage ['sælvɪʤ] *vt* **-vaged; -vaging** : sauver, récupérer

salvation [sæl'veɪʃən] *n* : salut *m*

salve ['sæv, 'sav] *n* : onguent *m*, pommade *f*

same ['seɪm] *adj* 1 : même 2 **be the ~ (as)** : être comme 3 **the ~ thing (as)** : la même chose (que) — ~ *pron* 1 **all the ~** : pareil 2 **the ~** : le même — ~ *adv* **the ~** : pareil

sample ['sæmpəl] *n* : échantillon *m* — ~ *vt* **-pled; -pling** : essayer

sanctify ['sæŋktəˌfaɪ] *vt* **-fied; -fying** : sanctifier

sanction ['sæŋkʃən] *n* : sanction *f* — ~ *vt* : sanctionner

sanctuary ['sæŋktʃʊˌɛri] *n, pl* **-aries** : sanctuaire *m*

sand ['sænd] *n* : sable *m* — ~ *vt* 1 : sabler (une route) 2 : poncer (du bois)

sandal ['sændəl] *n* : sandale *f*

sandpaper ['sændˌpeɪpər] *n* : papier *m* de verre — ~ *vt* : poncer

sandwich ['sændˌwɪtʃ] *n* : sandwich *m* — ~ *vt* **~ between** : mettre entre

sandy ['sændi] *adj* **sandier; -est** : sablonneux

sane ['seɪn] *adj* **saner; -est** 1 : sain d'esprit 2 SENSIBLE : raisonnable

sang → **sing**

sanitary ['sænəˌtɛri] *adj* 1 : sanitaire 2 HYGIENIC : hygiénique — **sanitary napkin** *n* : serviette *f* hygiénique — **sanitation** [ˌsænə'teɪʃən] *n* : système *m* sanitaire

sanity ['sænət̬i] *n* : équilibre *m* mental

sank → **sink**

Santa Claus ['sæntəˌklɔz] *n* : père *m* Noël

sap[1] ['sæp] *n* : sève *f* (d'un arbre)

sap[2] *vt* **sapped; sapping** : saper, miner

sapphire ['sæˌfaɪr] *n* : saphir *m*

sarcasm ['sɑrˌkæzəm] *n* : sarcasme *m* — **sarcastic** [sɑr'kæstɪk] *adj* : sarcastique

sardine [sɑr'di:n] *n* : sardine *f*

sash ['sæʃ] *n* : large ceinture *f* (d'une robe), écharpe *f* (d'un uniforme)

sat → **sit**

satellite ['sæt̬əˌlaɪt] *n* : satellite *m*

satin ['sætən] *n* : satin *m*

satire ['sæˌtaɪr] *n* : satire *f* — **satiric** [sə'tɪrɪk] *or* **satirical** [-ɪkəl] *adj* : satirique

satisfaction [ˌsæt̬əs'fækʃən] *n* : satisfaction *f* — **satisfactory** [ˌsæt̬əs'fæktəri] *adj* : satisfaisant — **satisfy** ['sæt̬əsˌfaɪ] *vt* **-fied; -fying** : satisfaire — **satisfying** ['sæt̬əsˌfaɪɪŋ] *adj* : satisfaisant

saturate ['sætʃəˌreɪt] *vt* **-rated; -rating** 1 : saturer 2 DRENCH : tremper

Saturday ['sæt̬ərˌdeɪ, -di] *n* : samedi *m*

Saturn ['sæt̬ərn] *n* : Saturne *f*

sauce ['sɔs] *n* : sauce *f* — **saucepan** ['sɔsˌpæn] *n* : casserole *f* — **saucer** ['sɔsər] *n* : soucoupe *f*

Saudi ['saʊdi] *or* **Saudi Arabian** ['saʊdiə'reɪbiən] *adj* : saoudien

sauna ['sɔnə, 'saʊnə] *n* : sauna *m*

saunter ['sɔntər, 'sɑn-] *vi* : se promener

sausage ['sɔsɪʤ] n : saucisse f (crue), saucisson m (cuit)
sauté [sɔ'teɪ, so:-] vt -téed or -téd; -téing : faire revenir
savage ['sævɪʤ] adj : sauvage, féroce — ~ n : sauvage mf — savagery ['sævɪʤri, -ʤəri] n, pl -ries : férocité f
save ['seɪv] vt saved; saving 1 RESCUE : sauver 2 RESERVE : garder 3 : gagner (du temps), économiser (de l'argent) 4 : sauvegarder (en informatique) — ~ prep EXCEPT : sauf
savior ['seɪvjər] n : sauveur m
savor ['seɪvər] vt : savourer — savory ['seɪvəri] adj : savoureux
saw[1] → see
saw[2] ['sɔ] n : scie f — ~ vt sawed; sawed or sawn ['sɔn]; sawing : scier — sawdust ['sɔ,dʌst] n : sciure f — sawmill ['sɔ,mɪl] n : scierie f
saxophone ['sæksə,fo:n] n : saxophone m
say ['seɪ] v said ['sɛd]; saying; says ['sɛz] vt 1 : dire 2 INDICATE : indiquer (se dit d'une montre, etc.) — vi 1 : dire 2 that is to ~ : c'est-à-dire — ~ n, pl says ['seɪz] 1 have no ~ : ne pas avoir son mot à dire 2 have one's ~ : dire son mot — saying ['seɪɪŋ] n : dicton m
scab ['skæb] n 1 : croûte f, gale f Can 2 STRIKEBREAKER : jaune mf
scaffold ['skæfəld, -,fo:ld] n : échafaudage m (en construction)
scald ['skɔld] vt : ébouillanter
scale[1] ['skeɪl] n : pèse-personne m, balance f
scale[2] n : écaille f (d'un poisson, etc.) — ~ vt scaled; scaling : écailler
scale[3] n : gamme f (en musique), échelle f (salariale)
scallion ['skæljən] n : ciboule f, échalote f
scallop ['skɑləp, 'skæ-] n : coquille f Saint-Jacques
scalp ['skælp] n : cuir m chevelu
scam ['skæm] n : escroquerie f
scan ['skæn] vt scanned; scanning 1 EXAMINE : scruter 2 SKIM : lire attentivement 3 : balayer (en informatique)
scandal ['skændəl] n : scandale m — scandalous ['skændələs] adj : scandaleux
Scandinavian [,skændə'neɪviən] adj : scandinave
scant ['skænt] adj : insuffisant
scapegoat ['skeɪp,go:t] n : bouc m émissaire
scar ['skɑr] n : cicatrice f — ~ v scarred; scarring vt : laisser une cicatrice sur — vi : se cicatriser
scarce ['skɛrs] adj scarcer; scarcest : rare — scarcely ['skɛrsli] adv : à peine — scarcity ['skɛrsəṭi] n, pl -ties : pénurie f
scare ['skɛr] vt scared; scaring 1 : faire peur à 2 be ~d of : avoir peur de — ~ n 1 FRIGHT : peur f 2 PANIC : panique f — scarecrow ['skɛr,kro:] n : épouvantail m
scarf ['skɑrf] n, pl scarves ['skɑrvz] or scarfs : écharpe f, foulard m
scarlet ['skɑrlət] adj : écarlate — scarlet fever n : scarlatine f
scary ['skɛri] adj scarier, -est : qui fait peur
scathing ['skeɪðɪŋ] adj : cinglant
scatter ['skæṭər] vt 1 STREW : éparpiller 2 DISPERSE : disperser — vi : se disperser
scavenger ['skævənʤər] n : charognard m, -gnarde f
scenario [sə'næri,o:, -'nɑr-] n, pl -ios : scénario m
scene ['si:n] n 1 : scène f 2 behind the ~s : dans les coulisses — scenery ['si:nəri] n, pl -eries 1 : décor m 2 LANDSCAPE : paysages mpl — scenic ['si:nɪk] adj : pittoresque
scent ['sɛnt] n 1 : arôme m 2 PERFUME : parfum m 3 TRAIL : piste f — scented ['sɛntəd] adj : parfumé
sceptic ['skɛptɪk] → skeptic
schedule ['skɛ,ʤu:l, -ʤəl, esp Brit 'ʃɛd-ju:l] n 1 : programme m 2 TIMETABLE : horaire m 3 behind ~ : en retard 4 on ~ : à l'heure — ~ vt -uled; -uling : prévoir
scheme ['ski:m] n 1 PLAN : plan m 2 PLOT : intrigue f — ~ vi schemed; scheming : conspirer
schizophrenia [,skɪtsə'fri:niə, ,skɪzə-, -'frɛ-] n : schizophrénie f
scholar ['skɑlər] n : savant m, -vante f; érudit m, -dite f — scholarship ['skɑlər,ʃɪp] n : bourse f
school[1] ['sku:l] n : banc m (de poissons)
school[2] n 1 : école f, lycée m 2 COLLEGE : université f 3 DEPARTMENT : faculté f — ~ vt : instruire — schoolboy ['sku:l,bɔɪ] n : écolier m — schoolgirl ['sku:l,gərl] n : écolière f
science ['saɪənts] n : science f — scientific [,saɪən'tɪfɪk] adj : scientifique — scientist ['saɪəntɪst] n : scientifique mf
scissors ['sɪzərz] npl : ciseaux mpl
scoff ['skɑf] vi ~ at : se moquer de
scold ['sko:ld] vt : gronder, réprimander
scoop ['sku:p] n 1 : pelle f 2 : exclusivité f (en journalisme) — ~ vt 1 : enlever (avec une pelle) 2 ~ out : évider 3 ~ up : ramasser
scooter ['sku:ṭər] n 1 : trottinette f 2 or motor ~ : scooter m
scope ['sko:p] n 1 RANGE : étendue f, portée f 2 OPPORTUNITY : possibilités fpl
scorch ['skɔrtʃ] vt : roussir
score ['skor] n, pl scores 1 : score m, pointage m Can (aux sports) 2 RATING : note f, résultat m 3 : partition f (en musique) 4 keep ~ : marquer les points — ~ vt scored; scoring 1 : marquer (un point) 2 : obtenir (une note)
scorn ['skɔrn] n : mépris m, dédain m — ~ vt : mépriser, dédaigner — scornful ['skɔrnfəl] adj : méprisant
scorpion ['skɔrpiən] n : scorpion m
scotch ['skɑtʃ] n or ~ whiskey : scotch m — Scottish ['skɑṭɪʃ] adj : écossais
scoundrel ['skaʊndrəl] n : chenapan m
scour ['skaʊər] vt 1 SCRUB : récurer 2 SEARCH : parcourir
scourge ['skərʤ] n : fléau m
scout ['skaʊt] n : éclaireur m, -reuse f; scout m, scoute f
scowl ['skaʊl] vi : faire la grimace — ~ n : air m renfrogné
scram ['skræm] vi scrammed; scramming : filer fam
scramble ['skræmbəl] vt -bled; -bling : brouiller, mêler — ~ n : bousculade f, ruée f — scrambled eggs npl : œufs mpl brouillés
scrap ['skræp] n 1 PIECE : bout m 2 or ~ metal : ferraille f 3 ~s npl LEFTOVERS : restes mpl — ~ vt scrapped; scrapping : mettre au rebut
scrapbook ['skræp,bʊk] n : album m de coupures de journaux
scrape ['skreɪp] v scraped; scraping vt 1 : racler 2 : s'écorcher (le genou, etc.) 3 or ~ off : enlever en grattant — vi 1 ~ against : érafler 2 ~ by : se débrouiller — ~ n 1 : éraflure f 2 PREDICAMENT : pétrin m fam — scraper ['skreɪpər] n : grattoir m
scratch ['skrætʃ] vt 1 : égratigner 2 MARK : rayer 3 : se gratter (la tête, etc.) 4 ~ out : biffer — ~ n 1 : éraflure f, égratignure f 2 from ~ : à partir de zéro
scrawny ['skrɔni] adj -nier; -niest : maigre
scream ['skri:m] vi : hurler, crier — ~ n : hurlement m, cri m
screech ['skri:tʃ] n 1 : cri m perçant 2 : crissement m (de pneus, etc.) — ~ vi 1 : pousser un cri 2 : crisser (se dit des pneus, etc.)
screen ['skri:n] n 1 : écran m (de télévision, etc.) 2 PARTITION : paravent m 3 or window ~ : moustiquaire f — ~ vt 1 SHIELD : protéger 2 HIDE : cacher 3 EXAMINE : passer au crible
screw ['skru:] n : vis f — ~ vt 1 : visser 2 ~ up RUIN : bousiller — screwdriver ['skru:,draɪvər] n : tournevis m
scribble ['skrɪbəl] v -bled; -bling : gribouiller, griffonner — ~ n : gribouillage m
script ['skrɪpt] n : scénario m (d'un film, etc.)
scroll ['skro:l] n : rouleau m (de parchemin) — ~ vi : défiler (en informatique)
scrub ['skrʌb] vt scrubbed; scrubbing SCOUR : récurer — ~ n : nettoyage m
scruple ['skru:pəl] n : scrupule m — scrupulous ['skru:pjələs] adj : scrupuleux
scrutiny ['skru:təni] n, pl -nies : analyse f attentive
scuffle ['skʌfəl] n : bagarre f
sculpture ['skʌlptʃər] n : sculpture f — sculptor ['skʌlptər] n : sculpteur m
scum ['skʌm] n : écume f
scurry ['skəri] vi -ried; -rying : se précipiter
scuttle ['skʌṭəl] vt -tled; -tling : saborder (un navire)
scythe ['saɪð] n : faux f
sea ['si:] n 1 : mer f 2 at ~ : en mer — ~ adj : de mer — seafood ['si:,fu:d] n : fruits mpl de mer — seagull ['si:,gʌl] n : mouette f
seal[1] ['si:l] n : phoque m
seal[2] n 1 STAMP : sceau m 2 CLOSURE : fermeture f (hermétique) — ~ vt : sceller, cacheter
seam ['si:m] n : couture f
search ['sərtʃ] vt : fouiller — vi ~ for : chercher — ~ n 1 : recherche f 2 EXAMINATION : fouille f
seashell ['si:,ʃɛl] n : coquillage m — seashore ['si:,ʃor] n : bord m de la mer — seasick ['si:,sɪk] adj be ~ : avoir le mal de mer — seasickness ['si:,sɪknəs] n : mal m de mer
season ['si:zən] n : saison f — ~ vt : assaisonner, épicer — seasonal ['si:zənəl] adj : saisonnier — seasoned ['si:zənd] adj : expérimenté — seasoning ['si:zənɪŋ] n : assaisonnement m
seat ['si:t] n 1 : siège m 2 : fond m (de pantalon) 3 take a ~ : asseyez-vous — ~ vt 1 be ~ed : s'asseoir 2 the bus ~s 30 : l'autobus peut accueillir 30 personnes — seat belt n : ceinture f de sécurité
seaweed ['si:,wi:d] n : algue f marine
secede [sɪ'si:d] vi -ceded; -ceding : faire sécession
secluded [sɪ'klu:dəd] adj : isolé — seclusion [sɪ'klu:ʒən] n : isolement m
second ['sɛkənd] adj : second, deuxième — ~ or secondly ['sɛkəndli] adv : deuxièmement — ~ n 1 : deuxième mf; second m, -conde f 2 MOMENT : seconde f 3 have ~s : prendre une deuxième portion (de nourriture) — ~ vt : affirmer, appuyer — secondary ['sɛkən,dɛri] adj : secondaire — secondhand ['sɛkənd'hænd] adj : d'occasion — second-rate ['sɛkənd'reɪt] adj : médiocre
secret ['si:krət] adj : secret — ~ n : secret m — secrecy ['si:krəsi] n, pl -cies : secret m
secretary ['sɛkrə,tɛri] n, pl -taries 1 : secrétaire mf 2 : ministre m (du gouvernement)
secrete [sɪ'kri:t] vt -creted; -creting : sécréter
secretive ['si:krəṭɪv, sɪ'kri:ṭɪv] adj : cachottier — secretly ['si:krətli] adv : en secret
sect ['sɛkt] n : secte f
section ['sɛkʃən] n : section f, partie f
sector ['sɛktər] n : secteur m
secular ['sɛkjələr] adj : séculier, laïque
secure [sɪ'kjʊr] adj -curer; -est : sûr, en sécurité — ~ vt -cured; -curing 1 FASTEN : attacher 2 GET : obtenir — security [sɪ'kjʊrəṭi] n, pl -ties 1 : sécurité f 2 GUARANTEE : garantie f 3 securities npl : valeurs fpl
sedan [sɪ'dæn] n : berline f
sedative ['sɛdəṭɪv] n : calmant m, sédatif m
sedentary ['sɛdən,tɛri] adj : sédentaire
seduce [sɪ'du:s, -'dju:s] vt -duced; -ducing : séduire — seduction [sɪ'dʌkʃən] n : séduction f — seductive [sɪ'dʌktɪv] adj : séduisant
see ['si:] v saw ['sɔ]; seen ['si:n]; seeing vt 1 : voir 2 UNDERSTAND : comprendre 3 ESCORT : accompagner 4 ~ through : mener à terme 5 ~ you later : au revoir — vi 1 : voir 2 UNDERSTAND : comprendre 3 let's ~ : voyons 4 ~ to : s'occuper de
seed ['si:d] n, pl seed or seeds 1 : graine f 2 SOURCE : germe m — seedling ['si:dlɪŋ] n : semis m, jeune plant m — seedy ['si:di] adj seedier; seediest SQUALID : miteux
seek ['si:k] v sought ['sɔt]; seeking vt 1 or ~ out : chercher 2 REQUEST : demander — vi : rechercher
seem ['si:m] vi : paraître, sembler, avoir l'air
seep ['si:p] vi : suinter
seesaw ['si:,sɔ] n : balançoire f, bascule f
seethe ['si:ð] vi seethed; seething : bouillonner (de rage)
segment ['sɛgmənt] n : segment m
segregate ['sɛgrɪ,geɪt] vt -gated; -gating : séparer — segregation [,sɛgrɪ'geɪʃən] n : ségrégation f
seize ['si:z] vt seized; seizing 1 GRASP : saisir 2 CAPTURE : prendre — seizure ['si:ʒər] n : attaque f, crise f (en médecine)
seldom ['sɛldəm] adv : rarement
select [sə'lɛkt] adj : privilégié — ~ vt : choisir, sélectionner — selection [sə'lɛkʃən] n : sélection f
self ['sɛlf] n, pl selves ['sɛlvz] 1 : moi m 2 her better ~ : son meilleur côté — self-addressed [,sɛlfə'drɛst] adj ~ envelope : enveloppe f affranchie — self-assured [,sɛlfə'ʃʊrd] adj : sûr de soi — self-centered [,sɛlf'sɛntərd] adj : égocentrique — self-confidence [,sɛlf'kɑnfədənts] n : confiance f en soi — self-confident [,sɛlf'kɑnfədənt] adj : sûr de soi — self-conscious [,sɛlf'kɑntʃəs] adj : gêné, timide — self-control [,sɛlfkən'tro:l] n : maîtrise f de soi — self-defense [,sɛlfdɪ'fɛnts] n : autodéfense f — self-employed [,sɛlfɪm'plɔɪd] adj : qui travaille à son compte — self-esteem [,sɛlfɪ'sti:m] n : amour-propre m — self-evident [,sɛlf'ɛvədənt] adj : qui va de soi — self-explanatory [,sɛlfɪk'splænə,tori] adj : explicite — self-help [,sɛlf'hɛlp] n : initiative f personnelle — self-important [,sɛlfɪm'pɔrtənt] adj : vaniteux — self-interest [,sɛlf'ɪntrəst, -tə,rɛst] n : intérêt m personnel — selfish ['sɛlfɪʃ] adj : égoïste — selfishness ['sɛlfɪʃnəs] n : égoïsme m — self-pity [,sɛlf'pɪṭi] n, pl -ties : apitoiement m sur soi-même — self-portrait [,sɛlf'pɔrtrət] n : autoportrait m — self-respect [,sɛlfrɪ'spɛkt] n : amour m propre — self-righteous [,sɛlf'raɪtʃəs] adj : suffisant — self-service [,sɛlf'sərvɪs] n : libre-service m — self-sufficient [,sɛlfsə'fɪʃənt] adj : autosuffisant — self-taught [,sɛlf'tɔt] adj : autodidacte
sell ['sɛl] v sold ['so:ld]; selling vt : vendre — vi : se vendre — seller ['sɛlər] n : vendeur m, -deuse f
selves → self
semantics [sɪ'mæntɪks] ns & pl : sémantique f
semblance ['sɛmblənts] n : semblant m, apparence f
semester [sə'mɛstər] n : semestre m
semicolon ['sɛmi,ko:lən, 'sɛ,maɪ-] n : point-virgule m
semifinal ['sɛmi,faɪnəl, 'sɛ,maɪ-] n : demi-finale f
seminary ['sɛmə,nɛri] n, pl -naries : séminaire m — seminar ['sɛmə,nɑr] n : séminaire m
senate ['sɛnət] n : sénat m — senator ['sɛnəṭər] n : sénateur m
send ['sɛnd] vt sent ['sɛnt]; sending 1 : envoyer, expédier 2 ~ away for : commander 3 ~ back : renvoyer (de la marchandise, etc.) 4 ~ for : appeler, faire venir — sender ['sɛndər] n : expéditeur m, -trice f
Senegalese [,sɛnəgə'li:z, -'li:s] adj : sénégalais
senile ['si:,naɪl] adj : sénile — senility [sɪ'nɪləṭi] n : sénilité f
senior ['si:njər] n 1 SUPERIOR : supérieur m 2 : étudiant m, -diante f de dernière année (en éducation) 3 or ~ citizen : personne f du troisième âge 4 be s.o.'s ~ : être plus âgé que qqn — ~ adj 1 : haut placé 2 ELDER : aîné, plus âgé — seniority [,si:'njɔrəṭi] n : ancienneté f
sensation [sɛn'seɪʃən] n : sensation f — sensational [sɛn'seɪʃənəl] adj : sensationnel
sense ['sɛnts] n 1 : sens m 2 FEELING : sensation f 3 COMMON SENSE : bon sens m 4 make ~ : être logique — ~ vt sensed; sensing : sentir — senseless ['sɛntsləs] adj : insensé — sensible ['sɛntsəbəl] adj : raisonnable, pratique — sensibility [,sɛntsə'bɪləṭi] n, pl -ties : sensibilité f — sensitive ['sɛntsəṭɪv] adj 1 : sensible 2 TOUCHY : susceptible — sensitivity [,sɛntsə'tɪvəṭi] n, pl -ties : sensibilité f — sensor ['sɛn,sɔr, 'sɛntsər] n : détecteur m — sensual ['sɛntʃʊəl] adj : sensuel — sensuous ['sɛnʃʊəs] adj : sensuel
sent → send
sentence ['sɛntənts, -ənz] n 1 : phrase f 2 JUDGMENT : sentence f, condamnation f — ~ vt -tenced; -tencing : condamner
sentiment ['sɛntəmənt] n 1 : sentiment m 2 BELIEF : opinion f, avis m — sentimental [,sɛntə'mɛntəl] adj : sentimental — sentimentality [,sɛntə,mɛn'tæləṭi] n, pl -ties : sentimentalité f
sentry ['sɛntri] n, pl -tries : sentinelle f
separation [,sɛpə'reɪʃən] n : séparation f — separate ['sɛpə,reɪt] v -rated; -rating vt 1 : séparer 2 DISTINGUISH : distinguer — vi : se séparer — ~ ['sɛprət, 'sɛpə-] adj 1 : séparé 2 DETACHED : à part 3 DISTINCT : distinct — separately ['sɛprətli, 'sɛpə-] adv : séparément
September [sɛp'tɛmbər] n : septembre m
sequel ['si:kwəl] n : continuation f, suite f
sequence ['si:kwənts] n 1 ORDER : ordre m, suite f 2 : série f, succession f (de nombres)
serene [sə'ri:n] adj : serein, calme — serenity [sə'rɛnəṭi] n : sérénité f
sergeant ['sɑrʤənt] n : sergent m
serial ['sɪriəl] adj : en série — ~ n : feuilleton m — series ['sɪr,i:z] n, pl : série f
serious ['sɪriəs] adj : sérieux — seriously ['sɪriəsli] adv 1 : sérieusement 2 GRAVELY : gravement 3 take ~ : prendre au sérieux
sermon ['sərmən] n : sermon m
serpent ['sərpənt] n : serpent m
servant ['sərvənt] n : domestique mf
serve ['sərv] v served; serving vi 1 : servir 2 ~ as : servir de — vt 1 : servir (une personne, etc.), desservir (une région, etc.) 2 ~ time : purger une peine — server ['sərvər] n 1 WAITER : serveur m, -veuse f 2 : serveur m (en informatique)
service ['sərvəs] n 1 : service m 2 CEREMONY : office m (en religion) 3 MAINTENANCE : entretien m 4 armed ~s : forces fpl armées — ~ vt -viced; -vicing : réviser (un véhicule, etc.) — serviceman ['sərvəs,mæn, -mən] n, pl -men [-mən, -,mɛn] : militaire m — service station n : station-service f, poste m d'essence — serving ['sərvɪŋ] n : portion f, ration f
session ['sɛʃən] n : séance f, session f
set ['sɛt] n 1 : ensemble m, série f, jeu m 2 : set m (au tennis) 3 or stage ~ : scène f, plateau m 4 or television ~ : poste m de télévision — ~ v set; setting vt 1 or ~ down : mettre, placer 2 : régler (une montre) 3 FIX : fixer (un rendez-vous, etc.) 4 ~ fire to : mettre le feu à 5 ~ free : mettre en liberté 6 ~ off : déclencher (une alarme), faire détoner (une bombe) 7 ~ out to do sth : se proposer de faire qqch 8 ~ up ASSEMBLE : installer 9 ~ up ESTABLISH : établir — vi 1 : prendre (se dit de la gélatine, etc.) 2 : se coucher (se dit du soleil) 3 ~ in BEGIN : commencer 4 ~ off or ~ out : partir (en voyage) — ~ adj 1 FIXED : fixe 2 READY : prêt — setback ['sɛt,bæk] n : revers m — setting ['sɛṭɪŋ] n 1 : réglage m (d'une machine) 2 MOUNTING : monture f (d'un bijou) 3 SCENE : décor m
settle ['sɛṭəl] v settled; settling vi 1 : se poser (se dit d'un oiseau), se déposer (se dit de la poussière) 2 ~ down RELAX : se calmer 3 ~ for : se contenter de 4 ~ in

: s'installer — vt 1 DECIDE : fixer, décider 2 RESOLVE : résoudre 3 PAY : régler (un compte) 4 CALM : calmer 5 COLONIZE : coloniser — **settlement** [ˈsɛtəlmənt] n 1 PAYMENT : règlement m 2 COLONY : colonie f, village m 3 AGREEMENT : accord m — **settler** [ˈsɛtələr] n : colonisateur m, -trice f; colon m

seven [ˈsɛvən] n : sept m — ~ adj : sept — **seven hundred** adj : sept cents — **seventeen** [ˌsɛvənˈti:n] n : dix-sept m — ~ adj : dix-sept — **seventeenth** [ˌsɛvənˈti:nθ] n 1 : dix-septième mf 2 April ~ : le dix-sept avril — ~ adj : dix-septième — **seventh** [ˈsɛvənθ] n 1 : septième mf 2 July ~ : le sept juillet — ~ adj : septième — **seventieth** [ˈsɛvəntiəθ] n : soixante-dixième mf — ~ adj : soixante-dixième — **seventy** [ˈsɛvənti] n, pl -ties : soixante-dix m — ~ adj : soixante-dix

sever [ˈsɛvər] vt -ered; -ering 1 : couper 2 BREAK : rompre

several [ˈsɛvrəl, ˈsɛvə-] adj & pron : plusieurs

severance [ˈsɛvrənts, ˈsɛvə-] n 1 : rupture f 2 ~ pay : indemnité f de départ

severe [səˈvɪr] adj -verer; -verest 1 : sévère 2 SERIOUS : grave — **severely** [səˈvɪrli] adv 1 : sévèrement 2 SERIOUSLY : gravement

sew [ˈso:] v sewed; sewn [ˈso:n] or sewed; sewing : coudre

sewer [ˈsu:ər] n : égout m — **sewage** [ˈsu:ɪʤ] n : eaux fpl d'égout

sewing [ˈso:ɪŋ] n : couture f

sex [ˈsɛks] n 1 : sexe m 2 INTERCOURSE : relations fpl sexuelles — **sexism** [ˈsɛkˌsɪzəm] n : sexisme m — **sexist** [ˈsɛksɪst] adj : sexiste — **sexual** [ˈsɛkʃuəl] adj : sexuel — **sexuality** [ˌsɛkʃuˈæləṭi] n : sexualité f — **sexy** [ˈsɛksi] adj sexier; sexiest : sexy

shabby [ˈʃæbi] adj -bier; -biest 1 WORN : miteux 2 UNFAIR : mal, injuste

shack [ˈʃæk] n : cabane f

shackles [ˈʃækəlz] npl : fers mpl, chaînes fpl

shade [ˈʃeɪd] n 1 : ombre f 2 : ton m (d'une couleur) 3 NUANCE : nuance f 4 or lampshade : abat-jour m 5 window ~ : store m — ~ vt shaded; shading : protéger de la lumière — **shadow** [ˈʃædo:] n : ombre f — **shadowy** [ˈʃædowi] adj INDISTINCT : vague — **shady** [ˈʃeɪdi] adj shadier; shadiest 1 : ombragé 2 DISREPUTABLE : suspect

shaft [ˈʃæft] n 1 : tige f (d'une flèche, etc.) 2 HANDLE : manche m 3 AXLE : arbre m 4 or mine ~ : puits m

shaggy [ˈʃægi] adj -gier; -est : poilu

shake [ˈʃeɪk] v shook [ˈʃʊk]; shaken [ˈʃeɪkən]; shaking vt 1 : secouer 2 MIX : agiter 3 ~ hands with s.o. : serrer la main à qqn 4 ~ one's head : secouer la tête 5 ~ up UPSET : ébranler — vi : trembler — ~ n 1 : secousse f 2 → handshake — **shaker** [ˈʃeɪkər] n 1 salt ~ : salière f 2 pepper ~ : poivrière f — **shaky** [ˈʃeɪki] adj shakier; shakiest 1 : tremblant 2 UNSTABLE : peu ferme

shall [ˈʃæl] v aux, past should [ˈʃʊd]; pres sing & pl shall 1 (expressing volition or futurity) → will 2 (expressing possibility or obligation) → should 3 ~ we go? : nous y allons?

shallow [ˈʃælo:] adj 1 : peu profond 2 SUPERFICIAL : superficiel

sham [ˈʃæm] n : faux-semblant m

shambles [ˈʃæmbəlz] ns & pl : désordre m

shame [ˈʃeɪm] n 1 : honte f 2 what a ~! : quel dommage! — ~ vt shamed; shaming : faire honte à — **shameful** [ˈʃeɪmfəl] adj : honteux

shampoo [ʃæmˈpu:] vt : se laver (les cheveux) — ~ n, pl -poos : shampooing m

shan't [ˈʃænt] (contraction of shall not) → shall

shape [ˈʃeɪp] v shaped; shaping vt 1 : façonner 2 DETERMINE : déterminer 3 be ~d like : avoir la forme de — vi or ~ up : prendre forme — ~ n 1 : forme f 2 get in ~ : se mettre en forme — **shapeless** [ˈʃeɪpləs] adj : informe

share [ˈʃɛr] n 1 : portion f, part f 2 : action f (d'une compagnie) — ~ v shared; sharing vt 1 : partager 2 DIVIDE : diviser — vi : partager — **shareholder** [ˈʃɛrˌho:ldər] n : actionnaire mf

shark [ˈʃɑrk] n : requin m

sharp [ˈʃɑrp] adj 1 : affilé 2 POINTY : pointu 3 ACUTE : aigu 4 HARSH : dur, sévère 5 CLEAR : net 6 : dièse (en musique) — ~ adv at two o'clock ~ : à deux heures pile — ~ n : dièse m (en musique) — **sharpen** [ˈʃɑrpən] vt : aiguiser (un couteau, etc.), tailler (un crayon) — **sharpener** [ˈʃɑrpənər] n 1 or knife ~ : aiguisoir m 2 or pencil ~ : taille-crayon m — **sharply** [ˈʃɑrpli] adv : brusquement

shatter [ˈʃæṭər] vt 1 : briser, fracasser 2 DEVASTATE : détruire — vi : se briser, se fracasser

shave [ˈʃeɪv] v shaved; shaved or shaven [ˈʃeɪvən]; shaving vt 1 : raser 2 SLICE : couper — vi : se raser — ~ n : rasage — **shaver** [ˈʃeɪvər] n : rasoir m

shawl [ˈʃɔl] n : châle m

she [ˈʃi:] pron : elle

sheaf [ˈʃi:f] n, pl sheaves [ˈʃi:vz] : gerbe f (de céréales), liasse f (de papiers)

shear [ˈʃɪr] vt sheared; sheared or shorn [ˈʃorn]; shearing : tondre — **shears** [ˈʃɪrz] npl : cisailles fpl

sheath [ˈʃi:θ] n, pl sheaths [ˈʃi:ðz, ˈʃi:θs] : fourreau m (d'épée), gaine f (de poignard)

shed[1] [ˈʃɛd] v shed; shedding vt 1 : verser (des larmes) 2 : perdre (ses poils, etc.) 3 ~ light on : éclairer — vi : perdre ses poils, muer

shed[2] n : abri m, remise f

she'd [ˈʃi:d] (contraction of she had or she would) → have, would

sheen [ˈʃi:n] n : lustre m, éclat m

sheep [ˈʃi:p] n, pl sheep : mouton m — **sheepish** [ˈʃi:pɪʃ] adj : penaud

sheer [ˈʃɪr] adj 1 PURE : pur 2 STEEP : escarpé

sheet [ˈʃi:t] n 1 : drap m (de lit) 2 : feuille f (de papier) 3 : plaque f (de glace, etc.)

shelf [ˈʃɛlf] n, pl shelves [ˈʃɛlvz] : étagère f, rayon m

shell [ˈʃɛl] n 1 : coquillage m 2 : carapace f (d'un crustacé, etc.) 3 : coquille f (d'œuf, etc.) 4 POD : cosse f 5 MISSILE : obus m — ~ vt 1 : décortiquer (des noix), écosser (des pois) 2 BOMBARD : bombarder

she'll [ˈʃi:l, ˈʃɪl] (contraction of she shall or she will) → shall, will

shellfish [ˈʃɛlˌfɪʃ] n : crustacé m

shelter [ˈʃɛltər] n 1 : abri m, refuge m 2 take ~ : se réfugier — ~ vt 1 PROTECT : protéger 2 HARBOR : abriter

shepherd [ˈʃɛpərd] n : berger m

sherbet [ˈʃərbət] n : sorbet m

sheriff [ˈʃɛrɪf] n : shérif m

sherry [ˈʃɛri] n, pl -ries : xérès m

she's [ˈʃi:z] (contraction of she is or she has) → be, have

shield [ˈʃi:ld] n : bouclier m — ~ vt : protéger

shier, shiest → shy

shift [ˈʃɪft] vt : bouger, changer — vi 1 : se déplacer, bouger 2 CHANGE : changer 3 or ~ gears : changer de vitesse — ~ n 1 : changement m 2 : équipe f (au travail)

shimmer [ˈʃɪmər] vi : briller, reluire

shin [ˈʃɪn] n : tibia m

shine [ˈʃaɪn] v shone [ˈʃo:n, esp Brit and Can ˈʃɒn] or shined; shining vi : briller — vt POLISH : cirer (des chaussures) — ~ n : éclat m

shingle [ˈʃɪŋgəl] n : bardeau m — **shingles** [ˈʃɪŋgəlz] npl : zona m

shiny [ˈʃaɪni] adj shinier; shiniest : brillant

ship [ˈʃɪp] n : bateau m, navire m — ~ vt shipped; shipping : expédier (par bateau), transporter (par avion) — **shipbuilding** [ˈʃɪpˌbɪldɪŋ] n : construction f navale — **shipment** [ˈʃɪpmənt] n : cargaison f, chargement m — **shipping** [ˈʃɪpɪŋ] n : transport m (maritime) — **shipwreck** [ˈʃɪpˌrɛk] n : naufrage m — ~ vt be ~ed : faire naufrage — **shipyard** [ˈʃɪpˌjɑrd] n : chantier m naval

shirt [ˈʃərt] n : chemise f

shiver [ˈʃɪvər] vi : frissonner — ~ n : frisson m

shoal [ˈʃo:l] n : banc m (de poissons, etc.)

shock [ˈʃɑk] n 1 : choc m 2 or electric ~ : décharge f (électrique) — ~ vt : choquer, scandaliser — **shock absorber** n : amortisseur m — **shocking** [ˈʃɑkɪŋ] adj : choquant

shoddy [ˈʃɑdi] adj -dier; -est : de mauvaise qualité

shoe [ˈʃu:] n : chaussure f, soulier m — **shoelace** [ˈʃu:ˌleɪs] n : lacet m — **shoemaker** [ˈʃu:ˌmeɪkər] n : cordonnier m, -nière f

shone → shine

shook → shake

shoot [ˈʃu:t] v shot [ˈʃɑt]; shooting vt 1 : tirer (une balle, etc.) 2 : lancer (un regard) 3 PHOTOGRAPH : photographier 4 FILM : tourner — vi 1 : tirer 2 ~ by : passer en trombe — ~ n : rejeton m, pousse f (d'une plante) — **shooting star** n : étoile f filante

shop [ˈʃɑp] n 1 : magasin m, boutique f 2 WORKSHOP : atelier m — ~ vi shopped; shopping 1 : faire des courses 2 go shopping : faire les magasins — **shopkeeper** [ˈʃɑpˌki:pər] n : commerçant m, -çante f; marchand m, -chande f — **shoplift** [ˈʃɑpˌlɪft] vt : voler à l'étalage — **shoplifter** [ˈʃɑpˌlɪftər] n : voleur m, -leuse f à l'étalage — **shopper** [ˈʃɑpər] n : personne f qui fait ses courses

shore [ˈʃor] n : rivage m, bord m

shorn → shear

short [ˈʃɔrt] adj 1 : court 2 : petit, de petite taille 3 CURT : brusque 4 a ~ time ago : il y a peu de temps 5 be ~ of : être à court de — ~ adv 1 fall ~ : ne pas atteindre 2 stop ~ : s'arrêter net — **shortage** [ˈʃɔrtɪʤ] n : manque m, carence f — **shortcake** [ˈʃɔrtˌkeɪk] n : tarte f sablée — **shortcoming** [ˈʃɔrtˌkʌmɪŋ] n : défaut m — **shortcut** [ˈʃɔrtˌkʌt] n : raccourci m — **shorten** [ˈʃɔrtən] vt : raccourcir — **shorthand** [ˈʃɔrtˌhænd] n : sténographie f — **short-lived** [ˈʃɔrtˈlɪvd, -ˈlaɪvd] adj : éphémère — **shortly** [ˈʃɔrtli] adv : bientôt — **shortness** [ˈʃɔrtnəs] n 1 : petite taille f 2 ~ of breath : manque m de souffle — **shorts** npl : short m, pantalons mpl courts — **shortsighted** [ˈʃɔrtˌsaɪṭəd] → nearsighted

shot [ˈʃɑt] n 1 : coup m (de feu) 2 : coup m, tir m (aux sports) 3 ATTEMPT : essai m, tentative f 4 PHOTOGRAPH : photo f 5 INJECTION : piqûre f 6 : verre m (de liqueur) — **shotgun** [ˈʃɑtˌgʌn] n : fusil m

should [ˈʃʊd] past of shall 1 if she ~ call : si elle appelle 2 I ~ have gone : j'aurais dû y aller 3 they ~ arrive soon : ils devraient arriver bientôt 4 what ~ we do? : qu'allons nous faire?

shoulder [ˈʃo:ldər] n 1 : épaule f 2 : accotement m (d'une chaussée) — **shoulder blade** n : omoplate f

shouldn't [ˈʃʊdənt] (contraction of should not) → should

shout [ˈʃaʊt] v : crier — ~ n : cri m

shove [ˈʃʌv] vt shoved; shoving : pousser, bousculer — ~ n give s.o. a ~ : pousser qqn

shovel [ˈʃʌvəl] n : pelle f — ~ vt -veled or -velled; -veling or -velling : pelleter

show [ˈʃo:] v showed; shown [ˈʃo:n] or showed; showing vt 1 : montrer 2 TEACH : enseigner 3 PROVE : démontrer 4 ESCORT : accompagner 5 : passer (une émission, un film, etc.) 6 ~ off : faire étalage de — vi 1 : se voir 2 ~ off : faire le fier 3 ~ up ARRIVE : arriver — ~ n 1 : démonstration f 2 EXHIBITION : exposition f 3 : spectacle m (de théâtre), émission f (de télévision, etc.) — **showdown** [ˈʃo:ˌdaʊn] n : confrontation f

shower [ˈʃaʊər] n 1 : douche f 2 : averse f (de pluie, etc.) 3 PARTY : fête f — ~ vt 1 SPRAY : arroser 2 ~ s.o. with : couvrir qqn de — vi : prendre une douche

showy [ˈʃo:i] adj showier; showiest : tape-à-l'œil

shrank → shrink

shrapnel [ˈʃræpnəl] ns & pl : éclats mpl d'obus

shred [ˈʃrɛd] n 1 : brin m, parcelle f 2 in ~s : en lambeaux — ~ vt shredded; shredding 1 : déchirer 2 GRATE : râper

shrewd [ˈʃru:d] adj : astucieux

shriek [ˈʃri:k] vi : pousser un cri perçant — ~ n : cri m perçant

shrill [ˈʃrɪl] adj : perçant, strident

shrimp [ˈʃrɪmp] n : crevette f

shrine [ˈʃraɪn] n : lieu m saint

shrink [ˈʃrɪŋk] v shrank [ˈʃræŋk]; shrunk [ˈʃrʌŋk] or shrunken [ˈʃrʌŋkən]; shrinking : rétrécir

shrivel [ˈʃrɪvəl] vi -eled or -elled; -eling or -elling or ~ up : se dessécher, se rider

shroud [ˈʃraʊd] n 1 : linceul m 2 VEIL : voile m — ~ vt : envelopper

shrub [ˈʃrʌb] n : arbuste m, arbrisseau m

shrug [ˈʃrʌg] vi shrugged; shrugging : hausser les épaules

shrunk → shrink

shudder [ˈʃʌdər] vi : frissonner, frémir — ~ n : frisson m

shuffle [ˈʃʌfəl] v -fled; -fling vt : mélanger (des papiers), battre (des cartes) — vi : marcher en traînant les pieds

shun [ˈʃʌn] vt shunned; shunning : éviter, esquiver

shut [ˈʃʌt] v shut; shutting vt 1 CLOSE : fermer 2 → turn off 3 ~ up CONFINE : enfermer — vi 1 or ~ down : fermer 2 ~ up : se taire — **shutter** [ˈʃʌṭər] n or window ~ : volet m (d'une fenêtre)

shuttle [ˈʃʌṭəl] n 1 : navette f (à l'aéroport, etc.) 2 → space shuttle — ~ vt -tled; -tling : transporter — **shuttlecock** [ˈʃʌṭəlˌkɑk] n : volant m

shy [ˈʃaɪ] adj shier or shyer [ˈʃaɪər]; shiest or shyest [ˈʃaɪəst] : timide, gêné — ~ vi shied; shying or ~ away : éviter — **shyness** [ˈʃaɪnəs] n : timidité f

sibling [ˈsɪblɪŋ] n : frère m, sœur f

sick [ˈsɪk] adj 1 : malade 2 be ~ VOMIT : vomir 3 be ~ of : en avoir assez de 4 feel ~ : avoir des nausées — **sicken** [ˈsɪkən] vt DISGUST : écœurer — **sickening** [ˈsɪkənɪŋ] adj : écœurant — **sick leave** n : congé m de maladie

sickle [ˈsɪkəl] n : faucille f

sickly [ˈsɪkli] adj -lier; -est : maladif — **sickness** [ˈsɪknəs] n : maladie f

side [ˈsaɪd] n 1 : bord m 2 : côté m (d'une personne), flanc m (d'un animal) 3 : côté m, camp m (de l'opposition, etc.) 4 ~ by ~ : côte à côte 5 take ~s : prendre parti — ~ adj : latéral — vi ~ with : prendre le parti de — **sideboard** [ˈsaɪdˌbord] n : buffet m — **sideburns** [ˈsaɪdˌbərnz] npl : favoris mpl — **side effect** n : effet m secondaire — **sideline** [ˈsaɪdˌlaɪn] n : travail m d'appoint — **sidewalk** [ˈsaɪdˌwɔk] n : trottoir m — **sideways** [ˈsaɪdˌweɪz] adv & adj : de côté — **siding** [ˈsaɪdɪŋ] n : revêtement m extérieur

siege [ˈsi:ʤ, ˈsi:ʒ] n : siège m

sieve [ˈsɪv] n : tamis m, crible m

sift [ˈsɪft] vt 1 : tamiser 2 or ~ through : examiner

sigh [ˈsaɪ] vi : soupirer — ~ n : soupir m

sight [ˈsaɪt] n 1 : vue f 2 SPECTACLE : spectacle m 3 : centre m d'intérêt (touristique) 4 catch ~ of : apercevoir — **sightseer** [ˈsaɪtˌsi:ər] n : touriste mf

sign [ˈsaɪn] n 1 : signe m 2 NOTICE : panneau m, enseigne f — ~ vt : signer (un chèque, etc.) — vi 1 : signer 2 ~ up ENROLL : s'inscrire

signal [ˈsɪgnəl] n : signal m — ~ v -naled or -nalled; -naling or -nalling vt 1 : faire signe à 2 INDICATE : signaler — vi 1 : faire des signes 2 : mettre son clignotant (dans un véhicule)

signature [ˈsɪgnəˌʧor] n : signature f

significance [sɪgˈnɪfɪkənts] n 1 : signification f, sens m 2 IMPORTANCE : importance f — **significant** [sɪgˈnɪfɪkənt] adj 1 : significatif 2 IMPORTANT : considérable — **significantly** [sɪgˈnɪfɪkəntli] adv : sensiblement — **signify** [ˈsɪgnəˌfaɪ] vt -fied; -fying : signifier — **sign language** n : langage m des signes — **signpost** [ˈsaɪnˌpo:st] n : poteau m indicateur

silence [ˈsaɪlənts] n : silence m — ~ vt -lenced; -lencing : faire taire — **silent** [ˈsaɪlənt] adj 1 : silencieux 2 : muet (se dit d'un film, etc.)

silhouette [ˌsɪləˈwɛt] n : silhouette f

silicon [ˈsɪlɪkən, -ˌkɑn] n : silicium m

silk [ˈsɪlk] n : soie f — **silky** [ˈsɪlki] adj silkier; -est : soyeux

sill [ˈsɪl] n : rebord m (d'une fenêtre), seuil m (d'une porte)

silly [ˈsɪli] adj -lier; -est : stupide, bête

silt [ˈsɪlt] n : limon m

silver [ˈsɪlvər] n 1 : argent m 2 → silverware — ~ adj : d'argent, en argent — **silverware** [ˈsɪlvərˌwær] n : argenterie f, coutellerie f Can — **silvery** [ˈsɪlvəri] adj : argenté

similar [ˈsɪmələr] adj : semblable, pareil — **similarity** [ˌsɪməˈlærəṭi] n, pl -ties : ressemblance f, similarité f

simmer [ˈsɪmər] vi : mijoter

simple [ˈsɪmpəl] adj -pler; -plest 1 : simple 2 EASY : facile — **simplicity** [sɪmˈplɪsəṭi] n : simplicité f — **simplify** [ˈsɪmpləˌfaɪ] vt -fied; -fying : simplifier — **simply** [ˈsɪmpli] adv 1 : simplement 2 ABSOLUTELY : absolument

simulate [ˈsɪmjəˌleɪt] vt -lated; -lating : simuler

simultaneous [ˌsaɪməlˈteɪniəs] adj : simultané

sin [ˈsɪn] n : péché m — ~ vi sinned; sinning : pécher

since [ˈsɪnts] adv 1 or ~ then : depuis 2 long ~ : il y a longtemps — ~ conj 1 : depuis que 2 BECAUSE : puisque, comme 3 it's been years ~ … : il y a des années que … — ~ prep : depuis

sincere [sɪnˈsɪr] adj -cerer; -cerest : sincère — **sincerely** [sɪnˈsɪrli] adv : sincèrement — **sincerity** [sɪnˈsɛrəṭi] n : sincérité f

sinful [ˈsɪnfəl] adj : immoral

sing [ˈsɪŋ] v sang [ˈsæŋ] or sung [ˈsʌŋ]; sung; singing : chanter

singer [ˈsɪŋər] n : chanteur m, -teuse f

single [ˈsɪŋgəl] adj 1 : seul, unique 2 UNMARRIED : célibataire 3 every ~ day : tous les jours 4 every ~ time : chaque fois — ~ vt -gled; -gling ~ out 1 SELECT : choisir 2 DISTINGUISH : distinguer

singular [ˈsɪŋgjələr] adj : singulier — ~ n : singulier m

sinister [ˈsɪnəstər] adj : sinistre

sink [ˈsɪŋk] v sank [ˈsæŋk] or sunk [ˈsʌŋk]; sunk; sinking vi 1 : couler 2 DROP : baisser, tomber — vt 1 : couler 2 ~ sth into : enfoncer qqch dans — ~ n 1 or bathroom ~ : lavabo m 2 or kitchen ~ : évier m

sinner [ˈsɪnər] n : pécheur m, -cheresse f

sip [ˈsɪp] vt sipped; sipping : boire à petites gorgées, siroter fam — ~ n : petite gorgée f

siphon [ˈsaɪfən] n : siphon m — ~ vt : siphonner

sir [ˈsər] n 1 (as a form of address) : monsieur m 2 (in titles) : sir m

siren [ˈsaɪrən] n : sirène f

sirloin [ˈsərˌlɔɪn] n : aloyau m

sissy [ˈsɪsi] n, pl -sies : poule f mouillée fam

sister [ˈsɪstər] n : sœur f — **sister-in-law** [ˈsɪstərɪnˌlɔ] n, pl sisters-in-law : belle-sœur f

sit [ˈsɪt] v sat [ˈsæt]; sitting vi 1 or ~ down : s'asseoir 2 LIE : être, se trouver 3 MEET : siéger 4 or ~ up : se redresser — vt : asseoir

site [ˈsaɪt] n 1 : site m, emplacement m 2 LOT : terrain m

sitting room → living room

situated [ˈsɪʧuˌeɪṭəd] adj : situé — **situation** [ˌsɪʧuˈeɪʃən] n : situation f

six [ˈsɪks] n : six m — ~ adj : six — **six hundred** adj : six cents — **sixteen** [sɪksˈti:n] n : seize m — ~ adj : seize — **sixteenth** [sɪksˈti:nθ] n 1 : seizième mf 2 October ~ : le seize octobre — ~ adj

: seizième — **sixth** ['sɪksθ, 'sɪkst] *n* 1 : sixième *mf* 2 **March ~** : le six mars — **~** *adj* : sixième — **sixtieth** ['sɪkstiəθ] *n* : soixantième *mf* — **~** *adj* : soixantième — **sixty** ['sɪksti] *n, pl* **-ties** : soixante *m* — **~** *adj* : soixante

size ['saɪz] *n* 1 : taille *f* (d'un vêtement), pointure *f* (de chaussures, etc.) 2 EXTENT : ampleur *f* — **~** *vt* **sized; sizing** *or* **~ up** : jauger, évaluer

sizzle ['sɪzəl] *vi* **-zled; -zling** : grésiller

skate ['skeɪt] *n* : patin *m* — **~** *vi* **skated; skating** : patiner, faire du patin — **skateboard** ['skeɪt,bord] *n* : planche *f* à roulettes — **skater** ['skeɪtər] *n* : patineur *m*, -neuse *f*

skeleton ['skɛlətən] *n* : squelette *m*

skeptical ['skɛptɪkəl] *adj* : sceptique

sketch ['skɛtʃ] *n* : esquisse *f*, croquis *m* — **~** *vt* : esquisser

skewer ['skju:ər] *n* : brochette *f*, broche *f*

ski ['ski:] *n, pl* **skis** : ski *m* — **~** *vi* **skied; skiing** : faire du ski

skid ['skɪd] *n* : dérapage *m* — **~** *vi* **skidded; skidding** : déraper, patiner

skier ['ski:ər] *n* : skieur *m*, skieuse *f*

skill ['skɪl] *n* 1 : habileté *f*, dextérité *f* 2 TECHNIQUE : technique *f* 3 **~s** *npl* : compétences *fpl* — **skilled** ['skɪld] *adj* : habile

skillet ['skɪlət] *n* : poêle *f* (à frire)

skillful *or Brit* **skilful** ['skɪlfəl] *adj* : habile, adroit

skim ['skɪm] *vt* **skimmed; skimming** 1 : écumer (de la soupe), écrémer (du lait) 2 : effleurer (une surface) 3 *or* **~ through** : parcourir (un livre, etc.) — **~** *adj* : écrémé

skimpy ['skɪmpi] *adj* **skimpier; skimpiest** 1 : maigre (se dit d'une portion) 2 : étriqué (se dit d'un vêtement)

skin ['skɪn] *n* 1 : peau *f* 2 : pelure *f* (de pomme, etc.) — **~** *vt* **skinned; skinning** 1 : dépouiller (un animal) 2 : s'écorcher (le genou, etc.) — **skin diving** *n* : plongée *f* sous-marine — **skinny** ['skɪni] *adj* **-nier; -est** : maigre

skip ['skɪp] *v* **skipped; skipping** *vi* : sautiller — *vt* OMIT : sauter — **~** *n* : petit saut *m*, petit bond *m*

skirmish ['skərmɪʃ] *n* : escarmouche *f*

skirt ['skərt] *n* : jupe *f*

skull ['skʌl] *n* : crâne *m*

skunk ['skʌŋk] *n* : mouffette *f*

sky ['skaɪ] *n, pl* **skies** : ciel *m* — **skylight** ['skaɪ,laɪt] *n* : lucarne *f* — **skyline** ['skaɪ,laɪn] *n* : horizon *m* — **skyscraper** ['skaɪ,skreɪpər] *n* : gratte-ciel *m*

slab ['slæb] *n* : dalle *f*, bloc *m*

slack ['slæk] *adj* 1 LOOSE : mou, lâche 2 CARELESS : négligent — **slacks** ['slæks] *npl* : pantalon *m* — **slacken** ['slækən] *vt* : relâcher

slain → **slay**

slam ['slæm] *n* : claquement *m* (de porte) — **~** *v* **slammed; slamming** *vt* 1 : claquer (une porte, etc.) 2 *or* **~ down** : flanquer 3 *or* **~ shut** : fermer brusquement — *vi* **~ into** : heurter

slander ['slændər] *vt* : calomnier, diffamer — **~** *n* : calomnie *f*, diffamation *f*

slang ['slæŋ] *n* : argot *m*

slant ['slænt] *n* : pente *f*, inclinaison *f* — **~** *vi* : pencher, s'incliner

slap ['slæp] *vt* **slapped; slapping** : gifler, donner une claque à — **~** *n* : gifle *f*, claque *f*

slash ['slæʃ] *vt* : entailler

slat ['slæt] *n* : lame *f*, lamelle *f*

slate ['sleɪt] *n* : ardoise *f*

slaughter ['slɔtər] *n* : massacre *m* — **~** *vt* 1 : abattre (des animaux) 2 MASSACRE : massacrer — **slaughterhouse** ['slɔtər,haʊs] *n* : abattoir *m*

slave ['sleɪv] *n* : esclave *mf* — **slavery** ['sleɪvəri] *n* : esclavage *m*

sled ['slɛd] *n* : traîneau *m*, luge *f*

sledgehammer ['slɛdʒ,hæmər] *n* : masse *f*

sleek ['sli:k] *adj* : lisse, luisant

sleep ['sli:p] *n* 1 : sommeil *m* 2 **go to ~** : s'endormir — **~** *vi* **slept** ['slɛpt]; **sleeping** : dormir — **sleeper** ['sli:pər] *n* **be a light ~** : avoir le sommeil léger — **sleepless** ['sli:pləs] *adj* **have a ~ night** : passer une nuit blanche — **sleepwalker** ['sli:p,wɔkər] *n* : somnambule *mf* — **sleepy** ['sli:pi] *adj* **sleepier; -est** 1 : somnolent 2 **be ~** : avoir sommeil

sleet ['sli:t] *n* : grésil *m* — **~** *vi* : grésiller

sleeve ['sli:v] *n* : manche *f* — **sleeveless** ['sli:vləs] *adj* : sans manches

sleigh ['sleɪ] *n* : traîneau *m*, carriole *f Can*

slender ['slɛndər] *adj* : svelte, mince

slept → **sleep**

slice ['slaɪs] *vt* **sliced; slicing** : trancher — **~** *n* : tranche *f*, rondelle *f*

slick ['slɪk] *adj* SLIPPERY : glissant

slide ['slaɪd] *v* **slid** ['slɪd]; **sliding** ['slaɪdɪŋ] *vi* : glisser — *vt* : faire glisser — **~** *n* 1 : glissoire *f* 2 : toboggan *m* (dans un terrain de jeu) 3 : diapositive *f* (en photographie) 4 DECLINE : baisse *f*

slier, sliest → **sly**

slight ['slaɪt] *adj* 1 SLENDER : mince 2 MINOR : léger — **~** *vt* : offenser — **slightly** ['slaɪtli] *adv* : légèrement, un peu

slim ['slɪm] *adj* **slimmer; slimmest** 1 : svelte 2 **a ~ chance** : une faible chance — **~** *v* **slimmed; slimming** : maigrir

slime ['slaɪm] *n* MUD : vase *f*, boue *f*

sling ['slɪŋ] *vt* **slung** ['slʌŋ]; **slinging** THROW : lancer — **~** *n* 1 : fronde *f* 2 : écharpe *f* (en médecine) — **slingshot** ['slɪŋ,ʃɑt] *n* : lance-pierres *m*

slip[1] ['slɪp] *v* **slipped; slipping** *vi* 1 SLIDE : glisser 2 **~ away** : partir furtivement 3 **~ up** : faire une gaffe — *vt* 1 : glisser 2 **~ into** : enfiler (un vêtement, etc.) — **~** *n* 1 MISTAKE : erreur *f* 2 : jupon *m* 3 **a ~ of the tongue** : un lapsus

slip[2] *n* **~ of paper** : bout *m* (de papier)

slipper ['slɪpər] *n* : pantoufle *f*

slippery ['slɪpəri] *adj* **-perier; -est** : glissant

slit ['slɪt] *n* 1 OPENING : fente *f* 2 CUT : incision *f* — **~** *vt* **slit; slitting** : couper

slither ['slɪðər] *vi* : ramper

sliver ['slɪvər] *n* : éclat *m* (de bois)

slogan ['slo:gən] *n* : slogan *m*

slope ['slo:p] *vi* **sloped; sloping** : pencher — **~** *n* : pente *f*

sloppy ['slɑpi] *adj* **-pier; -piest** 1 CARELESS : peu soigné 2 UNKEMPT : débraillé

slot ['slɑt] *n* 1 : fente *f* 2 GROOVE : rainure *f*

sloth ['slɔθ, 'slo:θ] *n* : paresse *f*

slouch ['slaʊtʃ] *vi* : marcher avec les épaules rentrées

slow ['slo:] *adj* 1 : lent 2 **be ~** : retarder (se dit d'une horloge) — **~** *adv* → **slowly** — **~** *vt* : retarder — *vi or* **~ down** : ralentir — **slowly** ['slo:li] *adv* : lentement — **slowness** ['slo:nəs] *n* : lenteur *f*

slug ['slʌg] *n* : limace *f* (mollusque)

sluggish ['slʌgɪʃ] *adj* : lent

slum ['slʌm] *n* : taudis *m*

slumber ['slʌmbər] *vi* : sommeiller — **~** *n* : sommeil *m*

slump ['slʌmp] *vi* 1 DROP : baisser, chuter 2 COLLAPSE : s'effondrer — **~** *n* : crise *f* (économique)

slung → **sling**

slur[1] ['slər] *n* : calomnie *f*, diffamation *f*

slur[2] *vt* **slurred; slurring** : mal articuler (ses mots)

slurp ['slərp] *v* : boire bruyamment

slush ['slʌʃ] *n* : neige *f* fondue, gadoue *f Can*

sly ['slaɪ] *adj* **slier** ['slaɪər]; **sliest** ['slaɪəst] 1 : rusé, sournois 2 **on the ~** : en cachette

smack[1] ['smæk] *vi* **~ of** : sentir

smack[2] *vt* 1 : donner une claque à 2 KISS : donner un baiser à — **~** *n* 1 SLAP : claque *f*, gifle *f* 2 KISS : gros baiser *m* — **~** *adv* : juste, exactement

small ['smɔl] *adj* : petit — **smallpox** ['smɔl,pɑks] *n* : variole *f*

smart ['smɑrt] *adj* 1 : intelligent 2 STYLISH : élégant

smash ['smæʃ] *n* 1 COLLISION : choc *m* 2 BANG, CRASH : fracas *m* — **~** *vt* BREAK : fracasser — *vi* 1 SHATTER : se briser 2 **~ into** : s'écraser contre

smattering ['smætərɪŋ] *n* : notions *fpl* vagues

smear ['smɪr] *n* : tache *f* — **~** *vt* 1 : barbouiller, faire des taches sur 2 **~ sth on** : enduire qqch de

smell ['smɛl] *v* **smelled** ['smɛld] *or* **smelt** ['smɛlt]; **smelling** : sentir — **~** *n* 1 : odorat *m* 2 ODOR : odeur *f* — **smelly** ['smɛli] *adj* **smellier; -est** : qui sent mauvais

smile ['smaɪl] *vi* **smiled; smiling** : sourire — **~** *n* : sourire *m*

smirk ['smərk] *n* : petit sourire *m* satisfait

smitten ['smɪtən] *adj* **be ~ with** : être épris de

smock ['smɑk] *n* : blouse *f*, sarrau *m*

smog ['smɑg, 'smɔg] *n* : smog *m*

smoke ['smo:k] *n* : fumée *f* — **~** *v* **smoked; smoking** : fumer — **smoke detector** *n* : détecteur *m* de fumée — **smoker** ['smo:kər] *n* : fumeur *m*, -meuse *f* — **smokestack** ['smo:k,stæk] *n* : cheminée *f* — **smoky** ['smo:ki] *adj* **smokier; -est** : enfumé

smolder ['smo:ldər] *vi* : couver

smooth ['smu:ð] *adj* : lisse (se dit d'une surface, etc.), calme (se dit de la mer), doux (se dit de la peau, etc.) — **~** *or* **~ out** *vt* : défroisser — **smoothly** ['smu:ðli] *adv* : sans heurts

smother ['smʌðər] *vt* 1 : recouvrir (un feu) 2 : étouffer (qqn)

smudge ['smʌdʒ] *vt* **smudged; smudging** : salir, faire des taches sur — **~** *n* : tache *f*, bavure *f*

smug ['smʌg] *adj* **smugger; smuggest** : suffisant

smuggle ['smʌgəl] *vt* **-gled; -gling** : faire passer en contrebande — **smuggler** ['smʌgələr] *n* : contrebandier *m*, -dière *f*

snack ['snæk] *n* : casse-croûte *m*, collation *f*

snag ['snæg] *n* : accroc *m* — **~** *vt* **snagged; snagging** : faire un accroc à (un bas)

snail ['sneɪl] *n* : escargot *m*

snake ['sneɪk] *n* : serpent *m*

snap ['snæp] *v* **snapped; snapping** *vi* 1 BREAK : se casser, se briser 2 **~ at** : répondre brusquement à — *vt* 1 BREAK : casser, briser 2 **~ one's fingers** : claquer des doigts 3 **~ open/shut** : s'ouvrir, se fermer d'un coup sec — **~** *n* 1 : claquement *m* 2 FASTENER : bouton-pression *m* 3 **be a ~** : être facile — **snappy** ['snæpi] *adj* **-pier; -piest** 1 FAST : vite 2 STYLISH : élégant — **snapshot** ['snæp,ʃɑt] *n* : instantané *m*

snare ['snær] *n* : piège *m*

snarl[1] ['snɑrl] *vi* TANGLE : enchevêtrer

snarl[2] *vi* GROWL : grogner — **~** *n* : grognement *m*

snatch ['snætʃ] *vt* : saisir

sneak ['sni:k] *vi* : se glisser, se faufiler — *vt* : faire furtivement — **sneakers** ['sni:kərz] *npl* : tennis *mpl France*, espadrilles *fpl Can* — **sneaky** ['sni:ki] *adj* **sneakier; -est** : sournois

sneer ['snɪr] *vi* : ricaner — **~** *n* : ricanement *m*

sneeze ['sni:z] *vi* **sneezed; sneezing** : éternuer — **~** *n* : éternuement *m*

snide ['snaɪd] *adj* : sarcastique

sniff ['snɪf] *vi* : renifler — **~** *n* : inhalation *f* — **sniffle** ['snɪfəl] *vi* **-fled; -fling** : renifler — **sniffles** ['snɪfəlz] *npl* **have the ~** : être enrhumé

snip ['snɪp] *n* : coup *m* de ciseaux — **~** *vt* **snipped; snipping** : couper

snivel ['snɪvəl] *vi* **-eled** *or* **-elled; -eling** *or* **-elling** : pleurnicher *fam*

snob ['snɑb] *n* : snob *mf* — **snobbish** ['snɑbɪʃ] *adj* : snob

snoop ['snu:p] *vi or* **~ around** : fouiner

snooze ['snu:z] *vi* **snoozed; snoozing** : sommeiller — **~** *n* : petit somme *m*, sieste *f*

snore ['snor] *vi* **snored; snoring** : ronfler — **~** *n* : ronflement *m*

snort ['snɔrt] *vi* : grogner (se dit d'un cochon, d'une personne) — **~** *n* : grognement *m*

snout ['snaʊt] *n* : museau *m*, groin *m*

snow ['sno:] *n* : neige *f* — **~** *vi* : neiger — **snowbank** ['sno:,bæŋk] *n* : banc *m* de neige *Can* — **snowfall** ['sno:,fɔl] *n* : chute *f* de neige — **snowflake** ['sno:,fleɪk] *n* : flocon *m* de neige — **snowman** ['sno:,mæn] *n* : bonhomme *m* de neige — **snowplow** ['sno:,plaʊ] *n* : chasse-neige *m* — **snowshoe** ['sno:,ʃu:] *n* : raquette *f* — **snowstorm** ['sno:,stɔrm] *n* : tempête *f* de neige — **snowy** ['sno:i] *adj* **snowier; -est** 1 : neigeux 2 : enneigé (se dit d'une montagne, etc.)

snub ['snʌb] *vt* **snubbed; snubbing** : rabrouer — **~** *n* : rebuffade *f*

snuff ['snʌf] *vt or* **~ out** : moucher (une chandelle)

snug ['snʌg] *adj* **snugger; snuggest** 1 : confortable, douillet 2 TIGHT : ajusté — **snuggle** ['snʌgəl] *vi* **-gled; -gling** : se blottir

so ['so:] *adv* 1 LIKEWISE : aussi 2 THUS : ainsi 3 THEREFORE : alors 4 *or* **~ much** : tant 5 *or* **~ very** : si 6 **and ~ on** : et cetera 7 **I think ~** : je pense que oui 8 **I told you ~** : je te l'avais bien dit — **~** *conj* 1 THEREFORE : donc 2 *or* **~ that** : pour que 3 **~ what?** : et alors? — **~** *adj* TRUE : vrai — **~** *pron* **or ~** : plus ou moins

soak ['so:k] *vt* 1 : tremper 2 **~ up** : absorber — **~** *n* : trempage *m*

soap ['so:p] *n* : savon *m* — **~** *vt* **~ up** : savonner — **soapy** ['so:pi] *adj* **soapier; -est** : savonneux

soar ['sor] *vi* 1 : planer 2 INCREASE : monter (en flèche)

sob ['sɑb] *vi* **sobbed; sobbing** : sangloter — **~** *n* : sanglot *m*

sober ['so:bər] *adj* 1 : sobre 2 SERIOUS : sérieux — **sobriety** [sə'braɪəti, so-] *n* 1 : sobriété *f* 2 SERIOUSNESS : sérieux *m*

so–called ['so:'kɔld] *adj* : présumé

soccer ['sɑkər] *n* : football *m France*, soccer *m Can*

social ['so:ʃəl] *adj* : social — **~** *n* : réunion *f* — **sociable** ['so:ʃəbəl] *adj* : sociable — **socialism** ['so:ʃə,lɪzəm] *n* : socialisme *m* — **socialist** ['so:ʃəlɪst] *n* : socialiste *mf* — **~** *adj* : socialiste — **socialize** ['so:ʃə,laɪz] *v* **-ized; -izing** *vt* : socialiser — *vi* **~ with** : fréquenter des gens — **society** [sə'saɪəti] *n, pl* **-eties** : société *f* — **sociology** [,so:si'ɑlədʒi] *n* : sociologie *f*

sock[1] ['sɑk] *n, pl* **socks** *or* **sox** : chaussette *f*

sock[2] *vt* : donner un coup de poing à

socket ['sɑkət] *n* 1 *or* **electric ~** : prise *f* de courant 2 *or* **eye ~** : orbite *f*

soda ['so:də] *n* 1 *or* **~ pop** : boisson *f* gazeuse, soda *m France*, liqueur *f Can* 2 *or* **~ water** : soda *m*

sodium ['so:diəm] *n* : sodium *m*

sofa ['so:fə] *n* : canapé *m*

soft ['sɔft] *adj* 1 : mou 2 SMOOTH : doux — **softball** ['sɔft,bɔl] *n* : balle-molle *f Can* — **soft drink** *n* : boisson *f* non alcoolisée, boisson *f* gazeuse — **soften** ['sɔfən] *vt* 1 : amollir, ramollir 2 EASE : adoucir, atténuer — *vi* 1 : se ramollir 2 EASE : s'adoucir — **softly** ['sɔftli] *adv* : doucement — **softness** ['sɔftnəs] *n* : douceur *f* — **software** ['sɔft,wær] *n* : logiciel *m*

soggy ['sɑgi] *adj* **-gier; -est** : détrempé

soil ['sɔɪl] *vt* : salir, souiller — **~** *n* DIRT : terre *f*

solace ['sɑləs] *n* : consolation *f*

solar ['so:lər] *adj* : solaire

sold → **sell**

solder ['sɑdər, 'sɔ-] *n* : soudure *f* — **~** *vt* : souder

soldier ['so:ldʒər] *n* : soldat *m*

sole[1] ['so:l] *n* : sole *f* (poisson)

sole[2] *n* : plante *f* (du pied), semelle *f* (d'un soulier)

sole[3] *adj* : seul — **solely** ['so:li] *adv* : uniquement

solemn ['sɑləm] *adj* : solennel — **solemnity** [sə'lɛmnəti] *n, pl* **-ties** : solennité *f*

solicit [sə'lɪsət] *vt* : solliciter

solid ['sɑləd] *adj* 1 : solide 2 UNBROKEN : continu 3 **~ gold** : or massif 4 **two ~ hours** : deux heures de suite — **~** *n* : solide *m* — **solidarity** [,sɑlə'dærəti] *n* : solidarité *f* — **solidify** [sə'lɪdə,faɪ] *v* **-fied; -fying** *vt* : solidifier — *vi* : se solidifier — **solidity** [sə'lɪdəti] *n, pl* **-ties** : solidité *f*

solitary ['sɑlə,tɛri] *adj* : solitaire — **solitude** ['sɑlə,tu:d, -,tju:d] *n* : solitude *f*

solo ['so:,lo:] *n, pl* **-los** : solo *m* — **soloist** ['so:loɪst] *n* : soliste *mf*

solution [sə'lu:ʃən] *n* : solution *f* — **soluble** ['sɑljəbəl] *adj* : soluble — **solve** ['sɑlv] *vt* **solved; solving** : résoudre — **solvent** ['sɑlvənt] *n* : solvent *m*

somber ['sɑmbər] *adj* : sombre

some ['sʌm] *adj* 1 (*of unspecified identity*) : un 2 (*of an unspecified amount*) : de, un peu de 3 (*of an unspecified number*) : certains 4 SEVERAL : quelques 5 **that was ~ game!** : ça c'était un match! — **~** *pron* 1 SEVERAL : certains, quelques-uns 2 **do you want ~?** : en voulez vous? — **~** *adv* **~ twenty people** : une vingtaine de personnes — **somebody** ['sʌmbədi, -,bɑdi] *pron* : quelqu'un — **someday** ['sʌm,deɪ] *adv* : un jour — **somehow** ['sʌm,haʊ] *adv* 1 : pour quelque raison 2 **~ or other** : d'une manière ou d'une autre — **someone** ['sʌm,wʌn] *pron* : quelqu'un

somersault ['sʌmər,sɔlt] *n* : culbute *f*

something ['sʌmθɪŋ] *pron* 1 : quelque chose 2 **~ else** : autre chose — **sometime** ['sʌm,taɪm] *adv* 1 : un jour, un de ces jours 2 **~ next month** : dans le courant du mois à venir — **sometimes** ['sʌm,taɪmz] *adv* : quelquefois, parfois — **somewhat** ['sʌm,hwʌt, -,hwɑt] *adv* : un peu — **somewhere** ['sʌm,hwɛr] *adv* 1 : quelque part 2 **~ around** : autour de 3 **~ else** → **elsewhere**

son ['sʌn] *n* : fils *m*

song ['sɔŋ] *n* : chanson *f*

son–in–law ['sʌnɪn,lɔ] *n, pl* **sons–in–law** : gendre *m*, beau-fils *m*

soon ['su:n] *adv* 1 : bientôt 2 SHORTLY : sous peu 3 **as ~ as** : aussitôt que 4 **~ after** : peu après 5 **~er or later** : tôt ou tard 6 **the ~er the better** : le plus tôt sera le mieux

soot ['sʊt, 'su:t, 'sʌt] *n* : suie *f*

soothe ['su:ð] *vt* **soothed; soothing** 1 : calmer, apaiser 2 RELIEVE : soulager

sophisticated [sə'fɪstə,keɪtəd] *adj* 1 : perfectionné 2 WORLDLY : sophistiqué

sophomore ['sɑf,mor, 'sɑfə,mor] *n* : étudiant *m*, -diante *f* de deuxième année

soprano [sə'præ,no:] *n, pl* **-nos** : soprano *mf*

sorcerer ['sɔrsərər] *n* : sorcier *m* — **sorcery** ['sɔrsəri] *n* : sorcellerie *f*

sordid ['sɔrdɪd] *adj* : sordide

sore ['sor] *adj* **sorer; sorest** 1 : douloureux 2 **~ loser** : mauvais perdant 3 **~ throat** : mal *m* de gorge — **~** *n* : plaie *f* — **sorely** ['sorli] *adv* : grandement — **soreness** ['sornəs] *n* : douleur *f*

sorrow ['sɑr,o:] *n* : chagrin *m*, peine *f*

sorry ['sɑri] *adj* **-rier; -est** 1 PITIFUL : lamentable 2 **feel ~ for** : plaindre 3 **I'm ~** : je suis désolé, je regrette

sort ['sɔrt] *n* 1 : genre *m*, sorte *f* 2 **a ~ of** : une espèce de — **~** *vt* : trier, classer — **sort of** *adv* 1 SOMEWHAT : plutôt 2 MORE OR LESS : plus ou moins

SOS [,ɛs,o:'ɛs] *n* : S.O.S. *m*

so–so ['so:'so:] *adv* : comme ci comme ça — **~** *adj* : moyen

soufflé [su:'fleɪ] *n* : soufflé *m*

sought → **seek**

soul ['so:l] *n* 1 : âme *f* 2 **not a ~** : pas un chat

sound[1] ['saʊnd] *adj* 1 HEALTHY : sain 2 FIRM : solide 3 SENSIBLE : logique 4 **a ~ sleep** : un sommeil profond 5 **safe and ~** : sain et sauf

sound[2] *n* 1 : son *m* 2 NOISE : bruit *m* — **~** *vt* : sonner, retentir — *vi* 1 : sonner 2 SEEM : sembler, paraître

sound[3] *n* CHANNEL : détroit *m* — **~** *vt* : sonder

soundproof ['saʊnd,pru:f] *adj* : insonorisé

soup ['su:p] *n* : soupe *f*

sour ['saʊər] *adj* : aigre — **~** *vt* : aigrir

source ['sors] *n* : source *f*, origine *f*

south ['saʊθ] *adv* : au sud, vers le sud — ~ *adj* : (du) sud — ~ *n* : sud *m* — **southeast** [saʊ'θi:st] *adv* : au sud-est, vers le sud-est — ~ *adj* : (du) sud-est — ~ *n* : sud-est *m* — **southeastern** [saʊ'θi:stərn] *adj* → **southeast** — **southerly** ['sʌðərli] *adv* & *adj* : (du) sud — **southern** ['sʌðərn] *adj* : du sud, méridional — **southwest** [saʊθ'west] *adv* : au sud-ouest, vers le sud-ouest — ~ *adj* : (du) sud-ouest — ~ *n* : sud-ouest *m* — **southwestern** [saʊθ'westərn] *adj* → **southwest**

souvenir [ˌsu:və'nɪr, 'su:vəˌ-] *n* : souvenir *m*

sovereign ['sɑvərən] *n* : souverain *m*, -raine *f* — ~ *adj* : souverain — **sovereignty** ['sɑvərənti] *n, pl* **-ties** : souveraineté *f*

sow[1] ['saʊ] *n* : truie *f*

sow[2] ['so:] *vt* **sowed; sown** ['so:n] *or* **sowed; sowing** : semer

sox → **sock**

soybean ['sɔɪˌbi:n] *n* : graine *f* de soja

spa ['spɑ] *n* : station *f* thermale

space ['speɪs] *n* **1** : espace *m* **2** ROOM, SPOT : place *f* — ~ *vt* **spaced; spacing** *or* ~ **out** : espacer — **spaceship** ['speɪsˌʃɪp] *n* : vaisseau *m* spatial — **space shuttle** *n* : navette *f* spatiale — **spacious** ['speɪʃəs] *adj* : spacieux, ample

spade[1] ['speɪd] *n* SHOVEL : bêche *f*, pelle *f*

spade[2] *n* : pique *f* (aux cartes)

spaghetti [spə'gɛti] *n* : spaghetti *mpl*

span ['spæn] *n* **1** PERIOD : espace *m* **2** : travée *f* (d'un pont) — ~ *vt* **spanned; spanning 1** : couvrir (une période) **2** CROSS : s'étendre sur

spaniel ['spænjəl] *n* : épagneul *m*

Spanish ['spænɪʃ] *adj* : espagnol — ~ *n* : espagnol *m* (langue)

spank ['spæŋk] *vt* : donner une fessée à

spare ['spær] *vt* **spared; sparing 1** PARDON : pardonner **2** SAVE : épargner **3 can you ~ a dollar?** : avez-vous un dollar à me prêter? **4 I can't ~ the time** : je n'ai pas le temps **5 ~ no expense** : ne pas ménager ses efforts — ~ *adj* **1** : de rechange **2** EXCESS : de trop — ~ *n or* ~ **part** : pièce *f* de rechange — **spare time** *n* : temps *m* libre — **sparing** ['spærɪŋ] *adj* : économe

spark ['spɑrk] *n* : étincelle *f* — ~ *vt* : éveiller, susciter — **sparkle** ['spɑrkəl] *vi* **-kled; -kling** : étinceler, scintiller — ~ *n* : scintillement *m* — **spark plug** *n* : bougie *f*

sparrow ['spæro:] *n* : moineau *m*

sparse ['spɑrs] *adj* **sparser; sparsest** : clairsemé, épars — **sparsely** ['spɑrsli] *adv* : peu

spasm ['spæzəm] *n* : spasme *m*

spat[1] ['spæt] → **spit**

spat[2] *n* QUARREL : prise *f* de bec

spatter ['spætər] *vt* : éclabousser

spawn ['spɔn] *vi* : frayer — *vt* : engendrer, produire — ~ *n* : frai *m*

speak ['spi:k] *v* **spoke** ['spo:k]; **spoken** ['spo:kən]; **speaking** *vi* **1** : parler **2 ~ out against** : dénoncer **3 ~ up** : parler plus fort **4 ~ up for** : défendre — *vt* **1** : dire **2** : parler (une langue) — **speaker** ['spi:kər] *n* **1** : personne *f* qui parle (une langue) **2** ORATOR : orateur *m*, -trice *f* **3** LOUDSPEAKER : haut-parleur *m*

spear ['spɪr] *n* : lance *f* — **spearhead** ['spɪrˌhɛd] *n* : fer *m* de lance — ~ *vt* : mener, être à la tête de — **spearmint** ['spɪrˌmɪnt] *n* : menthe *f* verte

special ['spɛʃəl] *adj* : spécial, particulier — **specialist** ['spɛʃəlɪst] *n* : spécialiste *mf* — **specialize** ['spɛʃəˌlaɪz] *vi* **-ized; -izing** : se spécialiser — **specially** ['spɛʃəli] *adv* : spécialement — **specialty** ['spɛʃəlti] *n, pl* **-ties** : spécialité *f*

species ['spi:ˌʃi:z, -ˌsi:z] *ns & pl* : espèce *f*

specify ['spɛsəˌfaɪ] *vt* **-fied; -fying** : spécifier — **specific** [spɪ'sɪfɪk] *adj* : précis, explicite — **specifically** [spɪ'sɪfɪkli] *adv* **1** : spécialement **2** EXPLICITLY : expressément

specimen ['spɛsəmən] *n* : spécimen *m*, échantillon *m*

speck ['spɛk] *n* **1** SPOT : tache *f* **2** BIT : brin *m* — **speckled** ['spɛkəld] *adj* : tacheté, moucheté

spectacle ['spɛktɪkəl] *n* **1** : spectacle *m* **2 ~s** *npl* GLASSES : lunettes *fpl* — **spectacular** [spɛk'tækjələr] *adj* : spectaculaire — **spectator** ['spɛkˌteɪtər] *n* : spectateur *m*, -trice *f*

specter *or* **spectre** ['spɛktər] *n* : spectre *m*

spectrum ['spɛktrəm] *n, pl* **-tra** [-trə] *or* **-trums 1** : spectre *m* **2** RANGE : gamme *f*

speculation [ˌspɛkjə'leɪʃən] *n* : conjectures *fpl*, spéculations *fpl*

speech ['spi:tʃ] *n* **1** : parole *f* **2** ADDRESS : discours *m* — **speechless** ['spi:tʃləs] *adj* : muet

speed ['spi:d] *n* **1** : vitesse *f* **2** VELOCITY : rapidité *f* — ~ *v* **sped** ['spɛd] *or* **speeded; speeding** *vi* **1** : faire un excès de vitesse **2 ~ off** : aller à toute vitesse — *vt or* ~ **up** : accélérer — **speed limit** *n* : limitation *f* de vitesse — **speedometer** [spɪ'dɑmətər] *n* : compteur *m* (de vitesse) — **speedy** ['spi:di] *adj* **speedier; -est** : rapide

spell[1] ['spɛl] *vt* **1** : écrire, orthographier **2** *or* ~ **out** : épeler **3** MEAN : signifier

spell[2] *n* ENCHANTMENT : sortilège *m*

spell[3] *n* : période *f* (de temps)

spellbound ['spɛlˌbaʊnd] *adj* : captivé

spelling ['spɛlɪŋ] *n* : orthographe *f*

spend ['spɛnd] *vt* **spent** ['spɛnt]; **spending 1** : dépenser (de l'argent) **2** : passer (ses vacances, etc.)

sperm ['spərm] *n, pl* **sperm** *or* **sperms** : sperme *m*

sphere ['sfɪr] *n* : sphère *f* — **spherical** ['sfɪrɪkəl, 'sfɛr-] *adj* : sphérique

spice ['spaɪs] *n* : épice *f* — ~ *vt* **spiced; spicing** : assaisonner — **spicy** ['spaɪsi] *adj* **spicier; -est** : épicé, piquant

spider ['spaɪdər] *n* : araignée *f*

spigot ['spɪgət, -kət] *n* : robinet *m*

spike ['spaɪk] *n* **1** : gros clou *m* **2** POINT : pointe *f* — **spiky** ['spaɪki] *adj* **-kier; -est** : pointu

spill ['spɪl] *vt* : renverser, répandre — *vi* : se répandre

spin ['spɪn] *v* **spun** ['spʌn]; **spinning** *vi* : tourner, tournoyer — *vt* **1** : faire tourner **2** : filer (de la laine) — ~ *n* **1** : tour *m* **2 go for a ~** : faire une balade (en auto)

spinach ['spɪnɪtʃ] *n* : épinards *mpl*

spinal cord ['spaɪnəl] *n* : moelle *f* épinière

spindle ['spɪndəl] *n* : fuseau *m* (en textile)

spine ['spaɪn] *n* **1** : colonne *f* vertébrale **2** : piquant *m* (d'un animal) **3** : dos *m* (d'un livre)

spinster ['spɪnstər] *n* : vieille fille *f*

spiral ['spaɪrəl] *adj* : en spirale — ~ *n* : spirale *f* — ~ *vi* **-raled** *or* **-ralled; -raling** *or* **-ralling** : aller en spirale

spire ['spaɪr] *n* : flèche *f*

spirit ['spɪrət] *n* **1** : esprit *m* **2 in good ~s** : de bonne humeur **3 ~s** *npl* : spiritueux *mpl* — **spirited** ['spɪrətəd] *adj* : animé — **spiritual** ['spɪrɪtʃʊəl, -tʃəl] *adj* : spirituel — **spirituality** [ˌspɪrɪtʃʊ'æləti] *n* : spiritualité *f*

spit[1] ['spɪt] *n* : broche *f*

spit[2] *v* **spit** *or* **spat** ['spæt]; **spitting** : cracher — ~ *n* SALIVA : salive *f*

spite ['spaɪt] *n* **1** : rancune *f* **2 in ~ of** : malgré — ~ *vt* **spited; spiting** : contrarier — **spiteful** ['spaɪtfəl] *adj* : rancunier

splash ['splæʃ] *vt* : éclabousser — *vi or* ~ **about** : patauger — ~ *n* **1** : éclaboussement *m* **2** : plouf *m* (bruit)

splatter ['splætər] → **spatter**

spleen ['spli:n] *n* : rate *f* (organe)

splendid ['splɛndəd] *adj* : splendide — ~ **splendor** *or Brit* **splendour** ['splɛndər] *n* : splendeur *f*

splint ['splɪnt] *n* : attelle *f*

splinter ['splɪntər] *n* : éclat *m* — ~ *vi* : se briser en éclats

split ['splɪt] *v* **split; splitting** *vt* **1** : fendre (du bois), déchirer (un pantalon) **2** *or* ~ **up** : diviser — *vi* ~ **up** : se séparer — ~ *n* **1** CRACK : fente *f* **2** *or* ~ **seam** : déchirure *f*

splurge ['splərdʒ] *vi* **splurged; splurging** : faire des folles dépenses

spoil ['spɔɪl] *vt* **spoiled** *or* **spoilt** ['spɔɪlt]; **spoiling 1** RUIN : gâcher **2** PAMPER : gâter — **spoils** ['spɔɪlz] *npl* : butin *m*

spoke[1] ['spo:k] → **speak**

spoke[2] *n* : rayon *m* (d'une roue)

spoken → **speak**

spokesman ['spo:ksmən] *n, pl* **-men** [-mən, -ˌmɛn] : porte-parole *m* — **spokeswoman** ['spo:ksˌwʊmən] *n, pl* **-women** [-ˌwɪmən] : porte-parole *f*

sponge ['spʌndʒ] *n* : éponge *f* — ~ *vt* **sponged; sponging** : éponger — **spongy** ['spʌndʒi] *adj* **spongier; -est** : spongieux

sponsor ['spɑntsər] *n* : parrain *m* (d'une cause, etc.) — ~ *vt* : patronner — **sponsorship** ['spɑntsərˌʃɪp] *n* : parrainage *m*, patronage *m*

spontaneity [ˌspɑntə'ni:əti, -'neɪ-] *n* : spontanéité *f* — **spontaneous** [spɑn'teɪniəs] *adj* : spontané

spooky ['spu:ki] *adj* **spookier; -est** : qui donne la chair de poule

spool ['spu:l] *n* : bobine *f*

spoon ['spu:n] *n* : cuillère *f* — **spoonful** ['spu:nˌfʊl] *n* : cuillerée *f*

sporadic [spə'rædɪk] *adj* : sporadique

sport ['sport] *n* **1** : sport *m* **2 be a good ~** : avoir l'esprit d'équipe — **sportsman** ['sportsmən] *n, pl* **-men** [-mən, -ˌmɛn] : sportif *m* — **sportswoman** ['sportsˌwʊmən] *n, pl* **-women** [-ˌwɪmən] : sportive *f* — **sporty** ['sporti] *adj* **sportier; -est** : sportif

spot ['spɑt] *n* **1** : tache *f* **2** DOT : pois *m* **3** PLACE : endroit *m*, lieu *m* **4 in a tight ~** : dans l'embarras **5 on the ~** INSTANTLY : immédiatement — ~ *vt* **spotted; spotting 1** STAIN : tacher **2** DETECT, NOTICE : apercevoir, repérer — **spotless** ['spɑtləs] *adj* : impeccable — **spotlight** ['spɑtˌlaɪt] *n* **1** : projecteur *m*, spot *m* **2 be in the ~** : être le centre de l'attention — **spotty** ['spɑti] *adj* **-tier; -est** : irrégulier

spouse ['spaʊs] *n* : époux *m*, épouse *f*

spout ['spaʊt] *vi* : jaillir — ~ *n* : bec *m* (d'une cruche)

sprain ['spreɪn] *n* : entorse *f*, foulure *f* — ~ *vt* : se faire une entorse à, se fouler (la cheville, etc.)

sprawl ['sprɔl] *vi* **1** : être affalé (dans un fauteuil, etc.) **2** EXTEND : s'étendre — ~ *n* : étendue *f*

spray[1] ['spreɪ] *n* BOUQUET : gerbe *f*, bouquet *m*

spray[2] *n* **1** MIST : gouttelettes *fpl* fines **2** *or* **aerosol ~** : vaporisateur *m*, bombe *f* **3** *or* **~ bottle** : atomiseur *m* — ~ *vt* : vaporiser, pulvériser

spread ['sprɛd] *v* **spread; spreading** *vt* **1** : propager (une nouvelle), répandre (de l'information) **2** *or* ~ **out** : écarter **3** : étaler, tartiner (avec de la confiture, etc.) — *vi* **1** : se propager (se dit d'une maladie) **2** *or* ~ **out** : s'étendre (se dit d'un feu) — ~ *n* **1** : propagation *f*, diffusion *f* **2** PASTE : pâte *f* à tartiner — **spreadsheet** ['sprɛdˌʃi:t] *n* : tableur *m*

spree ['spri] *n* **go on a spending ~** : faire de folles dépenses

sprightly ['spraɪtli] *adj* **-lier; -est** : vif, alerte

spring ['sprɪŋ] *v* **sprang** ['spræŋ] *or* **sprung** ['sprʌŋ]; **sprung; springing** *vi* **1** : sauter, bondir **2 ~ from** : surgir de — *vt* **1** ACTIVATE : actionner **2 ~ sth on s.o.** : surprendre qqn avec qqch — ~ *n* **1** : puits *m* **2** : printemps *m* (saison) **3** LEAP : bond *m*, saut *m* **4** RESILIENCE : élasticité *f* **5** : ressort *m* (mécanisme) **6** *or* **bedspring** : sommier *m* — **springboard** ['sprɪŋˌbord] *n* : tremplin *m* — **springtime** ['sprɪŋˌtaɪm] *n* : printemps *m* — **springy** ['sprɪŋi] *adj* **springier; -est** : élastique

sprinkle ['sprɪŋkəl] *v* **-kled; -kling** *vt* **1** : arroser **2** DUST : saupoudrer — ~ *n* : petite averse *f* — **sprinkler** ['sprɪŋk'lər] *n* : arroseur *m*

sprint ['sprɪnt] *vi* : courir — ~ *n* : sprint *m* (aux sports)

sprout ['spraʊt] *vi* : germer, pousser — ~ *n* : pousse *f*

spruce[1] ['spru:s] *vt* **spruced; sprucing ~ up** : embellir

spruce[2] *n* : épicéa *m*

spun → **spin**

spur ['spər] *n* **1** : éperon *m* **2** STIMULUS : incitation *f* **3 on the ~ of the moment** : sur le coup — ~ *vt* **spurred; spurring 1** *or* ~ **on** : éperonner (un cheval) **2 ~ on** MOTIVATE : motiver

spurn ['spərn] *vt* : repousser, rejeter

spurt[1] ['spərt] *vi* : jaillir — ~ *n* : jaillissement *m*, jet *m*

spurt[2] *n* **1** : sursaut *m* (d'énergie, etc.) **2 work in ~s** : travailler par à-coups

spy ['spaɪ] *vi* **spied; spying ~ on** : espionner — ~ *n* : espion *m*

squabble ['skwɑbəl] *n* : dispute *f*, querelle *f* — ~ *vi* **-bled; -bling** : se disputer, se chamailler

squad ['skwɑd] *n* : peloton *m* (militaire), brigade *f* (de police)

squadron ['skwɑdrən] *n* : escadron *m* (de soldats), escadre *f* (de navires ou d'avions)

squalid ['skwɑlɪd] *adj* : sordide

squalor ['skwɑlər] *n* : conditions *fpl* sordides

squander ['skwɑndər] *vt* : gaspiller

square ['skwær] *n* **1** : carré *m* **2** : place *f* (d'une ville) — ~ *adj* **squarer; squarest 1** : carré **2** EVEN : quitte — ~ *vt* **squared; squaring** : carrer (un nombre) — **square root** *n* : racine *f* carrée

squash[1] ['skwɑʃ, 'skwɔʃ] *vt* : écraser, aplatir

squash[2] *n, pl* **squashes** *or* **squash** : courge *f*

squat ['skwɑt] *vi* **squatted; squatting** : s'accroupir — ~ *adj* **squatter; squattest** : trapu

squawk ['skwɔk] *n* : cri *m* rauque — ~ *vi* : pousser des cris rauques

squeak ['skwi:k] *vi* : grincer — ~ *n* : grincement *m*

squeal ['skwi:l] *vi* **1** : pousser des cris aigus **2** : crisser (se dit des pneus), grincer (se dit des freins) **3 ~ on** : dénoncer — ~ *n* : petit cri *m* aigu

squeamish ['skwi:mɪʃ] *adj* : impressionnable, délicat

squeeze ['skwi:z] *vt* **squeezed; squeezing 1** : presser, serrer **2** : extraire (du jus) — ~ *n* : pression *f*, resserrement *m*

squid ['skwɪd] *n, pl* **squid** *or* **squids** : calmar *m*

squint ['skwɪnt] *vi* : loucher

squirm ['skwərm] *vi* : se tortiller

squirrel ['skwərəl] *n* : écureuil *m*

squirt ['skwərt] *vt* : lancer un jet de — *vi* : jaillir — ~ *n* : jet *m*

stab ['stæb] *n* **1** : coup *m* de couteau **2 ~ of pain** : élancement *m* **3 take a ~ at sth** : tenter de faire qqch — ~ *vt* **stabbed; stabbing 1** KNIFE : poignarder **2** THRUST : planter

stable ['steɪbəl] *n* **1** : étable *f* (pour le bétail) **2** *or* **horse ~** : écurie *f* — ~ *adj* **-bler; -est** : stable — **stability** [stə'bɪləti] *n, pl* **-ties** : stabilité *f* — **stabilize** ['steɪbəˌlaɪz] *vt* **-lized; -lizing** : stabiliser

stack ['stæk] *n* : tas *m*, pile *f* — ~ *vt* : entasser, empiler

stadium ['steɪdiəm] *n, pl* **-dia** [-diə] *or* **-diums** : stade *m*

staff ['stæf] *n, pl* **staffs** ['stæfs, 'stævz] *or* **staves** ['stævz, 'steɪvz] **1** : bâton *m* **2** *pl* **staffs** PERSONNEL : personnel *m*

stag ['stæg] *n, pl* **stags** *or* **stag** : cerf *m*

stage ['steɪdʒ] *n* **1** : scène *f* (au théâtre) **2** PHASE : étape *f* **3 the ~** : le théâtre — ~ *vt* **staged; staging 1** : mettre en scène **2** ORGANIZE : organiser

stagger ['stægər] *vi* : tituber, chanceler — *vt* **1** : échelonner **2 be ~ed by** : être stupéfié par — **staggering** ['stægərɪŋ] *adj* : stupéfiant

stagnant ['stægnənt] *adj* : stagnant — **stagnate** ['stægˌneɪt] *vi* **-nated; -nating** : stagner

stain ['steɪn] *vt* **1** : tacher **2** : teindre (du bois) — ~ *n* **1** : tache *f* **2** DYE : teinture *f* — **stainless steel** ['steɪnləs] *n* : acier *m* inoxydable

stair ['stær] *n* **1** STEP : marche *f* **2 ~s** *npl* : escalier *m* — **staircase** ['stærˌkeɪs] *n* : escalier *m* — **stairway** ['stærˌweɪ] *n* : escalier *m*

stake ['steɪk] *n* **1** POST : poteau *m*, pieu *m*, piquet *m* **2** INTEREST : intérêts *mpl* **3 be at ~** : être en jeu — ~ *vt* **staked; staking 1** BET : miser, parier **2 ~ a claim to** : revendiquer

stale ['steɪl] *adj* **staler; stalest 1** : rassis **2** OLD : vieux **3** STUFFY : vicié

stalk[1] ['stɔk] *n* : tige *f* (d'une plante)

stalk[2] *vt* : traquer, suivre

stall[1] ['stɔl] *n* **1** : stalle *f* (d'un cheval, etc.) **2** STAND : stand *m*, kiosque *m* — ~ *vi* : caler (se dit d'un moteur)

stall[2] *vt* : retarder

stallion ['stæljən] *n* : étalon *m*

stalwart ['stɔlwərt] *adj* **1** STRONG : robuste **2 ~ supporter** : partisan *m* inconditionnel

stamina ['stæmənə] *n* : résistance *f*

stammer ['stæmər] *vi* : bégayer — ~ *n* : bégaiement *m*

stamp ['stæmp] *n* **1** SEAL : cachet *m* **2** MARK : tampon *m* **3** *or* **postage ~** : timbre *m* — ~ *vt* **1** : affranchir (une lettre, etc.) **2** IMPRINT : estamper **3** MINT : frapper (la monnaie) **4 ~ one's feet** : taper des pieds

stampede [stæm'pi:d] *n* : débandade *f*, ruée *f*

stance ['stænts] *n* : position *f*

stand ['stænd] *v* **stood** ['stʊd]; **standing** *vi* **1** : être debout **2** BE : être, se trouver **3** CONTINUE : rester valable **4** LIE, REST : reposer **5 ~ back** : reculer **6 ~ out** : ressortir **7** *or* **~ up** : se mettre debout — *vt* **1** PLACE : mettre **2** ENDURE : supporter **3 ~ a chance** : avoir de bonnes chances — **stand by** *vt* **1** : s'en tenir à (une promesse, etc.) **2** SUPPORT : appuyer — **stand for** *vt* **1** MEAN : signifier **2** PERMIT : tolérer — **stand up** *vi* **1 ~ for** : défendre **2 ~ up to** : tenir tête à — **stand** *n* **1** RESISTANCE : résistance *f* **2** STALL : stand *m* **3** BASE : pied *m* **4** POSITION : position *f* **5 ~s** *npl* : tribune *f*

standard ['stændərd] *n* **1** : norme *f* **2** BANNER : étendard *m* **3** CRITERION : critère *m* **4 ~ of living** : niveau *m* de vie — ~ *adj* : standard

standing ['stændɪŋ] *n* **1** RANK : position *f*, standing *m* **2** DURATION : durée *f*

standpoint ['stændˌpɔɪnt] *n* : point *m* de vue

standstill ['stændˌstɪl] *n* **1 be at a ~** : être paralysé **2 come to a ~** : s'arrêter

stank → **stink**

stanza ['stænzə] *n* : strophe *f*

staple[1] ['steɪpəl] *n* : produit *m* de base — ~ *adj* : principal, de base

staple[2] *n* : agrafe *f* — ~ *vt* **-pled; -pling** : agrafer — **stapler** ['steɪplər] *n* : agrafeuse *f*

star ['stɑr] *n* : étoile *f* — ~ *v* **starred; starring** *vt* FEATURE : avoir pour vedette — *vi* ~ **in** : être la vedette de

starboard ['stɑrbərd] *n* : tribord *m*

starch ['stɑrtʃ] *vt* : amidonner — ~ *n* **1** : amidon *m* **2** : fécule *f* (aliment)

stardom ['stɑrdəm] *n* : célébrité *f*

stare ['stær] *vi* **stared; staring** : regarder fixement — ~ *n* : regard *m* fixe

starfish ['stɑrˌfɪʃ] *n* : étoile *f* de mer

stark ['stɑrk] *adj* **1** PLAIN : austère **2** HARSH : sévère, dur

starling ['stɑrlɪŋ] *n* : étourneau *m*

starry ['stɑri] *adj* **-rier; -est** : étoilé

start ['stɑrt] *vi* **1** : débuter, commencer **2** SET OUT : partir **3** JUMP : sursauter **4** *or* ~ **up** : démarrer — *vt* **1** : commencer **2** CAUSE : provoquer **3** *or* ~ **up** ESTABLISH : établir **4** *or* ~ **up** : mettre en marche (un moteur, etc.) — ~ *n* **1** : commencement *m*, début *m* **2 get an early ~** : commencer tôt **3 give s.o. a ~** : faire sursauter qqn — **starter** ['stɑrtər] *n* : démarreur *m* (d'un véhicule)

startle ['stɑrtəl] *vt* **-tled; -tling** : surprendre

starve ['stɑrv] *v* **starved; starving** *vi* : mourir de faim — *vt* : affamer — **starvation** [stɑr'veɪʃən] *n* : faim *f*
state ['steɪt] *n* **1** : état *m* **2 the States** : les États-Unis — **~** *vt* **stated; stating 1** SAY : déclarer **2** REPORT : exposer — **statement** ['steɪtmənt] *n* **1** : déclaration *f* **2** *or* **bank ~** : relevé *m* de compte — **statesman** ['steɪtsmən] *n, pl* **-men** [-mən, -ˌmɛn] : homme *m* d'État
static ['stæṭɪk] *adj* : statique — **~** *n* : parasites *mpl* (en radio, etc.)
station ['steɪʃən] *n* **1** : gare *f* (de train) **2** : chaîne *f* (de télévision), poste *m* (de radio) **3** → **fire station, police station** — **~** *vt* : poster, placer — **stationary** ['steɪʃəˌnɛri] *adj* : stationnaire
stationery ['steɪʃəˌnɛri] *n* : papeterie *f*, papier *m* à lettres
station wagon *n* : familiale *f*
statistic [stə'tɪstɪk] *n* : statistique *f*
statue ['stæˌtʃu:] *n* : statue *f*
stature ['stætʃər] *n* : stature *f*, taille *f*
status ['steɪṭəs, 'stæ-] *n* **1** : statut *m* **2** *or* **marital ~** : situation *f* (de famille) **3** *or* **social ~** : rang *m* (social)
statute ['stæˌtʃu:t] *n* : loi *f*, règle *f*
staunch ['stɔntʃ] *adj* : dévoué
stay[1] ['steɪ] *vi* **1** REMAIN : rester, demeurer **2** LODGE : séjourner **3 ~ awake** : rester éveillé **4 ~ in** : rester à la maison — **~** *n* : séjour *m*
stay[2] *n* SUPPORT : soutien *m*
stead ['stɛd] *n* **in s.o.'s ~** : à la place de qqn — **steadfast** ['stɛdˌfæst] *adj* **1** FIRM : ferme **2** LOYAL : fidèle — **steady** ['stɛdi] *adj* **steadier; -est 1** FIRM, SURE : ferme, stable **2** FIXED : fixe **3** CONSTANT : constant — **~** *vt* **steadied; steadying** : stabiliser
steak ['steɪk] *n* : bifteck *m*, steak *m*
steal ['sti:l] *v* **stole** ['sto:l]; **stolen** ['sto:lən]; **stealing** : voler
stealthy ['stɛlθi] *adj* **stealthier; -est** : furtif
steam ['sti:m] *n* **1** : vapeur *f* **2 let off ~** : se défouler — *vt* **1** : cuire à la vapeur **2** *or* **~ up** : s'embuer
steel ['sti:l] *n* **1** : acier *m* **2 ~ industry** : sidérurgie — **~** *adj* : en acier, d'acier
steep[1] ['sti:p] *adj* : raide, à pic
steep[2] *vt* : infuser (du thé, etc.)
steeple ['sti:pəl] *n* : clocher *m*, flèche *f*
steer[1] ['stɪr] *n* : bœuf *m*
steer[2] *vt* **1** : conduire (une voiture, etc.), gouverner (un navire) **2** GUIDE : diriger — **steering wheel** *n* : volant *m*
stem ['stɛm] *n* : tige *f* (d'une plante), pied *m* (d'un verre) — **~** *vi* **~ from** : provenir de
stench ['stɛntʃ] *n* : puanteur *f*
step ['stɛp] *n* **1** : pas *m* **2** RUNG, STAIR : marche *f* **3 ~ by ~** : petit à petit **4 take ~s** : prendre des mesures **5 watch your ~** : faites attention (à la marche) — **~** *vi* **stepped; stepping 1** : faire un pas **2 ~ back** : reculer **3 ~ down** RESIGN : se retirer **4 ~ in** : intervenir **5 ~ out** : sortir (pour un moment) **6 ~ this way** : par ici — **step up** *vt* INCREASE : augmenter
stepbrother ['stɛpˌbrʌðər] *n* : beau-frère *m* — **stepdaughter** ['stɛpˌdɔṭər] *n* : belle-fille *f* — **stepfather** ['stɛpˌfɑðər, -ˌfa-] *n* : beau-père *m*
stepladder ['stɛpˌlædər] *n* : escabeau *m*
stepmother ['stɛpˌmʌðər] *n* : belle-mère *f* — **stepsister** ['stɛpˌsɪstər] *n* : belle-sœur *f* —**stepson** ['stɛpˌsʌn] *n* : beau-fils *m*
stereo ['stɛriˌo:, 'stɪr-] *n, pl* **stereos** : stéréo *f* — **~** *adj* : stéréo
stereotype ['stɛrioˌtaɪp, 'stɪr-] *vt* **-typed; -typing** : stéréotyper — **~** *n* : stéréotype *m*
sterile ['stɛrəl] *adj* : stérile — **sterility** [stə'rɪləṭi] *n* : stérilité *f* — **sterilization** [ˌstɛrələ'zeɪʃən] *n* : stérilisation *f* — **sterilize** ['stɛrəˌlaɪz] *vt* **-ized; -izing** : stériliser
sterling silver ['stərlɪŋ] *n* : argent *m* fin
stern[1] ['stərn] *adj* : sévère
stern[2] *n* : poupe *f*
stethoscope ['stɛθəˌsko:p] *n* : stéthoscope *m*
stew ['stu:, 'stju:] *n* : ragoût *m* — **~** *vi* **1** : cuire **2** FRET : être préoccupé
steward ['stu:ərd, 'stju:-] *n* **1** : administrateur *m*, -trice *f* **2** : steward *m* (d'un avion, etc.) — **stewardess** ['stu:ərdəs, 'stju:-] *n* : hôtesse *f*
stick[1] ['stɪk] *n* **1** : bâton *m* **2** WALKING STICK : canne *f*
stick[2] *v* **stuck** ['stʌk]; **sticking** *vt* **1** : coller **2** STAB : enfoncer **3** PUT : mettre **4 ~ out** : sortir, tirer (la langue) — *vi* **1** : se coller **2** JAM : se bloquer **3 ~ around** : rester **4 ~ out** PROTRUDE : dépasser **5 ~ up for** : défendre — **sticker** ['stɪkər] *n* : autocollant *m* — **sticky** ['stɪki] *adj* **stickier; -est** : collant
stiff ['stɪf] *adj* **1** RIGID : rigide, raide **2** STILTED : guindé **3** : courbaturé (se dit des muscles) — **stiffen** ['stɪfən] *vt* : renforcer, raidir — *vi* : se durcir, se raidir — **stiffness** ['stɪfnəs] *n* : raideur *f*, rigidité *f*
stifle ['staɪfəl] *vt* **-fled; -fling** : étouffer
stigmatize ['stɪgməˌtaɪz] *vt* **-tized; -tizing** : stigmatiser
still ['stɪl] *adj* **1** : immobile **2** SILENT : tranquille — **~** *adv* **1** : encore, toujours **2** NEVERTHELESS : quand même, tout de même **3 sit ~!** : reste tranquille! — **~** *n* : quiétude *f*, calme *m* — **stillness** ['stɪlnəs] *n* : calme *m*, silence *m*
stilt ['stɪlt] *n* : échasse *f* — **stilted** ['stɪltəd] *adj* : forcé
stimulate ['stɪmjəˌleɪt] *vt* **-lated; -lating** : stimuler — **stimulant** ['stɪmjələnt] *n* : stimulant *m* — **stimulation** [ˌstɪmjə'leɪʃən] *n* : stimulation *f* — **stimulus** ['stɪmjələs] *n, pl* **-li** [-ˌlaɪ] : stimulant *m*
sting ['stɪŋ] *v* **stung** ['stʌŋ]; **stinging** : piquer — **~** *n* : piqûre *f* — **stinger** ['stɪŋər] *n* : dard *m*, aiguillon *m*
stingy ['stɪnʤi] *adj* **stingier; -est** : avare, pingre — **stinginess** ['stɪnʤinəs] *n* : avarice *f*
stink ['stɪŋk] *vi* **stank** ['stæŋk] *or* **stunk** ['stʌŋk]; **stunk; stinking** : puer — **~** *n* : puanteur *f*
stint ['stɪnt] *vi* **~ on** : lésiner sur — **~** *n* : période *f* (de travail)
stipulate ['stɪpjəˌleɪt] *vt* **-lated; -lating** : stipuler — **stipulation** [ˌstɪpjə'leɪʃən] *n* : stipulation *f*
stir ['stər] *v* **stirred; stirring** *vt* **1** : agiter, remuer **2** MOVE : émouvoir **3** INCITE : inciter **4** *or* **~ up** PROVOKE : susciter — *vi* : remuer, bouger — **~** *n* COMMOTION : émoi *m*
stirrup ['stərəp, 'stɪr-] *n* : étrier *m*
stitch ['stɪtʃ] *n* : point *m* (en couture, en médecine) — **~** *v* : coudre
stock ['stɑk] *n* **1** INVENTORY : réserve *f*, stock *m* **2** SECURITIES : actions *fpl*, valeurs *fpl* **3** ANCESTRY : lignée *f*, souche *f* **4** BROTH : bouillon *m* **5 out of ~** : épuisé **6 take ~ of** : évaluer — **~** *vt* : approvisionner — *vi* **~ up on** : s'approvisionner en — **stockbroker** ['stɑkˌbro:kər] *n* : agent *m* de change
stocking ['stɑkɪŋ] *n* : bas *m*
stock market *n* : Bourse *f*
stocky ['stɑki] *adj* **stockier; -est** : trapu
stodgy ['stɑʤi] *adj* **stodgier; -est 1** DULL : lourd **2** OLD-FASHIONED : vieux-jeu
stoic ['sto:ɪk] *n* : stoïque *mf* — **~** *or* **stoical** [-ɪkəl] *adj* : stoïque
stoke ['sto:k] *vt* **stoked; stoking** : alimenter (un feu, etc.)
stole[1] ['sto:l] → **steal**
stole[2] *n* : étole *f*
stolen → **steal**
stomach ['stʌmɪk] *n* : estomac *m* — **~** *vt* : supporter, tolérer — **stomachache** ['stʌmɪkˌeɪk] *n* : mal *m* de ventre
stone ['sto:n] *n* **1** : pierre *f* **2** : noyau *m* (d'un fruit) — **~** *vt* **stoned; stoning** : lapider — **stony** ['sto:ni] *adj* **stonier; -est** : pierreux
stood → **stand**
stool ['stu:l] *n* : tabouret *m*
stoop ['stu:p] *vi* **1** : se baisser, se pencher **2 ~ to** : s'abaisser à
stop ['stɑp] *v* **stopped; stopping** *vt* **1** PLUG : boucher **2** PREVENT : empêcher **3** HALT : arrêter, mettre fin à **4** CEASE : cesser de — *vi* **1** : s'arrêter, stopper **2** CEASE : cesser **3 ~ by** : passer — **~** *n* **1** : arrêt *m*, halte *f* **2 come to a ~** : s'arrêter **3 put a ~ to** : mettre fin à — **stoplight** ['stɑpˌlaɪt] *n* : feu *m* rouge — **stopper** ['stɑpər] *n* : bouchon *m*
store ['stor] *vt* **stored; storing** : emmagasiner, entreposer — **~** *n* **1** SUPPLY : réserve *f*, provision *f* **2** SHOP : magasin *m* — **storage** ['storɪʤ] *n* : entreposage *m* — **storehouse** ['storˌhaʊs] *n* : entrepôt *m* — **storekeeper** ['storˌki:pər] *n* : commerçant *m*, -çante *f* — **storeroom** ['storˌru:m, -ˌrʊm] *n* : magasin *m*, réserve *f*
stork ['stɔrk] *n* : cigogne *f*
storm ['stɔrm] *n* : orage *m*, tempête *f* — **~** *vi* **1** RAGE : tempêter **2 ~ out** : partir furieux — *vt* ATTACK : prendre d'assaut — **stormy** ['stɔrmi] *adj* **stormier; -est** : orageux
story[1] ['stori] *n, pl* **stories 1** TALE : conte *m* **2** ACCOUNT : histoire *f*, récit *m* **3** RUMOR : rumeur *f*
story[2] *n* FLOOR : étage *m*
stout ['staʊt] *adj* **1** RESOLUTE : tenace **2** STURDY : fort **3** FAT : corpulent
stove ['sto:v] *n* **1** : poêle *m* (pour chauffer) **2** RANGE : cuisinière *f*
stow ['sto:] *vt* **1** : ranger **2** LOAD : charger — *vi* **~ away** : voyager clandestinement
straddle ['strædəl] *vt* **-dled; -dling** : s'asseoir à califourchon sur
straggle ['strægəl] *vi* **-gled; -gling** : traîner — **straggler** ['strægələr] *n* : traînard *m*, -narde *f*
straight ['streɪt] *adj* **1** : droit **2** : raide (se dit des cheveux) **3** HONEST : franc — **~** *adv* **1** DIRECTLY : (tout) droit, directement **2** FRANKLY : carrément — **straightaway** [ˌstreɪtə'weɪ] *adv* : immédiatement — **straighten** ['streɪtən] *vt* **1** : redresser, rendre droit **2** *or* **~ up** : ranger — **straightforward** [streɪt'fɔrwərd] *adj* **1** FRANK : franc, honnête **2** CLEAR : clair, simple
strain ['streɪn] *vt* **1** : se forcer (la voix), se fatiguer (les yeux), se froisser (un muscle) **2** FILTER : égoutter **3 ~ oneself** : faire un grand effort — *vi* : s'efforcer — **~** *n* **1** STRESS : stress *m*, tension *f* **2** SPRAIN : foulure *f* — **strainer** ['streɪnər] *n* : passoire *f*
strait ['streɪt] *n* **1** : détroit *m* **2 in dire ~s** : aux abois
strand[1] ['strænd] *vt* **be left ~ed** : être abandonné
strand[2] *n* : fil *m*, brin *m*
strange ['streɪnʤ] *adj* **stranger; strangest 1** : étrange, bizarre **2** UNFAMILIAR : inconnu — **strangely** ['streɪnʤli] *adv* : étrangement — **strangeness** ['streɪnʤnəs] *n* : étrangeté *f* — **stranger** ['streɪnʤər] *n* : étranger *m*, -gère *f*
strangle ['stræŋgəl] *vt* **-gled; -gling** : étrangler
strap ['stræp] *n* **1** : courroie *f*, sangle *f* **2** *or* **shoulder ~** : bretelle *f* — **~** *vt* **strapped; strapping** : attacher — **strapless** ['stræpləs] *n* : sans bretelles — **strapping** ['stræpɪŋ] *adj* : robuste, costaud *fam*
strategy ['stræṭəʤi] *n, pl* **-gies** : stratégie *f* — **strategic** [strə'ti:ʤɪk] *adj* : stratégique
straw ['strɔ] *n* **1** : paille *f* **2 the last ~** : le comble
strawberry ['strɔˌbɛri] *n, pl* **-ries** : fraise *f*
stray ['streɪ] *n* : animal *m* errant — **~** *vi* **1** : errer, vagabonder **2** DEVIATE : s'écarter — **~** *adj* : errant, perdu
streak ['stri:k] *n* **1** : raie *f*, bande *f* **2** VEIN : veine *f*
stream ['stri:m] *n* **1** : ruisseau *m* **2** FLOW : flot *m*, courant *m* — **~** *vi* : couler — **streamer** ['stri:mər] *n* **1** : banderole *f* **2** : serpentin *m* (de papier) — **streamlined** ['stri:mˌlaɪnd] *adj* **1** : aérodynamique **2** EFFICIENT : efficace
street ['stri:t] *n* : rue *f* — **streetcar** ['stri:tˌkɑr] *n* : tramway *m* — **streetlight** ['stri:tˌlaɪt] *n* : réverbère *m*
strength ['strɛŋkθ] *n* **1** : force *f* **2** TOUGHNESS : résistance *f* **3** INTENSITY : intensité *f* **4 ~s and weaknesses** : qualités et faiblesses — **strengthen** ['strɛŋkθən] *vt* **1** : fortifier **2** REINFORCE : renforcer **3** INTENSIFY : intensifier
strenuous ['strɛnjuəs] *adj* **1** : énergique **2** ARDUOUS : ardu — **strenuously** ['strɛnjuəsli] *adv* : vigoureusement
stress ['strɛs] *n* **1** : stress *m*, tension *f* **2** EMPHASIS : accent *m* — **~** *vt* **1** EMPHASIZE : mettre l'accent sur **2** *or* **~ out** : stresser — **stressful** ['strɛsfəl] *adj* : stressant
stretch ['strɛtʃ] *vt* **1** : étirer (des muscles, un élastique, etc.) **2** EXTEND : tendre **3 ~ the truth** : exagérer — *vi* **1** : s'étirer **2 ~ out** EXTEND : s'étendre — **~** *n* **1** : étirement *m* **2** EXPANSE : étendue *f* **3** : période *f* (de temps) — **stretcher** ['strɛtʃər] *n* : civière *f*, brancard *m*
strew ['stru:] *vt* **strewed; strewed** *or* **strewn** ['stru:n]; **strewing** : éparpiller
stricken ['strɪkən] *adj* **~ with** : affligé de (une émotion), atteint de (une maladie)
strict ['strɪkt] *adj* : strict — **strictly** *adv* **~ speaking** : à proprement parler
stride ['straɪd] *vi* **strode** ['stro:d]; **stridden** ['strɪdən]; **striding** : marcher à grandes enjambées — **~** *n* **1** : grand pas *m*, enjambée *f* **2 make great ~s** : faire de grands progrès
strident ['straɪdənt] *adj* : strident
strife ['straɪf] *n* : conflit *m*
strike ['straɪk] *v* **struck** ['strʌk]; **struck; striking** *vt* **1** HIT : frapper **2** *or* **~ against** : heurter **3** *or* **~ out** DELETE : rayer **4** : sonner (l'heure) **5** IMPRESS : impressionner **6** : découvrir (de l'or, du pétrole) **7 it ~s me that ...** : il m'apparaît que ... **8 ~ up** START : commencer — *vi* **1** : frapper **2** ATTACK : attaquer **3** : faire grève — **~** *n* **1** BLOW : coup *m* **2** : grève *f* (des transports, etc.) **3** ATTACK : attaque *f* **4** : prise *f* *Can* (au baseball) — **striker** ['straɪkər] *n* : gréviste *mf* — **striking** ['straɪkɪŋ] *adj* : frappant, saisissant
string ['strɪŋ] *n* **1** : ficelle *f* **2** SERIES : suite *f* **3 ~s** *npl* : cordes *fpl* (d'un orchestre) — **~** *vt* **strung** ['strʌŋ]; **stringing** : enfiler — **string bean** *n* : haricot *m* vert
stringent ['strɪnʤənt] *adj* : rigoureux, strict
strip[1] ['strɪp] *v* **stripped; stripping** *vt* REMOVE : enlever — *vi* UNDRESS : se déshabiller
strip[2] *n* : bande *f*
stripe ['straɪp] *n* : rayure *f*, bande *f* — **striped** ['straɪpt, 'straɪpəd] *adj* : rayé, à rayures
strive ['straɪv] *vi* **strove** ['stro:v]; **striven** ['strɪvən] *or* **strived; striving 1 ~ for** : lutter pour **2 ~ to** : s'efforcer de
strode → **stride**
stroke ['stro:k] *vt* **stroked; stroking** : caresser — **~** *n* : attaque *f* (cérébrale)
stroll ['stro:l] *vi* : se promener — **~** *n* : promenade *f* — **stroller** ['stro:lər] *n* : poussette *f* (pour enfants)
strong ['strɔŋ] *adj* : fort, robuste — **stronghold** ['strɔŋˌho:ld] *n* : bastion *m* — **strongly** ['strɔŋli] *adv* **1** DEEPLY : profondément **2** TOTALLY : totalement **3** VIGOROUSLY : énergiquement
strove → **strive**
struck → **strike**
structure ['strʌktʃər] *n* : structure *f* — **structural** ['strʌktʃərəl] *adj* : structural
struggle ['strʌgəl] *vi* **-gled; -gling 1** : lutter, se débattre **2** STRIVE : s'efforcer — **~** *n* : lutte *f*
strung → **string**
strut ['strʌt] *vi* **strutted; strutting** : se pavaner
stub ['stʌb] *n* : mégot *m* (de cigarette), bout *m* (de crayon, etc.), talon *m* (de chèque) — **~** *vt* **stubbed; stubbing ~ one's toe** : se cogner le doigt de pied
stubble ['stʌbəl] *n* : barbe *f* de plusieurs jours
stubborn ['stʌbərn] *adj* **1** : têtu, obstiné **2** PERSISTENT : tenace
stuck → **stick** — **stuck–up** ['stʌk'ʌp] *adj* : prétentieux
stud[1] ['stʌd] *n* : étalon *m*
stud[2] *n* **1** NAIL : clou *m* **2** : montant *m* (en construction)
student ['stu:dənt, 'stju:-] *n* : élève *m*, élève *f* (au primaire); étudiant *m*, -diante *f* (universitaire) — **studio** ['stu:diˌo:, 'stju:-] *n, pl* **-dios** : studio *m*, atelier *m* — **study** ['stʌdi] *n, pl* **studies 1** : étude *f* **2** OFFICE : bureau *m* — **~** *v* **studied; studying** : étudier — **studious** ['stu:diəs, 'stju:-] *adj* : studieux
stuff ['stʌf] *n* **1** : affaires *fpl*, choses *fpl* **2** MATTER, SUBSTANCE : chose *f* — **~** *vt* **1** FILL : rembourrer **2** CRAM : fourrer — **stuffing** ['stʌfɪŋ] *n* : rembourrage *m* — **stuffy** ['stʌfi] *adj* **stuffier; -est 1** STODGY : ennuyeux **2** : bouché (se dit du nez) **3 ~ rooms** : pièces *fpl* mal aérées
stumble ['stʌmbəl] *vi* **-bled; -bling 1** : trébucher **2 ~ across** *or* **~ upon** : tomber sur
stump ['stʌmp] *n* **1** : moignon *m* (d'un membre) **2** *or* **tree ~** : souche *f* — **~** *vt* : laisser perplexe
stun ['stʌn] *vt* **stunned; stunning 1** : assommer (avec un coup) **2** ASTONISH : étonner
stung → **sting**
stunk → **stink**
stunning ['stʌnɪŋ] *adj* **1** : incroyable, sensationnel **2** STRIKING : frappant
stunt[1] ['stʌnt] *vt* : rabougrir
stunt[2] *n* : prouesse *f* (acrobatique)
stupid ['stu:pəd, 'stju:-] *adj* **1** : stupide **2** SILLY : bête — **stupidity** [stʊ'pɪdəṭi, stjʊ-] *n, pl* **-ties** : stupidité *f*
sturdy ['stərdi] *adj* **-dier; -est 1** : fort, résistant **2** ROBUST : robuste — **sturdiness** ['stərdinəs] *n* : solidité *f*
stutter ['stʌṭər] *vi* : bégayer — **~** *n* : bégaiement *m*
sty ['staɪ] *n* **1** *pl* **sties** PIGPEN : porcherie *f* **2** *pl* **sties** *or* **styes** : orgelet *m*
style ['staɪl] *n* **1** : style *m* **2** FASHION : mode *f* — **~** *vt* **styled; styling** : coiffer (les cheveux) — **stylish** ['staɪlɪʃ] *adj* : chic, élégant
suave ['swɑv] *adj* : raffiné et affable
subconscious [ˌsʌb'kɑntʃəs] *adj* : subconscient — **~** *n* : subconscient *m*
subdivision ['sʌbdəˌvɪʒən] *n* : subdivision *f*
subdue [səb'du:, -'dju:] *vt* **-dued; -duing 1** CONQUER : subjuguer **2** CONTROL : dominer **3** SOFTEN : atténuer — **subdued** [səb'du:d, -'dju:d] *adj* : atténué
subject ['sʌbʤɪkt] *n* **1** : sujet *m* **2** TOPIC : matière *f* — **~** *adj* **1** : asservi **2 ~ to** : sujet à — **~** [səb'ʤɛkt] *vt* **~ to** : soumettre à — **subjective** [səb'ʤɛktɪv] *adj* : subjectif
subjunctive [səb'ʤʌŋktɪv] *n* : subjonctif *m*
sublet ['sʌbˌlɛt] *vt* **-let; -letting** : sous-louer
sublime [sə'blaɪm] *adj* : sublime
submarine ['sʌbməˌri:n, ˌsʌbmə'-] *n* : sous-marin *m*
submerge [səb'mərʤ] *vt* **-merged; -merging** : submerger
submit [səb'mɪt] *v* **-mitted; -mitting** *vi* **1** YIELD : se rendre **2 ~ to** : se soumettre à — *vt* : soumettre — **submission** [səb'mɪʃən] *n* : soumission *f* — **submissive** [səb'mɪsɪv] *adj* : soumis
subordinate [sə'bɔrdənət] *adj* : subordonné — **~** *n* : subordonné *m*, -née *f* — **~** [sə'bɔrdənˌeɪt] *vt* **-nated; -nating** : subordonner
subpoena [sə'pi:nə] *n* : assignation *f*
subscribe [səb'skraɪb] *vi* **-scribed; -scribing ~ to** : s'abonner à (un magazine, etc.) — **subscriber** [səb'skraɪbər] *n* : abonné *m*, -née *f* — **subscription** [səb'skrɪpʃən] *n* : abonnement *m*
subsequent ['sʌbsɪkwənt, -səˌkwɛnt] *adj* **1** : subséquent, suivant **2 ~ to** : postérieur à — **subsequently** ['sʌbsɪˌkwɛntli, -ˌkwənt-] *adv* : par la suite
subservient [səb'sərviənt] *adj* : servile
subside [səb'saɪd] *vi* **-sided; -siding** : s'atténuer
subsidiary [səb'sɪdiˌɛri] *adj* : secondaire — **~** *n, pl* **-aries** : filiale *f*

subsidy [ˈsʌbsədi] n, pl -dies : subvention f — subsidize [ˈsʌbsəˌdaɪz] vt -dized; -dizing : subventionner
subsistence [səbˈsɪstənts] n : subsistance f — subsist [səbˈsɪst] vi : subsister
substance [ˈsʌbstənts] n : substance f
substandard [ˌsʌbˈstændərd] adj : inférieur
substantial [səbˈstæntʃəl] adj : substantiel — substantially [səbˈstæntʃəli] adv : considérablement
substitute [ˈsʌbstəˌtu:t, -ˌtju:t] n 1 : remplaçant m, -çante f; suppléant m, -pléante f 2 : succédané m (d'une chose) — ~ vt -tuted; -tuting : substituer, remplacer
subtitle [ˈsʌbˌtaɪtəl] n : sous-titre m
subtle [ˈsʌtəl] adj -tler; -tlest : subtil — subtlety [ˈsʌtəlti] n, pl -ties : subtilité f
subtraction [səbˈtrækʃən] n : soustraction f — subtract [səbˈtrækt] vt : soustraire
suburb [ˈsʌˌbərb] n 1 : quartier m résidentiel 2 the ~s : la banlieue — suburban [səˈbərbən] adj : de banlieue
subversive [səbˈvərsɪv] adj : subversif
subway [ˈsəbˌweɪ] n : métro m
succeed [səksəbsi:d] vt : succéder à — vi : réussir — success [səkˈsɛs] n : réussite f, succès m — successful [səkˈsɛsfəl] adj : réussi — successfully [səkˈsɛsfəli] adv : avec succès
succession [səkˈsɛʃən] n 1 : succession f 2 in ~ : successivement, de suite — successive [səkˈsɛsɪv] adj : successif — successor [səkˈsɛsər] n : successeur m
succinct [səkˈsɪŋkt, səˈsɪŋkt] adj : succinct
succumb [səˈkʌm] vi : succomber
such [ˈsʌtʃ] adj 1 : tel, pareil 2 ~ as : comme 3 ~ a pity! : quel dommage! — ~ pron 1 : tel 2 as ~ : comme tel — ~ adv 1 VERY : très 2 ~ a nice man! : un homme si gentil! 3 ~ that : de façon à ce que
suck [ˈsʌk] vt 1 or ~ on : sucer 2 or ~ up : absorber (un liquide), aspirer (avec une machine) — suckle [ˈsʌkəl] v -led; -ling vt : allaiter — vi : téter — suction [ˈsʌkʃən] n : succion f
sudden [ˈsʌdən] adj 1 : soudain, subit 2 all of a ~ : tout à coup — suddenly [ˈsʌdənli] adv : soudainement, subitement
suds [ˈsʌdz] npl : mousse f (de savon)
sue [ˈsu:] vt sued; suing : poursuivre en justice
suede [ˈsweɪd] n : daim m, suède m
suet [ˈsu:ət] n : graisse f de rognon
suffer [ˈsʌfər] vi : souffrir — suffering [ˈsʌfərɪŋ] n : souffrance f
suffice [səˈfaɪs] vi -ficed; -ficing : être suffisant, suffir — sufficient [səˈfɪʃənt] adj : suffisant — sufficiently [səˈfɪʃəntli] adv : suffisamment
suffix [ˈsʌˌfɪks] n : suffixe m
suffocate [ˈsʌfəˌkeɪt] v -cated; -cating vt : asphyxier, suffoquer — vi : s'asphyxier, suffoquer
suffrage [ˈsʌfrɪʤ] n : suffrage m
sugar [ˈʃʊgər] n : sucre m — sugarcane [ˈʃʊgərˌkeɪn] n : canne f à sucre — sugarhouse [ˈʃʊgərˌhaʊs] n : cabane f (à sucre) Can
suggestion [səgˈʤɛstʃən, sə-] n : suggestion f, proposition f — suggest [səgˈʤɛst, sə-] vt 1 : proposer, suggérer 2 INDICATE : laisser supposer
suicide [ˈsu:əˌsaɪd] n 1 : suicide m 2 commit ~ : se suicider — suicidal [ˌsu:əˈsaɪdəl] adj : suicidaire
suit [ˈsu:t] n 1 : complet m (d'homme), tailleur m (de femme) 2 : couleur f (aux cartes) — ~ vt : convenir à, aller à — suitable [ˈsu:təbəl] adj : convenable, approprié — suitcase [ˈsu:tˌkeɪs] n : valise f
suite [ˈswi:t] n : suite f
suitor [ˈsu:tər] n : prétendant m
sulfur or Brit **sulphur** [ˈsʌlfər] n : soufre m
sulk [ˈsʌlk] vi : bouder — sulky [ˈsʌlki] adj sulkier; -est : boudeur
sullen [ˈsʌlən] adj : maussade, morose
sulphur Brit → sulfur
sultry [ˈsʌltri] adj -trier; -est 1 : étouffant, lourd 2 SENSUAL : sensuel
sum [ˈsʌm] n : somme f — ~ vt summed; summing ~ up : résumer — summarize [ˈsʌməˌraɪz] v -rized; -rizing vt : résumer — vi : se résumer — summary [ˈsʌməri] n, pl -ries : sommaire m, résumé m
summer [ˈsʌmər] n : été m
summit [ˈsʌmət] n : sommet m, cime f
summon [ˈsʌmən] vt 1 : appeler (qqn), convoquer (une réunion) 2 : citer (en droit) — summons [ˈsʌmənz] n, pl summonses SUBPOENA : assignation f
sumptuous [ˈsʌmptʃʊəs] adj : somptueux
sun [ˈsʌn] n : soleil m — sunbathe [ˈsʌnˌbeɪð] vi -bathed; -bathing : prendre un bain de soleil — sunburn [ˈsʌnˌbərn] n : coup m de soleil
Sunday [ˈsʌnˌdeɪ, -di] n : dimanche m
sunflower [ˈsʌnˌflaʊər] n : tournesol m
sung → sing
sunglasses [ˈsʌnˌglæsəz] npl : lunettes fpl de soleil
sunk → sink
sunlight [ˈsʌnˌlaɪt] n : (lumière f du) soleil m — sunny [ˈsʌni] adj -nier; -est : ensoleillé — sunrise [ˈsʌnˌraɪz] n : lever m du soleil — sunset [ˈsʌnˌsɛt] n : coucher m du soleil — sunshine [ˈsʌnˌʃaɪn] n : (lumière f du) soleil m — suntan [ˈsʌnˌtæn] n : hâle m, bronzage m
super [ˈsu:pər] adj : super fam, génial
superb [sʊˈpərb] adj : superbe
superficial [ˌsu:pərˈfɪʃəl] adj : superficiel
superfluous [sʊˈpərflʊəs] adj : superflu
superintendent [ˌsu:pərɪnˈtɛndənt] n 1 : commissaire m (de police) 2 or building ~ : concierge mf 3 or school ~ : inspecteur m, -trice f
superior [sʊˈpɪriər] adj : supérieur — ~ n : supérieur m, -rieure f — superiority [sʊˌpɪriˈɔrəti] n, pl -ties : supériorité f
superlative [sʊˈpərlətɪv] n : superlatif m
supermarket [ˈsu:pərˌmɑrkət] n : supermarché m
supernatural [ˌsu:pərˈnætʃərəl] adj : surnaturel
superpower [ˈsu:pərˌpaʊər] n : superpuissance f
supersede [ˌsu:pərˈsi:d] vt -seded; -seding : remplacer, supplanter
superstition [ˌsu:pərˈstɪʃən] n : superstition f — superstitious [ˌsu:pərˈstɪʃəs] adj : superstitieux
supervise [ˈsu:pərˌvaɪz] vt -vised; -vising : surveiller, superviser — supervision [ˌsu:pərˈvɪʒən] n : surveillance f, supervision f — supervisor [ˈsu:pərˌvaɪzər] n : surveillant m, -lante f
supper [ˈsʌpər] n : dîner m, souper m Can
supplant [səˈplænt] vt : supplanter
supple [ˈsʌpəl] adj -pler; -plest : souple
supplement [ˈsʌpləmənt] n : supplément m — ~ [ˈsʌpləˌmɛnt] vt : compléter, augmenter
supply [səˈplaɪ] vt -plied; -plying 1 : fournir 2 ~ with : approvisionner en — ~ n, pl -plies 1 : provision f, réserve f 2 ~ and demand : l'offre et la demande 3 supplies npl : provisions fpl, vivres mpl 4 supplies npl : fournitures fpl (de bureau, etc.) — supplier [səˈplaɪər] n : fournisseur m, -seuse f
support [səˈport] vt 1 BACK : soutenir, appuyer 2 : subvenir aux besoins de (une famille, etc.) 3 PROP UP : supporter — ~ n 1 : appui m, soutien m 2 PROP : support m — supporter [səˈportər] n 1 : partisan m, -sane f 2 FAN : supporter m
suppose [səˈpo:z] vt -posed; -posing 1 : supposer 2 be ~d to do sth : être censé faire qqch — supposedly [səˈpo:zədli] adv : soi-disant
suppress [səˈprɛs] vt 1 : réprimer 2 WITHHOLD : supprimer
supreme [sʊˈpri:m] adj : suprême — supremacy [sʊˈprɛməsi] n, pl -cies : suprématie f
sure [ˈʃʊr] adj surer; surest 1 : sûr 2 make ~ that : s'assurer que — ~ adv 1 OF COURSE : bien sûr 2 it ~ is hot! : quelle chaleur! — surely [ˈʃʊrli] adv : sûrement
surfing [ˈsərfɪŋ] n : surf m
surface [ˈsərfəs] n 1 : surface f 2 AREA : superficie f — ~ vi -faced; -facing : faire surface, remonter à la surface — vt : revêtir (une chaussée)
surfboard [ˈsərfˌbord] n : planche f de surf
surfeit [ˈsərfət] n : excès m
surfing [ˈsərfɪŋ] n : surf m
surge [ˈsərʤ] vi surged; surging : déferler — ~ n 1 : déferlement m (de la mer), ruée f (de personnes, etc.) 2 INCREASE : augmentation f (subite)
surgeon [ˈsərʤən] n : chirurgien m, -gienne f — surgery [ˈsərʤəri] n, pl -geries : chirurgie f — surgical [ˈsərʤɪkəl] adj : chirurgical
surly [ˈsərli] adj -lier; -est : revêche, bourru
surname [ˈsərˌneɪm] n : nom m de famille
surpass [sərˈpæs] vt : surpasser
surplus [ˈsərˌplʌs] n : excédent m, surplus m
surprise [səˈpraɪz, sər-] n 1 : surprise f 2 take by ~ : prendre au dépourvu — ~ vt -prised; -prising : surprendre — surprising [səˈpraɪzɪŋ, sər-] adj : surprenant
surrender [səˈrɛndər] vt : rendre, céder — vi : se rendre — ~ n : capitulation f, reddition f
surround [səˈraʊnd] vt : entourer — surroundings [səˈraʊndɪŋz] npl : environs mpl, alentours mpl
surveillance [sərˈveɪlənts, -ˈveɪljənts, -ˈveɪənts] n : surveillance f
survey [sərˈveɪ] vt -veyed; -veying 1 : arpenter (un terrain) 2 INSPECT : inspecter 3 POLL : sonder — ~ [ˈsərˌveɪ] n, pl -veys 1 INSPECTION : inspection f 2 POLL : sondage m — surveyor [sərˈveɪər] n : arpenteur m, -teuse f
survive [sərˈvaɪv] v -vived; -viving vi : survivre — vt : survivre à — survival [sərˈvaɪvəl] n : survie f — survivor [sərˈvaɪvər] n : survivant m, -vante f
susceptible [səˈsɛptəbəl] adj ~ to : prédisposé à
suspect [ˈsʌsˌpɛkt, səˈspɛkt] adj : suspect — ~ [ˈsʌsˌpɛkt] n : suspect m, -pecte f — ~ [səˈspɛkt] vt 1 : douter de, se méfier de 2 ~ s.o. of : soupçonner qqn de
suspend [səˈspɛnd] vt : suspendre — suspenders [səˈspɛndərz] npl : bretelles fpl — suspense [səˈspɛnts] n 1 : incertitude f 2 : suspense m (au cinéma, etc.)
suspicion [səˈspɪʃən] n : soupçon m — suspicious [səˈspɪʃəs] adj 1 QUESTIONABLE : suspect 2 DISTRUSTFUL : soupçonneux
sustain [səˈsteɪn] vt 1 SUPPORT : soutenir 2 NOURISH : nourrir 3 SUFFER : subir
swagger [ˈswægər] vi : se pavaner
swallow[1] [ˈswɑlo:] vt 1 : avaler 2 or ~ up : engloutir — ~ n : gorgée f
swallow[2] n : hirondelle f
swam → swim
swamp [ˈswɑmp] n : marais m, marécage m — ~ vt : inonder — swampy [ˈswɑmpi] adj swampier; -est : marécageux
swan [ˈswɑn] n : cygne m
swap [ˈswɑp] vt swapped; swapping : échanger — ~ n : échange m
swarm [ˈswɔrm] n : essaim m (d'abeilles, etc.) — ~ vi ~ with : grouiller de
swat [ˈswɑt] vt swatted; swatting : écraser (un insecte)
sway [ˈsweɪ] n 1 : balancement m 2 INFLUENCE : influence f — ~ vi : se balancer — vt : influencer
swear [ˈswær] v swore [ˈswor]; sworn [ˈsworn]; swearing vi CURSE : jurer — vt VOW : jurer — swearword [ˈswærˌwərd] n : juron m
sweat [ˈswɛt] vi sweat or sweated; sweating : transpirer — ~ n : sueur f, transpiration f
sweater [ˈswɛtər] n : pull-over m France, chandail m
sweaty [ˈswɛti] adj sweatier; -est : en sueur
sweep [ˈswi:p] v swept [ˈswɛpt] sweeping vt 1 : balayer 2 or ~ aside : écarter — vi : balayer — ~ n 1 : coup m de balai 2 SCOPE : étendue f — sweeping [ˈswi:pɪŋ] adj 1 WIDE : large 2 EXTENSIVE : de grande portée
sweet [ˈswi:t] adj 1 : doux, sucré 2 PLEASANT : agréable, gentil — ~ n : bonbon m, dessert m — sweeten [ˈswi:tən] vt : sucrer — sweetener [ˈswi:tənər] n : édulcorant m — sweetheart [ˈswi:tˌhɑrt] n 1 : petit ami m, petite amie f 2 (used as a term of address) : chéri m, -rie f — sweetness [ˈswi:tnəs] n : douceur f — sweet potato n : patate f douce
swell [ˈswɛl] vi swelled; swelled or swollen [ˈswo:lən, ˈswʌl-]; swelling 1 or ~ up : enfler, gonfler 2 INCREASE : augmenter — ~ n : houle f (de la mer) — swelling [ˈswɛlɪŋ] n : enflure f, gonflement m
sweltering [ˈswɛltərɪŋ] adj : étouffant
swept → sweep
swerve [ˈswərv] vi swerved; swerving : faire une embardée — ~ n : embardée f
swift [ˈswɪft] adj : rapide — swiftly [ˈswɪftli] adv : rapidement
swim [ˈswɪm] vi swam [ˈswæm]; swum [ˈswʌm]; swimming 1 : nager 2 REEL : tourner — ~ n 1 : baignade f 2 go for a ~ : aller se baigner — swimmer [ˈswɪmər] n : nageur m, -geuse f
swindle [ˈswɪndəl] vt -dled; -dling : escroquer — ~ n : escroquerie f — swindler [ˈswɪndələr] n : escroc m
swine [ˈswaɪn] ns & pl : porc m
swing [ˈswɪŋ] v swung [ˈswʌŋ]; swinging vt : balancer, faire osciller — vi 1 : se balancer, osciller 2 SWIVEL : tourner — ~ n 1 : va-et-vient m, balancement m 2 : balançoire f (dans un terrain de jeu) 3 be in full ~ : battre son plein
swipe [ˈswaɪp] vt swiped; swiping 1 : passer dans un lecteur de cartes 2 STEAL : piquer fam
swirl [ˈswərl] vi : tourbillonner — ~ n : tourbillon m
swish [ˈswɪʃ] vi RUSTLE : faire un bruit léger
Swiss [ˈswɪs] adj : suisse
switch [ˈswɪtʃ] n 1 CHANGE : changement m 2 : interrupteur m (d'électricité), bouton m (d'une radio ou d'une télévision) — ~ vt 1 CHANGE : changer de 2 ~ on : ouvrir, allumer 3 ~ off : couper, fermer, éteindre — vi SWAP : échanger — switchboard [ˈswɪtʃˌbord] n or telephone ~ : standard m
swivel [ˈswɪvəl] vi -eled or -elled; -eling or -elling : pivoter
swollen → swell
swoop [ˈswu:p] vi ~ down on : s'abattre sur — ~ n : descente f en piqué
sword [ˈsord] n : épée f
swordfish [ˈsordˌfɪʃ] n : espadon m
swore, sworn → swear
swum → swim
swung → swing
syllable [ˈsɪləbəl] n : syllabe f
syllabus [ˈsɪləbəs] n, pl -bi [-ˌbaɪ] or -buses : programme m (d'études)
symbol [ˈsɪmbəl] n : symbole m — symbolic [sɪmˈbɑlɪk] adj : symbolique — symbolism [ˈsɪmbəˌlɪzəm] n : symbolisme m — symbolize [ˈsɪmbəˌlaɪz] vt -ized; -izing : symboliser
symmetry [ˈsɪmətri] n, pl -tries : symétrie f — symmetrical [səˈmɛtrɪkəl] adj : symétrique
sympathy [ˈsɪmpəθi] n, pl -thies 1 COMPASSION : sympathie f 2 UNDERSTANDING : compréhension f 3 CONDOLENCES : condoléances fpl — sympathetic [ˌsɪmpəˈθɛtɪk] adj 1 COMPASSIONATE : compatissant 2 UNDERSTANDING : compréhensif — sympathize [ˈsɪmpəˌθaɪz] vi -thized; -thizing ~ with 1 PITY : plaindre 2 UNDERSTAND : comprendre
symphony [ˈsɪmpfəni] n, pl -nies : symphonie f
symposium [sɪmˈpo:ziəm] n, pl -sia [-ziə] or -siums : symposium m
symptom [ˈsɪmptəm] n : symptôme m
synagogue [ˈsɪnəˌgɑg, -ˌgɔg] n : synagogue f
synchronize [ˈsɪŋkrəˌnaɪz, ˈsɪn-] vt -nized; -nizing : synchroniser
syndrome [ˈsɪnˌdro:m] n : syndrome m
synonym [ˈsɪnəˌnɪm] n : synonyme m — synonymous [səˈnɑnəməs] adj : synonyme
syntax [ˈsɪnˌtæks] n : syntaxe f
synthesis [ˈsɪnθəsɪs] n, pl -ses [-ˌsi:z] : synthèse f — synthetic [sɪnˈθɛtɪk] adj : synthétique
syringe [səˈrɪnʤ, ˈsɪrɪnʤ] n : seringue f
syrup [ˈsərəp, ˈsɪrəp] n : sirop m
system [ˈsɪstəm] n 1 : système m 2 BODY : organisme m 3 digestive ~ : appareil m digestif — systematic [ˌsɪstəˈmætɪk] adj : systématique

T

t [ˈti:] n, pl t's or ts [ˈti:z] : t m, vingtième lettre de l'alphabet
tab [ˈtæb] n 1 FLAP : languette f 2 keep ~s on : surveiller
table [ˈteɪbəl] n : table f — tablecloth [ˈteɪbəlˌklɔθ] n : nappe f — tablespoon [ˈteɪbəlˌspu:n] n : cuillère f à soupe
tablet [ˈtæblət] n 1 : bloc-notes m 2 PILL : comprimé m
tabloid [ˈtæˌblɔɪd] n : quotidien m populaire, tabloïde m
taboo [təˈbu:, tæ-] adj : tabou — ~ n, pl -boos : tabou m
tacit [ˈtæsɪt] adj : tacite
taciturn [ˈtæsɪˌtərn] adj : taciturne
tack [ˈtæk] vt 1 ATTACH : clouer 2 ~ on ADD : ajouter
tackle [ˈtakəl] n 1 GEAR : équipement m, matériel m 2 : plaquage m (au football) — ~ vt -led; -ling 1 : plaquer (au football) 2 CONFRONT : s'attaquer à
tacky [ˈtæki] adj tackier; tackiest 1 STICKY : collant 2 GAUDY : de mauvais goût
tact [ˈtækt] n : tact m — tactful [ˈtæktfəl] adj : plein de tact
tactical [ˈtæktɪkəl] adj : tactique — tactic [ˈtæktɪk] n : tactique f — tactics [ˈtæktɪks] ns & pl : tactique f
tactless [ˈtæktləs] adj : qui manque de tact
tadpole [ˈtædˌpo:l] n : têtard m
tag[1] [ˈtæg] n LABEL : étiquette f — ~ v tagged; tagging vt LABEL : étiqueter — vi ~ along : suivre
tag[2] vt : toucher (au jeu de chat)
tail [ˈteɪl] n 1 : queue f 2 ~s npl : pile f (d'une pièce de monnaie) — ~ vt FOLLOW : suivre
tailor [ˈteɪlər] n : tailleur m — ~ vt 1 : faire sur mesure (un vêtement) 2 ADAPT : adapter
taint [ˈteɪnt] vt : entacher, souiller
Taiwanese [ˌtaɪwəˈni:z, -ˈni:s] adj : taiwanais
take [ˈteɪk] v took [ˈtʊk]; taken [ˈteɪkən]; taking vt 1 : prendre 2 BRING : emmener 3 CARRY : porter 4 REQUIRE : demander 5 ACCEPT : accepter 6 BEAR : supporter 7 : passer (un examen) 8 I ~ it that : je suppose que 9 ~ a walk : se promener 10 ~ apart DISMANTLE : démonter 11 ~ back : retirer 12 ~ in ALTER : reprendre 13 ~ in UNDERSTAND : saisir 14 ~ in DECEIVE : tromper 15 ~ off REMOVE : enlever 16 ~ on : assumer (une responsabilité) 17 ~ over : prendre le pouvoir 18 ~ place : avoir lieu 19 ~ up SHORTEN : raccourcir 20 ~ up OCCUPY : prendre — vi 1 WORK : faire effet 2 ~ off DEPART : s'en aller 3 ~ off : décoller (se dit d'un avion) — ~ n 1 PROCEEDS : recette f 2 : prise f (au cinéma) — takeoff [ˈteɪkˌɔf] n : décollage m (d'un avion) — takeover [ˈteɪkˌo:vər] n : prise f de contrôle (d'une compagnie)
talcum powder [ˈtælkəm] n : talc m
tale [ˈteɪl] n : conte m, histoire f
talent [ˈtælənt] n : talent m — talented [ˈtæləntəd] adj : talentueux, doué

talk [ˈtɔk] *vt* **1** : parler **2 ~ about** : parler de **3 ~ to/with** : parler avec — *vi* **1** SPEAK : parler **2 ~ over** : parler de, discuter — **~** *n* **1** CONVERSATION : entretien *m*, conversation *f* **2** SPEECH : discours *m*, exposé *m* — **talkative** [ˈtɔkət̬ɪv] *adj* : bavard

tall [ˈtɔl] *adj* **1** : grand **2 how ~ are you?** : combien mesures-tu?

tally [ˈtæli] *n, pl* **-lies** : compte *m* — **~** *v* **-lied; -lying** *vt* RECKON : calculer — *vi* MATCH : correspondre

tambourine [ˌtæmbəˈri:n] *n* : tambourin *m*

tame [ˈteɪm] *adj* **tamer; tamest 1** : apprivoisé **2** : docile — **~** *vt* **tamed; taming** : apprivoiser, dompter

tamper [ˈtæmpər] *vi* **~ with** : forcer (une serrure), falsifier (un document)

tampon [ˈtæmˌpɑn] *n* : tampon *m* (hygiénique)

tan [ˈtæn] *v* **tanned; tanning** *vt* : tanner (du cuir) — *vi* : bronzer — **~** *n* **1** SUNTAN : bronzage *m* **2** : brun *m* clair (couleur)

tang [ˈtæŋ] *n* : goût *m* piquant

tangent [ˈtændʒənt] *n* : tangente *f*

tangerine [ˈtændʒəˌri:n, ˌtændʒəˈ-] *n* : mandarine *f*

tangible [ˈtændʒəbəl] *adj* : tangible

tangle [ˈtæŋgəl] *v* **-gled; -gling** *vt* : enchevêtrer — *vi* : s'emmêler — **~** *n* : enchevêtrement *m*

tango [ˈtæŋˌgo:] *n, pl* **-gos** : tango *m*

tank [ˈtæŋk] *n* **1** : réservoir *m*, cuve *f* **2** : char *m* (militaire) — **tanker** [ˈtæŋkər] *n* **1** *or* **oil ~** : pétrolier *m* **2** *or* **~ truck** : camion-citern *m*

tantalizing [ˈtæntəˌlaɪzɪŋ] *adj* : alléchant

tantrum [ˈtæntrəm] *n* **throw a ~** : piquer une crise

tap[1] [ˈtæp] *n* FAUCET : robinet *m* — **~** *vt* **tapped; tapping** : mettre sur écoute

tap[2] *v* **tapped; tapping** *vt* TOUCH : tapoter, taper — *vi* : taper légèrement — **~** *n* : petit coup *m*

tape [ˈteɪp] *n or* **adhesive ~** : ruban *m* adhésif — **~** *vt* **taped; taping 1** : coller avec un ruban adhésif **2** RECORD : enregistrer — **tape measure** *n* : mètre *m* ruban

taper [ˈteɪpər] *vi* **1** : s'effiler **2** *or* **~ off** : diminuer

tapestry [ˈtæpəstri] *n, pl* **-tries** : tapisserie *f*

tar [ˈtɑr] *n* : goudron *m* — **~** *vt* **tarred; tarring** : goudronner

tarantula [təˈræntʃələ, -ˈræntələ] *n* : tarentule *f*

target [ˈtɑrgət] *n* **1** : cible *f* **2** GOAL : objectif *m*, but *m*

tariff [ˈtærɪf] *n* : tarif *m* douanier

tarnish [ˈtɑrnɪʃ] *vt* : ternir — *vi* : se ternir

tarpaulin [tɑrˈpɔlən, ˈtɑrpə-] *n* : bâche *f*

tart[1] [ˈtɑrt] *adj* SOUR : aigre

tart[2] *n* : tartelette *f*

tartan [ˈtɑrtən] *n* : tartan *m*, tissu *m* écossais

task [ˈtæsk] *n* : tâche *f*

tassel [ˈtæsəl] *n* : gland *m*

taste [ˈteɪst] *v* **tasted; tasting** *vt* : goûter (à) — *vi* **~ like** : avoir le goût de — **~** *n* : goût *m* — **tasteful** [ˈteɪstfəl] *adj* : de bon goût — **tasteless** [ˈteɪstləs] *adj* **1** FLAVORLESS : sans goût **2** COARSE : de mauvais goût — **tasty** [ˈteɪsti] *adj* **tastier; tastiest** : savoureux

tattered [ˈtæt̬ərd] *adj* : en lambeaux

tattle [ˈtæt̬əl] *vi* **-tled; -tling ~ on s.o.** : dénoncer qqn

tattoo [tæˈtu:] *vt* : tatouer — **~** *n* : tatouage *m*

taught → **teach**

taunt [ˈtɔnt] *n* : raillerie *f* — **~** *vt* : railler

taut [ˈtɔt] *adj* : tendu

tavern [ˈtævərn] *n* : taverne *f*

tax [ˈtæks] *vt* **1** : imposer (une personne), taxer (de l'argent, des marchandises) **2** STRAIN : mettre à l'épreuve — **~** *n* : taxe *f*, impôt *m* — **taxable** [ˈtæksəbəl] *adj* : imposable — **taxation** [tækˈseɪʃən] *n* : taxation *f*, imposition *f* — **tax–exempt** [ˈtæksɪgˈzɛmpt, -ɛg-] *adj* : exempt d'impôts

taxi [ˈtæksi] *n, pl* **taxis** : taxi *m*

taxpayer [ˈtæksˌpeɪər] *n* : contribuable *mf*

tea [ˈti:] *n* : thé *m*

teach [ˈti:tʃ] *v* **taught** [ˈtɔt]; **teaching** *vt* **1** : enseigner (un sujet) **2 ~ s.o. to** : apprendre qqn à — *vi* : enseigner — **teacher** [ˈti:tʃər] *n* : instituteur *m*, -trice *f* (à l'école primaire); professeur *m* — **teaching** [ˈti:tʃɪŋ] *n* : enseignement *m*

teacup [ˈti:ˌkʌp] *n* : tasse *f* à thé

team [ˈti:m] *n* : équipe *f* — **~** *vi* **~ up with** : faire équipe avec — **~** *adj* : d'équipe — **teammate** [ˈti:mˌmeɪt] *n* : coéquipier *m*, -pière *f* — **teamwork** [ˈti:mˌwərk] *n* : travail *m* d'équipe

teapot [ˈti:ˌpɑt] *n* : théière *f*

tear[1] [ˈtær] *v* **tore** [ˈtor]; **torn** [ˈtorn]; **tearing** *vt* **1** RIP : déchirer **2 ~ down** : démolir **3 ~ off** *or* **~ out** : arracher **4 ~ up** : déchirer — *vi* **1** : se déchirer **2** RUSH : se précipiter — **~** *n* : déchirure *f*

tear[2] [ˈtɪr] *n* : larme *f* — **tearful** [ˈtɪrfəl] *adj* : larmoyant

tease [ˈti:z] *vt* **teased; teasing** : taquiner — **~** *n* : taquin *m*, -quine *f*

teaspoon [ˈti:ˌspu:n] *n* : petite cuillère *f*, cuillère *f* à café

technical [ˈtɛknɪkəl] *adj* : technique — **technicality** [ˌtɛknəˈkæləti] *n, pl* **-ties** : détail *m* technique — **technician** [tɛkˈnɪʃən] *n* : technicien *m*, -cienne *f*

technique [tɛkˈni:k] *n* : technique *f*

technological [ˌtɛknəˈlɑdʒɪkəl] *adj* : technologique — **technology** [tɛkˈnɑlədʒi] *n, pl* **-gies** : technologie *f*

tedious [ˈti:diəs] *adj* : fastidieux — **tedium** [ˈti:diəm] *n* : ennui *m*

teem [ˈti:m] *vi* **~ with** : foisonner de, abonder en

teenage [ˈti:nˌeɪdʒ] *or* **teenaged** [-ˌeɪdʒd] *adj* : adolescent, d'adolescence — **teenager** [ˈti:nˌeɪdʒər] *n* : adolescent *m*, -cente *f* — **teens** [ˈti:nz] *npl* : adolescence *f*

teepee → **tepee**

teeter [ˈti:t̬ər] *vi* : chanceler

teeth → **tooth** — **teethe** [ˈti:ð] *vi* **teethed; teething** : faire ses dents

telecommunication [ˌtɛləkəˌmju:nəˈkeɪʃən] *n* : télécommunication *f*

telegram [ˈtɛləˌgræm] *n* : télégramme *m*

telegraph [ˈtɛləˌgræf] *n* : télégraphe *m*

telephone [ˈtɛləˌfo:n] *n* : téléphone *m* — **~** *v* **-phoned; -phoning** *vt* : téléphoner à — *vi* : appeler, téléphoner

telescope [ˈtɛləˌsko:p] *n* : télescope *m*

televise [ˈtɛləˌvaɪz] *vt* **-vised; -vising** : téléviser — **television** [ˈtɛləˌvɪʒən] *n* **1** : télévision *f* **2** *or* **~ set** : téléviseur *m*

tell [ˈtɛl] *v* **told** [ˈto:ld]; **telling** *vt* **1** : dire **2** RELATE : raconter **3** DISTINGUISH : distinguer **4 ~ s.o. off** : réprimander qqn — *vi* **1** : dire **2** KNOW : savoir **3** SHOW : se faire sentir **4 ~ on s.o.** : dénoncer qqn — **teller** [ˈtɛlər] *n or* **bank ~** : caissier *m*, -sière *f*

temp [ˈtɛmp] *n* : intérimaire *mf;* occasionnel *m*, -nelle *f Can*

temper [ˈtɛmpər] *vt* MODERATE : tempérer — **~** *n* **1** MOOD : humeur *f* **2 lose one's ~** : se mettre en colère — **temperament** [ˈtɛmpərmənt, -prə-, -pərə-] *n* : tempérament *m* — **temperamental** [ˌtɛmpərˈmɛntəl, -prə-, -pərə-] *adj* : capricieux — **temperate** [ˈtɛmpərət] *adj* **1** MILD : tempéré **2** MODERATE : modéré

temperature [ˈtɛmpərˌtʃʊr, -prə-, -tʃər] *n* **1** : température *f* **2 have a ~** : avoir de la température

temple [ˈtɛmpəl] *n* **1** : temple *m* **2** : tempe *f* (en anatomie)

tempo [ˈtɛmˌpo:] *n, pl* **-pi** [-ˌpi:] *or* **-pos 1** : tempo *m* **2** PACE : rythme *m*

temporarily [ˌtɛmpəˈrɛrəli] *adv* : temporairement — **temporary** [ˈtɛmpəˌrɛri] *adj* : temporaire

tempt [ˈtɛmpt] *vt* : tenter — **temptation** [tɛmpˈteɪʃən] *n* : tentation *f*

ten [ˈtɛn] *n* : dix *m* — **~** *adj* : dix

tenacious [təˈneɪʃəs] *adj* : tenace — **tenacity** [təˈnæsət̬i] *n* : ténacité *f*

tenant [ˈtɛnənt] *n* : locataire *mf*

tend[1] [ˈtɛnd] *vt* : s'occuper de

tend[2] *vi* **~ to** : avoir tendance à — **tendency** [ˈtɛndəntsi] *n, pl* **-cies** : tendance *f*

tender[1] [ˈtɛndər] *adj* **1** : tendre **2** PAINFUL : douloureux

tender[2] *vt* : présenter — **~** *n* **1** : soumission *f* **2 legal ~** : cours *m* légal

tenderloin [ˈtɛndərˌlɔɪn] *n* : filet *m* (de porc, etc.)

tenderness [ˈtɛndərnəs] *n* : tendresse *f*

tendon [ˈtɛndən] *n* : tendon *m*

tenet [ˈtɛnət] *n* : principe *m*

tennis [ˈtɛnəs] *n* : tennis *m*

tenor [ˈtɛnər] *n* : ténor *m*

tense[1] [ˈtɛnts] *n* : temps *m* (en grammaire)

tense[2] *v* **tensed; tensing** *vt* : tendre — *vi or* **~ up** : se raidir — **~** *adj* **tenser; tensest** : tendu — **tension** [ˈtɛntʃən] *n* : tension *f*

tent [ˈtɛnt] *n* : tente *f*

tentacle [ˈtɛntɪkəl] *n* : tentacule *m*

tentative [ˈtɛntət̬ɪv] *adj* **1** HESITANT : hésitant **2** PROVISIONAL : provisoire

tenth [ˈtɛnθ] *n* **1** : dixième *mf* **2 September ~** : le dix septembre — **~** *adj* : dixième

tenuous [ˈtɛnjʊəs] *adj* : ténu

tepee [ˈti:ˌpi:] *n* : tipi *m*

tepid [ˈtɛpɪd] *adj* : tiède

term [ˈtərm] *n* **1** WORD : terme *m* **2** : trimestre *m* (scolaire) **3 be on good ~s** : être en bons termes — **~** *vt* : appeler, nommer

terminal [ˈtərmənəl] *adj* : terminal — **~** *n* **1** : borne *f* (en électricité) **2** *or* **computer ~** : terminal *m* **3** : terminus *m* (de train, de bus)

terminate [ˈtərməˌneɪt] *v* **-nated; -nating** *vi* : se terminer — *vt* : terminer — **termination** [ˌtərməˈneɪʃən] *n* : fin *f*

terminology [ˌtərməˈnɑlədʒi] *n, pl* **-gies** : terminologie *f*

termite [ˈtərˌmaɪt] *n* : termite *m*

terrace [ˈtɛrəs] *n* : terrasse *f*

terrain [təˈreɪn] *n* : terrain *m*

terrestrial [təˈrɛstriəl] *adj* : terrestre

terrible [ˈtɛrəbəl] *adj* : terrible, épouvantable — **terribly** [ˈtɛrəbli] *adv* : terriblement

terrier [ˈtɛriər] *n* : terrier *m*

terrific [təˈrɪfɪk] *adj* **1** FRIGHTFUL : terrible **2** EXCELLENT : formidable

terrify [ˈtɛrəˌfaɪ] *vt* **-fied; -fying** : terrifier — **terrifying** [ˈtɛrəˌfaɪɪŋ] *adj* : terrifiant

territory [ˈtɛrəˌtori] *n, pl* **-ries** : territoire *m* — **territorial** [ˌtɛrəˈtoriəl] *adj* : territorial

terror [ˈtɛrər] *n* : terreur *f* — **terrorism** [ˈtɛrərˌɪzəm] *n* : terrorisme *m* — **terrorist** [ˈtɛrərɪst] *n* : terroriste *mf* — **terrorize** [ˈtɛrərˌaɪz] *vt* **-ized; -izing** : terroriser

terse [ˈtərs] *adj* **terser; tersest** : concis, succinct

test [ˈtɛst] *n* **1** TRIAL : épreuve *f* **2** EXAM : examen *m*, test *m* **3 blood ~** : analyse *f* de sang — **~** *vt* **1** TRY : essayer **2** QUIZ : examiner, tester **3** : analyser (le sang, etc.), examiner (les yeux, etc.)

testament [ˈtɛstəmənt] *n* **1** WILL : testament *m* **2 the Old/New Testament** : l'Ancien, le Nouveau Testament

testicle [ˈtɛstɪkəl] *n* : testicule *m*

testify [ˈtɛstəˌfaɪ] *v* **-fied; -fying** : témoigner

testimony [ˈtɛstəˌmo:ni] *n, pl* **-nies** : témoignage *m*

test tube *n* : éprouvette *f*

tetanus [ˈtɛtənəs] *n* : tétanos *m*

tether [ˈtɛðər] *vt* : attacher

text [ˈtɛkst] *n* : texte *m* — **textbook** [ˈtɛkstˌbʊk] *n* : manuel *m* scolaire

textile [ˈtɛkˌstaɪl, ˈtɛkstəl] *n* : textile *m*

texture [ˈtɛkstʃər] *n* : texture *f*

than [ˈðæn] *conj* : que — **~** *prep* : que, de

thank [ˈθæŋk] *vt* **1** : remercier **2 ~ you** : merci — **thankful** [ˈθæŋkfəl] *adj* : reconnaissant — **thankfully** [ˈθæŋkfəli] *adv* **1** : avec reconnaissance **2** FORTUNATELY : heureusement — **thankless** [ˈθæŋkləs] *adj* : ingrat — **thanks** [ˈθæŋks] *npl* **1** : remerciements *mpl* **2 ~ to** : grâce à

Thanksgiving [θæŋksˈgɪvɪŋ, ˈθæŋksˌ-] *n* : jour *m* d'Action de Grâces

that [ˈðæt] *pron, pl* **those** [ˈðo:z] **1** : cela, ce, ça **2** (*more distant*) : celui-là, celle-là, ceux-là, celles-là **3** WHO : qui **4** (*used to introduce relative clauses*) : que **5 is ~ you?** : c'est toi? **6 ~ is** : c'est-à-dire — **~** *conj* **1** : que **2 in order ~** : afin que — **~** *adj, pl* **those 1** : ce, cet, cette, ces **2 ~ one** : celui-là, celle-là — **~** *adv* VERY : tellement, très

thaw [ˈθɔ] *vt* : dégeler (des aliments) — *vi* **1** : se dégeler **2** MELT : fondre — **~** *n* : dégel *m*

the [ðə, *before vowel sounds usu* ði:] *art* **1** : le, la, l', les **2** PER : le, la **3 ~ English** : les Anglais — **~** *adv* **1** : le **2 ~ sooner ~ better** : le plus tôt sera le mieux

theater *or* **theatre** [ˈθi:ət̬ər] *n* : théâtre *m* — **theatrical** [θiˈætrɪkəl] *adj* : théâtral

theft [ˈθɛft] *n* : vol *m*

their [ˈðɛr] *adj* : leur — **theirs** [ˈðɛrz] *pron* **1** : le leur, la leur, les leurs **2 some friends of ~** : des amis à eux

them [ˈðɛm] *pron* **1** (*used as direct object*) : les **2** (*used as indirect object*) : leur **3** (*used as object of a preposition*) : eux, elles

theme [ˈθi:m] *n* : thème *m*

themselves [ðəmˈsɛlvz, ðɛm-] *pron* **1** (*used reflexively*) : se **2** (*used emphatically*) : eux-mêmes, elles-mêmes **3** (*used after a preposition*) : eux, elles, eux-mêmes, elles-mêmes **4 by ~** : tous seuls, toutes seules

then [ˈðɛn] *adv* **1** : alors **2** NEXT : ensuite, puis **3** BESIDES : et puis — **~** *adj* : d'alors, de l'époque

theology [θiˈɑlədʒi] *n, pl* **-gies** : théologie *f*

theorem [ˈθi:ərəm, ˈθɪrəm] *n* : théorème *m* — **theoretical** [ˌθi:əˈrɛtɪkəl] *adj* : théorique — **theory** [ˈθi:əri, ˈθɪri] *n, pl* **-ries** : théorie *f*

therapeutic [ˌθɛrəˈpju:t̬ɪk] *adj* : thérapeutique — **therapist** [ˈθɛrəpɪst] *n* : thérapeute *mf* — **therapy** [ˈθɛrəpi] *n, pl* **-pies** : thérapie *f*

there [ˈðær] *adv* **1** *or* **over ~** : là-bas **2 down/up ~** : là-dessous, là-haut **3 in ~** : là-dedans **4 ~, it's done!** : voilà, c'est fini! **5 who's ~?** : qui est là? — **~** *pron* **1 ~ is/are** : il y a **2 ~ are three of us** : nous sommes trois — **thereabouts** *or* **thereabout** [ðærəˈbaʊts, -ˈbaʊt, ˈðærəˌ-] *adv* : dans les environs, par là — **thereafter** [ðærˈæftər] *adv* : par la suite — **thereby** [ðærˈbaɪ, ˈðærˌbaɪ] *adv* : ainsi — **therefore** [ˈðærˌfor] *adv* : donc, par conséquent

thermal [ˈθərməl] *adj* : thermal, thermique

thermometer [θərˈmɑmət̬ər] *n* : thermomètre *m*

thermos [ˈθərməs] *n* : thermos *mf*

thermostat [ˈθərməˌstæt] *n* : thermostat *m*

thesaurus [θɪˈsɔrəs] *n, pl* **-sauri** [-ˈsɔrˌaɪ] *or* **-sauruses** [-ˈsɔrəsəz] : dictionnaire *m* analogique, dictionnaire *m* des synonymes

these → **this**

thesis [ˈθi:sɪs] *n, pl* **theses** [ˈθiˌsi:z] : thèse *f*

they [ˈðeɪ] *pron* **1** : ils, elles **2 as ~ say** : comme on dit **3 there ~ are** : les voici — **they'd** [ˈðeɪd] (*contraction of* **they had** *or* **they would**) → **have, would** — **they'll** [ˈðeɪl, ˈðɛl] (*contraction of* **they shall** *or* **they will**) → **shall, will** — **they're** [ˈðɛr] (*contraction of* **they are**) → **be** — **they've** [ˈðeɪv] (*contraction of* **they have**) → **have**

thick [ˈθɪk] *adj* **1** : épais **2** DENSE : bête **3 a ~ accent** : un accent prononcé **4 two inches ~** : deux pouces d'épaisseur — **~** *n* **in the ~ of** : au plus fort de — **thicken** [ˈθɪkən] *vt* : épaissir (une sauce, etc.) — *vi* : s'épaissir — **thicket** [ˈθɪkət] *n* : fourré *m* — **thickness** [ˈθɪknəs] *n* : épaisseur *f*, grosseur *f*

thief [ˈθi:f] *n, pl* **thieves** [ˈθi:vz] : voleur *m*, -leuse *f*

thigh [ˈθaɪ] *n* : cuisse *f*

thimble [ˈθɪmbəl] *n* : dé *m* à coudre

thin [ˈθɪn] *adj* **thinner; thinnest 1** : mince **2** SPARSE : clairsemé **3** WATERY : clair (se dit d'une soupe, etc.) — **~** *v* **thinned; thinning** *vt* DILUTE : diluer — *vi* : s'éclaircir

thing [ˈθɪŋ] *n* **1** : chose *f* **2 ~s** *npl* BELONGINGS : affaires *fpl* **3 for one ~** : en premier lieu **4 how are ~s?** : comment ça va? **5 the important ~ is…** : l'important c'est…

think [ˈθɪŋk] *v* **thought** [ˈθɔt]; **thinking** *vt* **1** : penser **2** BELIEVE : croire **3 ~ up** : inventer — *vi* **1** : penser **2 ~ about** *or* **~ of** CONSIDER : penser à **3 ~ of** REMEMBER : se rappeler

thinness [ˈθɪnnəs] *n* : minceur *f*

third [ˈθərd] *adj* : troisième — **~** *or* **thirdly** [-li] *adv* : troisième, troisièmement — **~** *n* **1** : troisième *mf* (dans une série) **2** : tiers *m* (en mathématiques) **3 December ~** : le trois décembre — **Third World** *n* : le tiers-monde

thirst [ˈθərst] *n* : soif *f* — **thirsty** [ˈθərsti] *adj* **thirstier; thirstiest 1** : assoiffé **2 be ~** : avoir soif

thirteen [ˌθərˈti:n] *n* : treize *m* — **~** *adj* : treize — **thirteenth** [ˌθərˈti:nθ] *n* **1** : treizième *mf* **2 January ~** : le treize janvier — **~** *adj* : treizième

thirty [ˈθərt̬i] *n, pl* **-ties** : trente *m* — **~** *adj* : trente — **thirtieth** [ˈθərt̬iəθ] *n* **1** : trentième *mf* **2 May ~** : le trente mai — **~** *adj* : trentième

this [ˈðɪs] *pron, pl* **these 1** : ce, ceci **2** (*in comparisons*) : celui-ci, celle-ci, ceux-ci, celles-ci **3 ~ is your room** : voici ta chambre — **~** *adj, pl* **these** [ˈði:z] **1** : ce, cet, cette, ces **2 ~ one** : celui-ci, celle-ci **3 ~ way** : par ici — **~** *adv* : si, aussi

thistle [ˈθɪsəl] *n* : chardon *m*

thorn [ˈθɔrn] *n* : épine *f* — **thorny** [ˈθɔrni] *adj* **thornier; thorniest** : épineux

thorough [ˈθəˌro:] *adj* **1** : consciencieux **2** COMPLETE : complet — **thoroughly** [ˈθəroli] *adv* **1** : à fond **2** COMPLETELY : absolument — **Thoroughbred** [ˈθərəˌbrɛd] *n* : pur-sang *m* — **thoroughfare** [ˈθərəˌfær] *n* : voie *f* publique

those → **that**

though [ˈðo:] *conj* : bien que, quoique — **~** *adv* **1** : cependant, pourtant **2 as ~** : comme si

thought [ˈθɔt] → **think** — **~** *n* **1** : pensée *f* **2** IDEA : idée *f* — **thoughtful** [ˈθɔtfəl] *adj* **1** : pensif **2** KIND : aimable — **thoughtless** [ˈθɔtləs] *adj* **1** : irréfléchi **2** RUDE : manquer d'égard (envers qqn)

thousand [ˈθaʊzənd] *n, pl* **-sands** *or* **-sand** : mille *m* — **~** *adj* : mille — **thousandth** [ˈθaʊzəntθ] *n* : millième *mf* — **~** *adj* : millième

thrash [ˈθræʃ] *vi or* **~ about** : se débattre

thread [ˈθrɛd] *n* : fil *m* — **~** *vt* : enfiler (une aiguille, des perles, etc.) — **threadbare** [ˈθrɛdˈbær] *adj* : usé

threat [ˈθrɛt] *n* : menace *f* — **threaten** [ˈθrɛtən] *v* : menacer — **threatening** [ˈθrɛtənɪŋ] *adj* : menaçant

three [ˈθri:] *n* : trois *m* — **~** *adj* : trois — **three hundred** *adj* : trois cent

threshold [ˈθrɛʃˌho:ld, -ˌo:ld] *n* : seuil *m*

threw → **throw**

thrift [ˈθrɪft] *n* : économie *f* — **thrifty** [ˈθrɪfti] *adj* **thriftier; thriftiest** : économe

thrill [ˈθrɪl] *vt* : transporter (de joie) — **~** *n* : frisson *m* — **thriller** [ˈθrɪlər] *n* : thriller *m* — **thrilling** [ˈθrɪlɪŋ] *adj* : excitant

thrive [ˈθraɪv] *vi* **throve** [ˈθro:v] *or* **thrived; thriven** [ˈθrɪvən] **1** FLOURISH : réussir **2** PROSPER : prospérer

throat [ˈθro:t] *n* : gorge *f*

throb [ˈθrɑb] *vi* **throbbed; throbbing 1** : battre, palpiter **2** VIBRATE : vibrer **3 ~ with pain** : lanciner

throes [ˈθro:z] *npl* **1** : agonie *f* **2 in the ~ of** : en proie à

throne [ˈθro:n] *n* : trône *m*

throng [ˈθrɔŋ] *n* : foule *f*

through [ˈθru:] *prep* **1** : à travers **2** BECAUSE OF : à cause de **3** BY : par **4** DURING : pendant **5 Monday ~ Friday** : du lundi au vendredi **6** → **throughout** — **~** *adv* **1** : à travers **2** COMPLETELY : complètement **3 let ~** : laisser passer — **~** *adj* **1 be ~** : avoir terminé **2 ~ traffic** : trafic en transit — **throughout** [θru:ˈaʊt] *prep* **1** : partout dans **2** DURING : pendant

throw [ˈθro:] *vt* **threw** [ˈθru:]; **thrown** [ˈθro:n]; **throwing 1** : lancer (une balle, etc.) **2** CONFUSE : déconcerter **3 ~ a party** : organiser une fête **4 ~ away** *or* **~ out** : jeter — **~** *n* TOSS : lancer *m*, jet *m* — **throw up** *vt* : vomir, renvoyer *Can fam*, restituer *Can fam*

thrush [ˈθrʌʃ] *n* : grive *f* (oiseau)
thrust [ˈθrʌst] *vt* **thrust; thrusting 1** : enfoncer, planter **2 ~ upon** : imposer à — **~** *n* : poussée *f*
thud [ˈθʌd] *n* : bruit *m* sourd
thug [ˈθʌg] *n* : voyou *m*
thumb [ˈθʌm] *n* : pouce *m* — **~** *vt or* **~ through** : feuilleter — **thumbnail** [ˈθʌmˌneɪl] *n* : ongle *m* du pouce — **thumbtack** [ˈθʌmˌtæk] *n* : punaise *f*
thump [ˈθʌmp] *vt* : cogner — *vi* : battre fort (se dit du cœur) — **~** *n* : bruit *m* sourd
thunder [ˈθʌndər] *n* : tonnerre *m* — **~** *vi* : tonner — **~** *vt* SHOUT : vociférer — **thunderbolt** [ˈθʌndərˌboːlt] *n* : foudre *f* — **thunderous** [ˈθʌndərəs] *adj* : étourdissant — **thunderstorm** [ˈθʌndərˌstɔrm] *n* : orage *m*
Thursday [ˈθərzˌdeɪ, -di] *n* : jeudi *m*
thus [ˈðʌs] *adv* **1** : ainsi, donc **2 ~ far** : jusqu'à présent
thwart [ˈθwɔrt] *vt* : contrecarrer
thyme [ˈtaɪm, ˈθaɪm] *n* : thym *m*
thyroid [ˈθaɪˌrɔɪd] *n* : thyroïde *f*
tic [ˈtɪk] *n* : tic *m* (nerveux)
tick[1] [ˈtɪk] *n* : tique *f* (insecte)
tick[2] *n* **1** : tic-tac *m* (bruit) **2** CHECK : coche *f* — **~** *vi* : faire tic-tac — *vt* **1** *or* **~ off** CHECK : cocher **2 ~ off** ANNOY : agacer
ticket [ˈtɪkət] *n* **1** : billet *m* (d'avion, de train, etc.), ticket *m* (d'autobus, de métro) **2** *or* **parking ~** : contravention *f*
tickle [ˈtɪkəl] *v* **-led; -ling** *vt* **1** : chatouiller **2** AMUSE : amuser — *vi* : chatouiller — **~** *n* : chatouillement *m* — **ticklish** [ˈtɪkəlɪʃ] *adj* : chatouilleux
tidal wave [ˈtaɪdəl] *n* : raz-de-marée *m*
tidbit [ˈtɪdˌbɪt] *n* : détail *m* intéressant
tide [ˈtaɪd] *n* : marée *f* — **~** *vt* **tided; tiding ~ over** : dépanner
tidy [ˈtaɪdi] *adj* **-dier; -est** NEAT : propre — **~** *vt* **-died; -dying** *or* **~ up** : ranger
tie [ˈtaɪ] *n* **1** : attache *f*, cordon *m* **2** BOND : lien *m* **3** : match *m* nul (aux sports) **4** NECKTIE : cravate *f* — **~** *v* **tied; tying** *or* **tieing** *vt* **1** : attacher **2 ~ a knot** : faire un nœud — *vi* : faire match nul, être ex æquo
tier [ˈtɪr] *n* : étage *m*, gradin *m* (d'un stade)
tiger [ˈtaɪgər] *n* : tigre *m*
tight [ˈtaɪt] *adj* **1** : serré, étroit **2** TAUT : tendu **3** STINGY : avare **4 a ~ seal** : une fermeture étanche — **~** *adv* **closed ~** : bien fermé — **tighten** [ˈtaɪtən] *vt* : serrer, resserrer — **tightly** [ˈtaɪtli] *adv* : fermement, bien — **tightrope** [ˈtaɪtˌroːp] *n* : corde *f* raide — **tights** [ˈtaɪts] *npl* : collants *mpl*
tile [ˈtaɪl] *n* : carreau *m*, tuile *f* — **~** *vt* **tiled; tiling** : carreler, poser des tuiles sur
till[1] [ˈtɪl] *prep & conj* → **until**
till[2] *vt* : labourer
till[3] *n* : tiroir-caisse *m*
tilt [ˈtɪlt] *n* **1** : inclinaison *f* **2 at full ~** : à toute vitesse — **~** *vt* : pencher, incliner — *vi* : se pencher, s'incliner
timber [ˈtɪmbər] *n* **1** : bois *m* de construction **2** BEAM : poutre *f*
time [ˈtaɪm] *n* **1** : temps *m* **2** AGE : époque *f* **3** : rythme *m* (en musique) **4 at ~s** : parfois **5 at this ~** : en ce moment **6 for the ~ being** : pour le moment **7 from ~ to ~** : de temps à autre **8 have a good ~** : amusez-vous bien **9 on ~** : à l'heure **10 several ~s** : plusieurs fois **11 ~ after ~** : à maintes reprises **12 what ~ is it?** : quelle heure est-il? — **~** *vt* **timed; timing 1** SCHEDULE : prévoir, fixer **2** : chronométrer (une course, etc.) — **timeless** [ˈtaɪmləs] *adj* : éternel — **timely** [ˈtaɪmli] *adj* **-lier; -est** : opportun — **timer** [ˈtaɪmər] *n* : minuteur *m* (en cuisine) — **times** [ˈtaɪmz] *prep* **3 ~ 4 is 12** : 3 fois 4 égale 12 — **timetable** [ˈtaɪmˌteɪbəl] *n* : horaire *m*
timid [ˈtɪmɪd] *adj* : timide
tin [ˈtɪn] *n* **1** : étain *m* (métal) **2** *or* **~ can** : boîte *f* — **tinfoil** [ˈtɪnˌfɔɪl] *n* : papier *m* d'aluminium
tinge [ˈtɪnʤ] *vt* **tinged; tingeing** *or* **tinging** [ˈtɪnʤɪŋ] : teinter — **~** *n* : teinte *f*
tingle [ˈtɪŋgəl] *vi* **-gled; -gling** : picoter — **~** *n* : picotement *m*
tinker [ˈtɪŋkər] *vi* **~ with** : bricoler
tinkle [ˈtɪŋkəl] *vi* **-kled; -kling** : tinter — **~** *n* : tintement *m*
tint [ˈtɪnt] *n* : teinte *f* — **~** *vt* : teinter
tiny [ˈtaɪni] *adj* **-nier; -niest** : minuscule
tip[1] [ˈtɪp] *v* **tipped; tipping** *vt* **1** TILT : incliner **2** *or* **~ over** : renverser — *vi* : pencher
tip[2] *n* END : pointe *f*, bout *m* (d'un crayon)
tip[3] *n* ADVICE : conseil *m*, tuyau *m fam* — **~** *vt* **~ off** : prévenir
tip[4] *vt* : donner un pourboire à — **~** *n* GRATUITY : pourboire *m*
tipsy [ˈtɪpsi] *adj* **-sier; -est** : gris *fam*, éméché *fam*
tiptoe [ˈtɪpˌtoː] *n* **on ~** : sur la pointe des pieds — **~** *vi* **-toed; -toeing** : marcher sur la pointe des pieds
tire[1] [ˈtaɪr] *n* : pneu *m*
tire[2] *v* **tired; tiring** *vt* : fatiguer — *vi* : se fatiguer — **tired** [ˈtaɪrd] *adj* **1** : fatigué **2 be ~ of** : en avoir assez de — **tiresome** [ˈtaɪrsəm] *adj* : ennuyeux
tissue [ˈtɪˌʃuː] *n* **1** : tissu *m* (en biologie) **2** : mouchoir *m* en papier, papier *m* mouchoir *Can*
title [ˈtaɪtəl] *n* : titre *m* — **~** *vt* **-tled; -tling** : intituler
to [ˈtuː] *prep* **1** : à **2** TOWARD : vers **3** IN ORDER TO : afin de, pour **4** UP TO : jusqu'à **5 a quarter ~ three** : trois heures moins le quart **6 be nice ~ him** : sois gentil envers lui **7 ten ~ the box** : dix par boîte **8 two ~ four years old** : entre deux et quatre ans **9 want ~ do** : vouloir faire — **~** *adv* **1 come ~** : reprendre connaissance **2 go ~ and fro** : aller et venir
toad [ˈtoːd] *n* : crapaud *m*
toast [ˈtoːst] *vt* **1** : griller (du pain), toaster *Can* **2** : boire à la santé de (une personne) — **~** *n* **1** : toast *m*, pain *m* grillé, rôtie *f* **2 drink a ~ to** : porter un toast à — **toaster** [ˈtoːstər] *n* : grille-pain *m*
tobacco [təˈbækoː] *n, pl* **-cos** : tabac *m*
toboggan [təˈbɑgən] *n* : toboggan *m*, traîne *f Can*
today [təˈdeɪ] *adv* : aujourd'hui — **~** *n* : aujourd'hui *m*
toddler [ˈtɑdələr] *n* : bambin *m*, -bine *f*
toe [ˈtoː] *n* : orteil *m*, doigt *m* de pied — **toenail** [ˈtoːˌneɪl] *n* : ongle *m* d'orteil
together [təˈgɛðər] *adv* **1** : ensemble **2 ~ with** : ainsi que
toil [ˈtɔɪl] *n* : labeur *m* — **~** *vi* : peiner
toilet [ˈtɔɪlət] *n* BATHROOM : toilettes *fpl*, toilette *f Can* — **toilet paper** *n* : papier *m* hygiénique — **toiletries** [ˈtɔɪlətriz] *npl* : articles *mpl* de toilette
token [ˈtoːkən] *n* **1** SIGN : signe *m*, marque *f* **2** : jeton *m* (pour le métro, etc.)
told → **tell**
tolerable [ˈtɑlərəbəl] *adj* : tolérable — **tolerance** [ˈtɑlərənts] *n* : tolérance *f* — **tolerant** [ˈtɑlərənt] *adj* : tolérant — **tolerate** [ˈtɑləˌreɪt] *vt* **-ated; -ating** : tolérer
toll[1] [ˈtoːl] *n* **1** : péage *m* **2 death ~** : nombre *m* de morts **3 take a ~ on** : affecter
toll[2] *v* RING : sonner
tomato [təˈmeɪto, -ˈmɑ-] *n, pl* **-toes** : tomate *f*
tomb [ˈtuːm] *n* : tombeau *m* — **tombstone** [ˈtuːmˌstoːn] *n* : pierre *f* tombale
tomorrow [təˈmɑro] *adv* : demain — **~** *n* : demain *m*
ton [ˈtən] *n* : tonne *f*
tone [ˈtoːn] *n* **1** : ton *m* **2** BEEP : tonalité *f* — **~** *vt* **toned; toning** *or* **~ down** : atténuer
tongs [ˈtɑŋz, ˈtɔŋz] *npl* : pinces *fpl*
tongue [ˈtʌŋ] *n* : langue *f*
tonic [ˈtɑnɪk] *n* : tonique *m*
tonight [təˈnaɪt] *adv* : ce soir — **~** *n* : ce soir, cette nuit
tonsil [ˈtɑntsəl] *n* : amygdale *f*
too [ˈtuː] *adv* **1** ALSO : aussi **2** VERY : très
took → **take**
tool [ˈtuːl] *n* : outil *m* — **toolbox** [ˈtuːlˌbɑks] *n* : boîte *f* à outils
toot [ˈtuːt] *vi* : klaxonner — **~** *n* : coup *m* de klaxon
tooth [ˈtuːθ] *n, pl* **teeth** [ˈtiːθ] : dent *f* — **toothache** [ˈtuːθˌeɪk] *n* : mal *m* de dents — **toothbrush** [ˈtuːθˌbrʌʃ] *n* : brosse *f* à dents — **toothpaste** [ˈtuːθˌpeɪst] *n* : dentifrice *m*
top[1] [ˈtɑp] *n* **1** : haut *m* **2** SUMMIT : cime *f* **3** COVER : couvercle *m* **4 on ~ of** : sur — **~** *vt* **topped; topping 1** COVER : couvrir **2** SURPASS : dépasser — **~** *adj* **1** : de haut, du haut **2** LEADING : premier, principal **3 the ~ floor** : le dernier étage
top[2] *n* : toupie *f* (jouet)
topic [ˈtɑpɪk] *n* : sujet *m* — **topical** [ˈtɑpɪkəl] *adj* : d'actualité
topple [ˈtɑpəl] *v* **-pled; -pling** *vi* : basculer — *vt* : renverser
torch [ˈtɔrʧ] *n* : torche *f*
tore → **tear**[1]
torment [ˈtɔrˌmɛnt] *n* : tourment *m* — **~** [ˈtɔrˌmɛnt, tɔrˈ-] *vt* : tourmenter
torn → **tear**[1]
tornado [tɔrˈneɪdo] *n, pl* **-does** *or* **-dos** : tornade *f*
torpedo [tɔrˈpiːdo] *n, pl* **-does** : torpille *f* — **~** *vt* : torpiller
torrent [ˈtɔrənt] *n* : torrent *m*
torrid [ˈtɔrɪd] *adj* : torride
torso [ˈtɔrˌsoː] *n, pl* **-sos** *or* **-si** [-ˌsiː] : torse *m*
tortoise [ˈtɔrtəs] *n* : tortue *f* — **tortoiseshell** [ˈtɔrtəsˌʃɛl] *n* : écaille *f*
tortuous [ˈtɔrtʃuəs] *adj* : tortueux
torture [ˈtɔrʧər] *n* : torture *f* — **~** *vt* **-tured; -turing** : torturer
toss [ˈtɔs, ˈtɑs] *vt* : tirer, lancer — *vi* **~ and turn** : se tourner et se retourner — **~** *n* : lancer *m*
tot [ˈtɑt] *n* : petit enfant *m*
total [ˈtoːtəl] *adj* : total — **~** *n* : total *m* — **~** *vt* **-taled** *or* **-talled; -taling** *or* **-talling** : totaliser, additionner
totalitarian [ˌtoːˌtæləˈtɛriən] *adj* : totalitaire
touch [ˈtʌʧ] *vt* **1** : toucher **2** AFFECT : émouvoir **3 ~ up** : retoucher — *vi* : se toucher — **~** *n* **1** : toucher *m* (sens) **2** HINT : touche *f* **3 a ~ of** : un peu de **4 keep in ~** : demeurer en contact — **touchdown** [ˈtʌʧˌdaʊn] *n* **1** : atterrissage *m* (d'un avion) **2** : but *m* (au football américain) — **touchy** [ˈtʌʧi] *adj* **touchier; touchiest 1** : susceptible **2 a ~ subject** : un sujet épineux
tough [ˈtʌf] *adj* **1** : dur **2** STRONG : solide **3** STRICT : sévère **4** DIFFICULT : difficile — **toughen** [ˈtʌfən] *vt or* **~ up** : endurcir — *vi* : s'endurcir — **toughness** [ˈtʌfnəs] *n* : dureté *f*
tour [ˈtʊr] *n* **1** : tour *m* (d'une ville, etc.), visite *f* (d'un musée, etc.) **2 go on ~** : faire une tournée — **~** *vi* **1** TRAVEL : voyager **2** : être en tournée (se dit d'une équipe, etc.) — *vt* : visiter — **tourist** [ˈtʊrɪst, ˈtər-] *n* : touriste *mf*
tournament [ˈtərnəmənt, ˈtʊr-] *n* : tournoi *m*
tousle [ˈtaʊzəl] *vt* **-sled; -sling** : ébouriffer (les cheveux)
tout [ˈtaʊt] *vt* : vanter les mérites de
tow [ˈtoː] *vt* : remorquer — **~** *n* : remorquage *m*
toward [ˈtord, təˈwɔrd] *or* **towards** [ˈtordz, təˈwɔrdz] *prep* : vers
towel [ˈtaʊəl] *n* : serviette *f*
tower [ˈtaʊər] *n* : tour *f* — **~** *vi* **~ over** : dominer — **towering** [ˈtaʊərɪŋ] *adj* : imposant
town [ˈtaʊn] *n* **1** VILLAGE : village *m* **2** CITY : ville *f* — **township** [ˈtaʊnˌʃɪp] *n* **1** : municipalité *f* **2** : canton *m Can* (division territoriale)
tow truck [ˈtoːˌtrʌk] *n* : dépanneuse *f*, remorqueuse *f Can*
toxic [ˈtɑksɪk] *adj* : toxique
toy [ˈtɔɪ] *n* : jouet *m* — **~** *vi* **~ with** : jouer avec
trace [ˈtreɪs] *n* : trace *f* — **~** *vt* **traced; tracing 1** : tracer, calquer (un dessin) **2** FOLLOW : suivre **3** LOCATE : retrouver
track [ˈtræk] *n* **1** : piste *f* **2** FOOTPRINT : trace *f* **3** *or* **railroad ~** : voie *f* ferrée **4 keep ~ of** : suivre — **~** *vt* : suivre la trace de, suivre la piste de
tract[1] [ˈtrækt] *n* **1** EXPANSE : étendue *f* **2** : appareil *m* (en physiologie)
tract[2] *n* LEAFLET : brochure *f*
traction [ˈtrækʃən] *n* : traction *f*
tractor [ˈtræktər] *n* **1** : tracteur *m* **2** *or* **tractor–trailer** : semi-remorque *m*
trade [ˈtreɪd] *n* **1** PROFESSION : métier *m* **2** COMMERCE : commerce *m* **3** INDUSTRY : industrie *f* **4** EXCHANGE : échange *m* — **~** *v* **traded; trading** *vi* : faire du commerce — *vt* **~ sth for** : échanger qqch pour — **trademark** [ˈtreɪdˌmɑrk] *n* : marque *f* de fabrique
tradition [trəˈdɪʃən] *n* : tradition *f* — **traditional** [trəˈdɪʃənəl] *adj* : traditionnel
traffic [ˈtræfɪk] *n* **1** : circulation *f* (routière) **2 drug ~** : trafic *m* de drogue — **~** *vi* **-ficked; -ficking** : trafiquer — **traffic light** *n* : feu *m* (de signalisation)
tragedy [ˈtræʤədi] *n, pl* **-dies** : tragédie *f* — **tragic** [ˈtræʤɪk] *adj* : tragique
trail [ˈtreɪl] *vi* **1** DRAG : traîner **2** LAG : être à la traîne **3 ~ off** : s'estomper — *vt* **1** : traîner **2** PURSUE : suivre la piste de — **~** *n* **1** : trace *f*, piste *f* **2** PATH : sentier *m*, chemin *m* — **trailer** [ˈtreɪlər] *n* **1** : remorque *f* **2** CAMPER : caravane *f*, roulotte *f Can*
train [ˈtreɪn] *n* **1** : train *m* **2** : traîne *f* (d'une robe) **3** SERIES : suite *f*, série *f* **4 ~ of thought** : fil *m* des pensées — **~** *vt* **1** : former, entraîner (un athlète, etc.) **2** AIM : braquer — *vi* : s'entraîner (aux sports) — **trainer** [ˈtreɪnər] *n* **1** : entraîneur *m*, -neuse *f* (aux sports) **2** : dresseur *m*, -seuse *f* (d'animaux)
trait [ˈtreɪt] *n* : trait *m*
traitor [ˈtreɪtər] *n* : traître *m*, -tresse *f*
tramp [ˈtræmp] *vi* : marcher (d'un pas lourd) — **~** *n* VAGRANT : clochard *m*, -charde *f*
trample [ˈtræmpəl] *vt* **-pled; -pling** : piétiner
trampoline [ˌtræmpəˈliːn, ˈtræmpəˌ-] *n* : trampoline *m*
trance [ˈtrænts] *n* : transe *f*
tranquillity *or* **tranquility** [trænˈkwɪləti] *n* : tranquillité *f* — **tranquilizer** [ˈtræŋkwəˌlaɪzər] *n* : tranquillisant *m*
transaction [trænˈzækʃən] *n* : transaction *f*
transcribe [trænˈskraɪb] *vt* **-scribed; -scribing** : transcrire — **transcript** [ˈtrænˌskrɪpt] *n* : transcription *f*
transfer [trænt͡sˈfər, ˈtræntsˌfər] *v* **-ferred; -ferring** *vt* **1** : transférer **2** : muter (un employé) — *vi* **1** : être transféré **2** : changer (d'université) — **~** [ˈtræntsˌfər] *n* **1** : transfert *m*, mutation *f* **2** : virement *m* (de fonds)
transform [træntsˈfɔrm] *vt* : transformer — **transformation** [ˌtræntsfərˈmeɪʃən] *n* : transformation *f*
transfusion [træntsˈfjuːʒən] *n* : transfusion *f*
transgression [træntsˈgrɛʃən, trænz-] *n* : transgression *f* — **transgress** [træntsˈgrɛs, trænz-] *vt* : transgresser
transient [ˈtrænʧənt, ˈtrænsiənt] *adj* : transitoire, passager
transit [ˈtræntsɪt, ˈtrænzɪt] *n* **1** : transit *m* **2** TRANSPORTATION : transport *m* — **transition** [trænˈsɪʃən, -ˈzɪʃ-] *n* : transition *f* — **transitive** [ˈtræntsəṭɪv, ˈtrænzə-] *adj* : transitif — **transitory** [ˈtræntsəˌtori, ˈtrænzə-] *adj* : transitoire, passager
translate [træntsˈleɪt, trænz-; ˈtræntsˌ-, ˈtrænzˌ-] *vt* **-lated; -lating** : traduire — **translation** [træntsˈleɪʃən, trænz-] *n* : traduction *f* — **translator** [træntsˈleɪtər, trænz-; ˈtræntsˌ-, ˈtrænzˌ-] *n* : traducteur *m*, -trice *f*
translucent [træntsˈluːsənt, trænz-] *adj* : translucide
transmit [træntsˈmɪt, trænz-] *vt* **-mitted; -mitting** : transmettre — **transmission** [træntsˈmɪʃən, trænz-] *n* : transmission *f* — **transmitter** [træntsˈmɪṭər, trænz-; ˈtræntsˌ-, ˈtrænsˌ-] *n* : émetteur *m*
transparent [træntsˈpærənt] *adj* : transparent — **transparency** [træntsˈpærəntsi] *n, pl* **-cies** : transparence *f*
transplant [træntsˈplænt] *vt* : transplanter — **~** [ˈtræntsˌplænt] *n* : transplantation *f*
transport [træntsˈport, ˈtræntsˌ-] *vt* : transporter — **~** [ˈtræntsˌport] *n* : transport *m* — **transportation** [ˌtræntspərˈteɪʃən] *n* : transport *m*
transpose [træntsˈpoːz] *vt* **-posed; -posing** : transposer
trap [ˈtræp] *n* : piège *m* — **~** *vt* **trapped; trapping** : prendre au piège, attraper — **trapdoor** [ˈtræpˈdor] *n* : trappe *f*
trapeze [træˈpiːz] *n* : trapèze *m*
trappings [ˈtræpɪŋz] *npl* SIGNS : attributs *mpl*
trash [ˈtræʃ] *n* : déchets *mpl*, ordures *fpl*
trauma [ˈtrɔmə, ˈtraʊ-] *n* : traumatisme *m* — **traumatic** [trəˈmæṭɪk, trɔ-, traʊ-] *adj* : traumatisant
travel [ˈtrævəl] *vi* **-eled** *or* **-elled; -eling** *or* **-elling 1** : voyager **2** SPREAD : circuler, se répandre **3** MOVE : aller, rouler — **~** *n* : voyages *mpl* — **traveler** *or* **traveller** [ˈtrævələr] *n* : voyageur *m*, -geuse *f*
trawl [ˈtrɔl] *vi* : pêcher au chalut — **trawler** [ˈtrɔlər] *n* : chalutier *m*
tray [ˈtreɪ] *n* : plateau *m*
treachery [ˈtrɛʧəri] *n, pl* **-eries** : traîtrise *f* — **treacherous** [ˈtrɛʧərəs] *adj* **1** : traître **2** DANGEROUS : dangereux
tread [ˈtrɛd] *v* **trod** [ˈtrɑd]; **trodden** [ˈtrɑdən] *or* **trod; treading** *vt* **~ water** : nager sur place — *vi or* **~ on** : marcher sur — **~** *n* **1** STEP : pas *m* **2** : bande *f* de roulement (d'un pneu) — **treadmill** [ˈtrɛdˌmɪl] *n* : exerciseur *m*
treason [ˈtriːzən] *n* : trahison *f*
treasure [ˈtrɛʒər, ˈtreɪ-] *n* : trésor *m* — **~** *vt* **-sured; -suring** : tenir beaucoup à — **treasurer** [ˈtrɛʒərər, ˈtreɪ-] *n* : trésorier *m*, -rière *f* — **treasury** [ˈtrɛʒəri, ˈtreɪ-] *n, pl* **-suries 1** : trésorerie *f* **2 Treasury** : ministère *m* des Finances
treat [ˈtriːt] *vt* **1** : traiter **2 ~ s.o. to sth** : offrir qqch à qqn — **~** *n* : régal *m*, plaisir *m*
treatise [ˈtriːṭəs] *n* : traité *m*
treatment [ˈtriːtmənt] *n* : traitement *m*
treaty [ˈtriːṭi] *n, pl* **-ties** : traité *m*
treble [ˈtrɛbəl] *adj* **1** TRIPLE : triple **2** : de soprano (en musique) — **treble clef** *n* : clé *f* de sol
tree [ˈtriː] *n* : arbre *m*
trek [ˈtrɛk] *n* : randonnée *f*
trellis [ˈtrɛlɪs] *n* : treillis *m*, treillage *m*
tremble [ˈtrɛmbəl] *vi* **-bled; -bling** : trembler
tremendous [trɪˈmɛndəs] *adj* **1** HUGE : énorme **2** EXCELLENT : formidable
tremor [ˈtrɛmər] *n* : tremblement *m*
trench [ˈtrɛnʧ] *n* : tranchée *f*
trend [ˈtrɛnd] *n* **1** : tendance *f* **2** FASHION : mode *f* — **trendy** [ˈtrɛndi] *adj* **trendier; trendiest** : à la mode
trepidation [ˌtrɛpəˈdeɪʃən] *n* : inquiétude *f*
trespass [ˈtrɛspəs, -ˌpæs] *vi* : s'introduire illégalement
trial [ˈtraɪəl] *n* **1** HEARING : procès *m* **2** TEST : essai *m* **3** ORDEAL : épreuve *f* — **~** *adj* : d'essai
triangle [ˈtraɪˌæŋgəl] *n* : triangle *m* — **triangular** [traɪˈæŋgjələr] *adj* : triangulaire
tribe [ˈtraɪb] *n* : tribu *f* — **tribal** [ˈtraɪbəl] *adj* : tribal
tribulation [ˌtrɪbjəˈleɪʃən] *n* : tourment *m*
tribunal [traɪˈbjuːnəl, trɪ-] *n* : tribunal *m*
tribute [ˈtrɪbˌjuːt] *n* : hommage *m* — **tributary** [ˈtrɪbjəˌtɛri] *n, pl* **-taries** : affluent *m*
trick [ˈtrɪk] *n* **1** PRANK : farce *f*, tour *m* **2** KNACK : truc *m*, astuce *f* — **~** *vt* : duper — **trickery** [ˈtrɪkəri] *n* : tromperie *f*
trickle [ˈtrɪkəl] *vi* **-led; -ling** DRIP : dégouliner — **~** *n* : filet *m* (d'eau)
tricky [ˈtrɪki] *adj* **trickier; trickiest 1** SLY : rusé **2** DIFFICULT : difficile
tricycle [ˈtraɪsəkəl, -ˌsɪkəl] *n* : tricycle *m*
trifle [ˈtraɪfəl] *n* : bagatelle *f*, rien *m* — **trifling** [ˈtraɪflɪŋ] *adj* : insignifiant
trigger [ˈtrɪgər] *n* : détente *f*, gâchette *f* — **~** *vt* : déclencher
trillion [ˈtrɪljən] *n* : billion *m*
trilogy [ˈtrɪləʤi] *n, pl* **-gies** : trilogie *f*
trim [ˈtrɪm] *vt* **trimmed; trimming 1** CUT : tailler **2** ADORN : décorer — **~** *adj* **trimmer; trimmest 1** SLIM : mince **2** NEAT

: soigné — ~ n 1 HAIRCUT : coupe f 2 DECORATION : garniture f — **trimmings** ['trɪmɪŋs] npl : garniture f

Trinity ['trɪnəṭi] n : Trinité f

trinket ['trɪŋkət] n : babiole f

trio ['tri:,o:] n, pl **trios** : trio m

trip ['trɪp] v **tripped; tripping** vi : trébucher, s'enfarger Can — vt 1 : faire trébucher (une personne) 2 ACTIVATE : déclencher — ~ n 1 : voyage m 2 STUMBLE : trébuchement m

tripe ['traɪp] n : tripes fpl (d'un animal)

triple ['trɪpəl] v **-pled; -pling** : tripler — ~ n : triple m — ~ adj : triple — **triplets** ['trɪpləts] npl : triplés mpl — **triplicate** ['trɪplɪkət] n **in** ~ : en trois exemplaires

tripod ['traɪ,pɑd] n : trépied m

trite ['traɪt] adj **triter; tritest** : banal

triumph ['traɪəmpf] n : triomphe m — ~ vi : triompher — **triumphal** [traɪ'ʌmpfəl] adj : triomphal — **triumphant** [traɪ'ʌmpfənt] adj : triomphant

trivial ['trɪviəl] adj : insignifiant — **trivia** ['trɪviə] ns & pl : futilités fpl — **triviality** [,trɪvi'æləṭi] n, pl **-ties** : insignifiance f

trod, trodden → **tread**

trolley ['trɑli] n, pl **-leys** : tramway m

trombone [trɑm'bo:n] n : trombone m

troop ['tru:p] n 1 GROUP : bande f, groupe m 2 ~**s** npl : troupes fpl — **trooper** ['tru:pər] n 1 : soldat m 2 or **state** ~ : gendarme m France, policier m

trophy ['tro:fi] n, pl **-phies** : trophée m

tropic ['trɑpɪk] n 1 : tropique m 2 **the** ~**s** : les tropiques mpl — ~ or **tropical** ['trɑpɪkəl] adj : tropical

trot ['trɑt] n : trot m — ~ vi **trotted; trotting** : trotter

trouble ['trʌbəl] vt **-bled; -bling** 1 WORRY : inquiéter 2 BOTHER : déranger — ~ n 1 PROBLEMS : ennuis mpl 2 EFFORT : mal m, peine f 3 **be in** ~ : avoir des ennuis 4 **I had** ~ **doing it** : j'ai eu du mal à le faire — **troublemaker** ['trʌbəl,meɪkər] n : fauteur m, -trice f de troubles — **troublesome** ['trʌbəlsəm] adj : gênant, pénible

trough ['trɔf] n, pl **troughs** ['trɔfs, 'trɔvz] 1 : abreuvoir m (pour les animaux) 2 or **feeding** ~ : auge f

trousers ['traʊzərz] npl : pantalon m

trout ['traʊt] ns & pl : truite f

trowel ['traʊəl] n : truelle f (pour le mortier), déplantoir m (pour le jardinage)

truant ['tru:ənt] n : élève mf absentéiste

truce ['tru:s] n : trêve f

truck ['trʌk] n : camion m — **trucker** ['trʌkər] n : camionneur m, -neuse f; routier m

trudge ['trʌʤ] vi **trudged; trudging** : marcher péniblement

true ['tru:] adj **truer; truest** 1 FACTUAL : vrai 2 LOYAL : fidèle 3 GENUINE : authentique

truffle ['trʌfəl] n : truffe f

truly ['tru:li] adv : vraiment

trump ['trʌmp] n : atout m

trumpet ['trʌmpət] n : trompette f

trunk ['trʌŋk] n 1 STEM, TORSO : tronc m 2 : trompe f (d'un éléphant) 3 : coffre m (d'une voiture) 4 SUITCASE : malle f 5 ~**s** npl : maillot m de bain

trust ['trʌst] n 1 CONFIDENCE : confiance f 2 HOPE : espoir m 3 : trust m (en finances) 4 **in** ~ : par fidéicommis — ~ vt 1 HOPE : espérer 2 ~ **in** : faire confiance à — vt 1 ENTRUST : confier 2 **I** ~ **him** : j'ai confiance en lui — **trustee** [,trʌs'ti:] n : fidéicommissaire mf — **trustworthy** ['trʌst,wərði] adj : digne de confiance

truth ['tru:θ] n, pl **truths** ['tru:ðz, 'tru:θs] : vérité f — **truthful** ['tru:θfəl] adj : sincère, vrai

try ['traɪ] v **tried; trying** vt 1 ATTEMPT : essayer 2 : juger (un accusé) 3 TEST : éprouver, mettre à l'épreuve 4 TASTE : goûter — vi : essayer — ~ n, pl **tries** : essai m — **trying** ['traɪɪŋ] adj : pénible — **tryout** ['traɪ,aʊt] n : essai m

tsar ['zɑr, 'tsɑr, 'sɑr] → **czar**

T–shirt ['ti:,ʃərt] n : tee-shirt m, t-shirt m

tub ['tʌb] n 1 VAT : cuve f 2 CONTAINER : pot m 3 BATHTUB : baignoire f

tuba ['tu:bə, 'tju:-] n : tuba m

tube ['tu:b, 'tju:b] n 1 : tube m 2 or **inner** ~ : chambre f à air 3 **the** ~ : la télé

tuberculosis [tʊ,bərkjə'lo:səs, tjʊ-] n, pl **-loses** [-,si:z] : tuberculose f

tubing ['tu:bɪŋ, 'tju:-] n : tubes mpl — **tubular** ['tubjələr, 'tju:-] adj : tubulaire

tuck ['tʌk] vt 1 or ~ **away** : ranger 2 ~ **in** : rentrer (une chemise, etc.) — ~ n : pli m

Tuesday ['tu:z,deɪ, 'tju:z-, -di] n : mardi m

tuft ['tʌft] n : touffe f (de cheveux, d'herbe, etc.)

tug ['tʌg] vt **tugged; tugging** or ~ **at** : tirer sur — ~ n : petit coup m — **tugboat** ['tʌg,bo:t] n : remorqueur m — **tug–of–war** [,tʌgə'wɔr] n, pl **tugs–of–war** : lutte f à la corde

tuition [tʊ'ɪʃən, 'tju:-] n : frais mpl de scolarité

tulip ['tu:lɪp, 'tju:-] n : tulipe f

tumble ['tʌmbəl] vi **-bled; -bling** : tomber — ~ n : chute f — **tumbler** ['tʌmblər] n : verre m droit

tummy ['tʌmi] n, pl **-mies** : ventre m

tumor or Brit **tumour** ['tu:mər, 'tju:-] n : tumeur f

tumult ['tu:,mʌlt 'tju:-] n : tumulte m — **tumultuous** [tʊ'mʌlʧʊəs, tjʊ-] adj : tumultueux

tuna ['tu:nə 'tju:-] n, pl **-na** or **-nas** : thon m

tune ['tu:n, 'tju:n] n 1 MELODY : air m 2 **in** ~ : accordé, juste 3 **out of** ~ : désaccordé, faux — ~ v **tuned; tuning** vt 1 : accorder (un piano, etc.) 2 or ~ **up** : régler (un moteur) — vi ~ **in** : se mettre à l'écoute — **tuner** ['tu:nər, 'tju:-] n : accordeur m (de pianos, etc.)

tunic ['tu:nɪk, 'tju:-] n : tunique f

Tunisian [tu:'ni:ʒən, tju:'nɪziən] adj : tunisien

tunnel ['tʌnəl] n : tunnel m — ~ vi **-neled** or **-nelled; -neling** or **-nelling** : creuser un tunnel

turban ['tərbən] n : turban m

turbine ['tərbən, -,baɪn] n : turbine f

turbulent ['tərbjələnt] adj : turbulent — **turbulence** ['tərbjələnts] n : turbulence f

turf ['tərf] n : gazon m

turkey ['tərki] n, pl **-keys** : dinde f

Turkish ['tərkɪʃ] adj : turc — ~ n : turc m (langue)

turmoil ['tər,mɔɪl] n : désarroi m, confusion f

turn ['tərn] vt 1 : tourner 2 SPRAIN : tordre 3 ~ **down** REFUSE : refuser 4 ~ **down** LOWER : baisser 5 ~ **in** : rendre 6 ~ **into** : convertir en 7 ~ **off** : éteindre (la lumière, etc.), couper (le contact, etc.) 8 ~ **out** EXPEL : expulser 9 ~ **out** PRODUCE : produire 10 ~ **out** → **turn off** 11 or ~ **over** FLIP : retourner 12 ~ **over** TRANSFER : remettre 13 ~ **s.o.'s stomach** : soulever le cœur à qqn 14 ~ **up** RAISE : augmenter — vi 1 ROTATE : tourner 2 BECOME : devenir 3 SOUR : tourner 4 CHANGE : se transformer 5 HEAD : se diriger 6 or ~ **around** : se retourner 7 ~ **in** RETIRE : se coucher 8 ~ **in** DELIVER : livrer 9 ~ **into** : se changer en 10 ~ **out** COME : venir 11 ~ **out** RESULT : se terminer 12 ~ **out to be** : s'avérer, se révéler 13 ~ **up** APPEAR : se présenter — ~ n 1 ROTATION : tour m 2 CHANGE : changement m 3 CURVE : virage m 4 DEED : service m 5 **wait your** ~ : attendez votre tour

turnip ['tərnəp] n : navet m

turnout ['tərn,aʊt] n : participation f — **turnover** ['tərn,o:vər] n 1 REVERSAL : renversement m 2 : roulement m (du personnel) 3 **apple** ~ : chausson m aux pommes — **turnpike** ['tərn,paɪk] n : autoroute f à péage — **turntable** ['tərn,teɪbəl] n : platine f

turpentine ['tərpən,taɪn] n : térébenthine f

turret ['tərət] n : tourelle f

turtle ['tərṭəl] n : tortue f — **turtleneck** ['tərṭəl,nɛk] n : col m roulé, col m montant

tusk ['tʌsk] n : défense f (d'un animal)

tutor ['tu:ṭər, 'tju:-] n : précepteur m, -trice f; professeur m particulier — ~ vt : donner des cours particuliers à

tuxedo [,tək'si:,do:] n, pl **-dos** or **-does** : smoking m

TV [,ti:'vi:, 'ti:,vi:] → **television**

twang ['twæŋ] n : ton m nasillard (de la voix)

tweed ['twi:d] n : tweed m

tweet ['twi:t] n : pépiement m — ~ vi : pépier

tweezers ['twi:zərz] ns & pl : pince f à épiler

twelve ['twɛlv] n : douze m — ~ adj : douze — **twelfth** ['twɛlfθ] n 1 : douzième mf 2 **February** ~ : le douze février — ~ adj : douzième

twenty ['twʌnti, 'twɛn-] n, pl **-ties** : vingt m — ~ adj : vingt — **twentieth** ['twʌntiəθ, 'twɛn-] n 1 : vingtième mf 2 **March** ~ : le vingt mars — ~ adj : vingtième

twice ['twaɪs] adv 1 : deux fois 2 ~ **as much** : deux fois plus

twig ['twɪg] n : brindille f

twilight ['twaɪ,laɪt] n : crépuscule m

twin ['twɪn] n : jumeau m, -melle f — ~ adj : jumeau

twine ['twaɪn] n : ficelle f

twinge ['twɪnʤ] n : élancement m (de douleur)

twinkle ['twɪŋkəl] vi **-kled; -kling** 1 : scintiller (se dit des étoiles, etc.) 2 : pétiller (se dit des yeux) — ~ n : scintillement m (des étoiles), pétillement m (des yeux)

twirl ['twərl] vt : faire tournoyer — vi : tournoyer — ~ n : tournoiement m

twist ['twɪst] vt 1 TURN : tourner 2 SPRAIN : tordre 3 DISTORT : déformer — vi 1 : serpenter (se dit d'une route) 2 COIL : s'enrouler 3 ~ **and turn** : se tortiller 4 ~ **off** : dévisser — ~ n 1 TURN : tour m 2 BEND : tournant m 3 **a** ~ **of fate** : un coup du sort — **twister** ['twɪstər] → **tornado**

twitch ['twɪʧ] vi : se contracter — ~ n or **nervous** ~ : tic m (nerveux)

two ['tu:] n, pl **twos** : deux m — ~ adj : deux — **twofold** ['tu:'fo:ld] adj : double — ~ adv : doublement — **two hundred** adj : deux cents

tycoon [taɪ'ku:n] n : magnat m

tying → **tie**

type ['taɪp] n 1 KIND : type m 2 : caractère m (d'imprimerie) — ~ v **typed; typing** : taper (à la machine) — **typewriter** ['taɪp,raɪṭər] n : machine f à écrire, dactylo f Can

typhoon [taɪ'fu:n] n : typhon m

typical ['tɪpɪkəl] adj : typique — **typify** ['tɪpə,faɪ] vt **-fied; -fying** : être typique de

typist ['taɪpɪst] n : dactylo mf

typography [taɪ'pɑgrəfi] n : typographie f

tyranny ['tɪrəni] n, pl **-nies** : tyrannie f — **tyrant** ['taɪrənt] n : tyran m

tzar ['zɑr, 'tsɑr, 'sɑr] → **czar**

U

u ['ju:] n, pl **u's** or **us** ['ju:z] : u m, vingt et unième lettre de l'alphabet

udder ['ʌdər] n : pis m

UFO [,ju:,ɛf'o:, 'ju:,fo:] n (unidentified flying object), pl **UFO's** or **UFOs** : ovni m

ugly ['ʌgli] adj **-lier; -est** : laid — **ugliness** ['ʌglinəs] n : laideur f

ulcer ['ʌlsər] n : ulcère f

ulterior [,ʌl'tɪriər] adj ~ **motive** : arrière-pensée f

ultimate ['ʌltəmət] adj 1 : ultime, final 2 SUPREME : suprême — **ultimately** ['ʌltəmətli] adv 1 : finalement, en fin de compte 2 EVENTUALLY : par la suite

ultimatum [,ʌltə'meɪṭəm, -'mɑ-] n, pl **-tums** or **-ta** [-ṭə] : ultimatum m

ultraviolet [,ʌltrə'vaɪələt] adj : ultraviolet

umbilical cord [,ʌm'bɪlɪkəl] n : cordon m ombilical

umbrella [,ʌm'brɛlə] n : parapluie m

umpire ['ʌm,paɪr] n : arbitre m — ~ vt **-pired; -piring** : arbitrer

umpteenth ['ʌmp,tinθ, ,ʌmp'-] adj : énième

unable [,ʌn'eɪbəl] adj 1 : incapable 2 **be** ~ **to** : ne pas pouvoir

unabridged [,ʌnə'brɪʤd] adj : intégral

unacceptable [,ʌnɪk'sɛptəbəl] adj : inacceptable

unaccountable [,ʌnə'kaʊntəbəl] adj : inexplicable

unaccustomed [,ʌnə'kʌstəmd] adj **be** ~ **to** : ne pas avoir l'habitude de

unadulterated [,ʌnə'dʌltə,reɪṭəd] adj : pur, naturel

unaffected [,ʌnə'fɛktəd] adj 1 : indifférent 2 NATURAL : sans affectation

unafraid [,ʌnə'freɪd] adj : sans peur

unaided [,ʌn'eɪdəd] adj : sans aide

unanimous [jʊ'nænəməs] adj : unanime

unannounced [,ʌnə'naʊnst] adj : inattendu, sans se faire annoncer

unarmed [,ʌn'ɑrmd] adj : non armé, sans armes

unassuming [,ʌnə'su:mɪŋ] adj : modeste

unattached [,ʌnə'tæʧt] adj 1 : détaché 2 UNMARRIED : libre

unattractive [,ʌnə'træktɪv] adj : peu attrayant

unauthorized [,ʌn'ɔθə,raɪzd] adj : non autorisé

unavailable [,ʌnə'veɪləbəl] adj : indisponible

unavoidable [,ʌnə'vɔɪdəbəl] adj : inévitable

unaware [,ʌnə'wær] adj 1 : ignorant 2 **be** ~ **of** : ignorer, ne pas être conscient de

unbalanced [,ʌn'bæləntst] adj : déséquilibré

unbearable [,ʌn'bærəbəl] adj : insupportable

unbelievable [,ʌnbə'li:vəbəl] adj : incroyable

unbending [,ʌn'bɛndɪŋ] adj : inflexible

unbiased [,ʌn'baɪəst] adj : impartial

unborn [,ʌn'bɔrn] adj : qui n'est pas encore né

unbreakable [,ʌn'breɪkəbəl] adj : incassable

unbroken [,ʌn'bro:kən] adj 1 INTACT : intact 2 CONTINUOUS : continu

unbutton [,ʌn'bʌtən] vt : déboutonner

uncalled–for [,ʌn'kɔld,fɔr] adj : déplacé, injustifié

uncanny [ən'kæni] adj 1 STRANGE : mystérieux, troublant 2 REMARKABLE : remarquable

unceasing [,ʌn'si:sɪŋ] adj : incessant

uncertain [,ʌn'sərtən] adj : incertain — **uncertainty** [,ʌn'sərtənti] n, pl **-ties** : incertitude f

unchanged [,ʌn'ʧeɪnʤd] adj : inchangé — **unchanging** [,ʌn'ʧeɪnʤɪŋ] adj : immuable

uncivilized [,ʌn'sɪvə,laɪzd] adj : barbare

uncle ['ʌŋkəl] n : oncle m

unclear [,ʌn'klɪr] adj : peu clair

uncomfortable [,ʌn'kʌmpfərṭəbəl] adj 1 : inconfortable 2 AWKWARD : mal à l'aise

uncommon [,ʌn'kɑmən] adj : rare, peu commun

uncompromising [,ʌn'kɑmprə'maɪzɪŋ] adj : intransigeant

unconcerned [,ʌnkən'sərnd] adj : indifférent

unconditional [,ʌnkən'dɪʃənəl] adj : inconditionnel

unconscious [,ʌn'kɑnʃəs] adj : inconscient

uncontrollable [,ʌnkən'tro:ləbəl] adj : incontrôlable

unconventional [,ʌnkən'vɛnʧənəl] adj : peu conventionnel

uncouth [,ʌn'ku:θ] adj : grossier

uncover [,ʌn'kʌvər] vt : découvrir

undecided [,ʌndɪ'saɪdəd] adj : indécis

undeniable [,ʌndɪ'naɪəbəl] adj : indéniable

under ['ʌndər] adv 1 : en dessous 2 LESS : moins 3 or ~ **anesthetic** : sous anesthésie — ~ prep 1 BELOW, BENEATH : sous, en dessous de 2 ACCORDING TO : d'après, selon

underage [,ʌndər'eɪʤ] adj : mineur

underclothes ['ʌndər,klo:z, -,klo:ðz] npl → **underwear**

undercover [,ʌndər'kʌvər] adj : secret

underdeveloped [,ʌndərdɪ'vɛləpt] adj : sous-développé

underestimate [,ʌndər'ɛstə,meɪt] vt **-mated; -mating** : sous-estimer

undergo [,ʌndər'go:] vt **-went** [-'wɛnt]; **-gone** [-'gɔn]; **-going** : subir, éprouver

undergraduate [,ʌndər'græʤʊət] n : étudiant m, -diante f de premier cycle; étudiant m, -diante f qui prépare une licence France

underground [,ʌndər'graʊnd] adv : sous terre — ~ ['ʌndər,graʊnd] adj 1 : souterrain 2 SECRET : clandestin — ~ ['ʌndər,graʊnd] n SUBWAY : métro m

undergrowth ['ʌndər,gro:θ] n : sous-bois m, broussailles fpl

underhanded [,ʌndər'hændəd] adj SLY : sournois

underline ['ʌndər,laɪn] vt **-lined; -lining** : souligner

underlying [,ʌndər'laɪɪŋ] adj : sous-jacent

undermine [,ʌndər'maɪn] vt **-mined; -mining** : saper, miner

underneath [,ʌndər'ni:θ] prep : sous, au-dessous de — ~ adv : en dessous, dessous

underpants ['ʌndər,pænts] npl : caleçon m, slip m France

underpass ['ʌndər,pæs] n : voie f inférieure (de l'autoroute), passage m souterrain (pour piétons)

underprivileged [,ʌndər'prɪvlɪʤd] adj : défavorisé

undershirt ['ʌndər,ʃərt] n : maillot m de corps

understand [,ʌndər'stænd] vt **-stood** [-'stʊd]; **-standing** 1 : comprendre 2 BELIEVE : croire — **understandable** [,ʌndər'stændəbəl] adj : compréhensible — **understanding** [,ʌndər'stændɪŋ] n 1 : compréhension f 2 AGREEMENT : entente f, accord m — ~ adj : compréhensif

understudy ['ʌndər,stʌdi] n, pl **-dies** : doublure f (au théâtre)

undertake [,ʌndər'teɪk] vt **-took** [-'tʊk]; **-taken** [-'teɪkən]; **-taking** : entreprendre (une tâche), assumer (une responsabilité) — **undertaker** ['ʌndər,teɪkər] n : entrepreneur m de pompes funèbres — **undertaking** ['ʌndər,teɪkɪŋ, ,ʌndər'-] n : entreprise f

undertone ['ʌndər,to:n] n : voix f basse

undertow ['ʌndər,to:] n : courant m sous-marin

underwater [,ʌndər'wɔṭər, -'wɑ-] adj : sous-marin — ~ adv : sous l'eau

under way [,ʌndər'weɪ] adv : en cours, en route

underwear ['ʌndər,wær] n : sous-vêtements mpl

underwent → **undergo**

underworld ['ʌndər,wərld] n or **criminal** ~ : milieu m, pègre f

undesirable [,ʌndɪ'zaɪrəbəl] adj : indésirable

undisputed [,ʌndɪ'spju:ṭəd] adj : incontesté

undo [,ʌn'du:] vt **-did; -done; -doing** 1 UNFASTEN : défaire, détacher 2 ~ **a wrong** : réparer un tort

undoubtedly [,ʌn'daʊṭədli] adv : sans aucun doute

undress [,ʌn'drɛs] vt : déshabiller — vi : se déshabiller

undue [,ʌn'du:, -'dju:] adj : excessif, démesuré

undulate ['ʌnʤə,leɪt] vi **-lated; -lating** : onduler

unduly [,ʌn'du:li] adv : excessivement

unearth [,ʌn'ərθ] vt : déterrer

uneasy [,ʌn'i:zi] adj 1 : mal à l'aise, gêné 2 WORRIED : inquiet 3 UNSTABLE : précaire — **uneasily** [,ʌn'i:zəli] adv : avec inquiétude — **uneasiness** [,ʌn'i:zinəs] n : inquiétude f

uneducated [,ʌn'ɛʤə,keɪṭəd] adj : sans éducation

unemployed [ˌʌnɪm'plɔɪd] *adj* : en chômage, sans travail — **unemployment** [ˌʌnɪm'plɔɪmənt] *n* : chômage *m*

unequal [ˌʌn'i:kwəl] *adj* : inégal

uneven [ˌʌn'i:vən] *adj* **1** : inégal **2** ODD : impair

unexpected [ˌʌnɪk'spɛktəd] *adj* : inattendu, imprévu

unfailing [ˌʌn'feɪlɪŋ] *adj* **1** CONSTANT : infaillible **2** INEXHAUSTIBLE : inépuisable

unfair [ˌʌn'fær] *adj* : injuste — **unfairly** [ˌʌn'færli] *adv* : injustement — **unfairness** [ˌʌn'færnəs] *n* : injustice *f*

unfaithful [ˌʌn'feɪθfəl] *adj* : infidèle — **unfaithfulness** [ˌʌn'feɪθfəlnəs] *n* : infidélité *f*

unfamiliar [ˌʌnfə'mɪljər] *adj* **1** : inconnu, peu familier **2 be ~ with** : mal connaître

unfasten [ˌʌn'fæsən] *vt* : déboucler (une ceinture)

unfavorable [ˌʌn'feɪvərəbəl] *adj* : défavorable

unfeeling [ˌʌn'fi:lɪŋ] *adj* : insensible

unfinished [ˌʌn'fɪnɪʃd] *adj* : inachevé

unfit [ˌʌn'fɪt] *adj* : inapte, impropre

unfold [ˌʌn'fo:ld] *vt* **1** : déplier **2** REVEAL : dévoiler — *vi* **1** : se dérouler

unforeseen [ˌʌnfor'si:n] *adj* : imprévu

unforgettable [ˌʌnfər'gɛtəbəl] *adj* : inoubliable

unforgivable [ˌʌnfər'gɪvəbəl] *adj* : impardonnable

unfortunate [ˌʌn'fɔrtʃənət] *adj* **1** UNLUCKY : malheureux **2** REGRETTABLE : regrettable, fâcheux — **unfortunately** [ˌʌn'fɔrtʃənətli] *adv* : malheureusement

unfounded [ˌʌn'faʊndəd] *adj* : sans fondement

unfurl [ˌʌn'fərl] *vt* : déployer

unfurnished [ˌʌn'fərnɪʃt] *adj* : non meublé

ungainly [ˌʌn'geɪnli] *adj* : gauche

ungodly [ˌʌn'gɑdli, -'gɑd-] *adj* UNSEEMLY : indu, impossible

ungrateful [ˌʌn'greɪtfəl] *adj* : ingrat

unhappy [ˌʌn'hæpi] *adj* **-pier; -est 1** SAD : malheureux, triste **2** DISSATISFIED : mécontent — **unhappiness** [ˌʌn'hæpinəs] *n* : tristesse *f*

unharmed [ˌʌn'hɑrmd] *adj* : indemne

unhealthy [ˌʌn'hɛlθi] *adj* **-healthier; -healthiest 1** : insalubre, malsain **2** SICKLY : malade, maladif

unheard–of [ˌʌn'hərdəv] *adj* : sans précédent, inconnu

unhook [ˌʌn'hʊk] *vt* **1** REMOVE : décrocher **2** UNFASTEN : dégrafer

unhurt [ˌʌn'hərt] *adj* : indemne

unicorn ['ju:nəˌkɔrn] *n* : licorne *f*

unification [ˌju:nəfə'keɪʃən] *n* : unification *f*

uniform ['ju:nəˌfɔrm] *adj* : uniforme — **~** *n* : uniforme *m* — **uniformity** [ˌju:nə'fɔrməṭi] *n, pl* **-ties** : uniformité *f*

unify ['ju:nəˌfaɪ] *vt* **-fied; -fying** : unifier

unilateral [ˌju:nə'læṭərəl] *adj* : unilatéral

uninhabited [ˌʌnɪn'hæbəṭəd] *adj* : inhabité

union ['ju:njən] *n* **1** : union *f* **2** *or* **labor ~** : syndicat *m*

unique [jʊ'ni:k] *adj* : unique — **uniquely** [jʊ'ni:kli] *adv* : exceptionnellement

unison ['ju:nəsən, -zən] *n* **in ~** : à l'unisson

unit ['ju:nɪt] *n* **1** : unité *f* **2** GROUP : groupe *m*

unite [jʊ'naɪt] *v* **united; uniting** *vt* : unir — *vi* : s'unir — **unity** ['ju:nəṭi] *n, pl* **-ties** : unité *f*

universe ['ju:nəˌvərs] *n* : univers *m* — **universal** [ˌju:nə'vərsəl] *adj* : universel

university [ˌju:nə'vərsəṭi] *n, pl* **-ties** : université *f*

unjust [ˌʌn'dʒʌst] *adj* : injuste — **unjustified** [ˌʌn'dʒʌstəˌfaɪd] *adj* : injustifié

unkempt [ˌʌn'kɛmpt] *adj* : en désordre, négligé

unkind [ˌʌn'kaɪnd] *adj* : peu aimable, pas gentil — **unkindness** [ˌʌn'kaɪndnəs] *n* : méchanceté *f*

unknown [ˌʌn'no:n] *adj* : inconnu

unlawful [ˌʌn'lɔfəl] *adj* : illégal

unless [ən'lɛs] *conj* : à moins que, à moins de

unlike [ˌʌn'laɪk] *adj* : différent — **~** *prep* **1** : différent de **2** : contrairement à — **unlikelihood** [ˌʌn'laɪkliˌhʊd] *n* : improbabilité *f* — **unlikely** [ˌʌn'laɪkli] *adj* **-lier; -liest** : improbable

unlimited [ˌʌn'lɪməṭəd] *adj* : illimité

unload [ˌʌn'lo:d] *vt* : décharger

unlock [ˌʌn'lɑk] *vt* : ouvrir, débarrer *Can* (une porte, etc.)

unlucky [ˌʌn'lʌki] *adj* **-luckier; -luckiest 1** : malchanceux **2** : qui porte malheur (se dit d'un numéro)

unmarried [ˌʌn'mærid] *adj* : célibataire

unnecessary [ˌʌn'nɛsəˌsɛri] *adj* : inutile

unnerving [ˌʌn'nərvɪŋ] *adj* : déconcertant

unnoticed [ˌʌn'no:ṭəst] *adj* : inaperçu

unoccupied [ˌʌn'ɑkjəˌpaɪd] *adj* **1** IDLE : inoccupé **2** EMPTY : libre

unofficial [ˌʌnə'fɪʃəl] *adj* : officieux, non officiel

unpack [ˌʌn'pæk] *vi* : défaire ses bagages

unparalleled [ˌʌn'pærəˌlɛld] *adj* : sans égal, sans pareil

unpleasant [ˌʌn'plɛzənt] *adj* : désagréable

unplug [ˌʌn'plʌg] *vt* **-plugged; -plugging 1** UNCLOG : déboucher **2** DISCONNECT : débrancher

unpopular [ˌʌn'pɑpjələr] *adj* : impopulaire

unprecedented [ˌʌn'prɛsəˌdɛntəd] *adj* : sans précédent

unpredictable [ˌʌnprɪ'dɪktəbəl] *adj* : imprévisible

unprepared [ˌʌnpri'pærd] *adj* : mal préparé

unqualified [ˌʌn'kwɑləˌfaɪd] *adj* : non qualifié

unquestionable [ˌʌn'kwɛstʃənəbəl] *adj* : incontestable

unravel [ˌʌn'rævəl] *vt* **-eled** *or* **-elled; -eling** *or* **elling** : démêler, dénouer

unreal [ˌʌn'ri:l] *adj* : irréel — **unrealistic** [ˌʌnˌri:ə'lɪstɪk] *adj* : irréaliste

unreasonable [ˌʌn'ri:zənəbel] *adj* : déraisonnable

unrecognizable [ˌʌn'rɛkəgˌnaɪzəb'l] *adj* : méconnaissable

unrelated [ˌʌnrɪ'leɪṭəd] *adj* : sans rapport

unrelenting [ˌʌnrɪ'lɛntɪŋ] *adj* : implacable

unreliable [ˌʌnrɪ'laɪəbəl] *adj* : peu fiable, peu sûr

unrepentant [ˌʌnrɪ'pɛntənt] *adj* : impénitent

unrest [ˌʌn'rɛst] *n* : agitation *f*, troubles *mpl*

unripe [ˌʌn'raɪp] *adj* : pas mûr, vert

unrivaled *or* **unrivalled** [ˌʌn'raɪvəld] *adj* : sans égal, incomparable

unroll [ˌʌn'ro:l] *vt* : dérouler

unruly [ˌʌn'ru:li] *adj* : indiscipliné

unsafe [ˌʌn'seɪf] *adj* : dangereux

unsatisfactory [ˌʌnˌsæṭəs'fæktəri] *adj* : peu satisfaisant

unscrew [ˌʌn'skru:] *vt* : dévisser

unseemly [ˌʌn'si:mli] *adj* **-lier; -est** : inconvenant

unseen [ˌʌn'si:n] *adj* : invisible

unsettle [ˌʌn'sɛṭəl] *vt* **-tled; -tling** DISTURB : perturber — **unsettled** [ˌʌn'sɛṭəld] *adj* **1** UNSTABLE : instable **2** DISTURBED : troublé

unsightly [ˌʌn'saɪtli] *adj* : laid

unskilled [ˌʌn'skɪld] *adj* : non spécialisé — **unskillful** [ˌʌn'skɪlfəl] *adj* : malhabile

unsound [ˌʌn'saʊnd] *adj* : peu judicieux

unspeakable [ˌʌn'spi:kəbəl] *adj* **1** : indicible **2** TERRIBLE : atroce

unstable [ˌʌn'steɪbəl] *adj* : instable

unsteady [ˌʌn'stɛdi] *adj* **1** : instable **2** SHAKY : tremblant

unsuccessful [ˌʌnsək'sɛsfəl] *adj* **1** : infructueux **2 be ~** : échouer

unsuitable [ˌʌn'su:ṭəbəl] *adj* : qui ne convient pas, inapproprié — **unsuited** [ˌʌn'su:ṭəd] *adj* : inapte

unsure [ˌʌn'ʃʊr] *adj* **1** : incertain **2 be ~ of oneself** : manquer de confiance en soi

unsuspecting [ˌʌnsə'spɛktɪŋ] *adj* : qui ne se doute de rien

unthinkable [ˌʌn'θɪŋkəbəl] *adj* : impensable, inconcevable

untidy [ˌʌn'taɪdi] *adj* **-dier; -est** : en désordre

untie [ˌʌn'taɪ] *vt* **-tied; -tying** *or* **-tieing** : dénouer, défaire

until [ˌʌn'tɪl] *prep* **1** UP TO : jusqu'à **2** BEFORE : avant — **~** *conj* : jusqu'à ce que, avant que, avant de

untimely [ˌʌn'taɪmli] *adj* **1** : prématuré **2** INOPPORTUNE : déplacé

untoward [ˌʌn'tɔrd, -'to:ərd, -tə'wɔrd] *adj* : fâcheux

untroubled [ˌʌn'trʌbəld] *adj* **1** : tranquille **2 be ~ by** : ne pas être affecté par

untrue [ˌʌn'tru:] *adj* : faux

unused *adj* [ˌʌn'ju:zd, *in sense 1 usually* -'ju:st] **1** UNACCUSTOMED : pas habitué **2** NEW : neuf, nouveau

unusual [ˌʌn'ju:ʒʊəl] *adj* : peu commun, rare — **unusually** [ˌʌn'ju:ʒʊəli] *adv* : exceptionnellement

unveil [ˌʌn'veɪl] *vt* : dévoiler

unwanted [ˌʌn'wɑntəd] *adj* : non désiré

unwarranted [ˌʌn'wɔrəntəd] *adj* : injustifié

unwelcome [ˌʌn'wɛlkəm] *adj* : inopportun

unwell [ˌʌn'wɛl] *adj* : indisposé

unwieldy [ˌʌn'wi:ldi] *adj* : encombrant

unwilling [ˌʌn'wɪlɪŋ] *adj* : peu disposé — **unwillingly** [ˌʌn'wɪlɪŋli] *adv* : à contrecœur

unwind [ˌʌn'waɪnd] *v* **-wound; -winding** *vt* : dérouler — *vi* **1** : se dérouler **2** RELAX : se détendre

unwise [ˌʌn'waɪz] *adj* : imprudent

unworthy [ˌʌn'wərði] *adj* **~ of** : indigne de

unwrap [ˌʌn'ræp] *vt* **-wrapped; -wrapped** : déballer

up ['ʌp] *adv* **1** ABOVE : en haut **2** UPWARDS : vers le haut **3 farther ~** : plus loin **4 go ~** : augmenter, monter **5 speak ~** : parler plus fort **6 stand ~** : se lever **7 ~ until** : jusqu'à — **~** *adj* **1** AWAKE : levé **2** INCREASING : qui augmente **3** UP-TO-DATE : au courant, à jour **4** FINISHED : fini **5 be ~ for** : être prêt pour **6 what's ~?** : qu'est-ce qui se passe? — **~** *prep* **1** : en haut de **2 go ~** : monter **3 sail ~ the river** : remonter la rivière en bateau **4 ~ to** : jusqu'à — **~** *v* **upped; upping** *vt* : augmenter — *vi* **~ and leave** : partir sans mot dire

upbringing ['ʌpˌbrɪŋɪŋ] *n* : éducation *f*

upcoming [ˌʌp'kʌmɪŋ] *adj* : prochain, à venir

update [ˌʌp'deɪt] *vt* **-dated; -dating** : mettre à jour — **~** ['ʌpˌdeɪt] *n* : mise *f* à jour

upgrade ['ʌpˌgreɪd, ˌʌp'-] *vt* **-graded; -grading 1** IMPROVE : améliorer **2** PROMOTE : promouvoir

upheaval [ˌʌp'hi:vəl] *n* : bouleversement *m*

uphill [ˌʌp'hɪl] *adv* **go ~** : monter — **~** ['ʌpˌhɪl] *adj* **1** ASCENDING : qui monte **2** DIFFICULT : pénible

uphold [ˌʌp'ho:ld] *vt* **-held; -holding** : soutenir, maintenir

upholstery [ˌʌp'ho:lstəri] *n, pl* **-steries** : rembourrage *m*

upkeep ['ʌpˌki:p] *n* : entretien *m*

upon [ə'pɔn, ə'pɑn] *prep* **1** : sur **2 ~ leaving** : en partant

upper ['ʌpər] *adj* : supérieur

upper class *n* : aristocratie *f*

upper hand *n* **have the ~** : avoir le dessus

uppermost ['ʌpərˌmo:st] *adj* : le plus haut, le plus élevé

upright ['ʌpˌraɪt] *adj* : droit — **~** *n* : montant *m* (en construction)

uprising ['ʌpˌraɪzɪŋ] *n* : soulèvement *m*

uproar ['ʌpˌro:r] *n* : tumulte *m*

uproot [ˌʌp'ru:t, -'rʊt] *vt* : déraciner

upset [ˌʌp'sɛt] *vt* **-set; -setting 1** OVERTURN : renverser **2** DISRUPT : déranger **3** ANNOY : ennuyer — **~** *adj* **1** DISTRESSED : bouleversé **2** ANNOYED : ennuyé, vexé **3 have an ~ stomach** : avoir l'estomac dérangé — **~** ['ʌpˌsɛt] *n* : bouleversement *m*

upshot ['ʌpˌʃɑt] *n* : résultat *m*

upside down *adv* **1** : à l'envers **2 turn ~** : mettre sens dessus dessous — **upside–down** [ˌʌpˌsaɪd'daʊn] *adj* : à l'envers

upstairs [ˌʌp'stærz] *adv* : en haut — **~** ['ʌpˌstærz, ˌʌp'-] *adj* : d'en haut, à l'étage — **~** ['ʌpˌstærz, ˌʌp'-] *ns & pl* : étage *m*

upstart ['ʌpˌstɑrt] *n* : arriviste *mf*

upstream ['ʌp'stri:m] *adv* : en amont

up–to–date [ˌʌptə'deɪt] *adj* **1** : à jour **2** MODERN : moderne

uptown ['ʌp'taʊn] *adv* : dans les quartiers résidentiels

upturn ['ʌpˌtərn] *n* : amélioration *f*, reprise *f* (économique)

upward ['ʌpwərd] *or* **upwards** [-wərdz] *adv* **1** : vers le haut **2 ~ of** : plus de — **upward** *adj* : ascendant

uranium [jʊ'reɪniəm] *n* : uranium *m*

Uranus [jʊ'reɪnəs, 'jʊrənəs] *n* : Uranus *f*

urban ['ərbən] *adj* : urbain

urbane [ˌər'beɪn] *adj* : raffiné, courtois

urge ['ərdʒ] *vt* **urged; urging** : pousser, inciter — **~** *n* **1** DESIRE : envie *f* **2** IMPULSE : pulsion *f* — **urgency** ['ərdʒəntsi] *n, pl* **-cies** : urgence *f* — **urgent** ['ərdʒənt] *adj* **1** : urgent **2 be ~** : presser

urinal ['jʊrənəl, *esp Brit* jʊr'aɪnəl] *n* : urinoir *m*

urine ['jʊrən] *n* : urine *f* — **urinate** ['jʊrəˌneɪt] *vi* **-nated; -nating** : uriner

urn ['ərn] *n* : urne *f*

us ['ʌs] *pron* : nous

usable ['ju:zəbəl] *adj* : utilisable

usage ['ju:sɪdʒ, -zɪdʒ] *n* : usage *m*

use ['ju:z] *v* **used** ['ju:zd; *in phrase "used to" usually* 'ju:stu:]; **using** *vt* **1** : employer, utiliser, se servir de **2** CONSUME : consommer **3 ~ up** : épuiser — *vi* **she ~d to dance** : elle dansait avant — **~** ['ju:s] *n* **1** : emploi *m*, usage *m* **2** USEFULNESS : utilité *f* **3 in ~** : occupé **4 what's the ~?** : à quoi bon? — **used** ['ju:zd] *adj* **1** SECONDHAND : d'occasion **2 be ~ to** : avoir l'habitude de, être habitué à — **useful** ['ju:sfəl] *adj* : utile, pratique — **usefulness** ['ju:sfəlnəs] *n* : utilité *f* — **useless** ['ju:sləs] *adj* : inutile — **user** ['ju:zər] *n* : usager *m;* utilisateur *m*, -trice *f*

usher ['ʌʃər] *vt* **1** : conduire, accompagner **2 ~ in** : inaugurer — **~** *n* : huissier *m* (à un tribunal); placeur *m*, -ceuse *f* (au théâtre)

usual ['ju:ʒʊəl] *adj* **1** : habituel **2 as ~** : comme d'habitude — **usually** ['ju:ʒʊəli] *adv* : habituellement, d'habitude

usurp [jʊ'sərp, -'zərp] *vt* : usurper

utensil [jʊ'tɛntsəl] *n* : ustensile *m*

uterus ['ju:ṭərəs] *n, pl* **uteri** [-ˌraɪ] : utérus *m*

utility [ju:'tɪləṭi] *n, pl* **-ties 1** : utilité *f* **2** *or* **public ~** : service *m* public

utilize ['ju:ṭəlˌaɪz] *vt* **-lized; -lizing** : utiliser

utmost ['ʌtˌmo:st] *adj* **1** FARTHEST : extrême **2 of ~ importance** : de la plus haute importance — **~** *n* **do one's ~** : faire tout son possible

utopia [jʊ'to:piə] *n* : utopie *f* — **utopian** [jʊ'to:piən] *adj* : utopique

utter[1] ['ʌtər] *adj* : absolu, total

utter[2] *vt* : émettre (un son), pousser (un cri) — **utterance** ['ʌṭərənts] *n* : déclaration *f*, paroles *fpl*

utterly ['ʌtərli] *adv* : complètement

V

v ['vi:] *n, pl* **v's** *or* **vs** ['vi:z] : v *m*, vingt-deuxième lettre de l'alphabet

vacant ['veɪkənt] *adj* **1** AVAILABLE : libre **2** UNOCCUPIED : vacant — **vacancy** ['veɪkəntsi] *n, pl* **-cies 1** : chambre *f* disponible **2** : poste *m* vacant **3 no ~** : complet

vacate ['veɪˌkeɪt] *vt* **-cated; -cating** : quitter

vacation [veɪ'keɪʃən, və-] *n* : vacances *fpl*

vaccination [ˌvæksə'neɪʃən] *n* : vaccination *f* — **vaccinate** ['væksəˌneɪt] *vt* **-nated; -nating** : vacciner — **vaccine** [væk'si:n, 'vækˌ-] *n* : vaccin *m*

vacuum ['væˌkju:m, -kjəm] *n, pl* **vacuums** *or* **vacua** ['vækjʊə] : vide *m* — **~** *vt* : passer l'aspirateur sur — **vacuum cleaner** *n* : aspirateur *m*, balayeuse *f Can*

vagina [və'dʒaɪnə] *n, pl* **-nae** [-ˌni:, -ˌnaɪ] *or* **-nas** : vagin *m*

vagrant ['veɪgrənt] *n* : vagabond *m*, -bonde *f*

vague ['veɪg] *adj* **vaguer; vaguest** : vague

vain ['veɪn] *adj* **1** FUTILE : vain **2** CONCEITED : vaniteux

valentine ['vælənˌtaɪn] *n* : carte *f* de Saint-Valentin

valiant ['væljənt] *adj* : vaillant

valid ['væləd] *adj* : valable, valide — **validate** ['væləˌdeɪt] *vt* **-dated; -dating** : valider

valley ['væli] *n, pl* **-leys** : vallée *f*

valor *or Brit* **valour** ['vælər] *n* : bravoure *f*

value ['vælˌju:] *n* : valeur *f* — **~** *vt* **valued; valuing 1** : estimer, évaluer **2** APPRECIATE : apprécier — **valuable** ['væljʊəbəl, -jəbəl] *adj* **1** : de valeur **2** WORTHWHILE : précieux — **valuables** ['væljʊəbəlz, -jəbəlz] *npl* : objets *mpl* de valeur

valve ['vælv] *n* : valve *f* (d'un pneu), soupape *f*

vampire ['væmˌpaɪr] *n* : vampire *m*

van ['væn] *n* : camionnette *f*, fourgonnette *f*

vandal ['vændəl] *n* : vandale *mf* — **vandalism** ['vændəlˌɪzəm] *n* : vandalisme *m* — **vandalize** ['vændəlˌaɪz] *vt* **-ized; -izing** : saccager

vane ['veɪn] *n or* **weather ~** : girouette *f*

vanguard ['vænˌgɑrd] *n* : avant-garde *f*

vanilla [və'nɪlə, -'nɛ-] *n* : vanille *f*

vanish ['vænɪʃ] *vi* : disparaître

vanity ['vænəṭi] *n, pl* **-ties** : vanité *f*

vantage point ['væntɪdʒ] *n* : point *m* de vue

vapor ['veɪpər] *n* : vapeur *f*

variable ['vɛriəbəl] *adj* : variable — **~** *n* : variable *f* — **variant** ['vɛriənt] *n* : variante *f* — **variation** [ˌvɛri'eɪʃən] *n* : variation *f* — **varied** ['vɛrid] *adj* : varié, divers — **variety** [və'raɪəṭi] *n, pl* **-eties 1** DIVERSITY : variété *f* **2** SORT : espèce *f*, sorte *f* — **various** ['vɛriəs] *adj* : divers, varié

varnish ['vɑrnɪʃ] *n* : vernis *m* — **~** *vt* : vernir

vary ['vɛri] *v* **varied; varying** : varier

vase ['veɪs, 'veɪz, 'vɑz] *n* : vase *m*

vast ['væst] *adj* : vaste — **vastness** ['væstnəs] *n* : immensité *f*

vat ['væt] *n* : cuve *f*, bac *m*

vault ['vɔlt] *n* **1** ARCH : voûte *f* **2** *or* **bank ~** : chambre *f* forte

VCR [ˌvi:ˌsi:'ɑr] *n* (*v*ideo*c*assette *r*ecorder) : magnétoscope *m*

veal ['vi:l] *n* : veau *m*

veer ['vɪr] *vi* : virer

vegetable ['vɛdʒtəbəl, 'vɛdʒəṭə-] *adj* **1** : végétal **2 ~ soup** : soupe *f* aux légumes — **~** *n* : légume *m* — **vegetarian** [ˌvɛdʒə'tɛriən] *n* : végétarien *m*, -rienne *f* — **vegetation** [ˌvɛdʒə'teɪʃən] *n* : végétation *f*

vehement ['vi:əmənt] *adj* : véhément

vehicle ['vi:əkəl, 'vi:ˌhɪkəl] *n* : véhicule *m*

veil ['veɪl] *n* : voile *m* — **~** *vt* : voiler

vein ['veɪn] *n* **1** : veine *f* **2** : filon *m* (d'un minéral, etc.) **3** : nervure *f* (d'une feuille)

velocity [və'lɑsəṭi] *n, pl* **-ties** : vélocité *f*

velvet ['vɛlvət] *n* : velours *m* — **velvety** ['vɛlvəṭi] *adj* : velouté

vending machine ['vɛndɪŋ-] *n* : distributeur *m* automatique

vendor ['vɛndər] *n* : vendeur *m*, -deuse *f*

veneer [və'nɪr] *n* **1** : placage *m* (de bois) **2** FACADE : vernis *m*

venerable ['vɛnərəbəl] *adj* : vénérable — **venerate** ['vɛnəˌreɪt] *vt* **-ated; -ating** : vénérer

venereal [və'nɪriəl] *adj* : vénérien

venetian blind [və'ni:ʃən] *n* : store *m* vénitien

vengeance ['vɛndʒənts] *n* **1** : vengeance *f* **2 take ~ on** : se venger sur — **vengeful** ['vɛndʒfəl] *adj* : vengeur, vindicatif

venison ['vɛnəsən, -zən] *n* : venaison *f*

venom ['vɛnəm] *n* : venin *m* — **venomous** ['vɛnəməs] *adj* : venimeux

vent ['vɛnt] *vt* : décharger — **~** *n* **1** : orifice *m*, conduit *m* **2** *or* **air ~** : bouche *f* d'aération — **ventilate** ['vɛntəlˌeɪt] *vt* **-lated; -lating** : ventiler — **ventilation** [ˌvɛntəl'eɪʃən] *n* : ventilation *f*

venture ['vɛntʃər] *v* **-tured; -turing** *vt* RISK : risquer — *vi or* **~ out** : s'aventurer — **~** *n* : entreprise *f*

Venus ['vi:nəs] *n* : Vénus *f*

veranda *or* **verandah** [və'rændə] *n* : véranda *f*

verb ['vərb] *n* : verbe *m* — **verbal** ['vərbəl] *adj* : verbal — **verbatim** [vər'beɪṭəm] *adv & adj* : mot pour mot

verdict ['vərdɪkt] *n* : verdict *m*

verge ['vərʤ] *n* **1** EDGE : bordure *f* **2 on the ~ of** : sur le point de

verify ['vɛrə,faɪ] *vt* **-fied; -fying** : vérifier

vermin ['vərmən] *ns & pl* : vermine *f*

versatile ['vərsəṭəl] *adj* : polyvalent

verse ['vərs] *n* **1** STANZA : strophe *f* **2** POETRY : vers *mpl* **3** : verset *m* (de la Bible) — **versed** ['vərst] *adj* **be well ~ in** : être versé dans

version ['vərʒən] *n* : version *f*

versus ['vərsəs] *prep* : contre

vertebra ['vərṭəbrə] *n, pl* **-brae** [-,breɪ, -,bri:] *or* **-bras** : vertèbre *f*

vertical ['vərṭɪkəl] *adj* : vertical — **~** *n* : verticale *f*

vertigo ['vərṭɪ,go:] *n, pl* **-goes** *or* **-gos** : vertige *m*

very ['vɛri] *adv* **1** : très **2 ~ much** : beaucoup — **~** *adj* **1** EXACT : même **2 at the ~ least** : tout au moins **3 the ~ thought!** : quelle idée!

vessel ['vɛsəl] *n* **1** : vaisseau *m* **2** CONTAINER : récipient *m*

vest ['vɛst] *n* : gilet *m*

vestige ['vɛstɪʤ] *n* : vestige *m*

veteran ['vɛṭərən, 'vɛtrən] *n* : vétéran *m*, ancien combattant *m*

veterinarian [,vɛṭərə'nɛriən, ,vɛtrə-] *n* : vétérinaire *mf*

veto ['vi:ṭo] *n, pl* **-toes** : veto *m* — **~** *vt* : mettre son veto à

vex ['vɛks] *vt* **vexed; vexing** : vexer, contrarier

via ['vaɪə, 'vi:ə] *prep* : via, par

viable ['vaɪəbəl] *adj* : viable

vial ['vaɪəl] *n* : ampoule *f*

vibrant ['vaɪbrənt] *adj* : vibrant — **vibrate** ['vaɪ,breɪt] *vi* **-brated; -brating** : vibrer — **vibration** [vaɪ'breɪʃən] *n* : vibration *f*

vicar ['vɪkər] *n* : vicaire *m*

vice ['vaɪs] *n* : vice *m*

vice president *n* : vice-président *m*, -dente *f*

vice versa [,vaɪsɪ'vərsə, ,vaɪs'vər-] *adv* : vice versa

vicinity [və'sɪnəṭi] *n, pl* **-ties** : environs *mpl*

vicious ['vɪʃəs] *adj* **1** SAVAGE : brutal **2** MALICIOUS : méchant

victim ['vɪktəm] *n* : victime *f*

victor ['vɪktər] *n* : vainqueur *m* — **victorious** [vɪk'to:riəs] *adj* : victorieux — **victory** ['vɪktəri] *n, pl* **-ries** : victoire *f*

video ['vɪdi,o:] *n* : vidéo *f* — **~** *adj* : vidéo — **videocassette** [,vɪdiokə'sɛt] *n* : vidéocassette *f* — **videotape** ['vɪdio,teɪp] *n* : bande *f* vidéo — **~** *vt* **-taped; -taping** : enregistrer (sur magnétoscope)

vie ['vaɪ] *vi* **vied; vying** ['vaɪɪŋ] **~ for** : lutter pour

Vietnamese [vi,ɛtnə'mi:z, -'mi:s] *adj* : vietnamien

view ['vju:] *n* **1** : vue *f* **2** OPINION : opinion *f*, avis *m* **3 come into ~** : apparaître **4 in ~ of** : vu, étant donné — **~** *vt* **1** : voir **2** CONSIDER : considérer — **viewer** ['vju:ər] *n or* **television ~** : téléspectateur *m*, -trice *f* — **viewpoint** ['vju:,pɔɪnt] *n* : point *m* de vue

vigil ['vɪʤəl] *n* : veille *f* — **vigilance** ['vɪʤələnts] *n* : vigilance *f* — **vigilant** ['vɪʤələnt] *adj* : vigilant, attentif

vigor *or Brit* **vigour** ['vɪgər] *n* : vigueur *f* — **vigorous** ['vɪgərəs] *adj* : vigoureux

vile ['vaɪl] *adj* **viler; vilest 1** BASE : vil **2** AWFUL : abominable, exécrable

villa ['vɪlə] *n* : villa *f*

village ['vɪlɪʤ] *n* : village *m* — **villager** ['vɪlɪʤər] *n* : villageois *m*, -geoise *f*

villain ['vɪlən] *n* : scélérat *m*, -rate *f*; méchant *m*, -chante *f*

vindicate ['vɪndə,keɪt] *vt* **-cated; -cating** : justifier

vindictive [vɪn'dɪktɪv] *adj* : vindicatif

vine ['vaɪn] *n* : vigne *f*

vinegar ['vɪnɪgər] *n* : vinaigre *m*

vineyard ['vɪnjərd] *n* : vignoble *m*

vintage ['vɪntɪʤ] *n* **1** *or* **~ wine** : vin *m* de grand cru **2** *or* **~ year** : millésime *m*

vinyl ['vaɪnəl] *n* : vinyle *m*

violate ['vaɪə,leɪt] *vt* **-lated; -lating** : violer — **violation** [,vaɪə'leɪʃən] *n* : violation *f*

violence ['vaɪələnts] *n* : violence *f* — **violent** ['vaɪələnt] *adj* : violent

violet ['vaɪələt] *adj* : violet — **~** *n* **1** : violette *f* (plante) **2** : violet *m* (couleur)

violin [,vaɪə'lɪn] *n* : violon *m* — **violinist** [,vaɪə'lɪnɪst] *n* : violoniste *mf*

VIP [,vi:,aɪ'pi:] *n, pl* **VIPs** [-'pi:z] (*very important person*) : personnage *m* de marque

viper ['vaɪpər] *n* : vipère *f*

virgin ['vərʤən] *adj* : vierge — **~** *n* : vierge *f* — **virginity** [vər'ʤɪnəṭi] *n, pl* **-ties** : virginité *f*

virile ['vɪrəl, -,aɪl] *adj* : viril

virtual ['vərtʃuəl] *adj* : virtuel (en informatique) — **virtually** ['vərtʃuəli] *adv* : pratiquement

virtue ['vər,tʃu:] *n* **1** : vertu *f* **2 by ~ of** : en raison de

virtuoso [,vərtʃu'o:,so:, -,zo:] *n, pl* **-sos** *or* **-si** [-,si:, -,zi:] : virtuose *mf*

virtuous ['vərtʃuəs] *adj* : vertueux

virulent ['vɪrələnt, -jələnt] *adj* : virulent

virus ['vaɪrəs] *n* : virus *m*

visa ['vi:zə, -sə] *n* : visa *m*

viscous ['vɪskəs] *adj* : visqueux

vise *or Brit* **vice** ['vaɪs] *n* : étau *m*

visible ['vɪzəbəl] *adj* : visible — **visibility** [,vɪzə'bɪləṭi] *n, pl* **-ties** : visibilité *f*

vision ['vɪʒən] *n* : vision *f* — **visionary** ['vɪʒə,nɛri] *adj* : visionnaire

visit ['vɪzət] *vt* : rendre visite à (qqn), visiter (un lieu) — **~** *n* : visite *f* — **visitor** ['vɪzəṭər] *n* : visiteur *m*, -teuse *f*

visor ['vaɪzər] *n* : visière *f*

vista ['vɪstə] *n* : vue *f*

visual ['vɪʒuəl] *adj* : visuel — **visualize** ['vɪʒuə,laɪz] *vt* **-ized; -izing** : visualiser

vital ['vaɪṭəl] *adj* **1** : vital **2** ESSENTIAL : essentiel — **vitality** [vaɪ'tæləṭi] *n, pl* **-ties** : vitalité *f*

vitamin ['vaɪṭəmən] *n* : vitamine *f*

vivacious [və'veɪʃəs, vaɪ-] *adj* : vif, animé

vivid ['vɪvəd] *adj* : vivant, vif

vocabulary [vo:'kæbjə,lɛri] *n, pl* **-laries** : vocabulaire *m*

vocal ['vo:kəl] *adj* **1** : vocal **2** OUTSPOKEN : franc — **vocal cords** *npl* : cordes *fpl* vocales — **vocalist** ['vo:kəlɪst] *n* : chanteur *m*, -teuse *f*

vocation [vo'keɪʃən] *n* **1** : vocation *f* (religieuse) **2** OCCUPATION : profession *f*, métier *m* — **vocational** [vo'keɪʃənəl] *adj* : professionnel

vodka ['vɑdkə] *n* : vodka *m*

vogue ['vo:g] *n* **1** : vogue *f*, mode *f* **2 be in ~** : être à la mode

voice ['vɔɪs] *n* : voix *f* — **~** ['vɔɪs] *vt* **voiced; voicing** : exprimer, formuler

void ['vɔɪd] *adj* **1** NULL : nul **2 ~ of** : dépourvu de — **~** *n* : vide *m* — **~** *vt* ANNUL : annuler

volatile ['vɑləṭəl] *adj* : volatil, instable

volcano [vɑl'keɪ,no:, vɔl-] *n, pl* **-noes** *or* **-nos** : volcan *m* — **volcanic** [vɑl'kænɪk, vɔl-] *adj* : volcanique

volley ['vɑli] *n, pl* **-leys** : volée *f* — **volleyball** ['vɑli,bɔl] *n* : volley-ball *m*

volt ['vo:lt] *n* : volt *m* — **voltage** ['vo:ltɪʤ] *n* **1** : voltage *m* **2 high ~** : de haute tension

volume ['vɑljəm, -,ju:m] *n* : volume *m*

voluntary ['vɑlən,tɛri] *adj* **1** : volontaire **2** UNPAID : bénévole — **volunteer** [,vɑlən'tɪr] *n* : volontaire *mf* — **~** *vt* : offrir — *vi* : se porter volontaire

voluptuous [və'lʌptʃuəs] *adj* : voluptueux

vomit ['vɑmət] *n* : vomi *m* — **~** *v* : vomir

voracious [vɔ'reɪʃəs, və-] *adj* : vorace

vote ['vo:t] *n* **1** : vote *m* **2** SUFFRAGE : droit *m* de vote — **~** *v* **voted; voting** : voter — **voter** ['vo:ṭər] *n* : électeur *m*, -trice *f* — **voting** ['vo:ṭɪŋ] *n* : scrutin *m*, vote *m*

vouch ['vaʊtʃ] *vi* **~ for** : répondre de — **voucher** ['vaʊtʃər] *n* : bon *m*

vow ['vaʊ] *n* : vœu *m*, serment *m* — **~** *vt* : jurer

vowel ['vaʊəl] *n* : voyelle *f*

voyage ['vɔɪɪʤ] *n* : voyage *m*

vulgar ['vʌlgər] *adj* **1** COMMON : vulgaire **2** CRUDE : grossier — **vulgarity** [,vʌl'gærəṭi] *n, pl* **-ties** : vulgarité *f*

vulnerable ['vʌlnərəbəl] *adj* : vulnérable — **vulnerability** [,vʌlnərə'bɪləṭi] *n* : vulnérabilité *f*

vulture ['vʌltʃər] *n* : vautour *m*

vying → **vie**

W

w ['dʌbəl,ju:] *n, pl* **w's** *or* **ws** [-,ju:z] : w *m*, vingt-troisième lettre de l'alphabet

wad ['wɑd] *n* : tampon *m* (d'ouate, etc.), liasse *f* (de billets)

waddle ['wɑdəl] *vi* **-dled; -dling** : se dandiner

wade ['weɪd] *v* **waded; wading** *vi* : patauger — *vt or* **~ across** : traverser

wafer ['weɪfər] *n* : gaufrette *f*

waffle ['wɑfəl] *n* : gaufre *f*

waft ['wɑft, 'wæft] *vi* : flotter

wag ['wæg] *vt* **wagged; wagging** : agiter, remuer

wage ['weɪʤ] *n or* **wages** *npl* : salaire *m*, paie *f* — **~** *vt* **waged; waging ~ war** : faire la guerre

wager ['weɪʤər] *n* : pari *m* — **~** *v* : parier

wagon ['wægən] *n* : chariot *m*

wail ['weɪl] *vi* : se lamenter — **~** *n* : lamentation *f*

waist ['weɪst] *n* : taille *f* — **waistline** ['weɪst,laɪn] *n* : taille *f*

wait ['weɪt] *vi* : attendre — *vt* **1** AWAIT : attendre **2 ~ tables** : servir à table — **~** *n* **1** : attente *f* **2 lie in ~ for** : guetter — **waiter** ['weɪṭər] *n* : serveur *m*, garçon *m* — **waiting room** *n* : salle *f* d'attente — **waitress** ['weɪtrəs] *n* : serveuse *f*

waive ['weɪv] *vt* **waived; waiving** : renoncer à

wake[1] ['weɪk] *v* **woke** ['wo:k]; **woken** ['wo:kən] *or* **waked; waking** *vi or* **~ up** : se réveiller — *vt* : réveiller — **~** *n* : veillée *f* funèbre

wake[2] *n* **1** : sillage *m* (laissé par un bateau) **2 in the ~ of** : à la suite de

waken ['weɪkən] *vt* : réveiller — *vi* : se réveiller

walk ['wɔk] *vi* **1** : marcher, aller à pied **2** STROLL : se promener — *vt* **1** : faire à pied **2** : raccompagner (qqn), promener (un chien) — **~** *n* **1** : marche *f*, promenade *f* **2** PATH : chemin *m* **3** GAIT : démarche *f* (d'une personne) — **walker** ['wɔkər] *n* : marcheur *m*, -cheuse *f*; promeneur *m*, -neuse *f* — **walking stick** *n* : canne *f* — **walkout** ['wɔk,aʊt] *n* STRIKE : grève *f* — **walk out** *vi* **1** STRIKE : faire la grève **2** LEAVE : partir, sortir **3 ~ on** : quitter, abandonner

wall ['wɔl] *n* **1** : mur *m* (extérieur), paroi *f* (intérieure) **2** : remparts *mpl* (d'une ville)

wallet ['wɑlət] *n* : portefeuille *m*

Walloon [wɑ'lu:n] *adj* : wallon

wallop ['wɑləp] *vt* : donner une raclée à — **~** *n* : raclée *f*

wallow ['wɑ,lo:] *vi* **1** : se vautrer **2 ~ in** : s'apitoyer sur

wallpaper ['wɔl,peɪpər] *n* : tapisserie *f* — **~** *vt* : tapisser

walnut ['wɔl,nʌt] *n* **1** : noyer *m* (arbre) **2** : noix *f* (fruit)

walrus ['wɔlrəs, 'wɑl-] *n, pl* **-rus** *or* **-ruses** : morse *m*

waltz ['wɔlts] *n* : valse *f* — **~** *vi* : valser

wan ['wɑn] *adj* **wanner; wannest** : blême, pâle

wand ['wɑnd] *n* : baguette *f* (magique)

wander ['wɑndər] *vi* **1** : se promener, se balader **2** STRAY : errer — *vt* : parcourir — **wanderer** ['wɑndərər] *n* : vagabond *m*, -bonde *f*

wane ['weɪn] *vi* **waned; waning** : diminuer — **~** *n* **be on the ~** : être sur le déclin

want ['wɑnt, 'wɔnt] *vt* **1** DESIRE : vouloir **2** NEED : avoir besoin de **3** LACK : manquer de **4 ~ed** : recherché par la police — **~** *n* **1** NEED : besoin *m* **2** LACK : manque *m* **3** DESIRE : désir *m* **4 for ~ of** : faute de — **wanting** ['wɑntɪŋ, 'wɔn-] *adj* **be ~** : manquer

wanton ['wɑntən, 'wɔn-] *adj* **1** LEWD : lascif **2 ~ cruelty** : cruauté *f* gratuite

war ['wɔr] *n* : guerre *f*

ward ['wɔrd] *n* **1** : salle *f* (d'un hôpital, etc.) **2** : circonscription *f* électorale **3 ~ of the court** : pupille *f* — **~** *vt or* **~ off** : parer, éviter — **warden** ['wɔrdən] *n* **1** : gardien *m*, -dienne *f* **2** *or* **prison ~** : directeur *m*, -trice *f* de prison

wardrobe ['wɔrd,ro:b] *n* **1** CLOSET : armoire *f*, penderie *f* **2** CLOTHES : garde-robe *f*

warehouse ['wær,haʊs] *n* : entrepôt *m*, magasin *m* — **wares** ['wærz] *npl* : marchandises *fpl*

warfare ['wɔr,fær] *n* : guerre *f*

warhead ['wɔr,hɛd] *n* : ogive *f*

warily ['wærəli] *adv* : avec précaution

warlike ['wɔr,laɪk] *adj* : guerrier, belliqueux

warm ['wɔrm] *adj* **1** : chaud **2** LUKEWARM : tiède **3** CARING : chaleureux **4 I feel ~** : j'ai chaud — **~** *vt or* **~ up** : chauffer, réchauffer — *vi* **1** *or* **~ up** : se réchauffer **2 ~ to** : se prendre de sympathie pour (qqn), s'enthousiasmer pour (qqch) — **warm–blooded** ['wɔrm'blʌdəd] *adj* : à sang chaud — **warmhearted** ['wɔrm'hɑrṭəd] *adj* : chaleureux — **warmly** ['wɔrmli] *adv* **1** : chaleureusement **2 dress ~** : s'habiller chaudement — **warmth** ['wɔrmpθ] *n* **1** : chaleur *f* **2** AFFECTION : affection *f*

warn ['wɔrn] *vt* **1** : avertir **2** INFORM : aviser — **warning** ['wɔrnɪŋ] *n* **1** : avertissement *m* **2** NOTICE : avis *m*

warp ['wɔrp] *vt* **1** : voiler (bois, etc.) **2** DISTORT : déformer

warrant ['wɔrənt] *n* **1** : autorisation *f* **2 arrest ~** : mandat *m* d'arrêt — **~** *vt* : justifier — **warranty** ['wɔrənti, ,wɔrən'ti:] *n, pl* **-ties** : garantie *f*

warrior ['wɔriər] *n* : guerrier *m*, -rière *f*

warship ['wɔr,ʃɪp] *n* : navire *m* de guerre

wart ['wɔrt] *n* : verrue *f*

wartime ['wɔr,taɪm] *n* : temps *m* de guerre

wary ['wæri] *adj* **warier; -est 1** : prudent, circonspect **2 be ~ of** : se méfier de

was → **be**

wash ['wɔʃ, 'wɑʃ] *vt* **1** : laver, se laver **2 ~ away** : emporter — *vi* : se laver — **~** *n* **1** : lavage *m* **2** LAUNDRY : linge *m* sale — **washable** ['wɔʃəbəl, 'wɑ-] *adj* : lavable — **washcloth** ['wɔʃ,klɔθ, 'wɑʃ-] *n* : gant *m* de toilette, débarbouillette *f Can* — **washed–out** ['wɔʃt'aʊt, 'wɑʃt-] *adj* **1** : décoloré **2** EXHAUSTED : épuisé — **washer** ['wɔʃər, 'wɑ-] *n* **1** → **washing machine 2** : rondelle *f*, joint *m* — **washing machine** *n* : machine *f* à laver — **washroom** ['wɔʃ,ru:m, 'wɑʃ-, -,rʊm] *n* : toilettes *fpl*

wasn't ['wʌzənt] (*contraction of* **was not**) → **be**

wasp ['wɑsp] *n* : guêpe *f*

waste ['weɪst] *v* **wasted; wasting** *vt* : gaspiller, perdre — *vi or* **~ away** : dépérir — **~** *adj* : de rebut — **~** *n* **1** : gaspillage *m* (d'argent), perte *f* (de temps) **2** RUBBISH : déchets *mpl*, ordures *fpl* — **wastebasket** ['weɪst,bæskət] *n* : corbeille *f* à papier — **wasteful** ['weɪstfəl] *adj* : gaspilleur — **wasteland** ['weɪst,lænd, -lənd] *n* : terre *f* inculte

watch ['wɑtʃ] *vi* **1** : regarder **2** *or* **keep ~** : faire le guet **3 ~ out** : faire attention — *vt* **1** : regarder **2** *or* **~ over** : veiller — **~** *n* **1** : montre *f* **2** SURVEILLANCE : surveillance *f* — **watchdog** ['wɑtʃ,dɔg] *n* : chien *m* de garde, chienne *f* de garde — **watchful** ['wɑtʃfəl] *adj* : vigilant — **watchman** ['wɑtʃmən] *n, pl* **-men** [-mən, -,mɛn] : gardien *m*

water ['wɔṭər, 'wɑ-] *n* : eau *f* — **~** *vt* **1** : arroser (un jardin, etc.) **2** *or* **~ down** DILUTE : diluer, couper (du vin, etc.) — *vi* **1** : larmoyer (se dit des yeux) **2 my mouth is ~ing** : j'ai l'eau à la bouche — **watercolor** ['wɔṭər,kʌlər, 'wɑ-] *n* : aquarelle *f* — **watercress** ['wɔṭər,krɛs, cwɑ-] *n* : cresson *m* — **waterfall** ['wɔṭər,fɔl, 'wɑ-] *n* : chute *f* (d'eau), cascade *f* — **water lily** *n* : nénuphar *m* — **watermark** ['wɔṭər,mɑrk, 'wɑ-] *n* : filigrane *m* — **watermelon** ['wɔṭər,mɛlən, 'wɑ-] *n* : pastèque *f*, melon *m* d'eau — **waterproof** ['wɔṭər,pru:f, 'wɑ-] *adj* : imperméable — **watershed** ['wɔṭər,ʃɛd, 'wɑ-] *n* **1** : ligne *m* de partage des eaux **2** : moment *m* critique — **waterskiing** ['wɔṭər,ski:ɪŋ, 'wɑ-] *n* : ski *m* nautique — **watertight** ['wɔṭər,taɪt, wɑ-] *adj* : étanche — **waterway** ['wɔṭər,weɪ, 'wɑ-] *n* : cours *m* d'eau navigable — **waterworks** ['wɔṭər'wərks, wɑ-] *npl* : système *m* hydraulique — **watery** ['wɔṭəri, 'wɑ-] *adj* **1** : larmoyant (se dit des yeux) **2** DILUTED : trop liquide, dilué

watt ['wɑt] *n* : watt *m* — **wattage** ['wɑṭɪʤ] *n* : puissance *f* en watts

wave ['weɪv] *v* **waved; waving** *vi* **1** : faire un signe de la main **2** : flotter au vent (se dit d'un drapeau) — *vt* **1** SHAKE : agiter, brandir **2** CURL : onduler **3** SIGNAL : faire signe à — **~** *n* **1** : vague *f* (d'eau) **2** CURL : ondulation *f* **3** : onde *f* (en physique) **4** : geste *m* de la main **4** SURGE : vague *f* — **wavelength** ['weɪv,lɛŋkθ] *n* : longueur *f* d'onde

waver ['weɪvər] *vi* : vaciller, chanceler

wavy ['weɪvi] *adj* **wavier; -est** : ondulé

wax[1] ['wæks] *vi* : croître (se dit de la lune)

wax[2] *n* : cire *f* — **~** *vt* : cirer (le plancher, etc.), farter (des skis) — **waxy** ['wæksi] *adj* **waxier; -est** : cireux

way ['weɪ] *n* **1** : chemin *m* **2** MEANS : façon *f*, manière *f* **3 by the ~** : à propos **4 by ~ of** : par, via **5 come a long ~** : faire de grands progrès **6 get in the ~** : gêner le passage **7 get one's own ~** : arriver à ses fins **8 out of the ~** REMOTE : éloigné, isolé **9 which ~ did he go?** : où est-il passé?

we ['wi:] *pron* : nous

weak ['wi:k] *adj* : faible — **weaken** ['wi:kən] *vt* : affaiblir — *vi* : s'affaiblir, faiblir — **weakling** ['wi:klɪŋ] *n* : mauviette *f* — **weakly** ['wi:kli] *adv* : faiblement — **weakness** ['wi:knəs] *n* **1** : faiblesse *f* **2** FLAW : défaut *m*

wealth ['wɛlθ] *n* **1** : richesse *f* **2 a ~ of** : une profusion de — **wealthy** ['wɛlθi] *adj* **wealthier; -est** : riche

wean ['wi:n] *vt* : sevrer (un bébé)

weapon ['wɛpən] *n* : arme *f*

wear ['wær] *v* **wore** ['wor]; **worn** ['worn]; **wearing** *vt* **1** : mettre, porter **2 ~ oneself out** : s'épuiser **3** *or* **~ out** : user — *vi* **1** LAST : durer **2 ~ off** : diminuer **3 ~ out** : s'user, se détériorer — **~** *n* **1** USE : usage *m* **2** CLOTHES : vêtements *mpl* — **wear and tear** : usure *f*

weary ['wɪri] *adj* **-rier; -est** : fatigué, las — **~** *vt* **-ried; -rying** : lasser, fatiguer — **weariness** ['wɪrinəs] *n* : lassitude *f* — **wearisome** ['wɪrisəm] *adj* : fastidieux

weasel ['wi:zəl] *n* : belette *f*

weather ['wɛðər] *n* **1** : temps *m* **2 be under the ~** : ne pas être dans son assiette — **~** *vt* OVERCOME : surmonter — **weather–beaten** ['wɛðər,bi:tən] *adj* **1** : battu, usé (par les intempéries) **2** : hâlé (se dit d'un visage) — **weatherman** ['wɛðər,mæn] *n, pl* **-men** [-mən, -,mɛn] : météorologiste *mf* — **weather vane** *n* : girouette *f*

weave ['wi:v] *v* **wove** ['wo:v] *or* **weaved; woven** ['wo:vən] *or* **weaved; weaving** *vt* **1** : tisser **2 ~ one's way through** : se faufiler à travers — *vi* : tisser — **~** *n* : tissage *m*

web ['wɛb] *n* 1 : toile *f* (d'araignée) 2 : palmure *f* (d'un oiseau) 3 NETWORK : réseau *m* 4 **Web** → **World Wide Web**
webbed ['wɛbd] *adj* : palmé
webmaster ['wɛb,mæstər] *n* : webmestre *m*
wed ['wɛd] *v* **wedded; wedding** *vt* : se marier à, épouser — *vi* : marier
we'd ['wi:d] (*contraction of* **we had, we should,** *or* **we would**) → **have, should, would**
wedding ['wɛdɪŋ] *n* : mariage *m*, noces *fpl*
wedge ['wɛʤ] *n* 1 : cale *f* 2 PIECE : morceau *m* (de fromage), part *m* (de gâteau, etc.) — ~ *vt* **wedged; wedging** 1 : caler, fixer 2 CRAM : enfoncer
Wednesday ['wɛnz,deɪ, -di] *n* : mercredi *m*
wee ['wi:] *adj* 1 : très petit 2 **in the ~ hours** : aux petites heures (du matin)
weed ['wi:d] *n* : mauvaise herbe *f* — ~ *vt* 1 : désherber 2 **~ out** : se débarrasser de
week ['wi:k] *n* : semaine *f* — **weekday** ['wi:k,deɪ] *n* : jour *m* de semaine — **weekend** ['wi:k,ɛnd] *n* : fin *f* de semaine, weekend *m* — **weekly** ['wi:kli] *adv* : à la semaine, chaque semaine — ~ *adj* : hebdomadaire — ~ *n, pl* **-lies** : hebdomadaire *m*
weep ['wi:p] *vi* **wept** ['wɛpt]; **weeping** : pleurer — **weeping willow** *n* : saule *m* pleureur — **weepy** ['wi:pi] *adj* **weepier; -est** : au bord des larmes
weigh ['weɪ] *vt* 1 : peser 2 CONSIDER : considérer 3 **~ down** : accabler — *vi* 1 : peser 2 **~ on s.o.'s mind** : préoccuper qqn
weight ['weɪt] *n* 1 : poids *m* 2 IMPORTANCE : influence *f* 3 **gain ~** : engraisser 4 **lose ~** : maigrir — **weighty** ['weɪt̬i] *adj* **weightier; -est** 1 HEAVY : pesant, lourd 2 IMPORTANT : de poids
weird ['wɪrd] *adj* 1 : mystérieux 2 STRANGE : étrange, bizarre
welcome ['wɛlkəm] *vt* **-comed; -coming** : accueillir, souhaiter la bienvenue à — ~ *adj* 1 : bienvenu 2 **you're ~** : de rien, je vous en prie — ~ *n* : accueil *m*
weld ['wɛld] *vt* : souder — ~ *n* : soudure *f*
welfare ['wɛl,fær] *n* 1 WELL-BEING : bien-être *m* 2 AID : aide *f* sociale, assistance *f* publique
well[1] ['wɛl] *n* : puits *m* (d'eau, de pétrole, etc.) — ~ *vi or* **~ up** : monter, jaillir
well[2] *adv* **better** ['bɛt̬ər]; **best** ['bɛst] 1 : bien 2 **as ~** : aussi — ~ *adj* : bien — ~ *interj* 1 (*used to introduce a remark*) : bon, bien, enfin 2 (*used to express surprise*) : ça alors!, eh bien!
we'll ['wi:l, wɪl] (*contraction of* **we shall** *or* **we will**) → **shall, will**
well-being ['wɛl'bi:ɪŋ] *n* : bien-être *m* — **well-bred** ['wɛl'brɛd] *adj* : bien élevé, poli — **well-done** ['wɛl'dʌn] *adj* 1 : bien fait 2 : bien cuit (se dit de la viande, etc.) — **well-known** ['wɛl'no:n] *adj* : bien connu — **well-meaning** ['wɛl'mi:nɪŋ] *adj* : bien intentionné — **well-off** ['wɛl'ɔf] *adj* : prospère — **well-rounded** ['wɛl'raʊndəd] *adj* : complet — **well-to-do** [,wɛltə'du:] *adj* : riche, aisé
Welsh ['wɛlʃ] *adj* : gallois — ~ *n* : gallois *m* (langue)
welt ['wɛlt] *n* : zébrure *f*, marque *f* (sur la peau)
went → **go**
wept → **weep**
were → **be**
we're ['wɪr, 'wər, 'wi:ər] (*contraction of* **we are**) → **be**
weren't ['wərənt, 'wərnt] (*contraction of* **were not**) → **be**
west ['wɛst] *adv* : à l'ouest, vers l'ouest — ~ *adj* : ouest, d'ouest — ~ *n* 1 : ouest *m* 2 **the West** : l'Ouest *m*, l'Occident *m* — **westerly** ['wɛstərli] *adv* : vers l'ouest — ~ *adj* : à l'ouest, d'ouest — **western** ['wɛstərn] *adj* 1 : ouest, de l'ouest, occidental 2 **Western** : de l'Ouest, occidental — **Westerner** ['wɛstərnər] *n* : habitant *m*, -tante *f* de l'Ouest — **westward** ['wɛstwərd] *adv & adj* : vers l'ouest
wet ['wɛt] *adj* **wetter; wettest** 1 : mouillé 2 RAINY : pluvieux 3 **~ paint** : peinture *f* fraîche — ~ *vt* **wet** *or* **wetted; wetting** : mouiller, humecter
we've ['wi:v] (*contraction of* **we have**) → **have**
whack ['hwæk] *vt* : donner une claque à — ~ *n* : coup *m*, claque *f*
whale ['hweɪl] *n, pl* **whales** *or* **whale** : baleine *f*
wharf ['hwɔrf] *n, pl* **wharves** ['hwɔrvz] : quai *m*
what ['hwɑt, 'hwʌt] *adj* 1 (*used in questions and exclamations*) : quel 2 WHATEVER : tout — ~ *pron* 1 (*used in questions*) : qu'est-ce que, qu'est-ce qui 2 (*used in indirect statements*) : ce que, ce qui 3 **~ does it cost?** : combien est-ce que ça coûte? 4 **~ for?** : pourquoi? 5 **~ if** : et si — **whatever** [hwɑt'ɛvər, hwʌt-] *adj* 1 : n'importe quel 2 **there's no chance ~** : il n'y a pas la moindre possibilité 3 **nothing ~** : rien du tout — ~ *pron* 1 ANYTHING : (tout) ce que 2 (*used in questions*) : qu'est-ce que, qu'est-ce qui 3 **~ it may be** : quoi que ce soit — **whatsoever** [,hwɑtso'ɛvər, ,hwʌt-] *adj & pron* → **whatever**
wheat ['hwi:t] *n* : blé *m*
wheedle ['hwi:dəl] *vt* **-dled; -dling** : enjôler
wheel ['hwi:l] *n* 1 : roue *f* 2 *or* **steering ~** : volant *m* — ~ *vt* : pousser (quelque chose sur des roulettes) — **wheelbarrow** ['hwi:l,bær,o:] *n* : brouette *f* — **wheelchair** ['hwi:l,ʧær] *n* : fauteuil *m* roulant
wheeze ['hwi:z] *vi* **wheezed; wheezing** : respirer bruyamment
when ['hwɛn] *adv* : quand — ~ *conj* 1 : quand, lorsque 2 **the days ~ I go to the bank** : les jours où je vais à la banque — ~ *pron* : quand — **whenever** [hwɛn'ɛvər] *adv* : quand (donc) — ~ *conj* 1 : chaque fois que 2 **~ you like** : quand vous voulez
where ['hwɛr] *adv* 1 : où 2 **~ are you going?** : où vas-tu? — ~ *conj & pron* : où — **whereabouts** ['hwɛrə,baʊts] *adv* : où (donc) — ~ *ns & pl* **know s.o.'s ~** : savoir où se trouve qqn
whereas [hwɛr'æz] *conj* : alors que, tandis que
wherever [hwɛr'ɛvər] *conj* 1 : n'importe où 2 WHERE : où, où donc
whet ['hwɛt] *vt* **whetted; whetting** 1 : affûter, aiguiser (un couteau) 2 **~ one's appetite** : ouvrir l'appétit
whether ['hwɛðər] *conj* 1 : si 2 **we doubt ~ he'll show up** : nous doutons qu'il vienne 3 **~ you like it or not** : que cela te plaise ou non
which ['hwɪʧ] *adj* 1 : quel 2 **in ~ case** : auquel cas — ~ *pron* 1 (*used in questions*) : lequel, quel 2 (*used in relative clauses*) : qui, que — **whichever** [hwɪʧ'ɛvər] *adj* : peu importe quel — ~ *pron* : quel que
whiff ['hwɪf] *n* 1 PUFF : bouffée *f* 2 SMELL : odeur *f*
while ['hwaɪl] *n* 1 : temps *m*, moment *m* 2 **be worth one's ~** : valoir la peine 3 **in a ~** : sous peu — ~ *conj* 1 : pendant que 2 WHEREAS : tandis que, alors que 3 ALTHOUGH : bien que — ~ *vt* **whiled; whiling ~ away** : (faire) passer
whim ['hwɪm] *n* : caprice *m*, lubie *f*
whimper ['hwɪmpər] *vi* : gémir, pleurnicher *fam* — ~ *n* : gémissement *m*
whimsical ['hwɪmzɪkəl] *adj* : capricieux, fantasque
whine ['hwaɪn] *vi* **whined; whining** 1 WHIMPER : gémir 2 COMPLAIN : se plaindre — ~ *n* : gémissement *m*
whip ['hwɪp] *v* **whipped; whipping** *vt* 1 : fouetter 2 BEAT : battre (des œufs, etc.) — *vi* FLAP : battre, claquer — ~ *n* : fouet *m*
whir ['hwər] *vi* **whirred; whirring** : ronronner, vrombir
whirl ['hwərl] *vi* : tourner, tourbillonner — ~ *n* : tourbillon *m* — **whirlpool** ['hwərl,pu:l] *n* : tourbillon *m* (d'eau) — **whirlwind** ['hwərl,wɪnd] *n* : tourbillon *m* (de vent)
whisk ['hwɪsk] *vt* 1 : fouetter (des œufs) 2 *or* **~ away** : enlever — ~ *n* : fouet *m* (en cuisine)
whisker ['hwɪskər] *n* 1 : poil *m* de barbe 2 **~s** *npl* : barbe *f* (d'un homme), moustaches *fpl* (d'un chat, etc.)
whiskey *or* **whisky** ['hwɪski] *n, pl* **-keys** *or* **-kies** : whisky *m*
whisper ['hwɪspər] *v* : chuchoter — ~ *n* : chuchotement *m*
whistle ['hwɪsəl] *v* **-tled; -tling** : siffler — ~ *n* 1 : sifflement *m* (son) 2 : sifflet *m* (objet)
white ['hwaɪt] *adj* **whiter; -est** : blanc — ~ *n* 1 : blanc *m* (couleur) 2 *or* **~ person** : Blanc *m*, Blanche *f* — **white-collar** ['hwaɪt'kɑlər] *adj* : de bureau — **whiten** ['hwaɪtən] *v* : blanchir — **whiteness** ['hwaɪtnəs] *n* : blancheur *f* — **whitewash** ['hwaɪt,wɔʃ] *n* : lait *m* de chaux
whittle ['hwɪt̬əl] *vt* **-tled; -tling ~ down** : réduire
whiz *or* **whizz** ['hwɪz] *vi* **whizzed; whizzing** 1 BUZZ : bourdonner 2 **~ by** : passer à toute vitesse — ~ *or* **whizz** *n, pl* **whizzes** : expert *m*, as *m* — **whiz kid** *n* : jeune prodige *m*
who ['hu:] *pron* 1 (*used in direct and indirect questions*) : qui, qui est-ce qui 2 (*used in relative clauses*) : qui — **whoever** [hu:'ɛvər] *pron* 1 : qui que ce soit, quiconque 2 (*used in questions*) : qui
whole ['ho:l] *adj* 1 : entier 2 INTACT : intact 3 **a ~ lot** : beaucoup — ~ *n* 1 : tout *m*, ensemble *m* 2 **as a ~** : dans son ensemble 3 **on the ~** : en général — **wholehearted** ['ho:l'hɑrt̬əd] *adj* : sincère — **wholesale** ['ho:l,seɪl] *n* : vente *f* en gros — ~ *adj* : de gros — ~ *adv* : en gros — **wholesaler** ['ho:l,seɪlər] *n* : grossiste *mf* — **wholesome** ['ho:lsəm] *adj* : sain — **whole wheat** *adj* : de blé entier — **wholly** ['ho:li] *adv* : entièrement
whom ['hu:m] *pron* 1 (*used in direct and indirect questions*) : qui, à qui 2 (*used in relative clauses*) : que
whooping cough ['hu:pɪŋ] *n* : coqueluche *f*
whore ['hor] *n* : prostituée *f*
whose ['hu:z] *adj* 1 (*used in questions*) : de qui, à qui 2 (*used in relative clauses*) : dont — ~ *pron* : à qui
why ['hwaɪ] *adv* : pourquoi — ~ *n, pl* **whys** : pourquoi *m* — ~ *conj* : pourquoi — ~ *interj* (*used to express surprise*) : mais!, tiens!
wick ['wɪk] *n* : mèche *f*
wicked ['wɪkəd] *adj* 1 : méchant 2 MISCHIEVOUS : espiègle 3 TERRIBLE : terrible — **wickedness** ['wɪkədnəs] *n* : méchanceté *f*
wicker ['wɪkər] *n* : osier *m*
wide ['waɪd] *adj* **wider; widest** 1 : de large, de largeur 2 VAST : étendu, vaste — ~ *adv* 1 **~ apart** : très écarté 2 **far and ~** : partout 3 **open ~** : ouvrir grand (la bouche) — **wide-awake** ['waɪdə'weɪk] *adj* : éveillé, alerte — **widely** ['waɪdli] *adv* : largement — **widen** ['waɪdən] *vt* : élargir — **widespread** ['waɪd'sprɛd] *adj* : généralisé
widow ['wɪ,do:] *n* : veuve *f* — ~ *vt* : devenir veuf — **widower** ['wɪdowər] *n* : veuf *m*
width ['wɪdθ] *n* : largeur *f*
wield ['wi:ld] *vt* 1 : manier 2 EXERT : exercer
wife ['waɪf] *n, pl* **wives** ['waɪvz] : femme *f*, épouse *f*
wig ['wɪg] *n* : perruque *f*
wiggle ['wɪgəl] *v* **-gled; -gling** *vi* : remuer — *vt* : faire bouger (ses orteils, etc.)
wigwam ['wɪg,wɑm] *n* : wigwam *m*
wild ['waɪld] *adj* 1 : sauvage 2 UNRULY : indiscipliné 3 RANDOM : au hasard 4 FRANTIC : frénétique 5 OUTRAGEOUS : extravagant — ~ *adv* 1 → **wildly** 2 **run ~** : se déchaîner — **wild boar** *n* : sanglier *m* — **wilderness** ['wɪldərnəs] *n* : région *f* sauvage — **wildfire** ['waɪld,faɪr] *n* 1 : feu *m* de forêt 2 **spread like ~** : se répandre comme une traînée de poudre — **wildflower** ['waɪld,flaʊər] *n* : fleur *f* des champs — **wildlife** ['waɪld,laɪf] *n* : faune *f* — **wildly** ['waɪldli] *adv* 1 FRANTICALLY : frénétiquement 2 EXTREMELY : extrêmement
will[1] ['wɪl] *v, past* **would** ['wʊd]; *pres sing & pl* **will** *vt* WISH : vouloir — *v aux* 1 **tomorrow we ~ go shopping** : demain nous irons faire les magasins 2 **he ~ get angry over nothing** : il se fâche pour des riens 3 **I ~ go despite them** : j'irai malgré eux 4 **I won't do it** : je ne le ferai pas 5 **that ~ be the mailman** : ça doit être le facteur 6 **the back seat ~ hold three people** : le siège arrière peut accommoder trois personnes 7 **accidents ~ happen** : les accidents arrivent 8 **you ~ do as I say** : je t'ordonne de faire ce que je te dis
will[2] *n* 1 : volonté *f* 2 TESTAMENT : testament *m* 3 **free ~** : de son propre gré — **willful** *or* **wilful** ['wɪlfəl] *adj* 1 OBSTINATE : volontaire 2 INTENTIONAL : délibéré — **willing** ['wɪlɪŋ] *adj* 1 : complaisant 2 **be ~ to** : être prêt à, être disposé à — **willingly** ['wɪlɪŋli] *adv* : volontiers, de bon cœur — **willingness** ['wɪlɪŋnəs] *n* : bonne volonté *f*
willow ['wɪ,lo:] *n* : saule *m*
willpower ['wɪl,paʊər] *n* : volonté *f*
wilt ['wɪlt] *vi* : se faner
wily ['waɪli] *adj* **wilier; -est** : rusé, malin
win ['wɪn] *v* **won** ['wʌn]; **winning** *vi* : gagner — *vt* 1 : gagner, remporter 2 **~ over** : convaincre — ~ *n* : victoire *f*
wince ['wɪnts] *vi* **winced; wincing** : tressaillir — ~ *n* : tressaillement *m*
winch ['wɪnʧ] *n* : treuil *m*
wind[1] ['wɪnd] *n* 1 : vent *m* 2 BREATH : souffle *m* 3 : gaz *mpl* intestinaux 4 **get ~ of** : apprendre
wind[2] ['waɪnd] *v* **wound** ['waʊnd]; **winding** *vi* : serpenter — *vt* 1 COIL : enrouler 2 **~ a clock** : remonter une horloge
wind down *vi* RELAX : se détendre
windfall ['wɪnd,fɔl] *n* : bénéfice *m* inattendu
winding ['waɪndɪŋ] *adj* : sinueux
wind instrument *n* : instrument *m* à vent
windmill ['wɪnd,mɪl] *n* : moulin *m* à vent
window ['wɪn,do:] *n* : fenêtre *f* (d'une maison), vitre *f* (d'une voiture), guichet *m* (dans une banque, etc.), vitrine *f* (d'un magasin) — **windowpane** ['wɪn,do:,peɪn] *n* : vitre *f*, carreau *m* — **windowsill** ['wɪndo,sɪl] *n* : rebord *m* de fenêtre
windpipe ['wɪnd,paɪp] *n* : trachée *f*
windshield ['wɪnd,ʃi:ld] *n* 1 : pare-brise *m* 2 **~ wiper** : essuie-glace *m*
wind up ['waɪnd,ʌp] *vt* : terminer, conclure — *vi* : finir
windy ['wɪndi] *adj* **windier; -est** 1 : venteux 2 **it's ~** : il vente
wine ['waɪn] *n* : vin *m* — **wine cellar** *n* : cave *f* à vin
wing ['wɪŋ] *n* : aile *f*
wink ['wɪŋk] *vi* : faire un clin d'œil — ~ *n* 1 : clin *m* d'œil 2 **not sleep a ~** : ne pas fermer l'œil
winner ['wɪnər] *n* : gagnant *m*, -gnante *f* — **winning** ['wɪnɪŋ] *adj* : gagnant — **winnings** ['wɪnɪŋz] *npl* : gains *mpl*
winter ['wɪntər] *n* : hiver *m* — ~ *adj* : d'hiver — **wintergreen** ['wɪntər,gri:n] *n* : gaulthérie *f* — **wintertime** ['wɪntər,taɪm] *n* : hiver *m* — **wintry** ['wɪntri] *adj* **-trier; -est** : hivernal
wipe ['waɪp] *vt* **wiped; wiping** 1 : essuyer 2 **~ away** : effacer (un souvenir) 3 **~ out** : détruire — ~ *n* : coup *m* d'éponge
wire ['waɪr] *n* 1 : fil *m* métallique 2 : câble *m* (électrique ou téléphonique) — ~ *vt* **wired; wiring** 1 : faire l'installation électrique de 2 BIND : relier, attacher — **wireless** ['waɪrləs] *adj* : sans fil — **wiring** ['waɪrɪŋ] *n* : installation *f* électrique — **wiry** ['waɪri] *adj* **wirier** ['waɪriər]; **-est** : mince et musclé
wisdom ['wɪzdəm] *n* : sagesse *f* — **wisdom tooth** *n* : dent *f* de sagesse
wise ['waɪz] *adj* **wiser; wisest** 1 : sage 2 SENSIBLE : prudent — **wisecrack** ['waɪz,kræk] *n* : vanne *f* — **wisely** ['waɪzli] *adv* : sagement
wish ['wɪʃ] *vt* 1 : souhaiter, désirer 2 **~ s.o. well** : souhaiter le meilleur à qqn — *vi* 1 : souhaiter, vouloir 2 **as you ~** : comme vous voulez — ~ *n* 1 : souhait *m*, désir *m*, vœu *m* 2 **best ~es** *npl* : meilleurs vœux *mpl* — **wishful** ['wɪʃfəl] *adj* 1 : désireux 2 **~ thinking** : illusions *fpl*
wishy-washy ['wɪʃi,wɔʃi, -,wɑʃi] *adj* : faible, insipide
wisp ['wɪsp] *n* 1 : mèche *f* (de cheveux) 2 HINT : trace *f*, soupçon *m*
wistful ['wɪstfəl] *adj* : mélancolique
wit ['wɪt] *n* 1 CLEVERNESS : ingénuosité *f* 2 HUMOR : esprit *m* 3 **at one's ~'s end** : désespéré 4 **scared out of one's ~s** : mort de peur
witch ['wɪʧ] *n* : sorcière *f* — **witchcraft** ['wɪʧ,kræft] *n* : sorcellerie *f*
with ['wɪð, 'wɪθ] *prep* 1 : avec 2 **I'm going ~ you** : je vais avec toi 3 **it varies ~ the season** : ça varie selon la saison 4 **the girl ~ red hair** : la fille aux cheveux roux 5 **~ all his faults, he's still my friend** : malgré tous ses défauts, il est quand même mon ami
withdraw [wɪð'drɔ, wɪθ-] *v* **-drew** [-'dru:]; **-drawn** [-'drɔn]; **-drawing** *vt* : retirer, rétracter (une parole, etc.) — *vi* LEAVE : se retirer — **withdrawal** [wɪð'drɔəl, wɪθ-] *n* : retrait *m* — **withdrawn** [wɪð'drɔn, wɪθ-] *adj* : renfermé, replié sur soi-même
wither ['wɪðər] *vi* : se faner, se flétrir
withhold [wɪθ'ho:ld, wɪð-] *vt* **-held** [-'hɛld]; **-holding** : retenir (des fonds), refuser (la permission, etc.)
within [wɪð'ɪn, wɪθ-] *adv* : à l'intérieur — ~ *prep* 1 : dans, à l'intérieur de 2 (*in expressions of distance*) : à moins de 3 (*in expressions of time*) : en moins de 4 **~ reach** : à (la) portée de la main
without [wɪð'aʊt, wɪθ-] *adv* **do ~** : se passer de — ~ *prep* : sans
withstand [wɪθ'stænd, wɪð-] *vt* **-stood** [-'stʊd]; **-standing** 1 BEAR : supporter 2 RESIST : résister à
witness ['wɪtnəs] *n* 1 : témoin *m* 2 EVIDENCE : témoignage *m* 3 **bear ~** : témoigner — ~ *vt* 1 SEE : être témoin de 2 : servir de témoin lors de (une signature)
witty ['wɪt̬i] *adj* **-tier; -est** : ingénieux
wives → **wife**
wizard ['wɪzərd] *n* 1 : magicien *m*, sorcier *m* 2 **a math ~** : un génie en mathématiques
wobble ['wɑbəl] *vi* **-bled; -bling** 1 : branler, osciller 2 : trembler (se dit de la voix, etc.) — **wobbly** ['wɑbəli] *adj* : bancal
woe ['wo:] *n* 1 : affliction *f* 2 **~s** *npl* TROUBLES : peines *fpl* — **woeful** ['wo:fəl] *adj* : triste
woke, woken → **wake**
wolf ['wʊlf] *n, pl* **wolves** ['wʊlvz] : loup *m*, louve *f* — ~ *vt or* **~ down** : engloutir, engouffrer
woman ['wʊmən] *n, pl* **women** ['wɪmən] : femme *f* — **womanly** ['wʊmənli] *adj* : féminin
womb ['wu:m] *n* : utérus *m*
won → **win**
wonder ['wʌndər] *n* 1 MARVEL : merveille *f* 2 AMAZEMENT : émerveillement *m* — ~ *vi* : penser, songer — *vt* : se demander — **wonderful** ['wʌndərfəl] *adj* : merveilleux, formidable
won't ['wo:nt] (*contraction of* **will not**) → **will**
woo ['wu:] *vt* 1 COURT : courtiser, faire la cour à 2 : rechercher les faveurs de (un client, etc.)
wood ['wʊd] *n* 1 : bois *m* (matière) 2 *or* **~s** *npl* FOREST : bois *m* — ~ *adj* : de bois, en bois — **woodchuck** ['wʊd,ʧʌk] *n* : marmotte *f* d'Amérique — **wooded** ['wʊdəd] *adj* : boisé — **wooden** ['wʊdən] *adj* : en bois, de bois — **woodpecker** ['wʊd,pɛkər] *n* : pic *m* — **woodwind** ['wʊd,wɪnd] *n* : bois *m* (en musique) — **woodwork** ['wʊd,wərk] *n* : boiseries *fpl* (en menuiserie)
wool ['wʊl] *n* : laine *f* — **woolen** *or* **woollen** ['wʊlən] *adj* 1 : de laine, en laine 2 **~s** *npl* : lainages *mpl* — **woolly** ['wʊli] *adj* **-lier; -est** : laineux

woozy [ˈwu:zi] *adj* **-zier; -est** : qui a la tête qui tourne
word [ˈwərd] *n* **1** : mot *m* **2** NEWS : nouvelles *fpl* **3 ~s** *npl* : texte *m,* paroles *fpl* (d'une chanson, etc.) **4 have a ~ with s.o.** : parler avec qqn **5 keep one's ~** : tenir sa parole — ~ *vt* : formuler, rédiger — **wording** [ˈwərdɪŋ] *n* : termes *mpl* (d'un document) — **word processing** *n* : traitement *m* de texte — **word processor** *n* : machine *f* à traitement de textes — **wordy** [ˈwərdi] *adj* **wordier; -est** : prolixe
wore → **wear**
work [ˈwərk] *n* **1** LABOR : travail *m* **2** EMPLOYMENT : travail *m,* emploi *m* **3** : œuvre *f* (d'art, etc.) **4 ~s** *npl* FACTORY : usine *f* **5 ~s** *npl* MECHANISM : rouages *mpl* (d'une horloge, etc.) — ~ *v* **worked** [ˈwərkt] *or* **wrought** [ˈrɔt]; **working** *vt* **1** : faire travailler (qqn) **2** OPERATE : faire marcher — *vi* **1** : travailler **2** FUNCTION : fonctionner **3** SUCCEED : réussir — **workbench** [ˈwərk,bɛntʃ] *n* : établi *m* — **worked up** *adj* : nerveux — **worker** [ˈwərkər] *n* : travailleur *m,* -leuse *f;* employé *m,* -ployée *f* — **working** [ˈwərkɪŋ] *adj* **1** : qui travaille (se dit d'une personne), de travail (de sit d'un vêtement, etc.) **2 be in ~ order** : en état de marche — **working class** *n* : classe *f* ouvrière — **workman** [ˈwərkmən] *n, pl* **-men** [-mən, -,mɛn] : ouvrier *m* — **workmanship** [ˈwərkmən,ʃɪp] *n* : habileté *f,* dextérité *f* — **workout** [ˈwərk,aʊt] *n* : exercices *mpl* physiques — **work out** *vt* **1** DEVELOP : élaborer **2** SOLVE : résoudre — *vi* **1** TURN OUT : marcher **2** SUCCEED : fonctionner, bien tourner **3** EXERCISE : s'entraîner, faire de l'exercice — **workshop** [ˈwərk,ʃɑp] *n* : atelier *m* — **work up** *vt* **1** EXCITE : stimuler **2** GENERATE : produire
world [ˈwərld] *n* **1** : monde *m* **2 think the ~ of s.o.** : tenir qqn en haute estime — ~ *adj* : du monde, mondial — **worldly** [ˈwərldli] *adj* : matériel, de ce monde — **worldwide**[ˈwərldˈwaɪd] *adv* : partout dans le monde — ~ *adj* : mondial, universel
World Wide Web *n* : Web *m*
worm [ˈwərm] *n* **1** : ver *m* **2 ~s** *npl* : vers *mpl* (intestinaux)
worn → **wear** — **worn–out** [ˈwornˈaʊt] *adj* **1** USED : usé, fini **2** EXHAUSTED : épuisé, éreinté
worry [ˈwəri] *v* **-ried; -rying** *vt* : inquiéter, préoccuper — *vi* : s'inquiéter — ~ *n, pl* **-ries** : inquiétude *f,* souci *m* — **worried** [ˈwəri:d] *adj* : inquiet — **worrisome** [ˈwərisəm] *adj* : inquiétant
worse [ˈwərs] *adv* (*comparative of* **bad** *or of* **ill**) : moins bien, plus mal — ~ *adj* (*comparative of* **bad** *or of* **ill**) **1** : pire, plus mauvais **2 get ~** : s'empirer — ~ *n* **1 the ~** : le pire **2 take a turn for the ~** : s'aggraver, empirer — **worsen** [ˈwərsən] *vi* : empirer, rempirer *Can fam* — *vt* : aggraver
worship [ˈwərʃəp] *v* **-shiped** *or* **-shipped; -shiping** *or* **-shipping** *vt* : adorer, vénérer — *vi* : pratiquer une religion — ~ *n* : adoration *f,* culte *m* — **worshiper** *or* **worshipper** [ˈwərləpər] *n* : fidèle *mf* (en religion)
worst [ˈwərst] *adv* (*superlative of* **ill** *or of* **bad** *or* **badly**) : plus mal — ~ *adj* (*superlative of* **bad** *or of* **ill**) : pire, plus mauvais — ~ *n* **the ~** : le pire
worth [ˈwərθ] *n* **1** : valeur *f* (monétaire) **2** MERIT : mérite *m* **3 ten dollars' ~ of gas** : dix dollars d'essence — ~ *prep* **1 be ~ doing** : valoir l'effort **2 it's ~ $ 10** : cela vaut 10 $ — **worthless** [ˈwərθləs] *adj* **1** : sans valeur **2** USELESS : inutile — **worthwhile** [wərθˈhwaɪl] *adj* : qui en vaut la peine — **worthy** [ˈwərði] *adj* **-thier; -est** : digne
would [ˈwʊd] *past of* **will 1 he ~ often take his children to the park** : il amenait souvent ses enfants au parc **2 I ~ go if I had the money** : j'irais si j'avais les moyens **3 I ~ rather go alone** : je préférerais y aller seul **4 she ~ have won if she hadn't tripped** : elle aurait gagné si elle n'avait pas trébuché **5 ~ you kindly help them?** : auriez-vous la gentillesse de les aider? — **wouldn't** [ˈwʊdˈnt] (*contraction of* **would not**) → **would**
wound[1] [ˈwu:nd] *n* : blessure *f* — ~ *vt* : blesser
wound[2] [ˈwaʊnd] → **wind**
wove, woven → **weave**
wrangle [ˈræŋgəl] *vi* **-gled; -gling** : se disputer
wrap [ˈræp] *vt* **wrapped; wrapping 1** : envelopper, emballer **2** *or* **~ up** FINISH : conclure — ~ *n* → **wrapper** — **wrapper** [ˈræpər] *n* : papier *m,* emballage *m* — **wrapping** [ˈræpɪŋ] *n* : emballage *m*
wrath [ˈræθ] *n* : furie *f,* colère *f*
wreath [ˈri:θ] *n, pl* **wreaths** [ˈri:ðz, ˈri:θs] : couronne *f* (de fleurs, etc.)
wreck[ˈrɛk] *n* **1** WRECKAGE : épave *f* (d'un navire) **2** ACCIDENT : accident *m* (de voiture), écrasement *m* (d'avion) **3 be a nervous ~** : être à bout — ~ *vt* : détruire (une automobile), faire échouer (un navire) — **wreckage** [ˈrɛkɪʤ] *n* **1** : épave *f* (d'un navire) **2** : décombres *mpl* (d'un édifice)
wren [ˈrɛn] *n* : roitelet *m*
wrench [ˈrɛntʃ] *vt* PULL : tirer brusquement — ~ *n* **1** TUG : secousse *f* **2** *or* **monkey ~** : clef *f*
wrestle [ˈrɛsəl] *vi* **-tled; -tling** : lutter, pratiquer la lutte (aux sports) — **wrestler** [ˈrɛsələr] *n* : lutteur *m,* -teuse *f* — **wrestling** [ˈrɛsəlɪŋ] *n* : lutte *f* (sport)
wretch [ˈrɛtʃ] *n* : pauvre diable *m* — **wretched** [ˈrɛtʃəd] *adj* **1** : misérable **2 ~ weather** : temps *m* affreux
wriggle [ˈrɪgəl] *vi* **-gled; -gling** : gigoter
wring [ˈrɪŋ] *vt* **wrung** [ˈrʌŋ]; **wringing 1** *or* **~ out** : essorer (du linge) **2** TWIST : tordre
wrinkle [ˈrɪŋkəl] *n* : ride *f* — ~ *v* **-kled; -kling** *vt* : rider — *vi* : se rider
wrist [ˈrɪst] *n* : poignet *m* — **wristwatch** [ˈrɪst,wɑtʃ] *n* : montre-bracelet *f*
writ [ˈrɪt] *n* : ordonnance *f* (en droit)
write [ˈraɪt] *v* **wrote** [ˈro:t]; **written** [ˈrɪtən]; **writing** : écrire — **write down** *vt* : mettre par écrit, noter — **write off** *vt* CANCEL : annuler — **writer** [ˈraɪtər] *n* : écrivain *m,* écrivaine *f Can*
writhe [ˈraɪð] *vi* **writhed; writhing** : se tordre, se tortiller
writing [ˈraɪtɪŋ] *n* : écriture *f*
wrong [ˈrɔŋ] *n* **1** : mal *m* **2** INJUSTICE : tort *m* — ~ *adj* **wronger; wrongest 1** : mal **2** UNSUITABLE : inapproprié **3** INCORRECT : mauvais, faux **4 be ~** : se tromper, avoir tort **5 what's ~?** : qu'est-ce qui ne va pas? — ~ *adv* **1** : à tort **2** INCORRECTLY : mal — ~ *vt* **wronged; wronging** : faire du tort à — **wrongful** [ˈrɔŋfəl] *adj* **1** UNJUST : injustifié **2** UNLAWFUL : illégal — **wrongly** [ˈrɔŋli] *adv* : à tort
wrote → **write**
wroughtiron [ˈrɔt] *n* : fer *m* forgé
wrung → **wring**
wry [ˈraɪ] *adj* **wrier** [ˈraɪər]; **wriest** [ˈraɪəst] : narquois

x [ˈɛks] *n, pl* **x's** *or* **xs** [ˈɛksəz] : x *m,* vingt-quatrième lettre de l'alphabet
xenophobia [,zɛnəˈfo:biə, ,zi:-] *n* : xénophobie *f*
Xmas [ˈkrɪsməs] → **Christmas**
X ray [ˈɛks,reɪ] *n* **1** : rayon *m* X **2** *or* **~ photograph** : radiographie *f* — **x–ray** *vt* : radiographier
xylophone [ˈzaɪlə,fo:n] *n* : xylophone *m*

y [ˈwaɪ] *n, pl* **y's** *or* **ys** [ˈwaɪz] : y *m,* vingt-cinquième lettre de l'alphabet
yacht [ˈjɑt] *n* : yacht *m*
yam [ˈjæm] *n* SWEET POTATO : patate *f* douce
yank [ˈjæŋk] *vt* : tirer d'un coup sec — ~ *n* : coup *m* sec
yap [ˈjæp] *vi* **yapped; yapping 1** : japper **2** CHATTER : jacasser — ~ *n* : jappement *m*
yard [ˈjɑrd] *n* **1** : yard *m,* verge *f Can* (unité de mesure) **2** COURTYARD : cour *f* **3** : jardin *m* (d'une maison) — **yardstick** [ˈjɑrd,stɪk] *n* **1** : mètre *m* **2** CRITERION : critère *m*
yarn [ˈjɑrn] *n* **1** : fil *m* (à tisser) **2** TALE : histoire *f*
yawn [ˈjɔn] *vi* : bâiller — ~ *n* : bâillement *m*
year [ˈjɪr] *n* **1** : an *m,* année *f* **2 he's ten ~s old** : il a dix ans **3 I haven't seen them in ~s** : je ne les ai pas vus depuis des années — **yearbook** [ˈjɪr,bʊk] *n* : recueil *m* annuel, annuaire *m* — **yearly** [ˈjɪrli] *adv* **1** : annuellement **2 three times ~** : trois fois par an — ~ *adj* : annuel
yearn [ˈjərn] *vi* **~ for** : désirer ardemment — **yearning** [ˈjərnɪŋ] *n* : désir *m* ardent
yeast [ˈji:st] *n* : levure *f*
yell [ˈjɛl] *vi* : crier — *vt* : crier, hurler — ~ *n* : cri *m,* hurlement *m*
yellow [ˈjɛlo] *adj* : jaune — ~ *n* : jaune *m* — ~ *v* : jaunir — **yellowish** [ˈjɛloɪʃ] *adj* : jaunâtre
yelp [ˈjɛlp] *n* : glapissement *m* — ~ *vi* : glapir
yes [ˈjɛs] *adv* **1** : oui **2 you're not ready, are you? ~, I am** : vous n'êtes pas prêt? mais si, je le suis — ~ *n* : oui *m*
yesterday [ˈjɛstər,deɪ, -di] *adv* : hier — ~ *n* **1** : hier *m* **2 the day before ~** : avant-hier *m*
yet [ˈjɛt] *adv* **1** : encore **2 has he come ~?** : est-il déjà arrivé? **3 not ~** : pas encore **4 ~ more problems** : encore des problèmes **5** NEVERTHELESS : néanmoins — ~ *conj* : mais
yield [ˈji:ld] *vt* **1** PRODUCE : produire, rapporter **2 ~ the right of way** : céder le passage — *vi* **1** GIVE : céder **2** SURRENDER : se rendre — ~ *n* : rendement *m,* rapport *m*
yoga [ˈjo:gə] *n* : yoga *m*
yogurt [ˈjo:gərt] *n* : yaourt *m,* yogourt *m*
yoke[ˈjo:k] *n* : joug *m*
yolk [ˈjo:k] *n* : jaune *m* (d'œuf)
you [ˈju:] *pron* **1** (*used as subject — singular*) : tu (familier), vous (forme polie) **2** (*used as subject — plural*) : vous **3** (*used as the direct or indirect object of a verb*) : te (familier), vous (forme polie), vous (pluriel) **4** (*used as the object of a preposition*) : toi (familier), vous (forme polie), vous (pluriel) **5 ~ never know** : on ne sait jamais — **you'd** [ˈju:d, ˈjʊd] (*contraction of* **you had** *or* **you would**) → **have, would** — **you'll** [ˈju:l, ˈjʊl] (*contraction of* **you shall** *or* **you will**) → **shall, will**
young [ˈjʌŋ] *adj* **younger** [ˈjʌŋgər]; **youngest** [-gəst] **1** : jeune **2 my ~er brother** : mon frère cadet **3 she is the ~est** : elle est la plus jeune — ~ *npl* : jeunes *mfpl* (personnes), petits *mpl* (animaux) — **youngster** [ˈjʌŋkstər] *n* **1** : jeune *mf* **2** CHILD : enfant *mf*
your [ˈjʊr, ˈjo:r, jər] *adj* **1** (*familiar singular*) : ta, ton **2** (*formal singular*) : votre **3** (*familiar plural*) : tes **4** (*formal plural*) : vos **5 on ~ left** : à votre gauche
you're [ˈjʊr, ˈjoɪr, ˈjər, ˈjuɪər] (*contraction of* **you are**) → **be**
yours [ˈjʊrz, ˈjo:rz] *pron* **1** (*familiar singular*) : le tien, la tienne **2** (*formal singular*) : le vôtre, la vôtre **3** (*familiar plural*) : les tiens, les tiennes **4** (*formal plural*) : les vôtres
yourself [jərˈsɛlf] *pron, pl* **yourselves** [jərˈsɛlvz] **1** (*used reflexively*) : tu (familier), vous (forme polie), vous (pluriel) **2** (*used for emphasis*) : toi-même (familier), vous-même (forme polie), vous-mêmes (pluriel)
youth [ˈju:θ] *n, pl* **youths** [ˈju:ðz, ˈju:θs] **1** : jeunesse *f* **2** BOY : jeune *m* **3 today's ~** : les jeunes d'aujourd'hui — **youthful** [ˈju:θfəl] *adj* **1** : juvénile, de jeunesse **2** YOUNG : jeune
you've [ˈju:v] (*contraction of* **you have**) → **have**
yowl [ˈjæʊl] *vi* : hurler (se dit d'un chien ou d'une personne) — ~ *n* : hurlement *m*
yule [ˈju:l] *n* : Noël *m* — **yuletide** [ˈju:l,taɪd] *n* : temps *m* de Noël

Z

z [ˈzi:] *n, pl* **z's** *or* **zs** : z *m,* vingt-sixième lettre de l'alphabet
zany [ˈzeɪni] *adj* **-nier; -est** : farfelu *fam*
zeal [ˈzi:l] *n* : zèle *m,* ferveur *f* — **zealous** [ˈzɛləs] *adj* : zélé
zebra [ˈzi:brə] *n* : zèbre *m*
zed [ˈzɛd] *Brit* → **z**
zenith [ˈzi:nəθ] *n* : zénith *m*
zero [ˈzi:ro, ˈzɪro] *n, pl* **-ros** : zéro *m* — ~ *adj* : zéro, nul
zest [ˈzɛst] *n* **1** : enthousiasme *m,* entrain *m* **2** FLAVOR : piquant *m*
zigzag [ˈzɪg,zæg] *n* : zigzag *m* — ~ *vi* **-zagged; -zagging** : zigzaguer
zinc [ˈzɪŋk] *n* : zinc *m*
zip [ˈzɪp] *v* **zipped; zipping** *vt or* **~ up** : fermer avec une fermeture à glissière — *vi* SPEED : filer à toute allure — **zip code** *n* : code *m* postal — **zipper** [ˈzɪpər] *n* : fermeture *f* à glissière
zodiac [ˈzo:di,æk] *n* : zodiaque *m*
zone[ˈzo:n] *n* : zone *f*
zoo [ˈzu:] *n, pl* **zoos** : zoo *m* — **zoology** [zoˈɑləʤi, zu:-] *n* : zoologie *f*
zoom [ˈzu:m] *vi* : passer comme une trombe — ~ *n or* **~ lens** : zoom *m*
zucchini [zʊˈki:ni] *n, pl* **-ni** *or* **-nis** : courgette *f*

Common French Abbreviations

French Abbreviation and Expansion		English Equivalent	
AB, Alb.	Alberta	**AB, Alta.**	Alberta
ALÉNA	Accord de libre-échange nord-américain	**NAFTA**	North American Free Trade Agreement
AP	assistance publique (France)	—	welfare services
ap. J.-C.	après Jésus-Christ	**AD**	anno Domini
a/s	aux soins de	**c/o**	care of
av.	avenue	**ave.**	avenue
av. J.-C.	avant Jésus-Christ	**BC**	before Christ
avr.	avril	**Apr.**	April
BC	Colombie-Britannique	**BC, B.C.**	British Columbia
bd	boulevard	**blvd.**	boulevard
BD	bande dessinée	—	comic strip
BN	Bibliothèque nationale	—	national library
BP	boîte postale	**P.O.B.**	post office box
B.S.	bien-être social (Canada)	—	welfare services
c	centime	**c, ct.**	cent
C	centigrade, Celsius	**C**	centigrade, Celsius
CA	comptable agréé (Canada)	**CPA**	certified public accountant
CA	courant alternatif	**AC**	alternating current
c.-à-d.	c'est-à-dire	**i.e.**	that is
C.-B.	Colombie-Britannique	**BC, B.C.**	British Columbia
CC	courant continu	**DC**	direct current
CE	Communauté européenne	**EC**	European Community
CEE	Communauté européenne économique	**EEC**	European Economic Community
cg	centigramme	**cg**	centigram
Cie	compagnie	**Co.**	company
cm	centimètre	**cm**	centimeter
C.P.	case postale (Canada)	**P.O.B**	post office box
CV	curriculum vitae	**CV**	curriculum vitae
déc.	décembre	**Dec.**	December
dép., dépt.	département	**dept.**	department
DG	directeur général	**CEO**	chief executive officer
dim.	dimanche	**Sun.**	Sunday
dir.	directeur	**dir.**	director
DOM	Département(s) d'outre-mer	—	French overseas department
dr.	droite	**rt.**	right
Dr	docteur	**Dr.**	doctor
E	Est, est	**E**	East, east
ECG	électrocardiogramme	**EKG**	electrocardiogram
éd.	édition	**ed.**	edition
EPS	éducation physique et sportive	**PE**	physical education
etc.	et caetera, et cetera	**etc.**	et cetera
É.-U.	États-Unis	**US**	United States
F	Fahrenheit	**F**	Fahrenheit
F	franc	**fr.**	franc
FAB	franco à bord	**FOB**	free on board
févr.	février	**Feb.**	February
FMI	Fonds monétaire international	**IMF**	International Monetary Fund
g	gauche	**l., L**	left
g	gramme	**g**	gram
h	heure(s)	**hr.**	hour
HS	hors service	—	out of order
i.e.	c'est-à-dire	**i.e.**	that is
IPC	indice des prix à la consommation	**CPI**	consumer price index
Î.P.-É	île-du-Prince-Édouard	**PE, P.E.I.**	Prince Edward Island
janv.	janvier	**Jan.**	January
jeu.	jeudi	**Thurs.**	Thursday
juill.	juillet	**Jul.**	July
kg	kilogramme	**kg**	kilogram
km	kilomètre	**km**	kilometer
l	litre	**l**	liter
lun.	lundi	**Mon.**	Monday
m	mètre	**m.**	meter
M.	monsieur	**Mr.**	mister
mar.	mardi	**Tues.**	Tuesday
MB, Man.	Manitoba	**MB, Man.**	Manitoba
mer.	mercredi	**Wed.**	Wednesday
MLF	mouvement de libération des femmes	—	—
Mlle	Mademoiselle	**Ms., Miss**	—
Mme	Madame	**Ms., Mrs.**	—
MST	maladie sexuellement transmissible	**STD**	sexually transmitted disease
N	Nord, nord	**N**	North, north
Nº, nº	numéro	**no.**	number
NB, N.-B.	Nouveau-Brunswick	**NB, N.B.**	New Brunswick
n.d.	non disponible	**NA**	not available
NL, T.-N.-L.	Terre-Neuve et Labrador	**NL**	Newfoundland and Labrador
nov.	novembre	**Nov.**	November
NS, N.-É.	Nouvelle-Écosse	**NS, N.S.**	Nova Scotia
NT	Territoires du Nord-Ouest	**NT, N.T.**	Northwest Territories
NU	Nunavut	**Nu**	Nunavut
O	Ouest, ouest	**W**	West, west
oc	ondes courtes	**s-w**	short wave
oct.	octobre	**Oct.**	October
OIT	Organisation internationale du travail	**ILO**	International Labor Organization
OMS	Organisation mondiale de la santé	**WHO**	World Health Organization
ON, Ont.	Ontario	**ON, Ont.**	Ontario
ONG	organisation non gouvernementale	**NGO**	nongovernmental organization
ONU	Organisation des Nations Unies	**UN**	United Nations
OTAN	Organisation du traité de l'Atlantique Nord	**NATO**	North Atlantic Treaty Organization
OVNI, ovni	objet volant non identifié	**UFO**	unidentified flying object
p.	page	**p.**	page
PCV	paiement contre vérification	—	collect call
PDG	président-directeur général	**CEO**	chief executive officer
PE	Île-du-Prince-Édouard	**PE, P.E.I.**	Prince Edward Island
p. ex.	par exemple	**e.g.**	for example
PIB	produit intérieur brut	**GDP**	gross domestic product
PNB	produit national brut	**GNP**	gross national product
P.-S.	post-scriptum	**P.S.**	postscript
QC	Québec	**QC, Que.**	Quebec
QG	quartier général	**HQ**	headquarters
QI	quotient intellectuel	**IQ**	intelligence quotient
R-D	recherche-développement	**R and D**	research and development
réf.	référence	**ref.**	reference
RF	République Française	—	France
RN	route nationale	—	interstate highway
RV	rendez-vous	**rdv., R.V.**	rendezvous
s.	siècle	**c., cent.**	century
S	Sud, sud	**S, so.**	South, south
SA	société anonyme	**Inc.**	incorporated (company)
sam.	samedi	**Sat.**	Saturday
SARL	société à responsabilité limitée	**Ltd.**	limited (corporation)
Sask.	Saskatchewan	**SK, Sask.**	Saskatchewan
SDF	sans domicile fixe	—	homeless (person)
sept.	septembre	**Sept.**	September
SK	Saskatchewan	**SK, Sask.**	Saskatchewan
SM	Sa Majesté	**HM**	His Majesty, Her Majesty
SME	Système monétaire européen	—	European Monetary System
St	saint	**St.**	Saint
Ste	sainte	**St.**	Saint
SVP	s'il vous plaît	**pls.**	please
t	tonne	**t., tn.**	ton
tél.	téléphone	**tel.**	telephone
T.-N.	Terre-Neuve	**NF, Nfld.**	Newfoundland
T.N.-O.	Territoires du Nord-Ouest	**NT, N.T.**	Northwest Territories
TVA	taxe à valeur ajoutée	**VAT**	value-added tax
UE	Union européenne	**EU**	European Union
univ.	université	**U., univ.**	university
V., v.	voir	**vid.**	see
ven.	vendredi	**Fri.**	Friday
vol.	volume	**vol.**	volume
VPC	vente par correspondance	—	mail-order selling
W-C	water closet	**w.c.**	water closet
YT, Yuk.	Yukon	**YT, Y.T.**	Yukon Territory

Common English Abbreviations

ENGLISH ABBREVIATION AND EXPANSION		FRENCH EQUIVALENT	
AB	Alberta	**AB**	Alberta
AC	alternating current	**CA**	courant alternatif
AD	anno Domini (in the year of our Lord)	**ap. J.-C.**	après Jésus-Christ
AK	Alaska	—	Alaska
AL, Ala.	Alabama	—	Alabama
Alta.	Alberta	**Alb.**	Alberta
a.m., AM	ante meridiem (before noon)	—	du matin
Am., Amer.	America, American	—	Amérique, américain
anon.	anonymous	—	anonyme
Apr.	April	**avr.**	avril
AR	Arkansas	—	Arkansas
Ariz.	Arizona	—	Arizona
Ark.	Arkansas	—	Arkansas
asst.	assistant	—	assistant, -tante
atty.	attorney	—	avocat, -cate
Aug.	August	—	août
ave.	avenue	**av.**	avenue
AZ	Arizona	—	Arizona
B.A.	Bachelor of Arts (degree)	—	licence ès lettres
BC	before Christ	**av. J.-C.**	avant Jésus-Christ
BC, B.C.	British Columbia	**BC, C.-B.**	Colombie-Britannique
BCE	Before Common Era, Before Christian Era	—	avant notre ère
bldg.	building	**édif.**	édifice
blvd.	boulevard	**bd**	boulevard
Br., Brit.	Britain, British	—	Grande-Bretagne, britannique
Bro(s).	brother(s)	**F., Fr.**	frère(s)
B.S.	Bachelor of Science (degree)	**lic.**	licence ès sciences
c.	cent	—	cent (Canada), centime
c.	century	**s.**	siècle
c.	cup	—	tasse
C	Celsius, centigrade	**C**	Celsius, centigrade
CA, Cal., Calif.	California	—	Californie
Can., Canad.	Canada, Canadian	—	Canada, canadien
Capt.	captain	**Cap.**	capitaine
cent.	century	**s.**	siècle
CEO	chief executive officer	**DG, PDG**	directeur général, président-directeur général
cf.	compare	**cf.**	confer
cg	centigram	**cg**	centigramme
ch., chap.	chapter	**chap.**	chapitre
CIA	Central Intelligence Agency	—	—
cm	centimeter	**cm**	centimètre
Col.	colonel	**Col.**	colonel
Co.	company	**Cie.**	compagnie
co.	county	—	comté
CO	Colorado	—	Colorado
c/o	care of	**a/s**	aux soins de
COD	cash on delivery, collect on delivery	—	—
Col., Colo.	Colorado	—	Colorado
Conn.	Connecticut	—	Connecticut
corp.	corporation	—	corporation, société
CPI	consumer price index	**IPC**	indice des prix à la consommation
CPR	cardiopulmonary resuscitation	—	réanimation cardiopulmonaire
ct.	cent	—	cent (Canada), centime
CT	Connecticut	—	Connecticut
D.A.	District Attorney	—	—
DC	direct current	**CC**	courant continu
DC, D.C.	District of Columbia	—	—
DDS	doctor of dental surgery	—	chirurgien-dentiste
DE	Delaware	—	Delaware
Dec.	December	**déc.**	décembre
Del.	Delaware	—	Delaware
dir.	director	**dir.**	directeur
dept.	department	**dép., dépt.**	département
DJ	disc jockey	**DJ**	disc jockey
DMD	doctor of dental medicine	—	docteur en médecine dentaire

ENGLISH ABBREVIATION AND EXPANSION		FRENCH EQUIVALENT	
doz.	dozen	**douz., dz**	douzaine
Dr.	doctor	**Dr**	docteur
DVM	doctor of veterinary medicine	—	docteur en médecine vétérinaire
E	East, east	**E**	est
ea.	each	—	chacun, la pièce
ed.	edition	**éd.**	édition
e.g.	for example	**p. ex.**	par exemple
EKG	electrocardiogram	**ECG**	électrocardiogramme
EMT	emergency medical technician	—	technicien médical des services d'urgence
Eng.	England, English	**Angl., angl.**	Angleterre, anglais
esp.	especially	—	—
etc.	et cetera	**etc.**	et cætera, et cetera
EU	European Union	**UE**	Union européenne
F	Fahrenheit	**F**	Fahrenheit
FBI	Federal Bureau of Investigation	—	—
Feb.	February	**fév.**	février
FL, Fla.	Florida	—	Floride
Fri.	Friday	**ven.**	vendredi
ft.	feet, foot	—	pied(s)
g	gram	**g**	gramme
Ga., GA	Georgia	—	Georgie
gal.	gallon	—	—
G.B.	Great Britain	**GB, G-B**	Grande-Bretagne
GDP	gross domestic product	**PIB**	produit national brut
Gen.	general, General	**Gén.**	général
gm	gram	**g**	gramme
GNP	gross national product	**PNB**	produit national brut
gov.	governor	—	gouverneur
govt.	government	**gouv.**	gouvernement
HI	Hawaii	—	Hawaii
HM	His Majesty, Her Majesty	**SM**	Sa Majesté
hr.	hour	**h**	heure(s)
HS	high school	—	lycée
ht.	height	—	taille
Ia., IA	Iowa	—	Iowa
ID	Idaho	—	Idaho
i.e.	that is	**i.e.**	c'est-à-dire
IL, Ill.	Illinois	—	Illinois
IMF	International Monetary Fund	**FMI**	Fonds monétaire international
in.	inch	—	pouce
IN	Indiana	—	Indiana
Inc.	incorporated (company)	**SA**	société anonyme
Ind.	Indian, Indiana	—	Indiana
IQ	intelligence quotient	**QI**	quotient intellectuel
Jan.	January	**janv.**	janvier
Jul.	July	**juill.**	juillet
Jun.	June	—	juin
Jr., Jun.	Junior	—	fils
Kan., Kans.	Kansas	—	Kansas
kg	kilogram	**kg**	kilogramme
km	kilometer	**km**	kilomètre
KS	Kansas	—	Kansas
Ky., KY	Kentucky	—	Kentucky
l	liter	**l**	litre
l.	left	**g.**	gauche
La, LA	Louisiana	—	Louisiane
lb.	pound	—	livre
Ltd.	limited (corporation)	**SARL**	société à responsabilité limitée
m.	meter	**m.**	mètre
m.	mile	—	mille
m.	minute	**min.**	minute
MA	Massachusetts	—	Massachusetts
Maj.	major	**Maj.**	commandant
Mar.	March	—	mars
Mass.	Massachusetts	—	Massachusetts
MB, Man.	Manitoba	**MB, Man.**	Manitoba
Md., MD	Maryland	—	Maryland
M.D.	doctor of medicine	—	docteur en médecine
Me., ME	Maine	—	Maine
Mex.	Mexico, Mexican	—	Mexique, mexicain
mg	milligram	**mg**	milligramme
mi.	mile	—	mile, mille
MI, Mich.	Michigan	—	Michigan
min.	minute	**min**	minute

ENGLISH ABBREVIATION AND EXPANSION		FRENCH EQUIVALENT	
Minn.	Minnesota	—	Minnesota
Miss.	Mississippi	—	Mississippi
ml	milliliter	**ml**	millilitre
mm	millimeter	**mm**	millimètre
MN	Minnesota	—	Minnesota
mo.	month	—	mois
Mo., MO	Missouri	—	Missouri
Mon.	Monday	**lun.**	lundi
Mont.	Montana	—	Montana
mpg	miles per gallon	—	milles au gallon
mph	miles per hour	—	milles à l'heure
MS	Mississippi	—	Mississippi
mt.	mount, mountain	—	mont, montagne
MT	Montana	—	Montana
mtn.	mountain	—	montagne
N	North, north	**N**	Nord, nord
NA	not available	**n.d.**	non disponible
NASA	National Aeronautics and Space Administration	—	—
NATO	North Atlantic Treaty Organization	**OTAN**	Organisation du traité de l'Atlantique Nord
NB, N.B.	New Brunswick	**NB, N.-B.**	Nouveau-Brunswick
NC	North Carolina	—	Caroline du Nord
ND, N. Dak.	North Dakota	—	Dakota du Nord
NE	northeast	**NE**	nord-est
NE, Neb., Nebr.	Nebraska	—	Nebraska
Nev.	Nevada	—	Nevada
NGO	nongovernmental organization	**ONG**	organisation non gouvernementale
NH, N.H.	New Hampshire	—	New Hampshire
NJ, N.J.	New Jersey	—	New Jersey
NL	Newfoundland and Labrador	**NL, T.-N.-L.**	Terre-Neuve et Labrador
NM, N. Mex.	New Mexico	—	Nouveau-Mexique
no.	north	**N**	nord
no.	number	**N°, n°**	numéro
Nov.	November	**nov.**	novembre
NS, N.S.	Nova Scotia	**NS, N.-É.**	Nouvelle-Écosse
NT	Nunavut	**NT**	Nunavut
NT, N.T.	Northwest Territories	**NT, T. N.-O.**	Territoires du Nord-Ouest
NV	Nevada	—	Nevada
NW	northwest	**NO**	nord-ouest
NY, N.Y.	New York	**NY**	New York
O.	Ohio	—	Ohio
Oct.	October	**oct.**	octobre
OH	Ohio	—	Ohio
OK, Okla.	Oklahoma	—	Oklahoma
ON, Ont.	Ontario	**ON, Ont.**	Ontario
OR, Ore., Oreg.	Oregon	—	Oregon
oz.	ounce, ounces	—	once
p.	page	**p.**	page
Pa., PA	Pennsylvania	—	Pennsylvanie
pat.	patent	**pat.**	patent
P.D.	police department	—	services de police
PE	physical education	**EPS**	éducation physique et sportive
PE, P.E.I.	Prince Edward Island	**PE, Î. P.-É.**	Île-du-Prince-Édouard
Penn., Penna.	Pennsylvania	—	Pennsylvanie
pg.	page	**p.**	page
Ph.D.	doctor of philosophy	—	doctorat
pkg.	package	—	paquet
p.m., PM	post meridiem (after noon)	—	de l'après-midi, du soir
P.O.	post office	—	bureau de poste
pp.	pages	**pp.**	pages
pres.	president	—	président
prof.	professor	—	professeur
P.S.	postscript	**P.-S.**	post-scriptum
P.S.	public school	—	école publique
pt.	pint	—	pinte
pt.	point	**pt**	point
PTA	Parent-Teacher Association	—	—

ENGLISH ABBREVIATION AND EXPANSION		FRENCH EQUIVALENT	
PTO	Parent-Teacher Organization	—	—
q., qt.	quart	—	quart de gallon
QC, Que.	Quebec	**QC**	Québec
r.	right	**dr.**	droite
rd.	road	—	rue
RDA	recommended daily allowance	**AQR**	apport quotidien recommandé
Rev.	reverend	**Rév.**	révérend
RI, R.I.	Rhode Island	—	Rhode Island
rpm	revolutions per minute	**tr/min**	tours par minute
RR	railroad	—	chemin de fer
R.S.V.P.	please respond (répondez s'il vous plaît)	**RSVP**	répondez s'il vous plaît
rt.	right	**dr.**	droite
rte.	route	—	route
s.	second	**s**	seconde
S	South, south	**S**	Sud, sud
S.A.	South America	—	l'Amérique du Sud
Sat.	Saturday	**sam.**	samedi
SC, S.C.	South Carolina	—	Caroline du Sud
SD, S. Dak.	South Dakota	—	Dakota du Sud
SE	southeast	**SE**	sud-est
sec.	second	**s**	seconde
Sept.	September	**sept.**	septembre
Sgt.	sergeant	**Sgt.**	sergent
SK, Sask.	Saskatchewan	**SK, Sask.**	Saskatchewan
so.	south	**S**	sud
sq.	square	—	carré
Sr.	Senior	—	père
st.	street	—	rue
St.	saint	**St, Ste**	saint, sainte
STD	sexually transmitted disease	**MST**	maladie sexuellement transmissible
Sun.	Sunday	**dim.**	dimanche
SW	southwest	**SO**	sud-ouest
t.	teaspoon	—	cuillerée à café
t.	ton	**t**	tonne
T, tb., tbsp.	tablespoon	—	cuillerée (à soupe)
tel.	telephone	**tél.**	téléphone
Tenn.	Tennessee	—	Tennessee
Tex.	Texas	—	Texas
Thu., Thur., Thurs.	Thursday	**jeu.**	jeudi
TM	trademark	—	marque déposée
TN	Tennessee	—	Tennessee
tsp.	teaspoon	—	cuillerée à café
Tue., Tues.	Tuesday	**mar.**	mardi
TX	Texas	—	Texas
U.	university	**univ.**	université
UFO	unidentified flying object	**OVNI, ovni**	objet volant non identifié
UN	United Nations	**ONU**	Nations Unies
univ.	university	**univ.**	université
US	United States	**É.-U.**	États-Unis
USA	United States of America	**USA**	États-Unis d'Amérique
usu.	usually	—	—
UT	Utah	—	Utah
v.	versus	**vs**	versus
Va., VA	Virginia	—	Virginie
vol.	volume	**vol.**	volume
VP	vice president	—	vice-président, -dente
vs.	versus	**vs**	versus
Vt., VT	Vermont	—	Vermont
W	West, west	**O**	Ouest, ouest
WA, Wash.	Washington (state)	—	Washington
Wed.	Wednesday	**mer.**	mercredi
WI, Wis., Wisc.	Wisconsin	—	Wisconsin
wt.	weight	—	poids
WV, W. Va.	West Virginia	—	Virginie-Occidentale
WY, Wyo.	Wyoming	—	Wyoming
yd.	yard	—	—
yr.	year	—	an
YT, Y.T.	Yukon Territory	**YT, Yuk.**	Yukon

Numbers

Cardinal Numbers

NUMBER	ENGLISH	FRENCH	NUMBER	ENGLISH	FRENCH
1	one	un	24	twenty-four	vingt-quatre
2	two	deux	25	twenty-five	vingt-cinq
3	three	trois	26	twenty-six	vingt-six
4	four	quatre	27	twenty-seven	vingt-sept
5	five	cinq	28	twenty-eight	vingt-huit
6	six	six	29	twenty-nine	vingt-neuf
7	seven	sept	30	thirty	trente
8	eight	huit	40	forty	quarante
9	nine	neuf	50	fifty	cinquante
10	ten	dix	60	sixty	soixante
11	eleven	onze	70	seventy	soixante-dix
12	twelve	douze	80	eighty	quatre-vingts
13	thirteen	treize	90	ninety	quatre-vingt-dix
14	fourteen	quatorze	100	one hundred	cent
15	fifteen	quinze	101	one hundred and one	cent un
16	sixteen	seize	200	two hundred	deux cents
17	seventeen	dix-sept	1 000	one thousand	mille
18	eighteen	dix-huit	1 001	one thousand and one	mille un
19	nineteen	dix-neuf	2 000	two thousand	deux mille
20	twenty	vingt	100 000	one hundred thousand	cent mille
21	twenty-one	vingt et un	1 000 000	one million	un million
22	twenty-two	vingt-deux	1 000 000 000	one billion	un milliard
23	twenty-three	vingt-trois			

Ordinal Numbers

NUMBER	ENGLISH	FRENCH	NUMBER	ENGLISH	FRENCH
1st	first	premier, première	16th	sixteenth	seizième
2nd	second	deuxième *or* second	17th	seventeenth	dix-septième
3rd	third	troisième	18th	eighteenth	dix-huitième
4th	fourth	quatrième	19th	nineteenth	dix-neuvième
5th	fifth	cinquième	20th	twentieth	vingtième
6th	sixth	sixième	21st	twenty-first	vingt et unième
7th	seventh	septième	22nd	twenty-second	vingt-deuxième
8th	eighth	huitième	30th	thirtieth	trentième
9th	ninth	neuvième	40th	fortieth	quarantième
10th	tenth	dixième	50th	fiftieth	cinquantième
11th	eleventh	onzième	60th	sixtieth	soixantième
12th	twelfth	douzième	70th	seventieth	soixante-dixième
13th	thirteenth	treizième	80th	eightieth	quatre-vingtième
14th	fourteenth	quatorzième	90th	ninetieth	quatre-vingt-dixième
15th	fifteenth	quinzième	100th	hundredth	centième

Nations of the World

Africa/Afrique

ENGLISH	FRENCH
Algeria	Algérie
Angola	Angola
Benin	Bénin
Botswana	Botswana
Burkina Faso	Burkina Faso
Burundi	Burundi
Cameroon	Cameroun
Cape Verde	Cap-Vert
Central African Republic	République centrafricaine
Chad	Tchad
Comoro Islands	Comores, les îles
Congo, Democratic Republic of the	Congo, République démocratique du
Congo, Republic of the	Congo, République du
Djibouti	Djibouti
Egypt	Égypte
Equatorial Guinea	Guinée-Équatoriale
Eritrea	Érythrée
Ethiopia	Éthiopie
Gabon	Gabon
Gambia	Gambie
Ghana	Ghana
Guinea	Guinée
Guinea-Bissau	Guinée-Bissau
Ivory Coast	Côte-d'Ivoire
Kenya	Kenya
Lesotho	Lesotho
Liberia	Liberia
Libya	Libye
Madagascar	Madagascar
Malawi	Malawi
Mali	Mali
Mauritania	Mauritanie
Mauritius	Maurice, l'île
Morocco	Maroc
Mozambique	Mozambique
Namibia	Namibie
Niger	Niger
Nigeria	Nigeria
Rwanda	Rwanda
São Tomé and Principe	São Tomé et Príncipe
Senegal	Sénégal
Seychelles	Seychelles
Sierra Leone	Sierra Leone
Somalia	Somalie
South Africa, Republic of	Afrique du Sud, République de l'
Sudan	Soudan
Swaziland	Swaziland
Tanzania	Tanzanie
Togo	Togo
Tunisia	Tunisie
Uganda	Ouganda
Zambia	Zambie
Zimbabwe	Zimbabwe

Antarctica/Antarctique

No independent countries

Asia/Asie

ENGLISH	FRENCH
Afghanistan	Afghanistan
Armenia	Arménie
Azerbaijan	Azerbaïdjan
Bahrain	Bahreïn
Bangladesh	Bangladesh
Bhutan	Bhoutan
Brunei	Brunei
Cambodia	Cambodge
China	Chine
Cyprus	Chypre
East Timor	Timor-Oriental
Georgia, Republic of	Géorgie, République de
India	Inde
Indonesia	Indonésie
Iran	Iran
Iraq	Irak, Iraq
Israel	Israël
Japan	Japon
Jordan	Jordanie
Kazakhstan	Kazakhstan
Korea, North	Corée du Nord
Korea, South	Corée du Sud
Kuwait	Koweït
Kyrgyzstan	Kirghizistan
Laos	Laos
Lebanon	Liban
Malaysia	Malaisie, Malaysia
Maldive Islands	Maldives, les îles
Mongolia	Mongolie
Myanmar	Myanmar
Nepal	Népal
Oman	Oman
Pakistan	Pakistan
Philippines	Philippines
Qatar	Qatar
Saudia Arabia	Arabie Saoudite
Singapore	Singapour
Sri Lanka	Sri Lanka
Syria	Syrie
Taiwan	Taiwan, Taïwan
Tajikistan	Tadjikistan
Thailand	Thaïlande
Turkey	Turquie
Turkmenistan	Turkménistan
United Arab Emirates	Émirats arabes unis
Uzbekistan	Ouzbékistan
Vietnam	Viêt-nam
Yemen	Yémen

Europe

ENGLISH	FRENCH
Albania	Albanie
Andorra	Andorre
Austria	Autriche
Belarus	Biélorussi
Belgium	Belgique
Bosnia and Herzegovina	Bosnie-Herzégovine
Bulgaria	Bulgarie
Croatia	Croatie
Czech Republic	République tchèque
Denmark	Danemark
Estonia	Estonie
Finland	Finlande
France	France
Germany	Allemagne
Greece	Grèce
Hungary	Hongrie
Iceland	Islande
Ireland	Irlande
Italy	Italie
Latvia	Lettonie
Liechtenstein	Liechtenstein
Lithuania	Lituanie
Luxembourg	Luxembourg
Macedonia	Macédoine
Malta	Malte
Moldova	Moldavie
Monaco	Monaco
Netherlands	Pays-Bas

ENGLISH	FRENCH
Norway	Norvège
Poland	Pologne
Portugal	Portugal
Romania	Roumanie
Russian Federation	Fédération de Russie
San Marino	Saint-Marin
Serbia and Montenegro	Serbie-Monténégro
Slovakia	Slovaquie
Slovenia	Slovénie
Spain	Espagne
Sweden	Suède
Switzerland	Suisse
Ukraine	Ukraine
United Kingdom	Royaume-Uni
Vatican City	Vatican (État de la cité du)

North America/Amérique du Nord

ENGLISH	FRENCH
Antigua and Barbuda	Antigua et Barbuda
Bahamas	Bahamas
Barbados	Barbade
Belize	Belize
Canada	Canada
Costa Rica	Costa Rica
Cuba	Cuba
Dominica	Dominique
Dominican Republic	République dominicaine
El Salvador	Salvador
Grenada	Grenade
Guatemala	Guatemala
Haiti	Haïti
Honduras	Honduras
Jamaica	Jamaïque
Mexico	Mexique
Nicaragua	Nicaragua
Panama	Panamá
Saint Kitts-Nevis	Saint-Kitts-et-Nevis
Saint Lucia	Sainte-Lucie
Saint Vincent and the Grenadines	Saint-Vincent et les Grenadines
Trinidad and Tobago	Trinité-et-Tobago
United States of America	États-Unis d'Amérique

Oceania/Océanie

ENGLISH	FRENCH
Australia	Australie
Fiji	Fidji, les îles
Kiribati	Kiribati
Marshall Islands	Marshall, les îles
Nauru	Nauru
New Zealand	Nouvelle-Zélande
Papua New Guinea	Papouasie-Nouvelle-Guinée
Samoa	Samoa
Soloman Islands	Salomon, les îles
Tonga	Tonga
Tuvalu	Tuvalu
Vanuatu	Vanuatu

South America/Amérique Latine

ENGLISH	FRENCH
Argentina	Argentine
Bolivia	Bolivie
Brazil	Brésil
Chile	Chili
Colombia	Colombie
Ecuador	Équateur
Guyana	Guyana
Paraguay	Paraguay
Peru	Pérou
Suriname	Surinam, Suriname
Uruguay	Uruguay
Venezuela	Venezuela

Metric System

Length

Unit	Number of Meters	Approximate U.S. Equivalents
millimeter	0.001	0.039 inch
centimeter	0.01	0.39 inch
meter	1	39.37 inches
kilometer	1,000	0.62 mile

Longueur

Unité	Nombre de mètres	Équivalents approximatifs (E-U)
millimètre	0,001	0,039 pouce
centimètre	0,01	0,39 pouce
mètre	1	39,37 pouces
kilomètre	1 000	0,62 mille

Area

Unit	Number of Square Meters	Approximate U.S. Equivalents
square centimeter	0.0001	0.155 square inch
square meter	1	10.764 square feet
hectare	10,000	2.47 acres
square kilometer	1,000,000	0.3861 square mile

Superficie

Unité	Nombre de mètres carrés	Équivalents approximatifs (E-U)
centimètre carré	0,0001	0,155 pouce carré
mètre carré	1	10,764 pieds carrés
hectare	10 000	2,47 acres
kilomètre carré	1 000 000	0,3861 mille carré

Volume

Unit	Number of Cubic Meters	Approximate U.S. Equivalents
cubic centimeter	0.000001	0.061 cubic inch
cubic meter	1	1.307 cubic yards

Volume

Unité	Nombre de mètres cubes	Équivalents approximatifs (E-U)
centimètre cube	0,000001	0,061 pouce cube
mètre cube	1	1,307 yards cubes

Capacity

Unit	Number of liters	Approximate U.S. Equivalents		
		CUBIC	DRY	LIQUID
liter	1	61.02 cubic inches	0.908 quart	1.057 quart

Capacité

Unité	Nombre de litres	Équivalents approximatifs (E-U)		
		CUBE	À GRAIN	LIQUIDE
litre	1	61,02 pouces cubes	0,908 pinte	1,057 pintes

Mass and Weight

Unit	Number of Grams	Approximate U.S. Equivalents
milligram	0.001	0.015 grain
centigram	0.01	0.154 grain
gram	1	0.035 ounce
kilogram	1,000	2.2046 pounds
metric ton	1,000,000	1.102 short tons

Masse et poids

Unité	Nombre de grammes	Équivalents approximatifs (E-U)
milligramme	0,001	0,015 grain
centigramme	0,01	0,154 grain
gramme	1	0,035 once
kilogramme	1 000	2,2046 livres
tonne métrique	1 000 000	1,102 tonnes